WILEY
CPA
EXAM
REVIEW

2013

WILEY CPA EXAM REVIEW

Financial Accounting *and* Reporting

O. Ray Whittington, CPA, PhD

Patrick R. Delaney, CPA, PhD

WILEY

JOHN WILEY & SONS, INC.

CONTENTS

INTRODUCTION

FINANCIAL ACCOUNTING AND REPORTING

APPENDICES

INDEX   1067

PREFACE

Passing the CPA exam upon your first attempt is possible! The *Wiley CPA Examination Review* preparation materials provide you with the necessary materials (visit our website at www.wiley.com /cpa for more information). It's up to you to add the hard work and commitment. Together we can beat the pass rate on each section of about 45%. All Wiley CPA products are continuously updated to provide you with the most comprehensive and complete knowledge base. Choose your products from the Wiley preparation materials and you can proceed confidently. You can select support materials that are exam-based and user-friendly. You can select products that will help you pass!

Remaining current is one of the keys to examination success. Here is a list of what's new in this edition of the *Wiley CPA Examination Review Financial Accounting and Reporting* text.

- The new AICPA Content Specification Outlines on Financial Accounting and Reporting for the computerized CPA Examination beginning in 2012
- AICPA questions released in 2012
- The new task-based simulations
- Complete coverage of standards, especially

  - The newest FASB accounting standards
  - International accounting standards
  - SEC reporting requirements

The objective of this work is to provide you with the knowledge to pass the Financial Accounting and Reporting portion of the Uniform Certified Public Accounting (CPA) Exam. The text is divided up into fourteen areas of study called modules. Each module contains written text with discussion, examples, and demonstrations of the key exam concepts. Following each text area, actual American Institute of Certified Public Accountants (AICPA) unofficial questions and answers are presented to test your knowledge. We are indebted to the AICPA for permission to reproduce and adapt examination materials from past examinations. Author constructed questions and simulations are provided for new areas or areas that require updating. All author constructed questions and simulations are modeled after AICPA question formats. The multiple-choice questions are grouped into topical areas, giving candidates a chance to assess their areas of strength and weakness. Selection and inclusion of topical content is based upon current AICPA Content Specification Outlines. Only testable topics are presented. If the CPA exam does not test it, this text does not present it.

The CPA exam is one of the toughest exams you will ever take. It will not be easy. But if you follow our guidelines and focus on your goal, you will be thrilled with what you can accomplish.

Ray Whittington
November 2012

> **DON'T FORGET TO VISIT OUR WEBSITE AT WWW.WILEY.COM/CPA FOR SUPPLEMENTS AND UPDATES.**

ABOUT THE AUTHORS

Ray Whittington, PhD, CPA, CMA, CIA, is the dean of the Driehaus College of Business at DePaul University. Prior to joining the faculty at DePaul, Professor Whittington was the Director of Accountancy at San Diego State University. From 1989 through 1991, he was the Director of Auditing Research for the American Institute of Certified Public Accountants (AICPA), and he previously was on the audit staff of KPMG. He previously served as a member of the Auditing Standards Board of the AICPA and as a member of the Accounting and Review Services Committee and the Board of Regents of the Institute of Internal Auditors. Professor Whittington has published numerous textbooks, articles, monographs, and continuing education courses.

Patrick R. Delaney, deceased, was the dedicated author and editor of the *Wiley CPA Exam Review* books for twenty years. He was the Arthur Andersen LLP Alumni Professor of Accountancy and Department Chair at Northern Illinois University. He received his PhD in Accountancy from the University of Illinois. He had public accounting experience with Arthur Andersen LLP and was coauthor of *GAAP: Interpretation and Application*, also published by John Wiley & Sons, Inc. He served as Vice President and a member of the Illinois CPA Society's Board of Directors, and was Chairman of its Accounting Principles Committee; was a past president of the Rockford Chapter, Institute of Management Accountants; and had served on numerous other professional committees. He was a member of the American Accounting Association, American Institute of Certified Public Accountants, and Institute of Management Accountants. Professor Delaney was published in *The Accounting Review* and was a recipient of the Illinois CPA Society's Outstanding Educator Award, NIU's Excellence in Teaching Award, and Lewis University's Distinguished Alumnus Award. He was involved in NIU's CPA Review Course as director and instructor.

ABOUT THE CONTRIBUTOR

Natalie T. Churyk, PhD, CPA, is the Caterpillar Professor of Accountancy at Northern Illinois University. She teaches in the undergraduate and L.M.A.S. programs as well as developing and delivering continuing professional education in Northern Illinois University's CPA Review program. Professor Churyk has published in professional and academic journals. She serves on state and national committees relating to education and student initiatives and is a member of several editorial review boards. Professor Churyk is a coauthor on two textbooks: *Accounting and Auditing Research: Tools and Strategies* and *Mastering the Codification and eIFRS: A Case Approach*.

INTRODUCTION

To maximize the efficiency of your review program, begin by studying (not merely reading) chapters 1 through 5 of this volume. They have been carefully organized and written to provide you with important information to assist you in successfully completing the Financial Accounting and Reporting section of the CPA exam. Beyond providing a comprehensive outline to help you organize the material tested on the Financial Accounting and Reporting section of the exam, these chapters will assist you in organizing a study program to prepare for the Financial Accounting and Reporting portion. Self-discipline is essential.

Chapter 1: Beginning Your CPA Review Program

GENERAL COMMENTS ON THE EXAMINATION

The Uniform CPA Examination is delivered using computer-based testing (CBT). Computer-based testing has several advantages. You may take the exam one section at a time. As a result, your studies can be focused on that one section, improving your chances for success. In addition, the exam is no longer offered twice a year. During eight months of every year, you may take the exam on your schedule, six days a week and in the morning or in the afternoon.

Successful completion of the Uniform CPA Examination in Financial Accounting and Reporting is an attainable goal. Keep this point foremost in your mind as you study the first four chapters in this volume and develop your study plan.

Purpose of the Examination[1]

The Uniform CPA Examination is designed to test the entry-level knowledge and skills necessary to protect the public interest. An entry-level CPA is defined as one who has fulfilled the applicable jurisdiction's educational requirements and has the knowledge and skills typically possessed by a person with up to two years of experience. These knowledge and skills were identified through a Practice Analysis performed in 2008, which served as a basis for the development of the content specifications for the exam beginning in 2013.

The CPA examination is one of many screening devices to assure the competence of those licensed to perform the attest function and to render professional accounting services. Other screening devices include educational requirements, ethics examinations, and work experience.

The examination appears to test the material covered in accounting programs of the better business schools. It also appears to be based upon the body of knowledge essential for the practice of public accounting and the auditor of a medium-sized client. Since the examination is primarily a textbook or academic examination, you should plan on taking it as soon as possible after completing your accounting education.

Examination Content

Guidance concerning topical content of the Financial Accounting and Reporting section of the CPA exam can be found in a document prepared by the Board of Examiners of the AICPA entitled *Content and Skill Specifications for the Uniform CPA Exam.* We have included the content outlines for Financial Accounting and Reporting in Chapter 5. These outlines should be used as an indication of the topics' relative emphasis on the exam.

The Board's objective in preparing this detailed listing of topics tested on the exam is to help "in assuring the continuing validity and reliability of the Uniform CPA Examination." These outlines are an excellent source of guidance concerning the areas and the emphasis to be given each area on future exams.

The new Content and Skill Specification Outlines for the CPA examination, including the testing of International Financial Reporting Standards (IFRS), goes into effect January 1, 2013. In addition, the AICPA adopted CBT-e, which is a new computer platform. The major change from your standpoint is that simulations are smaller in size and a larger number of these "task-based simulations" are included on the Auditing and Attestation, Financial Accounting and Reporting, and Regulation exams. In addition, all simulations that test writing skills have been moved to the Business Environment and Concepts exam.

New accounting and auditing pronouncements, including those in the governmental and not-for-profit areas, are tested in the testing window six months after the pronouncement's *effective* date. If early application is permitted, a pronouncement is tested six months after the *issuance* date; candidates are also responsible for the old pronouncement until it is superseded. The AICPA posts content changes regularly on its Internet site at www.cpa-exam.org.

Nondisclosure and Computerization of Examination

Beginning May 1996, the Uniform CPA Examination became nondisclosed. For each exam section, candidates are required to agree to a *Statement of Confidentiality,* which states that they will not divulge the nature and content of any exam question. The CPA exam is computer-based, and candidates take the exam at Prometric sites in the 55 jurisdictions in which the exam is offered. The CPA exam is offered continually during the testing windows shown below.

Testing Window (Exam Available)	January through February	April through May	July through August	October through November
AICPA Review & Update (Exam Unavailable)	March	June	September	December

---

[1] More information may be obtained from the AICPA's *Uniform CPA Examination Candidate Bulletin*, which you can find on the AICPA's website at www.cpa-exam.org.

One or more exam sections may be taken during any exam window, and the sections may be taken in any desired order. **However, no candidate will be allowed to sit for the same section more than once during any given testing window.** In addition, a candidate must pass all four sections of the CPA exam within a "rolling" eighteen-month period, which begins on the date he or she passes a section. In other words, you must pass the other three sections of the exam within eighteen months of when you pass the first section. If you do not pass all sections within the eighteen-month period, credit for any section(s) passed outside the eighteen-month period will expire and the section(s) must be retaken.

Types of Questions

The computer-based Uniform CPA Examination consists of two basic question formats.

1. Multiple-Choice—questions requiring the selection of one of four responses to a short scenario.
2. Task-Based Simulations—short case studies that are used to assess knowledge and skills in a context approximating that found on the job through the use of realistic scenarios and tasks, and access to normally available and familiar resources.

The multiple-choice questions are much like the ones that have constituted a majority of the CPA examination for years. **And the good news is that these types of questions constitute 60% of the Financial Accounting and Reporting section.**

Process for Sitting for the Examination

While there are some variations in the process from state to state, the basic process for sitting for the CPA examination may be described as follows:

1. Apply to take the examination (request, complete, and submit an application).
2. Payment of examination fees.
3. Review the tutorial and sample tests.
4. Receive your Notice to Schedule.
5. Schedule your examination.
6. Take your examination(s).
7. Receive your Score Report(s).

Applying to Take the Examination

The right to practice public accounting as a CPA is governed by individual state statutes. While some rules regarding the practice of public accounting vary from jurisdiction to jurisdiction, all State Boards of Accountancy use the Uniform CPA Examination and AICPA advisory grading service as one of the requirements to practice public accounting. The State Boards of Accountancy determine the requirements to sit for the exam (e.g., education requirements and fees). For comparisons of requirements for various state boards and those policies that are uniform across jurisdictions, you should refer to the website of the National Association of State Boards of Accountancy (NASBA) at www.nasba.org.

A frequent problem candidates encounter is failure to apply by the deadline. **Apply to sit for the examination early. Also, you should use extreme care in filling out the application and mailing required materials to your State Board of Accountancy.** If possible, have a friend review your completed application before mailing with check and other documentation. The name on your application must appear exactly the same as it appears on the identification you plan to use at the testing center. Candidates miss a particular CPA examination window simply because of minor technical details that were overlooked (checks not signed, items not enclosed, question not answered on application, etc.). **Because of the very high volume of applications received in the more populous states, the administrative staff does not have time to call or write to correct minor details and will simply reject your application.**

The NASBA website has links to the registration information for all 55 jurisdictions. It is possible for candidates to sit for the examination at a Prometric site in any state or territory. Candidates desiring to do so should refer to the registration information for the applicable State Board of Accountancy.

Obtaining the Notice to Schedule

Once your application has been processed and you have paid all fees, you will receive a Notice to Schedule (NTS) from NASBA. The NTS will list the section(s) of the examination that you are approved to take. When you receive the NTS, verify that all information is correct. **Be certain that the name appearing on the NTS matches EXACTLY the name on the identification documents that you will use during check-in at the testing center. If the information is incorrect or the name does not match, immediately contact your board of accountancy or its designated agent to request a correction. You must bring your NTS with you to the examination.**

Exam Scheduling

Once you have been cleared to take the exam by the applicable state board, you will receive by mail a Notice to Schedule (NTS) and may then schedule to sit for one or more sections of the exam.

You have the following two options for scheduling your examination:

1. **Visit www.prometric.com/cpa on the Internet**

    This is the easiest and quickest way to schedule an examination appointment (or cancel and reschedule an appointment, if necessary). Simply go to the website, select "schedule your test," and follow the directions. It is advised that you print and keep for your records the confirmation number for your appointment.

2. **Call 800-580-9648 (Candidate Services Call Center)**

    Before you call, you must have your NTS in front of you, and have in mind several times, dates, and locations that would work for you. You will not receive written confirmation of your appointment. Be sure to write down the date, time, location, and confirmation number for each of your appointments.

You should also be aware that if you have to cancel or reschedule your appointment, you may be subject to a cancellation/rescheduling fee. The AICPA's *Uniform CPA Examination Candidate Bulletin* lists the rescheduling and cancellation fees.

To assure that you get your desired location and time period, it is imperative that you schedule early. To get your first choice of dates, you are advised to schedule at least 45 days in advance. You will not be scheduled for an exam fewer than 5 days before testing.

ATTRIBUTES OF EXAMINATION SUCCESS

Your primary objective in preparing for the Financial Accounting and Reporting section is to pass. Other objectives such as learning new and reviewing old material should be considered secondary. The six attributes of examination success discussed below are **essential**. You should study the attributes and work toward achieving/developing each of them **before** taking the examination.

1. **Knowledge of Material**

    Two points are relevant to "knowledge of material" as an attribute of examination success. **First,** there is a distinct difference between being familiar with material and knowing the material. Frequently candidates confuse familiarity with knowledge. Can you remember when you just could not answer an examination question or did poorly on an examination, but maintained to yourself or your instructor that you knew the material? You probably were only familiar with the material. On the CPA examination, familiarity is insufficient; you must know the material. Remember the exam will test your ability to analyze data, make judgments, communicate, perform research, and demonstrate understanding of the material. For example, you may be familiar with the concepts in accounting for leases (SFAS 13), but can you compute the present value of an annuity due under a lease agreement and record entries for the lessee and lessor? Once again, a major concern must be to know the material rather than just being familiar with it. Knowledgeable discussion of the material is required on the CPA examination. **Second,** the Financial Accounting and Reporting exam tests a literally overwhelming amount of material at a rigorous level. From an undergraduate point of view, the CPA examination in Financial Accounting and Reporting includes material from the following courses:

    Intermediate Financial (usually two semesters)
    Advanced Financial

Furthermore, as noted earlier, the CPA exam will test new material, sometimes as early as six months after issuance. In other words, you are not only responsible for material in the above courses, but also for all new developments in each of these areas.

    This text contains outlines of accounting topics from FASB pronouncements, financial accounting courses, etc. Return to the original material (e.g., FASB, your accounting textbooks, etc.) only if the outlines do not reinforce material you already know.

2. **Commitment to Exam Preparation**

    Your preparation for the CPA exam should begin at least two months prior to the date you plan to schedule your seating for an exam section. If you plan to take more than one section, you should start earlier. Over the course of your preparation, you will experience many peaks and valleys. There will be days when you feel completely prepared and there will also be days when you feel totally overwhelmed. This is not unusual and, in fact, should be expected.

    The CPA exam is a very difficult and challenging exam. How many times in your college career did you study months for an exam? Probably not too many. Therefore, candidates need to remain focused on the objective— succeeding on the CPA exam.

    Develop a personal study plan so that you are reviewing material daily. Of course, you should schedule an occasional study break to help you relax, but don't schedule too many breaks. Candidates who dedicate themselves to studying have a much greater chance of going through this process only one time. On the other hand, a lack of focus and piecemeal preparation will only extend the process over a number of exam sittings.

3. **Solutions Approach**

    The solutions approach is a systematic approach to solving the questions and simulations found on the CPA examination. Many candidates know the material fairly well when they sit for the CPA exam, but they do not know how to take the examination. Candidates generally neither work nor answer problems efficiently in terms of time or grades. The solutions approach permits you to avoid drawing "blanks" on CPA exam problems; using the solutions approach coupled with grading insights (see below) allows you to pick up a sizable number of points on test material with which you are not familiar. Chapter 3 outlines the solutions approach for multiple-choice questions and task-based simulations.

4. **Grading Insights**

Your score on each section of the exam is determined by the sum of points assigned to individual questions and simulations. Thus, you must attempt to maximize your points on each individual item.

The multiple-choice questions within each section are organized into three groups which are referred to as testlets. Each multiple-choice testlet is comprised of approximately 30 multiple-choice questions. The multiple-choice testlets vary in overall difficulty A testlet is labeled either "medium difficult" or "difficult" based on its makeup. A "difficult" testlet has a higher percentage of hard questions than a "medium difficult" testlet. Every candidate's first multiple-choice testlet in each section will be a "medium difficult" testlet. If a candidate scores well on the first testlet, he or she will receive a "difficult" second testlet. Candidates that do not perform well on the first testlet receive a second "medium difficult" testlet. Because the scoring procedure takes the difficulty of the testlet into account, candidates are scored fairly regardless of the type of testlets they receive.

Each multiple-choice testlet contains "operational" and "pretest" questions. The operational questions are the only ones that are used to determine your score. Pretest questions are not scored; they are being tested for future use as operational questions. However, you have no way of knowing which questions are operational and which questions are pretest questions. Therefore, you must approach each question as if it will be used to determine your grade.

Task-based simulations include more extensive scenarios and requirements. For example, the requirements may involve calculations, spreadsheet completion, journal entries, or research. The points assigned to the requirements will vary according to their difficulty. The task-based simulations make use of a number of commonly used tools such as spreadsheets and electronic research databases. Therefore, you need to become proficient in the use of these tools to maximize your score on the simulations.

CPA Exam scores are reported on a scale from 0 to 99. The total score is not a percent correct score. It is a combination of scores from the multiple-choice and simulation portions of the exam considering the relative difficulty of the items. A total score of 75 is required to pass each section.

The AICPA includes a tutorial and sample examinations on its website that allow you to get experience with the use of the actual computer tools used on the CPA exam. Also, more experience with computer testing can be obtained by using *Wiley CPA Exam Review Test Bank*.

5. **Examination Strategy**

Prior to sitting for the examination, it is important to develop an examination strategy (i.e., an approach to working efficiently throughout the exam.). Your ability to cope successfully with the 4 hours of examination in Financial Accounting and Reporting can be improved by

a. Recognizing the importance and usefulness of an examination strategy
b. Using Chapter 4, Taking the Examination and previous examination experience to develop a "personal strategy" for the exam
c. Testing your "personal strategy" on example examination questions under conditions similar to those at the test centers (using similar tools and databases and with a time limit)

6. **Examination Confidence**

You need confidence to endure the physical and mental demands of 4 hours of problem solving under tremendous pressure. Examination confidence results from proper preparation for the exam, which includes mastering the first five attributes of examination success. Examination confidence is necessary to enable you to overcome the initial frustration with problems for which you may not be specifically prepared.

This study manual, when properly used, contributes to your examination confidence. Build confidence by completing the questions contained herein.

Common Candidate Mistakes

The CPA Exam is a formidable hurdle in your accounting career. With a pass rate of about 40% on each section, the level of difficulty is obvious. The good news, though, is that about 75% of all candidates (first-time and reexam) sitting for each examination eventually pass. The authors believe that the first-time pass rate could be higher if candidates would be more careful. Seven common mistakes that many candidates make are

1. Failure to understand the exam question requirements
2. Misunderstanding the supporting text of the problem
3. Lack of knowledge of material tested, especially recently issued pronouncements
4. Failure to develop proficiency with computer-based testing and practice tools such as electronic research databases and spreadsheets
5. Inability to apply the solutions approach

6. Lack of an exam strategy (e.g., allocation of time)
7. Sloppiness and logical errors

These mistakes are not mutually exclusive. Candidates may commit one or more of the above items. Remind yourself that when you decrease the number of common mistakes, you increase your chances of successfully becoming a CPA. Take the time to read carefully the exam question requirements. Do not jump into a quick start, only to later find out that you didn't understand what information the examiners were asking for. Read slowly and carefully. Take time to recall your knowledge. Respond to the question asked. Apply an exam strategy such as allocating your time among all question formats. Do not spend too much time on the multiple-choice testlets, leaving no time to spend on preparing your simulation responses. Answer questions quickly but precisely, avoid common mistakes, and increase your score.

PURPOSE AND ORGANIZATION OF THIS REVIEW TEXTBOOK

This book is designed to help you prepare adequately for the Financial Accounting and Reporting examination. There is no easy way to prepare for the successful completion of the CPA Examination; however, through the use of this manual, your approach will be systematic and logical.

The objective of this book is to provide study materials supportive to CPA candidates. While no guarantees are made concerning the success of those using this text, this book promotes efficient preparation by

1. Explaining how to **maximize your score** through analysis of examination grading and illustration of the solutions approach.
2. **Defining areas tested** through the use of the content specification outlines. Note that predictions of future exams are not made. You should prepare yourself for all possible topics rather than gambling on the appearance of certain questions.
3. **Organizing your study program** by comprehensively outlining all of the subject matter tested on the examination in 14 easy-to-use study modules. Each study module is a manageable task which facilitates your exam preparation. Turn to Chapter 5 and peruse the contents to get a feel for the organization of this book.
4. **Providing CPA candidates with previous examination problems** organized by topic (e.g., consolidations, inventory, etc.) Questions have also been developed for new areas and in simulation format.
5. **Explaining the AICPA unofficial answers** to the examination questions included in this text. The AICPA publishes unofficial answers for all questions from exams administered prior to 1996 and for any released questions from exams administered on or after May 1996. However, no explanation is made of the approach that should have been applied to the examination questions to obtain these unofficial answers.

As you read the next few paragraphs which describe the contents of this book, flip through the chapters to gain a general familiarity with the book's organization and contents. Chapters 2, 3, and 4 are to help you maximize your score.

Chapter 2	Examination Grading
Chapter 3	The Solutions Approach
Chapter 4	Taking the Examination

Chapters 2, 3, and 4 contain material that should be kept in mind throughout your study program. Refer back to them frequently. Reread them for a final time just before you sit for the exam.

Chapter 5, Exam Content Overview, outlines and discusses the coverage of the Financial Accounting and Reporting section of the CPA examination. It also contains the AICPA Content Specification Outlines for all the Financial Accounting and Reporting topics tested in this section of the exam.

The Financial Accounting and Reporting Modules contain

1. AICPA Content Specification Outlines of the material tested on the Financial Accounting and Reporting section of the exam
2. Multiple-choice questions
3. Task-based simulations
4. AICPA unofficial answers with the author's explanations for the multiple-choice questions
5. Author's answers to task-based simulations

Also included at the end of this text is a complete Sample Financial Accounting and Reporting CPA Examination. The sample exam is included to enable candidates to gain experience in taking a "realistic" exam. While studying the modules, the candidate can become accustomed to concentrating on fairly narrow topics. By working through the sample examination near the end of their study programs, candidates will be better prepared for taking the actual examination. Because some task-based simulations require the use of research materials, it is useful to have the appropriate electronic research database (FASB Financial Accounting Research System or a printed copy of professional standards to complete the sample examination). **Remember that this research material will not be available to answer the multiple-choice questions.**

Other Textbooks

This text is a comprehensive compilation of study guides and outlines; it should not be necessary to supplement them with accounting textbooks and other materials for most topics. You probably already have some of these texts or earlier editions of them. In such a case, you must make the decision whether to replace them and trade familiarity (including notes therein, etc.), with the cost and inconvenience of obtaining the newer texts containing a more updated presentation.

Before spending time and money acquiring new texts, begin your study program with *CPA EXAMINATION REVIEW: FINANCIAL ACCOUNTING AND REPORTING* to determine your need for supplemental texts.

Ordering Other Textual Materials

You probably already have intermediate and advanced texts for financial accounting and reporting. If you cannot order desired texts through a local bookstore, write the publisher directly.

If you want to order AICPA materials, locate an AICPA educator member to order your materials, since educators are entitled to a discount and may place website or telephone orders.

> AICPA (CPA2Biz)
> Telephone: 888-777-7077
> website: www.CPA2Biz.com

A variety of supplemental CPA products are available from John Wiley & Sons, Inc. By using a variety of learning techniques, such as software, computer-based learning, and audio CDs, the candidate is more likely to remain focused during the study process and to retain information for a longer period of time. Visit our website at **www.wiley.com/cpa** for other products, supplements, and updates.

Working CPA Questions

The AICPA Content Outlines, study outlines, etc., will be used to acquire and assimilate the knowledge tested on the examination. This, however, should be only **one-half** of your preparation program. The other half should be spent practicing how to work questions and problems. Some candidates probably spend over 90% of their time reviewing material tested on the CPA exam. Much more time should be allocated to working questions and problems **under exam conditions**. Working examination questions and problems serves two functions. First, it helps you develop a solutions approach as well as solutions that will maximize your score. Second, it provides the best test of your knowledge of the material. At a minimum, candidates should work one of the more complex and difficult problems and simulations (e.g., pensions, statement of cash flows, consolidated financial statement worksheet) in each area or module.

The multiple-choice questions and answers can be used in many ways. First, they may be used as a diagnostic evaluation of your knowledge. For example, before beginning to review deferred taxes you may wish to answer 10 to 15 multiple-choice questions to determine your ability to answer CPA examination questions on deferred taxes. The apparent difficulty of the questions and the correctness of your answers will allow you to determine the necessary breadth and depth of your review. Additionally, exposure to examination questions prior to review and study of the material should provide motivation. You will develop a feel for your level of proficiency and an understanding of the scope and difficulty of past examination questions. Moreover, your review materials will explain concepts encountered in the diagnostic multiple-choice questions.

Second, the multiple-choice questions can be used as a poststudy or postreview evaluation. You should attempt to understand all concepts mentioned (even in incorrect answers) as you answer the questions. Refer to the explanation of the answer for discussion of the alternatives even though you selected the correct response. Thus, you should read the explanation of the unofficial answer unless you completely understand the question and all of the alternative answers.

Third, you may wish to use the multiple-choice questions as a primary study vehicle. This is probably the quickest but least thorough approach in preparing for the exam. Make a sincere effort to understand the question and to select the correct response before referring to the unofficial answer and explanation. In many cases, the explanations will appear inadequate because of your unfamiliarity with the topic. Always refer back to an appropriate study source, such as the outlines and text in this volume, your accounting textbooks, FASB pronouncements, etc.

The multiple-choice questions outnumber the task-based simulations by greater than 10 to 1 in this book. This is similar to the content of the new computer-based examination. One problem with so many multiple-choice questions is that you may overemphasize them. Candidates generally prefer to work multiple-choice questions because they are

1. Shorter and less time-consuming
2. Solvable with less effort
3. Less frustrating than task-based simulations

Another problem with the large number of multiple-choice questions is that you may tend to become overly familiar with the questions. The result may be that you begin reading the facts and assumptions of previously studied questions into the questions on your examination. Guard against this potential problem by reading each multiple-choice question with **extra** care.

Beginning with the introduction of the computer-based examination, the AICPA began testing with simulations. Simulations released by the AICPA, prepared by the authors, and revised from prior CPA exam problems are incorporated in the modules to which they pertain. (See the listing of question material at the beginning of Chapter 5.)

The questions and solutions in this volume provide you with an opportunity to diagnose and correct any exam-taking weaknesses prior to sitting for the examination. Continually analyze your incorrect solutions to determine the cause of the error(s) during your preparation for the exam. Treat each incorrect solution as a mistake that will not be repeated (especially on the examination). Also attempt to generalize your weaknesses so that you may change, reinforce, or develop new approaches to exam preparation and exam taking.

After you have finished reviewing for the Financial Accounting and Reporting section of the exam, work the complete sample exam provided in Appendix A.

SELF-STUDY PROGRAM

CPA candidates generally find it difficult to organize and to complete their own self-study programs. A major problem is determining **what** and **how** to study. Another major problem is developing the self-discipline to stick to a study program. Relatedly, it is often difficult for CPA candidates to determine how much to study (i.e., determining when they are sufficiently prepared).

The following suggestions will assist you in developing a **systematic, comprehensive,** and **successful** self-study program to help you complete the Financial Accounting and Reporting exam.

Remember that these are only suggestions. You should modify them to suit your personality, available study time, and other constraints. Some of the suggestions may appear trivial, but CPA candidates generally need all the assistance they can get to systemize their study programs.

Study Facilities and Available Time

Locate study facilities that will be conducive to concentrated study. Factors that you should consider include

1. Noise distraction
2. Interruptions
3. Lighting
4. Availability (e.g., a local library is not available at 5:00 A.M.)
5. Accessibility (e.g., your kitchen table vs. your local library)
6. Desk or table space

You will probably find different study facilities optimal for different times (e.g., your kitchen table during early morning hours and local libraries during early evening hours).

Next review your personal and professional commitments from now until the exam to determine regularly available study time. Formalize a schedule to which you can reasonably commit yourself. At the end of this chapter, you will find a detailed approach to managing your time available for the exam preparation program.

Self-Evaluation

The *CPA EXAMINATION REVIEW: FINANCIAL ACCOUNTING AND REPORTING* self-study program is partitioned into 14 topics or modules. Since each module is clearly defined and should be studied separately, you have the task of preparing for the Financial Accounting and Reporting section of the CPA exam by tackling 14 manageable tasks. Partitioning the overall project into 14 modules makes preparation psychologically easier, since you sense yourself completing one small step at a time rather than seemingly never completing one or a few large steps.

By completing the following "Preliminary Estimate of Your Knowledge of Subject" inventory, organized by the 14 modules in this program, you will tabulate your strong and weak areas at the beginning of your study program. This will help you budget your limited study time. Note that you should begin studying the material in each module by answering up to 1/4 of the total multiple-choice questions covering that module's topics (see instruction 4.A. in the next section). This "mini-exam" should constitute a diagnostic evaluation as to the amount of review and study you need.

PRELIMINARY ESTIMATE OF YOUR PRESENT KNOWLEDGE OF SUBJECT*

No.	Module	Proficient	Fairly proficient	Generally familiar	Not familiar
9	Basic Theory and Financial Reporting				
10	Inventory				
11	Fixed Assets				
12	Monetary Current Assets and Current Liabilities				
13	Present Value				
14	Deferred Taxes				
15	Stockholders' Equity				
16	Investments				

No.	Module	Proficient	Fairly proficient	Generally familiar	Not familiar
17	Statement of Cash Flows				
18	Business Combinations and Consolidations				
19	Derivative Instruments and Hedging Activities				
20	Miscellaneous				
21	Governmental Accounting				
22	Not-for-Profit Accounting				

*The number of modules in this text commences with number 9 to correspond with the numbering system used in our two-volume set.

Time Allocation

The study program below entails an average of 80 hours (Step 5. below) of study time. The breakdown of total hours is indicated in the left margin.

[2 1/2 hrs.]   1. Study Chapters 2-4 in this volume. These chapters are essential to your efficient preparation program. Time estimate includes candidate's review of the examples of the solutions approach in Chapters 2 and 3.

[1/2 hr.]   2. Begin Financial Accounting and Reporting by studying Chapter 5.

               3. Study one module at a time. The modules are listed above in the self-evaluation section.

               4. For each module

[14 hrs.]   A. First, review the listing of key terms at the end of the module. Then, work 1/4 of the multiple-choice questions (e.g., if there are 40 multiple-choice questions in a module, you should work every 4th question). Score yourself. This diagnostic routine will provide you with an index of your proficiency and familiarity with the type and difficulty of questions.

                       Time estimate: 3 minutes each, not to exceed 1 hour total.

[25 hrs.]   B. Study the outlines and illustrations. Refer to outlines of authoritative pronouncements per instructions. Also refer to your accounting textbooks and original authoritative pronouncements (this will occur more frequently for topics in which you have a weak background). The outlines for each module are broken into smaller sections that you refer you to multiple choice questions to test your comprehension of the material. You may find this organization useful in breaking your study into smaller bites.

                       Time estimate: 1 hour minimum per module, with more time devoted to topics less familiar to you.

[18 hrs.]   C. Work the remaining multiple-choice questions. Study the explanations of the multiple-choice questions you missed or had trouble answering.

                       Time estimate: 3 minutes to answer each question and 2 minutes to study the answer explanation of each question missed.

[8 hrs.]   D. Work the task-based simulations.

                       Time estimate: 15 minutes for each problem and 10 minutes to study the answer explanations for each item missed.

[5 hrs.]   E. Under simulated exam conditions, work the questions and simulations in Appendices B and C.

                       Time estimate: 5 hrs.

[7 hrs.]   F. Work through the sample CPA examination presented in Appendix A. The exam should be taken in one sitting. Take the examination under simulated exam conditions (i.e., in a strange place with other people present [e.g., your local municipal library or a computer lab]). Apply your solutions approach to each problem and your exam strategy to the overall exam. You should limit yourself to the time that you will have when taking the actual CPA exam section (4 hours for the Financial Accounting and Reporting section). Spend time afterwards grading your work and reviewing your effort.

                       Time estimate: 6-7 hours to take the exam and review it later.

5. The total suggested time of 80 hours is only an average. Allocation of time will vary candidate by candidate. Time requirements vary due to the diverse backgrounds and abilities of CPA candidates.

Allocate your time so you gain the most proficiency in the least time. Remember that while 80 hours will be required, you should break the overall project down into 14 more manageable tasks. Do not study more than one module during each study session.

Using Notecards

Below are one candidate's notecards on financial accounting and reporting topics which illustrate how key definitions, formulas, lists, etc. can be summarized on index cards for quick review. Since candidates can take these anywhere they go, they are a very efficient review tool.

Business Combinations
· _Must use purchase method_
· _FMV, differential may have goodwill CNI from date of combination_

Accounting Changes	_Prospective treat._	_Restate FS_
Δ in estimate	Y	N
Δ in principle	N	Y
Δ in reporting entity	N	Y

Prepared by Greg Graber, CPA, former student, Northern Illinois University

Level of Proficiency Required

What level of proficiency must you develop with respect to each of the topics to pass the exam? You should work toward a minimum correct rate on the multiple-choice questions of 80%. Working towards these correct rates or higher ones for Financial Accounting and Reporting will allow for a margin.

Warning: Disproportional study time devoted to multiple-choice (relative to simulations) can be disastrous on the exam. You should work a substantial number of task-based simulations under exam conditions, even though multiple-choice questions are easier to work and are used to gauge your proficiency. The authors believe that practicing task-based simulations will also improve your proficiency on the multiple-choice questions.

Multiple-Choice Feedback

One of the benefits of working through previous exam questions is that it helps you to identify your weak areas. Once you have graded your answers, your strong areas and weak areas should be clearly evident. Yet, the important point here is that you should not stop at a simple percentage evaluation. The percentage only provides general feedback about your knowledge of the material contained within that particular module. The percentage **does not** give you any specific feedback regarding the concepts which were tested. In order to get this feedback, you should look at the questions missed on an individual basis because this will help you gain a better understanding of **why** you missed the question.

This feedback process has been facilitated by the fact that within each module where the multiple-choice answer key appears, two blank lines have been inserted next to the multiple-choice answers. As you grade the multiple-choice questions, mark those questions which you have missed. However, instead of just marking the questions right and wrong, you should now focus on marking the questions in a manner which identifies **why** you missed the question. As an example, a candidate could mark the questions in the following manner: ✓ for math mistakes, x for conceptual mistakes, and ? for areas which the candidate was unfamiliar with. The candidate should then correct these mistakes by reworking through the marked questions.

The objective of this marking technique is to help you identify your weak areas and thus, the concepts which you should be focusing on. While it is still important for you to get between 75% and 80% correct when working multiple-choice questions, it is more important for you to understand the concepts. This understanding applies to both the questions answered correctly and those answered incorrectly. Remember, questions on the CPA exam will be different from the questions in the book, however, the concepts will be the same. Therefore, your preparation should focus on understanding concepts, not just getting the correct answer.

Conditional Candidates

If you have received conditional status on the examination, you must concentrate on the remaining section(s). Unfortunately, many candidates do not study after conditioning the exam, relying on luck to get them through the remaining section(s). Conditional candidates will find that material contained in Chapters 1–4 and the information contained in the appropriate modules will benefit them in preparing for the remaining section(s) of the examination.

PLANNING FOR THE EXAMINATION

Overall Strategy

An overriding concern should be an orderly, systematic approach toward both your preparation program and your examination strategy. A major objective should be to avoid any surprises or anything else that would rattle you during the examination. In other words, you want to be in complete control as much as possible. Control is of paramount importance from both positive and negative viewpoints. The presence of control on your part will add to your confidence and your ability to prepare for and take the exam. Moreover, the presence of control will make your preparation program more enjoyable (or at least less distasteful). On the other hand, a lack of organization will result in inefficiency in preparing and taking the examination, with a highly predictable outcome. Likewise, distractions during the examination (e.g., inadequate lodging, long drive) are generally disastrous.

In summary, establishing a systematic, orderly approach to taking the examination is of paramount importance. Follow these six steps:

1. Develop an overall strategy at the beginning of your preparation program (see below)
2. Supplement your overall strategy with outlines of material tested on the Financial Accounting and Reporting exam (see Chapter 5)
3. Supplement your overall strategy with an explicitly stated set of problem-solving procedures—the solutions approach
4. Supplement your overall strategy with an explicitly stated approach to each examination session (see Chapter 4)
5. Evaluate your preparation progress on a regular basis and prepare lists of things "to do" (see Weekly Review of Preparation Program Progress later in this section).
6. RELAX: You can pass the exam. About 40 to 45% of the candidates taking a section of the CPA examination pass. But if you take out the individuals that did not adequately prepare, these percentages increase substantially. You will be one of those who pass if you complete an efficient preparation program and execute well (i.e., solutions approach and exam strategy) while taking the exam.

The following outline is designed to provide you with a general framework of the tasks before you. You should tailor the outline to your needs by adding specific items and comments.

A. Preparation Program (refer to Self-Study Program discussed previously)

1. Obtain and organize study materials
2. Locate facilities conducive for studying and block out study time
3. Develop your solutions approach (including solving task-based simulations as well as multiple-choice questions)
4. Prepare an examination strategy
5. Study the material tested recently and prepare answers to actual exam questions on these topics under examination conditions
6. Periodically evaluate your progress

B. Physical Arrangements

1. Apply to and obtain acceptance from your state board
2. Schedule your testing location and time

C. Taking the Examination (covered in detail in Chapter 4)

1. Become familiar with location of the test center and procedures
2. Implement examination strategies and the solutions approach

Weekly Review of Preparation Program Progress

The following pages contain a hypothetical weekly review of program progress. You should prepare a similar progress chart. This procedure, which takes only about 5 minutes per week, will help you proceed through a more efficient, complete preparation program.

Make notes of materials and topics

1. That you have studied
2. That you have completed
3. That need additional study

Weeks to go	Comments on progress, "to do" items, etc.

12	1) Read Basic Theory and Financial Reporting Module 2) Made notecards 3) Worked the MC Questions and Task-based Simulations, on a sample basis 4) Need to work Task-based simulations using the solutions approach
11	1) Read Fixed Assets and Stockholders' Equity Modules 2) Made notecards 3) Read the SFAS and APB outlines that correspond to these topics 4) Briefly looked over the MC for both modules
10	1) Read Monetary Current Assets and Current Liabilities Module 2) Made notecards 3) Read the corresponding SFAS/APB outlines 4) Worked the MC Questions and Task-based simulations for Fixed Assets, Stockholders' Equity, and Monetary CA/CL
9	1) Read the Inventory and Statement of Cash Flows Modules 2) Made notecards 3) Skimmed the SFAS and APB outlines, taking notes of important areas 4) Worked the MC Questions and Task-based simulations
8	1) Read the Present Value Module 2) Made notecards 3) Studied the SFASs and APBs on leases and pensions 4) Completed the MC Questions and Task-based simulations
7	1) Read Deferred Taxes Module 2) Made notecards 3) Read the corresponding SFAS and APB outlines 4) Worked the MC Questions and Task-based simulations
6	1) Read the Derivative Instruments and Hedging Activities and Miscellaneous Modules 2) Made notecards 3) Read the corresponding SFAS and APB outlines 4) Worked the MC Questions and Task-based simulations for these modules 5) Confident with these mods; only need a quick review
5	1) Read Investments Module 2) Made notecards 3) Read the corresponding SFAS and APB outlines 4) Worked the MC Questions and Task-based simulations
4	1) Read the Business Combinations and Consolidations Module 2) Reviewed consolidations in an advanced accounting textbook 3) Made notecards 4) Worked the MC Questions and Task-based simulations
3	1) Took Financial Accounting and Reporting Sample Exam

| 2 | 1) | *Reviewed all prior topics, picking out a few MC for each topic and working them out* |
| | 2) | *Did a statement of cash flows* |

| 1 | 1) | *Reviewed notecards and SFAS and APB outlines* |
| | 2) | *Worked MC from Deferred Taxes and Stockholders' Equity Modules* |

| 0 | 1) | *Tried to relax and review topics* |

Time Management of Your Preparation

As you begin your CPA exam preparation, you obviously realize that there is a large amount of material to cover over the course of the next two to three months. Therefore, it is very important for you to organize your calendar, and maybe even your daily routine, so that you can allocate sufficient time to studying. An organized approach to your preparation is much more effective than a last week cram session. An organized approach also builds up the confidence necessary to succeed on the CPA exam.

An approach which we have already suggested is to develop weekly "to do" lists. This technique helps you to establish intermediate objectives and goals as you progress through your study plan. You can then focus your efforts on small tasks and not feel overwhelmed by the entire process. And as you accomplish these tasks you will see yourself moving one step closer to realizing the overall goal, succeeding on the CPA exam.

Note, however, that the underlying assumption of this approach is that you have found the time during the week to study and thus accomplish the different tasks. Although this is an obvious step, it is still a very important step. Your exam preparation should be of a continuous nature and not one that jumps around the calendar. Therefore, you should strive to find available study time within your daily schedule, which can be utilized on a consistent basis. For example, everyone has certain hours of the day which are already committed for activities such as jobs, classes, and, of course, sleep. There is also going to be the time you spend relaxing because CPA candidates should try to maintain some balance in their lives. Sometimes too much studying can be counterproductive. But there will be some time available to you for studying and working through the questions. Block off this available time and use it only for exam prep. Use the time to accomplish your weekly tasks and to keep yourself committed to the process. After awhile your preparation will develop into a habit and the preparation will not seem as overwhelming as it once did.

NOW IS THE TIME TO MAKE YOUR COMMITMENT

Chapter 2: Examination Grading

All State Boards of Accountancy use the AICPA advisory grading service. As your grade is to be determined by this process, it is very important that you understand the AICPA grading process and its **implications for your preparation program and for the solution techniques you will use during the examination**.

The AICPA has a full-time staff of CPA examination personnel under the supervision of the AICPA Board of Examiners, which has the responsibility for the CPA examination.

This chapter contains a description of the AICPA grading process, including a determination of the passing standard.

Setting the Passing Standard of the Uniform CPA Examination

As a part of the development of any licensing process, the passing score on the licensing examination must be established. This passing score must be set to distinguish candidates who are qualified to practice from those who are not. After conducting a number of studies of methods to determine passing scores, the Board of Examiners decided to use candidate-centered methods to set passing scores for the computer-based Uniform CPA Examination. In candidate-centered methods, the focus is on looking at actual candidate answers and making judgments about which sets of answers represent the answers of qualified entry-level CPAs. To make these determinations, the AICPA convened panels of CPAs to examine candidate responses and set the passing scores for multiple-choice questions and simulations. The data from these panels provide the basis for the development of question and problem points (relative weightings). **As with the previous pencil-and-paper exam, a passing score on the computer-based examination is 75%.**

Grading the Examination

All of the responses on the computer-based Financial Accounting and Reporting CPA exam are objective in nature. Obviously, this includes the responses to the multiple-choice questions. However, it also includes the responses to the requirements of simulations. Requirements of simulations include responses involving pull-down selection, entries into spreadsheets, form completion, graphical responses, and drag and drop. All of these responses are computer graded. Therefore, no consideration is given to any comments or explanations outside of the structured responses.

Multiple-Choice Grading

Financial Accounting and Reporting exams contain three multiple-choice testlets of 30 questions each. A few of these questions will be pretest questions that will not be considered in the candidate's score, but there is no way of determining which are the pretest questions. Also, the possible score on a question and on a testlet will vary based on the difficulty of the questions. The makeup of the second testlet provided to a candidate will be determined based upon the candidate's performance on the first testlet, and the makeup of the third testlet will be determined by the candidate's performance on the first two testlets. Therefore, you should not be discouraged if you get a difficult set of questions; it may merely mean that you performed very well on the previous testlet(s). Also, you will receive more raw points for hard and medium questions than for easy questions.

Your grade on the multiple-choice questions is based on the total number of correct answers weighted by their difficulty (and with no penalty for incorrect answers). As mentioned earlier, several of the multiple-choice questions are pretest items that are not included in the candidate's grade.

Task-Based Simulation Grading

As indicated previously, all of the responses to the simulations are computer graded. They will typically involve checking a box, selecting a response from a list, or dragging and dropping an answer.

Requesting a Score Review

For an additional fee, you may request a score review. A score review is a verification of your score making certain that the approved answer key was used. Because the AICPA grades your exam at least twice as a part of its normal process, it is unlikely that you will get an adjustment to your score. You should contact the applicable board of accountancy to request a score review.

NOW IS THE TIME TO MAKE YOUR COMMITMENT

Chapter 3: The Solutions Approach

The solutions approach is a systematic problem-solving methodology. The purpose is to assure efficient, complete solutions to CPA exam questions, some of which are complex and confusing relative to most undergraduate accounting questions. This is especially true with regard to the new Simulation type problems. Unfortunately, there appears to be a widespread lack of emphasis on problem-solving techniques in accounting courses. Most accounting books and courses merely provide solutions to specific types of problems. Memorization of these solutions for examinations and preparation of homework problems from examples is "cookbooking." "Cookbooking" is perhaps a necessary step in the learning process, but it is certainly not sufficient training for the complexities of the business world. Professional accountants need to be adaptive to a rapidly changing, complex environment. For example, CPAs have been called on to interpret and issue reports on new concepts such as price controls, energy allocations, and new taxes. These CPAs rely on their problem-solving expertise to understand these problems and to formulate solutions to them.

The steps outlined below are only one of many possible series of solution steps. Admittedly, the procedures suggested are **very** structured; thus, you should adapt the suggestions to your needs. You may find that some steps are occasionally unnecessary, or that certain additional procedures increase your problem-solving efficiency. Whatever the case, substantial time should be allocated to developing an efficient solutions approach before taking the examination. You should develop your solutions approach by working questions and problems.

Note that the steps below relate to any specific question or simulation; overall examination strategies are discussed in Chapter 4. Remember, the Financial Accounting and Reporting exam will consist of 3 multiple choice testlets containing 30 questions each, and 1 simulation testlet consisting of 7 task-based simulations.

Multiple-Choice Screen Layout

The following is a computer screenshot that illustrates the manner in which multiple-choice questions will be presented:

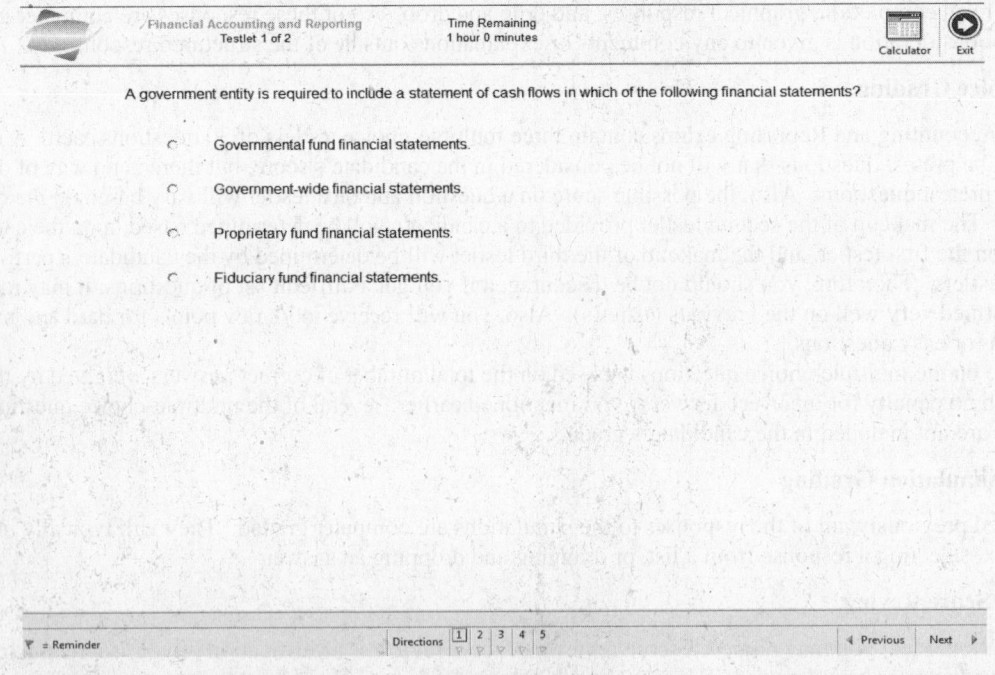

As indicated previously, multiple-choice questions will be presented in three individual testlets of 30 questions. Characteristics of the testlets of multiple-choice questions include the following:

1. You may move freely within a particular testlet from one question to the next or back to previous questions until you click on the "Exit" button. Once you have indicated that you have finished the testlet by clicking on the "Exit" button and reconfirmed, you can never return to that set of questions.
2. The button on the screen will allow you to "flag" a question for review if you wish to come back to it later.
3. A four-function computer calculator with an electronic tape is available as a tool.
4. The time remaining for the entire exam section is shown on the screen.
5. The questions will be shown at the bottom of the screen. You may navigate between questions by simply clicking on the question number.
6. The "Help" button will provide you with help in navigating and completing the testlet.

The previous screenshot was obtained from the AICPA's sample exam at www.cpa-exam.org. Candidates are urged to complete the tutorial and other example questions on the AICPA's website to obtain additional experience with computer-based testing.

Multiple-Choice Question Solutions Approach

1. **Work individual questions in order.**

   a. If a question appears lengthy or difficult, skip it until you can determine that extra time is available. Mark it for review to remind you to return to a question that you have skipped or need to review.

2. **Read the stem of the question without looking at the answers.**

   a. The answers are sometimes misleading and may cause you to misread or misinterpret the question.

3. **Read each question *carefully* to determine the topical area.**

   a. Study the requirements **first** so you know which data are important.
   b. Note keywords and important data.
   c. Identify pertinent information.
   d. Be especially careful to note when the requirement is an **exception** (e.g., "Which of the following is **not** characteristic of variables sampling?").
   e. If a set of data is the basis for two or more questions, read the requirements of each of the questions first before beginning to work the first question (sometimes it is more efficient to work the questions out of order).
   f. Be alert to read questions as they are, not as you would like them to be. You may encounter a familiar looking item; do not jump to the conclusion that you know what the answer is without reading the question completely.

4. **Anticipate the answer before looking at the alternative answers.**

   a. Recall the applicable principle (e.g., the criteria for identification of a capital lease).

5. **Read the answers and select the *best* alternative.**
6. **Click on the correct answer (or your educated guess).**
7. **After completing all of the questions including the ones flagged for review, click on the "Exit" button to close out the testlet. Remember, once you have closed out the testlet you can never return to it.**

Multiple-Choice Question Solutions Approach Example

A good example of the multiple-choice solutions approach follows, using an actual multiple-choice question from a previous CPA Exam.

Step 3:

Topical area? Bad debt expense

Step 4A:

Principle? Recognize that uncollectible accounts are debited to the allowance account

Inge Co. determined that the net value of its accounts receivable at December 31, 2008, based on an aging of the receivables, was $325,000. Additional information is as follows:

Allowance for uncollectible accounts--1/1/08	$ 30,000
Uncollectible accounts written off during 2008	18,000
Uncollectible accounts recovered during 2008	2,000
Accounts receivable at 12/31/08	350,000

For 2008, what would be Inge's uncollectible accounts expense?

a. $ 5,000
b. $11,000
c. $15,000
d. $21,000

Currently, all multiple-choice questions are scored based on the number correct, weighted by a difficulty rating (i.e., there is no penalty for guessing). The rationale is that a "good guess" indicates knowledge. Thus, you should answer all multiple-choice questions.

Task-Based Simulations

Simulations are case-based problems designed to

- Test integrated knowledge
- More closely replicate real-world problems

- Assess research, and other skills

Any of the following types of responses might be required on simulation parts:

- Drop-down selection
- Numeric and monetary inputs
- Formula answers
- Check box response
- Enter spreadsheet formulas
- Research results

The following screenshot illustrates a simulation that requires the candidate to complete a journal entry by selecting from a list of accounts and inputting amounts.

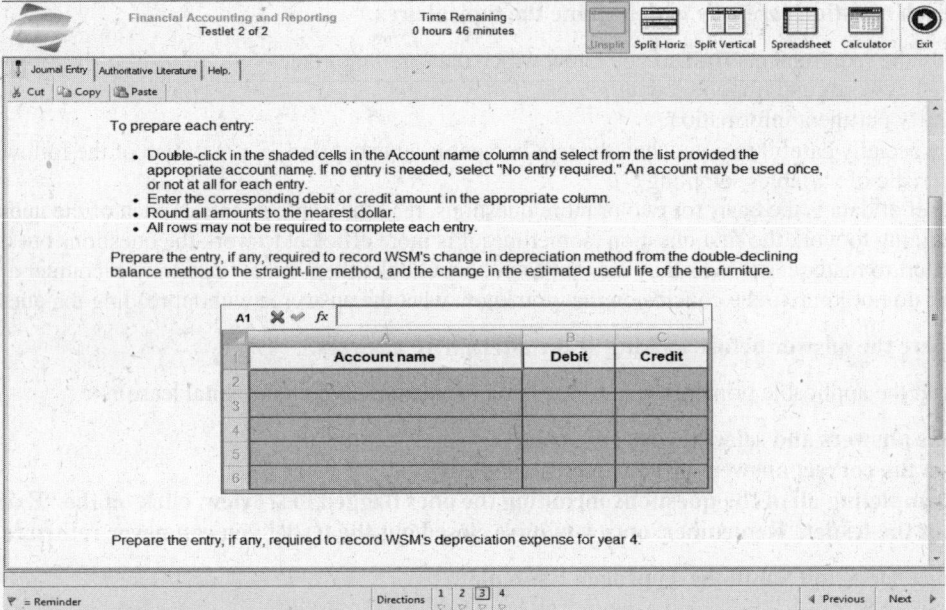

The following screenshot illustrates a simulation that requires selection from a pull-down list.

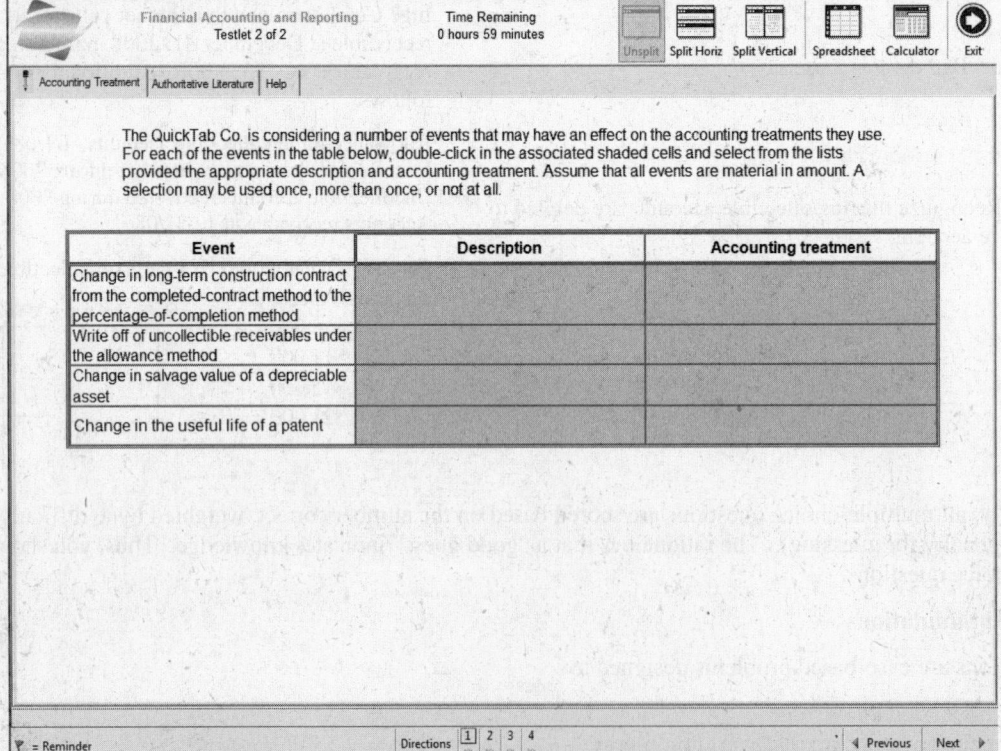

To complete the simulations, candidates are provided with a number of tools, including

- A four-function computer calculator with an electronic tape
- Scratch spreadsheet
- The ability to split windows horizontally or vertically to show two tabs on the screen (e.g., you can examine the situation tab in one window and a requirement tab in a second window)
- Access to professional literature databases to answer research requirements
- Copy and paste functions

In addition, the resource tab provides other resources that may be needed to complete the problem. For example, a resource tab might contain a present value table for use in answering a lease problem.

A window on the screen shows the time remaining for the entire exam and the "Help" button provides instructions for navigating the simulation and completing the requirements.

The AICPA has introduced a new simulation interface which is illustrated in this manual. You are urged to complete the tutorial and other sample tests that are on the AICPA's website (www.cpa-exam.org) to obtain additional experience with the interface and computer-based testing.

Task-Based Simulations Solutions Approach

The following solutions approach is suggested for answering simulations:

1. **Review the entire background and problem.** Get a feel for the topical area and related concepts that are being tested. Even though the format of the question may vary, the exam continues to test your understanding of applicable principles or concepts. Relax, take a deep breath, and determine your strategy for conquering the simulation.
2. **Identify the requirements of the simulation.** This step will help you focus in more quickly on the solution(s) without wasting time reading irrelevant material.
3. **Study the items to be answered.** As you do this and become familiar with the topical area being tested, you should review the concepts of that area. This will help you organize your thoughts so that you can relate logically the requirements of the simulation with the applicable concepts.
4. **Use the scratch paper (which will be provided) and the spreadsheet and calculator tools to assist you in answering the simulation.**

The following screenshots explain how the spreadsheet operates.

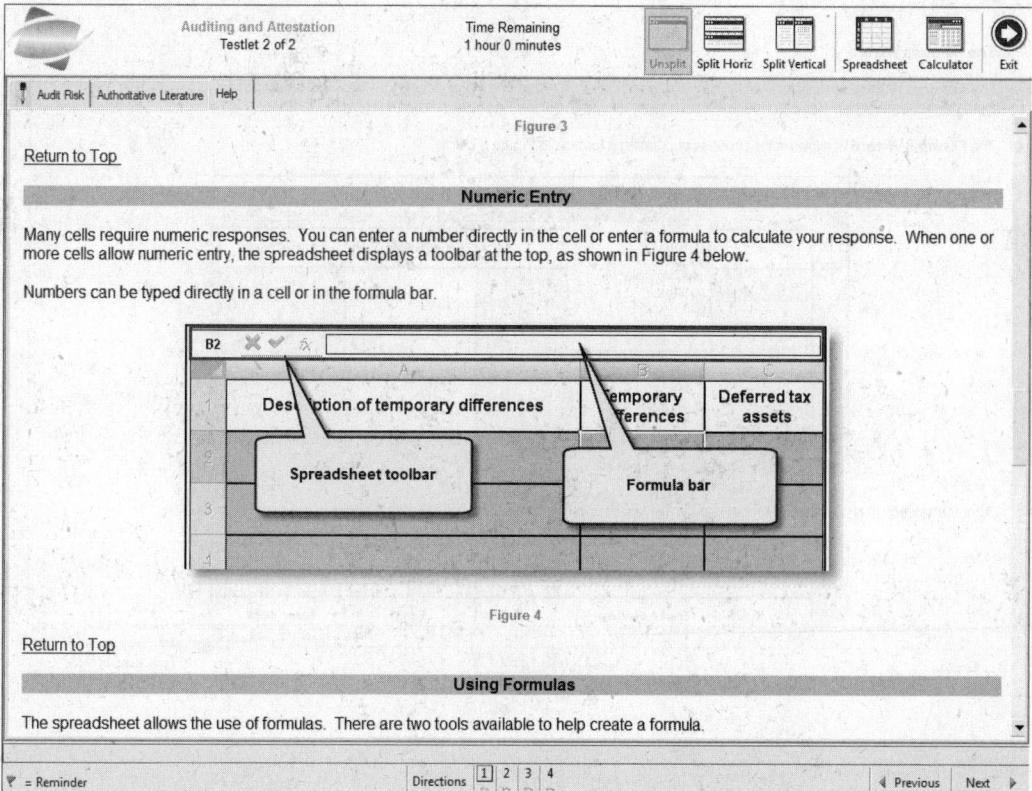

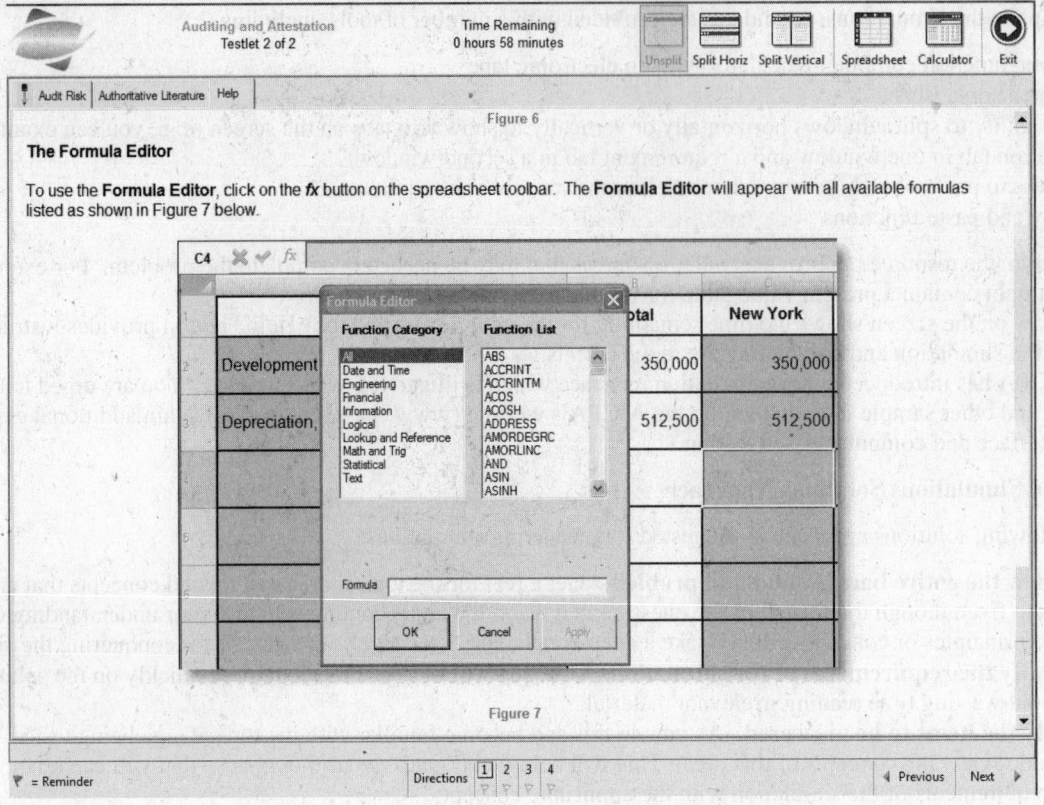

The Formula Editor

To use the **Formula Editor**, click on the *fx* button on the spreadsheet toolbar. The **Formula Editor** will appear with all available formulas listed as shown in Figure 7 below.

Figure 7

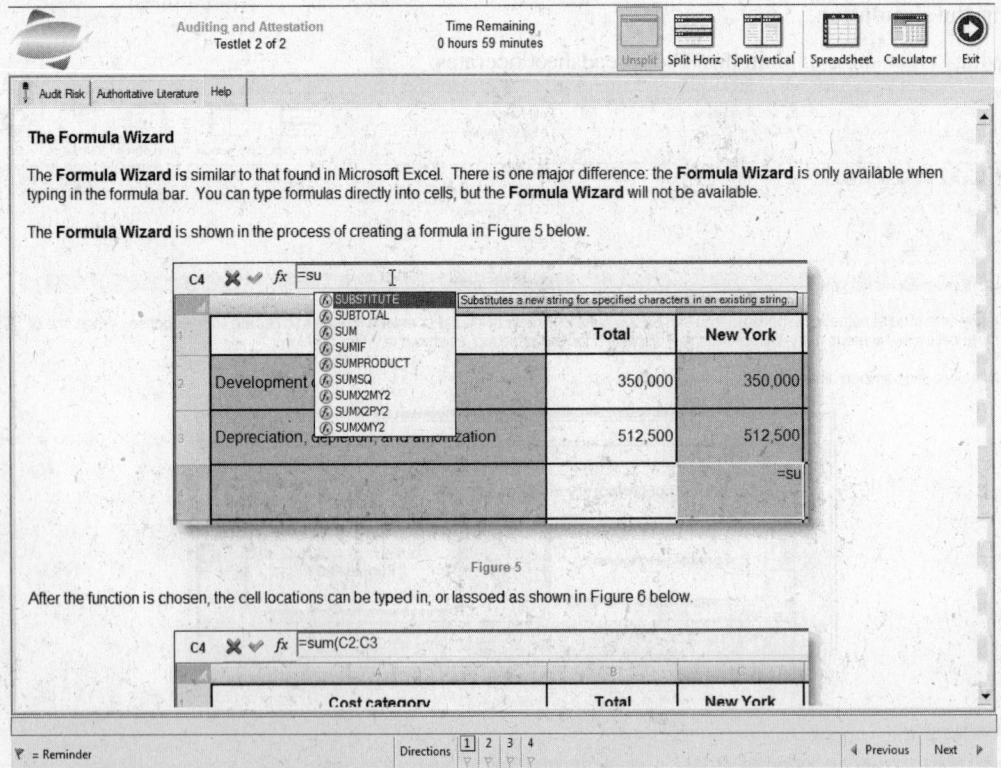

The Formula Wizard

The **Formula Wizard** is similar to that found in Microsoft Excel. There is one major difference: the **Formula Wizard** is only available when typing in the formula bar. You can type formulas directly into cells, but the **Formula Wizard** will not be available.

The **Formula Wizard** is shown in the process of creating a formula in Figure 5 below.

Figure 5

After the function is chosen, the cell locations can be typed in, or lassoed as shown in Figure 6 below.

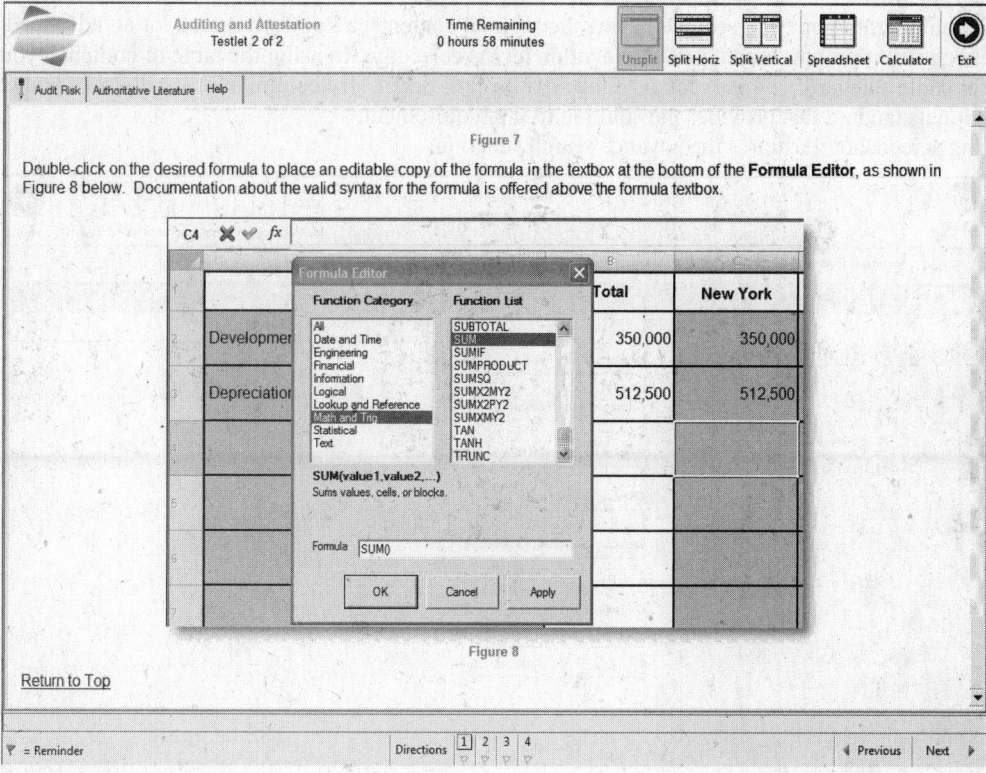

Figure 8

Research Simulations

One of the seven simulations on the Auditing and Attestation exam will be a research simulation. Research simulations require candidates to search the professional literature in electronic format and input the reference to the results. In the Financial Accounting and Reporting section the professional literature database includes

- The FASB Accounting Standards Codification

The following screenshot from the new research interface that was implemented in 2011.

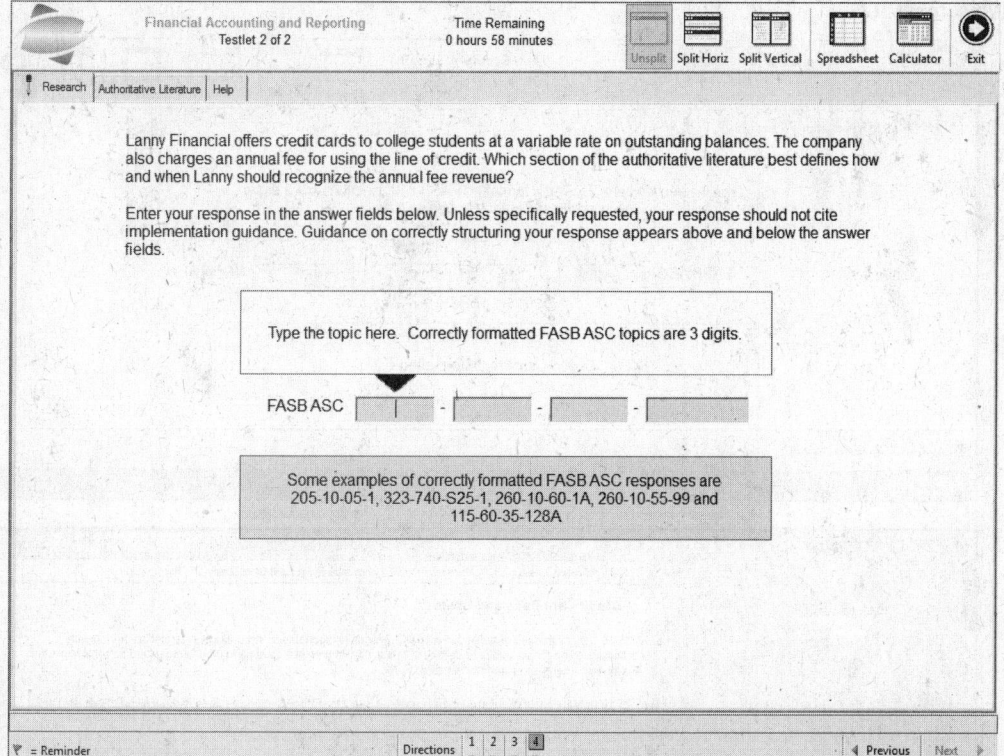

The professional literature may be searched using the table of contents, a keyword search, or an advanced search. **If you use the search function you must spell the term or terms** correctly. In using the table of contents, you simply click on the applicable standards and it expands to the next level of detail. By continuing to drill down you will get to the topic or professional standard that provides the solution to the requirement.

The following screenshot illustrates the advance search function.

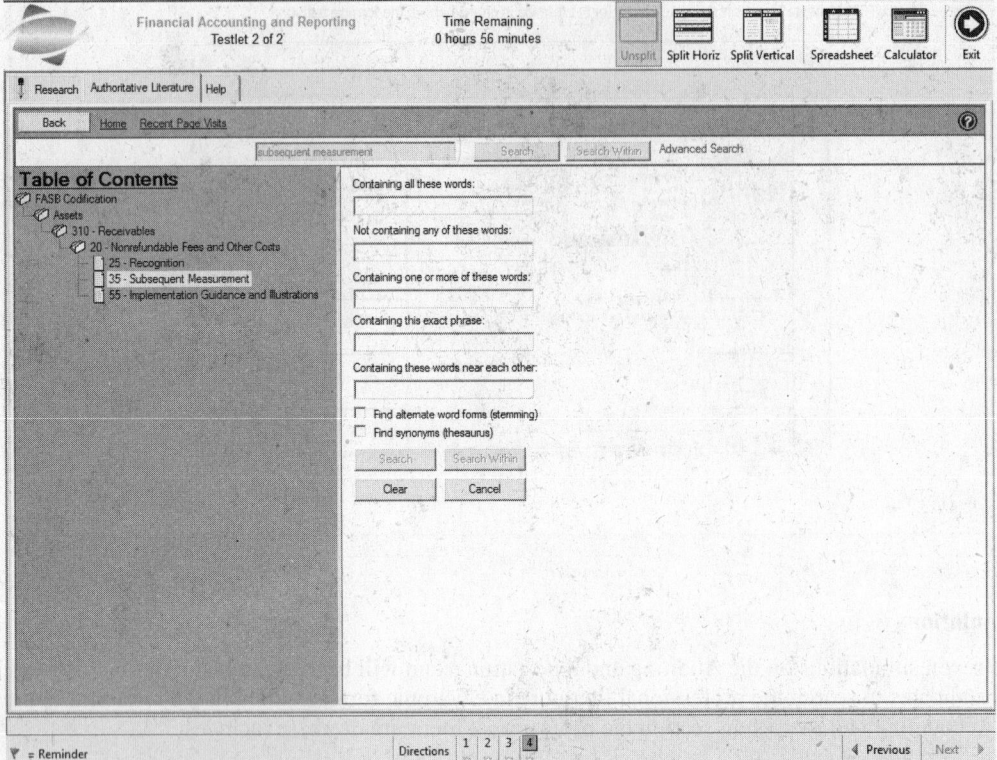

Once you have found the correct passage in the literature, you must input the citation in the answer box. To facilitate this process you should use the split screen function to view the literature in one screen and the answer box in the other as in the following screenshot.

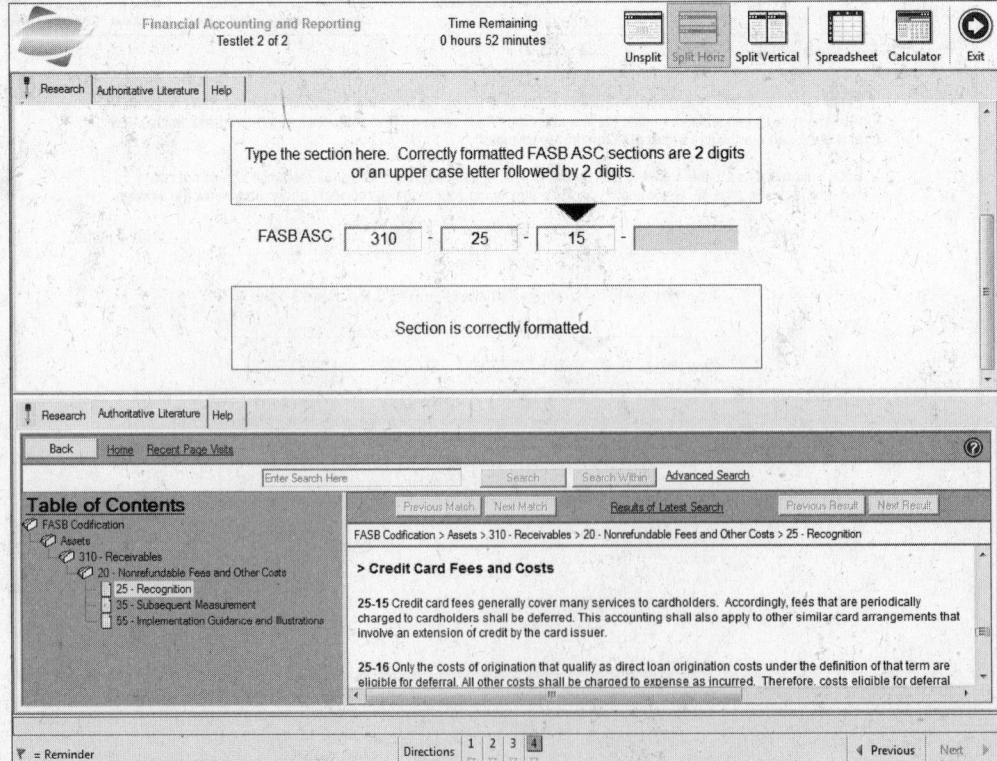

If possible, it is important to get experience using the FASB Accounting Standards Codification System to sharpen your research skills. This database is available from the FASB and many colleges and universities have licenses for use online. In addition, CPA candidates can get a free six-month subscription to the online package of professional literature used in the computerized CPA examination. Other students and recent graduates may subscribe at a special price. Subscriptions are available at www.cpa-exam.org. If that is not available, you should use the printed copy of the professional standards to answer the research simulations in the manual.

Chapter 5 of this manual contains guidance on how to perform research on the Accounting Standards Codification database.

Time Requirements for the Solutions Approach

Many candidates bypass the solutions approach, because they feel it is too time-consuming. Actually, the solutions approach is a time-saver and, more importantly, it helps you prepare better solutions to all questions and simulations.

Without committing yourself to using the solutions approach, try it step-by-step on several questions and simulations. After you conscientiously go through the step-by-step routine a few times, you will begin to adopt and modify aspects of the technique which will benefit you. Subsequent usage will become subconscious and painless. The important point is that you must try the solutions approach several times to accrue any benefits.

In summary, the solutions approach may appear foreign and somewhat cumbersome. At the same time, if you have worked through the material in this chapter, you should have some appreciation for it. Develop the solutions approach by writing down the steps in the solutions approach at the beginning of this chapter, and keep them before you as you work CPA exam questions and problems. Remember that even though the suggested procedures appear **very structured** and **time-consuming,** integration of these procedures into your own style of problem solving will help improve **your** solutions approach. The next chapter discusses strategies for the overall examination.

NOW IS THE TIME TO MAKE YOUR COMMITMENT

Chapter 4: Taking The Examination

This chapter is concerned with developing an examination strategy (e.g., how to cope with the environment at the Test Center, time management, etc.).

EXAMINATION STRATEGIES

Your performance during the examination is final and not subject to revision. While you may sit for the examination again if you are unsuccessful, the majority of your preparation will have to be repeated, requiring substantial, additional amounts of time. Thus, examination strategies (discussed in this chapter) that maximize your exam-taking efficiency are very important.

Getting "Psyched Up"

The CPA exam is quite challenging and worthy of your best effort. Explicitly develop your own psychological strategy to get yourself "up" for the exam. Pace your study program such that you will be able to operate at peak performance when you are actually taking the exam. Many candidates give up because they have a bad day or encounter a rough problem. A significant advantage of the computerized exam is that if you have scheduled early in a testing window and do not feel well, you can reschedule your sitting. However, once you start the exam you cannot retake it in the same testing window, so do not leave the exam early. Do the best you can.

Lodging, Meals, Exercise

If you must travel to the test center, make advance reservations for comfortable lodging convenient to the test center. Do not stay with friends, relatives, etc. Both uninterrupted sleep and total concentration on the exam are a must. Consider the following in making your lodging plans:

1. Proximity to the test center
2. Availability of meals and snacks
3. Recreational facilities

Plan your meal schedule to provide maximum energy and alertness during the day and maximum rest at night. Do not experiment with new foods, drinks, etc., around your scheduled date. Within reasonable limits, observe your normal eating and drinking habits. Recognize that overconsumption of coffee during the exam could lead to a hyperactive state and disaster. Likewise, overindulgence in alcohol to overcome nervousness and to induce sleep the night before might contribute to other difficulties the following morning.

Tenseness should be expected before and during the examination. Rely on a regular exercise program to unwind at the end of the day. As you select your lodging for the examination, try to accommodate your exercise pleasure (e.g., running, swimming, etc.).

To relieve tension or stress while studying, try breathing or stretching exercises. Use these exercises before and during the examination to start and to keep your adrenaline flowing. Remain determined not to have to sit for the section another time.

In summary, the examination is likely to be both rigorous and fatiguing. Expect it and prepare for it by getting in shape, planning methods of relaxation during the exam and in the evening before, and finally, building the confidence and competence to successfully complete the exam.

Test Center and Procedures

If possible, visit the test center before the examination to assure knowledge of the location. Remember: no surprises. Having a general familiarity with the center will lessen anxiety prior to the examination. Talking to a recent veteran of the examination will give you background for the general examination procedures. **You must arrive at the test center 30 minutes before your scheduled time.**

Upon completion of check-in at the test location, the candidate

- Is seated at a designated workstation
- Begins the exam after proctor launches the session
- Is monitored by a Test Center Administrator
- Is videotaped

If you have any remaining questions regarding examination procedure, call or write your state board or go to Prometric's website at www.prometric.com/cpa.

Allocation of Time

Budget your time. Time should be carefully allocated in an attempt to maximize points per minute. While you must develop your own strategy with respect to time allocation, some suggestions may be useful. First, consider the Financial Accounting and Reporting examination, which is 240 minutes long. Allocate 5 minutes to reading the instructions. When you begin the exam you will be given an inventory of the total number of testlets and simulations, including the suggested times. Budget your time based on this inventory.

Plan on spending about 1 ½ to 2 minutes working each of the individual multiple-choice questions. The time allocated to the simulations will vary. Plan on spending about 1¼ to 1½ hours on the simulations testlet.

Techniques for Time Management

The Financial Accounting and Reporting section contains three testlets of multiple-choice questions with 30 questions each. As you complete each testlet keep track of how you performed in relation to the AICPA suggested times. The Financial and Reporting section will also have a testlet with seven task-based simulations. After you finish the multiple-choice testlets, budget your time for the simulations based on your remaining time and the AICPA suggested times. Remember that you alone control watching your progress towards successfully completing this exam.

Examination Rules

1. Prior to the start of the examination, you will be required to accept a *Confidentiality and Break Policy Statement*.
2. You must not bring any personal/unauthorized items into the testing room. Such items include but are not limited to outerwear, hats, food, drinks, purses, briefcases, notebooks, pagers, watches, cellular telephones, recording devices, and photographic equipment. You will be asked to empty and turn your pockets inside out prior to every entry into the test room to confirm that you have no prohibited items. Lockers are provided for storage of personal items.
3. Breaks may be taken at any time between testlets. **However, your exam time continues to run while you take the break.**
4. If you need access to an item stored in the test center during a break such as food or medicine, you must inform the Test Center Administrator before you retrieve the item. You are not allowed to access a prohibited item.
5. Any reference during the examination to books or other materials or the exchange of information with other persons shall be considered misconduct sufficient to bar you from further participation in the examination.
6. Penalties will be imposed on any candidate who is caught cheating before, during, or after the examination. These penalties may include expulsion from the examination, denial of applications for future examinations, and civil or criminal penalties.
7. You may not leave the examination room with any notes about the examination.

Refer to the brochure *CPA Candidate Bulletin* for other rules.

CPA EXAM CHECKLIST

One week before you are scheduled to sit

___ 1. Look over major topical areas, concentrating on schedule formats and the information flow of the formats.

For example:
Accounting Changes and Error Correction
Income Statement Format
Long-Term Construction Accounting
Inventory Methods
Investments
Lessee-Lessor Accounting
Statement of Cash Flows
Derivatives and Hedging

___ 2. If time permits, work through a few questions in your weakest areas so that techniques/concepts are fresh in your mind.

___ 3. Assemble notecards and key outlines of major topical areas into a manageable "last review" notebook to be taken with you to the exam.

What to bring

___ 1. *Notice to Schedule (NTS)*—You must bring the proper NTS with you.
___ 2. *Identification*—Bring two valid forms of ID. One must be government issued. The name on the ID must match exactly the name on the NTS. The CPA Candidate bulletin lists valid primary and secondary IDs.
___ 3. *Hotel confirmation*—(if you must travel).
___ 4. *Cash*—Payment for anything by personal check is rarely accepted.
___ 5. *Major credit card*—American Express, Master Card, Visa, etc.
___ 6. *Alarm clock*—This is too important an event to trust to a hotel wake-up call that might be overlooked.
___ 7. *Clothing*—Should be comfortable and layered to suit the possible temperature range in the testing room.
___ 8. *Earplugs*—Even though examinations are being given, there may be constant activity in the testing room (e.g., people walking around, rustling of paper, clicking of keyboards, people

coughing, etc.). The use of earplugs may block out some of this distraction and help you concentrate better.

__ 9. *Other*—Any "Last review" materials.

Evenings before exams

1. Reviewing the evening before the exam could earn you the extra points needed to pass a section. Just keep this last-minute effort in perspective and **do not panic** yourself into staying up all night trying to cover every possible point. This could lead to disaster by sapping your body of the endurance needed to attack questions creatively during the next day.
2. Before taking the Financial Accounting and Reporting section, scan the general schedule formats to imprint the *flow* of information on your mind (e.g., income statement, statement of cash flows, and lease formats, etc.).
3. Read over **key** notecards or the most important outlines on topics in which you feel deficient.
4. Go over mnemonics and acronyms you have developed as study aids. Test yourself by writing out the letters on paper while verbally giving a brief explanation of what the letters stand for.
5. Scan outlines of SFAC 1, 2, 5, 6, 7 and any other notes pertinent to answering conceptual questions to imprint keywords.
6. **Set your alarm and get a good night's rest!** Being well rested will permit you to meet the day's challenge with a fresh burst of creative energy.

Exam taking strategy

1. Review the AICPA suggested times for the testlets to plan your time allocation during the exam.
2. Do not spend an excess amount of time on the introductory screens. If you take longer than 10 minutes on these screens, the test session will automatically terminate. If the exam session terminates, it will not be possible to restart the examination and you will have to reapply to take the section.
3. Report equipment/software issues to the test center staff immediately. Do not attempt to correct the problem yourself and do not use examination time thinking about it before reporting it. Remind the test center staff to file a report describing the problem. The test center staff should be able to handle any equipment or software problems. However, if you believe the problem was not handled appropriately, contact NASBA at candidatecare@nasba.org.
4. Report any concerns about test questions to test center staff after you have completed the session. The members of the test center staff know nothing about the CPA Examination content. The test center staff can report the issues to the AICPA. You should also report concerns about the questions in writing to the AICPA (FAX to [609] 671-2922). If possible, the question and testlet numbers should be included in the FAX.
5. In the event of a power outage or incident requiring a restart, the computer clock will stop and you will not lose examination time. Your responses up to the

time of the restart will not be lost as responses are saved at frequent intervals throughout the examination.

6. If you have questions about the examination software functions (e.g., the transfer function), you should read the instructions and "Help" tab information. The test center staff is not familiar with the functioning of the examination software and, therefore, will not be able to help you.
7. The crucial technique to use for multiple-choice questions is to read through each question stem **carefully,** noting keywords such as "fair value," "contingent," "other comprehensive income," etc. Then **read each choice** carefully before you start eliminating inappropriate answers. Often the first or second answer may **sound** correct, but a later answer may be more correct. Be discriminating! Reread the question and choose the **best** answer.
8. If you are struggling with questions beyond a minute or two, use the strategy of dividing multiple-choice questions into two categories.

   a. Questions for which you know you lack knowledge to answer: Drawing from any responses you have, narrow answers down to as few as possible, then make an educated guess.
   b. Questions for which you feel you should be getting the correct answer: Mark the question for review. Your mental block may clear, or you may spot a simple error in logic that will be corrected when you rereview the question.

9. Remember: **Never** change a first impulse answer later unless you are absolutely certain you are right. It is a proven fact that your subconscious often guides you to the correct answer.
10. Begin the tasked-based simulations, carefully monitoring your time. Read the information and requirement tabs and organize your thoughts around the concepts, mnemonics, acronyms, and buzzwords that are responsive to the requirements. Constantly compare your progress with the time remaining. Fight the urge to **complete** one simulation at the expense of others.
11. Each test may include a simulation requirement or question for which you may feel unprepared. Accept the challenge and go after the points! Draw from all your resources. Ask yourself how GAAP would be applied to similar situations, scan the simulation questions for clues, look for relationships in **all** the available resources given in the problem, try "backing into" the question from another angle, etc. Every simulation (no matter how impossible it may look at first glance) contains some points that are yours for the taking. Make your best effort. You may be on the right track and not even know it!
12. Constantly compare your progress with the time remaining. Never spend excessive amounts of time on one testlet or simulation.
13. The cardinal rule is **never,** but **never,** leave an answer blank.

After taking the examination

1. Retain the Confirmation of Attendance form issued after the examination because it provides valuable contact information.

2. Report any examination incidents/concerns in writing, even if the issues were already reported to test center staff.

3. If you feel that the circumstances surrounding your test administration prevented you from performing at a level consistent with your knowledge and skills, immediately contact NASBA at candidatecare@nasba.org.

HAVE YOU MADE YOUR COMMITMENT?

Chapter 5: Exam Content Overview

This chapter is written to help you review intermediate and advanced accounting (financial accounting) for the Financial Accounting and Reporting section of the exam. The AICPA Content Specification Outline of financial accounting coverage appears below.

The chapter is organized along the lines of the traditional intermediate and advanced accounting texts. The topics are arranged per the fourteen financial modules (on the previous pages). The objective is to provide you with the basic concepts, journal entries, and formulas for each topic and subtopic. Hopefully you will be able to expand, adapt, and apply the basics to specific problem situations as presented in multiple-choice questions and simulations appearing on the CPA exam. Keep in mind the importance of working questions and simulations under exam conditions as you study the basics set forth in this chapter. Refer to the multiple-choice questions, problems, and simulation problems on each of the financial accounting topics.

As you work through this chapter, remember that there are many possible series of journal entries and account titles that can be used in accounting for a specific type of economic transaction (e.g., long-term construction contracts). Reconcile the approach illustrated in the chapter with the approach you studied as an undergraduate per your intermediate or advanced text.

In this chapter, you will be referred frequently to the authoritative literature. As of July 1, 2009, the FASB Accounting Standards Codification is the single source of all US GAAP, except for the SEC authoritative literature. Task-based research simulations test research using the Accounting Standards Codification beginning in 2011.

AICPA CONTENT AND SKILLS SPECIFICATION

The AICPA Content and Skills Specifications for the Uniform CPA Exam set forth the coverage of topics on the Financial Accounting and Reporting exam. This outline was issued by the AICPA and is effective beginning in 2013. The first part of the outline describes the topical coverage of the Financial Accounting and Reporting exam, and the second part provides some insights into the skills tested on all sections of the Uniform CPA exam.

Content Specification Outlines (CSOs)

The Financial Accounting and Reporting section tests knowledge and understanding of the financial reporting framework used by business enterprises, not-for-profit organizations, and governmental entities. The financial reporting frameworks that are included in this section are those issued by the standard setters identified in the references to these CSOs, which include standards issued by the Financial Accounting Standards Board, the International Accounting Standards Board, the US Securities and Exchange Commission, and the Governmental Accounting Standards Board.

In addition to demonstrating knowledge and understanding of accounting principles, candidates are required to demonstrate the skills required to apply that knowledge in performing financial reporting and other tasks as certified public accountants. To demonstrate such knowledge and skills, candidates will be expected to perform the following tasks:

- Identify and understand the differences between financial statements prepared on the basis of accounting principles generally accepted in the United States of America (US GAAP) and International Financial Reporting Standards (IFRS).
- Prepare and/or review source documents including account classification, and enter data into subsidiary and general ledgers.
- Calculate amounts for financial statement components.
- Reconcile the general ledger to the subsidiary ledgers or underlying account details.
- Prepare account reconciliation and related schedules; analyze accounts for unusual fluctuations and make necessary adjustments.
- Prepare consolidating and eliminating entries for the period.
- Identify financial accounting and reporting methods and select those that are appropriate.
- Prepare consolidated financial statements, including balance sheets, income statements, and statements of retained earnings, equity, comprehensive income, and cash flows.
- Prepare appropriate notes to the financial statements.
- Analyze financial statements including analysis of accounts, variances, trends, and ratios.
- Exercise judgment in the application of accounting principles.
- Apply judgment to evaluate assumptions and methods underlying estimates, including fair value measures of financial statement components.
- Produce required financial statement filings in order to meet regulatory or reporting requirements (e.g. Form 10-Q, 10-K, Annual Report).
- Determine appropriate accounting treatment for new or unusual transactions and evaluate the economic substance of transactions in making the determinations.
- Research relevant professional literature.

The outline below specifies the knowledge in which candidates are required to demonstrate proficiency:

I. **Conceptual Framework, Standards, Standard Setting, and Presentation of Financial Statements (17%–23%)**

   A. Process by Which Accounting Standards Are Set and Roles of Accounting Standard-Setting Bodies

     1. US Securities and Exchange Commission (SEC)
     2. Financial Accounting Standards Board (FASB)
     3. International Accounting Standards Board (IASB)
     4. Governmental Accounting Standards Board (GASB)

   B. Conceptual Framework

     1. Financial reporting by business entities
     2. Financial reporting by not-for-profit (nongovernmental) entities
     3. Financial reporting by state and local governmental entities

   C. Financial Reporting, Presentation and Disclosures in General-Purpose Financial Statements

     1. Balance sheet
     2. Income statement
     3. Statement of comprehensive income
     4. Statement of changes in equity
     5. Statement of cash flows
     6. Notes to financial statements
     7. Consolidated and combined financial statements
     8. First-time adoption of IFRS

   D. SEC Reporting Requirements (e.g. Form 10-Q, 10-K)

   E. Other Financial Statement Presentations, Including Other Comprehensive Bases of Accounting (OCBOA)

     1. Cash basis
     2. Modified cash basis
     3. Income tax basis
     4. Personal financial statements
     5. Financial statements of employee benefit plans/trusts

II. **Financial Statement Accounts: Recognition, Measurement, Valuation, Calculation, Presentation, and Disclosures (27%–33%)**

   A. Cash and Cash Equivalents
   B. Receivables
   C. Inventory
   D. Property, Plant, and Equipment
   E. Investments

     1. Financial assets at fair value through profit or loss
     2. Available-for-sale financial assets
     3. Held-to-maturity investments
     4. Joint ventures

     5. Equity method investments (investments in associates)
     6. Investment property

   F. Intangible Assets—Goodwill and Other
   G. Payables and Accrued Liabilities
   H. Deferred Revenue
   I. Long-Term Debt (Financial Liabilities)

     1. Notes payable
     2. Bonds payable
     3. Debt with conversion features and other options
     4. Modifications and extinguishments
     5. Troubled debt restructurings by debtors
     6. Debt covenant compliance

   J. Equity
   K. Revenue Recognition
   L. Costs and Expenses
   M. Compensation and Benefits

     1. Compensated absences
     2. Deferred compensation arrangements
     3. Nonretirement postemployment benefits
     4. Retirement benefits
     5. Stock compensation (share-based payments)

   N. Income Taxes

III. **Specific Transactions, Events and Disclosures: Recognition, Measurement, Valuation, Calculation, Presentation, and Disclosures (27%–33%)**

   A. Accounting Changes and Error Corrections
   B. Asset Retirement and Environmental Obligations
   C. Business Combinations
   D. Consolidation (Including Off-Balance Sheet Transactions, Variable-Interest Entities and Non-controlling Interests)
   E. Contingencies, Commitments, and Guarantees (Provisions)
   F. Earnings Per Share
   G. Exit or Disposal Activities and Discontinued Operations
   H. Extraordinary and Unusual Items
   I. Fair Value Measurements, Disclosures, and Reporting
   J. Derivatives and Hedge Accounting
   K. Foreign Currency Transactions and Translation
   L. Impairment
   M. Interim Financial Reporting
   N. Leases
   O. Distinguishing Liabilities from Equity
   P. Nonmonetary Transactions (Barter Transactions)
   Q. Related Parties and Related Party Transactions
   R. Research and Development Costs
   S. Risks and Uncertainties
   T. Segment Reporting
   U. Software Costs
   V. Subsequent Events
   W. Transfers and Servicing of Financial Assets and Derecognition

IV.Governmental Accounting and Reporting (8%–12%)

  A. Governmental Accounting Concepts

    1. Measurement focus and basis of accounting
    2. Fund accounting concepts and applications
    3. Budgetary accounting

  B. Format and Content of Comprehensive Annual Financial Report (CAFR)

    1. Government-wide financial statements
    2. Governmental funds financial statements
    3. Proprietary funds financial statements
    4. Fiduciary funds financial statements
    5. Notes to financial statements
    6. Management's discussion and analysis
    7. Required supplementary information (RSI) other than Management's Discussion and Analysis
    8. Combining statements and individual fund statements and schedules
    9. Deriving government-wide financial statements and reconciliation requirements

  C. Financial Reporting Entity, Including Blended and Discrete Component Units

  D. Typical Items and Specific Types of Transactions and Events: Recognition, Measurement, Valuation, Calculation, and Presentation in Governmental Entity Financial Statements

    1. Net position and components thereof
    2. Fund balances and components thereof

    3. Capital assets and infrastructure assets
    4. General long-term liabilities
    5. Interfund activity, including transfers
    6. Nonexchange revenue transactions
    7. Expenditures
    8. Special items
    9. Encumbrances

  E. Accounting and Reporting for Governmental Not-for-Profit Organizations

V. Not-for-Profit (Nongovernmental) Accounting and Reporting (8%–12%)

  A. Financial Statements

    1. Statement of financial position
    2. Statement of activities
    3. Statement of cash flows
    4. Statement of functional expenses

  B. Typical Items and Specific Types of Transactions and Events: Recognition, Measurement, Valuation, Calculation, and Presentation in Financial Statements of Not-for-Profit Organizations

    1. Support, revenues, and contributions
    2. Types of restrictions on resources
    3. Types of net assets
    4. Expenses, including depreciation and functional expenses
    5. Investments

References—Financial Accounting and Reporting

- Financial Accounting Standards Board (FASB) Accounting Standards Codification
- Governmental Accounting Standards Board (GASB) Codification of Governmental Accounting and Financial Reporting Standards
- Standards Issued by the US Securities and Exchange Commission (SEC):

  - Regulation S-X of the Code of Federal Regulations (17 CFR Part 210)
  - Financial Reporting Releases (FRR)/Accounting Series Releases (ASR)
  - Interpretive Releases (IR)
  - SEC Staff Guidance in Staff Accounting Bulletins (SAB)
  - SEC Staff Guidance in EITF Topic D and SEC Staff Observer Comments
  - Regulation S-K of the Code of Federal Regulations

- International Accounting Standards Board (IASB) International Financial Reporting Standards (IFRS), International Accounting Standards (IAS), and Interpretations
- AICPA Auditing and Accounting Guides
- Codification of Statements on Auditing Standards

  - AU Section 623, Special Reports

- Current textbooks on accounting for business enterprises, not-for-profit organizations, and governmental entities
- FASB Concept Statements
- GASB Concept Statements
- IFRS Framework

Skill Specification Outlines (SSOs)

The Skill Specification Outlines (SSOs) identify the skills to be tested on the Uniform CPA Examination. There are three categories of skills, and the weightings will be implemented through the use of different question formats in the exam. For each of the question formats, a different set of tools will be available as resources to the candidates, who will need to use those tools to demonstrate proficiency in the applicable skills categories.

Weights

The percentage range assigned to each skill category will be used to determine the quantity of each type of question, as described below. The percentage range assigned to each skill category represents the approximate percentage to which that category of skills will be used in the different sections of the CPA Examination to assess proficiency. The ranges are designed to provide flexibility in building the examination, and the midpoints of the ranges for each section total 100%. No percentages are given for the bulleted descriptions included in these definitions. The presence of several groups within an area or several topics within a group does not imply equal importance or weight will be given to these bullets on an examination.

Skills Category	Weights (FAR, REG, AUD)	Weights (BEC)
Knowledge and Understanding	50%–60%	80%–90%
Application of the Body of Knowledge	40%–50%	—
Written Communication	—	10%–20%

Knowledge and Understanding. Multiple-choice questions will be used as the proxy for assessing knowledge and understanding and will be based upon the content topics as outlined in the CSOs. Candidates will not have access to the authoritative literature, spreadsheets, or database tools while answering these questions. A calculator will be accessible for the candidates to use in performing calculations to demonstrate their understanding of the principles or subject matter.

Application of the Body of Knowledge. Task-based simulations will be used as the proxy for assessing application of the body of knowledge and will be based upon the content topics as outlined in the CSOs. Candidates will have access to the authoritative literature, a calculator, spreadsheets, and other resources and tools which they will use to demonstrate proficiency in applying the body of knowledge.

Written Communication will be assessed through the use of responses to essay questions, which will be based upon the content topics as outlined in the CSOs. Candidates will have access to a word processor, which includes a spell-check feature.

Outlines

The outlines below provide additional descriptions of the skills that are represented in each category.

Knowledge and Understanding. Expertise and skills developed through learning processes, recall, and reading comprehension. Knowledge is acquired through experience or education and is the theoretical or practical understanding of a subject; knowledge is also represented through awareness or familiarity with information gained by experience of a fact or situation. Understanding represents a higher level than simple knowledge and is the process of using concepts to deal adequately with given situations, facts, or circumstances. Understanding is the ability to recognize and comprehend the meaning of a particular concept.

Application of the Body of Knowledge, Including Analysis, Judgment, Synthesis, Evaluation, and Research. Higher-level cognitive skills that require individuals to act or transform knowledge in some fashion. These skills are inextricably intertwined and thus are grouped into this single skill area.

- Assess the Business Environment

  - Business Process Evaluation: Assessing and integrating information regarding a business's operational structure, functions, processes, and procedures to develop a broad operational perspective; identify the need for new systems or changes to existing systems and/or processes.
  - Contextual Evaluation: Assessing and integrating information regarding client's type of business or industry.
  - Strategic Analysis—Understanding the Business: Obtaining, assessing and integrating information on the entity's strategic objectives, strategic management process, business environment, the nature of and value to customers, its products and services, extent of competition within its market space, etc.).
  - Business Risk Assessment: Obtaining, assessing and integrating information on conditions and events that could impede the entity's ability to achieve strategic objectives.
  - Visualize Abstract Descriptions: Organize and process symbols, pictures, graphs, objects, and other information.

- Research

  - Identify the appropriate research question.
  - Identify key search terms for use in performing electronic searches through large volumes of data.
  - Search through large volumes of electronic data to find required information.
  - Organize information or data from multiple sources.
  - Integrate diverse sources of information to reach conclusions or make decisions.
  - Identify the appropriate authoritative guidance in applicable financial reporting frameworks and auditing standards for the accounting issue being evaluated.

- Application of Technology

  - Using electronic spreadsheets to perform calculations, financial analysis, or other functions to analyze data.
  - Integration of technological applications and resources into work processes.
  - Using a variety of computer software and hardware systems to structure, utilize, and manage data.

- Analysis

  - Review information to determine compliance with specified standards or criteria.
  - Use expectations, empirical data, and analytical methods to determine trends and variances.
  - Perform appropriate calculations on financial and nonfinancial data.
  - Recognize patterns of activity when reviewing large amounts of data or recognize breaks in patterns.
  - Interpretation of financial statement data for a given evaluation purpose.
  - Forecasting future financial statement data from historical financial statement data and other information.
  - Integrating primary financial statements: using data from all primary financial statements to uncover financial transactions, inconsistencies, or other information.

- Complex Problem Solving and Judgment

  - Develop and understand goals, objectives, and strategies for dealing with potential issues, obstacles, or opportunities.
  - Analyze patterns of information and contextual factors to identify potential problems and their implications.
  - Devise and implement a plan of action appropriate for a given problem.
  - Apply professional skepticism, which is an attitude that includes a questioning mind and a critical assessment of information or evidence obtained.
  - Adapt strategies or planned actions in response to changing circumstances.
  - Identify and solve unstructured problems.
  - Develop reasonable hypotheses to answer a question or resolve a problem.
  - Formulate and examine alternative solutions in terms of their relative strengths and weaknesses, level of risk, and appropriateness for a given situation.
  - Develop creative ways of thinking about situations, problems, and opportunities to create insightful and sound solutions.
  - Develop logical conclusions through the use of inductive and deductive reasoning.
  - Apply knowledge of professional standards and laws, as well as legal, ethical, and regulatory issues.
  - Assess the need for consultations with other professionals when gray areas, or areas requiring specialized knowledge, are encountered.

- Decision Making

  - Specify goals and constraints.
  - Generate alternatives.
  - Consider risks.
  - Evaluate and select the best alternative.

- Organization, Efficiency, and Effectiveness

  - Use time effectively and efficiently.
  - Develop detailed work plans, schedule tasks and meetings, and delegate assignments and tasks.
  - Set priorities by determining the relevant urgency or importance of tasks and deciding the order in which they should be performed.
  - File and store information so that it can be found easily and used effectively.

Written Communication. The various skills involved in preparing written communication, including

- Basic writing mechanics, such as grammar, spelling, word usage, punctuation, and sentence structure.
- Effective business writing principles, including organization, clarity, and conciseness.
- Exchange technical information and ideas with coworkers and other professionals to meet goals of job assignment.
- Documentation:

  - Prepare documents and presentations that are concise, accurate, and supportive of the subject matter.
  - Document and cross-reference work performed and conclusions reached in a complete and accurate manner.

- Assist client to recognize and understand implications of critical business issues by providing recommendations and informed opinions.
- Persuade others to take recommended courses of action.
- Follow directions.

RESEARCHING FASB ACCOUNTING STANDARDS

Research components of simulations in the Financial Accounting and Reporting section will involve a research database. Beginning in 2011, that database will be the FASB Accounting Standards Codification (ASC)

Database Searching

Searching a database consists of the following five steps:

1. Define the issue. What is the research question to be answered?
2. Choose appropriate search technique. Select keywords that will locate the needed information or use the table of contents.
3. Execute the search. Enter the keyword(s) or click on the table of contents item and complete the search.
4. Evaluate the results. Evaluate the research to see if an answer has been found. If not, try a new search.
5. Select an answer by clicking on one of the citations provided in the answer selections on the right-hand side of the screen.

Advanced Searches

The advanced search screen allows you to use Boolean concepts to perform more precise searches. Examples of searches that can be performed in the advanced search mode include

1. Containing all these words—Allows you to retrieve sections that contain two or more specified words.
2. Not containing any of these words—Allows you to retrieve sections that do not contain specific words.
3. Containing one or more of these words—Allows you to retrieve sections that contain any one or more of the specified words.
4. Containing these words near each other—Allows you to retrieve sections that contain words near to each other.

The advanced search also allows you to select options for the search. One alternative allows you to retrieve alternative word terms. For example, using this approach with a search on the word "cost" would also retrieve sections containing the word "costing." A synonyms option allows you to retrieve sections that contain words that mean the same as the specified word. You also have the option to only search on the selected sections of the literature.

FINANCIAL ACCOUNTING AND REPORTING

As indicated previously, this manual consists of 14 modules designed to facilitate your study for the Financial Accounting and Reporting section of the Uniform CPA Examination. The table of contents at the right describes the content of each module.

Module 9: Basic Theory and Financial Reporting

Overview

This module covers **basic concepts** such as the conceptual framework and revenue recognition, **error correction** such as counterbalancing and classification errors, **accounting changes** such as changes in principle and changes in estimates, and **financial statements** such as the income statement and balance sheet.

US GAAP is the basis for financial reporting but it does not constitute a cohesive body of accounting theory. Concept Statements were issued to provide a theoretical framework for accounting standard development and a basis for financial reporting.

As of July 1, 2009, the Accounting Standards Codification (ASC) became the single source for US GAAP. **The relevant Accounting Standards Codification topic is indicated in the discussion with a cross-reference to the previous accounting literature (i.e., ARB, APB, SFAS, and SFAC).** Appendix A of this text includes an outline of the pre-Codification standards with a cross reference to the appropriate Codification topics to help candidates transition to the FASB's Accounting Standards Codification. Note these outlines appear in the following sequence: ARB, APB, SFAS, and SFAC. Turn to each outline as directed and study the outline while reviewing the related journal entries, computations, etc.

The AICPA began testing International Financial Reporting Standards (IFRS) on January 1, 2011. Coverage of international standards and outlines of the differences between US GAAP and IFRS are located at the end of each module.

A. Basic Concepts

Basic concepts include theory, income determination, accruals, deferrals, and revenue recognition.

1. Basic Accounting Theory

Effective July 1, 2009, the FASB's Accounting Standards Codification became the single source of US GAAP for nongovernmental entities.

a. The Accounting Standards Codification (ASC) replaced all previously issued non-SEC accounting literature. The Codification did not change GAAP, but merely restructured the existing accounting standards to provide one cohesive set of accounting standards.

(1) Included in the Codification is all GAAP, as well as relevant literature issued by the SEC.
(2) The FASB issues Accounting Standards Updates (ASUs) to update the Codification.

> **NOTE:** To help the CPA candidate transition to the Accounting Standards Codification, the Codification citation is shown first, and the cross-reference to previous GAAP citations are shown in parentheses.

b. Theory can be defined as a coherent set of hypothetical, conceptual, and pragmatic principles forming a general frame of reference for a field of inquiry; thus, accounting theory should be the basic principles of accounting rather than its practice (which GAAP describes or dictates).

(1) Although GAAP is the current basis for financial reporting, it does not constitute a cohesive body of accounting theory. Generally, authoritative pronouncements have been the result of a problem-by-problem approach that have dealt with specific problems as they occur and are not predicated on an underlying body of theory.

(2) Accounting has a definite need for conceptual theoretical structure if an authoritative body such as the FASB is to promulgate consistent standards.

(3) A body of accounting theory should be the foundation of the standard-setting process and should provide guidance where no authoritative GAAP exists.

(4) The FASB issued concept statements to develop a theoretical framework. As of December 2011, the FASB had issued eight concept statements to develop a frame of reference.

    (a) The purpose of the concept statements is "to set forth objectives and fundamental concepts that will be the basis for development of financial accounting and reporting guidance" (SFAC 8). In other words, the SFAC attempt to organize a framework that can serve as a reference point in formulating financial accounting standards.

> **NOTE:** The SFAC do not constitute authoritative GAAP and therefore are not part of the Codification.

    (b) Three concept statements have been superseded by other concept statements: SFAC 1 and SFAC 2 were superseded by SFAC 8, and SFAC 3 was superseded by SFAC 6. The remaining concept statements are as follows: SFAC 4, *Objectives of Financial Reporting of Nonbusiness Organizations*; SFAC 5, *Recognition and Measurement in Financial Statements*; SFAC 6, *Elements of Financial Statements*; SFAC 7, *Using Cash Flow Information and Present Value in Accounting Measurements*; and SFAC 8, *Conceptual Framework for Financial Reporting*.

    (c) SFAC 8 is the most recent attempt to develop accounting theory as a joint project between the FASB and the International Accounting Standards Board (IASB).

        1] SFAC 8 contains two chapters of the revised conceptual framework and replaces SFACs 1 and 2.

            a] Chapter 1, The Objective of General-Purpose Financial Reporting replaces SFAC 1.
            b] Chapter 3, Qualitative Characteristics of Useful Financial Information, replaces SFAC 2.

    (d) As additional phases of the joint project between the FASB and the IASB are completed, the revised concept statements will be included as new chapters to SFAC 8.

c. **Financial Reporting.** "The objective of general-purpose financial reporting is to provide financial information about the reporting entity that is useful to existing and potential investors, lenders, and other creditors in making decisions about providing resources to the entity" (SFAC 8).

> **NOTE:** Not all informational needs are met by accounting or financial reporting.

(1) The following diagram from SFAC 5 describes the information spectrum.

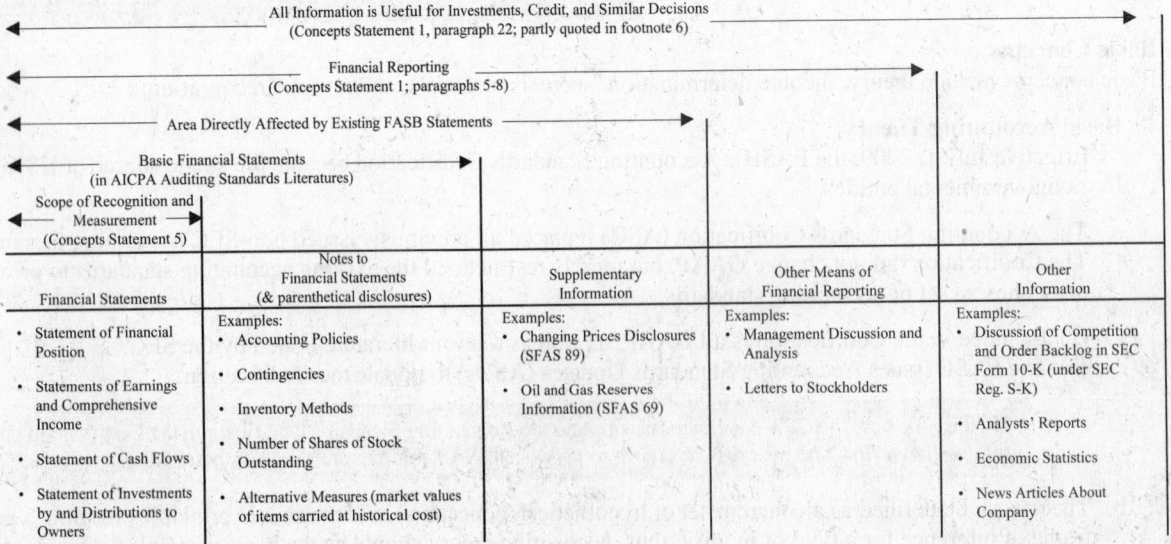

Financial Statements	Notes to Financial Statements (& parenthetical disclosures)	Supplementary Information	Other Means of Financial Reporting	Other Information
• Statement of Financial Position	Examples: • Accounting Policies	Examples: • Changing Prices Disclosures (SFAS 89)	Examples: • Management Discussion and Analysis	Examples: • Discussion of Competition and Order Backlog in SEC Form 10-K (under SEC Reg. S-K)
• Statements of Earnings and Comprehensive Income	• Contingencies	• Oil and Gas Reserves Information (SFAS 69)	• Letters to Stockholders	• Analysts' Reports
• Statement of Cash Flows	• Inventory Methods			• Economic Statistics
• Statement of Investments by and Distributions to Owners	• Number of Shares of Stock Outstanding			• News Articles About Company
	• Alternative Measures (market values of items carried at historical cost)			

* The SFAC 5 diagram has not been updated to reflect the issuance of SFAC 8.

d. **Components of the Conceptual Framework.** The components of the conceptual framework for financial accounting and reporting include objectives, qualitative characteristics, elements, recognition, measurement, financial statements, earnings, funds flow, and liquidity.

(1) The relationship between these components is illustrated in the following diagram from *Financial Statements and Other Means of Financial Reporting*, a FASB Invitation to Comment.

   (a) In the diagram below, components to the left are more basic and those to the right depend on components to their left. Components are closely related to those above or below them.
   (b) The most basic component of the conceptual framework is the objectives.

      1] The objectives underlie the other phases and are derived from the needs of those for whom financial information is intended.
      2] The objectives provide a focal point for financial reporting by identifying what types of information are relevant.

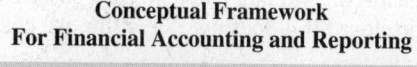

**Conceptual Framework
For Financial Accounting and Reporting**

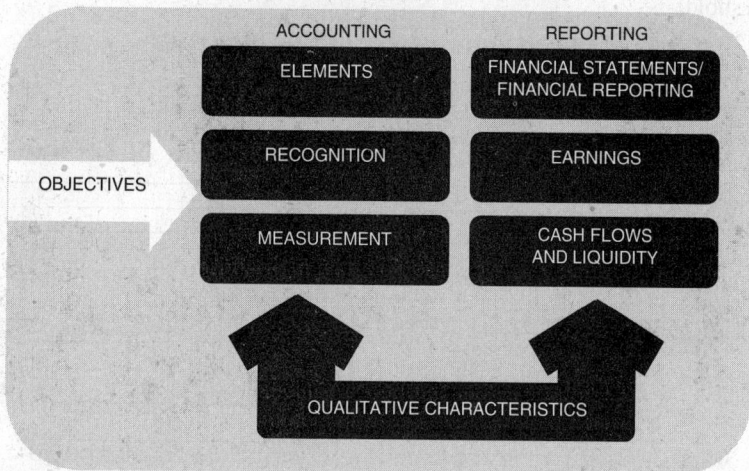

   (c) The qualitative characteristics also underlie most of the other phases.

      1] They are the criteria to be used in choosing and evaluating accounting and reporting policies.

   (d) Elements of financial statements are the components from which financial statements are created. They include assets, liabilities, equity, investments by owners, distributions to owners, comprehensive income, revenues, expenses, gains, and losses.
   (e) In order to be included in financial statements, an element must meet criteria for recognition and possess an attribute which is relevant and can be reliably measured.
   (f) Finally, reporting and display considerations are concerned with what information should be provided, who should provide it, and where it should be displayed.
   (g) How the financial statements (financial position, earnings, and cash flow) are presented is the focal point of this part of the conceptual framework project.

(2) **Objectives of Financial Reporting.** (See outline of SFAC 8, Chapter 1.) The objectives of general-purpose financial reporting focus on users of financial information.

   (a) The primary users of financial reporting are investors, lenders, and other creditors who must rely on reporting entities to provide information to them.

      1] Although management is also interested in financial information, management does not rely on general-purpose reports because information can be obtained internally.
      2] In addition, although other parties such as regulators and members of the public may use financial information, they are not considered primary users according to SFAC 8.

   (b) SFAC 8, Chapter 1, states that the objective of financial reporting is to provide

      1] Information that is useful to potential and existing investors, lenders, and other creditors (primary users)
      2] Information about the reporting entity's economic resources and claims against the reporting entity
      3] Changes in economic resources and claims
      4] Financial performance reflected by accrual accounting

5] Financial performance reflected by past cash flow

6] Changes in economic resources and claims not resulting from financial performance

(3) **Qualitative Characteristics.** (See outline of SFAC 8, Chapter 3.) The qualitative characteristics also underlie the conceptual framework, but in a different way. While the objectives provide an overall basis, the qualitative characteristics establish criteria for selecting and evaluating accounting alternatives which will meet the objectives. In other words, information must possess the qualitative characteristics if that information is to fulfill the objectives.

(a) SFAC 8 views these characteristics as a hierarchy of accounting qualities, as represented in the diagram below.

1] The diagram below reveals many important relationships. At the top is the cost-benefit constraint. If the benefits of information do not exceed the costs of providing that information, it would not be reported. At the bottom of the diagram is the materiality threshold. An item that is not material is not required to be disclosed. Although an item may possess the other qualitative characteristics for disclosure, it is not disclosed if it does not fall within the cost-benefit constraint or the materiality threshold.

A HIERARCHY OF ACCOUNTING QUALITIES

Primary Users of Accounting Information	Existing and Potential Investors, Lendors, and other Creditors

Pervasive Constraint —————————————————————
————————————— Benefits > Costs —————————————

Decision Usefulness

Fundamental Qualitative Characteristics	Relevance	←————————→	Faithful Representation

| Predictive Value | Confirmatory Value | | Complete | Neutral | Free from Error |

Enhancing Qualitative Characteristics

| Comparability (consistency helps achieve comparability) | | Verifiability | Timeliness | Understandability |

Threshold for Recognition —————————————— Materiality ——————————————
(Entity-specific and related to relevance)

(b) The two fundamental qualitative characteristics of accounting information are relevance and faithful representation.

1] Relevant information is capable of making a difference in a user's decision. Financial information is relevant if it has predictive value, confirmatory value, or both.

a] **Predictive value** requires that information be used to predict future outcomes.

b] **Confirmatory value** requires that information either confirms or changes prior evaluations.

c] An item is material if omitting it or misstating it could influence a user's decision. Therefore, the materiality threshold relates to the qualitative characteristic of relevance.

2] Information has the quality of **faithful representation** if the information depicts what it purports to represent. A faithful representation should be complete, neutral, and free from error.

a] Completeness requires that information is presented or depicted in a way that users can understand the item being depicted.

b] Neutrality requires that the item is depicted without bias either favorably or unfavorably to users.

c] Free from error means that there are no errors or omissions in the information reported.

(c) The enhancing qualitative characteristics of accounting information are comparability, verifiability, timeliness, and understandability.

    1] **Comparability** enables users to identify and understand similarities and differences between items.

        a] Consistency refers to the use of the same accounting methods in different periods. Consistency, therefore, helps achieve comparability because it helps the user make comparisons across different time periods.

    2] **Verifiability** occurs when different sources reach consensus or agreement on an amount of representation of an item. Direct verification occurs through direct observation; indirect verification occurs by using techniques such as checking formulas or recalculating amounts. Although forward-looking information cannot be verified, the underlying assumptions, methods, facts, and circumstances can be disclosed to help users determine if the information is useful.

    3] **Timelines** requires that information is available to a decision maker when it is useful to make the decision.

    4] **Understandability** involves classifying, characterizing, and presenting information clearly and concisely. Understandability assumes that a user has a reasonable knowledge of business and economic activities to comprehend financial reports.

(4) **Basic Elements.** (See outline of SFAC 6.) Elements of financial statements are the ten basic building blocks from which financial statements are constructed. These definitions are based upon the objectives of SFAC 8. They are intended to assure that users will receive decision-useful information about enterprise resources (assets), claims to those resources (liabilities and equity), and changes therein (the other seven elements). In order to be included in the statements, an item must qualify as an element, meet recognition criteria, and be measurable.

(a) The meaning of financial statement elements depends on the conceptual view of earnings which is adopted. Two basic views are the asset-liability view and the revenue-expense view.

    1] Under the **asset-liability view**, earnings are measured by the change (other than investments or withdrawals) in the net economic resources of an enterprise during a period. Therefore, definitions of assets and liabilities are the key under this view, and definitions of revenues, expenses, gains, and losses are secondary and are based on assets and liabilities.

    2] The **revenue-expense view** holds that earnings are a measure of an enterprise's effectiveness in using its inputs to obtain and sell outputs. Thus, definitions of revenues and expenses are basic to this view, and definitions of assets, liabilities, and other elements are derived from revenues and expenses.

(b) The definitions of all ten elements are contained in the outline of SFAC 6. Let us examine one definition in more detail.

EXAMPLE

"Assets are probable future economic benefits obtained or controlled by a particular entity as a result of past transactions or events." This definition is based on the objectives and qualities of SFAC 8. The overall thrust of the objectives—predicting and evaluating future cash flows—is reflected in the phrase "probable future economic benefits." "Control by a particular entity" is crucial if reporting an item as an asset is to have decision usefulness (or relevance). The quality of reliability is assured by the phrase "as a result of past transactions." Information is more verifiable, valid, and neutral (the components of reliability) if based on past transactions. A similar analysis can be applied to liabilities, equity, investments by owners, distributions to owners, comprehensive income, revenues; expenses, gains and losses.

(c) SFAC 6 also defines some other concepts in addition to the ten elements. Especially important among these eleven additional concepts are accrual accounting, realization, recognition, and matching.

    1] Realization and recognition are addressed by the FASB in SFAC 5.

    2] The definition of accrual accounting is important because SFAC 8 stated that accrual accounting should be used since it provides a better indication of future cash flows than the cash basis. This is true because accrual accounting records transactions with cash consequences (involving future cash flows) as they occur, not when the cash actually moves.

    3] Matching is referred to in most accounting literature as a principle, or fundamental law, of accounting.

(5) **Recognition and Measurement.** (See outline of SFAC 5.) Recognition principles establish criteria concerning when an element should be included in the statements, while measurement principles govern the valuation of those elements.

(a) SFAC 5 established four fundamental recognition criteria: definitions, measurability, relevance, and reliability. If an item meets the definition of an element, can be reliably measured, is capable of making a difference in user decisions, and is verifiable, neutral, and representationally faithful, it should be included in the financial statements.

(b) Five different attributes are used to measure assets and liabilities in present practice. These are discussed below in an excerpt from SFAC 5.

    1] **Historical cost (historical proceeds).** Property, plant, and equipment and most inventories are reported at their historical cost, which is the amount of cash, or its equivalent, paid to acquire an asset, commonly adjusted after acquisition for amortization or other allocations. Liabilities that involve obligations to provide goods or services to customers are generally reported at historical proceeds, which is the amount of cash, or its equivalent, received when the obligation was incurred and may be adjusted after acquisition for amortization or other allocations.

    2] **Current cost.** Some inventories are reported at their current (replacement) cost, which is the amount of cash, or its equivalent, that would have to be paid if the same or an equivalent asset were acquired currently.

    3] **Current market value.** Some investments in marketable securities are reported at their current market value, which is the amount of cash or its equivalent, that could be obtained by selling an asset in orderly liquidation. Current market value is also generally used for assets expected to be sold at prices lower than previous carrying amounts. Some liabilities that involve marketable commodities and securities, for example, the obligations of writers of options or sellers of common shares who do not own the underlying commodities or securities, are reported at current market value. Current market value is now referred to as fair value.

    4] **Net realizable (settlement) value.** Short-term receivables and some inventories are reported at their net realizable value, which is the nondiscounted amount of cash, or its equivalent, into which an asset is expected to be converted in due course of business less direct costs, if any, necessary to make that conversion. Liabilities that involve known or estimated amounts of money payable at unknown future dates, for example, trade payables or warranty obligations, generally are reported at their net settlement value, which is the nondiscounted amount of cash, or its equivalent, expected to be paid to liquidate an obligation in the due course of business, including direct costs, if any, necessary to make that payment.

    5] **Present (or discounted) value of future cash flows.** Long-term receivables are reported at their present or discounted value (discounted at the implicit or historical rate), which is the present value of future cash inflows into which an asset is expected to be converted in due course of business less present values of cash outflows necessary to obtain those inflows. Long-term payables are similarly reported at their present or discounted value (discounted at the implicit or historical rate), which is the present or discounted value of future cash outflows expected to be required to satisfy the liability in due course of business.

(c) SFAC 5 states that each of these attributes is appropriate in different situations and that all five attributes will continue to be used in the future.

(d) Similarly, SFAC 5 states that nominal units of money will continue to be the measurement unit. However, if inflation increases to a level where the FASB feels that financial statements become too distorted, another unit (such as units of constant purchasing power) could be adopted.

(e) SFAC 5 is based on the concept of financial capital maintenance. Two basic concepts of capital maintenance (financial and physical) can be used to separate return **on** capital (earnings) from return **of** capital (capital recovery). Remember, any capital which is "used up" during a period must be returned before earnings can be recognized. In other words, earnings is the amount an entity can distribute to its owners and be as well-off at the end of the year as at the beginning.

    1] One way "well-offness" can be measured is in terms of *financial capital.* This concept of capital maintenance holds that the capital to be maintained is measured by the amount of cash (possibly restated into constant dollars) invested by owners. Earnings may not be recognized until the dollar investment in net assets, measured in units of money or purchasing power, is returned. The financial capital maintenance concept is the traditional view which is reflected in most present financial statements.

    2] An alternative definition of "well-offness" is expressed in terms of *physical capital.* This concept holds that the capital to be maintained is the physical productive capacity of the enterprise. Earnings may not be recognized until the current replacement costs of assets with the same productive capabilities of the assets used up are returned. The physical capital maintenance concept supports current cost accounting. Again, the physical productive capacity may be measured in nominal or constant dollars.

EXAMPLE

Suppose an enterprise invests $10 in an inventory item. At year-end, the enterprise sells the item for $15. In order to replace the item at year-end, they would have to pay $12 rather than $10. To further simplify, assume the increase in replacement cost is due to specific price changes, and there is no general inflation.

The **financial capital** concept would maintain that the firm is as well-off once the dollar investment ($10) is returned. At that point, the financial capital is maintained and the remaining $5 is a return **on** capital, or income. The **physical capital** concept maintains that the firm is not as well-off until the physical capacity (a similar inventory item) is returned. Therefore, the firm must reinvest $12 to be as well-off. Then physical capital is maintained, and only the remaining $3 is a return **on** capital or income.

(f) SFAC 5 also gives specific guidance as to recognition of revenues and gains, and expenses and losses, as indicated below.

  1] Recognize **revenues** when realized or realizable (when related assets received or held are readily convertible to known amounts of cash or claims to cash) and earned
  2] Recognize **gains** when realized or realizable
  3] Recognize **expenses** when economic benefits are consumed in revenue-earning activities, or when future economic benefits are reduced or eliminated

    a] When economic benefits are consumed during a period, the expense may be recognized by matching (such as cost of goods sold), immediate recognition (such as selling and administrative salaries), or systematic and rational allocation (such as depreciation).

  4] Recognize **losses** when future economic benefits are reduced or eliminated

(g) Revenues, expenses, gains, and losses are used to compute **earnings**.

  1] Earnings is the extent to which revenues and gains associated with cash-to-cash cycles substantially completed during the period exceed expenses and losses directly or indirectly associated with those cycles.
  2] Earnings adjusted for cumulative accounting adjustments and other nonowner changes in equity (such as foreign currency translation adjustments) is **comprehensive income**.

    a] Per SFAC 5, comprehensive income would reflect all changes in the equity of an entity during a period, except investments by owners and distributions to owners. However, accounting standards only go part way in implementing this concept.

> **NOW REVIEW MULTIPLE-CHOICE QUESTIONS 1 THROUGH 17**

(6) **Cash Flow Information and Present Value.** (See outline of SFAC 7.) As discussed earlier, the attributes most often used to measure assets and liabilities include observable marketplace-determined amounts. These observable marketplace amounts (such as current cost) are generally more reliable and are determined more efficiently than measurements which employ estimates of future cash flows. However, when observable amounts are unavailable, accountants often turn to estimated cash flows to determine the carrying amount of an asset or liability. Since those cash flows often occur in one or more future periods, questions arise regarding whether the accounting measurement should reflect the present value or the undiscounted sum of those cash flows.

(a) In February 2000, the FASB issued SFAC 7, *Using Cash Flow Information and Present Value in Accounting Measurements.*

  1] SFAC 7 provides a framework for using future cash flows as the basis of an accounting measurement.

NOTE: SFAC 7 addresses measurement issues, not recognition questions.

EXAMPLE

SFAC 7 does not specify **when** fresh-start measurements are appropriate. Fresh-start measurements are defined by the FASB as measurements in periods following initial recognition that establish a new carrying amount unrelated to previous amounts and accounting conventions.

      2] SFAC 7 applies only to measurements at initial recognition, fresh-start measurements, and amortization techniques based on future cash flows.

      3] SFAC 7 does not apply to measurements based on the amount of cash or other assets paid or received, or on observation of fair values in the marketplace.

        a] If such observations or transactions are present, the measurement would be based on them, not on future cash flows. The marketplace assessment of present value is already embodied in the transaction price.

(b) The framework provides general principles governing the use of present value, especially when the amount of future cash flows, their timing, or both, are uncertain. The framework provided by SFAC 7 also describes the objective of present value in accounting measurements.

      1] The present value formula is a tool used to incorporate the time value of money in a measurement. Thus, it is useful in financial reporting whenever an item is measured using estimated future cash flows.

      2] The FASB defines present value as the current measure of an estimated future cash inflow or outflow, discounted at an interest rate for the number of periods between today and the date of the estimated cash flow.

      3] The objective of using present value in an accounting measurement is to capture, to the extent possible, the economic difference between sets of future cash flows.

(c) Assets with the same cash flows are distinguished from one another by the timing and uncertainty of those cash flows.

> **NOTE:** Accounting measurement based on undiscounted cash flows would measure assets with the same cash flows at the same amount.

EXAMPLE

An asset with a contractual cash flow of $28,000 due in ten days would be equal to an asset with an *expected* cash flow of $28,000 due in ten years.

      1] Present value helps to distinguish between cash flows that might otherwise appear similar.

      2] A present value measurement that incorporates the uncertainty in estimated cash flows always provides more relevant information than a measurement based on the undiscounted sum of those cash flows, or a discounted measurement that ignores uncertainty.

(d) To provide relevant information for financial reporting, present value must represent some observable measurement attribute of assets or liabilities. This attribute is fair value. Fair value is "the price that would be received to sell an asset or paid to transfer a liability in an orderly transaction between market participants at the measurement date under market conditions."

(e) **The only objective of present value, when used in accounting measurements at initial recognition and fresh-start measurements, is to estimate fair value.**

      1] In the absence of observed transaction prices, accounting measurements at initial recognition and fresh-start measurements should attempt to capture the elements that taken together would comprise a market price if one existed.

        a] Marketplace participants attribute prices to assets and liabilities. In doing so they distinguish the risks and rewards of one asset or liability from those of another. An observed market price encompasses the consensus view of all marketplace participants about an asset's or liability's utility, future cash flows, the uncertainties surrounding those cash flows, and the amount that marketplace participants demand for bearing those uncertainties.

        b] While the expectations of an entity's management are often useful and informative in estimating asset and liability values, the marketplace is the final judge of asset and liability values. An entity is required to pay the market's price when it acquires an asset or settles a liability in a current transaction, regardless of the intentions or expectations of the entity's management. Therefore, for measurements at initial recognition or for fresh-start measurements, fair value provides the most complete and representationally faithful measurement of the economic characteristics of an asset or a liability.

(f) A present value measurement that is able to capture the economic differences between various assets and liabilities would include the following elements according to SFAC 7:

1] An estimate of the future cash flow, or in more complex cases, series of future cash flows at different times.
2] Expectations about possible variations in the amount or timing of those cash flows.
3] The time value of money, represented by the risk-free rate of interest.
4] The price for bearing the uncertainty inherent in the asset or liability.
5] Other, sometimes unidentifiable factors, including illiquidity and market imperfections.

(g) SFAC 7 contrasts two approaches to computing present value. Either approach may be used to estimate the fair value of an asset or a liability, depending on the circumstances.

1] In the expected cash flow approach only the time value of money, represented by the risk-free rate of interest, is included in the discount rate; the other factors cause adjustments in arriving at risk-adjusted expected cash flows.
2] In a traditional approach to present value, adjustments for factors [2] – [5] are embedded in the discount rate.

(h) While techniques used to estimate future cash flows and interest rates vary due to situational differences, certain general principles govern any application of present value techniques in measuring assets. These are discussed in the outline of SFAC 7.

(i) Traditionally, accounting applications of present value have used a single set of estimated cash flows and a single interest rate, often described as "the rate commensurate with risk."

1] The *discount rate adjustment approach* assumes that a single interest rate convention can reflect all of the expectations about future cash flows and the appropriate risk premium. While the traditional approach may be adequate for some simple measurements, the FASB found that it does not provide the tools needed to address more complex problems.
2] The *expected cash flow (present value) approach* was found to be a more effective measurement tool than the discount rate adjustment approach in many situations. **The expected cash flow approach** uses all expectations about possible cash flows instead of the single most-likely cash flow. The expected cash flow approach focuses on direct analysis of the cash flows in question and on explicit assumptions about the range of possible estimated cash flows and their respective probabilities.

EXAMPLE

A cash flow might be $100, $200, or $300 with probabilities of 10%, 60%, and 30%, respectively. The expected cash flow is $220 ($100 × .1) + ($200 × .6) + ($300 × .3) = $220. However, the traditional approach would choose $200 as the best estimate or most-likely amount.

3] When the timing of cash flows is uncertain, the expected cash flow approach allows present value techniques to be utilized. The following example is from SFAC 7.

EXAMPLE

A cash flow of $1,000 may be received in one year, two years, or three years with probabilities of 10%, 60%, and 30%, respectively. Notice that the expected present value of $892.36 differs from the traditional notion of a best estimate of $902.73 (the 60% probability). The following shows the computation of expected present value:

Present value of $1,000 in one year at 5%	$952.38	
Probability	10.00%	$ 95.24
Present value of $1,000 in two years at 5.25%	$902.73	
Probability	60.00%	541.64
Present value of $1,000 in three years at 5.50%	$851.61	
Probability	30.00%	255.48
Expected present value		$892.36

---

a] An interest rate in a traditional present value computation is unable to reflect any uncertainties in the timing of cash flows.
b] By incorporating a range of possible outcomes (with their respective timing differences), the expected cash flow approach accommodates the use of present value techniques when the timing of cash flows is uncertain.

(j) An estimate of fair value should include an adjustment for risk.

    1] The risk adjustment is the price that marketplace participants are able to receive for bearing the uncertainties in cash flows.

    2] This assumes that the amount is identifiable, measurable, and significant.

    3] Present value measurements occur under conditions of uncertainty. In SFAC 7, the term **uncertainty** refers to the fact that the cash flows used in a present value measurement are estimates, rather than known amounts. Uncertainty has accounting implications because it has economic consequences. Business and individuals routinely enter into transactions based on expectations about uncertain future events. The outcome of those events will place the entity in a financial position that may be better or worse than expected, but until the uncertainties are resolved, the entity is **at risk**.

    4] In common usage, the word **risk** refers to any exposure to uncertainty in which that exposure has potential negative consequences. Risk is a relational concept. A particular risk can only be understood in context. In most situations, marketplace participants are said to be **risk adverse**. They prefer situations with less uncertainty relative to an expected outcome. Marketplace participants seek compensation for accepting uncertainty. This is referred to as a **risk premium**. They demand more compensation (a higher premium) to assume a liability with expected cash flows that are uncertain, than to assume a liability with cash flows of the same expected amount but no uncertainty. This phenomenon can be described with the financial axiom, "the greater the risk, the greater the return." The objective of including uncertainty and risk in accounting measurements is to imitate, to the extent possible, the market's behavior toward assets and liabilities with uncertain cash flows.

(k) If prices for an asset or liability or an essentially similar asset or liability can be observed in the marketplace, there is no need to use present value measurements. The marketplace assessment of present value is already embodied in the price. However, if observed prices are unavailable, present value measurements are often the best available technique with which to estimate what a price would be.

(l) The measurement of liabilities sometimes involves problems different from those encountered in the measurement of assets. Thus, measurement of liabilities may require different techniques in arriving at fair value. Liabilities can be held by individuals who sell their rights differently than they would sell other assets. Liabilities are sometimes settled through assumption by a third party. To estimate the liability's fair value, accountants must estimate the price necessary to pay the third party to assume the liability.

    1] The most relevant measure of a liability always reflects the credit standing of the entity obligated to pay. An entity's credit standing affects the interest rate at which it borrows in the marketplace. The initial proceeds of a loan, therefore, always reflect the entity's credit standing at that time. Likewise, the price at which others buy and sell the entity's loan includes their assessment of the entity's ability to repay. The failure to include changes in credit standing in the measurement of a liability ignores economic differences between liabilities.

(m) Present value techniques are also used in periodic reporting conventions knows collectively as **interest methods of allocation**. Financial statements usually attempt to represent changes in assets and liabilities from one period to the next. In principle, the purpose of all accounting allocations is to report changes in the value, utility, or substance of assets and liabilities over time.

    1] Accounting allocations attempt to relate the change in an asset or liability to some observable real-world phenomenon. An interest method of allocation relates changes in the reported amount with changes in the present value of a set of future cash inflows or outflows. However, allocation methods are only representations. They are not measurements of an asset or liability. The selection of a particular allocation method and the underlying assumptions always involves a degree of arbitrariness. As a result, no allocation method can be demonstrated to be superior to others in all circumstances. The FASB will continue to decide whether to require an interest method of allocation on a project-by-project basis. Refer to the outline of SFAC 7 for further information regarding the interest method of allocation.

> **NOW REVIEW MULTIPLE-CHOICE QUESTIONS 18 THROUGH 25**

2. **Income Determination** (See outlines of SFAC 5, 6, and 8.)

    a. The primary objective of accounting is to measure income. Income is a measure of management's efficiency in combining the factors of production into desired goods and services.

(1) Efficient firms with prospects of increased efficiency (higher profits) have greater access to financial capital and at lower costs. Their stock usually sells at a higher price-earnings ratio than the stock of a company with less enthusiastic prospects. The credit rating of the prospectively efficient company is probably higher than the prospectively less efficient company. Thus, the "cost of capital" will be lower for the company with the brighter outlook (i.e., lower stock dividend yield rates and/or lower interest rates).

b. The entire process of acquiring the factors of production, processing them, and selling the resulting goods and services produces revenue. The acquisition of raw materials is part of the revenue-producing process, as is providing warranty protection.

c. Under the accrual basis of accounting, revenue is generally recognized at the point of sale (ASC Topic 605) or as service is performed. The point of sale is when title passes: generally when seller ships (FOB shipping point) or when buyer receives (FOB destination).

(1) Three exceptions exist to the general revenue recognition rule: during production, at the point where production is complete, and at the point of cash collection. The table below compares the three exceptions with the general revenue recognition rule (point of sale).

Recognition basis/ source of GAAP	Accounting method	Criteria for use of basis	Reason(s) for departing from sale basis
• **Point of sale/ ASC Topic 605**	• Transactions approach (sales basis)	• Exchange has taken place • Earnings process is (virtually) complete	
• **During production basis/ASC Topic 605**	• Percentage-of-completion	• Long-term construction,* property, or service contract • Dependable estimates of extent of progress and cost to complete • Reasonable assurance of collectibility of contract price	• Availability of evidence of ultimate proceeds • Better measure of periodic income • Avoidance of fluctuations in revenues, expenses, and income
• **Completion-of-production basis/ ASC Topic 330**	• Net realizable value	• Immediate marketability at quoted prices • Unit interchangeability • Difficulty of determining costs	• Known or determinable revenues • Inability to determine costs and thereby defer expense recognition until sale
• **Cash collection basis/ASC Topic 605**	• Installment and cost recovery methods	• Absence of a reasonable basis for estimating degree of collectibility	• Level of uncertainty with respect to collection of the receivable precludes recognition of gross profit before cash is received

* Note that the "completed contract" method for construction contracts is not a departure from the sale basis.

SOURCE: Adapted from Henry R. Jaenicke, *Survey of Present Practices in Recognizing Revenues, Expenses, Gains, and Losses,* FASB, 1981.

(2) Under accrual accounting, expenses are recognized as related revenues are recognized, that is, (product) expenses are matched with revenues. Some (period) expenses, however, cannot be associated with particular revenues. These expenses are recognized as incurred.

   (a) **Product costs** are those which can be associated with particular sales (e.g., cost of sales). Product costs attach to a unit of product and become an expense only when the unit to which they attach is sold. This is known as associating "cause and effect."

   (b) **Period costs** are not particularly or conveniently assignable to a product. They become expenses due to the passage of time by

      1] Immediate recognition if the future benefit cannot be measured (e.g., advertising)

      2] Systematic and rational allocation if benefits are produced in certain future periods (e.g., asset depreciation)

   (c) Thus, income is the net effect of inflows of revenue and outflows of expense during a period of time. The period in which revenues and expenses are taken to the income statement (recognized) is determined by the above criteria.

(3) **Cash basis accounting**, in contrast to accrual basis accounting, recognizes income when cash is received and expenses when cash is disbursed. Cash basis accounting is subject to manipulation (i.e., cash receipts and expenses can be switched from one year to another by management). Another reason for adopting accrual basis accounting is that economic transactions have become more involved and multiperiod. An expenditure for a fixed asset may produce revenue for years and years.

NOW REVIEW MULTIPLE-CHOICE QUESTIONS 26 THROUGH 28

3. **Accruals and Deferrals**

    a. **Accrual**—accrual-basis recognition precedes (leads to) cash receipt/expenditure

       (1) Revenue—recognition of revenue earned, but not received
       (2) Expense—recognition of expense incurred, but not paid

    b. **Deferral**—cash receipt/expenditure precedes (leads to) accrual-basis recognition

       (1) Revenue—postponement of recognition of revenue; cash is received, but revenue is not earned
       (2) Expense—postponement of recognition of expense; cash is paid, but expense is not incurred
       (3) A deferral postpones recognition of revenue or expense by placing the amount in liability or asset accounts.
       (4) Two methods are possible for deferring revenues and expenses depending on whether real or nominal accounts are originally used to record the cash transaction.

EXAMPLE

BOOKKEEPING METHODS

Deferrals of Expense

	Expense method			**Asset method**	
When paid	Insurance expense	xx		Prepaid insurance	xx
	Cash		xx	Cash		xx
Year-end	Prepaid insurance	xx		Insurance expense	xx
	Insurance expense		xx	Prepaid insurance		xx
Reverse	Yes			No	

Deferrals of Revenue

	Revenue method			**Liability method**	
When received	Cash	xx		Cash	xx
	Rent revenue		xx	Unearned rent		xx
Year-end	Rent revenue	xx		Unearned rent	xx
	Unearned rent		xx	Rent revenue		xx
Reverse	Yes			No	

Accruals

	Expense			**Revenue**	
Adjustment	Wages expense	xx		Interest receivable	xx
	Wages payable		xx	Interest revenue		xx
Reverse	Yes			Yes	

---

    c. Entries are reversed for bookkeeping expediency. If accruals are reversed, the subsequent cash transaction is reflected in the associated nominal account. If accruals are not reversed, the subsequent cash transaction must be apportioned between a nominal and real account.

Cash	(amount received)
Revenue	(earned in current period)
Revenue receivable	(accrual at last year-end)

       (1) Accruals do not have two methods, but can be complicated by failure to reverse adjusting entries (also true for deferrals initially recorded in nominal accounts).

4. **Cash to Accrual**

    a. Many smaller companies use the **cash basis** of accounting, where revenues are recorded when cash is received and expenses are recorded when cash is paid (except for purchases of fixed assets, which are capitalized and depreciated). Often the accountant is called upon to convert cash basis accounting records to the accrual basis. This type of problem is also found on the CPA examination.

    b. When making journal entries to adjust from the cash basis to the accrual basis, it is important to identify two types of amounts:

       (1) The **current balance** in the given account (cash basis) and
       (2) The **correct balance** in the account (accrual basis).

         (a) The journal entries must adjust the account balances from their current amounts to the correct amounts.

c. It is also important to understand relationships between balance sheet accounts and income statement accounts.

  (1) When adjusting a balance sheet account from the cash basis to the accrual basis, the other half of the entry will generally be to the related income statement account. Thus, when adjusting accounts receivable, the related account is sales; for accounts payable, purchases; for prepaid rent, rent expense; and so on.

EXAMPLE

Assume a company adjusts to the accrual basis every 12/31; during the year, they use the cash basis. The 12/31/Y1 balance in accounts receivable, after adjustment, is $17,000. During year 2, whenever cash is collected, the company debits cash and credits sales. Therefore, the 12/31/Y2 balance in accounts receivable **before adjustment** is still $17,000. Suppose the **correct** 12/31/Y2 balance in accounts receivable is $28,000. The necessary entry is

    Accounts receivable   11,000
        Sales   11,000

This entry not only corrects the accounts receivable account, but also increases sales since unrecorded receivables means that there are also unrecorded sales. On the other hand, suppose the **correct** 12/31/Y2 balance of accounts receivable is $12,500. The necessary entry is

    Sales   4,500
        Accounts receivable   4,500

Sales is debited because during year 2, $4,500 more cash was collected on account than should be reported as sales. When cash is received on account the transaction is recorded as a credit to sales, not accounts receivable. This overstates the sales account.

EXAMPLE

Some problems do not require journal entries, but instead a computation of accrual amounts from cash basis amounts, as in the example below.

	12/31/Y1	12/31/Y2	Year 2
Rent payable	$4,000	$6,000	
Prepaid rent	8,000	4,500	
Cash paid for rent			$27,000

The rent expense can be computed using either T-accounts or a formula.

T-accounts are shown below.

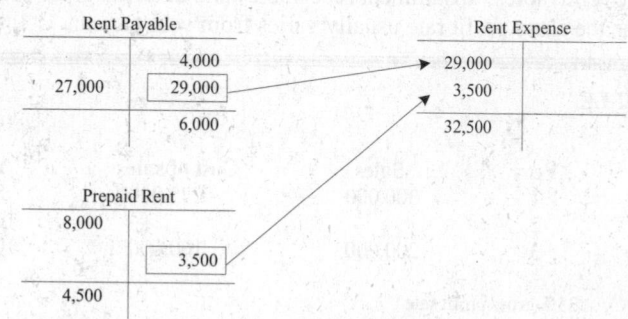

The use of a formula is illustrated next.

		Beginning		Ending		Ending		Beginning		
Payments	+	prepaid	+	payable	–	prepaid	–	payable	=	Expense
$27,000	+	8,000	+	6,000	–	4,500	–	4,000	=	$32,500

---

  (2) Formulas for conversion of various income statement amounts from the cash basis to the accrual basis are summarized in the following equations.

    (a) Since the accrual-basis numbers can be derived with T-accounts, you should not have to memorize the formulas.

Cash basis		Additions		Deductions		Accrual basis
Collections from sales	+	Ending AR (a) AR written off (b)	−	Beginning AR (c)	=	Sales
Collections from other revenues	+	Beginning unearned revenue (d) Ending revenue receivable (e)	−	Ending unearned revenue (f) Beginning revenue receivable (g)	=	Other revenues
Payments for purchases	+	Beginning inventory (h) Ending AP (i)	−	Ending inventory (j) Beginning AP (k)	=	Cost of goods sold
Payments for expenses	+	Beginning prepaid expenses (l) Ending accrued expenses payable (m)	−	Ending prepaid expenses (n) Beginning accrued expenses payable (o)	=	Operating expenses*

*Provision must also be made for depreciation expense and similar write-offs and bad debt expense.
(a) Ending AR and related sales have not yet been recorded
(b) AR written off reduced AR but did not result in cash collected
(c) Beginning AR was collected and recorded as sale during the period but was sale of the prior period
(d) Beginning unearned revenue was collected and recorded as revenue in the prior period but was earned in the current period
(e) Ending revenue receivable was earned during the period but has not yet been recorded because it has not been collected
(f) Ending unearned revenue was recorded upon collection as revenue but has not yet been earned
(g) Beginning revenue receivable was recorded during the current period upon collection as revenue but was earned last period
(h) Beginning inventory was sold during the period
(i) Ending AP and related purchases have not yet been recorded
(j) Ending inventory must be excluded from cost of goods sold
(k) Beginning AP reflects purchases last period which were not paid for or recorded until the current period
(l) Beginning prepaid expenses were recorded as expenses when paid in a prior period but are expenses of the current period
(m) Ending accrued expenses payable have not yet been recorded
(n) Ending prepaid expenses were recorded as expenses when paid this period but are expenses of future periods
(o) Beginning accrued expenses payable were recorded currently as expenses when paid but are expenses of the prior period

NOW REVIEW MULTIPLE-CHOICE QUESTIONS 29 THROUGH 53

5. Installment Sales

a. Revenue is recognized as cash is collected. Thus, revenue recognition takes place at the point of cash collection rather than the point of sale. Installment sales accounting can only be used where "collection of the sale price is not reasonably assured" (ASC Topic 605) (APB 10).

b. Under the installment sales method, gross profit is deferred to future periods and recognized proportionately to collection of the receivables. Installment receivables and deferred gross profit accounts must be kept separate by year, because the gross profit rate usually varies from year to year.

EXAMPLE

			Collections of	
Year	Sales	Cost of sales	Year 1	Year 3
1	300,000	225,000*	80,000	--
2	--	--	120,000	--
3	200,000	160,000**	100,000	100,000

    *25% gross profit rate
    **20% gross profit rate

To record sale	Year 1	Year 2	Year 3
Install AR-1	300,000	--	--
Install AR-3	--	--	200,000
Install sales	300,000	--	200,000

To record cash receipt			
Cash	80,000	120,000	200,000
Install AR-1	80,000	120,000	100,000
Install AR-3	--	--	100,000

To record CGS			
Install cost of sales	225,000	--	160,000
Inventory (or Purchases)	225,000	--	160,000

To defer gross profit	Year 1	Year 2	Year 3
Install sales	300,000	--	200,000
Install cost of sales	225,000	--	160,000
Deferred install GP-1	75,000	--	--
Deferred install GP-3	--	--	40,000
To recognize gross profit			
Deferred install GP-1	20,000[a]	30,000[b]	25,000[c]
Deferred install GP-3	--	--	20,000[d]
GP realized on install method	20,000	30,000	45,000

[a]$(25\% \times 80,000)$ [c]$(25\% \times 100,000)$

[b]$(25\% \times 120,000)$ [d]$(20\% \times 100,000)$

c. Summary of accounts used in installment sales accounting for year 3

BALANCE SHEET

Cash		Installment AR—Year 1		Installment AR—Year 3	
(B)		Ending balance from year 1 sales	(B)	(A)	(B)

Inventory (or Purchases)		Deferred Gross Profit—Year 1		Deferred Gross Profit— Year 3	
	(C)	(E)	Ending balance from year 1 installment sales	(E)	(D)

INCOME STATEMENT

Cost of Installment Sales		Installment Sales	
(C)	(D)	(D)	(A)

Realized Gross Profit on Installment Sales		Income Summary	
(F)	(E)		(F)

Explanation of Select Journal Entries

(A) To record installment sales year 3
(B) To record cash collected from year one and year three installment receivables
(C) To record cost of goods sold (perpetual or periodic) for year one and year three
(D) To close installment sales and cost of installment sales accounts
(E) To remove gross profit realized through collections from the deferred gross profit account
    (Gross profit rate for year one × Cash collections from year one receivables)
    (Gross profit rate for year three × Cash collections from year three receivables)
(F) To close realized gross profit at year-end

6. **Cost Recovery Method**

a. The cost recovery method is similar to the installment sales method in that gross profit on the sale is deferred. The difference is that no profit is recognized until the cumulative receipts exceed the cost of the asset sold.

> **EXAMPLE**
>
> In our installment sales example, the entire profit from year one sales ($75,000) would be recognized in year three. Profit on year three sales will be recognized in year four to the extent that in year four cash collections on year three sales exceed the $60,000 ($160,000 cost – $100,000 cash collected) unrecovered cost on year three sales.

b. If interest revenue was to be earned by the seller, it would likewise be deferred until the entire cost was recovered.

c. The cost recovery method is used when the uncertainty of collection is so great that even use of the installment method is precluded.

NOW REVIEW MULTIPLE-CHOICE QUESTIONS 54 THROUGH 66

7. **Franchise Agreements**

   a. ASC Topic 952 (SFAS 45—see outline) provides that the initial franchise fee be recognized as revenue by the franchiser **only** upon substantial performance of their initial service obligation.

   b. The amount and timing of revenue recognized depends upon whether the contract contains bargain purchase agreements, tangible property, and whether the continuing franchise fees are reasonable in relation to future service obligations.

   c. Direct franchise costs are deferred until the related revenue is recognized.

8. **Real Estate Transactions**

   a. Accounting treatment for real estate sales is provided by ASC Topics 360 and 976 (SFAS 66). Due to the variety of methods of financing real estate transactions, determining when the risks and rewards of ownership have been clearly transferred and when revenue should be recognized becomes very complex.

   b. Profit from real estate sales may be recognized in full, provided the profit is determinable and the earnings process is virtually complete. Additionally, the following four criteria must be met to recognize profit in full at the point of sale:

      (1) A sale is consummated.

      (2) The buyer's initial and continuing investments are adequate to demonstrate a commitment to pay for the property.

      (3) The seller's receivable is not subject to future subordination.

      (4) The seller has transferred to the buyer the usual risks and rewards of ownership in a transaction that is, in substance, a sale and does not have a substantial continuing involvement in the property.

   c. Depending on which combination of criteria is met, the real estate sales will be recorded using one of the following methods:

      (1) Deposit.

      (2) Cost recovery.

      (3) Installment.

      (4) Reduced profit.

      (5) Percentage-of-completion.

      (6) Full accrual.

         (a) The deposit and reduced profit methods require explanation. In accordance with the **deposit method**, payments received are recorded as a liability until the contract is canceled or a sale is achieved.

         (b) Under the **reduced profit method**, the seller recognizes a portion of profit at the time of sale with the remaining portion recognized in future periods. Profit recognized at the time of sale is determined by calculating the present value of the buyer's receivable and applying a formula. The reduced profit recognized at the time of sale is the gross profit less the present value of the receivable as determined above. The remaining profit is recognized in future periods. See the outline of SFAS 66.

9. **Multiple-Deliverable Revenue Arrangements**

   Another exception to the general revenue recognition principles is for multiple-deliverable revenue arrangements.

   a. If an entity has revenue generating activities to provide multiple products or services at different times, the arrangement should be evaluated to determine if there are separate units being delivered. Two conditions must be met for an item to be considered a separate unit of accounting:

      (1) The delivered item has value on a stand-alone basis (i.e., it can be sold separately by the vendor or customer) and

      (2) If the arrangement includes a right of return for the delivered item, the undelivered item must be substantially in control of the vendor.

      (3) If it meets both requirements, the revenue arrangement is divided into separate units based on the relative selling prices. Revenue recognition criteria are then applied to each of the separate units.

10. **Research or Development Accounted for on the Milestone Basis**

   a. The **milestone method** of accounting may be used in accounting for research and development arrangements in which revenue (payments) to the vendor is contingent on achieving one or more substantive milestones related to deliverables or units of accounting.

      (1) A substantive milestone is an uncertain event that can only be achieved based on the vendor's performance and

(a) It is commensurate with the vendor's performance or enhancement of value resulting from the vendor's performance.

(b) It relates solely to past performance.

(c) It is reasonable relative to all of the deliverables and payment terms.

(2) If all of these circumstances are met, the vendor may recognize the contingent revenue in its entirety in the period in which the milestone is achieved.

b. The notes to the financial statements should disclose its accounting policy for the recognition of milestone payments. In addition the following should be disclosed:

(1) A description of the overall arrangement.

(2) A description of each milestone and related contingent consideration.

(3) A determination of whether each milestone is considered substantive.

(4) The factors considered in determining whether the milestones are substantive.

(5) The amount of consideration recognized during the period for the milestone or milestones.

11. **Software Revenue Recognition**

a. Software products that require significant production, modification, or customization should be accounted for using ASC Topic 605 (ARB 45, *Long-Term Construction-Type Contracts*).

(1) Software products that are included with tangible products (i.e., hardware) and are required for the product's functionality are excluded from these software revenue recognition rules.

b. Software products that do not require significant production, modification, or customization should recognize revenue when all of the following criteria are met:

(1) Persuasive evidence of an arrangement exists.

(2) Delivery has occurred.

(3) Vendor's fee is fixed or determinable.

(4) Collectibility is probable.

c. The portion of the fee allocated to an element should be recognized using the same list of criteria.

(1) Delivery of an element is considered not to have occurred if other elements essential to the functionality of it are undelivered.

(2) No portion of the fee meets the criterion of collectibility if the portion of the fee allocable to delivered elements is subject to forfeiture, refund, or other concession if undelivered elements are not delivered.

d. Arrangement that includes multiple elements should allocate the fee to the elements based on vendor-specific objective evidence of fair value, regardless of stated prices in a contract.

(1) Multiple elements

(a) Arrangements consisting of multiple software deliverables including

1] Software products.

2] Upgrades/enhancements.

3] Postcontract customer service (PCS).

4] Services.

5] Elements deliverable on a when-and-if-available basis.

(2) Vendor-specific objective evidence of fair value

(a) Limited to

1] Price charged when the same element is sold separately.

2] Price established by management if not sold separately yet. It should be probable that the price will not change before being sold separately.

(b) Amount allocated to an undelivered element should not be adjusted. If it is probable that the amount allocated will result in a loss, ASC Topic 450, *Contingencies* (SFAS 5), should be followed.

(3) Insufficient vendor-specific objective evidence of fair value

(a) Defer revenue until whichever one of the following occurs first:

1] Sufficient vendor-specific objective evidence does exist.

2] All elements have been delivered.

(b) Exceptions

1] The PCS is the only undelivered element—recognize entire fee ratably.
2] Only undelivered element is services that don't require significant production, modification, or customization—recognize the entire fee over the period in which the services will be performed.
3] Arrangement is a subscription in substance—recognize entire fee ratably.
4] Fee based on the number of copies.

e. Separate accounting for service element of an arrangement is required if both of following criteria met

(1) Services not essential to functionality of any other element of the transaction.
(2) Services are described in the contract such that total price of the arrangement would be expected to vary as result of inclusion or exclusion of the services.

12. **Sales Basis Criteria for Selected Transactions**

a. Under GAAP, specific rules have been developed which are stated in the form of conditions which must be met before it is acceptable to recognize profit from "a sale in the ordinary course of business." Unfortunately, these rules represent a patchwork set of criteria for applying the sales basis of revenue recognition. This patchwork set of criteria contains many inconsistencies either in the results obtained or in the rationale justifying the criteria.

b. The table below summarizes the criteria which have been devised for applying the sales basis to selected transactions involving the sale of assets.

Recognition issue/ source of GAAP	Factors to be considered before recognizing revenue on the sale basis	Conditions that cause recognition to be delayed beyond time of sale
Sale with a right of return/ASC Topic 605 (SFAS 48)	• Whether economic substance of the transaction is a sale or a financing arrangement • Determination of sales price • Probability of collection of sales price • Seller's future obligations • Predictability of returns	• Sales price not fixed or determinable • Payment excused until product is sold • Payment excused if property stolen or damaged • Buyer without separate economic substance • Seller's obligation to bring about resale of the property • Inability to predict future returns
Product financing arrangement/ ASC Topic 470 (SFAS 49)	• Whether risks and rewards of ownership are transferred	• Agreement requires repurchase at specified prices or provides compensation for losses
Real estate sale/ ASC Topics 360 and 976 (SFAS 66)	• Probability of collection • Seller's continued involvement • Whether economic substance of the transaction is a sale of real estate or another type of transaction such as a service contract	• Inadequate buyer investment in the property • Seller's continuing obligations, such as participation in future losses, responsibility to obtain financing, construct buildings, or initiate or support operations
Sales-type lease/ ASC Topic 840 (SFAS 13)	• Transfer of benefits and risks of ownership • Probability of collection • Predictability of future unreimbursable costs	• Inability to meet conditions specified above for real estate sales • Inability to meet specified conditions (four criteria) indicating transfer of benefits and risks of ownership • Collectibility not predictable • Uncertainty about future unreimbursable costs
Sale of receivables with recourse/ ASC Topic 860 (SFAS 140)	• Isolation of transferred assets • Right to pledge or exchange transferred assets • Control of receivables	• Transferred assets can be reached by transferor or its creditors • Transferee's inability to pledge or exchange transferred assets • Control of receivables not surrendered due to repurchase or redemption agreement
Nonmonetary exchange/ASC Topic 845 (APB 29 and SFAS 153)	• Transaction has commercial substance	• Fair value not determinable • Exchange transaction to facilitate sales to customers • Transaction lacks commercial substance

Recognition issue/ source of GAAP	Factors to be considered before recognizing revenue on the sale basis	Conditions that cause recognition to be delayed beyond time of sale
• **Sale-leaseback transaction/ASC Topic 840 (SFAS 13)**	• Substance of the transaction • Portion of property leased back • Length of leaseback period	• All sale-leaseback transactions are financing transactions and not sales transactions unless leaseback covers only a small part of the property or is for a short period of time

SOURCE: Adapted from Henry R. Jaenicke, *Survey of Present Practices in Recognizing Revenues, Expenses, Gains, and Losses*, FASB, 1981.

13. **Reporting Start-up Costs**

ASC Topic 720-15 (Statement of Position (SOP) 98-5) provides the guidance for accounting for a company's start-up costs. These costs include those incurred during the course of undertaking one-time activities related to opening a new facility, introducing a new product or service, conducting business in a new territory, conducting business with a new class of customer or beneficiary, initiating a new process in an existing facility, commencing some new operation, or organizing a new entity. ASC Topic 720-15 requires start-up costs to be expensed rather than capitalized.

> **NOW REVIEW MULTIPLE-CHOICE QUESTIONS 67 THROUGH 73**

14. **Research Component—Accounting Standards Codification**

a. Basic concepts are included in the Financial Accounting Concepts (SFACs). However, the concept statements are not considered authoritative literature, and, therefore, are not included in the Accounting Standards Codification (ASC).

b. The Accounting Standards Codification database uses the following categories on the main menu: Presentation, Assets, Liabilities, Equity, Revenue, Expenses, Broad Transactions, Industry, and Master Glossary. Under each of these main categories are Topics. Topics are further divided into subtopics, sections, and subsections.

c. Citations in this text for information on a certain topic are cited as ASC Topic XXX. Complete citations for a specific rule are referenced by topic-subtopic-section-subsection. An example of a full research citation is ASC 350-10-25-1.

d. The following table lists the topical areas within the Codification.

Presentation
105 Generally Accepted Accounting Principles
205 Presentation of Financial Statements
210 Balance Sheet
215 Statement of Shareholder Equity
220 Comprehensive Income
225 Income Statement
230 Statement of Cash Flows
235 Notes to Financial Statements
250 Accounting Changes and Error Corrections
255 Changing Prices
260 Earnings per Share
270 Interim Reporting
272 Limited Liability Entities
274 Personal Financial Statements
275 Risks and Uncertainties
280 Segment Reporting

Assets
305 Cash and Cash Equivalents
310 Receivables
320 Investments—Debt and Equity Securities
323 Investments—Equity Method and Joint Ventures
325 Investments—Other
330 Inventory
340 Deferred Costs and Other Assets
350 Intangibles—Goodwill and Other
360 Property, Plant, and Equipment

Liabilities
405 Liabilities
410 Asset Retirement and Environmental Obligations
420 Exit or Disposal Cost Obligations
430 Deferred Revenue
440 Commitments
450 Contingencies
460 Guarantees
470 Debt
480 Distinguishing Liabilities from Equity

Equity
505 Equity

Revenue
605 Revenue

Expenses
705 Cost of Sales and Services
710 Compensation—General
712 Compensation—Nonretirement Postemployment Benefits
715 Compensation—Retirement Benefits
718 Compensation—Stock Compensation
720 Other Expenses
730 Research and Development
740 Income Taxes

Broad Transactions
- 805 Business Combinations
- 810 Consolidation
- 815 Derivatives and Hedging
- 820 Fair Value Measurements and Disclosures
- 825 Financial Instruments
- 830 Foreign Currency Matters
- 835 Interest

- 840 Leases
- 845 Nonmonetary Transactions
- 850 Related-Party Disclosures
- 852 Reorganizations
- 855 Subsequent Events
- 860 Transfers and Servicing

Industry
- 905 through 995

> **NOTE:** The accounting rules for development stage enterprises, franchising, not-for-profit entities, real estate, and software issues are located under "Industry" in the Codification. SEC content is included in each topic as appropriate and labeled "S." The SEC content is provided for convenience and is not the complete SEC literature.

e. Keywords for researching basic concepts are shown below.

Area franchise	Installment accounting	Sales type lease
Bargain purchase	Installment method	Sales value
Capital surplus	Net income	Security interest
Collectibility	Persuasive evidence arrangement	Seller obligation
Collection reasonably assured	Proceeds of sale	Services substantially performed
Consummated sale	Product financing	Significant customization
Consummation sale	Product financing arrangements	Significant production
Continuing franchise fees	Profit and loss	Software products
Continuing involvement	Profit on transactions	Specified prices resale
Culmination of earning process	Reasonable estimate returns	Sponsor purchase
Earned surplus	Recognizing revenue software	Sponsor repurchase
Fair value determinable	Related transaction purchase	Sponsor sells
Financial asset	Repurchase product	Substantial performance
Franchise fee revenue	Retained earnings	Substantially identical product
Franchisee	Return privilege expired	Transaction completed
Franchisor	Revenue recognized	Transfer financial asset
Full accrual method	Right of return	Unrealized profit
Initial franchise fee	Sales leaseback	Vendor specific evidence
Initial services	Sales price	

15. International Financial Reporting Standards (IFRS)

a. The International Accounting Standards Committee (IASC) issued International Accounting Standards (IAS) from 1973 to 2001. In addition, the IASC created a Standing Interpretations Committee (SIC) that provided further interpretive guidance on accounting issues not addressed in the standards. In 2001, the International Accounting Standards Board (IASB) replaced the IASC. The IASB adopted the existing International Accounting Standards (IAS) and interpretations issued by the Standing Interpretations Committee (SIC). Since 2001, the IASB is responsible for issuing International Financial Reporting Standards (IFRS), and the IFRS Interpretations Committee (IFRIC) is responsible for issuing interpretations of the standards. Therefore, the current international accounting guidelines are contained in the IAS and IFRS pronouncements, together with SIC and IFRIC interpretations.

b. It is often said that US GAAP employs a "rules"-based approach. In other words, the standards are usually explicit as to precise rules that must be followed for recognition, measurement, and financial statement presentation. IFRS, on the other hand, is considered a "principles"-based approach because it attempts to set general principles for recognition, measurement and reporting, and allows professional judgment in applying these principles. This principles-based approach should focus on a true and fair view or a fair representation of the financial information.

c. In 2002, the FASB and the IASB agreed to work toward convergence in the accounting standards. Therefore, you will find some IFRS accounting treatments identical, some similar, and others different from US GAAP. An effective study strategy is to study US GAAP and then learn the significant differences between US GAAP and IFRS. This compare/contrast strategy will help the candidate to remember which method is US GAAP and which method is IFRS. As you study this module, notice the differences in the following areas:

(1) **Vocabulary or definition differences.** Although the concepts of US GAAP and IFRS may be similar, vocabulary and definitions are often somewhat different.

(2) **Recognition and measurement differences.** Differences may exist in when and how an item is recognized in the financial statements. Alternative methods may be acceptable in US GAAP whereas only one method may be allowed for IFRS (or vice versa). In some instances, either IFRS or US GAAP may not require an item to be recognized in the financial statements. In addition, the amount recognized (measurement of the item) may be different in the two sets of standards.

(3) **Presentation and disclosure differences.** Presentation refers to the presentation of items on the financial statements, whereas disclosure refers to the additional information contained in the notes to financial statements. Again, differences exist as to whether an item must be presented in the financial statements or disclosed in the footnotes, as well as the types of information that must be disclosed.

(4) The table below highlights the major accounting differences between US GAAP and IFRS.

Major Differences— US GAAP versus IFRS

US GAAP	IFRS
Financial Statement Presentation	
No specific requirement regarding comparative information.	Requires comparative information for prior year.
Comprehensive income may be presented as a stand-alone statement or at the bottom of the income statement and changes in equity may be presented in the notes.	Requires a separate statement of comprehensive income and statement of changes in equity.
Presentation of certain items as extraordinary is required.	Extraordinary items are not allowed.
Revenue Recognition	
Construction contracts are accounted for using the percentage-of-completion method if certain criteria are met. Otherwise the completed-contract method is used.	Construction contracts are accounted for using the percentage-of-completion method if certain criteria are met. Otherwise, revenue recognition is limited to the costs incurred. The completed-contract method is not allowed.
Consolidated Financial Statements	
No exemption from consolidating subsidiaries in general-purpose financial statements.	Under certain restrictive situations a subsidiary (normally required to be consolidated) may be exempt from the requirement.
Noncontrolling interest measured at fair value.	Noncontrolling interest may be measured either at fair value or the proportionate share of the value of the identifiable assets and liabilities of the acquiree.
Monetary Current Assets and Current Liabilities	
Short-term obligations expected to be refinanced can be classified as noncurrent if the entity has the intent and ability to refinance.	Short-term obligations expected to be refinanced can be classified as noncurrent only if the entity has entered into an agreement to refinance prior to the balance sheet date.
Contingencies that are probable and can be reasonably estimated are accrued.	Contingencies that are probable and measurable are considered provisions and accrued.
Inventory	
LIFO cost flow assumption is an acceptable method.	The LIFO cost flow assumption is not allowed.
Inventories are valued at lower of cost of market (between a floor and a ceiling).	Inventories are valued at lower of cost or net realizable value.
Any impairment write-downs create a new cost basis; previously recognized impairment losses are not reversed.	Previously recognized impairment losses are reversed.
Fixed Assets	
Revaluation not permitted.	Revaluation of assets is permitted as an election for an entire class of assets but must be done consistently.
No separate accounting for investment property.	Separate accounting is prescribed for investment property versus property, plant, and equipment.
Unless the assets are "held for sale" they are valued using the cost model.	Investment property may be measured at fair value.

US GAAP	IFRS
Biological assets are not a separate category.	Biological assets are a separate category and not included in property, plant, and equipment.
There is no requirement to account for separate components of an asset.	If the major components of an asset have significantly different patterns of consumption or economic benefits, the entity must allocate the costs to the major components and depreciate them separately.
Impairment losses are not reversed.	Impairment losses may be reversed in future periods.

Financial Investments

US GAAP	IFRS
Compound (hybrid) financial instruments are not split into debt and equity components unless certain requirements are met, but they may be bifurcated into debt and derivative components.	Compound financial interests (e.g., convertible bonds) are split into debt, equity and, if applicable, derivative components.
Declines in fair value below cost may result in impairment loss solely based on a change in interest rate unless entity has the ability and intent to hold the debt till maturity.	Generally, only evidence of a credit default results in impairment loss for an available-for-sale debt instrument.
When impairment is recognized through the income statement, a new cost basis is established and such losses cannot be reversed.	Impairment losses in available-for-sale investments may be reversed in future periods.
Unless the fair value option is elected, loans and receivables are classified as either (1) held for investment, which is measured at amortized cost, or (2) held for sale, which is measured at lower of cost or fair value.	Loans and receivables are measured at amortized cost unless classified into the Fair Value Through Profit or Loss category or the Available-for-Sale category, both of which are carried at fair value.

Leases

US GAAP	IFRS
Operating leased assets are never recorded on the balance sheet.	Assets held by lessee under operating leases may be capitalized on the balance sheet if they meet certain requirements.
A lease for land and building that transfers ownership to the lessee or contains a bargain purchase option would be classified as a capital lease regardless of the relative value of the land. If the fair value of the land at inception represents 25% or more of the total fair value, the lessee must consider the components separately when evaluating the lease.	When land and buildings are leased, elements of the lease are considered separately when evaluating the lease unless the amount for the land element is immaterial.

Income Taxes

US GAAP	IFRS
Deferred tax assets are recognized in full but valuation allowances reduce them to the amount that is more likely than not to be realized.	Deferred tax assets are recognized only to the extent it is probable that they will be realized.

    d. **Underlying Concepts—The IASB *Framework***

       (1) The IASB *Framework for the Preparation and Presentation of Financial Statements* establishes the underlying concepts for preparing financial statements.

       (2) This framework addresses the objectives of financial statements, underlying assumptions, qualitative characteristics of financial statement information, definitions, recognition, measurement, and capital maintenance concepts.

       (3) Although the IASB *Framework* contains information similar to the Statement of Financial Accounting Concepts by the US Financial Accounting Standards Board (FASB), several important differences exist.

         (a) First, some terms and definitions are different.

         (b) Second, the elements of financial statements are not identical.

         (c) Candidates should become familiar with these subtle differences in the two sets of concepts.

       (4) The IASB *Framework* is not considered an accounting standard and therefore does not override any accounting treatment required by the International Accounting Standards (IAS) or International Financial Reporting Standards (IFRS). The *Framework* exists to assist in the development of future international accounting standards and to assist preparers in accounting for topics that do not have guidance in an existing standard.

       (5) In September 2010, the IASB completed two chapters on a joint conceptual framework project with the FASB.

         (a) The new conceptual framework contains Chapter 1, The Objective of General-Purpose Financial Reporting, and Chapter 3, Qualitative Characteristics of Useful Financial Information.

         (b) Because this is a joint project, the FASB and IASB chapters 1 and 3 are identical. You may refer to the information earlier in this chapter on those topics.

(c) However, until the remaining parts of the joint project are completed, there are subtle differences between the two frameworks. The most significant differences are terms, definitions, and elements of financial statements.

(6) FASB SFAC 6 contains ten elements of financial statements: assets, liabilities, equity, investments by owners, distributions to owners, comprehensive income, revenues, expenses, gains, and losses. The IASB *Framework* contains only five elements: assets, liabilities, equity, income, and expense.

> **NOTE:** There are several significant vocabulary differences regarding the elements of financial statements. With US GAAP, the term "income" is not a financial statement element. In US GAAP, the term income is used to describe a calculation of some type (e.g., income from continuing operations, net income) or to designate a specific type of income such as interest income. However, with IFRS, the term income is a financial statement element, and the items that are considered "income" are revenues and gains. IFRS uses the term "profit" whereas US GAAP uses the term "net income."

(7) The IASB *Framework*'s formal definitions of the five elements are shown below.

IASB *Framework*—Elements of Financial Statements	
Asset	An asset is a resource controlled by the entity as a result of past events and from which future economic benefits are expected to flow to the entity.
Liability	A liability is a present obligation of the entity arising from past events, the settlement of which is expected to result in an outflow from the entity of resources embodying economic benefits.
Equity	Equity is the residual interest in the assets of the entity after deducting all its liabilities.
Income	Income is increases in economic benefits during the accounting period in the form of inflows or enhancements of assets or decreases of liabilities that result in increases in equity, other than those relating to contributions from equity participants.
Expenses	Expenses are decreases in economic benefits during the accounting period in the form of outflows or depletions of assets or incurrence of liabilities that result in decreases in equity, other than those relating to distributions to equity participants.

(a) An important point to understand is that the definition of income includes both revenue and gains. Revenues arise in the normal course of business and are often referred to as sales, fees, interest, dividends, royalties, and rent. Gains are other items that meet the definition of income, which may or may not arise in the normal course of business. The IASB *Framework* indicates that gains are increases in economic benefits and are no different in nature from revenues. Therefore, they are not regarded as a separate element in the *Framework*. The *Framework* treats losses in the same way, as no different in nature from other expenses. However, the *Framework* also indicates that when gains or losses are reported in the income statement, they are usually displayed separately because this knowledge may be useful to the decision maker. Gains may be reported net of their related expenses, and losses may be reported net of their related income.

(8) The IASB *Framework* provides for capital maintenance adjustments. When assets or liabilities are revalued or restated, and there is a corresponding increase or decrease to equity, the definition of income or expense may not be met. Therefore, certain items may be included in equity as revaluation reserves.

(9) The IASB *Framework* defines recognition as the process of incorporating into the balance sheet or income statement an item that meets the definition of an element and satisfies the criteria for recognition.

(a) The two criteria for recognition are (1) it is probable that a future economic benefit will flow to the entity, and (2) the item has a cost or value that can be measured reliably.

(10) The *Framework* also outlines various bases of measurement such as historical cost, current cost, realizable (settlement) value, and present value. Current cost is the amount of cash or cash equivalent that would be paid if the same or equivalent asset were acquired currently. Realizable (settlement) value is the amount of cash that could be currently obtained by settling (e.g., selling) the asset in an orderly disposal. Although the measurement basis is commonly historical cost, certain accounts use different measurement methods.

e. **Revenue Recognition.** As indicated above, revenue is the gross inflow of economic benefits resulting from an entity's ordinary activities. These inflows must increase equity and not increase the contribution of owners or equity participants. Revenue is generated from the sale of goods, the rendering of services, and the use of an entity's assets by others. Various titles are used for revenue including sales, fees, interest, dividends, and royalties. Revenue is measured at the fair value of the consideration received or the receivable, net of trade discounts or rebates.

(1) Revenue is recognized from the sale of goods if all five of the following criteria are met:

   (a) The significant risks and rewards of ownership of the goods are transferred to the buyer,
   (b) The entity does not retain either a continuing managerial involvement or control over the goods,
   (c) The amount of revenue can be measured reliably,
   (d) It is probable that economic benefits will flow to the entity from the transaction, and
   (e) The costs incurred can be measured reliably.

(2) Revenue can be recognized from rendering services when the outcome of rendering services can be estimated reliably. This method is often referred to as the percentage-of-completion method.

> **NOTE:** Progress payments or advances from customers are not used to determine the state of completion. The outcomes can be estimated reliably if all the following criteria are met:
>
> 1. The amount of revenue can be measured reliably,
> 2. It is probable that economic benefits will flow to the entity,
> 3. The stage of completion at the end of the reporting period can be measured reliably, and
> 4. The costs incurred and the costs to complete the transaction can be measured reliably.

   (a) If the outcomes cannot be estimated reliably, then revenue should be recognized using the cost recovery method.

      1] The cost recovery method recognizes revenue only to the extent that the expenses recognized are recoverable.

> **NOTE:** IFRS does not permit use of the completed-contract method, which is allowed for US GAAP.

(3) Barter transactions are not recognized if the exchanged goods are similar in nature and value. If the goods are dissimilar, revenue is recognized at fair value of the goods received. If the fair value of the goods received cannot be measured, revenue is recognized at the fair value of goods or services given up.

(4) Interest income is recognized using the effective interest method. Royalties should be accrued as provided for in the contractual agreement. Dividends should be recognized when the shareholder has a right to receive the dividend payment.

f. **First-Time Adoption of IFRS.** There are a number of options available upon first-time adoption of IFRS, as described below.

(1) Generally the adoption involves restating assets, liabilities, and equity using IFRS principles. The "date of transition to IFRS" is defined as the beginning of the earliest period for which an entity presents full comparative information under IFRSs in its first IFRS financial statements. The "first IFRS reporting period" is defined as the latest reporting period covered by an entity's first IFRS financial statements.

(2) **Business combinations.** With respect to business combinations, the first-time adopter has the option of retrospectively adopting IFRS 3 for all periods presented, or adjusting the assets and liabilities through retained earnings in the period of adoption.

(3) **Plant, property, and equipment.** Unless an entity decides to use a fair value election, it will need to recalculate the life-to-date depreciation or amortization of any PPE or intangible assets under IFRS. This can be quite time-consuming. Alternatively, the entity may use various methods to determine the fair value of the assets and use those amounts as the deemed cost at the time of adoption. IFRS would then be used going forward. The fair value election may be applied on an individual item basis.

NOW REVIEW MULTIPLE-CHOICE QUESTIONS 74 THROUGH 83

KEY TERMS

Accounting Standards Codification (ASC). The single source for all US GAAP.

Accrual. Recognition precedes cash receipt/expenditure.

Accrual basis. Expenses are recognized as related revenues are recognized.

Cash basis. Recognizes income when cash is received and expenses when cash is disbursed.

Current cost. The amount of cash, or its equivalent, that would be paid if the same asset were to be acquired currently.

Current market value. The amount of cash, or its equivalent, that could be obtained by selling as asset in orderly liquidation.

Deferral. Cash receipt/expenditure precedes accrual-basis recognition.

Fair value. The price that would be received to sell an asset or paid to transfer a liability in an orderly transaction between market participants at the measurement date under current market conditions.

Historical cost. The amount of cash, or its equivalent, paid to acquire an asset.

Installment sales. Revenue is recognized as cash is collected.

Net realizable value. The nondiscounted amount of cash, or its equivalent, into which an asset is expected to be converted during the normal course of business less direct costs to make the conversion.

Period costs. Costs not particularly or conveniently assignable to a product.

Present value. The current measure of an estimated future cash inflow or outflow, discounted at an interest rate for the number of period between today and the date of the estimated cash outflow.

Product costs. Costs which can be associated with particular sales.

Realized (realizable). When related assets received or held are readily convertible into known amounts of cash or claims to cash.

Risk adverse. Market place participants prefer situations with less uncertainty relative to an expected outcome.

Start-up costs. The costs incurred during the course of undertaking on-time activities related to opening a new facility.

Multiple-Choice Questions (1-83)

A.1. Basic Accounting Theory

1. What are the Statements of Financial Accounting Concepts intended to establish?
   a. Generally accepted accounting principles in financial reporting by business enterprises.
   b. The meaning of "Present fairly in accordance with generally accepted accounting principles."
   c. The objectives and concepts for use in developing standards of financial accounting and reporting.
   d. The hierarchy of sources of generally accepted accounting principles.

2. According to the FASB conceptual framework, the objectives of financial reporting for business enterprises are based on
   a. Generally accepted accounting principles.
   b. Reporting for regulators.
   c. The need for conservatism.
   d. The needs of the users of the information.

3. According to the FASB conceptual framework, the relevance of providing information in financial statements is subject to the constraint of
   a. Comparability.
   b. Cost-benefit.
   c. Reliability.
   d. Faithful representation.

4. The enhancing qualitative characteristics of financial reporting are
   a. Relevance, reliability, and faithful representation.
   b. Cost-benefit and materiality.
   c. Comparability, verifiability, timeliness, and understandability.
   d. Completeness, neutrality, and freedom from error.

5. According to Statements of Financial Accounting Concepts, neutrality is an ingredient of

	Faithful representation	**Relevance**
a.	Yes	Yes
b.	Yes	No
c.	No	Yes
d.	No	No

6. According to the FASB conceptual framework, which of the following is an enhancing quality that relates to both relevance and faithful representation?
   a. Comparability.
   b. Confirmatory value.
   c. Predictive value.
   d. Freedom from error.

7. According to the FASB conceptual framework, the process of reporting an item in the financial statements of an entity is
   a. Allocation.
   b. Matching.
   c. Realization.
   d. Recognition.

8. Under FASB Statement of Financial Accounting Concepts 5, which of the following items would cause earnings to differ from comprehensive income for an enterprise in an industry **not** having specialized accounting principles?
   a. Unrealized loss on investments classified as available-for-sale securities.
   b. Unrealized loss on investments classified as trading securities.
   c. Loss on exchange of similar assets.
   d. Loss on exchange of dissimilar assets.

9. Under FASB Statement of Financial Accounting Concepts 5, comprehensive income excludes changes in equity resulting from which of the following?
   a. Loss from discontinued operations.
   b. Prior period error correction.
   c. Dividends paid to stockholders.
   d. Unrealized loss on securities classified as available-for-sale.

10. The fundamental qualitative characteristic of faithful representation has the components of
   a. Predictive value and confirmatory value.
   b. Comparability, consistency, and confirmatory value.
   c. Understandability, predictive value, and reliability.
   d. Completeness, neutrality, and freedom from error.

11. According to the FASB conceptual framework, which of the following statements conforms to the realization concept?
   a. Equipment depreciation was assigned to a production department and then to product unit costs.
   b. Depreciated equipment was sold in exchange for a note receivable.
   c. Cash was collected on accounts receivable.
   d. Product unit costs were assigned to cost of goods sold when the units were sold.

12. What is the underlying concept that supports estimating a fixed asset impairment charge?
   a. Substance over form.
   b. Consistency.
   c. Matching.
   d. Faithful representation.

13. What is the concept that supports the issuance of interim reports?
   a. Relevance.
   b. Materiality.
   c. Consistency.
   d. Faithful representation.

14. FASB's conceptual framework explains both financial and physical capital maintenance concepts. Which capital maintenance concept is applied to currently reported net income, and which is applied to comprehensive income?

	Currently reported net income	**Comprehensive income**
a.	Financial capital	Physical capital
b.	Physical capital	Physical capital
c.	Financial capital	Financial capital
d.	Physical capital	Financial capital

15. According to the FASB conceptual framework, an entity's revenue may result from

a. A decrease in an asset from primary operations.
b. An increase in an asset from incidental transactions.
c. An increase in a liability from incidental transactions.
d. A decrease in a liability from primary operations.

16. According to the FASB conceptual framework, which of the following is an essential characteristic of an asset?
a. The claims to an asset's benefits are legally enforceable.
b. An asset is tangible.
c. An asset is obtained at a cost.
d. An asset provides future benefits.

17. According to the FASB conceptual framework, which of the following attributes would **not** be used to measure inventory?
a. Historical cost.
b. Replacement cost.
c. Net realizable value.
d. Present value of future cash flows.

A.1.d. (6) Cash Flow Information and Present Value

18. According to SFAC 7, *Using Cash Flow Information and Present Value in Accounting Measurements*, the most relevant measurement of an entity's liabilities at initial recognition and fresh-start measurements should always reflect
a. The expectations of the entity's management.
b. Historical cost.
c. The credit standing of the entity.
d. The single most-likely minimum or maximum possible amount.

19. Which of the following is **not** covered by SFAC 7, *Using Cash Flow Information and Present Value in Accounting Measurements?*
a. Measurements at initial recognition.
b. Interest method of amortization.
c. Expected cash flow approach.
d. Determining when fresh-start measurements are appropriate.

20. In calculating present value in a situation with a range of possible outcomes all discounted using the same interest rate, the expected present value would be
a. The most-likely outcome.
b. The maximum outcome.
c. The minimum outcome.
d. The sum of probability-weighted present values.

21. A cash flow of $200,000 may be received by Lydia Nickels, Inc. in one year, two years, or three years, with probabilities of 20%, 50%, and 30%, respectively. The rate of interest on default risk-free investments is 5%. The present value factors are

> PV of 1, at 5%, for 1 year is .95238
> PV of 1, at 5%, for 2 years is .90703
> PV of 1, at 5%, for 3 years is .86384

What is the expected present value of Lydia Nickels' cash flow (in whole dollars)?
a. $181,406
b. $180,628
c. $ 90,703
d. $ 89,925

22. Which of the following statements regarding interest methods of allocations is **not** true?
a. The term "interest methods of allocation" refers both to the convention for periodic reporting and to the several approaches to dealing with changes in estimated future cash flows.
b. Interest methods of allocation are reporting conventions that use present value techniques in the absence of a fresh-start measurement to compute changes in the carrying amount of an asset or liability from one period to the next.
c. Interest methods of allocation are grounded in the notion of current cost.
d. Holding gains and losses are generally excluded from allocation systems.

23. Which of the following is **not** an objective of using present value in accounting measurements?
a. To capture the value of an asset or a liability in the context of a particular entity.
b. To estimate fair value.
c. To capture the economic difference between sets of future cash flows.
d. To capture the elements that taken together would comprise a market price if one existed.

24. On December 31, year 1, Brooks Co. decided to end operations and dispose of its assets within three months. At December 31, year 1, the net realizable value of the equipment was below historical cost. What is the appropriate measurement basis for equipment included in Brooks' December 31, year 1 balance sheet?
a. Historical cost.
b. Current reproduction cost.
c. Net realizable value.
d. Current replacement cost.

25. Which of the following accounting literature is not included in the FASB Accounting Standards Codification?
a. AICPA Statements of Position.
b. FASB Statements.
c. Accounting Research Bulletins.
d. Statements of Auditing Standards.

A.2. Income Determination

26. On October 1, year 1, Acme Fuel Co. sold 100,000 gallons of heating oil to Karn Co. at $3 per gallon. Fifty thousand gallons were delivered on December 15, year 1, and the remaining 50,000 gallons were delivered on January 15, year 2. Payment terms were: 50% due on October 1, year 1, 25% due on first delivery, and the remaining 25% due on second delivery. What amount of revenue should Acme recognize from this sale during year 1?
a. $ 75,000
b. $150,000
c. $225,000
d. $300,000

27. Amar Farms produced 300,000 pounds of cotton during the year 1 season. Amar sells all of its cotton to Brye Co., which has agreed to purchase Amar's entire production at the prevailing market price. Recent legislation assures that the market price will not fall below $.70 per pound during the next two years. Amar's costs of selling and distributing the cotton are immaterial and can be reasonably estimated. Amar reports its inventory at expected exit value. During year 1, Amar sold and delivered to Brye 200,000 pounds at the market price of $.70. Amar sold the remaining 100,000 pounds during year 2 at the market price of $.72. What amount of revenue should Amar recognize in year 1?

a. $140,000
b. $144,000
c. $210,000
d. $216,000

28. Lin Co., a distributor of machinery, bought a machine from the manufacturer in November year 1 for $10,000. On December 30, year 1, Lin sold this machine to Zee Hardware for $15,000, under the following terms: 2% discount if paid within thirty days, 1% discount if paid after thirty days but within sixty days, or payable in full within ninety days if not paid within the discount periods. However, Zee had the right to return this machine to Lin if Zee was unable to resell the machine before expiration of the ninety-day payment period, in which case Zee's obligation to Lin would be canceled. In Lin's net sales for the year ended December 31, year 1, how much should be included for the sale of this machine to Zee?

a. $0
b. $14,700
c. $14,850
d. $15,000

A.3. Accruals and Deferrals

29. Under a royalty agreement with another company, Wand Co. will pay royalties for the assignment of a patent for three years. The royalties paid should be reported as expense

a. In the period paid.
b. In the period incurred.
c. At the date the royalty agreement began.
d. At the date the royalty agreement expired.

30. Clark Co.'s advertising expense account had a balance of $146,000 at December 31, year 1, before any necessary year-end adjustment relating to the following:

- Included in the $146,000 is the $15,000 cost of printing catalogs for a sales promotional campaign in January year 2.
- Radio advertisements broadcast during December year 1 were billed to Clark on January 2, year 2. Clark paid the $9,000 invoice on January 11, year 2.

What amount should Clark report as advertising expense in its income statement for the year ended December 31, year 1?

a. $122,000
b. $131,000
c. $140,000
d. $155,000

31. An analysis of Thrift Corp.'s unadjusted prepaid expense account at December 31, year 2, revealed the following:

- An opening balance of $1,500 for Thrift's comprehensive insurance policy. Thrift had paid an annual premium of $3,000 on July 1, year 1.
- A $3,200 annual insurance premium payment made July 1, year 2.

- A $2,000 advance rental payment for a warehouse Thrift leased for one year beginning January 1, year 3.

In its December 31, year 2 balance sheet, what amount should Thrift report as prepaid expenses?

a. $5,200
b. $3,600
c. $2,000
d. $1,600

32. Roro, Inc. paid $7,200 to renew its only insurance policy for three years on March 1, year 1, the effective date of the policy. At March 31, year 1, Roro's unadjusted trial balance showed a balance of $300 for prepaid insurance and $7,200 for insurance expense. What amounts should be reported for prepaid insurance and insurance expense in Roro's financial statements for the three months ended March 31, year 1?

	Prepaid insurance	Insurance expense
a.	$7,000	$300
b.	$7,000	$500
c.	$7,200	$300
d.	$7,300	$200

33. Aneen's Video Mart sells one- and two-year mail order subscriptions for its video-of-the-month business. Subscriptions are collected in advance and credited to sales. An analysis of the recorded sales activity revealed the following:

	Year 1	Year 2
Sales	$420,000	$500,000
Less cancellations	20,000	30,000
Net sales	$400,000	$470,000
Subscriptions expirations:		
Year 1	$120,000	
Year 2	155,000	$130,000
Year 3	125,000	200,000
Year 4		140,000
	$400,000	$470,000

In Aneen's December 31, year 2 balance sheet, the balance for unearned subscription revenue should be

a. $495,000
b. $470,000
c. $465,000
d. $340,000

34. Regal Department Store sells gift certificates, redeemable for store merchandise, that expire one year after their issuance. Regal has the following information pertaining to its gift certificates sales and redemptions:

Unredeemed at 12/31/Y1	$ 75,000
Year 2 sales	250,000
Year 2 redemptions of prior year sales	25,000
Year 2 redemptions of current year sales	175,000

Regal's experience indicates that 10% of gift certificates sold will not be redeemed. In its December 31, year 2 balance sheet, what amount should Regal report as unearned revenue?

a. $125,000
b. $112,500
c. $100,000
d. $ 50,000

35. Wren Corp.'s trademark was licensed to Mont Co. for royalties of 15% of sales of the trademarked items. Royalties are payable semiannually on March 15 for sales in July through December of the prior year, and on September 15 for sales in January through June of the same year. Wren received the following royalties from Mont:

	March 15	September 15
Year 1	$10,000	$15,000
Year 2	12,000	17,000

Mont estimated that sales of the trademarked items would total $60,000 for July through December year 2. In Wren's year 2 income statement, the royalty revenue should be
- a. $26,000
- b. $29,000
- c. $38,000
- d. $41,000

36. In year 1, Super Comics Corp. sold a comic strip to Fantasy, Inc. and will receive royalties of 20% of future revenues associated with the comic strip. At December 31, year 2, Super reported royalties receivable of $75,000 from Fantasy. During year 3, Super received royalty payments of $200,000. Fantasy reported revenues of $1,500,000 in year 3 from the comic strip. In its year 3 income statement, what amount should Super report as royalty revenue?
- a. $125,000
- b. $175,000
- c. $200,000
- d. $300,000

37. Rill Co. owns a 20% royalty interest in an oil well. Rill receives royalty payments on January 31 for the oil sold between the previous June 1 and November 30, and on July 31 for oil sold between December 1 and May 31. Production reports show the following oil sales:

June 1, year 1 - November 30, year 1	$300,000
December 1, year 1 - December 31, year 1	50,000
December 1, year 1 - May 31, year 2	400,000
June 1, year 2 - November 30, year 2	325,000
December 1, year 2 - December 31, year 2	70,000

What amount should Rill report as royalty revenue for year 2?
- a. $140,000
- b. $144,000
- c. $149,000
- d. $159,000

38. Decker Company assigns some of its patents to other enterprises under a variety of licensing agreements. In some instances advance royalties are received when the agreements are signed, and in others, royalties are remitted within sixty days after each license year-end. The following data are included in Decker's December 31 balance sheet:

	Year 1	Year 2
Royalties receivable	$90,000	$85,000
Unearned royalties	60,000	40,000

During year 2 Decker received royalty remittances of $200,000. In its income statement for the year ended December 31, year 2, Decker should report royalty income of
- a. $195,000
- b. $215,000
- c. $220,000
- d. $225,000

39. Cooke Company acquires patent rights from other enterprises and pays advance royalties in some cases, and in others, royalties are paid within ninety days after year-end. The following data are included in Cooke's December 31 balance sheets:

	Year 1	Year 2
Prepaid royalties	$55,000	$45,000
Royalties payable	80,000	75,000

During year 2 Cooke remitted royalties of $300,000. In its income statement for the year ended December 31, year 2, Cooke should report royalty expense of
- a. $295,000
- b. $305,000
- c. $310,000
- d. $330,000

40. The premium on a three-year insurance policy expiring on December 31, year 3, was paid in total on January 1, year 1. The original payment was initially debited to a prepaid asset account. The appropriate journal entry has been recorded on December 31, year 1. The balance in the prepaid asset account on December 31, year 1, should be
- a. Zero.
- b. The same as it would have been if the original payment had been debited initially to an expense account.
- c. The same as the original payment.
- d. Higher than if the original payment had been debited initially to an expense account.

41. On January 1, year 1, Sip Co. signed a five-year contract enabling it to use a patented manufacturing process beginning in year 1. A royalty is payable for each product produced, subject to a minimum annual fee. Any royalties in excess of the minimum will be paid annually. On the contract date, Sip prepaid a sum equal to two years' minimum annual fees. In year 1, only minimum fees were incurred. The royalty prepayment should be reported in Sip's December 31, year 1 financial statements as
- a. An expense only.
- b. A current asset and an expense.
- c. A current asset and noncurrent asset.
- d. A noncurrent asset.

42. A retail store received cash and issued gift certificates that are redeemable in merchandise. The gift certificates lapse one year after they are issued. How would the deferred revenue account be affected by each of the following transactions?

	Redemption of certificates	Lapse of certificates
a.	No effect	Decrease
b.	Decrease	Decrease
c.	Decrease	No effect
d.	No effect	No effect

43. Jersey, Inc. is a retailer of home appliances and offers a service contract on each appliance sold. Jersey sells appliances on installment contracts, but all service contracts must be paid in full at the time of sale. Collections received for service contracts should be recorded as an increase in a
- a. Deferred revenue account.
- b. Sales contracts receivable valuation account.
- c. Stockholders' valuation account.
- d. Service revenue account.

A.4. Cash to Accrual

44. Ward, a consultant, keeps her accounting records on a cash basis. During year 2, Ward collected $200,000 in fees from clients. At December 31, year 1, Ward had accounts receivable of $40,000. At December 31, year 2, Ward had accounts receivable of $60,000, and unearned fees of $5,000. On an accrual basis, what was Ward's service revenue for year 2?

    a. $175,000
    b. $180,000
    c. $215,000
    d. $225,000

45. Zeta Co. reported sales revenue of $4,600,000 in its income statement for the year ended December 31, year 2. Additional information is as follows:

	12/31/Y1	12/31/Y2
Accounts receivable	$1,000,000	$1,300,000
Allowance for uncollectible accounts	(60,000)	(110,000)

Zeta wrote off uncollectible accounts totaling $20,000 during year 2. Under the cash basis of accounting, Zeta would have reported year 2 sales of

    a. $4,900,000
    b. $4,350,000
    c. $4,300,000
    d. $4,280,000

46. Marr Corp. reported rental revenue of $2,210,000 in its cash basis federal income tax return for the year ended November 30, year 2. Additional information is as follows:

Rents receivable—November 30, year 2	$1,060,000
Rents receivable—November 30, year 1	800,000
Uncollectible rents written off during the fiscal year	30,000

Under the accrual basis, Marr should report rental revenue of

    a. $1,920,000
    b. $1,980,000
    c. $2,440,000
    d. $2,500,000

47. The following information pertains to Eagle Co.'s year 1 sales:

Cash sales

Gross	$ 80,000
Returns and allowances	4,000

Credit sales

Gross	120,000
Discounts	6,000

On January 1, year 1, customers owed Eagle $40,000. On December 31, year 1, customers owed Eagle $30,000. Eagle uses the direct writeoff method for bad debts. No bad debts were recorded in year 1. Under the cash basis of accounting, what amount of net revenue should Eagle report for year 1?

    a. $ 76,000
    b. $170,000
    c. $190,000
    d. $200,000

48. The following balances were reported by Mall Co. at December 31, year 2 and year 1:

	12/31/Y2	12/31/Y1
Inventory	$260,000	$290,000
Accounts payable	75,000	50,000

Mall paid suppliers $490,000 during the year ended December 31, year 2. What amount should Mall report for cost of goods sold in year 2?

    a. $545,000
    b. $495,000
    c. $485,000
    d. $435,000

49. Class Corp. maintains its accounting records on the cash basis but restates its financial statements to the accrual method of accounting. Class had $60,000 in cash-basis pretax income for year 2. The following information pertains to Class's operations for the years ended December 31, year 2 and year 1:

	Year 2	Year 1
Accounts receivable	$40,000	$20,000
Accounts payable	15,000	30,000

Under the accrual method, what amount of income before taxes should Class report in its December 31, year 2 income statement?

    a. $25,000
    b. $55,000
    c. $65,000
    d. $95,000

50. On February 1, year 1, Tory began a service proprietorship with an initial cash investment of $2,000. The proprietorship provided $5,000 of services in February and received full payment in March. The proprietorship incurred expenses of $3,000 in February, which were paid in April. During March, Tory drew $1,000 against the capital account. In the proprietorship's financial statements for the two months ended March 31, year 1, prepared under the cash basis method of accounting, what amount should be reported as capital?

    a. $1,000
    b. $3,000
    c. $6,000
    d. $7,000

51. Compared to the accrual basis of accounting, the cash basis of accounting understates income by the net decrease during the accounting period of

	Accounts receivable	Accrued expenses
a.	Yes	Yes
b.	Yes	No
c.	No	No
d.	No	Yes

52. White Co. wants to convert its year 1 financial statements from the accrual basis of accounting to the cash basis. Both supplies inventory and office salaries payable increased between January 1, year 1, and December 31, year 1. To obtain year 1 cash basis net income, how should these increases be added to or deducted from accrual-basis net income?

	Supplies inventory	Office salaries payable
a.	Deducted	Deducted
b.	Deducted	Added
c.	Added	Deducted
d.	Added	Added

53. Before year 2, Droit Co. used the cash basis of accounting. As of December 31, year 2, Droit changed to the accrual basis. Droit cannot determine the beginning balance of supplies inventory. What is the effect of Droit's inability to determine beginning supplies inventory on its year 2 accrual-basis net income and December 31, year 2 accrual-basis owners' equity?

	Year 2 net income	12/31/Y2 owners' equity
a.	No effect	No effect
b.	No effect	Overstated
c.	Overstated	No effect
d.	Overstated	Overstated

A.5. Installment Sales

54. Gant Co., which began operations on January 1, year 1, appropriately uses the installment method of accounting. The following information pertains to Gant's operations for year 1:

Installment sales	$500,000
Regular sales	300,000
Cost of installment sales	250,000
Cost of regular sales	150,000
General and administrative expenses	50,000
Collections on installment sales	100,000

In its December 31, year 1 balance sheet, what amount should Gant report as deferred gross profit?
- a. $250,000
- b. $200,000
- c. $160,000
- d. $ 75,000

55. Since there is no reasonable basis for estimating the degree of collectibility, Astor Co. uses the installment method of revenue recognition for the following sales:

	Year 2	Year 1
Sales	$900,000	$600,000
Collections from:		
Year 1 sales	100,000	200,000
Year 2 sales	300,000	--
Accounts written off:		
Year 1 sales	150,000	50,000
Year 2 sales	50,000	--
Gross profit percentage	40%	30%

What amount should Astor report as deferred gross profit in its December 31, year 2 balance sheet for the year 1 and year 2 sales?
- a. $150,000
- b. $160,000
- c. $225,000
- d. $250,000

56. Luge Co., which began operations on January 2, year 1, appropriately uses the installment sales method of accounting. The following information is available for year 2:

Installment accounts receivable, December 31, year 2	$800,000
Deferred gross profit, December 31, year 2 (before recognition of realized gross profit for year 2)	560,000
Gross profit on sales	40%

For the year ended December 31, year 2, cash collections and realized gross profit on sales should be

	Cash collections	Realized gross profit
a.	$400,000	$320,000
b.	$400,000	$240,000
c.	$600,000	$320,000
d.	$600,000	$240,000

57. Dolce Co., which began operations on January 1, year 1, appropriately uses the installment method of accounting to record revenues. The following information is available for the years ended December 31, year 1 and year 2:

	Year 1	Year 2
Sales	$1,000,000	$2,000,000
Gross profit realized on sales made in:		
Year 1	150,000	90,000
Year 2	--	200,000
Gross profit percentages	30%	40%

What amount of installment accounts receivable should Dolce report in its December 31, year 2 balance sheet?
- a. $1,225,000
- b. $1,300,000
- c. $1,700,000
- d. $1,775,000

58. On December 31, year 1, Mill Co. sold construction equipment to Drew, Inc. for $1,800,000. The equipment had a carrying amount of $1,200,000. Drew paid $300,000 cash on December 31, year 1, and signed a $1,500,000 note bearing interest at 10%, payable in five annual installments of $300,000. Mill appropriately accounts for the sale under the installment method. On December 31, year 2, Drew paid $300,000 principal and $150,000 interest. For the year ended December 31, year 2, what total amount of revenue should Mill recognize from the construction equipment sale and financing?
- a. $250,000
- b. $150,000
- c. $120,000
- d. $100,000

59. On January 2, year 1, Blake Co. sold a used machine to Cooper, Inc. for $900,000, resulting in a gain of $270,000. On that date, Cooper paid $150,000 cash and signed a $750,000 note bearing interest at 10%. The note was payable in three annual installments of $250,000 beginning January 2, year 2. Blake appropriately accounted for the sale under the installment method. Cooper made a timely payment of the first installment on January 2, year 2, of $325,000, which included accrued interest of $75,000. What amount of deferred gross profit should Blake report at December 31, year 2?
- a. $150,000
- b. $172,500
- c. $180,000
- d. $225,000

60. For financial statement purposes, the installment method of accounting may be used if the
- a. Collection period extends over more than twelve months.
- b. Installments are due in different years.
- c. Ultimate amount collectible is indeterminate.
- d. Percentage-of-completion method is inappropriate.

61. According to the installment method of accounting, gross profit on an installment sale is recognized in income

a. On the date of sale.
b. On the date the final cash collection is received.
c. In proportion to the cash collection.
d. After cash collections equal to the cost of sales have been received.

62. Income recognized using the installment method of accounting generally equals cash collected multiplied by the
    a. Net operating profit percentage.
    b. Net operating profit percentage adjusted for expected uncollectible accounts.
    c. Gross profit percentage.
    d. Gross profit percentage adjusted for expected uncollectible accounts.

63. It is proper to recognize revenue prior to the sale of merchandise when

  I. The revenue will be reported as an installment sale.
  II. The revenue will be reported under the cost recovery method.

    a. I only.
    b. II only.
    c. Both I and II.
    d. Neither I nor II.

A.6. Cost Recovery Method

64. The following information pertains to a sale of real estate by Ryan Co. to Sud Co. on December 31, year 1:

Carrying amount	$2,000,000
Sales price:	
Cash	$ 300,000
Purchase money mortgage	2,700,000 3,000,000

The mortgage is payable in nine annual installments of $300,000 beginning December 31, year 2, plus interest of 10%. The December 31, year 2 installment was paid as scheduled, together with interest of $270,000. Ryan uses the cost recovery method to account for the sale. What amount of income should Ryan recognize in year 2 from the real estate sale and its financing?
    a. $570,000
    b. $370,000
    c. $270,000
    d. $0

65. Wren Co. sells equipment on installment contracts. Which of the following statements best justifies Wren's use of the cost recovery method of revenue recognition to account for these installment sales?
    a. The sales contract provides that title to the equipment only passes to the purchaser when all payments have been made.
    b. No cash payments are due until one year from the date of sale.
    c. Sales are subject to a high rate of return.
    d. There is no reasonable basis for estimating collectibility.

66. According to the cost recovery method of accounting, gross profit on an installment sale is recognized in income
    a. After cash collections equal to the cost of sales have been received.
    b. In proportion to the cash collections.
    c. On the date the final cash collection is received.
    d. On the date of sale.

A.7. Franchise Agreements

67. On December 31, year 1, Rice, Inc. authorized Graf to operate as a franchisee for an initial franchise fee of $150,000. Of this amount, $60,000 was received upon signing the agreement and the balance, represented by a note, is due in three annual payments of $30,000 each beginning December 31, year 2. The present value on December 31, year 1, of the three annual payments appropriately discounted is $72,000. According to the agreement, the nonrefundable down payment represents a fair measure of the services already performed by Rice; however, substantial future services are required of Rice. Collectibility of the note is reasonably certain. In Rice's December 31, year 1 balance sheet, unearned franchise fees from Graf's franchise should be reported as
    a. $132,000
    b. $100,000
    c. $ 90,000
    d. $ 72,000

68. Each of Potter Pie Co.'s twenty-one new franchisees contracted to pay an initial franchise fee of $30,000. By December 31, year 1, each franchisee had paid a nonrefundable $10,000 fee and signed a note to pay $10,000 principal plus the market rate of interest on December 31, year 2, and December 31, year 3. Experience indicates that one franchisee will default on the additional payments. Services for the initial fee will be performed in year 2. What amount of net unearned franchise fees would Potter report at December 31, year 1?
    a. $400,000
    b. $600,000
    c. $610,000
    d. $630,000

A.8. Real Estate Transactions

69. In which of the following examples of real estate transactions would the seller not transfer the usual risks and rewards of ownership?

  I. The buyer can compel the seller to repurchase the property.
  II. The seller guarantees the return of the buyer's investment.
  III. The seller is required to support operations of the buyer and will be reimbursed on a cost plus 5% basis.

    a. I.
    b. II.
    c. III.
    d. I and II.

70. Esker Inc. specializes in real estate transactions other than retail land sales. On January 1, year 1, Esker consummated a sale of property to Kame Ltd. The amount of profit on the sale is determinable and Esker is not obligated to perform any additional activities to earn the profit. Kame's initial and continuing investments were adequate to demonstrate a commitment to pay for the property. However, Esker's receivable may be subject to future subordination. Esker should account for the sale using the
    a. Deposit method.
    b. Reduced recovery method.
    c. Cost recovery method.
    d. Full accrual method.

A.9. Multiple-Deliverable Revenue Arrangements

71. Which of the following is one of the conditions that must exist for a company to recognize revenue on separate units under a multiple-deliverables arrangement?

    a. The delivered item has value on a stand-alone basis and can be sold separately.

    b. The delivered item is not returnable.

    c. Collection has occurred for all of the separate units.

    d. The separate units must be delivered within 90 days of the end of the accounting period.

A.10. Research or Development Accounted for on the Milestone Method

72. The milestone method of accounting may be used to recognize revenue for

    a. Multiple-deliverable products or services.

    b. Research and development arrangements.

    c. Long-term construction contracts.

    d. Franchise arrangements.

73. The milestone method of revenue recognition provides that if a substantive milestone is achieved, what amount of revenue is recognized?

    a. Revenue is recognized up to the amount of cash collected.

    b. A provisions rata share of revenue based upon the percentage delivered to date.

    c. Contingent revenue is recognized in its entirety.

    d. A percentage of total revenue based on the separate units delivered.

A.15. International Financial Reporting Standards (IFRS)

74. Which of the following organizations is responsible for setting International Financial Reporting Standards?

    a. Financial Accounting Standards Board.

    b. International Accounting Standards Committee.

    c. Financial Accounting Committee.

    d. International Accounting Standards Board.

75. According to the IASB *Framework for the Preparation and Presentation of Financial Statements,* the fundamental qualitative characteristic of relevance includes

    a. Predictive value and feedback value.

    b. Verifiability, neutrality, and representational faithfulness.

    c. Predictive value and confirmatory value.

    d. Comparability and timeliness.

76. According to the IASB *Framework*, the financial statement element that is defined as increases in economic benefits during the accounting period in the form of inflows or enhancements of assets or decreases of liabilities that result in increases in equity, other than those relating to contributions from equity participants, is

    a. Revenue.

    b. Income.

    c. Profits.

    d. Gains.

77. According to the IASB *Framework*, the two criteria required for incorporating items into the income statement or statement of financial position are that

    a. It meets the definition of relevance and faithful representation.

    b. It meets the definition of an element and can be measured reliably.

    c. It satisfies the criteria of capital maintenance.

    d. It meets the requirements of comparability and consistency.

78. If the outcome of rendering services cannot be estimated reliably, IFRS® requires the use of which revenue recognition method?

    a. Percentage-of-completion method.

    b. Completed contract method.

    c. Cost recovery method.

    d. Installment method.

79. Which of the following is not one of the criteria for revenue recognition for sales of goods under IFRS?

    a. The significant risks and rewards of ownership of goods are transferred.

    b. Payment has been received.

    c. The entity does not retain either a continuing managerial involvement or control over the goods.

    d. The costs incurred can be measured reliably.

80. Upon first-time adoption of IFRS, an entity may elect to use fair value as deemed cost for

    a. Biological assets related to agricultural activity for which there is **no** active market.

    b. Intangible assets for which there is **no** active market.

    c. Any individual item of property, plant, and equipment.

    d. Financial liabilities that are **not** held for trading.

81. Under IFRS, which of the following is the first step within the hierarchy of guidance to which management refers, and whose applicability it considers, when selecting accounting policies?

    a. Consider the most recent pronouncements of other standard-setting bodies to the extent they do **not** conflict with the IFRS or the IASB *Framework.*

    b. Apply a standard from IFRS if it specifically relates to the transaction, other event, or condition.

    c. Consider the applicability of the definitions, recognition criteria, and measurement concepts in the IASB *Framework.*

    d. Apply the requirements in IFRS dealing with similar and related issues.

82. On July 1, year 2, a company decided to adopt IFRS. The company's first IFRS reporting period is as of and for the year ended December 31, year 2. The company will present one year of comparative information. What is the company's date of transition to IFRS?

    a. January 1, year 1.

    b. January 1, year 2.

    c. July 1, year 2.

    d. December 31, year 2.

83. How should a first-time adopter of IFRS recognize the adjustments required to present its opening IFRS statement of financial position?

    a.   All of the adjustments should be recognized in profit or loss.

    b.   Adjustments that are capital in nature should be recognized in retained earnings and adjustments that are revenue in nature should be recognized in profit or loss.

    c.   Current adjustments should be recognized in profit or loss and noncurrent adjustments should be recognized in retained earnings.

    d.   All of the adjustments should be recognized directly in retained earnings or, if appropriate, in another category of equity.

Multiple-Choice Answers and Explanations

Answers

1. c __ __	19. d __ __	37. c __ __	55. d __ __	73. c __ __
2. d __ __	20. d __ __	38. b __ __	56. d __ __	74. d __ __
3. b __ __	21. b __ __	39. b __ __	57. c __ __	75. c __ __
4. c __ __	22. c __ __	40. b __ __	58. a __ __	76. b __ __
5. b __ __	23. a __ __	41. b __ __	59. a __ __	77. b __ __
6. a __ __	24. c __ __	42. b __ __	60. c __ __	78. c __ __
7. d __ __	25. d __ __	43. a __ __	61. c __ __	79. b __ __
8. a __ __	26. b __ __	44. c __ __	62. c __ __	80. c __ __
9. c __ __	27. c __ __	45. d __ __	63. d __ __	81. b __ __
10. d __ __	28. a __ __	46. d __ __	64. d __ __	82. a __ __
11. b __ __	29. b __ __	47. d __ __	65. d __ __	83. d __ __
12. d __ __	30. c __ __	48. a __ __	66. a __ __	
13. a __ __	31. b __ __	49. d __ __	67. d __ __	
14. c __ __	32. b __ __	50. c __ __	68. c __ __	
15. d __ __	33. c __ __	51. d __ __	69. d __ __	
16. d __ __	34. d __ __	52. b __ __	70. c __ __	
17. d __ __	35. a __ __	53. c __ __	71. a __ __	1st: __/83 = __%
18. c __ __	36. d __ __	54. b __ __	72. b __ __	2nd: __/83 = __%

Explanations

1. (c) The Statements of Financial Accounting Concepts (SFAC) were issued to establish a framework from which financial accounting and reporting standards could be developed. The SFAC provide the theory behind accounting and reporting and provide guidance when no GAAP exists. The SFAC are not included as GAAP.

2. (d) Per SFAC 8, the objectives of financial reporting focus on providing present and potential investors and creditors with information useful in making investment decisions. Financial statement users do not have the authority to prescribe the data they desire. Therefore, they must rely on external financial reporting to satisfy their information needs, and the objectives must be based on the needs of those users.

3. (b) The FASB conceptual framework has identified the cost-benefit constraint to the relevance of providing financial reports. Information is **not** disclosed if the costs of disclosure outweigh the benefits of providing the information. Comparability is an enhancing qualitative characteristic. Reliability is no longer part of the conceptual framework according to SFAC 8. Faithful representation is a fundamental qualitative characteristic.

4. (c) The enhancing qualitative characteristics of financial reporting are comparability (including consistency), verifiability, timeliness, and understandability. Answer (a) is incorrect because relevance and faithful representation are fundamental qualitative characteristics of financial information. Reliability is no longer listed as a fundamental quality. Answer (b) is incorrect because cost-benefit is a constraint, and materiality is a threshold for reporting useful information. Answer (d) is incorrect because completeness, neutrality, and freedom from error are characteristics of faithful representation, a fundamental qualitative characteristic.

5. (b) SFAC 8 defines neutrality as the quality of information which requires freedom from bias toward a predetermined result. Unbiased information would always be more faithfully represented than biased information. Other components of faithful representation include information to be verifiable and free from error. Neutrality is not an ingredient of relevance because relevance requires information to have predictive value and confirmatory value, or both.

6. (a) Per SFAC 8, comparability is an enhancing quality of financial reporting which relates to both relevance and faithful representation. Confirmatory value and predictive value only relate to relevance. Freedom from error only relates to faithful representation.

7. (d) Per SFAC 5, recognition is the process of formally recording or incorporating an item into the financial statements as an asset, liability, revenue, expense, or the like. According to SFAC 6, allocation is the process of assigning or distributing an amount according to a plan or formula, matching is the simultaneous recognition of revenues with expenses that are related directly or jointly to the same transactions or events, and realization is the process of converting noncash resources and rights into money.

8. (a) Per SFAC 5, earnings and comprehensive income have the same broad components—revenues, expenses, gains, and losses—but are not the same because certain classes of gains and losses are excluded from earnings. Changes in market values of investments in marketable equity securities classified as available-for-sale securities are included in comprehensive income, but are excluded from earnings until realized. Answers (b), (c), and (d) are incorrect because they would be included in both earnings and comprehensive income. Note that unrealized gains and losses on marketable equity securities classified as trading securities are included in earnings. This treatment is in accordance with SFAS 115.

9. (c) Per SFAC 6, comprehensive income includes all changes in equity during a period except those resulting from investments by owners and distributions to owners. Dividends paid to stockholders is a change in equity resulting from a distribution to owners, so it is excluded from comprehensive income. Answers (a), (b), and (d) are all included in comprehensive income because they **are** changes in equity, but are **not** investments by, or distributions to, owners.

10. (d) The fundamental qualitative characteristic of faithful representation has the components of completeness, neutrality, and freedom from error. Answer (a) is incorrect because predictive value and confirmatory value are the components of relevance. Answer (b) is incorrect because comparability and consistency are enhancing characteristics, and confirmatory value is a component of relevance. Answer (c) is incorrect, because understandability is an enhancing characteristic, predictive value is a component of relevance, and reliability is no longer a characteristic in the concept statements.

11. (b) According to SFAC 6, realization is the process of converting noncash resources and rights into money through the sale of assets for cash or claims to cash. When equipment is sold for a note receivable, money is realized since a note qualifies as a claim to cash. Answers (a) and (d) relate to cost allocation. Answer (c) is incorrect because accounts receivable represents a claim to cash. Realization occurs at the time of sale rather than when cash is collected.

12. (d) An estimate of an impairment charge to a fixed asset can only be a faithful representation if the entity has applied impairment rules properly, disclosed the process of arriving at the impairment estimate and disclosed any uncertainties that affect the impairment estimate. Assuming the above is true, and no other estimate is better than the derived estimate, then the estimate is comprised of the best available information. Therefore, it is a faithful representation.

13. (a) Relevant financial information is capable of making a difference if it has predictive value, confirmatory, value, or both. Predictive value requires information to be used to predict future outcomes. Confirmatory value requires that information either confirm or change prior expectations. An interim report provides both predictive value and confirmatory value because it provides a basis to forecast future earnings and it provides feedback about prior performance expectations. Therefore, interim reporting is relevant.

14. (c) Per SFAC 6, the major difference between financial and physical capital maintenance is related to the effects of price changes on assets held and liabilities owed during a period. The financial capital concept is applied in current GAAP. Under this concept, the effects of the price changes described above are considered "holding gains and losses," and are included in computing return on capital. Comprehensive income, which is described in SFAC 5, is "the change in equity of a business enterprise during a period from transactions and other events and circumstances from nonowner sources." It is also a measure of return on **financial** capital. The concept of physical capital maintenance seeks to measure the effects of price changes that are not currently captured under GAAP (e.g., replacement costs of nonmonetary assets). Under this concept, holding gains and losses are considered "capital maintenance adjustments" which would be included directly in equity and excluded from return on capital.

15. (d) Per SFAC 6, revenues are inflows of assets or settlements of liabilities, or both, during a period as a result of an entity's major or primary operations. Two essential characteristics of revenues are that revenues (1) arise from a company's primary earnings activities and (2) are recurring or continuing in nature. Therefore, answer (d) is correct because it meets the above criteria. Answers (b) and (c) are incorrect because they result from incidental transactions. Answer (a) is incorrect because a decrease of an asset is not a revenue.

16. (d) Per SFAC 6, the common quality shared by all assets is "service potential" or "future economic benefit." Per SFAC 6, assets commonly have other distinguishing features, such as being legally enforceable, tangible or acquired at a cost. These features, however, are not essential characteristics of assets.

17. (d) Per SFAC 5, five different attributes are used to measure assets and liabilities in present practice: historical cost, current (replacement) cost, current market value, net realizable value, and present value of future cash flows. Three of these (historical cost, replacement cost, and net realizable value) are used in measuring inventory at lower of cost or market. Present value of future cash flows is not used to measure inventory.

18. (c) The most relevant measure of a liability always reflects the credit standing of the entity obligated to pay, according to SFAC 7. Those who hold the entity's obligations as assets incorporate the entity's credit standing in determining the prices they are willing to pay.

19. (d) SFAC 7 provides a framework for using future cash flows as the basis for accounting measurements at initial recognition or fresh-start measurements and for the interest method of amortization. **FASB limited SFAC 7 to measurement issues** (how to measure) **and chose not to address recognition questions** (when to measure). SFAC 7 introduces the expected cash flow approach, which differs from the traditional approach by focusing on explicit assumptions about the range of possible estimated cash flows and their respective probabilities.

20. (d) The expected cash flow approach uses all expectations about possible cash flows in developing a measurement, rather than just the single most-likely cash flow. By incorporating a range of possible outcomes (with their respective timing differences), the expected cash flow approach accommodates the use of present value techniques when the timing of cash flows is uncertain. Thus, the expected cash flow is likely to provide a better estimate of fair value than the minimum, most-likely, or maximum taken alone. According to SFAC 7, expected present value refers to the sum of probability-weighted present values in a range of estimated cash flows, all discounted using the same interest rate convention.

21. (b) The computation of expected present value using a single interest rate is as follows:

PV of $200,000 in one year at 5%	$190,476	
Probability	20%	$38,095
PV of $200,000 in two years at 5%	$181,406	
Probability	50%	90,703
PV of $200,000 in three years at	$172,768	
5% Probability	30%	51,830
		$180,628

According to SFAC 7, expected present value refers to the sum of probability-weighted present values in a range of estimated cash flows, all discounted using the same interest rate convention.

22. (c) Like depreciation and amortization conventions, interest methods are grounded in notions of historical cost, not current cost.

23. (a) According to SFAC 7, the objective of using present value in an accounting measurement is to capture, to the extent possible, the economic difference between sets of future cash flows. The objective of present value, when used in accounting measurements at initial recognition and fresh-start measurements, is to estimate fair value. Stated differently, present value should attempt to capture the elements that taken together would comprise a market price, if one existed, that is fair value. Value-in-use and entity-specific measurements attempt to capture the value of an asset or liability in the context of a particular entity. An entity-specific measurement substitutes the entity's assumptions for those that marketplace participants would make.

24. (c) The Codification provides guidance on the determination of gain or loss on disposal of a component of a business. According to this guidance, such determination should be based on estimates of the net realizable value of the component. Since Brooks Co. plans to discontinue its entire operations, the appropriate measurement basis for its equipment is net realizable value. Historical cost and current reproduction and replacement costs are not appropriate measurement bases for assets once an entity has decided to discontinue its operations because these amounts do not reflect the entity's probable future benefit, which is a characteristic of assets per SFAC 6.

25. (d) The FASB Accounting Standards Codification includes all previous level A–D GAAP. The Codification includes the authoritative literature of the Financial Accounting Standards Board, the Emerging Issues Task Force Abstracts, Accounting Principles Board Opinions, Accounting Research Bulletins, Accounting Interpretations, AICPA Statements of Position, AICPA Audit and Accounting Guides, and Practice Bulletins. The FASB Accounting Standards Codification does not include the AICPA Statements of Auditing Standards. The auditing standards are included in the Professional Standards issued by the AICPA.

26. (b) Generally, sales revenue is recognized at the date of delivery, because that generally is the time at which a sale has occurred. At that point the two criteria for revenue recognition were met; the revenue is (1) realized or realizable and (2) it is earned (SFAC 6). Therefore, the amount of sales revenue recognized in year 1 is $150,000 ($50,000 × $3 = $150,000).

27. (c) Income generally accrues only at the time of sale, and gains may not be anticipated by reflecting assets at their **current** sales prices. Exception to this general rule is granted, however, for agricultural products that are homogenous and have an immediate marketability at quoted prices such as the cotton in this problem (ASC 905-330-30-1). When these inventories are stated at sales prices, they should be reduced by expenditures to be incurred in disposal. Amar Farms should, therefore, recognize revenue on the entire

300,000 pound crop in year 1 at the guaranteed (and prevailing) market price of $.70 per pound. This amounts to $210,000 (300,000 pounds × $.70 per pound = $210,000). Note that the additional $.02 per pound for the cotton sold in year 2 would be recognized in year 2, since its selling price exceeded the current (year 1) market price.

28. (a) Revenue from the sale of a product may be recognized at the time of sale only if **all** of the following conditions are met:

1. The seller's price is fixed or readily determinable.
2. The buyer has paid the seller or is obligated to pay the seller, the obligation not being contingent on resale of the product.
3. The buyer's obligation to the seller remains unchanged in the event of damage or destruction of the product.
4. The buyer is independent from the seller.
5. The seller does not have any significant obligations regarding resale of the product by the buyer.
6. The amount of future returns can be reasonably estimated.

Because the buyer, Zee, has the right to return the machine to the seller, Lin, condition (2) above has not been met. Therefore, the recognition of sales revenue and cost of sales is not allowable for this transaction.

29. (b) Under accrual accounting, events that change an entity's financial position are recorded in the period in which the events occur. This means revenues are recognized when earned rather than when cash is received, and expenses are recognized when incurred rather than when cash is paid. Therefore, when the royalties are paid, Wand should debit an asset account (prepaid royalties) rather than an expense account. The royalties paid should be reported as expense in the period incurred (by debiting royalty expense and crediting prepaid royalties).

30. (c) The balance in the advertising expense account on 12/31/Y1 before adjustment is $146,000. Since the sales promotional campaign is to be conducted in January, any associated costs are an expense of year 2. Thus, the $15,000 cost of printing catalogs should be removed from the advertising expense account and recorded as a prepaid expense as of 12/31/Y1. In addition, advertising expense must be increased by the $9,000 cost of December's radio advertisements, which are an expense of year 1 even though they were not billed to Clark or paid until year 2. The $9,000 must be accrued as an expense and a liability at 12/31/Y1. Therefore, year 1 advertising expense should total $140,000 ($146,000 – $15,000 + $9,000).

31. (b) The opening balance in prepaid expenses ($1,500) results from a one-year insurance premium paid on 7/1/Y1. Since this policy would have expired by 6/30/Y2, no part of the $1,500 is included in 12/31/Y2 prepaid expenses. The insurance premium paid on 7/1/Y2 ($3,200) would be partially expired (6/12) by 12/31/Y2. The remainder (6/12 × $3,200 = $1,600) would be a prepaid expense at year-end. The entire advance rental payment ($2,000) is a prepaid expense at 12/31/Y2 because it applies to year 3. Therefore, total 12/31/Y2 prepaid expenses are $3,600.

Prepaid insurance ($3,200 × 6/12)	$1,600
Prepaid rent	2,000
Total prepaid expenses	$3,600

32. (b) Apparently Roro records policy payments as charges to insurance expense and records prepaid insurance at the end of the quarter through an adjusting entry. The unadjusted trial balance amounts at 3/31/Y1 must represent the final two months of the old policy ($300 of prepaid insurance) and the cost of the new policy ($7,200 of insurance expense). An adjusting entry must be prepared to reflect the correct 3/31/Y1 balances. Since the new policy has been in force one month (3/1 through 3/31), thirty-five months remain unexpired. Therefore, the balance in prepaid insurance should be $7,000 ($7,200 × 35/36). Insurance expense should include the cost of the last two months of the old policy and the first month of the new policy [$300 + ($7,200 × 1/36) = $500]. Roro's adjusting entry would transfer $6,700 from insurance expense to prepaid insurance to result in the correct balances.

33. (c) At 12/31/Y2, the liability account unearned subscription revenue should have a balance which reflects all unexpired subscriptions. Of the year 1 sales, $125,000 expires during year 3 and would still be a liability at 12/31/Y2. Of the year 2 sales, $340,000 ($200,000 + $140,000) expires during year 3 and year 4, and therefore is a liability at 12/31/Y2. Therefore, the total liability is $465,000 ($125,000 + $340,000). This amount would have to be removed from the sales account and recorded as a liability in a 12/31/Y2 adjusting entry.

34. (d) Regal's unredeemed gift certificates at 12/31/Y1 are $75,000. During year 2, these certificates are either redeemed ($25,000) or expire by 12/31/Y2 ($75,000 – $25,000 = $50,000). Therefore, none of the $75,000 affects the 12/31/Y2 unearned revenue amount. During year 2, additional certificates totaling $250,000 were sold. Of this amount, $225,000 is expected to be redeemed in the future [$250,000 – (10% × $250,000)]. Since $175,000 of year 2 certificates were redeemed in year 2, 12/31/Y2 unearned revenue is $50,000 ($225,000 – $175,000).

35. (a) The requirement is to calculate Wren's royalty revenue for year 2. The 3/15/Y2 royalty receipt ($12,000) would not affect year 2 revenue because this amount pertains to revenues earned for July through December of year 1 and would have been accrued as revenue on 12/31/Y1. On 9/15/Y2, Wren received $17,000 in royalties for the first half of year 2. Royalties for the second half of year 2 will not be received until 3/15/Y3. However, the royalty payment to be received for the second six months (15% × $60,000 = $9,000) has been earned and should be accrued at 12/31/Y2. Therefore, year 2 royalty revenue is $26,000 ($17,000 + $9,000).

36. (d) The agreement states that Super is to receive royalties of 20% of revenues associated with the comic strip. Since Fantasy's year 3 revenues from the strip were $1,500,000, Super's royalty revenue is $300,000 ($1,500,000 × 20%). The other information in the problem about the receivable and cash payments is not needed to compute revenues. Super's year 3 summary entries would be

Cash	200,000		
Royalties rec.	75,000		
Royalty revenue		125,000	($200,000 – $75,000)
Royalties rec.	175,000		
Royalty revenue		175,000	($300,000 – $125,000)

37. (c) Royalty revenues should be recognized when earned, regardless of when the cash is collected. Royalty revenue earned from 12/1/Y1 to 5/31/Y2 is $80,000 ($400,000 × 20%). Of this amount, $10,000 ($50,000 × 20%) was earned in December of year 1, so the portion earned in the first five months of year 2 is $70,000 ($80,000 – $10,000). Royalty revenue earned from 6/1/Y2 to 11/30/Y2 is $65,000 ($325,000 × 20%). The amount earned from 12/1/Y2 to 12/31/Y2, which would be accrued at 12/31, is $14,000 ($70,000 × 20%). Therefore, year 2 royalty revenue is $149,000.

1/1/Y2 - 5/31/Y2	$70,000
6/1/Y2 - 11/30/Y2	65,000
12/1/Y2 - 12/31/Y2	14,000
	$149,000

38. (b) The requirement is to calculate the amount of royalty income to be recognized in year 2. Cash collected for royalties totaled $200,000 in year 2. However, this amount must be adjusted for changes in the related accounts, as follows:

Year 2 cash received	$200,000
Royalties receivable 12/31/Y1	(90,000)
Royalties receivable 12/31/Y2	85,000
Unearned royalties 12/31/Y1	60,000
Unearned royalties 12/31/Y2	(40,000)
Royalty income	$215,000

The beginning receivable balance ($90,000) is subtracted because that portion of the cash collected was recognized as revenue last year. The ending receivable balance ($85,000) is added because that amount is year 2 revenue, even though it has not yet been collected. The beginning balance of unearned royalties ($60,000) is added because that amount is assumed to be earned during the year. Finally, the ending balance of unearned royalties ($40,000) is subtracted since this amount was collected, but not earned as revenue, by 12/31/Y2.

39. (b) The requirement is to determine the amount of royalty expense to be recognized in year 2. Cash paid for royalties totaled $300,000 in year 2. However, this amount must be adjusted for changes in the related accounts, as follows:

Year 2 cash paid	$300,000
Royalties payable 12/31/Y1	(80,000)
Royalties payable 12/31/Y2	75,000
Prepaid royalties 12/31/Y1	55,000
Prepaid royalties 12/31/Y2	(45,000)
	$305,000

The beginning payable balance ($80,000) is subtracted because that portion of the cash paid was recognized as expense during the previous year. The ending payable balance ($75,000) is added because that amount has been accrued as year 2 expense, even though it has not yet been paid. The beginning balance of prepaid royalties ($55,000) is added because that amount is assumed to have expired during the year. Finally, the ending balance of prepaid royalties

($45,000) is subtracted since this amount was paid, but not incurred as an expense, by 12/31/Y2.

40. (b) When the insurance policy was initially purchased, the entire balance was debited to a prepaid asset account (i.e., prepaid insurance). The adjusting entry at December 31, year 1, to recognize the expiration of one year of the policy would be

Insurance expense	(1/3 of original pymt.)
Prepaid insurance	(1/3 of original pymt.)

After the adjusting entry, the prepaid asset account would contain 2/3 of the original payment. If the original payment had instead been debited to an expense account (i.e., insurance expense), then the adjusting entry at December 31, year 1 would be

Prepaid insurance	(2/3 of original pymt.)
Insurance expense	(2/3 of original pymt.)

This alternate approach would also result in 1/3 of the original payment being expensed in year 1 and 2/3 of the original payment being carried forward as a prepaid asset. Thus, answer (b) is correct. Answer (a) is incorrect because the premium paid was for a three-year policy, 2/3 of which had not yet expired and would therefore be carried forward in the prepaid asset account. Answer (c) is incorrect because 1/3 of the original payment was already expensed. Answer (d) is incorrect because the amount would be the same as it would have been if the original payment had been debited initially to an expense account (as explained for answer (b) above).

41. (b) Current assets are identified as resources that are reasonably expected to be realized in cash or sold or **consumed** during the normal operating cycle of the business. These resources include prepaid expenses such as royalties. Since the balance remaining in Sip Co.'s royalty prepayment (the payment relating to year 2 royalties) will be consumed within the next year, it should be reported as a current asset. Additionally, the payment relating to year 1 should be reported as an expense.

42. (b) At the time the gift certificates were issued, the following entry was made, reflecting the store's future obligation to honor the certificates:

Cash	xx	
Deferred revenue		xx

Upon redemption of the certificates, the obligation recorded in the deferred revenue account becomes satisfied and the revenue is earned. Similarly, as the certificates expire, the store is no longer under any obligation to honor the certificates and the deferred revenue should be taken into income. In both instances, the deferred revenue account must be reduced (debited) to reflect the earning of revenue. This is done through the following entry:

Deferred revenue	xx	
Revenue		xx

43. (a) The revenues from service contracts should be recognized on a pro rata basis over the term of the contract. This treatment allocates the contract revenues to the period(s) in which they are earned. Since the sale of a service contract does not culminate in the completion of the earnings process (i.e., does not represent the seller's

performance of the contract), payments received for such a contract should be recorded initially in a deferred revenue account.

44. (c) The following formula is used to adjust service revenue from the cash basis to the accrual basis:

$$\begin{array}{c}\text{Cash}\\\text{fees}\\\text{collected}\end{array} + \begin{array}{c}\text{End.}\\\text{AR}\end{array} - \begin{array}{c}\text{Beg.}\\\text{AR}\end{array} + \begin{array}{c}\text{Beg.}\\\text{unearned}\\\text{fees}\end{array} - \begin{array}{c}\text{End.}\\\text{unearned}\\\text{fees}\end{array} = \begin{array}{c}\text{Accrual}\\\text{basis}\\\text{service}\\\text{revenue}\end{array}$$

$200,000 + $60,000 − $40,000 + 0 − $5,000 = $215,000

As an alternative, T-accounts can be used.

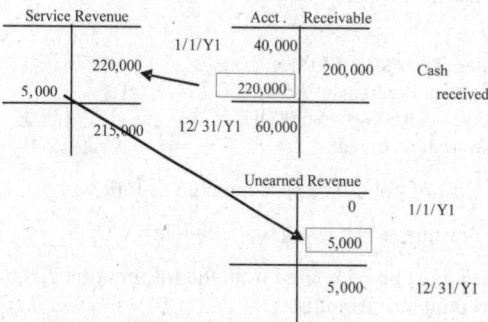

45. (d) To determine cash basis revenue, the solutions approach is to prepare a T-account for accounts receivable.

	Accounts Receivable		
12/31/Y1	1,000,000		
Sales	4,600,000	20,000	Write-offs
		?	Collections
12/31/Y2	1,300,000		

The missing amount for cash collections is $4,280,000. Another approach is to use the following formula:

Sales	+	Decrease (−increase) in AR	−	Write-offs	=	Collections
$4,600,000	−	$300,000	−	$20,000	=	$4,280,000

The increase in receivables ($300,000) means that cash collected during the period was less than sales during the period and therefore is deducted from sales revenue. The write-offs ($20,000) represent recognized sales that will never be collected in cash and therefore must also be deducted to compute collections.

46. (d) To determine rental revenue, the solutions approach is to prepare a T-account for rents receivable and rent revenues.

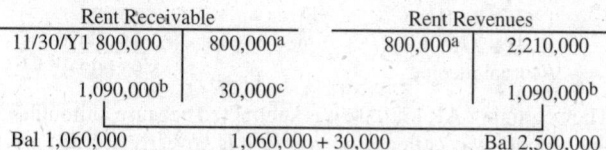

a To remove year 1 revenue from the $2,210,000 of cash collected and relieve rent receivable of collections from year 1 receivables.
b To recognize unrecorded rent earned including write-offs.
c To recognize write-offs. Debit would be to the allowance account.

47. (d) Under the cash basis method of accounting, revenue is recognized as it is collected. Cash sales after returns and allowances totaled $76,000 ($80,000 − $4,000). Net credit sales for year 1 were $114,000 ($120,000 credit sales − $6,000 discounts). As made evident by the following T-account, cash collections from credit sales must equal $124,000 ($40,000 + $114,000 − $30,000), since $10,000 in excess of current credit sales was received and reduced Accounts Receivable by this amount.

Accounts Receivable			
Bal. 1/1	40,000		
Net credit sales	114,000	?	Collections
Bal. 12/31	30,000		

A summary journal entry would be

Cash	124,000	
Sales discounts	6,000	
Accounts receivable		130,000

Total cash basis revenue for year 1 is $200,000 as shown below.

Cash sales ($80,000 – $4,000)	$ 76,000
Collections of credit sales [($40,000 +	
$120,000 – $30,000) – $6,000]	124,000
Total cash received	$200,000

48.   (a)   Cost of goods sold is computed as follows:

Beg. inv. + Net purchases – End. inv. = CGS

Net purchases must be computed from the information given using a T-account or a formula.

AP			
		50,000	12/31Y1
Payments	490,000	?	Purchases
		75,000	12/31Y2

The missing amount for purchases is $515,000. Another approach is to use the following formula:

Payments	+	Ending AP	–	Beginning AP	=	Purchases
$490,000	+	$75,000	–	$50,000	=	$515,000

This amount can be used to determine cost of goods sold

Beg. inventory	$290,000
+ Net purchases	515,000
Cost of goods available	805,000
– End. inventory	260,000
Cost of goods sold	$545,000

49.   (d)   Cash-basis income of $60,000 must be adjusted for changes in accounts receivable and accounts payable to compute accrual income

Cash-basis income	$ 60,000
12/31Y1 AR	(20,000)
12/31Y2 AR	40,000
12/31Y1 AP	30,000
12/31Y2 AP	(15,000)
Accrual income	$ 95,000

The beginning AR ($20,000) is subtracted because although this amount was collected in year 2, it is properly accrued as year 1 revenue. The ending AR is added because although not collected in year 2, it should be accrued as year 2 revenue. The beginning AP is added because although this amount was paid in year 2, it is properly accrued as year 1 expense. The ending AP is subtracted because although not paid in year 2, it should be accrued as year 2 expense.

50.   (c)   The ending balance in Tory's capital account on either the accrual or cash basis is computed as follows:

Beginning capital	+	Investments	+	Income	–	Drawings	=	Ending capital

Tory's beginning capital is his initial cash investment of $2,000. No other investments were made. Under the cash basis method of accounting, income is the excess of cash revenues ($5,000) over cash expenses ($0, since the expenses were not paid until after March 31). Therefore, cash basis income is $5,000. Drawings are $1,000. Therefore, ending capital is $6,000 ($2,000 + $0 + $5,000 – $1,000).

51.   (d)   The requirement of this question is to determine if a decrease in accounts receivable and/or a decrease in accrued expenses would result in **cash-basis income** being **lower** than accrual-basis income.

A decrease in the accounts receivable balance would generally mean that cash was collected. In accordance with the cash basis of accounting when cash is received it is recorded as revenue (Dr. Cash, Cr. Revenue), whereas under the accrual basis the revenue would have been recorded when the receivable was recorded (Dr. AR, Cr. Revenue). Thus, a decreased accounts receivable balance would result in increased revenue/income. Therefore, the answer for this account is No.

A decrease in the accrued expenses account would generally mean cash was paid on some expenses. Under the cash basis, when the cash is paid the expense is recorded (Dr. Expense, Cr. Cash), whereas under the accrual basis the expense would have been recorded when the accrued expense was recorded (Dr. Expense, Cr. Accrued Expense). Thus, a decreased accrued expenses account would result in increased expenses/lower income for the cash basis. Thus, the answer for this account is Yes.

52.   (b)   When a company operates on the accrual basis, supplies are inventoried and expensed as they are used. Under the cash method, however, supplies are expensed as they are paid for. Therefore if White Co. experiences an increase in supplies inventory during the year, this increase must be deducted from accrual income to get to the cash basis, because the cost of the supplies would be expensed at the time of purchase.

Office salaries payable works the opposite way. Under the accrual method, a liability would have been established resulting in additional expense over the amount of cash paid to employees. Under the cash method, no liability is accrued and the unpaid salaries are not expensed. Therefore, the increase must be added to the accrual basis net income.

53.   (c)   Prior to year 2, Droit Co. used the cash basis of accounting. Accordingly, Droit would have expensed all purchases of supplies as incurred. In contrast, under the accrual basis of accounting, the cost of unused supplies at each year-end would have been carried as an asset and, therefore, excluded from the current year's supplies expense. In year 2, the year Droit adopted the accrual basis of accounting, Droit would have inventoried unused supplies at December 31 and excluded those costs from year 2 net income. Since the cost of year 2's beginning balance of supplies was expensed during year 1, even though the supplies were not used until year 2, Droit's inability to determine the beginning supplies inventory would result in an understatement of supplies expense and overstatement of year 2 net income. However, since Droit properly inventoried supplies at December 31, year 2, its cumulative (inception-to-date) supplies expense would be properly stated. Therefore, Droit's inability to determine year 2's beginning supplies expense would have no impact on Droit's December 31, year 2 retained earnings.

54. (b) Under the installment method, gross profit is deferred at the time of sale and is recognized by applying the gross profit rate to subsequent cash collections. At the time of sale, gross profit of $250,000 is deferred ($500,000 installment sales less $250,000 cost of installment sales). The gross profit rate is 50% ($250,000 ÷ $500,000). Since year 1 collections on installment sales were $100,000, gross profit of $50,000 (50% × $100,000) is recognized in year 1. This would decrease the deferred gross profit account to a 12/31/Y1 balance of $200,000 ($250,000 – $50,000). Note that regular sales, cost of regular sales, and general and administrative expenses do not affect the deferred gross profit account.

55. (d) Under the installment sales method, gross profit is deferred to future periods and recognized proportionately to collection of the receivables. Therefore, at each year-end, deferred gross profit can be computed by multiplying the gross profit percentage by the accounts receivable balance, as indicated below.

	Year 2	**Year 1**
Sales	$900,000	$600,000
Year 1 Collections		(200,000)
Year 2 Collections	(300,000)	(100,000)
Year 1 Write-offs		(50,000)
Year 2 Write-offs	(50,000)	(150,000)
12/31/Y2 AR	$550,000	$100,000
Gross profit %	× 40%	× 30%
12/31/Y2 Deferred GP	$220,000	$ 30,000

Thus, total deferred gross profit at 12/31/Y2 is $250,000 ($220,000 + $30,000).

56. (d) Under the installment sales method, gross profit is deferred to future periods and is recognized proportionately as cash is collected. To determine cash collections in this case, first compute the year 2 installment sales by dividing deferred gross profit by the gross profit percentage ($560,000 ÷ 40% = $1,400,000). Then, the 12/31/Y2 installment accounts receivable is subtracted to determine cash collections ($1,400,000 – $800,000 = $600,000). Realized gross profit is then computed by multiplying cash collections by the gross profit percentage ($600,000 × 40% = $240,000).

57. (c) When using the installment method, gross profit realized is computed as indicated below.

Cash collections × GP% = GP realized

This equation can be rearranged as follows:

GP realized ÷ GP% = Cash collections

Therefore, cash collected to date on year 1 sales is $800,000 [($150,000 + $90,000) ÷ 30%], and on year 2 sales is $500,000 ($200,000 ÷ 40%). Installment accounts receivable at 12/31/Y2 is computed by subtracting cash collections from the original sales amount.

Installment AR – year 1 ($1,000,000 – $800,000)	$ 200,000
Installment AR – year 2 ($2,000,000 – $500,000)	1,500,000
Total 12/31/Y2 installment AR	$1,700,000

58. (a) The equipment sale is accounted for using the installment method. The gross profit percentage on the sale is 33 1/3% ($600,000 profit ÷ $1,800,000 selling price). Since $300,000 of the sales price is collected in year 2, gross profit of $100,000 is recognized (33 1/3% × $300,000). The **total** revenue recognized is $250,000 ($100,000 gross profit + $150,000 interest revenue).

59. (a) The machine sale is accounted for using the installment method, where gross profit is deferred and recognized in proportion to cash collected. Initially, the entire $270,000 gain is deferred. In year 1, $150,000 of the sales price was collected, and the gross profit percentage is 30% ($270,000 ÷ $900,000), so gross profit recognized was $45,000 (30% × $150,000). In year 2, $250,000 of the sales price was collected, so gross profit recognized was $75,000 (30% × $250,000). Therefore, at 12/31/Y2, deferred gross profit is $150,000 ($270,000 – $45,000 – $75,000). As a shortcut, you can compute the 12/31/Y2 note receivable balance ($750,000 – $250,000 = $500,000), and multiply by the 30% gross profit percentage (30% × $500,000 = $150,000). Note that the **interest** collected ($75,000) does not affect the computation because it is not a collection of sales price.

60. (c) The profit on a sale in the ordinary course of business is considered to be realized at the time of sale unless it is uncertain whether the sale price will be collected. The Board concluded that use of the installment method of accounting is not acceptable unless this uncertainty exists. Answers (a), (b), and (d) are incorrect because they do not involve the element of uncertainty regarding the collectibility of the sale price.

61. (c) According to the **installment method** of accounting, gross profit on an installment sale is recognized in income in proportion to the cash collection. The cash collected from a given year's sales is multiplied by that year's gross profit percentage to compute the amount of gross profit to be recognized. Answer (a) describes the **point-of-sale** recognition basis, while answer (d) describes the **cost recovery** method. Answer (b) does not describe any recognition basis currently used.

62. (c) The installment method of accounting is used when there is a high degree of uncertainty regarding the collectibility of the sale price. Under this method, sales revenues and the related cost of goods sold are recognized in the period of the sale. However, the gross profit is deferred to the periods in which cash is collected. Income recognized in the period of collection is generally computed by multiplying the cash collected by the gross margin percentage. The installment method is based upon deferral of the gross profit, not the net operating profit. The installment method is generally only applicable when the reporting company is unable to estimate the amount of uncollectible accounts.

63. (d) Under the installment method (case I) revenue (gross profit) is recognized **after** the sale, in proportion to cash collected. Under the cost recovery method (case II), revenue (gross profit) is again recognized **after** the sale, when cumulative receipts exceed the cost of the asset sold. Therefore, revenue is not recognized prior to the sale of merchandise in either case I or case II.

64. (d) Under the cost recovery method **no profit of any type** is recognized until the cumulative receipts (principal and interest) exceed the cost of the asset sold. This means that the entire gross profit ($3,000,000 – $2,000,000 = $1,000,000) and the year 2 interest received

($270,000) will be deferred until cash collections exceed $2,000,000. Therefore, no income is recognized in year 2.

65. (d) The **installment method** is used when collection of the selling price is not reasonably assured. However, when the uncertainty of collection is so great that even the use of the installment method is precluded, then the cost recovery method may be used. Having no reasonable basis for estimating collectibility would provide a great enough uncertainty to use the cost recovery method. It is important to note that anytime the installment method is used, some risk of 100% collection exists, but the risk must be extreme before the cost recovery method is employed.

66. (a) Installment methods of recognizing revenue are appropriate only when "collection of the sale price is not reasonably assured." Under the cost recovery method, gross profit is deferred and recognized only when the cumulative receipts exceed the cost of the asset sold.

67. (d) Franchise fee revenue is recognized when all material services have been substantially performed by the franchiser. Substantial performance means the franchiser has performed substantially all of required initial services and has no remaining obligation to refund any cash received. The $60,000 nonrefundable down payment applies to the initial services already performed by Rice. Therefore, the $60,000 may be recognized as revenue in year 1. The three remaining $30,000 installments relate to substantial future services to be performed by Rice. The present value of these payments ($72,000) is recorded as unearned franchise fees and recognized as revenue once substantial performance of the future services has occurred.

Cash	60,000	
Notes receivable	90,000	
Discount on notes receivable		18,000
Franchise revenue		60,000
Unearned franchise fees		72,000

68. (c) Initial franchise fees are not recognized as revenue until the franchisor makes substantial performance of the required services, and collection is reasonably assured. Since Potter Pie has not yet performed the required services, the initial franchise fee (21 × $30,000 = $630,000) is reported as **unearned franchise fees** at 12/31/Y1. The estimated uncollectible amount ($20,000) normally would be recorded as a debit to **bad debt expense** and a credit to **allowance for uncollectible accounts**. However, since no revenue has yet been recognized, it is inappropriate to record bad debt expense. Instead, **unearned franchise fees** is debited, because an unearned revenue should not be recorded when, in effect, no related asset has been received. Therefore, the **net** unearned franchise fees is $610,000 ($630,000 − $20,000).

69. (d) Items I and II do not transfer the risks and rewards of ownership to the buyer since both scenarios entitle the buyer to a return of his/her initial investment. Thus, the risks of ownership still remain with the seller. The economic substance of such arrangements is that of financing, leasing, or profit-sharing transactions. Item III transfers the risks and rewards of ownership since the seller will be reimbursed for cost plus a 5% profit on the support provided. Therefore, the seller is not required to support operations of the property at its **own** risk.

70. (c) The problem states that the sale has been consummated and that Kame's initial and continuing investments are adequate to demonstrate a commitment to pay for the property. However, the fact that Esker's receivable is subject to future subordination precludes recognition of the profit in full. Instead, the cost recovery method must be used to account for the sale. The deposit method is to be used

1. Until the sale is consummated, when all activities necessary for closing have been performed.
2. If the buyer's initial and continuing investments are not adequate to demonstrate a commitment to pay for the property and the seller is not reasonably assured of recovering the cost of the property if the buyer defaults.

The problem states that the sale has been consummated and that Kame's initial and continuing investments are adequate. Therefore, the deposit method will not be used to account for the sale. The reduced profit method is used only when the initial investment is adequate to demonstrate a commitment to pay for the property but the continuing investments are not. The continuing investments must also meet certain additional requirements for the reduced profit method to be used. Since Kame's continuing investments are adequate, the reduced profit method will not be used to account for the sale. The full accrual method may be used only if profit on the sale is determinable, the earning process is virtually complete, and all of the following:

1. A sale is consummated.
2. The buyer's initial and continuing investments are adequate to demonstrate a commitment to pay for the property.
3. The seller's receivable is not subject to future subordination.
4. The seller has transferred to the buyer the usual risks and rewards of ownership in a transaction that is, in substance, a sale and does not have a substantial continuing involvement in the property.

71. (a) The requirement is to identify the condition that must be met to apply separate accounting. For a multiple-deliverables arrangement, two conditions must be met for an item to be considered a separate unit of accounting: (1) The delivered item has value on a stand-alone basis, and (2) if the arrangement includes a right of return for the delivered item, the undelivered item must be substantially in the control of the vendor. Therefore answer (a) is correct.

72. (b) The requirement is to identify the subject matter of milestone accounting. Answer (b) is correct because the milestone method of accounting may be used to recognize revenue for research and development arrangements. Note that the milestone method is an option, but it is not required.

73. (c) The requirement is to identify the amount of revenue recognized under the milestone method. Answer (c) is correct because contingent revenue may be recognized in its entirety in the period the milestone is achieved.

74. (d) The requirement is to identify the body that sets international accounting standards. Answer (d) is correct because the International Accounting Standards Board (IASB) issues International Financial Reporting Standards.

75. (c) The requirement is to identify the qualitative characteristics of relevance. Answer (c) is correct because the IASB *Framework* provides that relevance includes the qualities of predictive value and confirmatory value. Answer (a) is incorrect because feedback value is not a characteristic of relevance. Answer (b) is incorrect because these qualities are the characteristics of reliability in FASB Concept Statement 1, which is superseded by SFAC 8. Answer (d) is incorrect because comparability and timeliness are enhancing characteristics in the IASB *Framework*.

76. (b) The requirement is to identify the element that is defined as increases in economic benefits in the form of inflows or enhancements of assets or decreases of liabilities that result in increases in equity other than those resulting from contributions from equity participants. Answer (b) is correct because the IASB *Framework* has five elements: asset, liability, equity, income, and expense. The definition given is that of income. Note that income includes both revenues and gains.

77. (b) The requirement is to identify the criteria under IFRS that must be met for an item to be included in financial statements. Answer (b) is correct because in order for an item to be recognized in the financial statements, IFRS requires that it meet the definition of an element and can be measured reliably.

78. (c) The requirement is to identify the revenue recognition method that must be used if the outcome of rendering services cannot be estimated reliably. Answer (c) is correct because if the outcome of rendering services cannot be measured reliably, IFRS requires use of the cost recovery method. Answer (a) is incorrect because the percentage-of-completion method is used when reliable estimates can be made. Answer (b) is incorrect because the completed contract method is not permissible under IFRS. Answer (d) is incorrect because the installment method is a revenue recognition method used under US GAAP, not IFRS.

79. (b) The requirement is to identify the item that is not one of the criteria for revenue recognition for sales of goods under IFRS. Answer (b) is correct because it is not required that payment has been received.

80. (c) The requirement is to identify the assets for which the entity may use fair value as deemed cost upon adoption of IFRS. Answer (c) is correct because the entity may use fair value as deemed cost for any individual item of property plant and equipment.

81. (b) The requirement is to identify the first step within the hierarchy of guidance to which management refers when selecting accounting policies. Answer (b) is correct because the highest level in the hierarchy is an IFRS standard applicable to the transaction. Answer (a), (c), and (d) are incorrect because they all represent lower levels in the hierarchy.

82. (a) The requirement is to identify the transition date. Answer (a) is correct because the "date of transition to IFRS" is defined as the beginning of the earliest period for which an entity presents full comparative information under IFRS.

83. (d) The requirement is to identify how adjustments are reflected upon adoption of IFRS. Answer (d) is correct because upon first-time adoption of IFRS, any adjustments required to present the opening balances of the statement of financial position should be recognized directly in retained earnings or, if appropriate, in another category of equity.

Simulations

Task-Based Simulation 1

Account Classifications		
	Authoritative Literature	Help

Suppose Winston incorporated and had the following accounts. Indicate how each of the following is classified on the financial statements. Below is a list of classifications.

Balance sheet classification
A. Current asset
B. Noncurrent asset
C. Current liability
D. Noncurrent liability
E. Owner's equity
F. Contra asset
G. Contra equity

Income statement classifications
H. Revenue
I. Expense
J. Contra revenue

		Balance sheet classification							**Income statement classification**		
		(A)	(B)	(C)	(D)	(E)	(F)	(G)	(H)	(I)	(J)
1.	Bonds payable, due in year 8	O	O	O	O	O	O	O	O	O	O
2.	Treasury stock	O	O	O	O	O	O	O	O	O	O
3.	Accounts payable	O	O	O	O	O	O	O	O	O	O
4.	Sales discounts	O	O	O	O	O	O	O	O	O	O
5.	Notes payable, due in nine months	O	O	O	O	O	O	O	O	O	O
6.	Inventory	O	O	O	O	O	O	O	O	O	O
7.	Accounts receivable	O	O	O	O	O	O	O	O	O	O
8.	Common stock	O	O	O	O	O	O	O	O	O	O
9.	Cost of goods sold	O	O	O	O	O	O	O	O	O	O
10.	Allowance for uncollectible accounts	O	O	O	O	O	O	O	O	O	O

Task-Based Simulation 2

Accrual Basis Worksheet		
	Authoritative Literature	Help

The following information pertains to Baron Flowers, a calendar-year sole proprietorship, which maintained its books on the cash basis during the year.

Baron Flowers
TRIAL BALANCE
December 31, year 2

	Dr.	Cr.
Cash	$ 25,600	
Accounts receivable, 12/31/Y1	16,200	
Inventory, 12/31/Y1	62,000	
Furniture & fixtures	118,200	
Land improvements	45,000	
Accumulated depreciation, 12/31/Y1		$ 32,400
Accounts payable, 12/31/Y1		17,000
Baron, Drawings		
Baron, Capital, 12/31/Y1		124,600
Sales		653,000
Purchases	305,100	
Salaries	174,000	
Payroll taxes	12,400	
Insurance	8,700	

	Dr.	Cr.
Rent	34,200	
Utilities	12,600	
Living expenses	13,000	
	$827,000	$827,000

Baron has developed plans to expand into the wholesale flower market and is in the process of negotiating a bank loan to finance the expansion. The bank is requesting year 2 financial statements prepared on the accrual basis of accounting from Baron. During the course of a review engagement, Muir, Baron's accountant, obtained the following additional information.

1. Amounts due from customers totaled $32,000 at December 31, year 2.
2. An analysis of the above receivables revealed that an allowance for uncollectible accounts of $3,800 should be provided.
3. Unpaid invoices for flower purchases totaled $30,500 and $17,000, at December 31, year 2, and December 31, year 1, respectively.
4. The inventory totaled $72,800 based on a physical count of the goods at December 31, year 2. The inventory was priced at cost, which approximates market value.
5. On May 1, year 2, Baron paid $8,700 to renew its comprehensive insurance coverage for one year. The premium on the previous policy, which expired on April 30, year 2, was $7,800.
6. On January 2, year 2, Baron entered into a twenty-five-year operating lease for the vacant lot adjacent to Baron's retail store for use as a parking lot. As agreed in the lease, Baron paved and fenced in the lot at a cost of $45,000. The improvements were completed on April 1, year 2, and have an estimated useful life of fifteen years. No provision for depreciation or amortization has been recorded. Depreciation on furniture and fixtures was $12,000 for year 2.
7. Accrued expenses at December 31, year 1 and year 2, were as follows:

	Year 1	Year 2
Utilities	$ 900	$1,500
Payroll taxes	1,100	1,600
	$2,000	$3,100

8. Baron is being sued for $400,000. The coverage under the comprehensive insurance policy is limited to $250,000. Baron's attorney believes that an unfavorable outcome is probable and that a reasonable estimate of the settlement is $300,000.
9. The salaries account includes $4,000 per month paid to the proprietor. Baron also receives $250 per week for living expenses.

Using the worksheet below, prepare the adjustments necessary to convert the trial balance of Baron Flowers to the accrual basis of accounting for the year ended December 31, year 2. Formal journal entries are not required to support your adjustments. However, use the numbers given with the additional information to cross-reference the postings in the adjustment columns on the worksheet.

Baron Flowers
WORKSHEET TO CONVERT TRIAL BALANCE TO ACCRUAL BASIS
December 31, year 2

Account title	Cash basis		Adjustments		Accrual basis*	
	Dr.	Cr.	Dr.	Cr.	Dr. *	Cr. *
Cash	25,600					
Accounts receivable	16,200					
Inventory	62,000					
Furniture & fixtures	118,200					
Land improvements	45,000					
Accumulated depreciation & amortization		32,400				
Accounts payable		17,000				
Baron, Drawings						
Baron, Capital		124,600				
Sales		653,000				
Purchases	305,100					
Salaries	174,000					
Payroll taxes	12,400					
Insurance	8,700					
Rent	34,200					
Utilities	12,600					

Account title	Cash basis		Adjustments		Accrual basis*	
	Dr.	Cr.	Dr.	Cr.	Dr. *	Cr. *
Living expenses	13,000					
	827,000	827,000				

* Completion of these columns is not required.

Task-Based Simulation 3

Concepts		
	Authoritative Literature	Help

This question consists of ten items that represent descriptions or definitions of the various elements of the FASB's *Statements of Financial Accounting Concepts*. Select the **best** answer for each item from the terms listed in A – L. A term may be used once, more than once, or not at all.

Terms

A.	Recognition	G.	Gains
B.	Comprehensive Income	H.	Net Income
C.	Faithful representation	I.	Earnings
D.	Revenues	J.	Realization
E.	Predictive Value	K.	Replacement Cost
F.	Comparability	L.	Current Market Value

Concept statement definitions   (A) (B) (C) (D) (E) (F) (G) (H) (I) (J) (K) (L)

1. Component of relevance.   ○ ○ ○ ○ ○ ○ ○ ○ ○ ○ ○ ○

2. Increases in net assets from incidental or peripheral transactions affecting an entity.   ○ ○ ○ ○ ○ ○ ○ ○ ○ ○ ○ ○

3. The process of converting noncash resources and rights into cash or claims to cash.   ○ ○ ○ ○ ○ ○ ○ ○ ○ ○ ○ ○

4. Enhancing qualitative characteristic of relevance **and** faithful representation.   ○ ○ ○ ○ ○ ○ ○ ○ ○ ○ ○ ○

5. The process of formally recording an item in the financial statements of an entity after it has met existing criteria and been subject to cost-benefit constraints and materiality thresholds.   ○ ○ ○ ○ ○ ○ ○ ○ ○ ○ ○ ○

6. All changes in net assets of an entity during a period except those resulting from investments by owners and distributions to owners.   ○ ○ ○ ○ ○ ○ ○ ○ ○ ○ ○ ○

7. Inflows or other enhancements of assets of an entity or settlements of its liabilities from delivering or producing goods, rendering services, or other activities that constitute the entity's ongoing operations.   ○ ○ ○ ○ ○ ○ ○ ○ ○ ○ ○ ○

8. The amount of cash, or its equivalent, that could be obtained by selling an asset in orderly liquidation.   ○ ○ ○ ○ ○ ○ ○ ○ ○ ○ ○ ○

9. The quality of information that helps users to increase the likelihood of correctly forecasting the outcome of past or present events.   ○ ○ ○ ○ ○ ○ ○ ○ ○ ○ ○ ○

10. A performance measure concerned primarily with cash-to-cash cycles.   ○ ○ ○ ○ ○ ○ ○ ○ ○ ○ ○ ○

Task-Based Simulation 4

Trial Balance Worksheet		
	Authoritative Literature	Help

The accounts listed below appeared in the December 31 trial balance of Jane Alexander Theater.

Equipment	192,000	
Accumulated depreciation equipment		60,000
Notes payable		90,000
Admissions revenue		380,000
Advertising expense	13,680	
Salaries expense	57,600	
Interest expense	1,400	

Additional information

1. The equipment has an estimated life of 16 years and a salvage value of $40,000 at the end of that time. (Use straight-line method.)
2. The note payable is a 90-day note given to the bank October 20 and bearing interest at 10%. (Use 360 days for denominator.)
3. In December, two thousand (2,000) coupon admission books were sold at $25 each. They could be used for admission any time after January 1.
4. Advertising expense paid in advance and included in Advertising Expense, $1,100.
5. Salaries accrued but unpaid, $4,700.

Using the attached Excel file, complete the adjustments, adjusted trial balance, and the income statement columns of the worksheet. For the # column, insert the number of adjustments. Add accounts as needed.

Jane Alexander Theater
December 31, 200X

a)	Trial balance		#	Adjustments		Adjusted trial balance		Income statement	
	Debit	Credit		Debit	Credit	Debit	Credit	Debit	Credit
Equipment	192,000								
Accumulated depreciation—equipment		60,000							
Notes payable		90,000							
Admissions revenue		380,000							
Advertising expense	13,680								
Salaries expense	57,600								
Interest expense	1,400								
Depreciation expense									
Interest payable									
Unearned admissions revenue									
Revenue									
Prepaid advertising									
Salaries payable									

Task-Based Simulation 5

Concepts		
	Authoritative Literature	Help

SFAC 5 provides guidance on measuring assets and liabilities. The following measurement methods are available to measure assets and liabilities, as shown in the list below. Identify the appropriate valuation method for each item.

Measurement methods

A. Historical cost or historical proceeds
B. Current cost
C. Current market value
D. Net realizable value or settlement rate
E. Present value of future cash flows

	Account	(A)	(B)	(C)	(D)	(E)
1.	Long-term receivables	○	○	○	○	○
2.	Available for sale securities	○	○	○	○	○
3.	Equipment	○	○	○	○	○
4.	Warranty obligations	○	○	○	○	○
5.	Short-term payables	○	○	○	○	○
6.	Accounts receivable	○	○	○	○	○
7.	Bonds payable, due in ten years	○	○	○	○	○
8.	Trading securities	○	○	○	○	○

Task-Based Simulation 6

Adjusting Entries		
	Authoritative Literature	Help

Indicate whether each of the following adjusting entries is an accrual or a deferral type entry.

				Accrual	Deferral
1.	Depreciation expense	xx			
	Accumulated deprecation		xx	○	○
2.	Interest receivable	xx			
	Interest revenue		xx	○	○
3.	Rent expense	xx			
	Prepaid rent		xx	○	○
4.	Unearned revenue	xx			
	Rent revenue		xx	○	○
5.	Wage expense	xx			
	Wages payable		xx	○	○

Task-Based Simulation 7

Revenue and Expense Recognition		
	Authoritative Literature	Help

Emco has the following transactions in year 1. Indicate the amount of revenue or expense recognized in year 1, year 2, and year 3 for each of these items. You may show expense recognitions in parentheses (xx).

	Amounts to be recognized		
	Year 1	Year 2	Year 3

1. Emco sells $5,000 of goods to a customer, FOB shipping point on 12/30/Y1.

2. Emco sells three pieces of equipment on a contract over a three-year period. The sales price of each piece of equipment is $10,000. Delivery of each piece of equipment is on February 10 of each year. In year 1, the customer paid a $20,000 down payment, and paid $5,000 per year in year 2 and year 3. Collectibility is reasonably assured.

3. In 1/1/Y1, Emco pays $9,000 for a membership to Wholesalers Association for a two-year membership in the trade association.

4. On 6/1/Y1, Emco signs a contract for $20,000 for goods to be sold on account. Payment is to be made in two installments of $10,000 each on 12/1/Y2 and 12/1/Y3. The goods are delivered on 10/1/Y1. Collection is reasonably assured, and the goods may not be returned.

5. Emco sells goods to a customer on July 1, year 1, for $50,000. If the customer does not sell the goods to retail customers by December 31, year 2, the goods can be returned to Emco. The customer sells the goods to retail customers on October 1, year 2.

Simulation Solutions

Task-Based Simulation 1

Account Classifications		
	Authoritative Literature	
		Help

	Balance sheet classification (A) (B) (C) (D) (E) (F) (G)	Income statement classification (H) (I) (J)
1. Bonds payable, due in year 8	○ ○ ○ ● ○ ○ ○	○ ○ ○
2. Treasury stock	○ ○ ○ ○ ○ ○ ●	○ ○ ○
3. Accounts payable	○ ○ ● ○ ○ ○ ○	○ ○ ○
4. Sales discounts	○ ○ ○ ○ ○ ○ ○	○ ○ ●
5. Notes payable, due in nine months	○ ○ ● ○ ○ ○ ○	○ ○ ○
6. Inventory	● ○ ○ ○ ○ ○ ○	○ ○ ○
7. Accounts receivable	● ○ ○ ○ ○ ○ ○	○ ○ ○
8. Common stock	○ ○ ○ ○ ● ○ ○	○ ○ ○
9. Cost of goods sold	○ ○ ○ ○ ○ ○ ○	○ ● ○
10. Allowance for uncollectible accounts	○ ○ ○ ○ ○ ● ○	○ ○ ○

Task-Based Simulation 2

Accrual Basis Worksheet		
	Authoritative Literature	
		Help

Baron Flowers
WORKSHEET TO CONVERT TRIAL BALANCE TO ACCRUAL BASIS
December 31, year 2

Account title	Cash basis Dr.	Cash basis Cr.	Adjustments Dr.	Adjustments Cr.	Accrual basis* Dr.*	Accrual basis* Cr.*
Cash	25,600				25,600	
Accounts receivable	16,200		(1) 15,800		32,000	
Inventory	62,000		(4) 10,800		72,800	
Furniture & fixtures	118,200				118,200	
Land improvements	45,000				45,000	
Accumulated depreciation & amortization		32,400		(6) 14,250		46,650
Accounts payable		17,000		(3) 13,500		30,500
Baron, Drawings			(9) 61,000		61,000	
Baron, Capital		124,600	(7) 2,000	(5) 2,600		125,200
Allowance for uncollectible accounts				(2) 3,800		3,800
Prepaid insurance			(5) 2,900		2,900	
Accrued expenses				(7) 3,100		3,100
Estimated liability from lawsuit				(8) 50,000		50,000
Sales		653,000		(1) 15,800		668,800
Purchases	305,100		(3) 13,500		318,600	
Salaries	174,000			(9) 48,000	126,000	
Payroll taxes	12,400		(7) 500		12,900	
Insurance	8,700			(5) 300	8,400	
Rent	34,200				34,200	
Utilities	12,600		(7) 600		13,200	

Account title	Cash basis		Adjustments		Accrual basis*	
	Dr.	Cr.	Dr.	Cr.	Dr.*	Cr.*
Living expenses	13,000			(9) 13,000		
Income summary—inventory			(4) 62,000	(4) 72,800		10,800
Uncollectible accounts			(2) 3,800		3,800	
Depreciation & amortization			(6) 14,250		14,250	
Estimated loss from lawsuit			(8) 50,000		50,000	
	827,000	827,000	237,150	237,150	938,850	938,850

* Completion of these columns was not required.

Explanations of adjustments

[1]   To convert year 2 sales to accrual basis.

    Accounts receivable balances:
       December 31, year 2 $32,000
       December 31, year 1   16,200
       Increase in sales $15,800

[2]   To record provision for uncollectible accounts.

[3]   To convert year 2 purchases to accrual basis.

    Accounts payable balances:
       December 31, year 2 $30,500
       December 31, year 1   17,000
       Increase in purchases $13,500

[4]   To record increase in inventory from 12/31/Y1 to 12/31/Y2.

    Inventory balances:
       December 31, year 2 $72,800
       December 31, year 1   62,000
       Increase in inventory $10,800

[5]   To adjust prepaid insurance.

    Prepaid balances:
       December 31, year 2 ($8,700 × 4/12) $2,900
       December 31, year 1 ($7,800 × 4/12)   2,600
       Decrease in insurance expense $ 300

[6]   To record year 2 depreciation and amortization expense.

    Cost of leasehold improvement $45,000
    Estimated life   15 years
    Amortization ($45,000 × 1/15 × 9/12)   2,250
    Depreciation expense on fixtures and equipment   12,000
        $14,250

[7]   To convert expenses to accrual basis.

	Balances December 31,		Increase
	Year 2	Year 1	in expenses
Utilities	$1,500	$ 900	$ 600
Payroll taxes	1,600	1,100	500
	$3,100	$2,000	$1,100

[8]   To record lawsuit liability at 12/31/Y2.

    Attorney's estimate of probable loss $300,000
    Amount covered by insurance   250,000
    Baron's estimated liability $ 50,000

[9]   To record Baron's drawings for year 2.

    Salary ($4,000 × 12) $48,000
    Living expenses   13,000
        $61,000

Task-Based Simulation 3

Concepts		
	Authoritative Literature	Help

Concept statement definitions	(A) (B) (C) (D) (E) (F) (G) (H) (I) (J) (K) (L)
1. Component of relevance.	(E) ●
2. Increases in net assets from incidental or peripheral transactions affecting an entity.	(G) ●
3. The process of converting noncash resources and rights into cash or claims to cash.	(J) ●
4. Enhancing qualitative characteristic of relevance **and** faithful representation.	(F) ●
5. The process of formally recording an item in the financial statements of an entity after it has met existing criteria and been subject to cost-benefit constraints and materiality thresholds.	(A) ●
6. All changes in net assets of an entity during a period except those resulting from investments by owners and distributions to owners.	(B) ●

Concept statement definitions	(A)	(B)	(C)	(D)	(E)	(F)	(G)	(H)	(I)	(J)	(K)	(L)
7. Inflows or other enhancements of assets of an entity or settlements of its liabilities from delivering or producing goods, rendering services, or other activities that constitute the entity's ongoing operations.	○	○	○	●	○	○	○	○	○	○	○	○
8. The amount of cash, or its equivalent, that could be obtained by selling an asset in orderly liquidation.	○	○	○	○	○	○	○	○	○	○	○	●
9. The quality of information that helps users to increase the likelihood of correctly forecasting the outcome of past or present events.	○	○	○	○	●	○	○	○	○	○	○	○
10. A performance measure concerned primarily with cash-to-cash cycles.	○	○	○	○	○	○	○	○	●	○	○	○

Explanations

1. **(E)** SFAC 5 states that "Relevance is a primary qualitative characteristic. To be relevant, information about an item must have feedback value or predictive value (or both) for users and must be timely."

2. **(G)** SFAC 6 states that "Gains are increases in equity (net assets) from peripheral or incidental transactions of an entity and from all other transactions and other events and circumstances affecting the entity except those that result from revenues or investments by owners."

3. **(J)** SFAC 5 states that "Revenues and gains are realized when products (goods or services), merchandise, or other assets are exchanged for cash or claims to cash."

4. **(F)** SFAC 8 states that "Comparability, including consistency, is an enhancing quality that interacts with relevance and faithful representation to contribute to the usefulness of information."

5. **(A)** SFAC 5 states that "Recognition is the process of formally recording or incorporating an item into the financial statements of an entity as an asset, liability, revenue, expense, or the like." SFAC 5 continues the recognition concept by stating, "An item and information about it should meet four fundamental recognition criteria to be recognized and should be recognized when the criteria are met, subject to a cost-benefit constraint and a materiality threshold."

6. **(B)** SFAC 5 states that "Comprehensive income is a broad measure of the effects of transactions and other events on an entity, comprising all recognized changes in equity (net assets) of the entity during a period from transactions and other events and circumstances except those resulting from investments by owners and distributions to owners."

7. **(D)** SFAC 6 defines revenues as "inflows or other enhancements of assets of an entity or settlements of its liabilities (or a combination of both) from delivering or producing goods, rendering services, or other activities that constitute the entity's ongoing major or central operations."

8. **(L)** SFAC 5 defines current market value as "the amount of cash, or its equivalent, that could be obtained by selling an asset in orderly liquidation."

9. **(E)** Predictive value is the quality of information that helps users to increase the likelihood of correctly forecasting the outcome of past or present events (SFAC 8).

10. **(I)** SFAC 5 states that "Earnings is a measure of performance during a period that is concerned primarily with the extent to which asset inflows associated with cash-to-cash cycles substantially completed (or completed) during the period exceed (or are less than) asset outflows associated, directly or indirectly, with the same cycles."

Task-Based Simulation 4

Trial Balance Worksheet		
	Authoritative Literature	Help

Jane Alexander Theater
December 31, 200X

a)	Trial balance		#	Adjustments		Adjusted trial balance		Income statement	
	Debit	Credit		Debit	Credit	Debit	Credit	Debit	Credit
Equipment	192,000					192,000			
Accumulated depreciation—equipment		60,000	1		9,500		69,500		
Notes payable		90,000					90,000		
Admissions revenue		380,000	3	50,000			330,000		330,000
Advertising expense	13,680		4		1,100	12,580		12,580	
Salaries expense	57,600		5	4,700		62,300		62,300	
Interest expense	1,400		2	1,800		3,200		3,200	
Depreciation expense			1	9,500		9,500		9,500	
Interest payable			2		1,800		1,800		
Unearned admissions revenue			3		50,000		50,000		
Prepaid advertising			4	1,100		1,100			
Salaries payable			5		4,700		4,700		

Task-Based Simulation 5

Concepts		
	Authoritative Literature	Help

Account	(A)	(B)	(C)	(D)	(E)
1. Long-term receivables	○	○	○	○	●
2. Available-for-sale securities	○	○	●	○	○
3. Equipment	●	○	○	○	○
4. Warranty obligations	○	○	○	●	○
5. Short-term payables	●	○	○	○	○
6. Accounts receivable	○	○	○	●	○
7. Bonds payable, due in ten years	○	○	○	○	●
8. Trading securities	○	○	●	○	○

Task-Based Simulation 6

Adjusting Entries		
	Authoritative Literature	Help

			Accrual	Deferral
1.	Depreciation expense	xx	○	●
	Accumulated deprecation	xx		
2.	Interest receivable	xx	●	○
	Interest revenue	xx		
3.	Rent expense	xx	○	●
	Prepaid rent	xx		
4.	Unearned revenue	xx	○	●
	Rent revenue	xx		
5.	Wage expense	xx	●	○
	Wages payable	xx		

Task-Based Simulation 7

Revenue and Expense Recognition		
	Authoritative Literature	Help

		Amounts to be recognized		
		Year 1	Year 2	Year 3
1.	Emco sells $5,000 of goods to a customer, FOB shipping point on 12/30/Y1.	5,000	--	--
2.	Emco sells three pieces of equipment on a contract over a three-year period. The sales price of each piece of equipment is $10,000. Delivery of each piece of equipment is on February 10 of each year. In year 1, the customer paid a $20,000 down payment, and paid $5,000 per year in year 2 and year 3. Collectibility is reasonably assured.	10,000	10,000	10,000
3.	In 1/1/Y1, Emco pays $9,000 for a membership to Wholesalers Association for a two-year membership in the trade association.	(4,500)	(4,500)	--
4.	On 6/1/Y1, Emco signs a contract for $20,000 for goods to be sold on account. Payment is to be made in two installments of $10,000 each on 12/1/Y2 and 12/1/Y3. The goods are delivered on 10/1/Y1. Collection is reasonably assured, and the goods may not be returned.	20,000	--	--
5.	Emco sells goods to a customer on July 1, year 1, for $50,000. If the customer does not sell the goods to retail customers by December 31, year 2, the goods can be returned to Emco. The customer sells the goods to retail customers on October 1, year 2.	--	50,000	--

Explanations

1.   When goods are sold FOB shipping point, title passes at the time the goods are shipped. Therefore, Emco may recognize revenue on 12/30/Y1 at the time the goods are shipped.

2.   Revenue is recognized when earned and realizable. This sale is not complete until each piece of equipment is delivered. Therefore, Emco should recognize $10,000 each year as the equipment is delivered, regardless of payment terms.

3.   Emco should match expenses to the year in which the benefits are received, which is over the two-year period.

4.   Because Emco delivered the goods in year 1, and collectibility is reasonably assured, Emco should recognize all revenue in year 1.

5.   Because there is a sale with a right of return, and the buyer may return the merchandise if it is not sold to a retail customer, recognition should be delayed until the right of return has expired.

B. Error Correction

1. Accountants must be in a position to anticipate, locate, and correct errors in their functions of systems and procedures design, controllership, and attestation.

   a. Errors which are discovered in the same year that they are made are corrected by

      (1) Determining the entry that was made
      (2) Determining the correct entry
      (3) Analyzing increases or decreases needed in affected accounts
      (4) Making the correct entry

   b. Errors in classification (e.g., sales expense instead of R&D expense) affect only one period.
   c. Nonsystematic errors in adjusting entries (e.g., an error in ending inventory of one period) affect two periods and are known as self-correcting (counterbalancing) errors.

   EXAMPLE

   Overstating ending inventory of year 1 will overstate the income of year 1 and understate the income of year 2.

   ---

   d. Other errors will affect the income of several periods, such as misrecording the cost of a long-lived asset (i.e., depreciation will be misstated for all periods).

2. The chart below shows four examples of counterbalancing errors.

Errors Which Will Self-Correct After Two Years
Omitting Accruals

Case #1

	12/31/Y1	12/31/Y2	1/1/Y3
Expense (wages)	Understated	Overstated	Correct
Net income	Overstated	Understated	Correct
Payable (wages)	Understated	Correct	Correct
Retained earnings	Overstated	Correct	Correct

Case #2

Revenue (interest)	Understated	Overstated	Correct
Net income	Understated	Overstated	Correct
Receivable (interest)	Understated	Correct	Correct
Retained earnings	Understated	Correct	Correct

Omitting Deferrals (Prepaids)

Case #3

Expense (insurance)	Overstated	Understated	Correct
Net income	Understated	Overstated	Correct
Prepaid asset	Understated	Correct	Correct
Retained earnings	Understated	Correct	Correct

Case #4

Revenue (unearned)	Overstated	Understated	Correct
Net income	Overstated	Understated	Correct
Liability (un. rev.)	Understated	Correct	Correct
Retained earnings	Overstated	Correct	Correct

NOTE: In all four cases the income statement errors have the opposite effect in year 1 and year 2. Also notice that by the end of year 2 the balance sheet accounts are correct. Therefore, even if the error is not discovered, the financial statements will be correct by the beginning of the third year.

3. When an error is discovered in a period subsequent to the period when the error occurred, an entry must be made to correct the accounts as if the error had not been made.

EXAMPLE

Assume the entry to accrue wage expense in the amount of $10,000 is omitted on 12/31/Y1. The effects that would be caused by such an omission may be categorized as follows:

	Year 1	Year 2	Year 3
Expense	Understated	Overstated	Correct
Income	Overstated	Understated	Correct
Wages payable	Understated	Correct	Correct
Retained earnings	Overstated	Correct	Correct

If the company follows the policy of reversing adjusting entries for accruals, then correction of the error any time during year 2 will require

| Adjustment to correct error | 10,000 | |
| Wage expense | | 10,000 |

The adjustment account, when closed to retained earnings, will correct for the 1/1/Y2 overstatement in retained earnings due to the overstatement of year 1 income. The credit to wage expense will reduce the expense account for year 2 to an amount equal to year 2 wages.

If the error was discovered in year 3, no entry would be required since the error self-corrects during year 2. The year 3 balances would be the same with or without the error.

NOTE: The requirements of error analysis questions vary considerably. When asked for the effect of errors, be careful to determine the effect rather than the correction; they are opposite. The effect of revenue overstatement on income is over or plus; therefore, the correction to income is to subtract. Also distinguish between correcting/adjusting entries (which can be made in the accounts to correct the current period) and "worksheet entries" which adjust amounts reported in prior periods (i.e., journal entries are not recorded to correct nominal accounts of prior periods).

4. Accounting errors are errors in recognition, measurement, presentation, or disclosure in the financial statements. An error can occur from mathematical mistakes, mistakes in applying GAAP, or oversight of facts that existed when the financial statements were prepared. A change in accounting principle from non-GAAP to GAAP is also a correction of an error.

a. An error in the financial statements is treated as a prior period adjustment by restating the prior period financial statements. The cumulative effect of the error is reflected in the carrying value of assets and liabilities at the beginning of the first period presented, with an offsetting adjustment to the opening balance in retained earnings for that period. Financial statements for each period are then adjusted to reflect the correction of the period-specific effects of the error.

b. Footnote disclosures should disclose that the previously issued financial statements were restated, along with a description of the error. The line item effects of the error and any per share amounts must also be disclosed for each period presented. The gross effects and net effects from applicable income taxes on the net income of the prior period must be disclosed, as well as the effects on retained earnings and net income. Footnote disclosures must also indicate the cumulative effect of the change on retained earnings or other components of equity or net assets at the beginning of the earliest period presented. Once the correction of the error is disclosed, the financial statements of subsequent years do not need to repeat the disclosures.

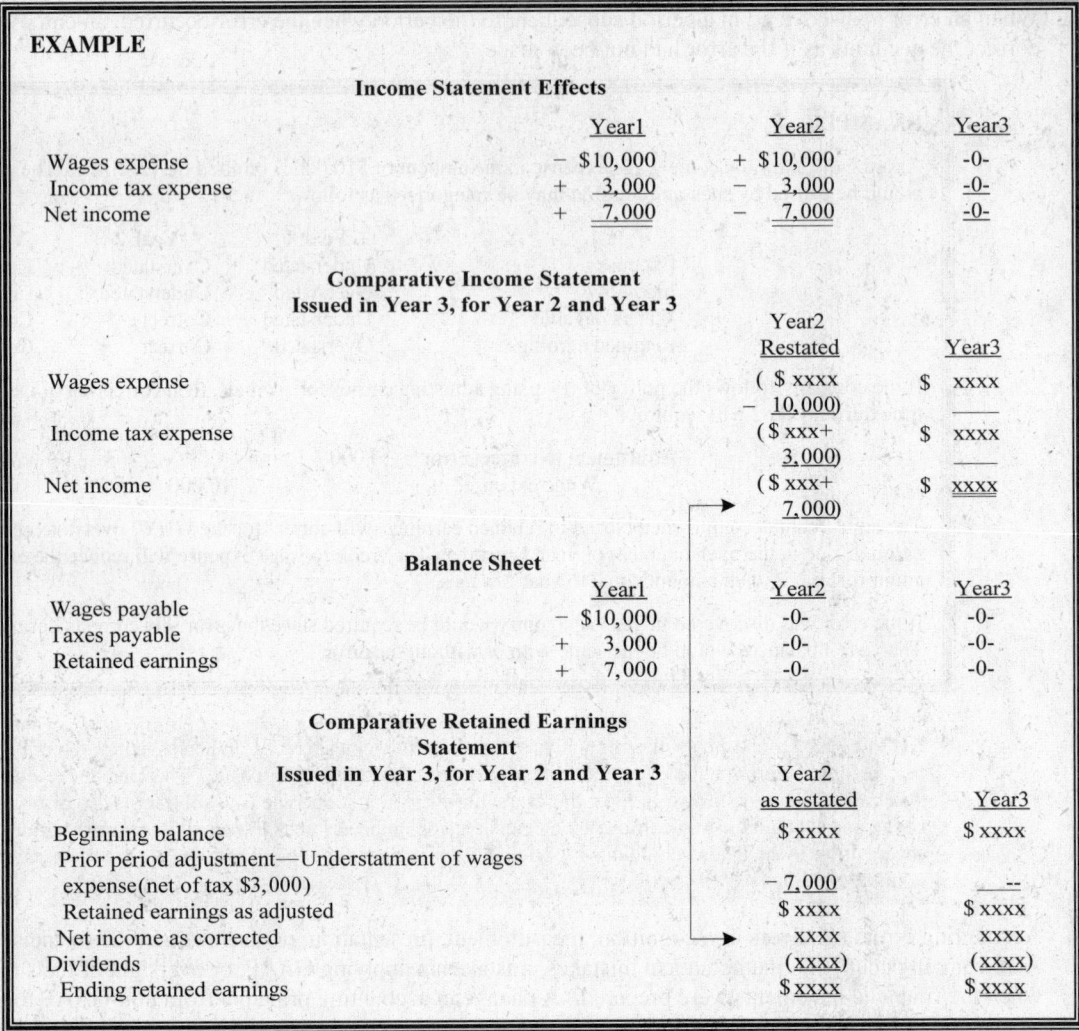

EXAMPLE

Income Statement Effects

	Year1	Year2	Year3
Wages expense	− $10,000	+ $10,000	-0-
Income tax expense	+ 3,000	− 3,000	-0-
Net income	+ 7,000	− 7,000	-0-

Comparative Income Statement
Issued in Year 3, for Year 2 and Year 3

	Year2 Restated	Year3
Wages expense	($ xxxx − 10,000)	$ xxxx
Income tax expense	($ xxx+ 3,000)	$ xxxx
Net income	($ xxx+ 7,000)	$ xxxx

Balance Sheet

	Year1	Year2	Year3
Wages payable	− $10,000	-0-	-0-
Taxes payable	+ 3,000	-0-	-0-
Retained earnings	+ 7,000	-0-	-0-

Comparative Retained Earnings Statement
Issued in Year 3, for Year 2 and Year 3

	Year2 as restated	Year3
Beginning balance	$ xxxx	$ xxxx
Prior period adjustment—Understatment of wages expense(net of tax $3,000)	− 7,000	--
Retained earnings as adjusted	$ xxxx	$ xxxx
Net income as corrected	xxxx	xxxx
Dividends	(xxxx)	(xxxx)
Ending retained earnings	$ xxxx	$ xxxx

5. Inventory errors have an impact on both the balance sheet and the income statement.

a. Inventory errors include a misstatement of the ending inventory balance, which is followed by a misstatement of the beginning balance for the next period, or an inventory error could be a misstatement of purchases for the period.

b. The analysis of inventory errors in a periodic inventory system is facilitated by setting up a statement of cost of goods sold. The statement of cost of goods sold shows the relationship between the inventory and purchases accounts and the impact of incorrect amounts.

c. The four examples shown below use the statement of cost of goods sold format to analyze different inventory errors. Items that are correct are identified by an "OK," while items that are incorrect are listed as overstated (over) or understated (under).

EXAMPLE

INVENTORY ERRORS

	Case #1 (Overstated Inventory Count)		Case #2 (Understated Inventory Count)	
	Year 1	Year 2	Year 1	Year 2
Beginning inventory	OK	Over	OK	Under
+ Purchases	OK	OK	OK	OK
Goods available for sale	OK	Over	OK	Under
− Ending inventory*	Over	OK	Under	OK
Cost of goods sold	Under	Over	Over	Under
Net income	Over	Under	Under	Over
Retained earnings	Over	OK	Under	OK
Accounts payable	OK	OK	OK	OK

* Determined by physical count.

	Case #3 (Overstated Purchases**)		Case #4 (Understated Purchases***)	
	Year 1	Year 2	Year 1	Year 2
Beginning inventory	OK	OK	OK	Under
+ Purchases	Over	Under	Under	Over
Goods available for sale	Over	Under	Under	OK
− Ending inventory*	OK	OK	Under	OK
Cost of goods sold	Over	Under	OK	OK
Net income	Under	Over	OK	OK
Retained earnings	Under	OK	OK	OK
Accounts payable	Over	OK	Under	OK

* Determined by physical count.
** Vendor shipped goods FOB destination. Goods were not received by 12/31, but recorded as purchases and not included in physical inventory count.
*** Vendor shipped goods FOB shipping point prior to 12/31, but not recorded as purchases or included in physical inventory count.

6. Research Component—Accounting Standards Codification

ASC Topic 250, found in the Presentation area of the Codification, outlines the accounting rules for accounting changes and error corrections. Keywords for researching accounting errors are shown below.

Correction error	Period-specific effects	Prior period adjustments error
Disclosure correction error	Prior period adjustment	Reporting correction error

7. International Financial Reporting Standards (IFRS)

Accounting for error correction is similar to US GAAP. A prior period error includes arithmetic mistakes, mistakes in applying accounting policies, and mistakes in recognition, measurement, presentation or disclosures in the financial statements. IFRS requires the entity to correct the error by restating the comparative amounts for prior periods. If the error occurred before the earliest period presented, then the opening balances of assets, liabilities, and equity should be restated for the earliest period presented. Similar to US GAAP, if it is impracticable to determine the periodic effects of the error, comparative information is restated from the earliest date practicable.

NOW REVIEW MULTIPLE-CHOICE QUESTIONS 1 THROUGH 15

Multiple-Choice Questions (1-15)

B.   Error Correction

1.   Loeb Corp. frequently borrows from the bank in order to maintain sufficient operating cash. The following loans were at a 12% interest rate, with interest payable maturity. Loeb repaid each loan on its scheduled maturity date.

Date of loan	Amount	Maturity date	Term of loan
11/1/Y1	$ 5,000	10/31/Y2	1 year
2/1/Y2	15,000	7/31/Y2	6 months
5/1/Y2	8,000	1/31/Y3	9 months

Loeb records interest expense when the loans are repaid. As a result, interest expense of $1,500 was recorded in year 2. If no correction is made, by what amount would year 2 interest expense be understated?

- a. $540
- b. $620
- c. $640
- d. $720

2.   During year 3, Paul Company discovered that the ending inventories reported on its financial statements were incorrect by the following amounts:

Year 1	$60,000 understated
Year 2	75,000 overstated

Paul uses the periodic inventory system to ascertain year-end quantities that are converted to dollar amounts using the FIFO cost method. Prior to any adjustments for these errors and ignoring income taxes, Paul's retained earnings at January 1, year 3, would be

- a.   Correct.
- b. $ 15,000 overstated.
- c. $ 75,000 overstated.
- d. $135,000 overstated.

3.   Tack, Inc. reported a retained earnings balance of $150,000 at December 31, year 1. In June year 2, Tack discovered that merchandise costing $40,000 had not been included in inventory in its year 1 financial statements. Tack has a 30% tax rate. What amount should Tack report as adjusted beginning retained earnings in its statement of retained earnings at December 31, year 2?

- a. $190,000
- b. $178,000
- c. $150,000
- d. $122,000

4.   Conn Co. reported a retained earnings balance of $400,000 at December 31, year 1. In August, year 2, Conn determined that insurance premiums of $60,000 for the three-year period beginning January 1, year 1, had been paid and fully expensed in year 1. Conn has a 30% income tax rate. What amount should Conn report as adjusted beginning retained earnings in its year 2 statement of retained earnings?

- a. $420,000
- b. $428,000
- c. $440,000
- d. $442,000

5.   Lore Co. changed from the cash basis of accounting to the accrual basis of accounting during year 2. The cumulative effect of this change should be reported in Lore's year 2 financial statements as a

- a.   Prior period adjustment resulting from the correction of an error.
- b.   Prior period adjustment resulting from the change in accounting principle.
- c.   Component of income before extraordinary item.
- d.   Component of income after extraordinary item.

6.   Bren Co.'s beginning inventory at January 1, year 1, was understated by $26,000, and its ending inventory was overstated by $52,000. As a result, Bren's cost of goods sold for year 1 was

- a.   Understated by $26,000.
- b.   Overstated by $26,000.
- c.   Understated by $78,000.
- d.   Overstated by $78,000.

7.   On January 2, year 2, Air, Inc. agreed to pay its former president $300,000 under a deferred compensation arrangement. Air should have recorded this expense in year 1 but did not do so. Air's reported income tax expense would have been $70,000 lower in year 1 had it properly accrued this deferred compensation. In its December 31, year 2 financial statements, Air should adjust the beginning balance of its retained earnings by a

- a. $230,000 credit.
- b. $230,000 debit.
- c. $300,000 credit.
- d. $370,000 debit.

8.   Net income is understated if, in the first year, estimated salvage value is excluded from the depreciation computation when using the

	Straight-line method	Production or use method
a.	Yes	No
b.	Yes	Yes
c.	No	No
d.	No	Yes

9.   At the end of year 1, Ritzcar Co. failed to accrue sales commissions earned during year 1 but paid in year 2. The error was not repeated in year 2. What was the effect of this error on year 1 ending working capital and on the year 2 ending retained earnings balance?

	Year 1 ending working capital	Year 2 ending retained earnings
a.	Overstated	Overstated
b.	No effect	Overstated
c.	No effect	No effect
d.	Overstated	No effect

10.   On December 31, year 1, special insurance costs were incurred and unpaid, but were not recorded. If these insurance costs were related to a particular job order in work in process that was not completed during the period, what is the effect of the omission on accrued liabilities and retained earnings in the December 31, year 1 balance sheet?

	Accrued liabilities	Retained earnings
a.	No effect	No effect
b.	No effect	Overstated
c.	Understated	No effect
d.	Understated	Overstated

11. Which of the following errors could result in an overstatement of both current assets and stockholders' equity?

    a.   An understatement of accrued sales expenses.

    b.   Noncurrent note receivable principal is misclassified as a current asset.

    c.   Annual depreciation on manufacturing machinery is understated.

    d.   Holiday pay expense for administrative employees is misclassified as manufacturing overhead.

12. Galaxy Corporation had the following financial statement information:

	Year 2	Year 1
Revenue	$135,000	$100,000
Expenses	98,000	65,000
Net income	37,000	35,000

	12/31/Y2	12/31/Y1
Total assets	$157,000	$105,000
Total liabilities	50,000	35,000
Total owners' equity	107,000	70,000

Galaxy failed to record $12,000 of accrued wages at the end of year 1. The wages were recorded and paid in January year 2. Assuming that the correct accruals were made on December 31, year 2, what are the corrected balances in the year 1 and year 2 restated financial statements?

	Year 1 net income	Dec. 31, year 1 total liabilities	Dec. 31, year 2 total owners' equity
a.	$23,000	$23,000	$ 95,000
b.	$47,000	$47,000	$107,000
c.	$23,000	$35,000	$ 95,000
d.	$23,000	$47,000	$107,000

13. Justin Corporation discovered an error in their year 1 financial statements after the statements were issued. This requires that

    a.   The cumulative effect of the error is reported on the year 2 income statement as a cumulative effect of change in accounting principle.

    b.   The cumulative effect of the error is reported in the year 2 beginning balance of each related account.

    c.   The financial statements are restated to reflect the correction of period-specific effects of the error.

    d.   An adjustment to beginning retained earnings in year 2 with a footnote disclosure describing the error.

14. During year 2, Kelly Corporation discovered that ending inventory reported in its year 1 financial statements was understated by $10,000. How should Kelly account for this understatement?

    a.   Adjust the beginning inventory balance in year 2 by $10,000.

    b.   Restate the financial statements with corrected balances for all periods presented.

    c.   Adjust the ending balance in the year 2 retained earnings account.

    d.   Make no entry because the error will self-correct.

15. Jackson Company uses IFRS to report its financial results. During the current year, the company discovered it had overstated sales in the prior year. How should the company handle this issue?

    a.   Adjust sales for the current period.

    b.   Spread the adjustment over the current and future periods.

    c.   Present the cumulative effect of the overstatement as an item in the current period income statement.

    d.   Restate the prior year financial statements presented for comparative purposes.

Multiple-Choice Answers and Explanations

Answers

1.	a	__ __	5.	a	__ __	8.	b	__ __	11.	d	__ __	14.	b	__ __
2.	c	__ __	6.	c	__ __	9.	d	__ __	12.	d	__ __	15.	d	__ __
3.	b	__ __	7.	b	__ __	10.	c	__ _.	13.	c	__ __	1st: __/15 = __%
4.	b	__ __										2nd: __/15 = __%

Explanations

1.　(a)　The correct amount of year 2 interest expense is $2,040, as computed below.

11/1/Y1 note	
Interest from 1/1/Y2 to 10/31/Y2	
($5,000 × 12% × 10/12)	$ 500
2/1/Y2 note	
Interest from 2/1/Y2 to 7/31/Y2	
($15,000 × 12% × 6/12)	900
5/1/Y2 note	
Interest from 5/1/Y2 to 12/31/Y2	
($8,000 × 12% × 8/12)	640
Total year 2 interest	$2,040

Since interest expense of $1,500 was recorded, year 2 interest expense was understated by $540 ($2,040 – $1,500).

2.　(c)　The error in understating the year 1 ending inventory would have self-corrected by 1/1/Y3 (year 1 income understated by $60,000; year 2 income overstated by $60,000). The error in overstating the year 2 ending inventory would **not** have been corrected by 1/1/Y3. This error overstates both year 2 income and the 1/1/Y3 retained earnings balance by $75,000.

3.　(b)　A correction of an error is treated as a prior period adjustment, recorded in the year the error is discovered, and is reported in the financial statements as an adjustment to the beginning balance of retained earnings. The adjustment is reported net of the related tax effect. In this case the net-of-tax effect is $28,000 [$40,000 – ($30% × $40,000)]. This should **increase** beginning retained earnings because the understatement of 12/31/Y1 inventory would have resulted in an overstatement of cost of goods sold and therefore an understatement of retained earnings. Thus, the adjustment 1/1/Y2 retained earnings is $178,000 ($150,000 + $28,000). Tack's journal entry to record the adjustment is

Inventory	40,000	
Retained earnings		28,000
Taxes payable		12,000

4.　(b)　A correction of an error is treated as a prior period adjustment and is reported in the financial statements as an adjustment to the beginning balance of retained earnings in the year the error is discovered. The adjustment is reported net of the related tax effect. In year 1, insurance expense of $60,000 was recorded. The correct year 1 insurance expense was $20,000 ($60,000 × 1/3). Therefore, before taxes, 1/1/Y2 retained earnings is understated by $40,000. The net of tax effect is $28,000 [$40,000 – (30% × $40,000)], so the adjusted beginning retained earnings is $428,000 ($400,000 + $28,000).

5.　(a)　A change in accounting principle is a change from one **generally accepted** principle to another **generally accepted** principle. A correction of an error is the correction of a mathematical mistake, a mistake in the application of an accounting principle, an oversight or misuse of existing facts, or **a change from an unacceptable principle to a generally accepted one**. Therefore, a switch from the cash basis (unacceptable) to the accrual basis (acceptable) is a correction of an error reported as a prior period adjustment.

6.　(c)　The requirement is to determine the effect of inventory errors on cost of goods sold. The effect of the errors on Bren's year 1 cost of goods sold (CGS) is illustrated below.

BI		
+ 　P	– $26,000	CGS understated $26,000
GAFS		
– 　EI	(+ $52,000)	CGS understated 　52,000
CGS		CGS understated $78,000

Beginning inventory is the starting point for the CGS computation, so BI errors have a direct effect on CGS. The understatement of BI ($26,000) causes an **understatement** of goods available for sale (GAFS) and thus of CGS. Ending inventory is subtracted in the CGS computation, so EI errors have an inverse effect on CGS. The overstatement of EI ($52,000) means that too much was subtracted in the CGS computation, causing another **understatement** of CGS. Therefore, CGS is understated by a total of $78,000.

7.　(b)　The failure to record the $300,000 of deferred compensation expense in year 1 is considered an error. The profession requires that the correction of an error be treated as a prior period adjustment. Thus, the requirement is to determine the retroactive adjustment that should be made to the beginning balance of the retained earnings for year 2 (**including** any income tax effect). The net adjustment to beginning retained earnings would be a debit for $230,000 ($300,000 less the income tax benefit of $70,000).

8.　(b)　The depreciable base used to compute depreciation expense under both the straight-line and production methods is equal to the cost less estimated salvage value of the asset. Depreciation expense is overstated and net income is, therefore, understated when the estimated salvage value is excluded from the depreciation computation under both of these methods.

9.　(d)　The entry Ritzcar should have made to accrue sales commissions earned but unpaid at the end of its year 1 fiscal year is

Commission expense	xxx	
Commissions payable		xxx

Since Commissions payable is a current liability, the year 1 ending working capital is overstated due to Ritzcar's failure to record this entry. Since this error was not repeated at the end of Ritzcar's year 2 fiscal year, the income impact of the year 1 error "self-corrected" during year 2, when Ritzcar recorded both the earned but unpaid year 1 commissions plus the year 2 earned commissions. Therefore, the year 2 ending retained earnings would not be impacted by the error.

10. (c) A liability is accrued when an obligation to pay or perform services has been incurred. This is the case even if the liability will not be satisfied until a future date. Therefore, accrued liabilities will be understated on the December 31, year 1 balance sheet because the special insurance costs were not recorded. However, there will be no effect on the December 31, year 1 balance of retained earnings because these costs relate to work in process, and work in process does not affect net income currently. Please note that if the special insurance costs related to goods that were sold, cost of goods sold would have been understated that would have caused both net income and retained earnings to be overstated.

11. (d) The classification of holiday pay expense for administrative employees as manufacturing overhead would result in the capitalization of some or all of these costs as a component of ending inventory, while these costs should be expensed as incurred. This error could overstate ending inventory, a current asset. The overstatement of ending inventory also understates the cost of goods sold (Beginning inventories + Net purchases – Ending inventories = Cost of goods sold), and overstates net income and stockholders' equity. The understatement of accrued sales expenses would not affect current assets. The misclassification of the noncurrent note receivable principal as a current asset would have no impact on stockholders' equity. The understatement of depreciation on **manufacturing** machinery would understate the overhead added to inventories, a current asset.

12. (d) The entry for the 12/31/year 1 wage accrual should have been

Wages expense	12,000	
Wages payable		12,000

Failure to accrue wage expense results in an understatement of wage expense and an understatement of wages payable by $12,000 in year 1. As a result, net income and retained earnings are overstated by $12,000 in year 1. The wages were expensed and paid in year 2. Therefore, wage expense for year 2 is overstated, and year 2 net income is understated by $12,000. This is a counterbalancing error, and ending retained earnings in year 2 would be correct. Although this is a self-correcting error, the financial statements must be restated with period-specific effects. The restated financial statements are

Galaxy Corporation
RESTATED FINANCIAL STATEMENTS

	Year 2	Year 1
Revenue	$135,000	$100,000
Expenses	86,000	77,000
Net income	49,000	23,000
Total assets	$157,000	$105,000
Total liabilities	50,000	47,000
Total owners' equity	107,000	58,000

13. (c) The financial statements of all periods should be restated and corrections made to reflect any period-specific effects of the error. Answer (a) is incorrect because this is an error, not a change in accounting principle. Answer (b) is incorrect because although the asset accounts may be adjusted to reflect correction of an error, income statement effects must also be disclosed. Answer (d) is incorrect because the financial statements must be restated for all periods presented.

14. (b) The financial statements must be restated for all periods presented with period-specific effects disclosed. Answer (a) is incorrect because although beginning inventory may be adjusted, prior years' financial statements must also be restated. Answer (c) is incorrect because correcting the balance of ending retained earnings is not sufficient disclosure for error correction. Answer (d) is incorrect because even though it is a self-correcting error, financial statements must be restated with period-specific effects of the error.

15. (d) The requirement is to identify how an overstatement of sales in prior year financial statement should be treated under IFRS. Answer (d) is correct because the overstatement is an error which must be accounted for by restating the prior year financial statements.

Simulations

Task-Based Simulation 1

Corrected Financial Statements		
	Authoritative Literature	Help

Situation

Cord Corp., a nonpublic enterprise, requires audited financial statements for credit purposes. After making normal adjusting entries, but before closing the accounting records for the year ended December 31, year 2, Cord's controller prepared the following financial statements for year 2:

Cord Corp.
STATEMENT OF FINANCIAL POSITION
December 31, year 2

Assets	
Cash	$1,225,000
Marketable equity securities	125,000
Accounts receivable	460,000
Allowance for doubtful accounts	(55,000)
Inventories	530,000
Property and equipment	620,000
Accumulated depreciation	(280,000)
Total assets	$2,625,000
Liabilities and Stockholders' Equity	
Accounts payable and accrued liabilities	$1,685,000
Income tax payable	110,000
Common stock, $20 par	300,000
Additional paid-in capital	75,000
Retained earnings	455,000
Total liabilities and stockholders' equity	$2,625,000

Cord Corp.
STATEMENT OF INCOME
For the Year Ended December 31, year 2

Net sales	$1,700,000
Operating expenses:	
Cost of sales	570,000
Selling and administrative	448,000
Depreciation	42,000
Total operating expenses	1,060,000
Income before income tax	640,000
Income tax expense	192,000
Net income	$ 448,000

Cord's tax rate for all income items was 30% for all affected years, and it made estimated tax payments when due. Cord has been profitable in the past and expects results in the future to be similar to year 2. During the course of the audit, the following additional information (not considered when the above statements were prepared) was obtained:

1. The investment portfolio consists of short-term investments, classified as available-for-sale, for which total market value equaled cost at December 31, year 1. On February 2, year 2, Cord sold one investment with a carrying value of $100,000 for $130,000. The total of the sale proceeds was credited to the investment account.

2. At December 31, year 2, the market value of the remaining securities in the portfolio was $142,000.

3. The $530,000 inventory total, which was based on a physical count at December 31, year 2, was priced at cost. Subsequently, it was determined that the inventory cost was overstated by $66,000. At December 31, year 2, the inventory's market value approximated the adjusted cost.

4. Pollution control devices costing $48,000, which is high in relation to the cost of the original equipment, were installed on December 29, year 2, and were charged to repairs in year 1.

5. The original equipment referred to in Item 4, which had a remaining useful life of six years on December 29, year 1, is being depreciated by the straight-line method for both financial and tax reporting.

6. A lawsuit was filed against Cord in October year 2 claiming damages of $250,000. Cord's legal counsel believes that an unfavorable outcome is probable, and a reasonable estimate of the court's award to the plaintiff is $60,000, which will be paid in year 3 if the case is settled.

7. Cord determined that its accumulated benefits obligation under the pension plan exceeded the fair value of plan assets by $40,000 at December 31, year 2. Cord has unrecognized prior service cost of $50,000 at December 31, year 2. Cord funds the total pension expense each year.

Complete the following amounts in the corrected financial statements for Cord Corp.

Cord Corp. STATEMENT OF FINANCIAL POSITION December 31, year 2	
Assets	
Cash	
Marketable equity securities	
Accounts receivable	
Allowance for doubtful accounts	
Inventories	
Deferred tax asset	
Property and equipment	
Accumulated depreciation	
Total assets	
Liabilities and Stockholders' Equity	
Accounts payable and accrued liabilities	
Income tax payable	
Estimated liability from lawsuit	
Pension liability	
Common stock, $20 par	
Additional paid-in capital	
Retained earnings	
Other comprehensive income	
Total liabilities and stockholders' equity	
Net sales	
Operating expenses:	
Cost of sales	
Selling and administrative	
Depreciation	
Pension cost	
Total operating expenses	
Other income/loss:	
Gain (loss) on marketable securities	
Estimated loss from lawsuit	
Income before income tax	
Income tax expense	
Net income	

Task-Based Simulation 2

Effect of Error		
	Authoritative Literature	Help

Situation

Klaus Corporation had $580,000 in inventory, which was based on a physical count at December 31, year 1. The inventory was priced at cost. In February year 2, it was determined that the inventory cost was overstated by $50,000.

Indicate the effects of the inventory overstatement in the year 1 and year 2 financial statements by completing the following table. Mark each item overstate, understate, or OK.

	Year 1 Effects			Year 2 Effects		
	(Overstate)	(Understate)	(OK)	(Overstate)	(Understate)	(OK)
Inventory on balance sheet	O	O	O	O	O	O
Cost of goods sold	O	O	O	O	O	O
Net income	O	O	O	O	O	O
Retained earnings	O	O	O	O	O	O

Task-Based Simulation 3

Research		
	Authoritative Literature	Help

Assume that you are assigned to the audit of Young Corporation. Young has determined that it issued financial statements in the prior year with a material error in the application of an accounting principle. Which section of the Professional Standards addresses the issue of how to account for this situation?

Enter your response in the answer fields below.

Task-Based Simulation 4

Concepts		
	Authoritative Literature	Help

Situation

The auditors of Cardiff Company have found the errors in the company's accounting records.
Identify whether each of the following statements is True or False.

		(T)	(F)
1.	Accounting errors are reported as adjustments to the end of the year retained earnings in the current year's financial statements.	O	O
2.	A self-correcting error need not be reported as an error if it has corrected itself in the current year.	O	O
3.	A change in depreciation method is treated as an error when adjusting the financial statements for the current year.	O	O
4.	An accounting error is treated as a prior period adjustment.	O	O
5.	A change in the useful lives of assets in calculating depreciation is treated as an accounting error and accumulated depreciation is adjusted to reflect this error.	O	O

Task-Based Simulation 5

Analysis of Error		
	Authoritative Literature	Help

Situation

The auditors of Cardiff Company have found the following errors in the company's accounting records.
Indicate how the error will affect the current year's financial statements by choosing an "O" in the column for overstate and "U" in the column for understate.

		Assets (O) (U)	Liabilities (O) (U)	Retained earnings (O) (U)	Net income (O) (U)	Other comprehensive income (O) (U)
1.	Cardiff fails to record a sale on account for $8,000.	O O	O O	O O	O O	O O
2.	The inventory was miscounted at year-end and overstated by $5,000.	O O	O O	O O	O O	O O
3.	Cardiff fails to record depreciation expense of $3,500 for the year.	O O	O O	O O	O O	O O
4.	The company receives a utility bill for $400 on December 29, but fails to record the bill.	O O	O O	O O	O O	O O

	Assets		Liabilities		Retained earnings		Net income		Other comprehensive income	
	(O)	(U)	(O)	(U)	(O)	(U)	(O)	(U)	(O)	(U)
5. Available-for-sale securities were not marked to market. Later analysis reveals that the securities increased in value by $4,000 as of the end of the current year. Cardiff does not elect the fair value option for any of its available-for-sale securities.	O	O	O	O	O	O	O	O	O	O
6. Cardiff fails to accrue wages of $17,000 at the end of the year.	O	O	O	O	O	O	O	O	O	O
7. Trading securities were not marked to market. Later analysis reveals that the securities declined in value by $8,000 as of the end of the current year.	O	O	O	O	O	O	O	O	O	O

Task-Based Simulation 6

Research		
	Authoritative Literature	Help

   Assume that you are assigned to the audit of Hughes Corporation. Hughes is attempting to determine whether an error in the prior year's financial statement is material. Which section of the Professional Standards provides guidance on this matter?
   Enter your response in the answer fields below.

Simulation Solutions

Task-Based Simulation 1

Corrected Financial Statements		
	Authoritative Literature	Help

The best way to calculate the new financial statement amounts is to make the required adjusting entries to correct the account balances as shown below.

Cord Corp.
ADJUSTING JOURNAL ENTRIES
December 31, year 2
(Explanations not required)

	Dr.		Cr.	
(1)				
Marketable equity securities	$ 30,000			
Realized gain on sale of marketable equity securities			$ 30,000	[a]
(2)				
Unrealized loss on marketable equity securities (other comprehensive income)	13,000			
Adjustment to reduce marketable equity securities to market value			13,000	[b]
(3)				
Cost of sales	66,000			
Inventories			66,000	
(4)				
Property and equipment	48,000			
Income tax payable			14,400	[c]
Retained earnings			33,600	[c]
(5)				
Depreciation	8,000			
Accumulated depreciation			8,000	[d]
(6)				
Estimated loss from lawsuit	60,000			
Estimated liability from lawsuit			60,000	
(7)				
Deferred pension cost	40,000			
Additional pension liability			40,000	
(8)				
Deferred tax asset	21,900	[i]		
Income tax payable	13,200	[ii]		
Income tax expense			35,100	[iii]

Supporting Computations for Number 8

Corrected total income tax expense for year 2

Income before income tax, as reported		$640,000
Add adjustment increasing income		
Realized gain on sale of securities		30,000 [1]
		670,000
Deduct adjustments decreasing income		
Increase cost of sales for inventory overstatement	$66,000	
Depreciation on pollution control devices	8,000	74,000
Adjusted taxable income before income tax		$596,000

Corrected current portion income tax expense and income taxes payable ($596,000 × 30%) $178,800

Deferred income tax benefits—based on following temporary differences:

Lawsuit expected to be settled in year 3	$60,000	[6]
Unrealized loss on short-term marketable equity securities	13,000	[2]
Total future deductible amounts	$73,000	

[i] Deferred tax benefit of future deductible amounts ($73,000 × 30%)		21,900
Corrected total income tax expense		$156,900
[ii] Income tax expense as reported (all current, no deferred)		$192,000
Corrected income tax payable and income tax expense		178,800
		$ 13,200
[iii] Income tax expense, as reported		$192,000
Corrected total income tax expense		156,900
		$ 35,100

Explanations of amounts

[a] Gain on sale of marketable equity securities

Selling price		$130,000
Cost		100,000
Gain		$ 30,000

[b] Adjustment to reduce marketable equity securities to market value

Marketable equity securities, at cost

Balance, 2/2/Y2 as reported		$125,000
Adjustment for recording error		30,000
Adjusted balance, 12/31/Y2		155,000
Market valuation, 12/31/Y2		142,000
Adjustment required, 12/31/Y2		$ 13,000

[c] Prior year adjustment for pollution control devices

Cost of installation, 12/29/Y1		$ 48,000
Deduct income tax effect ($48,000 × 30%)		14,400
Credit adjustment to retained earnings, 1/1/Y2		$ 33,600

[d] Depreciation for year 2 on pollution control devices

Cost of the installation on 12/29/Y1		$ 48,000
Depreciation for year 2 ($48,000 ÷ 6 years)		$ 8,000

Cord Corp.
STATEMENT OF FINANCIAL POSITION
December 31, year 2

Assets

Cash	$1,225,000
Marketable equity securities	142,000
Accounts receivable	460,000
Allowance for doubtful accounts	(55,000)
Inventories	464,000
Deferred tax asset	21,900
Deferred pension cost	40,000
Property and equipment	668,000
Accumulated depreciation	(288,000)
Total assets	$2,677,900

Liabilities and Stockholders' Equity

Accounts payable and accrued liabilities	$1,685,000
Income tax payable	111,200
Estimated liability from lawsuit	60,000
Pension liability	40,000
Common stock, $20 par	300,000
Additional paid-in capital	75,000
Retained earnings	419,700
Other comprehensive income	(13,000)
Total liabilities and stockholders' equity	$2,677,900

Calculation of corrected retained earnings:

Previous retained earnings (incorrect)	455,000
Less: Net income for year 2 (incorrect)	(448,000)
Beginning of year retained earnings (correct)	7,000
Net income (corrected)	379,100
Prior period adjustment for accounting error in expense pollution control devices in year 1	33,600
Corrected retained earnings	419,700

Cord Corp.
STATEMENT OF INCOME
For the Year Ended December 31, year 2

Net sales	$1,700,000
Operating expenses:	
Cost of sales	(636,000)
Selling and administrative	(448,000)
Depreciation	(50,000)
Total operating expenses	(1,134,000)
Other income/loss:	
Gain (loss) on marketable securities	30,000
Estimated loss from lawsuit	(60,000)
Income before income tax	536,000
Income tax expense	(156,900)
Net income	379,100

Task-Based Simulation 2

Effect of Error		
	Authoritative Literature	Help

	Year 1 Effects			Year 2 Effects		
	(Overstate)	(Understate)	(OK)	(Overstate)	(Understate)	(OK)
Inventory on balance sheet	●	○	○	○	○	●
Cost of goods sold	○	●	○	●	○	○
Net income	●	○	○	○	●	○
Retained earnings	●	○	○	○	○	●

Task-Based Simulation 3

Research		
	Authoritative Literature	Help

ASC	250	10	45	23

Task-Based Simulation 4

Concepts		
	Authoritative Literature	Help

	(T)	(F)
1. Accounting errors are reported as adjustments to the end of the year retained earnings in the current year's financial statements.	○	●
2. A self-correcting error need not be reported as an error if it has corrected itself in the current year.	○	●
3. A change in depreciation method is treated as an error when adjusting the financial statements for the current year.	○	●
4. An accounting error is treated as a prior period adjustment.	●	○
5. A change in the useful lives of assets in calculating depreciation is treated as an accounting error and accumulated depreciation is adjusted to reflect this error.	○	●

Explanations

1. False. Accounting errors require an adjustment to the beginning of the year retained earnings in the current year financial statements.

2. False. A self-correcting error would require an adjustment to correct comparative year financial statements. Adjustments to comparative years should be made to reflect retroactive application of the prior period adjustment to the accounts affected.

3. False. A change in depreciation method is treated as accumulative effect of change in accounting principle.

4. True. Correction of errors involve restatements of prior periods.

5. False. A change in the useful lives of an asset is treated on a prospective basis, and depreciation for the current year is calculated based on book value divided by the estimated number of years remaining.

Task-Based Simulation 5

Analysis of Error		
	Authoritative Literature	Help

	Assets (O) (U)	Liabilities (O) (U)	Retained earnings (O) (U)	Net income (O) (U)	Other comprehensive income (O) (U)
1. Cardiff fails to record a sale on account for $8,000.	○ ●	○ ○	○ ●	○ ●	○ ○
2. The inventory was miscounted at year-end and overstated by $5,000.	● ○	○ ○	● ○	● ○	○ ○
3. Cardiff fails to record depreciation expense of $3,500 for the year.	● ○	○ ○	● ○	● ○	○ ○
4. The company receives a utility bill for $400 on December 29, but fails to record the bill.	○ ○	○ ●	● ○	● ○	○ ○
5. Available-for-sale securities were not marked to market. Later analysis reveals that the securities increased in value by $4,000 as of the end of the current year. Cardiff does not elect the fair value option for any of its available-for-sale securities.	○ ●	○ ○	○ ○	○ ○	○ ●
6. Cardiff fails to accrue wages of $17,000 at the end of the year.	○ ○	○ ●	● ○	● ○	○ ○
7. Trading securities were not marked to market. Later analysis reveals that the securities declined in value by $8,000 as of the end of the current year.	● ○	○ ○	● ○	● ○	○ ○

Explanations

1. Cardiff should have debited Accounts Receivable and credited Sales. Therefore, accounts receivable is understated, and retained earnings is understated.

2. Cardiff has overstated ending inventory, which understates cost of goods sold. Understating cost of goods sold results in income being overstated for the period. Net income flows into retained earnings, and thus, retained earnings is also overstated in the current period.

3. Cardiff should have debited Depreciation Expense and credited Accumulated Depreciation. By not making this entry, depreciation expense is too low, overstating net income, and overstating retained earnings. Accumulated depreciation is also too low, which overstates assets.

4. The entry would be to debit Utility Expense and credit Accounts Payable. Failing to make this entry would understate expenses, which results in overstated net income, overstated retained earnings, and understated liabilities.

5. The unrealized gain on available-for-sale securities is not recognized in net income, but is recognized as an unrealized gain in other comprehensive income. Failing to mark to market when an available-for-sale security has increased in value would result in understating assets and understating other comprehensive income for the period.

6. The journal entry to accrue wages is to debit Wage Expense and credit Wages Payable. Failure to accrue wages results in expenses being understated, which in turn, overstates net income and overstates retained earnings for the period. Failure to accrue wages also results in liabilities being understated.

7. The unrealized gains and losses from trading securities should be included in net income for the period. Failure to mark to market and recognize the loss would result in assets being overstated, net income being overstated, and retained earnings being overstated for the period.

Task-Based Simulation 6

Research	Authoritative Literature	Help

ASC	250	10	45	27

C. Accounting Changes

Accounting changes include a change in accounting principle, a change in estimate, or a change in the reporting entity. The correction of an error in previous financial statements is not an accounting change. The statement further defines two important terms: restatement and retrospective application. A **restatement** is the process of revising previously issued financial statements to correct an error. A **retrospective application** is the application of a different accounting principle to previously issued financial statements, as if that principle had always been used. Retrospective application is required for changes in accounting principle and changes in reporting entity.

1. Changes in Accounting Principles

a. An entity may change accounting principle only if the change is required by a newly issued accounting pronouncement, or if the entity can justify the use of the alternative accounting principle because it is **preferable**.

b. A change in accounting principle is accounted for through retrospective application of the new accounting principle to all prior periods, unless it is impracticable to do so. Retrospective changes require the following:

(1) The cumulative effects of the change are presented in the carrying amounts of assets and liabilities as of **the beginning of the first period presented**.

(2) An offsetting adjustment is made to the opening balance of retained earnings for that period (the beginning of the first period presented).

(3) Financial statements for each individual prior period presented are adjusted to reflect the **period-specific effects** of applying the new accounting principle.

   (a) Only the **direct effects** of the change are recognized in prior periods. An example of a direct effect is an adjustment to an inventory balance due to a change in inventory valuation method. Related changes, such as the effect on deferred taxes or an impairment adjustment, are also considered direct effects and must be recognized in prior periods.

   (b) **Indirect effects** are any changes to current or future cash flows that result from making a change in accounting principle. An example of an indirect effect is a change in a profit sharing or royalty payment based on revenue or net income. Any indirect effects of the change are reported in the period in which the accounting change is made.

   (c) If the cumulative effect of applying the accounting change can be determined but the period-specific effects on all prior periods cannot be determined, the cumulative effect is applied to the carrying amounts of assets and liabilities at the beginning of the earliest period to which it can be applied or calculated. An offsetting adjustment is then made to the opening balance of retained earnings for that period.

EXAMPLE

Wagner Corporation began operations on January 1, year 1. On January 1, year 3, Wagner changes from the weighted-average method of accounting for inventory to the FIFO method. Wagner provides a profit-sharing plan for its employees. The bonus or profit-sharing plan allows all employees to share in a 5% bonus based on earnings before income taxes and bonus. The income tax rate for all periods is 30%. Assume there are no book/tax differences or deferred taxes. All taxes and bonuses are accrued at the end of each year on December 31 and paid in January of the following year.

Assume that Wagner's accounting records are adequate to determine the effects of the change in accounting principle for each year. Ending inventory for the weighted-average and FIFO methods are shown below.

Ending Inventory

	Weighted-average method	FIFO method
12-31-Y1	1,000	1,200
12-31-Y2	2,000	2,500
12-31-Y3	2,400	3,200

The income statements for year 1 through year 3 calculated using weighted-average method are shown below.

Wagner Corporation
Income Statements

	For the period ending 12-31-Y3 (before change)	For the period ending 12-31-Y2 (before change)	For the period ending 12-31-Y1 (before change)
Sales	$15,000	$12,000	$ 8,000
Less: Cost of good sold	(8,900)	(7,000)	(5,000)
Gross profit	6,100	5,000	3,000
Sales, general & admin. expenses	(3,500)	(3,000)	(2,000)

Earnings before bonus and income taxes	2,600	2,000	1,000
Bonus compensation expense	(130)	(100)	(50)
Earnings before income taxes	2,470	1,900	950
Income tax expense	(741)	(570)	(285)
Net income	$ 1,729	$ 1,330	$ 665

Balance sheets calculated using the weighted-average inventory method before the change to FIFO for year 1-year 3 are shown below.

Wagner Corporation
Balance Sheets

	Dec. 31, year 3 (before change)	Dec. 31, year 2 (before change)	Dec. 31, year 1 (before change)
Cash	$ 1,900	$ 1,000	$ 1,000
Inventory	2,400	2,000	1,000
Plant, property, and equipment	11,000	10,000	10,000
Total assets	15,300	13,000	12,000
Accounts payable	1,370	1,000	1,665
Accrued bonus liability	130	100	50
Income tax liability	741	570	285
Total liabilities	2,241	1,670	2,000
Common stock	500	500	500
Additional paid-in capital	8,835	8,835	8,835
Retained earnings	3,724	1,995	665
Total liabilities and owners' equity	$15,300	$13,000	$12,000

To account for the change in accounting for inventory, the new accounting method is applied retrospectively. Retrospective application requires restatement of the financial statements for the period-specific effects. The period-specific effects for Wagner include the direct effects on inventory, cost of goods sold, income tax expense, and income tax liability for each period. The change in bonus compensation expense and accrued bonus liability are indirect effects and are accounted for in the year of the change, which is the current year, year 3.

To calculate the adjustments in inventory and cost of goods sold for each year, use a T-account. First, calculate the purchases for each year using the weighted-average method.

Inventory
(Weighted-average method)

1-1-Y1	-0-		
Purchases	6,000	5,000	CGS
12-31-Y1	1,000		
Purchases	8,000	7,000	CGS
12-31-Y2	2,000		
Purchases	9,300	8,900	CGS
12-31-Y3	2,400		

Then, using the amount of purchases for each period and the information given in the problem for ending inventory using the FIFO method, calculate the adjusted cost of goods sold for each period using the FIFO method.

Inventory
(FIFO method)

1-1-Y1	-0-		
Purchases	6,000	4,800	CGS
12-31-Y1	1,200		
Purchases	8,000	6,700	CGS
12-31-Y2	2,500		
Purchases	9,300	8,600	CGS
12-31-Y3	3,200		

After you have calculated the period-specific effects on ending inventory and cost of goods sold, prepare an adjusted income statement for each period.

The adjusted income statement for the period ending December 31, year 1, is shown below.

Wagner Corporation—Income Statement
For the year ending 12-31-Y1

	For the period ending 12-31-Y1 as originally reported	For the period ending 12-31-Y1 as adjusted	Effect of the change
Sales	$ 8,000	$ 8,000	$ --
Less: Cost of good sold	(5,000)	(4,800)	(200)
Gross profit	3,000	3,200	200
Sales, general & admin. expenses	(2,000)	2,000	--
Earnings before bonus and income taxes	1,000	1,200	200
Bonus compensation expense*	(50)	(50)*	--
Earnings before income taxes	950	1,150	200
Income tax expense	(285)	(345)	(60)
Net income	$ 665	$ 805	$ 140

* Bonus expense is an indirect effect of the change; therefore, bonus expense is not adjusted retrospectively. Instead, the indirect effects of the bonus are adjusted in the current year, year 3.

Wagner Corporation—Income Statement
For the year ending 12-31-Y2

	For the period ending 12-31-Y2 as originally reported	For the period ending 12-31-Y2 as adjusted	Effect of the change
Sales	$ 12,000	$ 12,000	$ --
Less: Cost of good sold	(7,000)	(6,700)	(300)
Gross profit	5,000	5,300	300
Sales, general & admin. expenses	(3,000)	3,000	--
Earnings before bonus and income taxes	2,000	2,300	300
Bonus compensation expense*	(100)	(100)*	--
Earnings before income taxes	1,900	2,200	300
Income tax expense	(570)	(660)	(90)
Net income	$ 1,330	$ 1,540	$ 210

* Bonus expense is an indirect effect of the change; therefore, it is adjusted and expensed in the current year, year 3.

Wagner Corporation—Income Statement
For the year ending 12-31-Y3

	For the period ending 12-31-Y3 current year before adjustment	For the period ending 12-31-Y3 as adjusted
Sales	$15,000	$15,000
Less: Cost of good sold	(8,900)	(8,600)
Gross profit	6,100	6,400
Sales, general & admin. expenses	(3,500)	(3,500)
Earnings before bonus and income taxes	2,600	2,900
Bonus compensation expense*	(130)	(170)*
Earnings before income taxes	2,470	2,730
Income tax expense	(741)	819
Net income	$ 1,729	$ 1,911

* Bonus compensation expense for year 3 is calculated as follows:

Year 3	Earnings before bonus and taxes	$2,900	× 5%	$145
Year 2	Adjustment to earnings before bonus and taxes	300	× 5%	15
Year 1	Adjustment to earnings before bonus and taxes	200	× 5%	10
	Total bonus compensation expense for year 3 (adjusted for effects of the accounting change)			$170

The adjusted income statements for year 1 through year 3, presented on a comparative basis are shown below.

Wagner Corporation
Income Statement

	For the period ending 12-31-Y3	For the period ending 12-31-Y2 as adjusted	For the period ending 12-31-Y1 as adjusted
Sales	$15,000	$12,000	$ 8,000
Less: Cost of good sold	(8,600)	(6,700)	(4,800)
Gross profit	6,400	5,300	3,200
Sales, general & admin. expenses	(3,500)	(3,000)	(2,000)
Earnings before bonus and income taxes	2,900	2,300	1,200
Bonus compensation expense	(170)	(100)	(50)
Earnings before income taxes	2,730	2,200	1,150
Income tax expense	(819)	(660)	(345)
Net income	$ 1,911	$ 1,540	$ 805

The balance sheet is presented on a comparative basis for two years. Therefore, the assets and liabilities must be retrospectively adjusted for the period-specific effects as of December 31, year 2, the first year presented. In addition, any previous years' adjustment are shown as an adjustment to retained earnings for the earliest year presented.

Wagner Corporation—Balance Sheet
December 31, year 2

	Dec. 31, year 2 as originally reported	Dec. 31, year 2 as adjusted
Cash	$ 1,000	$ 1,000
Inventory	2,000	2,500
Plant, property, and equipment	10,000	10,000
Total assets	13,000	13,500
Accounts payable	1,000	1,000
Accrued bonus liability	100	100
Income tax liability	570	720*
Total liabilities	1,670	1,820
Common stock	500	500
Additional paid-in capital	8,835	8,835
Retained earnings	1,995	2,345**
Total liabilities and owners' equity	$13,000	$13,500

* Tax liability is adjusted for the increase in income tax expense and income tax liability for year 1 and year 2 ($60 in year 1 and $90 in year 2, for a total of $150 increase in income tax liability).
** Retained earnings is adjusted as follows:

Retained earnings
(with adjustments)

665	NI year 1, as originally reported
140	Adjustment to NI for year 1
805	Bal. in R/E, 12-31-Y1 adjusted
1,330	NI year 2, as originally reported
210	Adjustment to NI for year 2
2,345	Bal. in R/E, 12-31-Y2 after adjustments
1,911	Net income in year 3 using FIFO method
4,256	Bal. in R/E, 12-31-Y3

The balance sheet presented on a comparative basis for two years, is as follows:

Wagner Corporation
Comparative Balance Sheets

	Dec. 31, year 3	Dec. 31, year 2 (as adjusted)
Cash	$ 1,900	$ 1,000
Inventory	3,200	2,500
Plant, property, and equipment	11,000	10,000
Total assets	16,100	13,500
Accounts payable	1,370	1,000
Accrued bonus liability	170*	100
Income tax liability	969**	720**
Total liabilities	2,509	1,820

	Dec. 31, year 3	Dec. 31, year 2 (as adjusted)
Common stock	500	500
Additional paid-in capital	8,835	8,835
Retained earnings	4,256	2,345**
Total liabilities and owners' equity	$16,100	$13,500

* Bonus liability calculation

Bonus liability will be accrued in year 3 and paid in year 4. Therefore, the bonus liability at the end of December 31, year 3, is calculated as follows:

Year 3	Earnings before bonus and taxes	$2,900	×	5%	$145
Year 2	Adjustment to earnings before bonus and taxes	300	×	5%	15
Year 1	Adjustment to earnings before bonus and taxes	200	×	5%	10
	Total bonus compensation liability as of 12-31-Y3 (adjusted for effects of the accounting change)				$170

** Tax liability calculation

Because the change in accounting method occurred in year 3, the tax liability resulting from the change will be accrued in year 3 and paid in January, year 4. The tax liability on the balance sheet is calculated as follows:

Year 3	Earnings before income taxes	$2,730	×	30%	$819
Year 2	Adjustment to earnings before income taxes	300	×	30%	90
Year 1	Adjustment to earnings before income taxes	200	×	30%	60
	Total tax liability for year 3 (adjusted for effects of the accounting change)				$969

c. If it is impracticable to determine the cumulative effect to any of the prior periods, the new accounting principle is applied as if the change was made prospectively at the earliest date practicable. It is considered impracticable only if one of the following three conditions is met:

(1) After making every reasonable effort to apply the new principle to the previous period, the entity is unable to do so.
(2) Retrospective application requires assumptions about management's intentions in a prior period that cannot be independently substantiated.
(3) Retrospective application requires significant estimates, and it is impossible to obtain objective information about the estimates.

d. Notes to the financial statements to describe a change in accounting principle must include

(1) The nature and reason for the change, and explanation as to why the new method is preferable
(2) The method of applying the change
(3) A description of the prior period information that is retrospectively adjusted
(4) The effect of the change on income from continuing operations, net income, and any other affected financial statement line item, and any affected per share amounts for the current period and all periods adjusted retrospectively
(5) The cumulative effect of the change on retained earnings or other components of equity or net assets as of the earliest period presented
(6) If retrospective application is impracticable, the reason, and a description of how the change was reported
(7) A description of the indirect effects of the change, including amounts recognized in the current period, and related per share amounts
(8) Unless impracticable, the amounts of the indirect effects of the change and the per share amounts for each prior period presented

e. Disclosures are also required for interim periods. In the year of the change to the new accounting principle, interim financial statements should disclose the effect of the change on income from continuing operations, net income, and related per share amounts for the postchange interim periods.

f. Once the change in method is disclosed, financial statements in subsequent periods do not need to repeat the disclosures.

NOW REVIEW MULTIPLE-CHOICE QUESTIONS 1 THROUGH 18

2. **Changes in Accounting Estimates**

   a. Changes in accounting estimates are accounted for on a prospective basis. The financial statements are not re-stated or retrospectively adjusted. The change is accounted for in the current period and future periods.

   b. If a change in accounting estimate is effected by a change in principle (e.g., a change in depreciation method), it is treated as a change in estimate.

      (1) In cases where an entity effects a change in estimate by changing an accounting principle, the footnote disclosures required by a change in accounting principle apply and must be included in the notes to the financial statements.

EXAMPLE

Gonzalez Corporation acquires equipment on January 1, year 1, for $100,000. Gonzalez depreciates the equipment using the double-declining balance method. The equipment has a ten-year life and a $20,000 salvage value. In January, year 3, Gonzalez changes its depreciation method to straight-line.

This change in depreciation method is considered a change in estimate effected by a change in accounting principle. According to ASC Topic 250, it is accounted for in the current year and future years.

Step 1: Calculate accumulated depreciation and book value at the beginning of the year of the change in depreciation method.

Double declining balance method

The double-declining rate is $\dfrac{1}{10} \times 2 = 20\%$

Year	Book value at beginning of year	Depreciation rate	Depreciation expense
Year 1	$100,000	20%	$20,000
Year 2	$ 80,000	20%	16,000
Accum. Depr. Jan. 1, year 3			$36,000

To calculate book value on January 1, year 3:

Historical cost	$100,000
– Accum. depr.	36,000
Book value 1-1-Y3	$ 64,000

Step 2: Calculate depreciation expense for current year and future years using the new method.

($64,000 BV – $20,000 salvage value) ÷ 8 years remaining life = $5,500 depreciation expense per year

Journal entry for year 3

In year 3 and in future years, the following depreciation entry is recorded:

Depreciation expense	5,500	
Accumulated depreciation		5,500

---

3. **Changes in Reporting Entities**

   a. Another type of accounting change is a change in reporting entity. A change in reporting entity occurs when a change in the structure of the organization is made which results in financial statements that represent a different or changed entity.

      (1) Some examples of a change in reporting entity include presenting consolidated statements in place of individual statements, a change in subsidiaries, or a change in the use of the equity method for an investment.

   b. When there is a change in reporting entity, the change is retrospectively applied to the financial statements of all prior periods presented. Previously issued interim statements are also presented on a retrospective basis. Footnote disclosures for change in reporting entity include the nature and reason for the change, net income, other comprehensive income, and any related per share amounts for all periods presented.

4. **Correction of an Error**

   a. A correction of an error in previously issued financial statements requires a prior period adjustment by restating the financial statements. Prior period adjustments are covered in the previous section of this module.

TYPES OF ACCOUNTING CHANGES

Type of accounting change	Definition	Financial statement treatment	Financial statement disclosure
1. Change in accounting principle	Change from the use of one generally accepted accounting principle to another generally accepted accounting principle	**Retrospective application:** Report cumulative effect of change in the carrying amounts of assets and liabilities as of the beginning of the first period presented, with an offsetting adjustment to the opening balance of retained earnings for that period. Financial statements for each period are adjusted to reflect period-specific effects of the change for direct effects.	Disclose the nature and reason for the change; method of applying the change; description of prior period information that is retrospectively adjusted; effect of the change on income from continuing operations, net income, and any other financial statement line item; per share amounts for current period and adjusted periods; and a description of the indirect effects of the change and related per share amounts.
2. Change in estimate	Change of estimated FS amount based on new information or experience	**Prospective:** Report in the period of the change and future periods. Do not adjust financial statements of previous periods.	Disclose the effect on income from continuing operations, net income, and related per share amounts if the change affects several future periods.
3. Change in reporting entity	Change that results in the financial statements representing a different entity	**Retrospective application:** Report financial statements of all periods to show financial information for the new reporting entity for those periods.	Disclose the type of change and the reasons for the change, the related effects on income before extraordinary items, net income, other comprehensive income, and related per share effects on EPS for all periods presented.

> **NOW REVIEW MULTIPLE-CHOICE QUESTIONS 19 THROUGH 26**

5. **International Financial Reporting Standards (IFRS)**

   a. **Change in accounting principle.** The rules for accounting changes are also similar to US GAAP.

      (1) Accounting changes may occur only when a change is required by an IFRS, or there is a voluntary change in accounting methods.

         (a) In the case of a new IFRS pronouncement, the transition rules in the new IFRS statement should be followed.
         (b) A voluntary change in accounting method may only be made if it provides reliable and more relevant information about the transactions, entity's financial position, performance, or cash flows.

            1] A voluntary change in accounting method is given retrospective application by applying the policy as if the new policy had always been applied. Retrospective application provides that the opening balance of equity is adjusted for the earliest period presented, and that other amounts are disclosed for each prior period as if the new accounting policy had always been applied.
            2] If it is impracticable to determine the effects of the change, then the change may be applied on a prospective basis.

      (2) Disclosures include the title of the IFRS requiring the change, the nature of the change, the amount of the adjustments to each financial statement line item, and effects on earnings per share.

   b. **Change in accounting estimate.** A change in accounting estimate occurs due to uncertainties in measuring items on the financial statements. Changes in estimates include changes in estimates for bad debts, inventory obsolescence, the fair value of financial assets or liabilities, the useful life of a depreciable asset, or warranty obligations. A change in estimate is accounted for on a prospective basis in the period of the change (current period) and future periods.

> **NOW REVIEW MULTIPLE-CHOICE QUESTIONS 27 THROUGH 29**

KEY TERMS

Prospective application. The change is accounted for in the current period and future periods.

Restatement. The process of revising previously issued financial statements to correct an error.

Retrospective application. The application of a different accounting principle to previously issued financial statements, as if that principle had always been used.

Multiple-Choice Questions (1-29)

C.1. Changes in Accounting Principles (SFAS 154)

1. On January 1, year 1, Bray Company purchased for $240,000 a machine with a useful life of ten years and no salvage value. The machine was depreciated by the double-declining balance method and the carrying amount of the machine was $153,600 on December 31, year 2. Bray changed to the straight-line method on January 1, year 3. Bray can justify the change. What should be the depreciation expense on this machine for the year ended December 31, year 3?

    a. $15,360
    b. $19,200
    c. $24,000
    d. $30,720

Items 2 and 3 are based on the following:

On January 1, year 1, Warren Co. purchased a $600,000 machine, with a five-year useful life and no salvage value. The machine was depreciated by an accelerated method for book and tax purposes. The machine's carrying amount was $240,000 on December 31, year 2. On January 1, year 3, Warren changed to the straight-line method for financial reporting purposes. Warren can justify the change. Warren's income tax rate is 30%.

2. In its year 3 income statement, what amount should Warren report as the cumulative effect of this change?

    a. $120,000
    b. $ 84,000
    c. $ 36,000
    d. $0

3. On January 1, year 3, what amount should Warren report as deferred income tax liability as a result of the change?

    a. $120,000
    b. $ 72,000
    c. $ 36,000
    d. $0

4. On January 2, year 3, to better reflect the variable use of its only machine, Holly, Inc. elected to change its method of depreciation from the straight-line method to the units of production method. The original cost of the machine on January 2, year 1, was $50,000, and its estimated life was ten years. Holly estimates that the machine's total life is 50,000 machine hours.

Machine hours usage was 8,500 during year 1 and 3,500 during year 2.

Holly's income tax rate is 30%. Holly should report the accounting change in its year 3 financial statements as a(n)

    a. Cumulative effect of a change in accounting principle of $2,000 in its income statement.
    b. Entry for current year depreciation expense on the income statement and treated on a prospective basis.
    c. Cumulative effect of a change in accounting principle of $1,400 in its income statement.
    d. Adjustment to beginning retained earnings of $1,400.

5. The effects of a change in accounting principle should be recorded on a prospective basis when the change is from the

    a. Cash basis of accounting for vacation pay to the accrual basis.
    b. Straight-line method of depreciation for previously recorded assets to the double-declining balance method.
    c. Presentation of statements of individual companies to their inclusion in consolidated statements.
    d. Completed-contract method of accounting for long-term construction-type contracts to the percentage-of-completion method.

6. When a company changes from the straight-line method of depreciation for previously recorded assets to the double-declining balance method, which of the following should be used?

	Cumulative effects of change in accounting principle	Retrospective application
a.	No	No
b.	No	Yes
c.	Yes	Yes
d.	Yes	No

Items 7 and 8 are based on the following:

During year 3, Orca Corp. decided to change from the FIFO method of inventory valuation to the weighted-average method. Inventory balances under each method were as follows:

	FIFO	Weighted-average
January 1, year 3	$71,000	$77,000
December 31, year 3	79,000	83,000

Orca's income tax rate is 30%.

7. In its year 3 financial statements, what amount should Orca report as the gain or loss on the cumulative effect of this accounting change?

    a. $2,800
    b. $4,000
    c. $4,200
    d. $0

8. In accordance with the Codification, Orca should report the effect of this accounting change as a(n)

    a. Prior period adjustment.
    b. Component of income from continuing operations.
    c. Retrospective application to previous year's financial statements.
    d. Component of income after extraordinary items.

9. On January 1, year 3, Roem Corp. changed its inventory method to FIFO from LIFO for both financial and income tax reporting purposes. The change resulted in a $500,000 increase in the January 1, year 3 inventory, which is the only change that could be calculated from the accounting records. Assume that the income tax rate for all years is 30%. Retrospective application would result in

    a. An increase in ending inventory in the year 2 balance sheet.

b. A decrease in ending inventory in the year 3 balance sheet.

c. A decrease in net income in year 2.

d. A gain from cumulative effect of change on the income statement in year 3.

10. Which of the following would receive treatment as a cumulative effect on an accounting change on the income statement?

	LIFO to weighted-average	FIFO to weighted-average
a.	Yes	Yes
b.	Yes	No
c.	No	No
d.	No	Yes

11. On August 31, year 3, Harvey Co. decided to change from the FIFO periodic inventory system to the weighted-average periodic inventory system. Harvey is on a calendar year basis. The cumulative effect of the change is determined

a. As of January 1, year 3.

b. As of August 31, year 3.

c. During the eight months ending August 31, year 3, by a weighted-average of the purchases.

d. As of the earliest period presented if practicable.

12. In year 3, Brighton Co. changed from the individual item approach to the aggregate approach in applying the lower of FIFO cost or market to inventories. The change should be reported in Brighton's financial statements as a

a. Change in estimate on a prospective basis.

b. Cumulative effect of change in accounting principle on the current year income statement.

c. Retrospective application to the earliest period presented if practicable.

d. Prior period adjustment with a separate disclosure.

13. On January 1, year 3, Poe Construction, Inc. changed to the percentage-of-completion method of income recognition for financial statement reporting but not for income tax reporting. Poe can justify this change in accounting principle. As of December 31, year 2, Poe compiled data showing that income under the completed-contract method aggregated $700,000. If the percentage-of-completion method had been used, the accumulated income through December 31, year 2, would have been $880,000. Assuming an income tax rate of 40% for all years, the cumulative effect of this accounting change should be reported by Poe as

a. An increase in construction-in-progress for $180,000 in the year 2 balance sheet.

b. A decrease in the beginning balance of retained earnings for $108,000 in year 3.

c. A cumulative effect adjustment of $108,000 on the year 3 income statement.

d. An increase in ending retained earnings of $180,000 in year 2.

14. The effect of a change in accounting principle that is inseparable from the effect of a change in accounting estimate should be reported

a. By restating the financial statements of all prior periods presented.

b. As a correction of an error.

c. As a component of income from continuing operations, in the period of change and future periods if the change affects both.

d. As a separate disclosure after income from continuing operations, in the period of change and future periods if the change affects both.

15. Which of the following is considered a direct effect of a change in accounting principle?

a. Deferred taxes.

b. Profit sharing.

c. Royalty payments.

d. None of the above.

16. Indirect effects from a change in accounting principle should be reported

a. Retrospectively to the earliest period presented.

b. As a cumulative change in accounting principle in the current period.

c. In the period in which the accounting change occurs.

d. As a prior period adjustment.

17. If it is impracticable to determine the cumulative effect of an accounting change to any of the prior periods, the accounting change should be accounted for

a. As a prior period adjustment.

b. On a prospective basis.

c. As a cumulative effect change on the income statement.

d. As an adjustment to retained earnings in the first period presented.

18. If the cumulative effect of applying an accounting change can be determined but the period-specific effects on all periods cannot be determined, the cumulative effect of the change should be applied to

a. The end balance of retained earnings of the earliest period presented.

b. Net income of the current year.

c. Retained earnings of the current year.

d. The carrying value of the assets and liabilities at the beginning of the earliest period to which it can be applied.

C.2. Change in Accounting Estimates

19. On January 1, year 1, Taft Co. purchased a patent for $714,000. The patent is being amortized over its remaining legal life of fifteen years expiring on January 1, year 16. During year 4, Taft determined that the economic benefits of the patent would not last longer than ten years from the date of acquisition. What amount should be reported in the balance sheet for the patent, net of accumulated amortization, at December 31, year 4?

a. $428,400

b. $489,600

c. $504,000

d. $523,600

20. On January 1, year 1, Flax Co. purchased a machine for $528,000 and depreciated it by the straight-line method using an estimated useful life of eight years with no salvage value. On January 1, year 4, Flax determined that the machine had a useful life of six years from the date of acquisition and will have a salvage value of $48,000. An accounting change was made in year 4 to reflect these additional data. The accumulated depreciation for this machine should have a balance at December 31, year 4, of

- a. $292,000
- b. $308,000
- c. $320,000
- d. $352,000

21. How should the effect of a change in accounting estimate be accounted for?

- a. By restating amounts reported in financial statements of prior periods.
- b. By reporting pro forma amounts for prior periods.
- c. As a prior period adjustment to beginning retained earnings.
- d. In the period of change and future periods if the change affects both.

22. During year 2, Krey Co. increased the estimated quantity of copper recoverable from its mine. Krey uses the units of production depletion method. As a result of the change, which of the following should be reported in Krey's year 2 financial statements?

	Cumulative effect of a change in accounting principle	Pro forma effects of retroactive application of new depletion base
a.	Yes	Yes
b.	Yes	No
c.	No	No
d.	No	Yes

23. Oak Co. offers a three-year warranty on its products. Oak previously estimated warranty costs to be 2% of sales. Due to a technological advance in production at the beginning of year 3, Oak now believes 1% of sales to be a better estimate of warranty costs. Warranty costs of $80,000 and $96,000 were reported in year 1 and year 2, respectively. Sales for year 3 were $5,000,000. What amount should be presented in Oak's year 3 financial statements as warranty expense?

- a. $ 50,000
- b. $ 88,000
- c. $100,000
- d. $138,000

24. For year 1, Pac Co. estimated its two-year equipment warranty costs based on $100 per unit sold in year 1. Experience during year 2 indicated that the estimate should have been based on $110 per unit. The effect of this $10 difference from the estimate is reported

- a. In year 2 income from continuing operations.
- b. As an accounting change, net of tax, below year 2 income from continuing operations.
- c. As an accounting change requiring year 1 financial statements to be restated.
- d. As a correction of an error requiring year 1 financial statements to be restated.

C.3. Change in Reporting Entity (ASC Topic 250)

25. A company has included in its consolidated financial statements this year a subsidiary acquired several years ago that was appropriately excluded from consolidation last year. This should be reported as

- a. An accounting change that should be reported prospectively.
- b. An accounting change that should be reported retrospectively.
- c. A correction of an error.
- d. Neither an accounting change nor a correction of an error.

26. Which of the following statements is correct regarding accounting changes that result in financial statements that are, in effect, the statements of a different reporting entity?

- a. Cumulative-effect adjustments should be reported as separate items on the financial statements pertaining to the year of change.
- b. No restatements or adjustments are required if the changes involve consolidated methods of accounting for subsidiaries.
- c. No restatements or adjustments are required if the changes involve the cost or equity methods of accounting for investments.
- d. The financial statements of all prior periods presented are adjusted retrospectively.

C.5. International Financial Reporting Standards (IFRS)

27. IFRS requires changes in accounting principles to be reported

- a. On a prospective basis.
- b. On a retrospective basis.
- c. By restating the financial statements.
- d. By a cumulative adjustment on the income statement.

28. Under IFRS, changes in accounting policies are

- a. Permitted if the change will result in a more reliable and more relevant presentation of the financial statements.
- b. Permitted if the entity encounters new transactions, events, or conditions that are substantively different from existing or previous transactions.
- c. Required for material transactions, if the entity had previously accounted for similar, though immaterial, transactions under an unacceptable accounting method.
- d. Required if an alternate accounting policy gives rise to a material change in assets, liabilities, or the current year net income.

29. Under IFRS, a voluntary change in accounting method may only be made by a company if

- a. A new standard mandates the change in method.
- b. Management prefers the new method.
- c. The new method provides reliable and more relevant information.
- d. There is no prohibition of the method in the standards.

Multiple-Choice Answers and Explanations

Answers

1. b	__ __	8. c	__ __	15. a	__ __	22. c	__ __	29. c	__ __
2. d	__ __	9. a	__ __	16. c	__ __	23. a	__ __		
3. d	__ __	10. c	__ __	17. b	__ __	24. a	__ __		
4. b	__ __	11. d	__ __	18. d	__ __	25. b	__ __		
5. b	__ __	12. c	__ __	19. b	__ __	26. d	__ __		
6. a	__ __	13. a	__ __	20. a	__ __	27. b	__ __	1st: __/29 = __%
7. d	__ __	14. c	__ __	21. d	__ __	28. a	__ __	2nd: __/29 = __%

Explanations

1. **(b)** A change in depreciation method is a change in method that is not distinguishable from a change in estimate, and is accounted for as a change in estimate. The change is reported on a prospective basis in the current year and future years. Book value as of 1/1/Y3 = $153,600/8 years remaining = $19,200 depreciation expense in year 3.

2. **(d)** Zero. A change in depreciation method is a change in method that is not distinguishable from a change in estimate, and is accounted for as a change in estimate. The change is reported on a prospective basis in the current year and future years. A change in depreciation method is no longer given cumulative effect treatment on the income statement.

3. **(d)** Zero. A change in depreciation method is a change in method that is not distinguishable from a change in estimate, and is accounted for as a change in estimate. The change is reported on a prospective basis in the current year and future years. Because a change in depreciation method is no longer given cumulative effect treatment on the income statement, there are no deferred income tax liability effects.

4. **(b)** A change in depreciation method is a change in method that is not distinguishable from a change in estimate, and is accounted for as a change in estimate. The change is reported on a prospective basis in the current year and future years.

5. **(b)** The requirement is to determine which accounting change should be reported on a prospective basis. A change in depreciation method is a change in principle that is not distinguishable from a change in estimate, and is accounted for as a change in estimate. The change is reported on a prospective basis in the current year and future years. A change from the cash basis to the accrual basis of accounting is a change from non-GAAP to GAAP accounted for as the correction of an error. A change in reporting entity requires retrospective application to the earliest year presented if practicable. A change in the method of accounting for long-term contracts requires retrospective application to the earliest year presented if practicable.

6. **(a)** The requirement is to determine whether a change in depreciation method from straight-line to double-declining balance should be reported as a cumulative effect of a change in accounting principle and receive retrospective application. A change in depreciation method is a change in method that is not distinguishable from a change in estimate, and is accounted for as a change in estimate. The change is reported on a prospective basis in the current year and future

years. Therefore, it does not receive cumulative effect treatment or retrospective treatment.

7. **(d)** A change in inventory method no longer receives cumulative effect treatment on the income statement. Instead, the accounting change is given retrospective application to the earliest period presented, if practicable. Therefore, the answer is zero.

8. **(c)** A change in inventory method no longer receives cumulative effect treatment on the income statement. Instead, the accounting change is given retrospective application to the earliest period presented, if practicable.

9. **(a)** Retrospective application requires applying the new principle to the earliest period presented if practicable. Because year 3 beginning inventory is the previous year's ending inventory, the new principle can be applied to the year 2 financial statements. This would result in an increase in ending inventory in the balance sheet for year 2, a decrease in cost of goods sold in year 2, and an increase in the beginning inventory, which would result in a higher cost of goods sold and a lower net income for year 3.

10. **(c)** A change in inventory method is given retrospective application to the earliest period presented, if practicable.

11. **(d)** Retrospective application requires the change to be calculated for the earliest period presented if practicable.

12. **(c)** A change in inventory method no longer receives cumulative effect treatment on the income statement. The accounting change is given retrospective application to the earliest period presented, if practicable.

13. **(a)** The requirement is to indicate how a change in accounting principle from the completed-contract method to the percentage-of-completion method should be reported. A change in the method of accounting for long-term contracts requires retrospective application to the earliest year practicable. This results in a $180,000 increase in income for year 2. The assets would be adjusted for the earliest period affected, and construction-in-progress would increase by $180,000. Net income for year 2 would increase by $108,000 ($180,000 less 40% tax effects), and the deferred tax liability account would increase in year 2 by $72,000.

14. **(c)** The effect of a change in accounting principle which is inseparable from the effect of a change in accounting estimate should be accounted for as a change in accounting estimate. Changes in estimate should be accounted for in the period of change and also in any affected future periods as a component of income from continuing operations. Financial statements are only restated for changes due to an error. Errors include mathematical mistakes, mistakes in applying accounting principles, oversights or misuse of available facts, and changes from unacceptable accounting principles to GAAP. The situation described in this question does not meet the description of an error.

15. **(a)** Deferred taxes is a direct effect from the change in accounting principle, and its effects should be recorded in the earliest period presented, if practicable. Profit sharing and royalty payments are indirect effects and should be reported in the period of the change.

16. **(c)** Indirect effects of a change in accounting principle should be reported in the period in which the accounting change occurs. Direct effects are reported retrospectively to the earliest period presented, if practicable. Answers (b) and (d) are incorrect since accounting changes are no longer treated as cumulative effect changes or prior period adjustments.

17. **(b)** If it is impracticable to determine the cumulative effect of an accounting change to any of the prior periods, the accounting change should be accounted for on a prospective basis. Answer (a) is incorrect because accounting changes are no longer treated as prior period adjustments. Answer (c) is incorrect because accounting changes are no longer treated as cumulative effect changes on the income statement. Answer (d) is incorrect because the change would not be to retained earnings in the first period presented.

18. **(d)** If the cumulative effect of applying an accounting change can be determined, but the period-specific effects on all periods cannot be determined, the cumulative effect of the change should be applied to the carrying value of the assets and liabilities at the beginning of the earliest period to which it can be determined.

19. **(b)** This situation is a change in accounting estimate and should be accounted for currently and prospectively. From 1/1/Y1 to 12/31/Y3, patent amortization was recorded using a fifteen-year life. Yearly amortization was $47,600 ($714,000 ÷ 15), accumulated amortization at 12/31/Y3 was $142,800 ($47,600 × 3), and the book value of the patent at 12/31/Y3 was $571,200 ($714,000 − $142,800). Beginning in year 4, this book value must be amortized over its remaining useful life of 7 years (10 years − 3 years). Therefore, year 4 amortization is $81,600 ($571,200 ÷ 7) and the 12/31/Y4 book value is $489,600 ($571,200 − $81,600).

20. **(a)** From 1/1/01 to 12/31/Y3, depreciation was recorded using an eight-year life. Yearly depreciation was $66,000 ($528,000 ÷ 8), and accumulated depreciation at 12/31/Y1 was $198,000 (3 × $66,000). In year 4, the estimated useful life was changed to six years total with a salvage value of $48,000. Therefore, the 12/31/Y3 book value ($528,000 − $198,000 = $330,000) is depreciated down to the $48,000 salvage value over a remaining useful life of three years (six years total − three years already recorded). Depreciation expense for year 4 is $94,000 [($330,000 − $48,000) ÷ 3], increasing accumulated depreciation to $292,000 ($198,000 + $94,000).

21. **(d)** Changes in accounting estimate are to be accounted for in the period of change and in future periods if the change affects both (i.e., **prospectively**). Pro forma amounts are presented for changes in accounting principle accounted for using the **current** (cumulative effect) approach. Answers (a) and (c) are incorrect because they apply to **retroactive**-type changes in principle and error correction, respectively.

22. **(c)** The effect of a change in accounting estimate should be accounted for in (a) the period of change if the change affects that period only, or (b) the period of change and future periods if the change affects both. The Codification further states that a change in an estimate should not be accounted for by restating amounts reported in financial statements of prior periods or by reporting pro forma amounts for prior periods.

23. **(a)** A change in estimated warranty costs due to technological advances in production qualifies as a change in accounting estimate. Changes in estimate are treated prospectively; there is no retroactive restatement, and the new estimate is used in current and future years. Therefore, in year 3, Oak should use the new estimate of 1% and report warranty expense of $50,000 ($5,000,000 × 1%).

24. **(a)** A change in equipment warranty costs based on additional information obtained through experience qualifies as a change in accounting estimate. Changes in estimate should be accounted for in the period of change as a component of income from continuing operations and in future periods if necessary. No restatement is required for a change in estimate.

25. **(b)** An accounting change that is a change in reporting entity is given retrospective application to the earliest period presented, if practicable. The term "restatement" refers only to correction of errors in previously issued financial statements.

26. **(d)** An accounting change that is a change in reporting entity is given retrospective application to the earliest period presented, if practicable. The term "restatement" refers only to correction of errors in previously issued financial statements.

27. **(b)** The requirement is to identify the item that describes how changes in accounting principles are reported under IFRS. Answer (b) is correct because IFRS requires changes in accounting principles to be reported by giving retrospective application to the earliest period presented. Answer (a) is incorrect because a change in accounting estimate is accounted for on a prospective basis in the current and future periods. Answer (c) is incorrect because restatement is required for errors in the financial statements. Answer (d) is incorrect because cumulative adjustments on the income statement are not permitted.

28. **(a)** The requirement is to select the item that describes when changes in accounting policies are permitted or required. Answer (a) is correct because changes are permitted if it will result in a more reliable and more relevant presentation of the financial statements.

29. **(c)** The requirement is to identify the circumstances that may justify a voluntary change in accounting method. Answer (c) is correct because the new method must provide reliable and more relevant information.

Simulations

Task-Based Simulation 1

Accounting Changes		
	Authoritative Literature	Help

Situation

On January 2, year 3, Quo, Inc. hired Reed to be its controller. During the year, Reed, working closely with Quo's president and outside accountants, made changes in accounting policies, corrected several errors dating from year 2 and before, and instituted new accounting policies.

Quo's year 3 financial statements will be presented in comparative form with its year 2 financial statements.

Items 1 through 10 represent Quo's transactions.

List A represents possible classifications of these transactions as: a change in accounting principle, a change in accounting estimate, a correction of an error in previously presented financial statements, or neither an accounting change nor an accounting error.

List B represents the general accounting treatment for these transactions. These treatments are

- Retrospective application approach—Apply the new accounting principle to all prior periods presented showing the cumulative effect of the change in the carrying value of assets and liabilities at the beginning of the first period presented, and adjust financial statements presented to reflect period-specific effects of the change.
- Retroactive restatement approach—Restate the year 2 financial statements and adjust year 2 beginning retained earnings if the error or change affects a period prior to year 2 financial statements.
- Prospective approach—Report year 3 and future financial statements on the new basis, but do **not** restate year 2 financial statements.

For each item, select one from List A and one from List B.

List A (Select one treatment)
A. Change in accounting principle.
B. Change in accounting estimate.
C. Correction of an error in previously presented financial statements.
D. Neither an accounting change nor an accounting error.

List B (Select one approach)
X. Retrospective application approach.
Y. Retroactive restatement approach.
Z. Prospective approach.

	List A Treatment (A) (B) (C) (D)	List B Approach (X) (Y) (Z)
1. Quo manufactures heavy equipment to customer specifications on a contract basis. On the basis that it is preferable, accounting for these long-term contracts was switched from the completed-contract method to the percentage-of-completion method.	○ ○ ○ ○	○ ○ ○
2. As a result of a production breakthrough, Quo determined that manufacturing equipment previously depreciated over fifteen years should be depreciated over twenty years.	○ ○ ○ ○	○ ○ ○
3. The equipment that Quo manufactures is sold with a five-year warranty. Because of a production breakthrough, Quo reduced its computation of warranty costs from 3% of sales to 1% of sales.	○ ○ ○ ○	○ ○ ○
4. Quo changed from LIFO to FIFO to account for its finished goods inventory.	○ ○ ○ ○	○ ○ ○
5. Quo changed from FIFO to average cost to account for its raw materials and work in process inventories.	○ ○ ○ ○	○ ○ ○
6. Quo sells extended service contracts on its products. Because related services are performed over several years, in year 3 Quo changed from the cash method to the accrual method of recognizing income from these service contracts.	○ ○ ○ ○	○ ○ ○

	List A Treatment (A) (B) (C) (D)	List B Approach (X) (Y) (Z)
7. During year 3, Quo determined that an insurance premium paid and entirely expensed in year 2 was for the period January 1, year 2, through January 1, year 4.	O O O O	O O O
8. Quo changed its method of depreciating office equipment from an accelerated method to the straight-line method to more closely reflect costs in later years.	O O O O	O O O
9. Quo instituted a pension plan for all employees in year 3 and adopted the accounting standards related to pensions. Quo had not previously had a pension plan.	O O O O	O O O
10. During year 3, Quo increased its investment in Worth, Inc. from a 10% interest, purchased in year 2, to 30%, and acquired a seat on Worth's board of directors. As a result of its increased investment, Quo changed its method of accounting for investment in subsidiary from the cost adjusted for fair value method to the equity method. Quo did not elect to use the fair value method to report its 30% investment in Worth.	O O O O	O O O

Task-Based Simulation 2

Calculations		
	Authoritative Literature	Help

Kent has $500,000 in equipment and machinery that was acquired on January 2, year 1. Kent has been using the double-declining balance method to depreciate the equipment over an estimated 10-year economic life with no salvage. On January 1, year 3, Kent decides to change to the straight-line method with no salvage. Kent has a 40% tax rate.

Calculate the following amounts:

1. Accumulated depreciation as of 12/31/Y2

2. Depreciation expense for year 3

3. Accumulated depreciation as of 12/31/Y3

4. Indicate the amount of the accounting change shown net of tax if appropriate

Task-Based Simulation 3

Classification/ Disclosure		
	Authoritative Literature	Help

Clark made the following changes in its accounting policies.

- Clark changed its depreciation method for its production machinery from the double-declining balance method to the straight-line method effective January 1, year 3.
- Clark appropriately changed the salvage values used in computing depreciation for its office equipment.
- Clark appropriately changed the specific subsidiaries constituting the group of companies for which consolidated financial statements are presented.

For each of the items that Clark changed, identify whether Clark should show the following by choosing Yes or No in the appropriate columns.

Change item	Cumulative effect of change in principle in net income of the period of change		Pro forma effects of retroactive application for all prior periods presented currently		Retrospective application to financial statements of all prior periods presented currently	
	Yes	No	Yes	No	Yes	No
1. Clark changed its depreciation method for its production machinery from the double-declining balance method to the straight-line method effective January 1, year 3.	○	○	○	○	○	○
2. Clark appropriately changed the salvage values used in computing depreciation for its office equipment.	○	○	○	○	○	○
3. Clark appropriately changed the specific subsidiaries constituting the group of companies for which consolidated financial statements are presented.	○	○	○	○	○	○

Task-Based Simulation 4

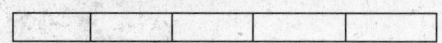

Assume that you are assigned to the audit of Clark Corporation. Clark is considering changing the depreciation method for its production machinery from the double-declining balance method to the straight-line method. Which section of the Professional Standards provides guidance on the nature of this type of change?

Enter your response in the answer fields below.

Task-Based Simulation 5

Situation

Falk Co. began operations in January, year 2. On January 2, year 3, Falk Co. hired a new controller. During the year, the controller, working closely with Falk's president and outside accountants, made changes in existing accounting policies, instituted new accounting policies, and corrected several errors dating from prior to year 3.

Falk's financial statements for the year ended December 31, year 3, will not be presented in comparative form with its year 2 financial statements.

List A represents possible classifications of these transactions as a change in accounting principle, a change in accounting estimate, correction of an error in previously presented financial statements, or neither an accounting change nor an error correction.

List B represents the general accounting treatment required for these transactions. These treatments are

- Retrospective application approach—Apply the new accounting principle to all prior periods presented showing the cumulative effect of the change in the carrying value of assets and liabilities at the beginning of the first period presented, and adjust financial statements presented to reflect period-specific effects of the change.
- Retroactive restatement approach—Adjust year 3 beginning retained earnings if the error or change affects a period prior to year 3.
- Prospective approach—Report year 3 and future financial statements on the new basis, but do not adjust beginning retained earnings or include the cumulative effect of the change in the year 3 income statements.

List A—Type of change (Select one)	List B—General accounting treatment (Select one)
A. Change in accounting principle.	X. Retroactive application approach.
B. Change in accounting estimate.	Y. Retroactive restatement approach.
C. Correction of an error in previously presented financial statements.	Z. Prospective approach.
D. Neither an accounting change nor an error correction.	

For **Items 1 and 2,** select a classification for each transaction from List A and the general accounting treatment required to report the change from List B.

	List A Type of change (A) (B) (C) (D)	List B Accounting treatment (X) (Y) (Z)
1. Falk manufactures customized equipment to customer specifications on a contract basis. Falk changed its method of accounting for these long-term contracts from the completed-contract method to the percentage-of-completion method because Falk is now able to make reasonable estimates of future construction costs.	○ ○ ○ ○	○ ○ ○
2. Based on improved collection procedures, Falk changed the percentage of credit sales used to determine the allowance for uncollectible accounts from 2% to 1%.	○ ○ ○ ○	○ ○ ○

Task-Based Simulation 6

Accounting Change		
	Authoritative Literature	Help

On January 1, year 3, Posey changed from the average cost method to the FIFO method to account for its inventory. Ending inventory for each method was as follows:

Year	Average cost	FIFO
Year 2	$5,000	$ 7,000
Year 3	$9,000	$14,000

Posey's income statement information calculated by the average cost method was as follows:

Posey Corporation
INCOME STATEMENT

	Before adjustments for the year ending 12-31-Y3	Before adjustment for the year ending 12-31-Y2
Sales	$130,000	$100,000
Cost of goods sold	90,000	70,000
Gross profit	40,000	30,000
Operating expense	20,000	17,000
Earnings before taxes	20,000	13,000
Tax expense	8,000	5,200
Net income	12,000	7,800

Assume that Posey has no book/tax differences or deferred taxes. Posey accrues tax expense on December 31 of each year and pays the tax in January of the following year. The income tax rate is 40%.

Prepare an adjusted income statement for year 3 and year 2 after the change to the FIFO inventory method.

Posey Corporation
INCOME STATEMENT

	Adjusted for the year ending 12-31-Y3	Adjusted for the year ending 12-31-Y2
Sales		
Cost of goods sold		
Gross profit		
Operating expense		
Earnings before taxes		
Tax expense		
Net income		

Indicate the adjusted balances on the December 31 balance sheet for each year.

	December 31, year 3	December 31, year 2
Inventory		
Income tax liability		
Retained earnings		

Task-Based Simulation 7

Research		
	Authoritative Literature	**Help**

Assume that you are assigned to the audit of Wilson Construction Company. Wilson is considering changing its method of accounting from the completed-contract method to the percentage-of-completion method. Which section of the Professional Standards addresses the issue of how to account for the indirect effects of the change?

Enter your response in the answer fields below.

Simulation Solutions

Task-Based Simulation 1

Accounting Changes		
	Authoritative Literature	Help

		List A Treatment (A) (B) (C) (D)	List B Approach (X) (Y) (Z)
1.	Quo manufactures heavy equipment to customer specifications on a contract basis. On the basis that it is preferable, accounting for these long-term contracts was switched from the completed-contract method to the percentage-of-completion method.	● ○ ○ ○	● ○ ○
2.	As a result of a production breakthrough, Quo determined that manufacturing equipment previously depreciated over fifteen years should be depreciated over twenty years.	○ ● ○ ○	○ ○ ●
3.	The equipment that Quo manufactures is sold with a five-year warranty. Because of a production breakthrough, Quo reduced its computation of warranty costs from 3% of sales to 1% of sales.	○ ● ○ ○	○ ○ ●
4.	Quo changed from LIFO to FIFO to account for its finished goods inventory.	● ○ ○ ○	● ○ ○
5.	Quo changed from FIFO to average cost to account for its raw materials and work in process inventories.	● ○ ○ ○	● ○ ○
6.	Quo sells extended service contracts on its products. Because related services are performed over several years, in year 3 Quo changed from the cash method to the accrual method of recognizing income from these service contracts.	○ ○ ● ○	○ ● ○
7.	During year 3, Quo determined that an insurance premium paid and entirely expensed in year 2 was for the period January 1, year 2, through January 1, year 4.	○ ○ ● ○	○ ● ○
8.	Quo changed its method of depreciating office equipment from an accelerated method to the straight-line method to more closely reflect costs in later years.	○ ● ○ ○	○ ○ ●
9.	Quo instituted a pension plan for all employees in year 3 and adopted the accounting standards related to pensions. Quo had not previously had a pension plan.	○ ○ ○ ●	○ ○ ●
10.	During year 3, Quo increased its investment in Worth, Inc. from a 10% interest, purchased in year 2, to 30%, and acquired a seat on Worth's board of directors. As a result of its increased investment, Quo changed its method of accounting for investment in subsidiary from the cost adjusted for fair value method to the equity method.	○ ○ ○ ●	○ ● ○

Explanations

1. **(A, X)** This situation represents a change in the method of accounting for long-term construction-type contracts and requires retrospective application for all periods presented.

2. **(B, Z)** This situation is not a change in accounting principle but is a change in an estimate and should be handled prospectively.

3. **(B, Z)** This situation is a change in an estimate. The change in the percentage of warranty costs is not a change in accounting principle. Changes in estimate are handled prospectively.

4. **(A, X)** This situation is a change from one acceptable accounting principle to another and requires retrospective application.

5. **(A, X)** This situation is a change from one acceptable accounting method to another and requires the retrospective application approach.

6. **(C, Y)** The use of the cash method is considered an error since that method is generally **not** acceptable. The switch to an acceptable method (accrual) is considered the correction of an error and requires the retroactive restatement approach.

7. **(C, Y)** The write-off of the insurance premium was an error. Since comparative financial statements are prepared, past years must be corrected using the retroactive restatement approach even though this error is self-correcting after two years.

8. **(B, Z)** This situation is a change in method which is considered a change in estimate effected by a change in principle. Per SFAS 154, a change in depreciation method requires prospective application.

9. **(D, Z)** Since the company did not previously account for pensions this situation is simply the adoption of an appropriate accounting principle for pensions. No change in principle occurs.

10. **(D, Y)** Quo's increase in ownership interest (10% to 30%) and its acquisition of a seat on Worth's board of directors has given Quo the ability to exercise significant influence in the operating decisions of Worth. If Quo does not elect to use the fair value option to report its 30% investment in Worth, Quo will use the equity method to account for its investment in Worth. The cost adjusted for fair value method is no longer applicable due to the change in Quo's investment in Worth. However, the change from the cost adjusted for fair value method to the equity method is not a change in accounting principle. A change in accounting principle occurs when an accounting principle different from the one used previously for reporting purposes is adopted. For a change to occur, a choice between two or more accounting principles must exist. In this case, the change in Quo's situation allows the equity method to account for the investment. Quo's current economic situation is clearly different and this necessitates the adoption of a different accounting principle. Consequently, this is not an accounting change. However, the investment account should be retroactively restated to reflect balances as if the equity method had always been used.

Task-Based Simulation 2

Calculations		
	Authoritative Literature	Help

1. Accumulated depreciation as of 12/31/Y2 $180,000

2. Depreciation expense for year 3 $ 40,000

3. Accumulated depreciation as of 12/31/Y3 $220,000

4. Indicate the amount of the accounting change shown net of tax if appropriate $ 0

Explanations

1. Before change, Kent used double-declining balance and 10-year life

Year 1	$1/10 \times 2 \times \$500,000$ book value	=	$100,000	depreciation expense
Year 2	$1/10 \times 2 \times \$400,000$ new book value	=	$ 80,000	depreciation expense
	Accumulated depreciation 12/31/Y1		$180,000	

2. To calculate depreciation expense for year 3:

Historical cost	$500,000
– Accum. depreciation	(180,000)
Book value	$320,000

($320,000 – $0 salvage) ÷ 8 years remaining life = $40,000 depreciation expense

3. To calculate accumulated depreciation as of 12/31/Y3:

Year 1	$100,000
Year 2	80,000
Year 3	40,000
Accum. depr. 12/31/Y3	$220,000

4. Accounting change net of tax – zero. Accounting standards treat changes in depreciation method as a change in estimate effected by a change in method. Therefore, a change in depreciation is accounted for on a prospective basis.

Task-Based Simulation 3

Classification/ Disclosure		
	Authoritative Literature	Help

	Change item	Cumulative effect of change in principle in net income of the period of change		Pro forma effects of retroactive application for all prior periods presented currently		Retrospective application to financial statements of all prior periods presented currently	
		Yes	No	Yes	No	Yes	No
1.	Clark changed its depreciation method for its production machinery from the double-declining balance method to the straight-line method effective January 1, year 3.	○	●	○	●	○	●
2.	Clark appropriately changed the salvage values used in computing depreciation for its office equipment.	○	●	○	●	○	●
3.	Clark appropriately changed the specific subsidiaries constituting the group of companies for which consolidated financial statements are presented.	○	●	○	●	●	○

Explanations

1. (N, N, N) Clark's change in depreciation method is a change in accounting estimate effected by a change in accounting principle. This change would be accounted for on a prospective basis in the current year and future periods.

2. (N, N, N) Clark's change in salvage values is a change in accounting estimate. Clark would not report a cumulative effect, nor pro forma effects, nor would prior period financial statements be restated.

3. (N, N, Y) Clark's change in the specific subsidiaries constituting the group of companies for which consolidated financial statements are presented is a change in reporting entity. The change in reporting entity requires the change to be retrospectively applied to the financial statements of all prior periods presented to show financial information for the new reporting entity.

Task-Based Simulation 4

Research		
	Authoritative Literature	Help

ASC	250	10	45	18

Task-Based Simulation 5

Accounting Treatment		
	Authoritative Literature	Help

		List A Type of Change (A) (B) (C) (D)	List B Accounting Treatment (X) (Y) (Z)
1.	Falk manufactures customized equipment to customer specifications on a contract basis. Falk changed its method of accounting for these long-term contracts from the completed-contract method to the percentage-of-completion method because Falk is now able to make reasonable estimates of future construction costs.	● ○ ○ ○	● ○ ○
2.	Based on improved collection procedures, Falk changed the percentage of credit sales used to determine the allowance for uncollectible accounts from 2% to 1%.	○ ● ○ ○	○ ○ ●

Explanations

1. (A, X) Changing from using the completed-contract method to the percentage-of-completion method is a change in accounting principle. Therefore, retrospective application to all periods presented is required.

2. (B, Z) The percentage of net credit sales used in determining the amount to be added to the allowance for uncollectible accounts is an estimate made by management. Changing the percentage is a change in accounting estimate, which is treated prospectively.

Task-Based Simulation 6

Accounting Change		
	Authoritative Literature	Help

Posey Corporation
INCOME STATEMENT

	Adjusted for the year ending 12-31-Y3	Adjusted for the year ending 12-31-Y2
Sales	$130,000	$100,000
Cost of goods sold	87,000	68,000
Gross profit	43,000	32,000
Operating expenses	20,000	17,000
Earnings before taxes	23,000	15,000
Income tax expense (40%)	9,200	6,000
Net income	13,800	9,000

	December 31, year 3	December 31, year 2
Inventory	$14,000	$7,000
Income tax liability	10,000	6,000

Explanations

To calculate cost of goods sold using FIFO method, you must first calculate purchases using the average cost method. Using T-accounts for analysis, the amounts are as shown below.

Inventory
(Weighted-average method)

1-1-Y2	-0-		
Purchases	75,000	70,000	CGS
12-31-Y2	5,000		
Purchases	94,000	90,000	CGS
12-31-Y3	9,000		

Inventory
(FIFO method)

1-1-Y2	-0-	68,000	CGS
Purchases	75,000		
12-31-Y2	7,000	87,000	CGS
Purchases	94,000		
12-31-Y3	14,000		

Income tax liability for December 31, year 3, is calculated as

Year 3 earnings before taxes 23,000 × 40% =	$ 9,200
Year 2 adjustment to earnings before taxes 2,000 × 40%	+ 800
Total income tax liability at 12-31-Y3	$10,000

Retained earnings as of December 31, year 3, is calculated as

Adjusted NI year 2	$ 9,000
Adjusted NI year 3	13,800
Retained earnings 12/31/Y3	$22,800

Task-Based Simulation 7

Research			
	Authoritative Literature	**Help**	

ASC	250	10	45	8

D. Financial Statements

1. Income and Retained Earnings Statement Formats

Income statements may be prepared using a multiple-step or single-step form. The income (earnings) and comprehensive income statement illustrated below for Totman Company includes separate categories for continuing operations, discontinued operations, and extraordinary items. The purpose of these separate categories is to enable users to assess future cash flows. Retrospective application is required for all changes in accounting principle. Other comprehensive income is required and may be disclosed in several methods (covered later in this module).

a. The Totman Company statement is a combined statement of income and comprehensive income.

EXAMPLE

Totman Company
STATEMENT OF EARNINGS AND COMPREHENSIVE INCOME
For the Year Ended December 31, Year 2

Sales		$2,677
Cost of goods sold		1,489
Gross margin on sales		1,188
Operating expenses		
Selling expenses	$ 220	
Administrative expenses	255	475
Operating income		713
Other revenues and gains		
Interest revenue	$ 5	
Equity in Huskie Co. earnings	15	
Gain on sale of available-for-sale securities	45	65
Other expenses and losses		
Interest expense	(60)	
Loss from permanent impairment of value of manufacturing facilities	(120)	(180)
Income from continuing operations before provision for income taxes		598
Provision for income taxes		
Current	$ 189	
Deferred	50	239
Income from continuing operations		359(a)
Discontinued operations:		
Loss from operations of discontinued Division Z, including loss on disposal of $230	(1,265)	
Income tax benefit	(466)	(799)(b)
Income (loss) before extraordinary item		(440)
Extraordinary item: Loss due earthquake (less applicable income taxes of $30)		(45)(b)
Net earnings (loss)		(485)(a)
Other comprehensive income:		
Foreign currency translation adjustments (less applicable income taxes of $6)		26
Unrealized gains on securities:		
Unrealized holding gains arising during period (Less applicable income taxes of $43)	179	
Less: reclassification adjustment (less applicable income taxes of $10) for gain		
included in net income	(35)	144
Other comprehensive income		170
Comprehensive income		$ (315)

See Note #5 below applies to the section from Sales through Provision for income taxes.

Note:

1. Assumes a tax rate of 40% on applicable items
2. (a) indicates where earnings per share (EPS) amounts would be necessary on the face of the IS. (b) EPS may be shown on the face of the income statement or in the notes. On the CPA exam, rather than memorizing these, simply calculate an EPS number for all numbers starting with income from continuing operations through net earnings.
3. Footnote explanations would also be required for many of the above events and transactions.
4. In the multiple-step format above, the Securities and Exchange Commission (SEC) requires that public companies place impairment losses in operating income instead of under "Other expenses and losses."
5. This is the format for a multiple-step income statement. A single-step income statement would differ only for the portion of the statement shown below. Otherwise, the single-step statement format is the same.

Revenues		
Sales	$2,677	
Interest	5	
Gain on sale of available-for-sale securities	45	
Equity in Huskie Co. earnings	15	
Total revenues		$2,742
Expenses		
Cost of goods sold	1,489	
Selling expenses	220	
Administrative expenses	255	
Interest expense	60	
Loss from permanent impairment of value of manufacturing facilities	120	
Total expenses		2,144
Income from continuing operations before provision for income taxes		598

b. The following chart summarizes the various category definitions and their placement on the income statement and retained earnings statement. These categories are all discussed in various parts of this module.

Income Statement and Retained Earnings Statement Categories

	Description	Definition	Placement on income statement or statement of retained earnings
1.	Unusual or Infrequent Items	An unusual or infrequent event considered to be material that does not qualify as extraordinary	Placed as part of income from continuing operations after normal recurring revenues and expenses
2.	Discontinued Operations*	Results from disposal of a business component	Placed as a separate category after income from continuing operations
3.	Extraordinary Items*	An unusual and infrequent nonrecurring event which has material effects	Placed as a separate category after discontinued operations
4.	Change in Accounting Principle:	Change from one generally accepted accounting principle to another	No longer on income statement. **Retrospective application:** Report cumulative effect of change in the carrying amounts of assets and liabilities as of the beginning of the first period presented, with an offsetting adjustment to the opening balance of retained earnings for that period. Financial statements for each period are adjusted to reflect period-specific effects of the change for direct effects.
5.	Correction of an Error	A correction of a material error from a prior period	Report as prior period adjustment by restating the prior-period financial statements. Cumulative effect of the error on prior periods is reflected in the carrying value of assets and liabilities at the beginning of the first period, with an offsetting adjustment made to the opening balance of retained earnings for that period. Financial statements are adjusted to reflect correction of period-specific effects of the error.

* These items are all presented net of applicable income tax effects.

2. **Unusual or Infrequent Items**

   a. Items that are unusual or infrequent but not both should not be presented as extraordinary items. However, they are often presented in a separate section in the income statement above income before extraordinary items. A common example of such items is a "restructuring charge."

      (1) A restructuring is a program that is planned and controlled by management and materially changes either the scope of the business undertaken by the company, or the manner in which that business is conducted. Examples include

         (a) Sale or termination of a line of business
         (b) Closure of business activities in a particular location
         (c) Relocation of business activities from one location to another
         (d) Changes in management structure, or
         (e) Fundamental reorganizations that affect the nature and focus of operations

(2) Another unusual or infrequent item is accounting for the costs of exit and disposal activities (which include, among other items, restructurings). A liability for a cost associated with an exit or disposal activity should be recognized and measured initially at fair value in the period in which the liability is incurred. The fair value is usually determined as the present value of the estimated future payments discounted at the credit-adjusted, risk-free rate of interest.

   (a) In the unusual circumstance when fair value cannot be reasonably estimated, the liability shall be initially recognized in the period in which fair value can be reasonably estimated. Examples of such liabilities include

   1] Onetime termination benefits provided to current employees that are involuntarily terminated
   2] Costs to terminate a contract that is not a capital lease
   3] Costs to consolidate facilities or relocate employees

   (b) The recognition of the liability and expense for onetime termination benefits depends on whether the employees are required to provide services beyond the minimum retention period. If so, the expense is recognized over the period that the services are provided. If they are not required to provide future services, the liability is recognized when the plan is communicated to the employees.
   (c) In periods subsequent to initial measurement, changes to the liability shall be measured using the credit-adjusted risk-free rate that was used to measure the liability initially.
   (d) Costs associated with an exit or disposal activity that does not involve discontinued operations shall be included in income from continuing operations before income taxes. The footnotes to the financial statements should provide extensive disclosure of the activities.

3. **Discontinued Operations**
   a. As shown on the Totman Co. income statement, "Discontinued operations" is broken out separately. The "Loss from discontinued operations" includes the loss or income of the component for the period, and the gain or loss on its disposal. Income taxes or tax benefit are deducted from or added to that amount to determine the gain or loss after taxes.
   b. To qualify for treatment as discontinued operations the assets must comprise a component of the entity with operations and cash flows that are clearly distinguished, operationally and for financial reporting purposes, from the rest of the entity. A component may be a reportable or operating segment, a reporting unit, a subsidiary, or an asset group.
   c. To be reported as discontinued operations, two requirements must be met: (1) the operations and cash flows of the component have been (or will be) eliminated from the ongoing operations of the entity as a result of the disposal, and (2) the entity will not have any significant involvement in the operations of the component after disposal.
   d. Many of the assets disposed of as discontinued operations are long-lived assets. Accordingly, the component is classified as discontinued operations in the first period that it meets the criteria as being "held for sale":

   (1) Management commits to a plan of disposal.
   (2) The assets are available for sale.
   (3) An active program to locate a buyer has been initiated.
   (4) The sale is probable.
   (5) The asset is being actively marketed for sale at a fair price.
   (6) It is unlikely that the disposal plan will significantly change.

   (a) Long-lived assets classified as "held for sale" are reported at the lower of their carrying amounts or fair values less costs to sell. Therefore, the gain or loss on disposal of discontinued operations is the actual gain or loss if disposal occurs in the same period that the component meets the criteria to be classified as "held for sale."
   (b) If the criteria to classify the component as "held for sale" is met in a period before it is disposed of, the amount of the loss (if applicable) on disposal is an estimated loss resulting from the write-down of the group of assets to their estimated fair values. Estimated gains cannot be initially recognized.
   (c) However, if the component is held for sale over several reporting periods, estimated gains can be recognized based on new information but are limited to the amount of losses previously recognized.
   (d) Thus, the assets can be written up but not above their carrying amounts when they met the criteria as being held for sale.

   e. When "discontinued operations" are disclosed in a comparative income statement, the income statement presented for each previous year must be adjusted retroactively to enhance comparability with the current year's income statement. Accordingly, the revenues, cost of goods sold, and operating expenses (including income taxes) for the discontinued component are removed from the revenues, cost of goods sold, and operating expenses of continuing operations and are netted into one figure, that is, "Income (loss) from discontinued operations."

(1) The following excerpt from a comparative income statement shows the proper disclosure (year 1 figures assumed).

	Year 2	Year 1
Discontinued operations:		
Loss from operations of discontinued Division Z, including loss on		
disposal in year 2 of $230	$699	$990
Income tax benefit	466	300

NOW REVIEW MULTIPLE-CHOICE QUESTIONS 1 THROUGH 32

4. **Comprehensive Income**

a. **Reporting.** Comprehensive income is the sum of net earnings (loss) and other comprehensive income. It requires disclosure of **changes during a period** of the following components of other comprehensive income: unrealized gains and losses on available-for-sale investments and foreign currency items, including any reclassification adjustments and any adjustments necessary to recognize the funding status of pension plans or other postemployment benefits.

b. This standard allows the management of an enterprise two choices for presenting **other comprehensive income**. These are as follows:

(1) At the bottom of income statement, continue from net income to arrive at a comprehensive income. An entity shall present the following:

(a) A total amount for net income and its components.
(b) A total amount for other comprehensive income and its components.
(c) Total comprehensive income.

(2) In a separate statement that may start with net income, (illustrated below) and that **directly** follows the statement of income. An entity shall present the following:

(a) Net income and it's components in the statement of net income.
(b) Comprehensive and its components along with total comprehensive income.

The accumulated (total) comprehensive income shall be presented separately from retained earnings and additional paid in capital in the statement of financial position. The changes in the accumulated balances are to be presented in the notes to the financial statements or on the face of the financial statements. (See the balance sheet on the following page and the statement of changes in stockholders' equity at the beginning of Module 15).

c. **Reclassification adjustments.** As unrealized gains (losses) recorded and reported in other comprehensive income for the current or prior periods are later realized, they are recognized and reported in net income. To avoid double counting it is necessary to reverse the unrealized amounts that have been recognized.

EXAMPLE

Assume that an available-for-sale security was sold April 1, year 2, for a $45 gain. Assume that Totman did not elect the fair value option. There was $30 of unrealized gain that arose in years prior to year 2 and is in **accumulated other** comprehensive income. The other $15 unrealized gain was reported in the first quarter statements and is part of the $179 reported below under other comprehensive income for year 2.

Totman Company
STATEMENT OF EARNINGS AND COMPREHENSIVE INCOME
For the Year Ended December 31, year 2

Sales		$2,677
Operating income		713
Other revenues and gains		
Interest revenue	$ 5	
Equity in Huskie Co. earnings	15	
Gain on sale of available-for-sale securities	45	65

Other expenses and losses		
Interest expense	(60)	
Loss from permanent impairment of value of manufacturing facilities	(120)	(180)
Income from continuing operations before provision for income taxes		598
Provision for income taxes		
Current	$ 189	
Deferred	50	239
Income from continuing operations		359
Net earnings (loss)		(485)
Other comprehensive income:		
Foreign currency translation adjustments (less applicable income taxes of $6)		26
Unrealized gains on securities:		
Unrealized holding gains arising during period (less applicable income taxes of $43)	179	
Less: Reclassification adjustment (less applicable income taxes of $10) for gain included in net income	(35)	144
Other comprehensive income		170
Comprehensive income		$ (315)

The reclassification adjustment to avoid double counting is $45 less a tax effect of $10 or $35 net. Since the $45 was realized in the current period, a realized gain of $45 was reported in the income from continuing operations under other revenues and gains above before provisions for income taxes of $598. The $10 of income tax on the $45 is reported as part of provision for income taxes in the current portion of income tax expense of $189. Recall that all items reported above the provision for income taxes are reported "gross," not net of taxes as in the case of items such as discontinued operations. Also, note the tax effects reported under other comprehensive income are **deferred** since the unrealized components are not recognized for tax purposes until realized.

d. **Balance sheet.** Accumulated other comprehensive income is reported in the stockholders' equity section of the balance sheet. When an entity has components of other comprehensive income, the total of these is closed to the balance sheet account entitled **accumulated other comprehensive income,** not retained earnings. In the case above, the other comprehensive income of $170 for the period would need to be closed to accumulated other comprehensive income, not retained earnings. The net loss is closed to retained earnings.

> **NOW REVIEW MULTIPLE-CHOICE QUESTIONS 33 THROUGH 46**

5. **Balance Sheets (Statements of Financial Position)**

a. Balance sheets or statements of financial position present assets, liabilities, and stockholders' equity. The balance sheet reports the effect of transactions at a point in time, whereas the statement of earnings (income) and comprehensive income, statement of retained earnings, and statement of cash flows report the effect of transactions over a period of time. An example of balance sheet classification and presentation is illustrated by the comprehensive balance sheet on the previous page.

b. Distinction between current and noncurrent assets and liabilities is almost universal.

(1) *Current assets*—Current assets is used to designate cash and other assets or resources commonly identified as those that are reasonably expected to be realized in cash or sold or consumed during the normal operating cycle of the business.

(2) *Current liabilities*—Current liabilities is used principally to designate obligations whose liquidation is reasonably expected to require the use of existing resources properly classifiable as current assets, or the creation of other current liabilities.

EXAMPLE

Totman Company
BALANCE SHEET
December 31, Year 2

Assets				Liabilities and Stockholders' Equity		
Current assets:				*Current liabilities:*		
Cash and bank deposits:				Commercial paper and other short-term notes	$xxx	
Restricted to current bond maturity	$xxx			Accounts payable	xxx	
Unrestricted	xxx	$xxx		Salaries, wages, and commissions	xxx	
Short-term investments:				Taxes withheld from employees	xxx	
Marketable securities (Trading)		xxx		Income taxes payable	xxx	
Refundable income taxes		xxx		Dividends payable	xxx	
Receivables from affiliates		xxx		Rent revenue collected in advance	xxx	
Accounts receivable	xxx			Other advances from customers	xxx	
Less allowance for doubtful accounts	(xxx)	xxx		Current portion of long-term debt	xxx	
Notes receivable due in year 3		xxx		Current obligations under capital leases	xxx	
Installment notes due in year 3		xxx		Deferred tax liability	xxx	
Interest receivable		xxx		Short-term portion of accrued warranty	xxx	
Creditors' accounts with debit balances		xxx		Other accrued liabilities	xxx	
Advances to employees		xxx		Total current liabilities		$xxx
Inventories (carried at lower of cost or market by FIFO)						
Finished goods	xxx			*Noncurrent liabilities:*		
Work in process	xxx			Notes payable due after year 3	xxx	
Raw materials	xxx	xxx		Plus unamortized note premium	xxx	$xxx
Prepaid expenses:				Long-term bonds:		
Prepaid rent	xxx			10% debentures due in year 13	xxx	
Prepaid insurance	xxx	xxx		9-1/2% collateralized obligations maturing serially to year 5	xxx	
Total current assets		$xxx		8% convertible subordinated debentures due in year 18	xxx	
				Less unamortized discounts net of premiums	(xxx)	xxx
Long-term investments:				Accrued pension cost		xxx
Investments in marketable securities (available-for-sale)	xxx			Obligations under capital leases		xxx
Investments in bonds (held-to-maturity)	xxx			Deferred tax liability		xxx
Investments in unused land	xxx			Long-term portion of accrued warranty		xxx
Cash surrender value of officers' life insurance policies	xxx			Total noncurrent liabilities		$xxx
Sinking fund for bond retirement	xxx			Total liabilities		$xxx
Plant expansion fund	xxx			*Capital stock:*		
Total long-term investments		$xxx		$12.50 convertible preferred stock, $100 stated value, 200,000 shares authorized, 175,000 outstanding	xxx	
Property, plant, and equipment:				12% cumulative preferred stock, $100 stated value, callable at $115, 100,000 shares authorized and outstanding	xxx	
Land	xxx			Common stock, $10 stated value, 500,000 shares authorized, 450,000 issued, 15,000 held in treasury	xxx	
Buildings	xxx			Common stock subscribed 10,000 shares	xxx	
Machinery and equipment	xxx			Less: Subscriptions receivable	(xxx)	xxx
Furniture and fixtures	xxx					
Leasehold improvements	xxx					
Leased assets	xxx					
Less accumulated depreciation and amortization	(xxx)					
Total property, plant, and equipment		$xxx		*Additional paid-in capital:*		
				From 12% cumulative preferred	xxx	
Intangible assets net of amortization:				From common stock	xxx	
Goodwill	xxx			From treasury stock transactions	xxx	
Patents	xxx			From stock dividends	xxx	
Trademarks	xxx			From expiration of stock options	xxx	
Total intangible assets, net		$xxx		Warrants outstanding	xxx	xxx
Other assets:				*Retained earnings:*		
Installment notes due after year 3	xxx			Appropriated for bond indebtedness	xxx	
Unamortized bond issue costs	xxx			Free and unappropriated	xxx	xxx
Equipment to be disposed of	xxx					
Total other noncurrent assets		$xxx		*Accumulated other comprehensive income:*		xxx*
Total assets		$xxx		Total stockholders' equity		
				Less: Treasury stock at cost		
				Total liabilities and stockholders' equity		

* Assumes components thereof are disclosed either in a statement of changes in stockholders' equity or in the notes to FS.

> **NOTE:** Current assets include those expected to be
>
> 1. Realized in cash
> 2. Sold
> 3. Consumed
>
> Current liabilities are those expected to
>
> 1. Use current assets
> 2. Create other current liabilities
>
> The operating cycle is the average time between acquisition of materials and final cash realization.

> **NOW REVIEW MULTIPLE-CHOICE QUESTIONS 47 THROUGH 53**

6. **Other Financial Statement Concepts**

   a. **Disclosures.** Related-party disclosures are covered by ASC Topic 850 (SFAS 57). Additional disclosures required for specific situations were specified at the end of most pronouncements.

   b. **Accounting policies** must be set forth as the initial footnote to the statements. Disclosures are required of

      (1) Accounting principles used when alternatives exist
      (2) Principles peculiar to a particular industry
      (3) Unusual or innovative applications of accounting principles

   c. **Subsequent events.** Subsequent events are those occurring after the balance sheet date but before the financial statements are issued or available to be issued. Financial statements are issued when they are distributed to shareholders and other users. Financial statements are "available to be issued" when they are in a form and format that is complete and complies with GAAP and all necessary approvals for issuance have been obtained.

      (1) An entity that is an SEC filer or is a conduit bond obligor for conduit debt securities traded in a public market must evaluate subsequent events through the date the financial statements are issued. All other entities must evaluate subsequent events through the date that the financial statements are available to be issued. There are two types of subsequent events: recognized and nonrecognized.

      (2) A recognized subsequent event is one in which the condition existed at the balance sheet date and, therefore, is recognized in the financial statements.

      > **EXAMPLE**
      >
      > Recognized events include an estimate for warranty liability, an estimate of a contingent liability due to a lawsuit, or an estimate of allowance for uncollectible accounts.

         (a) If a recognized subsequent event is settled after the balance sheet date but before the financial statements are issued or available to be issued, then the settlement amounts should be used as the liability in the balance sheet.

      (3) A nonrecognized subsequent event is one in which the condition did NOT exist at the balance sheet date, but arose AFTER the balance sheet date. In such cases, the event is NOT recognized in the financial statements. However, if the event is such that the financial statements would be misleading, then a footnote disclosure should be made indicating the nature of the event and an estimate of the financial statement effects.

      (4) An entity that is an SEC filer is not required to disclose the date through which subsequent events are evaluated. However, a non-SEC filer must also disclose the date through which the subsequent events were evaluated and whether that date is the date the financial statements are issued or available to be issued. The provisions of ASC Topics 855 apply both interim and annual reports for all subsequent events that are not addressed by other areas of the Codification.

> **NOW REVIEW MULTIPLE-CHOICE QUESTIONS 54 THROUGH 64**

   d. **Fair value measurements.** Fair value measurements are required for certain assets and liabilities (investments, derivatives, asset impairments, asset retirement obligations, goodwill, business combinations, troubled debt restructuring).

(1) Applying the fair value measurement approach involves the following six steps:

    (a) Identify the asset or liability to be measured.
    (b) Determine the principal or most advantageous market.
    (c) Determine the valuation premise.
    (d) Determine the appropriate valuation technique (*market, income, or cost approach*).
    (e) Obtain inputs for valuation (*Level 1, Level 2, or Level 3*).
    (f) Calculate the fair value of the asset.

(2) Fair value is the price that would be received to sell an asset or paid to transfer a liability in an orderly transaction between market participants at the measurement date (at exit price) under current market conditions. An orderderly transaction is a transaction that allows for normal marketing activities that are usual and customary. In other words, it is not a forced transaction or sale.

(3) The fair value measurement assumes that the asset or liability is sold or transferred in the principal market, or if no principal market exists, the most advantageous market. The **principal market** is a market in which the greatest volume and level of activity occurs. The **most advantageous market** maximizes price received for the asset or minimizes the amount paid to transfer the liability. Market participants in the principal or most advantageous market should have the following characteristics:

    (a) Be independent of the reporting entity (not related parties),
    (b) Be knowledgeable,
    (c) Able to transact, and
    (d) Willing to transact (i.e., motivated, but not compelled to transact).

(4) The price in the principal or most advantageous market shall **not** be adjusted for transaction costs, such as costs to sell. However, the cost to sell is used to determine which market is the most advantageous. If location is a characteristic of the asset or liability, the price **is adjusted** for costs necessary to transport the asset or liability to the market.

EXAMPLE 1

(Adapted from ASC 820-10-55-42 through 45A)

Company A is valuing a trading security to fair value at year-end. The stock is traded on two stock exchanges, the NYSE and NASDAQ. The price quoted on December 31, year 1, on the NYSE is $50 per share, and the brokerage fees are $4 per share. The price quoted on the NASDAQ is $48 per share with brokerage fees of $1 per share.

a. Assume the NYSE is the principal market. The fair value would be $50 because the FV is the price in the principal market for the asset.

b. Assume that there is no principal market, and the stock is exchanged equally on both markets. The fair value would be the price in the most advantageous market. The NYSE price would allow Company A to receive $46 per share for the stock ($50 – $4). The NASDAQ price would allow company A to receive $47 per share for the stock ($48 – $1 per share). Therefore, the NASDAQ price would maximize the price received for the asset, and the NASDAQ market would be considered the most advantageous market. The fair value of $48 per share would be the fair value of the stock.

NOTE: Although the selling fees may be used to determine the most advantageous market, selling costs or brokerage fees are NOT used in calculating the fair value.

EXAMPLE 2

(Adapted from SFAS 157, Appendix A)

Company B is valuing a commodity at year-end. The commodity is traded on an open-exchange, and the price quoted at December 31, year 1, is $10,000. Transportation costs to deliver the goods to market are $500. The fair value of the commodity is $9,500 ($10,000 less the cost to transfer the goods to market of $500).

---

(5) Fair value measurement also assumes the highest and best use of the nonfinancial asset.

NOTE: For financial assets and financial liabilities, the highest and best use concept is not relevant since they do not have alternative uses and their fair values do not depend upon their use within a group.

The **highest and best use** will maximize the value of the asset or group of assets. The use of the asset must be physically possible, legally permissible, and financially feasible at the measurement date. The highest and best use of the asset is then used to determine the valuation premise used to measure fair value as follows:

(a) If the asset provides maximum value by using it with other assets as a group. The fair value of the asset is the price that would be received to sell the asset assuming the asset is used with other assets as a group.

(b) If the asset provides maximum value on a stand-alone basis, the fair value of the asset is the price that would be received in a current transaction to sell the asset stand-alone.

(6) Three valuation techniques can be used to measure fair value: the market approach, the income approach, and the cost approach. The **market approach** uses prices and relevant information from market transactions for identical or comparable assets or liabilities. The **income approach** converts future amounts to a single current (discounted) amount. The **cost approach** relies on the current replacement cost to replace the asset with a comparable asset, adjusted for obsolescence.

(a) If a firm changes its valuation technique or approach for measuring fair value, the change is accounted for as a change in accounting estimate and treated on a prospective basis. The disclosure provisions for a change in accounting estimate are not required for revisions or changes to valuation techniques used in fair value measurements.

(b) Applying the market approach, income approach, and the cost approach requires gathering information to value the asset or liability. A fair value hierarchy is used to prioritize the inputs to valuation techniques. The fair value hierarchy is referred to as Level 1, Level 2, and Level 3, with the fair value hierarchy based on the lowest level of input. The lowest level that is practical should be used to value the asset or liability.

1] Level 1 uses quoted prices (unadjusted prices) from active markets for identical assets or liabilities. Quoted prices in active markets provide the most reliable evidence of fair value and should be used without adjustment whenever available. Examples of Level 1 inputs are stock quotations from the New York Stock Exchange, quotations from dealer markets such as NASDAQ or the market from US Treasury securities, brokered markets wherein brokers match buyers and sellers, and principal-to-principal markets. The fair value of a security measured within Level 1 is the quoted price times the quantity held, and it is not adjusted for the quantity of shares (blockage factor) held.

2] Level 2 inputs are directly or indirectly observable inputs other than quoted prices of Level 1. Examples of Level 2 inputs include quoted prices for similar assets or liabilities in active markets, quoted prices for identical or similar assets that are in markets where few transaction occur, the prices are not current, or prices vary substantially over time. Level 2 inputs also include observable inputs such as yield curves, bank prime rates, interest rates, volatilities, prepayment speeds, loss severities, credit risks, and default rates.

3] Level 3 inputs are unobservable inputs. Level 3 inputs may only be used to measure fair value if observable inputs are not available (i.e., there is little market activity for the asset or liability). These unobservable inputs may reflect the reporting entity's own assumptions about the market and are based on the best information available. Example of Level 3 inputs would include pricing a three-year option using the historical volatility on shares, valuing an asset retirement obligation using expected cash flows estimated by the company, or valuing a reporting unit using a firm's financial forecasts for cash flows or earnings.

e. **The fair value option for reporting financial assets and financial liabilities.** An election can be made to value certain financial assets and financial liabilities at fair value. A financial asset is cash, evidence of an ownership interest in an entity, or a contract that conveys a right to receive cash or another financial instrument or to exchange financial instruments on favorable terms. A financial liability is a contract that imposes an obligation to deliver cash or another financial instrument.

(1) The fair value option applies to all financial assets including available-for-sale, held-to-maturity, and equity method investments. The fair value option also applies to certain financial liabilities, firm commitments that involve financial instruments, written loan commitments, nonfinancial insurance contracts that can be settled by paying a third party, warranties that can be settled by paying a third party, and a host financial instrument that is an embedded nonfinancial derivative instrument separated from a nonfinancial hybrid instrument.

(2) The fair value method does **not** apply to consolidations, pensions, share-based payments, stock options, other postemployment benefits (OPEB), exit or disposal activities, leases, or financial instruments that are a component of equity.

(3) The fair value is the price that would be received to sell an asset or paid to transfer a liability in an orderly transaction between market participants at the measurement date under current market conditions.

(4) A company can elect to measure the applicable financial assets or financial liabilities at fair value on the date an eligible item is first recognized, the date the entity enters into a firm commitment, the date financial assets cease to qualify for fair value treatment due to specialized accounting rules.

    (a) For companies using the equity method of accounting, a company can elect to measure the investment at fair value on the date the percentage of ownership changes and the entity is no longer required to consolidate.

    (b) For debt modifications, the fair value option can be elected on the date the debt is modified. **Once the fair value option is elected, it is irrevocable.**

(5) The fair value election can be made on an instrument-by-instrument basis. For example, a company has two available-for-sale securities, Security A and Security B. The company can account for Security A using the cost adjusted fair value method for available-for-sale securities and it can elect the fair value option and account for Security B at fair value. **However, if the fair value option is elected, it must be applied to the entire instrument and not a portion of the instrument**. For example, if there are multiple advances to a borrower for a single contract, it must be applied to the entire balance of the contract. If the fair value option is applied to an investment in an entity that would normally use the equity method, it must be applied to all debt and equity interests in that entity.

    (a) Similarly, if the fair value option is elected for insurance contracts, it must be applied to all claims and obligations for that contract.

    (b) If the fair value option is elected, any unrealized gains and losses are reported in earnings for the period. Therefore, any unrealized gains and losses on an available-for-sale security would be reported on the income statement rather than in other comprehensive income. For a held-to-maturity security, the company would no longer report the investment at amortized cost. Instead, the held-to-maturity security would be marked to fair value at the end of the period, and the resulting unrealized gain or loss would be reported on the income statement. The rules remain in effect for classifying items on the statement of cash flows as operating or investing activities.

(6) If a reporting entity holds a group of financial assets and financial liabilities that are exposed to market and credit risks of counterparties, the reporting entity may apply fair value to the net position if the following conditions are met:

    (a) The group of financial assets and financial liabilities are managed on the basis of net exposure;
    (b) Information about the group is provided on a net basis; and
    (c) The reporting entity has elected or is required to measure the group at fair value.

(7) Additional financial statement disclosures are required if the fair value option is elected. Two methods are permissible for balance sheet disclosure: (1) present the aggregate fair value and non–fair value amounts in the same line with amounts measured at fair value parenthetically disclosed, or (2) present two separate line items for fair value and non–fair value carrying amounts.

f. **Disclosures for fair value measurements.** Additional footnote disclosures are required for fair value measurements. Fair value measurements are reported by class of assets or liabilities. The class is determined on the basis of the nature and risks of the assets or liability.

(1) For assets and liabilities that are measured at fair value on a **recurring** basis, the following disclosures are required for each major class of assets and liabilities:

    (a) The fair value measurement at the end of the reporting date.
    (b) The level within the fair value hierarchy used, segregating the fair value measurements, which use Levels 1, 2, and 3 inputs.
    (c) The amount of any transfers between Level 1 and Level 2 of the fair value hierarchy and the reason for the transfer along with the entity's transfer policy. Transfers into and out of each level are disclosed separately.
    (d) For fair value measures using significant other observable inputs (Level 2) and significant unobservable inputs (Level 3), a description of valuation techniques used, the inputs used to determine fair values of each class of assets or liabilities. If there is a change in valuation techniques, the reason for the change must be disclosed.
    (e) For fair value measurements using unobservable inputs (Level 3) a reconciliation of the beginning and ending balance, showing

        1] Total gains and losses for the period realized and unrealized, presenting gains and losses in earnings and gains and losses in other comprehensive income, and a description of where those gains or losses are included in the income statement, or in other comprehensive income.

        2] Purchases, sales, issues, and settlements shown separately.

        3] Transfers in and out of Level 3 are shown separately with reasons for the transfers, along with the entity's transfer policy.

    (f) For fair value measurements using unobservable inputs (Level 3) the amount of total gains or losses for the period included in earnings from unrealized gains and losses for those assets and liabilities still held at the end of the reporting period and the line item in the statement of income (or activities) where the gains and losses are recognized.

    (g) For fair value measurements using unobservable inputs (Level 3) a description of the valuation processes (policies, procedures, and analyses of change from period to period), the sensitivity of the measurement, and any interrelationships.

    (h) For fair value measurements, a description of nonfinancial assets with a current use differing from the highest and best use.

(2) For assets and liabilities that are measured at fair value on a **nonrecurring** basis, the following information must be disclosed in interim and annual period financial statements:

    (a) The fair value measurement at the end of the reporting period and the reasons for the measurement.

    (b) The level within the fair value hierarchy, Level 1, 2, and 3.

    (c) For fair value measurements categorized within Level 2 or Level 3 of the fair value hierarchy, the inputs and valuation techniques used to measure fair value.

    (d) For fair value measurements using significant unobservable inputs (Level 3), a description of valuation processes (policies, procedures, and analyses of change from period to period).

    (e) For fair value measurements a description of nonfinancial assets with a current use differing from the highest and best use.

NOW REVIEW MULTIPLE-CHOICE QUESTIONS 65 THROUGH 76

---

g. **Development stage enterprise accounting** should follow generally accepted accounting principles. The only additional disclosure required is that cumulative amounts from inception of losses, revenues, expenses, and cash flows should be shown in the income statement and statement of cash flows. Furthermore, the stockholders' equity section of the balance sheet should include cumulative net losses termed "deficit accumulated during development stage." These statements should be identified as those of a development stage enterprise. (More detailed coverage appears in Module 11.)

h. **Constant dollar accounting.** The accounting standards encourage, but do not require, a business enterprise that prepares its financial statements in US dollars and in accordance with US generally accepted accounting principles to disclose supplementary information on the effects of changing prices. This statement presents requirements to be followed by enterprises that voluntarily elect to disclose this information.

(1) Constant dollar accounting is a method of reporting financial statement elements in dollars which have the same purchasing power. This method is often described as accounting in units of current purchasing power.

    (a) Purchasing power indicates the ability of a dollar to command goods and services.

EXAMPLE

If the inflation rate during a given year for a group of items is 10%, then 110 end-of-year dollars are needed to purchase the same group of items which cost $100 at the beginning of the year. Similarly, a machine purchased at the beginning of that year for $1,000 would be presented in a year-end constant dollar balance sheet at a restated cost of $1,100. This represents the basic thrust of constant dollar accounting: the adjustment of historical data (nominal dollars) for changes in the general price level.

---

(2) The adjustment of nominal dollar data is facilitated by the use of the Consumer Price Index, which reflects the average change in the retail prices of a wide variety of consumer goods. The adjustment is made by multiplying historical cost by the TO/FROM ratio.

$$\begin{matrix} \text{Historical cost} \\ \text{(nominal dollars)} \end{matrix} \times \frac{\text{Price level adjusting to}}{\text{Price level adjusting from}} = \text{Restated historical cost (constant dollar)}$$

EXAMPLE

An asset was purchased on 12/31/Y1 for $20,000 and the Consumer Price Index was 100 on 12/31/Y1, 110 on 12/31/Y2, and 120 on 12/31/Y3. Restatement for end-of-year balance sheets would be

12/31/Y1	$20,000	×	$\frac{100}{100}$	=	$20,000
12/31/Y2	$20,000	×	$\frac{110}{100}$	=	$22,000
12/31/Y3	$20,000	×	$\frac{120}{100}$	=	$24,000
		or			
	$22,000	×	$\frac{120}{110}$	=	$24,000

---

(3) The preparation of constant dollar financial statements requires the classification of balance sheet items as either monetary or nonmonetary.

(a) Items are monetary if their amounts are fixed by statute or contract in terms of numbers of dollars. Examples include cash, accounts and notes receivable, accounts and notes payable, and bonds payable.

  1] By contract or statute, these items are already stated in current dollars and require no restatement.

(b) Nonmonetary items, on the other hand, do require restatement to current dollars. Inventory, property, plant, and equipment, and unearned service revenue are examples of nonmonetary items.

  1] Under some increasingly popular loan arrangements, when the repayment of loan principal is adjusted by an index, the receivable/payable is classified as a nonmonetary item.

NOTE: The holding of a nonmonetary asset such as land during a period of inflation need not result in a loss of purchasing power because the value of that land can "flow" with the price level (hence, the need for restatement). However, if a monetary asset such as cash is held during a period of inflation with no interest, purchasing power is lost because the cash will be able to purchase less goods and services at year-end than at the beginning of the year. This type of loss is simply called a "purchasing power loss." Holding a monetary liability has the opposite effect. Therefore, if a firm's balance sheet included more monetary liabilities than monetary assets throughout a given year, a purchasing power **gain** would result, since the firm could pay its liabilities using cash which is "worth less" than the cash it borrowed.

(c) A simple example can illustrate both the restatement process and the effect of holding monetary assets. Assume that the Static Company has the following balance sheet at the beginning of period 1:

EXAMPLE

Static Co.
End of Period 1
Consumer Price Index = 110

Cash	$1,000	Common Stock	$2,200[b]
Land	1,000		
	$2,000		$2,000

Further assume
- Index increases to 110 by the end of year 1
- No transactions have taken place, land and common stock would be restated to end-of-year dollars.
- Cash is still stated at $1,000.
- To have the same level of purchasing power that was present at the beginning of the year, Static Co. should also have cash of $1,100 at year-end. The fact that the company held $1,000 cash throughout the year has resulted in a $100 purchasing power loss. The balance sheet at the end of period 1 would therefore be

Static Co.
End of Period 1
Consumer Price Index = 110

Cash	$1,000	Common Stock	$2,200[b]
Land	1,100[a]	Retained Earnings	(100)[c]
	$2,100		$2,100

---

[a]$\$1,000 \times \dfrac{110}{100}$ [b]$\$2,000 \times \dfrac{110}{100}$ [c]Purchasing power loss $\$1,000 - \left(\$1,000 \times \dfrac{110}{100}\right)$

What if the entity had acquired equipment costing $1,000 at the beginning of the year by issuing a $1,000 note payable? At the end of the year, under constant dollar accounting, the equipment would be carried at $1,100 and the note payable would be still reported at $1,000. What would the net purchasing power gain (loss) be? The answer is zero because the loss of $100 is offset by a $100 gain from holding the note payable.

i. **Current cost accounting** is a method of valuing and reporting assets, liabilities, revenues, and expenses at their current cost at the balance sheet date or at the date of their use or sale.

(1) It is important to distinguish between constant dollar and current cost accounting. Constant dollar accounting is concerned only with changes in the unit of measure—from nominal dollars to units of general purchasing power. Current cost accounting discards historical cost as a reporting model.

(2) Preparation of a current cost income statement requires an understanding of certain basic current cost concepts. **Current cost income from continuing operations** is sales revenue less expenses on a current cost basis. **Realized holding gains** (the difference between current cost and historical cost of assets consumed) are then added to arrive at **realized income,** which will always be equal to historical cost net income. Finally, **unrealized holding gains** (increases in the current cost of assets held throughout the year) are included to result in **current cost net income.**

EXAMPLE

Bell Company went into business on 1/1/Y1. Year 1 sales revenue was $200,000 and purchases totaled $150,000. Inventory with a historical cost of $100,000 was sold when its current cost was $160,000. Ending inventory (historical cost, $50,000) had a year-end current cost of $80,000. No other revenue was realized or expenses incurred during year 1. Historical and current cost income statements for year 1 are presented below.

Bell Company
INCOME STATEMENTS

Historical cost		**Current cost**	
Sales	$ 200,000	Sales	$ 200,000
Less CGS	(100,000)	Less CGS	(160,000)
		Cur. cost income from cont. oper.	40,000
		Realized holding gains (160,000 – 100,000)	60,000
Net income	$ 100,000	Realized income	100,000
		Unrealized holding gains (80,000 – 50,000)	30,000
		Current cost net income	$ 130,000

Year 1 journal entries for Bell Company in current cost system would be as follows:

a)	Inventory	150,000		d)	Cost of goods sold	160,000	
	Cash		150,000		Inventory		160,000
b)	Inventory	90,000		e)	Realizable holding gain	90,000	
	Realizable				Realized holding gain		60,000
	holding gain		90,000		Unrealized holding gain		30,000
c)	Cash	200,000					
	Sales revenue		200,000				

---

(3) In general, sales and some expense amounts (salaries, rent, etc.) will be the same under historical and current cost systems. However, whenever an expense represents the use or consumption of an asset whose current cost has changed since its acquisition (as with the inventory in the Bell Company example), that expense must be expressed at the current cost of the asset when used. Realized holding gains are computed by comparing the current cost of assets when used or consumed with their historical cost. Unrealized holding gains for the period are determined by identifying changes in the current cost of assets held throughout the year (not used or consumed).

NOTE: Holding gains do not reflect changes in the general purchasing power. In other words, holding gains are not reported net of general inflation when the reporting model is current cost/nominal dollar.

(4) **Current cost/constant dollars.** The relationship measured is current cost, but the measuring unit is restated dollars. Changes in both the general and specific price levels are separately recorded.

NOW REVIEW MULTIPLE-CHOICE QUESTIONS 77 THROUGH 87

j. **Risks and uncertainties.** Disclosure is required in financial statements about the risks and uncertainties existing as of the date of those statements. The four areas of disclosure are

(1) Nature of operations

    (a) Major products/services and principal markets served.
    (b) Industries operating within and relative importance of each industry, including basis of determination (assets, revenue, or earnings).

> **NOTE:** Quantification not required and words such as predominantly, equally, major, or other may be used.

(2) Use of estimates in preparation of financial statements.

    (a) This fact must be disclosed by an explanation that management must use estimates.
    (b) The purpose is to alert users clearly to pervasiveness of estimates.

(3) Certain significant estimates:

    (a) Potential impact of estimates to value assets, liabilities, gains, or losses when

        1] Reasonably possible the estimate will change in the near term.
        2] Effect of change would be material to financial statements.

> **NOTE:** Near term is defined as not to exceed one year from date of financial statements.

    (b) Contingencies.
    (c) Disclosure of factors causing the estimate to be sensitive to change is encouraged, but not required.
    (d) Materiality is measured by the effect that using a different estimate would have on the financial statements.

(4) Current vulnerability due to concentrations.

    (a) Before issuance of financial statements, management knows that concentrations:

        1] Exist at balance sheet date.
        2] Make entity vulnerable to risk of near-term severe impact.
        3] Reasonably possible events could cause severe impact in near future.

> **NOTE:** Severe impact is defined as higher than materiality and would have a significant financially disruptive effect on the normal functioning of the entity.

    (b) Examples are concentrations in

        1] Volume of business transacted with a particular customer, supplier, lender, grantor, or contributor.
        2] Revenue from particular products, services, or fund-raising events.
        3] Available sources of supply of materials, labor, or services, or of licenses or other rights used in the entity's operations.
        4] Market or geographical area in which an entity conducts its operations.

    (c) Disclose the percentage of labor covered by a collective bargaining agreement and the percentage covered whose agreement expires within one year.
    (d) Describe for operations outside of home country, the carrying value of net assets and location.

7. **Comparative Financial Statements**

    The Totman Company balance sheet and income statement illustrated in this module are presented for a single year. Most companies present comparative financial statements. Comparative financial statements present not only the current year's information, but prior periods also. The purpose of comparative financial statements is to enable users to evaluate trends which may reveal information about the company's future performance. The SEC requires that a two-year comparative balance sheet and a three-year comparative income statement and statement of cash flows be presented.

8. **Other Comprehensive Bases of Accounting (OCBOA)**

   a. Financial statements may be prepared in conformity with a comprehensive basis of accounting other than generally accepted accounting principles (GAAP) or international accounting standards. The four types of OCBOA include

      (1) **Cash-basis** financial statements—In pure cash-basis financial statements the only asset is cash; revenue is recognized when cash is received; and expenses are recognized when they are paid. The pure basis is rarely used.

      (2) **Modified cash-basis** financial statements—Modified cash basis financial statements are cash basis statements with modifications that have substantial support. For example, fixed assets, inventories, and the related liabilities are typically recorded in modified cash-basis financial statements. Modifications that have substantial support involve presenting the items as they would be in GAAP financial statements providing that the presentation is not illogical. As an example, an illogical modification would involve recording inventories but not recording the accounts payable related to the inventories.

      (3) **Tax-basis** financial statements—Tax-basis financial statements are statements prepared on the basis of tax laws and regulations. When financial statements are prepared on an income tax basis, the financial statements should not simply repeat items and amounts reported in the tax return. Thus, items such as nontaxable municipal interest and the nondeductible portion of travel and entertainment expense should be **fully** reflected in the tax-basis income statement.

      (4) **Regulatory-basis** financial statements—Regulatory financial statements are prepared based on rules established by a regulatory agency.

   b. OCBOA financial statements should not include titles such as "balance sheet" and "statement of income" (unmodified) because these terms are reserved for GAAP-basis statements. Titles such as "balance sheet—tax basis," "statement of revenues and expenses—income tax basis," "statement of assets and liabilities—modified cash basis," and "statement of cash receipts and disbursements" are appropriate. In addition, the notes to the financial statements should disclose the differences between the OCBOA- and GAAP-basis financial statements, as well as the other information normally included in GAAP-basis financial statements.

9. **Prospective Financial Information**

   a. Definitions

      (1) **Prospective financial information**—any financial information about the future.
      (2) **Responsible party**—person(s), usually management, who are responsible for assumptions underlying the information.
      (3) Users of prospective financial information

         (a) General—use of financial statements by parties with whom responsible party is not negotiating directly.
         (b) Limited use—use of prospective financial information by the responsible party only or by responsible party and third parties with whom responsible party is negotiating directly.

      (4) **Financial forecast**—prospective FS that present the knowledge and belief of responsible party in terms of expected financial position, results of operations, and cash flows

         (a) May be prepared for **general** or **limited** use.
         (b) Monetary amounts are expressed as a single-point estimate of results or range.

      (5) **Financial projection**—prospective FS that present the knowledge and belief of responsible party, based on one or more **hypothetical** assumptions, the enterprise's financial position, results of operations, and cash flows.

         (a) Assumptions **not necessarily** expected to occur.
         (b) May contain a single-point estimate of results or a range of dollars.
         (c) May be prepared only for **limited** use.

   b. Reasons for preparation are to

      (1) Obtain external financing.
      (2) Consider a change in accounting or operations.
      (3) Prepare budgets.

   c. Process for preparing forecasts and projections may consist of any of the following:

      (1) Formal system.
      (2) Carrying out a work program that outlines steps followed in preparation.
      (3) Documented procedures, methods, and practices used in preparation.

d. Financial forecasts and projections should reflect **a reasonably objective basis** as a result of preparing them

(1) In good faith.
(2) With due care by qualified personnel.
(3) In accordance with GAAP.
(4) With the highest quality information that is reasonably available.
(5) Using information that is in accordance with plans of the entity.
(6) Identifying key factors as basis for assumptions.

    (a) Key factors are important matters for which outcomes are expected to depend.

(7) Using appropriate assumptions.

    (a) Quality of these is crucial.
    (b) **Hypothetical** assumptions used in projections do **not** need to meet a strict reasonableness test; they must, however, be appropriate in light of the purpose of the projection.

(8) Providing ways to determine relative effect of variations in main assumptions (i.e., sensitivity analysis).
(9) Documenting forecast/projection and process used.
(10) Providing for comparison of forecast/projection with attained results.
(11) Providing adequate review of the responsible party at appropriate levels of authority in the organization.
(12) Prospective financial statement disclosures include.

    (a) Summary of significant accounting policies.
    (b) Summary of significant assumptions.

NOW REVIEW MULTIPLE-CHOICE QUESTIONS 88 THROUGH 97

---

10. **SEC Reporting Requirements**

a. Unless exempt by regulation, companies with assets of more than $10 million and 500 or more shareholders and securities that trade on a national securities exchange or an over-the-counter market must have the securities registered.

b. Companies with registered securities (termed issuers) must follow SEC rules and regulations. Securities regulations include, but are not limited to

(1) **Regulation S-X** describes the form and content of financial statements filed with the SEC.
(2) **Regulation S-K** describes the requirements for information and forms required by Regulation S-X.
(3) **Regulation AB** describes reporting requirements for asset-backed securities.
(4) **Regulation Fair Disclosure (FD)** mandates that publicly traded companies disclose material information to all investors simultaneously.

c. Companies with registered securities (termed issuers) must file the following reports with the SEC:

(1) **Form S-1/F-1**-registration statement for US/ foreign companies.
(2) **Form 8-K/6-K**- information about material events for US/foreign companies.
(3) **Form 10-K/20F**-annual report for US/foreign companies.

    (a) A foreign registrant can omit the reconciliation between US GAAP and home-country GAAP (e.g. IFRS) if the foreign-based company follows IFRS as issued by the IASB.

(4) **Form 10-Q**- quarterly reports.
(5) **Schedule 14A**- proxy statement.

d. Information statements (**Form 8-K**) provide information about material events that affect the company, such as mergers and acquisitions, changes in directors or CEO, other major changes in operations or status, changes in auditors, etc. The Form 8-K must be filed within 4 business days of the occurrence of the events.

EXAMPLE

ITEM 7.01. REGULATION FD DISCLOSURE[*]

On May 26, 2011, management of Rand Logistics, Inc. ("Rand") presented to institutional investors a summary of Rand's business, historical financial performance, and future earnings guidance at the CJS Securities 2nd Annual Midwest Investor Conference. The presentation is attached as Exhibit 99.1 and is incorporated by reference herein.

[*]SEC Edgar Filing

(1) The 8-K includes the following information (*Italicized items may be omitted*):

    (a) Item 1.01, Entry into a Material Definitive Agreement.

    (b) Item 1.02, Termination of a Material Definitive Agreement.

    (c) Item 1.03, Bankruptcy or Receivership.

    (d) *Item 2.01, Completion of Acquisition or Disposition of Assets.*

    (e) *Item 2.02, Results of Operations And Financial Condition.*

    (f) *Item 2.03, Creation of A Direct Financial Obligation or an Obligation Under an Off-Balance Sheet Arrangement of a Registrant.*

    (g) Item 2.04, Triggering Events That Accelerate or Increase a Direct Financial Obligation or an Obligation Under an Off-Balance Sheet Arrangement.

    (h) *Item 2.05, Costs Associated with Exit or Disposal Activities.*

    (i) *Item 2.06, Material Impairments.*

    (j) *Item 3.01, Notice of Delisting or Failure to Satisfy a Continued Listing Rule or Standard; Transfer of Listing.*

    (k) *Item 3.02, Unregistered Sales of Equity Securities.*

    (l) Item 3.03, Material Modification to Rights of Security Holders.

    (m) *Item 4.01, Changes in Registrant's Certifying Accountant.*

    (n) *Item 4.02, Non-Reliance on Previously Issued Financial Statements or a Related Audit Reports or Completed Interim Review.*

    (o) *Item 5.01, Changes in Control of Registrant.*

    (p) *Item 5.02, Departure of Directors or Principal Officers; Election of Directors; Appointment of Principal Officers.*

    (q) Item 5.03, Amendments to Articles of Incorporation or Bylaws; Change in Fiscal Year.

    (r) *Item 5.04, Temporary Suspension of Trading Under Registrant's Employee Benefit Plans; and*

    (s) *Item 5.05, Amendments to the Registrant's Code of Ethics, or Waiver of a Provision of the Code of Ethics.*

    (t) Section 5.06, Change in Shell Company Status.

    (u) Item 5.07, Submission of Matters to a Vote of Security Holders.

    (v) Item 6.01, ABS Informational and Computational Material.

    (w) Item 6.02, Change of Servicer or Trustee.

    (x) Item 6.03, Change In Credit Enhancement or Other External Support.

    (y) Item 6.04, Failure to Make a Required Distribution.

    (z) Item 6.05, Securities Act Updating Disclosure.

    (aa) Item 7.01, Regulation FD Disclosure.

    (bb) Item 8.01, Other Events.

    (cc) Item 9, Financial Statements and Exhibits.

  e. A quarterly report (**Form 10-Q**) provides quarterly information similar to that in the 10-K but is less detail. It includes quarterly financial statements that are reviewed (not audited) by public accountants. The company files three Form 10-Qs every year and the Form 10-K contains the quarterly results for the fourth quarter. Form 10-Qs are due 40 days after the end of the fiscal quarter for accelerated filers and 45 days after the end of the fiscal quarter for all other companies.

  f. An annual report (**Form 10-K**) provides a comprehensive picture of a company's performance, including audited financial statements. The 10-K includes the following sections:

Item No.	Reg. S-K No. (unless otherwise noted)	Description
Part I		
1	101	Business
1A	503(c)	Risk factors
2	102	Properties
3	103	Legal proceedings
4	104	Removed
Part II		
5	201, 701, 703	Market for common equity and related matters
6	301	Selected financial data
7	303	Management's discussion and analysis
7A	305	Quantitative and qualitative disclosures about market risk
8	302	Financial statements and supplementary data
9	304 (b)	Changes in and disagreement with auditors
9A	307, 308	Controls and procedures

Item No.	Reg. S-K No. (unless otherwise noted)	Description
Part III		
10	401, 405,406,407(c)(3), (d)(4), (d)(5)	Directors and executive officers (may be omitted)
11	402	Executive compensation (may be omitted)
12	201(d)	Security ownership of owners and management (may be omitted)
13	404	Relationships and related transactions (may be omitted)
14	9 (e) of Schedule 14A	Principal accountant fees and services
Part IV		
15	302 and 601 of Reg. S-K, Reg. S-X	Exhibits, financial statement schedules
Other		
	Reg. AB1112(b), 1114(b), 1117, 1119, 1122, 1123	Substitute information to be included

* SOURCE: Modified by Natalie T. Churyk, NIU CPA Review

Form 10-Ks are due 60 days after the end of the fiscal year for large accelerated filers (more than $700 million of aggregate worldwide market value of voting and nonvoting common stock), 75 days after the end of the fiscal year for accelerated files (between $70 million of aggregated worldwide market value of voting and nonvoting common stock), and 90 days after the end of the fiscal year for all other companies.

g. SEC releases and administrative interpretations include, but are not limited to, the following:

(1) Accounting and Auditing Enforcement Releases (AAERs) that announce enforcement actions of the SEC's reporting and disclosure requirements.
(2) Accounting Series Releases (ASRs), issued from 1937-1982, are the predecessor of Financial Reporting Releases. The ASRs still in effect are codified.
(3) Financial Reporting Releases (FRRs) update the SEC Codification of Financial Reporting Policies and Regulations S-K and S-X.
(4) *Staff Accounting Bulletins (SABs) are unofficial interpretations relating to accounting and disclosure practices. SEC staff follow SABs when administering disclosure requirements.
(5) *Staff Legal Bulletins summarize the Commission staff's views related to SEC regulations and federal securities laws.
(6) *Staff no-action, Interpretive, and Exemptive letters are published SEC staff responses to interpretation inquires.

   *Items (4), (5) and (6) are not legally binding.

11. **Financial Statements of Trusts**

   a. Trusts are entities formed to hold assets for the benefit of the beneficiaries. They are administered by trustees. Trusts generally present the following financial statements:

   (1) A statement of assets and liabilities.
   (2) A statement of operations.
   (3) A statement of changes in net assets.

   b. The financial statements of a trust are generally presented on the accrual basis and the assets are generally presented at their fair values.

> **NOW REVIEW MULTIPLE-CHOICE QUESTIONS 98 THROUGH 104**

12. **Research Component—Accounting Standards Codification**

   a. The rules for presentation of financial statements are located in the category labeled "Presentation" in the Accounting Standards Codification. The topics are numbered in the 200 series. Note that discontinued operations are included under the rules of Topic 205. Treatment of extraordinary items is found in Topic 225. Below is a list of topics related to financial statement disclosures:

   Presentation
205	Presentation of Financial Statements
210	Balance Sheet
215	Statement of Shareholder Equity
220	Comprehensive Income

Presentation

225	Income Statement
230	Statement of Cash Flows
235	Notes to Financial Statements
250	Accounting Changes and Error Corrections
255	Changing Prices
260	Earnings Per Share
270	Interim Reporting
275	Risks and Uncertainties
280	Segment Reporting

b. Other topics covered in the module are located under the category "Broad Transactions" and include the following topics:

Broad Transactions

820	Fair Value Measurements and Disclosures
825	Financial Instruments
850	Related-Party Disclosures
855	Subsequent Events

c. Keywords for research financial statements and related disclosures are shown below.

Accounting policies	Disposal of segment	Period-specific effects
Balance sheet	Earned surplus	Principal market
Capital stock	External revenue	Prior period adjustments
Capital surplus	Extraordinary items	Pro forma amounts
Cash flow estimation	Fair value hierarchy	Pro forma effects
Change in accounting	Fair value option	Profit and loss
Change in principle	Financial position	Purchasing power gain/loss
Changes in entity	Highest and best use	Reclassification adjustments
Changes in equity	Impairment loss	Reconciliations of totals
Changes in estimates	Inclusive net income	Recurring operations
Classifications net income	Income approach	Reportable segment
Comparative financial statements	Income statement	Results of operations
Comparative purposes	Infrequency of occurrence	Retroactive adjustment
Component held for sale	Interim period information	Retrospective application
Component of an entity	Market approach	Segment item
Comprehensive income	Measure impairment loss	Surplus statement
Correction of error	Monetary asset	Translation adjustment
Cost approach	Monetary liability	Unusual nature
Current assets	Nature products services	Valuation techniques
Current cost purchasing power	Net income period	Working capital
Current liabilities	Obligations operating cycle	
Disclosure accounting policies	Operating cycle	
Discontinued operation	Operating segment	
Disposal activity	Other comprehensive income	

13. **International Financial Reporting Standards (IFRS)**

a. **Financial statements.** IAS 1 provides that a complete set of financial statements must be prepared annually. A complete set of financial statements includes a statement of financial position, a statement of comprehensive income, a statement of changes in equity, a statement of cash flows, and notes containing significant accounting policies and explanations.

(1) The headings on the financial statements should include the name of the entity, the title of the statement, and the date of the statement.

(2) The financial statements should present a "true and fair view" of the company. IFRS must be used unless there is a rare circumstance where the use of IFRS would produce misleading financial statements.

(3) Whenever an entity retrospectively applies an accounting policy, retrospectively restates its financial statements, or reclassifies items, three years of statements of financial position are required for comparative purposes. Presentation and classification of items on the financial statements should be consistent for the periods presented.

(4) The accrual basis of accounting is used to prepare the financial statements, with the assumption that the entity is a going concern.

(a) Assets and liabilities may not be offset against each other unless specifically permitted by an IFRS.
(b) Similarly, income and expenses may not be offset unless specifically permitted.
(c) Offsets may be used for valuation purposes, such as contra accounts (allowance for uncollectible accounts or accumulated depreciation).
(d) Items on the financial statements should be presented separately for each material class of similar items. If an item is not material, it may be aggregated with other items.

b. **Statement of financial position**.

(1) Assets are classified as current and noncurrent.

(a) An asset is current if it is expected to be realized or held for consumption in the normal course of the entity's operating cycle, held primarily for trading purposes, expected to be realized within 12 months of the end of the period, or is cash or a cash equivalent that is not restricted.
(b) Noncurrent assets include tangible, intangible, operating, and financial assets that are long term, such as held-to-maturity investments, investment property, property and equipment, intangible assets, assets held for sale, and miscellaneous assets.

(2) Liabilities are classified as current and noncurrent.

(a) A liability is current if it is expected to be settled in the normal course of business during the operating cycle, due to be settled within 12 months, held primarily for trading purposes, or does not have an unconditional right to defer settlement beyond 12 months.

1] However, certain payables such as trade payables and accruals for operating costs are classified as current liabilities regardless of the settlement date.

(b) Interest-bearing liabilities are classified based upon whether they are due within 12 months.

1] However, if an agreement to refinance the liability on a long-term basis is executed prior to the financial statement date, the liability may be classified as noncurrent.

NOTE: This is different from US GAAP, where if there is the intent and ability to refinance before the issuance of the financial statements, reclassification is permitted.

a] An executed agreement prior to the balance sheet is not required.

2] For IFRS, if the agreement to refinance is made after the balance sheet date, then the liability must be classified as current at the balance sheet date. Similar to US GAAP, if a long-term debt becomes callable due to violation of a loan covenant, the liability must be classified as a current liability.

(3) For shareholders' equity the financial statements must disclose the number of shares of common stock authorized, issued, and outstanding. If there are preference shares (e.g., preferred stock), they must be reported separately including the number of shares authorized, issued, and outstanding. Preference shares that are redeemable at the option of the holder must be classified as liabilities. Treasury shares repurchased are stated at cost and shown as a reduction to shareholders' equity. Accumulated other comprehensive income is reported in the shareholder's equity section of the balance sheet, and noncontrolling interests are disclosed as a separate item in the equity section of the balance sheet.

(4) Although IAS 1 does not require a specific format for the statement of financial position, the following categories should be displayed:

(a) Property, plant, and equipment
(b) Investment property
(c) Intangible assets
(d) Financial assets
(e) Investments accounted for using the equity method
(f) Biological assets
(g) Inventories
(h) Trade and other receivables
(i) Cash and cash equivalents
(j) The total assets classified as held for sale and assets included in disposal groups classified as held for sale under IFRS 5
(k) Trade and other payables
(l) Provisions
(m) Financial liabilities
(n) Liabilities and assets for current tax
(o) Deferred tax liabilities and deferred tax assets

    (p) Liabilities included in disposal groups classified as held for sale

    (q) Noncontrolling interest

    (r) Issued capital and reserves attributable to owners of the parent

c. **The income statement.** IAS 1 requires that at a minimum, the following items should be included on an income statement:

    (1) Revenue (referred to as income)

    (2) Finance costs (interest expense)

    (3) Share of profits and losses of associates and joint ventures accounted for using equity method

    (4) Tax expense

    (5) Discontinued operations

    (6) Profit or loss

    (7) Noncontrolling interest in profit and loss

    (8) Net profit (loss) attributable to equity holders in the parent

      (a) If an entity acquires less than 100% of a subsidiary, the income statement should indicate the profit or loss attributable to the noncontrolling interest and the owners of the parent.

      (b) A significant difference between US GAAP and IFRS is that IFRS does not permit the classification of items as "extraordinary items" on the income statement. Any gains or losses should be reported as income or expense.

        1] In addition, operating expenses may be classified either by nature or by function. Classification by nature is based on the character of the expense, such as salaries and wages, raw materials used, interest expense, tax expense, and depreciation of assets. Classification by function is based on the purpose of the expenditure, such as manufacturing, distribution, or administration. If the entity classifies expenses by function, cost of sales must be stated separately from other expenses. (Note that in US GAAP, expenses are classified by function, e.g., cost of goods sold, operating expenses, etc.).

        2] For IFRS, finance costs (interest expense) must be identified separately regardless of which classification scheme is used.

      (c) Operating expenses are normally classified as distribution costs (selling expenses) and general and administrative expenses.

        1] If an item is material in amount and of such a size, nature, or incidence that disclosure is important to understand the performance of the entity, then the item should be disclosed separately.

EXAMPLE

Examples of those disclosures include write-downs of inventories; write-downs of plant, property, and equipment; restructuring costs; costs of litigation settlements; and reversals of provisions.

      (d) The treatment of discontinued operations is similar to US GAAP. If an asset is classified as held for sale or is part of a disposal group, it is valued at the lower of carrying value or fair value less costs to sell. The write-down net of tax is included in discontinued operations in the income statement. For discontinued operations, several calculations are required.

        1] First, the revenues, expenses, pretax profit or loss, and the related income tax expense are calculated.

        2] Second, the gain or loss on disposal or remeasurement is calculated with the related income tax expense.

        3] Finally, the total of these two amounts is determined (net of tax) and must be disclosed on the income statement.

        4] The footnote disclosures must include the pretax profit or loss, gain or loss on disposal, and tax effects, as well as the net cash flows from operating, investing, and financing activities.

d. **Statement of comprehensive income.** The statement of comprehensive income may be presented in either one statement or in two statements.

    (1) The two-statement approach presents a separate income statement, and then presents a second statement, which begins with profit or loss and displays the components of comprehensive income.

      (a) Items that are included in comprehensive income are changes in revaluation surplus for plant, property, and equipment, actuarial gains and losses on defined benefit plans, gains and losses from foreign currency translations, gains and losses on remeasuring available-for-sale financial assets, and the effective portion of gains and losses on hedging instruments used as cash flow hedges.

(b) Each component of comprehensive income should be stated separately on the statement of comprehensive income.

e. **Statement of cash flows.** The accounting rules for the Statement of Cash Flows are similar to US GAAP. For IFRS, cash flows include the inflows and outflows of both cash and cash equivalents. Cash equivalents include cash on hand, bank balances for immediate use, other demand deposits, and short-term investments with maturities of three months or less. Both the direct method and indirect method are acceptable methods for preparing the statement of cash flows. However, for the indirect method, operating activities may be presented using a modified approach. This modified indirect method shows revenues and expenses in operating activities, and then reports the changes in working capital accounts.

(1) As in US GAAP, the statement of cash flows is divided into three parts: operating, investing, and financing activities. At the bottom of the statement of cash flows, a reconciliation must be made with the amounts in the statement of cash flows and the cash and cash equivalents reported in the statement of financial position.

(2) The most significant difference between IFRS and US GAAP is where certain items are presented on the statement of cash flows.

> **EXAMPLE**
>
> Interest and dividends received may be reported on the statement of cash flows as operating or investing activities. Interest and dividends paid may be reported either in the operating activities or the financing activities sections.

(a) Although the entity has discretion on where interest and dividends are reported, it must be reported on a consistent basis.

(b) Cash from the purchase and sale of trading securities are classified as operating activities.

(c) Cash advances and loans (bank overdrafts) are also usually classified as operating activities.

(d) Taxes paid on income must be disclosed separately in operating activities. However, cash flows from certain taxes may be classified elsewhere if they are related to investing or financing activities.

(e) In addition, the effects of noncash transactions are not reported on the statement of cash flows. Instead, significant noncash activities must be disclosed in the notes to the financial statements.

NOW REVIEW MULTIPLE-CHOICE QUESTIONS 105 THROUGH 115

KEY TERMS

Accounting Series Releases (ASRs). The predecessor of Financial Reporting Releases.

Active market. A market in which transactions for the asset or liability take place with sufficient frequency and volume to provide pricing information on an ongoing basis.

Cash basis financial statement. The only asset is cash, revenue is recognized when cash is received; and expenses are recognized when they are paid.

Change in accounting principle. Change from one generally accepted accounting principle to another.

Constant dollar accounting. A method of reporting financial statement elements in dollar which have the same purchasing power.

Correction of an error. A correction of a material error from a prior period.

Cost approach. A valuation technique that reflects the amount that would be required currently to replace the service capacity of an asset.

Current assets. Cash and other assets or resources that are reasonably expected to be realized in cash or sold or consumed during the normal operating cycle of the business.

Current cost accounting. A method of valuing and reporting assets, liabilities, revenues, and expenses at their current cost at the balance sheet date or at the date of their use or sale.

Current liabilities. Obligations whose liquidation is reasonably expected to require the use of existing resources properly classifiable as current assets, or the creation of other current liabilities.

Discontinued operation. Results from disposal of a business component.

Discount rate adjustment technique. A present value technique that uses a risk-adjusted discount rate and contractual, promised, or most likely cash flows.

Expected cash flow. The probability-weighted average of possible future cash flows.

Extraordinary items. An unusual and infrequent event which has material effects.

Fair value. The price that would be received to sell an asset or paid to transfer a liability in an orderly transaction between market participants at the measurement date under current market conditions.

Fair value option for reporting financial assets and financial liabilities. An election can be made to value certain financial assets and financial liabilities at fair value.

Financial forecast. Prospective financial statements that present the knowledge and belief of responsible party in terms of expected financial position, results of operations, and cash flows.

Financial projection. Prospective financial statements that present the knowledge and belief of responsible party, based on one or more **hypothetical** assumptions, the enterprise's financial position, results of operations, and cash flows.

Financial Reporting Releases (FRRs). Update the SEC Codification of Financial Reporting Policies and Regulations S-K and S-X.

Form S-1/F-1. Registration statement for US/foreign companies.

Form 8-K/6-K. Information about material events for US/foreign companies.

Form 10-K/20F. Annual report for US/foreign companies.

Form 10-Q. Quarterly reports.

Highest and best use. The use of a nonfinancial asset by market participants that would maximize the value of the asset or the group of assets and liabilities within which the asset would be used.

Income approach. A valuation technique that converts future amounts to a single current amount. The fair value measurement is determined on the basis of the value indicated by current market expectations about those future amounts.

Level 1 inputs. Quoted prices in active markets for identical assets or liabilities that the reporting entity can access at the measurement date.

Level 2 inputs. Inputs other than quoted prices included in Level 1 that are observable for the asset or liability, either directly or indirectly.

Level 3 inputs. Unobservable inputs for the asset or liability.

Market approach. A valuation technique that uses prices and other relevant information generated by market transactions involving identical or comparable assets, liabilities, or a group of assets and liabilities, such as a business.

Modified cash-basis financial statements. Cash basis financial statements with modifications that have substantial support.

Most advantageous market. The market that maximizes the price that would be received to sell the asset or minimizes the amount to be paid to transfer the liability taking into account transaction costs and transportation cost.

Observable inputs. Inputs that are developed using market data and that refect the assumptions that market participants would use when pricing the asset or liability.

Present value. A tool used to link future amounts to a present amount using a discount rate.

Principle market. A market in which the greatest volume and level of activity occurs.

Prospective financial information. Any financial information about the future.

Realized holding gains. The difference between current cost and historical cost of asset consumed.

Regulation AB. Describes reporting requirements for asset-backed securities.

Regulation Fair Disclosure (FD). Mandates that publicly traded companies disclose material information to all investors simultaneously.

Regulation S-X. Describes the form and content of financial statements filed with the SEC.

Regulation S-K. Describes the requirements for information and forms required by Regulation S-X.

Regulatory-basis financial statements. Based on rules established by a regulatory agency.

Responsible party. Person(s), usually management, who are responsible for assumptions underlying the information.

Restructuring. A program that is planned and controlled by management and materially changes either (1) the scope of the business or (2) the manner in which the business is conducted.

Risk premium. Compensation sought by risk-averse market participants for bearing the uncertainty inherent in the cash flows of an asset or a liability.

Schedule 14A. Proxy statement.

Staff Accounting Bulletin. Unofficial interpretations relating to accounting and disclosure practices.

Staff Legal Bulletins. Summarize the Commission staff's views related to SEC regulations and federal securities laws.

Staff no-action, Interpretive, and Exemptive letters. Published SEC staff responses to interpretation inquiries.

Subsequent events. Events occurring after the balance sheet date but before the financial statements are issued or available to be issued.

Systematic risk. The common risk shared by an asset or a liability with the other items in a diversified portfolio.

Tax-basis financial statements. Prepared on the basis of tax laws and regulations.

Unrealized holding gains. Increases in the current cost of assets held throughout the year.

Unsystematic risk. The risk specific to a particular asset or liability.

Unusual or infrequent items. An unusual or infrequent event considered to be material that does not qualify as extraordinary.

Multiple-Choice Questions (1-116)

D.1. Income and Retained Earnings Statements

1. In Baer Food Co.'s year 1 single-step income statement, the section titled "Revenues" consisted of the following:

Net sales revenue		$187,000
Results from discontinued operations:		
Loss from discontinued component		
Z including loss on disposal of		
$1,200	$16,400	
Less tax benefit	4,000	(12,400)
Interest revenue		10,200
Gain on sale of equipment		4,700
Extraordinary gain		1,500
Total revenues		$191,000

In the revenues section of the year 1 income statement, Baer Food should have reported total revenues of

- a. $216,300
- b. $215,400
- c. $203,700
- d. $201,900

Items 2 and 3 are based on the following:

Vane Co.'s trial balance of income statement accounts for the year ended December 31, year 2, included the following:

	Debit	Credit
Sales		$575,000
Cost of sales	$240,000	
Administrative expenses	70,000	
Loss on sale of equipment	10,000	
Sales commissions	50,000	
Interest revenue		25,000
Freight out	15,000	
Loss on early retirement of long-term		
debt	20,000	
Uncollectible accounts expense	15,000	
Totals	$420,000	$600,000

Other information

Finished goods inventory:

January 1, year 2	$400,000
December 31, year 2	360,000

Vane's income tax rate is 30%. In Vane's year 2 multiple-step income statement,

2. What amount should Vane report as the cost of goods manufactured?

- a. $200,000
- b. $215,000
- c. $280,000
- d. $295,000

3. What amount should Vane report as income after income taxes from continuing operations?

- a. $126,000
- b. $129,500
- c. $140,000
- d. $147,000

4. Brock Corp. reports operating expenses in two categories: (1) selling, and (2) general and administrative. The adjusted trial balance at December 31, year 1, included the following expense and loss accounts:

Accounting and legal fees	$120,000
Advertising	150,000
Freight-out	80,000
Interest	70,000
Loss on sale of long-term investment	30,000
Officers' salaries	225,000
Rent for office space	220,000
Sales salaries and commissions	140,000

One-half of the rented premises is occupied by the sales department.

Brock's total selling expenses for year 1 are

- a. $480,000
- b. $400,000
- c. $370,000
- d. $360,000

5. The following costs were incurred by Griff Co., a manufacturer, during year 1:

Accounting and legal fees	$ 25,000
Freight-in	175,000
Freight-out	160,000
Officers salaries	150,000
Insurance	85,000
Sales representatives salaries	215,000

What amount of these costs should be reported as general and administrative expenses for year 1?

- a. $260,000
- b. $550,000
- c. $635,000
- d. $810,000

6. Which of the following should be included in general and administrative expenses?

	Interest	Advertising
a.	Yes	Yes
b.	Yes	No
c.	No	Yes
d.	No	No

7. In Yew Co.'s year 1 annual report, Yew described its social awareness expenditures during the year as follows:

> The Company contributed $250,000 in cash to youth and educational programs. The Company also gave $140,000 to health and human service organizations, of which $80,000 was contributed by employees through payroll deductions. In addition, consistent with the Company's commitment to the environment, the Company spent $100,000 to redesign product packaging.

What amount of the above should be included in Yew's income statement as charitable contributions expense?

- a. $310,000
- b. $390,000
- c. $410,000
- d. $490,000

8. During year 1 both Raim Co. and Cane Co. suffered losses due to the flooding of the Mississippi River. Raim is located two miles from the river and sustains flood losses every two to three years. Cane, which has been located fifty miles from the river for the past twenty years, has never before had flood losses. How should the flood losses be reported in each company's year 1 income statement?

	Raim	**Cane**
a.	As a component of income from continuing operations	As an extraordinary item
b.	As a component of income from continuing operations	As a component of income from continuing operations
c.	As an extraordinary item	As a component of income from continuing operations
d.	As an extraordinary item	As an extraordinary item

9. Witt Co. incurred the following infrequent losses during year 1:

- $175,000 from a major strike by employees.
- $150,000 from an earthquake (unusual).
- $125,000 from the abandonment of equipment used in the business.

In Witt's year 1 income statement, the total amount of infrequent losses **not** considered extraordinary should be

a. $275,000
b. $300,000
c. $325,000
d. $450,000

10. Kent Co. incurred the following infrequent losses during year 1:

- A $300,000 loss was incurred on disposal of one of four dissimilar factories.
- A major currency devaluation caused a $120,000 exchange loss on an amount remitted by a foreign customer.
- Inventory valued at $190,000 was made worthless by a competitor's unexpected product innovation.

In its year 1 income statement, what amount should Kent report as losses that are **not** considered extraordinary?

a. $610,000
b. $490,000
c. $420,000
d. $310,000

11. Midway Co. had the following transactions during year 1:

- $1,200,000 pretax loss on foreign currency exchange due to a major unexpected devaluation by the foreign government.
- $500,000 pretax loss from discontinued operations of a division.
- $800,000 pretax loss on equipment damaged by a hurricane. This was the first hurricane ever to strike in Midway's area. Midway also received $1,000,000 from its insurance company to replace a building, with a carrying value of $300,000, that had been destroyed by the hurricane.

What amount should Midway report in its year 1 income statement as extraordinary loss before income taxes?

a. $ 100,000
b. $1,300,000
c. $1,800,000
d. $2,500,000

12. Ocean Corp.'s comprehensive insurance policy allows its assets to be replaced at current value. The policy has a $50,000 deductible clause. One of Ocean's waterfront warehouses was destroyed in a winter storm. Such storms occur approximately every four years. Ocean incurred $20,000 of costs in dismantling the warehouse and plans to replace it. The following data relate to the warehouse:

Current carrying amount	$ 300,000
Replacement cost	1,100,000

What amount of gain should Ocean report as a separate component of income before extraordinary items?

a. $1,030,000
b. $ 780,000
c. $ 730,000
d. $0

13. Purl Corporation's income statement for the year ended December 31, year 1, shows the following:

Income before income tax and extraordinary item	$900,000
Gain on life insurance coverage—included in the above $900,000 income amount	100,000
Extraordinary item—loss due to earthquake damage	300,000

Purl's tax rate for year 1 is 40%. How much should be reported as the provision for income tax in Purl's year 1 income statement?

a. $200,000
b. $240,000
c. $320,000
d. $360,000

14. Thorpe Co.'s income statement for the year ended December 31, year 2, reported net income of $74,100. The auditor raised questions about the following amounts that had been included in net income:

Unrealized loss on decline in market value of noncurrent investments in stock classified as available-for-sale (net of tax)	$ (5,400)
Gain on early retirement of bonds payable (net of $11,000 tax effect)	22,000
Adjustment to profits of prior years for errors in depreciation (net of $3,750 tax effect)	(7,500)
Loss from fire (net of $7,000 tax effect)	$(14,000)

The loss from the fire was an infrequent but not unusual occurrence in Thorpe's line of business. Thorpe's December 31, year 2 income statement should report net income of

a. $65,000
b. $66,100
c. $81,600
d. $87,000

15. On January 1, year 1, Brecon Co. installed cabinets to display its merchandise in customers' stores. Brecon expects to use these cabinets for five years. Brecon's year 1 multistep income statement should include

a. One-fifth of the cabinet costs in cost of goods sold.
b. One-fifth of the cabinet costs in selling, general, and administrative expenses.
c. All of the cabinet costs in cost of good sold.
d. All of the cabinet costs in selling, general, and administrative expenses.

16. A material loss should be presented separately as a component of income from continuing operations when it is

   a.   An extraordinary item.
   b.   A discontinued component of the business.
   c.   Unusual in nature and infrequent in occurrence.
   d.   Not unusual in nature but infrequent in occurrence.

17. During year 1, Peg Construction Co. recognized substantial gains from

   • An increase in value of a foreign customer's remittance caused by a major foreign currency revaluation.
   • A court-ordered increase in a completed long-term construction contract's price due to design changes.

Should these gains be included in continuing operations or reported as an extraordinary item in Peg's year 1 income statement?

	Gain from major currency revaluation	Gain from increase in contract's price
a.	Continuing operations	Continuing operations
b.	Extraordinary item	Continuing operations
c.	Extraordinary item	Extraordinary item
d.	Continuing operations	Extraordinary item

18. An extraordinary item should be reported separately on the income statement as a component of income

	Net of income taxes	Before discontinued operations of a component of a business
a.	Yes	Yes
b.	Yes	No
c.	No	No
d.	No	Yes

19. In year 5, hail damaged several of Toncan Co.'s vans. Hailstorms had frequently inflicted similar damage to Toncan's vans. Over the years, Toncan had saved money by not buying hail insurance and either paying for repairs, or selling damaged vans and then replacing them. In year 5, the damaged vans were sold for less than their carrying amount. How should the hail damage cost be reported in Toncan's year 5 financial statements?

   a.   The actual year 5 hail damage loss as an extraordinary loss, net of income taxes.
   b.   The actual year 5 hail damage loss in continuing operations, with **no** separate disclosure.
   c.   The expected average hail damage loss in continuing operations, with **no** separate disclosure.
   d.   The expected average hail damage loss in continuing operations, with separate disclosure.

D.2. Unusual or Infrequent Items

20. A transaction that is unusual in nature and infrequent in occurrence should be reported separately as a component of income

   a.   After cumulative effect of accounting changes and before discontinued operations.
   b.   After cumulative effect of accounting changes and after discontinued operations.
   c.   Before cumulative effect of accounting changes and before discontinued operations.
   d.   Before cumulative effect of accounting changes and after discontinued operations.

21. In year 1, Teller Co. incurred losses arising from its guilty plea in its first antitrust action, and from a substantial increase in production costs caused when a major supplier's workers went on strike. Which of these losses should be reported as an extraordinary item?

	Antitrust action	Production costs
a.	No	No
b.	No	Yes
c.	Yes	No
d.	Yes	Yes

22. In open market transactions, Gold Corp. simultaneously sold its long-term investment in Iron Corp. bonds and purchased its own outstanding bonds. The broker remitted the net cash from the two transactions. Gold's gain on the purchase of its own bonds exceeded its loss on the sale of the Iron bonds. Gold should report the

   a.   Net effect of the two transactions as an extraordinary gain.
   b.   Net effect of the two transactions in income before extraordinary items.
   c.   Effect of its own bond transaction gain in income before extraordinary items, and report the Iron bond transaction as a loss in income before extraordinary items.
   d.   Effect of its own bond transaction as an extraordinary gain, and report the Iron bond transaction loss in income before extraordinary items.

23. Under ASC 220, *Comprehensive Income,* corrections of errors are reported in

   a.   Other comprehensive income.
   b.   Other income/(expense).
   c.   Retained earnings.
   d.   Stockholders' equity.

24. Service Corp. incurred costs associated with relocating employees in a restructuring of its operations. How should the company account for these costs?

   a.   Measured at fair value and recognized over the next two years.
   b.   Measured at fair value and recognized when the liability is incurred.
   c.   Recognized when the costs are paid.
   d.   Measured at fair value and treated as a prior period adjustment.

D.3. Discontinued Operations

25. On January 1, year 1, Deer Corp. met the criteria for discontinuance of a business component. For the period January 1 through October 15, year 1, the component had revenues of $500,000 and expenses of $800,000. The assets of the component were sold on October 15, year 1, at a loss for which no tax benefit is available. In its income statement for the year ended December 31, year 1, how should Deer report the component's operations from January 1 to October 15, year 1?

   a. $500,000 and $800,000 should be included with revenues and expenses, respectively, as part of continuing operations.
   b. $300,000 should be reported as part of the loss on operations and disposal of a component.
   c. $300,000 should be reported as an extraordinary loss.
   d. $500,000 should be reported as revenues from operations of a discontinued component.

26. Which of the following criteria is not required for a component's results to be classified as discontinued operations?

a. Management must have entered into a sales agreement.
b. The component is available for immediate sale.
c. The operations and cash flows of the component will be eliminated from the operations of the entity as a result of the disposal.
d. The entity will not have any significant continuing involvement in the operations of the component after disposal.

27. On November 1, year 2, management of Herron Corporation committed to a plan to dispose of Timms Company, a major subsidiary. The disposal meets the requirements for classification as discontinued operations. The carrying value of Timms Company was $8,000,000 and management estimated the fair value less costs to sell to be $6,500,000. For year 2, Timms Company had a loss of $2,000,000. How much should Herron Corporation present as loss from discontinued operations before the effect of taxes in its income statement for year 2?

a. $0
b. $1,500,000
c. $2,000,000
d. $3,500,000

28. On December 1, year 2, Greer Co. committed to a plan to dispose of its Hart business component's assets. The disposal meets the requirements to be classified as discontinued operations. On that date, Greer estimated that the loss from the disposition of the assets would be $700,000 and Hart's year 2 operating losses were $200,000. Disregarding income taxes, what net gain (loss) should be reported for discontinued operations in Greer's year 2 income statement?

a. $0
b. $(200,000)
c. $(700,000)
d. $(900,000)

29. A component of Ace, Inc. was discontinued during year 2. Ace's loss on disposal should

a. Exclude the associated employee relocation costs.
b. Exclude operating losses for the period.
c. Include associated employee termination costs.
d. Exclude associated lease cancellation costs.

30. When a component of a business has been discontinued during the year, this component's operating losses of the current period should be included in the

a. Income statement as part of revenues and expenses.
b. Income statement as part of the loss on disposal of the discontinued component.
c. Income statement as part of the income (loss) from continuing operations.
d. Retained earnings statement as a direct decrease in retained earnings.

31. When a component of a business has been discontinued during the year, the loss on disposal should

a. Include operating losses of the current period.
b. Exclude operating losses during the period.
c. Be an extraordinary item.
d. Be an operating item.

32. On January 1, year 2, Shine Co. agreed to sell a business component on March 1, year 2. The gain on the disposal should be

a. Presented as an extraordinary gain.
b. Presented as an adjustment to retained earnings.
c. Netted with the loss from operations of the component as a part of discontinued operations.
d. None of the above.

D.4. Comprehensive Income

33. What is the purpose of reporting comprehensive income?

a. To report changes in equity due to transactions with owners.
b. To report a measure of overall enterprise performance.
c. To replace net income with a better measure.
d. To combine income from continuing operations with income from discontinued operations and extraordinary items.

34. During year 1, the "other revenues and gains" section of Totman Company's Statement of Earnings and Comprehensive Income contains $5,000 in interest revenue, $15,000 equity in Harpo Co. earnings, and $25,000 gain on sale of available-for-sale securities. Assuming the sale of the securities increased the current portion of income tax expense by $10,000, determine the amount of Totman's reclassification adjustment to other comprehensive income.

a. $ 5,000
b. $ 2,500
c. $35,000
d. $15,000

35. Which of the following is **not** an acceptable option of reporting other comprehensive income and its components?

I. In a separate statement of comprehensive income.
II. In a statement of earnings and comprehensive income.
III. In a statement of changes in stockholders' equity.

a. I only.
b. II only.
c. III only.
d. I and II.

36. Accumulated other comprehensive income should be reported on the balance sheet as a component of

	Retained earnings	Additional paid-in capital
a.	No	Yes
b.	Yes	Yes
c.	Yes	No
d.	No	No

37. Which of the following changes during a period is not a component of other comprehensive income?

a. Unrealized gains or losses as a result of a debt security being transferred from held-to-maturity to available-for-sale.
b. Stock dividends issued to shareholders.
c. Foreign currency translation adjustments.
d. Pension liability adjustments.

38. A company buys ten shares of securities at $2,000 each on December 31, year 1. The securities are classified as available for sale. The company does not elect to use the fair value option for reporting its available-for-sale securities. The fair value of the securities increases to $2,500 on December 31, year 2, and to $2,750 on December 31, year 3. On December 31, year 3, the company sells the securities. Assume no dividends are paid and that the company has a tax rate of 30%. What is the amount of the reclassification adjustment for other comprehensive income on December 31, year 3?

    a. $ 7,500
    b. $ (7,500)
    c. $ 5,250
    d. $ (5,250)

39. A company buys ten shares of securities at $1,000 each on January 15, year 1. The securities are classified as available-for-sale. The fair value of the securities increases to $1,250 per share as of December 31, year 1. The company does not elect to use the fair value option for reporting available-for-sale securities. Assume no dividends are paid and that the company has a 30% tax rate. What is the amount of the holding gain arising during the period that is classified in other comprehensive income for the period ending December 31, year 1?

    a. 0
    b. $1,750
    c. $2,500
    d. $7,500

40. Searles does not elect the fair value option for recording financial assets and liabilities. What amount of comprehensive income should Searles Corporation report on its statement of income and comprehensive income given the following net of tax figures that represent changes during a period?

Pension liability adjustment recognized in OCI	$ (3,000)
Unrealized gain on available-for-sale securities	15,000
Reclassification adjustment, for securities gain included in net income	(2,500)
Stock warrants outstanding	4,000
Net income	77,000

    a. $86,500
    b. $89,000
    c. $89,500
    d. $90,500

41. If ($2,450) net of tax is the reclassification adjustment included in other comprehensive income in the year the securities are sold, what is the gain (loss) that is included in income from continuing operations before income taxes? Assume a 30% tax rate.

    a. $(2,450)
    b. $(3,500)
    c. $ 2,450
    d. $3,500

42. Which of the following changes during a period is **not** a component of other comprehensive income?

    a. Pension liability adjustment for funded status of plan.
    b. Treasury stock, at cost.
    c. Foreign currency translation adjustment.
    d. Reclassification adjustment, for securities gain included in net income.

43. Which of the following is true?

    a. Separate EPS amounts must be presented for both other comprehensive income and comprehensive income.
    b. Separate EPS amounts must be presented for other comprehensive income but not for comprehensive income.
    c. Separate EPS amounts must be presented for comprehensive income but not for other comprehensive income.
    d. Separate EPS amounts are not required to be presented for either other comprehensive income or comprehensive income.

44. Which of the following options for displaying comprehensive income is(are) allowed by FASB?

    I. A continuation from net income at the bottom of the income statement.
    II. A separate statement that begins with net income.
    III. In the statement of changes in stockholders' equity.

    a. I only.
    b. II only.
    c. II and III.
    d. I and II.

45. Assume a company does not elect the fair value option for reporting financial assets and liabilities. Which of the following is not classified as other comprehensive income?

    a. An adjustment to pension liability to record the funded status of the plan.
    b. Subsequent decreases of the fair value of available-for-sale securities that have been previously written down as impaired.
    c. Decreases in the fair value of held-to-maturity securities.
    d. None of the above.

46. When a full set of general-purpose financial statements are presented, comprehensive income and its components should

    a. Appear as a part of discontinued operations, extraordinary items, and cumulative effect of a change in accounting principle.
    b. Be reported net of related income tax effect, in total and individually.
    c. Appear in a supplemental schedule in the notes to the financial statements.
    d. Be displayed in a financial statement that has the same prominence as other financial statements.

D.5. Balance Sheets

Items 47 through 49 are based on the following:

The following trial balance of Mint Corp. at December 31, year 1, has been adjusted except for income tax expense.

	Dr.	Cr.
Cash	$ 600,000	
Accounts receivable, net	3,500,000	
Cost in excess of billings on long-term contracts	1,600,000	
Billings in excess of costs on long-term contracts		$ 700,000
Prepaid taxes	450,000	
Property, plant, and equipment, net	1,480,000	

	Dr.	Cr.
Note payable—noncurrent		1,620,000
Common stock		750,000
Additional paid-in capital		2,000,000
Retained earnings—unappropriated		900,000
Retained earnings—restricted for note payable		160,000
Earnings from long-term contracts		6,680,000
Costs and expenses	5,180,000	
	$12,810,000	$12,810,000

Other financial data for the year ended December 31, year 1, are

- Mint uses the percentage-of-completion method to account for long-term construction contracts for financial statement and income tax purposes. All receivables on these contracts are considered to be collectible within twelve months.
- During year 1, estimated tax payments of $450,000 were charged to prepaid taxes. Mint has not recorded income tax expense. There were no temporary or permanent differences, and Mint's tax rate is 30%.

In Mint's December 31, year 1 balance sheet, what amount should be reported as

47. Total retained earnings?
   a. $1,950,000
   b. $2,110,000
   c. $2,400,000
   d. $2,560,000

48. Total noncurrent liabilities?
   a. $1,620,000
   b. $1,780,000
   c. $2,320,000
   d. $2,480,000

49. Total current assets?
   a. $5,000,000
   b. $5,450,000
   c. $5,700,000
   d. $6,150,000

50. Mirr, Inc. was incorporated on January 1, year 1, with proceeds from the issuance of $750,000 in stock and borrowed funds of $110,000. During the first year of operations, revenues from sales and consulting amounted to $82,000, and operating costs and expenses totaled $64,000. On December 15, Mirr declared a $3,000 cash dividend, payable to stockholders on January 15, year 2. No additional activities affected owners' equity in year 1. Mirr's liabilities increased to $120,000 by December 31, year 1. On Mirr's December 31, year 1 balance sheet, total assets should be reported at
   a. $885,000
   b. $882,000
   c. $878,000
   d. $875,000

51. The following changes in Vel Corp.'s account balances occurred during year 1:

	Increase
Assets	$89,000
Liabilities	27,000
Capital stock	60,000
Additional paid-in capital	6,000

Except for a $13,000 dividend payment and the year's earnings, there were no changes in retained earnings for year 1. What was Vel's net income for year 1?
   a. $ 4,000
   b. $ 9,000
   c. $13,000
   d. $17,000

52. When preparing a draft of its year 1 balance sheet, Mont, Inc. reported net assets totaling $875,000. Included in the asset section of the balance sheet were the following:

Treasury stock of Mont, Inc. at cost, which approximates market value on December 31	$24,000
Idle machinery	11,200
Cash surrender value of life insurance on corporate executives	13,700
Allowance for decline in market value of noncurrent equity investments	8,400

At what amount should Mont's net assets be reported in the December 31, year 1 balance sheet?
   a. $851,000
   b. $850,100
   c. $842,600
   d. $834,500

53. In analyzing a company's financial statements, which financial statement would a potential investor primarily use to assess the company's liquidity and financial flexibility?
   a. Balance sheet.
   b. Income statement.
   c. Statement of retained earnings.
   d. Statement of cash flows.

D.6.a. Disclosures

54. During year 1, Jones Company engaged in the following transactions:

Salary expense to key employees who are also principal owners	$100,000
Sales to affiliated enterprises	250,000

Which of the two transactions would be disclosed as related-party transactions in Jones' year 1 financial statements?
   a. Neither transaction.
   b. The $100,000 transaction only.
   c. The $250,000 transaction only.
   d. Both transactions.

55. Dean Co. acquired 100% of Morey Corp. prior to year 2. During year 2, the individual companies included in their financial statements the following:

	Dean	Morey
Officers' salaries	$ 75,000	$50,000
Officers' expenses	20,000	10,000
Loans to officers	125,000	50,000
Intercompany sales	150,000	--

What amount should be reported as related-party disclosures in the notes to Dean's year 2 consolidated financial statements?

a. $150,000
b. $155,000
c. $175,000
d. $330,000

56. Which type of material related-party transaction requires disclosure?

    a. Only those not reported in the body of the financial statements.
    b. Only those that receive accounting recognition.
    c. Those that contain possible illegal acts.
    d. All those other than compensation arrangements, expense allowances, and other similar items in the ordinary course of business.

57. Financial statements shall include disclosures of material transactions between related parties except

    a. Nonmonetary exchanges by affiliates.
    b. Sales of inventory by a subsidiary to its parent.
    c. Expense allowance for executives which exceed normal business practice.
    d. A company's agreement to act as surety for a loan to its chief executive officer.

58. Dex Co. has entered into a joint venture with an affiliate to secure access to additional inventory. Under the joint venture agreement, Dex will purchase the output of the venture at prices negotiated on an arm's-length basis. Which of the following is(are) required to be disclosed about the related-party transaction?

I. The amount due to the affiliate at the balance sheet date.
II. The dollar amount of the purchases during the year.

    a. I only.
    b. II only.
    c. Both I and II.
    d. Neither I nor II.

59. What is the purpose of information presented in notes to the financial statements?

    a. To provide disclosures required by generally accepted accounting principles.
    b. To correct improper presentation in the financial statements.
    c. To provide recognition of amounts **not** included in the totals of the financial statements.
    d. To present management's responses to auditor comments.

D.6.b.   *Accounting Policies*

60. Which of the following information should be included in Melay, Inc.'s year 1 summary of significant accounting policies?

    a. Property, plant, and equipment is recorded at cost with depreciation computed principally by the straight-line method.
    b. During year 1, the Delay component was sold.
    c. Business component year 1 sales are Alay $1M, Belay $2M, and Celay $3M.
    d. Future common share dividends are expected to approximate 60% of earnings.

61. Which of the following information should be disclosed in the summary of significant accounting policies?

a. Refinancing of debt subsequent to the balance sheet date.
b. Guarantees of indebtedness of others.
c. Criteria for determining which investments are treated as cash equivalents.
d. Adequacy of pension plan assets relative to vested benefits.

62. Swift Corp. prepares its financial statements for its fiscal year ending December 31, year 1. Swift estimates that its product warranty liability is $28,000 at December 31, year 1. On February 12, year 2, before the financial statements were issued, Swift received information about a product defect that will require a recall of all units sold in year 1. It is expected the product recall will cost an additional $40,000 in warranty repairs. What should Swift present in its December 31, year 1 financial statements?

    a. A footnote disclosure explaining the product recall.
    b. A footnote disclosure listing the estimated amount of $40,000 in warranty repairs and an explanation of the recall.
    c. An estimated warranty liability of $68,000.
    d. No disclosure is necessary.

63. Colter Corp. has a fiscal year-end of December 31, year 1. On that date, Colter reported total assets of $600,000. On February 1, year 2, before the year 1 financial statements were issued, Colter lost $250,000 of inventory due to a fire. The inventory was a total loss and was uninsured. How should Colter present this information in its December 31, year 1 financial statements?

    a. Colter should disclose the loss in a footnote to its year 1 financial statements.
    b. Colter should report an extraordinary loss in its year 1 income statement.
    c. Colter should report an allowance for lost inventory in its year 1 balance sheet.
    d. Colter should not report the loss.

64. Which of the following is a true statement regarding disclosures for subsequent events?

    a. Recognize a loss for all recognized and unrecognized subsequent events in the current year financial statements.
    b. Recognize a gain or loss for any recognized subsequent event in the current year financial statements.
    c. Recognize a loss for a recognized subsequent event in the financial statements in the year when the subsequent event occurs.
    d. Recognize a loss for a recognized subsequent event in the current year financial statements.

D.6.d.   *Fair Value Measurements*

65. The fair value of an asset should be based upon

    a. The replacement cost of an asset.
    b. The price that would be received to sell the asset at the measurement date under current market conditions.
    c. The original cost of the asset plus an adjustment for obsolescence.
    d. The price that would be paid to acquire the asset.

66. Which of the following describes a principal market for establishing fair value of an asset?

a.   The market that has the greatest volume and level of activity for the asset.

b.   Any broker or dealer market that buys or sells the asset.

c.   The most observable market in which the price of the asset is minimized.

d.   The market in which the amount received would be maximized.

67. Which of the following is true for valuing an asset to fair value?

a.   The price of the asset should be adjusted for transaction costs.

b.   The fair value of the asset should be adjusted for costs to sell.

c.   The fair value price is based upon an entry price to purchase the asset.

d.   The price should be adjusted for transportation costs to transport the asset to its principal market.

68. Which of the following would meet the qualifications as market participants in determining fair value?

a.   A liquidation market in which sellers are compelled to sell.

b.   A subsidiary of the reporting unit interested in purchasing assets similar to those being valued.

c.   An independent entity that is knowledgeable about the asset.

d.   A broker or dealer that wishes to establish a new market for the asset.

69. Which of the following is an assumption used in fair value measurements?

a.   The asset must be in-use.

b.   The asset must be considered in-exchange.

c.   The most conservative estimate must be used.

d.   The asset is in its highest and best use.

70. The fair value of an asset at initial recognition is

a.   The price paid to acquire the asset.

b.   The price paid to acquire the asset less transaction costs.

c.   The price paid to transfer or sell the asset.

d.   The book value of the asset acquired.

71. Which of the following is not a valuation technique used in fair value estimates?

a.   Income approach.

b.   Residual value approach.

c.   Market approach.

d.   Cost approach.

72. Valuation techniques for fair value that include the Black-Scholes-Merton formula, a binomial model, or discounted cash flows are examples of which valuation technique?

a.   Income approach.

b.   Market approach.

c.   Cost approach.

d.   Exit value approach.

73. The market approach valuation technique for measuring fair value requires which of the following?

a.   Present value of future cash flows.

b.   Prices and other relevant information of transactions from identical or comparable assets.

c.   The price to replace the service capacity of the asset.

d.   The weighted-average of the present value of future cash flows.

74. A change in valuation techniques used to measure fair value should be reported as

a.   A change in accounting principle with retrospective restatement.

b.   An error correction with restatement of the financial statements of previous periods.

c.   A change in accounting estimate reported on a prospective basis.

d.   An extraordinary item on the current year's income statement.

75. When measuring fair value, which level has the highest priority for valuation inputs?

a.   Level 1.

b.   Level 2.

c.   Level 3.

d.   Level 4.

76. Which of the following are observable inputs used for fair value measurements?

I.   Bank prime rate.
II. Default rates on loans.
III. Financial forecasts.

a.   I only.

b.   I and II only.

c.   I and III only.

d.   I, II and III.

D.6.f.   Constant Dollar Accounting

77. A company that wishes to disclose information about the effect of changing prices should report this information in

a.   The body of the financial statements.

b.   The notes to the financial statements.

c.   Supplementary information to the financial statements.

d.   Management's report to shareholders.

78. Lewis Company was formed on January 1, year 1. Selected balances from the historical cost balance sheet at December 31, year 2, were as follows:

Land (purchased in year 1)	$120,000
Investment in nonconvertible bonds (purchased in year 1, and expected to be held to maturity)	60,000
Long-term debt	80,000

The average Consumer Price Index was 100 for year 1, and 110 for year 2. In a supplementary constant dollar balance sheet (adjusted for changing prices) at December 31, year 2, these selected account balances should be shown at

	Land	Investment	Long-term debt
a.	$120,000	$60,000	$88,000
b.	$120,000	$66,000	$88,000
c.	$132,000	$60,000	$80,000
d.	$132,000	$66,000	$80,000

79. The following items were among those that appeared on Rubi Co.'s books at the end of year 1:

Merchandise inventory	$600,000
Loans to employees	20,000

What amount should Rubi classify as monetary assets in preparing constant dollar financial statements?

a. $0
b. $ 20,000
c. $600,000
d. $620,000

80. In its financial statements, Hila Co. discloses supplemental information on the effects of changing prices. Hila computed the increase in current cost of inventory as follows:

Increase in current cost (nominal dollars)	$15,000
Increase in current cost (constant dollars)	$12,000

What amount should Hila disclose as the inflation component of the increase in current cost of inventories?

a. $ 3,000
b. $12,000
c. $15,000
d. $27,000

81. When computing purchasing power gain or loss on net monetary items, which of the following accounts is classified as nonmonetary?

a. Advances to unconsolidated subsidiaries.
b. Allowance for uncollectible accounts.
c. Unamortized premium on bonds payable.
d. Accumulated depreciation of equipment.

82. During a period of inflation in which a liability account balance remains constant, which of the following occurs?

a. A purchasing power gain, if the item is a nonmonetary liability.
b. A purchasing power gain, if the item is a monetary liability.
c. A purchasing power loss, if the item is a nonmonetary liability.
d. A purchasing power loss, if the item is a monetary liability.

D.6.i. Current Cost Accounting

83. The following information pertains to each unit of merchandise purchased for resale by Vend Co.:

March 1, year 1

Purchase price	$ 8
Selling price	$ 12
Price level index	110

December 31, year 1

Replacement cost	$ 10
Selling price	$ 15
Price level index	121

Under current cost accounting, what is the amount of Vend's holding gain on each unit of this merchandise?

a. $0
b. $0.80
c. $1.20
d. $2.00

84. Kerr Company purchased a machine for $115,000 on January 1, year 1, the company's first day of operations. At the end of the year, the current cost of the machine was $125,000. The machine has no salvage value, a five-year

life, and is depreciated by the straight-line method. For the year ended December 31, year 1, the amount of the current cost depreciation expense which would appear in supplementary current cost financial statements is

a. $14,000
b. $23,000
c. $24,000
d. $25,000

85. At December 31, year 1, Jannis Corp. owned two assets as follows:

	Equipment	Inventory
Current cost	$100,000	$80,000
Recoverable amount	$ 95,000	$90,000

Jannis voluntarily disclosed supplementary information about current cost at December 31, year 1. In such a disclosure, at what amount would Jannis report total assets?

a. $175,000
b. $180,000
c. $185,000
d. $190,000

86. Could current cost financial statements report holding gains for goods sold during the period and holding gains on inventory at the end of the period?

	Goods sold	Inventory
a.	Yes	Yes
b.	Yes	No
c.	No	Yes
d.	No	No

87. Manhof Co. prepares supplementary reports on income from continuing operations on a current cost basis. How should Manhof compute cost of goods sold on a current cost basis?

a. Number of units sold times average current cost of units during the year.
b. Number of units sold times current cost of units at year-end.
c. Number of units sold times current cost of units at the beginning of the year.
d. Beginning inventory at current cost plus cost of goods purchased less ending inventory at current cost.

D.6.j. Risks and Uncertainties

88. Which of the following are examples of concentrations that create vulnerabilities and therefore would require disclosure of risks and uncertainties?

I. Market in which an entity conducts its operations.
II. Available sources of supply of materials used in operations of an entity.
III. Volume of business transacted with a certain contributor.

a. I and II.
b. II and III.
c. I and III.
d. I, II, and III.

89. Which of the following is required to be disclosed regarding the risks and uncertainties that exist?

a. Factors causing an estimate to be sensitive.
b. The potential impact of estimates about values of assets and liabilities when it is reasonably possible that the estimate will change in the near future.
c. The potential impact of estimates about values of assets and liabilities when it is remotely possible that the estimate will change in the near future.
d. A description of the operations both within and outside of the home country.

D.8. Other Comprehensive Bases of Accounting

90. Which of the following accounting bases may be used to prepare financial statements in conformity with a comprehensive basis of accounting other than generally accepted accounting principles?

I. Basis of accounting used by an entity to file its income tax return.
II. Cash receipts and disbursements basis of accounting.

a. I only.
b. II only.
c. Both I and II.
d. Neither I nor II.

91. Income tax basis financial statements differ from those prepared under GAAP in that income tax basis financial statements

a. Do **not** include nontaxable revenues and nondeductible expenses in determining income.
b. Include detailed information about current and deferred income tax liabilities.
c. Contain **no** disclosures about capital and operating lease transactions.
d. Recognize certain revenues and expenses in different reporting periods.

92. In financial statements prepared on the income tax basis, how should the nondeductible portion of expenses such as meals and entertainment be reported?

a. Included in the expense category in the determination of income.
b. Included in a separate category in the determination of income.
c. Excluded from the determination of income but included in the determination of retained earnings.
d. Excluded from the financial statements.

93. If a company uses the modified cash basis of accounting, the modifications from the pure cash basis should have substantial support. In this context substantial support requires

a. The financial statements have only minor modifications from GAAP.
b. The modifications must be the same as those required by tax law.
c. The modifications must be the same as GAAP and not illogical.
d. No modifications are allowed.

D.9. Prospective Financial Information

94. Which of the following is false?

a. Prospective financial information may be prepared for general or limited users.
b. The responsible party is the only limited user.

c. The financial projection may contain assumptions not necessarily expected to occur.
d. The financial projection may be expressed as a range of dollars.

95. Prospective financial information is defined as

a. Any financial information about the past, present, or future.
b. Any financial information about the present or future.
c. Any financial information about the future related to the day-to-day operations.
d. Any financial information about the future.

96. To achieve a reasonably objective basis, financial forecasts and projections should be prepared

I. In accordance with GAAP.
II. Using information that is in accordance with the plans of the entity.
III. With due professional care.

a. I and III.
b. II and III.
c. I, II, and III.
d. I and II.

97. Which of the following disclosures should prospective financial statements include?

	Summary of significant accounting policies	Summary of significant assumptions
a.	Yes	Yes
b.	Yes	No
c.	No	Yes
d.	No	No

D.10. SEC Reporting Requirements

98. Which of the following is the SEC form used by issuer companies to file as an annual report with the SEC?

a. Form 10-Q.
b. Form 8-K.
c. Form 10-K.
d. Form S-1.

99. Which of the following best describes the content of the SEC Form 10-Q?

a. Quarterly audited financial information and other information about the company.
b. Annual audited financial information and nonfinancial information about the company.
c. Disclosure of material events that affect the company.
d. Quarterly reviewed financial information and other information about the company.

100. Which of the following is the SEC form used by issuer companies to file as a quarterly report with the SEC?

a. Form 10-Q.
b. Form 8-K.
c. Form 10-K.
d. Form S-1.

101. A company is required to file quarterly financial statements with the United States Securities and Exchange Commission on Form 10-Q. The company operates in an industry that is not subject to seasonal fluctuations that could have a significant impact on its financial condition. In addition to the most recent quarter-end, for which of the following periods is the company required to present balance sheets on Form 10-Q?

- a. The end of the corresponding fiscal quarter of the preceding fiscal year.
- b. The end of the preceding fiscal year and the end of the corresponding fiscal quarter of the preceding fiscal years.
- c. The end of the preceding fiscal year.
- d. The end of the preceding fiscal year and the end of the prior two fiscal years.

102. A company is an accelerated filer that is required to file Form 10-K with the United States Securities and Exchange Commission (SEC). What is the maximum number of days after the company's fiscal year-end that the company has to file Form 10-K with the SEC?

- a. 60 days.
- b. 75 days.
- c. 90 days.
- d. 120 days.

103. SEC's regulation S-X describes

- a. The requirements for information and forms required by other regulations.
- b. The reporting requirements for asset backed securities.
- c. The form and content of financial statements to be filed with the SEC.
- d. A mandate that publicly traded companies disclose material information to all investors simultaneously.

104. Crafty Inc is a publicly traded company. Recently, Crafty entered into a material long-term lease agreement. Which SEC form discloses information about material events?

- a. Form S-1
- b. Form 8-K
- c. Form 10-K
- d. Form 10Q

D.11. Financial Statements of Trust

105. Which financial statements should be presented for a trust?

- I. Statement of assets and liabilities.
- II. Statement of operations.
- III. Statement of cash flows.
- IV. Statement of changes in net assets.

- a. I only.
- b. I and II only.
- c. I, II, and IV.
- d. I, III and IV.

106. What is the basis of accounting and at what amount are assets measured on the financial statements of a trust?

	Basis of accounting	Measurement
a.	Cash	Cost
b.	Cash	Fair value
c.	Accrual	Cost
d.	Accrual	Fair value

D.13. International Financial Reporting Standards (IFRS)

107. Galaxy Corporation prepares its financial statements in accordance with IFRS. Galaxy intends to refinance a $10,000 note payable due on February 20, year 2. The company expects the note to be refinanced for a period of five years. Under what circumstances can Galaxy report the note payable as a noncurrent liability on its December 31, year 1 statement of financial position?

- a. If Galaxy has the intent and ability to refinance before December 31, year 1.
- b. If Galaxy has executed an agreement to refinance before December 31, year 1.
- c. If Galaxy has executed an agreement to refinance prior to the issuance of the financial statements in March year 2.
- d. If Galaxy has the intent and ability to refinance before the issuance of the financial statements in March year 2.

108. Largo Corporation prepares its financial statements in accordance with IFRS. Which of the following items is required disclosure on the income statement?

- a. Revenues, cost of goods sold, and advertising expense.
- b. Finance costs, tax expense, and income.
- c. Operating expenses, nonoperating expenses, and extraordinary items.
- d. Gross profit, operating profits, and net profits.

109. Which of the following may not be disclosed on the income statement for a company that prepares its financial statements in accordance with IFRS?

- a. Gain or loss.
- b. Tax expense.
- c. Gain or loss from extraordinary items.
- d. Gain or loss from discontinued operations.

110. Glenda Corporation prepares its financial statements in accordance with IFRS. Glenda must report finance costs on the statement of cash flows

- a. In operating activities.
- b. Either in operating activities or financing activities.
- c. In financing activities.
- d. In investing activities or financing activities.

111. Larimer Corporation prepares its financial statements in accordance with IFRS. Larimer acquired equipment by issuing 5,000 shares of its common stock. How should this transaction be reported on the statement of cash flows?

- a. As an outflow of cash from investing activities and inflow of cash from financing activities.
- b. As an inflow of cash from financing activities and an outflow of cash from operating activities.
- c. At the bottom of the statement of cash flows as a significant noncash transaction.
- d. In the notes to the financial statements as a significant noncash transaction.

112. For IFRS purposes, cash advances and loans from bank overdrafts should be reported on the statement of cash flows as

- a. Operating activities.
- b. Investing activities.
- c. Financing activities.
- d. Other significant noncash activities.

113. Which of the following are acceptable methods for reporting comprehensive income under IFRS?

  I. One comprehensive income statement.
 II. Two statements: an income statement and a comprehensive income statement.
III. In the statement of owner's equity.

    a.   I only.
    b.   I and II only.
    c.   I, II, and III.
    d.   I and III only.

114. Which of the following is true about financial statement requirements under IFRS?
    a.   Prior year comparative financial statements are required.
    b.   Income statements for three years are required.
    c.   Balance sheets for three years are required.
    d.   There are no specific requirements regarding comparative financial statements.

115. Under IFRS, operating expenses on the income statement may be classified by

	Nature	Function
a.	Yes	Yes
b.	Yes	No
c.	No	Yes
d.	No	No

116. Under IFRS, the statement of cash flows may be presented on the

	Direct Basis	Indirect Basis
a.	Yes	Yes
b.	Yes	No
c.	No	Yes
d.	No	No

Multiple-Choice Answers and Explanations

Answers

1. d	__ __	21. c	__ __	41. d	__ __	61. c	__ __	81. d	__ __	101. c	__ __
2. a	__ __	22. c	__ __	42. b	__ __	62. c	__ __	82. b	__ __	102. b	__ __
3. a	__ __	23. c	__ __	43. d	__ __	63. a	__ __	83. d	__ __	103. c	__ __
4. a	__ __	24. b	__ __	44. d	__ __	64. d	__ __	84. c	__ __	104. b	__ __
5. a	__ __	25. b	__ __	45. c	__ __	65. b	__ __	85. a	__ __	105. c	__ __
6. d	__ __	26. a	__ __	46. d	__ __	66. a	__ __	86. a	__ __	106. d	__ __
7. a	__ __	27. d	__ __	47. b	__ __	67. d	__ __	87. a	__ __	107. b	__ __
8. a	__ __	28. d	__ __	48. a	__ __	68. c	__ __	88. d	__ __	108. b	__ __
9. b	__ __	29. c	__ __	49. c	__ __	69. d	__ __	89. b	__ __	109. c	__ __
10. a	__ __	30. b	__ __	50. a	__ __	70. a	__ __	90. c	__ __	110. b	__ __
11. a	__ __	31. a	__ __	51. b	__ __	71. b	__ __	91. d	__ __	111. d	__ __
12. c	__ __	32. c	__ __	52. a	__ __	72. a	__ __	92. a	__ __	112. a	__ __
13. c	__ __	33. b	__ __	53. a	__ __	73. b	__ __	93. c	__ __	113. b	__ __
14. d	__ __	34. d	__ __	54. c	__ __	74. c	__ __	94. b	__ __	114. a	__ __
15. b	__ __	35. d	__ __	55. c	__ __	75. a	__ __	95. d	__ __	115. a	__ __
16. d	__ __	36. d	__ __	56. d	__ __	76. b	__ __	96. c	__ __	116. a	__ __
17. a	__ __	37. b	__ __	57. b	__ __	77. c	__ __	97. a	__ __		
18. b	__ __	38. d	__ __	58. c	__ __	78. c	__ __	98. c	__ __		
19. b	__ __	39. b	__ __	59. a	__ __	79. b	__ __	99. d	__ __	1st: __/116 = __%
20. d	__ __	40. a	__ __	60. a	__ __	80. a	__ __	100. a	__ __	2nd: __/116 = __%

Explanations

1.   (d)   Baer Food's year 1 revenues should include net sales revenue ($187,000), interest revenue ($10,200), and gain on sale of equipment ($4,700), for a total of $201,900. Discontinued operations (loss of $12,400) and the extraordinary gain ($1,500) are both special items that should be reported as separate components of income, after **income from continuing operations**. Therefore, these items should **not** be included in the revenues section of the income statement (which is placed **before** income from continuing operations).

2.   (a)   To directly compute cost of goods manufactured (CGM), the formula is

> Beginning work in process
> + Direct materials used
> + Direct labor
> + Factory overhead
> − Ending work in process
> Cost of goods manufactured

However, none of these elements are given in this problem, so CGM must be computed indirectly, using the cost of sales formula

	Beginning finished goods	$400,000
+	Cost of goods manufactured	+ CGM
−	Ending finished goods	−360,000
	Cost of sales	$240,000

Solving for the missing amount, CGM is $200,000.

3.   (a)   All of the revenues, gains, expenses, and losses given in this problem are components of income from continuing operations. Income before income taxes is $180,000, as computed below.

Revenues ($575,000 + $25,000)	$600,000
Expenses and losses ($240,000 + $70,000 + $10,000 + $50,000 + $15,000 + $15,000 + $20,000)	420,000
Income before income taxes	$180,000

To compute income from continuing operations (after taxes), income taxes ($180,000 × 30% = $54,000) must also be deducted ($180,000 − $54,000 = $126,000).

4.   (a)   The requirement is to compute the amount of expenses to be included in selling expenses for year 1. Advertising ($150,000) and sales salaries and commissions ($140,000) are clearly selling expenses, as is the rent for the office space occupied by the sales department ($220,000 × 1/2 = $110,000). Additionally, freight-out ($80,000) is a selling expense because shipping the goods **from** the point of sale to the customer is the final effort in the selling process. The total selling expense is, therefore, $480,000 ($150,000 + $140,000 + $110,000 + $80,000). The remaining expenses given are general and administrative expenses, except for interest and the loss on sale of long-term investment, which are nonoperating items (other expenses and losses).

5.   (a)   Operating expenses are usually divided into two categories, **selling expenses** and **general and administrative (G&A) expenses**. Selling expenses are related to the sale of a company's products, while G&A expenses are related to the company's general operations. Therefore, Griff should include the following costs in G&A expense:

Accounting and legal fees	$ 25,000
Officers' salaries	150,000
Insurance	85,000
G&A expense	$260,000

Freight-in ($175,000) is an inventoriable cost which should be reflected in cost of goods sold and ending inventory.

Freight-out, the cost of delivering goods to customers ($160,000), is included in selling expenses. Sales representatives salaries ($215,000) is also a selling expense.

6. (d) Interest expense is generally considered to be a nonoperating item and is therefore included in **other expenses and losses**. Operating expenses are usually divided into two categories, **selling expenses** and **general and administrative expenses**. Since advertising expense is directly related to the sale of the company's products, it is included in selling expenses. Therefore, neither of the expenses given are general and administrative expenses.

7. (a) Charitable contributions expense should include all expenses incurred in year 1 by Yew Co. which involve charitable contributions to other entities. The total charitable contributions expense is $310,000, consisting of the $250,000 donated to youth and educational programs and the $60,000 ($140,000 – $80,000) donated to health and human service organizations. The other $80,000 was given to these organizations **by the employees,** with the company merely acting as an agent collecting that amount through payroll deductions and forwarding it on to the organizations. The expenditure for redesigning product packaging ($100,000) would be properly classified as research and development expense.

8. (a) Extraordinary items are material gains or losses which are both **unusual** in nature and **infrequent** in occurrence. For Raim Co., which sustains flood losses every two to three years, the year 1 flood loss is not infrequent, and should be recognized as a component of income from continuing operations. For Cane Co., the year 1 flood loss is both unusual and infrequent, so it should be recognized as an extraordinary item.

9. (b) Extraordinary items are material items which are **both unusual** in nature and **infrequent** in occurrence. The effect of a strike ($175,000) and a gain or loss from sale or abandonment of equipment ($125,000) is **not** considered extraordinary. The loss from the earthquake would be considered unusual and infrequent. Therefore the $150,000 loss is extraordinary, and the total amount of infrequent losses **not** considered extraordinary is $300,000 ($175,000 + $125,000).

10. (a) Extraordinary items are material items which are **both unusual** in nature and **infrequent** in occurrence. Disposals of plant assets, foreign currency losses, and inventory losses are not considered to be unusual in nature, and thus are not extraordinary. Items that may qualify as extraordinary items include some casualties, expropriations, and prohibitions under a new law. In Kent Co.'s year 1 income statement, losses not considered extraordinary amount to $610,000. The factory disposal ($300,000) is classified as discontinued operations because the operations carried on there are dissimilar from operations carried on at the other factories. The $120,000 foreign currency loss and $190,000 inventory loss are not extraordinary because they are not unusual in nature.

11. (a) Extraordinary items are material gains or losses which are both **unusual** in nature and **infrequent** in occurrence. Foreign currency losses ($1,200,000) and losses due to discontinued operations ($500,000) are not considered to be unusual in nature and thus are not extraordinary. Items

that may qualify as extraordinary include some casualties, expropriations, prohibitions under a new law, and extinguishment of debt. Midway's casualty loss appears to be extraordinary because the hurricane was the first ever to strike in Midway's area. The net pretax loss was $100,000 [$800,000 equipment loss – $700,000 building gain ($1,000,000 – $300,000)].

12. (c) A gain (loss) must be recognized when a nonmonetary asset is involuntarily converted into monetary assets even if the company reinvests the monetary assets in replacement nonmonetary assets. The gain or loss is the difference between the insurance proceeds ($1,100,000 replacement cost – $50,000 deductible = $1,050,000) and the carrying amount of the assets destroyed or used up as a result of the casualty loss. The warehouse (carrying amount of $300,000) was destroyed, and cash of $20,000 was used to cover removal costs. Therefore, the gain is $730,000 [$1,050,000 – ($300,000 + $20,000)]. It is **not** an extraordinary item because storms similar to the one that destroyed the warehouse occur frequently (every four years).

13. (c) In this situation, the provision for income tax (income tax expense) will be the amount of the tax liability to the government determined without including the extraordinary loss. This amount is determined by applying the 40% tax rate to pretax accounting income before extraordinary items adjusted for any permanent differences. Accounting income before taxes is $900,000, but that amount includes a gain on life insurance coverage ($100,000). A gain on life insurance coverage is a **permanent** difference because it is included in accounting income but will **never** be included in taxable income. Therefore, the amount of accounting income which will be subject to taxes is $800,000 ($900,000 – $100,000), and the provision for income taxes is $320,000 ($800,000 × 40%). The tax savings from the extraordinary loss ($300,000 × 40% = $120,000) will not affect the provision for income taxes because the extraordinary item must be reported together with its tax effect (extraordinary loss of $180,000; net of tax).

14. (d) Net income as reported ($74,100) properly included the gain on early retirement of bonds payable ($22,000) and the loss from fire ($14,000). The fact that the gain and loss were reported net of taxes in the income statement was incorrect, but does not cause the net income amount to be in error. However, the other two items should **not** be reported in the income statement at all. An unrealized loss on **noncurrent** investments in stock ($5,400) is reported in other comprehensive income, not in net income. A correction of an error ($7,500) is treated as a prior period adjustment. It is reported in the financial statements as an adjustment to the beginning balance of retained earnings, rather than in the income statement. Since both of these items were subtracted in the computation of reported net income, they must be added back to compute the correct net income of $87,000 ($74,100 + $5,400 + $7,500).

15. (b) In year 1, Brecon Co. would report one fifth of the cabinet costs as depreciation expense in selling, general, and administrative expenses. Four fifths of the cabinet cost would remain capitalized as fixed assets at the end of year 1. The cabinets are considered fixed assets and not a part of cost of goods sold.

16. **(d)** A material gain or loss that is unusual in nature or infrequent in occurrence, but not both, should be presented as a separate component of income or loss from continuing operations. Both discontinued operations and extraordinary items are reported separately **after** income from continuing operations.

17. **(a)** For an item to qualify as an extraordinary item it must be **both** unusual in nature and infrequent in occurrence. The above criteria must take into account the environment in which the entity operates. An entity with sales in different countries will experience foreign currency revaluations on a regular basis, so a currency revaluation would not be infrequent in occurrence and it is not an extraordinary item. Gains from increases in contract prices are neither infrequent nor unusual, so they cannot qualify as extraordinary items.

18. **(b)** Extraordinary items are reported **net of income taxes** as a separate component of income **after** discontinued operations.

19. **(b)** Extraordinary items are events and transactions that are distinguished by both their unusual nature and the infrequency of their occurrence. Losses from hail damage are both common and frequent for Toncan. Estimates of the losses would not be presented in the financial statements. No amount is recorded until a loss actually occurs.

20. **(d)** A transaction that is unusual in nature and infrequent in occurrence is considered an extraordinary item. An extraordinary item is reported **after** discontinued operations.

21. **(c)** Extraordinary items are events and transactions that are distinguished by both their unusual nature and the infrequency of their occurrence. Teller Co.'s loss arising from its **first** antitrust action meets both of these criteria (particularly since they pleaded guilty) and should therefore be reported as an extraordinary item. The strike against Teller's major supplier, however, should not be reported as an extraordinary item because it is usual in nature but may be expected to recur as a consequence of customary and continuing business activities.

22. **(c)** Extraordinary items are material items which are **both unusual** in nature and **infrequent** in occurrence. Therefore, the loss on sale of a bond investment is not extraordinary. Neither item is treated as extraordinary.

23. **(c)** Corrections of errors shall continue to be reported net of tax in retained earnings as an adjustment of the beginning balance.

24. **(b)** Costs of exit activities (including restructuring charges) should be measured and recognized at fair value when they are incurred.

25. **(b)** The operating loss of $300,000 ($500,000 revenues less $800,000 expenses) relates to a discontinued component, so it is part of discontinued operations, **not** continuing operations. It is combined with the loss from disposal on the income statement. **Discontinued operations** is a category distinct from **extraordinary items**.

26. **(a)** Management is not required to have entered into a sales agreement. It is sufficient if management is committed to a disposal plan that is reasonable. The other items are all required for presentation as discontinued operations.

27. **(d)** In discontinued operations, presentation of the income or loss from operations of the component and the gain or loss on disposal is required. Since the company met the requirements for "held for sale" status in year 2, the subsidiary should be written down to its fair value less cost to sell. This would result in a loss of $1,500,000 ($8,000,000 carrying amount – $6,500,000 fair value). Therefore, the loss from discontinued operations would be $3,500,000 ($2,000,000 loss from operations + $1,500,000 loss on planned disposal).

28. **(d)** The loss from discontinued operations would equal the loss from operations plus the estimated loss from disposal of the component.

29. **(c)** Costs of termination benefits, lease termination, and consolidating facilities or relocating employees related to a disposal activity that involves discontinued operations should be included in the results of discontinued operations.

30. **(b)** The requirement is to determine how a discontinued component's operating losses for the current period should be classified in the financial statements. The "income (loss) from operations" is combined with the loss on disposal.

31. **(a)** Gains or losses from the operation of a discontinued business component realized for the period are combined with the loss of disposal to determine the loss from discontinued operations.

32. **(c)** Discontinued operations should include the gain or loss on disposal plus the results of operations during the period.

33. **(b)** The purpose of reporting comprehensive income is to report a measure of overall enterprise performance by displaying all changes in equity of an enterprise that result from recognized transactions and other economic events of the period other than transactions with owners in their capacity as owners. An enterprise should continue to display an amount for net income with equal prominence to the comprehensive income amount displayed.

34. **(d)** Once unrealized items recorded and reported in the current or prior period are recognized as realized and reported in net income, it is necessary to reverse them out of other comprehensive income. The reclassification adjustment is to avoid double counting. The reclassification adjustment in this situation is $15,000 ($25,000 gain on AFS securities, net of $10,000 tax).

35. **(c)** The FASB allows two presentation formats [answer choices (a) and (b)].

36. **(d)** The accumulated balance of other comprehensive income should be reported as a component of equity, separate from retained earnings and additional paid-in capital.

37. **(b)** Comprehensive income is defined as the change in equity of a business during a period from transactions of nonowner sources. Stockholders are owners of the corporation or entity, therefore, transactions between the entity and shareholder are not a component of comprehensive income.

38. **(d)** Assuming the fair value option is not elected, the calculation of holding gains recognized in other comprehensive income is as follows:

	Before tax	Income tax	Net of tax
Year ended 12/31/Y2	$5,000	$1,500	$3,500
Year ended 12/31/Y3	2,500	750	1,750
Total gain	$7,500	$2,250	$5,250

The reclassification adjustment should be shown net of tax, so ($5,250) is the adjustment amount. $5,250 had been previously added to other comprehensive income when the gains occurred. The $5,250 needs to be taken out in order to avoid counting the gains twice. The securities have been sold so the gains are now realized and will be part of net income.

39. (b) The gain for the period is 10 shares times the increase in fair value, which is $250. This gain of $2,500 must be shown net of tax, so the holding gain is $1,750.

40. (a) Comprehensive income is computed as follows:

Net income		77,000
Other comprehensive income net of tax:		
Unrealized gain on securities	15,000	
Less: Reclassification adjustment	(2,500)	12,500
Pension liability adjustment		(3,000)
Other comprehensive income		9,500
Comprehensive income		86,500

Notice that stock warrants outstanding are not included as part of comprehensive income.

41. (d) If $2,450 (net of tax) is being deducted from other comprehensive income as a reclassification adjustment, $2,450 must be the amount of unrealized gains (net of tax) that have been recognized in other comprehensive income. The realized gains will then be recognized in income from continuing operations before tax. The gains before tax effects are $3,500 ($2,450 ÷ 70%).

42. (b) Comprehensive income disclosures include the changes during a period of the following components of other comprehensive income: unrealized gains and losses on available-for-sale investments and foreign currency items, including any reclassification adjustments, and the pension liability adjustment required to recognize the funded status of the plan. Treasury stock is deducted from stockholders' equity and **not** a component of other comprehensive income.

43. (d) Separate EPS calculations are not required for other comprehensive income or comprehensive income.

44. (d) The FASB allows comprehensive income to be shown at the bottom of the income statement as a continuation of net income or in a separate statement beginning with net income. Presenting comprehensive income in the statement of changes in stockholders' equity is not an allowable method.

45. (c) If the fair value option is not elected, held-to-maturity securities are reported at amortized cost. Any decreases or increases in fair value are reported neither in net income nor as part of other comprehensive income. Answers (a) and (b) are incorrect because an adjustment to pension liability to record the funded status of the plan, and subsequent decreases of the fair value of available-for-sale securities that have been previously written down as impaired are included in other comprehensive income. Answer (d) is incorrect because decreases in the fair value of held-to-maturity securities are not part of other comprehensive income.

46. (d) Comprehensive income (net income plus other comprehensive income) should be displayed in a financial statement that has the same prominence as other financial statements. Answer (a) is incorrect because the FASB prefers that comprehensive income be displayed either at the bottom of the income statement, continuing from net income to arrive at a comprehensive income figure (equals net income plus other comprehensive income), or in a separate statement of comprehensive income. Answer (b) is incorrect because components of other comprehensive income may be displayed net of related tax effects or before related tax effects with one amount shown for the aggregate income tax effect. Answer (c) is incorrect because comprehensive income can be displayed in the two methods preferred by the FASB (mentioned above) or in the statement of changes in stockholders' equity.

47. (b) Total retained earnings includes both unappropriated retained earnings and restricted retained earnings. Therefore, before closing entries, total retained earnings is $1,060,000 ($900,000 + $160,000). Before computing year 1 net income, tax expense must be recorded. Earnings ($6,680,000) less costs and expenses ($5,180,000) result in pretax income of $1,500,000. Since the tax rate is 30%, tax expense is $450,000 (30% × $1,500,000). Therefore, an adjustment is necessary to debit **income tax expense** and credit **prepaid taxes** for $450,000. After the adjustment, net income is $1,050,000 ($6,680,000 – $5,180,000 – $450,000). After closing entries, total retained earnings is $2,110,000 ($1,060,000 + $1,050,000).

48. (a) The only liabilities included in the trial balance are billings in excess of costs on long-term contracts ($700,000) and note payable-noncurrent ($1,620,000). Only the note is noncurrent. Billings in excess of costs on long-term contracts is similar to unearned revenue and is always reported as a current liability.

49. (c) Current assets listed in the trial balance are cash ($600,000), accounts receivable ($3,500,000), cost in excess of billings on long-term contracts ($1,600,000) and prepaid taxes ($450,000). However, income tax expense has not yet been recorded. Earnings ($6,680,000) less costs and expenses ($5,180,000) result in pretax income of $1,500,000. Since the tax rate is 30%, tax expense is $450,000 (30% × $1,500,000). Therefore, an adjustment is necessary to debit **income tax expense** and credit **prepaid taxes** for $450,000. Total current assets, after this adjustment, are $5,700,000.

Cash	$ 600,000
Accounts receivable	3,500,000
Cost in excess of billings	1,600,000
	$5,700,000

50. (a) Mirr began operations on 1/1/Y1 with the following balance sheet elements:

Assets	=	Liabilities	+	Owners' equity
$860,000	=	$110,000	+	$750,000

During year 1, liabilities increased to $120,000, and owners' equity increased to $765,000 [$750,000 beginning balance + $18,000 net income ($82,000 revenues – $64,000 expenses) – $3,000 dividends declared]. Therefore, 12/31/Y1 assets must be $885,000.

Assets	=	Liabilities	+	Owners' equity
Assets	=	$120,000	+	$765,000
Assets	=	$885,000		

51. (b) The requirement is to determine the net income for year 1 by analyzing changes in the balance sheet. Recall the accounting equation: Assets – Liabilities = Stockholders' equity. By inserting the changes given into this formula, we find an increase of $62,000 exists in the entire stockholders' equity section ($89,000 – $27,000 = $62,000). Stockholders' equity is composed of capital stock, additional paid-in capital and retained earnings. Because increases in the other two balances are given that total $66,000 ($60,000 + $6,000), the retained earnings balance must have decreased by $4,000 ($66,000 – $62,000). When dividends are paid, this reduces retained earnings, while Vel Corp. net income increases the balance of retained earnings. For the equation to balance, the changes in retained earnings account must reduce total stockholders' equity by $4,000. Therefore, if $13,000 in dividends are paid, which reduce retained earnings, and total retained earnings are to be reduced by $4,000, then net income, which increases retained earnings, must be $9,000. This creates the $4,000 difference needed to make the equation balance ($89,000 – $27,000 = $66,000 – $4,000). The following shows the analysis of the retained earnings account:

Retained earnings (beg.)	$	xxx
Net income (plug)		**9,000**
Dividends		(13,000)
Retained earnings (decrease)	$	(4,000)

52. (a) Idle machinery ($11,200) and cash surrender value of life insurance ($13,700) are both assets. The allowance for decline in market value of noncurrent marketable equity securities ($8,400) is a contra asset that is properly included in the asset section of the balance sheet (as a deduction). The only item listed which should **not** be included in the asset section of the balance sheet is the treasury stock ($24,000). Although the treasury stock account has a debit balance, it is not an asset; instead, it is reported as a contra equity account. Therefore, the $24,000 must be excluded from the asset section, reducing the net asset amount to $851,000 ($875,000 – $24,000).

53. (a) Although the statement of cash flows provides information about liquidity, solvency, and financial flexibility, a potential investor would **primarily** use the balance sheet to assess liquidity and financial flexibility. The balance sheet helps users analyze the company's ability to use current assets to pay current liabilities (liquidity) and the company's ability to alter the amounts and timing of future cash flows to adapt to unexpected needs or to take advantage of opportunities (flexibility).

54. (c) Financial statements must include disclosures of material transactions between related parties. Compensation arrangements in the ordinary course of business, however, are specifically excluded from this disclosure requirement. Therefore, only the $250,000 sale to affiliated enterprises must be disclosed.

55. (c) Disclosure of material transactions between related parties is required except for (1) compensation agreements, expense allowances, and other similar items in the ordinary course of business, and (2) transactions which are eliminated in the preparation of consolidated or combined

financial statements. The officers' salaries and officers' expenses fall into category (1), while the intercompany sales fall into category (2). Therefore, only the loans to officers ($125,000 + $50,000 = $175,000) are reported as related-party disclosures.

56. (d) Disclosure of material transactions between related parties is required except for (1) compensation agreements, expense allowances, and other similar items in the ordinary course of business and (2) transactions eliminated in the preparation of consolidated or combined financial statements.

57. (b) Disclosure of any material related-party transactions is required except

1. Compensation agreements, expense allowances, and similar items in the ordinary course of business.
2. Transactions that are eliminated in the preparation of consolidated or combined financial statements.

Since sales of inventory between subsidiary and parent are eliminated in preparing consolidated financial statements, such sales need not be disclosed as a related-party transaction. Nonmonetary exchanges by affiliates are not specifically exempted from disclosure, and therefore must be disclosed as related-party transactions. Compensation arrangements, expense allowances, and similar items in the ordinary course of business need not be disclosed as related-party transactions. However, in this case the allowances are in excess of normal business practice and therefore must be disclosed. Surety and guaranty agreements between related parties are not specifically exempted from disclosure and therefore must be disclosed as related-party transactions.

58. (c) Disclosures of material transactions shall include (1) nature of relationship(s), (2) description of transaction(s), including those assigned zero or nominal amounts, (3) dollar amounts of transactions for each income statement period and effect of any change in method of establishing terms, and (4) amounts due to/from related parties, including terms and manner of settlement.

59. (a) The users of the information are the focus of financial reporting. GAAP requires disclosures in the notes to facilitate the users' understanding of the financial statements. Answer (b) is incorrect because the financial statements should be properly presented in accordance with GAAP; thus no improper presentation should exist. Answer (c) is incorrect because the totals of the financial statements should include all items; thus, no items would be excluded. Answer (d) is incorrect because management's responses to the auditor's comments would be contained in the management letter, which is a separate report typically presented to the audit committee or the board of directors.

60. (a) The requirement is to determine which information should be included in the summary of significant accounting policies. Disclosure of accounting policies should identify and describe the accounting principles followed by the reporting entity and methods of applying those principles. Answer (a) is correct because the method of recording and depreciating assets is an example of such a required disclosure. Answers (b) and (c) are incorrect because both represent detail presented elsewhere in the financial statements. Answer (d) is incorrect because it is an estimate of earnings rather than an accounting policy.

61.   (c)   Disclosure of accounting policies should identify and describe the accounting principles followed by the reporting entity and methods of applying those principles. The criteria for determining which investments are treated as cash equivalents is an example of how the entity applies accounting principles. These disclosures should not duplicate details presented elsewhere as part of the financial statements. Answers (a), (b), and (d) are not disclosures of accounting **policies,** and also would be presented elsewhere in the financial statements.

62.   (c)   This is a recognized subsequent event in the financial statement because Swift records an estimate for warranty liability. Prior to issuing the financial statements, Swift must make an adjustment for warranty liability for the product recall. Therefore, warranty liability should be $68,000 on the year 1 balance sheet.

63.   (a)   This is an unrecognized subsequent event that did not exist as of the balance sheet date of December 31, year 1. Therefore, there should be no adjustment of the year 1 financial statements. However, since the inventory loss is material in amount and the loss is uninsured, to prevent the financial statements from being misleading, Colter should disclose the loss in a footnote to the year 1 financial statements.

64.   (d)   A loss for a recognized subsequent event should be reported in the current year financial statements. Therefore, answer (d) is correct. Answer (a) is incorrect because a loss would not be recognized in the current year for an unrecognized subsequent event. However, a footnote disclosure would be required for the unrecognized subsequent event if the event is material and the financial statements would be misleading if the event were not disclosed. Answer (b) is incorrect because gains are not recognized until realized. Answer (c) is incorrect because recognized subsequent events result in a loss recognized in the current year and a corresponding adjustment to record the liability.

65.   (b)   The definition of fair value is the price that would be received to sell an asset in an orderly transaction between market participants at the measurement date under current market conditions. Answer (a) is incorrect because it is an entry price, not an exit price. Answer (c) is incorrect because assets that require to be revalued to fair value should be based on an exit value, not an adjusted historic cost. Answer (d) is incorrect because the price paid to acquire the asset is an entry price, not an exit price.

66.   (a)   The principal market is the market in which the reporting entity would sell the asset or transfer the liability with the greatest volume and level of activity for the asset or liability. Answers (b) and (c) are incorrect because they do not meet the definition of principal market. Answer (d) is incorrect because it describes the most advantageous market.

67.   (d)   If location is an attribute of the asset, the price in the principal market should be adjusted for costs to transport the asset to its principal or most advantageous market. Answers (a) and (b) are incorrect because prices are not adjusted for transaction costs such as selling costs. Answer (c) is incorrect because fair values are not based upon entry prices to the market.

68.   (c)   Market participants are buyers and sellers in the principal market or most advantageous market for the asset or liability. Market participants should be independent, knowledgeable, able to transact for the asset, and willing to transact (i.e., motivated but not compelled to do so). Answer (a) is incorrect because market participants should not be compelled to sell. Answer (b) is incorrect because it is not an independent, unrelated party. Answer (d) is incorrect because the dealer is establishing a new market and is not in the principal market that exists for the asset.

69.   (d)   A fair value measurement assumes the highest and best use of the asset that is physically possible, legally permissible, and financially feasible. Answers (a) and (b) are incorrect because to determine the valuation premise, the asset can be classified as either in-use or in-exchange. Answer (c) is incorrect because for valuation purposes, the highest and best use would maximize the value of the asset.

70.   (a)   The fair value at initial recognition is the transaction price that represents the price paid to acquire the asset (an entry price). Answer (b) is incorrect because transaction costs are not included. Answer (c) is incorrect because it is an exit price. Answer (d) is incorrect because it is not a fair value measure.

71.   (b)   There are three approaches to valuation techniques for fair value: the market approach, the income approach, and the cost approach. There is no technique called the residual value approach.

72.   (a)   The income approach uses valuation techniques to convert future amounts to a single present value amount. Therefore, Black-Scholes-Merton, binomial models, or discounted cash flow models are examples of the income approach. Answers (b) and (c) are incorrect because these approaches do not use present value techniques. Answer (d) is incorrect because there is no exit value approach.

73.   (b)   The market approach valuation technique uses prices and other relevant information generated by market transactions involving identical or comparable assets or liabilities. Answer (a) is incorrect because it refers to the income approach. Answer (c) is incorrect because it refers to the cost approach. Answer (d) is incorrect because it is not a technique for any of the permissible valuation techniques.

74.   (c)   A change in valuation technique used to measure fair value should be reported as a change in accounting estimate. The change is reported on a prospective basis; however, the disclosures for change in accounting estimate are not required for a change in valuation technique. Answers (a), (b), and (d) are incorrect.

75.   (a)   The fair value hierarchy prioritizes the inputs to valuation techniques into three levels: Level 1, Level 2, and Level 3. The highest priority is given to Level 1 inputs, which are quoted prices in active markets for identical assets and liabilities. Answers (b) and (c) are incorrect, because these levels are lower priority than Level 1. Answer (d) is incorrect because there is no Level 4 input.

76.   (b)   The bank prime rate and the default rates are both observable inputs. A financial forecast is developed by an entity and is an unobservable input or Level 3 input. Therefore, answers (a), (c), and (d) are incorrect.

77.   (c)   The Codification encourages, but does not require, business enterprises to disclose **supplementary information** on the effects of changing prices. The statement presents requirements to be followed by enterprises that voluntarily elect to disclose this information. Answers (a) and (b) are incorrect because the information is not reported in the body of the financial statements or in the notes to the financial statements. Answer (d) is incorrect because management's report to shareholders identifies management's responsibilities, including responsibilities for the internal control system, and would not include information about changing prices.

78. **(c)**   The requirement is to determine the amounts to be reported for three balance sheet accounts in a supplementary **constant dollar** balance sheet. In a constant dollar balance sheet, **nonmonetary** items are restated to the current price level, while monetary items are **not** restated because they are already stated in current dollars. The investment in bonds and the long-term debt are monetary items since their amounts are fixed by contract in terms of number of dollars. Therefore, these items are not restated and are reported at $60,000 and $80,000, respectively. The land, however, is a nonmonetary item and its cost ($120,000) must be restated to current dollars by using the TO/FROM ratio (110/100), resulting in an adjusted amount of $132,000 ($120,000 × 110/100).

79. **(b)**   The account "loans to employees" is a monetary asset account since its payment amount is fixed at some point in the future. Conversely, merchandise inventory is considered a nonmonetary asset account since its value will change based on relative price levels in the future. The total value of monetary assets is the balance of the loans to employees account, or $20,000.

80. **(a)**   The increase in current cost (nominal dollars) of $15,000 is the **total** increase in current cost, including any increase caused by inflation. The effect of changes in the general price level is **not** separated from the effect of changes in specific value. The increase in current cost (constant dollars) of $12,000 is the increase in current cost after eliminating any increase caused by inflation. Therefore, the inflation component of the increase in current cost of inventories is $3,000 ($15,000 – $12,000).

81. **(d)**   The requirement is to determine which item is classified as nonmonetary when computing the purchasing power gain or loss on net monetary items. A monetary item is one that is fixed or determinable without reference to future prices. Accumulated depreciation is not a monetary item. Advances to unconsolidated subsidiaries, allowance for doubtful accounts, and unamortized premium on bonds payable are all monetary items.

82. **(b)**   A purchasing power gain or loss is the net gain or loss determined by restating in units of constant purchasing power the opening and closing balances of, and transactions in, **monetary** assets and liabilities. During a period of rising prices, monetary liabilities give rise to purchasing power gains because they will be settled with cash which can be used to purchase relatively fewer goods or services at a future time.

83. **(d)**   Current cost accounting is a method of valuing and reporting assets, liabilities, revenues, and expenses at their current cost at the balance sheet date or at the date of their use or sale. A holding gain is recorded as an increase in an item's value. At December 31, year 1, Vend Co. is holding merchandise which is currently valued at $10 per

unit (replacement cost), while the original recorded value of the merchandise was $8 per unit (purchase price). Therefore, the holding gain is $2 per unit.

84. **(c)**   The requirement is to calculate the amount of current cost depreciation expense which would appear in supplementary current cost financial statements. Depreciation is to be measured based on the **average** current cost of the asset during the period of use. The average current cost of this machine during year 1 is $120,000 [($115,000 + $125,000) ÷ 2]. Therefore, year 1 depreciation expense is $24,000 ($120,000 ÷ 5-year useful life).

85. **(a)**   Current cost for inventories and equipment is measured at the lower of current cost or recoverable amount. For equipment, recoverable amount ($95,000) is lower than current cost; for inventory, current cost ($80,000) is lower than recoverable amount. Therefore, the total amount to be reported for these assets is $175,000 ($95,000 + $80,000).

86. **(a)**   Increases or decreases in the current cost of inventory result from the difference between the measures of assets at their entry dates (beginning of year or purchase date) and measures of assets at their exit dates (end of year or date of use/sale). Based on this definition, holding gains would be reported both when inventory is sold during the year (realized gains), and when inventory is held at the end of the year (unrealized gains).

87. **(a)**   The current cost of goods sold is computed by multiplying the average cost of units produced or purchased during the year times the number of units sold.

88. **(d)**   The market in which an entity conducts its operations, the available sources of supply of materials used in operations of an entity, and the volume of business transacted with a certain contributor are all examples of concentrations that create vulnerabilities that are required to be disclosed.

89. **(b)**   The potential impact of estimates about values of assets and liabilities when it is reasonably possible that the estimate will change in the near future is a required disclosure regarding significant risks and uncertainties. Factors causing an estimate to be sensitive is not a required disclosure, only recommended. The potential impact of estimates about values of assets and liabilities when it is remotely possible that the estimate will change in the near future is not a required disclosure. It is only a required disclosure if it is reasonably possible that the estimates will change in the near future. Only a description of operations outside the home country is a required disclosure.

90. **(c)**   Other than generally accepted accounting principles, the only other bases which may be used to prepare financial statements in conformity with a comprehensive basis of accounting are the **cash basis** and a **basis of accounting used to file an income tax return**.

91. **(d)**   When financial statements are prepared using an income tax basis, two accounting methods can be used: (1) modified cash basis—hybrid method of IRS and (2) accrual basis—IRS. The modified cash basis reflects the use of accrual basis for inventories, cost of goods sold, sales, and depreciation, if these are significant. The accrual basis uses accruals and deferrals with several exceptions (e.g., prepaid income, warranty expense). When financial statements are prepared on an income tax basis, the financial statements should not simply repeat items and amounts reported in the tax return. Thus, items such as nontaxable municipal interest and the nondeductible portion of travel and entertainment expense should be fully reflected in the income statement on the basis used for tax purposes, with footnote disclosure of the differences between the amounts reported in the income statements and tax return.

92. (a) In financial statements prepared on the income tax basis, the nondeductible portion of meals and entertainment expense should be included with the deductible portion as a total amount of travel and entertainment expense. Additionally, the nondeductible portion should be footnoted. Answer (a) is the best answer among the alternatives given, although it does not indicate that a footnote is required.

93. (c) The requirement is to identify the statement that best describes appropriate modifications in cash basis financial statements. Answer (c) is correct because the modifications should be the same as GAAP and not illogical. Answer (a) is incorrect because modified cash basis financial statements may have substantial modifications from GAAP. Answer (b) is incorrect because the modifications are not required to be the same as those required by tax law. Answer (d) is incorrect because modifications are allowed.

94. (b) The responsible party is not the only limited user. Third parties with whom the responsible party is negotiating directly are also limited users. Answer (a) is incorrect because prospective financial information may be prepared for general or limited use. Answer (c) is incorrect because it is true that assumptions not necessarily expected to occur may be included in the financial projection. Answer (d) is incorrect because the financial projection may be expressed as a range of dollars.

95. (d) Prospective financial information is defined as any financial information about the future.

96. (c) Financial forecasts and projections must be prepared in accordance with GAAP, with the plans of the entity, and with due professional care in order to achieve a reasonably objective basis.

97. (a) Prospective financial statements include information on the purpose of the statements, assumptions, and significant accounting policies.

98. (c) The requirement is to identify the form used to file as an annual report with the SEC. Answer (c) is correct because Form 10-K is the title of the annual report required to be filed annually by issuer companies. Answer (a) is incorrect because this is the title of the quarterly financial report. Answer (b) is incorrect because Form 8-K is the information report that may be filed any time during the year. Answer (d) is incorrect because a Form S-1 is an initial registration form for securities under the Securities Act of 1933.

99. (d) The requirement is to identify the content of the SEC Form 10-Q. Answer (d) is correct because the Form 10-Q presents reviewed quarterly information and other information about the company. Answer (a) is incorrect because the information is reviewed, not audited. Answer (b) is incorrect because this describes the Form 10-K. Answer (c) is incorrect because this describes the Form 8-K.

100. (a) The requirement is to identify the form used to file as a quarterly report with the SEC. Answer (a) is correct because Form 10-Q is the title of the quarterly report required to be filed by issuer companies.

101. (c) The requirement is to identify the balance sheet required in the Form 10-Q. Answer (c) is correct because the SEC requires that a Form 10-Q contain an interim balance sheet as of the end of the most recent fiscal quarter and a balance sheet as of the end of the preceding fiscal year. An interim balance sheet for the fiscal quarter of the preceding year does not need to be provided unless it is necessary for understanding the impact of seasonal fluctuations.

102. (b) The requirement is to identify the deadline for filing a Form 10-K for an accelerated filer. Answer (b) is correct because the maximum number of days for an accelerated filer to file a 10-K with the SEC is 75 days after the company's fiscal year-end. However, a large accelerated filer with $700 million of public float has a deadline of 60 days, and nonaccelerated filers have a deadline of 90 days.

103. (c) Answer (c) is correct because SEC's regulation S-X describes the form and content of financial statements to be filed with the SEC. Answer (a) is incorrect because Regulation S-K describes the requirements for information and forms required by Regulation S-X. Answer (b) is incorrect because Regulation AB describes the reporting requirements for asset-backed securities. Answer (d) is incorrect because Regulation FD mandates that publicly traded companies disclose material information to all investors simultaneously.

104. (b) Answer (b) is correct because Form 8-K discloses information about material events for US Companies. Answer (a) is incorrect because an S-1 is a registration statement for US Companies. Answer (c) is incorrect because Form 10-K is an annual report for US Companies Answer (d) is incorrect because Form 10-Q is a quarterly report.

105. (c) The requirement is to identify the financial statements of a trust. A statement of assets and liabilities, a statement of operations, and a statement of changes in net assets are generally presented for a trust.

106. (d) The requirement is to identify the accounting and measurement bases for a trust. The financial statements of a trust should be presented on the accrual basis and the assets are generally measured at their fair values.

107. (b) The requirement is to identify the circumstances in which Galaxy may present the note as a noncurrent liability. Answer (b) is correct because IFRS requires that Galaxy must have executed an agreement to refinance at the balance sheet date in order to classify the debt as a noncurrent liability. Inasmuch as no agreement existed at the balance sheet date, the note payable must be classified as a current liability. Therefore, answers (a), (c), and (d) are incorrect.

108. (b) The requirement is to identify the item required to be disclosed on the income statement. The correct answer is (b) because the income statement may be prepared by presenting expenses either by nature or by function. The minimum required disclosures on the income statement include income, finance costs, share of profits and losses using the equity method, tax expense, discontinued operations, profit or loss, noncontrolling interests in profits and losses, and the net profit (loss) attributable to equity holders of the parent. Therefore, answers (a), (c), and (d) are incorrect.

109. (c)   The requirement is to identify the item that may not be disclosed on the income statement under IFRS. Answer (c) is correct because gain or loss from extraordinary items is not allowed on an income statement prepared using IFRS. Answers (a), (b), and (d) are items that are disclosed on the income statement.

110. (b)   The requirement is to identify where the finance costs are presented in the statement of cash flows. Answer (b) is correct because under IFRS finance costs (interest expense) may be reported in either the operating or financing section of the statement of cash flows. However, once it is disclosed in a particular section, it must be reported on a consistent basis. Therefore, answers (a), (c), and (d), are incorrect.

111. (d)   The requirement is to identify how the transaction should be reported on the statement of cash flows. Answer (d) is correct because this transaction did not involve an exchange of cash; therefore, it is not included on the statement of cash flows. IFRS requires that significant noncash transactions be reported in the notes to the financial statements. (Note that for US GAAP, if there are only a few significant noncash transactions, they may be reported at the bottom of the statement of cash flows, or they may be reported in a separate schedule in the notes to the financial statements.)

112. (a)   The requirement is to identify how cash advances and loans from bank overdrafts should be reported on the statement of cash flows. Answer (a) is correct because IFRS requires cash advances and loans from bank overdrafts to be classified as operating activities.

113. (b)   The requirement is to identify the acceptable methods for presenting other comprehensive income. Answer (b) is correct because IFRS provides that comprehensive income may be presented in either one statement or in two statements. (US GAAP allows the presentation in all three ways.)

114. (a)   The requirement is to identify the true statement about IFRS requirements for financial statements. Answer (a) is correct because IFRS requires the presentation of prior year financial statements for comparative purposes.

115. (a)   The requirement is to identify the manner in which operating expenses may be classified on the income statement under IFRS. Answer (a) is correct because they may be classified by nature or function.

116. (a)   The requirement is to identify how the statement of cash flows may be presented. Answer (a) is correct because the statement may be presented on the direct or the indirect basis.

Simulations

Task-Based Simulation 1

Concepts		
	Authoritative Literature	**Help**

Situation

Lim Corporation is preparing its financial statements and has given the project to its new entry-level accountant, Sam. Indicate whether each of the following statements made by Sam is True or False.

	True	False
1. The gain or loss from discontinued operations is placed in a separate category under other income or loss.	○	○
2. The gain or loss from infrequent or unusual items is given extraordinary treatment and disclosed on the income statement after discontinued operations.	○	○
3. Exit and disposal activities are classified as discontinued operations.	○	○
4. A component of a company can be classified as discontinued in the first period that it meets the criteria as being held for sale.	○	○
5. A correction of an error is included in the cumulative effect of change in accounting principle on the income statement.	○	○
6. Other comprehensive income may be presented at the bottom of the income statement.	○	○
7. Separate earnings per share amounts must be presented for both other comprehensive income and comprehensive income.	○	○
8. Prospective financial information includes information on the purpose of the statements, assumptions, and significant accounting policies.	○	○

Task-Based Simulation 2

Financial Statement Classification		
	Authoritative Literature	**Help**

The outline presented below represents the various classifications suggested by the chief accountant for the balance sheet.

Assets	**Liabilities**	**Owner's equity**	**Other**
A. Current	G. Current	J. Preferred stock	N. Items excluded from the balance sheet
B. Investments	H. Long-term	K. Common stock	
C. Plant and equipment	I. Other liabilities	L. Paid-in capital excess of par	X. Contra valuation account
D. Intangibles		M. Retained earnings	
E. Deferred charges			
F. Other assets			

Items 1 through 18 represent accounts of the Craven Corporation. Determine how each account would be classified from the list above. If the account is a contra or valuation account, mark "X" before the letter. For example: "Allowance for Doubtful Accounts" would be "X–A." An answer may be selected once, more than once, or not at all.

	Assets (A-F)	Liabilities (G, H, I)	Owner's equity (J, K, L, M)	Other (N or X)
1. Dividend payable (on Craven's preferred stock).				
2. Plant construction in progress by the company.				
3. Factory building (retired from use and held for sale).				
4. Land (held for possible future building site).				
5. Merchandise inventory (held by Craven Corporation on consignment).				
6. Stock dividend distributable (in common stock to common stockholders and to be issued at par).				

	Assets (A-F)	Liabilities (G, H, I)	Owner's equity (J, K, L, M)	Other (N or X)
7. Office supplies inventory.				
8. Sinking fund cash (First National Bank, Trustee).				
9. Installment sales accounts receivable (average collection period eighteen months). All sales are installment sales.				
10. Temporary decline in inventory value.				
11. Advances to officers (indefinite repayment date).				
12. Estimated warranty costs. The warranty costs are for a one-year warranty on parts and labor.				
13. Inventory of small tools used in the business.				
14. Treasury stock under par value method.				
15. Common stock subscribed (Craven Corporation's stock).				
16. Convertible bonds.				
17. Securities held as collateral.				
18. Bank overdraft (only account with bank).				

Task-Based Simulation 3

Balance Sheet		
	Authoritative Literature	Help

Situation

You have been asked to assist the chief accountant of the Stephen King Corporation in the preparation of a balance sheet. Presented below is the balance sheet of Stephen King Corporation for the current year, year 2.

Stephen King Corporation
BALANCE SHEET
December 31, Year 2

Current assets		$ 435,000
Investments		640,000
Property, plant, and equipment		1,720,000
Intangible assets		305,000
		$3,100,000
Current liabilities	$ 330,000	
Long-term liabilities	1,000,000	
Stockholders' equity	1,770,000	
	$3,100,000	

Consider the following information:

1. The current assets section includes: cash $100,000, accounts receivable $170,000 less $10,000 for allowance for doubtful accounts, inventories $180,000, and unearned revenue $5,000. The cash balance is composed of $114,000, less a bank overdraft of $14,000. Inventories are stated on the lower of FIFO cost or market.
2. The investments section includes: the cash surrender value of a life insurance contract $40,000; investment in common stock, short-term (trading) $80,000 and long-term (available-for-sale) $270,000; and bond sinking fund $250,000. The cost and fair value of investments in common stock are the same.
3. Property, plant, and equipment includes: buildings $1,040,000 less accumulated depreciation $360,000; equipment $450,000 less accumulated depreciation $180,000; land $500,000; and land held for future use $270,000.
4. Intangible assets include: a franchise $165,000; goodwill $100,000; and discount on bonds payable $40,000.
5. Current liabilities include: accounts payable $90,000; notes payable—short term $80,000 and long-term $120,000; and taxes payable $40,000.
6. Long-term liabilities are compose solely of 10% bonds payable due in year 11.
7. Stockholders' equity has: preferred stock, no par value, authorized 200,000 shares, issued 70,000 shares for $450,000; and common stock, $1.00 par value, authorized 400,000 shares, issued 100,000 shares at an average price of $10. In addition, the corporation has retained earnings of $320,000.
8. The company's management does not elect to use the fair value option for any of its financial assets or liabilities.

Complete the corrected balance sheet. To make it a more realistic exam experience use Excel.

	A	B	C	D	E
1	**Stephen King Corporation**				
2	**Balance Sheet**				
3	**December 31, year 2**				
4					
5	Current assets:				
6	Cash				
7	Trading securities				
8	Accounts receivable (net of $xxx allowance for doubtful accounts)				
9	Inventories (lower of FIFO cost or market)				
10					
11	Total current assets				
12					
13	Investments:				
14	Available-for-sale securities				
15	Bond sinking fund				
16	Land held for future use				
17	Cash surrender value of life insurance contract				
18					
19	Total investments				
20					
21	Property, plant, and equipment:				
22	Land				
23	Buildings (net of accumulated depreciation of $xxx)				
24	Equipment (net of accumulated depreciation of $xxx)				
25					
26	Total property, plant, and equipment				
27					
28	Intangible assets:				
29	Franchise				
30	Goodwill				
31					
32	Total intangible assets				
33	Total assets				
34					
35	Current liabilities:				
36	Accounts payable				
37	Notes payable				
38	Taxes payable				
39	Bank overdraft				
40	Unearned revenue				
41					
42	Total current liabilities				
43					
44	Long-term liabilities:				
45	Notes payable				
46	Bonds payable, 10% due in year 11 (less discount of $xxx)				
47					
48	Total long-term liabilities				
49	Total liabilities				
50					

	A	B	C	D	E
51	Stockholders' equity:				
52	Paid-in capital				
53	Preferred stock, no par, authorized xxx shares, issued xxx shares				
54	Common stock, $1.00 par value, authorized xxx shares, issued xxx shares				
55	Paid-in capital in excess of par value common				
56					
57	Total paid-in capital				
58					
59	Retained earnings				
60					
61	Total stockholders' equity				
62	Total liabilities and stockholders' equity				

Task-Based Simulation 4

Research		
	Authoritative Literature	Help

Assume that you are assigned to the audit of Russell Corporation. The CFO of Russell is trying to determine how to classify items within comprehensive income. Which section of the Professional Standards addresses the issue of how to classify items in comprehensive income?

Enter your response in the answer fields below.

Task-Based Simulation 5

Journal Entries		
	Authoritative Literature	Help

Situation

Hillside had the following selected account balances as of December 31, year 1.

Accounts receivable	$250,000
Notes receivable	75,000
Prepaid rent	168,000
Supplies	60,000
Inventory	420,000
Equipment (historical cost)	640,000
Accounts payable	176,000
Salaries payable	15,000
Accumulated depreciation	174,000

The following information was received from Hillside's accountant. Adjusting entries have not yet been made.

1. It is estimated that $16,000 of accounts will not be collectible. A provision for uncollectible accounts has never been made by Hillside.
2. Supplies remaining at the end of the year were $37,000.
3. Equipment is depreciated over 20 years with a $60,000 salvage value.
4. Accrued salaries at 12/31/Y1 were $37,500.
5. The note receivable was signed by the customer on November 1, year 1. It is a 6-month note with an interest rate of 12%, with the principle and interest paid at maturity.
6. Rent was paid on August 1, year 1, for 24 months and recorded in a prepaid rent account.
7. Hillside does not elect to use the fair value option for any of its financial assets or liabilities.

Prepare the adjusting journal entries necessary for each item. If no entry is necessary, write "no entry."

Task-Based Simulation 6

Calculations		
	Authoritative Literature	Help

Situation

Hillside had the following selected account balances as of December 31, year 1.

Accounts receivable	$250,000
Notes receivable	75,000
Prepaid rent	168,000
Supplies	60,000
Inventory	420,000
Equipment (historical cost)	640,000
Accounts payable	176,000
Salaries payable	15,000
Accumulated depreciation	174,000

The following information was received from Hillside's accountant. Adjusting entries have not yet been made.

1. It is estimated that $16,000 of accounts will not be collectible. A provision for uncollectible accounts has never been made by Hillside.
2. Supplies remaining at the end of the year were $37,000.
3. Equipment is depreciated over 20 years with a $60,000 salvage value.
4. Accrued salaries at 12/31/Y1 were $37,500.
5. The note receivable was signed by the customer on November 1, year 1. It is a 6-month note with an interest rate of 12%, with the principle and interest paid at maturity.
6. Rent was paid on August 1, year 1, for 24 months and recorded in a prepaid rent account.
7. Hillside does not elect to use the fair value option for any of its financial assets or liabilities.

Determine the adjustments necessary for December 31, and indicate the adjusted balances of the selected accounts at December 31, year 1.

Accounts receivable (net)	
Notes receivable	
Prepaid rent	
Supplies	
Inventory	
Equipment	
Accounts payable	
Salaries payable	
Accumulated depreciation	

Task-Based Simulation 7

Classification/ Disclosures		
	Authoritative Literature	Help

Griffin Co. is in the process of preparing its financial statements for the year ended December 31, year 4.

Items 1 through 6 represent various transactions that occurred during year 4. The following **two** responses are required for each item:

Compute the amount of gain, loss, or adjustment to be reported in Griffin's year 4 financial statements. Disregard income taxes. On the CPA exam, a list of numeric answer choices would be provided to select from.

Select from the list below the financial statement category in which the gain, loss, or adjustment should be presented. A category may be used once, more than once, or not at all.

Financial Statement Categories
A. Income from continuing operations.
B. Extraordinary item.
C. Cumulative effect of change in accounting principle.
D. Prior period adjustment to beginning retained earnings.
E. Separate component of other comprehensive income.

Amount   (A) (B) (C) (D) (E)

1. On June 30, year 4, after paying the semiannual interest due and recording amortization of bond discount, Griffin redeemed its fifteen-year, 8% $1,000,000 par bonds at 102. The bonds, which had a carrying amount of $940,000 on January 1, year 4, had originally been issued to yield 10%. Griffin uses the effective interest method of amortization, and had paid interest and recorded amortization on June 30. Compute the amount of gain or loss on redemption of the bonds and select the proper financial statement category.   _____   ○ ○ ○ ○ ○

2. As of January 1, year 4, Griffin decided to change the method of computing depreciation on its sole piece of equipment from the sum-of-the-years' digits method to the straight-line method. The equipment, acquired in January year 1 for $520,000, had an estimated life of five years and a salvage value of $20,000. Compute the amount of depreciation expense for year 4 and select the proper financial statement category.   _____   ○ ○ ○ ○ ○

3. In October year 4, Griffin paid $375,000 to a former employee to settle a lawsuit out of court. The lawsuit had been filed in year 3, and at December 31, year 3, Griffin recorded a liability from the lawsuit based on legal counsel's estimate that the loss from the lawsuit would be between $250,000 and $750,000. Compute the amount of gain or loss from settlement of the lawsuit and select the proper financial statement category.   _____   ○ ○ ○ ○ ○

4. In November year 4, Griffin purchased two marketable securities, I and II, which it bought and held principally to sell in the near term by February 28, year 5. Relevant data is as follows: _____

	Cost	Fair value 12/31/Y4	2/28/Y5
I	$125,000	$145,000	$155,000
II	235,000	205,000	230,000

○ ○ ○ ○ ○

Compute the amount of holding gain or loss at December 31, year 4, and select the proper financial statement category, assuming Griffin classifies the securities as trading securities.

5. During year 4, Griffin received $1,000,000 from its insurance company to cover losses suffered during a hurricane. This was the first hurricane ever to strike in Griffin's area. The hurricane destroyed a warehouse with a carrying amount of $470,000, containing equipment with a carrying amount of $250,000, and inventory with a carrying amount of $535,000 and a fair value of $600,000. Compute the amount of gain or loss from the financial statement category.   _____   ○ ○ ○ ○ ○

6. At December 31, year 4, Griffin prepared the following worksheet summarizing the translation of its wholly owned foreign subsidiary's financial statements into dollars. Griffin purchased the foreign subsidiary for $324,000 on January 2, year 4. On that date, the carrying amounts of the subsidiary's assets and liabilities equaled their fair values.   _____   ○ ○ ○ ○ ○

	Foreign currency amounts	Applicable exchange rates	Dollars
Net assets January 2, year 4 (date of purchase)	720,000	$.45	$324,000
Net income, year 4	250,000	.42	105,000
Net assets at December 31, year 4	970,000		$429,000
Net assets at December 31, year 4	970,000	.40	$388,000

Compute the amount of the foreign currency translation adjustment and select the proper financial statements category.

Task-Based Simulation 8

Research		
	Authoritative Literature	Help

    Assume that you are assigned to the audit of Jane Corporation. Jane has committed itself to a formal plan for sale of a business component that meets the requirements for presentation as discontinued operations. Which section of the Professional Standards addresses the issue of how to account for the costs that will be incurred to relocate employees of the discontinued component?

    Enter your response in the answer fields below.

Task-Based Simulation 9

Classifications		
	Authoritative Literature	Help

    The illustrations below represent accounting transactions that affect the recognition of income for an accounting period. Their classification is the subject of this objective format matching question.

    For each of the ten illustrations below, select the best classification from those listed A–I below. A classification may be used once, more than once, or not at all.

Classification

A.	Change in reporting entity	F.	Discontinued Operations—Gain or loss from discontin-
B.	Correction of an error		ued operations
C.	Change in accounting principle	G.	Not an accounting change
D.	Change in estimate	H.	Part of net income before extraordinary items
E.	Extraordinary item	I.	Discontinued Operations—Gain or loss on disposal

		(A)	(B)	(C)	(D)	(E)	(F)	(G)	(H)	(I)
1.	Newly acquired assets are depreciated using the sum-of-the-years' digits method, previously recorded assets are depreciated using the straight-line method.	O	O	O	O	O	O	O	O	O
2.	Accounting for acquisition of a 100% owned subsidiary.	O	O	O	O	O	O	O	O	O
3.	Reported as a restatement of all periods presented.	O	O	O	O	O	O	O	O	O
4.	Write-down of inventory due to obsolescence.	O	O	O	O	O	O	O	O	O
5.	Gains or losses on the disposal of the net assets of a component are included in this calculation.	O	O	O	O	O	O	O	O	O
6.	Changing from the gross profit method for determining year-end inventory balances to dollar value LIFO.	O	O	O	O	O	O	O	O	O
7.	Accounting for existing construction contracts is changed from completed contract to percentage-of-completion.	O	O	O	O	O	O	O	O	O
8.	The effects of a change in estimate and a change in principle are inseparable for the same event.	O	O	O	O	O	O	O	O	O
9.	The excess of cash paid over the carrying value to extinguish bonds.	O	O	O	O	O	O	O	O	O
10.	Income or loss of the component for the period of disposal included in this calculation.	O	O	O	O	O	O	O	O	O

Task-Based Simulation 10

Multistep Income Statement		
	Authoritative Literature	Help

Situation

Presented below is information related to American Horse Company for year 2.

Retained earnings balance, January 1, year 2	$ 980,000
Sales for the year	25,000,000
Cost of goods sold	17,000,000
Interest revenue	70,000
Selling and administrative expenses	4,700,000
Write-off of goodwill (not tax deductible)	820,000
Income taxes for year 2	905,000
Gain on the sale of investments (normal recurring)	110,000
Loss due to flood damage—extraordinary item (net of tax)	390,000
Loss on the disposition of the wholesale division	615,000
Loss on operations of the wholesale division	200,000
Income tax benefit from discontinued wholesale division	285,000
Dividends declared on common stock	250,000
Dividends declared on preferred stock	70,000

American Horse Company decided to discontinue its entire wholesale operations and to retain its manufacturing operations. On September 15, American Horse sold the wholesale operations to Rogers Company. During year 2, there were 300,000 shares of common stock outstanding all year.

Prepare a multistep income statement.

American Horse Company **INCOME STATEMENT** *For the Year Ended December 31, Year 2*		
Sales		$25,000,000
Net income		
Earnings per share		
Net income		

Task-Based Simulation 11

Research		
	Authoritative Literature	Help

Assume that you are assigned to the audit of Clark Corporation. Clark has incurred a significant loss that may meet the definition of an extraordinary item. Which section of the Professional Standards provides guidance on the definition of an extraordinary item?

Enter your response in the answer fields below.

Task-Based Simulation 12

Financial Statement Classification		
	Authoritative Literature	Help

Select from the list of financial statement categories below the category in which the item should be presented. A financial statement category may be selected once, more than once, or not at all. Assume management does not elect to use the fair value option for any financial assets or liabilities.

Financial Statement Categories

A. Income from continuing operations, with **no** separate disclosure.
B. Income from continuing operations, with separate disclosure (either on the face of statement or in the notes).
C. Other comprehensive income for the period.
D. Extraordinary items.
E. Separate component of stockholders' equity.
F. None of the above categories include this item.

Item	(A)	(B)	(C)	(D)	(E)	(F)
1. An increase in the unrealized excess of cost over market value of marketable equity securities classified as trading-type securities.	○	○	○	○	○	○
2. The accumulated amount of the unrealized excess of cost over market value of available-for-sale marketable equity securities.	○	○	○	○	○	○
3. Income from operations of a discontinued component in the component's disposal year.	○	○	○	○	○	○
4. A gain on remeasuring a foreign subsidiary's financial statements from the local currency into the functional currency.	○	○	○	○	○	○
5. A loss on translating a foreign subsidiary's financial statements from the functional local currency into the reporting currency during this period.	○	○	○	○	○	○
6. A loss caused by a major earthquake in an area previously considered to be subject to only minor tremors.	○	○	○	○	○	○
7. The probable receipt of $1,000,000 from a pending lawsuit.	○	○	○	○	○	○
8. The purchase of research and development services. There were no other research and development activities.	○	○	○	○	○	○

Task-Based Simulation 13

Calculate Net Income and Earnings Per Share		
	Authoritative Literature	Help

Situation

Rap Corp. has 100,000 shares of common stock outstanding. In year 2, the company reports income from continuing operations before taxes of $1,210,000.

Additional transactions not considered in the $1,210,000 are as follows:

1. In year 2, Rap Corp. sold equipment for $40,000. The machine had originally cost $80,000 and had accumulated depreciation of $36,000. The gain or loss is considered ordinary.
2. The company discontinued operations of one of its subsidiaries during the current year at a loss of $190,000 before taxes. Assume that this transaction meets the criteria for discontinued operations. The loss of operations of the discontinued subsidiary was $90,000 before taxes; the loss from disposal of the subsidiary was $100,000 before taxes.
3. In year 2, the company reviewed its accounts receivable and determined that $26,000 of accounts receivable that had been carried for years appeared unlikely to be collected.
4. An internal audit discovered that amortization of intangible assets was understated by $35,000 (net of tax) in a prior period. The amount was charged against retained earnings.
5. The company sold its only investment in common stock during the year at a gain of $145,000. The gain is taxed at a total effective rate of 40%. Assume that the transaction meets the requirements of an extraordinary item.

Complete the table below for the calculation of net income and earnings per share. Assume the income tax rate is 38% for income from continuing operations.

Rap Corp. INCOME STATEMENT For the Year Ended December 31, Year 2			
Income from continuing operations before income tax			
Income tax			
Income from continuing operations			
Discontinued operations:			
Income before extraordinary item			
Extraordinary item:			
Net income			
Per share of common stock:			
Income from continuing operations			
Discontinued operations, net of tax			
Income before extraordinary item			
Extraordinary item, net of tax			
Net income			

Simulation Solutions

Task-Based Simulation 1

Concepts		
	Authoritative Literature	Help

	True	False
1. The gain or loss from discontinued operations is placed in a separate category under other income or loss.	○	●
2. The gain or loss from infrequent or unusual items is given extraordinary treatment and disclosed on the income statement after discontinued operations.	○	●
3. Exit and disposal activities are classified as discontinued operations.	○	●
4. A component of a company can be classified as discontinued in the first period that it meets the criteria as being held for sale.	●	○
5. A correction of an error is included in the cumulative effect of change in accounting principle on the income statement.	○	●
6. Other comprehensive income may be presented at the bottom of the income statement.	●	○
7. Separate earnings per share amounts must be presented for both other comprehensive income and comprehensive income.	○	●
8. Prospective financial information includes information on the purpose of the statements, assumptions, and significant accounting policies.	●	○

Explanations

1. **(F)** Discontinued operations are placed in a separate category after income from continuing operations and before extraordinary items.

2. **(F)** An item must be **both** infrequent and unusual to be treated as an extraordinary item.

3. **(F)** Exit and disposal activities that are not in connection with a component of the entity that qualifies for discontinued operations or extraordinary treatment should be reported as unusual or infrequent income/loss in income from continuing operations before income taxes.

4. **(T)** A component must be classified as discontinued when it meets the criteria.

5. **(F)** A correction of an error requires restatement of the financial statements.

6. **(T)** Flexibility is allowed for presentation.

7. **(F)** Separate EPS amounts are only required for gains/losses from continuing operations, discontinued operations, extraordinary items, and cumulative effect of accounting changes.

8. **(T)** The notes to prospective financial statements must include those disclosures.

Task-Based Simulation 2

Financial Statement Classification		
	Authoritative Literature	Help

	Assets (A-F)	Liabilities (G, H, I)	Owner's equity (J, K, L, M)	Other (N or X)
1. Dividend payable (on Craven's preferred stock).		G		
2. Plant construction in progress by the company.	C			
3. Factory building (retired from use and held for sale).	F			
4. Land (held for possible future building site).	B			
5. Merchandise inventory (held by Craven Corporation on consignment).				N

		Assets (A-F)	Liabilities (G, H, I)	Owner's equity (J, K, L, M)	Other (N or X)
6.	Stock dividend distributable (in common stock to common stockholders and to be issued at par).			K	
7.	Office supplies inventory.	A			
8.	Sinking fund cash (First National Bank, Trustee).	B			
9.	Installment sales accounts receivable (average collection period eighteen months). All sales are installment sales.	A			
10.	Temporary decline in inventory value.				N
11.	Advances to officers (indefinite repayment date).	F			
12.	Estimated warranty costs. The warranty costs are for a one-year warranty on parts and labor.		G		
13.	Inventory of small tools used in the business.	C			
14.	Treasury stock under par value method.				X-K
15.	Common stock subscribed (Craven Corporation's stock).			K	
16.	Convertible bonds.		H		
17.	Securities held as collateral.				N
18.	Bank overdraft (only account with bank).		G		

Explanations

1. **(G)** When a corporation declares a cash or property dividend, the amount to be paid becomes a liability of the corporation. The dividends payable amount would be classified as a current liability on the balance sheet. It is important to note that dividends payable represent the amount distributed to stockholders as a return on their investment. Dividends are not expenses.

2. **(C)** When an item of property, plant, or equipment is being constructed by the company that intends to use it, all of the relevant costs related to the construction should be included in the asset. The asset would be classified as plant and equipment.

3. **(F)** A factory building that has been retired from use and held for sale should be classified as an **other asset** rather than as property, plant and equipment. The property, plant and equipment account should include only those tangible assets that are being used in operations.

4. **(B)** Land that is held for speculative or investment purposes should be classified as an investment rather than as property, plant, and equipment. The property, plant, and equipment account should represent only those assets being used in current operations.

5. **(N)** Consigned inventory is excluded from the balance sheet because it is not owned by Craven. Consigned inventory represents an arrangement whereby the owner of the goods transfers physical possession to an agent (Craven). The agent (consignee) will attempt to sell the goods on the owner's behalf. The inventory remains an asset of its owner.

6. **(K)** A stock dividend distributable represents a dividend to be distributed to shareholders in the form of additional shares of the corporation's stock. Each shareholder will receive a proportional share of additional stock. The declaration of a stock dividend does not result in a liability, as it does not result in any of the corporation's assets being paid. Thus, a stock dividend distributable would be classified as an addition in the stockholders' equity section in the common stock account.

7. **(A)** Current assets represent cash or other assets that are expected to be used within the operating cycle. Office supplies inventory represents an asset that could be expected to be used within the operating cycle.

8. **(B)** Generally, a fund is a group of assets set aside for a future nonoperating purpose. A sinking fund contains assets to be used in the future to retire bonds. These assets are generally invested while waiting to be used and are noncurrent.

9. **(A)** An installment sales accounts receivable results when the corporation makes a sale to a customer and does not receive payment in full on the date of sale. Since this company normally sells on the installment basis, its operating cycle becomes eighteen months. Its receivables are current assets because their average life falls within the operating cycle.

10. **(N)** Temporary decline in inventory value is a loss and appears on the income statement.

11. **(F)** Advances to officers are considered nontrade receivables. These types of receivables should be reported separately on the balance sheet as other assets.

12. **(G)** A warranty is a guarantee made by the seller to the purchaser against defects in the product's quality. Estimated warranty expense for a given period can be estimated as a percentage of sales. The percentage is based on past warranty experience. The estimated warranty cost represents the warranty expenditures in the future for past sales and is a current liability.

13. **(C)** Property, plant, and equipment consists of items used in the normal operations of a business. The inventory of small tools represents tools **used** in the business and are not for sale.

14. **(X-K)** Treasury stock is a corporation's own stock which has been issued and reacquired by the corporation. Treasury stock may be accounted for under the cost or par value method. When the par value method is used, treasury stock would be recorded on the balance sheet as a reduction or contra to the common stock account.

15. **(K)** Common stock subscribed represents stock subscriptions that have not been fully paid. The stock is not considered to be issued until the full price is paid. This account should be classified as an increase in the common stock and it is offset in stockholders' equity by a contra account for the balance of the subscription due.

16. **(H)** A convertible bond is a bond which may be converted to another form of the corporation's securities during a specified time frame. A bond is typically classified as a long-term liability on the balance sheet.

17. **(N)** Corporations do not own securities they hold as collateral. The corporation will retain the securities only in the event of a default on the receivable the securities are collateralizing. Thus, the securities are excluded from the balance sheet of Craven and they appear on the balance sheets of their owners.

18. **(G)** A bank overdraft occurs when a check is written for a greater amount than the balance in the bank account. A bank overdraft should be classified as a current liability. It should not be offset against other cash account balances unless the cash account is in the same bank.

Task-Based Simulation 3

Balance Sheet		
	Authoritative Literature	Help

	A	B	C	D	E
1	**Stephen King Corporation**				
2	**Balance Sheet**				
3	**December 31, year 2**				
4					
5	Current assets:				
6	Cash				$ 114,000
7	Trading securities				80,000
8	Accounts receivable (net of $10,000 allowance for doubtful accounts)				160,000
9	Inventories (lower of FIFO cost or market)				180,000
10					
11	Total current assets				534,000
12					
13	Investments:				
14	Available-for-sale securities				270,000
15	Bond sinking fund				250,000
16	Land held for future use				270,000
17	Cash surrender value of life insurance contract				40,000
18					
19	Total investments				830,000
20					
21	Property, plant, and equipment:				
22	Land				500,000
23	Buildings (net of accumulated depreciation of $360,000)				680,000
24	Equipment (net of accumulated depreciation of $180,000)				270,000
25					
26	Total property, plant, and equipment				1,450,000
27					
28	Intangible assets:				
29	Franchise				165,000
30	Goodwill				100,000
31					
32	Total intangible assets				265,000
33	Total assets				$3,079,000
34					

	A	B	C	D	E
35	Current liabilities:				
36	Accounts payable		$ 90,000		
37	Notes payable		80,000		
38	Taxes payable		40,000		
39	Bank overdraft		14,000		
40	Unearned revenue		5,000		
41					
42	Total current liabilities		229,000		
43					
44	Long-term liabilities:				
45	Notes payable		120,000		
46	Bonds payable, 10% due in year 11 (less discount of $40,000)		960,000		
47					
48	Total long-term liabilities		1,080,000		
49	Total liabilities		$1,309,000		
50					
51	Stockholders' equity:				
52	Paid-in capital				
53	Preferred stock, no par, authorized 200,000 shares, issued 70,000 shares		450,000		
54	Common stock, $1.00 par value, authorized 40,000 shares, issued 100,000 shares		100,000		
55	Paid-in capital in excess of par value common		900,000		
56					
57	Total paid-in capital		$1,450,000		
58					
59	Retained earnings		320,000		
60					
61	Total stockholders' equity		1,770,000		
62	Total liabilities and stockholders' equity		$3,079,000		

Task-Based Simulation 4

Research

	Authoritative Literature	Help

ASC	220	10	45	13

Task-Based Simulation 5

Journal Entries

	Authoritative Literature	Help

1. Bad debt expense 16,000
    Allowance for uncollectible account 16,000

2. Supplies expense 23,000
    Supplies 23,000
    [remaining = 23,000 (60,000 – 37,000)]

3. Depreciation expense 29,000
    Accumulated depreciation 29,000
    (640,000 – 60,000) ÷ 20 years = 29,000 per year

4. Salary expense 37,500
    Salaries payable 37,500

5. Interest receivable 1,500
    Interest income 1,500
    75,000 × 12% × 2/12 = 1,500

6.   Rent expense   35,000
     Prepaid rent   35,000
     $168,000 \div 24$ mo. = 7,000 per month $\times$ 5 months =
     35,000

Task-Based Simulation 6

Calculations

Authoritative Literature	Help

Accounts receivable (net)	234,000	(1)
Notes receivable	75,000	(2)
Prepaid rent	133,000	(3)
Supplies	37,000	(4)
Inventory	420,000	(5)
Equipment (historical cost)	640,000	(6)
Accounts payable	176,000	(7)
Salaries payable	52,500	(8)
Accumulated depreciation	203,000	(9)

Explanations

1. $250,000 − $16,000 allowance for uncollectible accounts = $234,000

2.   No change. Interest receivable is recorded in a separate account.

3. $168,000 − $35,000 = $133,000

4.   Given in the problem.

5.   No adjustments were made to inventory.

6.   Equipment is at historical cost.

7.   No change.

8. $15,000 + $37,500 = $52,500

9. $174,000 + $29,000 = $203,000

Task-Based Simulation 7

Classification/ Disclosures

Authoritative Literature	Help

1.   **($73,000, A)** The net carrying amount of the bonds redeemed is determined by adjusting the carrying amount of the bonds at the beginning of the year for any partial year amortization of corresponding premiums or discounts and for any unamortized issue costs. In this example, Griffin would determine its discount amortization by computing the difference between its bond interest expense and its bond interest paid as of June 30, year 4.

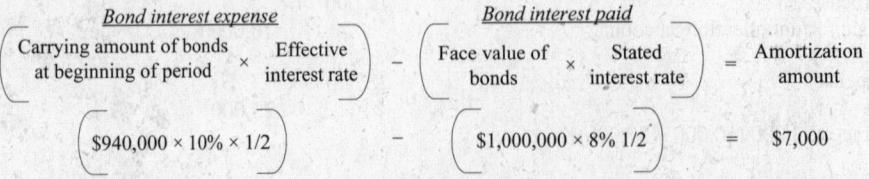

This amount is added to the carrying amount of the bonds at the beginning of the year to determine the net carrying amount: $940,000 + $7,000 = $947,000. This amount is subtracted from the reacquisition price to determine the loss on redemption: $1,020,000 ($1,000,000 × 1.02) − $947,000 = $73,000. Gains or losses from early redemption of bonds are treated as gains or losses in determining net income. Early extinguishment of debt is not generally considered an extraordinary item.

2.   **($50,000, A)** The accounting change is accounted for on a prospective basis. Therefore, it is necessary to calculate the book value of the asset as of the beginning of the year of the change.

SYD

Year 1	$500,000 × 5/15 =	$166,667
Year 2	$500,000 × 4/15 =	$133,333
Year 3	$500,000 × 3/15 =	$100,000
		$400,000

On January 1, year 4, the book value is calculated as follows:

Historical cost	$520,000
– Accumulated depreciation	(400,000)
Book value 1/1/Y4	$120,000

Straight-line depreciation for year 4 and future years is calculated as

($120,000 BV – $20,000 salvage value) ÷ 2 years remaining life = $50,000 per year

The depreciation expense would be shown as a part of the calculation of income from continuing operations.

3. (**[$125,000], A**) Since an accrual was made for Griffin's contingent liability in year 3, one must first determine the amount of the liability recorded. If a range of possible losses exists and no amount within the range is more likely than any other amount, an accrual should be made for the minimum amount of the loss, in this case $250,000. As Griffin accrued a $250,000 liability and loss in year 3, the year 4 loss would be $125,000 ($250,000 – $375,000). Such a loss would be classified under income from continuing operations as it is incurred in conjunction with ordinary operations (amount paid to employee). Such a loss would not be extraordinary as it does not meet the criteria of being both unusual in nature and infrequent in occurrence.

4. (**[$10,000], A**) Trading securities are securities that are bought and held principally for the purpose of selling them in the near term. As Griffin purchased these securities to sell in the near term, any unrealized holding gain or loss would appear as income from continuing operations on the income statement. The holding gain or loss from marketable equity securities held in the trading portfolio is computed as of December 31, year 4, by comparing the cost of the securities at the purchase date with the fair market value at the end of the year.

	Cost	FV 12/31/Y4	Gain (loss)
I	$125,000	$145,000	$ 20,000
II	235,000	205,000	(30,000)
			$(10,000)

5. (**[$255,000], B**) The amount of gain or loss from the hurricane would be computed by adding the carrying amounts of the assets destroyed and comparing this amount with the amount of insurance recovery. For Griffin, an extraordinary loss would result as follows:

Insurance recovery	$1,000,000
Warehouse	470,000
Equipment	250,000
Inventory	535,000
Total carrying value	$1,255,000
Extraordinary loss	$ (255,000)

As this hurricane is unusual in that it is not related to the normal activities of the entity and infrequent in occurrence in that it is not expected to occur again in the foreseeable future (this was the first hurricane ever in Griffin's area), the $255,000 loss would be classified as an extraordinary loss.

6. (**$41,000, E**) To compute the translation adjustment for year 4, both net asset figures in dollars must be compared. The $429,000 represents the translation at the date of purchase plus the translation of net income at a weighted-average exchange rate. The $388,000 represents the net assets at the translated rate at the balance sheet date. The $41,000 difference is the translation adjustment necessary to make the balance sheet balance. This translation adjustment should not be included in net income, but shall be reported as a separate component of other comprehensive income.

Task-Based Simulation 8

Research			
	Authoritative Literature	Help	

ASC	420	10	25	14

Task-Based Simulation 9

Classifications	
Authoritative Literature	**Help**

		(A)	(B)	(C)	(D)	(E)	(F)	(G)	(H)	(I)
1.	Newly acquired assets are depreciated using the sum-of-the-years' digits method; previously recorded assets are depreciated using the straight-line method.	○	○	○	○	○	○	●	○	○
2.	Accounting for the acquisition of a 100% owned subsidiary.	●	○	○	○	○	○	○	○	○
3.	Reported as a restatement of all periods presented.	○	●	○	○	○	○	○	○	○
4.	Write-down of inventory due to obsolescence.	○	○	○	○	○	○	○	●	○
5.	Gains or losses on the disposal of the net assets of a component are included in this calculation.	○	○	○	○	○	○	○	○	●
6.	Changing from the gross profit method for determining year-end inventory balances to dollar value LIFO.	○	●	○	○	○	○	○	○	○
7.	Accounting for existing construction contracts is changed from completed contract to percentage-of-completion.	○	○	●	○	○	○	○	○	○
8.	The effects of a change in estimate and a change in principle are inseparable for the same event.	○	○	○	●	○	○	○	○	○
9.	The excess of cash paid over the carrying value to extinguish bonds.	○	○	○	○	○	○	○	●	○
10.	Income or loss of the component for the period of disposal included in this calculation.	○	○	○	○	○	●	○	○	○

Explanations

1.   (G) The acquisition of assets does not necessitate that the same method of depreciation be used for the newly acquired assets as for the existing assets. Therefore, no change in accounting principle has occurred because the previously recorded assets will continue to be depreciated using the straight-line method.

2.   (A) Accounting for the acquisition of a 100% owned subsidiary is properly accounted for as a change in reporting entity.

3.   (B) All corrections of errors should be treated as a restatement of the prior period financial statements. This requires prompt recording of the error in the year in which the error was discovered, and reporting the effects of the error in the financial statements as an adjustment to the carrying value of the assets and liabilities as of the beginning of the first period presented with an offsetting adjustment to the opening balance of retained earnings for that period. Financial statements for each individual period are adjusted to reflect the correction of the period-specific effects of the error.

4.   (H) For an item to qualify as an extraordinary item it must be both unusual in nature and infrequent in occurrence. Clearly, the write-down of inventory due to obsolescence does not qualify for extraordinary treatment; therefore, it should be disclosed separately in the income statement before extraordinary items.

5.   (I) Gains or losses on the disposal of net assets is included in the calculation of gain or loss on disposal of discontinued operations. Therefore, the total gain or loss on disposal should consist of the following two calculations: the net asset gain or loss mentioned above and the income or loss from operations from the measurement date to the disposal date (the phaseout period).

6.   (B) The use of the gross profit method to determine year-end inventory balances is not proper GAAP. Therefore, if a situation such as this existed, it should be treated as a correction of an error.

7.   (C) The change from one generally accepted accounting principle to another is considered a change in accounting principle. Since both the completed contract method and the percentage-of-completion methods are recognized GAAP, the change from one to the other is properly accounted for as a change in accounting principle, and accounted for on a retrospective basis.

8.   (D) When it is impossible to determine whether a change in accounting principle or a change in estimate has occurred, the change should be considered as a change in estimate.

9.   (H) Gains or losses on extinguishment of debt are no longer treated as extraordinary items.

10.   (F) Income or loss from operations is properly included in the calculation of the gain or loss on the discontinued operations. Therefore, this calculation includes both the income or loss from operations and the gain or loss on the disposal of net assets. The gain or loss on the disposal should also be disclosed parenthetically or in the notes to the financial statements.

Task-Based Simulation 10

Multistep Income Statement		
	Authoritative Literature	Help

American Horse Company INCOME STATEMENT For the Year Ended December 31, Year 1		
Sales		$ 25,000,000
Less cost of goods sold		(17,000,000)
Gross profit		$ 8,000,000
Less selling and administrative expenses		(4,700,000)
Income from operations		$ 3,300,000
Other revenue and gains		
Interest revenue	$ 70,000	
Gain on the sale of investments	110,000	$180,000
Other expenses and losses		
Write-off of goodwill		(820,000)
Income from continuing operations before income taxes		$ 2,660,000
Income taxes		(905,000)
Income from continuing operations		$ 1,755,000
Discontinued operations		
Loss on discontinued wholesale division, including loss on disposal of $200,000	$815,000	
Income tax benefit	(285,000)	
Loss on discontinued operation (net of tax)		(530,000)
Income before extraordinary item		$ 1,225,000
Extraordinary loss from flood damage, net of tax		(390,000)
Net income		$ 835,000
Earnings per share		
Income from continuing operations		$ 5.62[a]
Discontinued operations:		(1.77)
Income before extraordinary item		3.85[b]
Extraordinary loss (net of tax)		(1.30)
Net income		$ 2.55[c]

a $\dfrac{\$1,755,000 - \$70,000}{300,000 \text{ shares}} = \$5.62$

b $\dfrac{\$1,225,000 - \$70,000}{300,000 \text{ shares}} = \$3.85$

c $\dfrac{\$835,000 - \$70,000}{300,000 \text{ shares}} = \$2.55$

Task-Based Simulation 11

Research		
	Authoritative Literature	Help

ASC	225	20	45	2

Task-Based Simulation 12

Financial Statement Classification		
	Authoritative Literature	Help

		(A)	(B)	(C)	(D)	(E)	(F)
1.	An increase in the unrealized excess of cost over market value of marketable equity securities classified as trading-type securities.	○	●	○	○	○	○
2.	The accumulated amount of the unrealized excess of cost over market value of available-for-sale marketable equity securities.	○	○	○	○	●	○
3.	Income from operations of a discontinued component in the component's disposal year.	○	○	○	○	○	●
4.	A gain on remeasuring a foreign subsidiary's financial statements from the local currency into the functional currency.	○	●	○	○	○	○
5.	A loss on translating a foreign subsidiary's financial statements from the functional local currency into the reporting currency during this period.	○	○	●	○	○	○
6.	A loss caused by a major earthquake in an area previously considered to be subject to only minor tremors.	○	○	○	●	○	○
7.	The probable receipt of $1,000,000 from a pending lawsuit.	○	○	○	○	○	●
8.	The purchase of research and development services. There were no other research and development activities.	○	●	○	○	○	○

Explanations

1. **(B)** Changes in the market value of (trading type) marketable securities shall be included in the determination of income from continuing operations of the period in which the change in market value occurs.

2. **(E)** The accumulated changes in the valuation (unrealized excess of cost over market value) of **available-for-sale** marketable equity securities shall be reported as accumulated other comprehensive income.

3. **(F)** Results of operations of a component that has been or will be discontinued should be reported **separately** as a component of income, after income from continuing operations but before extraordinary items.

4. **(B)** A foreign subsidiary must **remeasure** its financial statements when its functional currency (the currency of the primary economic environment in which the entity operates) is different from its local currency (the currency currently used by the entity). The effect of the remeasurement process (gain or loss) should be recognized currently in income. Aggregate gain or loss for the period should also be disclosed either in the financial statements or in the notes.

5. **(C)** When translating a foreign subsidiary's financial statements from functional currency to reporting currency, a translation adjustment will result. The translation adjustment is not included in net income but is reported as a component of comprehensive income and called other comprehensive income.

6. **(D)** Extraordinary items are events and transactions that are **both** unusual and infrequent. The earthquake in this problem occurred in an area previously considered subject to only minor tremors. Therefore, the earthquake would be considered an extraordinary event. Extraordinary items should be shown separately on the income statement, after income from continuing operations.

7. **(F)** The question indicates that it is probable that the company will **receive** $1,000,000 from a pending lawsuit. Thus, the $1,000,000 is a **gain** contingency. Contingencies that may result in **gains** are not reflected in the accounts, as doing so might result in the recognition of revenue before its realization. Adequate disclosure of the gain contingency should be made, but care should be taken to avoid misleading implications as to the likelihood of realization.

8. **(B)** The cost of research and development services performed by others on behalf of the enterprise are included in R&D costs. R&D costs are charged to expense when incurred and thus are included in income from continuing operations of that period. In addition, separate disclosure of the total R&D costs for the period should be made either in the financial statements or in the notes.

Task-Based Simulation 13

Calculate Net Income and Earnings Per Share	Authoritative Literature	Help

Rap Corp. INCOME STATEMENT For the Year Ended December 31, Year 2			
Income from continuing operations before income tax		$1,180,000	
Income tax		(448,400)	
Income from continuing operations		$ 731,600	
Discontinued operations:			
Loss from discontinued operations (including loss from disposal of $100,000)	$(190,000)		
Income tax benefit	72,200		
Loss from discontinued operations (net of tax)		117,800	
Income before extraordinary item		$ 613,800	
Extraordinary item:			
Gain on sale of investment	145,000		
Less applicable taxes	58,000	87,000	
Net income		$ 700,800	
Per share of common stock:			
Income from continuing operations		$ 7.32	
Discontinued operations, net of tax		(1.18)	
Income before extraordinary item		6.14	
Extraordinary item, net of tax		0.87	
Net income ($700,800/100,000)		$ 7.01	

Module 10: Inventory

Overview

Inventory is defined as tangible personal property (1) held for sale in the ordinary course of business, (2) in the process of production for such sale, or (3) to be used currently in the production of items for sale.

Inventory is tested on the Financial Accounting and Reporting section of the exam. The primary topics covered by questions on the exam are

1. **Ownership of goods:** The determination of which items are to be included in inventory taking into account items such as shipping terms and consignments.
2. **Cost:** The determination of which costs are to be assigned to inventory such as freight and overhead.
3. **Cost flow assumptions:** The determination of costs assigned to cost of goods sold and inventory under the various cost flow methods such as LIFO and FIFO.
4. **Valuation:** The determination of how and when inventories should reflect their market values using rules such as LCM.

A. Determining Inventory and Cost of Goods Sold

1. The primary basis of accounting for inventories is cost, which includes the cash or other fair value of consideration given in exchange for it. Inventory cost is a function of two variables

   a. The number of units included in inventory, and
   b. The costs attached to those units.

2. The units to be included in inventory are those which the firm owns; ownership is usually determined by legal title.
3. The costs to be included in inventory include all costs necessary to prepare the goods for sale. Normal costs for freight-in, handling costs, and normal spoilage are included in inventory.

   a. For a manufacturing entity, the cost of inventory includes direct materials, direct labor, and both direct and indirect factory overhead. These costs are then allocated to the work in progress and finished goods inventory account. Variable production overhead is allocated to each unit of production based on the actual use of the production facilities. Fixed overhead is allocated based on the normal capacity of the production facilities. The normal capacity of the production facility is the production expected to be achieved over a number of periods or seasons under normal circumstances, taking into account the loss of capacity resulting from planned maintenance. The range of normal capacity will vary based on business and industry-specific factors. The actual level of production may be used if it approximates normal capacity. Unallocated fixed overhead costs are recognized as an expense in the period in which they are incurred.

      (1) Any abnormal costs for freight-in, handling costs, and spoilage are treated as current period expenses, and are not allocated to inventory.
      (2) Interest on inventories routinely produced, or repetitively produced in large quantities, is not capitalized as part of inventory cost.

   b. For a merchandising concern, the costs to be included in inventory include the purchase price of the goods, freight-in, insurance, warehousing, and any other costs incurred in the preparation of these goods for sale. The amount used as a purchase price for the goods will vary depending upon whether the gross or net method is used in the recording of purchases.

      (1) If the gross method is used to record the purchases, then any subsequent discount taken is shown as purchase discount which is netted against the purchases account in determining cost of goods sold.

(2) If the net method is used to record purchases, then any purchase discounts offered are assumed taken and the purchase account reflects the net price. If subsequent to the recording of the purchases the discount is not taken (i.e., payment is tendered after the discount period has elapsed), a purchase discounts lost account is debited. The balance in the purchase discounts lost account does **not** enter into the determination of cost of goods sold; this amount is treated as a period expense.

> **NOTE:** Regardless of the method used, purchases are always recorded net of any allowable **trade discounts**. These are discounts that are allowed to the entity because of its being a wholesaler, a good customer, or merely the fact that the item is on sale at a reduced price.

> **NOTE:** Interest paid to vendors is not included in the cost of inventory.

4. The determination of cost of goods sold and inventory under each of the cost flow assumptions depends upon the method used to record the inventory: periodic or perpetual.

   a. **Periodic system.** Inventory is counted periodically and then priced. The ending inventory is usually recorded in the cost of goods sold (CGS) entry.

Ending inventory (EI)	xx	
CGS	(plug)	
Beginning inventory (BI)		xx
Purchases		xx

   (1) CGS = Purchases – (the change in inventory). For example, if ending inventory decreases, all of the purchases and some of the beginning inventory have been sold. If ending inventory increases, not all of the purchases have been sold.

   b. **Perpetual system.** A running total is kept of the units on hand (and possibly their value) by recording all increases and decreases as they occur. When inventory is purchased, the inventory account, rather than purchases, is debited. As inventory is sold, the following entry is recorded.

CGS	(cost)	
Inventory		(cost)

NOW REVIEW MULTIPLE-CHOICE QUESTIONS 1 THROUGH 13

B. Inventory Valuation and Cost-Flow Methods

1. Specific identification	8. Last-in, first-out (LIFO)
2. Weighted-average	9. Dollar-value LIFO
3. Simple average	10. Gross profit
4. Moving average	11. Standard costs
5. Lower of cost or market	12. Direct (variable) costing
6. Losses on purchase commitments	13. Market
7. First-in, first-out (FIFO)	14. Cost apportionment by relative sales value

1. Specific Identification

   a. The seller determines which item is sold.

> **EXAMPLE**
>
> A seller has for sale four identical machines costing $260, $230, $180, and $110. Since the machines are identical, a purchaser will have no preference as to which machine s/he receives when purchased.

> **NOTE:** The seller is able to manipulate income as s/he can sell any machine (and charge the appropriate amount to CGS). Significant dollar value items are frequently accounted for by specific identification.

   b. The use of the specific identification method is appropriate when there is a relatively small number of significant dollar value items in inventory.

2. Weighted-Average

a. The seller averages the cost of all items on hand and purchased during the period. The units in ending inventory and units sold (CGS) are costed at this average cost.

EXAMPLE

	Cost	Units	
Beginning inventory	$200	100	($2.00 unit)
Purchase 1	315	150	($2.10 unit)
Purchase 2	85	50	($1.70 unit)
	$600	300	

Weighted-average cost $600/300 = $2.00 unit

---

3. Simple Average

a. The seller does not weight the average for units purchased or in beginning inventory (e.g., the above $2.00, $2.10, and $1.70 unit costs would be averaged to $1.93).

b. The method is fairly accurate if all purchases, production runs, and beginning inventory quantities are equal.

4. Moving Average

a. The average cost of goods on hand must be recalculated any time additional inventory is purchased at a unit cost different from the previously calculated average cost of goods on hand.

EXAMPLE

	Dollar cost of units on hand	Units on hand	Inventory unit cost
Beginning inventory	$200	100	$2.00
Sale of 50 units @ $2.00 = $100	100	50	2.00
Purchase of 150 units for $320	420	200	2.10
Sale of 50 units @ $2.10 = $105	315	150	2.10
Purchase of 50 units for $109	424	200	2.12

NOTE: Sales do not change the unit price because they are taken out of inventory at the average price.

b. Moving average may only be used with perpetual systems which account for changes in value with each change in inventory (and not with perpetual systems only accounting for changes in the number of units).

NOW REVIEW MULTIPLE-CHOICE QUESTIONS 14 THROUGH 17

---

5. Lower of Cost or Market

a. "A departure from the cost basis of pricing the inventory is required when the utility of the goods is no longer as great as its cost." The following steps should be used to apply the lower of cost or market rule:

(1) Determine market

(a) Market is replacement cost limited to

1] **Ceiling**—which is net realizable value (selling price less selling costs and costs to complete).
2] **Floor**—which is net realizable value less normal profit.

NOTE: If replacement cost is greater than net realizable value, market equals net realizable value. Likewise, market equals net realizable value minus normal profit if replacement cost is less than net realizable value minus normal profit.

(2) Determine cost

NOTE: The floor and ceiling have nothing to do with cost

(3) Select the lower of cost or market either for each individual item or for inventory as a whole (compute total market and total cost, and select lower).

EXAMPLE

LOWER OF COST OR MARKET EXAMPLE

Item	Cost	Replacement cost	Selling price	Selling cost	Normal profit
A	$10.50	$10.25	$15.00	$2.50	$2.50
B	5.75	5.25	8.00	1.50	1.00
C	4.25	4.75	5.50	1.00	1.50

Item	Replacement cost	NRV (ceiling)	NRV-Profit (floor)	Designated market value	Cost	LCM
A	$10.25	$12.50	$10.00	$10.25	$10.50	$10.25
B	5.25	6.50	5.50	5.50	5.75	5.50
C	4.75	4.50	3.00	4.50	4.25	4.25

Item A—Market is replacement cost, $10.25, because it is between the floor ($10.00) and the ceiling ($12.50). Lower of cost or market is $10.25.

Item B—Market is limited to the floor, $5.50 ($8.00 – $1.50 – $1.00) because the $5.25 replacement cost is beneath the floor. Lower of cost or market is $5.50.

Item C—Market is limited to the ceiling, $4.50 ($5.50 – $1.00) because the $4.75 replacement cost is above the ceiling. Lower of cost or market is $4.25.

---

b. Observations about the lower of cost or market rule

(1) The floor limitation on market prevents recognition of more than normal profit in future periods (if market is less than cost).
(2) The ceiling limitation on market prevents recognition of a loss in future periods (if market is less than cost).
(3) Cost or market applied to individual items will always be as low as, and usually lower than, cost or market applied to the inventory as a whole. They will be the same when all items at market or all items at cost are lower.
(4) Once inventory has been written down there can be no recovery from the write-down until the units are sold. Recall that this differs from marketable securities where recoveries of prior write-downs are required to be taken into the income stream.

c. Methods of recording the write-down

(1) If market is less than cost at the end of any period, there are two methods available to record the market decline. The entry to establish the ending inventory can be made using the market figure. The difficulty with this procedure is that it forces the loss to be included in the cost of goods sold, thus overstating the cost of goods sold by the amount of the loss.

NOTE: Under this method the loss is not separately disclosed.

(2) An alternative treatment is to debit the inventory account for the actual cost (not market) of goods on hand, and then to make the following entry to give separate recognition to the market decline.

Loss due to market decline   xx
    Inventory   xx

NOW REVIEW MULTIPLE-CHOICE QUESTIONS 18 THROUGH 22

6. **Losses on Purchase Commitments**

a. **Purchase commitments** (PC) result from legally enforceable contracts to purchase specific quantities of goods at fixed prices in the future. When there is a decline in market value below the contract price at the balance sheet date and the contracts are noncancellable, an unrealized loss has occurred and, if material, should be recorded in the period of decline.

Estimated loss on PC   (excess of PC over mkt.)
    Accrued loss on PC   (excess of PC over mkt.)

b. If further declines in market value are estimated to occur before delivery is made, the amount of the loss to be accrued should be increased to include this additional decline in market value. The loss is taken to the income statement; the accrued loss on PC is a liability account and shown on the balance sheet.

When the goods are subsequently received

Purchases	xx	
Accrued loss on PC	xx	
Cash		xx

c. If a partial or full recovery occurs before the inventory is received, the accrued loss account would be reduced by the amount of the recovery. Likewise, an income statement account, "Recovery on Loss of PC," would be credited.

> **NOW REVIEW MULTIPLE-CHOICE QUESTIONS 23 THROUGH 24**

7. First-In, First-Out (FIFO)

a. The goods from beginning inventory and the earliest purchases are assumed to be the goods sold first.
b. In a period of rising prices, cost of goods sold is made up of the earlier, lower-priced goods resulting in a larger profit (relative to LIFO). The ending inventory is made up of more recent purchases and thus represents a more current value (relative to LIFO) on the balance sheet.

> **NOTE:** This cost-flow assumption may be used even when it does not match the physical flow of goods.

c. Whenever the FIFO method is used, the results of inventory and cost of goods sold are the same at the end of the period under either a perpetual or a periodic system.

8. Last-In, First-Out (LIFO)

a. Under this cost-flow method, the most recent purchases are assumed to be the first goods sold; thus, ending inventory is assumed to be composed of the oldest goods. Therefore, the cost of goods sold contains relatively current costs (resulting in the matching of current costs with sales).

> **NOTE:** This cost-flow assumption usually does not parallel the physical flow of goods.

b. LIFO is widely adopted because it is acceptable for tax purposes and because in periods of rising prices it reduces tax liability due to the lower reported income (resulting from the higher cost of goods sold).
c. LIFO smoothes out fluctuations in the income stream relative to FIFO because it matches current costs with current revenues.
d. A primary disadvantage of LIFO is that it results in large profits if inventory decreases because earlier, lower valued layers are included in the cost of goods sold. This is generally known as a LIFO liquidation.

   (1) Another disadvantage is the cost involved in maintaining separate LIFO records for each item in inventory.

e. If LIFO is used for tax purposes, it must be used for financial reporting purposes. This is known as the **LIFO conformity rule**.

   (1) Under current tax law, inventory layers may be added using the (1) earliest acquisition costs, (2) weighted-average unit cost for the period, or (3) latest acquisition costs.

> **NOTE:** In solving questions on the CPA Exam, use the earliest acquisition costs unless you are instructed to use one of the other alternatives.

f. When a company uses LIFO for external reporting purposes and another inventory method for internal purposes, a **LIFO Reserve** account is used to reduce inventory from the internal valuation to the LIFO valuation. LIFO Reserve is a contra account to inventory, and is adjusted up or down at year-end with a corresponding increase or decrease to **Cost of Goods Sold**.

9. Dollar-Value LIFO

a. Dollar-value LIFO is LIFO applied to **pools** of inventory items rather than to **individual** items. Thus, the cost of keeping inventory records is less under dollar-value LIFO than under unit LIFO.

(1) Because the LIFO conformity rule (if LIFO is used for tax, it must also be used for external financial state- ments) also applies to dollar-value LIFO, companies using dollar-value LIFO define their LIFO pools so as to conform with IRS regulations.

(2) Under these regulations, a LIFO pool can contain all of the inventory items for a natural business unit, or a multiple pool approach can be elected whereby a business can group similarly used inventory items into several groups or pools.

b. The advantage of using inventory pools is that an involuntary liquidation of LIFO layers is less likely to occur because of the increased number of items in the pool (if the level of one item decreases it can be offset by in- creases in the levels of other items), and because the pools can be adjusted for changes in product composition or product mix.

c. Like unit LIFO, dollar-value LIFO is a layering method. Unlike unit LIFO, dollar-value LIFO determines in- creases or decreases in ending inventory in terms of dollars of the same purchasing power rather than in terms of units. Dollar-value LIFO seeks to determine the real dollar change in inventory.

(1) Ending inventory is deflated to base-year cost by dividing ending inventory by the current year's conversion price index and comparing the resulting amount with the beginning inventory, which has also been stated in base-year dollars. The difference represents the layer which, after conversion, must be added or subtracted to arrive at the appropriate value of ending inventory.

> **NOTE:** The individual layers in a dollar-value LIFO inventory are valued as follows:
>
> $ value LIFO = Inventory at base-year prices × Conversion price index

d. In applying dollar-value LIFO, manufacturers develop their own indexes while retailers and wholesalers use published figures. In computing the conversion price index, the **double-extension technique** is used, named so because each year the ending inventory is extended at both base-year prices and current-year prices. The index, computed as follows, measures the change in the inventory prices since the base year.

$$\frac{\text{EI at end-of-year prices}}{\text{EI at base-year prices}} = \text{Conversion price index}$$

EXAMPLE

To illustrate the computation of the index, assume that the base-year price of products A and B is $3 and $5, respectively, and at the end of the year, the price of product A is $3.20 and B, $5.75, with 2,000 and 800 units on hand, respectively. The index for the year is 110%, computed as follows:

	EI at end-of-year prices	÷	EI at base-year prices	=	Conversion price index
Product A	2,000 @ $3.20 = $ 6,400		2,000 @ $3 = $ 6,000		
Product B	800 @ $5.75 = $ 4,600		800 @ $5 = $ 4,000		
	$11,000		$10,000		1.10 (or 110%)

---

e. Steps in dollar-value LIFO

Manufacturers	**Retailers and wholesalers**
1. Compute the conversion price index	1. Determine index from appropriate pub- lished source
2. Compare BI at base-year prices to EI at base-year prices to determine the	2. Divide EI by conversion price index to restate to base-year prices
a. New inventory layer added, or b. Old inventory layer removed (LIFO liquidation)	3. Same as 2 for manufacturers
3. If there is an increase at base-year prices, value this new layer by multiplying the layer (stated in base-year dollars) by the conversion price index. If there is a de- crease at base-year prices, the remaining layers are val- ued at the index in effect when the layer was first added.	4. Same as 3 for manufacturers

EXAMPLE

Assume the following:

	EI at end-of-year prices	+	Conversion price index	=	EI at base-year prices		Change as measured in base-year dollars
Year 1 (base)	$100,000		1.00		$100,000		
Year 2	121,000		1.10		110,000	>	$10,000
Year 3	150,000		1.20		125,000	>	15,000
Year 4	135,000		1.25		108,000	>	(17,000)

In both year 2 and year 3, ending inventory in terms of base-year dollars increased 10,000 and 15,000 base-year dollars, respectively. Since layers are added every year that ending inventory at base-year prices is greater than the previous year's ending inventory at base-year prices, the ending inventory for year 3 would be computed as follows:

Ending inventory, Year 3

	Base-year prices	×	Index	=	EI at dollar-value LIFO cost
Year 1 (base)	$100,000		1.00		$100,000
Year 2 layer	10,000		1.10		11,000
Year 3 layer	15,000		1.20		18,000
Ending inventory	$125,000				$129,000

NOTE: Each layer added is multiplied by the conversion price index in effect when the layer was added. Thus, the year 2 layer is multiplied by the year 2 index of 1.10 and the year 3 layer is multiplied by the year 3 index of 1.20.

In year 4, ending inventory decreased by 17,000 base-year dollars. Therefore, a LIFO liquidation has occurred whereby 17,000 base-year dollars will have to be removed from the previous year's ending inventory. Because LIFO is being used, the liquidation affects the most recently added layer first and then, if necessary, the next most recently added layer(s). Ending inventory in year 4 is composed of

	Base-year prices	×	Index	=	EI at dollar-value LIFO cost
Year 1 (base)	$100,000		1.00		$100,000
Year 2 layer	8,000		1.10		8,800
Ending inventory	$108,000				$108,800

NOTE: The liquidation of 17,000 base-year dollars in year 4 caused the entire year 3 layer of 15,000 base-year dollars to be liquidated as well as 2,000 base-year dollars from year 2. Also note that the remaining 8,000 base-year dollars in the year 2 layer is still multiplied by the year 2 index of 1.10.

f. **Link-chain technique.** The computations for application of the double-extension technique can become very arduous even if only a few items exist in the inventory. Also, consider the problems that arise when there is a constant change in the inventory mix or in situations in which the breadth of the inventory is large.

(1) The link-chain method was originally developed for (and limited to) those companies that wanted to use LIFO but, because of a substantial change in product lines over time, were unable to recreate or keep the historical records necessary to make accurate use of the double-extension method.

(2) The link-chain method is the process of developing a single cumulative index. Technological change is allowed for by the method used to calculate each current year index. The index is derived by double extending a representative sample (generally thought to be between 50% and 75% of the dollar value of the pool) at both beginning-of-year prices and end-of-year prices. This annual index is then applied (multiplied) to the previous period's cumulative index to arrive at the new current year cumulative index.

EXAMPLE

How the links and cumulative index are computed.

End of period	Ratio of end of period prices to beginning prices*	Cumulative index number**
0	--	1.000
1	1.10	1.100
2	1.05	1.155
3	1.07	1.236

$$* \quad \frac{\text{End of period prices}}{\text{Beginning of period prices}} = \text{Index number for \textbf{this period only}}$$

** Multiply the cumulative index number at the beginning of the period by the ratio computed with the formula shown above.

(a) The ending inventory is divided by the cumulative index number to derive the ending inventory at base period prices. An increase (layer) in base period dollars for the period is priced using the newly derived index number.

> **NOW REVIEW MULTIPLE-CHOICE QUESTIONS 25 THROUGH 35**

10. Gross Profit

a. Ending inventory is estimated by using the gross profit (GP) percentage to convert sales to cost of goods presumed sold.

b. Since ending inventory is only estimated, the gross method is not acceptable for either tax or annual financial reporting purposes.

c. Its major uses are to estimate ending inventory for internal use, for use in interim financial statements, and for establishing the amount of loss due to the destruction of inventory by fire, flood, or other catastrophes.

EXAMPLE

Suppose the inventory of the Luckless Company has been destroyed by fire and the following information is available from duplicate records stored at a separate facility: beginning inventory of $30,000, purchases for the period of $40,000, sales of $60,000, and an average GP percentage of 25%. The cost of the inventory destroyed is computed as follows:

	Beginning inventory	$30,000
+	Purchases	40,000
	Goods available	70,000
−	Cost of goods sold	45,000*
	Inventory destroyed	$25,000

* Cost of goods sold is computed as (1) sales of $60,000 − ($60,000 × 25%) or (2) sales of $60,000 × 75%.

---

d. If you need to convert a GP rate on cost to a markup (MU) rate on the selling price, divide the GP rate on cost by 1 **plus** the GP rate on cost, that is, if the GP rate on cost is 50%, then .50/(1 + .50) = 33 1/3% is the MU rate on the selling price.

e. If you need to convert a MU rate on the selling price to a GP rate on cost, divide the MU rate on the selling price by 1 **minus** the MU rate on the selling price, that is, if the MU rate on the selling price is 20%, then .20/(1 − .20) = 25% GP rate on cost.

f. Always be cautious about gross profit rates (on cost or the selling price).

11. Standard Costs

a. Standard costs are predetermined costs in a cost accounting system, generally used for control purposes.

b. Inventory may be costed at standard only if variances are reasonable (i.e., not large).

(1) Large debit (unfavorable) variances would indicate inventory (and cost of sales) were undervalued, whereas large credit (favorable) variances would indicate inventory is overvalued.

12. **Direct (Variable) Costing**

   a. Direct costing is not an acceptable method for valuing inventory (ARB 43, chap 4).
   b. Direct costing considers only variable costs as product costs and fixed production costs as period costs. In contrast, absorption costing considers both variable and fixed manufacturing costs as product costs.

13. **Market**

   a. Inventory is usually valued at market value when market is lower than cost. However, occasionally, inventory will be valued at market even if it is above cost. This usually occurs with

   (1) Precious metals with a fixed market value
   (2) Industries such as meatpacking where costs cannot be allocated and

      (a) Quoted market prices exist
      (b) Goods are interchangeable (e.g., agricultural commodities)

14. **Cost Apportionment by Relative Sales Value**

   a. Basket purchases and similar situations require cost allocation based on relative value.

   > **EXAMPLE**
   >
   > A developer may spend $400,000 to acquire land, survey, curb and gutter, pave streets, etc. for a subdivision. Due to location and size, the lots may vary in selling price. If the total of all selling prices were $600,000, the developer could cost each lot at 2/3 (400/600; COST/RETAIL ratio) of its selling price.

   NOW REVIEW MULTIPLE-CHOICE QUESTIONS 36 THROUGH 37

C. Items to Include in Inventory

1. Goods shipped FOB shipping point which are in transit should be included in the inventory of the buyer since title passes to the buyer when the carrier receives the goods.
2. Goods shipped FOB destination should be included in the inventory of the seller until the goods are received by the buyer since title passes to the buyer when the goods are received at their final destination.

   NOTE: The more complicated UCC rules concerning transfer of title should be used for the law portion, not the financial accounting and reporting portion, of the exam.

D. Consignments

1. Consignors consign their goods to consignees who are sales agents of the consignors. Consigned goods remain the property of the consignor until sold. Therefore, any unsold goods (including a proportionate share of freight costs incurred in shipping the goods to the consignee) must be included in the consignor's inventory.
2. Consignment sales revenue should be recognized by the consignor when the consignee sells the consigned goods to the ultimate customer. Therefore, no revenue is recognized at the time the consignor ships the goods to the consignee.

   NOTE: Sales commission made by the consignee would be reported as a selling expense by the consignor and would **not** be netted against the sales revenue recognized by the consignor.

   NOTE: The UCC rules concerning consignments should be used for the law portion, not the financial accounting and reporting portion, of the exam.

E. Ratios
The two ratios below relate to inventory.

1. **Inventory turnover**—Measures the number of times inventory was sold and reflects inventory order and investment policies

$$\frac{\text{Cost of goods sold}}{\text{Average inventory}}$$

2. **Number of days' supply in average inventory**—Number of days inventory is held before sale; reflects on efficiency of inventory policies

$$\frac{365}{\text{Inventory turnover}}$$

NOW REVIEW MULTIPLE-CHOICE QUESTIONS 38 THROUGH 50

F. Long-Term Construction Contracts

1. Long-term contracts are accounted for by two methods: completed-contract method and percentage-of-completion method.

   a. **Completed-contract method**—Recognition of contract revenue and profit at contract completion. All related costs are deferred until completion and then matched to revenues.

      (1) The completed-contract method is preferable in circumstances in which estimates cannot meet the criteria for reasonable dependability or one of the above conditions does not exist.
      (2) The advantage of the completed-contract method is that it is based on results, not estimates, and the disadvantage is that current performance is not reflected and income recognition may be irregular.

   b. **Percentage-of-completion**—Recognition of contract revenue and profit during construction based on expected total profit and estimated progress towards completion in the current period. All related costs are recognized in the period in which they occur.

      (1) The use of the percentage-of-completion method depends on the ability to make reasonably dependable estimates of contract revenues, contract costs, and the extent of progress toward completion. For entities which customarily operate under contractual arrangements and for whom contracting represents a significant part of their operations, the **presumption** is that they have the ability to make estimates that are sufficiently dependable to justify the use of the percentage-of-completion method of accounting.
      (2) The percentage-of-completion method is **preferable** in circumstances in which reasonably dependable estimates can be made and in which all of the following conditions exist:

         (a) Contracts executed by the parties normally include provisions that clearly specify the enforceable rights regarding goods or services to be provided and received by the parties, the consideration to be exchanged, and the manner and terms of settlement.
         (b) The buyer can be expected to satisfy obligations under the contract.
         (c) The contractor can be expected to perform contractual obligation.

      (3) The advantage of percentage-of-completion is periodic recognition of income, and the disadvantage is dependence on estimates.
      (4) In practice, various procedures are used to measure the extent of progress toward completion under the percentage-of-completion method, but the most widely used one is **cost-to-cost** which is based on the assumed relationship between a unit of input and productivity. Under cost-to-cost, either revenue and/or profit to be recognized in the current period can be determined by the following formula:

$$\text{Revenue (profit)} = \left(\frac{\text{Cost to date}}{\substack{\text{Total expected} \\ \text{cost based on} \\ \text{latest estimate}}} \times \substack{\text{Contract price} \\ \text{(Expected profit)}} \right) - \substack{\text{Revenue (profit)} \\ \text{recognized in} \\ \text{previous periods}}$$

NOTE: Revenue and profit are two different terms. Profit is calculated by subtracting construction expenses from revenue. Revenue is the contract price. Therefore, pay particular attention to what item the CPA exam asks you to calculate.

2. The ledger account titles used in the following discussion are unique to long-term construction contracts. In practice, there are numerous account titles for the same item (e.g., "billings on LT contracts" vs. "partial billings on construction in progress") and various methodologies for journalizing the same transactions (e.g., separate revenue and expense control accounts in lieu of an "income on LT contracts" account). The following example has been simplified to highlight the main concepts.

EXAMPLE

Assume a 3-year contract at a contract price of $500,000 as well as the following data:

	Year 1	Year 2	Year 3
Cost incurred this year	$135,000	$225,000	$ 45,000
Prior years' costs	-0-	135,000	360,000
Estimated costs to complete	$315,000	40,000	-0-
Total costs	$450,000	400,000	$405,000
Progress billings made during the year	$200,000	$200,000	$100,000
Collection of billings each year	$175,000	$200,000	$125,000

From the above information, the following may be determined.

Percent of completion (costs to date/total costs)
Year 1: $135,000/$450,000 = 30%
Year 2: $360,000/$400,000 = 90%
Year 3: $405,000/$405,000 = 100%

	Year 1	Year 2	Year 3
Total revenue	$ 500,000	$ 500,000	$ 500,000
× Percent of completion	× 30%	× 90%	× 100%
Total revenue to be recognized by end of year	$ 150,000	$ 450,000	$ 500,000
− Revenue recognized in prior periods	--	(150,000)	$(450,000)
Current year's revenue (to be recognized)	$ 150,000	$ 300,000	$ 50,000
Contract price	$ 500,000	$ 500,000	$ 500,000
− Total estimated costs	(450,000)	(400,000)	(405,000)
Estimated profit	$ 50,000	$ 100,000	$ 95,000
× Percent of completion	× 30%	× 90%	× 100%
Total profit to be recognized by end of year	$ 15,000	$ 90,000	$ 95,000
− Profit recognized in prior periods	--	(15,000)	(90,000)
Current year's profit (to be recognized)	$ 15,000	$ 75,000	$ 5,000

		Percentage-of-completion		Completed-contract	
Year 1 Costs	Construction in progress	135,000		135,000	
	Cash		135,000		135,000
Year 1 Progress billings	Accounts receivable	200,000		200,000	
	Billings on LT contracts		200,000		200,000
Year 1 Cash collected	Cash	175,000		175,000	
	Accounts receivable		175,000		175,000
Year 1 Profit recognition	Construction expenses	135,000		none	
	Construction in progress	15,000			
	Construction revenue		150,000		
Year 2 Costs	Construction in progress	225,000		225,000	
	Cash		225,000		225,000
Year 2 Progress billings	Accounts receivable	200,000		200,000	
	Billings on LT contracts		200,000		200,000
Year 2 Cash collected	Cash	200,000		200,000	
	Accounts receivable		200,000		200,000
Year 2 Profit recognition	Construction expenses	225,000		none	
	Construction in progress	75,000			
	Construction revenue		300,000		
Year 3 Costs	Construction in progress	45,000		45,000	
	Cash		45,000		45,000
Year 3 Progress billings	Accounts receivable	100,000		100,000	
	Billings on LT contracts		100,000		100,000
Year 3 Cash collected	Cash	125,000		125,000	
	Accounts receivable		125,000		125,000

Year 3 Profit recognition and closing of special accounts	Construction expenses	45,000		
	Construction in progress	5,000		
	Construction revenue		50,000	
	Billings on LT contracts	500,000		
	Const. in progress		500,000	
	Construction expenses			405,000
	Const. in progress			405,000
	Billings on LT contracts			500,000
	Construction revenue			500,000

3. The "construction in progress" (CIP) account is a cost accumulation account similar to "work in process" for job-order costing, except that the percentage-of-completion method includes interim profits in the account. The "billings on LT contracts" account is similar to an unearned revenue account. At each financial statement date, the "construction in progress" account should be netted against the "billings on LT contracts" account on a project-by-project basis, resulting in a net current asset and/or a net current liability.

EXAMPLE

Under the percentage of completion method in the above example, a net current asset of $50,000 [($135,000 + $15,000 + $225,000 + $75,000) – ($200,000 + $200,000)] would be reported at the end of year 2. A net current liability of $40,000 would result under the completed-contract method [($200,000 + $200,000) – ($135,000 + $225,000)] for the same year.

SUMMARY OF ACCOUNTS USED IN CONSTRUCTION ACCOUNTING
(NO LOSS EXPECTED OR INCURRED)

Balance sheet

Construction in Progress		A/P, Materials, etc.		Income statement — Construction Revenue	
(A)	(E)	(A)			(D)
(F)	(G)				(F)

Accounts Receivable		Billings on LT Contracts		Construction Expenses	
(B)	(C)	(D)	(B)	(E)	
		(G)		(F)	

Cash	
(C)	

Explanation of Journal Entries

Both methods	**Completed-contract method**	**Percentage-of-completion method**
(A) To record accumulated costs	(D) To record revenue upon completion and to close billings account	(F) To record recognition of interim revenue and expense
(B) To record progress billings	(E) To record expenses upon completion and to close construction in progress account	(G) To close construction-in-progress and billings accounts at project completion
(C) To record cash collections		

Balance Sheet Classification*

Current asset	**Current liability**
Projects where CIP at year-end** > Billings	Projects where billings > CIP at year-end**
	Estimated loss on uncompleted contract***

* Evaluate and classify on a project-by-project basis.

** Construction in progress including income (when percentage-of-completion method is used) or loss recognized.

*** When recognizing and reporting losses, it is necessary to use a current liability account instead of reducing CIP in those cases in which a contract's billings exceed its accumulated costs.

---

4. **Contract losses**

a. In any year when a **percentage-of-completion** contract has an expected loss on the entire contract, the amount of the loss reported in that year is the total expected loss on the entire contract **plus** all profit previously recognized.

> **EXAMPLE**
>
> If the expected costs yet to be incurred at the end of year two were $147,000, the total expected loss is $7,000 [$500,000 – ($135,000 + $225,000 + $147,000)] and the total loss reported in year two would be $22,000 ($7,000 + $15,000).

b. Similarly, under the **completed-contract** method, total expected losses on the entire contract are recognized as soon as they are estimated. The loss recognized is similar to that for percentage-of-completion except the amount is for the expected loss on the entire contract.

> **EXAMPLE**
>
> In the aforementioned example, the loss to be recognized is only $7,000 (the entire loss on the contract expected in year two) because interim profits have not been recorded.

c. Journal entries and a schedule for profit or loss recognized on the contract under the percentage-of-completion method follow.

> **EXAMPLE**
>
> | Journal entry at end of year 2 | Percentage-of-completion | Completed-contract |
> |---|---|---|
> | Construction expenses | 227,000* | |
> | Construction in progress (loss) | 22,000 | |
> | Construction revenue | 205,000** | |
> | Loss on uncompleted LT contracts | | 7,000 |
> | Construction in progress (loss) | | 7,000 |
> | * Year 2 costs | | $225,000 |
> | Loss attributable to year 3: | | |
> | Year 3 revenue ($500,000 – $150,000 – | | |
> | $205,000) | $145,000 | |
> | Year 3 costs (expected) | 147,000 | 2,000 |
> | Total | | $227,000 |
>
> ** ($360,000/$507,000) (Costs to date/Total estimated costs) = 71% (rounded); (71% × $500,000) – $150,000 = $205,000
>
> **PERCENTAGE-OF-COMPLETION METHOD**
>
> | | Year 1 | Year 2 | Year 3 |
> |---|---|---|---|
> | Contract price: | $500,000 | $500,000 | $500,000 |
> | Estimated total costs: | | | |
> | Costs incurred this year | $135,000 | $225,000 | $144,000*** |
> | Prior year's costs | -- | 135,000 | 360,000 |
> | Estimated cost yet to be incurred | 315,000 | 147,000 | -- |
> | Estimated total costs for the three-year period, actual for year 3 | $450,000 | $507,000 | $504,000 |
> | Estimated total income (loss) for three-year period, actual for year 3 | $ 15,000 | $ (7,000) | $ (4,000) |
> | Income (loss) on entire contract previously recognized | -- | 15,000 | (7,000) |
> | Amount of estimated income (loss) recognized in the current period, actual for year 3 | $ 15,000 | $ (22,000) | $ 3,000 |
>
> *** Assumed

NOW REVIEW MULTIPLE-CHOICE QUESTIONS 51 THROUGH 61

G. Research Component—Accounting Standards Codification

1. The authoritative literature for inventory is found primarily in two places in the Codification: Topic 330 and Topic 605.

    a. Topic 330 contains the definition of inventory, the significance of inventories, the basis of accounting, cost flows, and application of lower of cost or market.

b. Topic 605 focuses on long-term construction contracts and the percentage-of-completion and completed-contract methods.

c. Although the weighted-average, moving-average, and gross profit methods of accounting for inventory are acceptable methods, few, if any, references are made to these methods in the accounting literature.

(1) The only references to methods are first-in first-out, average and last-in first-out.

> **NOTE:** Typing the keywords with correct hyphenation should produce faster and more accurate results.

Accumulated costs billings	Expected losses contract	Mark-up inventory
Basis consistently applied	Finished goods	Net realizable value
Clearly reflects income	Firm purchase commitments	Percentage-of-completion method
Completed-contract method	First-in first-out	Physical deterioration
Contract costs loss	Held for sale	Raw materials
Contracts in process	Inventory obsolescence	Utility of goods
Cost or market	Last-in first-out	Work in process
Cost principle inventories	Lower of cost or market	

H. International Financial Reporting Standards (IFRS)

1. IFRS accounting for inventory differs from US GAAP in three areas: cost flow assumption, valuation of inventory at year-end, and capitalization of interest.

   a. With IFRS, the LIFO cost flow assumption is not permissible. Specific ID is required for inventory of goods that are not interchangeable, or goods that are produced and segregated for specific projects. FIFO and weighted-average methods are acceptable methods under IFRS for other types of inventory. The retail method may only be used for certain industries. In addition, the gross profit method can be used to estimate ending inventory when a physical count is not possible.

   b. Inventories are carried at the lower of cost or net realizable value (LCNRV). An exception to the LCNRV rule applies to agricultural inventories (biological assets) which are carried at fair value less costs to sell at the point of harvest.

      (1) Recall that in US GAAP, lower of cost or market (LCM) is used to value inventories. Market is defined as replacement cost, subject to a ceiling and floor. The ceiling is net realizable value (NRV), and the floor is NRV less a normal profit margin. Once inventory is written down, a loss may not be recovered.

      (2) Although IFRS uses a similar valuation concept, IFRS values inventory at the lower of cost or net realizable value (LCNRV). Note that the calculations are different from US GAAP. NRV is calculated as estimated selling price less estimated costs of completion and sale. Generally, LCNRV is applied on an item-by-item basis. However, under IFRS if there are groups of items that have similar characteristics, they may be grouped for the application of LCNRV.

EXAMPLE

Assume the following facts for an inventory:

Historical cost	$100
Estimated selling price	90
Estimated costs to complete and sell	5
NRV	$ 85

To apply LCNRV to this example, you compare the cost of $100 to the estimated selling price less estimated costs to complete and sell ($90 – $5). NRV is $85. Therefore, the LCNRV is $85. The inventory would be written down to $85 with a corresponding expense on the income statement. If the inventory value at the end of Year 2 was $90, a recovery of the loss would be recorded by debiting Inventory and crediting an income account.

> **NOTE:** If LCM were applied under US standards, additional information would be needed. Specifically, US GAAP would require the replacement cost and the normal profit margin in order to arrive at the ceiling and the floor.

   c. Rules for capitalization of interest are also different.

      (1) US GAAP allows no capitalization of interest for inventories that are routinely manufactured or otherwise produced in quantities on a repetitive basis.

(2) Similar to US GAAP, IFRS does not allow interest or financing costs to be capitalized as an inventory cost if it is paid under normal credit terms. However, IFRS allows interest costs to be capitalized if there is a lengthy production period to prepare the goods for sale.

> **NOW REVIEW MULTIPLE-CHOICE QUESTIONS 62 THROUGH 68**

KEY TERMS

Absorption costing. Considers both variable and fixed manufacturing costs as product costs.

Ceiling. Which is net realizable value (selling price less selling costs and costs to complete).

Completed-contract method. Recognition of contract revenue and profit at contract completion.

Direct (Variable) costing. Considers only variable costs as product costs and fixed production costs as period costs.

Dollar-value LIFO. LIFO applied to pools of inventory items rather than to individual items.

First-In, First-Out (FIFO). The goods from beginning inventory and the earliest purchases are assumed to be the goods sold first.

Floor. Which is net realizable value less normal profit.

FOB destination. Title passes to the buyer when the goods are received at their final destination.

FOB shipping point. Title passes to the buyer when the carrier receives the goods.

Gross method. Any subsequent discount taken is shown as purchase discount which is netted against the purchases account in determining cost of goods sold.

Inventory turnover. Measures the number of times inventory was sold and reflects inventory order and investment policies.

Last-In, First-Out (LIFO). The most recent purchases are assumed to be the first goods sold; thus, ending inventory is assumed to be composed of the oldest goods.

LIFO conformity rule. If LIFO is used for tax purposes, it must be used for financial reporting purposes.

LIFO reserve. The account used to reduce inventory from the internal valuation to the LIFO valuation.

Moving-average. The average cost of goods on hand must be recalculated any time additional inventory is purchased at a unit cost different from the previously calculated average cost of goods on hand.

Net method. Any purchase discounts offered are assumed taken and the purchase account reflects the net price.

Number of days' supply in average inventory. Number of days inventory is held before sale; reflects on efficiency of inventory policies.

Percentage-of-completion. Recognition of contract revenue and profit during construction based on expected total profit and estimated progress towards completion in the current period.

Periodic system. Inventory is counted periodically and then priced.

Perpetual system. A running total is kept of the units on hand (and possibly their value) by recording all increases and decreases as they occur.

Purchase commitments. Result from legally enforceable contracts to purchase specific quantities of goods at fixed prices in the future.

Simple average. The seller does not weight the average for units purchased or in beginning inventory.

Specific identification. The seller determines which item is sold.

Standard costs. Predetermined costs in a cost accounting system, generally used for control purposes.

Trade discounts. These are discounts that are allowed to the entity because of its being a wholesaler, a good customer, or merely the fact that the item is on sale at a reduced price.

Weighted-average. The seller averages the cost of all items on hand and purchased during the period. The units in ending inventory and units sold (CGS) are costed at this average cost.

Multiple-Choice Questions (1-68)

A. Determining Inventory and Cost of Goods Sold

1. The following information applied to Fenn, Inc. for year 2:

Merchandise purchased for resale	$400,000
Freight-in	10,000
Freight-out	5,000
Purchase returns	2,000

Fenn's year 2 inventoriable cost was
  a. $400,000
  b. $404,000
  c. $408,000
  d. $413,000

2. On December 28, year 2, Kerr Manufacturing Co. purchased goods costing $50,000. The terms were FOB destination. Some of the costs incurred in connection with the sale and delivery of the goods were as follows:

Packaging for shipment	$1,000
Shipping	1,500
Special handling charges	2,000

These goods were received on December 31, year 2. In Kerr's December 31, year 2 balance sheet, what amount of cost for these goods should be included in inventory?
  a. $54,500
  b. $53,500
  c. $52,000
  d. $50,000

3. On June 1, year 2, Pitt Corp. sold merchandise with a list price of $5,000 to Burr on account. Pitt allowed trade discounts of 30% and 20%. Credit terms were 2/15, n/40 and the sale was made FOB shipping point. Pitt prepaid $200 of delivery costs for Burr as an accommodation. On June 12, year 2, Pitt received from Burr a remittance in full payment amounting to
  a. $2,744
  b. $2,940
  c. $2,944
  d. $3,140

4. The following information was taken from Cody Co.'s accounting records for the year ended December 31, year 2:

Decrease in raw materials inventory	$ 15,000
Increase in finished goods inventory	35,000
Raw material purchased	430,000
Direct labor payroll	200,000
Factory overhead	300,000
Freight-out	45,000

There was no work in process inventory at the beginning or end of the year. Cody's year 2 cost of goods sold is
  a. $895,000
  b. $910,000
  c. $950,000
  d. $955,000

5. The following information pertains to Deal Corp.'s year 2 cost of goods sold:

Inventory, 12/31/Y1	$ 90,000
Year 2 purchases	124,000
Year 2 write-off of obsolete inventory	34,000
Inventory, 12/31/Y2	30,000

The inventory written off became obsolete due to an unexpected and unusual technological advance by a competitor. In its year 2 income statement, what amount should Deal report as cost of goods sold?
  a. $218,000
  b. $184,000
  c. $150,000
  d. $124,000

6. How should the following costs affect a retailer's inventory?

	Freight-in	Interest on inventory loan
a.	Increase	No effect
b.	Increase	Increase
c.	No effect	Increase
d.	No effect	No effect

7. According to the net method, which of the following items should be included in the cost of inventory?

	Freight costs	Purchase discounts not taken
a.	Yes	No
b.	Yes	Yes
c.	No	Yes
d.	No	No

8. The following information pertained to Azur Co. for the year:

Purchases	$102,800
Purchase discounts	10,280
Freight in	15,420
Freight out	5,140
Beginning inventory	30,840
Ending inventory	20,560

What amount should Azur report as cost of goods sold for the year?
  a. $102,800
  b. $118,220
  c. $123,360
  d. $128,500

9. When allocating costs to inventory produced for the period, fixed overhead should be based upon
  a. The actual amounts of goods produced during the period.
  b. The normal capacity of production facilities.
  c. The highest production levels in the last three periods.
  d. The lowest production level in the last three periods.

10. Per the Codification, what is considered the normal capacity of production facilities?
  a. The average production over the previous five-year period.

b. Actual production for the period.
c. Actual production for the period plus loss of capacity for planned maintenance.
d. A range that may vary based on business and industry-specific factors.

11. How should unallocated fixed overhead costs be treated?

a. Allocated to finished goods and cost of goods sold based on ending balances in the accounts.
b. Allocated to raw materials, work in process, and finished goods, based on the ending balances in the accounts.
c. Recognized as an expense in the period in which they are incurred.
d. Allocated to work in process, finished goods, and cost of goods sold based on ending balances in the accounts.

12. When manufacturing inventory, what is the accounting treatment for abnormal freight-in costs?

a. Charge to expense for the period.
b. Charge to the finished goods inventory.
c. Charge to raw materials inventory.
d. Allocate to raw materials, work in process, and finished goods.

13. On December 15, year 2, Flanagan purchased goods costing $100,000. The terms were FOB shipping point. Costs incurred by Flanagan in connection with the purchase and delivery of the goods were as follows:

Normal freight charges	$3,000
Handling costs	2,000
Insurance on shipment	500
Abnormal freight charges for express shipping	1,200

The goods were received on December 17, year 2. What is the amount that Flanagan should charge to inventory and to current period expense?

	Inventory	Current period expense
a.	$3,000	$3,700
b.	$5,000	$1,700
c.	$5,500	$1,200
d.	$6,700	$0

B. Inventory Valuation and Cost-Flow Methods

14. Bach Co. adopted the dollar-value LIFO inventory method as of January 1, year 2. A single inventory pool and an internally computed price index are used to compute Bach's LIFO inventory layers. Information about Bach's dollar value inventory follows:

	Inventory	
	At base	**At dollar**
Date	**year cost**	**value LIFO**
1/1/Y1	$90,000	$90,000
Year 1 layer	20,000	30,000
Year 2 layer	40,000	80,000

What was the price index used to compute Bach's year 2 dollar value LIFO inventory layer?

a. 1.09
b. 1.25
c. 1.33
d. 2.00

15. Nest Co. recorded the following inventory information during the month of January:

	Units	Unit cost	Total cost	Units on hand
Balance on 1/1	2,000	$1	$2,000	2,000
Purchased on 1/8	1,200	3	3,600	3,200
Sold on 1/23	1,800			1,400
Purchased on 1/28	800	5	4,000	2,200

Nest uses the LIFO method to cost inventory. What amount should Nest report as inventory on January 31 under each of the following methods of recording inventory?

	Perpetual	Periodic
a.	$2,600	$5,400
b.	$5,400	$2,600
c.	$2,600	$2,600
d.	$5,400	$5,400

B.2. Weighted-Average

16. The weighted-average for the year inventory cost flow method is applicable to which of the following inventory systems?

	Periodic	Perpetual
a.	Yes	Yes
b.	Yes	No
c.	No	Yes
d.	No	No

B.4. Moving Average

17. During January year 2, Metro Co., which maintains a perpetual inventory system, recorded the following information pertaining to its inventory:

	Units	Unit cost	Total cost	Units on hand
Balance on 1/1/Y2	1,000	$1	$1,000	1,000
Purchased on 1/7/Y2	600	3	1,800	1,600
Sold on 1/20/Y2	900			700
Purchased on 1/25/Y2	400	5	2,000	1,100

Under the moving-average method, what amount should Metro report as inventory at January 31, year 2?

a. $2,640
b. $3,225
c. $3,300
d. $3,900

B.5. Lower of Cost or Market

18. Based on a physical inventory taken on December 31, year 2, Chewy Co. determined its chocolate inventory on a FIFO basis at $26,000 with a replacement cost of $20,000. Chewy estimated that, after further processing costs of $12,000, the chocolate could be sold as finished candy bars for $40,000. Chewy's normal profit margin is 10% of sales. Under the lower of cost or market rule, what amount should Chewy report as chocolate inventory in its December 31, year 2 balance sheet?

a. $28,000
b. $26,000
c. $24,000
d. $20,000

19. Reporting inventory at the lower of cost or market is a departure from the accounting principle of
- a. Historical cost.
- b. Consistency.
- c. Conservatism.
- d. Full disclosure.

20. The original cost of an inventory item is below both replacement cost and net realizable value. The net realizable value less normal profit margin is below the original cost. Under the lower of cost or market method, the inventory item should be valued at
- a. Replacement cost.
- b. Net realizable value.
- c. Net realizable value less normal profit margin.
- d. Original cost.

21. Which of the following statements are correct when a company applying the lower of cost or market method reports its inventory at replacement cost?

I. The original cost is less than replacement cost.
II. The net realizable value is greater than replacement cost.

- a. I only.
- b. II only.
- c. Both I and II.
- d. Neither I nor II.

22. The original cost of an inventory item is above the replacement cost and the net realizable value. The replacement cost is below the net realizable value less the normal profit margin. As a result, under the lower of cost or market method, the inventory item should be reported at the
- a. Net realizable value.
- b. Net realizable value less the normal profit margin.
- c. Replacement cost.
- d. Original cost.

B.6. Losses on Purchase Commitments

23. On January 1, year 2, Card Corp. signed a three-year noncancelable purchase contract, which allows Card to purchase up to 500,000 units of a computer part annually from Hart Supply Co. at $.10 per unit and guarantees a minimum annual purchase of 100,000 units. During year 2, the part unexpectedly became obsolete. Card had 250,000 units of this inventory at December 31, year 2, and believes these parts can be sold as scrap for $.02 per unit. What amount of probable loss from the purchase commitment should Card report in its year 2 income statement?
- a. $24,000
- b. $20,000
- c. $16,000
- d. $ 8,000

24. Thread Co. is selecting its inventory system in preparation for its first year of operations. Thread intends to use either the periodic weighted-average method or the perpetual moving-average method, and to apply the lower of cost or market rule either to individual items or to the total inventory. Inventory prices are expected to generally increase throughout year 2, although a few individual prices will decrease. What inventory system should Thread select if it wants to maximize the inventory carrying amount at December 31, year 2?

	Inventory method	Cost or market application
a.	Perpetual	Total inventory
b.	Perpetual	Individual item
c.	Periodic	Total inventory
d.	Periodic	Individual item

B.7. & B.8. First-In, First-Out (FIFO), and Last-In, First-Out (LIFO)

25. Marsh Company had 150 units of product A on hand at January 1, year 2, costing $21 each. Purchases of product A during the month of January were as follows:

	Units	Unit cost
Jan. 10	200	$22
18	250	23
28	100	24

A physical count on January 31, year 2, shows 250 units of product A on hand. The cost of the inventory at January 31, year 2, under the LIFO method is
- a. $5,850
- b. $5,550
- c. $5,350
- d. $5,250

26. During January year 2, Metro Co., which maintains a perpetual inventory system, recorded the following information pertaining to its inventory:

	Units	Unit cost	Total cost	Units on hand
Balance on 1/1/Y2	1,000	$1	$1,000	1,000
Purchased on 1/7/Y2	600	3	1,800	1,600
Sold on 1/20/Y2	900			700
Purchased on 1/25/Y2	400	5	2,000	1,100

Under the LIFO method, what amount should Metro report as inventory at January 31, year 2?
- a. $1,300
- b. $2,700
- c. $3,900
- d. $4,100

27. Drew Co. uses the average cost inventory method for internal reporting purposes and LIFO for financial statement and income tax reporting. At December 31, year 2, the inventory was $375,000 using average cost and $320,000 using LIFO. The unadjusted credit balance in the LIFO Reserve account on December 31, year 2, was $35,000. What adjusting entry should Drew record to adjust from average cost to LIFO at December 31, year 2?

		Debit	Credit
a.	Cost of goods sold	$55,000	
	Inventory		$55,000
b.	Cost of goods sold	$55,000	
	LIFO reserve		$55,000
c.	Cost of goods sold	$20,000	
	Inventory		$20,000
d.	Cost of goods sold	$20,000	
	LIFO reserve		$20,000

28. A company decided to change its inventory valuation method from FIFO to LIFO in a period of rising prices. What was the result of the change on ending inventory and net income in the year of the change?

	Ending inventory	Net income
a.	Increase	Increase
b.	Increase	Decrease
c.	Decrease	Decrease
d.	Decrease	Increase

29. Generally, which inventory costing method approximates most closely the current cost for each of the following?

	Cost of goods sold	Ending inventory
a.	LIFO	FIFO
b.	LIFO	LIFO
c.	FIFO	FIFO
d.	FIFO	LIFO

30. During periods of rising prices, a perpetual inventory system would result in the same dollar amount of ending inventory as a periodic inventory system under which of the following inventory cost flow methods?

	FIFO	LIFO
a.	Yes	No
b.	Yes	Yes
c.	No	Yes
d.	No	No

B.9. Dollar-Value LIFO

31. On January 1, year 1, Poe Company adopted the dollar-value LIFO inventory method. Poe's entire inventory constitutes a single pool. Inventory data for year 1 and year 2 are as follows:

Date	Inventory at current year cost	Inventory at base year cost	Relevant price index
1/1/Y1	$150,000	$150,000	1.00
12/31/Y1	220,000	200,000	1.10
12/31/Y2	276,000	230,000	1.20

Poe's LIFO inventory value at December 31, year 2, is

a. $230,000
b. $236,000
c. $241,000
d. $246,000

32. Brock Co. adopted the dollar-value LIFO inventory method as of January 1, year 1. A single inventory pool and an internally computed price index are used to compute Brock's LIFO inventory layers. Information about Brock's dollar-value inventory follows:

Date	At base year cost	Inventory At current year cost	At dollar value LIFO
1/1/Y1	$40,000	$40,000	$40,000
Year 1 layer	5,000	14,000	6,000
12/31/Y1	45,000	54,000	46,000
Year 2 layer	15,000	26,000	?
12/31/Y2	$60,000	$80,000	?

What was Brock's dollar-value LIFO inventory at December 31, year 2?

a. $80,000
b. $74,000

c. $66,000
d. $60,000

33. Estimates of price-level changes for specific inventories are required for which of the following inventory methods?
a. Conventional retail.
b. Dollar-value LIFO.
c. Weighted-average cost.
d. Average cost retail.

34. When the double-extension approach to the dollar-value LIFO inventory method is used, the inventory layer added in the current year is multiplied by an index number. Which of the following correctly states how components are used in the calculation of this index number?
a. In the numerator, the average of the ending inventory at base year cost and at current year cost.
b. In the numerator, the ending inventory at current year cost, and, in the denominator, the ending inventory at base year cost.
c. In the numerator, the ending inventory at base year cost, and, the denominator, the ending inventory at current year cost.
d. In the denominator, the average of the ending inventory at base year cost and at current year cost.

35. Jones Wholesalers stocks a changing variety of products. Which inventory costing method will be most likely to give Jones the lowest ending inventory when its product lines are subject to specific price increases?
a. Specific identification.
b. Weighted-average.
c. Dollar-value LIFO.
d. FIFO periodic.

B.10. Gross Profit

36. Dart Company's accounting records indicated the following information:

Inventory, 1/1/Y2	$ 500,000
Purchases during year 2	2,500,000
Sales during year 2	3,200,000

A physical inventory taken on December 31, year 2, resulted in an ending inventory of $575,000. Dart's gross profit on sales has remained constant at 25% in recent years. Dart suspects some inventory may have been taken by a new employee. At December 31, year 2, what is the estimated cost of missing inventory?

a. $ 25,000
b. $100,000
c. $175,000
d. $225,000

B.14. Cost Apportionment by Relative Sales Value

37. On July 1, year 2, Casa Development Co. purchased a tract of land for $1,200,000. Casa incurred additional cost of $300,000 during the remainder of year 2 in preparing the land for sale. The tract was subdivided into residential lots as follows:

Lot class	Number of lots	Sales price per lot
A	100	$24,000
B	100	16,000
C	200	10,000

Using the relative sales value method, what amount of costs should be allocated to the Class A lots?

- a. $300,000
- b. $375,000
- c. $600,000
- d. $720,000

C. Items to Include in Inventory

38. Herc Co.'s inventory at December 31, year 2, was $1,500,000 based on a physical count priced at cost, and before any necessary adjustment for the following:

- Merchandise costing $90,000, shipped FOB shipping point from a vendor on December 30, year 2, was received and recorded on January 5, year 3.
- Goods in the shipping area were excluded from inventory although shipment was not made until January 4, year 3. The goods, billed to the customer FOB shipping point on December 30, year 2, had a cost of $120,000.

What amount should Herc report as inventory in its December 31, year 2 balance sheet?

- a. $1,500,000
- b. $1,590,000
- c. $1,620,000
- d. $1,710,000

39. Kew Co.'s accounts payable balance at December 31, year 2, was $2,200,000 before considering the following data:

- Goods shipped to Kew FOB shipping point on December 22, year 2, were lost in transit. The invoice cost of $40,000 was not recorded by Kew. On January 7, year 3, Kew filed a $40,000 claim against the common carrier.
- On December 27, year 2, a vendor authorized Kew to return, for full credit, goods shipped and billed at $70,000 on December 3, year 2. The returned goods were shipped by Kew on December 28, year 2. A $70,000 credit memo was received and recorded by Kew on January 5, year 3.
- Goods shipped to Kew FOB destination on December 20, year 2, were received on January 6, year 3. The invoice cost was $50,000.

What amount should Kew report as accounts payable in its December 31, year 2 balance sheet?

- a. $2,170,000
- b. $2,180,000
- c. $2,230,000
- d. $2,280,000

40. Lewis Company's usual sales terms are net sixty days, FOB shipping point. Sales, net of returns and allowances, totaled $2,300,000 for the year ended December 31, year 2, before year-end adjustments. Additional data are as follows:

- On December 27, year 2, Lewis authorized a customer to return, for full credit, goods shipped and billed at $50,000 on December 15, year 2. The returned goods were received by Lewis on January 4, year 3, and a $50,000 credit memo was issued and recorded on the same date.

- Goods with an invoice amount of $80,000 were billed and recorded on January 3, year 3. The goods were shipped on December 30, year 2.
- Goods with an invoice amount of $100,000 were billed and recorded on December 30, year 2. The goods were shipped on January 3, year 3.

Lewis' adjusted net sales for year 2 should be

- a. $2,330,000
- b. $2,280,000
- c. $2,250,000
- d. $2,230,000

41. On January 1, year 2, Dell, Inc. contracted with the city of Little to provide custom built desks for the city schools. The contract made Dell the city's sole supplier and required Dell to supply no less than 4,000 desks and no more than 5,500 desks per year for two years. In turn, Little agreed to pay a fixed price of $110 per desk. During year 2, Dell produced 5,000 desks for Little. At December 31, year 2, 500 of these desks were segregated from the regular inventory and were accepted and awaiting pickup by Little. Little paid Dell $450,000 during year 2. What amount should Dell recognize as contract revenue in year 2?

- a. $450,000
- b. $495,000
- c. $550,000
- d. $605,000

D. Consignments

42. On October 20, year 2, Grimm Co. consigned forty freezers to Holden Co. for sale at $1,000 each and paid $800 in transportation costs. On December 30, year 2, Holden reported the sale of ten freezers and remitted $8,500. The remittance was net of the agreed 15% commission. What amount should Grimm recognize as consignment sales revenue for year 2?

- a. $ 7,700
- b. $ 8,500
- c. $ 9,800
- d. $10,000

43. The following items were included in Opal Co.'s inventory account at December 31, year 2:

Merchandise out on consignment, at sales price, including 40% markup on selling price	$40,000
Goods purchased, in transit, shipped FOB shipping point	36,000
Goods held on consignment by Opal	27,000

By what amount should Opal's inventory account at December 31, year 2, be reduced?

- a. $103,000
- b. $ 67,000
- c. $ 51,000
- d. $ 43,000

44. On December 1, year 2, Alt Department Store received 505 sweaters on consignment from Todd. Todd's cost for the sweaters was $80 each, and they were priced to sell at $100. Alt's commission on consigned goods is 10%. At December 31, year 2, five sweaters remained. In its December 31, year 2 balance sheet, what amount should Alt report as payable for consigned goods?

- a. $49,000
- b. $45,400

    c. $45,000

    d. $40,400

45. Southgate Co. paid the in-transit insurance premium for consignment goods shipped to Hendon Co., the consignee. In addition, Southgate advanced part of the commissions that will be due when Hendon sells the goods. Should Southgate include the in-transit insurance premium and the advanced commissions in inventory costs?

	Insurance premium	Advanced commissions
a.	Yes	Yes
b.	No	No
c.	Yes	No
d.	No	Yes

46. Jel Co., a consignee, paid the freight costs for goods shipped from Dale Co., a consignor. These freight costs are to be deducted from Jel's payment to Dale when the consignment goods are sold. Until Jel sells the goods, the freight costs should be included in Jel's

    a.   Cost of goods sold.

    b.   Freight-out costs.

    c.   Selling expenses.

    d.   Accounts receivable.

    e.   Ratios

E.   Ratios

47. Heath Co.'s current ratio is 4:1. Which of the following transactions would normally increase its current ratio?

    a.   Purchasing inventory on account.

    b.   Selling inventory on account.

    c.   Collecting an account receivable.

    d.   Purchasing machinery for cash.

48. During year 2, Rand Co. purchased $960,000 of inventory. The cost of goods sold for year 2 was $900,000, and the ending inventory at December 31, year 2, was $180,000. What was the inventory turnover for year 2?

    a.   6.4

    b.   6.0

    c.   5.3

    d.   5.0

49. In a comparison of year 2 to year 1, Neir Co.'s inventory turnover ratio increased substantially although sales and inventory amounts were essentially unchanged. Which of the following statements explains the increased inventory turnover ratio?

    a.   Cost of goods sold decreased.

    b.   Accounts receivable turnover increased.

    c.   Total asset turnover increased.

    d.   Gross profit percentage decreased.

50. Selected data pertaining to Lore Co. for the calendar year 2 is as follows:

Net cash sales	$ 3,000
Cost of goods sold	18,000
Inventory at beginning of year	6,000
Purchases	24,000
Accounts receivable at beginning of year	20,000
Accounts receivable at end of year	22,000

Lore would use which of the following to determine the average days' sales in inventory?

	Numerator	Denominator
a.	365	Average inventory
b.	365	Inventory turnover
c.	Average inventory	Sales divided by 365
d.	Sales divided by 365	Inventory turnover

F.   Long-Term Construction Contracts

51. Cord Builders, Inc. has consistently used the percentage-of-completion method of accounting for construction-type contracts. During year 1 Cord started work on a $9,000,000 fixed-price construction contract that was completed in year 3. Cord's accounting records disclosed the following:

	December 31	
	Year 1	Year 2
Cumulative contract costs incurred	$3,900,000	$6,300,000
Estimated total cost at completion	7,800,000	8,100,000

How much income would Cord have recognized on this contract for the year ended December 31, year 2?

    a. $100,000

    b. $300,000

    c. $600,000

    d. $700,000

52. State Co. recognizes construction revenue and expenses using the percentage-of-completion method. During year 1, a single long-term project was begun, which continued through year 2. Information on the project follows:

	Year 1	Year 2
Accounts receivable from construction contract	$100,000	$300,000
Construction expenses	105,000	192,000
Construction in progress	122,000	364,000
Partial billings on contract	100,000	420,000

Profit recognized from the long-term construction contract in year 2 should be

    a. $ 50,000

    b. $108,000

    c. $128,000

    d. $228,000

53. Lake Construction Company has consistently used the percentage-of-completion method of recognizing income. During year 1, Lake entered into a fixed-price contract to construct an office building for $10,000,000. Information relating to the contract is as follows:

	At December 31,	
	Year 1	Year 2
Percentage of completion	20%	60%
Estimated total cost at completion	$7,500,000	$8,000,000
Income recognized (cumulative)	500,000	1,200,000

Contract costs incurred during year 2 were

    a. $3,200,000

    b. $3,300,000

    c. $3,500,000

    d. $4,800,000

54. Hansen Construction, Inc. has consistently used the percentage-of-completion method of recognizing income.

During year 2, Hansen started work on a $3,000,000 fixed-price construction contract. The accounting records disclosed the following data for the year ended December 31, year 2:

Costs incurred	$ 930,000
Estimated cost to complete	2,170,000
Progress billings	1,100,000
Collections	700,000

How much loss should Hansen have recognized in year 2?
- a. $230,000
- b. $100,000
- c. $ 30,000
- d. $0

Items 55 and 56 are based on the following data pertaining to Pell Co.'s construction jobs, which commenced during year 2:

	Project 1	Project 2
Contract price	$420,000	$300,000
Costs incurred during year 2	240,000	280,000
Estimated costs to complete	120,000	40,000
Billed to customers during year 2	150,000	270,000
Received from customers during year 2	90,000	250,000

55. If Pell used the completed contract method, what amount of gross profit (loss) would Pell report in its year 2 income statement?
- a. $ (20,000)
- b. $ 0
- c. $ 340,000
- d. $ 420,000

56. If Pell used the percentage-of-completion method, what amount of gross profit (loss) would Pell report in its year 2 income statement?
- a. $(20,000)
- b. $ 20,000
- c. $ 22,500
- d. $ 40,000

57. Which of the following is used in calculating the income recognized in the fourth and final year of a contract accounted for by the percentage-of-completion method?

	Actual total costs	Income previously recognized
a.	Yes	Yes
b.	Yes	No
c.	No	Yes
d.	No	No

58. A company used the percentage-of-completion method of accounting for a five-year construction contract. Which of the following items will the company use to calculate the income recognized in the third year?

	Progress billings to date	Income previously recognized
a.	Yes	No
b.	No	Yes
c.	No	No
d.	Yes	Yes

59. The calculation of the income recognized in the third year of a five-year construction contract accounted for using the percentage-of-completion method includes the ratio of
- a. Total costs incurred to date to total estimated costs.

- b. Total costs incurred to date to total billings to date.
- c. Cost incurred in year three to total estimated costs.
- d. Costs incurred in year three to total billings to date.

60. When should an anticipated loss on a long-term contract be recognized under the percentage-of-completion method and the completed-contract method, respectively?

	Percentage-of-completion	Completed-contract
a.	Over life of project	Contract complete
b.	Immediately	Contract complete
c.	Over life of project	Immediately
d.	Immediately	Immediately

61. In accounting for a long-term construction contract using the percentage-of-completion method, the progress billings on contracts account is a
- a. Contra current asset account.
- b. Contra noncurrent asset account.
- c. Noncurrent liability account.
- d. Revenue account.

H. International Financial Reporting Standards (IFRS)

62. Brady Corporation values its inventory at the lower of cost or net realizable value as required by IFRS. Brady has the following information regarding its inventory:

Historical cost	$1,000
Estimated selling price	900
Estimated costs to complete and sell	50
Replacement cost	800

What is the amount for inventory that Brady should report on the balance sheet under the lower of cost or net realizable value method?
- a. $1,000
- b. $ 900
- c. $ 850
- d. $ 750

63. A company determined the following values for its inventory as of the end of its fiscal year:

Historical cost	$100,000
Current replacement cost	70,000
Net realizable value	90,000
Net realizable value less a normal profit margin	85,000
Fair value	95,000

Under IFRS, what amount should the company report as inventory on its balance sheet?
- a. $70,000
- b. $85,000
- c. $90,000
- d. $95,000

64. Under IFRS, which of the following inventory items are not valued at the lower of cost or net realizable value?
- a. Manufactured inventory items.
- b. Retail inventory items.
- c. Biological inventory items.
- d. Industrial inventory items.

65. Under IFRS, the specific identification method of accounting for inventory is required for
- a. All inventory items.
- b. Inventory items which are interchangeable.

    c.   Inventory items that are not interchangeable and goods that are produced and segregated for specific projects.

    d.   Biological (agricultural) inventories.

66. The information provided below is for an item in Harris Corporation's inventory at year end. Harris presents its financial statements in accordance with IFRS:

Historical cost	$1,200
Estimated selling price	1,300
Estimated completion and selling costs	150
Replacement cost	1,100

What should be the value of this inventory item in the company's financial statements?

    a. $1,100

    b. $1,150

    c. $1,200

    d. $1,300

67. Which of the following is not true about accounting for inventory under IFRS?

    a.   FIFO is allowed.

    b.   Interest costs may be capitalized if there is a lengthy production period to prepare goods for sale.

    c.   The weighted-average method is acceptable.

    d.   Inventories are always valued at net realizable value.

68. Which of the following methods of accounting for inventory is not allowed under IFRS?

    a.   LIFO.

    b.   Specific identification.

    c.   FIFO.

    d.   Weighted-average.

Multiple-Choice Answers and Explanations

Answers

1.	c __ __	15.	b __ __	29.	a __ __	43.	d __ __	57.	a __ __
2.	d __ __	16.	b __ __	30.	a __ __	44.	c __ __	58.	b __ __
3.	c __ __	17.	b __ __	31.	c __ __	45.	c __ __	59.	a __ __
4.	b __ __	18.	c __ __	32.	c __ __	46.	d __ __	60.	d __ __
5.	c __ __	19.	a __ __	33.	b __ __	47.	b __ __	61.	a __ __
6.	a __ __	20.	d __ __	34.	b __ __	48.	b __ __	62.	c __ __
7.	a __ __	21.	b __ __	35.	c __ __	49.	d __ __	63.	c __ __
8.	b __ __	22.	b __ __	36.	a __ __	50.	b __ __	64.	c __ __
9.	b __ __	23.	c __ __	37.	c __ __	51.	a __ __	65.	c __ __
10.	d __ __	24.	a __ __	38.	d __ __	52.	a __ __	66.	b __ __
11.	c __ __	25.	c __ __	39.	a __ __	53.	b __ __	67.	d __ __
12.	a __ __	26.	b __ __	40.	d __ __	54.	b __ __	68.	a __ __
13.	c __ __	27.	d __ __	41.	c __ __	55.	a __ __	1st: __/68 = __%
14.	d __ __	28.	c __ __	42.	d __ __	56.	b __ __	2nd: __/68 = __%

Explanations

1. (c) Inventoriable costs include all costs necessary to prepare goods for sale. For a merchandising concern these costs include the purchase price of the goods, freight-in, insurance, warehousing, and any costs necessary to get the goods to the point of sale (except interest on any loans obtained to purchase the goods). In this problem, inventoriable costs total $408,000.

Purchase price less returns ($400,000 – $2,000)	$398,000
Freight-in	10,000
	$408,000

Note that freight-out is a **selling expense,** not an inventoriable cost, as the diagram below indicates.

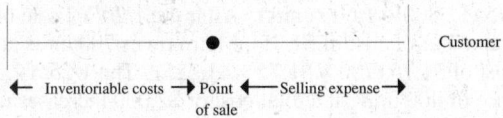

2. (d) When the shipping terms are FOB destination, the seller bears **all** costs of transporting the goods to the buyer. Therefore, the seller is responsible for the payment of packaging costs ($1,000), shipping costs ($1,500), and the special handling charges ($2,000). The only amount to be included as the buyer's cost of the inventory purchased is the purchase price ($50,000).

3. (c) Purchases are always recorded net of trade discounts. When more than one trade discount is applied to a list price, it is called a chain discount. Chain discounts are applied in steps; each discount applies to the previously discounted price. The cost, net of trade discounts, is $2,800 [$5,000 – (30% × $5,000) = $3,500; and $3,500 – (20% × $3,500) = $2,800]. Payment was made within the discount period, so the net purchase price is $2,744 [$2,800 – (2% × $2,800)]. The remittance from Burr would also include reimbursement of the $200 of delivery costs. Since the terms were FOB shipping point, Burr is responsible for paying this amount, and must reimburse Pitt, who prepaid the freight. Thus, the total remittance is $2,944 ($2,744 + $200).

4. (b) Three computations must be performed: raw materials used, cost of goods manufactured, and cost of goods sold.

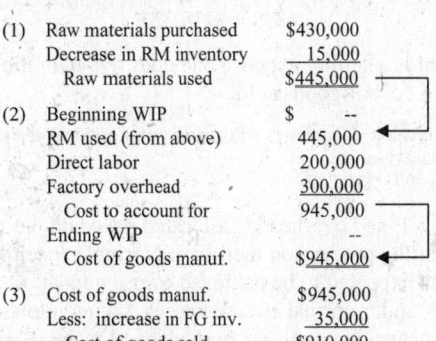

(1)	Raw materials purchased	$430,000
	Decrease in RM inventory	15,000
	Raw materials used	$445,000
(2)	Beginning WIP	$ --
	RM used (from above)	445,000
	Direct labor	200,000
	Factory overhead	300,000
	Cost to account for	945,000
	Ending WIP	--
	Cost of goods manuf.	$945,000
(3)	Cost of goods manuf.	$945,000
	Less: increase in FG inv.	35,000
	Cost of goods sold	$910,000

The decrease in RM inventory is added when computing RM used because RM were used in excess of those purchased. The increase in FG inventory is deducted when computing cost of goods sold because it represents the portion of goods manufactured which were not sold. The freight-out is irrelevant for this question because freight-out is a selling expense and therefore does not affect cost of goods sold.

5. (c) To compute cost of goods sold, the solutions approach is to set up a T-account for inventory

	Inventory		
12/31/Y1	90,000		
Purchases	124,000	34,000	Write-off
		?	Cost of goods sold
12/31/Y2	30,000		

Purchases increase inventory, while the write-off and cost of goods sold decrease inventory. Cost of goods sold can be computed as $150,000 using the T-account. An alternate solutions approach is to use the CGS computation

BI	$ 90,000	
+ Purchases	124,000	
CGAS	214,000	
– EI	(30,000)	
	$184,000	$34,000 recognized as inventory loss*
		$150,000 recognized as CGS

* Theoretically correct treatment.

6. (a) The cost of inventory should include all expenditures (direct and indirect) incurred to bring an item to its existing condition and location. Freight-in charges are thus appropriately included in inventory costs. Interest cost shall not be capitalized for assets that are in use or ready for their intended use in the earnings activities of the enterprise. Thus, interest on an inventory loan should not be included in inventory (it should be expensed as incurred).

7.   (a)   The cost of inventory should include all expenditures (direct and indirect) incurred to bring an item to its existing condition and location. Freight charges are thus appropriately included in inventory costs. Under the net purchase method, purchase discounts not taken are recorded in a Purchase Discounts Lost account. When this method is used, purchase discounts lost are considered a financial (i.e., "other") expense, and are thus excluded from the cost of inventory.

8.   (b)   Azur should report cost of goods sold calculated as

Cost of goods sold (CGS) = Beg. Inventory + Net purchases* + Freight in – Ending Inventory

CGS = $ 30,840 + $92,520** + $15,420 – $20,560

CGS = $118,220

Freight out is a selling expense and does not enter the calculation of cost of goods sold.

  * Net purchase = Purchases – Purchase returns and allowances – Purchase discounts
 ** ($102,800 – $10,280)

9.   (b)   Fixed overhead is allocated based on the normal capacity of the production facilities. Normal capacity is the production expected to be achieved over a number of periods or seasons under normal circumstances, taking into account the loss of capacity resulting from planned maintenance. Answer (a) is incorrect, because the actual amount of production may only be used if it approximates normal capacity. Answers (c) and (d) are incorrect because the accounting standards do not specify a formula to calculate normal capacity.

10.   (d)   Normal capacity refers to a range in production levels that will vary based on business and industry-specific factors. Normal capacity is the production expected to be achieved over a number of periods or seasons under normal circumstances, taking into account the loss of capacity resulting from planned maintenance. Answer (a) is incorrect because the Codification does not specify a formula for calculating normal capacity. Answers (b) and (c) are incorrect because actual production may only be used if it approximates normal capacity.

11.   (c)   Unallocated fixed overhead costs are recognized as an expense in the period in which they are incurred. Therefore, answers (a), (b), and (d) are incorrect.

12.   (a)   Any abnormal costs for freight, handling costs, and wasted material are required to be treated as current period charges, and not a part of inventory cost. Therefore, answers (b), (c), and (d) are incorrect.

13.   (c)   Inventoriable costs include all costs necessary to prepare goods for sale. For a merchandising concern, these include the purchase price of the goods, freight-in, insurance, warehousing, and any costs necessary to get the goods to the point of sale. Abnormal freight and handling should be charged to expense of the period. Therefore, the normal costs

for inventory are $5,500 ($3,000 + $2,000 + $500) and the abnormal freight of $1,200 is charged to current expense of the period.

14.   (d)   Ending inventory at dollar value LIFO is calculated as the base year inventory times the index. Therefore, the index used can be calculated as 2.00 = ($80,000 EI at dollar value LIFO/$40,000 base year cost).

15.   (b)   The inventory valuations are calculated as follows:

Valuations of ending inventory under LIFO perpetual

1,400 units at $1.00	=	$1,400
800 units at $5.00	=	4,000
Total		$5,400

Value of ending inventory under LIFO periodic

2,000 units at $1.00	=	$2,000
200 units at $3.00	=	600
Total		$2,600

16.   (b)   The requirement is to determine whether the weighted-average inventory method is applicable to a periodic and/or a perpetual inventory system. The weighted-average method computes a weighted-average unit cost of inventory for the entire period and is used with periodic records. The moving-average method requires that a new unit of cost be computed each time new goods are purchased and is used with perpetual records.

17.   (b)   The moving-average method requires that a new unit cost be computed each time goods are purchased. The new unit cost is used to cost all sales of inventory until the next purchase. After the 1/7/Y2 purchase, Metro owns 1,600 units (1,000 + 600) at a total cost of $2,800 ($1,000 + $1,800). Therefore, the moving-average unit cost at that time is $1.75 ($2,800 ÷ 1,600 units). After the 1/20/Y2 sale of 900 units (at a unit of cost of $1.75), Metro owns 700 units at a unit cost of $1.75 (700 × $1.75 = $1,225). The 1/25/Y2 purchase of 400 units at a total cost of $2,000 increases inventory to its 1/31/Y2 balance of $3,225 ($1,225 + $2,000). The new unit cost (not required) is $2.93 ($3,225 ÷ 1,100).

18.   (c)   The lower of cost or market (LCM) is used for financial reporting of inventories. The market value of inventory is defined as the replacement cost (RC), as long as it is less than the ceiling (net realizable value, or NRV) and more than the floor (NRV less a normal profit, or NRV – NP). In this case, the amounts are

Ceiling: NRV = $40,000 est. sell. price	
– $12,000 disp. cost =	$28,000
Floor: NRV – NP = $28,000 – (10% × $40,000)	$24,000
RC:	$20,000

Since RC falls below the floor, the floor (NRV – NP) is the designated market value. Once market value is designated, LCM can be determined by simply determining the lower of cost ($26,000) or market ($24,000). Therefore, inventory is reported at $24,000.

19.   (a)   SFAC 5 establishes five different attributes on which assets can be measured. The attribute used should be determined by the nature of the item and the relevance and reliability of the attribute measured. The five attributes are historical cost, current cost, current market value, net realizable value, and present value. Historical cost is defined as the amount of cash, or its equivalent, paid to acquire an asset. Reporting inventory at lower of cost or market is a departure from the historical cost principle as the inventory could potentially be carried at the market value if lower. Although, reporting inventory at lower of cost or market does not create a departure from conservatism as this method carries at inventory the lowest or most conservative value. The use of LCM does not violate the principle of consistency either, as it would be reported on this basis continually. Finally the use of LCM would not violate the principle of full disclosure as its use would be discussed in the footnotes.

20. (d) Inventory is to be valued at the lower of cost or market. Under this method, market is replacement cost provided that replacement cost is lower than net realizable value (ceiling) and higher than net realizable value less the normal profit margin (floor). The question does not specify whether replacement cost is above or below net realizable value, but since the original cost is below **both** of these values, that information is irrelevant.

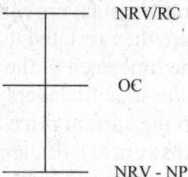

Either NRV or RC will be designated as the market value of the inventory, and since the original cost is below **both** of these values, the inventory will be valued at its original cost. Answer (c) is incorrect because NRV – NP represents the market floor. Answers (a) and (b) are incorrect because they are both **above** the original cost.

21. (b) Lower of cost or market (LCM) is used for financial reporting of inventories. The market value of inventory is defined as the replacement cost (RC) as long as it is less than the ceiling (net realizable value, or NRV) and more than the floor (NRV less a normal profit, or NRV – NP). Therefore, if inventory is reported at RC, RC must be less than original cost (meaning statement I is **not** correct), and RC must be less than NRV (meaning statement II **is** correct) and greater than NRV – NP.

22. (b) Inventory is priced at market when market value is less than cost. Market value is defined as current replacement cost, subject to a ceiling of net realizable value (NRV) and a floor of net realizable value minus a normal profit margin.

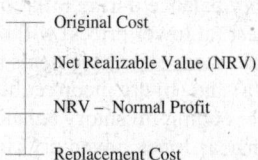

In this situation, replacement cost lies outside of (below) the floor and ceiling limitations. Therefore, NRV less a normal profit margin (the floor), will be used as the market to determine LCM. Since original cost is greater than market, market will be used to price the inventory for the period.

23. (c) The requirement is to determine the amount of probable loss from the purchase commitment that Card should report in its year 2 income statement. When there is a decline in market value below the contract price at the balance sheet

date and the contract is noncancelable, an unrealized loss should be recorded in the period of decline and reported in the income statement. In this case, Card has a contract to purchase a minimum of 100,000 units both in year 3 and year 4 at $.10 per unit. The $20,000 loss (200,000 × $.10) on these obsolete units should be reduced by the amount Card believes is realizable from the sale of these units. Therefore, the loss on **purchase commitment** is $16,000 [$20,000 – (200,000 × .02)]. Additionally, Card Corp. would need to record a loss of $20,000 ($.08 × 250,000) from **inventory obsolescence**.

24. (a) To maximize its inventory carrying amount at December 31, year 2, Thread should use the perpetual moving-average method with the lower of cost or market rule applied to the total inventory. First, when using the perpetual moving-average method, the cost of sales throughout the year are determined using the average cost of purchases up to the time of the sale. On the other hand, under the periodic weighted-average method, the cost of each item is the weighted-average of **all** units purchased during the year. During a period of rising prices, the perpetual moving-average method results in a lower cost of goods sold and a higher ending inventory because the cost of items sold throughout the year is the average of the earlier, lower prices. Second, the application of the lower of cost or market rule to the total inventory will result in a higher ending inventory because market values lower than cost are offset against market values higher than cost.

25. (c) The requirement is to determine the cost of the 1/31/Y2 inventory, using the LIFO method. LIFO stands for last-in, first-out; this means that the cost of the units purchased most recently are included in cost of goods sold. Therefore, the 1/31/Y2 inventory consists of the 250 units that were purchased at the earliest date(s). Thus, the 1/31/Y2 inventory would consist of the 150 units on hand at 1/1/Y2 (150 × $21 = $3,150) plus an additional 100 units purchased at the earliest purchase date in January (January 10; 100 × $22 = $2,200). The total value of the inventory at 1/31/Y2 would be $5,350 ($3,150 + $2,200).

26. (b) LIFO stands for last-in, first-out; this means that it is assumed that any units sold are the units most recently purchased. In a perpetual system, LIFO is applied at the time of each sale rather than once a year as in a periodic system. Using LIFO, the 900 units sold on 1/20/Y2 would consist of the 600 units purchased on 1/7/Y2 and 300 of the 1,000 units in the 1/1/Y2 balance. This would leave in inventory 700 units from the 1/1/Y2 balance. After the 1/25/Y2 purchase, inventory included those 700 units plus the 400 units purchased on 1/25/Y2. Therefore, ending inventory is $2,700 [(700 × $1) + (400 × $5)].

27. (d) When a company uses LIFO for external reporting purposes and another inventory method for internal purposes, a **LIFO Reserve** account is used to reduce inventory from the internal valuation to the LIFO valuation. LIFO Reserve is a contra account to inventory, and is adjusted up or down at year-end with a corresponding increase or decrease to **Cost of Goods Sold**. In this case, the LIFO Reserve account must be adjusted from a balance of $35,000 to a balance of $55,000 ($375,000 – $320,000). Therefore, LIFO Reserve is credited for $20,000 ($55,000 – $35,000) with a corresponding debit to Cost of Goods Sold.

28. (c) In a change **to** LIFO, no recognition is given to any cumulative effect associated with the change because it is usually not determinable. Thus, the effect on ending inventory and net income is the result solely of current year effects. In a period of rising prices, LIFO will result in a **lower ending inventory** amount than FIFO because the earlier lower costs are assumed to remain in ending inventory. LIFO will also result in a **lower net income** because the more recent higher costs are assigned to cost of goods sold.

29. (a) The inventory costing method which most closely approximates the current cost for cost of goods sold is LIFO, while the method which more accurately reflects ending inventory is FIFO. Under LIFO, the most recent purchases are assumed to be the first goods sold; thus, cost of goods sold contains relatively current costs. On the other hand, since FIFO assumes that the goods from beginning inventory and the earliest purchases are sold first, the ending inventory is made up of more recent purchases and thus represents a more current value.

30. (a) Under the FIFO method, the first goods purchased are considered to be the first goods used or sold. Ending inventory is thus made up of the latest (most recent) purchases. Whenever the FIFO method is used, the ending inventory is the same whether a perpetual or periodic system is used. This is true even during periods of rising or falling prices because the inventory flow is always in chronological order. Under the LIFO method, the latest (most recent) purchases are considered to be the first goods used or sold. Ending inventory is thus made up of the first (oldest) purchases. When a periodic method is used, the first/last purchase determination is made only at the end of the year, based upon the actual chronological order of all purchases. When a perpetual method is used, however, the first/last purchase determination is made continuously throughout the year. When inventory levels get low under the perpetual method, early purchase costs will often be assigned to goods sold, a situation that is much less likely to occur in a periodic system. Therefore, in times of either rising or falling prices, LIFO ending inventory is usually different under a periodic system than under a perpetual system.

31. (c) When using dollar-value LIFO, the ending inventory at current year cost must first be converted to base year cost. This amount is given at 12/31/Y2 ($230,000), but it could be computed as follows: $276,000 ÷ 1.20 = $230,000. The next step is to determine the incremental LIFO layers at base year cost. The 1/1/Y1 (base year) layer is $150,000, the year 1 layer is $50,000 ($200,000 – $150,000), and the year 2 layer is $30,000 ($230,000 – $200,000). Finally, the LIFO layers are restated using the price index in effect at the time each layer was added.

	Base cost		Ending inventory at DV LIFO cost
1/1/Y1 layer	$150,000	× 1.00 =	$150,000
Year 1 layer	50,000	× 1.10 =	55,000
Year 2 layer	30,000	× 1.20 =	36,000
	$230,000		$241,000

32. (c) When using dollar-value LIFO, the ending inventory at current year cost must first be converted to base year cost. The 12/31/Y2 inventory at base year cost is given as $60,000. Since the 12/31/Y1 inventory at base year cost was $45,000 ($40,000 base layer and $5,000 year 1 layer), a

new layer of $15,000 was added in year 2 ($60,000 – $45,000). This layer must be restated using the year 2 price index. The year 2 price index is computed using the double-extension technique, as illustrated below.

$$\frac{\text{EI at year-end prices}}{\text{EI at base year prices}} = \frac{\$80,000}{\$60,000} = \underline{1.33}$$

Therefore, the 12/31/Y2 inventory using dollar-value LIFO is $66,000 as computed below.

	Base cost		DV LIFO
Base layer	$40,000		$40,000
Year 1 layer	5,000		6,000
Year 2 layer	15,000	× 1.33	20,000
			$66,000

33. (b) The requirement is to determine which inventory method requires estimates of price level changes for specific inventories. In accordance with the dollar-value LIFO method, the ending inventory is first converted to the base year cost so that the incremental layers can be determined. The incremental layers are then restated using the price index which was in effect at the time each of the layers were added to the inventory. Thus, the specific layers of the ending inventory are adjusted to the current price level. Therefore, answer (b) is correct. Answers (a), (c), and (d) are incorrect because these methods do not specifically adjust for price level changes.

34. (b) The requirement is to determine the appropriate use of ending inventory at current year cost and ending inventory at base year cost in calculating the dollar-value LIFO index. The index number used to convert the current year's inventory layer is calculated as follows:

$$\text{Index} = \frac{\text{Ending inventory at current year cost}}{\text{Ending inventory at base year cost}}$$

This index indicates the relationship between current and base year prices as a percentage, and when multiplied by the new layer (which is the increase in inventory in base year dollars), it will convert the layer to current dollars.

35. (c) During periods of rising prices, the inventory costing methods which will give Jones the lowest ending inventory balance are LIFO methods, because inventory items that were purchased at the earliest date (when prices were lower) will remain in inventory and the most recently purchased and more expensive items will be expensed through cost of goods sold. Any FIFO method will produce a higher ending inventory balance during inflation since the items purchased earliest (at lower prices) will be expensed through CGS, while the more expensive items remain in inventory. Answers (a) and (b) are incorrect because neither will give Jones a lower ending inventory balance than dollar-value LIFO, particularly as Jones' inventory changes (because dollar-value LIFO allows the LIFO "layers" to be made up of similar, not necessarily identical, items).

36. (a) The gross profit method can be used to estimate the cost of missing inventory. The first step is to compute the cost of goods available for sale.

Beginning inventory	$ 500,000
Purchases	2,500,000
Cost of goods available for sale	$3,000,000

The second step is to estimate cost of goods sold based on the gross profit percentage.

Sales	$3,200,000
Estimated gross profit ($3,200,000 × 25%)	(800,000)
Cost of goods sold ($3,200,000 × 75%)	$2,400,000

Note that a shortcut is to realize that if gross profit is 25% of sales, cost of goods sold must be 75% of sales. The third step is to compute estimated ending inventory.

Cost of goods available for sale	$ 3,000,000
Estimated cost of goods sold	(2,400,000)
Estimated ending inventory	$ 600,000

Since the actual count of ending inventory at December 31 was only $575,000, the estimated shortage in inventory is $25,000 ($600,000 – $575,000).

37. **(c)** The total cost of acquiring the land and preparing it for sale ($1,200,000 + $300,000 = $1,500,000) should be allocated to the residential lots based on their relative sales value, as computed below.

Lot class	# of lots		Sales price		Total sales value
A	100	×	$24,000	=	$2,400,000
B	100	×	16,000	=	1,600,000
C	200	×	10,000	=	2,000,000
					$6,000,000

Total cost		Fraction allocated to Class A		Allocated cost
$1,500,000	×	($2,400/$6,000)	=	$600,000

38. **(d)** Before adjustment, the inventory based on a physical count was $1,500,000. The $90,000 of merchandise shipped FOB shipping point by a vendor on 12/30/Y2 should also be included in Herc's 12/31/Y2 inventory because Herc, the buyer, owns the goods while in transit under these terms. The goods in the shipping area (cost, $120,000) are also owned by Herc because they were not shipped until year 3 and Herc still retains the risks of ownership until that point. Therefore, 12/31/Y2 inventory is $1,710,000 ($1,500,000 + $90,000 + $120,000).

39. **(a)** Before adjustment, the balance in the Accounts Payable account is $2,200,000. The $40,000 of goods lost in transit from a vendor were shipped FOB **shipping point**. This means the buyer owns the goods while they were in transit; therefore, Kew should record the purchase and accounts payable in year 2. Kew, not the vendor, is ultimately responsible for the lost goods (note that Kew, not the vendor, is suing the common carrier). The $70,000 return that was recorded on 1/5/Y3 should have been recorded in year 2 when the return was authorized (December 27, year 2). Therefore, Kew should reduce 12/31/Y2 Accounts Payable by $70,000. The $50,000 of goods received on 1/6/Y3 were properly recorded in year 3, since the terms were FOB destination (the buyer does not own the goods until they are physically received). Therefore, no adjustment is necessary for this amount. Kew should report 12/31/Y2 Accounts Payable at $2,170,000 ($2,200,000 + $40,000 – $70,000).

40. **(d)** Net sales is $2,300,000, subject to three possible adjustments. The goods returned ($50,000) should be recorded as a return in year 2, when Lewis authorized the return. Since this return was not recorded until year 3, year 2

sales must be adjusted downward. The goods shipped on 12/30/Y2 ($80,000) were recorded as a sale in year 3. Since the terms were FOB shipping point, the sale must be recorded in year 2 when the goods were shipped; therefore, year 2 sales must be adjusted upward. The goods shipped on 1/3/Y3 ($100,000) should not be recorded as a sale until year 3. Since the sale was recorded in year 2, year 2 sales must be adjusted downward. Therefore, adjusted net sales for year 2 should be $2,230,000 ($2,300,000 – $50,000 + $80,000 – $100,000).

41. **(c)** Generally, goods are considered sold when legal title to the goods passes to the buyer. In certain situations, however, the transfer of title criteria does not reflect the underlying economics of the situation. In this situation, although transfer of legal title may not have occurred for the 500 segregated desks, the economic substance of the transaction is that the seller no longer retains the risks of ownership. Therefore, all 5,000 desks (including the 500 segregated and accepted desks) are considered sold in year 2, and revenue of $550,000 is recognized (5,000 × $110). Note that the amount of cash collected ($450,000) does not affect the amount of revenue recognized in this case.

42. **(d)** A consignor recognizes sales revenue from consignments when the consignee sells the consigned goods to the ultimate customer. Sales commissions earned by the consignee ($10,000 × 15% = $1,500) are reported as a selling expense by the consignor and are **not** netted against sales revenue. Therefore, sales revenue is reported at the total selling price of $10,000 (10 × $1,000). Note that the transportation costs ($800) do not affect sales either; one-fourth (10/40) is reflected in cost of goods sold and three-fourths (30/40) is included in ending inventory.

43. **(d)** No adjustment is necessary for the goods in transit ($36,000). The goods were shipped **FOB shipping point,** which means the buyer (Opal) owns the goods while in transit. Therefore, Opal properly included these goods in 12/31/Y2 inventory. The merchandise **out** on consignment is owned by the consignor (Opal) and should be included in Opal's inventory **at cost** [$40,000 – (40% × $40,000) = $24,000]. Therefore, inventory must be reduced by $16,000 for this item ($40,000 – $24,000). The goods **held** on consignment ($27,000) are owned by the consignor, not Opal; therefore, inventory must be reduced $27,000 for this item. The total reduction in inventory is $43,000 ($16,000 + $27,000).

44. **(c)** Alt sold 500 of the consigned sweaters (505 – 5) at $100 each, resulting in total sales of $50,000 (500 × $100). Alt must report a payable to Todd for this amount, less Alt's commission [$50,000 – (10% × $50,000) = $45,000]. Alt does not owe Todd anything for the unsold sweaters until they are sold.

45. **(c)** Inventoriable costs include all costs necessary to prepare goods for sale. These costs include the purchase price or manufacturing cost of the goods, freight, and any other costs necessary to get the goods to the point of sale. The in-transit insurance premium would therefore be included in inventory costs. Commissions paid to the consignee are selling expenses in the period the consigned goods are sold that are not required to ready the goods for sale. These costs, therefore, are not included in inventory.

46. **(d)**   In a consignment, the manufacturer or wholesaler is referred to as the consignor and the dealer or retailer is referred to as the consignee. In such an arrangement, title to the goods remains with the consignor until they are sold to a third party. Jel's payment of reimbursable freight costs results in an account receivable from Dale, which Jel will subtract from the sale proceeds it remits to Dale. Answers (a), (b), and (c) are incorrect because the consignee, Jel, generally does not bear any costs associated with the sale of consigned goods.

47. **(b)**   The formula to compute the current ratio is

$$\text{Current ratio} = \frac{\text{Current assets}}{\text{Current liabilities}}$$

The following entries would be recorded when inventory is sold on account:

Accounts receivable	} Sales price
Sales	of merchandise
Cost of goods sold	} Cost of
Inventory	merchandise

Since the selling price (increase to AR) is normally higher than the cost of the merchandise sold (decrease to merchandise inventory) the sale would normally cause a net increase in current assets, and therefore, a net increase in the current ratio. When the existing current ratio is greater than one, increases of equal amounts to the numerator (inventory, a component of current assets) and denominator (accounts payable, a component of current liabilities) will reduce the ratio. When an account receivable is collected, cash (a current asset) is increased by the same amount that accounts receivable (another current asset) is decreased. Thus, the transaction has no impact on the current ratio. When machinery (a noncurrent asset) is purchased for cash (a current asset), there is a **decrease** in the current ratio.

48. **(b)**   The formula for inventory turnover is

$$\frac{\text{Cost of goods sold}}{\text{Average inventory}}$$

Average inventory is equal to beginning inventory plus ending inventory, divided by two. Since beginning inventory is not given, it must be computed using the cost of goods sold relationship

Cost of goods sold	$ 900,000
+ Ending inventory	180,000
Cost of goods available for sale	$1,080,000
− Purchases	− 960,000
Beginning inventory	$ 120,000

Therefore, average inventory is $150,000 [($120,000 + $180,000) ÷ 2], and inventory turnover is 6.0 times ($900,000 ÷ 150,000).

49. **(d)**   The solutions approach is to create a numerical example that conforms to the facts given in the question. The inventory turnover ratio is calculated as follows:

$$\frac{\text{Cost of goods sold}}{\text{Average inventory}}$$

If we assume that cost of goods sold has increased from 100 to 150 and average inventory has remained unchanged at 50 then the following ratios result:

$$\frac{\text{Cost of goods sold}}{\text{Average inventory}} \quad \frac{100}{50} = 2 \quad \frac{150}{50} = 3$$

Thus, if cost of goods sold increases while inventory remains unchanged, then the inventory turnover ratio will increase.

In addition, we must examine the effects of the increase in cost of goods sold on the gross profit percentage when sales remain constant. Assuming the same facts as above, and sales of $200, we get the following results:

Sales	200	200
− Cost of goods sales	− 100	− 150
Gross profit	100	50

Thus, as cost of goods sold increases, the gross profit and the gross profit percentage will decrease.

Answer (a) is incorrect because a decrease in cost of goods sold will cause the inventory ratio to increase. Answers (b) and (c) are incorrect because they are not related to inventory turnover.

50. **(b)**   Average days' sales in inventory measures the number of days inventory is held before sale; it reflects on efficiency of inventory policies. It is computed using the following formula:

$$\frac{365}{\text{Inventory turnover}}$$

51. **(a)**   The total expected income on the contract at 12/31/Y2 is $900,000 ($9,000,000 − $8,100,000). The formula for recognizing profit under the percentage-of-completion method is

$$\frac{\text{Cost to date}}{\text{Total expected costs}} \times \frac{\text{Expected}}{\text{profit}} = \frac{\text{Profit recog-}}{\text{nized to date}}$$

$$\frac{\$6,300,000}{\$8,100,000} \times \$900,000 = \$700,000$$

This result is the **total** profit on the contract in year 1 and year 2. The year 1 profit recognized must be subtracted from $700,000 to determine the year 2 profit. At 12/31/Y1, the total expected income on the contract was $1,200,000 ($9,000,000 − $7,800,000). The income recognized in year 1 was $600,000, as computed below.

$$\frac{\$3,900,000}{\$7,800,000} \times \$1,200,000 = \$600,000$$

Therefore, year 2 income is $700,000 less $600,000, or $100,000.

52. **(a)**   Profit to be recognized using the percentage-of-completion method is generally computed as follows:

$$\left(\frac{\text{Cost to date}}{\text{Total expected cost}} \times \frac{\text{Expected}}{\text{profit}} \right) - \frac{\text{Profit recognized}}{\text{in previous periods}}$$

Not enough information is given in this problem to perform this computation, so year 2 profit must be computed indirectly. Since only construction expenses and profit are debited to the construction-in-progress (CIP account), year 1 profit must have been $17,000 ($122,000 CIP less $105,000 const. exp.). Cumulative profit recognized by the end of year 2 must be $67,000 [$364,000 CIP less $297,000 cumulative const. exp. ($105,000 + $192,000)]. Therefore, year 2 profit was $50,000 ($67,000 − $17,000).

CIP		
Year 1 Exp.	105,000	
Year 1 Profit	?	Year 1 Profit = $17,000
Year 1 End. bal	122,000	
Year 2 Exp.	192,000	
Year 2 Profit	?	Year 2 Profit = $50,000
Year 2 End. bal.	364,000	

53. (b) Based on the information given, it must be assumed that costs incurred are used to measure the extent of progress toward project completion. At 12/31/Y1, the project was 20% complete and total estimated costs were $7,500,000. Therefore, costs incurred as of 12/31/Y1 were 20% of $7,500,000, or $1,500,000. At 12/31/Y2, the project was 60% complete and total estimated costs were $8,000,000. Therefore, costs incurred as of 12/31/Y2 are 60% of $8,000,000 or $4,800,000. The costs incurred during year 2 were $4,800,000 less $1,500,000, or $3,300,000.

54. (b) The requirement is to determine the amount of loss to recognize in year 2 on a long-term, fixed-price construction contract. Under both the percentage-of-completion method and the completed-contract method, an expected **loss** on a contract must be recognized in **full** in the period in which the expected loss is discovered. Therefore, Hanson must recognize a loss of $100,000 in year 2.

Expected contract revenue	$3,000,000
Expected contract costs ($930,000 + $2,170,000)	3,100,000
Expected loss	$ (100,000)

55. (a) The expected income on project 1 [$420,000 – ($240,000 + $120,000) = $60,000] is **not** recognized until the project is completed under the completed contract method. However, under the completed contract method, an expected **loss** on a contract must be recognized in full in the period in which it is discovered. Project 2 has an expected loss of ($20,000) [$300,000 – ($280,000 + $40,000)] which must be recognized immediately in year 2.

56. (b) Construction companies that use the percentage-of-completion method in accounting for long-term construction contracts usually recognize gross profit according to the cost-to-cost method.

$$\frac{\text{Costs to date}}{\text{Total estimated costs}} \times \text{Estimated profit} = \text{Gross profit to date}$$

Pell would recognize gross profit of $40,000 on project 1

$$\frac{\$240,000}{\$240,000 + \$120,000} \times [\$420,000 - (\$240,000 + \$120,000)] = \$40,000$$

Note that prior years' gross profit need not be subtracted from $40,000 because the project commenced during year 2. Under both the percentage-of-completion method and the completed-contract method, an expected **loss** must be recognized in full in the period in which the expected loss is discovered. Project 2 has an expected loss of ($20,000) [$300,000 – ($280,000 + $40,000)] which must be recognized in full in year 2. The net gross profit recognized on the two projects is $20,000 ($40,000 profit less ($20,000) loss).

57. (a) In the **final year** of a contract accounted for by the percentage-of-completion method, the percentage of completion is 100%, since costs to date equal total costs.

Therefore, the formula to calculate income to be recognized in the final year is simply

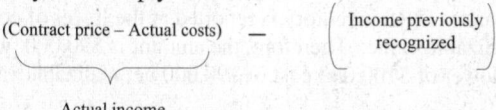

Therefore both **actual total costs** and **income previously recognized** are used in calculating income.

58. (b) Under the percentage-of-completion method of accounting for long-term contracts, the cost-to-cost formula is used to compute the amount of income to be recognized in a particular year. The formula to calculate current income is as follows:

$$\left(\frac{\text{Cost to date}}{\text{Total expected cost}} \times \text{Expected profit}\right) - \text{Profit recognized in previous periods}$$

Progress billings do not impact the amount of income recognized.

59. (a) The requirement is to determine the ratio to be used to calculate income in the third year using the percentage-of-completion method. Income may be recognized on a cost-to-cost basis when the percentage-of-completion method is used.

$$\left(\frac{\text{Cost to date}}{\text{Total expected cost}} \times \text{Expected profit}\right) - \text{Profit recognized in previous periods}$$

Answers (b) and (d) are incorrect because billings to date are not used as a basis for recognizing revenues. Answer (c) is incorrect as the cost-to-cost calculation requires a cumulative calculation so changes in expected costs and expected income can be adjusted for; thus, costs incurred in year three would be an incorrect basis for recognition of income.

60. (d) An anticipated loss on a long-term contract should be recognized immediately under **both** the percentage-of-completion and the completed-contract methods.

61. (a) The requirement is to determine the proper classification for the progress billings on contracts account under the percentage-of-completion method. In the construction industry, operating cycles for construction contracts generally exceed one year. Therefore, the predominant practice is to classify all contract-related assets and liabilities as current. On the balance sheet, the Construction in Progress (CIP) account is netted with the contra account, progress billings. If CIP exceeds billings, the excess is reported as a current asset [answer (a)]. If billings exceed CIP, the excess is reported as a current liability. Answers (b) and (c) are incorrect because the accounts related to construction contracts are classified as current. Answer (d) is incorrect because progress billings is not used as a basis for recognizing revenues.

62. (c) The requirement is to calculate the amount that should be presented for inventory. Answer (c) is correct because the lower of cost or net realizable value method requires net realizable value to be calculated as the estimated selling price less estimated costs of completion and estimated costs to sell. Therefore, the NRV is $850 ($900 – $50). The lower of cost or net realizable value is determined by comparing the cost of $1,000 to the NRV of $850, and using the lower amount. Inventory should be reported at $850.

63. (c)   The requirement is to determine the amount that should be reported as inventory. Answer (c) is correct because under IFRS inventory is reported at the lower of cost or net realizable value. Therefore, the amount is $90,000, which is the lower of $100,000 cost or $90,000 net realizable value.

64. (c)   The requirement is to identify the inventory items that are not valued at the lower of cost or net realizable value under IFRS. Answer (c) is correct because biological inventory items are valued at fair value less the cost to sell at the point of harvest.

65. (c)   The requirement is to identify when the specific identification method is required under IFRS. Answer (c) is correct because the specific identification method is required for inventory items that are not interchangeable and goods that are produced and segregated for specific projects.

66. (b)   The requirement is to determine the value of the inventory item under IFRS. Answer (b) is correct because under IFRS, inventory is presented at the lower of cost ($1,200) or net realizable value ($1,300 selling price – $150 estimated completion and selling costs). Therefore, the item should be valued at $1,050.

67. (d)   The requirement is to identify the statement that is not correct about accounting for inventories under IFRS. Answer (d) is correct because inventories are not always valued at net realizable value. They are valued at the lower of cost or net realizable value.

68. (a)   The requirement is to identify the method of accounting that is not allowed under IFRS. Answer (a) is correct because the LIFO method is not allowed under IFRS. All of the other methods are allowed.

Simulations

Task-Based Simulation 1

Concepts		
	Authoritative Literature	Help

Indicate whether each of the following is included in the cost of inventory.

		Included	Not included
1.	Merchandise purchased for resale	O	O
2.	Freight-out	O	O
3.	Direct materials	O	O
4.	Sales returns	O	O
5.	Packaging for shipment to customer	O	O
6.	Factory overhead	O	O
7.	Interest on inventory loan	O	O
8.	Purchase discounts not taken	O	O
9.	Freight-in	O	O
10.	Direct labor	O	O

Task-Based Simulation 2

Journal Entries		
	Authoritative Literature	Help

Blaedon uses the periodic inventory method for inventories. Prepare the journal entries for each of the following transactions. Blaedon uses the gross method for recording inventory transactions.

1. On January 5, year 2, purchased $17,000 of garden tillers on account from Bestbuilt Tillers, terms 2/10, n/30, FOB destination. Freight charges were $200.

2. On January 10, year 2, returned garden tillers worth $2,000 to Bestbuilt Tillers due to defects.

3. On January 14, year 2, paid for the remaining tillers purchased in **1.**

4. On January 28, year 2, purchased $30,000 of lawn mowers from Lawn Giant, terms 3/10, n/30, FOB shipping point. The freight charges were $820.

5. On February 6, year 2, paid for the lawn mowers purchased in part **4.** from Lawn Giant.

Task-Based Simulation 3

Calculations		
	Authoritative Literature	Help

Situation

A client, Blaedon Co., sells lawn mowers and garden tillers. The garden tillers are purchased from Bestbuilt Tillers and sold to customers without modification. The lawn mowers, however, are purchased from several contractors. Blaedon then makes ongoing design refinements to the mowers before selling them to customers.

The lawn mowers cost $200. Blaedon then makes the design refinements at a cost of $85 per lawn mower. Blaedon stores the lawn mowers in its own warehouse and sells them directly to retailers at a list price of $500. Blaedon uses the FIFO inventory method. Approximately two-thirds of new lawn mower sales involve trade-ins. For each used lawn mower traded in and returned to Blaedon, retailers receive a $40 allowance regardless of whether the trade-in was associated with a sale of a year 2 or year 3 model. Blaedon's net realizable value on a used lawn mower averages $25.

At December 31, year 2, Blaedon's inventory of new lawn mowers includes both year 2 and year 3 models. When the year 3 model was introduced in September year 2, the list price of the remaining year 2 model lawn mowers was reduced below cost. Blaedon is experiencing rising costs.

Blaedon has contacted your firm for advice on how to report the carrying value of inventory, the impact of the decline in value on the year 2 models, and the effects of using the FIFO method on their December 31, year 2 financial statements.

Assume that Blaedon had the following information regarding the garden tiller inventory:

Purchases	$210,000
Purchase discounts	38,000
Purchase returns	17,500
Freight-in	12,100
Freight-out	18,000
Beginning inventory	42,900
Ending inventory	34,250

Calculate the following items:

1. Goods available for sale

2. Costs of goods sold

Task-Based Simulation 4

Research		
	Authoritative Literature	Help

Assume that you are assigned to the audit of the inventories of Litton Corporation. Research the Professional Standards for the section that provides guidance on the items that should be included in the cost of inventory. Enter your response in the answer fields below.

Task-Based Simulation 5

Calculation of Gross Profit		
	Authoritative Literature	Help

Situation

London, Inc. began operation of its construction division on October 1, year 1, and entered into contracts for two separate projects. The Beta project contract price was $600,000 and provided for penalties of $10,000 per week for late completion. Although during year 2 the Beta project had been on schedule for timely completion, it was completed four weeks late in August year 3. The Gamma project's original contract price was $800,000. Change orders during year 3 added $40,000 to the original contract price.

The following data pertains to the separate long-term construction projects in progress:

	Beta	Gamma
As of September 30, year 2:		
Costs incurred to date	$360,000	$410,000
Estimated costs to complete	40,000	410,000
Billings	315,000	440,000
Cash collections	275,000	365,000
As of September 30, year 3:		
Costs incurred to date	450,000	720,000
Estimated costs to complete	--	180,000
Billings	560,000	710,000
Cash collections	560,000	625,000

Additional information

- London accounts for its long-term construction contracts using the percentage-of-completion method for financial reporting purposes and the completed-contract method for income tax purposes.
- Enacted income tax rates are 25% for year 2 and 30% for future years.
- London's income before income taxes from all divisions, before considering revenues from long-term construction projects, was $300,000 for the year ended September 30, year 2. There were no other temporary or permanent differences.

Prepare a schedule showing London's gross profit (loss) recognized for the years ended September 30, year 2, and year 3, under the percentage-of-completion method.

London Inc.
SCHEDULE OF GROSS PROFIT (LOSS)

	Beta		Gamma
For the Year Ended September 30, year 2:			
Estimated gross profit (loss):			
Contract price			
Less total costs			
Estimated gross profit (loss)			
Percent complete:			
Costs incurred to date			
Total costs			
Percent complete			
Gross profit (loss) recognized			
For the Year Ended September 30, year 3:			
Estimated gross profit (loss):			
Contract price			
Less total costs			
Estimated gross profit (loss)			
Percent complete:			
Costs incurred to date			
Total costs			
Percent complete			
Gross profit (loss) recognized			
Less gross profit (loss) recognized in prior year			
Gross profit (loss) recognized			

Task-Based Simulation 6

Financial Statement Disclosures		
	Authoritative Literature	Help

Situation

London, Inc. began operation of its construction division on October 1, year 1, and entered into contracts for two separate projects. The Beta project contract price was $600,000 and provided for penalties of $10,000 per week for late completion. Although during year 2 the Beta project had been on schedule for timely completion, it was completed four weeks late in August year 3. The Gamma project's original contract price was $800,000. Change orders during year 3 added $40,000 to the original contract price.

The following data pertains to the separate long-term construction projects in progress:

	Beta	Gamma
As of September 30, year 2:		
Costs incurred to date	$360,000	$410,000
Estimated costs to complete	40,000	410,000
Billings	315,000	440,000
Cash collections	275,000	365,000
As of September 30, year 3:		
Costs incurred to date	450,000	720,000
Estimated costs to complete	--	180,000
Billings	560,000	710,000
Cash collections	560,000	625,000

Additional information

- London accounts for its long-term construction contracts using the percentage-of-completion method for financial reporting purposes and the completed-contract method for income tax purposes.
- Enacted income tax rates are 25% for year 2 and 30% for future years.
- London's income before income taxes from all divisions, before considering revenues from long-term construction projects, was $300,000 for the year ended September 30, year 2. There were no other temporary or permanent differences.

Prepare the following schedule showing London's balances in the following accounts at September 30, year 2, under the percentage-of-completion method:

- Accounts receivable
- Costs and estimated earnings in excess of billings
- Billings in excess of costs and estimated earnings

London Inc.
SCHEDULE OF SELECTED BALANCE SHEET ACCOUNTS
September 30, year 2

Accounts receivable		
Costs and estimated earnings in excess of billings:		
Construction in progress		
Less: Billings		
Costs and estimated earnings in excess of billings		
Billings in excess of costs and estimated earnings		
Estimated loss on contract		

Task-Based Simulation 7

Research		
	Authoritative Literature	Help

Assume that you are assigned to the audit of Cole Construction Company. Cole constructs buildings under long-term contracts using the completed contract basis of accounting. Cole has determined that a loss is anticipated on its contract with Hale corporation. Which section of the Professional Standards provides guidance on how this situation should affect Cole's financial statements? Enter your response in the answer fields below.

Task-Based Simulation 8

Inventory Concepts		
	Authoritative Literature	Help

Items 1 through 13 represent True or False statements concerning inventory accounting methods. Indicate whether each statement is true or false by clicking on the appropriate response.

	True	False
1. The gross margin method uses historical sales margins to estimate the cost of inventory.	○	○
2. The dollar-value LIFO method preserves old inventory costs by charging current costs to cost of goods sold.	○	○
3. Inventory should be reported at the lower of cost or market and it may be based on the values of individual items, categories, or the total inventory.	○	○
4. A loss on a purchase commitment should be recorded when the contract price is greater than the market and it is anticipated that a loss will occur when the contract is completed.	○	○
5. Under the dollar-value LIFO method, increases and decreases in a layer would be measured based upon the change in the total dollar value of the layer.	○	○
6. The link-chain method uses a cumulative index to value the base cost of ending inventory.	○	○
7. The price index for dollar-value LIFO is a measure of changes in price levels between the current year and the base year.	○	○
8. Under the LIFO method, an inventory liquidation will result in higher profits in a period of rising prices.	○	○
9. A holding gain results from holding an item while the market value experiences a decline.	○	○
10. During a period of rising prices, the LIFO cost flow assumption results in a higher net income as compared to FIFO.	○	○
11. In a period of rising prices, when a company changes from FIFO to LIFO the net income will tend to decline as will working capital.	○	○
12. The use of LIFO for book and tax purposes will result in a lower tax payment in a period of rising prices.	○	○
13. Under the LIFO method, the cost of goods sold balance would be the same whether a perpetual or periodic inventory system is used.	○	○

Task-Based Simulation 9

Cost Flow Concepts		
	Authoritative Literature	Help

Below are statements describing inventory and cost flow methods. Identify which method matches each description by clicking on the correct term and placing it in the space provided. You may use a term once, more than once, or not at all.

Terms
Specific identification
Weighted-average
Simple average
Moving-average
First-in, first-out
Last-in, first-out
Dollar-value LIFO
Gross profit

Method

1. During a period of rising prices, this method results in a higher net income. _____

2. This method most closely matches the physical flow of inventory. _____

3. Method that uses historical sales margins to estimate ending inventory. _____

4. Method that is appropriate when there is a relatively small number of significant dollar value items in inventory. _____

5. Average cost must be calculated each time additional inventory is purchased. _____

6. Method that averages the cost of all items on hand and purchased during the period. _____

7. This method results in the lowest ending inventory in a period of rising prices. _____

8. Method that uses a price index to measure changes in inventory. _____

9. If used for tax purposes, this method must also be used for financial reporting purposes. _____

10. The cost of goods sold balance is the same whether a perpetual or periodic inventory system is used. _____

Task-Based Simulation 10

Schedule of Ending Inventory		
	Authoritative Literature	Help

Situation

York Co. sells one product, which it purchases from various suppliers. York's trial balance at December 31, year 2, included the following accounts:

Sales (33,000 units @ $16)	$528,000
Sales discounts	7,500
Purchases	368,900
Purchase discounts	18,000
Freight-in	5,000
Freight-out	11,000

York Co.'s inventory purchases during year 2 were as follows:

	Units	Cost per unit	Total cost
Beginning inventory, January 1	8,000	$8.20	$ 65,600
Purchases, quarter ended March 31	12,000	8.25	99,000
Purchases, quarter ended June 30	15,000	7.90	118,500
Purchases, quarter ended September 30	13,000	7.50	97,500
Purchases, quarter ended December 31	7,000	7.70	53,900
	55,000		$434,500

Additional information

York's accounting policy is to report inventory in its financial statements at the lower of cost or market, applied to total inventory. Cost is determined under the last-in, first-out (LIFO) method.

York has determined that, at December 31, year 2, the replacement cost of its inventory was $8 per unit and the net realizable value was $8.80 per unit. York's normal profit margin is $1.05 per unit.

From this information, complete the following schedules.

York Co.
SUPPORTING SCHEDULE OF ENDING INVENTORY
December 31, Year 2

Inventory at cost (LIFO):

	Units	Cost per unit	Total cost
Beginning inventory, January 1			
Purchases, quarter ended March 31			
Purchases, quarter ended June 30			
Totals			

York Co.
SCHEDULE OF COST OF GOODS SOLD
For the Year Ended December 31, Year 2

Beginning inventory		
Add: Purchases		
Less: Purchase discounts		
Add: Freight-in		
Goods available for sale		
Less: Ending inventory		
Cost of goods sold		

Task-Based Simulation 11

Research		
	Authoritative Literature	Help

Assume that you are assigned to the audit of Heath Corporation. Heath is considering changing its method of costing inventory. Which section of the Professional Standards provides guidance on the appropriate methods for determining inventory cost? Enter your response in the answer fields below.

Simulation Solutions

Task-Based Simulation 1

	Included	Not included
1. Merchandise purchased for resale	●	○
2. Freight-out	○	●
3. Direct materials	●	○
4. Sales returns	○	●
5. Packaging for shipment to customer	○	●
6. Factory overhead	●	○
7. Interest on inventory loan	○	●
8. Purchase discounts not taken	○	●
9. Freight-in	●	○
10. Direct labor	●	○

Explanations

1. Merchandise purchased for resale is a part of inventory.

2. Freight-out is part of selling expense.

3. Direct materials are part of work in process, which is an inventory account for manufacturers.

4. Sales returns are a contra account to sales, and are not part of inventory.

5. Packaging for shipment to customer is part of selling expenses.

6. Factory overhead is part of work in process, which is an inventory account for manufacturing firms.

7. Interest on inventory loan is an operating expense. Interest cost should not be capitalized for assets that are in use or ready for their intended use in the earnings activities of the enterprise.

8. Purchase discounts lost are considered a financing expense and are excluded from the cost of inventory.

9. Freight-in is part of getting the goods in place to sell and should be included in inventory.

10. Direct labor is part of work in process, and is an inventory account for manufacturing firms.

Task-Based Simulation 2

1. On January 5, year 2, purchased $17,000 of garden tillers on account from Bestbuilt Tillers, terms 2/10, n/30, FOB destination. Freight charges were $200.

Purchases	17,000	
Accounts payable		17,000

2. On January 10, year 2, returned garden tillers worth $2,000 to Bestbuilt Tillers due to defects.

Accounts payable	2,000	
Purchase returns		2,000

3. On January 14, year 2, paid for the remaining tillers purchased in **1.**

Accounts payable	15,000	
Purchase discounts		300*
Cash		14,700

   * 15,000 × .02 = 300

4. On January 28, year 2, purchased $30,000 of lawn mowers from Lawn Giant, terms 3/10, n/30, FOB shipping point. The freight charges were $820.

Purchases	30,000	
Freight-in	820	
Accounts payable		30,820

5. On February 6, year 2, paid for the lawn mowers purchased in part **4.** from Lawn Giant.

Accounts payable	30,000	
Purchase discounts		900
Cash		29,100
(This assumes the freight bill is paid separately to		
the freight company)		

Task-Based Simulation 3

Calculations		
	Authoritative Literature	**Help**

Assume that Blaedon had the following information regarding the garden tiller inventory:

Purchases	$210,000
Purchase discounts	38,000
Purchase returns	17,500
Freight-in	12,100
Freight-out	18,000
Beginning inventory	42,900
Ending inventory	34,250

Calculate the following items:

1. Goods available for sale   209,500

2. Costs of goods sold   175,250

Explanations

Beginning inventory		42,900
Purchases	210,000	
–Purchase discounts	(38,000)	
–Purchase returns	(17,500)	
Net purchases	154,500	
+Freight-in	12,100	
		166,600
Goods available for sale		209,500
–Ending inventory		(34,250)
Cost of goods sold		175,250

Task-Based Simulation 4

Research		
	Authoritative Literature	**Help**

ASC	330	10	30	1

Task-Based Simulation 5

Calculation of Gross Profit		
	Authoritative Literature	Help

London Inc.
SCHEDULE OF GROSS PROFIT (LOSS)

	Beta	Gamma
For the Year Ended September 30, Year 2:		
Estimated gross profit (loss):		
Contract price	$600,000	$800,000
Less total costs	400,000	820,000
Estimated gross profit (loss)	$200,000	$ (20,000)
Percent complete:		
Costs incurred to date	$360,000	$410,000
Total costs	400,000	820,000
Percent complete	90%	50%
Gross profit (loss) recognized	$180,000	$ (20,000)
For the Year Ended September 30, Year 3:		
Estimated gross profit (loss):		
Contract price	$560,000	$840,000
Less total costs	450,000	900,000
Estimated gross profit (loss)	$110,000	$ (60,000)
Percent complete:		
Costs incurred to date	$450,000	$720,000
Total costs	450,000	900,000
Percent complete	100%	80%
Gross profit (loss) recognized	110,000	(60,000)
Less gross profit (loss) recognized in prior year	180,000	(20,000)
Gross profit (loss) recognized	$ (70,000)	$ (40,000)

Explanations

- This problem consists of three related requirements concerning long-term construction contracts. The candidates must compute gross profit recognized for two years using the percentage-of-completion method, compute balances in various accounts, and reconcile financial statement income and taxable income.
- Using the percentage-of-completion method, gross profit is recognized periodically based on progress toward completion of the project using the following formula.

$$\frac{\text{Costs to date}}{\text{Total estimated costs}} \times \begin{array}{c}\text{Estimated}\\ \text{profit}\end{array} = \begin{array}{c}\text{Gross profit}\\ \text{to date}\end{array}$$

For the Beta project, London would recognize gross profit of $180,000 the first year.

$$\frac{\$360,000}{(\$360,000 + \$40,000)} \times [\$600,000 - (\$360,000 + \$40,000)] = \$180,000$$

The estimates available at 9/30/Y2 are used above.

- By the end of the second year, the Beta project is complete and has resulted in actual gross profit of $110,000 ($560,000 revenues less $450,000 costs). Since gross profit of $180,000 was recognized the first year, a loss of $70,000 must be recognized the second year [$110,000 − $180,000 = $(70,000)]. The loss of $70,000 is in effect an adjustment of the excessive gross profit recognized the first year. Instead of restating the prior period, the prior period misstatement is absorbed in the current period, as is appropriate for a change in estimate.
- Under both the percentage-of-completion method and the completed contract method, for financial accounting purposes, an expected **loss** on a contract must be recognized in full in the period in which the expected loss is discovered. At the end of the first year, London has an expected loss on the Gamma contract [$800,000 − ($410,000 + $410,000) = $(20,000)] that must be recognized immediately.
- By the end of the second year, the expected loss on the Gamma contract has increased to $60,000 [$840,000 − ($720,000 + $180,000)]. Since a loss of $20,000 was recognized the first year, an additional loss of $40,000 must be recognized in the second year to bring the cumulative loss recognized up to the new estimate of $60,000.
- Financial Statement Disclosures require the computation of the 9/30/Y2 balances of accounts receivable, costs and estimated earnings in excess of billings, and billings in excess of costs and estimated earnings. At 10/1/Y1, the balances in all three accounts were $0 since the construction division began operations on that date.

Task-Based Simulation 6

Financial Statement Disclosures		
	Authoritative Literature	Help

London Inc.
SCHEDULE OF SELECTED BALANCE SHEET ACCOUNTS
September 30, Year 2

Accounts receivable		$115,000
Costs and estimated earnings in excess of billings:		
Construction in progress	$540,000	
Less: Billings	315,000	
Costs and estimated earnings in excess of billings		225,000
Billings in excess of costs and estimated earnings		30,000
Estimated loss on contract		20,000

Explanations

- This problem consists of three related requirements concerning long-term construction contracts. The candidates must compute gross profit recognized for two years using the percentage-of-completion method, compute balances in various accounts, and reconcile financial statement income and taxable income.
- Using the percentage-of-completion method, gross profit is recognized periodically based on progress toward completion of the project using the following formula.

$$\frac{\text{Costs to date}}{\text{Total estimated costs}} \times \text{Estimated profit} = \text{Gross profit to date}$$

For the Beta project, London would recognize gross profit of $180,000 the first year.

$$\frac{\$360,000}{(\$360,000 + \$40,000)} \times [\$600,000 - (\$360,000 + \$40,000)] = \$180,000$$

The estimates available at 9/30/Y2 are used above.

- By the end of the second year, the Beta project is complete and has resulted in actual gross profit of $110,000 ($560,000 revenues less $450,000 costs). Since gross profit of $180,000 was recognized the first year, a loss of $70,000 must be recognized the second year [$110,000 − $180,000 = $(70,000)]. The loss of $70,000 is in effect an adjustment of the excessive gross profit recognized the first year. Instead of restating the prior period, the prior period misstatement is absorbed in the current period, as is appropriate for a change in estimate.
- Under both the percentage-of-completion method and the completed contract method, for financial accounting purposes, an expected **loss** on a contract must be recognized in full in the period in which the expected loss is discovered. At the end of the first year, London has an expected loss on the Gamma contract [$800,000 − ($410,000 + $410,000) = $(20,000)] that must be recognized immediately.
- By the end of the second year, the expected loss on the Gamma contract has increased to $60,000 [$840,000 − ($720,000 + $180,000)]. Since a loss of $20,000 was recognized the first year, an additional loss of $40,000 must be recognized in the second year to bring the cumulative loss recognized up to the new estimate of $60,000.
- Financial Statement Disclosures require the computation of the 9/30/Y2 balances of accounts receivable, costs and estimated earnings in excess of billings, and billings in excess of costs and estimated earnings. At 10/1/Y1, the balances in all three accounts were $0 since the construction division began operations on that date.
- **Accounts receivable** is increased by billings

    Accounts receivable
        Billings on LT contracts

    It is decreased by cash collections

    Cash
        Accounts receivable

    Therefore, 9/30/Y2 AR is computed by adding the billings on the two projects ($315,000 + $440,000 = $755,000) and subtracting the collections on the two projects ($275,000 + $365,000 = $640,000). The 9/30/Y2 balance is $115,000 ($755,000 − $640,000).

- **Construction-in-progress** is debited for costs incurred and profit recognized. **Billings on LT contracts** is credited for billings made. In the balance sheet, the two accounts are netted on a project-by-project basis, resulting in a net current asset and/or a net current liability. At 9/30/Y2, the costs incurred on the Beta project ($360,000) and the estimated earnings ($180,000 from item two of this solution guide) exceed billings ($315,000) by $225,000.

- On the Gamma project billings ($440,000) exceed costs ($410,000) by $30,000. There is no estimated earnings on this project because it is expected, at 9/30/Y2, to result in a $20,000 loss. This estimated loss does not affect the excess of billings over costs and estimated earnings because it is reported separately as a current liability.

Task-Based Simulation 7

Research			
	Authoritative Literature	**Help**	

ASC	605	35	25	46

Task-Based Simulation 8

Inventory Concepts		
	Authoritative Literature	**Help**

	True	False
1. The gross margin method uses historical sales margins to estimate the cost of inventory.	●	○
2. The dollar-value LIFO method preserves old inventory costs by charging current costs to cost of goods sold.	●	○
3. Inventory should be reported at the lower of cost or market and it may be based on the values of individual items, categories, or the total inventory.	●	○
4. A loss on a purchase commitment should be recorded when the contract price is greater than the market and it is anticipated that a loss will occur when the contract is completed.	●	○
5. Under the dollar-value LIFO method, increases and decreases in a layer would be measured based upon the change in the total dollar value of the layer.	●	○
6. The link-chain method uses a cumulative index to value the base cost of ending inventory.	●	○
7. The price index for dollar-value LIFO is a measure of changes in price levels between the current year and the base year.	●	○
8. Under the LIFO method, an inventory liquidation will result in higher profits in a period of rising prices.	●	○
9. A holding gain results from holding an item while the market value experiences a decline.	○	●
10. During a period of rising prices, the LIFO cost flow assumption results in a higher net income as compared to FIFO.	○	●
11. In a period of rising prices, when a company changes from FIFO to LIFO the net income will tend to decline as will working capital.	●	○
12. The use of LIFO for book and tax purposes will result in a lower tax payment in a period of rising prices.	●	○
13. Under the LIFO method, the cost of goods sold balance would be the same whether a perpetual or periodic inventory system is used.	○	●

Explanations

1. **(T)** The gross margin method uses historical margins on sales to estimate the cost of inventory. This method is typically used for interim reporting only because it may not be precise enough for the year-end financial statements.

2. **(T)** The dollar-value LIFO method groups inventory into layers and charges the most recent items to cost of goods sold before using older layers which have older inventory costs.

3. **(T)** Inventory should be carried at the lower of cost or market. In determining the lower of cost or market it may be based on the values of individual items, item categories, or even total inventory.

4. **(T)** When the market price of a contract to purchase goods falls below the contract price and it is foreseeable that the contract will result in a loss, then a loss on the purchase commitment should be recorded.

5. **(T)** The dollar-value LIFO method measures changes in inventory layers based upon the total dollar value change in the layer.

6.   (T) The link-chain method uses a cumulative index to compute the base cost of inventory. The cumulative index is equal to the current year's prices divided by the prior year's prices, multiplied by the prior year's cumulative index. The link-chain method is only used in limited circumstances.

7.   (T) A price index provides a measure of the changes in price between base year and the current year. The price index is generally used to compute changes in inventory levels.

8.   (T) In a period of rising prices, a liquidation of older inventory, which carries lower costs, will result in a decline in the cost of goods sold and higher profits.

9.   (F) A holding gain results from holding an item while the market value **increases**. Thus, the holding gain would be equal to the current market value less the value on the books.

10.   (F) During a period of rising prices, the LIFO method will result in higher priced items being charged to cost of goods sold, thus lowering net income. It is the FIFO method which would produce a higher net income because the cost of goods sold would reflect the older or lower cost goods.

11.   (T) A change from FIFO to LIFO will tend to result in a decrease in net income and working capital. This is because the LIFO method will put the more recent/higher priced items on the income statement (last in) and the older/less expensive goods will be carried in inventory. Thus, net income will be lower due to higher cost of goods sold, and working capital will be lower due to the lower inventory asset balance.

12.   (T) The LIFO method results in the most recently purchased inventory items being expensed first. In a period of rising prices this would result in a lower net income and thus a lower taxes payable. The IRS allows the use of LIFO for tax only if it is also used for external reporting purposes as well.

13.   (F) The cost of goods sold would be different because a periodic system will compute the cost of goods sold based on the total goods sold and total purchases for a period, whereas a perpetual one will match each good sold with the most recent purchase on an ongoing basis.

Task-Based Simulation 9

Cost Flow Concepts		
	Authoritative Literature	**Help**

		Method
1. During a period of rising prices, this method results in a higher net income.		FIFO
2. This method most closely matches the physical flow of inventory.		FIFO
3. Method that uses historical sales margins to estimate ending inventory.		Gross profit
4. Method that is appropriate when there is a relatively small number of significant dollar value items in inventory.		Specific identification
5. Average cost must be calculated each time additional inventory is purchased.		Moving-average
6. Method that averages the cost of all items on hand and purchased during the period.		Weighted-average
7. This method results in the lowest ending inventory in a period of rising prices.		LIFO
8. Method that uses a price index to measure changes in inventory.		Dollar-value LIFO
9. If used for tax purposes, this method must also be used for financial reporting purposes.		LIFO
10. The cost of goods sold balance is the same whether a perpetual or periodic inventory system is used.		FIFO

Task-Based Simulation 10

Schedule of Ending Inventory		
	Authoritative Literature	Help

York Co.
SUPPORTING SCHEDULE OF ENDING INVENTORY
December 31, Year 2

Inventory at cost (LIFO):

	Units	Cost per unit	Total cost
Beginning inventory, January 1	8,000	$8.20	$ 65,600
Purchases, quarter ended March 31	12,000	8.25	99,000
Purchases, quarter ended June 30	2,000	7.90	15,800
	22,000		$180,400

York Co.
SCHEDULE OF COST OF GOODS SOLD
For the Year Ended December 31, Year 2

Beginning inventory	$ 65,600	
Add: Purchases	368,900	
Less: Purchase discounts	(18,000)	
Add: Freight-in	5,000	
Goods available for sale	421,500	
Less: Ending inventory	(176,000)	[1]
Cost of Goods Sold	$245,500	

[1] Inventory at market:
22,000 units @ $8 = $176,000

Explanations

- This problem requires preparation of a cost of goods sold (CGS) schedule with a supporting schedule of ending inventory at lower of cost or market (LCM). York uses the direct method for LCM, which means the LCM amount is used directly in the CGS computation with no separate disclosure of any LCM loss.
- The cost of goods sold schedule can be prepared first, leaving the last two lines (ending inventory and CGS) blank for now. The computation starts with **beginning inventory** plus **cost of goods purchased** equals **cost of goods available for sale** (cost of goods purchased is **purchases** less **purchase discounts** plus **freight-in**). **Freight-out** is a selling expense which does not affect CGS.
- When determining LCM, the market value of inventory is defined as the **replacement cost,** as long as it is less than the ceiling [**net realizable value** (NRV)] and more than the floor (**NRV less a normal profit**).
- There are 22,000 units in ending inventory (55,000 units available less 33,000 units sold). Using LIFO, the earliest units in are assumed to remain in ending inventory. Therefore, ending inventory consists of the 8,000 units from beginning inventory, plus the 12,000 units purchased in the first quarter, plus 2,000 more units from second quarter purchases to get up to the 22,000 unit total. The cost of ending inventory is $180,400 [(8,000 × $8.20) + (12,000 × $8.25) + (2,000 × $7.90)].
- The replacement cost of the inventory is $176,000 (22,000 × $8).
- The ceiling (NRV) is $193,600 (22,000 × $8.80).
- The floor (NRV less a normal profit) is $170,500 [22,000 × ($8.80 – $1.05)].
- Because replacement cost ($176,000) falls between the floor ($170,500) and the ceiling ($193,600), the replacement cost of $176,000 is the designated market value.
- Since the designated market value of $176,000 is less than cost ($180,400), the LCM valuation of ending inventory is $176,000. This amount can be put into the cost of goods sold schedule, resulting in CGS of $245,500.

  - Value inventory at LCM
    Market is replacement with limits
      Market must ≤ NRV and
      Market must ≥ NRV – normal profit
  - Market is replacement cost in this situation
    Replacement cost ($176,000) falls between above limits
  - Inventory reported at market because < cost

Task-Based Simulation 11

Research			
	Authoritative Literature	Help	

ASC	330	10	30	9

Module 11: Fixed Assets

Overview

Fixed assets are defined as the capitalized amount of expenditures made to acquire tangible property which will be used for a period of more than one year. Tangible property includes property that physically exists. Intangible assets are nonphysical assets.

Fixed and intangible asset concepts are tested on the Financial Accounting and Reporting section of the exam. The primary topics covered include

1. Fixed and intangible asset acquisitions including the costs to be capitalized.
2. Self-constructed assets including capitalization of interest.
3. Asset exchanges including how to account for exchanges that lack commercial substance or include some monetary amount.
4. Asset cost allocation including depreciation, amortization, and depletion methods and impairment.

A. Acquisition Cost

1. **Fixed assets** represent the capitalized amount of expenditures made to acquire tangible property which will be used for a period of more than one year. Their cost, therefore, is deferred to future periods in compliance with the matching principle.
2. **Tangible property** includes land, buildings, equipment, or any other property that physically exists.

   a. All of the costs necessary to get the asset to the work site and to prepare it for use are capitalized, including the cost of negotiations, sales taxes, finders' fees, razing an old building, shipment, installation, preliminary testing, and so forth.

      (1) When capitalizing such costs it is necessary to associate them with the asset which is being prepared for use. Thus, the cost of razing an old building is added to the cost of acquiring the land on which the building stood.

3. Charges for self-constructed fixed assets include direct materials, direct construction labor, variable overhead, and a fair share of fixed overhead.
4. Assets received through donation should be recorded at fair value with a corresponding credit to revenue; if fair value is not determinable, book value should be used.

   a. If the entity incurs a liability associated with future retirement of the asset, the fair value (present value) of that obligation should be added to the carrying value of the asset.

239

B. Capitalization of Interest

1. The capitalization of interest is part of the cost of certain assets. Only assets which require a period of time to be prepared for use qualify for interest capitalization.

   a. These include assets constructed for sale produced as discrete projects (e.g., ships) and assets constructed for a firm's own use, whether by the entity itself or by an outsider.

   > **EXAMPLE**
   >
   > A building purchased by an entity **would not** qualify, but one constructed over a period of time **would**.

   (1) Other assets that do **not** qualify include those in use or ready for use and ones not being used in the earnings activities of a firm (e.g., idle land).

2. The amount of interest to be capitalized is the amount which could have been avoided if the project had not been undertaken. This amount includes amortization of any discount, premium, or issue costs; but, it shall not exceed the actual interest incurred during the period. The amount of "avoidable" interest is computed as

   Average accumulated expenditures during construction   ×   Interest rate   ×   Construction period

3. The interest rate used is the rate on specific borrowings for the asset, or a weighted-average of other borrowings when a specific rate is not available. Capitalized interest should be compounded.

   a. This is usually accomplished by including the interest capitalized in a previous period in the calculation of average accumulated expenditures of subsequent periods.
   b. Furthermore, noninterest-bearing payables (e.g., trade payables and accruals) are excluded in determining these expenditures.
   c. In practice, both the weighted-average interest rate and the average accumulated expenditures have been computed on the following bases: monthly, quarterly, semiannual, and annual.

4. The interest capitalization period begins when, and continues as long as, all three of the following conditions are met:

   a. Expenditures for the asset have been made
   b. Activities necessary to get the asset ready for its intended use are in progress
   c. Interest cost is being incurred

5. The period ends when the asset is substantially complete. Brief interruptions and delays do not suspend interest capitalization, while suspension of the activities will.

> **NOTE:** In no case should the amount capitalized exceed the interest actually incurred.

> **EXAMPLE**
>
> **Interest Capitalization**
>
> Assume the company is constructing an asset which qualifies for interest capitalization. By the beginning of July $3,000,000 had been spent on the asset, and an additional $800,000 was spent during July. The following debt was outstanding for the entire month.
>
> 1. A loan of $2,000,000, interest of 1% per month, specifically related to the asset.
> 2. A note payable of $1,500,000, interest of 1.5% per month.
> 3. Bonds payable of $1,000,000, interest of 1% per month.
>
> The amount of interest to be capitalized is computed below.
>
> **Average accumulated expenditures** (for the month of July) = ($3,000,000 + $3,800,000) ÷ 2 = $3,400,000
>
> | Avoidable interest | | | Actual interest | | |
> |---|---|---|---|---|---|
> | $2,000,000 × 1% | = | $20,000 | $2,000,000 × 1% | = | $20,000 |
> | 1,400,000 × 1.3%* | = | 18,200 | 1,500,000 × 1.5% | = | 22,500 |
> | | | | 1,000,000 × 1% | = | 10,000 |
> | $3,400,000 | | $38,200 | $4,500,000 | | $52,500 |
>
> $38,200 < $52,500 ∴ $38,200 is capitalized

Amount of interest to be capitalized is $38,200

Asset	38,200	
Interest expense		38,200

* The average rate on other borrowings is ($22,500 + $10,000) ÷ ($1,500,000 + $1,000,000) = 1.3%. Notice that a specific rate is used to the extent possible and the average rate is used only on any excess. Alternatively, the rate on all debt may be used.

6. Interest on expenditures made to acquire land on which a building is to be constructed qualifies for interest capitalization. The capitalization period begins when activities necessary to construct the building commence and ends when the building is substantially complete. Interest so capitalized becomes part of the cost of the building. Thus, it is charged to expense as the building is depreciated.

7. Frequently, the funds borrowed to finance the construction project are temporarily invested until needed. The interest earned on these funds must be recognized as revenue and may not be offset against the interest expense to be capitalized.

8. The diagram below outlines the requirements pertaining to capitalization of interest.

SUMMARY OF ACCOUNTING FOR INTEREST CAPITALIZATION

Capitalization of Interest During Construction

Qualifying Assets:
Capitalize means to include an expenditure in an asset's cost.
Interest costs, when material, incurred in acquiring the following types of assets, shall be capitalized

1. Assets constructed or produced for a firm's own use
   a. Including construction by outside contractors requiring progress payments
2. Assets intended for lease or sale that are produced as discrete projects
   a. For example, ships and real estate developments
3. But **not** on
   a. Routinely produced inventories (e.g., widgets)
   b. Assets ready for their intended use when acquired
   c. Assets not being used nor being readied for use (e.g., idle equipment)
   d. Land, unless it is being developed (e.g., as a plant site, real estate development, etc.). Then capitalized interest resulting from land expenditure (cash outlay) is added to building.

When to Capitalize Interest (All three must be met):
1. Expenditures for asset have been made
2. Activities intended to get asset ready are in progress
3. Interest cost is being incurred

Applicable Interest (Net of discounts, premiums, and issue costs):
1. Interest obligations having explicit rates
2. Imputed interest on certain payables/receivables
3. Interest related to capital leases

How Much Interest Cost Is Capitalized?

$$\left(\begin{array}{l}\text{Accumulated expenditures beg. of period (C - I - P ** bal.) +} \\ \text{Accumulated expenditures end of period (C - I - P bal.)}\end{array}\right) \div 2 \times \text{Portion of year} = \text{Weighted-average accumulated expenditures}$$

$$\text{Weighted-average accumulated expenditures} \times \left(\begin{array}{c}\text{Interest*} \\ \text{rate}\end{array}\right) = \text{Amount capitalized (cannot exceed total interest incurred)}$$

* AICPA questions have given the specific borrowing rate on debt incurred to finance a project and indicated that expenditures were incurred evenly throughout the year. ASC Topic 835 (SFAS 34) requires that the firm's weighted-average borrowing rate be used after the amount of a specific borrowing is exhausted. Alternatively, only the firm's weighted-average borrowing rate may be used on all expenditures.

** C-I-P-Construction-in-Progress

Qualifications:
1. Amount of interest to be capitalized cannot exceed total interest costs incurred during the entire reporting period
2. Interest earned on temporarily invested borrowings may not be offset against interest to be capitalized

a. **Rationale** for interest capitalization

    (1) To reflect asset's acquisition cost

    (2) To match asset's cost with revenue of periods that benefit from its use

> **NOW REVIEW MULTIPLE-CHOICE QUESTIONS 1 THROUGH 5**

C. Nonmonetary Exchanges

1. A nonmonetary exchange is a reciprocal transfer wherein the transferor has no substantial continuing involvement in the asset, and the risks and rewards of ownership are transferred.

2. The guidance on nonmonetary exchanges does not apply to (1) business combinations, (2) transfers of nonmonetary assets between companies under common control, (3) acquisition of nonmonetary assets or services for the issuance of capital stock, (4) stock issued or received in stock dividends or stock splits, (5) transfer of assets in exchange for equity interests, (6) a pooling of assets in joint undertaking for gas or oil, (7) exchanging part of an operating interest owned for a part of another operating interest owned by another party, and (8) certain transfers of financial assets.

3. Nonmonetary exchanges are usually recorded using the fair value of the asset exchanged.

    a. If one of the parties could have elected to receive cash instead of the nonmonetary asset, the amount of cash that could have been received is evidence of the fair value of the assets exchanged.

    b. If the fair value (FV) of the asset given up cannot be determined, assume it is equal to the fair value of the asset received.

    c. Three exceptions exist to the fair value treatment:

        (1) If fair value is not determinable;

        (2) If it is an exchange transaction to facilitate sales to customers; or

        (3) The transaction lacks commercial substance.

            (a) A transaction has **commercial substance** if the configuration of cash flows are significantly different as a result of the exchange. The configuration of cash flows includes the risk, timing, and the amount of future cash flows.

            (b) Cash flows from tax effects are not considered in determining if the transaction has commercial substance.

        (4) In these three exceptions, the transaction is measured using the recorded amount (book value) of the asset exchanged.

        (5) For exception (1) when neither of the fair values is determinable, the exchange is accounted for at book value, and no gain or loss is recognized. For exceptions (2) and (3), the transaction is measured using the recorded amount (book value) of the exchanged asset, and any losses are recognized. When book values are used, a part of the gain may be recognized when boot is received.

4. The exchange of nonmonetary assets (such as inventory, property, and equipment) for other nonmonetary assets requires special consideration of two amounts.

    a. Gain or loss, if any

    b. Fair market value of the nonmonetary assets received

> **EXAMPLE**
>
> Gain or loss on a nonmonetary exchange is computed as follows:
>
>   Fair value of the asset given – Book value of the asset given = Gain (loss)

    (1) The asset received is generally recorded at the fair value of the asset surrendered (or the FV of the asset received if "more clearly evident"). Some exceptions do exist. Remember, however, that the asset given up will always be removed from the books at book value.

5. The following rules apply in recording nonmonetary exchanges:

    a. Losses are always recognized

    b. Gains are recognized if the exchange is measured at fair value.

    c. If any of the three conditions for exception to fair value treatment are met, use book value (recorded amount) of the asset exchanged. If no boot is involved, no gain is recognized. If boot is given, no gain is recognized, and the new asset is recorded at the book value of the exchanged asset plus the boot given. If boot is received, a portion of the gain is recognized.

d. The following chart summarizes the process involved in accounting for nonmonetary exchanges. Refer to this chart as you work through the following examples.

ACCOUNTING FOR NONMONETARY EXCHANGES
Concepts Summary

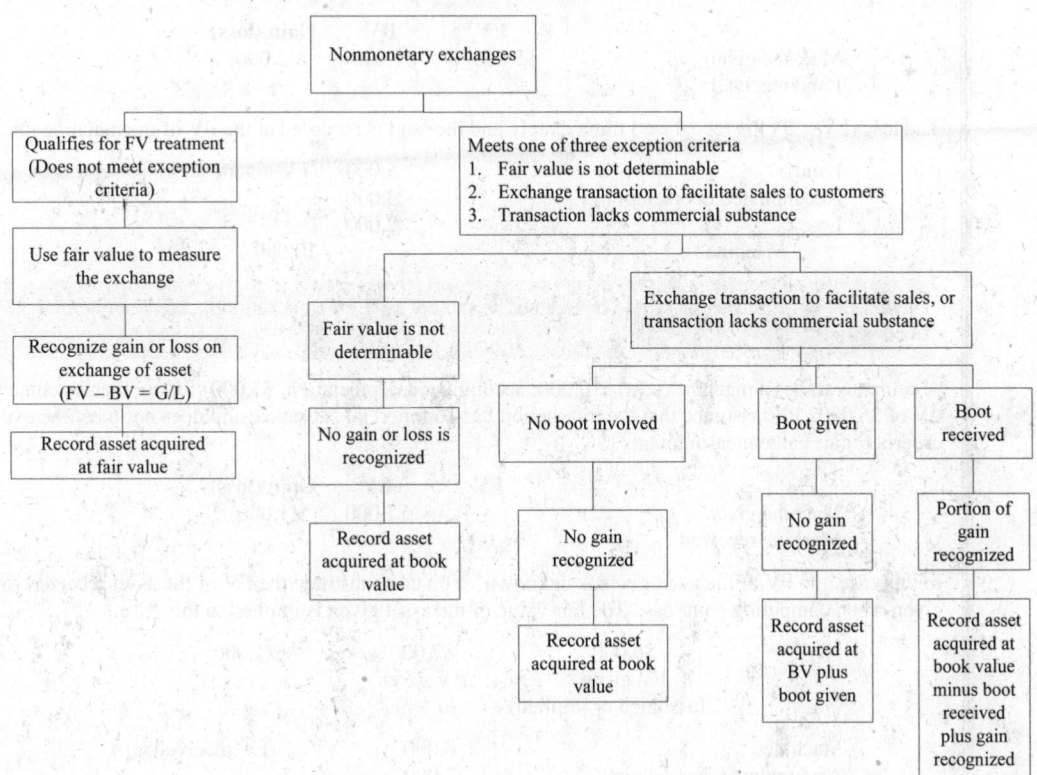

* For tax purposes losses are not recognized on exchanges of similar assets; they are adjustments to the asset's basis as are gains.

6. **FV is not determinable.** When fair value of the asset given up or the asset received is not determinable, book value is used to record the exchanged asset.

EXAMPLE

A company trades a machine (cost, $10,000; accumulated depreciation, $3,000) for land. Neither the FV of the machine or the land is determinable.

Land	7,000	(BV given)
Accumulated depreciation	3,000	
Machine		10,000

Since FV is unknown, no gain can be computed, and the asset received is recorded at the BV of the asset given up ($10,000 – $3,000).

---

7. **Loss situations.** Normally, an exchanged asset is valued at fair value of the asset exchanged, or the fair value of the asset received, whichever is more clearly evident. When the fair value is less than the book value, a loss occurs. Because losses are recognized immediately, the treatment in a loss situation is the same for all nonmonetary exchanges, regardless of whether it meets the exception criteria.

EXAMPLE

Situation 1. Loss, no boot involved.

A company trades a machine with a FV of $5,000 (cost, $10,000; accumulated depreciation, $3,000) for land. It is assumed that the transaction has commercial substance and does not meet the exception criteria to fair value measurement.

	FV	BV	Gain (loss)
Machine given	$5,000	$7,000	$(2,000)
Land received			

The loss (FV – BV) is recognized immediately and the land is recorded at the FV of the machine given up.

Land	5,000	(FV given)
Accumulated depreciation	3,000	
Loss	2,000	
Machine		10,000

NOTE: This transaction would be treated the same way if the transaction lacked commercial substance.

A company trades a machine (cost, $10,000; accumulated depreciation, $3,000) for another machine with a FV of $6,000. It is assumed that the transaction has commercial substance and does not meet the exception criteria to fair value measurement.

	FV	BV	Gain (loss)
Machine given		$7,000	$(1,000)
Machine received	$6,000		

In this case, the FV of the asset given is unknown. You can substitute the FV of the asset received for FV given when computing gain/loss. The fair value of the asset given is implied in this case.

$$\underset{\substack{\text{FV given} \\ \text{(assumed or implied)}}}{\$6,000} - \underset{\text{BV given}}{\$7,000} = \underset{\text{Loss}}{\$(1,000)}$$

Machine	6,000	(FV received)
Accumulated depreciation	3,000	
Loss	1,000	
Machine		10,000

NOTE: If the treatment lacked commercial substance, the entries would be the same because of the loss.

Situation 2. Loss, boot given.

A company trades a machine with a FV of $6,000 (cost, $10,000; accumulated depreciation, $3,000) and $500 cash for land. It is assumed that the transaction has commercial substance and does not meet the exception criteria to fair value measurement.

	Boot	FV	BV	Gain (loss)
Machine given	$500	$6,000	$7,000	$(1,000)
Land received				

Gain (loss) still equals FV less BV. Boot given is added to the value of the asset given.

Land	6,500	(FV given + Boot given)
Accumulated depreciation	3,000	
Loss	1,000	
Machine		10,000
Cash		500

Assume the FV of the machine was unknown, but the FV of the land received was known to be $6,000.

	Boot	FV	BV	Gain (loss)
Machine given	$500		$7,000	$(1,500)
Land received		$6,000		

To compute gain (loss), you can assume FV given is equal to FV received less boot given ($6,000 – $500).

$$\underset{\substack{\text{FV given}\\\text{(assumed)}}}{\$5,500} - \underset{\text{BV given}}{\$7,000} = \underset{\text{Loss}}{\$(1,500)}$$

Land	6,000	(FV received)
Accumulated depreciation	3,000	
Loss	1,500	
Machine		10,000
Cash		500

> **NOTE:** If the transaction lacked commercial substance, the entries would be the same because of the loss.

Situation 3. Loss, boot received.

A company trades a machine with a FV of $6,000 (cost, $10,000; accumulated depreciation, $3,000) for land and $500 cash.

	Boot	FV	BV	Gain (loss)
Machine given		$6,000	$7,000	$(1,000)
Land received	$500			

Boot received is deducted from the value of the asset given.

Land	5,500	(FV given – Boot received)
Accumulated depreciation	3,000	
Cash	500	
Loss	1,000	
Machine		10,000

Now assume the FV of the machine is unknown but the FV of the land received is known to be $6,000.

	Boot	FV	BV	Gain (loss)
Machine given			$7,000	$(500)
Land received	$500	$6,000		

In this case, you can assume FV given is equal to FV received **plus** the boot received ($6,000 + $500).

$$\underset{\substack{\text{FV given}\\\text{(assumed)}}}{\$6,500} - \underset{\text{BV given}}{\$7,000} = \underset{\text{Loss}}{\$(500)}$$

Land	6,000	(FV received)
Accumulated depreciation	3,000	
Cash	500	
Loss	500	
Machine		10,000

8. Gain Situations

> ### EXAMPLE
>
> #### Situation 1. Gain, fair value measurement.
>
> A company trades a computer with a FV of $12,000 (cost, $11,000; accumulated depreciation, $4,000) for a building. The transaction has commercial substance and does not meet any of the exception criteria; therefore the transaction should be valued at fair value.
>
> | | FV | BV | Gain (loss) |
> |---|---|---|---|
> | Computer given | $12,000 | $7,000 | $5,000 |
> | Building received | | | |
>
> Since the transaction has commercial substance, the earnings process is considered complete and the entire gain is recognized.
>
> | | | |
> |---|---|---|
> | Building | 12,000 | (FV received) |
> | Accumulated depreciation | 4,000 | |
> | Computer | | 11,000 |
> | Gain | | 5,000 |

> **NOTE:** If boot had been involved, the accounting would be similar to that illustrated in the loss situation.

Situation 2. Gain, transaction lacks commercial substance, no boot involved.

A company trades equipment with a FV of $12,000 (cost, $11,000; accumulated depreciation, $4,000) for another piece of equipment. The configuration of cash flows of the asset exchanged does not significantly differ from the cash flows of the new asset.

	FV	BV	Gain (loss)
Equipment given	$12,000	$7,000	$5,000
Equipment received			

Since this transaction lacks commercial substance, the earnings process is **not** considered complete and no gain is recognized. The asset received is debited at the book value (**not** fair value) of the asset given.

Equipment	7,000		(BV given)
Accumulated depreciation	4,000		
Equipment		11,000	

The unrecognized gain of $5,000 will be deferred; it will be recognized as the equipment received is depreciated (lower depreciation results than if FV had been used) and/or sold or disposed of in a subsequent transaction.

Situation 3. Gain, transaction lacks commercial substance, boot given.

A company trades a machine (cost, $10,000; accumulated depreciation, $2,000) and $4,000 in cash for another machine with a FV of $16,000. The configuration of cash flows of the asset exchanged does not significantly differ from the cash flows of the new asset.

	Boot	FV	BV	Gain (loss)
Machine given	$4,000		$8,000	$4,000
Machine received		$16,000		

As in the loss situation, the FV of the asset given can be assumed equal to the FV received less the boot given ($16,000 – $4,000).

$$\underset{\substack{\text{FV given}\\\text{(assumed)}}}{\$12,000} - \underset{\text{BV given}}{\$8,000} = \underset{\text{Gain}}{\$4,000}$$

Boot given is added to the value of the asset given (in this case, book value). Gain is still unrecognized.

Machine	12,000		(BV given + Boot given)
Accumulated depreciation	2,000		
Machine		10,000	
Cash		4,000	

Below are alternative ways to calculate the asset received.

FV received	$16,000	BV given	$ 8,000
Gain deferred	(4,000)	Cash paid	4,000
	12,000		12,000

Situation 4. Gain, transaction lacks commercial substance, boot received.

An exception to nonrecognition of gain on exchange for a transaction lacking commercial substance arises when boot is received in the exchange. This type of earnings process is assumed complete for the portion related to the boot received (i.e., "sale" portion), but is **not** assumed complete for the portion related to the asset received (i.e., "exchange" portion). Therefore, a gain is recognized only for that portion related to the boot. Gain recognized is computed as follows:

$$\left(\frac{\text{Boot received}}{\text{Boot received} + \text{FV of asset received}} \right) \times \text{Total gain} = \text{Gain recognized}$$

If the FV of the asset received is not given, it may be determined by subtracting the boot received from the FV of the asset given up.

A company trades a machine with a FV of $12,000 (cost, $9,000; accumulated depreciation, $2,000) for a different machine and $2,000 cash.

| | Boot received | **Machine** | | Gain (loss) |
		FV	BV	
Given		$12,000	$7,000	$5,000
Received	$2,000	?	?	

Since boot was received, the portion of the gain relating to the boot must be recognized.

$$\left(\frac{\$2,000}{\$2,000 + \$10,000*} \right) \times (\$5,000) = \$833$$

* The FV of the asset received ($10,000) was derived by deducting boot received from the FV of the machine given.

$12,000	$2,000	$10,000
FV given	− Boot received	= FV received
		(assumed)

Thus, only $833 of the gain will be recognized. The machine received would be recorded at its BV given less boot received, plus gain recognized ($7,000 − $2,000 + $833 = $5,833). Alternatively this could be calculated by taking its FV less the gain deferred [$10,000 − ($5,000 gain − $833 gain recognized)].

Cash	2,000		
Machine (received)	5,833		
Accumulated depreciation	2,000	$\left(\begin{array}{c} \text{BV given} - \text{Boot received} \\ + \text{Gain recognized} \end{array} \right)$ or $\left(\begin{array}{c} \text{FV received} - \\ \text{Gain deferred} \end{array} \right)$	
Machine (given)		9,000	
Gain		833	

NOW REVIEW MULTIPLE-CHOICE QUESTIONS 6 THROUGH 19

D. Purchase of Groups of Fixed Assets (Basket Purchase)

1. Cost should be allocated based on relative market value.

$$\text{Cost of all assets acquired} \times \frac{\text{Market value of A}}{\text{Market value of all assets acquired}}$$

EXAMPLE

Purchase of Asset 1 with a FMV of $60,000, Asset 2 with a FMV of $120,000, and Asset 3 with a FMV of $20,000 all for $150,000 cash.

	FMV	Relative FMV	Total cost	Allocated cost
Asset 1	$ 60,000	60/200	$150,000	$45,000
Asset 2	120,000	120/200	150,000	90,000
Asset 3	20,000	20/200	150,000	15,000
Total FMV	$200,000			

Journalized:

Asset 1	$45,000	
Asset 2	90,000	
Asset 3	15,000	
Cash		$150,000

E. Capital vs. Revenue Expenditures

1. Capital expenditures and revenue expenditures are charges that are incurred after the acquisition cost has been determined and the related fixed asset is in operation.

   a. **Capital expenditures** are not normal, recurring expenses; they benefit the operations of more than one period. The cost of major rearrangements of assets to increase efficiency is an example of a capital expenditure.

   b. **Revenue expenditures** are normal recurring expenditures. However, some expenditures that meet the test for capital expenditures are expensed because they are immaterial (e.g., less than $50).

2. Expenditures to improve the efficiency or extend the asset life should be capitalized and charged to future periods.

   a. A subtle distinction is sometimes made between an improvement in efficiency and an extension of the asset life. Some accountants feel improvements in efficiency should be charged to the asset account, and improvements extending the asset life should be charged to the accumulated depreciation account. The rationale is that improvements extending the asset life will need to be depreciated over an extended period of time, requiring revision of depreciation schedules.

3. The chart on the following page summarizes the appropriate treatment of expenditures related to fixed assets.

> **NOW REVIEW MULTIPLE-CHOICE QUESTIONS 20 THROUGH 24**

F. Depreciation

1. **Depreciation** is the annual charge to income for asset use during the period. Since depreciation is a noncash expense, it does not provide resources for the replacement of assets. It is simply a means of spreading asset costs to periods in which the assets produce revenue.

   a. Essentially, the "depreciation base" is allocated over the asset's useful life in a rational and systematic manner. The meaning of the key terms is as follows:

      (1) **Systematic**—Formula or plan
      (2) **Rational**—Representational faithfulness (fits with reality)
      (3) **Allocation**—Not a process of valuation

2. The objective is to match asset cost with revenue produced. The depreciation base is cost less salvage value (except for the declining balance method which ignores salvage value). The cost of an asset will include any reasonable cost incurred in bringing an asset to an enterprise and getting it ready for its intended use. The useful life can be limited by

   a. Technological change
   b. Normal deterioration
   c. Physical usage

      (1) The first two indicate depreciation is a function of time whereas the third indicates depreciation is a function of the level of activity. Other depreciation methods include inventory, retirement, replacement, group, composite, etc.

3. Depreciation methods based on time are

   a. Straight-line (SL)
   b. Accelerated

      (1) Declining balance (DB)

         (a) Most common is double-declining balance (DDB)

      (2) Sum-of-the-years' digits (SYD)

4. **Straight-line** and **accelerated** depreciation are illustrated by the following example:

EXAMPLE

$10,000 asset, four-year life, $2,000 salvage value.

Year	Straight line	DDB	SYD
1	$2,000	$5,000	$3,200
2	$2,000	$2,500	$2,400
3	$2,000	$ 500*	$1,600
4	$2,000	--	$ 800

$$\text{Straight-line} \rightarrow \quad \frac{\$10,000 - \$2,000}{4}$$

DDB   Twice the straight-line rate ($2 \times 25\%$) times the net book value at beginning of each year, but not below salvage value (salvage value is not deducted for depreciation base).

SYD   4/10**, 3/10, 2/10, 1/10 of ($10,000 – $2,000).

* $10,000 – ($5,000 + 2,500) = $2,500 Book value at beginning of year three. $2,500 – 2,000 salvage value = $500.

** $\dfrac{n(n+1)}{2} = \dfrac{4 \times 5}{2} = 10$

COSTS SUBSEQUENT TO ACQUISITION OF PROPERTY, PLANT, AND EQUIPMENT

Type of expenditure	Characteristics	Expense when incurred	Capitalize — Debit (credit) to asset	Capitalize — Debit (credit) to accum. deprec.	Other
1. Additions	• Extensions, enlargements, or expansions made to an existing asset		x		
2. Repairs and maintenance					
a. Ordinary	• Recurring, relatively small expenditures				
	1. Maintain normal operating condition	x			
	2. **Do not** add materially to use value	x			
	3. **Do not** extend useful life	x			
b. Extraordinary (major)	• Not recurring, relatively large expenditures				
	1. Primarily increase the quality and/or output of services		x		
	2. Primarily extend the useful life			x	
3. Replacements and improvements	• Major component of asset is removed and replaced with the same type of component with comparable performance capabilities (replacement) or a different type of component having superior performance capabilities (betterment)				
a. Book value of old component is known	• Old component amounts		(x)	x	• Recognize any proceeds and loss (or gain) on old asset
	• New component outlay		x		
b. Book value of old component is **not** known	• Primarily increases the use value		x		
	• Primarily extends the useful life			x	
4. Reinstallations and rearrangements	• Provide greater efficiency in production or reduce production costs				
	1. Material costs, benefits extend into future accounting periods		x		
	2. No measurable future benefit	x			

a. Straight-line and accelerated depreciation methods are illustrated by the following graphs:

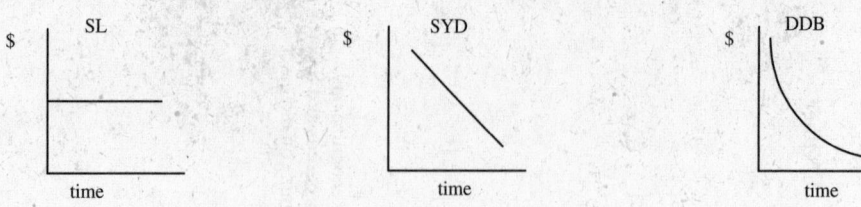

b. Accelerated depreciation is justified by

   (1) Increased productivity when asset is new
   (2) Increasing maintenance charges with age
   (3) Risk of obsolescence

c. Accelerated depreciation methods result in a better matching of costs and revenues when one or more of these factors are present.

5. **Physical usage depreciation** is based on activity (e.g., machine hours) or output (e.g., finished widgets).

$$\text{Annual depreciation} = \frac{\text{Current activity or output}}{\text{Total expected activity or output}} \times \text{Depreciation base}$$

> **EXAMPLE**
>
> A machine costs $60,000. The machine's total output is expected to be 500,000 units. If 100,000 units are produced in the first year, $12,000 of depreciation would be incurred (100/500 × $60,000).

NOTE: Physical usage depreciation results in a varying charge (i.e., not constant). Also physical usage depreciation is based on asset activity rather than expiration of time.

6. **Inventory depreciation** is a method typically used in situations where there are many low-cost tangible assets, such as hand tools for a manufacturer or utensils for a restaurant.

a. Using this method, an inventory of the assets is taken at the beginning and the end of the year. Valuation of these assets is based on appraisal value. Depreciation is calculated as follows:

$$= \text{Beginning inventory} + \text{Cost of acquisitions} - \text{Ending inventory}$$

b. The inventory method is advantageous in situations involving such small assets because it is not practical to maintain separate depreciation schedules for them. On the other hand, this method is often criticized because it is not systematic and rational.

7. **Composite (group) depreciation** averages the service life of a number of property units and depreciates the group as if it were a single unit.

a. The term "group" is used when the assets are similar; "composite" when they are dissimilar.
b. The depreciation rate is the following ratio:

$$\frac{\text{Sum of annual SL depreciation of individual assets}}{\text{Total asset cost}}$$

c. Thus, composite depreciation is a weighted-average of a group of assets—usually of a similar nature, expected life, etc.

> **EXAMPLE**
>
> Three types of assets (A, B, and C) are depreciated under the composite method.
>
> | Asset type | Asset cost | Salvage value | Depreciation base | Useful life (yrs.) | SL annual depreciation |
> |---|---|---|---|---|---|
> | A | $ 45,000 | $15,000 | $ 30,000 | 5 | $ 6,000 |
> | B | 90,000 | 50,000 | 40,000 | 4 | 10,000 |
> | C | 145,000 | 25,000 | 120,000 | 3 | 40,000 |
> | | $280,000 | $90,000 | $190,000 | | $56,000 |

$$\text{Depreciation or composite rate} = \frac{\$56,000}{\$280,000} = 20\%$$

$$\text{Composite life} = 3.39 \text{ years } (\$190,000 \div \$56,000)$$

NOTE: The composite life is the depreciation base divided by the annual depreciation.

(1) Depreciation is recorded until the book value of the composite group is depreciated to the salvage value of the then remaining assets. As assets are retired the composite group salvage value is reduced.

NOTE: Gains and losses are not recognized on disposal (i.e., gains and losses are netted into accumulated depreciation). This latter practice also affects the length of time required to reduce the book value (cost less accumulated depreciation) to the group salvage value.

The entry to record a retirement is

Cash, other consideration	(amount received)	
Accumulated depreciation	(plug)	
Asset		(original cost)

8. **Changes in depreciation.** A change in depreciation method is a change in accounting estimate effected by a change in accounting principle. Therefore, a change in depreciation method is treated as a change in accounting estimate.

   a. Changes in depreciation estimates also include changes in the expected useful life or salvage value. Changes in accounting estimates are accounted for on a prospective basis in the current and future periods. Make the change prospectively from the beginning of the year in which the change in estimate occurs. The procedure for straight-line depreciation is

      (1) Divide the periods remaining (from the beginning of the year of change) into
      (2) The remaining depreciation base (i.e., undepreciated cost to date less revised salvage value)

9. **Fractional year depreciation.** Many conventions exist for accounting for depreciation for midyear asset acquisitions. They include

   a. A whole year's depreciation in year of acquisition and none in year of disposal
   b. One-half year's depreciation in year of acquisition and year of disposal
   c. Depreciation to nearest whole month in both year of acquisition and year of disposal

   NOTE: CPA exam questions generally specify the convention to be followed.

NOW REVIEW MULTIPLE-CHOICE QUESTIONS 25 THROUGH 37

G. Disposals and Impairment of Value

1. The entry to record the disposal (sale) of an asset is

Cash	(amount received)	
Accumulated depreciation	(old asset)	
Old asset		(cost)
Gain or loss	(loss)	(gain)

   a. Remember to record depreciation for disposed assets up to the point of disposal.

EXAMPLE

Jimco, a manufacturer of sports equipment, purchased a machine for $6,000 on 1/1/Y1. The machine had an eight-year life, a $600 salvage value, and was depreciated using the straight-line method. Thus, depreciation was charged at a rate of $56.25 per month [($6,000 cost – $600 salvage) ÷ (8 yrs × 12 mos/yr)]. If Jimco sells the asset on 9/1/Y6 for $3,000, the following entries must be made to record year 6 depreciation and to record the sale:

Depreciation expense	450	
Accumulated depreciation ($56.25 × 8 mos)		450
Cash	3,000	
Accumulated depreciation ($56.25 × 68 mos)	3,825	
Equipment		6,000
Gain on sale of equip. [$3,000 cash − ($6,000 − $3,825)CV]		825

2. In some cases, assets are intended to be **disposed of** in a future reporting period rather than held for use. If management has adopted such a plan for disposal, a loss is recognized if the fair value minus selling costs (NRV) is less than the recorded carrying value.

EXAMPLE

Assume that the asset in the above example has not been sold yet. However, management intends to dispose of it in the next year at NRV of $1,500. The entry to record management's intents would be as follows:

Loss on planned disposition*	675	
Equipment to be disposed of	1,500	
Accumulated depreciation	3,825	
Equipment		6,000

* 1,500 − (6,000 − 3,825)

---

   a. Fixed assets intended for disposal are not subsequently depreciated. The equipment to be disposed of would be classified as other assets on the balance sheet.

   b. **Losses on fixed assets to be disposed of can be recovered** due to changes in the fair value or selling costs associated with the asset. This write-up, however, **cannot** exceed the carrying amount prior to recognition of impairment. If the NRV for this asset increases in the next period, the maximum recovery (gain) that could be recognized is $675.

3. **Assets that are intended to be held and used** should be tested for impairment. Impairment occurs when the carrying amount of a long-lived asset or asset group exceeds its fair value. However, an impairment loss is recognized only if the carrying amount of the asset is not recoverable. The carrying value is considered not recoverable if it exceeds the sum of the expected value of the undiscounted cash flows.

   a. The loss on impairment recognized is the difference between the asset's fair value and its carrying value. In determining the fair value, the principal or most advantageous market for the asset should be used consistent with the asset's highest and best use. The in-use valuation premise assumes the highest value of the asset is achieved by using it in the business with other assets. An in-exchange premise assumes that the highest value of the asset is the amount received to sell the asset stand-alone.

EXAMPLE

Assume that the asset in the previous example is not to be sold. A test for impairment indicates that the net undiscounted cash flows from the machine are $2,000. Since the carrying value is equal to $2,175 ($6,000 − $3,825), the asset is impaired as of 9/1/Y6. If the machine's fair value at this date is $1,400, its carrying value is reduced, as shown below.

Loss on impairment [($6,000 − $3,825) CV − $1,400 FV]	775	
Accumulated depreciation		775

It will continue to be depreciated at $50.00 per month for its remaining useful life ($1,400 ÷ 28 mos = $50.00). At 12/31/Y8, when the asset is fully depreciated, Jimco retires it and writes the machine off with the following entry:

Accumulated depreciation	6,000	
Equipment		6,000

NOTE: The entire cost has been depreciated because upon impairment of the asset it was determined that the equipment did not have a salvage value.

   b. When management has alternative courses of action to recover the carrying amount of the assets or a particular course has multiple outcomes in terms of cash flow, ASC 360-10-35-30 (SFAS 144) indicates that probability-weighted cash flow approach should be considered. **Recoveries of previously recognized impairment losses may not be recognized in subsequent periods.**

H. Depletion

1. **Depletion** is "depreciation" of natural resources. The depletion base is the total cost of the property providing the natural resources. This includes all development costs such as exploring, drilling, excavating, and other preparatory costs.

   a. The depletion base is usually allocated by the ratio of extracted units over the total expected recoverable units.

   $$\frac{\text{Units extracted}}{\text{Total expected recoverable units}} \times \text{Depletion base}$$

   b. The unit depletion rate is frequently revised due to the uncertainties surrounding the recovery of natural resources. The revised unit rate in any year takes the following form:

   $$\frac{\text{Orig. cost} + \text{Addl. cost incurred} - \text{Resid. value} - \text{Depletion taken in prev. yrs.}}{\text{Units withdrawn currently} + \text{Estimated units recoverable at year-end}}$$

   > **NOTE:** The adjustment is being made prospectively (i.e., the remaining undepleted cost is being expensed over the remaining recoverable units).

   c. Depletion on resources extracted during an accounting period is allocated between inventory and cost of goods sold.

   > **NOW REVIEW MULTIPLE-CHOICE QUESTIONS 38 THROUGH 57**

I. Insurance

1. **Loss account for fixed assets.** When an insured loss occurs, an insurance loss account should be set up and charged for all losses. These losses include decreases in asset value, earned insurance premiums, etc. The account should be credited for any payments from the insurance company. The remainder is closed to revenue and expense summary.
2. **Coinsurance.** This area is tested on the Business Environment and Concepts section of the exam.

J. Goodwill and Other Intangible Assets

1. Intangible assets are nonphysical assets. Intangible assets normally include only noncurrent intangibles (e.g., accounts receivable are not considered intangibles). Examples of intangible assets include copyrights, leaseholds, organizational costs, trademarks, franchises, patents, and goodwill. These intangibles may be categorized according to the following characteristics:

   a. Identifiability. Separately identifiable or lacking specific identification.
   b. Manner of acquisition. Acquired singly, in groups, or in business combinations; or developed internally.
   c. Expected period of benefit. Limited by law or contract, related to human or economic factors, or indefinite or indeterminate duration.
   d. Separability from enterprise. Rights transferable without title, salable, or inseparable from the entire enterprise.

2. **Acquisition of intangibles.** Purchased intangibles should be recorded at cost, which represents the fair value of the intangible at time of acquisition. Internally developed intangibles are written off as research and development expense; an exception is the cost to register a patent.
3. **Acquisition of goodwill and allocation to reporting units.** Goodwill is recorded only when an entire business is purchased. Purchase of goodwill as part of acquiring a business is discussed in the Investment and Business Combinations and Consolidations modules.

   a. In a business acquisition, the recognized goodwill should be assigned to one or more reporting units. In essence, the goodwill assigned to a reporting unit is the difference between the fair value of the unit and the value of its individual assets and liabilities. A reporting unit can be an operating segment or one level below.

EXAMPLE

Allocation of Goodwill to a Reporting Unit

Dunn Corporation acquired all of the assets of Yeager Corporation for $12,000,000 cash. The assets were seen as relating to three different reporting units (operating segments)—Communications, Technology, and Consulting. The fair value of the Communications reporting unit at the date of acquisition was $4,700,000. Goodwill associated with the unit would be assigned based on a comparison of its total fair value to the value of its assets and liabilities as shown below.

Communications Reporting Unit (In 000s)

	Fair value
Cash	$ 200
Accounts receivable	900
Net Equipment	2,700
Patents	1,000
Customer contracts	700
Current liabilities	(1,100)
Fair value of net assets	$ 4,400

The amount of goodwill assigned to the reporting unit would be $300,000 ($4,700,000 – $4,400,000), the excess of the fair value of the reporting unit over the value of its net assets. Goodwill would be assigned to the other two reporting units in a similar manner.

---

4. **Amortization of intangibles.** Intangible assets that have a definite useful life are amortized by crediting the intangible account directly (ordinarily, contra accounts are not used).

Amortization expense   xx

Intangible asset   xx

a. The method of amortization of intangibles should mirror the pattern that the asset is consumed. If the pattern cannot be reliably determined, the straight-line basis should be used.

EXAMPLE

Determination of Useful Life of an Intangible Asset

Yeager Communications owns several radio stations and has $5,000,000 recorded as the carrying value of broadcast rights. The rights have a legal life of 7 more years but may be extended upon appropriate application for an indefinite period. Since the company has the right and intent to extend the rights indefinitely, the useful life of the asset should be considered indefinite and the rights should not be amortized.

---

5. **Impairment of intangible assets.** An intangible asset that is amortized should be tested for impairment.

a. An intangible asset that is determined to have an indefinite useful life should not be amortized. However, it should be reevaluated every reporting period to determine if facts and circumstances have changed creating a limited life and requiring it to be amortized. Also, such intangible assets should be tested for impairment annually or more frequently if facts and circumstances indicate that impairment may have occurred. In assessing impairment, an entity may choose to qualitatively assess (a likelihood of more than 50%) whether a quantitative impairment assessment is necessary. Events and circumstances to be qualitatively examined include, but are not limited to: cost increases negatively effecting future cash flows; financial performance declines; legal, regulatory, or contractual changes; entity specific events; industry and market deterioration; and other macroeconomic conditions. If it is **not** more likely than not that the events and circumstances lead to impairment, then a quantitative assessment is unnecessary. However, if the qualitative assessment reveals that it is more likely than not that the indefinite-lived intangible asset is impaired, a quantitative assessment (described below) is necessary.

(1) If the carrying value of the intangible asset exceeds its fair value, an impairment loss should be recorded in the amount of the difference.

EXAMPLE

Impairment of an Intangible Asset with an Indefinite Life

Wilson Company acquired a trademark for a major consumer product several years ago for $50,000. At the time it was expected that the asset had an indefinite life. During its annual impairment test of this asset, the company determined that unexpected competition has entered the market that will significantly reduce the future sales of the product. Based on an analysis of cash flows, the trademark is determined to have a fair market value of $30,000 and is expected to continue to have an indefinite useful life. The $20,000 ($50,000 – $30,000) impairment loss should be recognized as shown below.

Impairment loss	20,000	
Trademark		20,000

6. **Impairment of goodwill.** The goodwill assigned to a reporting unit should be examined for impairment on an annual basis and between annual tests in certain circumstances. The annual examination may be performed any time during the company's fiscal year as long as it is done at the same time every year. Different reporting units may be examined at different times during the year. An entity has the option to first qualitatively determine if it is more likely than not (greater than 50%) that the fair value of a reporting unit is less than its carrying value, including goodwill. Circumstances to be examined include, but are not limited to, examination of: macroeconomic conditions, industry and market considerations, cost factors, overall financial performance, entity-specific events, reporting unit events, and share price decreases. If it is found that it is **not** more likely than not that the fair value of the reporting unit is less than its carrying value, the goodwill impairment tests are deemed unnecessary. Then entity can choose to bypass the qualitative assessment and proceed directly to the first step of the goodwill impairment test. The test of impairment is a two-step process as described below.

a. Compare the fair value of the reporting unit with its carrying amount.

   (1) To determine fair value, a valuation premise should be used that is consistent with the asset's highest and best use. The valuation premise can either be an in-use or an in-exchange premise. An in-use premise is used if the asset is used in a business in combination with other assets, such as a reporting unit.

   (a) If the carrying amount of the unit is greater than zero and exceeds its fair value, the second step is performed.
   (b) If the carrying amount of the unit is zero or negative, step 2 of the goodwill impairment test should be performed if it is more likely than not that a goodwill impairment exists.

b. Compare the implied fair value of the reporting unit goodwill with the carrying amount of that goodwill.

   (1) The implied fair value of goodwill is determined in the same manner as the amount of goodwill recognized in a business combination. That is, all assets in the segment are valued, and the excess of the fair value of the reporting unit as a whole over the amounts assigned to its assets and liabilities is the implied goodwill.

   (a) If the implied value of goodwill is less than its carrying amount, goodwill is written down to its implied value and an impairment loss is recognized.

EXAMPLE

Test of Impairment of Goodwill

Dunn Corporation is performing the test of impairment of the Communications reporting unit at 9/30/Y1. In performing the first step in the test of impairment, the Communications reporting unit is valued through a multiple of earnings approach at $4,450,000. The carrying amount of the unit at 9/30/Y1 is $4,650,000, requiring the second step to be performed. The fair value of the assets and liabilities are valued as shown below.

Communications Reporting Unit
Estimated Fair Values 9/30/Y1 (In 000s)

	Fair value
Cash	$ 150
Accounts receivable	1,000
Net Equipment	2,600
Patents	950
Customer contracts	800
Current liabilities	(1,100)
Fair value of net assets	$ 4,400

The implied value of goodwill is $50,000 ($4,450,000 – $4,400,000) and this is less than the carrying amount of $300,000. Therefore, an impairment of goodwill should be recognized as shown below.

Impairment loss	250,000	
Goodwill—Communications		250,000

NOW REVIEW MULTIPLE-CHOICE QUESTIONS 58 THROUGH 68

K. Reporting on the Costs of Start-Up Activities

Start-up costs, including organization costs, are to be expensed as incurred. Start-up costs are defined as one-time activities related to opening a new facility or new class of customer, initiating a new process in an existing facility, or some new operation. In practice, these are referred to as preopening costs, preoperating costs, and organization costs. Routine ongoing efforts to improve existing quality of products, services, or facilities, are not start-up costs.

L. Research and Development Costs

1. R&D costs are expensed as incurred except for intangibles or fixed assets purchased from others having alternative future uses. These should be capitalized and amortized over their useful life. Thus, the cost of patents and R&D equipment purchased from third parties may be deferred and amortized over the asset's useful life. Internally developed R&D may not be deferred.
2. Finally, R&D done under contract for others is not required to be expensed. The costs incurred would be matched with revenue using the completed-contract or percentage-of-completion method.

M. Computer Software Costs

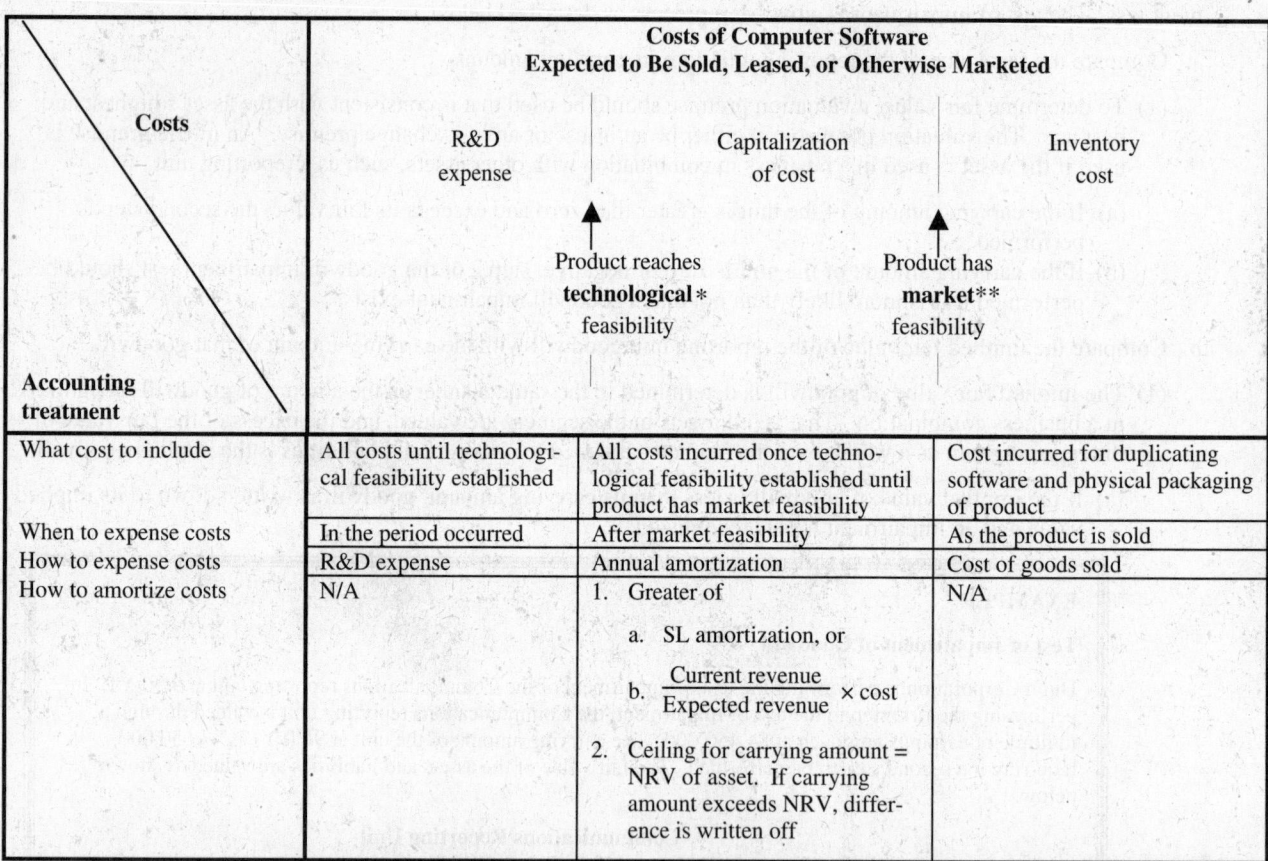

* Software creation process includes a detail program design.
** Product ready for release to customers.

1. **Software developed for sale or lease.** If software is developed for sale or lease, the costs incurred to internally create software should be expensed as research and development until technological feasibility is established. Thereafter, all costs should be capitalized and reported at the lower of unamortized cost or net realizable value. Capitalization should cease when the software is available for general release to customers.

   a. The annual amortization of capitalized computer software costs will be the greater of the ratio of current revenues to anticipated total revenues or the straight-line amortization which is based on the estimated economic life.
   b. Once the software is available for general release to customers, the inventory costs should include costs for duplicating software and for physically packaging the product.
   c. The cost of maintenance and customer support should be charged to expense in the period incurred.

2. **Software developed for internal use.** Software must meet two criteria to be accounted for as internally developed software.

   a. First, the software's specifications must be designed or modified to meet the reporting entity's internal needs, including costs to customize purchased software.

   b. Second, during the period in which the software is being developed, there can be no plan or intent to market the software externally, although development of the software can be jointly funded by several entities that each plan to use the software internally.

      (1) In order to justify capitalization of related costs, it is necessary for management to conclude that it is probable that the project will be completed and that the software will be used as intended.

         (a) Absent that level of expectation, costs must be expensed currently as research and development costs are required to be.

         (b) Entities which historically were engaged in both research and development of software for internal use and for sale to others would have to carefully identify costs with one or the other activity, since the former would (if all conditions are met) be subject to capitalization, while the latter might be expensed as research and development costs until technological feasibility had been demonstrated.

   b. Under terms of the standard, cost capitalization commences when an entity has completed the conceptual formulation, design, and testing of possible project alternatives, including the process of vendor selection for purchased software, if any. These early-phase costs (referred to as "preliminary project stage") are analogous to research and development costs and must be expensed as incurred. These cannot be later restored to an asset account if the development proves to be successful.

   c. Costs incurred subsequent to the preliminary stage, and which meet the criteria under GAAP as long-lived assets, can be capitalized and amortized over the asset's expected economic life. Capitalization of costs will begin when both of two conditions are met.

      (1) First, management having the relevant authority authorizes and commits to funding the project and believes that it is probable that it will be completed and that the resulting software will be used as intended.

      (2) Second, the conceptual formulation, design, and testing of possible software project alternatives (i.e., the preliminary project stage) have been completed.

N. Development Stage Enterprises

1. A **development stage enterprise** is defined as one devoting substantially all of its efforts to establishing a new business and (1) planned principal operations have not commenced, or (2) planned principal operations have commenced, but there has been no significant revenue.

   > **NOTE:** Generally accepted accounting principles are to be followed in preparing the financial statements of a development stage enterprise. Therefore, no special treatment is allowed concerning capitalization or deferral of costs; only costs that may be deferred for an established enterprise may be capitalized by a development stage enterprise.

   a. The balance sheet should show cumulative losses since inception under stockholders' equity.

   b. The income statement and statement of cash flows should include both current period and cumulative amounts, since inception, of revenues, expenses, losses, and cash flows.

   c. The financial statements must be identified as those of a development stage enterprise.

   > **NOTE:** The first fiscal year after the development stage, a disclosure is required in the financial statements stating that the entity was previously in the development stage.

> **NOW REVIEW MULTIPLE-CHOICE QUESTIONS 69 THROUGH 84**

O. Research Component—Accounting Standards Codification

Research on fixed assets is found in several locations in the accounting standards. The most basic accounting rules for fixed assets are in ASC Topic 360, titled *Property, Plant, and Equipment*. Other accounting standards may apply to fixed assets. The following table lists these standards with the corresponding ASC topic numbers and relevant account issues.

Topic number	Topic	Accounting issue(s)
250	Accounting Changes	Changes in Depreciation
280	Segment Reporting	Defining a Reporting Unit
350	Intangibles—Goodwill and Other	Valuation, Impairment
360	Property, Plant, and Equipment	Cost, Measurement, Impairment, Disclosures
410	Asset Retirement Obligations	Capitalizing Costs of Retirement Obligation
720	Other Expenses (Including Start-Up Costs)	Start-Up Activities/Costs
730	Research and Development	Capitalizing R&D
805	Business Combinations	Valuation in Business Combination
820	Fair Value Measurements and Disclosures	Fair Value Measures
835	Interest (Capitalization of Interest)	Capitalization of Interest
845	Nonmonetary Transactions	Exchanges of Nonmonetary Assets
915	Development Stage Enterprises	Accounting for Development Stage Enterprises
958	Not-For-Profit Entities	Donated Assets
985	Software	Capitalizing Software Costs

P. International Financial Reporting Standards (IFRS)

1. Some of the most significant differences between US GAAP and IFRS exist in the area of accounting for fixed assets. Items which are classified as noncurrent assets under US GAAP may be classified differently under IFRS. Specifically, noncurrent assets must be identified in categories such as plant, property, and equipment, investment property, intangible assets, and biological assets.

2. Plant, Property, and Equipment

   a. Plant, property, and equipment are tangible items which are expected to be used during more than one period, and used in the production or supply of goods or services, for rental to others, or for administrative purposes. Plant, property, and equipment are recorded at cost.

      (1) Cost includes the purchase price net of discounts and rebates, the expenditures to bring the asset to its required location and condition, delivery and handling, site preparation, installation, assembly costs, professional fees, and the estimate of the cost of obligations required for the asset's disposal (decommissioning or site restoration).

      (2) Similar to US GAAP, costs of self-constructed assets include material, labor, and interest costs.

   b. After an asset is initially recognized at cost, it is subsequently measured using either the cost model or the revaluation model. Long-lived assets are divided into classes, and a decision is made for each class on which valuation method is applied.

   > **NOTE:** A different valuation model can be used for different classes of assets but not individual assets within a class. Examples of classes of assets include land, equipment, motor vehicles, land and buildings, ships, aircraft, and furniture and fixtures.

      (1) The cost model provides that the asset is carried at cost less an accumulated depreciation and less any accumulated impairment loss.

         (a) The depreciation method chosen should reflect the pattern of economic benefits expected to be consumed. The straight-line, declining balance, and units of production methods are acceptable depreciation methods. A change in depreciation method is considered a change in accounting estimate and is accounted for on a prospective basis.

      (2) Under the revaluation model, the carrying amount of the asset is the fair value at the date of revaluation less any subsequent accumulated depreciation and subsequent accumulated impairment loss. The revaluation model should be applied to assets whose value can be reliably measured. There is no rule regarding the frequency or date of revaluation; therefore, annual revaluations are not required. However, when revaluation is performed, it must be performed for the entire class of assets.

         (a) Revaluation to fair value usually involves obtaining appraisals. When a class of assets is revalued, the asset account is written up or down, and the adjustment is recorded to the revaluation surplus account which is reported in other comprehensive income for the period.

         (b) If the revaluation model is used, accumulated depreciation can be adjusted proportionately, or the accumulated depreciation account can be eliminated and the asset shown net.

         (c) When an asset is disposed of, a gain or loss is recognized and reported on the income statement. Any balance in the revaluation surplus account is transferred directly to retained earnings (not to profit or loss).

3. **Investment Property**

   a. Investment property is defined as property held to earn rentals, for capital appreciation, or both. To qualify as investment property, it may not be used in the production or supply of goods or services or for administrative purposes, nor can it be held for sale in the ordinary course of business.

      (1) Investment property includes land or a building and can be held by the owner or by a lessee under a financing lease.
      (2) Examples of investment property also include land held for long-term appreciation, land held for an undetermined future use, buildings owned by the entity, or a vacant building held to be leased under an operating lease.

   b. Investment property is recognized when it is probable that the future economic benefits of the property will flow to the entity and the cost of the property can be measured reliably. Investment property is measured at cost. After initial recognition, the investment property is measured under the fair value model or the cost model, with certain exceptions.

      (1) Under the fair value model, investment property is initially measured at fair value. Changes in fair value are recognized in profit or loss in the period of the change. Notice that this is different treatment than for plant, property, and equipment, where the revaluation is recorded in other comprehensive income.

         (a) If the fair value model is used, no depreciation is recorded.
         (b) The fair value is the price at which the property could be exchanged between knowledgeable parties in an arm's-length transaction.

      (2) The cost model requires investment property to be carried on the balance sheet at cost less accumulated depreciation and less accumulated impairment losses. If an entity chooses the cost model, it must still disclose fair values in the notes to the financial statements.

   c. Another difference between IFRS and US GAAP involves investment property leased under operating leases. Under IFRS, an entity has the option to record investment property leased under an operating lease as an asset on the balance sheet if the lessee can reliably measure the fair value of the lease. Once this option is selected for one leased property, other investment property must also be accounted for using the fair value model.

   d. Investment property does not include property used in the business, property being constructed or developed for others, property under construction that will be future investment property, and property held for sale in the normal course of business.

4. **Intangible Assets**

   a. Intangible assets either have no physical substance or have a value that is not represented by its physical substance. Intangible assets are categorized as either identifiable or unidentifiable.

      (1) An asset is identifiable if meets one of the two criteria: (1) it is based on contractual or legal rights, or (2) it can be separated from the entity and sold, transferred, licensed, rented, or exchanged.

         (a) Notice this is similar to US GAAP where an identifiable intangible must meet the legal, contractual, or separability criteria.

      (2) Identifiable intangibles include patents, copyrights, brand names, customer lists, trade names, computer software, formulae, licenses, and franchises.

   b. Accounting for intangibles under IFRS depends upon whether the intangible assets were acquired or internally developed.

      (1) If the intangible assets were acquired, the intangible asset is recorded at cost.
      (2) If the intangible assets were acquired in a business combination, newly identified intangibles are recognized at fair value separately from goodwill.
      (3) Internally generated intangibles are initially recognized at the cost of development. However, to be recognized, they must meet the definition of identifiable assets (i.e., they must have future economic benefits and can be measured reliably).

         (a) Although internally generated goodwill may provide future economic benefits, it cannot be measured reliably. Therefore, internally generated goodwill is not recognized as an asset.
         (b) Similarly, expenditures on research may not result in probable future economic benefits; therefore, research expenditures are treated as an expense of the period.
         (c) Development is the application of research findings for the production of new products or technology. Development costs may be recognized as an intangible asset if the following six criteria are met: (1) technological feasibility of completing the asset for use or sale has been achieved; (2) the entity intends

to complete and use or sell the asset; (3) the entity has the ability to use or sell the asset; (4) the entity understands how the asset will generate probable future economic benefits; (5) technical, financial, and other resources are available to complete development of the asset; (6) the entity has the ability to reliably measure the expenditures. If all six conditions are not met, development costs should be expensed in the current period. Once development costs are expensed, they cannot be capitalized in the future.

   c. Intangible assets may use either the cost model or the revaluation model.

     (1) Similar to plant, property, and equipment, the cost model requires the asset to be recorded at its cost less any accumulated amortization or accumulated impairment losses.

     (2) The revaluation model requires that the fair value must be determined in an active market. Therefore, only intangible assets that are traded with active market prices may be valued using the revaluation model. The revaluation model requires gains and losses on revaluation to be recorded in other comprehensive income.

   d. The useful life of an intangible asset is either finite or indefinite. Intangible assets with finite lives are amortized over the useful life; intangible assets with indefinite lives are not amortized, but tested for impairment annually (at the reporting date).

5. **Impairment of Assets**

   a. An entity should determine at each reporting date if there are conditions that would cause an asset to be impaired.

     (1) Asset impairment exists if the carrying value of the asset is greater than its recoverable amount.

       (a) The recoverable amount is the greater of the net selling price or its value in use.

     (2) An impairment loss for an asset accounted for at historical cost is recognized as an expense of the current period. The loss may be included with depreciation expense or identified separately on the income statement.

     (3) If the revaluation model was used, an impairment adjustment may be treated as a reversal of an upward revaluation. Once the entire revaluation account is eliminated, the excess charge is recognized in expense of the period. Hence, the revaluation account cannot have a debit balance.

   b. Intangible assets with finite lives are tested for impairment when the asset's carrying value is more than its recoverable amount. However, if an intangible asset has an indefinite life, a test for impairment must be made annually.

     (1) If an intangible asset's carrying value is more than its recoverable amount, the asset is considered impaired.

       (a) The recoverable amount is the greater of the net selling price (fair value less costs of disposal) or its value in use.

       (b) The value in use is determined by estimating the future cash flows expected from the continued use of the asset and its disposal.

     (2) Impairments of intangible assets carried at historical cost are recognized as charges against the current period profit or loss.

     (3) If the revaluation method was used for long-lived assets, any increase in value was recorded in a revaluation account in other comprehensive income. Therefore, the impairment adjustment is used to reverse any previous revaluation adjustment. Once the revaluation account is reduced to zero, the impairment is then charged to expense of the period.

   c. An important difference between US GAAP and IFRS is that IFRS allows reversals of previously recognized impairments if the historical cost method is used.

     (1) If the cost method is used, a reversal of impairment losses may be recognized in the income statement up to the amount of the impairments previously recognized.

     (2) However, if the revaluation method is used, the recovery of impairments would be recognized in other comprehensive income.

6. **Biological Assets**

   a. Biological assets (agricultural assets) are living animals or plants and must be disclosed as a separate item on the balance sheet. Biological assets are recognized when a future economic benefit is probable, the entity controls the asset as a result of past events, and the cost or fair value can be measured reliably. Agricultural produce should be measured as fair value less costs to sell at harvest.

NOW REVIEW MULTIPLE-CHOICE QUESTIONS 85 THROUGH 102

KEY TERMS

Capital expenditures are not normal, recurring expenses; they benefit the operations of more than one period.

Capitalize. To include an expenditure in an asset's cost.

Commercial substance. A transaction lacks commercial substance if the configuration of cash flows is significantly different as a result of the exchange.

Depletion. "Depreciation" of natural resources.

Depreciation is the annual charge to income for asset use during the period.

Development stage enterprise. One devoting substantially all of its efforts to establishing a new business and (1) planned principal operations have not commenced, or (2) planned principal operations have commenced, but there has been no significant revenue.

Fixed assets. The capitalized amount of expenditures made to acquire tangible property which will be used for a period of more than one year.

Impairment. Occurs when the carrying amount of a long-lived asset or asset group exceeds its fair value.

Intangible assets. Nonphysical assets.

Nonmonetary exchange is a reciprocal transfer wherein the transferor has no substantial continuing involvement in the asset, and the risks and rewards of ownership are transferred.

Revenue expenditures are normal recurring expenditures.

Start-up costs. One-time activities related to opening a new facility or new class of customer, initiating a new process in an existing facility, or some new operation.

Tangible property. Property that physically exists.

Multiple-Choice Questions (1-102)

A.   Acquisition Cost

1. Merry Co. purchased a machine costing $125,000 for its manufacturing operations and paid shipping costs of $20,000. Merry spent an additional $10,000 testing and preparing the machine for use. What amount should Merry record as the cost of the machine?
- a. $155,000
- b. $145,000
- c. $135,000
- d. $125,000

2. On December 1, year 4, Boyd Co. purchased a $400,000 tract of land for a factory site. Boyd razed an old building on the property and sold the materials it salvaged from the demolition. Boyd incurred additional costs and realized salvage proceeds during December year 4 as follows:

Demolition of old building	$50,000
Legal fees for purchase contract and recording ownership	10,000
Title guarantee insurance	12,000
Proceeds from sale of salvaged materials	8,000

In its December 31, year 4 balance sheet, Boyd should report a balance in the land account of
- a. $464,000
- b. $460,000
- c. $442,000
- d. $422,000

B.   Capitalization of Interest

3. Cole Co. began constructing a building for its own use in January year 4. During year 4, Cole incurred interest of $50,000 on specific construction debt, and $20,000 on other borrowings. Interest computed on the weighted-average amount of accumulated expenditures for the building during year 4 was $40,000. What amount of interest cost should Cole capitalize?
- a. $20,000
- b. $40,000
- c. $50,000
- d. $70,000

4. Clay Company started construction of a new office building on January 1, year 4, and moved into the finished building on July 1, year 5. Of the building's $2,500,000 total cost, $2,000,000 was incurred in year 4 evenly throughout the year. Clay's incremental borrowing rate was 12% throughout year 4, and the total amount of interest incurred by Clay during year 4 was $102,000. What amount should Clay report as capitalized interest at December 31, year 4?
- a. $102,000
- b. $120,000
- c. $150,000
- d. $240,000

5. During year 4, Bay Co. constructed machinery for its own use and for sale to customers. Bank loans financed these assets both during construction and after construction was complete. How much of the interest incurred should be reported as interest expense in the year 4 income statement?

	Interest incurred for machinery for own use	Interest incurred for machinery held for sale
a.	All interest incurred	All interest incurred
b.	All interest incurred	Interest incurred after completion
c.	Interest incurred after completion	Interest incurred after completion
d.	Interest incurred after completion	All interest incurred

C.   Nonmonetary Exchanges

6. On July 1, year 4, Balt Co. exchanged a truck for twenty-five shares of Ace Corp.'s common stock. On that date, the truck's carrying amount was $2,500, and its fair value was $3,000. Also, the book value of Ace's stock was $60 per share. On December 31, year 4, Ace had 250 shares of common stock outstanding and its book value per share was $50. What amount should Balt report in its December 31, year 4 balance sheet as investment in Ace?
- a. $3,000
- b. $2,500
- c. $1,500
- d. $1,250

7. A nonmonetary exchange is recognized at fair value of the assets exchanged unless
- a.   Exchange has commercial substance.
- b.   Fair value is not determinable.
- c.   The assets are similar in nature.
- d.   The assets are dissimilar.

8. In a nonmonetary exchange, which of the following situations will require the asset to be recognized at the recorded value of the asset relinquished?
- a.   A delivery truck exchanged for a delivery van that can deliver four times the quantity of goods to customers.
- b.   The exchanged item is intended to facilitate sales to customers.
- c.   The cash flows from the new asset will be significantly different from cash flows of the exchanged asset.
- d.   The assets are both productive assets.

9. For purposes of nonmonetary exchanges, the configuration of cash flows includes which of the following?
- a.   The implicit rate, maturity date of loan, and amount of loan.
- b.   The risk, timing, and amount of cash flows of the assets.
- c.   The entity-specific value of the asset which is equal to the fair value of the asset exchanged.
- d.   The estimated present value of the assets exchanged.

10. When determining the commercial substance of the exchange, which of the following items is not considered?
- a.   Cash flow of exchanged asset.
- b.   Cash flow of new asset.
- c.   Cash flow from tax effects on the exchange to avoid taxes.

d.   Cash flow from potential sale of new equipment at a later date.

11. On March 31, year 4, Winn Company traded in an old machine having a carrying amount of $16,800, and paid a cash difference of $6,000 for a new machine having a total cash price of $20,500. The cash flows from the new machine are expected to be significantly different than the cash flows from the old machine. On March 31, year 4, what amount of loss should Winn recognize on this exchange?

a. $0
b. $2,300
c. $3,700
d. $6,000

12. Amble, Inc. exchanged a truck with a carrying amount of $12,000 and a fair value of $20,000 for a truck and $2,500 cash. The cash flows from the new truck are not expected to be significantly different from the cash flows of the old truck. The fair value of the truck received was $17,500. At what amount should Amble record the truck received in the exchange?

a. $ 7,000
b. $ 9,500
c. $10,500
d. $17,500

13. In an exchange of assets that is deemed to lack commercial substance, Transit Co. received equipment with a fair value equal to the carrying amount of equipment given up. Transit also contributed cash. As a result of the exchange, Transit recognized

a.   A loss equal to the cash given up.
b.   A loss determined by the proportion of cash paid to the total transaction value.
c.   A gain determined by the proportion of cash paid to the total transaction value.
d.   Neither gain **nor** loss.

14. May Co. and Sty Co. exchanged nonmonetary assets. The exchange did not result in the expected cash flows of the assets being significantly different for either May or Sty. May paid cash to Sty in connection with the exchange. To the extent that the amount of cash exceeds a proportionate share of the carrying amount of the asset surrendered, a realized gain on the exchange should be recognized by

	May	Sty
a.	Yes	Yes
b.	Yes	No
c.	No	Yes
d.	No	No

15. Vik Auto and King Clothier exchanged goods, held for resale, with equal fair values. Each will use the other's goods to promote their own products. The retail price of the car that Vik gave up is less than the retail price of the clothes received. Assuming the transaction has commercial substance, what profit should Vik recognize for the nonmonetary exchange?

a.   A profit is **not** recognized.
b.   A profit equal to the difference between the retail prices of the clothes received and the car.
c.   A profit equal to the difference between the retail price and the cost of the car.
d.   A profit equal to the difference between the fair value and the cost of the car.

16. Yola Co. and Zaro Co. are fuel oil distributors. To facilitate the delivery of oil to their customers, Yola and Zaro exchanged ownership of 1,200 barrels of oil without physically moving the oil. Yola paid Zaro $20,000 to compensate for a difference in the grade of oil. On the date of the exchange, cost and market values of the oil were as follows:

	Yola Co.	Zaro Co.
Cost	$100,000	$126,000
Market values	130,000	150,000

In Zaro's income statement, what amount of gain should be reported from the exchange of the oil?

a. $0
b. $ 3,200
c. $20,000
d. $24,000

17. An entity disposes of a nonmonetary asset in a nonreciprocal transfer. A gain or loss should be recognized on the disposition of the asset when the fair value of the asset transferred is determinable and the nonreciprocal transfer is to

	Another entity	A stockholder of the entity
a.	No	Yes
b.	No	No
c.	Yes	No
d.	Yes	Yes

18. On July 1, year 4, one of Rudd Co.'s delivery vans was destroyed in an accident. On that date, the van's carrying value was $2,500. On July 15, year 4, Rudd received and recorded a $700 invoice for a new engine installed in the van in May year 4, and another $500 invoice for various repairs. In August, Rudd received $3,500 under its insurance policy on the van, which it plans to use to replace the van. What amount should Rudd report as gain (loss) on disposal of the van in its year 4 income statement?

a. $1,000
b. $ 300
c. $0
d. $ (200)

19. Lano Corp.'s forest land was condemned for use as a national park. Compensation for the condemnation exceeded the forest land's carrying amount. Lano purchased similar, but larger, replacement forest land for an amount greater than the condemnation award. As a result of the condemnation and replacement, what is the net effect on the carrying amount of forest land reported in Lano's balance sheet?

a.   The amount is increased by the excess of the replacement forest land's cost over the condemned forest land's carrying amount.
b.   The amount is increased by the excess of the replacement forest land's cost over the condemnation award.
c.   The amount is increased by the excess of the condemnation award over the condemned forest land's carrying amount.
d.   No effect, because the condemned forest land's carrying amount is used as the replacement forest land's carrying amount.

D.   Purchase of Groups of Fixed Assets

20. On July 1, year 4, Town Company purchased for $540,000 a warehouse building and the land on which it is located. The following data were available concerning the property:

	Current appraised value	Seller's original cost
Land	$200,000	$140,000
Warehouse building	300,000	280,000
	$500,000	$420,000

Town should record the land at
a. $140,000
b. $180,000
c. $200,000
d. $216,000

E. Capital vs. Revenue Expenditures

21. During year 4, King Company made the following expenditures relating to its plant building:

Continuing and frequent repairs	$40,000
Repainted the plant building	10,000
Major improvements to the electrical wiring system	32,000
Partial replacement of roof tiles	14,000

How much should be charged to repair and maintenance expense in year 4?
a. $96,000
b. $82,000
c. $64,000
d. $54,000

22. On June 18, year 4, Dell Printing Co. incurred the following costs for one of its printing presses:

Purchase of collating and stapling attachment	$84,000
Installation of attachment	36,000
Replacement parts for overhaul of press	26,000
Labor and overhead in connection with overhaul	14,000

The overhaul resulted in a significant increase in production. Neither the attachment nor the overhaul increased the estimated useful life of the press. What amount of the above costs should be capitalized?
a. $0
b. $ 84,000
c. $120,000
d. $160,000

23. A building suffered uninsured fire damage. The damaged portion of the building was refurbished with higher quality materials. The cost and related accumulated depreciation of the damaged portion are identifiable. To account for these events, the owner should
a. Reduce accumulated depreciation equal to the cost of refurbishing.
b. Record a loss in the current period equal to the sum of the cost of refurbishing and the carrying amount of the damaged portion of the building.
c. Capitalize the cost of refurbishing and record a loss in the current period equal to the carrying amount of the damaged portion of the building.
d. Capitalize the cost of refurbishing by adding the cost to the carrying amount of the building.

24. Derby Co. incurred costs to modify its building and to rearrange its production line. As a result, an overall reduc-

tion in production costs is expected. However, the modifications did not increase the building's market value, and the rearrangement did not extend the production line's life. Should the building modification costs and the production line rearrangement costs be capitalized?

	Building modification costs	Production line rearrangement costs
a.	Yes	No
b.	Yes	Yes
c.	No	No
d.	No	Yes

F. Depreciation

25. On January 2, year 4, Lem Corp. bought machinery under a contract that required a down payment of $10,000, plus twenty-four monthly payments of $5,000 each, for total cash payments of $130,000. The cash equivalent price of the machinery was $110,000. The machinery has an estimated useful life of ten years and estimated salvage value of $5,000. Lem uses straight-line depreciation. In its year 4 income statement, what amount should Lem report as depreciation for this machinery?
a. $10,500
b. $11,000
c. $12,500
d. $13,000

26. Turtle Co. purchased equipment on January 2, year 2, for $50,000. The equipment had an estimated five-year service life. Turtle's policy for five-year assets is to use the 200% double-declining depreciation method for the first two years of the asset's life, and then switch to the straight-line depreciation method. In its December 31, year 4 balance sheet, what amount should Turtle report as accumulated depreciation for equipment?
a. $30,000
b. $38,000
c. $39,200
d. $42,000

27. Rago Company takes a full year's depreciation expense in the year of an asset's acquisition, and no depreciation expense in the year of disposition. Data relating to one of Rago's depreciable assets at December 31, year 5, are as follows:

Acquisition year	Year 2
Cost	$110,000
Residual value	20,000
Accumulated depreciation	72,000
Estimated useful life	5 years

Using the same depreciation method as used in year 2, year 3, and year 4, how much depreciation expense should Rago record in year 5 for this asset?
a. $12,000
b. $18,000
c. $22,000
d. $24,000

28. On January 2, year 1, Union Co. purchased a machine for $264,000 and depreciated it by the straight-line method using an estimated useful life of eight years with no salvage value. On January 2, year 4, Union determined that the machine had a useful life of six years from the date of acquisition and will have a salvage value of $24,000. An accounting change was made in year 4 to reflect the additional data. The accumulated depreciation for this machine should have a balance at December 31, year 4, of

a. $176,000
b. $160,000
c. $154,000
d. $146,000

29. Weir Co. uses straight-line depreciation for its property, plant, and equipment, which, stated at cost, consisted of the following:

	12/31/Y4	12/31/Y3
Land	$ 25,000	$ 25,000
Buildings	195,000	195,000
Machinery and equipment	695,000	650,000
	915,000	870,000
Less accumulated depreciation	400,000	370,000
	$515,000	$500,000

Weir's depreciation expense for year 4 and year 3 was $55,000 and $50,000, respectively. What amount was debited to accumulated depreciation during year 4 because of property, plant, and equipment retirements?

a. $40,000
b. $25,000
c. $20,000
d. $10,000

30. On January 1, year 1, Crater, Inc. purchased equipment having an estimated salvage value equal to 20% of its original cost at the end of a ten-year life. The equipment was sold December 31, year 5, for 50% of its original cost. If the equipment's disposition resulted in a reported loss, which of the following depreciation methods did Crater use?

a. Double-declining balance.
b. Sum-of-the-years' digits.
c. Straight-line.
d. Composite.

31. A depreciable asset has an estimated 15% salvage value. At the end of its estimated useful life, the accumulated depreciation would equal the original cost of the asset under which of the following depreciation methods?

	Straight-line	Productive output
a.	Yes	No
b.	Yes	Yes
c.	No	Yes
d.	No	No

32. In which of the following situations is the units-of-production method of depreciation most appropriate?

a. An asset's service potential declines with use.
b. An asset's service potential declines with the passage of time.
c. An asset is subject to rapid obsolescence.
d. An asset incurs increasing repairs and maintenance with use.

33. A machine with a five-year estimated useful life and an estimated 10% salvage value was acquired on January 1, year 1. On December 31, year 4, accumulated depreciation, using the sum-of-the-years' digits method, would be

a. (Original cost less salvage value) multiplied by 1/15.

b. (Original cost less salvage value) multiplied by 14/15.
c. Original cost multiplied by 14/15.
d. Original cost multiplied by 1/15.

34. Spiro Corp. uses the sum-of-the-years' digits method to depreciate equipment purchased in January year 1 for $20,000. The estimated salvage value of the equipment is $2,000 and the estimated useful life is four years. What should Spiro report as the asset's carrying amount as of December 31, year 3?

a. $1,800
b. $2,000
c. $3,800
d. $4,500

35. The following graph depicts three depreciation expense patterns over time.

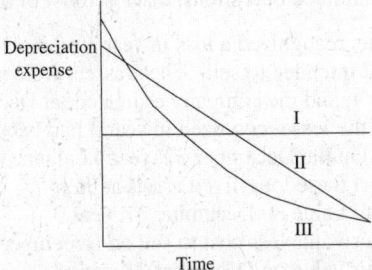

Which depreciation expense pattern corresponds to the sum-of-the-years' digits method and which corresponds to the double-declining balance method?

	Sum-of-the-years' digits	Double-declining balance
a.	III	II
b.	II	I
c.	I	III
d.	II	III

36. Which of the following uses the straight-line depreciation method?

	Group depreciation	Composite depreciation
a.	No	No
b.	Yes	No
c.	Yes	Yes
d.	No	Yes

37. A company using the composite depreciation method for its fleet of trucks, cars, and campers retired one of its trucks and received cash from a salvage company. The net carrying amount of these composite asset accounts would be decreased by the

a. Cash proceeds received and original cost of the truck.
b. Cash proceeds received.
c. Original cost of the truck less the cash proceeds.
d. Original cost of the truck.

G. Disposals and Impairment of Value

38. During year 4, the management of West Inc. decided to dispose of some of its older equipment and machinery. By year-end, December 31, year 4, these assets had not been sold, although the company was negotiating their sale to another company. On the December 31, year 4 balance sheet of West Inc., this equipment and machinery should be reported at

a. Fair value.

b.   Carrying amount.
c.   The lower of carrying amount or fair value.
d.   The lower of carrying amount or fair value less cost to sell.

39. At December 31, year 4, Matson Inc. was holding long-lived assets that it intended to sell. The assets do not constitute a separate component of the company. The company appropriately recognized a loss in year 4 related to these assets. On Matson's income statement for the year ended December 31, year 4, this loss should be reported as a(n)

a.   Extraordinary item.
b.   Component of income from continuing operations before income taxes.
c.   Separate component of selling or general and administrative expenses, disclosed net of tax benefit.
d.   Component of the gain (loss) from sale of discontinued operations, disclosed net of income taxes.

40. Taft Inc. recognized a loss in year 3 related to long-lived assets that it intended to sell. These assets were not sold during year 4, and the company estimated, at December 31, year 4, that the loss recognized in year 3 had been more than recovered. On the December 31, year 4 balance sheet, Taft should report these long-lived assets at their

a.   Fair value on December 31, year 3.
b.   Fair value less cost to sell on December 31, year 3.
c.   Fair value on December 31, year 4.
d.   Carrying amount on December 31, year 3.

41. Cranston Inc. reported an impairment loss of $150,000 on its income statement for the year ended December 31, year 3. This loss was related to long-lived assets which Cranston intended to use in its operations. On the company's December 31, year 3 balance sheet, Cranston reported these long-lived assets at $920,000 and, as of December 31, year 3, Cranston estimated that these long-lived assets would be used for another five years. On December 31, year 4, Cranston determined that the fair values of its impaired long-lived assets had increased by $25,000 over their fair values at December 31, year 3. On the company's December 31, year 4 balance sheet, what amount should be reported as the carrying amount for these long-lived assets? Assume straight-line depreciation and no salvage value for the impaired assets.

a. $761,000
b. $736,000
c. $945,000
d. $756,000

42. Assets intended to be held and used for productive purposes may suffer from impairment in each of the following circumstances **except**

a.   A change in the way the assets are used or physical change in the assets.
b.   Asset costs incurred exceed the original amounts planned.
c.   Discounted expected future cash flows and interest charges are less than the carrying amount of the assets.
d.   A significant adverse change in legal factors that might affect the assets' fair value.

43. Synthia, Inc., a clothing manufacturer, purchased a sewing machine for $10,000 on July 1, year 2. The machine had a ten-year life, a $500 salvage value, and was depreciated

using the straight-line method. On December 31, year 4, a test for impairment indicates that the undiscounted cash flows from the sewing machine are less than its carrying value. The machine's actual fair value on December 31, year 4 is $3,000. What is Synthia's loss on impairment on December 31, year 4?

a. $6,500
b. $4,750
c. $4,625
d. $4,150

44. With regard to impaired assets, the FASB standards provide for

	Recognition of loss upon impairment	Restoration of previously recognized impairment losses
a.	Yes	Yes
b.	Yes	No
c.	No	Yes
d.	No	No

45. Scarbrough Company had purchased equipment for $280,000 on January 1, year 1. The equipment had an eight-year useful life and a salvage value of $40,000. Scarbrough depreciated the equipment using the straight-line method. In August year 4, Scarbrough questioned the recoverability of the carrying amount of this equipment. At August 31, year 4, the expected net future cash inflows (undiscounted) related to the continued use and eventual disposal of the equipment total $175,000. The equipment's fair value on August 31, year 4, is $150,000. After any loss on impairment has been recognized, what is the carrying value of Scarbrough's equipment as of August 31, year 4?

a. $175,000
b. $170,000
c. $150,000
d. $130,000

46. Linx Corporation acquired equipment on January 1, year 3, for $100,000. The equipment had a ten-year useful life and no salvage value. On December 31, year 4, the following information was obtained regarding the equipment:

Expected value of undiscounted cash flows	$72,000
Fair value estimated with in-use valuation premise	$74,000
Fair value estimated with in-exchange valuation premise	$70,000

What is the amount of impairment loss that Linx should report in its year 4 income statement?

a. $ 6,000
b. $ 8,000
c. $10,000
d. $0

47. Conner Corporation has equipment with a carrying value of $160,000 on December 31, year 4, after recording depreciation expense for year 4. The following information was available on December 31, year 4:

Value of similar equipment for sale in market	$140,000
Present value of estimated future cash flows discounted at 10%	$130,000
Estimated undiscounted cash flows of equipment	$135,000

At what amount should the equipment be presented on the December 31, year 4 balance sheet?

    a. $160,000
    b. $140,000
    c. $135,000
    d. $130,000

48. Dahle Corporation has equipment with a carrying value of $450,000 on December 31, year 4. The following information was available on December 31, year 4:

Expected net cash flows (undiscounted)	$420,000
Expected net cash flows discounted at 7%	$400,000
Fair value, using the assets with other assets	$415,000
Fair value, assuming the assets are sold stand-alone	$428,000

What is the impairment loss that Dahle must report in its year 4 income statement for this equipment?

    a. $50,000
    b. $35,000
    c. $30,000
    d. $22,000

49. Under the reporting requirements for impaired assets, impairment losses for assets to be held and used shall be reported

    a.   As an extraordinary item.
    b.   As a component of discontinued operations.
    c.   As a component of income from continuing operations.
    d.   As a change in accounting estimate.

50. During December year 4, Bubba Inc. determined that there had been a significant decrease in the market value of its equipment used in its manufacturing process. At December 31, year 4, Bubba compiled the information below.

Original cost of the equipment	$500,000
Accumulated depreciation	300,000
Expected net future cash inflows (undiscounted) related to the continued use and eventual disposal of the equipment	175,000
Fair value of the equipment	125,000

What is the amount of impairment loss that should be reported on Bubba's income statement prepared for the year ended December 31, year 4?

    a. $ 75,000
    b. $ 25,000
    c. $325,000
    d. $375,000

51. Marjorie, Inc. acquired a machine for $320,000 on August 31, year 1. The machine has a five-year life, a $50,000 salvage value, and was depreciated using the straight-line method. On May 31, year 4, a test for recoverability reveals that the expected net future undiscounted cash inflows related to the continued use and eventual disposal of the machine total $150,000. The machine's actual fair value on May 31, year 4, is $135,000, with no salvage value. Assuming a loss on impairment is recognized May 31, year 4, what is Marjorie's depreciation expense for June year 4?

    a. $6,352
    b. $5,000
    c. $4,500
    d. $3,148

52. Which of the following statements is(are) correct about the carrying amount of a long-lived asset after an impairment loss has been recognized? Assume the long-lived asset is being held for use in the business and that the asset is depreciable.

  I. The reduced carrying amount of the asset may be increased in subsequent years if the impairment loss has been recovered.
  II. The reduced carrying amount of the asset represents the amount that should be depreciated over the asset's remaining useful life.

    a.   I only.
    b.   II only.
    c.   Both I and II.
    d.   Neither I nor II.

53. According to ASC Topic 360, if a long-lived asset is determined to be impaired, how is the loss calculated?

    a.   Future discounted cash flows less asset's carrying (book) value.
    b.   Future undiscounted cash flows less asset's carrying (book) value.
    c.   Fair value less asset's carrying (book) value.
    d.   Cash outflows needed to obtain cash inflows.

54. In accordance with ASC Topic 360, long-lived assets are required to be reviewed for impairment

    a.   At the balance sheet date, every three years.
    b.   When the asset is fully depreciated.
    c.   When circumstances indicate that the carrying amount of an asset might not be recoverable.
    d.   At the balance sheet date, every year.

55. During December year 4, Toni Corp. determined that there had been a significant decrease in the market value of its equipment used in its roofing business. At December 31, year 4, Toni compiled the information below.

Original cost of equipment	$800,000
Accumulated depreciation	450,000
Expected net future cash inflows (undiscounted) related to the continued use and eventual disposal of the equipment	300,000
Fair value of the equipment	250,000

What is the amount of the impairment loss that should be reported on Toni's income statement prepared for the year ended December 31, year 4?

    a. $ 50,000
    b. $100,000
    c. $150,000
    d. $200,000

56. Miller Company acquired a machine for $420,000 on June 30, year 2. The machine has a seven-year life, no salvage value, and was depreciated using the straight-line method. On August 31, year 4, a test for recoverability reveals that the expected net future undiscounted cash inflows related to the continued use and eventual disposal of the machine total $275,000. The machine's actual fair value on August 31, year 4, is $261,000. Assuming a loss on impairment is recognized August 31, year 4, what is Miller's depreciation expense for September year 4?

    a. $4,000
    b. $4,350

c. $4,500
d. $5,000

H.   Depletion

57. In January year 4, Vorst Co. purchased a mineral mine for $2,640,000 with removable ore estimated at 1,200,000 tons. After it has extracted all the ore, Vorst will be required by law to restore the land to its original condition at an estimated cost of $220,000. The present value of the estimated restoration costs is $180,000. Vorst believes it will be able to sell the property afterwards for $300,000. During year 4, Vorst incurred $360,000 of development costs preparing the mine for production and removed and sold 60,000 tons of ore. In its year 4 income statement, what amount should Vorst report as depletion?
   a. $135,000
   b. $144,000
   c. $150,000
   d. $159,000

J.   Intangible Assets

58. On December 31, year 3, Byte Co. had capitalized software costs of $600,000 with an economic life of four years. Sales for year 4 were 10% of expected total sales of the software. At December 31, year 4, the software had a net realizable value of $480,000. In its December 31, year 4 balance sheet, what amount should Byte report as net capitalized cost of computer software?
   a. $432,000
   b. $450,000
   c. $480,000
   d. $540,000

59. On January 2, year 4, Judd Co. bought a trademark from Krug Co. for $500,000. Judd retained an independent consultant, who estimated the trademark's remaining life to be fifty years. Its unamortized cost on Krug's accounting records was $380,000. In Judd's December 31, year 4 balance sheet, what amount should be reported as accumulated amortization?
   a. $ 7,600
   b. $ 9,500
   c. $10,000
   d. $12,500

60. On January 2, year 4, Paye Co. purchased Shef Co. at a cost that resulted in recognition of goodwill of $200,000. During the first quarter of year 4, Paye spent an additional $80,000 on expenditures designed to maintain goodwill. In its December 31, year 4 balance sheet, what amount should Paye report as goodwill?
   a. $180,000
   b. $200,000
   c. $252,000
   d. $280,000

61. Northern Airline purchased airline gate rights at Newark International Airport for $2,000,000 with a legal life of five years. However, Northern has the ability and right to extend the rights every ten years for an indefinite period of time. Over what period of time should Northern amortize the gate rights?
   a.   5 years.
   b.   15 years.

c.   40 years.
d.   The rights should not be amortized.

62. On January 2, year 1, Lava, Inc. purchased a patent for a new consumer product for $90,000. At the time of purchase, the patent was valid for fifteen years; however, the patent's useful life was estimated to be only ten years due to the competitive nature of the product. On December 31, year 4, the product was permanently withdrawn from sale under governmental order because of a potential health hazard in the product. What amount should Lava charge against income during year 4, assuming amortization is recorded at the end of each year?
   a. $ 9,000
   b. $54,000
   c. $63,000
   d. $72,000

63. What does ASC Topic 350 require with respect to accounting for goodwill?
   a.   Goodwill should be amortized over a five-year period.
   b.   Goodwill should be amortized over its expected useful life.
   c.   Goodwill should be recorded and never adjusted.
   d.   Goodwill should be recorded and periodically evaluated for impairment.

64. Which of the following statements concerning patents is correct?
   a.   Legal costs incurred to successfully defend an internally developed patent should be capitalized and amortized over the patent's remaining economic life.
   b.   Legal fees and other direct costs incurred in registering a patent should be capitalized and amortized on a straight-line basis over a five-year period.
   c.   Research and development contract services purchased from others and used to develop a patented manufacturing process should be capitalized and amortized over the patent's economic life.
   d.   Research and development costs incurred to develop a patented item should be capitalized and amortized on a straight-line basis over seventeen years.

65. Under ASC Topic 350, goodwill should be tested periodically for impairment
   a.   For the entity as a whole.
   b.   At the subsidiary level.
   c.   At the industry segment level.
   d.   At the operating segment level or one level below.

66. On July 12, year 4, Carver, Inc. acquired Jones Company in a business combination. As a result of the combination, the following amounts of goodwill were recorded for each of the three reporting units of the acquired company.

Retailing	$30,000
Service	$20,000
Financing	$40,000

Near the end of year 4 a new major competitor entered the company's market and Carver was concerned that this might cause a significant decline in the value of goodwill. Accordingly, Carver computed the implied value of the goodwill for the three major reporting units at December 31, year 4, as follows:

Retailing	$25,000
Service	$10,000
Financing	$60,000

Determine the amount of impairment of goodwill that should be recorded by Carver at December 31, year 4.

a. $0
b. $10,000
c. $15,000
d. $25,000

67. Sloan Corporation is performing its annual test of the impairment of goodwill for its Financing reporting unit. It has determined that the fair value of the unit exceeds it carrying value. Which of the following is correct concerning this test of impairment?

a. Impairment is not indicated and no additional analysis is necessary.
b. Goodwill should be written down as impaired.
c. The assets and liabilities should be valued to determine if there has been an impairment of goodwill.
d. Goodwill should be retested at the entity level.

68. Wilson Corporation is performing the test of impairment of its Technology reporting unit at 9/30/Y4. In the first step of the process, Wilson has valued the unit using a multiple of earnings approach at $2,000,000. The carrying value of the net assets of the Technology unit is $2,100,000. What should Wilson do with this information?

a. Record an impairment loss of $100,000.
b. Record no impairment loss.
c. Value goodwill individually.
d. Perform step two of the test of impairment.

K.   Reporting on the Costs of Start-Up Activities

69. Brunson Corp., a major US winery, begins construction of a new facility in Italy. Following are some of the costs incurred in conjunction with the start-up activities of the new facility:

Production equipment	$815,000
Travel costs of salaried employees	40,000
License fees	14,000
Training of local employees for production and maintenance operations	120,000
Advertising costs	85,200

What portion of the organizational costs will be expensed?

a. $975,000
b. $160,000
c. $0
d. $139,200

70. On January 1, year 4, Kew Corp. incurred organization costs of $24,000. What portion of the organization costs will Kew defer to years subsequent to year 4?

a. $23,400
b. $19,200
c. $ 4,800
d. $0

71. Which of the following statements is(are) correct regarding the treatment of start-up activities related to the opening of a new facility?

I. Costs of raising capital should be expensed as incurred.
II. Costs of acquiring or constructing long-lived assets and getting them ready for their intended use should be expensed as incurred.
III. Cost of research and development should be expensed as incurred.

a. I only.
b. III only.
c. Both I and III.
d. I, II, and III.

L.   Research and Development Costs (ASC Topic 730)

72. Cody Corp. incurred the following costs during year 4:

Design of tools, jigs, molds, and dies involving new technology	$125,000
Modification of the formulation of a process	160,000
Troubleshooting in connection with breakdowns during commercial production	100,000
Adaptation of an existing capability to a particular customer's need as part of a continuing commercial activity	110,000

In its year 4 income statement, Cody should report research and development expense of

a. $125,000
b. $160,000
c. $235,000
d. $285,000

73. In year 4, Ball Labs incurred the following costs:

Direct costs of doing contract research and development work for the government to be reimbursed by governmental unit	$400,000

Research and development costs not included above were

Depreciation	$300,000
Salaries	700,000
Indirect costs appropriately allocated	200,000
Materials	180,000

What was Ball's total research and development expense in year 4?

a. $1,080,000
b. $1,380,000
c. $1,580,000
d. $1,780,000

74. West, Inc. made the following expenditures relating to Product Y:

• Legal costs to file a patent on Product Y—$10,000. Production of the finished product would not have been undertaken without the patent.
• Special equipment to be used solely for development of Product Y—$60,000. The equipment has no other use and has an estimated useful life of four years.
• Labor and material costs incurred in producing a prototype model—$200,000.
• Cost of testing the prototype—$80,000.

What is the total amount of costs that will be expensed when incurred?

a. $280,000
b. $295,000
c. $340,000
d. $350,000

75. Brill Co. made the following expenditures during year 4:

Costs to develop computer software for internal use in Brill's general management information system	$100,000
Costs of market research activities	75,000

What amount of these expenditures should Brill report in its year 4 income statement as research and development expenses?

a. $175,000
b. $100,000
c. $ 75,000
d. $0

76. On January 1, year 4, Jambon purchased equipment for use in developing a new product. Jambon uses the straight-line depreciation method. The equipment could provide benefits over a ten-year period. However, the new product development is expected to take five years, and the equipment can be used only for this project. Jambon's year 4 expense equals

a. The total cost of the equipment.
b. One-fifth of the cost of the equipment.
c. One-tenth of the cost of the equipment.
d. Zero.

M.   Computer Software Costs (ASC Topic 985)

Items 77 and 78 are based on the following:

During year 4, Pitt Corp. incurred costs to develop and produce a routine, low-risk computer software product, as follows:

Completion of detailed program design	$13,000
Costs incurred for coding and testing to establish technological feasibility	10,000
Other coding costs after establishment of technological feasibility	24,000
Other testing costs after establishment of technological feasibility	20,000
Costs of producing product masters for training materials	15,000
Duplication of computer software and training materials from product masters (1,000 units)	25,000
Packaging product (500 units)	9,000

77. In Pitt's December 31, year 4 balance sheet, what amount should be reported in inventory?

a. $25,000
b. $34,000
c. $40,000
d. $49,000

78. In Pitt's December 31, year 4 balance sheet, what amount should be capitalized as software cost, subject to amortization?

a. $54,000
b. $57,000
c. $59,000
d. $69,000

79. On December 31, year 3, Bit Co. had capitalized costs for a new computer software product with an economic life of five years. Sales for year 4 were 30% of expected total sales of the software. At December 31, year 4, the software had a net realizable value equal to 90% of the capitalized cost. What percentage of the original capitalized cost should

be reported as the net amount on Bit's December 31, year 4 balance sheet?

a. 70%
b. 72%
c. 80%
d. 90%

80. Which of the following statements is incorrect regarding internal-use software?

a. The application and development costs of internal-use software should be amortized on a straight-line basis unless another systematic and rational basis is more representative of its costs.
b. Internal-use software is considered to be software that is marketed as a separate product or as part of a product or process.
c. The costs of testing and installing computer hardware should be capitalized as incurred.
d. The costs of training and application maintenance should be expensed as incurred.

81. Which of the following statements is(are) correct regarding the proper accounting treatment for internal-use software costs?

I. Preliminary costs should be capitalized as incurred.
II. Application and development costs should be capitalized as incurred.

a. I only.
b. II only.
c. Both I and II.
d. Neither I nor II.

82. What is the proper accounting treatment for the following stages of internal-use software costs?

	Preliminary stage costs	Post-implementation costs
a.	Capitalized as incurred	Capitalized as incurred
b.	Expensed as incurred	Capitalized as incurred
c.	Capitalized as incurred	Expensed as incurred
d.	Expensed as incurred	Expensed as incurred

N.   Development Stage Enterprises (ASC Topic 915)

83. Financial reporting by a development stage enterprise differs from financial reporting for an established operating enterprise in regard to footnote disclosures

a. Only.
b. And expense recognition principles only.
c. And revenue recognition principles only.
d. And revenue and expense recognition principles.

84. A development stage enterprise

a. Issues an income statement that shows only cumulative amounts from the enterprise's inception.
b. Issues an income statement that is the same as an established operating enterprise, but does **not** show cumulative amounts from the enterprise's inception as additional information.
c. Issues an income statement that is the same as an established operating enterprise, and shows cumulative amounts from the enterprise's inception as additional information.
d. Does **not** issue an income statement.

P. International Financial Reporting Standards (IFRS)

85. For companies that prepare financial statements in accordance with IFRS, plant, property, and equipment should be valued using which models?

- a. The cost model or the revaluation model.
- b. The cost model or the fair value model.
- c. The cost model or the fair value through profit or loss model.
- d. The revaluation model or the fair value model.

86. Which is true about the revaluation model for valuing plant, property, and equipment?

- a. Revaluation of assets must be made on the last day of the fiscal year.
- b. Revaluation of assets must be made on the same date each year.
- c. There is no rule for the frequency or date of revaluation.
- d. Revaluation of assets must be made every two years.

87. When the revaluation model is used for reporting plant, property, and equipment, the gain or loss should be included in

- a. Income for the period.
- b. Gain from revaluation on the income statement.
- c. A revaluation surplus account is other comprehensive income.
- d. An extraordinary gain or loss on the income statement.

88. Linden Corporation has investment property that is held to earn rental income. Linden prepares its financial statements in accordance with IFRS. Linden uses the fair value model for reporting the investment property. Which of the following is true?

- a. Changes in fair value are reported as profit or loss in the current period.
- b. Changes in fair value are reported as other comprehensive income for the period.
- c. Changes in fair value are reported as an extraordinary gain on the income statement.
- d. Changes in fair value are reported as deferred revenue for the period.

89. Under IFRS, what valuation methods are used for intangible assets?

- a. The cost model or the fair value model.
- b. The cost model or the revaluation model.
- c. The cost model or the fair value through profit or loss model.
- d. The revaluation model or the fair value model.

90. Pinkerton Corp. uses the cost model for intangible assets. On April 10, year 3, Pinkerton acquired assets for $100,000. On December 31, year 3, it was determined that the recoverable amount for these intangible assets was $80,000. On December 31, year 4, it was determined that the intangible assets had a recoverable amount of $84,000. What is the impairment gain or loss recognized in year 3 and year 4 on the income statement?

	Year 3	Year 4
a.	$20,000 loss	$16,000 loss
b.	$20,000 loss	$0
c.	$20,000 loss	$ 4,000 gain
d.	$0	$0

91. Under IFRS when accounting for plant, property, and equipment, a company

- a. Must use the cost model for presenting the assets.
- b. May elect to use the cost model or the revaluation model on any individual asset.
- c. May elect to use the cost model or the revaluation model on any asset class.
- d. Must use the cost model for land.

92. Under the IFRS revaluation model for accounting for plant, property, and equipment

- a. Assets must be revaluated quarterly.
- b. Assets must be revaluated annually.
- c. Assets must be revaluated biannually.
- d. There are no rules regarding the frequency of revaluation.

93. Wilson Company maintains its records under IFRS. During the current year Wilson sold a piece of equipment used in production. The equipment had been accounted for using the revaluation method and details of the accounts and sale are presented below.

Sales price	$100,000
Equipment book value (net)	90,000
Revaluation surplus	20,000

Which of the following is correct regarding recording the sale?

- a. The gain that should be recorded in profit and loss is $30,000.
- b. The gain that should be recorded in other comprehensive income is $10,000.
- c. The gain that should be recorded in other comprehensive income is $30,000.
- d. The gain that should be recorded in profit and loss is $10,000; the $20,000 revaluation surplus should be transferred to retained earnings.

94. Under IFRS, an entity that acquires an intangible asset may use the revaluation model for subsequent measurement only if

- a. The useful life of the intangible asset can be reliably determined.
- b. An active market exists for the intangible asset.
- c. The cost of the intangible asset can be measured reliably.
- d. The intangible asset is a monetary asset.

95. Under IFRS, which of the following is a criterion that must be met in order for an item to be recognized as an intangible asset other than goodwill?

- a. The item's fair value can be measured reliably.
- b. The item is part of the entity's activities aimed at gaining new scientific or technical knowledge.
- c. The item is expected to be used in the production or supply of goods or services.
- d. The item is identifiable and lacks physical substance.

96. An entity purchases a trademark and incurs the following costs in connection with the trademark:

One-time trademark purchase price	$100,000
Nonrefundable VAT taxes	5,000
Training sales personnel on the use of the new trademark	7,000
Research expenditures associated with the purchase of the new trademark	24,000
Legal costs incurred to register the trademark	10,500
Salaries of the administrative personnel	12,000

Applying IFRS and assuming that the trademark meets all of the applicable initial asset recognition criteria, the entity should recognize an asset in the amount of

    a. $100,000
    b. $115,500
    c. $146,500
    d. $158,500

97. Under IFRS, when an entity chooses the revaluation model as its accounting policy for measuring property, plant, and equipment, which of the following statements is correct?

    a. When an asset is revalued, the entire class of property, plant, and equipment to which that asset belongs must be revalued.
    b. When an asset is revalued, individual assets within a class of property, plant, and equipment to which that asset belongs can be revalued.
    c. Revaluations of property, plant, and equipment must be made at least every three years.
    d. Increases in an asset's carrying value as a result of the first revaluation must be recognized as a component of profit or loss.

98. On January 1, year 1, an entity acquires for $100,000 a new piece of machinery with an estimated useful life of 10 years. The machine has a drum that must be replaced every five years and costs $20,000 to replace. Continued operation of the machine requires an inspection every four years after purchase; the inspection cost is $8,000. The company uses the straight-line method of depreciation. Under IFRS, what is the depreciation expense for year 1?

    a. $10,000
    b. $10,800
    c. $12,000
    d. $13,200

99. Taylor Company uses IFRS for financial reporting purposes. Which of the following is true about accounting for the development costs of the company?

    a. Development costs must be expensed.
    b. Development costs are always deferred and expensed against future revenues.
    c. Development costs may be capitalized as an intangible asset in very restrictive situations.
    d. Development costs are recorded in other comprehensive income.

100. Under IFRS, intangible assets with indefinite lives are tested for impairment

    a. Quarterly at the quarterly reporting date.
    b. Annually at the annual reporting date.
    c. Biannually at the reporting date.
    d. There are no guidelines defining when intangible assets are tested for impairment.

101. Under IFRS, an intangible asset is considered to be impaired if its carrying value is greater than its recoverable amount. The recoverable amount is

    a. Its historical cost.
    b. Its net selling price.
    c. The greater of its net selling price or its value in use.
    d. Its replacement cost.

102. Which of the following is true about biological assets under IFRS?

    a. Biological assets are only found in Biotech companies.
    b. Biological assets are living animals or plants and must be disclosed as a separate item on the balance sheet.
    c. Biological assets must be valued at cost.
    d. Biological assets do not generally have future economic benefits.

Multiple-Choice Answers and Explanations

Answers

1. a __ __	22. d __ __	43. c __ __	64. a __ __	85. a __ __
2. a __ __	23. c __ __	44. b __ __	65. d __ __	86. c __ __
3. b __ __	24. b __ __	45. b __ __	66. c __ __	87. c __ __
4. a __ __	25. a __ __	46. a __ __	67. a __ __	88. a __ __
5. d __ __	26. b __ __	47. b __ __	68. d __ __	89. b __ __
6. a __ __	27. a __ __	48. d __ __	69. b __ __	90. c __ __
7. b __ __	28. d __ __	49. c __ __	70. d __ __	91. c __ __
8. b __ __	29. b __ __	50. a __ __	71. b __ __	92. d __ __
9. b __ __	30. c __ __	51. b __ __	72. d __ __	93. d __ __
10. c __ __	31. d __ __	52. b __ __	73. b __ __	94. b __ __
11. b __ __	32. a __ __	53. c __ __	74. c __ __	95. d __ __
12. c __ __	33. b __ __	54. c __ __	75. d __ __	96. b __ __
13. a __ __	34. c __ __	55. b __ __	76. a __ __	97. a __ __
14. c __ __	35. d __ __	56. c __ __	77. b __ __	98. d __ __
15. d __ __	36. c __ __	57. b __ __	78. c __ __	99. c __ __
16. b __ __	37. b __ __	58. b __ __	79. a __ __	100. b __ __
17. d __ __	38. d __ __	59. c __ __	80. b __ __	101. c __ __
18. b __ __	39. b __ __	60. b __ __	81. b __ __	102. b __ __
19. a __ __	40. d __ __	61. d __ __	82. d __ __	
20. d __ __	41. b __ __	62. c __ __	83. a __ __	1st: __/102 = __%
21. c __ __	42. c __ __	63. d __ __	84. c __ __	2nd: __/102 = __%

Explanations

1. (a) The cost of machinery includes all expenditures incurred in acquiring the asset and preparing it for use. Cost includes the purchase price, freight and handling charges, insurance on the machine while in transit, cost of special foundations, and costs of assembling, installation, and testing. All of the costs given in this problem are properly recorded as the cost of the machine. Therefore the cost to be recorded is $155,000 ($125,000 + $20,000 + $10,000).

2. (a) Any cost involved in preparing land for its ultimate use (such as a factory site) is considered part of the cost of the land. Before the land can be used as a building site, it must be purchased (involving costs such as purchase price, legal fees, and title insurance) and the old building must be razed (cost of demolition less proceeds from sale of scrap). The total balance in the land account should be $464,000.

Purchase price	$400,000
Legal fees	10,000
Title insurance	12,000
Net cost of demolition ($50,000 – $8,000)	42,000
	$464,000

3. (b) The amount of interest cost which should be capitalized during building construction is the **lower** of **avoidable interest** or **actual interest**. Avoidable interest equals the interest computed on the weighted-average amount of accumulated expenditures on the building ($40,000). Since actual interest is $70,000 ($50,000 + $20,000), the amount capitalized should be $40,000.

4. (a) The requirement is to calculate the amount of capitalized interest at 12/31/Y4. The requirements for capitalization of interest are met if: (1) expenditures for the asset have been made, (2) activities that are necessary to get the asset ready for its intended use are in progress, and (3) interest cost is being incurred. The amount to be capital-

ized is the lower of avoidable interest or actual interest. Avoidable interest is the average accumulated expenditures multiplied by the appropriate interest rate or rates. Since $2,000,000 was spent on the building evenly throughout the year, the average accumulated expenditures were $1,000,000 ($2,000,000 ÷ 2) and the avoidable interest was $120,000 ($1,000,000 × 12%). Since actual interest ($102,000) is less than avoidable interest, the actual interest cost is capitalized.

5. (d) Certain assets for which interest costs incurred in their production should be capitalized rather than expensed. Assets which "qualify" for interest capitalization are those constructed or otherwise produced for an enterprise's own use and those intended for sale or lease that are constructed or otherwise produced as **discrete projects**. The capitalization period shall end when the asset is substantially complete and ready for its intended use. Based upon these criteria, the interest costs associated with the machinery for Bay's own use should be capitalized during the construction period and expensed after completion. Additionally, all costs associated with the machinery held for sale should be expensed because the machinery does not meet the "discrete project" criterion.

6. (a) When the investment was acquired, it was recorded at cost—the fair market value of the asset surrendered to acquire it. The July 1 entry was

Inv. in Ace stock	3,000	
Truck		2,500
Gain on disposal		500 ($3,000 – $2,500)

The investment would be reported in the 12/31/Y4 balance sheet at $3,000. The book value of Ace's stock does not affect the amount recorded on Balt's books.

7. (b) A nonmonetary exchange is recognized at fair value unless the fair value is not determinable, the exchange transaction is to facilitate sales to customers, or the exchange transactions lacks commercial substance. Answer (a) is incorrect, because the exchange must **lack** commercial substance. Answers (c) and (d) are incorrect because there is no longer the distinction of similar or dissimilar assets in nonmonetary exchanges.

8. (b) A nonmonetary exchange is recognized at fair value unless the fair value is not determinable, the exchange transaction is to facilitate sales to customers, or the exchange transactions lacks commercial substance. Answers (a) and (c) are incorrect; these transactions have commercial substance because there is a significant change in the entity's cash flows as a result of the exchange.

9. (b) An entity's cash flows are expected to change significantly if the configuration of the cash flows of the asset received differs significantly from the configuration of the cash flows of the asset transferred. The configuration includes the risk, timing, and amount of the cash flows.

10. (c) In determining cash flows from a transaction, the effect of taxes is not considered unless it serves a legitimate business purpose other than tax avoidance. In assessing the commercial substance of an exchange, tax cash flows arising solely to avoid taxes are not considered. Other cash flows from the nonmonetary exchange are considered.

11. (b) The cash price of the new machine represents its fair market value (FMV). The FMV of the old machine can be determined by subtracting the cash portion of the purchase price ($6,000) from the total cost of the new machine: $20,500 – $6,000 = $14,500. Since the book value of the machine ($16,800) exceeds its FMV on the date of the trade-in ($14,500), the difference of $2,300 must be recognized as a loss.

12. (c) Because the cash flows of the exchanged assets will not be significantly different, the transaction lacks commercial substances. Therefore, book value is used to record the transition. When the assets are exchanged, boot is received, and a gain results, the exchange is treated as part sale and part exchange. The earnings process is assumed to be complete for the portion relating to the boot received. The gain recognized is computed as follows:

$$\frac{\text{Boot received}}{\text{Boot received} + \text{FMV of assets received}} \times \text{Total gain} = \text{Gain recognized}$$

Total Gain = (17,500 + 2,500) – 12,000 = 8,000

Assets received by Amble — Book value of asset given up by Amble

The gain recognized would be calculated as follows:

$$\frac{2,500}{17,500 + 2,500} \times 8,000 = \$1,000 \text{ gain recognized}$$

The asset acquired is recorded at the **book** value of the asset surrendered plus the gain recognized less boot received ($12,000 + $1,000 – $2,500 = $10,500). The journal entry is

Truck (new)	10,500	
Cash	2,500	
Truck (old)		12,000
Gain on sale		1,000

13. (a) If a loss is indicated by the terms of the transaction, the entire loss on the exchange should be recognized. In this case, a loss results because Transit received an asset whose fair value equaled the book value of the asset given up and paid cash. Therefore, Transit gave up more than they received, the difference being the loss.

14. (c) Transactions lacking commercial substance are recorded at book value. When the exchange of nonmonetary assets includes an amount of monetary consideration, the receiver of monetary consideration has realized a partial gain on the exchange. To determine the partial gain to be recognized, first compute the total gain which is the difference between the fair market value of the nonmonetary asset given up and its book value. Then multiply the ratio of the **monetary** consideration received to the **total** consideration received (i.e., monetary consideration plus the estimated fair market value of the asset received) times the total gain. The result is the realized gain to be recognized. The entity paying the monetary consideration should **not** recognize any gain until the earnings process is culminated. Note, however, that **all losses** on sales or exchanges are recognized immediately.

15. (d) Nonmonetary exchanges of assets that are deemed to have commercial substance are accounted for on the basis of fair values, and both gains and losses recognized. The gain (or loss) for Vik is calculated as the difference between the fair value and cost of the car. Note that the retail/list price of an asset is not always representative of the fair value of the asset. An asset can often be purchased for less than the retail/list price.

16. (b) This transaction qualifies as an exception to fair value measurement and should be measured at book value. However, when these assets are exchanged, and boot is received and a gain results, the exchange is treated as part sale and part exchange. The earnings process is assumed to be complete for the portion relating to the boot received. The gain recognized is computed as follows:

$$\frac{\text{Boot received}}{\text{Boot received} + \text{FMV of assets received}} \times \text{Total gain} = \text{Gain recognized}$$

Total gain = (130,000 + 20,000) – 126,000 = 24,000

Assets received by Zaro — Book value of asset given up by Zaro

In this case, it would be calculated as follows:

$$\frac{20,000}{(20,000 + 130,000)} \times 24,000 = \$3,200$$

17. (d) A transfer of a nonmonetary asset in a nonreciprocal transfer should be recorded at the fair value of the asset transferred, with a gain or loss recognized on the disposition, whether the transfer is made to a stockholder or to another entity.

18. (b) A gain (loss) must be recognized when a nonmonetary asset is involuntarily converted into monetary assets even if the company reinvests the monetary assets in replacement nonmonetary assets. The gain or loss is the difference between the insurance proceeds received ($3,500) and the carrying value of the asset destroyed. The unadjusted carrying value ($2,500) must be adjusted for the capital expenditure ($700) which has not yet been recorded. When a major component of an asset like an engine is replaced, the preferred treatment is to take the old component off the books (with a loss recognized) and record the new component. When the book value of the component is unknown (as in this case), the cost of the new component ($700) is simply debited to the accumulated depreciation account. This increases the van's carrying value to $3,200 ($2,500 + $700), which means the gain is $300 ($3,500 – $3,200). Note that the $500 invoice should be recorded as repairs expense, and therefore does not affect the van's carrying value.

19. **(a)** Involuntary conversions of nonmonetary assets to monetary assets are monetary transactions for which gain or loss shall be recognized even though an enterprise reinvests or is obligated to reinvest the monetary assets in replacement nonmonetary assets. Accordingly, Lano would record the condemnation and replacement of the forest land as two separate transactions. Lano should recognize a gain on the condemnation and subsequently record the replacement land at the total purchase price. The net effect of these events is to increase the amount of forest land on Lano's balance sheet by the excess of the replacement land's cost over the condemned land's carrying amount, as shown below.

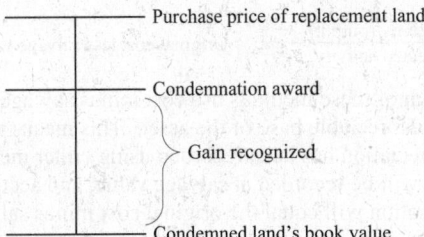

20. **(d)** The requirement is to determine the amount at which land acquired in a group purchase of fixed assets should be recorded. The total cost ($540,000) of the land and building should be allocated based on their relative fair value (FV). Current appraised value is a better indicator of FV than the seller's original cost. Therefore, the land should be recorded at $216,000.

$$\frac{\text{FV land}}{\text{Total FV of assets purchased}} \times \text{Purchase price of group assets}$$

$$\frac{200,000}{500,000} \times 540,000 = \$216,000$$

There is no problem in recording the land at more than its appraised value since value is only an estimate of FV.

21. **(c)** The requirement is to calculate the amount to be charged to repair and maintenance expense in year 4. Generally, a cost should be capitalized if it improves the asset and expensed if it merely maintains the asset at its current level. Continuing and frequent repairs ($40,000) should be expensed. Similarly, the cost of repainting the plant building ($10,000) and the cost of partially replacing the roof tiles ($14,000) should be expensed. These are ordinary, regularly occurring expenditures which maintain, rather than improve, the plant building. The work on the electrical wiring system ($32,000) is capitalized instead of expensed since it is a major improvement. Therefore, the total amount expensed is $64,000 ($40,000 + $10,000 + $14,000).

22. **(d)** The cost of the attachment ($84,000) should be capitalized because it is an **addition**. The cost of installing the attachment ($36,000) is also capitalized because this expenditure was required to get the attachment ready for its

intended use. The overhaul costs ($26,000 + $14,000 = $40,000) are also capitalized. Even though the overhaul did not increase useful life, it is a capital expenditure because it increased productivity. The total amount capitalized is $160,000 ($84,000 + $36,000 + $40,000).

23. **(c)** When an entity suffers a casualty loss to an asset, the accounting loss is recorded at the net carrying value of the damaged asset, if known. In this case, the cost and related accumulated depreciation are identifiable. The entity should therefore recognize a loss in the current period equal to the carrying amount of the damaged portion of the building. The refurbishing of the building, which is an economic event separate from the fire damage, should be treated similarly to the purchase of other assets or betterments. The cost of refurbishing the building should therefore be capitalized and depreciated over the shorter of the refurbishment's useful life or the useful life of the building.

Loss	xxx	(Plug)
Acc. depr.	xxx	
Building		xxx
Building	xxx	
Cash		xxx

Answer (a) is incorrect because in order to reduce the accumulated depreciation account, the useful life of the asset must be extended. In this case, there is no mention of this fact. Answer (d) is incorrect because it fails to recognize the casualty loss and properly remove the cost and accumulated depreciation on the damaged portion of the building from the accounting records.

NOTE: If the components of the damaged portion are not identifiable, the following entry would be made:

Loss	xxx	
Cash		xxx

24. **(b)** Generally, a cost should be capitalized if it improves the efficiency of the asset or extends its useful life and expensed if it merely maintains the asset at its current level. Since an overall reduction in production costs is expected, efficiency must have been improved by the steps taken by Derby. In this problem, it appears that both the building modification and the production line rearrangement contributed to the improved efficiency in the production process. Therefore, both costs should be capitalized.

25. **(a)** Machinery is recorded at its historical cost, which is measured by the cash or **cash equivalent price** of obtaining the machine and preparing it for use. The journal entry to record this acquisition would be

Machinery	110,000	(cash equiv.)
Discount on N.P.	20,000	($130,000 – $110,000)
Notes payable		120,000 (24 × $5,000)
Cash		10,000

The $20,000 discount represents future interest expense (the cost associated with paying for the asset over two years instead of immediately) rather than part of the cost of the machine. Straight-line depreciation for year 4 is computed as follows:

(Cost – Salvage value)	×	1/useful life	=	Depr. expense
($110,000 – $5,000)	×	1/10	=	$10,500

26. **(b)** The formula for 200% double-declining balance (DDB) depreciation is

(Beginning-of-year book value) × DDB rate = Depreciation expense

The DDB rate is two times the straight-line rate (in this case, $1/5 × 2 = 2/5$ or 40%). Therefore, depreciation for the first two years is

Year 2:	$50,000 × 40%	=	$20,000
Year 3:	($50,000 – $20,000) × 40%	=	12,000
			$32,000

In year 4, Turtle switches to the straight-line method. The book value ($50,000 – $32,000 = $18,000) would be depreciated over the remaining three years (five years less two gone by). Therefore, year 4 depreciation is $6,000 ($18,000 × 1/3) and 12/31/Y4 accumulated depreciation is $38,000 ($32,000 + $6,000).

27. (a) The requirement is to calculate the amount of depreciation expense to be recorded in year 5. After three years (year 2-year 4), accumulated depreciation is $72,000. Therefore, the method that was used was the sum-of-the-years' digits (SYD) method. Using this method, after three years the balance in accumulated depreciation would be 12/15 of the depreciable base (5/15 + 4/15 + 3/15). The depreciable base is the cost ($110,000) less the residual value ($20,000), or $90,000. Thus, using the SYD method, accumulated depreciation at 12/31/Y4 would be $72,000 ($90,000 × 12/15), which matches the amount given in the problem. Year 5 depreciation expense, using the SYD method is $12,000 ($90,000 × 2/15).

28. (d) From 1/2/Y1 to 12/31/Y3, depreciation was recorded using an eight-year life. Yearly depreciation was $33,000 ($264,000 ÷ 8), and accumulated depreciation at 12/31/Y3 was $99,000 (3 × $33,000). In year 4, the estimated useful life was changed to six years total with a salvage value of $24,000. Therefore, the 12/31/Y3 book value ($264,000 – $99,000 = $165,000) is depreciated down to the $24,000 salvage value over a remaining useful life of three years (6 years total – 3 years already recorded). The year 4 depreciation expense is $47,000 [($165,000 – $24,000) ÷ 3], increasing accumulated depreciation to $146,000 ($99,000 + $47,000).

29. (b) The solutions approach is to set up a T-account for **accumulated depreciation** and solve for the unknown.

Accumulated Depreciation			
		370,000	12/31/Y3
Year 4 retirements	?	55,000	Year 4 depr. expense
		400,000	12/31/Y4

The 12/31/Y3 and 12/31/Y4 balances were given in the schedule. The year 4 depreciation expense would be recorded by debiting the expense account and crediting accumulated depreciation. The accumulated depreciation would be debited for the property, plant, and equipment retirements. To balance the T-account, the debit must be $25,000. Alternatively, an equation can be used as shown below.

$370,000 + $55,000 – X	=	$400,000
425,000 – X	=	400,000
X	=	25,000
370,000	=	12/31/Y3 balance
55,000	=	Year 4 depreciation expense
400,000	=	12/31/Y4 balance
X	=	retirements

30. (c) After reviewing the different methods, you might realize that the method with the highest carrying amount would result in a loss as shown below, where C is equal to the asset's original cost.

Gain/loss = Proceeds – Carrying amount
= 50% C – [C – 50% (C – S)]
= 50% C – [C – 50% (C – 20%C)]
= .5C – [1.00C – .5(1.00C – .2C)]
= .5C – [.6C]
Carrying amount > Proceeds
∴ Loss

Straight-line depreciation would result in the highest carrying value.

31. (d) The formula to compute straight-line depreciation is

$$\frac{\text{Original cost less salvage value}}{\text{Estimated useful life}}$$

The formula to determine depreciation using the productive output method is

$$\frac{\text{Current activity (output)}}{\text{Total expected activity}} \times \text{Original cost less salvage value}$$

Note that both of these methods use cost minus salvage value as the depreciable base of the asset. This means that after all depreciation has been recorded using either method, the net asset will be recorded at salvage value, and accumulated depreciation will equal the original cost minus salvage value.

32. (a) Depreciation is a method of allocating the cost of an asset in a systematic and rational manner. Since the units-of-production method of depreciation is most appropriate when depreciation is a function of activity, answer (a) is correct. Answer (b) is incorrect because this situation warrants the use of a depreciation method based on the passage of time. Answers (c) and (d) are incorrect because both support the use of an accelerated method of depreciation.

33. (b) Under the sum-of-the-years' digits (SYD) method, depreciation expense is computed by applying declining fractions to the depreciable cost of the asset. The denominator is the sum of the years in the life of the asset (1 + 2 + 3 + 4 + 5 = 15 in this case). Annual depreciation would be computed as follows:

Year 1	Original cost less salvage value	×	5/15
Year 2	Original cost less salvage value	×	4/15
Year 3	Original cost less salvage value	×	3/15
Year 4	Original cost less salvage value	×	2/15
Total	Original cost less salvage value	×	14/15

Accumulated depreciation at December 31, year 4, would be (original cost less salvage value) multiplied by 14/15.

34. (c) Sum-of-the-years' digits (SYD) depreciation = (Cost less Salvage value) × Applicable fraction.

Where applicable fraction = $\dfrac{\text{Number of years of estimated life remaining as of the beginning of the year}}{\text{SYD}}$

and

$$SYD = \dfrac{N(n+1)}{2} \quad \text{Where n = estimated useful life}$$

Calculated as

Year 1 = $18,000* ×	$\dfrac{4}{10}$	= $7,200
Year 2 = $18,000* ×	$\dfrac{3}{10}$	= $5,400
Year 3 = $18,000* ×	$\dfrac{2}{10}$	= $3,600

* ($20,000 – $2,000)

On December 31, year 3, the carrying amount of Spiro's asset equals $3,800 (the asset's cost of $20,000 minus accumulated depreciation of $16,200**).

** ($7,200 + $5,400 + $3,600)

35. **(d)** Line I represents depreciation expense that stays constant over time (i.e., straight-line). Both sum-of-the-years' digits and double-declining balance are accelerated depreciation methods, and hence the depreciation expense for these two methods does not stay constant over time. Line II represents depreciation expense that decreases at a constant rate (i.e., a linear function) and thus would be the pattern of depreciation for sum-of-the-years' digits. Line III represents depreciation expense that decreases at a decreasing rate (i.e., a nonlinear function) and thus would be the pattern of depreciation for the double-declining balance method.

36. **(c)** Composite (group) depreciation averages the service life of a number of property units and depreciates the group as if it were a single unit. The term "group" is used when the assets are similar; the term "composite" is used when they are dissimilar. The mechanical application of both of these methods is identical. The depreciation rate is the following ratio:

$$\dfrac{\text{Sum of annual SL depreciation of individual assets}}{\text{Total asset cost}}$$

Thus, both group and composite depreciation utilize the straight-line depreciation method.

37. **(b)** The solutions approach is to prepare the journal entry that would be made when an asset is retired under the composite depreciation method.

Cash	(cash proceeds)
Accumulated depreciation	(plug)
Truck	(original cost)

The net decrease in the carrying amount of the assets is the credit to the asset account less the plug to accumulated depreciation. This amount would be equal to the **cash proceeds received**.

38. **(d)** When management plans to dispose of long-lived assets and limited-lived intangibles, the assets shall be reported at the lower of carrying amount or fair value less cost to sell.

39. **(b)** Losses associated with long-lived assets which are to be disposed of are to be reported as a component of income from continuing operations before income taxes for entities preparing income statements. Losses on long-lived assets to be disposed of are neither unusual nor infrequent occurrences. These losses are not part of selling or general and administrative expenses and they are not disclosed net of tax. Discontinued operations result from disposal of a separate business component.

40. **(d)** In year 3, Taft recognized a loss on the long-lived assets that were to be sold and changed the carrying amount of these assets to fair value less cost to sell. In year 4, the assets have still not been sold. The loss recognized has been more than recovered. Subsequent revisions in estimates of fair value less cost to sell shall be reported as adjustments of the carrying amount of an asset to be disposed of. However, the carrying amount may not be increased above the carrying amount prior to impairment. The same amount recognized as a loss in year 3 would be recognized as a recovery (gain) in the year 4 income statement.

41. **(b)** The reduced carrying amount of Cranston's assets ($920,000) should be accounted for as their new cost, and this amount should be depreciated over the remaining useful life of five years. Restoration of previously recognized impairment losses is prohibited. Therefore, Cranston should report .80 × $920,000 or $736,000 as the carrying amount of its impaired long-lived assets on its December 31, year 4 balance sheet.

42. **(c)** The requirement is to determine when an asset is impaired. An asset is impaired when the sum of the expected future cash flows is less than the carrying amount of the asset. The expected future cash flows are **not** discounted and do not consider interest charges. Answer (c) refers to one way to measure a loss once it has been determined that an asset has been impaired.

43. **(c)** The loss on impairment is calculated by subtracting the machine's actual fair value from its carrying value at the date of impairment.

$10,000	Initial cost of machine	$10,000	Cost on 7/1/Y2
– 500	Salvage value	– 2,375	Accumulated depreciation
$ 9,500	Depreciable base	$ 7,625	Carrying value on 12/31/Y4
÷ 10	Year life	– 3,000	Actual fair value on 12/31/Y4
$950	Depreciation per year	$ 4,625	Loss on impairment
× 2.5	Years (7/1/Y2–12/31/Y4)		
$ 2,375	Accumulated depreciation		

44. **(b)** When an asset has been determined to be impaired, it is written down to fair value and loss on impairment is recognized. Restoration of previously recognized impairment losses is prohibited.

45. **(b)** A long-lived asset is considered impaired if the future cash flows expected to result from the use of the asset and its eventual disposition are less than the carrying amount of the asset. If deemed impaired, the asset's carrying value is reduced to fair value and a loss on impairment is recognized for the difference (Carrying value – Fair value). In this case, the asset is **not** impaired, as the net cash inflows of $175,000 are greater than the 8/31/Y4 carrying amount (book value) of $170,000. Therefore, the carrying amount of the asset ($170,000) remains unchanged.

46. **(a)** The requirement is to determine the amount of impairment loss. The impairment loss recognized is the difference between the asset's fair value and its carrying value. On December 31, year 4, the carrying value of the equipment is $80,000 after recording depreciation expense for the current year. ($100,000/Y4 years = $10,000 per year × 2 years = $20,000 accumulated depreciation). The fair value is determined by using the principal or most advantageous market assuming the highest and best use of the asset. Since the in-use valuation premise is $74,000, the asset is assumed to be in its highest and best use using an in-use valuation premise. Therefore, the impairment loss recognized in year 4 would be the carrying value of $80,000 less the fair value of $74,000 = $6,000.

47. **(b)** The requirement is to determine the amount that should be presented for the equipment. An impairment loss is recognized if the carrying value of the asset exceeds the sum of the undiscounted cash flows. Since the carrying value of $160,00 exceeds the sum of the estimated undiscounted cash flows of $135,000, an impairment loss must be measured. The impairment loss is measured by comparing the fair value of the asset to the carrying value. The fair value of the asset is determined by using the lowest level input available. In this situation, a Level 1 input is not available. The value of similar equipment for sale in the market is a Level 2 input because it is a directly or indirectly observable input. The present value of future cash flows is a Level 3 input, and should only be used when Level 1 or Level 2 inputs are not available. Therefore, the asset should be presented at its fair value of $140,000, which uses a Level 2 input to appropriately measure fair value of the equipment.

48. **(d)** The requirement is to determine the impairment loss on the equipment. An impairment loss is recognized when the carrying value of an asset exceeds the expected undiscounted cash flows of the asset. In this case, the undiscounted expected cash flows are $420,000 and are less than the carrying value. Therefore, an impairment loss is measured as the difference between the fair value of the asset and its carrying value. The fair value of the asset should be measured based on the lowest level priority input, and assuming the highest and best use of the asset. The highest and best use of the asset occurs when the asset is sold as standalone for $428,000. Therefore, the impairment loss recognized for year 4 is $428,000 fair value less $450,000 carrying value, or $22,000.

49. **(c)** An impairment loss for assets to be held and used shall be reported as a component of income from continuing operations before income taxes for entities presenting an income statement and in the statement of activities of a not-for-profit organization. Although there is no requirement to report a subtotal such as "income from operations," entities that present such a subtotal must include the impairment loss in that subtotal.

50. **(a)** The undiscounted expected future cash flows ($175,000) are less than the carrying amount of the equipment ($200,000). Therefore, the equipment is deemed impaired. The impairment loss is calculated in the following way:

Carrying amount of the equipment on December 31, year 4	$200,000
Fair value of the equipment on December 31, year 4	125,000
Impairment loss reported on year 4 income statement	$ 75,000

51. **(b)** After an impairment loss is recognized, the reduced carrying amount of the asset shall be accounted for as its new cost. This new cost (the fair value of the asset at the date of impairment, or $135,000) shall be depreciated over the asset's remaining useful life (twenty-seven months). Therefore, the depreciation expense for June is $5,000 ($135,000 ÷ 27 months × 1 month).

52. **(b)** Recoveries of impairment losses shall not be recognized.

53. **(c)** The loss due to impairment of long-lived assets is measured by deducting the asset's fair value from the carrying (book) value.

54. **(c)** Long-lived assets and limited-lived intangibles must be reviewed for impairment whenever circumstances and situations change such that there is an indication that the carrying amount might not be recoverable. A specific time frame for review of asset impairment, every year or every three years, is not required.

55. **(b)** The undiscounted expected future cash flows ($300,000) are less than the carrying amount of the equipment ($350,000). Thus, the equipment is determined to be impaired. The impairment loss is calculated as follows:

Carrying value - 12/31/Y4	$350,000
Fair value - 12/31/Y4	250,000
Impairment loss reported on year 4 income statement	$100,000

56. **(c)** After an impairment loss is recognized, the reduced carrying amount of the asset shall be accounted for as its new cost. This new cost (the fair value of the asset at the date of impairment, or $261,000) shall be depreciated over the asset's remaining useful life (58 months). Therefore, the depreciation expense for September is $4,500 ($261,000 ÷ 58 months × 1 month).

57. **(b)** The depletion charge per unit is the **depletion base** (net cost of the resource) divided by the **estimated units of the resource**. Vorst's depletion base is $2,880,000, as computed below.

Cost of mine	$2,640,000
Development cost	360,000
Restoration cost	180,000
Residual value	(300,000)
	$2,880,000

Note that the present value of the restoration costs are recorded. The depletion charge is $2.40 per ton ($2,880,000 ÷ 1,200,000 tons). Since 60,000 tons were removed and sold, depletion of $144,000 (60,000 × $2.40) is included in Vorst's year 4 income statement. Note that the amount of depletion included in the income statement depends on the tons **sold**. If more tons were removed than sold, part of the depletion would be included in the cost of ending inventory rather than in the income statement.

58. (b) The software should be valued at the lower of its unamortized cost or its net realizable value. The software's unamortized cost is $450,000, which is equal to $600,000 – $150,000 ($600,000/4). Answer (c) is incorrect because the software's unamortized cost is less than its net realizable value.

59. (c) Judd Company would record the trademark at its cost of $500,000. The unamortized cost on the seller's books ($380,000) is irrelevant to the buyer. The trademark has a remaining useful life of fifty years. Therefore, the year 4 amortization expense and 12/31/Y4 accumulated amortization is $10,000 ($500,000 ÷ 50 years).

60. (b) A company should record as an asset the cost of intangible assets such as goodwill **acquired from other entities**. **Costs of developing** intangible assets such as goodwill "which are not specifically identifiable, have indeterminate lives, or are inherent in a continuing business and related to an entity as a whole" should be expensed when incurred. Therefore, only the $200,000 (and not the additional $80,000) should be capitalized as goodwill. Goodwill should not be amortized.

61. (d) In determining the useful life of an intangible, consideration should be given to the legal, regulatory or contractual life, including rights to extension. Since Northern has the ability and intent to renew the rights indefinitely, the intangible should not be amortized.

62. (c) Before year 4, Lava would record total amortization of $27,000 [($90,000 × 1/10) × 3 years], resulting in a 12/31/Y3 carrying amount of $63,000 ($90,000 – $27,000). Since the patent became worthless at 12/31/Y4 due to government prohibition of the product, the entire carrying amount ($63,000) should be charged against income in year 4 as an impairment loss.

63. (d) Goodwill should not be amortized. Instead, goodwill remains at the amount established at the time of the business combination unless it is determined to be impaired. Goodwill should be tested for impairment annually, or more often if events and circumstances indicate that goodwill may be impaired.

64. (a) Costs incurred in connection with securing a patent, as well as attorney's fees and other unrecovered costs of a successful legal suit to protect the patent, can be capitalized as part of patent costs. Therefore, answer (a) is correct because legal fees and other costs incurred to successfully defend a patent should be amortized along with the acquisition cost over the remaining economic life of the patent. Answer (b) is incorrect because legal fees and other direct costs incurred in registering a patent should be capitalized and amortized on a straight-line basis over its economic life, not five years. Answers (c) and (d) are incorrect because research and development costs related to the development of the product, process or idea that is subsequently patented must be expensed as incurred, not capitalized and amortized.

65. (d) Goodwill is allocated to reporting units which are operating segments of the business or one level below. Goodwill is also tested for impairment at the level of the reporting unit.

66. (c) Goodwill impairment is determined at the level of the individual reporting unit. It is the difference between the carrying amount of goodwill and its implied value. The carrying amounts of goodwill of the Retailing and Service reporting units are greater than their implied values. Therefore, an impairment loss should be recognized in the amount of $15,000 ($30,000 + $20,000) – ($25,000 + $10,000).

67. (a) There are two steps in the test of impairment of goodwill. The first is to compare the carrying value of the reporting unit to its fair value. If the fair value exceeds the carrying value there is no need to perform the second step of valuing the unit's assets and liabilities. Goodwill is never tested at the entity level.

68. (d) Since the fair value of the reporting unit is less than its carrying amount, the second step in the test should be performed. The assets and liabilities of the unit should be valued and compared to value of the total unit. The implied value of goodwill is the difference. The impairment is equal to the difference between the implied value and the carrying amount of the goodwill.

69. (b) Start-up activities are defined broadly as those onetime activities related to opening a new facility as well as introducing a new product or service and conducting business in a new territory. Certain costs that may be incurred in conjunction with start-up activities are not subject to these provisions. These costs include the costs of acquiring long-lived assets such as production equipment, costs of advertising, and license fees. Answer (b) which includes the costs of training local employees ($120,000) and travel costs of salaried employees ($40,000) is the correct answer.

70. (d) Organization costs are those incurred in the formation of a corporation. These costs should be expensed as incurred. The rationale is that uncertainty exists concerning the future benefit of these costs in future years. Thus, they are properly recorded as an expense in year 4.

71. (b) The costs of raising capital and the costs of acquiring or constructing long-lived assets and getting them ready for their intended use are not expensed as incurred. Such costs should be accounted for in accordance with other existing authoritative accounting literature. Research and development (R&D) costs are expensed as incurred.

72. (d) Among those items listed as being part of R&D costs are design of tools, jigs, molds, and dies involving new technology ($125,000) and modification of the formulation of a process ($160,000), for a total R&D expense of $285,000. Included in the items **not** being part of R&D costs are troubleshooting breakdowns during production ($100,000), and adaptation of existing capability for a specific customer ($110,000).

73. (b) All R&D costs must be expensed when incurred. However, R&D costs incurred when performing R&D work under contract for other entities are specifically excluded from the reporting requirements. Generally such costs are deferred and matched with revenue under the completed-contract or percentage-of-completion method. The other costs listed would all be expensed in year 4. Therefore, Ball's year 4 research and development expense is $1,380,000 ($300,000 + $700,000 + $200,000 + $180,000).

74. (c) All R&D costs are to be charged to expense when incurred. Specifically R&D costs include designing, constructing, and testing preproduction prototypes, and the cost of R&D equipment (unless it has alternative future uses). Therefore, $340,000 ($60,000 + $200,000 + $80,000) is classified as R&D costs and expensed. The legal costs incurred to obtain a patent ($10,000) are capitalized in the patents account.

75. **(d)** The FASB excludes from its definitions of research and development expense the acquisition, development, or improvement of a product or process for use in its **selling or administrative activities**. Both costs given in this problem relate to selling or administrative activities, so the expenditures of $175,000 would not be reported as research and development expense.

76. **(a)** Research and development costs are expensed as incurred except for fixed assets, intangible assets, or materials purchased that have alternative future uses. Jambon purchased equipment to be used for research and development, but the equipment can only be used for that project. Therefore, the cost of the equipment must be expensed in year 4 as it has no alternative future uses.

77. **(b)** Costs incurred in creating a computer software product should be charged to research and development expense when incurred until **technological feasibility** has been established for the product. Technological feasibility is established upon completion of a detailed program design or working model. In this case, $23,000 would be recorded as expense ($13,000 for completion of detailed program design and $10,000 for coding and testing to establish technological feasibility). Costs incurred from the point of technological feasibility until the time when product costs are incurred are capitalized as software costs. In this situation, $59,000 is capitalized as software cost ($24,000 + $20,000 + $15,000). Product costs that can be easily associated with the inventory items are reported as inventory (in this case, $25,000 for duplication of computer software and training materials and $9,000 of packaging costs, for a total of $34,000).

78. **(c)** Costs incurred in creating a computer software product should be charged to research and development expense when incurred until **technological feasibility** has been established. Technological feasibility is established upon completion of a detailed program design or working model. In this case, $23,000 would be recorded as expense ($13,000 for completion of detailed program design and $10,000 for coding and testing to establish technological feasibility). Costs incurred from the point of technological feasibility until the time when product costs are incurred are capitalized as software costs. In this situation, $59,000 is capitalized as software cost ($24,000 + $20,000 + $15,000). Product costs that can be easily associated with the inventory items are reported as inventory (in this case, $25,000 for duplication of computer software and training materials and $9,000 of packaging costs, for a total of $34,000).

79. **(a)** The annual amortization of capitalized software costs shall be the greater of

1. The ratio of the software's current sales to its expected total sales, or
2. The straight-line method over the economic life of the product.

In this case, the ratio of current to expected total sales is 30% (given). The annual straight-line rate is 20% per year (1 ÷ economic life of five years). The 30% amortization should be recorded in year 4, since it is the higher of the two. The unamortized cost on the 12/31/Y4 balance sheet

should, therefore, be 70% (100% – 30% amortization). Note that the unamortized cost of capitalized software products must be compared to the net realizable value of those assets at each balance sheet date. Any excess of the amortized cost over the net realizable value must be written off. In this case, the net realizable value (90%) was **above** the unamortized cost (70%), so no additional write-off was required.

80. **(b)** Internal-use software is software having the following characteristics: (1) The software is acquired, internally developed, or modified solely to meet the entity's internal needs, and (2) during the software's development or modification, no substantive plan exists to market the software externally.

81. **(b)** Application and development costs create probable future benefit. Therefore, they should be capitalized as incurred. However, preliminary costs are similar to research and development costs and are expensed as incurred, not capitalized.

82. **(d)** Preliminary costs are similar to research and development costs; therefore, they are expensed as incurred. Postimplementation costs such as training are not considered software development costs at all and are expensed as incurred.

83. **(a)** A development stage enterprise shall follow the same revenue and expense recognition principles and issue the same basic financial statements as an established operating enterprise, but shall disclose certain additional information. A development stage company shall use the same generally accepted accounting principles that apply to established operating enterprises to govern the recognition of revenue and to determine whether a cost is to be capitalized or expensed as incurred.

84. **(c)** A development stage enterprise shall issue the same basic financial statements as an established operating enterprise, but shall disclose certain additional information. An income statement, in addition to showing amounts of revenues and expenses for each period covered by the income statement, shall include the cumulative amounts from the enterprise's inception.

85. **(a)** The requirement is to identify the models that may be used to value plant, property, and equipment. Answer (a) is correct because IFRS allows the use of the cost model or the revaluation model for reporting plant, property, and equipment.

86. **(c)** The requirement is to identify the true statement about the revaluation model. Answer (c) is correct because IFRS does not provide requirements as to the frequency or date of revaluation of plant, property, and equipment.

87. **(c)** The requirement is to identify where the gain or loss should be presented. Answer (c) is correct because when the revaluation method is used for reporting plant, property, and equipment under IFRS, any gain or loss is recorded in a revaluation surplus account which is classified as other comprehensive income.

88. **(a)** The requirement is to identify the true statement regarding use of the fair value model. Answer (a) is correct because the fair value model requires that investment property be measured at fair value, and any changes in fair value are recognized in profit or loss of the period.

89. **(b)** The requirement is to identify the acceptable valuation methods for intangible assets. Answer (b) is correct because under IFRS, intangible assets can be measured using either the cost model or the revaluation model.

90. **(c)** The requirement is to determine the impairment gain or loss reported in the financial statements. Answer (c) is correct because if the cost model is used to record intangible assets, the impairment loss is recognized as a loss in the current period. If the cost model is used, a reversal of impairment losses may be recognized in the income statement up to the amount of the impairment loss previously recognized. Therefore, an impairment loss of $20,000 is recognized in year 3, and a gain of $4,000 is recognized in year 4.

91. **(c)** The requirement is to identify the statement that is true about accounting for plant, property, and equipment under IFRS. Answer (c) is correct because a company may elect to use the cost model or the revaluation model on any asset class.

92. **(d)** The requirement is to identify the correct statement about the revaluation model. Answer (d) is correct because there are no rules under IFRS regarding the frequency of revaluation.

93. **(d)** The requirement is to identify the correct statement about recording the sale. Answer (d) is correct because the gain of $10,000 ($100,000 book value – $90,000 book value) should be recorded in profit and loss for the period; the balance in the revaluation surplus account should be transferred to retained earnings.

94. **(b)** The requirement is to identify the circumstances that allow the entity to use the revaluation model. Answer (b) is correct because the revaluation method can only be used if there is an active market for the intangible asset.

95. **(d)** The requirement is to identify the criterion that must be met in order for an item to be recognized as an intangible asset other than goodwill. Answer (d) is correct because the asset must be identifiable and lack physical substance.

96. **(b)** The requirement is to determine the amount that should be recognized in the financial statements for the trademark. Answer (b) is correct because the trademark amount should include the purchase price ($100,000) plus the VAT taxes ($5,000) plus the legal cost incurred to register the trademark ($10,500), which is equal to $115,500. The research expenditures, training costs, and salaries should be expensed.

97. **(a)** The requirement is to identify the correct statement regarding the use of the revaluation model. Answer (a) is correct because when an asset is revalued, the entire class must be revalued. Answer (b) is incorrect because the entire class must be revalued. Answer (c) is incorrect because there are no rules regarding the frequency of revaluation. Answer (d) is incorrect because the revaluation surplus is presented in other comprehensive income, not profit or loss.

98. **(d)** The requirement is to calculate depreciation for the asset. Answer (d) is correct because IFRS requires each major component to be depreciated over its respective useful life. The machinery cost $72,000 ($100,000 – $20,000 – $8,000) would be depreciated over 10 years. The drum would be depreciated over 5 years, and the inspection would be depreciated over 4 years. Therefore, depreciation for year 1 would be calculated as $13,200 [($72,000/10) + ($20,000/5) + ($8,000/4)].

99. **(c)** The requirement is to identify the correct statement regarding accounting for development costs under IFRS. Answer (c) is correct because development costs can be capitalized only if six criteria are met.

100. **(b)** The requirement is to identify the rule regarding testing intangible assets with indefinite lives for impairment under IFRS. Answer (b) is correct because intangible assets with indefinite lives must be tested for impairment annually at the annual reporting date.

101. **(c)** The requirement is to identify the definition of recoverable amount under IFRS. Answer (c) is correct because recoverable amount is defined as the greater of net selling price or value in use.

102. **(b)** The requirement is to identify the true statement about biological assets under IFRS. Answer (b) is correct because biological assets are living animals or plants and must be disclosed as a separate item on the balance sheet.

Simulations

Task-Based Simulation 1

Concepts		
	Authoritative Literature	Help

For **items 1 through 6,** determine for each item whether the expenditure should be capitalized or expensed as a period cost.

		Capitalize	Expense
1.	Freight charges paid for goods held for resale.	○	○
2.	In-transit insurance on goods held for resale purchased FOB shipping point.	○	○
3.	Interest on note payable for goods held for resale.	○	○
4.	Installation of equipment.	○	○
5.	Testing of newly purchased equipment.	○	○
6.	Cost of current year service contract on equipment.	○	○

Task-Based Simulation 2

Asset Valuation		
	Authoritative Literature	Help

Situation

- Link Co. purchased an office building and the land on which it is located by paying $800,000 cash and assuming an existing mortgage of $200,000. The property is assessed at $960,000 for realty tax purposes, of which 60% is allocated to the building.
- Link leased construction equipment under a seven-year capital lease requiring annual year-end payments of $100,000. Link's incremental borrowing rate is 9%, while the lessor's implicit rate, which is not known to Link, is 8%. Present value factors for an ordinary annuity for seven periods are 5.21 at 8% and 5.04 at 9%. Fair value of the equipment is $515,000.
- Link paid $50,000 and gave a plot of undeveloped land with a carrying amount of $320,000 and a fair value of $450,000 to Club Co. in exchange for a plot of undeveloped land with a fair value of $500,000. The land was carried on Club's books at $350,000. This transaction is considered to lack commercial substance; the configuration of cash flows from the land acquired is not expected to be significantly different from the configuration of cash flows of the land exchanged.

Calculate the following amounts to be recorded by Link.

Amount

1. Building.
2. Leased equipment.
3. Land received from Club on Link's books.
4. Land received from Link on Club's books.

Task-Based Simulation 3

Depreciation Calculations		
	Authoritative Literature	Help

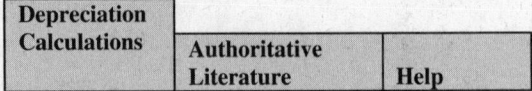

On January 2, year 3, Gray purchased a manufacturing machine for $864,000. The machine has an eight-year estimated life and a $144,000 estimated salvage value. Gray expects to manufacture 1,800,000 units over the life of the machine. During year 4, Gray manufactured 300,000 units.

Calculate depreciation expense on the manufacturing machine for year 4 for each method listed.

Amount

1. Straight-line.

2. Double-declining balance.

3. Sum-of-the-years' digits.

4. Units of production.

Task-Based Simulation 4

Research		
	Authoritative Literature	Help

Assume that you are assigned to the audit of Lopez Corporation. Lopez has discontinued one of its business components, and the CFO of Lopez has asked you whether this should be reported as discontinued operations on the income statement. Which section of the Professional Standards provides the conditions that must exist for the component to be presented as discontinued operations?

Enter your response in the answer fields below.

Task-Based Simulation 5

Capitalized Costs		
	Authoritative Literature	Help

Situation

Selected accounts included in the property, plant, and equipment section of Carlton Corporation's balance sheet at December 31, year 3, had the following balances:

Land	$ 400,000
Land improvements	130,000
Buildings	2,000,000
Machinery and equipment	800,000

During year 4, the following transactions occurred:

1. A tract of land was acquired for $200,000 as a potential future building site from Alison Corp.
2. A plant facility consisting of land and building was acquired from Kaufman Company in exchange for 20,000 shares of Carlton's common stock. On the acquisition date, Carlton's stock had a closing market price of $42 per share on a national stock exchange. The plant facility was carried on Kaufman's books at $178,000 for land and $520,000 for the building at the exchange date. Current appraised values for the land and the building, respectively, are $200,000 and $800,000. The building has an expected life of forty years with a $20,000 salvage value.
3. Items of machinery and equipment were purchased from Apex Equipment at a total cost of $400,000. Additional costs were incurred as follows: freight and unloading, $13,000; installation, $26,000. The equipment has a useful life of ten years with no salvage value.
4. Expenditures totaling $120,000 were made for new parking lots, street, and sidewalks at the corporation's various plant locations. These expenditures had an estimated useful life of fifteen years.
5. Research and development costs were $110,000 for the year.

Indicate the capitalized cost of each asset acquired during year 4, and the depreciation expense recorded for each of the acquired items in year 4.

	Capitalized cost	Depreciation/amortization expense for year 4
Land acquired from Alison Corp.		
Land acquired from Kaufman		
Building acquired from Kaufman		
Machinery and equipment acquired from Apex Equipment		
Land improvements		
Research and development		

Task-Based Simulation 6

Disposal of Assets		
	Authoritative Literature	**Help**

Situation

Selected accounts included in the property, plant, and equipment section of Carlton Corporation's balance sheet at December 31, year 7, had the following balances:

Land	$ 400,000
Land improvements	130,000
Buildings	2,000,000
Machinery and equipment	800,000

During year 4, the following transactions occurred:

1. A machine costing $16,000 on January 1, year 1, was scrapped on June 30, year 8. Straight-line depreciation had been recorded on the basis of a 10-year life with no salvage value.
2. A machine was sold for $48,000 on July 1, year 8. Original cost of the machine was $74,000 on January 1, year 5, and it was depreciated on the straight-line basis over an estimated useful life of eight years and a salvage value of $2,000.

Calculate the gain or loss on the disposal of each asset. Place your answer in the appropriate column.

Item	Amount of gain	Amount of loss
Scrapped machine on 6/30/Y8		
Sale of machine on 7/1/Y8		

Prepare the journal entries for the sale of the machine on July 1, year 8. Select your account titles from the following list. Assume depreciation is recorded at the date of disposal for any equipment sold.

Cash
Accumulated depreciation
Equipment
Gain on sale of equipment
Loss on sale of equipment
Depreciation expense

	Debit	Credit

Task-Based Simulation 7

Research		
	Authoritative Literature	**Help**

Assume that you are assigned to the audit of Carson Corporation. Carson has determined that the value of a major productive asset has been impaired. Which section of the Professional Standards provides guidance on how the impairment loss should be presented in Carson's income statement?

Enter your response in the answer fields below.

Task-Based Simulation 8

Concepts		
	Authoritative Literature	**Help**

Indicate whether each of the following statements is True or False.

		True	False
1.	An intangible asset that is determined to have an indefinite life should be amortized over 40 years.	○	○
2.	If the carrying value of the intangible asset exceeds its fair value, an impairment loss must be recognized.	○	○
3.	The impairment test for goodwill must be performed at the end of each fiscal year for each reporting unit.	○	○
4.	When a company borrows funds to finance a construction project and temporarily invests this cash, the interest expense should be offset against the interest expense to be capitalized.	○	○
5.	A company may capitalize interest on inventories it regularly produces for resale to customers.	○	○
6.	Gains are never recognized when similar assets are exchanged.	○	○
7.	In nonmonetary exchanges, losses are only recognized when cash is received in the transactions.	○	○
8.	If the fair value of the asset is unknown in a nonmonetary exchange and no gain can be computed, the asset is recorded at the fair market value of the asset given up.	○	○
9.	A capital expenditure is charged against income over the useful life of the asset.	○	○
10.	Expenditures to improve the efficiency or extend the useful life of an asset should be capitalized.	○	○

Task-Based Simulation 9

Intangible Assets		
	Authoritative Literature	Help

Situation

During year 4, Broca Co. had the following transactions:

- On January 2, Broca purchased the net assets of Amp Co. for $360,000. The fair value of Amp's identifiable net assets was $172,000. Broca believes that, due to the popularity of Amp's consumer products, the life of the resulting goodwill is unlimited.
- On February 1, Broca purchased a franchise to operate a ferry service from the state government for $60,000 and an annual fee of 1% of ferry revenues. The franchise expires after five years. Broca received $20,000 of ferry revenues in year 4.
- On April 5, Broca was granted a patent that had been applied for by Amp. During year 4, Broca incurred legal costs of $51,000 to register the patent and an additional $85,000 to successfully prosecute a patent infringement suit against a competitor. Broca estimates the patent's economic life to be ten years.

Broca has determined that it is appropriate to amortize these intangibles on the straight-line basis over the maximum period permitted by generally accepted accounting principles, taking a full year's amortization in the year of acquisition.

Complete the following schedule for Broca's intangible assets and the related income statement expenses.

Broca Co. SCHEDULE FOR INTANGIBLE ASSETS AND AMORTIZATION EXPENSE December 31, Year 4			
Item	**Valuation before adjusting entries**	**Amortization expense for the year**	**Valuation on 12/31/Y4**
Goodwill			
Franchise (net)			
Patent (net)			

Complete the following schedule for Broca's expenses.

Broca Co.	
EXPENSES RESULTING FROM INTANGIBLES	
For the Year Ended December 31, Year 4	
Amortization:	
Franchise	
Patent	
Franchise fee	
Total expenses	

Task-Based Simulation 10

Goodwill Impairment		
	Authoritative Literature	Help

Jane Corporation is performing its annual test of the impairment of the goodwill related to its Technology reporting unit. The carrying value of goodwill allocated to the unit is $500,000. Using a multiple of revenue, Jane has determined the fair value of the Technology reporting unit to be $1,700,000 at 12/31/Y4, and the fair value and carrying value of the assets and liabilities were determined as follows:

	(In 000s)	
	Carrying value	**Fair value**
Cash	$ 200	$ 200
Accounts receivable	250	250
Inventory	350	400
Net Equipment	700	700
Patents	400	450
Goodwill	500	?
Accounts payable	(200)	(200)
Long-term debt	(300)	(300)
	1,900	

1. Calculate the following amounts related to the impairment of goodwill.

   Implied Goodwill   [   ]

   Impairment of Goodwill   [   ]

2. Prepare the related journal entry if there is an impairment of goodwill for the Technology reporting unit.

Task-Based Simulation 11

Research		
	Authoritative Literature	Help

Assume that you are assigned to the audit of Dumas Corporation. Dumas has decided to self construct a productive asset. Which section of the Professional Standards provides guidance on whether the asset qualifies for capitalization of interest? Enter your response in the answer fields below.

Simulation Solutions

Task-Based Simulation 1

Concepts		
	Authoritative Literature	Help

		Capitalize	Expense
1.	Freight charges paid for goods held for resale.	●	○
2.	In-transit insurance on goods held for resale purchased FOB shipping point.	●	○
3.	Interest on note payable for goods held for resale.	○	●
4.	Installation of equipment.	●	○
5.	Testing of newly purchased equipment.	●	○
6.	Cost of current year service contract on equipment.	○	●

Explanations

Items 1 through 6 represent questions concerning expenditures for goods held for resale and equipment and whether these expenditures should be capitalized or expensed as a period cost. The general concept that determines whether expenditures should be product costs and, therefore, capitalized or expensed as period costs is whether or not these expenditures "attach" themselves to the assets of inventory or equipment. Costs that "attach" themselves to assets are those that are directly connected with bringing the goods or equipment to the place of business of the buyer and converting such goods to a salable (inventory) or usable (equipment) condition.

1. **(C)** Freight charges are directly connected with bringing the goods to the place of business of the buyer.

2. **(C)** Insurance charges are directly connected with bringing the goods to the place of business of the buyer.

3. **(E)** Only interest costs related to continued assets constructed for internal use or assets produced as discrete products for sale or lease should be capitalized. The informational benefit of capitalization does not justify the cost of the accounting for the interest as a product cost.

4. **(C)** Direct cost of bringing the equipment to the buyer.

5. **(C)** Direct cost of converting the equipment to a usable condition.

6. **(E)** Does not relate to bringing the equipment to the buyer or putting it into a usable condition.

Task-Based Simulation 2

Asset Valuation		
	Authoritative Literature	Help

1. **($600,000)** Since the land and building were purchased together, the cost of each must be allocated based on the relative market value. The land and building were purchased together for a total cost of $1,000,000 ($800,000 cash + $200,000 mortgage assumption). For property tax purposes, the building is deemed to be 60% of the value of the land and building. Therefore, the cost of the building should be recorded at $600,000 ($1,000,000 × 60%).

2. **($504,000)** As the lease is classified as a capital lease, Link must record an asset and liability based on the present value of the minimum lease payments. However, the leased assets cannot be recorded at an amount greater than the fair value. To determine the minimum value of the lease payments, Link should discount the future payments using the **lesser** of the lessee's (Link's) incremental borrowing rate (9%) or the lessor's implicit rate if **known** by the lessee. Therefore, since Link does not know the lessor's implicit rate, Link's rate of 9% should be used. The recorded value would be $100,000 × 5.04 = $504,000, which is less than the fair value.

3. **($370,000)** In recording a nonmonetary exchange, if the transaction lacks commercial substance, the asset received is recorded at the book value of the asset given up plus any boot given when gains and losses are not recognized. The following fact pattern exists for Link:

	Boot	**FV**	**BV**	**Gain (Loss)**
Land given	50,000	450,000	320,000	130,000
Land received		500,000		

Link will record the land received from Club at the book value of the land given up plus the boot given ($320,000 + 50,000 = $370,000).

An alternative method to calculate the value to record the land at is to subtract the deferred gain from the fair value of the land received ($500,000 − 130,000 = $370,000).

4. ($315,000) On Club's books the following situation exists:

	Boot	**FV**	**BV**	**Gain (Loss)**
Land given		500,000	350,000	150,000
Land received	50,000	450,000		

An exception to the nonrecognition of gain on similar assets exists when boot is received. The earnings process is considered complete for the portion related to the boot received, but not complete for the portion related to the asset received. A gain is recognized only for the portion related to the boot. The gain is computed as follows:

$$\frac{\text{Boot received}}{\text{Boot received} + \text{FMV of assets received}} \times \text{Total gain} = \text{Gain recognized}$$

$$\frac{50,000}{50,000 + 450,000} \times 150,000 = \$15,000$$

The land received will be recorded at its fair value less the gain deferred.

$$\$450,000 − (150,000 − 15,000) = \$315,000$$

An alternative method is to record the land received at the book value of the land given less the boot received plus the gain recognized, as follows:

$$\$350,000 − 50,000 + 15,000 = \$315,000$$

Task-Based Simulation 3

Depreciation Calculations		
	Authoritative Literature	Help

1. ($90,000) Under the straight-line method of depreciation, the depreciation expense would be calculated as follows:

$$\frac{\text{Cost-salvage value}}{\text{Estimated life}} = \frac{\$864,000 − 144,000}{8} = \$90,000$$

Depreciation expense would be $90,000 for all eight years, year 3-2016.

2. ($162,000) The double-declining balance method is calculated by taking two times the straight-line rate times the net book value at the beginning of each year, but not below the salvage value. Furthermore the salvage value is not deducted to arrive at the depreciable base. The calculation would be as follows:

	NBV		**Depreciation expense**
Year 3	$864,000 × (1/8 × 2)	=	$216,000
Year 4	($864,000 − 216,000) × (1/8 × 2)	=	$162,000

3. ($140,000) Under the sum-of-the-years' digits method, the depreciation expense is calculated as follows:

$$\text{Year 3} \quad 8 \div \frac{8(8+1)}{2} \times (\$864,000) − \$144,000) = \$160,000$$

$$\text{Year 4} \quad (7 \div 36) \times (\$864,000 − \$144,000) = \$140,000$$

4. ($120,000) The units of production method is a type of physical usage depreciation that is based on activity. The formula is as follows:

$$\frac{\text{Current activity/output}}{\text{Total expected activity/output}} \times \text{Depreciable base} = \text{Annual depreciation}$$

Depreciation expense for year 4 is calculated as follows:

$$\frac{300,000 \text{ units}}{1,800,000 \text{ units}} \times (\$864,000 − \$144,000) = \$120,000$$

Task-Based Simulation 4

Research			
	Authoritative Literature	Help	

ASC	205	20	45	1

Task-Based Simulation 5

Capitalized Costs		
	Authoritative Literature	Help

	Capitalized cost	Depreciation/amortization expense for year 4
Land acquired from Alison Corp.	$200,000	0
Land acquired from Kaufman	168,000	0
Building acquired from Kaufman	672,000	16,300
Machinery and equipment acquired from Apex Equipment	439,000	43,900
Land improvements	120,000	8,000
Research and development	0	0

Explanations

- Allocation of the land and building for purchase from Kaufman: FMV = 20,000 shares × $42 per share = $840,000.
- Allocate based on relative fair values. Therefore, land is $840,000 × $200,000/$1,000,000 = $168,000; Building is $840,000 × $800,000/$1,000,000 = $672,000. Land is not depreciated. Building is depreciated ($672,000 – $20,000)/40 years = $16,300.
- Items of machinery and equipment should capitalize all costs to get the asset in its intended and useful place.
- Land improvements are depreciated over fifteen years. $120,000/15 years = $8,000 per year.
- Research and development costs should be expensed as incurred. They are not capitalized, and they are not depreciated.

Task-Based Simulation 6

Disposal of Assets		
	Authoritative Literature	Help

Item	Amount of gain	Amount of loss
Scrapped machine on 6/30/Y8		$4,000
Sale of machine on 7/1/Y8	$5,500	

	Debit	Credit
Depreciation expense	4,500	
Accumulated depreciation		4,500
Cash	48,000	
Accumulated depreciation	31,500	
Equipment		74,000
Gain on sale of equipment		5,500

Task-Based Simulation 7

Research			
	Authoritative Literature	Help	

ASC	360	10	45	4

Task-Based Simulation 8

Concepts		
	Authoritative Literature	Help

		True	False
1.	An intangible asset that is determined to have an indefinite life should be amortized over 40 years.	○	●
2.	If the carrying value of the intangible asset exceeds its fair value, an impairment loss must be recognized.	●	○
3.	The impairment test for goodwill must be performed at the end of each fiscal year for each reporting unit.	○	●
4.	When a company borrows funds to finance a construction project and temporarily invests this cash, the interest expense should be offset against the interest expense to be capitalized.	○	●
5.	A company may capitalize interest on inventories it regularly produces for resale to customers.	○	●
6.	Gains are never recognized when similar assets are exchanged.	○	●
7.	In nonmonetary exchanges, losses are only recognized when cash is received in the transactions.	○	●
8.	If the fair value of the asset is unknown in a nonmonetary exchange and no gain can be computed, the asset is recorded at the fair market value of the asset given up.	○	●
9.	A capital expenditure is charged against income over the useful life of the asset.	●	○
10.	Expenditures to improve the efficiency or extend the useful life of an asset should be capitalized.	●	○

Explanations

1. **(F)** Intangible assets that have indefinite lives are not amortized.

2. **(T)** The recorded values of intangibles are impaired if they are above fair value.

3. **(F)** The impairment test for goodwill can be performed anytime during the year, but it must be performed at the same time every year.

4. **(F)** Interest earned on temporary investments from borrowed funds used to finance construction projects should be recognized as interest revenue and not netted against interest expense during the period.

5. **(F)** A company may not capitalize interest on funds borrowed to finance routinely produced inventory.

6. **(F)** Recognition of gain is required unless the transaction lacks commercial substance.

7. **(F)** Losses on nonmonetary exchanges are recognized.

8. **(F)** In a nonmonetary exchange, if the fair value is unknown and no gain can be computed, the asset is recorded at the book value of the asset given up.

9. **(T)** Capital expenditures are amortized over the useful life of the asset.

10. **(T)** Expenditures to improve capital assets should be capitalized.

Task-Based Simulation 9

Intangible Assets		
	Authoritative Literature	Help

Broca Co.
SCHEDULE FOR INTANGIBLE ASSETS AND AMORTIZATION EXPENSE
December 31, Year 4

Item	Valuation before adjusting entries		Amortization expense for the year	Valuation on 12/31/Y4
Goodwill	188,000	[1]	-0-	188,000
Franchise (net)	60,000	[2]	12,000	48,000
Patent (net)	136,000	[3]	13,600	122,400

Explanations

Broca Co.
SUPPORTING CALCULATIONS FOR INTANGIBLES
December 31, Year 4

Goodwill	$188,000 [1]
Franchise, net of accumulated amortization of $12,000	48,000 [2]
Patent, net of accumulated amortization of $13,600	122,400 [3]

[1]	Cash paid	$ 360,000
	Value of net assets	(172,000)
	Goodwill	188,000
[2]	Franchise	$ 60,000
	Amortization over 5 years	(12,000)
	Balance	$ 48,000
[3]	Legal costs ($51,000 + $85,000)	$ 136,000
	Amortization over 10 years	(13,600)
	Balance	$ 122,400

[1]   Goodwill calculation

In a purchase, the net assets acquired are recorded at their FV. The excess of the cost of the investment ($360,000) over the FV of the net assets acquired ($172,000) is allocated to goodwill ($360,000 – $172,000 = $188,000). Intangible assets with an indeterminate or unlimited life, such as this goodwill, are not amortized. The goodwill is reported in the 12/31/Y4 balance at its cost.

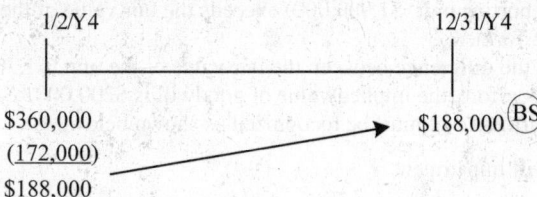

[2]   Franchise fee

The franchise acquired on 2/1/Y4 is recorded at its cost of $60,000. Since Broca amortizes these intangibles on a straight-line basis, and takes a full year's amortization in the year of acquisition, year 4 amortization is $12,000 ($60,000 × 1/5), and the franchise is reported at cost less accumulated amortization at 12/31/Y4 ($60,000 – $12,000 = $48,000). In addition to the amortization expense, there is also an annual fee that must be expensed, equal to 1% of ferry revenues.

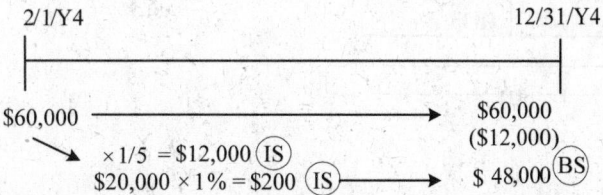

[3]   Patents are initially recorded at cost of acquisition, which is purchase price for a purchased patent, or legal and other costs of registration ($51,000) for an internally generated patent. Legal fees incurred in **successfully** defending the

patent ($85,000) are also capitalized because such fees help establish the legal right of the holder to any future benefits that will be derived from the patent. Therefore, this patent is capitalized at a total amount of $136,000 ($51,000 + $85,000). Since Broca amortizes these intangibles on a straight-line basis and takes a full-year's amortization in the year of acquisition, amortization is $13,600 ($136,000 x1/Y4). The patent is reported at cost less accumulated amortization at 12/31/Y4 ($136,000 – $13,600 = $122,400).

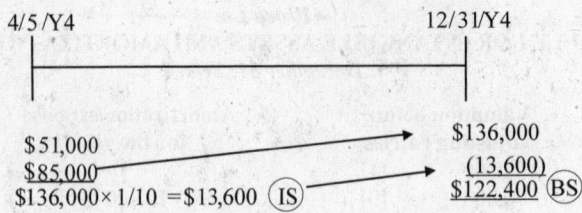

Broca Co.
EXPENSES RESULTING FROM INTANGIBLES
For the Year Ended December 31, Year 4

Amortization:		
	Franchise	12,000
	Patent	13,600
		$25,600
Franchise fee		200
($20,000 × 1%)		
Total expenses		$25,800

Task-Based Simulation 10

Goodwill Impairment		
	Authoritative Literature	Help

1.   Implied goodwill $200,000

   Impairment of goodwill $300,000

Explanations

1. Goodwill acquired through a business combination is the only type of goodwill that is recognized. Such goodwill is not amortized but is tested periodically for impairment. Internally generated goodwill is not recorded. Expenditures to develop, maintain, or enhance goodwill are expensed as incurred.

Since the carrying value of the reporting unit ($1,900,000) exceeds the fair value of the unit ($1,700,000), the second step in the test of impairment should be performed.

The implied value of goodwill is the difference between the fair value of the unit ($1,700,000) and the fair value of its assets and liabilities ($1,500,000). Therefore, the implied value of goodwill is $200,000. Since the carrying value of goodwill is $500,000, there is a $300,000 impairment that must be recognized as shown below.

2. Journal entry required for goodwill impairment

Impairment loss	$300,000	
Goodwill		$300,000

To recognize impairment of goodwill for the Technology reporting unit at 12/31/Y4.

Task-Based Simulation 11

Research		
	Authoritative Literature	Help

ASC	835	20	15	5

Module 12: Monetary Current Assets and Current Liabilities

Overview

This study module reviews accounting for current assets (except inventory which is presented in Module 10) and short-term investments (which are presented in Module 16). The primary topics covered on the Financial Accounting Reporting Section of the exam include

1. Cash and bank reconciliations.
2. Receivables with respect to initial recording, bad debts, borrowing, factoring, transferring, servicing, and securitizing.

This module also reviews current liabilities. The primary topics tested on the exam include accounting for payroll and contingencies (e.g., warranties, lawsuits.) Additionally, this module covers ratio analysis for solvency (e.g. current ratio) and operational efficiency (e.g. inventory turnover).

A. Cash

The definition of **cash** includes both cash (cash on hand and demand deposits) and cash equivalents (short-term, highly liquid investments).

1. **Cash equivalents** have to be readily convertible into cash and so near maturity that they carry little risk of changing in value due to interest rate changes. Generally this will include only those investments with original maturities of three months or less from the **date of purchase** by the enterprise.

   a. Common examples of cash equivalents include Treasury bills, commercial paper, and money market funds. Unrestricted cash and cash equivalents available for general use are presented as the first current asset.

2. Cash set aside for special uses is usually disclosed separately. The entry to set up a special fund is

   | Special cash fund | xx | |
   | Cash | | xx |

3. Cash restricted as to use (e.g., not transferable out of a foreign country) should be disclosed separately, but not as a current asset if it cannot be used in the next year (this is true of special funds also).
4. Imprest (petty) cash funds are generally included in the total cash figure, but unreimbursed expense vouchers are excluded.

B. Bank Reconciliations

1. Bank reconciliations are prepared by bank depositors when they receive their monthly bank statements. The reconciliation is made to determine any required adjustments to the cash balance. Two types of reconciling items are possible.

   a. Reconciling items not requiring adjustment on the books (type A)

      (1) There are three type A reconciling items. They do not require adjusting journal entries.

         (a) Outstanding checks
         (b) Deposits in transit
         (c) Bank errors

   b. Reconciling items requiring adjustment on the books (type B)

      (1) All other reconciling items (type B) require adjusting journal entries. Examples of type B reconciling items include

(a) Unrecorded returned nonsufficient funds (NSF) checks
(b) Unrecorded bank charges
(c) Errors in the cash account
(d) Unrecorded bank collections of notes receivable

2. Two types of formats are used in bank reconciliations.

Format 1	Format 2
Balance per bank	Balance per bank
+(−) A adjustments	+(−) A adjustments
Correct cash balance	+(−) B adjustments
	Balance per books
Balance per books	+(−) B adjustments
+(−) B adjustments	Correct cash balance
Correct cash balance	

a. Type A and B adjustments can be either added or subtracted depending upon the type of format and the nature of the item.
b. Reconciling items must be analyzed to determine whether they are included in (1) the balance per bank, and/or (2) the balance per books.

   (1) If they are included in one, but not the other, an adjustment is required.

      (a) For instance, the $1,800 deposit in transit in the following example is included in the balance per books but not in the balance per bank. Thus, it must be added to the balance per bank to reconcile to the correct cash balance.
      (b) Deposits in transit do not require an adjusting journal entry. Analyze all reconciling items in this manner, but remember, only journalize type B reconciling items.

SAMPLE BANK RECONCILIATION (FORMAT 1)

Per bank statement	$ 4,702
Deposits in transit	1,800
Outstanding checks	(1,200)
Bank error	50
Correct cash balance	$ 5,352
Per books	$ 5,332
Service charges	(5)
Note collected by bank	150
Customer's NSF check	(170)
Deposit of July 10 recorded as $749 instead of $794	45
Correct cash balance	$ 5,352

NOTE: The balance per bank and balance per books each are reconciled directly to the corrected balance.

c. **Adjusting journal entries.** All of the items in the per books section of a bank reconciliation (type B) require adjusting entries. The entries for the above example appear below.

Miscellaneous expense	5		AR	170	
Cash		5	Cash		170
Cash	150		Cash	45	
Notes receivable		150	AR (or sales)		45

3. **Four-column cash reconciliation**

a. Unlike the bank reconciliation above, which is as of a specific date, a four-column cash reconciliation, also known as a "proof of cash," reconciles bank and book cash balances over a specified time period.
b. A proof of cash consists of four columns: beginning of the period bank reconciliation, receipts, disbursements, and end-of-the-period bank reconciliation. Thus, the proof of cash cross-foots as well as foots.

SAMPLE PROOF OF CASH (FORMAT 2)

	Bank reconciliation June 30, Year 1	Receipts	Disbursements	Bank reconciliation July 31, Year 1
Balance per bank statement	$3,402	$25,200	$23,900	$ 4,702
Deposits in transit				
June 30, year 1	1,610	(1,610)		
July 31, year 1		1,800		1,800
Outstanding checks				
June 30, year 1	(450)		(450)	
July 31, year 1			1,200	(1,200)
Service charges			(5)	5
Note collected by bank		(150)		(150)
Customer's NSF check			(170)	170
Deposit of July 10 recorded as $749				
instead of $794		(45)		(45)
Bank error			(50)	50
Balance per books	$4,562	$25,195	$24,425	$ 5,332

(1) There are no type B reconciling items in the beginning reconciliation column. This is because the $4,562 has been adjusted when the June bank statement was reconciled.

(2) Figures appearing in the center columns have unlike signs if they are adjacent and like signs if they are not adjacent to amounts in the side columns.

c. The purpose of the proof of cash is to disclose any cash misstatements, such as unrecorded disbursements and receipts within a month, which would not be detected by a bank reconciliation.

> **EXAMPLE**
>
> If the center two columns each required a negative $1,000 to make the top line reconcile with the bottom line, there may be unrecorded receipts and deposits of $1,000.

NOW REVIEW MULTIPLE-CHOICE QUESTIONS 1 THROUGH 6

C. Receivables

Accounts receivable should be disclosed in the balance sheet at net realizable value (gross amount less estimated uncollectibles) by source (e.g., trade, officer, etc.). Officer, employee, and affiliate company receivables should be separately disclosed. Unearned interest and finance charges should be deducted from gross receivables.

1. Anticipation of Sales Discounts

a. Cash discounts are generally recognized as expense when cash payment is received within the discount period. As long as cash discounts to be taken on year-end receivables remain constant from year to year, there is no problem. If, however, discounts on year-end receivables fluctuate, a year-end allowance can be set up or sales can be recorded net of the discounts.

(1) The entries to record sales at net are shown below in comparison to the sales recorded at **gross**.

		Sales at net		Sales at gross	
a.	Sale	AR (net)		AR (gross)	
		Sales	(net)	Sales	(gross)
b.	Cash receipt within discount period	Cash (net)		Sales disc. (disc.)	
		AR	(net)	Cash (net)	
				AR	(gross)
c.	Cash receipt after discount period	Cash (gross)		Cash (gross)	
		AR	(net)	AR	(gross)
		Disc. not taken	(disc.)		

(a) The rationale for the net method is that sales are recorded at the cash equivalent amount and receivables nearer realizable value.

NOTE: Under both the net and gross methods, sales and accounts receivable are recorded net of trade discounts for the same reason.

(b) If a sales discount allowance method is used, the entry below is made with the gross method entries. The entry should be reversed.

Sales discounts   (expected disc. on year-end AR)
   Allowance for sales disc.   (expected disc. on year-end AR)

(c) Similarly, when using the **"net method,"** an entry should be made to pick up discounts not expected to be taken on year-end receivables. Generally, however, these latter adjustments are not made, because they are assumed to be about the same each period.

2. **Bad Debts Expense**

There are two approaches to bad debts.

- Direct write-off method
- Allowance method

a. Under the **direct write-off method**, bad debts are considered expenses in the period in which they are written off.

> **NOTE:** The direct write-off method is not considered acceptable under GAAP, unless the amounts are immaterial.

(1) The direct write-off method is the method required for tax purposes.

Bad debts expense   (uncollectible AR)
   AR   (uncollectible AR)

b. The **allowance method** seeks to estimate the amount of uncollectible receivables, and establishes a contra valuation account (allowance for bad debts) for the amount estimated to be uncollectible.

(1) The adjusting entry to set up the allowance is

Bad debts expense   (estimated)
   Allowance for bad debts   (estimated)

(2) The entry to write off bad debts is

Allowance for bad debts   (uncollectible AR)
   AR   (uncollectible AR)

(a) There are two methods to determine the annual charge to bad debts expense.

1] **Annual sales**

a] Charging bad debts expense for 1% of annual sales is based on the theory that bad debts are a function of sales; this method emphasizes the income statement.

b] When bad debts expense is estimated as a function of sales, any balance in the allowance account is ignored in making the adjusting entry. Bad debts expense under this method is simply the total amount computed (i.e., Sales × Percentage).

2] **Year-end AR**

a] Charging bad debts on year-end AR is based on the theory that bad debts are a function of AR collections during the period; this method emphasizes the balance sheet.

b] A bad debts percentage can be applied to total AR or subsets of AR. Often an aging schedule is prepared for this purpose. An AR aging schedule classifies AR by their age (e.g., 30, 60, 90, 120, etc., days overdue).

c] When bad debts expense is estimated using outstanding receivables, the expense is the amount needed to adjust the allowance account to the amount computed (i.e., AR × Percentage[s]). Thus, bad debts expense under this method is the amount computed less any credit balance currently in the allowance account (or plus any debit balance).

(3) **Net accounts receivable** is the balance in accounts receivable less the allowance for bad debts.

> **NOTE:** Net receivables **do not change** when a specific account is written off since both accounts receivable and the allowance account are reduced by the same amount.

(4) The policy for charging off uncollectible trade accounts receivable must be disclosed for receivables that have a contractual maturity of one year or less and arise from the sale of goods or services.

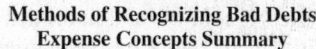

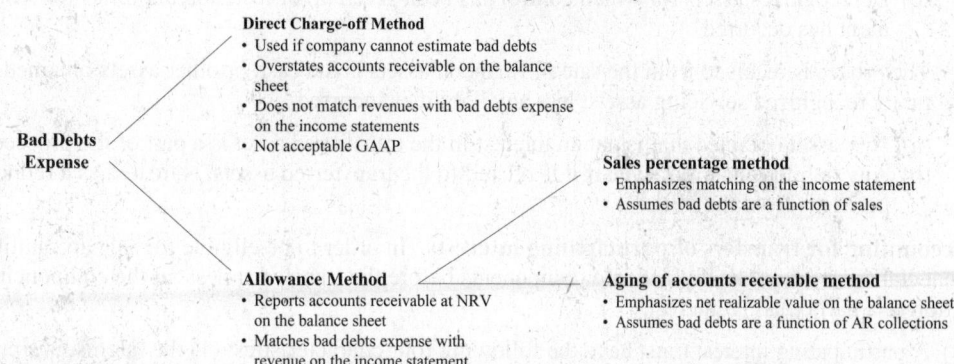

Methods of Recognizing Bad Debts
Expense Concepts Summary

Bad Debts Expense

Direct Charge-off Method
• Used if company cannot estimate bad debts
• Overstates accounts receivable on the balance sheet
• Does not match revenues with bad debts expense on the income statements
• Not acceptable GAAP

Sales percentage method
• Emphasizes matching on the income statement
• Assumes bad debts are a function of sales

Allowance Method
• Reports accounts receivable at NRV on the balance sheet
• Matches bad debts expense with revenue on the income statement

Aging of accounts receivable method
• Emphasizes net realizable value on the balance sheet
• Assumes bad debts are a function of AR collections

> **NOW REVIEW MULTIPLE-CHOICE QUESTIONS 7 THROUGH 23**

---

3. **Transfers and servicing of financial assets (ASC Topic 860).** Transfers of financial assets include the transfer of an entire financial asset, a group of financial assets, or a participating interest in an entire financial asset. Specifically, this topic includes servicing arrangements, recourse arrangements, guarantees, agreements to purchase or redeem transferred financial assets, options written or held, derivative financial instruments that are entered into with contemplation of a transfer, arrangements to provide financial support, pledges of collateral, and transferor's beneficial interests in the transferred financial asset.

   a. The major types of transfers include

   (1) **Securitizations**—Purchasing and selling securities that are collateralized by a pool of assets, such as a group of receivables.
   (2) **Factoring**—Selling receivables at a discount to obtain immediate cash.
   (3) **Transfers of receivables with recourse**—Selling receivables at a discount to obtain immediate cash but retaining the risk of loss if the customer does not pay the amount owed.
   (4) **Repurchase agreements**—An agreement to sell an asset to a lender and later repurchase the asset. These agreements are in effect using the asset as collateral for a loan.
   (5) **Loan participations**—A situation where a group of financial institutions (called participating interest holders) purchases a share of a financial instruments (e.g., a loan).
   (6) **Banker's acceptances**—An order from a customer of a bank for the payment of a specified sum of money (like a post-dated check) that may be bought and sold.

   b. The important determination in accounting for transfers of assets is whether the transaction is accounted for as a sale of the asset or a secured loan with the asset as collateral.

   (1) A transfer may be accounted for as a sale only when the transferor surrenders control of the financial asset(s) and all of the following conditions are met:

      (a) The transferred financial asset(s) are isolated and beyond the reach of the transferor and its creditors, even in bankruptcy or receivership.
      (b) The transferee can pledge or exchange the asset(s) without unreasonable constraints or conditions.
      (c) The transferor does not maintain effective control over the transferred financial asset(s) or a third-party beneficial interest in the asset(s).

   > **EXAMPLE**
   >
   > The transferor may not have a repurchase or redemption agreement, an agreement to cause the holder to return the asset (other than a cleanup call), or an agreement that requires the transferor to repurchase the financial asset at a favorable price wherein it is probable that the repurchase will occur.

   (2) Transfers of financial assets are disaggregated into separate components of assets and liabilities. Each entity involved in the transaction

    (a) Recognizes only the assets it controls and liabilities it incurs after the transaction has occurred, and

    (b) Derecognizes assets for which control has been given up or lost, and liabilities for which extinguishment has occurred.

(3) The proceeds received from the sale of financial assets is the cash or other assets obtained, including separately recognized servicing assets, less any liabilities incurred.

    (a) Any asset obtained that is not an interest in the transferred asset is a part of the proceeds of the sale.

    (b) Any liability incurred, even if it is related to the transferred assets, is treated as a reduction of the proceeds from the sale.

c. **Accounting for transfers of participating interests.** In order to be eligible for sale accounting, the entire financial asset cannot be divided into components before the transfer, unless all the components meet the definition of a participating interest.

(1) A participating interest must have the following four characteristics: (1) the interest is a proportionate ownership interest in an entire financial asset; (2) all cash flows received from the asset are divided proportionately among the participating interest holders based upon their share of ownership; (3) the rights of each participating interest holder have the same priority (i.e., in transfers, bankruptcy, or receivership); and (4) no party has the right to pledge or exchange the financial asset unless all participating interest holders agree.

(2) When a transfer of a participating interest(s) qualifies as a sale, the transferor should

    (a) Allocate the carrying amount of the entire financial asset(s) between the participating interest(s) sold and the participating interest that continues to be held by the transferor. Relative fair values at the date of transfer are used to allocate the carrying amount.

    (b) Derecognize the participating interest(s) sold.

    (c) Recognize and measure at fair value servicing assets, servicing liabilities, and any other assets obtained or liabilities incurred in the sale.

    (d) Recognize any gain or loss on the sale in earnings.

    (e) Report any participating interest that continues to be held as the difference between the previous carrying amount and the amount derecognized.

(3) If the transfer of a financial asset does not meet the criteria for a sale, the transferor and transferee account for the transfer as a secured borrowing with the financial asset(s) pledged as collateral.

d. **Factoring of receivables.** This category of financing is the most significant in terms of accounting implications. **Factoring** traditionally involves the outright sale of receivables to a financing institution known as a factor. These arrangements usually involve (1) notification to the customer to forward future payments to the factor and (2) transfer of receivables **without recourse**, which means that the factor assumes the risk of loss from noncollection. Thus, once a factoring arrangement is completed, the entity has no further involvement with the receivables, unless the customer decides to return the merchandise. In its simplistic form, the receivables are sold and the difference between the cash received and the carrying value of the receivables is recognized as a gain or loss.

(1) Factoring **without** recourse provides two financial benefits to the business: it permits the entity to obtain cash earlier, and the risk of bad debts is transferred to the factor.

    (a) The factor is compensated for each of the aspects of the transaction.

    (b) Interest is charged based on the anticipated length of time between the date the factoring is consummated and the expected collection date of the receivables sold, and a fee is charged based upon the anticipated bad debt losses.

EXAMPLE

Thirsty Corp., on July 1, year 1, enters into an agreement with Rich Company (the factor) to sell a group of its receivables **without recourse**. A total face value of $200,000 of accounts receivable are involved. The factor charges 20% interest computed on the weighted-average time to maturity of the receivables of thirty-six days plus a 3% fee.

The entries required by the transferor are as follows:

Cash	190,055	
Interest expense (or prepaid) ($200,000 \times .20 \times 36/365$)	3,945	
Factoring fee ($200,000 \times .03$)	6,000	
Accounts receivable		200,000

The interest expense and factor's fee can be combined into a $9,945 loss on the sale of receivables.

(c) Merchandise returns will normally be the responsibility of the transferor, who must then make the appropriate settlement with the factor.

1] To protect against the possibility of merchandise returns which diminish the total amount of the receivables to be collected, a factor will often holdback a portion of the amount of the receivables factored in addition to taking the interest and fee.

2] The transferor will charge any merchandise returns to a "factor's holdback receivable" account that is created when the receivables are factored. At the end of the return privilege period, any remaining holdback will become due and payable to the borrower.

EXAMPLE

Accounting by the transferor for the transfer of receivables without recourse

1. Thirsty Corp., on July 1, year 1, enters into an agreement with Rich Company to sell a group of its receivables **without recourse**. A total face value of $200,000 accounts receivable are involved. Rich (the factor) charges 20% interest computed on the weighted-average time to maturity of the receivables of thirty-six days plus a 3% fee. A 5% holdback is also retained.
2. Thirsty's customers return for credit $4,800 of merchandise.
3. The customer return privilege period expires and the remaining holdback is paid to the transferor.

The entries required are as follows:

1. Cash	180,055	
Loss on sale of receivables	9,945*	
Factor's holdback receivable (200,000 × .05)	10,000	
Accounts receivable		200,000

* ($3,945 interest expense + $6,000 factoring fee)

2. Sales returns and allowances	4,800	
Factor's holdback receivable		4,800
3. Cash	5,200	
Factor's holdback receivable		5,200

(d) Factoring transfers title to the receivables. Thus, if there is a **without recourse** provision, the removal of these receivables from the borrower's balance sheet is clearly warranted.

(2) Factoring arrangements may also involve factoring **with** recourse.

(a) In a with-recourse arrangement, if the customer does not pay the factor, the transferor must pay the factor the amount due on the account.

(b) The rules for transfer of receivables with recourse vary by jurisdiction; therefore, transfers with recourse may or may not qualify for sale treatment.

(c) If the factoring with recourse arrangement qualifies as a sale, the recourse liability is treated as reduction of the proceeds received in the transfer.

1] In computing the gain or loss to be recognized at the date of the transfer of the receivables, the borrower (transferor) must take into account the anticipated chargebacks from the transferee for bad debts expected to be incurred. This action requires an estimate by the transferor, based on past experience.

2] Adjustments should also be made at the time of sale for the estimated effects of any accelerated payments by customers (where the receivables are interest-bearing or where cash discounts are available).

EXAMPLE

Accounting by the transferor for the transfer of receivables with recourse

1. Thirsty Corp., on July 1, year 1, enters into an agreement with Rich Company to sell a group of its receivables with a face value of $200,000. Rich Company (the factor) charges 20% interest computed on the weighted-average time to maturity of the receivables of thirty-six days and a 3% fee. A 5% holdback is also retained.
2. Assume Thirsty Corp. surrenders control of the receivables, per ASC Topic 860, Thirsty's future obligation for uncollectible accounts is reasonably estimable, and Rich Co. does not have a unilateral ability to require Thirsty to repurchase the receivables.
3. The factor accepts the receivables **subject to recourse** for nonpayment. The recourse obligation has a fair value of $10,000.

Fair Values

Cash proceeds	180,055
Factor's holdback receivable	10,000
Recourse obligation	(10,000)
Net proceeds	180,055
Less: Carrying value of receivables	(200,000)
Loss on sale of receivables	(19,945)

The entries required to record the sale are

Cash	180,055	
Factor's holdback receivable (200,000 × .05)	10,000	
Loss on sale of receivables	19,945	
Accounts receivable		200,000
Recourse obligation		10,000

(d) The accounts receivable are removed from the transferor's books because they have been sold. The loss on sale of receivables is the sum of the interest charged by the factor ($3,945), the factor's fee ($6,000), and the fair value of the recourse obligation ($10,000), which is the estimated amount of uncollectible accounts.

(e) Because the transaction resulted in a "sale" rather than a borrowing, the "interest" and "fee" elements relate directly to the sale transaction. In a sale, these components are in essence part of a negotiated price for the receivables.

(f) If, subsequent to the sale of the receivables, the actual experience relative to the recourse terms differs from the provision made at the time of the sale, a change in an accounting estimate results. It is reflected as an additional gain or loss in the subsequent period. These changes are not corrections of errors or retroactive adjustments.

(g) If the above transfer did not meet the requirements for sale treatment, it would be accounted for as a secured borrowing.

(3) The chart below summarizes the accounting for the transfer of receivables.

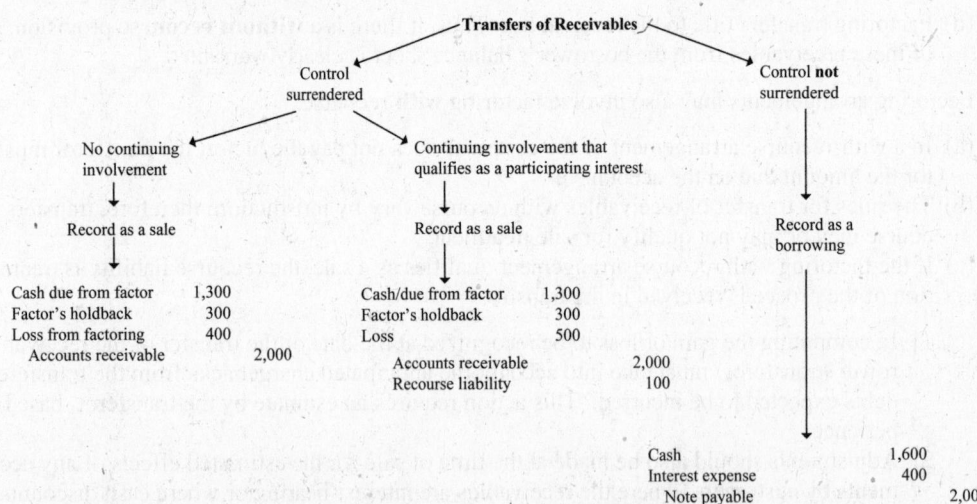

e. **Servicing of financial assets.**

(1) Servicing of financial assets may involve any one or all of the following activities:

    (a) Collecting payments

    (b) Paying taxes and insurance

    (c) Monitoring delinquencies

    (d) Foreclosing

    (e) Investing

    (f) Remitting fees

    (g) Accounting

(2) Although inherent in transfers of most financial assets, **servicing** is a distinct asset or liability only when separated contractually from the underlying financial asset. The servicing asset usually results either from

separate purchase or assumption of the servicing rights, or from securitization with retained servicing. The servicer's obligations are specified in the contract.

(3) Typically, the servicing contract results in an asset because the benefits are more than adequate compensation for the cost of servicing. The benefits include fees, late charges, float, and other income.

(4) If the benefits do not provide fair compensation, the servicing contract is a liability. The fair value of a servicing contract is based on its value in the market and is not based on the internal cost structure of the servicer. Thus, the concept of adequate compensation is judged by requirements that would be imposed by a new or outside servicer. In cases where there is not a reliable market for the contract, present value methods may be used to value the servicing contract.

(5) In summary, the servicer should record the servicing contract based on the following criteria:

(a) More than adequate—resulting in a recorded asset
(b) Adequate compensation—resulting in no asset or liability
(c) Less than adequate—resulting in a recorded liability

(6) Servicing assets or servicing liabilities are to be accounted for separately as follows:

(a) Assets are reported separately from liabilities. They are not netted.
(b) Initially measure servicing assets that are retained by the transferor by allocating the carrying amount based on relative fair values at the date of transfer.
(c) Initially measure at fair value all purchased assets, assumed liabilities, and liabilities undertaken in a sale or securitization.
(d) Account separately for interest-only strips (future interest income from serviced assets that exceed servicing fees).
(e) Measure servicing assets and servicing liabilities using one of two methods: amortization method, or fair value method. An election must be made to use the fair value method for each class of servicing assets and servicing liabilities. Once the election is made to value using the fair value method, the election cannot be reversed.
(f) Report servicing assets and servicing liabilities on the balance sheet in one of two ways:

1] Display separate line items for amounts valued at fair value and amounts measured by amortization method, **or**
2] Display aggregate amounts for all servicing assets and servicing liabilities, and disclose parenthetically the amount that is measured at fair value that is included in the aggregate amount.

(7) The **amortization method** requires servicing assets and servicing liabilities to be initially recorded at fair value. Assets are then amortized in proportion to, and over the period of, receipt of estimated net servicing income or net servicing loss. At the end of each period, the assets are assessed for impairment or increased obligation based on fair value. Over time, the asset is tested for impairment which is recognized in a valuation allowance account. Liabilities are amortized in proportion to, and over the period of, the net servicing loss. In cases where changes have increased the fair value above the book value, an increased liability and a loss should be recognized.

(8) Under the **fair value method,** servicing assets and servicing liabilities are initially recorded at fair value. The fair value is measured at each reporting date. Changes in fair value are reported in earnings in the period in which the change in fair value occurs.

(9) Required disclosures for **all** servicing assets and servicing liabilities include management's basis for determining classes, a description of risks, the instruments used to mitigate income statement effect of changes in fair value, the amount of contractually specified servicing fees, late fees, and ancillary fees for each period, and quantitative and qualitative information about assumptions used to estimate fair value.

(a) For servicing assets and liabilities subsequently measured at fair value, disclosures must also be provided showing the beginning and ending balances, additions, disposals, changes in fair value inputs or assumptions used, and changes in fair value.
(b) For servicing assets and liabilities that use the amortization method, disclosures must include the beginning and ending balances, additions, disposals, amortization, application of valuation allowance to adjust carrying value, and other changes that affect the balance, as well as a description of the changes. In addition, the fair value at the beginning and end of each period should be disclosed if it is practicable to estimate the value. The activity in the valuation account, including beginning and ending balances, recoveries made, and write-downs charged against the allowance for each period should also be disclosed.

f. **Securitizations.** As described above, securitization is the transformation of financial assets into securities (asset-backed securities). Various assets including mortgages, credit cards, trade receivables, loans, and leases are grouped and securitized. These groupings of relatively homogeneous assets are then pooled and divided into securities with cash flows that can be quite different from those of the original individual assets. With an established market, most of these securities cost less than the alternative use of the assets as collateral for borrowing. Thus, the benefits of most securitizations include lower financing costs, increased liquidity, and lower credit risk.

(1) The transferor (also called issuer or sponsor) forms a securitization mechanism to buy the assets and to issue the securities. Sometimes, another transfer is made to a trust and the trust issues the securities. These different structures are generally referred to as one-tier or two-tier respectively. The securitization mechanism then generates beneficial interests in the assets or resulting cash flows which are sold. The form of the securities chosen depends on such things as the nature of the assets, income tax considerations, and returns to be received.

(2) Various financial components (assets or liabilities) arise from securitizations. Examples include servicing contracts, interest-only strips, retained interests, recourse obligations, options, swaps, and forward contracts. All controlled assets and liabilities must be recognized.

EXAMPLE

Sale of loans with servicing contract and an interest-strip of 1% (transferor retains 1% of the interest paid).

(This problem is adapted from ASC 860-10-65-3)

Facts given:	
Cash proceeds	$16,000
Loan's book value	15,000
Fair value of servicing asset	1,200
Fair value of interest strip	800

Net Proceeds	
Cash proceeds	$16,000
Servicing asset	1,200
Interest strip	800
Net proceeds	18,000
Less: Carrying amount of loans	(15,000)
Gain on sale of loans	3,000

Journal entry

Cash	16,000	
Servicing asset	1,200	
Interest strip	800	
Loans		15,000
Gain on sale		3,000

---

(3) The transferor generally wants to take the assets off the balance sheet. This result can be accomplished if the transaction results in a sale. The key criterion in this case is to be sure that the assets are beyond control of the transferor even in bankruptcy.

g. **Secured borrowings.** In a **secured borrowing** arrangement, receivables are pledged as collateral for a loan. The customers whose accounts have been pledged are not aware of this event, and their payments are still remitted to the borrower. The pledged accounts merely serve as security to the lender, giving comfort that sufficient assets exist which will generate cash flows adequate in amount and timing to repay the debt. However the debt is paid by the borrower whether or not the pledged receivables are collected and whether or not the pattern of such collections matches the payments due on the debt.

EXAMPLE

Thirsty Corp., on July 1, year 1, enters into an agreement with Rich Company (the factor) to sell a group of its receivables **with recourse**. A total face value of $200,000 of accounts receivable are involved. The factor charges 20% interest computed on the weighted-average time to maturity of the receivables of thirty-six days plus a 3% fee. Assume the transfer does not qualify as a sale.

Since the transfer does not qualify as a sale, it is treated as a secured borrowing. The borrower's entry will be

Cash	190,055	
Interest expense (or prepaid)	3,945	
Factoring fee	6,000	
Factor borrowing payable		200,000

---

    (1) The accounts receivable remain on the borrower's books. Both the accounts receivable and the factor borrowing payable should be cross-referenced in the balance sheet.

    (2) In a secured borrowing, the assets of the borrowing entity continue to be shown as assets in its financial statements but must be identified as having been pledged. This identification can be accomplished either parenthetically or by footnote disclosures. Similarly, the related debt should be identified as having been secured by the receivables or other asset.

EXAMPLE

Proper disclosure for pledged receivable shown parenthetically on the balance sheet

Current assets:
    Accounts receivable, net of allowance for doubtful accounts of $600,000
        ($3,500,000 of which has been pledged as collateral for bank loans)   8,450,000
Current liabilities:
    Bank loans payable (secured by pledged accounts receivable)   2,700,000

---

    h. **Accounting for collateral.** The method of accounting for a collateral agreement depends both on control of the assets and on the liabilities incurred under the agreement.

        (1) Ordinarily, the transferor should carry the collateral as an asset and the transferee should not record the pledged asset.

        (2) If the transferee, however, has control of the asset, the secured party should record the asset at fair value and also the liability to return it. The transferor should reclassify the asset (probably as a receivable) and report it separately in the balance sheet.

        (3) If the transferor defaults and is not entitled to the return of the collateral, it should be derecognized. If not already recognized, the transferee should record collateral as an asset at fair value.

4. **Disclosures.** Additional disclosures required for receivables, off-balance-sheet credit exposure, and foreclosed and repossessed assets include the following:

    a. Accounting policies for loans and trade receivables
    b. Assets serving as collateral
    c. Nonaccrual and past due financing receivables
    d. Accounting policies for off-balance sheet credit exposures
    e. Foreclosed and repossessed assets
    f. Allowance for credit losses
    g. Impaired loans
    h. Loss contingencies
    i. Risks and uncertainties
    j. Fair value disclosures
    k. Credit quality information
    l. Modifications

NOW REVIEW MULTIPLE-CHOICE QUESTIONS 24 THROUGH 46

D. Current Liabilities

    Current liabilities are "obligations whose liquidation is reasonably expected to require the use of existing resources properly classifiable as current assets, or the creation of other current liabilities."

1. **Examples of current liabilities** (as they fall within the above definition)

    a. Trade accounts and notes payable
    b. Loan obligations—Including current portions of long-term debt. This is not true if the current portion of long-term debt will not require the use of current assets (e.g., be paid from a sinking fund which is not classified as current).
    c. Short-term obligations expected to be refinanced cannot be reclassified as noncurrent liabilities unless there is both an intent and an ability to refinance.
    d. Dividends payable—Cash dividends are a liability when declared. They cannot be rescinded.
    e. Accrued liabilities—Adjusting entries to reflect the use of goods or services before paying for them. Will pay in future periods even though the expense is incurred in this period (e.g., interest, payroll, rent expenses).

        Expense account   xx
             Liability (usually current) account   xx

f. Payroll—There are two entries to record payroll. The first records the employee's payment and deductions on behalf of the employee. The second is to record the employer's taxes.

Payroll expense	xx (gross pay)	
Payroll payable, cash		xx (net pay)
Income taxes payable		xx
FICA taxes payable		xx
Union dues payable		xx
Medical insurance payable		xx
Payroll tax expense	xx	
FICA taxes payable		xx
Federal unemployment tax payable		xx
State unemployment tax payable		xx

g. Property taxes. Generally, there is a monthly accrual for property taxes over the fiscal period of the taxing authority. If taxes are payable at the end of the tax authority's fiscal period, the monthly accrual would be

Property tax expense	xx
Property tax payable	xx

(1) If the taxes were paid at the beginning of the period, the entry to record the prepayment would be followed by monthly entries to expense the prepayment.

Prepaid property taxes	xx		Property tax expense	xx
Cash		xx	Prepaid property taxes	xx

(2) If taxes are due, but not paid at the beginning of the year, the liability should be recorded and the deferred charge expensed over the fiscal year of the taxing body.

Deferred property taxes	xx		Property tax expense	xx
Property tax payable		xx	Deferred property taxes	xx

h. Bonus arrangements

Bonus expense	xx
Bonus payable	xx

(1) Set up equations to describe the terms of the bonus agreement. The general forms of the equations follow:

$$B = P(NI - B - T)$$
$$T = R(NI - B)$$
$$B = \text{Bonus}$$
$$P = \text{Bonus or profit sharing rate (10\%)}$$
$$NI = \text{Net income (\$150,000)}$$
$$T = \text{Taxes}$$
$$R = \text{Tax rate (40\%)}$$

EXAMPLE

Work through the above equations using the data in parentheses.

$$T = .40(150,000 - B)$$
$$T = 60,000 - .4B$$
$$B = .10(150,000 - B - T)$$
$$B = .10(150,000 - B - 60,000 + .4B)$$
$$B = 15,000 - .1B - 6,000 + .04B$$
$$1.06B = 9,000$$
$$B = \$8,491$$

---

i. Advances from customers—Record as deferred revenue and recognize as revenue when earned

Cash	xx		Deferred revenue	xx
Deferred revenue		xx	Revenue	xx

NOW REVIEW MULTIPLE-CHOICE QUESTIONS 47 THROUGH 76

2. **Contingencies**

   a. **Definitions**—An obligation may be either determinable (fixed) or contingent in accordance with the following definitions.

      (1) **Determinable liabilities**—The amount of cash and time of payment are known and reasonably precise. Such liabilities are usually evidenced by written contracts but may also arise from implied agreements or imposed legal statutes. Examples include notes payable and liabilities for various taxes as shown above.

      (2) **Contingent liabilities**—Such obligations **may** exist but are dependent on uncertain future events. A contingency is defined as an existing condition, situation, or set of circumstances involving uncertainty as to possible gain or loss to an enterprise that will ultimately be resolved when one or more future events occur or fail to occur.

   b. **Recording and disclosing contingencies**—The accounting problems related to contingencies involve the following issues.

      (1) When is it appropriate to record and report the effects of a contingency in the financial statements? Should the financial impact of the contingency be reported in the period when the contingency is still unresolved or in the period in which the contingency is resolved?

      (2) For contingencies not recorded and reported on the financial statements before they are resolved, what disclosures, if any, are needed in the footnotes to the financial statements?

   c. A loss contingency should be accrued if it is **probable** that an asset has been impaired or a liability has been incurred at the balance sheet date **and** the amount of the loss is **reasonably estimable**. When loss contingencies are accrued, a debit should be made to an expense or to a loss account and a credit should be made to either a liability or to a contra asset account.

> **NOTE:** To accrue a loss contingency means that the financial effects are reported in the financial statements **before** the contingency is resolved.

      (1) When making the decision concerning the accrual of a loss contingency, the term **probable** relates to the likelihood of a future event taking place or failing to take place which would resolve the uncertainty. However, the likelihood of a future event taking place or failing to take place may not always be judged to be probable. The likelihood of the future event taking place or failing to take place may instead be judged to be **reasonably possible** or **remote**. In these last two situations, it is **not** appropriate to accrue the loss contingency as of the balance sheet date, although footnote disclosure may be necessary. Footnote disclosure will be discussed later in this section.

      (2) In addition to being probable, the accrual of a loss contingency also requires that the amount of the loss be **reasonably estimable**. In most situations, a single amount can be estimated, and this represents the loss that is accrued. In other situations, the loss may be estimated in terms of a range, for example, the range of loss may be $100,000 to $500,000. In these situations, the amount of loss to accrue is the best estimate within the range. For example, if the best estimate within the range is $200,000, the loss should be accrued in the amount of $200,000. However, if no number in the range is a better estimate of the loss than any other number in the range, the lower number in the range is accrued as the loss. Thus, $100,000 would be accrued if no other number in the range from $100,000 to $500,000 were a better estimate of the loss than any other number in the range.

EXAMPLE

The accounting problems related to contingencies involve the following issues:

- Collectibility of receivables (Bad debts expense/Allowance for uncollectible accounts),
- Obligations related to product warranties and product defects (Warranty expense/Warranty liability), and
- Premiums offered to customers (Premium expense/Premium liability)

      (a) These contingencies are usually accrued because it is **probable** that some receivables will not be collected, that some of the products sold will be defective and may need warranty work, and that some customers will take advantage of premiums offered by the company.

      (b) In addition, the **amounts** in each case can usually be **estimated** because of past experience with each of these situations.

EXAMPLE

Product warranty loss contingency.

Facts related to the illustration for ABC Company.

Year	Sales	Actual warranty expenditures	Estimated warranty costs related to dollar sales
Year 1	$500,000	$15,000	Year of sale 4%
Year 2	$700,000	$47,000	Year after sale 6%

In year 1, ABC should accrue a loss contingency related to product warranties for $50,000 [$500,000 × (4% + 6%)]. The entry would appear as follows:

Warranty expense	50,000	
Liability for product warranty		50,000

The **actual** warranty expenditures in year 1 would be recorded in the following manner. (Note that the actual expenditures reduce the liability and have no effect on the expense account.)

Liability for product warranty	15,000	
Cash, parts inventory, etc.		15,000

ABC's income statement for year 1 would report an expense for $50,000 related to its product warranty, and its December 31, year 1 balance sheet would report a current liability for product warranty of $35,000 ($50,000 – $15,000). In year 2, ABC should accrue a loss contingency related to product warranties for $70,000 [$700,000 × (4% + 6%)]. The entry would appear as follows:

Warranty expense	70,000	
Liability for product warranty		70,000

The actual warranty expenditures for year 2 would be recorded in the following manner. (Again, note that the actual expenditures only affect the liability account.)

Liability for product warranty	47,000	
Cash, parts inventory, etc.		47,000

ABC's income statement for year 2 should report an expense related to product warranties of $70,000, and its December 31, year 2 balance sheet should report a current liability for product warranty of $58,000 (the 1/1/Y2 balance of $35,000 + the year 2 expense of $70,000 less the actual warranty expenditures of $47,000 in year 2).

EXAMPLE

Premium (e.g., towels, knives, and other prizes) **contingency accrual**.

Companies often have premium liability for outstanding coupons when it is probable that some of the coupons will be redeemed and the amount can be estimated. The expense should be accrued in the period of sale based on the estimated redemption rate.

Premium plan expense	xx	
Premium plan liability		xx

As coupons are actually redeemed by customers, the liability is reduced.

Premium plan liability	xx	
Premiums		xx

EXAMPLE

Environmental Liabilities [e.g., Asset Retirement Obligation (ARO)]

Companies often have environmental liabilities related to nuclear facilities, oil and gas properties, mining facilities, or landfills and these liabilities are often estimable. The cost associated with the ARO is initially measured at fair value and is included in the carrying amount of the associated asset. A related liability is also recorded.

Landfill	xx	
Asset retirement obligation		xx

The cost of the ARO is allocated over the asset's life.

Depreciation expense	xx	
Accumulated deprecation		xx

Interest is accrued (accretion expense).

Interest expense	xx	
Asset retirement obligation		xx

An entry is made to record the retirement of the settlement

Asset retirement obligation	xx	
Loss on settlement of ARO	xx	
Cash		xx

(3) Loss contingencies that may be accrued (depending upon whether or not the two conditions of probable and reasonably estimable are satisfied) include the following events.

- Threat of expropriation of assets
- Pending or threatened litigation
- Actual or possible claims and assessments
- Guarantees of indebtedness of others
- Obligations of commercial banks under "Standby letters of credit," and
- Agreements to repurchase receivables (or the related property) that have been sold

(a) **Litigation**—The one event listed above that appears frequently on the exam involves pending litigation. If the loss from litigation is reasonably estimable, and it is probable as of the balance sheet date that the lawsuit will be lost, the loss should be accrued.

EXAMPLE

Litigation

Assume that XYZ Company is presently involved in litigation involving patent infringement that allegedly occurred during year 1. The financial statements for year 1 are being prepared, and XYZ's legal counsel believes it is probable that XYZ will lose the lawsuit and that the damages will be in the range from $500,000 to $800,000 with the most likely amount being $700,000. Based upon XYZ's legal counsel, it should accrue the loss contingency in the following manner at December 31, year 1.

Loss from litigation	700,000	
Liability from litigation		700,000

The $700,000 loss from litigation should be reported on XYZ's year 1 income statement, and the liability should be reported on the December 31, year 1 balance sheet.

If XYZ settles the litigation in year 2 by paying damages of $600,000, the following journal entry should be made.

Liability from litigation	700,000	
Cash		600,000
Recovery of loss from litigation		100,000

The above entry results in a loss recovery for year 2 because the damages were settled for less than their estimated amount. This situation is not unusual because the loss contingency related to the litigation was based upon an estimate. Note that the loss recovery cannot exceed the estimated loss, which in this case was $700,000. It would be incorrect to revise the year 1 financial statements so that the loss contingency reflected the actual damages of $600,000. When the financial statements for year 1 were issued, the best estimate of loss was $700,000. This estimate is not revised subsequent to the issuance of the year 1 financial statements.

Since loss contingencies involving litigation are only accrued if the conditions of probable and reasonably estimable are present, you should be aware of what is reported if either or both of these conditions are not present. For XYZ's case, suppose that its legal counsel believed it was only **reasonably possible** (not probable) as of the balance sheet date, December 31, year 1, that XYZ would lose its lawsuit. In this situation, it would **not** be appropriate for XYZ to accrue a loss at December 31, year 1. However, because XYZ's legal counsel believes it is reasonably possible to lose the lawsuit, XYZ should disclose this litigation in its footnotes for its year 1 financial statements. The range of loss, noted before as being from $500,000 to $800,000, would also be disclosed in the footnote. In year 2, when the actual damages of $600,000 are known, XYZ would record a loss of this amount and report it on its year 2 income statement.

If XYZ's legal counsel believed that it was **remote** as of December 31, year 1, that the lawsuit would be lost, no accrual or disclosure of the litigation would be necessary.

(4) Loss contingencies that are not accrued or even disclosed in the footnotes include the following events.

- Risk of loss or damage of enterprise property by fire, explosion, or other hazards
- General or unspecified business risks
- Risk of loss from catastrophes assumed by property and casualty insurance companies including reinsurance companies

(a) Losses that result from the above events are recorded and reported in the period when the event occurs that causes the loss.

EXAMPLE

If XYZ's factory is destroyed by fire in year 1, the loss from this event should be recorded and reported in year 1. If the damages from the fire amount to $1,000,000, and XYZ's insurance company reimburses XYZ $800,000, XYZ's loss is $200,000. If XYZ does not insure for fire with an insurance company, XYZ's loss for year 1 would be $1,000,000.

---

d. **Compensated absences**—Knowledge of the conditions that must be present in order to accrue a loss contingency is helpful in the accounting for compensated absences (vacation, sick leave pay, etc.).

(1) An employer shall accrue a liability for employees' compensation for future absences if all of the following conditions are met:

(a) The employer's obligation relating to employees' rights to receive compensation for future absences is attributable to employees' **services already rendered**
(b) The obligation relates to rights that **vest or accumulate**
(c) Payment of the compensation is **probable**
(d) The amount can be reasonably **estimated**

NOTE: The last two criteria are the general criteria for recognizing a loss contingency.

EXAMPLE

Assume MNO Company employees earn two weeks of paid vacation for each year of employment. Unused vacation time can be accumulated and carried forward to succeeding years, and will be paid at the salary level in effect when the vacation is taken. As of December 31, year 11 when John Baker's salary was $600 per week, John Baker had earned eighteen weeks vacation time and had used twelve weeks of accumulated vacation time. At December 31, year 11, MNO should report a liability for John Baker's accumulated vacation time of $3,600 (six weeks of accumulated vacation time times $600 per week). The journal entry at December 31, year 11, would appear as follows (assume previous year's entry was reversed).

Salary and wages expense	3,600	
Accrued liability for compensated absences		3,600

---

e. **Gain contingencies**—The discussion relating to contingencies has focused on the accounting for loss contingencies. On the other hand, contingencies exist that may also result in possible **gains**.

(1) Contingencies that might result in gains usually are not reflected in the accounts since to do so might be to recognize revenue prior to its realization. This means that any gains that result from gain contingencies should be recorded and reported in the period during which the contingency is resolved.

(a) For example, the plaintiff in a lawsuit should not record or report the expected damages to be received until the lawsuit has been decided.

E. Fair Value Option

As discussed in Module 9D, a company can elect the fair value option for reporting financial assets and financial liabilities. The fair value option also applies to firm commitments that would otherwise not be recognized at inception that only involve financial instruments. Nonfinancial insurance contracts and warranties may only be reported at fair value if the obligation can be settled by paying a third party to provide the goods and services.

NOW REVIEW MULTIPLE-CHOICE QUESTIONS 77 THROUGH 103

F. Ratios

1. **Solvency**—Measures short-term viability

   a. **Acid-test (quick) ratio**—Measures ability to pay current liabilities from cash and near-cash items

   $$\frac{\text{Cash, Net receivables, Marketable securities}}{\text{Current liabilities}}$$

   b. **Current ratio**—Measures ability to pay current liabilities from cash, near-cash, and cash flow items

   $$\frac{\text{Current assets}}{\text{Current liabilities}}$$

2. **Operational efficiency**—Measures utilization of assets

   a. **Receivable turnover**—Measures how rapidly cash is collected from credit sales

   $$\frac{\text{Net credit sales}}{\text{Average net receivables}}$$

   b. **Number of days' sales in average receivables**—Average length of time receivables are outstanding, which reflects credit and collection policies

   $$\frac{365}{\text{Receivable turnover}}$$

   c. **Inventory turnover**—Indicates how rapidly inventory is sold

   $$\frac{\text{Cost of goods sold}}{\text{Average inventory}}$$

   d. **Number of days' supply in average inventory**—Measures the number of days inventory is held before sale and therefore reflects the efficiency of the entity's inventory policies

   $$\frac{365}{\text{Inventory turnover}}$$

   e. **Length of operating cycle**—Measures length of time from purchase of inventory to collection of cash

   $$\begin{array}{c}\text{Number of days'} \\ \text{supply in average} \\ \text{inventory}\end{array} + \begin{array}{c}\text{Number of days'} \\ \text{sales in average} \\ \text{receivables}\end{array}$$

NOW REVIEW MULTIPLE-CHOICE QUESTIONS 104 THROUGH 111

G. Research Component—Accounting Standards Codification

1. Basic concepts regarding balance sheet classification of current assets and current liabilities are found in ASC Section 210-10-45, which is contained under the heading "Presentation" in the Codification. Specific rules for monetary current assets and current liabilities are located throughout the Codification as shown in the following table.

Topic number	Topic	Accounting issues
305	Cash and cash equivalents	Classification and disclosures
310	Receivables	A/R, bad debts
405	Liabilities	Cross referencing to specific issues
440	Commitments	Unconditional purchase obligations
450	Contingencies	Contingent liabilities
470	Debt	Liability issues
720	Compensation—general	Compensated absences
820	Fair value measurements	Measuring FV
825	Financial instruments	FV option
835	Interest	Interest rates, imputed interest, interest calculations and disclosures
860	Transfers and servicing	Factoring, pledging, assigning A/R

2. Keywords for research are listed below.

Agreement to refinance	Estimated or accrued amounts	Refinance obligation
Appropriated retained earnings	Examples loss contingencies	Remote
Beneficial interests	Extinguished debt	Retained interests
Benefits of servicing	Extinguished liability	Rights that vest
Classification current liabilities	Fair value retained interests	Sale of financial assets
Collateral	Financial assets	Sale of receivables
Collateral pledged	Financial assets exchange	Securitization
Compensation future absences	Financial liability	Securitized financial assets
Contingency	Loss contingency	Servicing fees
Control transferred assets	Operating cycle	SPE
Current assets	Ordinary operations	Transferor surrendered control
Current liabilities	Primary obligor	Transfers financial assets
Debtor security interest	Probable	Undivided interests
Deduction from receivables	Probable future events	Unilateral ability
Derecognize assets	Proceeds	With recourse
Derecognize liability	Reasonably possible	Without recourse
Estimated loss	Recourse	Working capital

H. International Financial Reporting Standards (IFRS)

1. Normally, assets are reported as current and noncurrent, and liabilities are reported as current and noncurrent on the balance sheet. If a liquidity presentation provides more relevant and reliable information, then balance sheet items may be reported based on their liquidity without segregation.

   a. In a balance sheet segregated between current and noncurrent items, an asset is classified as current (1) when the entity expects to realize the asset or to consume or sell it within 12 months or the normal operating cycle, or (2) it holds the asset primarily for the purpose of trading. A liability is classified as current when it expects to settle the liability within the normal operating cycle, the liability will be settled within 12 months after the reporting period, or it holds the liability for the purpose of trading.

2. IFRS defines the terms financial assets and financial liabilities.

   a. A financial asset is any asset that is cash, an equity instrument of another entity, a contractual right to receive cash or another financial asset, a contractual right to exchange a financial instrument, or a contract that will be settled in the reporting entity's own equity instruments.

      (1) IFRS 9 requires that financial assets be measured at amortized cost or fair value based on the entity's business model for managing the financial asset and the contractual cash flow characteristics of the financial asset.

         (a) A financial asset should be measured at amortized cost if the business model's objective is to hold the asset in order to collect contractual cash flows, and the terms of the contract indicate specific dates for the payment of principal and interest on the principle amount outstanding.
         (b) An entity may also elect at initial recognition to value a financial asset at fair value through profit or loss (FVTPL).

   b. A financial liability is any liability that is a contractual obligation to deliver cash or another financial asset, a contractual obligation to exchange financial instruments under potentially unfavorable conditions, or a contract that may be settled in the entity's own equity instruments.

      (1) Financial liabilities are measured at either amortized cost using the effective interest method, or an election may be made to value the financial liability at fair value through profit or loss (FVTPL).

3. There are two important areas where IFRS differ from US GAAP.

   a. The first relates to short-term obligations expected to be refinanced. Under US GAAP, short-term obligations expected to be refinanced may be reported in the noncurrent liability section of the balance sheet if the company has the intent and ability to refinance. However, IFRS requires obligations expected to be refinanced to be reported as current liabilities unless there is an agreement to refinance in place prior to the balance sheet date.

b. The second area in which the terminology and rules are different is "provisions" and "contingencies." Under IFRS, a "provision" is a liability that is uncertain in timing or amount. Provisions are made for items such as taxes payable, compensated absences, bad debts, warranties, and other estimated liabilities. A "contingency," however, depends upon some future uncertainty or event.

(1) A contingent asset is a possible asset that arises from past events that will be confirmed only by occurrence or nonoccurrence of uncertain future events that are not within the control of the reporting entity. As with US GAAP, a contingent asset is not recognized, but it is disclosed if the economic benefits are probable.

(2) Under IFRS, a contingent liability does not have the same definition as in the US standards. Recall that under US GAAP, the accounting for a contingency depends on whether the outcome is probable, reasonably possible, or remote, and whether the contingency is measureable. In contrast, under IFRS if the outcome is probable and measureable, it is not considered a contingency. Instead, it is classified as a "provision."

(3) Under IFRS, the term contingency is used to describe an event which is not recognized because it is not probable that an outflow will be required or the amount cannot be measured reliably.

(4) If an item qualifies as a contingency, the notes to the financial statements should include an estimate of the financial effect, and indication of the uncertainties, and the possibility of reimbursement. If the possibility of the event occurring is remote, no disclosure is required in the notes to the financial statements.

(5) It should be noted that the "probable" threshold test for determining whether a provision should be made is "more likely than not" which is defined as a probability over 50%.

NOW REVIEW MULTIPLE-CHOICE QUESTIONS 112 THROUGH 116

KEY TERMS

Acid-test (quick) ratio. Measures ability to pay current liabilities from cash and near-cash items.

Allowance method. Seeks to estimate the amount of uncollectible receivables, and establishes a contra valuation account (allowance for bad debts) for the amount estimated to be uncollectible.

Amortization method. Requires servicing assets and servicing liabilities to be initially recorded at fair value. Assets are then amortized in proportion to, and over the period of, receipt of estimated net servicing income or net servicing loss.

Banker's acceptance. An order from a customer of a bank for the payment of specified sum of money (like a post-dated check) that may be bought and sold.

Cash. Includes both cash (cash on hand and demand deposits) and cash equivalents (short-term, highly liquid investments).

Cash equivalents. Readily convertible into cash and so near maturity that they carry little risk of changing in value due to interest rate changes.

Contingent liabilities. Obligations may exist but are dependent on uncertain future events.

Current liabilities. Obligations whose liquidation is reasonably expected to require the use of existing resources properly classifiable as current assets, or the creation of other current liabilities.

Current ratio. Measures ability to pay current liabilities form cash, near-cash, and cash flow items.

Determinable liabilities. The amount of cash and time of payment are known and reasonably precise.

Direct write-off method. Bad debts are considered expenses in the period in which they are written off.

Factoring. Selling receivables at a discount to obtain immediate cash. Traditionally involves the outright sale of receivables to a financing institution know as a factor.

Fair value method. Servicing assets and servicing liabilities are initially recorded at fair value. The fair value is measured at each reporting date.

Inventory turnover. Indicated how rapidly inventory is sold.

Length of operating cycle. Measures length of time from purchase of inventory to collection of cash.

Loan participations. A situation where a group of financial institutions (called participating interest holders) purchases a share of a financial instruments (e.g., a loan).

Net realizable value. Gross amount of receivables less estimated uncollectibles.

Number of days' sales in average receivables. Average length of time receivables are outstanding, which reflects credit and collection policies.

Number of days' supply in average inventory. Measures the number of days inventory is held before sale and therefore reflects the efficiency of the entity's inventory policies.

Operation efficiency. Measures utilization of assets.

Probable. The likelihood of a future event taking place or failing to take place which would resolve the uncertainty.

Receivable turnover. Measures how rapidly cash is collected from credit sales.

Repurchase agreements. An agreement to sell an asset to a lender and later repurchase the asset. These agreements are in effect using the asset as collateral for a loan.

Secured borrowing. Receivables are pledged as collateral for a loan.

Securitizations. Purchasing and selling securities that are collateralized by a pool of assets, such as a group of receivables.

Servicing. A distinct asset or liability only when separated contractually from the underlying.

Solvency. Measures short-term viability.

Transfers of receivables with recourse. Selling receivables at a discount to obtain immediate cash but retaining the risk of loss if the customer does not pay the amount owned.

Transfer of receivables without recourse. The factor assumes the risk of loss from noncollection.

A. Cash

1. Burr Company had the following account balances at December 31, year 2:

Cash in banks	$2,250,000
Cash on hand	125,000
Cash legally restricted for additions to plant (expected to be disbursed in year 3)	1,600,000

Cash in banks includes $600,000 of compensating balances against short-term borrowing arrangements. The compensating balances are not legally restricted as to withdrawal by Burr. In the current assets section of Burr's December 31, year 2 balance sheet, total cash should be reported at

  a. $1,775,000
  b. $2,250,000
  c. $2,375,000
  d. $3,975,000

2. Ral Corp.'s checkbook balance on December 31, year 2, was $5,000. In addition, Ral held the following items in its safe on that date:

Check payable to Ral Corp., dated January 2, year 3, in payment of a sale made in December year 2, not included in December 31 checkbook balance	$2,000
Check payable to Ral Corp., deposited December 15 and included in December 31 checkbook balance, but returned by bank on December 30 stamped "NSF." The check was redeposited on January 2, year 3, and cleared on January 9	500
Check drawn on Ral Corp.'s account, payable to a vendor, dated and recorded in Ral's books on December 31 but not mailed until January 10, year 3	300

The proper amount to be shown as Cash on Ral's balance sheet at December 31, year 2, is

  a. $4,800
  b. $5,300
  c. $6,500
  d. $6,800

3. Trans Co. had the following balances at December 31, year 2:

Cash in checking account	$ 35,000
Cash in money market account	75,000
US Treasury bill, purchased 11/1/year 2, maturing 1/31/year 3	350,000
US Treasury bill, purchased 12/1/year 2, maturing 3/31/year 3	400,000

Trans's policy is to treat as cash equivalents all highly liquid investments with a maturity of three months or less when purchased. What amount should Trans report as cash and cash equivalents in its December 31, year 2 balance sheet?

  a. $110,000
  b. $385,000
  c. $460,000
  d. $860,000

4. On October 31, year 2, Dingo, Inc. had cash accounts at three different banks. One account balance is segregated solely for a November 15, year 2 payment into a bond sinking fund. A second account, used for branch operations, is overdrawn. The third account, used for regular corporate operations, has a positive balance. How should these accounts be reported in Dingo's October 31, year 2 classified balance sheet?

  a. The segregated account should be reported as a noncurrent asset, the regular account should be reported as a current asset, and the overdraft should be reported as a current liability.
  b. The segregated and regular accounts should be reported as current assets, and the overdraft should be reported as a current liability.
  c. The segregated account should be reported as a noncurrent asset, and the regular account should be reported as a current asset net of the overdraft.
  d. The segregated and regular accounts should be reported as current assets net of the overdraft.

B. Bank Reconciliations

5. In preparing its August 31, year 2 bank reconciliation, Apex Corp. has available the following information:

Balance per bank statement, 8/31/Y2	$18,050
Deposit in transit, 8/31/Y2	3,250
Return of customer's check for insufficient funds, 8/31/Y2	600
Outstanding checks, 8/31/Y2	2,750
Bank service charges for August	100

At August 31, year 2, Apex's correct cash balance is

  a. $18,550
  b. $17,950
  c. $17,850
  d. $17,550

6. Poe, Inc. had the following bank reconciliation at March 31, year 2:

Balance per bank statement, 3/31/Y2	$46,500
Add deposit in transit	10,300
	56,800
Less outstanding checks	12,600
Balance per books, 3/31/Y2	$44,200

Data per bank for the month of April year 2 follow:

Deposits	$58,400
Disbursements	49,700

All reconciling items at March 31, year 2, cleared the bank in April. Outstanding checks at April 30, year 2, totaled $7,000. There were no deposits in transit at April 30, year 2. What is the cash balance per books at April 30, year 2?

  a. $48,200
  b. $52,900
  c. $55,200
  d. $58,500

C. Receivables

7. On the December 31, year 2 balance sheet of Mann Co., the current receivables consisted of the following:

Trade accounts receivable	$ 93,000
Allowance for uncollectible accounts	(2,000)
Claim against shipper for goods lost in transit (November year 2)	3,000
Selling price of unsold goods sent by Mann on consignment at 130% of cost (**not** included in Mann's ending inventory)	26,000
Security deposit on lease of warehouse used for storing some inventories	30,000
Total	$150,000

At December 31, year 2, the correct total of Mann's current net receivables was

a. $ 94,000
b. $120,000
c. $124,000
d. $150,000

8. The following information relates to Jay Co.'s accounts receivable for year 2:

Accounts receivable, 1/1/Y2	$ 650,000
Credit sales for year 2	2,700,000
Sales returns for year 2	75,000
Accounts written off during year 2	40,000
Collections from customers during year 2	2,150,000
Estimated future sales returns at 12/31/Y2	50,000
Estimated uncollectible accounts at 12/31/Y2	110,000

What amount should Jay report for accounts receivable, before allowances for sales returns and uncollectible accounts, at December 31, year 2?

a. $1,200,000
b. $1,125,000
c. $1,085,000
d. $ 925,000

9. Frame Co. has an 8% note receivable dated June 30, year 1, in the original amount of $150,000. Payments of $50,000 in principal plus accrued interest are due annually on July 1, year 2, year 3, and year 4. In its June 30, year 2 balance sheet, what amount should Frame report as a current asset for interest on the note receivable?

a. $0
b. $ 4,000
c. $ 8,000
d. $12,000

10. On December 1, year 2, Tigg Mortgage Co. gave Pod Corp. a $200,000, 12% loan. Pod received proceeds of $194,000 after the deduction of a $6,000 nonrefundable loan origination fee. Principal and interest are due in sixty monthly installments of $4,450, beginning January 1, year 3. The repayments yield an effective interest rate of 12% at a present value of $200,000 and 13.4% at a present value of $194,000. Tigg does not elect the fair value option for recording the note to Pod. What amount of accrued interest receivable should Tigg include in its December 31, year 2 balance sheet?

a. $4,450
b. $2,166
c. $2,000
d. $0

11. On Merf's April 30, year 2 balance sheet a note receivable was reported as a noncurrent asset and its accrued in-

terest for eight months was reported as a current asset. Which of the following terms would fit Merf's note receivable?

a. Both principal and interest amounts are payable on August 31, year 2, and August 31, year 3.
b. Principal and interest are due December 31, year 2.
c. Both principal and interest amounts are payable on December 31, year 2, and December 31, year 3.
d. Principal is due August 31, year 3, and interest is due August 31, year 2, and August 31, year 3.

12. On August 15, year 2, Benet Co. sold goods for which it received a note bearing the market rate of interest on that date. The four-month note was dated July 15, year 2. Note principal, together with all interest, is due November 15, year 2. Assume Benet did not elect the fair value option for reporting the note. When the note was recorded on August 15, which of the following accounts increased?

a. Unearned discount.
b. Interest receivable.
c. Prepaid interest.
d. Interest revenue.

C.1. Anticipation of Sales Discounts

13. Delta, Inc. sells to wholesalers on terms of 2/15, net 30. Delta has no cash sales but 50% of Delta's customers take advantage of the discount. Delta uses the gross method of recording sales and trade receivables. An analysis of Delta's trade receivables balances at December 31, year 2, revealed the following:

Age		Amount	Collectible
0 - 15	days	$100,000	100%
16 - 30	days	60,000	95%
31 - 60	days	5,000	90%
Over 60 days		2,500	$500
		$167,500	

In its December 31, year 2 balance sheet, what amount should Delta report for allowance for discounts?

a. $1,000
b. $1,620
c. $1,675
d. $2,000

14. Fenn Stores, Inc. had sales of $1,000,000 during December, year 2. Experience has shown that merchandise equaling 7% of sales will be returned within thirty days and an additional 3% will be returned within ninety days. Returned merchandise is readily resalable. In addition, merchandise equaling 15% of sales will be exchanged for merchandise of equal or greater value. What amount should Fenn report for net sales in its income statement for the month of December year 2?

a. $900,000
b. $850,000
c. $780,000
d. $750,000

C.2. Bad Debts Expense

15. At January 1, year 2, Jamin Co. had a credit balance of $260,000 in its allowance for uncollectible accounts. Based on past experience, 2% of Jamin's credit sales have been uncollectible. During year 2 Jamin wrote off $325,000 of uncollectible accounts. Credit sales for year 2 were $9,000,000. In its December 31, year 2 balance sheet, what amount should Jamin report as allowance for uncollectible accounts?

- a. $115,000
- b. $180,000
- c. $245,000
- d. $440,000

16. The following accounts were abstracted from Roxy Co.'s unadjusted trial balance at December 31, year 2:

	Debit	Credit
Accounts receivable	$1,000,000	
Allowance for uncollectible accounts		8,000
Net credit sales		$3,000,000

Roxy estimates that 3% of the gross accounts receivable will become uncollectible. After adjustment at December 31, year 2, the allowance for uncollectible accounts should have a credit balance of

- a. $90,000
- b. $82,000
- c. $38,000
- d. $30,000

17. In its December 31 balance sheet, Butler Co. reported trade accounts receivable of $250,000 and related allowance for uncollectible accounts of $20,000. What is the total amount of risk of accounting loss related to Butler's trade accounts receivable, and what amount of that risk is off-balance-sheet risk?

	Risk of accounting loss	Off-balance-sheet risk
a.	$0	$0
b.	$230,000	$0
c.	$230,000	$20,000
d.	$250,000	$20,000

18. Inge Co. determined that the net value of its accounts receivable at December 31, year 2, based on an aging of the receivables, was $325,000. Additional information is as follows:

Allowance for uncollectible accounts—1/1/Y2	$ 30,000
Uncollectible accounts written off during year 2	18,000
Uncollectible accounts recovered during year 2	2,000
Accounts receivable at 12/31/Y2	350,000

For year 2, what would be Inge's uncollectible accounts expense?

- a. $ 5,000
- b. $11,000
- c. $15,000
- d. $21,000

19. The following information pertains to Tara Co.'s accounts receivable at December 31, year 2:

Days outstanding	Amount	Estimated % uncollectible
0 – 60	$120,000	1%
61 – 120	90,000	2%
Over 120	100,000	6%
	$310,000	

During year 2, Tara wrote off $7,000 in receivables and recovered $4,000 that had been written off in prior years. Tara's December 31, year 1 allowance for uncollectible accounts was $22,000. Under the aging method, what amount

of allowance for uncollectible accounts should Tara report at December 31, year 2?

- a. $ 9,000
- b. $10,000
- c. $13,000
- d. $19,000

20. A method of estimating uncollectible accounts that emphasizes asset valuation rather than income measurement is the allowance method based on

- a. Aging the receivables.
- b. Direct write-off.
- c. Gross sales.
- d. Credit sales less returns and allowances.

21. Which method of recording uncollectible accounts expense is consistent with accrual accounting?

	Allowance	Direct write-off
a.	Yes	Yes
b.	Yes	No
c.	No	Yes
d.	No	No

22. When the allowance method of recognizing uncollectible accounts is used, the entry to record the write-off of a specific account

- a. Decreases both accounts receivable and the allowance for uncollectible accounts.
- b. Decreases accounts receivable and increases the allowance for uncollectible accounts.
- c. Increases the allowance for uncollectible accounts and decreases net income.
- d. Decreases both accounts receivable and net income.

23. A company uses the allowance method to recognize uncollectible accounts expense. What is the effect at the time of the collection of an account previously written off on each of the following accounts?

	Allowance for uncollectible accounts	Uncollectible accounts expense
a.	No effect	Decrease
b.	Increase	Decrease
c.	Increase	No effect
d.	No effect	No effect

C.3. Transfers and Servicing of Financial Assets (ASC Topic 860)

24. Which of the following is a method to generate cash from accounts receivables?

	Assignment	Factoring
a.	Yes	No
b.	Yes	Yes
c.	No	Yes
d.	No	No

25. Gar Co. factored its receivables. Control was surrendered in the transaction which was on a without recourse basis with Ross Bank. Gar received cash as a result of this transaction, which is best described as a

- a. Loan from Ross collateralized by Gar's accounts receivable.
- b. Loan from Ross to be repaid by the proceeds from Gar's accounts receivable.

   c.   Sale of Gar's accounts receivable to Ross, with the risk of uncollectible accounts retained by Gar.

   d.   Sale of Gar's accounts receivable to Ross, with the risk of uncollectible accounts transferred to Ross.

Items 26 through 28 are based on the following:

Taylored Corp. factored $400,000 of accounts receivable to Rich Corp. on July 1, year 2. Control was surrendered by Taylored. Rich accepted the receivables subject to recourse for nonpayment. Rich assessed a fee of 2% and retains a holdback equal to 5% of the accounts receivable. In addition, Rich charged 15% interest computed on a weighted-average time to maturity of the receivables of forty-one days. The fair value of the recourse obligation is $12,000.

26. Taylored will receive and record cash of
   a. $385,260
   b. $357,260
   c. $365,260
   d. $377,260

27. Which of the following statements is correct?
   a.   Rich should record an asset of $8,000 for the recourse obligation.
   b.   Taylored should record a liability and corresponding loss of $12,000 related to the recourse obligation.
   c.   Taylored should record a liability of $12,000, but no loss, related to the recourse obligation.
   d.   No entry for the recourse obligation should be made by Taylored or Rich until the debtor fails to pay.

28. Assuming all receivables are collected, Taylored's cost of factoring the receivables would be
   a. $ 8,000
   b. $34,740
   c. $42,740
   d. $14,740

29. Which of the following is used to account for probable sales discounts, sales returns, and sales allowances?

	Due from factor	Recourse liability
a.	Yes	No
b.	Yes	Yes
c.	No	Yes
d.	No	No

30. Scarbrough Corp. factored $600,000 of accounts receivable to Duff Corp. on October 1, year 2. Control was surrendered by Scarbrough. Duff accepted the receivables subject to recourse for nonpayment. Duff assessed a fee of 3% and retains a holdback equal to 5% of the accounts receivable. In addition, Duff charged 15% interest computed on a weighted-average time to maturity of the receivables of fifty-four days. The fair value of the recourse obligation is $9,000. Scarbrough will receive and record cash of
   a. $529,685
   b. $538,685
   c. $547,685
   d. $556,685

31. Synthia Corp. factored $750,000 of accounts receivable to Thomas Company on December 3, year 2. Control was surrendered by Synthia. Thomas accepted the receivables subject to recourse for nonpayment. Thomas assessed a fee of 2% and retains a holdback equal to 4% of the accounts receivable. In addition, Thomas charged 12% interest computed on a weighted-average time to maturity of the receivables of fifty-one days. The fair value of the recourse obligation is $15,000. Assuming all receivables are collected, Synthia's cost of factoring the receivables would be
   a. $12,575
   b. $15,000
   c. $27,575
   d. $42,575

32. Bannon Corp. transferred financial assets to Chapman, Inc. The transfer meets the conditions to be accounted for as a sale. As the transferor, Bannon should do each of the following, **except**
   a.   Remove all assets sold from the balance sheet.
   b.   Record all assets received and liabilities incurred as proceeds from the sale.
   c.   Measure the assets received and liabilities incurred at cost.
   d.   Recognize any gain or loss on the sale.

33. If financial assets are exchanged for cash or other consideration, but the transfer does not meet the criteria for a sale, the transferor and the transferee should account for the transaction as a

	Secured borrowing	Pledge of collateral
a.	No	Yes
b.	Yes	Yes
c.	Yes	No
d.	No	No

34. All but one of the following are required before a transfer of receivables can be recorded as a sale.
   a.   The transferred receivables are beyond the reach of the transferor and its creditors.
   b.   The transferor has not kept effective control over the transferred receivables through a repurchase agreement.
   c.   The transferor maintains continuing involvement.
   d.   The transferee can pledge or sell the transferred receivables.

35. Which of the following is not an objective for each entity accounting for transfers of financial assets?
   a.   To derecognize assets when control is gained.
   b.   To derecognize liabilities when extinguished.
   c.   To recognize liabilities when incurred.
   d.   To derecognize assets when control is given up.

36. Which of the following is false?
   a.   A servicing asset shall be assessed for impairment based on its fair value.
   b.   A servicing liability shall be assessed for increased obligation based on its fair value.
   c.   An obligation to service financial assets may result in the recognition of a servicing asset or servicing liability.
   d.   A servicing asset or liability should be amortized for a period of five years.

37. Fusion Corporation uses the amortization method to account for its servicing assets. Which of the following statements is true?
   a.   Increases in fair value are reported in other comprehensive income.

b. Increases in fair value are reported in earnings of the period.

c. The assets are measured at fair value at the end of each reporting period.

d. The assets are measured for impairment at the end of each reporting period.

38. According to ASC Topic 860, which of the following statements is true regarding servicing assets and servicing liabilities?

I. Either the amortization method or the fair value method can be used.

II. Once the fair value method is elected, the election cannot be reversed.

III. Changes in fair value are reported in other comprehensive income for the period.

   a. I only.

   b. I and II.

   c. II only.

   d. I and III.

39. Binsar Corporation transfers a financial asset but continues to hold an interest in the servicing asset. How should the interest in the servicing asset that continues to be held be measured at the date of the transfer?

   a. At the present value of future cash flows.

   b. At fair value.

   c. At the difference between the previous carrying amount and the amount derecognized.

   d. At net realizable value.

40. Which of the following is true?

   a. A debtor may not grant a security interest in certain assets to a lender to serve as collateral with recourse.

   b. A debtor may not grant a security interest in certain assets to a lender to serve as collateral without recourse.

   c. The arrangement of having collateral transferred to a secured party is known as a pledge.

   d. Secured parties are never permitted to sell collateral held under a pledge.

Items 41 through 43 are based on the following:

Company ABC sells loans with a $2,200 fair value and a carrying amount of $2,000. ABC Company obtains an option to purchase similar loans and assumes a recourse obligation to repurchase loans. ABC Company also agrees to provide a floating rate of interest to the transferee company. The fair values are listed.

Fair values	
Cash proceeds	$2,100
Interest rate swap	140
Call option	80
Recourse obligation	(120)

41. What is the gain (loss) on the sale?

   a. $ 320

   b. $ 200

   c. $(100)

   d. $ 120

42. The journal entry to record the transfer for ABC Company includes

   a. A debit to call option.

b. A credit to interest rate swap.

c. A debit to loans.

d. A credit to cash.

43. Assume for this problem that ABC Company agreed to service the loans without explicitly stating the compensation. The fair value of the service is $50. What are the net proceeds received and the gain (loss) on the sale?

	Net proceeds received	**Gain (loss)**
a.	$2,200	$ 200
b.	$2,250	$ 250
c.	$2,150	$ 150
d.	$2,200	$(250)

44. In accordance with accounting for transfers and servicing, financial assets subject to prepayment should be measured

   a. Like investments in debt securities classified as held-to-maturity.

   b. At cost.

   c. Like investments in debt securities classified as available-for-sale or trading.

   d. At fair value.

45. In accordance with accounting for transfers and servicing, all of the following would be disclosed except

   a. Policy for requiring collateral or other security due to repurchase agreements or securities lending transactions.

   b. Cash flows between the securitization special-purpose entity (SPE) and the transferor.

   c. Accounting policies for measuring interests that continue to be held.

   d. Description of assets or liabilities with estimable fair values.

46. Taft Inc. borrowed $1,000,000 from Wilson Company on July 2, year 8. As part of the loan agreement, Taft granted Wilson a security interest in land that originally cost $750,000 when it was acquired by Taft in year 1. The land had a fair value of $900,000 on July 2, year 8. In June year 9, Taft defaulted on its loan to Wilson, and the land was transferred to Wilson in full settlement of the debt on June 30. The land had a fair value of $950,000 on June 30, year 9. What amount should Wilson record for land on June 30, year 9?

   a. $0

   b. $750,000

   c. $900,000

   d. $950,000

D.1. Examples of Current Liabilities

47. Lyle, Inc. is preparing its financial statements for the year ended December 31, year 2. Accounts payable amounted to $360,000 before any necessary year-end adjustment related to the following:

- At December 31, year 2, Lyle has a $50,000 debit balance in its accounts payable to Ross, a supplier, resulting from a $50,000 advance payment for goods to be manufactured to Lyle's specifications.

- Checks in the amount of $100,000 were written to vendors and recorded on December 29, year 2. The checks were mailed on January 5, year 3.

What amount should Lyle report as accounts payable in its December 31, year 2 balance sheet?

    a. $510,000
    b. $410,000
    c. $310,000
    d. $210,000

48. Rabb Co. records its purchases at gross amounts but wishes to change to recording purchases net of purchase discounts. Discounts available on purchases recorded from October 1, year 1, to September 30, year 2, totaled $2,000. Of this amount, $200 is still available in the accounts payable balance. The balances in Rabb's accounts as of and for the year ended September 30, year 2, before conversion are

Purchases	$100,000
Purchase discounts taken	800
Accounts payable	30,000

What is Rabb's accounts payable balance as of September 30, year 2, after the conversion?
    a. $29,800
    b. $29,200
    c. $28,800
    d. $28,200

49. On March 1, year 1, Fine Co. borrowed $10,000 and signed a two-year note bearing interest at 12% per annum compounded annually. Interest is payable in full at maturity on February 28, year 3. What amount should Fine report as a liability for accrued interest at December 31, year 2?
    a. $0
    b. $1,000
    c. $1,200
    d. $2,320

50. On September 1, year 1, Brak Co. borrowed on a $1,350,000 note payable from Federal Bank. The note bears interest at 12% and is payable in three equal annual principal payments of $450,000. On this date, the bank's prime rate was 11%. The first annual payment for interest and principal was made on September 1, year 2. At December 31, year 2, what amount should Brak report as accrued interest payable?
    a. $54,000
    b. $49,500
    c. $36,000
    d. $33,000

51. In its year 2 financial statements, Cris Co. reported interest expense of $85,000 in its income statement and cash paid for interest of $68,000 in its cash flow statement. There was no prepaid interest or interest capitalization either at the beginning or end of year 2. Accrued interest at December 31, year 1, was $15,000. What amount should Cris report as accrued interest payable in its December 31, year 2 balance sheet?
    a. $ 2,000
    b. $15,000
    c. $17,000
    d. $32,000

52. Ames, Inc. has $500,000 of notes payable due June 15, year 3. Ames signed an agreement on December 1, year 2, to borrow up to $500,000 to refinance the notes payable on a long-term basis with no payments due until year 4. The financing agreement stipulated that borrowings may not exceed 80% of the value of the collateral Ames was providing. At the date of issuance of the December 31, year 2 financial

statements, the value of the collateral was $600,000 and is not expected to fall below this amount during year 3. In Ames' December 31, year 2 balance sheet, the obligation for these notes payable should be classified as

	Short-term	Long-term
a.	$500,000	$0
b.	$100,000	$400,000
c.	$ 20,000	$480,000
d.	$0	$500,000

53. A company issued a short-term note payable with a stated 12% rate of interest to a bank. The bank charged a .5% loan origination fee and remitted the balance to the company. The effective interest rate paid by the company in this transaction would be
    a.   Equal to 12.5%.
    b.   More than 12.5%.
    c.   Less than 12.5%.
    d.   Independent of 12.5%.

54. Cali, Inc. had a $4,000,000 note payable due on March 15, year 3. On January 28, year 3, before the issuance of its year 2 financial statements, Cali issued long-term bonds in the amount of $4,500,000. Proceeds from the bonds were used to repay the note when it came due. How should Cali classify the note in its December 31, year 2 financial statements?
    a.   As a current liability, with separate disclosure of the note refinancing.
    b.   As a current liability, with no separate disclosure required.
    c.   As a noncurrent liability, with separate disclosure of the note refinancing.
    d.   As a noncurrent liability, with no separate disclosure required.

55. On December 31, year 2, Largo, Inc. had a $750,000 note payable outstanding, due July 31, year 3. Largo borrowed the money to finance construction of a new plant. Largo planned to refinance the note by issuing long-term bonds. Because Largo temporarily had excess cash, it prepaid $250,000 of the note on January 12, year 3. In February year 3, Largo completed a $1,500,000 bond offering. Largo will use the bond offering proceeds to repay the note payable at its maturity and to pay construction costs during year 3. On March 3, year 3, Largo issued its year 2 financial statements. What amount of the note payable should Largo include in the current liabilities section of its December 31, year 2 balance sheet?
    a. $750,000
    b. $500,000
    c. $250,000
    d. $0

56. Rice Co. salaried employees are paid biweekly. Advances made to employees are paid back by payroll deductions. Information relating to salaries follows:

	12/31/Y1	12/31/Y2
Employee advances	$24,000	$ 36,000
Accrued salaries payable	40,000	?
Salaries expense during the year		420,000
Salaries paid during the year (gross)		390,000

In Rice's December 31, year 2 balance sheet, accrued salaries payable was

a. $94,000
b. $82,000
c. $70,000
d. $30,000

57. Fay Corp. pays its outside salespersons fixed monthly salaries and commissions on net sales. Sales commissions are computed and paid on a monthly basis (in the month following the month of sale), and the fixed salaries are treated as advances against commissions. However, if the fixed salaries for salespersons exceed their sales commissions earned for a month, such excess is not charged back to them. Pertinent data for the month of March year 2 for the three salespersons are as follows:

Salesperson	Fixed salary	Net sales	Commission rate
A	$10,000	$ 200,000	4%
B	14,000	400,000	6%
C	18,000	600,000	6%
Totals	$42,000	$1,200,000	

What amount should Fay accrue for sales commissions payable at March 31, year 2?
a. $70,000
b. $68,000
c. $28,000
d. $26,000

58. Lime Co.'s payroll for the month ended January 31, year 2, is summarized as follows:

Total wages	$10,000
Federal income tax withheld	1,200

All wages paid were subject to FICA. FICA tax rates were 7% each for employee and employer. Lime remits payroll taxes on the 15th of the following month. In its financial statements for the month ended January 31, year 2, what amounts should Lime report as total payroll tax liability and as payroll tax expense?

	Liability	Expense
a.	$1,200	$1,400
b.	$1,900	$1,400
c.	$1,900	$ 700
d.	$2,600	$ 700

59. Under state law, Acme may pay 3% of eligible gross wages or it may reimburse the state directly for actual unemployment claims. Acme believes that actual unemployment claims will be 2% of eligible gross wages and has chosen to reimburse the state. Eligible gross wages are defined as the first $10,000 of gross wages paid to each employee. Acme had five employees, each of whom earned $20,000 during year 2. In its December 31, year 2 balance sheet, what amount should Acme report as accrued liability for unemployment claims?
a. $1,000
b. $1,500
c. $2,000
d. $3,000

60. Pine Corp. is required to contribute, to an employee stock ownership plan (ESOP), 10% of its income after deduction for this contribution but before income tax. Pine's income before charges for the contribution and income tax was $75,000. The income tax rate is 30%. What amount should be accrued as a contribution to the ESOP?

a. $7,500
b. $6,818
c. $5,250
d. $4,773

61. Able Co. provides an incentive compensation plan under which its president receives a bonus equal to 10% of the corporation's income before income tax but after deduction of the bonus. If the tax rate is 40% and net income after bonus and income tax was $360,000, what was the amount of the bonus?
a. $36,000
b. $60,000
c. $66,000
d. $90,000

62. Ivy Co. operates a retail store. All items are sold subject to a 6% state sales tax, which Ivy collects and records as sales revenue. Ivy files quarterly sales tax returns when due, by the twentieth day following the end of the sales quarter. However, in accordance with state requirements, Ivy remits sales tax collected by the twentieth day of the month following any month such collections exceed $500. Ivy takes these payments as credits on the quarterly sales tax return. The sales taxes paid by Ivy are charged against sales revenue.

Following is a monthly summary appearing in Ivy's first quarter year 2 sales revenue account:

	Debit	Credit
January	$ --	$10,600
February	600	7,420
March	--	8,480
	$600	$26,500

In its March 31, year 2 balance sheet, what amount should Ivy report as sales taxes payable?
a. $ 600
b. $ 900
c. $1,500
d. $1,590

63. Hudson Hotel collects 15% in city sales taxes on room rentals, in addition to a $2 per room, per night, occupancy tax. Sales taxes for each month are due at the end of the following month, and occupancy taxes are due fifteen days after the end of each calendar quarter. On January 3, year 3, Hudson paid its November year 2 sales taxes and its fourth quarter year 2 occupancy taxes. Additional information pertaining to Hudson's operations is

Year 2	Room rentals	Room nights
October	$100,000	1,100
November	110,000	1,200
December	150,000	1,800

What amounts should Hudson report as sales taxes payable and occupancy taxes payable in its December 31, year 2 balance sheet?

	Sales taxes	Occupancy taxes
a.	$39,000	$6,000
b.	$39,000	$8,200
c.	$54,000	$6,000
d.	$54,000	$8,200

64. On July 1, year 2, Ran County issued realty tax assessments for its fiscal year ended June 30, year 3. On September 1, year 2, Day Co. purchased a warehouse in Ran

County. The purchase price was reduced by a credit for accrued realty taxes. Day did not record the entire year's real estate tax obligation, but instead records tax expenses at the end of each month by adjusting prepaid real estate taxes or real estate taxes payable, as appropriate. On November 1, year 2, Day paid the first of two equal installments of $12,000 for realty taxes. What amount of this payment should Day re-cord as a debit to real estate taxes payable?

a. $ 4,000
b. $ 8,000
c. $10,000
d. $12,000

65. Kemp Co. must determine the December 31, year 2 year-end accruals for advertising and rent expenses. A $500 advertising bill was received January 7, year 3, comprising costs of $375 for advertisements in December year 2 issues, and $125 for advertisements in January year 3 issues of the newspaper.

A store lease, effective December 16, year 1, calls for fixed rent of $1,200 per month, payable one month from the effective date and monthly thereafter. In addition, rent equal to 5% of net sales over $300,000 per calendar year is payable on January 31 of the following year. Net sales for year 2 were $550,000.

In its December 31, year 2 balance sheet, Kemp should report accrued liabilities of

a. $12,875
b. $13,000
c. $13,100
d. $13,475

66. On May 1, year 2, Marno County issued property tax assessments for the fiscal year ended June 30, year 3. The first of two equal installments was due on November 1, year 2. On September 1, year 2, Dyur Co. purchased a four-year-old factory in Marno subject to an allowance for accrued taxes. Dyur did not record the entire year's property tax obligation, but instead records tax expenses at the end of each month by adjusting prepaid property taxes or property taxes payable, as appropriate. The recording of the November 1, year 2 payment by Dyur should have been allocated between an increase in prepaid property taxes and a decrease in property taxes payable in which of the following percentages?

	Percentage allocated to	
	Increase in pre-paid property taxes	Decrease in property taxes payable
a.	66 2/3%	33 1/3%
b.	0%	100%
c.	50%	50%
d.	33 1/3%	66 2/3%

67. Black Co. requires advance payments with special orders for machinery constructed to customer specifications. These advances are nonrefundable. Information for year 2 is as follows:

Customer advances—balance 12/31/Y1	$118,000
Advances received with orders in year 2	184,000
Advances applied to orders shipped in year 2	164,000
Advances applicable to orders cancelled in year 2	50,000

In Black's December 31, year 2 balance sheet, what amount should be reported as a current liability for advances from customer?

a. $0
b. $ 88,000
c. $138,000
d. $148,000

68. Marr Co. sells its products in reusable containers. The customer is charged a deposit for each container delivered and receives a refund for each container returned within two years after the year of delivery. Marr accounts for the containers not returned within the time limit as being retired by sale at the deposit amount. Information for year 3 is as follows:

Container deposits at December 31, year 2, from deliveries in

Year 1	$150,000	
Year 2	430,000	$580,000
Deposits for containers delivered in year 3		780,000

Deposits for containers returned in year 3 from deliveries in

Year 1	$ 90,000	
Year 2	250,000	
Year 3	286,000	626,000

In Marr's December 31, year 3 balance sheet, the liability for deposits on returnable containers should be

a. $494,000
b. $584,000
c. $674,000
d. $734,000

69. Kent Co., a division of National Realty, Inc., maintains escrow accounts and pays real estate taxes for National's mortgage customers. Escrow funds are kept in interest-bearing accounts. Interest, less a 10% service fee, is credited to the mortgagee's account and used to reduce future escrow payments. Additional information follows:

Escrow accounts liability, 1/1/Y2	$ 700,000
Escrow payments received during year 2	1,580,000
Real estate taxes paid during year 2	1,720,000
Interest on escrow funds during year 2	50,000

What amount should Kent report as escrow accounts liability in its December 31, year 2 balance sheet?

a. $510,000
b. $515,000
c. $605,000
d. $610,000

70. Cobb Company sells appliance service contracts agreeing to repair appliances for a two-year period. Cobb's past experience is that, of the total dollars spent for repairs on service contracts, 40% is incurred evenly during the first contract year and 60% evenly during the second contract year. Receipts from service contract sales for the two years ended December 31, year 2, are as follows:

Year 1	$500,000
Year 2	600,000

Receipts from contracts are credited to unearned service contract revenue. Assume that all contract sales are made evenly during the year. What amount should Cobb report as unearned service contract revenue at December 31, year 2?

a. $360,000
b. $470,000
c. $480,000
d. $630,000

71. Toddler Care Co. offers three payment plans on its twelve-month contracts. Information on the three plans and the number of children enrolled in each plan for the September 1, year 2 through August 31, year 3 contract year follows:

Plan	Initial payment per child	Monthly fees per child	Number of children
#1	$500	$ --	15
#2	200	30	12
#3	--	50	9
			36

Toddler received $9,900 of initial payments on September 1, year 2, and $3,240 of monthly fees during the period September 1 through December 31, year 2. In its December 31, year 2 balance sheet, what amount should Toddler report as deferred revenues?
a. $3,300
b. $4,380
c. $6,600
d. $9,900

72. A retail store received cash and issued gift certificates that are redeemable in merchandise. The gift certificates lapse one year after they are issued. How would the deferred revenue account be affected by each of the following transactions?

	Redemption of certificates	Lapse of certificates
a.	Decrease	No effect
b.	Decrease	Decrease
c.	No effect	No effect
d.	No effect	Decrease

73. On March 31, year 2, Dallas Co. received an advance payment of 60% of the sales price for special-order goods to be manufactured and delivered within five months. At the same time, Dallas subcontracted for production of the special-order goods at a price equal to 40% of the main contract price. What liabilities should be reported in Dallas' March 31, year 2 balance sheet?

	Deferred revenues	Payables to subcontractor
a.	None	None
b.	60% of main contract price	40% of main contract price
c.	60% of main contract price	None
d.	None	40% of main contract price

74. In June year 2, Northan Retailers sold refundable merchandise coupons. Northan received $10 for each coupon redeemable from July 1 to December 31, year 2, for merchandise with a retail price of $11. At June 30, year 2, how should Northan report these coupon transactions?
a. Unearned revenues at the merchandise's retail price.
b. Unearned revenues at the cash received amount.
c. Revenues at the merchandise's retail price.
d. Revenues at the cash received amount.

75. Delect Co. provides repair services for the AZ195 TV set. Customers prepay the fee on the standard one-year service contract. The year 1 and year 2 contracts were identical, and the number of contracts outstanding was substantially the same at the end of each year. However, Delect's December 31, year 2 deferred revenues' balance on unperformed service contracts was significantly less than the balance at December 31, year 1. Which of the following situations might account for this reduction in the deferred revenue balance?
a. Most year 2 contracts were signed later in the calendar year than were the year 1 contracts.
b. Most year 2 contracts were signed earlier in the calendar year than were the year 1 contracts.
c. The year 2 contract contribution margin was greater than the year 1 contract contribution margin.
d. The year 2 contribution margin was less than the year 1 contract contribution margin.

76. Brad Corp. has unconditional purchase obligations associated with product financing arrangements. These obligations are reported as liabilities on Brad's balance sheet, with the related assets also recognized. In the notes to Brad's financial statements, the aggregate amount of payments for these obligations should be disclosed for each of how many years following the date of the latest balance sheet?
a. 0
b. 1
c. 5
d. 10

D.2. Contingencies

77. On January 17, year 2, an explosion occurred at a Sims Co. plant causing extensive property damage to area buildings. Although no claims had yet been asserted against Sims by March 10, year 2, Sims' management and counsel concluded that it is likely that claims will be asserted and that it is reasonably possible Sims will be responsible for damages. Sims' management believed that $1,250,000 would be a reasonable estimate of its liability. Sims' $5,000,000 comprehensive public liability policy has a $250,000 deductible clause. In Sims' December 31, year 1 financial statements, which were issued on March 25, year 2, how should this item be reported?
a. As an accrued liability of $250,000.
b. As a footnote disclosure indicating the possible loss of $250,000.
c. As a footnote disclosure indicating the possible loss of $1,250,000.
d. No footnote disclosure or accrual is necessary.

78. Brite Corp. had the following liabilities at December 31, year 2:

Accounts payable	$55,000
Unsecured notes, 8%, due 7/1/Y3	400,000
Accrued expenses	35,000
Contingent liability	450,000
Deferred income tax liability	25,000
Senior bonds, 7%, due 3/31/Y3	1,000,000

The contingent liability is an accrual for possible losses on a $1,000,000 lawsuit filed against Brite. Brite's legal counsel expects the suit to be settled in year 4, and has estimated that

Brite will be liable for damages in the range of $450,000 to $750,000.

The deferred income tax liability is not related to an asset for financial reporting and is expected to reverse in year 4.

What amount should Brite report in its December 31, year 2 balance sheet for current liabilities?

a. $ 515,000
b. $ 940,000
c. $1,490,000
d. $1,515,000

79. On February 5, year 3, an employee filed a $2,000,000 lawsuit against Steel Co. for damages suffered when one of Steel's plants exploded on December 29, year 2. Steel's legal counsel expects the company will lose the lawsuit and estimates the loss to be between $500,000 and $1,000,000. The employee has offered to settle the lawsuit out of court for $900,000, but Steel will not agree to the settlement. In its December 31, year 2 balance sheet, what amount should Steel report as liability from lawsuit?

a. $2,000,000
b. $1,000,000
c. $ 900,000
d. $ 500,000

80. On November 5, year 2, a Dunn Corp. truck was in an accident with an auto driven by Bell. Dunn received notice on January 12, year 3, of a lawsuit for $700,000 damages for personal injuries suffered by Bell. Dunn Corp.'s counsel believes it is probable that Bell will be awarded an estimated amount in the range between $200,000 and $450,000, and that $300,000 is a better estimate of potential liability than any other amount. Dunn's accounting year ends on December 31, and the year 2 financial statements were issued on March 2, year 3. What amount of loss should Dunn accrue at December 31, year 2?

a. $0
b. $200,000
c. $300,000
d. $450,000

81. During year 2, Haft Co. became involved in a tax dispute with the IRS. At December 31, year 2, Haft's tax advisor believed that an unfavorable outcome was probable. A reasonable estimate of additional taxes was $200,000 but could be as much as $300,000. After the year 2 financial statements were issued, Haft received and accepted an IRS settlement offer of $275,000. What amount of accrued liability should Haft have reported in its December 31, year 2 balance sheet?

a. $200,000
b. $250,000
c. $275,000
d. $300,000

82. Management can estimate the amount of loss that will occur if a foreign government expropriates some company assets. If expropriation is reasonably possible, a loss contingency should be

a. Disclosed but not accrued as a liability.
b. Disclosed and accrued as a liability.
c. Accrued as a liability but not disclosed.
d. Neither accrued as a liability nor disclosed.

83. Invern, Inc. has a self-insurance plan. Each year, retained earnings is appropriated for contingencies in an amount equal to insurance premiums saved less recognized losses from lawsuits and other claims. As a result of a year 2 accident, Invern is a defendant in a lawsuit in which it will probably have to pay damages of $190,000. What are the effects of this lawsuit's probable outcome on Invern's year 2 financial statements?

a. An increase in expenses and no effect on liabilities.
b. An increase in both expenses and liabilities.
c. No effect on expenses and an increase in liabilities.
d. No effect on either expenses or liabilities.

84. In year 1, a personal injury lawsuit was brought against Halsey Co. Based on counsel's estimate, Halsey reported a $50,000 liability in its December 31, year 1 balance sheet. In November year 2, Halsey received a favorable judgment, requiring the plaintiff to reimburse Halsey for expenses of $30,000. The plaintiff has appealed the decision, and Halsey's counsel is unable to predict the outcome of the appeal. In its December 31, year 2 balance sheet, Halsey should report what amounts of asset and liability related to these legal actions?

	Asset	Liability
a.	$30,000	$50,000
b.	$30,000	$0
c.	$0	$20,000
d.	$0	$0

85. During January year 2, Haze Corp. won a litigation award for $15,000 that was tripled to $45,000 to include punitive damages. The defendant, who is financially stable, has appealed only the $30,000 punitive damages. Haze was awarded $50,000 in an unrelated suit it filed, which is being appealed by the defendant. Counsel is unable to estimate the outcome of these appeals. In its year 2 financial statements, Haze should report what amount of pretax gain?

a. $15,000
b. $45,000
c. $50,000
d. $95,000

86. In May year 1 Caso Co. filed suit against Wayne, Inc. seeking $1,900,000 damages for patent infringement. A court verdict in November year 5 awarded Caso $1,500,000 in damages, but Wayne's appeal is not expected to be decided before year 7. Caso's counsel believes it is probable that Caso will be successful against Wayne for an estimated amount in the range between $800,000 and $1,100,000, with $1,000,000 considered the most likely amount. What amount should Caso record as income from the lawsuit in the year ended December 31, year 5?

a. $0
b. $ 800,000
c. $1,000,000
d. $1,500,000

87. During year 2, Smith Co. filed suit against West, Inc. seeking damages for patent infringement. At December 31, year 2, Smith's legal counsel believed that it was probable that Smith would be successful against West for an estimated amount in the range of $75,000 to $150,000, with all amounts in the range considered equally likely. In March year 3, Smith was awarded $100,000 and received full payment thereof. In its year 2 financial statements, issued in February year 3, how should this award be reported?

a. As a receivable and revenue of $100,000.
b. As a receivable and deferred revenue of $100,000.
c. As a disclosure of a contingent gain of $100,000.
d. As a disclosure of a contingent gain of an undetermined amount in the range of $75,000 to $150,000.

88. In year 2, a contract dispute between Dollis Co. and Brooks Co. was submitted to binding arbitration. In year 2, each party's attorney indicated privately that the probable award in Dollis' favor could be reasonably estimated. In year 3, the arbitrator decided in favor of Dollis. When should Dollis and Brooks recognize their respective gain and loss?

	Dollis' gain	Brooks' loss
a.	Year 2	Year 2
b.	Year 2	Year 3
c.	Year 3	Year 2
d.	Year 3	Year 3

89. Eagle Co. has cosigned the mortgage note on the home of its president, guaranteeing the indebtedness in the event that the president should default. Eagle considers the likelihood of default to be remote. How should the guarantee be treated in Eagle's financial statements?

a. Disclosed only.
b. Accrued only.
c. Accrued and disclosed.
d. Neither accrued nor disclosed.

90. North Corp. has an employee benefit plan for compensated absences that gives employees 10 paid vacation days and 10 paid sick days. Both vacation and sick days can be carried over indefinitely. Employees can elect to receive payment in lieu of vacation days; however, no payment is given for sick days not taken. At December 31, year 2, North's unadjusted balance of liability for compensated absences was $21,000. North estimated that there were 150 vacation days and 75 sick days available at December 31, year 2. North's employees earn an average of $100 per day. In its December 31, year 2 balance sheet, what amount of liability for compensated absences is North required to report?

a. $36,000
b. $22,500
c. $21,000
d. $15,000

91. Ross Co. pays all salaried employees on a Monday for the five-day workweek ended the previous Friday. The last payroll recorded for the year ended December 31, year 2, was for the week ended December 25, year 2. The payroll for the week ended January 1, year 3, included regular weekly salaries of $80,000 and vacation pay of $25,000 for vacation time earned in year 2 not taken by December 31, year 2. Ross had accrued a liability of $20,000 for vacation pay at December 31, year 1. In its December 31, year 2 balance sheet, what amount should Ross report as accrued salary and vacation pay?

a. $64,000
b. $68,000
c. $69,000
d. $89,000

92. Gavin Co. grants all employees two weeks of paid vacation for each full year of employment. Unused vacation time can be accumulated and carried forward to succeeding years and will be paid at the salaries in effect when vacations are taken or when employment is terminated. There was no employee turnover in year 2. Additional information relating to the year ended December 31, year 2, is as follows:

Liability for accumulated vacations at 12/31/Y1	$35,000
Pre-year 2 accrued vacations taken from 1/1/Y2 to 9/30/Y2 (the authorized period for vacations)	20,000
Vacations earned for work in year 2 (adjusted to current rates)	30,000

Gavin granted a 10% salary increase to all employees on October 1, year 2, its annual salary increase date. For the year ended December 31, year 2, Gavin should report vacation pay expense of

a. $45,000
b. $33,500
c. $31,500
d. $30,000

93. At December 31, year 2, Taos Co. estimates that its employees have earned vacation pay of $100,000. Employees will receive their vacation pay in year 3. Should Taos accrue a liability at December 31, year 2, if the rights to this compensation accumulated over time or if the rights are vested?

	Accumulated	Vested
a.	Yes	No
b.	No	No
c.	Yes	Yes
d.	No	Yes

94. If the payment of employees' compensation for future absences is probable, the amount can be reasonably estimated, and the obligation relates to rights that accumulate, the compensation should be

a. Accrued if attributable to employees' services not already rendered.
b. Accrued if attributable to employees' services already rendered.
c. Accrued if attributable to employees' services whether already rendered or not.
d. Recognized when paid.

95. During year 1, Gum Co. introduced a new product carrying a two-year warranty against defects. The estimated warranty costs related to dollar sales are 2% within twelve months following the sale and 4% in the second twelve months following the sale. Sales and actual warranty expenditures for the years ended December 31, year 1 and year 2, are as follows:

	Sales	Actual warranty expenditures
Year 1	$150,000	$2,250
Year 2	250,000	7,500
	$400,000	$9,750

What amount should Gum report as estimated warranty liability in its December 31, year 2 balance sheet?

a. $ 2,500
b. $ 4,250
c. $11,250
d. $14,250

96. Vadis Co. sells appliances that include a three-year warranty. Service calls under the warranty are performed by an independent mechanic under a contract with Vadis. Based on experience, warranty costs are estimated at $30 for each machine sold. When should Vadis recognize these warranty costs?

    a.   Evenly over the life of the warranty.
    b.   When the service calls are performed.
    c.   When payments are made to the mechanic.
    d.   When the machines are sold.

97. Lute Corporation sells furnaces that include a three-year warranty. Lute can contract with a third party to provide these warranty services. Lute elects the fair value option for reporting financial liabilities. At what amount should Lute record the warranty liability on the balance sheet?

    a.   The cost of expected warranty services.
    b.   The present value of expected warranty costs.
    c.   The fair value of the contract to settle the warranty services.
    d.   The fair value of the contract to settle less the cost to provide services.

98. Case Cereal Co. frequently distributes coupons to promote new products. On October 1, year 2, Case mailed 1,000,000 coupons for $.45 off each box of cereal purchased. Case expects 120,000 of these coupons to be redeemed before the December 31, year 2, expiration date. It takes thirty days from the redemption date for Case to receive the coupons from the retailers. Case reimburses the retailers an additional $.05 for each coupon redeemed. As of December 31, year 2, Case had paid retailers $25,000 related to these coupons and had 50,000 coupons on hand that had not been processed for payment. What amount should Case report as a liability for coupons in its December 31, year 2 balance sheet?

    a. $35,000
    b. $29,000
    c. $25,000
    d. $22,500

99. Dunn Trading Stamp Co. records stamp service revenue and provides for the cost of redemptions in the year stamps are sold to licensees. Dunn's past experience indicates that only 80% of the stamps sold to licensees will be redeemed. Dunn's liability for stamp redemptions was $6,000,000 at December 31, year 1. Additional information for year 2 is as follows:

Stamp service revenue from stamps sold to licensees	$4,000,000
Cost of redemptions (stamps sold prior to 1/1/Y2)	2,750,000

If all the stamps sold in year 2 were presented for redemption in year 3, the redemption cost would be $2,250,000. What amount should Dunn report as a liability for stamp redemptions at December 31, year 2?

    a. $7,250,000
    b. $5,500,000
    c. $5,050,000
    d. $3,250,000

100. Chemrite Inc. reported a total asset retirement obligation of $350,000 in last year's balance sheet. This year, Chemrite acquired a new chemical manufacturing facility subject to unconditional retirement obligations. Two measures of the obligation are the discounted cash flow estimate of $82,000 and the undiscounted cash flow estimate of $105,000. Accretion expense equaled $23,000. What amount should Chemrite report for the asset retirement obligation in this year's balance sheet?

    a. $350,000
    b. $373,000
    c. $455,000
    d. $478,000

Miscellaneous

Items 101 and 102 are based on the following:

The following trial balance of Trey Co. at December 31, year 2, has been adjusted except for income tax expense.

	Debit	Credit
Cash	$ 550,000	
Accounts receivable, net	1,650,000	
Prepaid taxes	300,000	
Accounts payable		$ 120,000
Common stock		500,000
Additional paid-in capital		680,000
Retained earnings		630,000
Foreign currency translation adjustment	430,000	
Revenues		3,600,000
Expenses	2,600,000	
	$5,530,000	$5,530,000

Additional information

- During year 2, estimated tax payments of $300,000 were charged to prepaid taxes. Trey has not yet recorded income tax expense. There were no differences between financial statement and income tax income, and Trey's tax rate is 30%.
- Included in accounts receivable is $500,000 due from a customer. Special terms granted to this customer require payment in equal semiannual installments of $125,000 every April 1 and October 1.

101. In Trey's December 31, year 2 balance sheet, what amount should be reported as total current assets?

    a. $1,950,000
    b. $2,200,000
    c. $2,250,000
    d. $2,500,000

102. In Trey's December 31, year 2 balance sheet, what amount should be reported as total retained earnings?

    a. $1,029,000
    b. $1,200,000
    c. $1,330,000
    d. $1,630,000

103. The following is Gold Corp.'s June 30, year 2 trial balance:

Cash overdraft		$ 10,000
Accounts receivable, net	$ 35,000	
Inventory	58,000	
Prepaid expenses	12,000	
Land held for resale	100,000	
Property, plant, and equipment, net	95,000	
Accounts payable and accrued expenses		32,000
Common stock		25,000
Additional paid-in capital		150,000
Retained earnings		83,000
	$300,000	$300,000

Additional information

- Checks amounting to $30,000 were written to vendors and recorded on June 29, year 2, resulting in a cash overdraft of $10,000. The checks were mailed on July 9, year 2.
- Land held for resale was sold for cash on July 15, year 2.
- Gold issued its financial statements on July 31, year 2.

In its June 30, year 2 balance sheet, what amount should Gold report as current assets?

a. $225,000
b. $205,000
c. $195,000
d. $125,000

104. Mill Co.'s trial balance included the following account balances at December 31, year 2:

Accounts payable	$15,000
Bonds payable, due year 3	25,000
Discount on bonds payable, due year 3	3,000
Dividends payable 1/31/Y3	8,000
Notes payable, due year 4	20,000

What amount should be included in the current liability section of Mill's December 31, year 2 balance sheet?

a. $45,000
b. $51,000
c. $65,000
d. $78,000

F. Ratios

Items 105 and 106 are based on the following:

Rey, Inc.
SELECTED FINANCIAL DATA
December 31,

	Year 2	Year 1
Cash	$ 170,000	$ 90,000
Accounts receivable (net)	450,000	400,000
Merchandise inventory	540,000	420,000
Short-term marketable securities	80,000	40,000
Land and building (net)	1,000,000	1,000,000
Mortgage payable—current portion	60,000	50,000
Accounts payable and accrued liabilities	240,000	220,000
Short-term notes payable	100,000	140,000

Net credit sales totaled $3,000,000 and $2,000,000 for the years ended December 31, year 2 and year 1, respectively.

105. At December 31, year 2, Rey's quick (acid-test) ratio was

a. 1.50 to 1.
b. 1.75 to 1.
c. 2.06 to 1.
d. 3.10 to 1.

106. For year 2, Rey's accounts receivable turnover was

a. 1.13
b. 1.50
c. 6.67
d. 7.06

107. Which of the following ratios is(are) useful in assessing a company's ability to meet currently maturing or short-term obligations?

	Acid-test ratio	Debt to equity ratio
a.	No	No
b.	No	Yes
c.	Yes	Yes
d.	Yes	No

108. North Bank is analyzing Belle Corp.'s financial statements for a possible extension of credit. Belle's quick ratio is significantly better than the industry average. Which of the following factors should North consider as a possible limitation of using this ratio when evaluating Belle's creditworthiness?

a. Fluctuating market prices of short-term investments may adversely affect the ratio.
b. Increasing market prices for Belle's inventory may adversely affect the ratio.
c. Belle may need to sell its available-for-sale investments to meet its current obligations.
d. Belle may need to liquidate its inventory to meet its long-term obligations.

109. On December 30, year 2, Vida Co. had cash of $200,000, a current ratio of 1.5:1 and a quick ratio of .5:1. On December 31, year 2, all cash was used to reduce accounts payable. How did these cash payments affect the ratios?

	Current ratio	Quick ratio
a.	Increased	Decreased
b.	Increased	No effect
c.	Decreased	Increased
d.	Decreased	No effect

110. Tod Corp. wrote off $100,000 of obsolete inventory at December 31, year 2. The effect of this write-off was to decrease

a. Both the current and acid-test ratios.
b. Only the current ratio.
c. Only the acid-test ratio.
d. Neither the current nor the acid-test ratios.

111. The following computations were made from Clay Co.'s year 2 books:

Number of days' sales in inventory	61
Number of days' sales in accounts receivable	33

What was the number of days in Clay's year 2 operating cycle?

a. 33
b. 47
c. 61
d. 94

112. On December 31, year 2, Northpark Co. collected a receivable due from a major customer. Which of the following ratios would be increased by this transaction?

    a. Inventory turnover ratio.
    b. Receivable turnover ratio.
    c. Current ratio.
    d. Quick ratio.

H. International Financial Reporting Standards (IFRS)

113. On March 22, year 1, Cole Corporation received notification of legal action against the firm. Cole's attorneys determine that it is probable the company will lose the suit, and the loss is estimated at $2,000,000. Cole's accountants believe this amount is material and should be disclosed. Cole prepares its financial statements in accordance with IFRS. How should the estimated loss be disclosed in Cole's financial statements at December 31, year 1?

    a. As a loss recorded in other comprehensive income.
    b. As a contingent liability reported in the balance sheet and a loss on the income statement.
    c. As a provision for loss reported in the balance sheet and a loss on the income statement.
    d. In the footnotes to the financial statements as a contingency.

114. Roland Corp. signed an agreement with Linx, which requires that if Linx does not meet certain contractual obligations, Linx must forfeit land worth $40,000 to Roland. Roland's accountants believe that Linx will not meet its contractual obligations, and it is probable Roland will receive the land by the end of year 2. Roland uses IFRS for reporting purposes. How should Roland report the land?

    a. As investment property in the asset section of the balance sheet.
    b. As a contingent asset in the current asset section of the balance sheet.
    c. In a footnote disclosure if the economic benefits are probable.
    d. As a contingent asset and other comprehensive income for the period.

115. Under IFRS, if a long-term debt becomes callable due to the violation of a loan covenant

    a. The debt may continue to be classified as long-term if the company believes the covenant can be renegotiated.
    b. The debt must be reclassified as current.
    c. Cash must be reserved to pay the debt.
    d. Retained earnings must be restricted in the amount of the debt.

116. Under IFRS, which of the following accounts would not be considered a "provision"?

    a. Warranty liabilities.
    b. Bad debts.
    c. Taxes payable.
    d. Note payable.

117. Under IFRS, a contingency is described as

    a. An estimated liability.
    b. An event which is not recognized because it is not probable that an outflow will be required or the amount cannot be reasonably estimated.

    c. The same as it is described by US generally accepted accounting principles.
    d. A potentially large liability.

Multiple-Choice Answers and Explanations

Answers

1. c __ __	21. b __ __	41. b __ __	61. b __ __	81. a __ __	101. a __ __
2. a __ __	22. a __ __	42. a __ __	62. b __ __	82. a __ __	102. c __ __
3. c __ __	23. c __ __	43. c __ __	63. b __ __	83. b __ __	103. a __ __
4. a __ __	24. b __ __	44. c __ __	64. b __ __	84. d __ __	104. a __ __
5. a __ __	25. d __ __	45. d __ __	65. d __ __	85. a __ __	105. b __ __
6. a __ __	26. c __ __	46. d __ __	66. d __ __	86. a __ __	106. d __ __
7. a __ __	27. b __ __	47. a __ __	67. b __ __	87. d __ __	107. d __ __
8. c __ __	28. d __ __	48. a __ __	68. c __ __	88. c __ __	108. a __ __
9. c __ __	29. a __ __	49. d __ __	69. c __ __	89. a __ __	109. a __ __
10. c __ __	30. b __ __	50. c __ __	70. d __ __	90. d __ __	110. b __ __
11. d __ __	31. c __ __	51. d __ __	71. c __ __	91. d __ __	111. d __ __
12. b __ __	32. c __ __	52. c __ __	72. b __ __	92. c __ __	112. b __ __
13. a __ __	33. b __ __	53. b __ __	73. c __ __	93. c __ __	113. c __ __
14. a __ __	34. c __ __	54. c __ __	74. b __ __	94. b __ __	114. c __ __
15. a __ __	35. a __ __	55. c __ __	75. b __ __	95. d __ __	115. b __ __
16. d __ __	36. d __ __	56. c __ __	76. c __ __	96. d __ __	116. d __ __
17. b __ __	37. d __ __	57. c __ __	77. b __ __	97. c __ __	117. b __ __
18. b __ __	38. b __ __	58. d __ __	78. c __ __	98. a __ __	
19. a __ __	39. c __ __	59. a __ __	79. d __ __	99. c __ __	1st: __/117 = __%
20. a __ __	40. c __ __	60. b __ __	80. c __ __	100. c __ __	2nd: __/117 = __%

Explanations

1.   (c)   Cash on hand ($125,000) and cash in banks ($2,250,000) are both reported as cash in the current asset section of the balance sheet because they are both unrestricted and readily available for use. Cash legally restricted for additions to plant ($1,600,000) is not available to meet current operating needs, and therefore should be excluded from current assets. Instead, it should be shown in the long-term asset section of the balance sheet as an investment.

2.   (a)   To be classified as cash, the item must be readily available for current needs with no legal restrictions limiting its use. A postdated check is not acceptable for deposit and therefore is not considered cash. Thus, the $2,000 check was correctly excluded from the 12/31 checkbook balance and no adjustment is necessary. An NSF check should not be included in cash until it has been redeposited and has cleared the bank. At 12/31, the NSF check ($500) had not yet been redeposited, so it was incorrectly included in the 12/31 checkbook balance, and an adjustment must be made. The check which was not mailed until 1/10/Y3 ($300) should not be subtracted from cash until the company gives up physical control of that amount. Therefore, $300 must be added back to the checkbook balance. As a result of these adjustments, the correct cash balance is $4,800 ($5,000 – $500 + $300).

3.   (c)   The definition of cash includes both cash (cash on hand and demand deposits) and cash equivalents (short-term, highly liquid investments). Cash equivalents have to be readily convertible into cash and so near maturity that they carry little risk of changing in value due to interest rate changes. This will include only those investments with original maturities of three months or less from the date of purchase by the enterprise. Common examples of cash equivalents include treasury bills, commercial paper, and money market funds. Trans should report a total of $460,000 ($35,000 + $75,000 + $350,000) on its December

ber 31, year 2 balance sheet. The US treasury bill purchased on 12/1/Y2 is not included in the calculation because its original maturity is not within three months or less from the date of purchase.

4.   (a)   Cash which is segregated and deposited into a bond sinking fund is presented in a classified balance sheet as a noncurrent asset because its use is restricted. Bank overdrafts are presented as current liabilities, unless other accounts at the **same bank** contain sufficient cash to offset the overdraft. The operating account that has a positive balance, should be presented as a current asset.

5.   (a)   To determine the correct 8/31/Y2 cash balance, a partial bank reconciliation should be prepared. The balance per bank statement ($18,050) must be adjusted for any items which the bank has not yet recorded and also for any bank errors (none in this problem).

Balance per bank statement	$18,050
Deposits in transit	3,250
Outstanding checks	(2,750)
Correct balance	$18,550

The deposits in transit and outstanding checks represent transactions that the company has recorded, but the bank has not yet recorded. The insufficient funds check ($600) and bank service charge ($100) are both items which the bank has recorded but the company has not. They would be adjustments to the **book balance**, not the **bank balance**.

6.   (a)   The balance per books at 3/31/Y2 is $44,200. The amount would be increased by cash receipts per books and decreased by cash disbursements per books. Cash receipts per the bank in April were $58,400, but this amount includes the $10,300 in transit at 3/31. Therefore, cash receipts per books in April are $48,100 ($58,400 – $10,300). Cash disbursements per the bank in April were $49,700.

This amount includes the 3/31 outstanding checks ($12,600) but does **not** include the 4/30 outstanding checks ($7,000). Therefore, April cash disbursements per books is $44,100 ($49,700 – $12,600 + $7,000). The cash balance per books at 4/30/Y2 is $48,200 ($44,200 at 3/31/Y2, plus $48,100 receipts, less $44,100 disbursements). An alternative solutions approach is to first compute the 4/30/Y2 bank balance ($46,500 + $58,400 – $49,700 = $55,200), and then adjust for outstanding checks ($55,200 – $7,000 = $48,200).

7.   (a)   The 12/31/Y2 current net receivables would include the trade receivables, net of the allowance account ($93,000 – $2,000 = $91,000). The claim against a shipper for goods lost in transit ($3,000) is also a valid receivable at year-end. Therefore, the total current net receivables are $94,000 ($91,000 + $3,000). The **unsold** goods on consignment do not represent a receivable until sold. Therefore, the $26,000 should be removed from receivables and sales and the cost ($26,000 ÷ 130% = $20,000) should be removed from cost of goods sold and reported as ending inventory. The security deposit ($30,000) should be reported as a **long-term** receivable.

8.   (c)   The solutions approach is to set up a T-account for accounts receivable.

AR			
1/1/Y2	650,000		
Credit sales	2,700,000	75,000	Sales returns
		40,000	Write-offs
		2,150,000	Collections
12/31/Y2	1,085,000		

Credit sales are debited to **AR** and credited to **sales**. Sales returns are debited to **sales returns** and credited to **AR**; write-offs are debited to the **allowance for doubtful accounts** and credited to **AR**; and cash collections are debited to **cash** and credited to **AR**. The estimated future sales returns ($50,000) and estimated uncollectible accounts ($110,000) do not affect the accounts receivable account but are instead recorded in separate allowance accounts. Since the requirement is to determine accounts receivable **before** these allowances, the balance of accounts receivable should include only sales returns and write-offs for year 2.

9.   (c)   Accrued interest receivable at 6/30/Y3 is interest revenue which has been earned by 6/30/Y3, but has not yet been received by that date. Interest was last received on 7/1/Y2; the accrued interest receivable includes interest revenue earned from 7/1/Y2 through 6/30/Y3 (a full year). The original balance of the note receivable was $150,000 but the 7/1/Y2 principal payment of $50,000 reduced this balance to $100,000. Therefore, the 6/30/Y3 interest receivable is $8,000 ($100,000 × 8%).

10.   (c)   Loan origination fees are recognized over the life of the related loan as an adjustment of yield. These fees are recorded as a discount on the note receivable. Therefore, Tigg's 12/1/Y2 entry is

Notes receivable	200,000	
Discount on NR		6,000
Cash		194,000

Using the effective interest method, Tigg's 12/31/Y2 adjusting entry is

Int. receivable	2,000	
Discount on NR	166	
Int. revenue		2,166

The interest receivable is

Face value	×	Stated rate	×	Time		
$200,000	×	12%	×	1/12	=	$2,000

The interest revenue is

Carrying amount	×	Effective rate	×	Time		
$194,000	×	13.4%	×	1/12	=	$2,166

11.   (d)   A current asset is an asset that can be reasonably expected to be converted into cash, sold or consumed in operations, within a single operating cycle or within a year if more than one cycle is completed each year. A noncurrent asset is an asset that cannot be expected to be converted to cash, sold or consumed within a single operating cycle or within one year, whichever is longer. Because accrued interest was reported as a current asset on the year 2 balance sheet, it can be assumed interest will be received on August 31, year 2, since current assets are received within one year. Also, because the note receivable was reported as a noncurrent asset it can be assumed that the principal will not be collected within the next twelve months. Principal that is not due until August 31, year 3, coincides with reporting the note as a noncurrent asset.

12.   (b)   Upon receipt of the interest-bearing note for the sale of goods, Benet would record the following entry:

Notes receivable	(face value)
Interest receivable	(interest from 7/15 to 8/15)
Sales	(face + interest)

Note that the interest that accrued on the note from July 15 to August 15 represents part of the sales price of the merchandise (rather than interest income) because Benet did not hold the note during this period. On November 15, Benet will record the following entry:

Cash	(Plug)
Note receivable	(face value)
Interest revenue	(interest from 8/15 to 11/15)
Interest receivable	(interest from 7/15 to 8/15)

13.   (a)   If material, an allowance for discounts must be reported at year-end in order to match the discounts with the related sales and to report receivables at their collectible amount. At 12/31/Y2, $100,000 of the accounts receivable have the potential to be discounted by 2% because they are less than fifteen days old (terms 2/15, net 30). Since 50% of the customers are expected to take advantage of the 2% discount, the allowance for discounts should be $1,000 [($100,000 × 50%) × 2%]. None of the other categories require a discount allowance because they are older than the maximum age of fifteen days to receive the 2% discount.

14.   (a)   When revenue is recognized from sales and a right of return exists, sales revenue must be reduced to reflect estimated returns. In this case, sales of $1,000,000 must be reduced by estimated returns of $100,000 [(7% + 3%) × $1,000,000], resulting in net sales of $900,000. The estimated exchanges (15%) will not result in a future reduction of sales.

15.   (a)   To compute the 12/31/Y2 allowance for uncollectible accounts, the solutions approach is to set up a T-account for the allowance.

```
              Allowance for U.A.
                   |  260,000   1/1/Y2
                   |  180,000   Expense (2% × 9,000,000)
Write-offs  325,000|
                   |  115,000   12/31/Y2
```

The 1/1/Y2 balance is increased by bad debts expense recorded (2% × credit sales of $9,000,000) and decreased by write-offs of specific uncollectible accounts.

16. **(d)** The balance in the allowance for doubtful accounts should reflect the amount of accounts receivable that are estimated to be uncollectible. Since it is estimated that 3% of the gross accounts receivable will become uncollectible, the allowance account should have a 12/31/Y2 balance of $30,000 (3% × $1,000,000). Note that **bad debt expense** of $38,000 would be recorded for year 2, as indicated below.

```
                       Allowance
Bal. before adj.  8,000 |
                        |    ?       Bad debt expense ($38,000)
                        |  30,000    12/31/Y2 (3% × $1,000,000)
```

17. **(b)** The total amount of risk of accounting loss related to Butler's trade accounts receivable is $230,000 ($250,000 trade accounts receivable – $20,000 uncollectible amount). The accounting loss cannot exceed the amount of the account receivable recognized as an asset in the balance sheet ($230,000). Off-balance-sheet risk refers to a potential loss that may exceed the amount recognized as an asset. There is no off-balance-sheet risk in this example.

18. **(b)** The solutions approach is to set up a T-account for the allowance for doubtful accounts.

```
                          Allowance
                          |  30,000   1/1/Y2
Year 2 Write-offs  18,000 |   2,000   Year 2 Recoveries
                          |  14,000   12/31/Y2 Before adj.
                          |    ?      Unc. accts. expense
                          |  25,000   12/31/Y2
```

In year 2, $18,000 of accounts were written off as uncollectible (debit allowance, credit AR). Also, $2,000 of AR were recovered (debit AR, credit allowance; then, debit cash, credit AR), leaving a balance in the allowance account of $14,000 ($30,000 – $18,000 + $2,000). The desired 12/31/Y2 balance is $25,000 ($350,000 AR less $325,000 net value per aging schedule). Therefore, to increase the allowance from $14,000 to $25,000, uncollectible accounts expense of $11,000 must be recorded.

19. **(a)** When an aging schedule is used to estimate uncollectibles, the total uncollectibles computed is the amount used for the ending balance in the allowance account. As computed below, the 12/31/Y2 allowance for uncollectible accounts should be $9,000.

$$
\begin{array}{rcl}
\$120,000 \times 1\% & = & \$1,200 \\
90,000 \times 2\% & = & 1,800 \\
100,000 \times 6\% & = & \underline{6,000} \\
& & \underline{\$9,000}
\end{array}
$$

The other information given (12/31/Y1 allowance, write-offs, and recoveries) would be used to determine the bad debt expense adjustment, not the allowance balance. In this case, apparently due to a change in estimate, the bad debt expense adjustment would actually be a credit (to offset the necessary debit to the allowance account).

```
              Allowance for U.A.
                   |  22,000   12/31/Y1
Write-offs   7,000 |   4,000   Recoveries
                   |  19,000
Adjustment  10,000 |
                   |   9,000   12/31/Y2
```

20. **(a)** The aging of receivables method of estimating uncollectible accounts is based on the theory that bad debts are a function of accounts receivable collections during the period. The aging of receivables method emphasizes reporting accounts receivable at their net realizable value. It is a "balance-sheet" approach, which stresses the collectibility (valuation) of the receivable balance. Once the balance of the allowance account required to reduce net accounts receivable to their realizable value has been computed, bad debts expense is merely the amount needed to adjust the allowance account to the computed balance. Answer (b) is incorrect because under the direct write-off method, bad debts are considered expenses in the period in which they are written off; no consideration is given to the valuation of accounts receivable. Answers (c) and (d) are incorrect because both of these methods are based on the theory that bad debts are a function of sales. Thus, these methods emphasize reporting the bad debts expense amount accurately on the income statement.

21. **(b)** A primary objective of accrual accounting is to record the cash consequences of events that change an entity's financial position in the period in which the events occur. This means recognizing revenues when earned rather than when cash is received, and recognizing expenses when incurred rather than when cash is paid. Expenses are incurred when they help the firm earn revenue. Under the allowance method, uncollectible accounts expense is recognized in the same period as the related revenue. The same credit decisions that enabled the entity to earn revenue caused it to incur uncollectible accounts expense. Therefore, under accrual accounting that expense should be recognized in the same period. On the other hand, when the direct write-off method is used, the uncollectible accounts expense is generally recognized after the period in which the revenue is recognized; after the event (credit decision) which changed financial position. Therefore, the direct write-off method is **not** consistent with accrual accounting.

22. **(a)** When the allowance method for recognizing uncollectible accounts is used, the entry to write off a specific account is

```
Allowance for unc. accts.           xxx
    Accts. receivable                       xxx
```

Answer (a) is correct because this entry decreases both accounts.

23. **(c)** When an account receivable that was previously written off is collected, two entries must be made. The first entry reverses the write-off and reestablishes the receivable.

```
Accounts receivable                             xxx
    Allowance for uncollectible accounts               xxx
```

The second entry records the cash receipt.

```
Cash                                xxx
    Accounts receivable                     xxx
```

The credit to the allowance account in the first entry increases its balance. Uncollectible accounts expense, however, is not affected by this transaction.

24. (b) An **assignment** of accounts receivable is a financing arrangement whereby the owner of the receivables (assignor) obtains a loan from the lender (assignee) by pledging the accounts receivable as collateral. A **factoring** of accounts receivable is basically a sale of, or borrowing on, the receivables. "Factors" are intermediaries that buy receivables from companies (for a fee) and then collect payments directly from the customers. Thus, both of these are methods of generating cash from accounts receivable.

25. (d) When receivables are factored and control is surrendered the transaction is treated as a **sale**. A transfer in which control is surrendered will not be treated as a borrowing. The risk of uncollectible accounts is **not** retained by the seller in a sale without recourse.

26. (c) Taylored will receive the value of the receivables ($400,000), reduced by $20,000 for the amount of the holdback ($400,000 × .05), $8,000 withheld as fee income ($400,000 × .02), and $6,740 withheld as interest expense ($400,000 × .15 × 41/365). Answer (c) is therefore correct ($400,000 – $8,000 – $6,740 – $20,000).

27. (b) A sale of receivables with recourse is recorded using a financial components approach because the seller has a continuing involvement. Under this approach the seller would reduce receivables, recognize assets obtained and liabilities incurred, and record gain or loss. The entry would be

Cash	$365,260	
Factor's holdback	20,000	
Loss	26,740*	
Accounts receivable		$400,000
Recourse liability		12,000

* ($6,740 + $8,000 + $12,000)

28. (d) If all receivables are collected, Taylored would eliminate its recourse liability and the corresponding loss. The costs incurred by Taylored would include a fee of $8,000 ($400,000 × .02) and interest expense of $6,740 ($400,000 × .15 × 41/365) for a total of $14,740.

29. (a) The seller uses a Due from Factor or Factor's Holdback account to account for probable sales discounts, sales returns, and sales allowances. The Recourse liability account is recorded to indicate probable uncollectible accounts.

30. (b) Scarbrough will receive the value of the receivables ($600,000), reduced by $30,000 for the amount of the holdback ($600,000 × .05), $18,000 withheld as fee income ($600,000 × .03), and $13,315 withheld as interest expense ($600,000 × .15 × 54/365). Answer (b) is therefore correct ($538,685 = 600,000 – $30,000 – $18,000 – $13,315).

31. (c) If all receivables are collected, Synthia would eliminate its recourse liability and the corresponding loss. The costs incurred by Synthia would include a fee of $15,000 ($750,000 × .02) and interest expense of $12,575 ($750,000 × .12 × 51/365) for a total of $27,575.

32. (c) The transferor, Bannon, should measure the assets received and liabilities incurred at fair value, not at cost.

The transferee, Chapman, should record any assets obtained and liabilities incurred at fair value.

33. (b) If financial assets are exchanged for cash or other consideration, but the transfer does not meet the criteria to be accounted for as a sale, both the transferor and the transferee should account for the transfer as a secured borrowing and a pledge of collateral.

34. (c) A sale occurs if the seller surrenders control of the receivables transferred. Control is deemed to have been surrendered by the seller only if all three conditions listed in (a), (b), and (d) are met. Answer (c) is used to determine whether a recourse liability is recorded as part of the sale, not whether a transaction can be recorded as a sale.

35. (a) To derecognize assets when control is gained is not an objective in accounting for transfers of financial assets. When control is gained, the assets should be recognized. Answer (b) is incorrect because an objective is to derecognize liabilities when extinguished. A liability no longer exists, and it should be removed from the balance sheet. Answer (c) is incorrect because recognizing liabilities when incurred is an objective. Answer (d) is incorrect because derecognizing assets when control is given up is an objective in accounting for transfers of financial assets.

36. (d) A servicing asset or liability should be amortized in proportion to and over the period of estimated net servicing income or net servicing loss. Answer (a) is incorrect because a servicing asset shall be assessed for impairment based on its fair value. Answer (b) is incorrect because a servicing liability shall be assessed for increased obligation based on its fair value. Answer (c) is incorrect because an obligation to service financial assets may result in the recognition of a servicing asset or a servicing liability.

37. (d) The assets must be measured for impairment at the end of each reporting period. Answer (a) is incorrect because increases in fair value are not reported under the amortization method. Answer (a) is also incorrect because when using the fair value method, changes in fair value are reported in earnings, not in other comprehensive income. Answers (b) and (c) are incorrect because these rules refer to the fair value method.

38. (b) Answer (b) is correct. Either the amortization method or the fair value method can be used for servicing assets and servicing liabilities. However, if the fair value method is elected, the election cannot be reversed. Changes in fair value are reported in earnings in the period in which the change occurs.

39. (c) When a company transfers a financial asset but continues to hold an interest in the servicing asset, the transferor should report the interest that continues to be held as the difference between the previous carrying amount and the amount derecognized. Answers (a), (b), and (d) are incorrect because they represent incorrect values.

40. (c) The arrangement of having collateral transferred to a secured party is known as a pledge. Answer (a) is incorrect because a debtor may grant a security interest in certain assets to a lender to serve as collateral with recourse. Answer (b) is incorrect because a debtor may grant a security interest in certain assets to a lender to serve as collateral without recourse. Answer (d) is incorrect because secured parties are sometimes permitted to sell collateral held under a pledge.

41. (b) Net proceeds from the sale are equal to $2,200.

Net proceeds

Cash received	$2,100
Plus: Interest rate swap	140
Call option	80
Less: Recourse obligation	(120)
Net proceeds	$2,200

The gain is computed as follows:

Net proceeds	$2,200
Carrying amount of loans sold	2,000
Gain on sale	$ 200

42. (a) The journal entry to record the transfer for ABC Company is as follows:

Cash	2,100	
Interest rate swap	140	
Call option	80	
Loans		2,000
Recourse obligation		120
Gain on sale		200

Answer (b) is incorrect because is should be a debit to interest rate swap, not a credit. Answer (c) is incorrect because loans should be credited. It was on ABC Company's books as an asset and must be taken off. Answer (d) is incorrect because cash is being received, so it must be debited.

43. (c) ABC Company must report a servicing obligation of $50. The calculation of net proceeds is

Cash received	$2,100
Plus: Interest rate swap	140
Call option	80
Less: Recourse obligation	(120)
Servicing obligation	(50)
Net proceeds	$2,150

The gain is

Net proceeds	$2,150
Carrying amount of loans sold	2,000
Gain on sale	$ 150

44. (c) Financial assets subject to prepayment should be measured like investments in debt securities classified as available-for-sale or trading.

45. (d) Answers (a), (b), and (c) are required disclosures. Answer (d) is the correct answer as disclosure is only required of assets and liabilities with nonestimable fair values.

46. (d) If the debtor defaults under the terms of the secured contract and is no longer entitled to redeem the pledged asset, it (Taft) shall derecognize the pledged asset, and the secured party (Wilson) shall recognize the collateral as its asset initially measured at fair value.

47. (a) Before adjustment, the balance in the Accounts Payable account is $360,000. This amount is net of a $50,000 debit balance in Lyle's account payable to Ross resulting from a $50,000 advance payment for goods to be manufactured to Lyle's specifications. The $50,000 should be reclassified as a current asset, **Advance to Suppliers**. The checks recorded on 12/29/Y2 incorrectly reduced the accounts payable balance by $100,000. The $100,000 reduction should not have been recorded until the checks were mailed on 1/5/Y3. The 12/31/Y2 accounts payable must be increased by $100,000. Therefore, the corrected 12/31/Y2 accounts payable is $510,000.

Unadjusted AP	$360,000
Reclassification of advance	50,000
Error correction	100,000
	$510,000

48. (a) When purchases are recorded using the net method, purchases and accounts payable are recorded at an amount net of the cash discounts, and the failure to take advantage of a discount is recorded in a Purchase Discounts Lost account. Therefore, when Rabb changes to the net method, gross accounts payable ($30,000) must be adjusted down to the net amount. Since $200 of discounts are still available in the accounts payable balance, the net accounts payable at 9/30/Y2 is $29,800 ($30,000 – $200). The journal entry is

Purchase discounts lost	1,000	
Purchase discounts	800	
Accts. payable	200	
Purchases		2,000

49. (d) Accrued interest payable at 12/31/Y2 is interest expense which has been incurred by 12/31/Y2, but has not yet been paid by that date. The note was issued on 3/1/Y1 and interest is payable in full at maturity on 2/28/Y3. Therefore, there is one year and ten months of unpaid interest at 12/31/Y2 (3/1/Y1 to 12/31/Y2). Interest for the first year is $1,200 ($10,000 × 12%). Since interest is compounded annually, the new principal amount for the second year includes the original principal ($10,000) plus the first year's interest ($1,200). Therefore, accrued interest for the ten months ended 12/31/Y2 is $1,120 ($11,200 × 12% × 10/12), and total accrued interest at 12/31/Y2 is $2,320 ($1,200 + $1,120).

50. (c) Accrued interest payable at 12/31/Y2 is interest expense which has been incurred by 12/31/Y2, but has not yet been paid by that date. Interest was last paid on 9/1/Y2; the accrued interest payable includes interest expense incurred from 9/1/Y2 through 12/31/Y2 (four months). The original balance of the note payable was $1,350,000 but the 9/1/Y2 principal payment of $450,000 reduced this balance to $900,000. Therefore, the interest payable at 12/31/Y2 is $36,000 ($900,000 × 12% × 4/Y3). The prime rate (11%) does not affect the computation because it is not the stated rate on this note.

51. (d) The solutions approach is to analyze the interest payable T-account for year 2, assuming all interest payments flow through interest payable.

Interest Payable			
		15,000	12/31/Y1
Year 2 Int. paid	68,000	85,000	Year 2 Expense
		?	12/31/Y2

The beginning interest payable balance ($15,000) is increased by interest expense (debit interest expense, credit interest payable for $85,000) and decreased by interest paid (debit interest payable, credit cash for $68,000), resulting in a 12/31/Y2 balance of $32,000 ($15,000 + $85,000 – $68,000).

52. (c) All of the notes are due 6/15/Y3, and normally the entire amount would be classified as current. However, a short-term obligation can be reclassified as long-term if the enterprise intends to refinance the obligation on a long-term basis **and** the intent is supported by the ability to refinance. Ames demonstrated its ability by entering into a financing agreement before the statements are issued. The amount to be excluded from current liabilities cannot exceed the amount available for refinancing under the agreement. Ames expects to be able to refinance at least $480,000 (80% × $600,000) of the notes. Therefore, that amount can be classified as long-term, while the remaining $20,000 must be classified as short-term.

53. (b) The effective rate of interest paid on a note is computed as follows:

$$\text{Effective interest rate} = \frac{\text{Interest paid}}{\text{Cash received}}$$

In this case, let's assume the short-term note payable was in the amount of $100,000. The effective interest rate would be 12.56%.

$$\frac{(100{,}000 \times .12) + (\$100{,}000 \times .005)}{\$99{,}500} = 12.56$$

This is because the loan origination fee increases the interest paid on the note and reduces the net cash received from the note.

54. (c) The $4,000,000 note payable is due March 15, year 3 and normally would be classified as a current liability in the December 31, year 2 financial statements. However, a short-term obligation can be reclassified as long-term if the enterprise intends to refinance the obligation on a long-term basis and the intent is supported by the ability to refinance. Cali demonstrated its ability to refinance by actually issuing bonds and refinancing the note prior to the issuance of the December 31, year 2 financial statements. Since the proceeds from the bonds exceeded the amount needed to retire the note, the entire $4,000,000 notes payable would be classified as a noncurrent liability, with separate disclosure of the note refinancing.

55. (c) The notes payable ($750,000) are due 7/31/Y3, and would normally be included in 12/31/Y2 current liabilities. However, a short-term obligation can be reclassified as long-term if the enterprise intends to refinance the obligation on a long-term basis and the intent is supported by the ability to refinance. Largo demonstrated its ability to refinance by actually issuing $1,500,000 of bonds in February year 3 before the 12/31/Y2 financial statements were issued on 3/3/Y3. The bond proceeds will be used to retire the note at maturity. The amount excluded from current liabilities cannot exceed the amount actually refinanced. Since Largo prepaid $250,000 of the note on 1/12/Y3 with excess cash, that amount must be included in 12/31/Y2 current liabilities. Only the remaining $500,000 can be excluded from current liabilities.

56. (c) A key to solving this problem is understanding that the employee advances do **not** affect the accrued salaries payable. When advances are made to employees, they are a cash payment separate from the payroll function. The advances made, therefore, are not reflected in salaries expense ($420,000) or **gross** salaries paid ($390,000). There-

fore, the solutions approach is to analyze the salaries payable T-account for year 2 (disregarding the employee advances).

Salaries Payable

	40,000	12/31/Y1
Year 2 sal. paid 390,000	420,000	Year 2 sal. expense
	?	12/31/Y2

The beginning salaries payable balance ($40,000) is increased by salaries expense ($420,000) and decreased by salaries paid ($390,000), resulting in a 12/31/Y2 balance of $70,000.

57. (c) No sales commission is due to salesperson A because his commissions earned ($200,000 × 4% = $8,000) are less than his fixed salary ($10,000). Note that the excess of the fixed salary over commissions earned is not charged back against A. Commissions totaling $28,000 are due to salespersons B and C as computed below.

	Commissions earned		Fixed salary paid	Commissions payable
B	(6% × $400,000)	−	$14,000	$10,000
C	(6% × $600,000)	−	$18,000	18,000
				$28,000

58. (d) Lime's payroll tax liability includes amounts withheld from payroll checks [$1,200 of federal income taxes withheld and $700 of the **employees'** share of FICA ($10,000 × 7%)] plus the **employer's** share of FICA (an additional $700). Therefore, the total payroll tax liability is $2,600 ($1,200 + $700 + $700). The amount recorded as payroll tax expense consists only of the employer's share of FICA ($700), since no unemployment taxes are mentioned in the problem.

59. (a) The contingent unemployment claims liability is both probable and reasonably estimable, so it must be accrued at 12/31/Y2. Acme's reasonable estimate of its probable liability is 2% of eligible gross wages. Eligible gross wages are the first $10,000 of gross wages paid to each of the five employees (5 × $10,000 = $50,000), so the accrued liability should be $1,000 (2% × $50,000). Note that the 3% rate is not used because Acme has chosen the option to reimburse the state directly, and its best estimate of this liability is based on 2%, not 3%.

60. (b) To compute the amount of the contribution, the requirements described in the problem must be translated into an equation. The contribution must equal 10% of income **after** deduction of the contribution, but **before** income tax. Therefore, the tax rate (30%) does not enter into the computation. The equation is solved below.

$$C = .10 \times (\$75{,}000 - C)$$
$$C = \$7{,}500 - .10C$$
$$1.1C = \$7{,}500$$
$$C = \$7{,}500 \div 1.1$$
$$C = \$6{,}818$$

The amount to be accrued as an expense and liability is $6,818.

61. (b) If net income **after** bonus and income tax is $360,000, income before taxes can be computed by dividing **$360,000** by **1 minus the tax rate**.

$$\text{Income before taxes} = \frac{\$360{,}000}{1 - .40} = \underline{\$600{,}000}$$

The bonus is equal to 10% of income **before** income tax but **after** the bonus. The $600,000 computed above **is** income before tax but after all other expenses including the bonus. Therefore, the bonus must be $60,000 (10% × $600,000). Note that this problem is different from other bonus problems because usually the income before taxes and bonus ($660,000 in this case) is given as the starting point, rather than net income.

62. **(b)** To determine the correct amount for sales revenue, Ivy must divide the total of sales and sales taxes by 100% plus the sales tax percentage (6%) as indicated below.

Month	Total		Percentage		Sales revenue
Jan.	$10,600	÷	106%	=	$10,000
Feb.	$ 7,420	÷	106%	=	7,000
March	$ 8,480	÷	106%	=	8,000
Total					$25,000

Sales taxes payable would include all sales taxes collected, less any sales taxes already remitted.

January sales taxes ($10,600 – $10,000)	$ 600
*February sales taxes ($7,420 – $7,000)	420
March sales taxes ($8,480 – $8,000)	480
Total	$1,500
Less taxes remitted	600
Sales taxes payable	$ 900

> * Note February sales taxes were not remitted since they did not exceed $500.

63. **(b)** As of 12/31/Y2 the October sales taxes should have been paid, so there would be no 12/31/Y2 current liability for those taxes. However, at 12/31/Y2 sales taxes payable must be reported for the November room rentals as they were not paid until 1/3/Y3 and the December room rentals [15% × ($110,000 + $150,000) = $39,000]. The fourth quarter occupancy taxes were not paid until 1/3/Y3, so they would also represent a current liability at 12/31/Y2 [(1,100 + 1,200 + 1,800) × $2 = $8,200].

64. **(b)** When the warehouse was purchased on 9/1/Y2, it would be recorded at its total cost before any credit for accrued realty taxes. The offsetting credits would be to **cash** for the net amount paid, and to **real estate taxes payable** for two months' taxes ($12,000 × 2/6 = $4,000). At the end of September and of October, Day would record property tax expense each month as follows:

Real estate tax expense	2,000	
Real estate taxes payable		2,000

Therefore, at October 31, Day has a balance of $8,000 in the payable account ($4,000 + $2,000 + $2,000). On 11/1/Y2, Day would record the semiannual payment as follows:

Real estate taxes payable	8,000	
Prepaid real estate taxes	4,000	
Cash		12,000

The prepaid real estate taxes would then be expensed $2,000 per month at the end of November and December.

65. **(d)** An accrued liability is an expense which has been incurred, but has not been paid. Of the $500 advertising bill, $375 had been incurred as an expense as of 12/31/Y2 and should be reported as an accrued liability at that time. For the store lease, the fixed portion ($1,200 per month) is payable on the 16th of each month for the pre-

ceding month. Therefore, on 12/16/Y2, rent was paid for the period 11/16/Y2 to 12/15/Y2. An additional one-half month's rent expense (1/2 × $1200 = $600) has been incurred but not paid as of 12/31/Y2. The variable portion of the rent [5% × ($550,000 – $300,000), or $12,500] was incurred during year 2, but will not be paid until 1/31/Y3. It, too, is an accrued liability at 12/31/Y2. Total 12/31/Y2 accrued liabilities are $13,475.

Advertising	$ 375
Fixed rent (1/2 × $1,200)	600
Variable rent [5% × ($550,000 – $300,000)]	12,500
Total	$13,475

66. **(d)** The solutions approach to this problem is to construct a time line documenting the events in the question.

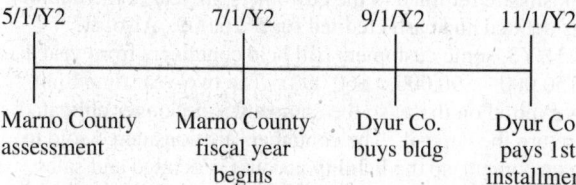

Note that on May 1, year 2, the County has merely determined the amount of property tax owed by each property owner, and no entries would be made by companies subject to property taxes on that date. The fiscal year year 3 taxes are for the period from July 1, year 2, to June 30, year 3. On September 1, year 2, the date on which Dyur purchased the building, two months of the fiscal year had passed, and the property tax expense related to those months was borne by the seller. At October 31, year 2, Dyur would have a liability for four months of property taxes (even though only the months of September and October would have been expensed by Dyur). On November 1, year 2, four months of the fiscal year had passed, and Dyur paid taxes for the first six months of the fiscal year. The entry recorded upon the payment would be

Property taxes payable	(four months)	
Prepaid property taxes	(two months)	
Cash		(six months)

The payment would therefore be allocated as two-sixths (33 1/3%) to an increase in prepaid property taxes and four-sixths (66 2/3%) to a decrease in property taxes payable.

67. **(b)** To determine the 12/31/Y2 balance of the liability for customer advances, the solutions approach is to set up a T-account for the liability.

Customer Advances		
	118,000	12/31/Y1
	184,000	Year 2 adv.
Year 2 adv. applied 164,000		received
Year 2 cancellations 50,000		
	88,000	12/31/Y2

When advances are received ($184,000), cash is debited and the liability account is credited. When advances are applied to orders shipped ($164,000), the liability account is debited and sales is credited. When an order is cancelled ($50,000), the liability account is debited and a revenue account is credited, since the advance payments are nonrefundable. Thus, the customer advances balance on 12/31/Y2 is $88,000.

68. **(c)** The solutions approach is to set up a T-account for the liability.

Liability for Deposits			
		580,000	12/31/Y2 balance
		780,000	Year 3 deliveries
Year 3 returns	626,000		
Year 2 sales	60,000		
		674,000	12/31/Y3 balance

When customers pay the deposit for a container, cash is debited and the liability is credited. Therefore, at 12/31/Y2 the liability consists of deposits for containers still held by customers from the last two years ($580,000). During year 3, the liability was increased for deposits on containers delivered ($780,000). When containers are returned, the deposits are returned to the customers; in year 3, the liability was debited and cash credited for $626,000. Also, at 12/31/Y3, some customers still held containers from year 1 ($150,000 – $90,000 = $60,000). The two-year time limit has expired on these, so the company is no longer obligated to return the deposit. The containers are considered sold to the customers, so the liability account is debited and sales credited for $60,000. This results in a 12/31/Y3 balance of $674,000.

69. **(c)** To compute the escrow liability, the solutions approach is to use a T-account.

Escrow Liability			
		700,000	1/1/Y2
Taxes paid	1,720,000	1,580,000	Receipts
		45,000	Net interest
		605,000	12/31/Y2

Escrow payments received ($1,580,000) would increase the liability because these amounts are payable to taxing authorities. Taxes paid ($1,720,000) decrease the liability. The net interest credited to the escrow accounts [$50,000 – (10% × $50,000) = $45,000] would increase the liability, resulting in a 12/31/Y2 balance of $605,000.

70. **(d)** All contract sales are made **evenly** during the year. Therefore, the year 1 contracts range from one year expired (if sold on 12/31/Y1) to two years expired (if sold on 1/1/Y1), for an average of one and one-half years expired [(2+1)/2]. Similarly, the year 2 contracts range from zero years expired to one year expired, for an average of one-half year expired [(0+1)/2]. The average **unearned** portion of the year 1 contracts is one-half year (two years – one and one-half years), the last half of the second contract year. The amount of unearned revenue related to year 1 contracts is computed as follows:

$$\$500,000 \times 60\% \times 1/2 = \underline{\$150,000}$$

The average **unearned** portion of the year 2 contracts is one and one-half years (two years – one-half year), the last half of the first contract year and all of the second contract year. The amount of unearned revenue related to the year 2 contracts is computed as follows:

Year 2:	$600,000 × 40% × ½		$120,000
	$600,000 × 60%	=	360,000
			$480,000

Therefore, the total unearned revenue is $630,000 ($150,000 + $480,000).

71. **(c)** Revenue is earned by Toddler Care Co. as time goes by and care is provided. Therefore, revenue should be recognized on a straight-line basis regardless of the timing of cash receipts. The monthly fees can simply be recognized on a monthly basis, but the initial payment must be deferred and recognized as revenue on a straight-line basis over the twelve-month period. The 12/31/Y2 deferred revenues are $6,600, as computed below.

Plan	Initial fees	Year 2 revenue (4/Y3)	12/31/Y2 def. rev. (8/Y3)
1	15 × $500 = $7,500	$2,500	$5,000
2	12 × $200 = $2,400	800	1,600
3	$ 0	0	0
	$9,900	$3,300	$6,600

Since the total initial payments received are given ($9,900), a shortcut is to multiply that amount by 8/Y3 ($9,900 × 8/12 = $6,600).

72. **(b)** When a company issues gift certificates for cash, the following journal entry is made:

Cash	(amount of certificate)	
Deferred revenue		(amount of certificate)

When the gift certificates are subsequently redeemed, the following journal entry is made:

Deferred revenue	(amount of certificate)	
Revenue		(amount of certificate)

However, if the gift certificates are not redeemed and lapse, the following journal entry is made:

Deferred revenue	(amount of certificate)	
Gain on lapse of certificates		(amount of certificate)

Please note that although different accounts are credited depending on whether the certificates are redeemed or lapse, the Deferred Revenue account is decreased in both cases.

73. **(c)** Revenues are generally recognized when they are both **realized** or **realizable** and **earned**. Therefore, Dallas Co. should report a liability for deferred revenues equal to the advance payment of 60% of the main contract price. One of three essential characteristics of a liability is that the transaction or other event obligating the entity has already happened. Since the subcontractor had not produced the special-order goods as of March 31, Dallas should not record a liability at that time. Therefore, no payable to the subcontractor would be reported for this activity as of March 31.

74. **(b)** At June 30, year 2, Northan Retailers should report the coupon transactions as unearned revenues because the sale of the coupons is not the culmination of the earnings process (i.e., Northan must allow customers to exchange the coupons for merchandise or refund the cost of the coupons at some later date). The unearned revenues should be recorded at the amount of the cash received by debiting cash and crediting an unearned revenue account. The retail price of the merchandise for which coupons may be redeemed does not impact the monetary amount of Northan's liability to its customers, and each coupon redeemed will ultimately result in the recognition of sales of $10, the amount of cash previously received.

75. (b) The requirement is to determine the situation that might account for the reduction in the deferred revenue balance. When a service contract is purchased by a customer and the fee prepaid, deferred revenue is recognized at the date of payment. Revenue cannot be recorded because revenue has not yet been earned. Revenue is only recorded when services are performed under the contract. The deferred revenue balance is reduced by the **actual** amount of revenue earned when services are performed under the services contract. If more contracts were signed earlier in one year than another year, there is a greater period of time in which to perform actual services. As previously stated, when actual services are performed, the deferred revenue balance is decreased. Therefore, the more actual services that are performed, the greater the reduction in the deferred revenue balance. If more year 2 contracts were signed later in year 2 than year 1, the deferred revenue balance in year 2 would be larger than year 1. There would be less time to perform actual services, therefore less actual revenue would be recognized, creating a larger deferred revenue balance at year-end. There is no contribution margin recognized on service contracts.

76. (c) The aggregate amount of payments for unconditional purchase obligations that have been recognized on the purchaser's balance sheet shall be disclosed for each of the **five** years following the date of the latest balance sheet presented.

77. (b) A loss contingency should be accrued if it is **probable** that a liability has been incurred at the balance sheet date and the amount of the loss is reasonably estimable. With respect to unfiled claims, the enterprise must consider both the probability that a claim will be filed and the probability of an unfavorable outcome. Although it is probable that claims will be asserted against Sims, it is only **reasonably possible** that the claims will be successful. Therefore, this contingent liability should not be accrued, but should be disclosed. The potential loss to be disclosed is $250,000, since the additional amount above the deductible would be covered by the insurance policy, and therefore is not a loss or liability for Sims.

78. (c) Current liabilities are obligations whose liquidation is reasonably expected to require the use of current assets or the creation of other current liabilities. This means that generally, current liabilities are the liabilities that are due within one year of the balance sheet date. Clearly, accounts payable ($55,000) and accrued expenses ($35,000) are current liabilities. Notes payable ($400,000) and bonds payable ($1,000,000) are usually considered to be long-term, but the maturity dates given (7/1/Y3 and 3/1/Y3 respectively) indicate they are current liabilities at 12/31/Y2. The contingent liability ($450,000) and deferred tax liability ($25,000) will not be settled until year 4 and therefore should be classified as long-term at 12/31/Y2. Thus, the 12/31/Y2 current liabilities total is $1,490,000 as follows:

Accounts payable	$ 55,000
Accrued expenses	35,000
Unsecured notes 8%—due 7/1/Y3	400,000
Senior bonds 7%—due 3/1/Y3	1,000,000
Total current liabilities	$1,490,000

79. (d) The lawsuit damages must be accrued as a loss contingency because an unfavorable outcome is **probable**

and the amount of the loss is **reasonably estimable**. When a range of possible loss exists, the best estimate within the range is accrued. When no amount within the range is a better estimate than any other amount, the dollar amount at the low end of the range is **accrued** (in this case, $500,000) and the dollar amount of the high end of the range is **disclosed**.

80. (c) A loss contingency should be accrued if it is **probable** that a liability has been incurred at the balance sheet date and the amount of the loss is **reasonably estimable**. This loss must be accrued because it meets both criteria. Notice that even though the lawsuit was not initiated until 1/12/Y3, the liability was incurred on 11/5/Y2 when the accident occurred. When some amount within an estimated range is a better estimate than any other amount in the range, that amount is accrued. Therefore, a loss of $300,000 should be accrued. If no amount within the range is a better estimate than any other amount, the amount at the low end of the range is accrued and the amount at the high end is disclosed.

81. (a) The additional tax liability must be accrued as a loss contingency because an unfavorable outcome is **probable** and the amount of the loss is **reasonably estimable**. Since $200,000 is the reasonable estimate, that amount should be accrued by debiting Income Tax Expense and crediting Income Tax Payable. The possibility of the liability being as high as $300,000 would be disclosed in the notes. The settlement offer of $275,000 is not accrued at 12/31/Y2 because prior to financial statement issuance, Haft was unaware of the offer, and $200,000 was the best estimate. In year 3, when the settlement offer was accepted, Haft would record an additional $75,000 of expense and liability.

82. (a) A loss contingency is accrued if it is **probable** that a liability has been incurred at the balance sheet date and the amount of the loss is reasonably estimable. If no accrual is made for a loss contingency because one or both of the conditions above are not met, disclosure of the contingency shall be made when it is at least **reasonably possible** that a loss was incurred. Therefore, this loss should be disclosed, but not accrued as a liability.

83. (b) Invern's appropriation of retained earnings for contingencies is merely a reclassification of retained earnings on the balance sheet which tells the readers of the financial statements that such amounts are generally not available to pay dividends. This appropriation has no effect on the income statement. When a loss contingency is probable (as in this instance) **and** reasonably estimable ($190,000 in this instance), accrual of the loss is required. Therefore, Invern must accrue both a liability and an expense of $190,000. Note that Invern will also reclassify $190,000 of appropriated retained earnings into the "general" retained earnings.

84. (d) At 12/31/Y2, Halsey's contingent liability of $50,000 is no longer probable due to the favorable judgment and the inability to predict the outcome of the appeal. Therefore, no liability should be reported in the balance sheet. **Gain** contingencies are not reflected in the accounts until realized, so the $30,000 asset is not reported in the 12/31/Y2 balance sheet, either.

85. (a) Gain contingencies are not recognized in the income statement until realized. As only $15,000 of the litigation awards has been resolved as of December 31, year 2, Haze should report only $15,000 as a gain in its year 2 financial statements.

86. (a) Gain contingencies are not reflected in the accounts until realized. Since the case is unresolved at 12/31/Y5, none of this contingent gain should be recorded as income in year 5. Adequate disclosure should be made of the gain contingency, but care should be taken to avoid misleading implications as to the likelihood of realization.

87. (d) Gain contingencies are not reflected in the accounts until realized. Since the case was unresolved at 12/31/Y2, none of this contingent gain can be recorded as a receivable and/or revenue in year 2. Since the contingency is probable, it should be disclosed along with the 12/31/Y2 estimate of a range of $75,000 to $150,000. A gain contingency would not be accrued as a receivable. The amount disclosed should be the range because all amounts within the range are considered equally likely.

88. (c) An estimated loss from a loss contingency shall be accrued by a charge to income if **both** of the following conditions are met:

1. Information available indicates that it is **probable** that an asset has been impaired or a liability has been incurred.
2. The amount of the loss can be **reasonably estimated**.

However, gain contingencies are only recognized when a specific event actually occurs, not prior to the event, because to do so would recognize the gain prior to its realization. Therefore, Brooks should recognize the loss in year 2 due to the fact that the event is probable and can be reasonably estimated. Dollis, on the other hand, cannot recognize the gain until year 3, the year they receive the actual award.

89. (a) Eagle Co. has a contingent liability where the possibility of loss is **remote**. Loss contingencies are accrued when they are **probable** and **reasonably estimable**. All others are disclosed unless remote. However, some contingencies, such as guarantees of others' debts, standby letters of credit by banks, and agreements to repurchase receivables, are disclosed even if remote. Eagle's contingent liability is **not** accrued, because it is not probable. It **is** disclosed for two reasons: it is a guarantee of other's debt, and it is a related-party transaction.

90. (d) An accrual of a liability for future vacation pay is required if all the conditions below are met.

1. Obligation arises from employee services already performed.
2. Obligation arises from rights that vest or accumulate.
3. Payment is probable.
4. Amount can be reasonably estimated.

The criteria are met for the vacation pay (150 × $100 = $15,000), so North is required to report a $15,000 liability. The same criteria apply to accrual of a liability for future sick pay, **except** that if sick pay benefits accumulate but do not vest, accrual is **permitted** but not **required** because its payment is contingent upon future employee sickness.

Therefore, no liability is **required** for these sick pay benefits (75 × $100 = $7500). Note that the unadjusted balance of the liability account ($21,000) does not affect the computation of the required 12/31/Y2 liability.

91. (d) The week ended 1/1/Y3 included four days in year 2 and one day in year 3. The pay due for this week won't be paid until the following Monday (1/4/Y3). Therefore, Ross has a liability for four days' accrued salaries at 12/31/Y2 (4/5 × $80,000 = $64,000). The entire $25,000 of vacation pay is an accrued liability at 12/31/Y2 because it represents vacation time earned by employees in year 2 but not taken by 12/31/Y2. Therefore, the total accrued salary and vacation pay is $89,000 ($64,000 + $25,000).

92. (c) An employer is required to accrue a liability for employees' rights to receive compensation for future absences, such as vacations, when certain conditions are met. The Statement does **not**, however, specify how such liabilities are to be measured. Since vacation time is paid by Gavin Co. at the salaries in effect when vacations are taken or when employment is terminated, Gavin adjusts its vacation liability and expense to current salary levels. Gavin's year 2 vacation pay expense consists of vacations earned for work in year 2 (adjusted to current rates) of $30,000 plus the amount necessary to adjust its pre-year 2 vacation liability for the 10% salary increase. The amount of this adjustment is equal to 10% of the preexisting liability balance at December 31, year 2 [($35,000 − $20,000) × 10% = $1,500]. Therefore, total vacation pay expense for the period is equal to $31,500 ($30,000 + $1,500).

93. (c) An employer shall accrue a liability for employees' future absences if **all** of the following conditions are met: (1) the employer's obligation relates to employees' service already rendered, (2) the employees' rights vest **or** accumulate, (3) payment of the compensation is probable, and (4) the amount can be reasonably estimated. All of these conditions are met whether Taos Co.'s employees' rights either accumulate or vest.

94. (b) Accrual of a liability for employees' compensation for future absences is required if all of the conditions below are met.

1. Obligation arises from employee services already performed.
2. Obligation arises from rights that vest or accumulate.
3. Payment is probable.
4. Amount can be reasonably estimated.

95. (d) The solutions approach is to set up a T-account for warranty liability.

	Warranty Liability		
Year 1 payments	2,250	9,000	Year 1 exp. (6% × $150,000)
Year 2 payments	7,500	15,000	Year 2 exp. (6% × $250,000)
		14,250	12/31/Y2 liability

Each year warranty expense is estimated at 6% of sales and recorded by debiting the expense account and crediting the liability. As warranty expenditures are made, the liability is debited and cash is credited. Note that the total estimated warranty cost for **both** years (2% + 4% = 6%) is recorded in the year of sale in compliance with the matching principle.

96. (d) The warranty expense of $30 for each machine sold, although it will be incurred over the three-year warranty period, is directly related to the sales revenue as an integral and inseparable part of the sale and recognized at the time of the sale. The warranty costs make their contribution to revenue in the year of sale by making the product more attractive to the customer. Therefore, in accordance with the matching principle, the warranty costs should be expensed when the machines are sold with a corresponding credit to accrued liability. Answers (a) and (b) are incorrect; this is a sales warranty approach in which the warranty is sold separately from the product. The revenue is recognized on the straight-line basis and they are expensed as incurred. Answer (c) is incorrect because this describes a cash basis method.

97. (c) Warranty services can be recorded at the fair value only if the contract can be settled by a third party. Therefore, the fair value is considered the settlement amount of the contract.

98. (a) Case expects 120,000 coupons to be redeemed at a total cost of $.50 per coupon ($.45 + $.05). Therefore, total expected redemptions are $60,000 (120,000 × $.50). By 12/31/Y2, $25,000 has been paid on coupon redemptions, so a liability of $35,000 must be established ($60,000 − $25,000). Note that this liability would include both payments due for the 50,000 coupons on hand, and payments due on coupons to be received within the first thirty days after the expiration date.

99. (c) Dunn records stamp service revenue and provides for the cost of redemptions in the year stamps are sold. Therefore, Dunn's entries are

To record sales of stamps

Cash	4,000,000	
Stamp service revenue		4,000,000

To record cost of redemptions

Liability for stamp reds.	2,750,000	
Inventory		2,750,000

To provide for cost of future redemptions

Cost of redemptions	1,800,000	
Liability for stamp reds.		
(80% × $2,250,000)		1,800,000

The 12/31/Y2 liability balance is $5,050,000 as shown below.

Liability for Stamp Redemptions		
	6,000,000	12/31/Y1
Redemptions 2,750,000	1,800,000	Provision for reds.
	5,050,000	12/31/Y2

100. (c) The asset retirement obligation (ARO) is recorded at its fair value in the period in which it is incurred. Subsequently, it is adjusted for revisions in estimates and the passage of time. The beginning balance in the asset retirement obligation account is $350,000. The fair value of the additional unconditional retirement obligations incurred during the year was $82,000 and increases the ARO. The $23,000 accretion expense is the expense recognized on the ARO due to the passage of time and will increase the ARO. ($350,000 + $82,000 + $23,000 = $455,000).

101. (a) Current assets listed in the trial balance are cash ($550,000), accounts receivable ($1,650,000), and prepaid

taxes ($300,000). However, part of the AR must be reclassified, and income tax expense has not yet been recorded. Included in AR is $500,000 due from a customer, for which $250,000 is collectible in year 3 (2 × $125,000) and $250,000 is collectible in year 4. The portion collectible in year 4 should be reclassified as a noncurrent asset. Revenues ($3,600,000) less expenses ($2,600,000) result in pretax income of $1,000,000. Since the tax rate is 30%, tax expense is $300,000 (30% × $1,000,000). Therefore, an adjustment is necessary to debit **income tax expense** and credit **prepaid taxes** for $300,000. Total current assets, after reclassification and adjustment, are $1,950,000 [answer (a)] as calculated below.

Cash	$ 550,000
AR ($1,650,000 − $250,000)	1,400,000
Prepaid taxes ($300,000 − $300,000)	--
	$1,950,000

102. (c) Before closing entries, retained earnings is $630,000. Year 2 net income is revenues ($3,600,000) less expenses ($2,600,000) and income tax expense [30% × ($3,600,000 − $2,600,000) = $300,000]. After adjusting for income tax expense, net income is $700,000 [$3,600,000 − ($2,600,000 + $300,000)]. After closing entries, 12/31/Y2 retained earnings is $1,330,000 ($630,000 + $700,000). The foreign currency translation adjustment ($430,000) does not affect retained earnings; it is reported as a separate component of stockholders' equity.

103. (a) Current assets are cash and other assets that are expected to be converted into cash, sold, or consumed either in one year, or in the operating cycle, whichever is longer. Generally included in this category are cash, temporary investments, short-term receivables, inventories, and prepaid expenses. In this situation, there are two special items. Cash must be adjusted because checks that were not mailed until July 9 were recorded June 29. To compute the correct June 30 cash balance, this $30,000 of checks must be added back to the cash balance, turning the $10,000 overdraft into a $20,000 positive balance [(− $10,000) + $30,000 = $20,000]. Also, land held for resale ($100,000) must be included in current assets because, like inventory, at June 30 it is expected to be sold for cash within the next year. Therefore, June 30 current assets total $225,000.

Cash	$ 20,000
AR, net	35,000
Inventory	58,000
Prepaid expenses	12,000
Land held for resale	100,000
	$225,000

104. (a) Current liabilities are obligations whose liquidation is reasonably expected to require the use of current assets or the creation of other current liabilities. This means that generally, current liabilities are liabilities due within one year of the balance sheet date. Clearly, accounts payable ($15,000) and dividends payable ($8,000) are current liabilities. Generally, bonds payable are a long-term liability; however, since these bonds are due in year 3, they must be reported as a current liability at 12/31/Y2 ($25,000 fair value less $3,000 discount, or $22,000). Therefore, total current liabilities are $45,000 ($15,000 + $8,000 + $22,000). The notes payable ($20,000) are classified as long-term because they are not due until year 4.

105. (b) The quick (acid-test) ratio is quick assets (cash, temporary investments in marketable equity securities, and net receivables) divided by current liabilities. The quick ratio measures the ability to pay current liabilities from cash and near-cash items. In this case, quick assets total $700,000 ($170,000 + $450,000 + $80,000) and current liabilities total $400,000 ($60,000 + $240,000 + $100,000), resulting in a quick ratio of 1.75 to 1 ($700,000 ÷ $400,000).

106. (d) The formula to compute accounts receivable turnover is

$$\frac{\text{Net credit sales}}{\text{Average accounts receivable}}$$

The average receivable is the sum of the beginning and ending net accounts receivable divided by 2. The year 2 beginning accounts receivable equals the year 1 ending balance in accounts receivable. Average accounts receivable is $425,000 [($450,000 + $400,000) ÷ 2]. Applying the formula, the year 2 accounts receivable turnover is 7.06 times ($3,000,000 ÷ $425,000).

107. (d) Ratios that are useful in assessing a company's ability to meet currently maturing or short-term obligations are referred to as solvency ratios. The acid-test ratio is classified as a solvency ratio, and it measures the ability to pay current liabilities from cash and near-cash items. The acid-test ratio is

$$\frac{\text{Cash + Net receivables + Marketable securities}}{\text{Current liabilities}}$$

The debt to equity ratio is a leverage ratio that measures the relative amount of leverage or debt a company has. The debt to equity ratio is

$$\frac{\text{Total liabilities}}{\text{Common stockholders' equity}}$$

Therefore, answer (d) is correct because the acid-test ratio is useful in assessing a company's ability to meet currently maturing or short-term obligations while the debt to equity ratio is not.

108. (a) The quick (acid-test) ratio measures the ability to pay current liabilities from cash and near-cash items.

$$\text{Quick ratio} = \frac{\text{Cash, Net receivables, Marketable securities}}{\text{Current liabilities}}$$

Fluctuating market prices of short-term investments may adversely affect Belle's quick ratio and creditworthiness. Inventory and available-for-sale investment items do not affect the quick ratio.

109. (a) The solutions approach is to create a numerical example that conforms to the facts given in the question. Assume the following:

$$\text{Current ratio} = \frac{\$900,000}{\$600,000} = 1.5 \text{ to } 1$$

$$\text{Quick ratio} = \frac{\$300,000}{\$600,000} = .5 \text{ to } 1$$

Payments of accounts payable decrease both cash (a current and quick asset) and accounts payable (a current liability). After payment the following

$$\text{Current ratio} = \frac{900 - 200}{600 - 200} = \frac{700}{400} = 1.75 \text{ to } 1$$

$$\text{Quick ratio} = \frac{300 - 200}{600 - 200} = \frac{100}{400} = .25 \text{ to } 1$$

Subtracting equal amounts from the numerator and the denominator of a ratio **greater than one** will **increase** the ratio. Subtracting equal amounts from the numerator and the denominator of a ratio **less than one** will **decrease** the ratio. Therefore, the current ratio will increase while the quick ratio decreases.

110. (b) The formula to compute the current ratio is

$$\text{Current ratio} = \frac{\text{Current assets}}{\text{Current liabilities}}$$

The write-off of inventory would decrease current assets and the current ratio. The formula to compute the acid-test (quick) ratio is

$$\text{Acid-test ratio} = \frac{\text{Cash, Net receivables, Marketable securities}}{\text{Current liabilities}}$$

The write-off of inventory has no effect on the acid-test ratio.

111. (d) The number of days in the operating cycle measures the length of time from purchase of inventory to collection of cash. The formula is

$$\left(\begin{array}{c}\text{Number of days'}\\\text{sales in inventories}\end{array}\right) + \left(\begin{array}{c}\text{Number of days' sales}\\\text{in accts. receivable}\end{array}\right) = \left(\begin{array}{c}\text{Number of days in}\\\text{operating cycle}\end{array}\right)$$

$$61 \text{ days} \quad + \quad 33 \text{ days} \quad = \quad \underline{94 \text{ days}}$$

Note that the number of days' sales in inventories measures the number of days from the purchase of inventory to the sale of inventory, while the number of days' sales in accounts receivable measures the number of days from the sale of inventory to the collection of cash.

112. (b) Collection of a receivable results in an increase in cash and a decrease in the accounts receivable balance. The accounts receivable turnover ratio is computed by dividing net credit sales by the average net accounts receivable balance. Collection of a receivable reduces the average net accounts receivable balance. Thus the receivable turnover ratio increases. Since this transaction does not affect cost of goods sold or inventory, the inventory turnover ratio is unaffected. Neither the current ratio nor the quick ratio is affected by the collection; neither current assets nor quick assets would change as a result of the collection.

113. (c) The requirement is to identify how the estimated loss should be disclosed in the financial statements. Answer (c) is correct because IFRS defines a provision as a liability that is uncertain in timing or amount. Provisions are made for estimated liabilities and recorded as a loss in earnings for the period if the outcome is probable and measurable. Answer (a) is incorrect because the loss should be recorded in the current period income statement. Answer (b) is incorrect because under IFRS, a contingency depends on some future uncertainty or event, it is not probable that an outflow will be required to settle, or the amount cannot be measured with reliability. If an item qualifies as a contingency, it is disclosed in the notes to the financial statements. Answer (d) is incorrect because contingencies are disclosed in the footnotes.

114. (c) The requirement is to identify how Roland should report the land. Answer (c) is correct because IFRS provides that a contingent asset is a possible asset that arises from past events, and is confirmed only by the occurrence of uncertain future events that are not within the control of the reporting entity. A contingent asset is not recognized, but it is disclosed in the notes to the financial statements if the economic benefits are probable. Answer (a) is incorrect because it does not meet the definition of an asset. Answers (b) and (d) are incorrect because contingent assets are not recognized in the balance sheet.

115. (b) The requirement is to identify the response to a violation of a loan covenant on a long-term debt under IFRS. Answer (b) is correct because the debt must be reclassified as current.

116. (d) The requirement is to identify the account that would not be considered a "provision." Answer (d) is correct because provisions are accounts that are uncertain as to amount or timing. They involve estimated amounts, such as warranty liabilities, bad debts, and taxes. A note payable is not uncertain as to amount or timing.

117. (b) The requirement is to identify the description of a contingency under IFRS. Answer (b) is correct because a contingency is described as an event which is not recognized in the financial statements because it is not probable that an outflow will be required or the amount cannot be reasonably estimated.

Simulations

Task-Based Simulation 1

Concepts		
	Authoritative Literature	Help

Chester Company has transactions involving current assets and current liabilities. Complete the various components of the simulation for Chester. Determine whether each statement is True or False.

		True	False
1.	The balance in "factor's holdback" (due from factor) is reported as an expense of the period.	○	○
2.	In a specific assignment of receivables, collections on the assigned accounts are generally remitted to the assignor.	○	○
3.	Factors are banks or finance companies that purchase receivables for a fee and then collect the remittances directly from the selling company.	○	○
4.	A transfer of receivables with recourse may be accounted for as a sale, provided the transferee can require the transferor to repurchase the receivables.	○	○
5.	In a transfer of receivables with recourse accounted for as a borrowing, the difference between the receivables and the total of the factor's holdback plus the proceeds is a financing cost that should be amortized to interest expense over the term of the receivables.	○	○

Task-Based Simulation 2

Journal Entries		
	Authoritative Literature	Help

Lake Company has the following items relating to the transfer of accounts and notes receivable. For each item, match the transaction with the appropriate journal entry. Entries may be used once, more than once, or not at all.

Journal entries

A. Cash   xxx
   Interest expense   xxx
      Liability on discounted NR   xxx
      Interest revenue   xxx

D. Cash   xxx
   Factor's holdback   xxx
   Loss on sale of AR   xxx
      AR   xxx

B. Cash   xxx
   Factor's holdback   xxx
   Interest expense (discount)   xxx
      Liability on transferred AR   xxx

E. Parenthetical or note disclosure only.

C. Cash   xxx
   Finance charge   xxx
   AR assigned   xxx
      Note payable   xxx
      AR   xxx

F. Cash   xxx
   Loss on sale of NR   xxx
      NR   xxx
      Interest revenue   xxx

		(A)	(B)	(C)	(D)	(E)	(F)
1.	Lake transfers receivables by surrendering control. Collection is to be made by the purchaser (factor), who assumes risk of loss.	○	○	○	○	○	○
2.	Lake specifically assigns a portion of its receivables as collateral for a loan. Collections from the assigned receivables will be used to repay the loan and interest.	○	○	○	○	○	○
3.	Lake pledges its receivables as collateral to secure a loan and the debtor collects the proceeds.	○	○	○	○	○	○
4.	Lake sells accounts receivable to a factor in a transaction considered a borrowing.	○	○	○	○	○	○
5.	Lake transfers a note receivable by surrendering control over it. The transfer was on a without recourse basis.	○	○	○	○	○	○
6.	Lake pledges its accounts receivable as security for a loan.	○	○	○	○	○	○

Task-Based Simulation 3

Reporting Requirements		
	Authoritative Literature	
		Help

Items 1 through 6 are based on the following:

Lorn Company is preparing its financial statements for the year ended December 31, year 2.

Items 1 through 6 represent various commitments and contingencies of Lorn at December 31, year 2, and events subsequent to December 31, year 2, but prior to the issuance of the year 2 financial statements. For each item, select from the following list the reporting requirement. A reporting requirement may be selected once, more than once, or not at all.

Reporting requirement

D. Disclosure only   B. Both accrual and disclosure
A. Accrual only   N. Neither accrual nor disclosure

		(D)	(A)	(B)	(N)
1.	On December 1, year 2, Lorn was awarded damages of $75,000 in a patent infringement suit it brought against a competitor. The defendant did not appeal the verdict, and payment was received in January year 3.	O	O	O	O
2.	A former employee of Lorn has brought a wrongful-dismissal suit against Lorn. Lorn's lawyers believe the suit to be without merit.	O	O	O	O
3.	At December 31, year 2, Lorn had outstanding purchase orders in the ordinary course of business for purchase of a raw material to be used in its manufacturing process. The market price is currently higher than the purchase price and is not anticipated to change within the next year.	O	O	O	O
4.	A government contract completed during year 2 is subject to renegotiation. Although Lorn estimates that it is reasonably possible that a refund of approximately $200,000 – $300,000 may be required by the government, it does not wish to publicize this possibility.	O	O	O	O
5.	Lorn has been notified by a governmental agency that it will be held responsible for the cleanup of toxic materials at a site where Lorn formerly conducted operations. Lorn estimates that it is probable that its share of remedial action will be approximately $500,000.	O	O	O	O
6.	On January 5, year 3, Lorn redeemed its outstanding bonds and issued new bonds with a lower rate of interest. The reacquisition price was in excess of the carrying amount of the bonds.	O	O	O	O

Task-Based Simulation 4

Research		
	Authoritative Literature	
		Help

Sarah Young, the partner on the audit of Lee Company, has asked you to perform some research. Lee company intends to refinance a short-term note with a long-term note due in 5 years. Sarah wants to know the criteria to reclassify the short-term debt as long-term. Place the citation for the excerpt from professional standards that provides this information in the answer box below.

Task-Based Simulation 5

Concepts		
	Authoritative Literature	
		Help

Identify which of the following items are disclosed as cash or cash equivalents on the balance sheet.

		Cash	Not cash
1.	Checking accounts	O	O
2.	Treasury stock	O	O
3.	Treasury bills	O	O
4.	Money market funds	O	O

	Cash	Not cash
5. Petty cash	○	○
6. Trading securities	○	○
7. Savings accounts	○	○
8. Sinking fund cash	○	○
9. Compensating balances against long-term borrowings	○	○
10. Cash restricted for new building	○	○
11. Postdated checks for customers	○	○
12. Available-for-sale securities	○	○

Task-Based Simulation 6

Uncollectible Accounts		
	Authoritative Literature	Help

Situation

Sigma Co. began operations on January 1, year 1. On December 31, year 1, Sigma provided for uncollectible accounts based on 1% of annual credit sales. On January 1, year 2, Sigma changed its method of determining its allowance for uncollectible accounts by applying certain percentages to the accounts receivable aging as follows:

Days past invoice date	Percent deemed to be uncollectible
0–30	1
31–90	5
91–180	20
Over 180	80

In addition, Sigma wrote off all accounts receivable that were over one year old. The following additional information relates to the years ended December 31, year 2, and year 1:

	Year 2	Year 1
Credit sales	$3,000,000	$2,800,000
Collections	2,915,000	2,400,000
Accounts written off	27,000	None
Recovery of accounts previously written off	7,000	None
Days past invoice date at 12/31		
0–30	300,000	250,000
31–90	80,000	90,000
91–180	60,000	45,000
Over 180	25,000	15,000

Complete the following schedules showing the calculation of the allowance for uncollectible accounts at December 31, year 2 and the calculation for uncollectible accounts expense for year 2.

Sigma Company
SCHEDULE OF CALCULATION OF ALLOWANCE FOR UNCOLLECTIBLE ACCOUNTS
December 31, Year 2

	Amounts of accounts receivable	Percentage of uncollectible accounts	Estimate of uncollectible accounts
0 to 30 days			
31 to 90 days			
91 to 180 days			
Over 180 days			
Total accounts receivable			
Total allowance for uncollectible accounts			

Schedule of Uncollectible Accounts Expense

Balance December 31, year 1	
Write-offs during year 2	
Recoveries during year 2	
Balance before year 2 provision	
Required allowance at December 31, year 2	
Year 2 Provision	

Task-Based Simulation 7

Journal Entries		
	Authoritative Literature	Help

Situation

Sigma Corp. has the following information regarding its allowance for uncollectible accounts.

Allowance for Uncollectible Accounts and Provision for Uncollectible Accounts

Balance December 31, year 1	$ 28,000
Write-offs during year 2	(27,000)
Recoveries during year 2	7,000
Balance before year 2 provision	8,000
Required allowance at December 31, year 2	39,000
Year 2 Provision	$ 31,000

Prepare the journal entries for the write-offs and recoveries for year 2, and for the provision for uncollectible accounts expense at December 31, year 2.

Write-offs

Recoveries

Uncollectible accounts expense at December 31, year 2

Task-Based Simulation 8

Transfer of Receivables		
	Authoritative Literature	Help

Jarvis enters into an agreement with First Finance Corporation to sell a group of receivables without recourse. The total face value of the receivables is $150,000. First Finance Corp. will charge 15% interest on the weighted-average time to maturity of the receivables of 45 days plus a 2% fee.

Prepare the journal entry to record the transfer of the receivables.

Task-Based Simulation 9

Research		
	Authoritative Literature	**Help**

    Tammy Yee, the partner on the audit of Huber Corporation, has asked you to perform some research. The company has factored some accounts receivable. Tammy wants to know the criteria to determine when control has been surrendered in a transfer of receivables. Place the citation for the excerpt from professional standards that provides this information in the answer box below.

Solutions to Simulations

Task-Based Simulation 1

Concepts		
	Authoritative Literature	**Help**

	True	False
1. The balance in "factor's holdback" (due from factor) is reported as an expense of the period.	○	●
2. In a specific assignment of receivables, collections on the assigned accounts are generally remitted to the assignor.	●	○
3. Factors are banks or finance companies that purchase receivables for a fee and then collect the remittances directly from the selling company.	○	●
4. A transfer of receivables with recourse may be accounted for as a sale, provided the transferee can require the transferor to repurchase the receivables.	○	●
5. In a transfer of receivables with recourse accounted for as a borrowing, the difference between the receivables and the total of the factor's holdback plus the proceeds is a financing cost that should be amortized to interest expense over the term of the receivables.	●	○

Explanations

1. **(F)** "Factor's holdback" accounts for the proceeds retained by the factor to cover estimated sales discounts, sales returns, and sales allowances. When all amounts have been collected by the factor, the balance in factor's margin is returned to the seller. Therefore, this account is a receivable reported as a current asset on the balance sheet.

2. **(T)** A specific assignment of receivables bestows more formal rights upon the assignee (lender) in that the AR do not simply collateralize the loan, but collections on the assigned accounts are actually remitted to the assignor who remits them to the assignee (lender).

3. **(F)** Once a company sells receivables to a factor it normally has no further involvement with the receivables. The factor usually collects the remittances directly from the **customer**.

4. **(F)** Transfers of receivables in which the transferee can require the transferor to repurchase the receivables may not be considered a sale.

5. **(T)** The difference between the amount of receivables sold to a factor in a borrowing transaction and the total of the factor's holdback plus the proceeds is recorded in a "Discount on Transferred AR" or interest expense account. This account represents interest cost and should be recognized over the term of the receivables. If interest expense is debited, an adjusting entry to defer some of the interest as "Discount" would be required if some of the discount pertains to a later period.

Task-Based Simulation 2

Journal Entries		
	Authoritative Literature	**Help**

	(A)	(B)	(C)	(D)	(E)	(F)
1. Lake transfers receivables by surrendering control. Collection is to be made by the purchaser (factor), who assumes risk of loss.	○	○	○	●	○	○
2. Lake specifically assigns a portion of its receivables as collateral for a loan. Collections from the assigned receivables will be used to repay the loan and interest.	○	○	●	○	○	○
3. Lake pledges its receivables as collateral to secure a loan and the debtor collects the proceeds.	○	○	○	○	●	○
4. Lake sells accounts receivable to a factor in a transaction considered a borrowing.	○	●	○	○	○	○
5. Lake transfers a note receivable by surrendering control over it. The transfer was on a without recourse basis.	○	○	○	○	○	●
6. Lake pledges its accounts receivable as security for a loan.	○	○	○	○	●	○

Explanations

1. **(D)** In this transaction, receivables are factored by surrendering control and without recourse. This constitutes an outright sale of the receivables in that title, risk of loss, and rights to future benefits are all transferred. Therefore, a loss on the transaction is recognized.

2. **(C)** In a specific assignment of receivables, AR assigned are identified by placing them in an AR assigned account. A finance charge is assessed on assignment transactions that are borrowings.

3. **(E)** When AR are pledged, the receivables serve as collateral for a loan but the proceeds are not remitted to the lender. In this case, the amount of AR pledged is reported at the balance sheet date either parenthetically or in the notes.

4. **(B)** In this transaction, considered a borrowing, receivables are considered to be factored with recourse. Thus, the transaction is viewed as a loan collateralized by AR and the amount of the proceeds plus the factor's holdback and interest charged should be reported as a liability.

5. **(F)** A note discounted on which control is surrendered and the terms include without recourse is considered a sales transaction upon which a loss should be recognized. Notes receivable should be credited.

6. **(E)** A general assignment of receivables is another term for pledging AR, and thus should be disclosed parenthetically or in the notes to the financial statements (no journal entry).

Task-Based Simulation 3

Reporting Requirements		
	Authoritative Literature	Help

	(D)	(A)	(B)	(N)
1. On December 1, year 2, Lorn was awarded damages of $75,000 in a patent infringement suit it brought against a competitor. The defendant did not appeal the verdict, and payment was received in January year 3.	○	○	●	○
2. A former employee of Lorn has brought a wrongful-dismissal suit against Lorn. Lorn's lawyers believe the suit to be without merit.	○	○	○	●
3. At December 31, year 2, Lorn had outstanding purchase orders in the ordinary course of business for purchase of a raw material to be used in its manufacturing process. The market price is currently higher than the purchase price and is not anticipated to change within the next year.	○	○	○	●
4. A government contract completed during year 2 is subject to renegotiation. Although Lorn estimates that it is reasonably possible that a refund of approximately $200,000 – $300,000 may be required by the government, it does not wish to publicize this possibility.	●	○	○	○
5. Lorn has been notified by a governmental agency that it will be held responsible for the cleanup of toxic materials at a site where Lorn formerly conducted operations. Lorn estimates that it is probable that its share of remedial action will be approximately $500,000.	○	○	●	○
6. On January 5, year 3, Lorn redeemed its outstanding bonds and issued new bonds with a lower rate of interest. The reacquisition price was in excess of the carrying amount of the bonds.	●	○	○	○

Explanations

1. **(B)** Contingencies that might result in gains usually are not reflected in the accounts since to do so might be to recognize revenue prior to its realization. Since this gain contingency was resolved before the issuance of the financial statements, it is handled similar to an ordinary transaction that occurred prior to the year-end and is accrued in the year of its occurrence.

　　However, disclosure of the contingencies that might result in gains is made in the notes to financial statements.

2. **(N)** To accrue an estimated loss from a loss contingency it is necessary that it is probable that an asset has been impaired or a liability has been incurred and that the amount of loss can be reasonably estimated. Since Lorn's lawyers believe the suit to be without merit, neither condition has been met.

　　Disclosure is also required of some loss contingencies that do not meet the accrual requirements if there is a **reasonable possibility** that a loss may be incurred. Again, this condition has not been met.

3. **(N)** The conditions described in this question would be considered general or unspecified business risks that do not meet the conditions for accrual or disclosure.

4. **(D)** The words "reasonably possible" require the disclosure of this item. No accrual need be made since the question does not state it is **probable** that an asset has been impaired or a liability incurred and that the amount of loss can be reasonably estimated.

5. (B) The word "probable" and the inclusion of the estimated amount of $500,000 mean that this situation meets the criteria of (1) a probable incurrence of a liability and (2) a reasonable estimate of an amount.

6. (D) Disclosure is made for commitments such as an obligation to reduce debts. Since the entire transaction took place in the next accounting period it does not meet the conditions for an accrual in the current period even though it would be disclosed in a footnote.

Task-Based Simulation 4

Research		
	Authoritative Literature	Help

ASC	470	10	45	14

Task-Based Simulation 5

Concepts		
	Authoritative Literature	Help

		Cash	Not Cash
1.	Checking accounts	●	○
2.	Treasury stock	○	●
3.	Treasury bills	●	○
4.	Money market funds	●	○
5.	Petty cash	●	○
6.	Trading securities	○	●
7.	Savings accounts	●	○
8.	Sinking fund cash	○	●
9.	Compensating balances against long-term borrowings	○	●
10.	Cash restricted for new building	○	●
11.	Postdated checks for customers	○	●
12.	Available-for-sale securities	○	●

Task-Based Simulation 6

Uncollectible Accounts		
	Authoritative Literature	Help

Schedule to calculate allowance for uncollectible accounts

Sigma Company
SCHEDULE OF CALCULATION OF ALLOWANCE FOR UNCOLLECTIBLE ACCOUNTS
December 31, Year 2

	Amounts of accounts receivable	Percentage of uncollectible accounts	Estimate of uncollectible accounts
0 to 30 days	$300,000	× 1%	$ 3,000
31 to 90 days	80,000	× 5%	4,000
91 to 180 days	60,000	× 20%	12,000
Over 180 days	25,000	× 80%	20,000
Total accounts receivable	$465,000		
Total allowance for un-collectible accounts			$39,000

Explanations

1. This problem consists of two related parts: part a. requires a calculation of the allowance for uncollectible accounts at 12/31/Y2 using an aging approach, and part b. requires a computation of the year 2 provision for uncollectible accounts (uncollectible accounts expense). The solutions approach is to quickly review the basics of accounting for uncollectible accounts, visualize the solution format, and begin. Some candidates may benefit from preparation of T-accounts (see item 4. below).

2. When using the aging approach, the **total** uncollectible accounts (in other words, the required ending balance in the allowance account) is estimated by applying a different percentage to the various age categories. The percentage increases as the age of the receivables increases because the older a receivable is, the less likely is its ultimate collection.

2.1 In this case, Sigma estimates that 1% of its receivables in the zero-thirty days age category will prove to be uncollectible. Therefore, of that $300,000 of accounts receivable, it is estimated that $3,000 (1% × $300,000) will be uncollectible. Similar computations are performed for the other age categories, resulting in an estimate that $39,000 of the $465,000 accounts receivable will prove to be uncollectible. This is the required 12/31/Y2 balance in the allowance account.

3. When using the aging approach, the first step is to compute the required ending balance in the allowance account (as discussed in items 2. and 2.1 above). The second step is to compute the uncollectible accounts expense necessary to bring the **unadjusted** allowance balance up to the **required** allowance balance.

3.1 The only item affecting the allowance account in year 1 was the recording of uncollectible accounts expense of $28,000 (1% × $2,800,000 credit sales). Therefore, the 1/1/Y2 balance in this account is $28,000. No adjustment is necessary for the change in the method of estimating this expense (from percent of sales to aging schedule) because any such change is handled prospectively.

> **NOTE:** Using the aging percents given also results in a $28,000 balance at 1/1/Y2. Even if the result was different, though, no adjustment is necessary.

3.2 During year 2, this $28,000 credit balance was decreased by write-offs of $27,000 (debit allowance, credit AR) and increased by $7,000 of recoveries (debit AR, credit allowance; and debit cash, credit AR). Therefore, the 12/31/Y2 balance in the allowance account, before adjustment, is $8,000 ($28,000 − $27,000 + $7,000).

3.3 To increase the allowance account from $8,000 (see 3.2 above) to $39,000 (see 2.1 above), a provision for uncollectible accounts (uncollectible accounts expense) of $31,000 must be recorded for year 2.

4. Some candidates may benefit from the preparation of T-accounts for the allowance account and accounts receivable. These T-accounts are provided below.

T-accounts for year 1

```
                    AR
Sales    2,800,000  | 2,400,000  Collections

12/31/Y1   400,000  |

                 Allowance
                    |  28,000    Provision
                    |  28,000    12/31/Y1
```

Computation of year 2 provision

Balance December 31, year 1	$ 28,000
Write-offs during year 2	(27,000)
Recoveries during year 2	7,000
Balance before year 2 provision	8,000
Required allowance at December 31, year 2	39,000
Year 2 Provision	$ 31,000

Task-Based Simulation 7

Journal Entries		
	Authoritative Literature	Help

Write-offs

Allowance for uncollectible accounts	27,000	
Accounts receivable		27,000

Recoveries

Accounts receivable	7,000	
Allowance for uncollectible accounts		7,000

To reinstate the account receivable

Cash	7,000	
Accounts receivable		7,000

To show payment on the account

Uncollectible accounts expense at December 31, year 2

Uncollectible accounts expense	31,000	
Allowance for uncollectible accounts		31,000

Task-Based Simulation 8

Transfer of Receivables		
	Authoritative Literature	Help

Cash	144,226	
Interest expense (150,000 × .15 × 45/365)	2,774	
Factoring fee (2% × 150,000)	3,000	
Accounts receivable		150,000

Task-Based Simulation 9

Research		
	Authoritative Literature	Help

ASC	860	10	40	5

Module 13: Present Value

Overview

This module begins by reviewing the basic concepts related to time value of money such as present and future value. The module then covers four major topics in which time value of money applications are used extensively:

1. **Bonds** payable and bond investments including initial accounting, sales, conversions, warrants, and extinguishments.
2. **Debt** restructure including settlement, modification of terms, and impairment.
3. **Pensions** including defined contribution plans, defined benefit plans, and other post employment benefits.
4. **Leases** including operating leases and capital leases for both lessees and lessor.

All of these topics are tested on the Financial Accounting and Reporting section of the exam to varying degrees.

A. Fundamentals

The concepts of time value of money are essential for successful completion of the CPA exam. Time value of money concepts are central to capital budgeting, leases, pensions, bonds, and other topics. You must understand the mechanics as well as the concepts. After studying the next few pages, work the multiple-choice questions entitled "Fundamentals." Note that the following abbreviations are used in the text that follows.

$$i = \text{interest rate}$$

$$n = \text{number of periods or rents}$$

On the CPA exam, you do not have to know the complex formulas that are used to compute time value of money factors (TVMF). The factors will be given to you or enough information will be given to you so that you can easily compute them (see section A.8. TVMF Applications). Your main focus of attention should be centered on under-standing which TVMF should be used in a given situation.

1. **Future Value (FV) of an Amount** (future value of $1)

   a. The future value of an amount is the amount that will be available at some point in the future if an amount is deposited today and earns compound interest for "n" periods.

      (1) The most common application is savings deposits.

      > **EXAMPLE**
      >
      > If you deposited $100 today at 10%, you would have $110 [$100 + ($100 × 10%)] at the end of the first year, $121[$100 + ($110 × 10%)] at the end of the second year, etc. The compounding feature allows you to earn interest on interest. In the second year of the example you earn $11 interest: $10 on the original $100 and $1 on the first year's interest of $10.

2. **Present Value (PV) of a Future Amount** (present value of $1)

   a. The present value of a future amount is the amount you would pay now for an amount to be received "n" periods in the future given an interest rate of "i."

      (1) A common application would be the money you would lend today for a noninterest-bearing note receivable in the future.

      > **EXAMPLE**
      >
      > If you were lending money at 10%, you would lend $100 for a $110 note due in one year or for a $121 note due in two years.

   b. The present value of $1 is the inverse of the future value of $1. Thus, given a future value of $1 table, you have a present value of $1 by dividing each value into 1.00.

      > **EXAMPLE**
      >
      > Look at the present value of $1 and future value of $1 tables on the next page. The future value of $1 at 10% in five years is 1.611. Thus, the present value of $1 in five years would be 1.00 ÷ 1.611 which is .621 (check the table). Conversely, the future value of $1 is found by dividing the present value of $1 into 1.00, that is, 1.00 ÷ .621 = 1.611.

3. **Compounding**

   a. When interest is compounded more than once a year, two extra steps are needed.

      (1) First, **multiply** "n" by the number of times interest is compounded annually. This will give you the total number of interest periods.
      (2) Second, **divide** "i" by the number of times interest is compounded annually. This will give you the appropriate interest rate for each interest period.

      > **EXAMPLE**
      >
      > If the 10% was compounded semiannually, the amount of $100 at the end of one year would be $110.25 [$(1.05)^2$] instead of $110.00. The extra $.25 is 5% of the $5.00 interest earned in the first half of the year.

4. **Future Value of an Ordinary Annuity**

   a. The **future value of an ordinary annuity** is the amount available "n" periods in the future as a result of the deposit of an amount (A) at the end of every period "1" through "n."
   b. Compound interest is earned at the rate of "i" on the deposits.

      (1) A common application is a bond sinking fund. A deposit is made at the end of the first period and earns compound interest for n-1 periods (not during the first period, because the deposit is made at the end of the first period). The next to the last payment earns one period's interest, that is, n – (n-1) = 1. The last payment earns no interest, because it is deposited at the end of the last (nth) period.

NOTE: In the FUTURE AMOUNT OF AN ORDINARY ANNUITY TABLE, all of the factors for any "n" row are based on one less interest period than the number of payments.

TIME VALUE OF MONEY FACTOR (TVMF) TABLES

Future Value (Amount) of $1

n	6%	8%	10%	12%	15%
1	1.060	1.080	1.100	1.120	1.150
2	1.124	1.166	1.210	1.254	1.323
3	1.191	1.260	1.331	1.405	1.521
4	1.262	1.360	1.464	1.574	1.749
5	1.338	1.469	1.611	1.762	2.011

Present Value of $1

n	6%	8%	10%	12%	15%
1	.943	.926	.909	.893	.870
2	.890	.857	.826	.797	.756
3	.840	.794	.751	.712	.658
4	.792	.735	.683	.636	.572
5	.747	.681	.621	.567	.497

Future Value (Amount) of an Ordinary Annuity of $1

n	6%	8%	10%	12%	15%
1	1.000	1.000	1.000	1.000	1.000
2	2.060	2.080	2.100	2.120	2.150
3	3.184	3.246	3.310	3.374	3.473
4	4.375	4.506	4.506	4.641	4.993
5	5.637	5.867	6.105	6.353	6.742

Present Value of an Ordinary Annuity of $1

n	6%	8%	10%	12%	15%
1	.943	.926	.909	.893	.870
2	1.833	1.783	1.736	1.690	1.626
3	2.673	2.577	2.487	2.402	2.283
4	3.465	3.312	3.170	3.037	2.855
5	4.212	3.993	3.791	3.605	3.352

5. **Present Value of an Ordinary Annuity**

   a. The present value of an ordinary annuity is the value today, given a discount rate, of a series of future payments.

   (1) A common application is the capitalization of lease payments by either lessors or lessees. Payments "1" through "n" are assumed to be made at the end of years "1" through "n," and are discounted back to the present.

EXAMPLE

Assume a five-year lease of equipment requiring payments of $1,000 at the end of each of the five years, which is to be capitalized. If the discount rate is 10%, the present value is $3,791 ($1,000 × 3.791).

The behavior of the present value of the lease payment stream over the five-year period is shown below. Note that the liability (principal amount) grows by interest in the amount of 10% during each period and decreases by $1,000 at the end of each period.

1	2	3	4	5

$3,791 + 380 Int. = $4,171
            − 1,000 Payment
            $3,171 + 320 Int. = $3,491
                     − 1,000 Payment
                     $2,491 + 250 Int. = $2,741
                               − 1,000 Payment
                               $1,741 + 170 Int. = $1,911
                                       − 1,000 Payment
                                       $ 911 + 91 Int. = $1,002 Payment
                                             − 1,000
                                               2*

* Due to rounding

6. **Distinguishing a Future Value of an Annuity from a Present Value of an Annuity**

    a. Sometimes confusion arises in distinguishing between the future value (amount) of an annuity and the present value of an annuity. These two may be distinguished by determining whether the total dollar amount in the problem comes at the beginning (e.g., cost of equipment acquired for leasing) or at the end (e.g., the amount needed to retire bonds) of the series of payments as illustrated as follows.

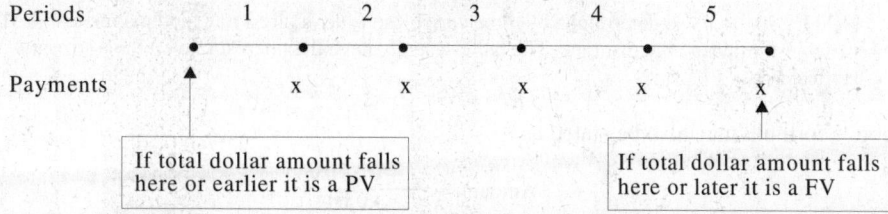

> **NOTE:** If the total amount comes at the end of the series of payments, it is a **future value** of annuity situation. If the total amount comes at the beginning of the series of payments, it is a **present value** of annuity situation. The total dollar amount may be given in the problem or you may have to compute it; either way, it makes no difference in determining whether a problem involves a present value or future value situation.

> **NOTE:** Some students feel the need to "convert" all time value of money problems into either present value or future value problems, depending on which they're most comfortable with. This process involves more work and more chance for errors, because an additional TVMF equation must be solved in the conversion. This is inefficient, and unnecessary if you are able to correctly identify between the two initially. Become proficient at determining present value and future value situations, so that you may efficiently select the correct TVMF from the corresponding table. Drawing a timeline for the facts in each problem will help you determine if you need to solve for a present value or a future value.

7. **Annuities Due**

    a. In some cases, the payments or annuities may not conform to the assumptions inherent in the annuity tables. For example, the payments might be made at the beginning of each of the five years instead of at the end of each year. This is an annuity due (annuity in advance) in contrast to an ordinary annuity (annuity in arrears). Both annuity due and ordinary annuity payments are represented by the "x's" in the illustration below.

Periods	1	2	3	4	5
Annuity	x	x	x	x	x
Annuity Due	x	x	x	x	x

> **EXAMPLE**
>
> If the payments in the 5-period lease example presented previously were made at the beginning of the period, the present value of the first payment which is made today is $1,000 (i.e., the TVMF is 1.00). The remaining 4 payments comprise an ordinary annuity for 4 periods as you can see on the above diagram. Always use time diagrams to analyze application of annuities.

    b. To convert either a future value of an ordinary annuity or the present value of an ordinary annuity factor to an annuity due factor, multiply the ordinary annuity factor times $(1 + i)$.

> **EXAMPLE**
>
> For the above lease example, you would find the present value of an ordinary annuity factor for n = 5 which is 3.993. Then multiply 3.993 by 1.08 to arrive at the annuity due factor, 4.312. The present value of the payments would be $4,312 (4.312 × $1,000).

> **NOTE:** The present value of the annuity due in the above example is $319 greater than the present value of the ordinary annuity because the payments are moved closer to the present.

8. **TVMF Applications**

a. The basic formula to use is

$$FV \text{ or } PV = TVMF \times Amount$$

b. If an annuity is involved, the amount is the periodic payment or deposit; if not, it is a single sum.

> **NOTE:** FV or PV is determined by three variables: time, interest rate, and payment. TVMF represents two variables: time and interest rate. The tables usually have the interest rate on the horizontal axis and time on the vertical axis.

c. The above formula may also be stated as

$$Amount = \frac{FV \text{ or } PV}{TVMF}$$

EXAMPLE

If we need to accumulate $12,210 in five years to repay a loan, we could determine the required annual deposit with the above formula. If the savings rate were 10%, we would divide the FV ($12,210) by the TVMF of the future value of annuity, n=5, i=.10 (6.105) and get $2,000. Thus, $2,000 deposited at the end of each of five years earning 10% will result in $12,210. This formula may also be used to find future values of an amount, present values of amounts, and annuities in the same manner.

Another variation of the formula is

$$TVMF = \frac{FV \text{ or } PV}{Amount}$$

EXAMPLE

We may be offered a choice between paying $3,312 in cash or $1,000 a year at the end of each of the next four years. We determine the interest rate by dividing the annual payment into the present value of the annuity to obtain the TVMF (3.312) for n=4. We then find the interest rate which has the same or similar TVMF (in this case 8%). Alternatively, using the above formula, we may know the interest rate but not know the number of payments. Given the TVMF, we can determine "n" by looking in the TVMF table under the known interest rate. Remember the TVMF reflects two variables: time and interest rate.

> **NOW REVIEW MULTIPLE-CHOICE QUESTIONS 1 THROUGH 5**

9. **Notes Receivable and Payable**

a. This section assumes that the entity does not elect the fair value option for accounting for receivables or payables (see section A.12 "Fair Value Option"). Short-term notes receivable and notes payable that arise from transactions with customers and suppliers in the normal course of business and are due in one year are classified as current liabilities. These short-term notes are recorded at their maturity value.

b. Notes receivable and notes payable due in more than one year (long-term notes) should be recorded at their present values. Upon receipt or issuance of a long-term note, record the net value of the note receivable or payable (i.e., note plus or minus premium or discount) at

   (1) Cash received or paid

      (a) Assumes no other rights or privileges

   (2) Established exchange price (fair value) or property or services received or provided

      (a) If not determinable, determine present value with imputed interest rate

c. Record interest revenue (on notes receivable) or interest expense (on notes payable) as the effective rate of interest times the net receivable or payable during the period.

d. **Note exchanged for cash only**

(1) When a note is exchanged for cash and no other rights or privileges are exchanged, the present value of the note is equivalent to the cash exchanged.

   (a) The cash exchanged, however, may not be equal to the face amount of the note (the amount paid at maturity).

(2) When the face amount of a note does not equal its present value, the difference is either a discount or a premium.

   (a) A discount results when the face of the note exceeds its present value, and a premium results when the present value of the note exceeds its face (see section B.1. in this module for a more detailed discussion of discounts and premiums).

e. **Note exchanged for cash and unstated rights and privileges**

   (1) In the preceding discussion, notes were issued solely for cash, and no other rights or privileges were exchanged. The accounting treatment differs, however, when a note is issued for cash and unstated rights and/or privileges are also exchanged. The cash exchanged for such a note consists of two elements:

   (a) The present value of the note, and
   (b) The present value of the unstated right or privilege.

   (2) Proper accounting for this situation requires that one of the two present values above be determined. Once this is done, the remaining present value is simply the difference between the face amount of the note and the present value that was determined.

EXAMPLE

On January 1, year 1, Zilch Company borrowed $200,000 from its major customer, Martha Corporation. The borrowing is evidenced by a note payable due in three years. The note is noninterest-bearing. In consideration for the borrowing, Zilch Company agrees to supply Martha Corporation's inventory needs for the loan period at favorable prices. This last feature of the transaction is the unstated right or privilege; that is, the ability of Martha to purchase inventory at less than regular prices.

The present value of the note (assuming it is easier to determine) should be based upon the interest rate Zilch would have to pay in a normal borrowing of $200,000 (i.e., in a transaction that did not include unstated rights or privileges). Assume that Zilch would have to pay interest at 12% in a normal borrowing. The present value of $200,000 discounted for three years at 12% is $142,400 ($200,000 × .712). The difference between the face amount of the note, $200,000, and its present value of $142,400 represents the present value of the unstated right or privilege. The amount of this present value is $57,600.

The entries below show how both Zilch and Martha should account for this transaction during year 1.

Zilch			Martha		
1/1/Y1			**1/1/Y1**		
Cash	142,400		Note receivable	200,000	
Discount on note payable	57,600		Discount on note receivable		57,600
Note payable		200,000	Cash		142,400
Cash	57,600		Advance payments on inventory	57,600	
Deferred revenue		57,600	Cash		57,600
12/31/Y1			**12/31/Y1**		
Interest expense	17,088*		Discount on note receivable	17,088	
Discount on note			Interest income		17,088
payable		17,088			
* $142,400 × .12 = $17,088					
Deferred revenue	xx		Inventory (purchases)	xx	
Sales		xx	Advance payments on		
			inventory		xx

The amounts represented by "xx" in the entries above depend upon the amount of goods acquired by Martha during year 1.

On the December 31, year 1 balance sheets of both Zilch and Martha, the above notes should be disclosed in the noncurrent liability (Zilch) and asset (Martha) sections net of the unamortized discount applicable to each note.

f. **Note exchanged in a noncash transaction**

(1) In addition to notes issued for cash, a note may also be received or issued in a noncash transaction; that is, for goods, property, or services. The problem created in this situation is how to determine the note's present value in the absence of cash.

(a) One way to solve this problem is to assume that the stated rate or contractual rate stated on the note represents a fair rate of return to the supplier for the use of the related funds. If the interest rate is presumed to be fair, then the face amount of the note is presumed to equal its present value. Interest revenue (expense) is computed by multiplying the interest rate stated on the face of the note by the face of the note. There is no discount or premium to consider because the face of the note is assumed to be equal to its present value.

(b) The assumption that the interest rate on the face of the note is fair is not always valid. The assumption is not valid if

1] The interest rate is not stated (usually, this means the note is noninterest-bearing), or
2] The stated rate is unreasonable (this refers to both unreasonably low and high rates), or
3] The stated face amount of the note is materially different from the current cash sales price for the same or similar items, or from the fair value of the note at the date of the transaction.

(c) When the interest rate is not fair, the face amount of the note does not equal its present value. In the absence of cash, the present value of a note is determined according to the following priorities:

1] First, determine if the goods, property, or services exchanged have a reliable fair value. If they do, the fair value is presumed to be the present value of the note.
2] If a reliable fair value does not exist for the goods, property, or services exchanged, then determine if the note has a fair value. If it does, the note's fair value is equal to the present value of the note.
3] Finally, if fair values do not exist for either the goods, property, or services or for the note, then an interest rate must be **imputed**. This imputed interest rate is then used to determine the present value of the note. The imputed interest rate represents the **debtor's** incremental borrowing rate.

EXAMPLE

The situation where the interest rate on a note is not fair, yet the fair value of the property exchanged is known.

Doink Co. sold a building on January 1, year 4, which originally cost $7,000,000 and which had a book value of $4,000,000 for a $14,000,000 (face amount) noninterest-bearing note due in three years. Since zero interest is not considered to be a fair rate of return, the face amount of Doink's note does not equal its present value. In Doink's case, the face of its note is $14,000,000. The present value of the note is the unknown and must be calculated.

To determine the present value of Doink's $14,000,000 noninterest-bearing note, you should first see if the building sold had a reliable fair value at the date it was sold. Assume that Doink's building could have been sold on January 1, year 4, for $10,000,000 in a straight cash transaction. Given the information about the building, its fair value of $10,000,000 on January 1, year 4, represents the note's present value. Since the face of the note is $14,000,000 and its present value is $10,000,000, the $4,000,000 difference represents the discount. Doink should record this transaction in the following manner:

Note receivable	14,000,000	
Accumulated depreciation	3,000,000	
Building		7,000,000
Gain on sale of building		6,000,000
Discount on note receivable		4,000,000

NOTE: It is important that you note how the gain is calculated in the entry above. The gain is the difference between the present value of the note ($10,000,000) and the book value of the property sold ($4,000,000). The difference between the face amount of the note ($14,000,000) and its present value ($10,000,000) represents the discount of $4,000,000. This discount should be amortized to interest income using the effective interest method. However, before this discount can be amortized, the interest rate must be determined. In situations like this, the interest rate can be determined by reference to present value tables. In Doink's situation, the present value of the note, $10,000,000, divided by its face amount, $14,000,000, results in the number .714. This number represents a factor from the present value of $1 table. Since Doink's note is for 3 periods, the factor .712 in the present value of $1 table is under the 12% interest rate. Thus, Doink's interest rate is approximately 12%.

If the building sold by Doink did not have a reliable fair value on January 1, year 4, the next step would be to determine if the note had a fair value on that date.

Finally, if the building sold by Doink did not possess a reliable fair value on January 1, year 4, and the note did not have a fair value on that date, the present value of Doink's note would have to be determined by **imputation**. This means that Doink would determine the present value of its note by reference to the incremental borrowing rate of the company which acquired its building.

(2) The following diagram represents the forementioned relationships and procedures for determining the present value of a note receivable or payable (monetary assets and liabilities) and the amount of a discount/premium.

ACCOUNTING FOR MONETARY ASSETS AND LIABILITIES WHICH HAVE MATURITIES GREATER THAN ONE YEAR FROM THE BALANCE SHEET DATE

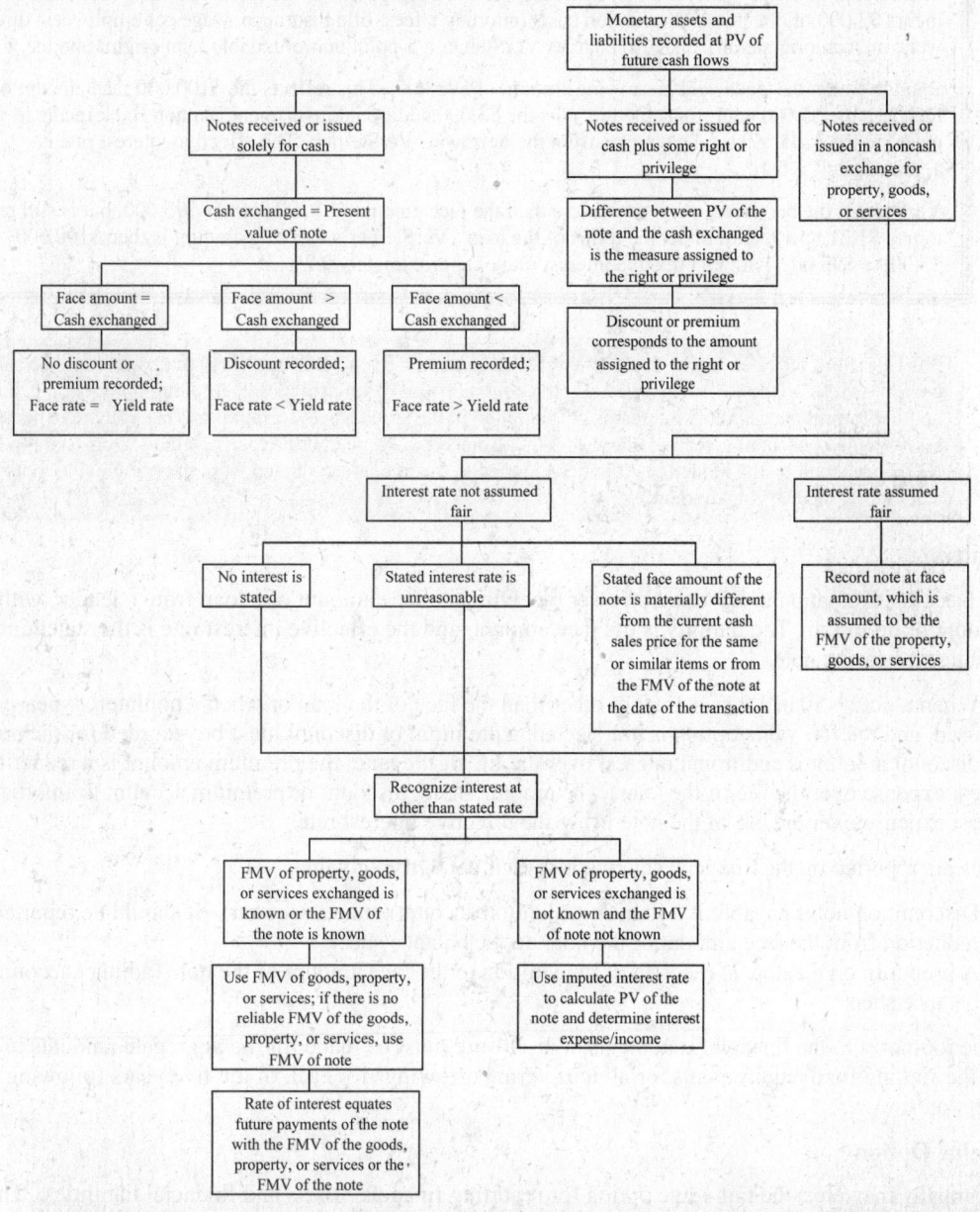

NOW REVIEW MULTIPLE-CHOICE QUESTIONS 6 THROUGH 18

10. **Loan Origination Costs and Fees**

  a. Sometimes the lender incurs various loan origination costs when originating or acquiring a loan. The lender shall defer and recognize these costs over the life of the loan only when the costs relate directly to the loan, and would not have been incurred but for the loan. Otherwise, the costs are considered indirect and are charged to expense as incurred.

  b. Sometimes the lender charges the borrower a nonrefundable loan origination fee. Both lender and borrower shall defer and recognize the nonrefundable fee over the life of the loan. The fee is frequently assessed in the form of points, where a point is 1% of the face amount of the loan.

EXAMPLE

Assume that Bannon Bank grants a ten-year loan to VerSteiner, Inc. in the amount of $100,000 with a stated interest rate of 8%. Payments are due monthly, and are computed to be $1,213. In addition, Bannon Bank incurs $3,000 of direct loan origination costs (attorney's fees, title insurance, wages of employees' direct work on loan origination), and also charges VerSteiner a 5-point nonrefundable loan origination fee.

Bannon Bank, the lender, has a carrying amount of $98,000. This reflects the $100,000 face amount of the loan less the $5,000 nonrefundable fee, plus the $3,000 additional investment Bannon Bank incurs to generate the $145,560 total payments from the borrower, VerSteiner. The effective interest rate is approximately 8.5%.

VerSteiner, the borrower, receives 5% less than the face amount of $100,000, or $95,000, but is still required to pay $1,213 per month under the terms of the loan. VerSteiner's carrying amount is then $100,000 – $5,000 = $95,000, with an effective interest rate of approximately 9.2%.

NOTE: Both the rates can be derived with a financial calculator. It is not likely that you would be asked to compute these on the CPA exam because the computerized exam provides a simple four-function calculator, and the formula to calculate interest is not included in the spreadsheet formulas. What you are expected to know is the concept of effective interest. You also need to know that the loan origination costs are to be added to the principal, by the lender, and any fee charged to the client is deducted from the principal by both parties in calculating the carrying amount.

11. **Disclosures**

  a. The basic loan situation involves a borrower receiving the face amount of a loan from a lender, with no related discount or premium. The liability is the face amount, and the effective interest rate is the stated interest rate on the interest-bearing note.

  (1) When a note is issued for an amount other than the face of the loan or when a noninterest-bearing note is used, and the fair value option is not elected, a premium or discount must be recorded for the note. The discount amount is additional interest over the life of the note; the premium amount is a reduction in interest expense over the life of the loan. The amount in the discount or premium account is amortized to interest expense over the life of the note using the effective interest rate.

  b. Notes are reported on the financial statement at their net carrying value.

  (1) Discount on notes payable is a liability valuation account (contra account). It should be reported as a direct reduction from the face amount of the note on the balance sheet.

  (2) A premium on the note is reported as an addition to the face amount of the note (adjunct account) on the balance sheet.

  c. In the footnotes to the financial statements, a disclosure must be made for the aggregate amounts of maturities and the sinking fund requirements for all long-term borrowings for each of the five years following the balance sheet date.

12. **Fair Value Option**

  a. A company may elect the fair value option for reporting financial assets and financial liabilities. The financial liability is reported at fair value at the end of each reporting period, and the resulting gain or loss is reported in earnings of the period. A company may calculate interest expense in various ways, but must disclose in the notes to the financial statements the method used to determine interest expense.

NOW REVIEW MULTIPLE-CHOICE QUESTIONS 19 THROUGH 25

13. **Research Component—Accounting Standards Codification**

    a. The authoritative literature on payables and receivables is found in several locations in the Codification: Topics 310, 825, and 835. ASC Topic 835 addresses the valuation of the note, determining appropriate interest rates, amortization of discounts and premiums, and financial statement presentation of the discount and premium account.
    b. A list of keywords that may be helpful in your research is shown below.

Determining present value	Indirect costs loan	Note issued
Direct costs loan	Loan origination fees	Note received
Disclosure long-term borrowings	Maturities long-term	Points fees
Effective interest note	Noncash transaction note	Present value note
Exchange price note	Nonrefundable fees loan	

14. **International Financial Reporting Standards (IFRS)**

    a. IAS 23 requires borrowing costs to be capitalized if they meet certain criteria. Borrowing costs must be capitalized if they are related to the acquisition, construction, or production of a qualifying asset.

    (1) A qualifying asset is one that takes a substantial period of time to get ready for its intended use. Qualifying assets include inventory, plant, property, and equipment, intangible assets, or investment property.
    (2) Borrowing costs that do not meet the rules for capitalization are expensed in the current period. Note that finance costs (interest expense) must be disclosed separately in the income statement.

KEY TERMS

Future value. The amount that will be available at some point in the future if an amount is deposited today and earns compound interest for "n" periods.

Future value of an ordinary annuity. The amount available "n" periods in the future as a result of the deposit of an amount (A) at the end of every period "1" through "n."

Present value. The amount you would pay now for an amount to be received "n" periods in the future given an interest rate of "i."

Present value of an ordinary annuity. The value today, given a discount rate, of a series of future payments.

Multiple-Choice Questions (1-25)

A. Fundamentals

1. On March 15, year 1, Ashe Corp. adopted a plan to accumulate $1,000,000 by September 1, year 5. Ashe plans to make four equal annual deposits to a fund that will earn interest at 10% compounded annually. Ashe made the first deposit on September 1, year 1. Future value and future amount factors are as follows:

Future value of $1 at 10% for 4 periods	1.46
Future amount of ordinary annuity of $1 at 10% for four periods	4.64
Future amount of annuity in advance of $1 at 10% for four periods	5.11

Ashe should make four annual deposits (rounded) of
- a. $250,000
- b. $215,500
- c. $195,700
- d. $146,000

2. On July 1, year 1, James Rago signed an agreement to operate as a franchisee of Fast Foods, Inc. for an initial franchise fee of $60,000. Of this amount, $20,000 was paid when the agreement was signed and the balance is payable in four equal annual payments of $10,000 beginning July 1, year 2. The agreement provides that the down payment is not refundable and no future services are required of the franchisor. Rago's credit rating indicates that he can borrow money at 14% for a loan of this type. Information on present and future value factors is as follows:

Present value of $1 at 14% for four periods	0.59
Future amount of $1 at 14% for four periods	1.69
Present value of an ordinary annuity of $1 at 14% for four periods	2.91

Rago should record the acquisition cost of the franchise on July 1, year 1 at
- a. $43,600
- b. $49,100
- c. $60,000
- d. $67,600

3. On November 1, year 1, a company purchased a new machine that it does not have to pay for until November 1, year 3. The total payment on November 1, year 3, will include both principal and interest. Assuming interest at a 10% rate, the cost of the machine would be the total payment multiplied by what time value of money concept?
- a. Present value of annuity of $1.
- b. Present value of $1.
- c. Future amount of annuity of $1.
- d. Future amount of $1.

4. For which of the following transactions would the use of the present value of an annuity due concept be appropriate in calculating the present value of the asset obtained or liability owed at the date of incurrence?
- a. A capital lease is entered into with the initial lease payment due one month subsequent to the signing of the lease agreement.
- b. A capital lease is entered into with the initial lease payment due upon the signing of the lease agreement.

- c. A ten-year 8% bond is issued on January 2 with interest payable semiannually on July 1 and January 1 yielding 7%.
- d. A ten-year 8% bond is issued on January 2 with interest payable semiannually on July 1 and January 1 yielding 9%.

5. Jole Co. lent $10,000 to a major supplier in exchange for a noninterest-bearing note due in three years and a contract to purchase a fixed amount of merchandise from the supplier at a 10% discount from prevailing market prices over the next three years. The market rate for a note of this type is 10%. On issuing the note, Jole should record

	Discount on note receivable	Deferred charge
a.	Yes	Yes
b.	Yes	No
c.	No	Yes
d.	No	No

A.9. Notes Receivable and Payable

6. On December 30, year 1, Chang Co. sold a machine to Door Co. in exchange for a noninterest-bearing note requiring ten annual payments of $10,000. Door made the first payment on December 30, year 1. The market interest rate for similar notes at date of issuance was 8%. Information on present value factors is as follows:

Period	Present value of $1 at 8%	Present value of ordinary annuity of $1 at 8%
9	0.50	6.25
10	0.46	6.71

In its December 31, year 1 balance sheet, what amount should Chang report as note receivable?
- a. $45,000
- b. $46,000
- c. $62,500
- d. $67,100

Items 7 and 8 are based on the following:

On January 2, year 1, Emme Co. sold equipment with a carrying amount of $480,000 in exchange for a $600,000 noninterest-bearing note due January 2, year 4. There was no established exchange price for the equipment. The prevailing rate of interest for a note of this type at January 2, year 1, was 10%. The present value of $1 at 10% for three periods is 0.75.

7. In Emme's year 1 income statement, what amount should be reported as interest income?
- a. $ 9,000
- b. $45,000
- c. $50,000
- d. $60,000

8. In Emme's year 1 income statement, what amount should be reported as gain (loss) on sale of machinery?
- a. $(30,000) loss.
- b. $ 30,000 gain.
- c. $120,000 gain.
- d. $270,000 gain.

9. On December 31, year 1, Jet Co. received two $10,000 notes receivable from customers in exchange for services rendered. On both notes, interest is calculated on the outstanding balance at the interest rate of 3% compounded annually and payable at maturity. The note from Hart Corp., made under customary trade terms, is due in nine months and the note from Maxx, Inc. is due in five years. The market interest rate for similar notes on December 31, year 1, was 8%. The compound interest factors are as follows:

Future value of $1 due in nine months at 3%	1.0225
Future value of $1 due in five years at 3%	1.1593
Present value of $1 due in nine months at 8%	.944
Present value of $1 due in five years at 8%	.680

Jet does not elect the fair value option for reporting its financial assets. At what amounts should these two notes receivable be reported in Jet's December 31, year 1 balance sheet?

	Hart	**Maxx**
a.	$ 9,440	$6,800
b.	$ 9,652	$7,820
c.	$10,000	$6,800
d.	$10,000	$7,883

10. Leaf Co. purchased from Oak Co. a $20,000, 8%, five-year note that required five equal annual year-end payments of $5,009. The note was discounted to yield a 9% rate to Leaf. At the date of purchase, Leaf recorded the note at its present value of $19,485. Leaf does not elect the fair value option for reporting its financial liabilities. What should be the total interest revenue earned by Leaf over the life of this note?

- a. $5,045
- b. $5,560
- c. $8,000
- d. $9,000

Items 11 and 12 are based on the following:

House Publishers offered a contest in which the winner would receive $1,000,000, payable over twenty years. On December 31, year 1, House announced the winner of the contest and signed a note payable to the winner for $1,000,000, payable in $50,000 installments every January 2. Also on December 31, year 1, House purchased an annuity for $418,250 to provide the $950,000 prize monies remaining after the first $50,000 installment, which was paid on January 2, year 2.

11. In its December 31, year 1 balance sheet, what amount should House report as note payable—contest winner, net of current portion?

- a. $368,250
- b. $418,250
- c. $900,000
- d. $950,000

12. In its year 1 income statement, what should House report as contest prize expense?

- a. $0
- b. $ 418,250
- c. $ 468,250
- d. $1,000,000

13. On December 31, year 1, Roth Co. issued a $10,000 face value note payable to Wake Co. in exchange for services rendered to Roth. The note, made at usual trade terms, is due in nine months and bears interest, payable at maturity, at the annual rate of 3%. The market interest rate is 8%. The compound interest factor of $1 due in nine months at 8% is .944. At what amount should the note payable be reported in Roth's December 31, year 1 balance sheet?

- a. $10,300
- b. $10,000
- c. $ 9,652
- d. $ 9,440

14. On January 1, year 1, Parke Company borrowed $360,000 from a major customer evidenced by a noninterest-bearing note due in three years. Parke agreed to supply the customer's inventory needs for the loan period at lower than fair value. At the 12% imputed interest rate for this type of loan, the present value of the note is $255,000 at January 1, year 1. What amount of interest expense should be included in Parke's year 1 income statement?

- a. $43,200
- b. $35,000
- c. $30,600
- d. $0

15. Pie Co. uses the installment sales method to recognize revenue. Customers pay the installment notes in twenty-four equal monthly amounts, which include 12% interest. What is an installment note's receivable balance six months after the sale?

- a. 75% of the original sales price.
- b. Less than 75% of the original sales price.
- c. The present value of the remaining monthly payments discounted at 12%.
- d. Less than the present value of the remaining monthly payments discounted at 12%.

16. On July 1, year 1, a company obtained a two-year 8% note receivable for services rendered. At that time the market rate of interest was 10%. The face amount of the note and the entire amount of the interest are due on June 30, year 3. Interest receivable at December 31, year 1, was

- a. 5% of the face value of the note.
- b. 4% of the face value of the note.
- c. 5% of the July 1, year 1, present value of the amount due June 30, year 3
- d. 4% of the July 1, year 1, present value of the amount due June 30, year 3.

17. Which of the following is reported as interest expense?

- a. Pension cost interest.
- b. Postretirement health-care benefits interest.
- c. Imputed interest on noninterest-bearing note.
- d. Interest incurred to finance construction of machinery for own use.

18. Norton Corp. does not elect the fair value option for recording its financial liabilities. The discount resulting from the determination of a note payable's present value should be reported on its balance sheet as a(n)

- a. Addition to the face amount of the note.
- b. Deferred charge separate from the note.
- c. Deferred credit separate from the note.
- d. Direct reduction from the face amount of the note.

A.10. Loan Origination Costs and Fees

19. In calculating the carrying amount of a loan, the lender adds to the principal

	Direct loan origination costs incurred by the lender	Loan origination fees charged to the borrower
a.	Yes	Yes
b.	Yes	No
c.	No	Yes
d.	No	No

20. Duff, Inc. borrowed from Martin Bank under a ten-year loan in the amount of $150,000 with a stated interest rate of 6%. Payments are due monthly, and are computed to be $1,665. Martin Bank incurs $4,000 of direct loan origination costs and $2,000 of indirect loan origination costs. In addition, Martin Bank charges Duff, Inc. a four-point nonrefundable loan origination fee.

Martin Bank, the lender, has a carrying amount of
   a. $144,000
   b. $148,000
   c. $150,000
   d. $152,000

21. Martin Bank grants a ten-year loan to Duff, Inc. in the amount of $150,000 with a stated interest rate of 6%. Payments are due monthly, and are computed to be $1,665. Martin Bank incurs $4,000 of direct loan origination costs and $2,000 of indirect loan origination costs. In addition, Martin Bank charges Duff, Inc. a four-point nonrefundable loan origination fee.

Duff, the borrower, has a carrying amount of
   a. $144,000
   b. $148,000
   c. $150,000
   d. $152,000

22. On December 1, year 1, Money Co. gave Home Co. a $200,000, 11% loan. Money paid proceeds of $194,000 after the deduction of a $6,000 nonrefundable loan origination fee. Principal and interest are due in sixty monthly installments of $4,310, beginning January 1, year 2. The repayments yield an effective interest rate of 11% at a present value of $200,000 and 12.4% at a present value of $194,000. What amount of income from this loan should Money report in its year 1 income statement?
   a. $0
   b. $1,833
   c. $2,005
   d. $7,833

23. On July 1, year 2, Marseto Corporation borrows $100,000 on a 10%, five-year interest-bearing note. At December 31, year 2, the fair value of the note is determined to be $97,500. Marseto elects the fair value option for reporting its financial liabilities. On its December 31, year 2 financial statements, what amounts should be presented for this note?

	Interest Expense	Note Payable	Gain (Loss)
a.	$10,000	$100,000	$0
b.	$10,000	$ 97,500	$ 2,500
c.	$ 5,000	$ 97,500	$ 2,500
d.	$0	$ 97,500	$(7,500)

24. On January 1, year 2, Connor Corporation signed a $100,000 noninterest-bearing note due in three years at a discount rate of 10%. Connor elects to use the fair value option for reporting its financial liabilities. On Decem-

ber 31, year 2, Connor's credit rating and risk factors indicated that the rate of interest applicable to its borrowings was 9%. The present value factors at 10% and 9% are presented below.

PV factor 10%, 3 periods	.751
PV factor 10%, 2 periods	.826
PV factor 10%, 1 period	.909
PV factor 9%, 3 periods	.772
PV factor 9%, 2 periods	.842
PV factor 9%, 1 period	.917

At what amount should Connor present the note on the December 31, year 2 balance sheet?
   a. $75,100
   b. $77,200
   c. $82,610
   d. $84,200

25. On January 1, year 2, London Corporation borrowed $500,000 on a 8%, noninterest-bearing note due in four years. The present value of the note on January 1, year 2, was $367,500. London Corporation elects the fair value method for reporting its financial liabilities. On December 31, year 2, it is determined the fair value of the note is $408,150. At what amount should the discount on notes payable be presented on the balance sheet on December 31, year 2?
   a. $132,500
   b. $103,100
   c. $ 91,850
   d. $0

Multiple-Choice Answers and Explanations

Answers

1.	c	__ __	7.	b	__ __	13.	b	__ __	19.	b	__ __	25.	d	__ __
2.	b	__ __	8.	a	__ __	14.	c	__ __	20.	b	__ __			
3.	b	__ __	9.	d	__ __	15.	c	__ __	21.	a	__ __			
4.	b	__ __	10.	b	__ __	16.	b	__ __	22.	c	__ __			
5.	a	__ __	11.	b	__ __	17.	c	__ __	23.	c	__ __	1st: __/25 = __%		
6.	c	__ __	12.	c	__ __	18.	d	__ __	24.	d	__ __	2nd: __/25 = __%		

Explanations

1. **(c)** The desired fund balance on September 1, year 5, ($1,000,000) is a **future amount**. The series of four equal annual deposits is an **annuity in advance,** as illustrated in the diagram below.

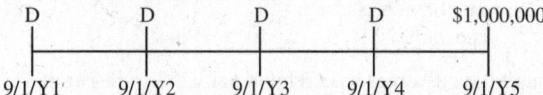

This is an annuity in advance, rather than an ordinary annuity, because the last deposit (9/1/Y4) is made one year prior to the date the future amount is needed. Therefore, these are beginning-of-year payments. The deposit amount is computed by dividing the future amount by the factor for the future amount of an annuity in advance.

$$\$1,000,000 \div 5.11 = \$195,700$$

2. **(b)** The requirement is to determine the acquisition cost of a franchise. The cost of this franchise is the down payment of $20,000 plus the present value of the four equal annual payments of $10,000. The annual payments represent an annuity, so the $10,000 annual payment is multiplied by the present value factor of 2.91. Therefore, the franchise cost is $49,100 ($20,000 + $29,100). The journal entry is

Franchise	49,100	
Discount on notes payable	10,900	
Notes payable		40,000
Cash		20,000

3. **(b)** The requirement is to determine what time value of money concept would be used to determine the cost of a machine when a payment (principal plus interest) is to be made in two years. Answer (b) is correct because the cost of the machine is to be recorded immediately; therefore, the cost of the present value of a lump-sum payment would be used. Answer (c) is incorrect because a future amount would be used in computing the payment and not the cost of the machine. Also, a lump-sum payment is involved and not an annuity. Answer (d) is incorrect because a future amount would be used in computing the payment and not the cost. Answer (a) is incorrect because a lump-sum payment is involved, not an annuity.

4. **(b)** The requirement is the situation which illustrates an annuity due. An annuity due (annuity in advance) is a series of payments where the first payment is made at the beginning of the first period, in contrast to an ordinary annuity (annuity in arrears), in which the first payment is made at the end of the first period. Answer (b) is correct because the initial lease payment is due immediately (at the beginning of the first period). Answers (a), (c), and (d) all illus-

trate situations in which the first lease or interest payment occurs at the end of the first period. Note that in answers (c) and (d), the stated rate and yield rate of the bonds differ; while this would affect the present value of the bonds, it has no effect on the classification as an annuity due or an ordinary annuity.

5. **(a)** In recording the transaction recognition should be given to both the imputed interest rate and the deferred charge related to the merchandise discount. Answer (b) is incorrect because the deferred charge should also be recognized. Answer (c) is incorrect because a discount on the noninterest-bearing note should also be recognized. Answer (d) is incorrect because both the discount and the deferred charge should be recognized.

6. **(c)** If the FMV of the machine and the FMV of the note are not known, the transaction should be recorded at the PV of the note by imputing interest at the prevailing rate (8%) for similar notes. This series of ten payments is an **annuity in advance,** because the first payment is due immediately on 12/30/Y1. However, the problem requires the amount to be reported for the note receivable on **12/31/Y1,** after the first payment is received. The remaining nine payments are an ordinary annuity, as illustrated in the diagram below.

PV = ?

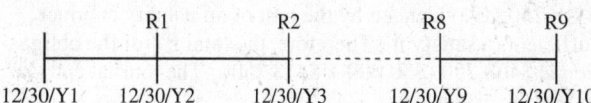

In a PV computation, one must look at the first rent to see if it is an ordinary annuity or annuity in advance. If the first rent occurs one period after the computation date, it is an ordinary annuity. Therefore, the PV to be reported for the note receivable at 12/31/Y1 is $62,500 (10,000 × 6.25).

7. **(b)** The $600,000 noninterest-bearing note should be recorded at its present value of $450,000 ($600,000 × .75). The journal entry is

Loss on sale of equip.	30,000		
Note receivable	600,000		
Discount on NR		150,000 }	450,000
Equipment (net)		480,000	

At 12/31/Y1, interest income would be recognized using the effective interest method. Using this method, interest is computing by multiplying the book value of the note ($600,000 − $150,000 = $450,000) by the effective interest rate ($450,000 × 10% = $45,000).

8.   (a)   The $600,000 noninterest-bearing note should be recorded at its present value of $450,000 ($600,000 × .75). The journal entry is

Loss on sale of equip.	30,000		
Note receivable	600,000		
Discount on NR		150,000 }	450,000
Equipment (net)		480,000	

The loss is recognized because the fair value of the note received ($450,000) is $30,000 less than the carrying amount of the equipment sold ($480,000).

9.   (d)   Receivables bearing an unreasonably low stated interest rate should be recorded at their present value. However, this rule does **not** apply to receivables arising through the normal course of business that mature in less than one year. Therefore, the Hart receivable would be recorded at face value ($10,000), since it matures in nine months. The Maxx receivable would be recorded at its present value, since it matures in five years. The Maxx receivable will result in a lump-sum collection of $11,593 ($10,000 × 1.1593), so its present value is $7,883 ($11,593 × .680).

10.   (b)   The total interest revenue earned over the life of the note equals the excess of the cash received over the cash paid to acquire the note. The cash received over the five years is $25,045 (5 receipts of $5,009 each). The cash paid to acquire the $20,000 note was $19,485. Therefore, the total interest revenue is $5,560 ($25,045 – $19,485).

11.   (b)   The $1,000,000 note is payable $50,000 in year 1 (current portion) and $950,000 after year 1 (long-term portion). This noninterest-bearing long-term note should be recorded at its present value, which can be measured as the amount required to purchase an annuity sufficient to provide the funds to satisfy the obligation. Therefore, the note payable, net of current portion, should be reported at $418,250.

12.   (c)   The contest prize expense must be recognized at the present value of the obligation incurred as a result of the contest. The obligation consists of $50,000 payable in two days, and $950,000 payable over the next nineteen years. The $950,000 long-term portion has a present value of $418,250, as evidenced by the cost of an annuity contract sufficient to satisfy it. Therefore, the total PV of the obligation is $468,250 ($50,000 + $418,250). The journal entry to record the expense is

Contest prize expense	468,250	
Discount on NP	531,750	
Notes payable		1,000,000

13.   (b)   All receivables and payables are subject to present value measurement techniques and interest imputation, if necessary, with certain exceptions. One exception is normal course of business receivables and payables maturing in less than one year. Therefore this note payable, due in nine months at usual trade terms, would be reported at face value ($10,000) rather than at present value ($10,225 × .944 = $9,652).

14.   (c)   The requirement is to determine the amount of interest expense to be recognized in year 1 from a noninterest-bearing note. Parke Company is able to borrow on a noninterest basis because they agree to sell their product at less than the fair value. In this type of situation, the note payable is recorded at present value, and the difference between the present value and the cash received is recorded

as **unearned sales revenue** (to be recognized when the product is sold at less than fair value). The initial journal entry is

Cash	360,000		
Discount on NP	105,000		
Note payable		360,000 }	255,000
Unearned sales revenue		105,000	

When interest expense is recognized at the end of year 1, the effective interest method must be used. Using this method, interest expense is computed by multiplying the book value of the liability ($360,000 – $105,000 = $255,000) by the effective interest rate (12%), resulting in interest expense of $30,600.

15.   (c)   The entry made to record an installment sale (ignoring the cost of sale and inventory) is as follows:

Note receivable	(Sale price)
Installment sales	(PV of note @ 12%)
Discount on notes	
receivable	(Plug)

Although the customer would have paid 25% (six out of twenty-four months) of the total payments due under the terms of the installment sale, the **net** carrying value of the note (equal to the principal balance of the note less the unamortized discount) is equal to the present value of the remaining monthly payments discounted at 12%. Under the effective interest method, the carrying value of the note will at all times be equal to the present value of the remaining installment payments, regardless of whether the note is recorded gross or net in Pie Co.'s accounts.

16.   (b)   When a note is issued with a stated rate (8% in this case) below the market rate (10% in this case), the note will be issued at a discount. The entry for the recipient of the note on July 1 would be as follows:

Notes receivable	xxx	
Disc. on notes rec.		xxx
Service revenue		xxx

On December 31, the company must accrue interest on the note. The following entry would be made:

Interest receivable	(6 months at stated rate)
Disc. on notes rec.	(6 months amortization)
Interest revenue	(6 months interest at market rate)

Note that interest receivable is debited for an amount based upon the **stated** (face) rate of the note. This is because the stated rate will determine the amount of cash interest that will be received upon maturity of the note. Since the bond was held for six months (7/1/Y1 to 12/31/Y1) as of 12/31/Y1, the amount of the receivable would be determined as follows:

Interest receivable	=	Face value of note	×	Stated rate	×	Period held
	=	Face value × 8% × (6/12 months)				
	=	4% × Face value				

17.   (c)   When a noninterest-bearing note is issued, interest must be imputed on the note and amortized to interest expense over the life of the note using the effective interest rate. Answers (a) and (b) are incorrect because interest on pension cost and postretirement health-care benefits is included as a component of future benefit obligation. Answer (d) is incorrect because interest incurred to finance construction of machinery for a company's own use may be capitalized and amortized.

18. **(d)** **Discount on notes payable** is a liability valuation account. It should be reported as a direct reduction from the face amount of the note (contra account). A **premium on notes payable** would be reported as an addition to the face amount of the note. A discount is not recorded as a separate asset because it does not provide any future economic benefit. It is not a deferred credit separate from the note because it is a debit, not a credit, and because it is inseparable from the note. Thus, a discount on notes payable should be reported on the balance sheet as a direct reduction from the face amount of the note.

19. **(b)** In calculating the carrying amount of a loan, loan origination costs are added to the principal by the lender. Any fee charged to the borrower is **deducted** from the principal by both parties (the lender and the borrower) in calculating the carrying amount.

20. **(b)** The lender's carrying amount of the loan is calculated by adding the direct loan origination costs to the principal and deducting the loan origination fee charged to the borrower. Indirect loan origination costs are charged to expense as incurred, and are not considered when calculating the carrying amount of the loan. Therefore, Martin Bank has a carrying amount of $148,000 [$150,000 principal plus $4,000 direct loan origination costs minus $6,000 ($150,000 × 0.04) nonrefundable loan origination fee]. The $2,000 indirect loan origination costs are expensed in the period incurred.

21. **(a)** Duff, Inc., the borrower, receives 4% less than the face amount of $150,000. Duff's carrying amount is, therefore, $150,000 – $6,000, or $144,000. Loan origination fees charged to the borrower are deducted from the principal in calculating the carrying amount.

> **NOTE:** Loan origination fees are frequently assessed in the form of points, where a point is 1% of the face amount of the loan.

22. **(c)** Money Co. made a cash outflow of $194,000 for the $200,000 loan Money gave to Home Co. The book value of the loan is $194,000 on Money's books. Money will receive an effective interest rate of 12.4% on its cash outflow. Income from the loan would be calculated by multiplying the book value, times the effective interest rate, and the number of months of the year (in this case just one—December). $194,000 × .124 × 1/12 = $2,004.67. The stated rate is 11% and is not used in the calculation. Money Co. will receive equal monthly installments over the sixty-month life of the loan. Money Co. will effectively earn 12.4% on its initial cash outflow of $194,000, because Home Co. will repay principal for the total loan amount of $200,000.

23. **(c)** The requirement is to determine the amounts presented in the financial statements. If the fair value option is elected for reporting financial liabilities, the liability would be reported on the balance sheet at its fair value of $97,500, with a resulting gain of $2,500 ($100,000 – $97,500) on the income statement. The interest expense for the period would be calculated as $100,000 × 10% × 6/12 = $5,000. Answers (a) and (b) are incorrect because interest is

calculated for the amount of time the loan is outstanding. In this case, the loan was outstanding for six months. Answer (d) is incorrect because if interest expense were netted against the gain of $2,500 the total expense or loss would be $2,500 for the period ($5,000 interest expense less $2,500 gain on note payable).

24. **(d)** The requirement is to determine the amount at which the note should be presented on the balance sheet. On January 1, year 2, the note payable would be recorded at its present value of $75,100 (PV factor of 10% for 3 periods .751 × $100,000 = $75,100). At December 31, year 2, the note would be revalued to fair value using the appropriate interest rate of 9%. At December 31, year 2, the note is valued at the PV factor of 9% for 2 periods. Therefore, the note would be valued at $84,200 (.842 × $100,000).

25. **(d)** The requirement is to determine the amount to be presented on the balance sheet. When the fair value option is elected, any effects of discounts or premiums are removed from the financial statements, and the accounting rules for reporting discounts and premiums no longer apply.

Simulations

Task-Based Simulation 1

Present Value Concepts		
	Authoritative Literature	Help

Assume that you are the accountant for Kern Corporation and are working on various debt accounting issues. Use the following responses to define the terms in the table that follows.

Responses to be selected
A. Effective interest rate × Net receivable or payable balance at the beginning of the period
B. Periodic interest is computed on principal balance and interest earned to date
C. Represents the debtor's incremental borrowing rate
D. Series of payments/receipts which occur at beginning of the period
E. The difference between the present value of the note and the cash exchanged when the market rate of interest < rate on note
F. Periodic interest is computed based on the principal balance only
G. Maturity value of note and interest payments discounted to the present value
H. This will result when face rate of the note < yield rate
I. The amount which will be available in the future as a result of consecutive payments/receipts at the end of each period—compounded at a specified interest rate
J. Series of payments/receipts which are made at the end of the period
K. No premium or discount exists

	(A)	(B)	(C)	(D)	(E)	(F)	(G)	(H)	(I)	(J)	(K)
1. Annuity due	O	O	O	O	O	O	O	O	O	O	O
2. Imputed interest rate	O	O	O	O	O	O	O	O	O	O	O
3. Fair value of note	O	O	O	O	O	O	O	O	O	O	O
4. Note issued at a discount	O	O	O	O	O	O	O	O	O	O	O
5. Premium on a note	O	O	O	O	O	O	O	O	O	O	O
6. Simple interest method	O	O	O	O	O	O	O	O	O	O	O
7. Interest revenue/expense	O	O	O	O	O	O	O	O	O	O	O
8. Future value of annuity	O	O	O	O	O	O	O	O	O	O	O
9. Face of note equals present value of the note	O	O	O	O	O	O	O	O	O	O	O

Task-Based Simulation 2

Balance Sheet Disclosures		
	Authoritative Literature	Help

Situation

Kern, Inc. had the following long-term receivable account balances at December 31, year 3:

Note receivable from the sale of an idle building	$750,000
Note receivable from an officer	200,000

Transactions during year 4 and other information relating to Kern's long-term receivables follow:

- The $750,000 note receivable is dated May 1, year 3, bears interest at 9%, and represents the balance of the consideration Kern received from the sale of its idle building to Able Co. Principal payments of $250,000 plus interest are due annually beginning May 1, year 4. Able made its first principal and interest payment on May 1, year 4. Collection of the remaining note installments is reasonably assured.
- The $200,000 note receivable is dated December 31, year 1, bears interest at 8%, and is due on December 31, year 6. The note is due from Frank Black, president of Kern, Inc., and is collateralized by 5,000 shares of Kern's common stock. Interest is payable annually on December 31, and all interest payments were made through December 31, year 4. The quoted market price of Kern's common stock was $45 per share on December 31, year 4.
- On April 1, year 4, Kern sold a patent to Frey Corp. in exchange for a $100,000 noninterest-bearing note due on April 1, year 6. There was no established exchange price for the patent, and the note had no ready market. The prevailing interest rate for this type of note was 10% at April 1, year 4. The present value of $1 for two periods at 10% is 0.826. The patent had a carrying amount of $40,000 at January 1, year 4, and the amortization for the year ended December 31, year 4, would have been $8,000. Kern is reasonably assured of collecting the note receivable from Frey.

- On July 1, year 4, Kern sold a parcel of land to Barr Co. for $400,000 under an installment sale contract. Barr made a $120,000 cash down payment on July 1, year 4, and signed a four-year 10% note for the $280,000 balance. The equal annual payments of principal and interest on the note will be $88,332, payable on July 1 of each year from year 5 through year 8. The fair value of the land at the date of sale was $400,000. The cost of the land to Kern was $300,000. Collection of the remaining note installments is reasonably assured.

Complete the following section of the long-term receivables on the balance sheet.

Kern, Inc. **LONG-TERM RECEIVABLES SECTION** **OF BALANCE SHEET** *December 31, Year 4*		
9% note receivable from sale of idle building, due in annual installments of $250,000 to May 1, year 6, less current installment		
8% note receivable from officer, due December 31, year 6 collateralized by 5,000 shares of Kern, Inc. common stock with a fair value of $225,000		
Noninterest-bearing note from sale of patent, net of 10% imputed interest due April 1, year 6		
Installment contract receivable, due in annual installments of $88,332 to July 1, year 8, less current installment		
Total long-term receivables		

Task-Based Simulation 3

Research		
	Authoritative Literature	Help

Assume that you are assigned to the audit of Kern Corporation. On July 1, year 1, Kern borrows $100,000 on a noninterest-bearing, three-year note and receives $85,000 in proceeds. Which section of the Professional Standards provides guidance on how to determine the present value of the note?

Enter your response in the answer fields below.

Task-Based Simulation 4

Amortization Table		
	Authoritative Literature	Help

Situation

Assume that you are the CPA for Dawson Corporation. On January 1, year 1, Catrina Corporation sold to Dawson Corporation equipment that originally cost $320,000, with accumulated depreciation of $75,000 for a noninterest-bearing note with a face value of $300,000 due January 1, year 5. The fair value of the equipment is not readily determinable but the market rate for a note of this type is 6%. Dawson depreciates equipment over a five-year life with no residual value. The present value of the note is $239,630.

Prepare an amortization table and calculate the interest income and carrying value of the note for Catrina for year 1 and year 2. Indicate whether the note has a premium or discount by completing the correct columns in the schedule. (For a more realistic exam experience, complete the problem using a spreadsheet program, such as Excel.)

Year	Interest income	Premium on note	Discount on note	Carrying value

Task-Based Simulation 5

Research		
	Authoritative Literature	Help

On January 1, year 1, Layton Corporation sold to Dart Corporation equipment that cost Layton $200,000 (3 years ago) for a noninterest-bearing note with a face value of $280,000 due June 20, year 4. The current fair value of the equipment is not readily determinable but the market interest rate for this type of note is 6%. Which section of the Professional Standards provides guidance about how the equipment should be valued on Dart's financial statements when it is purchased?

Enter your response in the answer fields below.

Simulation Solutions

Task-Based Simulation 1

Present Value Concepts		
	Authoritative Literature	Help

		(A)	(B)	(C)	(D)	(E)	(F)	(G)	(H)	(I)	(J)	(K)
1.	Annuity due	○	○	○	●	○	○	○	○	○	○	○
2.	Imputed interest rate	○	○	●	○	○	○	○	○	○	○	○
3.	Fair value of note	○	○	○	○	○	○	●	○	○	○	○
4.	Note issued at a discount	○	○	○	○	○	○	○	●	○	○	○
5.	Premium on a note	○	○	○	○	●	○	○	○	○	○	○
6.	Simple interest method	○	○	○	○	○	●	○	○	○	○	○
7.	Interest revenue/expense	●	○	○	○	○	○	○	○	○	○	○
8.	Future value of annuity	○	○	○	○	○	○	○	○	●	○	○
9.	Face of note equals present value of the note	○	○	○	○	○	○	○	○	○	○	●

Explanations

1. **(D)** An annuity due (annuity in advance) represents a series of payments made or received at the beginning of the period.

2. **(C)** An imputed interest rate is used when the rate on a note is not fair and the fair value of the items being exchanged is not readily determinable. An imputed interest rate represents the rate at which the debtor could obtain financing from a different source; this is known as the debtor's incremental borrowing rate.

3. **(G)** The fair value of a note is equal to the maturity value and the interest payments discounted to the present value. The present value represents the amount you would pay now for an amount to be received in the future. Thus, answer G is the correct response, as the present value equals the current fair value of the principal and interest amounts.

4. **(H)** When a note is exchanged for cash and no other rights or privileges exist, the present value of the note will equal the cash received if the stated rate on the note equals the market yield rate. However, if the stated rate is less than the market rate, then the note will be issued at a discount to compensate.

5. **(E)** A premium on a note occurs when the interest rate on a note is greater than the market yield rate. The market bids up the price of the bond above par until the effective interest rate on the note equals the market yield rate.

6. **(F)** The simple interest method computes interest based upon the amount of principal only. Interest is computed as Principal × Interest × Time. The compound interest method computes interest on principal and any interest earned and not withdrawn.

7. **(A)** The interest revenue or expense on a note is computed by taking the effective interest rate times the net receivable or payable balance.

8. **(I)** An annuity is a periodic payment or receipt made in consecutive intervals over time compounded at a stated interest rate. The future value of an annuity represents the total of the periodic payments and accumulated interest at some point in the future.

9. **(K)** When a note is exchanged for cash and no other rights or privileges exist, the present value of the note will be equal to the cash exchanged if the stated rate of interest equals the market yield rate. No premium or discount exists if the stated rate on the note equals the market yield rate.

Task-Based Simulation 2

Balance Sheet Disclosures		
	Authoritative Literature	Help

Kern, Inc. LONG-TERM RECEIVABLES SECTION OF BALANCE SHEET December 31, Year 4		
9% note receivable from sale of idle building, due in annual installments of $250,000 to May 1, year 6, less current installment	$250,000	[1]
8% note receivable from officer, due December 31, year 6 collateralized by 5,000 shares of Kern, Inc. common stock with a fair value of $225,000	200,000	
Noninterest-bearing note from sale of patent, net of 10% imputed interest, due April 1, year 6	88,795	[2]
Installment contract receivable, due in annual installments of $88,332 to July 1, year 8, less current installment	219,668	[3]
Total long-term receivables	$758,463	

Explanation of amounts

[1] Long-term portion of 9% note receivable at 12/31/Y4

Face amount, 5/1/Y3	$750,000
Less installment received 5/1/ Y4	250,000
Balance, 12/31/ Y4	500,000
Less installment due 5/1/ Y5	250,000
Long-term portion, 12/31/Y4	$250,000

[2] Noninterest-bearing note, net of imputed interest at 12/31/ Y4

Face amount, 4/1/ Y4	$100,000
Less imputed interest [$100,000 – $82,600 ($100,000 × 0.826)]	17,400
Balance, 4/1/ Y4	82,600
Add interest earned to 12/311/ Y4 [$82,600 × 10% × 9/12]	6,195
Balance, 12/31/ Y4	$ 88,795

[3] Long-term portion of installment contract receivable at 12/31/ Y4

Contract selling price, 7/1/ Y4	$400,000
Less cash down payment	120,000
Balance, 12/31/ Y4	280,000
Less installment due 7/1/ Y5 [$88,332 – $28,000 ($280,000 × 10%)]	60,332
Long-term portion, 12/31/ Y4	$219,668

Task-Based Simulation 3

Research		
	Authoritative Literature	Help

ASC	835	30	25	4

Task-Based Simulation 4

Amortization Table		
	Authoritative Literature	Help

Amortization Table (Off in Year 5 due to rounding).

Year	Interest income	Premium on note	Discount on note	Carrying value
1/1/ year 1			$62,370	$237,630
12/31/ year 1	$14,258		48,112	251,888
12/31/ year 2	15,113		32,999	267,001
12/31/ year 3	16,020		16,979	283,021
			rounding	
12/31/ year 4	16,981		(2)	300,002

Task-Based Simulation 5

Research		Authoritative Literature	Help	
ASC	835	30	25	2

B. Bonds

1. **Bonds Payable and Bond Investments**

    a. Investment in bonds and bonds payable are discussed together to contrast their treatment.[1] Bonds generally provide for periodic fixed interest payments at a contract rate of interest. At issuance, or thereafter, the market rate of interest for the particular type of bond may be above, the same, or below the contract rate.

    (1) If the market rate exceeds the contract rate, the book value will be less than the maturity value. The difference (discount) will make up for the contract rate being below the market rate.

    (2) Conversely, when the contract rate exceeds the market rate, the bond will sell for more than maturity value to bring the effective rate to the market rate. This difference (premium) will make up for the contract rate being above the market rate.

    (3) When the contract rate equals the market rate, the bond will sell for the maturity value.

    b. The market value of a bond is equal to the maturity value and interest payments discounted to the present.

    > **NOTE:** You may have to refer to the discussion of time value of money concepts in the previous section before working with the subsequent material. Finally, when solving bond problems, candidates must be careful when determining the number of months to use in the calculation of interest and discount/premium amortization. For example, candidates frequently look at a bond issue with an interest date of September 1 and count three months to December 31. This error is easy to make because candidates focus only on the fact that September is the ninth month instead of also noting whether the date is at the beginning or end of the month. Candidates should also be aware that bond issues that mature on a single date are called term bonds, and bond issues that mature in installments are called serial bonds.

2. **Accounting for Bonds**

    a. A company may elect the fair value option for reporting financial assets and financial liabilities. If the fair value option is elected for a bond, the measurement of the financial liability should include adjustments for nonperformance risk, credit risk, or instrument-specific credit risk.

    (1) The election to value a financial liability at fair value should be made on the date the entity initially recognizes the item.

    (2) Although the fair value option may be made on an instrument-by-instrument basis, it must be applied to the entire instrument.

    b. If the fair value option is elected for a financial liability, the bond is not reported with a discount or premium. In addition, if the fair value option is elected for a bond, the effective interest method is not required for measuring interest expense.

    (1) Interest expense may be calculated using various methods, but the company must disclose in the notes to the financial statements the manner in which interest expense was measured.

    (2) Any gain or loss in revaluing the bond to fair value should be included on the income statement for the current period.

    (3) Two methods are allowed for disclosing financial liabilities on the balance sheet.

        (a) The first method is to disclose the total fair value and non–fair value amounts in the aggregate, with a parenthetical disclosure of the amounts measured at fair value.

        (b) The second method of disclosure is to present two separate line items to display the fair value and non–fair value carrying amounts separately.

    (4) In addition, the standards require footnote disclosure of the difference between the aggregate fair value and the aggregate unpaid principal balance.

    (5) If the fair value of a liability is significantly affected by instrument-specific credit risk, disclosures must also indicate the estimated amount of gains and losses from fair value changes that are attributable to changes in the credit risk.

    c. If an entity does not elect the fair value option, the bond is recorded at its issue price, and the effective interest method is used to amortize any premium or discount on the bond. The remainder of this module will focus on the pricing of the bond using the effective interest method of amortizing a bond.

---

[1] Coverage in this module focuses on a bond's book or carrying value. Issues concerning FV, holding gains and losses, and financial statement presentation of bond investments are covered with other marketable debt securities in Module 16, Investments.

EXAMPLE

Bond Valuation Example

$10,000 in bonds, interest at 6% contract rate, paid semiannually, maturing in six years, and market rate of 5%.

- Find present value of maturity value. Use present value of $1 factor. Discount $10,000 back 12 periods at 2 1/2% interest (Factor = .7436). (Semiannual compounding is going to be required to discount the semiannual payments so it is also assumed here.)

$$\$10,000 \quad \times \quad .7436 \quad = \quad \$7,436$$

- Find the present value of the annuity of twelve $300 interest payments. Use present value of an ordinary annuity of $1 factor for twelve periods at 2 1/2% interest (Factor = 10.26).

$$\$300 \quad \times \quad 10.26 \quad = \quad \$3,078$$

- Today's value is $10,514 (7,436 + 3,078)

The $514 premium is to be recognized over the life of the bond issue. It is a reduction of interest expense on the books of the issuer and a reduction of interest revenue on the books of the investor. Amortization is to be on the present value basis.

---

    d. The following summarizes when bonds are issued/acquired at a premium or discount:

ISSUE/ACQUISITION PRICE OF BONDS—PRESENT VALUE OF INTEREST ANNUITY PLUS THE PRESENT VALUE OF THE MATURITY AMOUNT USING THE YIELD OR MARKET RATE

Face amount	Premium	Discount
Yield rate = Face rate	Yield rate < Face rate	Yield rate > Face rate

3. Journal Entries

EXAMPLE

Bond Journal Entries
The issuer's books will be illustrated at gross (including a premium or discount account) and the investor's books will be illustrated at net (no discount or premium account).

The investor may record the bonds either net or gross, but the issuer records at gross.
In the past, CPA examination problems and solutions have followed the net method on the books of the investor.

		Issuer			**Investor**		
a.	Issue and	Cash	10,514		Bond invest.	10,514	
	Acquisition	Bonds pay.		10,000	Cash		10,514
		Bonds prem.		514			
b.	First int.	Interest exp.	300		Cash	300	
	payment	Cash		300	Interest rev.		300
c.	Premium—	Bond prem.	37.15*		Interest rev.	37.15	
	Amortization	Interest exp.		37.15	Bond invest.		37.15*

* Interest receipt (payment) minus effective interest = 300 − 262.85 = 37.15

  Effective interest = net book value times effective rate = 10,514 × .025 = 262.85

---

    a. Entry a. assumes that the bonds are issued on the interest payment date. If bonds are purchased between interest payment dates, the purchaser will also include accrued interest through the purchase date in the total cash paid for the bonds.

    b. The payment of this accrued interest on the purchase date will serve to reduce the subsequent receipt of interest income (which covers a time period longer than the time the purchaser held the bond). Subsequent interest payments are recorded the same as entry b. shown above. The amount of subsequent amortization (entry c. above) changes. Interest to be recorded under the interest method is always computed by

$$\text{Effective interest rate} \times \text{Net book value}$$

    c. This formula is true of all applications of the interest method. The effective rate of interest times net book value is the actual interest revenue or expense for the period. The difference between the actual interest and the amount received or paid is the amortization. The amortization table below shows the effective interest amounts and premium amortizations for the first 4 periods.

EXAMPLE

Effective Interest Table and Journal Entries

Period	3% cash interest	2 1/2% effective interest	Decrease in book value	Book value of bonds
0				$10,514.00
1	$300[a]	$262.85[b]	$37.15[c]	10,476.85[d]
2	300	261.92	38.08	10,438.77
3	300	260.97	39.03	10,399.74
4	300	259.99	40.01	10,359.73

(a) 3% × $10,000　　　　(c) $300 – $262.85
(b) 2 1/2% × $10,514.00　(d) $10,514.00 – $37.15

Since the interest is paid semiannually, interest (including premium amortization) is recorded every six months. The journal entries for periods 2, 3, and 4 are

	Issuer				**Investor**		
Period 2	Interest expense	261.92			Cash	300.00	
	Bond premium	38.08			Interest rev.		261.92
	Cash		300.00		Bond invest.		38.08
Period 3	Interest expense	260.97			Cash	300.00	
	Bond premium	39.03			Interest rev		260.97
	Cash		300.00		Bond invest.		39.03
Period 4	Interest expense	259.99			Cash	300.00	
	Bond premium	40.01			Interest rev.		259.99
	Cash		300.00		Bond invest		40.01

NOTE: The interest (revenue and expense) decreases over time. This is because the net book value (which is also the present value) is decreasing from the maturity value plus premium to the maturity value. Thus, the effective rate is being multiplied by a smaller amount each six months.

NOTE: The change in interest each period is the prior period's premium amortization times the effective rate.

EXAMPLE

Change in Interest

The interest in period 3 is $.95 less than in period 2, and $38.08 of premium was amortized in period 2. The effective rate of 2½% (every six months) times $38.08 is $.95. Thus, if the interest changes due to the changing level of net book value, the change in interest will be equal to the change in the net book value times the effective rate of interest.

---

d. Another complication may arise if the year-end does not coincide with the interest dates. In such a case, an adjusting entry must be made. The proportional share of interest payable or receivable should be recognized along with the amortization of discount or premium. The amortization of discount or premium should be straight-line within the amortization period.

EXAMPLE

Assume that in the above example, both issuer and investor have reporting periods ending three months after the issuance of the bonds.

	Issuer				**Investor**		
Entries on the	Interest expense	150			Interest receivable	150	
closing date	Interest payable		150		Interest revenue		150
	Bond premium	18.57			Interest revenue	18.57	
	Interest expense		18.57		Bond investment		18.57

Reverse at beginning of new period and make regular entry at next interest payment date.

e. If bonds are sold (bought) between interest dates, premium/discount amortization must be computed for the period between sale (purchase) date and last (next) interest date. This is accomplished by straight-lining the six-month amount which was calculated using the effective interest method.

EXAMPLE

Sale of bonds between interest dates

The investor sold $5,000 of bonds in the above example, two months after issuance, for $5,250 plus interest.

1. The bond premium which must be amortized to the point of sale ($5,000 for two months) is $1/2 \times 1/3 \times$ 37.15 or $6.19.

Interest revenue	6.19	
Investment		6.19

2. The sale is recorded. The investment account was $5,257 before amortization of $6.19. The cash received would be $5,250 plus $50 interest ($1/2 \times 1/3 \times 300). The loss is a forced figure.

Cash	5,300.00	
Loss	.81	
Interest revenue		50.00
Investment		5,250.81 [($10,514.00/2) – $6.19]

3. Check the interest revenue recorded ($50.00 – $6.19) to the interest earned: $5,257 \times 2\ 1/2\% \times 1/3$ (which equals $43.81).

---

f. Bonds issue costs are treated as deferred charges and amortized on a straight-line basis over the life of the bond.

4. **Comparison of Effective Interest and Straight-Line Amortization Methods**

Method of Amortization	Interest Revenue/Expense	Interest Rate**
Effective interest method	Changes each period*	Constant each period
Straight-line method	Constant each period	Changes each period

* Carrying amount of the bond investment or bonds payable at the beginning of the interest period multiplied times the yield rate
** Interest revenue/expense for a period divided by the carrying amount of the bond investment or bond liability at the beginning of the interest period

a. The following table summarizes the various behavior patterns related to the use of the effective interest method:

	Amortization of	
Description	Discount	Premium
Interest revenue/expense	↑Increases each period	↓Decreases each period
Amount of amortization	↑Increases each period	↑Increases each period
Carrying amount of bonds payable/investment in bonds	↑Increases each period	↓Decreases each period

NOW REVIEW MULTIPLE-CHOICE QUESTIONS 1 THROUGH 30

5. **Convertible Bonds**

a. Bonds are frequently issued with the right to convert the bonds into common stock. When issued, no value is apportioned to the conversion feature. Two approaches are possible to account for bond conversions:

(1) Valuing the transaction at cost (book value of the bonds)

(a) Conversion under the cost method would result in debits to bonds payable and bond premium (or a credit to bond discount) equal to the book value of the bonds, and credits to common stock and paid-in excess of par equal to the book value.

(b) In practice, conversations are usually recorded at book value.

NOTE: Under the cost conversion method no gain (loss) is recorded, as no gain (loss) should result from an equity transaction.

(2) Valuing at market (of the stocks or bonds), whichever is more reliable.

(a) At market, assuming market value exceeds book value, the entries would be

Issuer		**Investor**	
Loss on redemption	(plug)	Stock invest	(mkt)
Bonds payable	(book value)	Invest in bonds	(carrying value)
Bond premium	(book value)	Gain on conversion	(plug)
Common stock	(par)		
Paid-in excess of par	(mkt-par)		

(b) On the issuer's books, the debit (credit) to the loss (gain) account (ordinary) would be for the difference between the market value of the stock (bonds) and the book value of the bonds.

(c) The conversion is treated as the culmination of an earnings process; thus the loss (gain) should be recognized.

(d) The bonds and the related accounts must be written off, and paid-in excess of par is credited for the excess of the market value of the stock (bonds) over the stock's par value.

(e) On the investor's books, the gain (loss) would also be the difference between the market value the stock (bonds) and the book value of the bonds.

> **NOTE:** In both cases that the accrued interest and discount or premium amortization must be recorded prior to the conversion

b. To induce conversion, firms sometimes change the original conversion privilege or give additional considerations to the bondholders.

(1) The fair value of these "sweeteners" should be recognized as an expense (ordinary in nature) upon conversion, determined as the excess of the FV of all securities and consideration transferred over the FV of the securities issuable per the original conversion terms.

> **NOW REVIEW MULTIPLE-CHOICE QUESTIONS 31 THROUGH 34**

6. **Debt Issued with Detachable Purchase Warrants**

a. The proceeds of debt issued with detachable stock purchase warrants are allocated between the debt and stock warrants based on relative market values.

EXAMPLE

Units of one bond and one warrant (to buy 10 shares of stock at $50/share) are issued for $1,030. Thereafter, warrants trade at $40 and the bonds at $960. The relative market value of the warrants is 4% (40/1,000) and the relative market value of the bonds is 96% (960/1,000). Thus, $41.20 (.04 × $1,030) of the issue price is assigned to the warrants.

Cash	1,030.00	
Bond discount	11.20	
Bonds payable		1,000.00
Paid-in capital—stock warrants		41.20

If one warrant was subsequently exercised

Cash	500.00	
Paid-in capital—stock warrants	41.20	
Common stock		(par of 10 shs)
Paid-in excess		(plug)

Alternatively, the example above could have indicated the market value of the stock (e.g., $54) rather than the market values of the bonds and warrants. In such a case, one would value the warrants based on the difference between option price and market price, for example, [$54 (market) – $50 (option)] × 10 shares = $40 value for the warrants.

> **NOTE:** The effect of requiring allocation of the cash received to the stock warrants. The final effect is to increase interest costs on the bond issue by reducing the premium or increasing the discount.

> **NOTE:** The allocation to equity shown above is only applicable where the purchase warrants are **detachable**. In contrast, no allocation is made to equity if the bonds are issued with **nondetachable** stock purchase warrants. Detachable warrants are often traded separately from the debt and therefore have a readily determinable market value of their own. The inseparability of nondetachable warrants prevents the determination of a separate market value; therefore, no allocation to equity is permitted.

7. **Extinguishment of Debt**

   a. Debt is considered extinguished whenever the debtor pays the creditor and is relieved of all obligations relating to the debt.

      (1) Typical examples of this are the calling of a bond by the debtor, requiring the bondholder to sell the bond to the issuing corporation at a certain date and stated price, and the open market repurchase of a debt issue.
      (2) Refunding of debt (replacement of debt with other debt) is also considered an extinguishment.
      (3) However, troubled debt restructures (situations where creditors agree to grant relief to debtors) and debt conversions initiated by the debt holders are not.
      (4) Additionally, when the debtor is legally released from being the primary obligor of the debt either judicially or by the creditor, and it is probable the debtor will make no further payments on it, the debt is considered extinguished.

   b. All gains (losses) resulting from the extinguishment of debt should be recognized in the period of extinguishment.

      (1) The gain (loss) is the difference between the bond's reacquisition price and its net book value (face value plus [minus] any unamortized premium [discount] and issue costs).

         (a) The rule is not affected by the reissuance of debt before or after the refunding.
         (b) Furthermore, this rule applies to convertible bonds when reacquired with cash. The gain or loss is considered an ordinary gain or loss, and is a separate item in net income before extraordinary items.

   c. Because most companies use debt refinancing as a normal risk management tool, early extinguishment of debt is no longer considered an extraordinary item. If, however, the company can meet the criteria for extraordinary (infrequent in occurrence and unusual in nature), the early extinguishment of debt may be considered for extraordinary treatment.

Loss or gain	xx	xx
Bonds payable	xx	
Bond premium	xx	
Unamortized issue costs		xx
Bond discount		xx
Cash		xx

> **NOW REVIEW MULTIPLE-CHOICE QUESTIONS 35 THROUGH 39**

8. **Research Component—Accounting Standards Codification**

   The Codification lists Liabilities as Topic 405. This topic lists the various issues related to liabilities and provides for cross-references for topics related to debt. Topic 470, entitled *Debt*, contains subtopics that outline the rules for debt with conversion and other options, product financing, modifications and extinguishments, and troubled debt restructuring by debtors. ASC Topic 835 outlines the rules relating to interest on debt.

> **NOW REVIEW MULTIPLE-CHOICE QUESTIONS 40 THROUGH 42**

9. **International Financial Reporting Standards (IFRS)**

   a. Similar to US accounting standards, IAS 39 provides that financial liabilities are initially measured at fair value, and subsequently measured at amortized cost using the effective interest method.

      (1) An option can be made to value financial liabilities at fair value.

   b. Financial instruments with characteristics of both debt and equity are referred to as "compound instruments."

      (1) Accounting for compounds instruments is another area where IFRS differs from US GAAP. Convertible bonds, bonds with detachable warrants, and other compound instruments must be separated into their components of debt and equity.

(a) The liability component is initially recorded at fair value, and the residual value is assigned to the equity component.

(b) Each component is presented in the appropriate section of the balance sheet. IFRS refers to the fair value option as "Fair Value through Profit or Loss" (FVTPL).

(c) If the fair value option is elected for a financial liability, then the liability is revalued at the end of the reporting period and the resulting gain or loss is recognized in profit or loss for the period.

> ## NOW REVIEW MULTIPLE-CHOICE QUESTIONS 43 THROUGH 45

KEY TERMS

Discount. The difference between the net proceeds, after expense, received upon issuance of debt and the amount repayable at its maturity.

Premium. The excess of the net proceeds, after expense, received upon issuance of debt over the amount repayable at its maturity.

Serial bands. Bond issues that mature in installments.

Term bonds. Bond issues that mature on a single date.

Warrant. A security that gives the holder the right to purchase shares of common stock in accordance with the terms of the instrument, usually upon payment of a specified amount.

Multiple-Choice Questions (1-45)

B.1.-4. Bonds

1. Hancock Co.'s December 31, year 1 balance sheet contained the following items in the long-term liabilities section:

Unsecured

9.375% registered bonds ($25,000 maturing annually beginning in year 5)	$275,000
11.5% convertible bonds, callable beginning in year 9, due year 21	125,000

Secured

9.875% guaranty security bonds, due year 21	$275,000
10.0% commodity backed bonds ($50,000 maturing annually beginning in year 6)	200,000

What are the total amounts of serial bonds and debenture bonds?

	Serial bonds	Debenture bonds
a.	$475,000	$400,000
b.	$475,000	$125,000
c.	$450,000	$400,000
d.	$200,000	$650,000

2. Blue Corp.'s December 31, year 1 balance sheet contained the following items in the long-term liabilities section:

9 3/4% registered debentures, callable in year 12, due in year 17	$700,000
9 1/2% collateral trust bonds, convertible into common stock beginning in year 10 due in year 20	600,000
10% subordinated debentures ($30,000 maturing annually beginning in year 7)	300,000

What is the total amount of Blue's term bonds?
a. $ 600,000
b. $ 700,000
c. $1,000,000
d. $1,300,000

3. Bonds payable issued with scheduled maturities at various dates are called

	Serial bonds	Term bonds
a.	No	Yes
b.	No	No
c.	Yes	No
d.	Yes	Yes

4. The following information pertains to Camp Corp.'s issuance of bonds on July 1, year 1:

Face amount	$800,000
Term	Ten years
Stated interest rate	6%
Interest payment dates	Annually on July 1
Yield	9%

	At 6%	At 9%
Present value of one for ten periods	0.558	0.422
Future value of one for ten periods	1.791	2.367
Present value of ordinary annuity of one for ten periods	7.360	6.418

What should be the issue price for each $1,000 bond?
a. $1,000
b. $ 864
c. $ 807
d. $ 700

5. Perk, Inc. issued $500,000, 10% bonds to yield 8%. Bond issuance costs were $10,000. How should Perk calculate the net proceeds to be received from the issuance?
a. Discount the bonds at the stated rate of interest.
b. Discount the bonds at the market rate of interest.
c. Discount the bonds at the stated rate of interest and deduct bond issuance costs.
d. Discount the bonds at the market rate of interest and deduct bond issuance costs.

6. The market price of a bond issued at a discount is the present value of its principal amount at the market (effective) rate of interest
a. Less the present value of all future interest payments at the market (effective) rate of interest.
b. Less the present value of all future interest payments at the rate of interest stated on the bond.
c. Plus the present value of all future interest payments at the market (effective) rate of interest.
d. Plus the present value of all future interest payments at the rate of interest stated on the bond.

7. On July 1, year 1, Eagle Corp. issued 600 of its 10%, $1,000 bonds at 99 plus accrued interest. The bonds are dated April 1, year 1, and mature on April 1, year 11. Interest is payable semiannually on April 1 and October 1. What amount did Eagle receive from the bond issuance?
a. $579,000
b. $594,000
c. $600,000
d. $609,000

8. During year 1, Lake Co. issued 3,000 of its 9%, $1,000 face value bonds at 101 1/2. In connection with the sale of these bonds, Lake paid the following expenses:

Promotion costs	$ 20,000
Engraving and printing	25,000
Underwriters' commissions	200,000

What amount should Lake record as bond issue costs to be amortized over the term of the bonds?
a. $0
b. $220,000
c. $225,000
d. $245,000

9. Dixon Co. incurred costs of $3,300 when it issued, on August 31, year 1, five-year debenture bonds dated April 1, year 1. What amount of bond issue expense should Dixon report in its income statement for the year ended December 31, year 1?
a. $ 220
b. $ 240
c. $ 495
d. $3,300

10. On November 1, year 1, Mason Corp. issued $800,000 of its ten-year, 8% term bonds dated October 1, year 1. The bonds were sold to yield 10%, with total proceeds of $700,000 plus accrued interest. Interest is paid every April 1 and October 1. Mason does not elect the fair value option for reporting financial liabilities. What amount should Mason report for interest payable in its December 31, year 1 balance sheet?

a. $17,500
b. $16,000
c. $11,667
d. $10,667

11. Which one of the following is a true statement for a firm electing the fair value option for valuing its bonds payable?

a. The effective interest method of amortization must be used to calculate interest expense.
b. Discount or premium is disclosed in the notes to the financial statements.
c. The fair value of the bond and the principal obligation value must be disclosed.
d. If the fair value option is elected, it must be applied to all bonds.

12. On January 1, year 2, Southern Corporation received $107,720 for a $100,000 face amount, 12% bond, a price that yields 10%. The bonds pay interest semiannually. Southern elects the fair value option for valuing its financial liabilities. On December 31, year 2, the fair value of the bond is determined to be $106,460. Southern recognized interest expense of $12,000 in its year 2 income statement. What was the gain or loss recognized on the year 2 income statement to report this bond at fair value?

a. $1,260 gain
b. $6,460 gain
c. $12,000 loss
d. $13,260 loss

13. On July 1, year 1, Day Co. received $103,288 for $100,000 face amount, 12% bonds, a price that yields 10%. Assuming management does not elect the fair value option, interest expense for the six months ended December 31, year 1, should be

a. $6,197
b. $6,000
c. $5,164
d. $5,000

14. On January 2, year 1, West Co. issued 9% bonds in the amount of $500,000, which mature on January 2, year 11. The bonds were issued for $469,500 to yield 10%. Interest is payable annually on December 31. West uses the interest method of amortizing bond discount and does not elect the fair value option for reporting financial liabilities. In its June 30, year 1 balance sheet, what amount should West report as bonds payable?

a. $469,500
b. $470,475
c. $471,025
d. $500,000

15. Webb Co. has outstanding a 7%, ten-year $100,000 face-value bond. The bond was originally sold to yield 6% annual interest. Webb uses the effective interest rate method to amortize bond premium, and does not elect the fair value option for reporting financial liabilities. On June 30, year 1, the carrying amount of the outstanding bond was $105,000.

What amount of unamortized premium on bond should Webb report in its June 30, year 2 balance sheet?

a. $1,050
b. $3,950
c. $4,300
d. $4,500

16. For the issuer of a ten-year term bond, the amount of amortization using the interest method would increase each year if the bond was sold at a

	Discount	**Premium**
a.	No	No
b.	Yes	Yes
c.	No	Yes
d.	Yes	No

17. On January 2, year 1, Nast Co. issued 8% bonds with a face amount of $1,000,000 that mature on January 2, year 7. The bonds were issued to yield 12%, resulting in a discount of $150,000. Nast incorrectly used the straight-line method instead of the effective interest method to amortize the discount. Nast does not elect the fair value option for reporting financial liabilities. How is the carrying amount of the bonds affected by the error?

	At December 31, Year 1	**At January 2, Year 7**
a.	Overstated	Understated
b.	Overstated	No effect
c.	Understated	Overstated
d.	Understated	No effect

18. The following information relates to noncurrent investments that Fall Corp. placed in trust as required by the underwriter of its bonds:

Bond sinking fund balance, 12/31/Y1	$ 450,000
Year 1 additional investment	90,000
Dividends on investments	15,000
Interest revenue	30,000
Administration costs	5,000
Carrying amount of bonds payable	1,025,000

What amount should Fall report in its December 31, year 2 balance sheet related to its noncurrent investment for bond sinking fund requirements?

a. $585,000
b. $580,000
c. $575,000
d. $540,000

19. Witt Corp. has outstanding at December 31, year 1, two long-term borrowings with annual sinking fund requirements and maturities as follows:

	Sinking fund requirements	**Maturities**
Year 2	$1,000,000	$ --
Year 3	1,500,000	2,000,000
Year 4	1,500,000	2,000,000
Year 5	2,000,000	2,500,000
Year 6	2,000,000	3,000,000
	$8,000,000	$9,500,000

In the notes to its December 31, year 1 balance sheet, how should Witt report the above data?

a. No disclosure is required.
b. Only sinking fund payments totaling $8,000,000 for the next five years detailed by year need to be disclosed.

c. Only maturities totaling $9,500,000 for the next five years detailed by year need to be disclosed.

d. The combined aggregate of $17,500,000 of maturities and sinking fund requirements detailed by year should be disclosed.

20. On March 1, year 1, a company established a sinking fund in connection with an issue of bonds due in year 12. At December 31, year 3, the independent trustee held cash in the sinking fund account representing the annual deposits to the fund and the interest earned on those deposits. How should the sinking fund be reported in the company's balance sheet at December 31, year 3?

a. The cash in the sinking fund should appear as a current asset.

b. Only the accumulated deposits should appear as a noncurrent asset.

c. The entire balance in the sinking fund account should appear as a current asset.

d. The entire balance in the sinking fund account should appear as a noncurrent asset.

21. An issuer of bonds uses a sinking fund for the retirement of the bonds. Cash was transferred to the sinking fund and subsequently used to purchase investments. The sinking fund

I. Increases by revenue earned on the investments.
II. Is **not** affected by revenue earned on the investments.
III. Decreases when the investments are purchased.

a. I only.
b. I and III.
c. II and III.
d. III only.

22. On July 2, year 1, Wynn, Inc., purchased as a short-term investment a $1,000,000 face value Kean Co. 8% bond for $910,000 plus accrued interest to yield 10%. The bonds mature on January 1, year 8, pay interest annually on January 1, and are classified as trading securities. On December 31, year 1, the bonds had a market value of $945,000. On February 13, year 2, Wynn sold the bonds for $920,000. In its December 31, year 1 balance sheet, what amount should Wynn report for short-term investments in trading debt securities?

a. $910,000
b. $920,000
c. $945,000
d. $950,000

23. On July 1, year 1, East Co. purchased as a long-term investment $500,000 face amount, 8% bonds of Rand Corp. for $461,500 to yield 10% per year. The bonds pay interest semiannually on January 1 and July 1. East does not elect the fair value option for reporting these securities. In its December 31, year 1 balance sheet, East should report interest receivable of

a. $18,460
b. $20,000
c. $23,075
d. $25,000

24. On October 1, year 1, Park Co. purchased 200 of the $1,000 face value, 10% bonds of Ott, Inc., for $220,000, including accrued interest of $5,000. The bonds, which mature on January 1, year 8, pay interest semiannually on

January 1 and July 1. Park used the straight-line method of amortization and appropriately classified the bonds as held-to-maturity. On Park's December 31, year 2 balance sheet, the bonds should be reported at

a. $215,000
b. $214,400
c. $214,200
d. $212,000

25. On July 1, year 1, York Co. purchased as a held-to-maturity investment $1,000,000 of Park, Inc.'s 8% bonds for $946,000, including accrued interest of $40,000. The bonds were purchased to yield 10% interest. The bonds mature on January 1, year 8, and pay interest annually on January 1. York uses the effective interest method of amortization. In its December 31, year 1 balance sheet, what amount should York report as investment in bonds?

a. $911,300
b. $916,600
c. $953,300
d. $960,600

26. In year 1, Lee Co. acquired, at a premium, Enfield, Inc. ten-year bonds as a long-term investment. At December 31, year 2, Enfield's bonds were quoted at a small discount. Which of the following situations is the most likely cause of the decline in the bonds' market value?

a. Enfield issued a stock dividend.

b. Enfield is expected to call the bonds at a premium, which is less than Lee's carrying amount.

c. Interest rates have declined since Lee purchased the bonds.

d. Interest rates have increased since Lee purchased the bonds.

27. An investor purchased a bond as a held-to-maturity investment on January 2. Assume the fair value option is not elected for these securities. The investor's carrying value at the end of the first year would be highest if the bond was purchased at a

a. Discount and amortized by the straight-line method.

b. Discount and amortized by the effective interest method.

c. Premium and amortized by the straight-line method.

d. Premium and amortized by the effective interest method.

28. An investor purchased a bond as a long-term investment on January 1. Annual interest was received on December 31. The investor's interest income for the year would be highest if the bond was purchased at

a. Par.
b. Face value.
c. A discount.
d. A premium.

29. On March 1, year 1, Clark Co. issued bonds at a discount. Clark incorrectly used the straight-line method instead of the effective interest method to amortize the discount. Clark does not elect the fair value option to report these securities. How were the following amounts, as of December 31, year 1, affected by the error?

	Bond carrying amount	Retained earnings
a.	Overstated	Overstated
b.	Understated	Understated
c.	Overstated	Understated
d.	Understated	Overstated

30. Jent Corp. purchased bonds at a discount of $10,000. Subsequently, Jent sold these bonds at a premium of $14,000. During the period that Jent held this investment, amortization of the discount amounted to $2,000. Jent did not elect the fair value option to report these bonds. What amount should Jent report as gain on the sale of bonds?

   a. $12,000
   b. $22,000
   c. $24,000
   d. $26,000

B.5. Convertible Bonds

31. On July 1, year 1, after recording interest and amortization, York Co. converted $1,000,000 of its 12% convertible bonds into 50,000 shares of $1 par value common stock. On the conversion date the carrying amount of the bonds was $1,300,000, the market value of the bonds was $1,400,000, and York's common stock was publicly trading at $30 per share. Using the book value method, what amount of additional paid-in capital should York record as a result of the conversion?

   a. $ 950,000
   b. $1,250,000
   c. $1,350,000
   d. $1,500,000

32. On March 31, year 1, Ashley, Inc.'s bondholders exchanged their convertible bonds for common stock. The carrying amount of these bonds on Ashley's books was less than the market value but greater than the par value of the common stock issued. If Ashley used the book value method of accounting for the conversion, which of the following statements correctly states an effect of this conversion?

   a. Stockholders' equity is increased.
   b. Additional paid-in capital is decreased.
   c. Retained earnings is increased.
   d. An extraordinary loss is recognized.

Items 33 and 34 are based on the following:

On January 2, year 1, Chard Co. issued ten-year convertible bonds at 105. During year 4, these bonds were converted into common stock having an aggregate par value equal to the total face amount of the bonds. At conversion, the market price of Chard's common stock was 50% above its par value.

33. On January 2, year 1, cash proceeds from the issuance of the convertible bonds should be reported as

   a. Contributed capital for the entire proceeds.
   b. Contributed capital for the portion of the proceeds attributable to the conversion feature and as a liability for the balance.
   c. A liability for the face amount of the bonds and contributed capital for the premium over the face amount.
   d. A liability for the entire proceeds.

34. Depending on whether the book value method or the market value method was used, Chard would recognize gains or losses on conversion when using the

	Book value method	Market value method
a.	Either gain or loss	Gain
b.	Either gain or loss	Loss
c.	Neither gain **nor** loss	Loss
d.	Neither gain **nor** loss	Gain

B.6. Debt Issued with Detachable Purchase Warrants

35. On December 30, year 1, Fort, Inc. issued 1,000 of its 8%, ten-year, $1,000 face value bonds with detachable stock warrants at par. Each bond carried a detachable warrant for one share of Fort's common stock at a specified option price of $25 per share. Immediately after issuance, the market value of the bonds without the warrants was $1,080,000 and the market value of the warrants was $120,000. In its December 31, year 1 balance sheet, what amount should Fort report as bonds payable?

   a. $1,000,000
   b. $ 975,000
   c. $ 900,000
   d. $ 880,000

36. On December 31, year 1, Moss Co. issued $1,000,000 of 11% bonds at 109. Each $1,000 bond was issued with fifty detachable stock warrants, each of which entitled the bondholder to purchase one share of $5 par common stock for $25. Immediately after issuance, the market value of each warrant was $4. On December 31, year 1, what amount should Moss record as discount or premium on issuance of bonds?

   a. $ 40,000 premium.
   b. $ 90,000 premium.
   c. $110,000 discount.
   d. $200,000 discount.

37. On March 1, year 1, Evan Corp. issued $500,000 of 10% nonconvertible bonds at 103, due on February 28, year 11. Each $1,000 bond was issued with thirty detachable stock warrants, each of which entitled the holder to purchase, for $50, one share of Evan's $25 par common stock. On March 1, year 1, the market price of each warrant was $4. By what amount should the bond issue proceeds increase stockholders' equity?

   a. $0
   b. $15,000
   c. $45,000
   d. $60,000

38. Main Co. issued bonds with detachable common stock warrants. Only the warrants had a known market value. The sum of the fair value of the warrants and the face amount of the bonds exceeds the cash proceeds. This excess is reported as

   a. Discount on bonds payable.
   b. Premium on bonds payable.
   c. Common stock subscribed.
   d. Contributed capital in excess of par—stock warrants.

39. When bonds are issued with stock purchase warrants, a portion of the proceeds should be allocated to paid-in capital for bonds issued with

	Detachable stock purchase warrants	Nondetachable stock purchase warrants
a.	No	Yes
b.	No	No
c.	Yes	No
d.	Yes	Yes

B.7. Extinguishment of Debt

40. On June 30, year 1, King Co. had outstanding 9%, $5,000,000 face value bonds maturing on June 30, year 6. Interest was payable semiannually every June 30 and December 31. King did not elect the fair value option for reporting its financial liabilities. On June 30, year 1, after amortization was recorded for the period, the unamortized bond premium and bond issue costs were $30,000 and $50,000, respectively. On that date, King acquired all its outstanding bonds on the open market at 98 and retired them. At June 30, year 1, what amount should King recognize as gain before income taxes on redemption of bonds?

- a.　$ 20,000
- b.　$ 80,000
- c.　$120,000
- d.　$180,000

41. On January 1, year 1, Fox Corp. issued 1,000 of its 10%, $1,000 bonds for $1,040,000. These bonds were to mature on January 1, year 11 but were callable at 101 any time after December 31, year 4. Interest was payable semiannually on July 1 and January 1. Fox did not elect the fair value option for reporting its financial liabilities. On July 1, year 6, Fox called all of the bonds and retired them. Bond premium was amortized on a straight-line basis. Before income taxes, Fox's gain or loss in year 6 on this early extinguishment of debt was

- a.　$30,000 gain.
- b.　$12,000 gain.
- c.　$10,000 loss.
- d.　$ 8,000 gain.

42. On January 1, year 13, Hart, Inc. redeemed its fifteen-year bonds of $500,000 par value for 102. They were originally issued on January 1, year 1, at 98 with a maturity date of January 1, year 16. The bond issue costs relating to this transaction were $20,000. Hart did not elect the fair value option for reporting its financial liabilities. Hart amortizes discounts, premiums, and bond issue costs using the straight-line method. What amount of loss should Hart recognize on the redemption of these bonds?

- a.　$16,000
- b.　$12,000
- c.　$10,000
- d.　$0

B.9. International Financial Reporting Standards (IFRS)

43. On February 1, year 1, Blake Corporation issued bonds with a fair value of $1,000,000. Blake prepares its financial statements in accordance with IFRS. What methods may Blake use to report the bonds on its December 31, year 1 statement of financial position?

　I. Amortized cost.
　II. Fair value method.
　III. Fair value through profit or loss.

- a.　I only
- b.　II only.
- c.　I and III only.
- d.　III only.

44. Under IFRS, issued convertible bonds are

- a.　Separated into debt and equity components with the liability component recorded at fair value and the residual assigned to the equity component.
- b.　Always recorded using the fair value option.
- c.　Recorded at face value for the liability along with the associated premium or discount.
- d.　Recorded at face value without consideration of a premium or discount.

45. Grim Corporation reports under IFRS. Grim issued 2,000 $1,000 convertible bonds at par, with an annual interest rate of 6% when the market was 8%. The bonds are due in 5 years and each $1,000 bond is convertible into 3 shares of common stock. At what amount would Grim record the liability component of the bond?

- a.　$　479,125
- b.　$1,840,285
- c.　$2,000,000
- d.　$2,006,000

Multiple-Choice Answers and Explanations

Answers

1. a	11. c	21. a	31. b	41. d	
2. d	12. a	22. c	32. a	42. a	
3. c	13. c	23. b	33. d	43. c	
4. c	14. b	24. d	34. c	44. a	
5. d	15. c	25. a	35. c	45. b	
6. c	16. b	26. d	36. c		
7. d	17. b	27. d	37. d		
8. d	18. b	28. c	38. a		
9. b	19. d	29. c	39. c	1st: __/45 = __%	
10. b	20. d	30. b	40. b	2nd: __/45 = __%	

Explanations

1. (a) Serial bonds are bond issues that mature in installments (usually on the same date each year over a period of years). In this case, serial bonds total $475,000 ($275,000 + $200,000). **Debenture** bonds are bonds that are **not** secured by specifically designated collateral, but rather by the general assets of the corporation. The unsecured bonds total $400,000 ($275,000 + $125,000).

2. (d) Term bonds are bond issues that mature on a single date, as opposed to **serial bonds,** which mature in installments. In this case, the 9 3/4% bonds and the 9 1/2% bonds are term bonds ($700,000 + $600,000 = $1,300,000), while the 10% bonds are serial bonds ($300,000).

3. (c) Serial bonds are bond issues that mature in installments (i.e., on the same date each year over a period of years). Term bonds, on the other hand, are bond issues that mature on a single date.

4. (c) The issue price of each bond is equal to the present value (PV) of the maturity value plus the PV of the interest annuity. The PV must be computed using the yield rate (9%). The computation is

Amount		PV factor		PV
$1,000	×	.422	=	$422
60	×	6.418	=	385
				$807

The annuity interest amount above ($60) is the principal ($1,000) times the stated cash rate (6%).

5. (d) The question asks for net proceeds to be received from the issuance. The market value of a bond is equal to the maturity value and the interest payments discounted at the market rate of interest. The net proceeds will be the market value of the bond less the bond issuance costs.

6. (c) The market price of a bond issued at any amount (par, premium, or discount) is equal to the present value of all of its future cash flows, discounted at the current market (effective) interest rate. The market price of a bond issued at a discount is equal to the present value of both its principal and periodic future cash interest payments at the stated (cash) rate of interest, discounted at the current market (effective) rate.

7. (d) To determine the net cash received from the bond issuance, the solutions approach is to prepare the journal entry for the issuance

Cash	?	
Discount on BP	6,000	
Bonds payable		600,000
Interest expense		15,000

The bonds were issued at 99 ($600,000 × 99% = $594,000), so the discount is $6,000 ($600,000 – $594,000). The accrued interest covers the three months from 4/1 to 7/1 ($600,000 × 10% × 3/12 = $15,000). The cash received includes the $594,000 for the bonds and the $15,000 for the accrued interest, for a total of $609,000.

8. (d) Engraving and printing costs, legal and accounting fees, commissions, promotion costs, and other similar costs should be recorded as bond issue costs and amortized over the term of the bonds. All the costs given are bond issue costs, so the amount reported as bond issue costs is $245,000 ($20,000 + $25,000 + $200,000).

9. (b) Bond issue costs are treated as deferred charges and amortized on a straight-line basis over the life of the bond. These five-year bonds were issued five months late (4/1/Y1 to 8/31/Y1), so they will be outstanding only fifty-five months (60 – 5). During year 1, the bonds were outstanding for four months (8/31/Y1 to 12/31/Y1). Therefore, the bond issue costs must be amortized for four months out of fifty-five months total, resulting in bond issue expense of $240 ($3,300 × 4/55).

10. (b) Interest payable reported in the 12/31/Y1 balance sheet would consist of interest due from the bond date (10/1/Y1) to the year-end (12/31/Y1); in other words, three months' interest. The formula for interest payable is

Face value	×	Stated rate	×	Time period	=	Interest payable
$800,000	×	8%	×	3/12	=	$16,000

This amount would result from two entries.

Issuance

Cash	705,333	
Discount on BP	100,000	
Bonds payable		800,000
Int. payable		5,333
		($800,000 × 8% × 1/12)

Adjusting entry

Interest expense	11,667	($700,000 × 10% × 2/12)
Int. payable		10,667
		($800,000 × 8% × 2/12)
Discount on BP		1,000

11. (c) Answer (a) is incorrect because various methods may be used to measure interest expense. Answer (b) is incorrect because when the fair value option is elected, the effects of discount or premiums are removed from the balance sheet. Answer (d) is incorrect because the fair value option may be applied on an instrument-by-instrument basis.

12. (a) Interest expense can be measured using various methods. In this situation, Southern recognized interest expense by debiting interest expense for $12,000 and crediting cash for $12,000, which represents the coupon interest paid on the bond. Therefore, interest expense was recognized on the income statement as a separate line item. The change in fair value from January 1, year 2, to December 31, year 2, would, therefore, be recognized as a gain or loss to revalue the bond's carrying value to fair value. The change in value is calculated as beginning of year carrying value of $107,720 less end of year carrying value of 106,460, or $1,260. Since the value of the liability decreased, this indicates a gain of $1,260 that would be recognized on the year 2 income statement.

13. (c) A bond premium must be amortized using the interest method or the straight-line method if the results are not materially different. To use the straight-line method, the amount of time the bonds will be outstanding must be known. Since this time period is not given, the interest method must be used. Under the interest method, interest expense is computed as follows:

BV of bonds	×	Yield rate	×	Time period	=	Interest expense
$103,288	×	10%	×	6/12	=	$5,164

The interest payable at 12/31/Y1 is $6,000 ($100,000 × 12% × 6/12), so the 12/31/Y1 journal entry is

Interest expense	5,164	
Premium on BP	836	
Interest payable		6,000

14. (b) Under the effective interest method, interest expense is computed as follows:

BV of bonds	×	Yield rate	×	Time period	=	Interest expense
$469,500	×	10%	×	6/12	=	$23,475

The cash interest payable is computed below.

FV of bonds	×	Stated rate	×	Time period	=	Interest payable
$500,000	×	9%	×	6/12	=	$22,500

The bond discount amortization is the difference between these two amounts computed above ($23,475 – $22,500 = $975). This amortization would increase the carrying amount of the bonds to $470,475 ($469,500 original carrying amount + $975 amortization).

15. (c) Under the effective interest method, interest expense is computed as follows:

BV of bonds	×	Yield rate	×	Time period	=	Interest payable
$105,000	×	6%	×	12/12	=	$6,300

The cash interest payable is computed as follows:

FV of bonds	×	Stated rate	×	Time period	=	Cash interest
$100,000	×	7%	×	12/12	=	$7,000

The bond premium amortization is the difference between these two amounts ($7,000 – $6,300 = $700). Therefore, the unamortized premium at 6/30/Y2 is $4,300 ($5,000 – $700).

16. (b) The requirement is to determine whether the amount of amortization increases each year using the interest method when a bond is sold either at a discount or premium or both. Using the interest method, interest expense for the period is based on the carrying value of the bond multiplied by the effective rate of interest. Cash interest paid for the period equals the face value of the bond multiplied by the stated rate of interest. The difference between these two resulting figures is the amortization of the discount or premium each period. The solutions approach is to prepare a table for a bond issued at a discount and at a premium and examine the direction of the successive amortization amounts. Consider $100,000 of 8% bonds issued on January 1, year 1, due on January 1, year 6, with interest payable each July 1 and January 1. Investors wish to obtain a yield of 10% on the issue. The amortization for the first two periods is as follows:

Dates	Credit cash	Debit interest expense	Credit bond discount	Carrying value of bonds
1/1/Y1				$92,278
7/1/Y1	$4,000	$4,614	$614	92,892
1/1/Y2	4,000	4,645	645	93,537

Assume the same facts, except the investors wish to obtain a yield of only 6% on the issue.

Dates	Credit cash	Debit interest expense	Debit bond premium	Carrying value of bonds
1/1/Y1				$108,530
7/1/Y1	$4,000	$3,256	$744	107,786
1/1/Y2	4,000	3,234	766	107,020

The above tables show that when bonds are sold at either a discount or a premium, the amount of amortization using the interest method will increase each year.

17. (b) Using the effective interest method, interest expense is computed as the **carrying amount** of the bonds multiplied by the **effective rate** of interest. Cash interest paid equals the **face value** of the bonds multiplied by the **stated rate** of interest. The difference between interest expense and cash interest paid is discount amortization. When bonds are issued at a discount, the carrying amount increases each year, so interest expense increases each year, which causes a larger difference between interest expense and interest paid. Therefore, under the effective interest method, the discount amortization amount increases yearly. Under the straight-line method, discount amortization is constant each period. After one year, the incorrect use of the straight-line method would overstate the carrying amount of the bonds since more discount would have been amortized than under the effective interest method. By the time the bonds mature at 1/2/Y7, the entire discount would have been amortized under both methods, so the carrying amount would be the same for both methods.

18. (b) The 12/31/Y1 bond sinking fund balance ($450,000) was increased by the additional investment ($90,000), dividends ($15,000), and interest ($30,000). It was decreased by administration costs ($5,000), resulting in a 12/31/Y2 balance of $580,000 ($450,000 + $90,000 + $15,000 + $30,000 – $5,000).

19. (d) Disclosure is required at the balance sheet date of future payments for sinking fund requirements and maturity amounts of long-term debt during each of the next five years. Therefore, the combined aggregate of $17,500,000 of maturities and sinking fund requirements detailed by year should be disclosed.

20. (d) Companies sometimes place assets in segregated funds for special needs. These funds may become unavailable for normal operations due to debt covenants or other contractual requirements. Funds segregated for long-term needs, such as the bond sinking fund established in this problem, are reported as investments in the noncurrent section of the balance sheet. When interest is earned on investments held in a bond sinking fund, the following journal entry would be made:

Bond sinking fund cash   (revenue earned)
    Bond sinking fund revenue   (revenue earned)

The debit to the bond sinking fund increases the balance of the fund. The amount credited to bond sinking fund revenue is reported in the "Other Income (Expense)" section of the income statement.

21. (a) Businesses occasionally accumulate a fund of cash and/or investments for a specific purpose, such as the retirement of bonds in this problem. These funds are referred to as "sinking funds." The sinking fund is increased when periodic additions are made to the fund and when revenue is earned on the investments held in the fund. When cash is used to purchase investments, the components of the fund change (i.e., cash is invested and replaced by bonds or other securities), but the total fund balance is not affected.

22. (c) Debt and equity securities that are classified as **trading securities** are reported at fair market value, with unrealized gains and losses included in earnings. Therefore, at 12/31/Y1 Wynn would recognize an unrealized holding gain of $35,000 ($945,000 – $910,000) on the income statement, and report the securities at their fair market value of $945,000. Securities classified as trading securities are reported at fair market value on the balance sheet.

23. (b) Interest **receivable** on an investment in bonds is computed using the basic interest formula

Face value	×	Stated rate	×	Time period	=	Interest receivable
$500,000	×	8%	×	6/12	=	$20,000

Note that interest **revenue** is $23,075 ($461,500 × 10% × 6/12) using the interest method.

24. (d) The bonds should be recorded at an original cost of $215,000 ($220,000 less accrued interest of $5,000). The premium of $15,000 is amortized using the straight-line method over the period from the 10/1/Y1 date of purchase to the 1/1/Y8 maturity date (seventy-five months). By 12/31/Y2, amortization has been recorded for fifteen months (10/1/Y1 to 12/31/Y2), so total amortization is $3,000

($15,000 × 15/75). Therefore, the bonds should be reported on the 12/31/Y2 balance sheet at $212,000 ($215,000 – $3,000).

25. (a) When using the interest method of amortization, interest revenue is computed as follows:

BV of bonds	×	Yield rate	×	Time period	=	Interest expense
$906,000	×	10%	×	6/12	=	$45,300

The initial BV is the total amount paid less the accrued interest ($946,000 – $40,000 = $906,000). The amount of interest receivable for the six months is computed below.

FV of bonds	×	Stated rate	×	Time period	=	Interest receivable
$1,000,000	×	8%	×	6/12	=	$40,000

The discount amortized at 12/31/Y1 is the difference in these two amounts ($45,300 – $40,000 = $5,300). This increases the book value of the investment to $911,300 ($906,000 + $5,300).

26. (d) The requirement is to determine the most likely cause of the decline in the bonds' market value. When the bonds were acquired at a premium, they sold above their face value. This meant that the stated rate of the bonds was greater than the market rate of interest on an alternative investment of equal risk. Thus, the investors paid more than the face value to acquire the bonds. However, when bonds are quoted at a discount, the stated rate of the bonds is less than the market rate. Therefore, the market rate of interest has increased since Lee purchased the bonds.

27. (d) At any point in time, an investor's carrying value of a bond held as a long-term investment is equal to the par value of the bond, plus the amount of the unamortized premium, or less the amount of the unamortized discount. A bond purchased at a premium, thus, has a higher carrying value at any point in time than if it had been purchased at a discount. This is logical since its initial cost is also higher when purchased at a premium.

Having determined that the bond purchased at a premium will result in the highest carrying value, we must now determine which amortization method will result in the higher carrying value at the end of the first year. Under the straight-line method, the periodic amortization is constant; it is computed by dividing the total premium by the number of periods involved. Under the effective interest method, the periodic amortization changes over the term of the bond. A review of amortization tables for bonds issued at a premium will demonstrate that the periodic amortization of the premium is lowest in the first period, but increases over subsequent periods. Therefore, the straight-line method would result in higher amortization of the premium at the end of the first year than under the effective interest method. The higher amortization would result in a smaller unamortized premium and lower, overall carrying value at the end of the first year under the straight-line method than under the effective interest method.

28. (c) The requirement is to determine the purchase price of a bond which will yield the highest interest income for the investor. If the bond's market rate of interest on the date of acquisition is different than the stated rate, the bonds will sell at a premium or discount. If the market rate of interest is higher than the bond's stated rate, the purchase price will be lower than the face value (i.e., discounted). The discount will be recognized over the life of the investment as an addition to interest income. Annual interest income will equal the cash interest received plus the discount amortization for the year. If the bonds are purchased at par (face value), the interest income will equal the cash interest received. The interest income for a bond purchased at a premium would equal the cash interest received less the premium amortization for the year.

29. (c) When a company uses the effective interest method to amortize a discount on bonds payable, interest expense (which is based on the carrying value of the bonds) is lower in earlier years when compared to interest expense under the straight-line method. Therefore, the straight-line method results in higher interest expense, lower net income, and **understated** retained earnings. Since more interest expense is recorded under the straight-line method, amortization of the discount on bonds payable will be greater under the straight-line method when compared to the effective-interest method. Therefore, the carrying amount of the bonds under the straight-line method is **overstated**.

30. (b) The gain on sale of the bond investment is the excess of the selling price over the carrying amount. The selling price was $14,000 **above** face value. The bonds were purchased at a discount of $10,000, but after amortization of $2,000 the carrying amount at the time of sale was $8,000 **below** face value. Therefore, the selling price exceeded the carrying amount by $22,000 ($14,000 premium + $8,000 remaining discount).

31. (b) Using the book value method, the common stock is recorded at the carrying amount of the converted bonds, less any conversion expenses. Since there are no conversion expenses in this case, the common stock is recorded at the $1,300,000 carrying amount of the converted bonds. The par value of the stock issued is $50,000 (50,000 × $1), so additional paid-in capital (APIC) of $1,250,000 ($1,300,000 – $50,000) is recorded. The entry is

Bonds payable	1,000,000	
Premium on B.P.	300,000	
Common stock		50,000
APIC		1,250,000

Note that when the book value method is used, the fair value is not considered, and no gain or loss is recognized.

32. (a) Under the book value method, the common stock will be recorded at the book value of the bonds at the date of conversion. Thus, no gain or loss is recognized on the conversion. The conversion entry credits common stock and APIC, which increases stockholders' equity. The amount of additional paid-in capital is the difference between the book value of the bonds and the par value of the stock. The effect of the conversion would be to increase the APIC. The conversion has no effect on retained earnings. No gain or loss is recognized.

33. (d) Convertible debt securities which may be converted into common stock at the option of the holder, and whose issue price is not significantly greater than face value, should be reported as debt upon issuance for the entire proceeds of the bonds. This reasoning is based on the inseparability of the debt and the conversion option, and the mu-

tually exclusive options of the holder (i.e., holding either bonds or stock). Contributed capital would be recorded only upon conversion of the bonds to common stock.

34. (c) When the **book value method** of accounting for the conversion of bonds into common stock is used, the common stock will be recorded at the book value of the bonds at the date of conversion. Thus, no gain or loss is recognized on the conversion. When the **market value method** of accounting for the conversion is used, the following journal entry would be made on the books of the issuer (assuming market value > book value):

Loss on redemption	(plug)
Bonds payable	(book value)
Common stock	(par)
APIC-common stock	(mkt.-par)

The debit to the loss account would be for the difference between the market value of the stock and the book value of the bonds. The market value method assumes a culmination of the earnings process, and a gain or loss on the conversion may be recognized. In this case, the market value of the stock exceeds the book value of the bonds, and a loss is recognized.

35. (c) The proceeds of bonds issued with **detachable** warrants are allocated between the bonds and the warrants based upon their relative fair value at the time of issuance. In this case, the portion allocated to the bonds is $900,000, calculated as follows:

$$\frac{\$1,080,000}{\$1,080,000 + \$120,000} = 90\%; 90\% \times \$1,000,000 = \$900,000$$

Therefore, the bonds payable are reported at $900,000 (face value $1,000,000 less discount $100,000).

36. (c) The proceeds from the issuance of debt with **detachable** stock warrants should be allocated between the debt and equity elements. 1,000 bonds ($1,000,000 ÷ $1,000) were issued with fifty detachable stock warrants each, for a total of 50,000 warrants. Paid-in capital from stock warrants is $200,000 (50,000 × $4). Since the bonds and warrants were issued for $1,090,000 ($1,000,000 × 109%), the portion of the proceeds allocated to the bonds is $890,000 ($1,090,000 – $200,000) and the discount is $110,000 ($1,000,000 – $890,000). Note that if a fair value is given for the **bonds without warrants,** ASC Subtopic 470-20 states that the proceeds should be allocated between the bonds and warrants based on their relative fair value at the time of issuance.

37. (d) The proceeds from the issuance of debt with **detachable** stock warrants should be allocated between the debt and equity elements. 500 bonds ($500,000 ÷ $1,000) were issued with thirty detachable stock warrants each, for a total of 15,000 warrants. Paid-in capital from stock warrants is $60,000 (15,000 × $4). Note that if a fair value was given for the **bonds without warrants,** ASC Subtopic 470-20 states that the proceeds should be allocated between the bonds and warrants based on their relative fair value at the time of issuance.

38. (a) The solutions approach is to set up the original journal entry on the books of the issuer. The entry would be made as follows:

Cash	(proceeds)	
Discount on bonds payable	(plug)	
Bonds payable		(face)
APIC—Stock warrants		(fair value

Since the APIC—Stock warrants account is already stated at market value, any remaining difference must be allocated to the **bonds**. Bonds payable would be credited only at their face (par) value. Therefore, Discount on bonds payable is debited for the excess of the fair value of the warrants and the face amount of the bonds over cash proceeds.

39.   (c)   Bonds issued with stock purchase warrants are, in substance, composed of two elements: a debt element, and a stockholders' equity element. Proceeds from bonds issued with **detachable** stock purchase warrants should be allocated between the bonds and the warrants on the basis of their relative fair market values. Detachable warrants trade separately from the debt; thus, a market value is available. The amount allocated to the warrants should be accounted for as paid-in capital. Bonds issued with **nondetachable** stock purchase warrants must be surrendered in order to exercise the warrants. Since this inseparability prevents the determination of individual market values, no allocation is permitted.

40.   (b)   A gain or loss on redemption of bonds is the difference between the **cash paid** ($5,000,000 × 98% = $4,900,000) and the **net book value of the bonds**. To compute the net book value, premium or discount and bond issue costs must be considered. Book value is $4,980,000 ($5,000,000 face value, less $50,000 bond issue costs, plus $30,000 premium). Therefore the gain or redemption is $80,000 ($4,980,000 book value less $4,900,000 cash paid).

41.   (d)   The gain on early extinguishment of debt is the excess of the book value of the bonds at the time of retirement over the cash paid ($1,000,000 × 101% = $1,010,000). On 1/1/Y1, the original balance in the premium account was $40,000 ($1,040,000 – $1,000,000). At 7/1/Y1, the premium had been amortized for five and one-half years, or eleven six-month periods (1/1/Y1 to 7/1/Y6). Since the bond term was ten years, or twenty six-month periods, the total premium amortized was $22,000 ($40,000 × 11/20). Therefore, the unamortized premium was $18,000 ($40,000 – $22,000) and the book value of the bonds was $1,018,000 ($1,000,000 + $18,000). A shortcut approach is to take the 1/1/Y1 book value ($1,040,000) and subtract the amortization ($22,000) to determine the 7/1/Y6 book value of $1,018,000. The gain is $8,000 ($1,018,000 book value less $1,010,000 cash paid).

42.   (a)   The total bond discount and bond issue costs were $30,000 at the time of issuance [(.02 × $500,000) + $20,000]. By 1/1/Y13, twelve years have passed since the bonds were issued on 1/1/Y1. Since the bonds have a fifteen-year life, 12/15 of the discount and issue costs have been amortized, leaving 3/15 unamortized (3/15 × $30,000 = $6,000). When bonds are retired, the bonds and unamortized premium or discount, and/or issue costs must be removed from the books. In this situation, the difference between the net book value of the bonds ($500,000 – $6,000 = $494,000) and the cash paid ($500,000 × 1.02 = $510,000) is recognized as a loss ($510,000 – $494,000 = $16,000).

43.   (c)   The requirement is to identify the method(s) that may be used to report the bonds. Answer (c) is correct be-

cause IFRS provides that financial liabilities may be reported at amortized cost or at the fair value through profit or loss (FVTPL). If FVTPL is elected, the resulting gain or loss is recognized in profit or loss for the period.

44.   (a)   Answer (a) is correct because under IFRS, an issued convertible bond is separated into debt and equity components with the liability component recorded at fair value and the residual assigned to the equity component.

45.   (b)   Under IFRS, Grim should bifurcate the convertible bond into its debt and equity components. Answer (b) is correct. To do this, discount the bond at market interest rates as in US GAAP. The liability component is the discounted amount and the equity component is the residual of the cash received less the discounted amount. Calculations are as follows:

Face amount of the bonds: 2,000 × $1,000	=	$2,000,000
Present value of $1 for the principal ($2,000,000 × 0.68058)	=	$1,361,160
Present value of an ordinary annuity for the interest ($120,000 × 3.99271)	=	$ 479,125
Value of the liability	=	$1,840,285
Value of the equity ($2,000,000 – $1,840,285)	=	$ 159,715

Journal entry at issuance:

Cash	2,000,000	
Bonds payable		1,840,285
Equity—conversion option		159,715

Simulations

Task-Based Simulation 1

Concepts		
	Authoritative Literature	Help

Parker Co. $50 par value common stock has always traded above par. During year 1, Parker had several transactions that affected the following balance sheet accounts:

   I.   Bond discount
  II.   Bond premium
 III.   Bond payable
  IV.   Common stock
   V.   Additional paid-in capital
  VI.   Retained earnings

For each of the following items, determine whether the transaction Increased, Decreased, or had No effect for each of the items in the chart.

	Bond discount	Bond premium	Bonds payable	Common stock	Additional paid-in capital	Retained earnings
1. Parker issued bonds payable with a nominal interest rate that was less than the market rate of interest.						
2. Parker issued convertible bonds, which are common stock equivalents, for an amount in excess of the bonds' face amount.						
3. Parker issued common stock when the convertible bonds described in item **2.** were submitted for conversion. Each $1,000 bond was converted into twenty common shares. The book value method was used for the early conversion.						
4. Parker issued bonds with nondetachable warrants for an amount equal to the face amount of the bonds. The stock warrants do not have a determinable value.						
5. Parker issued bonds, with detachable stock warrants, for an amount equal to the face amount of the bonds. The stock warrants have a determinable value.						
6. Parker redeemed a bond issued at 8% at a discount for an amount that was 102% of face value.						
7. Parker issued bonds payable with a nominal rate of interest that is higher than the market rate.						
8. Parker called a bond that was issued at 105 at a time when the market value of the bond was less than its carrying value.						

Task-Based Simulation 2

Bond Valuation and Amortization		
	Authoritative Literature	Help

Situation

On January 2, year 1, Parker Co. issued 6% bonds with a face value of $400,000 when the market interest rate was 8%. The bonds are due in ten years, and interest is payable every June 30 and December 31. Parker does not elect the fair value option for reporting its financial liabilities.

Use the following present value and present value annuity tables to calculate the selling price of the bond on January 2, year 1. Round your final answer to the nearest dollar.

Present Value Ordinary Annuity of $1

Periods	3%	4%	6%	8%	12%	16%
5 periods	4.5797	4.4518	4.2124	3.9927	3.6048	3.2743
10 periods	8.5302	8.1109	7.3601	6.7101	5.6502	4.8337
20 periods	14.8775	13.5903	11.4699	9.8181	7.4694	5.9288

Present Value of $1

Periods	3%	4%	6%	8%	12%	16%
5 periods	.8626	.8219	.7473	.6806	.5674	.4761
10 periods	.7441	.6756	.5584	.4632	.3220	.2267
20 periods	.5537	.4564	.3118	.2145	.1037	.0514

Selling price of the bond [   ]

Prepare the amortization schedule for the bond through December 31, year 1. Round all numbers to the nearest dollar.

Date	Interest paid	Interest expense	Amortization of discount	Discount on bond payable	Carrying value of bond payable
1/2/Y1					
6/30/Y1					
12/31/Y1					

Task-Based Simulation 3

Journal Entries		
	Authoritative Literature	Help

Situation

On January 2, year 1, Parker Co. issued 6% bonds with a face value of $400,000 when the market interest rate was 8%. The bonds are due in ten years, and interest is payable every June 30 and December 31. Parker does not elect the fair value option for reporting its financial liabilities.

1. Prepare the journal entries for the bond issue on January 2, year 1.

2. Prepare the journal entry for the interest payment on June 30, year 1.

Task-Based Simulation 4

Research		
	Authoritative Literature	Help

On January 1, year 1, Sutton Corporation purchased equipment by issuing a note to the supplier with a face value of $280,000 due June 30, year 4. The interest rate on the note is significantly below the market rate for notes with similar terms and risk. Which section of the Professional Standards provides guidance on how the note should be valued on Sutton's financial statements when it is executed?

Enter your response in the answer fields below.

Task-Based Simulation 5

Concepts		
	Authoritative Literature	Help

Indicate whether each item is True or False.

		True	False
1.	Bond issue costs should be treated as deferred charges and amortized over the life of the bond.	○	○
2.	Early extinguishment of debt is treated as an extraordinary item.	○	○
3.	Losses from extinguishment of debt should be amortized over the remaining life of the debt.	○	○
4.	The straight-line method of amortization should be used for bonds due in less than five years.	○	○
5.	Bonds that mature on a single date are called serial bonds.	○	○
6.	The effective interest is calculated by multiplying the maturity value of the bond by the coupon rate.	○	○
7.	A bond premium represents a reduction of interest expense on the books of the issuer.	○	○
8.	When the contract or coupon rate is greater than the effective rate, the bonds will sell at a premium.	○	○

Task-Based Simulation 6

Journal Entries		
	Authoritative Literature	Help

Situation

On January 1, year 5, Castle issued $400,000 of 6% bonds. The bonds were issued at 98 and pay interest semiannually on July 1 and December 31 each year.

On September 1, year 5, Castle issued for $530,000 cash, 500 7% five-year nonconvertible bonds dated September 1, year 5. Each $1,000 bond had a detachable stock purchase warrant to purchase 20 shares of $3 par value stock for $10 per share. Immediately after issuance, the warrants had a market value of $45,000, and the bonds were selling at 102 without the warrant.

On January 1, year 1, Castle issued 100 ten-year convertible bonds. Each $1,000 bond is convertible into 20 shares of Castle's $10 par value common stock. The bonds were issued at 105 when the common stock traded for $40 per share. The bonds pay interest annually. The conversion features of the bond are not beneficial. On October 1, year 5, half of the bonds were tendered for conversion when the common stock was trading at $62 per share. Castle uses the book value method to account for the conversion. At the time of conversion, the bonds had a carrying value of $104,300. Castle does not elect the fair value option for reporting these financial liabilities.

Prepare the journal entries for the bond transactions during year 5.

1. January 1, year 5 Issue bonds

2. September 1, year 5 Issue bonds with detachable warrants

3. October 1, year 5 Conversion of bonds

Task-Based Simulation 7

Research		
	Authoritative Literature	**Help**

Assume that you are assigned to the audit of Lake Corporation. Lake is contemplating issuing bonds with detachable stock warrants. Which section of the Professional Standards provides guidance on how to account for the issuance of bonds with detachable warrants?

Enter your response in the answer fields below.

Simulation Solutions

Task-Based Simulation 1

Concepts		
	Authoritative Literature	**Help**

		Bond discount	Bond premium	Bonds payable	Common stock	Additional paid-in capital	Retained earnings
1.	Parker issued bonds payable with a nominal interest rate that was less than the market rate of interest.	Increase	No effect	Increase	No effect	No effect	No effect
2.	Parker issued convertible bonds, which are common stock equivalents, for an amount in excess of the bonds' face amount.	No effect	Increase	Increase	No effect	No effect	No effect
3.	Parker issued common stock when the convertible bonds described in item 2. were submitted for conversion. Each $1,000 bond was converted into twenty common shares. The book value method was used for the early conversion.	No effect	Decrease	Decrease	Increase	Increase	No effect
4.	Parker issued bonds, with nondetachable warrants for an amount equal to the face amount of the bonds. The stock warrants do not have a determinable value.	No effect	No effect	Increase	No effect	No effect	No effect
5.	Parker issued bonds, with detachable stock warrants, for an amount equal to the face amount of the bonds. The stock warrants have a determinable value.	Increase	No effect	Increase	No effect	Increase	No effect
6.	Parker redeemed a bond issued at 8% at a discount for an amount that was 102% of face value.	Decrease	No effect	Decrease	No effect	No effect	Decrease
7.	Parker issued bonds payable with a nominal rate of interest that is higher than the market rate.	No effect	Increase	Increase	No effect	No effect	No effect
8.	Parker called a bond that was issued at 105 at a time when the market value of the bond was less than its carrying value.	No effect	Decrease	Decrease	No effect	No effect	Increase

Explanations

1. Since the nominal rate of interest was less than the market rate of interest, the bonds sold at a discount. In other words, the investors paid less than the face value to acquire the bonds. The journal entry to record the transaction is

Cash	xx	
Discount on bonds payable	xx	
Bonds payable		xx

Therefore, the issuance of the bonds would increase both bonds payable and discount on bonds payable.

2. Convertible debt securities which may be converted into common stock at the option of the holder, and whose issue price is not significantly greater than face value, should be reported as debt upon issuance for the entire proceeds of the bonds. This reasoning is based on the inseparability of the debt and the conversion option, and the mutually exclusive options of the holder (i.e., holding either bonds or stock). The journal entry to record the transaction is

Cash	xx	
Premium on bonds payable		xx
Bonds payable		xx

Therefore, the issuance of the convertible bonds would increase both bonds payable and premium on bonds payable.

3. When the book value method of accounting for the conversion of bonds into common stock is used, the common stock will be recorded at the book value of the bonds at the date of conversion. Thus, no gain or loss is recognized on the conversion. The journal entry to record the transaction is

Bonds payable	xx	
Premium on bonds payable	xx	
Common stock		xx
Additional paid-in capital		xx

Therefore, the conversion of the bonds would decrease bonds payable and premium on bonds payable while increasing common stock and additional paid-in capital.

4. Nondetachable warrants are not valued separately from the bond. Therefore, the entry to record the bond is

Cash	xx	
Bonds payable		xx

5. The proceeds of bonds issued with detachable warrants are allocated between the bonds and the warrants based upon their relative fair market values at the time of issuance. In this case, the bonds, with detachable stock warrants, were issued for an amount equal to the face amount of the bonds. Since part of the proceeds is allocated to the stock warrants, the bonds were issued at a discount. The journal entry to record the transaction is

Cash	xx	
Discount on bonds payable	xx	
Bonds payable		xx
Additional paid-in capital—Stock warrants		xx

Therefore, the issuance of the bonds, with detachable stock warrants, would increase bonds payable, discount on bonds payable, and additional paid-in capital.

6. The bond was sold at a discount. Therefore, when the bond is redeemed, the bonds payable and the discount account must be removed from the records. The net carrying amount is less than the reacquisition price. Therefore, there is a loss on the extinguishment of debt. It will be an ordinary loss on the income statement. The journal entry for the transaction is

Bonds payable	xx	
Loss on bond	xx	
Discount on bond		xx
Cash		xx

7. Since the nominal rate of interest is greater than the market rate, the bonds sold at a premium. In other words, the investors paid more than face value for the bond. The journal entry to record the transaction is

Cash	xx	
Bonds payable		xx
Premium on bond		xx

8. The net carrying value is greater than the market value of the bond (reacquisition price). Therefore, there is a gain on the redemption of the bond. The journal entry for this transaction is

Premium on bonds payable	xx	
Bonds payable	xx	
Cash		xx
Gain on extinguishment of debt		xx

Task-Based Simulation 2

Bond Valuation and Amortization		
	Authoritative Literature	**Help**

PVA of $12,000 at 4% for 20 periods   +   PV of $400,000 at 4% after 20 periods

(13.5903 × 12,000)   +   (.4564 × $400,000)

163,083.60   +   183,560

=   345,643.60

Rounds to 345,644

Date	Interest paid	Interest expense	Amortization of discount	Discount on bond payable	Carrying value of bond payable
1/2Y1	0	0	0	54,356	345,644
6/30/Y1	12,000	13,826	1,826	52,530	347,470
12/31/Y1	12,000	13,899	1,899	50,631	349,369

1. The discount on bonds is (face – carrying value). The carrying value is $345,644, the issue price. Therefore, the discount account is $54,356 ($400,000 – $345,644).

2. The carrying amount at date of issue is the issue price, $345,644.

3. The cash interest payment is $12,000 and is given in the problem. This represents a semiannual interest rate of 3% ($400,000 × 3% = $12,000).

4. The interest expense is $13,826 ($345,644 × 4%) and is given in the problem.

5. Amortization of discount is interest expense minus cash interest payment ($13,826 – $12,000) = $1,826.

6. The discount is amortized by $1,826. The discount account approaches zero as the bond approaches maturity date. Therefore, the discount on 6/30/Y1 is $52,530 ($54,356 – $1,826).

7. The new carrying amount on 6/30/Y1 is $347,470 ($345,644 + $1,826).

8. The cash interest payment is the same as the previous period. It is always coupon interest rate times the face of the bond (3% × $400,000) = $12,000.

9. Interest expense is the carrying value times the effective rate. $13,899 = ($347,470 × 4%).

10. Amortization is the difference between the cash payment and the interest expense. $1,899 ($13,899 – $12,000).

11. Discount on bonds is $50,631 ($52,530 – $1,899).

12. Carrying amount is $349,369 ($347,470 + $1,899).

Task-Based Simulation 3

Journal Entries		
	Authoritative Literature	Help

1. January 2, year 1	Cash	345,644	
	Discount on bonds payable	54,356	
	Bonds payable		400,000
2. June 30, year 1	Interest expense	13,826	
	Cash		12,000
	Discount on bonds payable		1,826

The computation of the issue price of the bond is illustrated in Simulation 2.

Task-Based Simulation 4

Research		
	Authoritative Literature	Help

ASC	835	30	25	10

Task-Based Simulation 5

Concepts		
	Authoritative Literature	Help

Indicate whether each item is True or False.

		True	False
1.	Bond issue costs should be treated as deferred charges and amortized over the life of the bond.	●	○
2.	Early extinguishment of debt is treated as an extraordinary item.	○	●
3.	Losses from extinguishment of debt should be amortized over the remaining life of the debt.	○	●
4.	The straight-line method of amortization should be used for bonds due in less than five years.	○	●
5.	Bonds that mature on a single date are called serial bonds.	○	●
6.	The effective interest is calculated by multiplying the maturity value of the bond by the coupon rate.	○	●
7.	A bond premium represents a reduction of interest expense on the books of the issuer.	●	○
8.	When the contract or coupon rate is greater than the effective rate, the bonds will sell at a premium.	●	○

Explanations

1. **(T)** Bond issue costs are amortized over the bond life.

2. **(F)** Early extinguishment of debt does not receive routine treatment as an extraordinary item. It must meet the test for an extraordinary item (infrequent and usual) in order to receive extraordinary treatment.

3. **(F)** Losses shall be recognized in the period of extinguishment.

4. **(F)** The effective amortization method should be used.

5. **(F)** Bonds that mature on a single date are called term bonds.

6. **(F)** The effective interest in calculated by the carrying value times the effective rate.

7. **(T)** As the premium is amortized, interest expense is decreased.

8. **(T)** When a bond pays a higher rate than the market, it will sell for a premium.

Task-Based Simulation 6

Journal Entries		
	Authoritative Literature	Help

1. January 1, year 5 Issue bonds

Cash	392,000	
Discount on bonds	8,000	
Bonds payable		400,000

2. September 1, year 5 Issue bonds with detachable warrants

Cash	530,000	
Discount on bonds	12,973	
Bonds payable		500,000
Additional paid-in capital—warrants		42,973

3. October 1, year 5 Conversion of bonds

Bonds payable	50,000	
Premium on bonds payable	2,150	
Common stock		10,000
Additional paid-in capital		42,150

Explanations

1. Cash received from the sale of the bonds is equal to $392,000 (98% × $400,000). Bonds payable is recorded at $400,000 (face value), and the difference is recorded as discount, $8,000 ($400,000 – $392,000).

2. The sales price of the bonds and the warrants was $530,000. The sales price is allocated to the two instruments based on relative fair value. After issuance, the bonds sold for $510,000 (102% × $500,000) and the warrants sold for $45,000 for a total value of $555,000. The price allocated to the warrants is $42,973 [$530,000 × ($45,000/$555,000)], and the price allocated to the bonds is $487,027 [$530,000 × ($510,000/$555,000)].

3. At the time of conversion, the bonds had a carrying value of $104,300 ($100,000 face value + $4,300 unamortized premium). In recording the conversion, bonds payable would be reduced by the face value of the bonds converted, $50,000 (50% × $100,000), and premium on bonds payable would be reduced by $2,150 (50% × $4,300). The common stock account would be increased for the par value of the stock issued, $10,000 (1,000 shares × $10). The difference between the carrying value of the bonds issued and the par value of the stock would be recorded as additional paid-in capital, $42,150 ($52,150 – $10,000).

Task-Based Simulation 7

Research		
	Authoritative Literature	Help

ASC	470	20	25	2

C. Debt Restructure

1. Creditors may grant relief to debtors. Two types of restructure are described. The first is a settlement of the debt at less than the carrying amount and the second is a continuation of the debt with a modification of terms.

   a. ASC 310 addresses the accounting by creditors for impairment of certain loans. Impaired loans include all loans that are restructured in a troubled debt restructuring involving a modification of terms. Two requirements must be met for a creditor to classify a restructuring as a troubled debt restructuring

      (1) The restructuring constitutes a concession
      (2) The debtor is experiencing financial difficulties

   b. An election can also be made to value certain financial assets or financial liabilities at fair value. Included in the list of eligible items is modification of debt. If the fair value option is elected, the debt is revalued at fair value and any resulting gain or loss is recognized in earnings for the period. If the fair value option is not elected, then the rules of ASC Topic 470 (SFAS 15) apply for the debtor, and the rules of ASC Topic 310 (SFAS 114) apply to the creditor. The remainder of this chapter will focus on the rules when the fair value option is **not** elected and when the restructuring qualifies as a troubled debt restructuring.

2. **Settlement of Debt**

   a. **Debtors.** If the debt is settled by the exchange of assets, a gain is recognized for the difference between the carrying amount of the debt and the consideration given to extinguish the debt. Such gains are no longer extraordinary.

      (1) If a noncash asset is given, a separate gain or loss is recorded to revalue the noncash asset to fair value (FV) as the basis of the noncash asset given. Thus, a two-step process is used: (1) revalue the noncash asset to FV and (2) determine the restructuring gain. If stock is issued to settle the liability, record the stock at FV.

   b. **Creditors**

      (1) Assets received in full settlement are recorded at FV

         (a) The excess of receivable over asset FV is an ordinary loss
         (b) Subsequently account for the assets as if purchased for cash

---

EXAMPLE

Settlement of Debt. Debtor company transfers land in full settlement of its loan payable.

Loan payable (5 years remaining)		$90,000
Accrued interest payable on loan		10,000
Land:		
Book value		70,000
Fair value		80,000

Debtor				**Creditor**		
1. Land	10,000		1. Land	80,000	
Gain on transfer of			Loss on settlement	20,000	
assets		10,000	Loan receivable		90,000
2. Loan payable	90,000		Interest receivable		10,000[*]
Interest payable	10,000				
Land		80,000			
Gain on settlement					
of debt		20,000			

[*] If the creditor was a bank or other finance company, this amount would be included as part of Loan receivable.

---

3. **Modification of Terms**

   a. **Debtors.** If the debt is continued with a modification of terms, it is necessary to compare the total future cash flows of the restructured debt (both principal and stated interest) with the prerestructured carrying value.

      (1) If the total amount of future cash flows is greater than the carrying value, no adjustment is made to the carrying value of the debt; however, a new effective interest rate must be computed.

         (a) This rate makes the present value of the total future cash flows equal to the present carrying value of debt (principal and accrued interest).

(2) If the total future cash flows of the restructured debt are less than the present carrying value, the current debt should be reduced to the amount of the future cash flows and a gain should be recognized.

    (a) No interest expense would be recognized in subsequent periods because the loan was written down below its carrying value.

    (b) All payments including those designated as interest would be applied to the principal amount.

(3) If the restructuring consists of part settlement and part modification of payments, first account for the part settlement per the above, and then account for the modification of payments per the above.

b. **Creditors**

(1) Under ASC 310 (SFAS 114), a creditor measures impairment based on the present value of expected future cash flows discounted at the loan's effective interest rate.

    (a) The effective interest rate for a loan restructured in a troubled debt restructuring is based on the original contractual rate, not the rate specified in the restructuring agreement.

    (b) As a practical expedient, a creditor may measure impairment based on a loan's observable market price, or the fair value of the collateral if the loan is collateral dependent.

        1] A loan is collateral dependent if the repayment of the loan is expected to be provided solely by the underlying collateral.

(2) If the measure of the impaired loan is less than the recorded investment in the loan (including accrued interest, net deferred loan fees or costs, and unamortized premium or discount), a creditor shall recognize an impairment by creating a valuation allowance with a corresponding charge to bad debt expense or by adjusting an existing valuation allowance for the impaired loan with a corresponding charge or credit to bad debt expense.

(3) The present value of an impaired loan's expected future cash flows will change from one reporting period to the next because of the passage of time and also may change because of revised estimates in the amount or timing of those cash flows. No guidance is provided on how the creditor should recognize the change in the present value.

(4) The following example of the treatment of modification of terms for creditors demonstrates the accounting for the **debtor** under ASC Topic 470 (SFAS 15) and for the **creditor** under ASC Topic 310 (SFAS 114).

EXAMPLE

Modification of Terms—Gain/Loss Recognized—Using the previous example with a loan payable of $90,000 and accrued interest payable on the loan of $10,000, assume the interest rate on above loan is 5% and the following modification of terms is made:

1. Interest rate is reduced to 4%.
2. The accrued interest is forgiven.
3. The principal at date of restructure is reduced to $80,000.

          Debtor

Future cash flows (after restructuring):	
Principal	$ 80,000
Interest (5 years × $80,000 × 4%;	
$3,200 per year)	+ 16,000
Total cash to be repaid	$ 96,000
Amount prior to restructure	
($90,000 principal + $10,000 accrued	–
interest)	100,000
Gain to be recognized	$ 4,000

Analysis of Debtor's Loan Payable Account			
		90,000	Loan payable before modification of terms
Gain	4,000	10,000	Additional amount payable from accrued interest
4% modified interest	3,200*	96,000	Balance after restructure
payments in years 1-5	3,200		
	3,200		
	3,200		
	3,200		

* Note that the $3,200 is recorded as a reduction of principal, not as an interest expense.

Creditor

Present value of future cash flows (after restructuring) discounted at
the original effective interest rate of 5% for the 5 years remaining:

Principal ($80,000 × .78353)**	$ 62,682
Interest ($80,000 × 4% × 4.32948)***	13,854
Present value of future cash flows	$ 76,536
Recorded investment in loan by creditor	$100,000
Present value of future cash flows after restructuring	76,536
Impairment loan loss to be recognized by creditor	$ 23,464

** PV of 1 for 5 periods at 5%.
*** PV of ordinary annuity for 5 periods at 5%.

Debtor (ASC Topic 470 [SFAS 15])			**Creditor (ASC Topic 310 [SFAS 114])**		
Beginning of Year 1			**Beginning of Year 1**		
Interest payable	10,000		Bad debt expense	23,464	
Loan payable	4,000		Loan receivable		10,000
Loan payable		10,000	Accrued interest receivable		10,000
Gain on restructure of debt		4,000	Valuation allowance for impaired		
			loans		3,464

(The accrued interest is added to the loan payable to arrive at the prerestructure carrying value. The gain reduces the loan payable to the total future cash flows of the restructured debt.)

(This entry reduces the principal to $80,000 forgives the accrued interest, and recognizes a loss on impairment.)

End of Year 1			**End of Year 1**		
Loan payable	3,200		Cash	3,200	
Cash		3,200	Valuation allowance for impaired loans	627	
			Interest revenue/bad debts expense		3,827*

* [($80,000 − $3,464)] × 5% = $3,827

End of Year 2			**End of Year 2**		
Loan payable	3,200		Cash	3,200	
Cash		3,200	Valuation allowance for impaired loans	658	
			Interest revenue/bad debts expense		3,858*

* [$80,000 − ($3,464 − $627)] × 5% = $3,858

End of Year 3			**End of Year 3**		
Loan payable	3,200		Cash	3,200	
Cash		3,200	Valuation allowance for impaired loans	691	
			Interest revenue/bad debts expense		3,891*

* [$80,000 − ($3,464 − $627 − $658)] × 5% = $3,891

End of Year 4			**End of Year 4**		
Loan payable	3,200		Cash	3,200	
Cash		3,200	Valuation allowance for impaired loans	726	
			Interest revenue/bad debts expense		3,926*

* [$80,000 − ($3,464 − $627 − $658 − $691)] × 5% = $3,926

End of Year 5			**End of Year 5**		
Loan payable	3,200		Cash	3,200	
Cash		3,200	Valuation allowance for impaired loans	762	
			Interest revenue/bad debts expense		3,962*

* [$80,000 − ($3,464 − $627 − $658 − $691 − $726)] × 5% = $3,962

Loan payable	80,000		Cash	80,000	
Cash		80,000	Loan receivable		80,000

NOTE: This example does not include any future changes in the amount and timing of future cash flows, due to the complexity of the accounting.

EXAMPLE

Modification of Terms—No Gain Recognized by Debtor

Assume the $90,000 principal is reduced to $85,000. The interest rate of 5% is reduced to 4%.

Future cash flows (after restructuring):	
Principal	$ 85,000
Interest (5 years × $85,000 × 4%)	17,000
Total cash to be repaid	$102,000
Amount prior to restructure:	
($90,000 principal + $10,000 accrued interest)	– 100,000
Interest expense/revenue to be recognized over 5 years	$ 2,000

NOTE: A new effective interest rate must be computed so that the PV of future payments = $100,000. A trial and error approach would be used. For the exam, you need to be prepared to describe this process and the related entries, but you will not have to make such a computation.

End of Year 1-5

	Debtor	
Loan payable	xxxx	
Interest expense	xxx	
Cash		3,400

End of Year 5

Loan payable	85,000	
Cash		85,000

NOTE: x's equal different amounts each year based on effective interest rate computed.

By Creditor—The creditor would account for the modification in the same way as in the previous example that shows the ASC Topic 310 (SFAS 114) approach. That is, the original effective rate would be used to measure the loss.

---

c. To summarize the two basic situations

(1) **Settlement of debt:** The debtor transfers assets or grants an equity interest to the creditor in full satisfaction of the claim. Both debtor and creditor account for the fair values of assets transferred and equity interest granted. A gain or loss is recognized on the asset transferred. The debtor recognizes a gain and the creditor recognizes a loss for the difference between the recorded value of the debt and the fair values accounted for.

(2) **Restructuring of the debt:** Under ASC Topic 470 (SFAS 15), the terms of the debt are modified in order to reduce or defer cash payments that the debtor is obligated to make to the creditor, but the debt itself is continued. The debtor accounts for the modification of terms as a reduction in interest expense from the date of restructuring until maturity. Gains and losses will generally not be recognized unless the total future cash payments specified by the new terms are less than the recorded amount of the debt. Then the debtor would recognize a gain for the difference. Under ASC Topic 310 (SFAS 114), the creditor accounts for a restructuring using the original effective rate to measure losses.

d. Refer to the outlines of ASC Topic 470 (SFAS 15) and ASC Topic 310 (SFAS 114) for the disclosure requirements.

3. **Impairment**

a. **Debtors.** The debtor still has a legal obligation to repay the debt, so no entry is made for impairment on the debtor's accounting records.

b. **Creditors.** If the creditor determines that, based on current information and events, it is probable that they will be unable to collect all amounts due on an outstanding note receivable, then the note is considered to be impaired. The criteria for determining uncollectibility of a note should be based on the creditor's normal review procedures.

(1) When a note receivable is considered to be impaired, a loss should be recorded at the time the impairment is discovered. The loss will be based upon the difference between the current carrying value of the note and

the present value of the expected future cash flows from the impaired note, discounted at the loan's contractual rate.

EXAMPLE

On January 1, year 1, Spot Corporation issued a $100,000, three-year noninterest-bearing note to yield 10%, to Grover Corporation. The amortization schedule using the effective interest method for the note is calculated as follows:

Date	10% interest	Carrying value	
1/1/Y1	--	$ 75,132	(present value of 100,000 at 10% for 3 periods, 100,000 × .75132)
12/31/Y1	7,513	82,645	(75,132 + 7,513)
12/31/Y2	8,265	90,910	(82,645 + 8,265)
12/31/Y3	9,090	100,000	(90,910 + 9,090)

On December 31, year 1, Spot Co. management determines that it is probable that Grover Co. will be unable to repay the entire note. It appears as though only $75,000 will be repaid. Using the effective interest method, the impairment is calculated as follows:

Carrying value at 12/31/Y1	$82,645
Present value of future receipts	
($75,000, 10%, 2 periods = $75,000 × .82645)	61,984
Impairment at 12/31/Y1	$20,661

The loss due to the impairment of the Grover Co. note will be recorded on Spot Corporation's (the creditor's) books as follows:

Bad debt expense	20,661	
Allowance for doubtful accounts		20,661

The debtor, Grover Co., should not record anything, as it still has a legal obligation to repay the entire $100,000. The future interest revenue recorded by Spot Co. will be based upon the new carrying value of $61,984. If there is a significant change in the expected future cash flows, then the impairment should be recalculated and the allowance adjusted accordingly.

---

4. **Research Component—Accounting Standards Codification**

   a. The Accounting Standards Codification addresses debt restructure in ASC Subtopics 470-50, 470-60, and 310-40.
   b. When researching impaired loans, it is important that you first distinguish whether you are taking the perspective of the debtor or the creditor. Using the word debtor or creditor in your search string may help to find the appropriate sites more quickly.
   c. ASC Topic 825 applies only if the entity elects the fair value option for accounting for a debt modification.
   d. Keywords for researching in this area are shown below.

Carrying amount payable	Impairment loan	Restructuring
Fair value collateral	Measure impaired loan	Restructuring payables
Future cash flows impairment	Modification terms	Troubled debt restructurings
Impaired loan	Original contract rate	

5. **International Financial Reporting Standards (IFRS)**

   IFRS 9 provides that a modification of debt, or an exchange of an original liability with a new financial liability with substantially different terms, are accounted for as an extinguishment of the original liability and the recognition of a new financial liability.

NOW REVIEW MULTIPLE-CHOICE QUESTIONS 1 THROUGH 8

KEY TERMS

Debt. A receivable or payable (collectively referred to as debt) represents a contractual right to receive money or a contractual obligation to pay money on demand or on fixed or determinable dates that is already included as an asset or liability in the creditor's or debtor's balance sheet at the time of the restructuring.

Effective interest rate. The rate of return implicit in the loan, that is, the contractual interest rate adjusted for any net deferred loan fees or costs, premium, or discount existing at the origination or acquisition of the loan.

Fair value. The price that would be received to sell an asset or paid to transfer a liability in an orderly transaction between market participants at the measurement date.

Probable. The future event or events are likely to occur.

Recorded investment. The amount of the investment in a loan, which is not net of a valuation allowance, but which does reflect any direct write-down of the investment.

Troubled debt restructuring. A restructuring of a debt constitutes a troubled debt restructuring if the creditor for economic or legal reasons related to the debtor's financial difficulties grants a concession to the debtor that it would not otherwise consider.

Multiple-Choice Questions (1-8)

C. Debt Restructure

1. For a troubled debt restructuring involving only a modification of terms, which of the following items specified by the new terms would be compared to the carrying amount of the debt to determine if the debtor should report a gain on restructuring?

    a. The total future cash payments.
    b. The present value of the debt at the original interest rate.
    c. The present value of the debt at the modified interest rate.
    d. The amount of future cash payments designated as principal repayments.

Items 2 and 3 are based on the following:

The following information pertains to the transfer of real estate pursuant to a troubled debt restructuring by Knob Co. to Mene Corp. in full liquidation of Knob's liability to Mene:

Carrying amount of liability liquidated	$150,000
Carrying amount of real estate transferred	100,000
Fair value of real estate transferred	90,000

2. What amount should Knob report as a gain (loss) on restructuring of payables?

    a. $(10,000)
    b. $0
    c. $50,000
    d. $60,000

3. What amount should Knob report as a gain (loss) on transfer of real estate?

    a. $(10,000)
    b. $0
    c. $50,000
    d. $60,000

4. On October 15, year 3, Kam Corp. informed Finn Co. that Kam would be unable to repay its $100,000 note due on October 31 to Finn. Finn agreed to accept title to Kam's computer equipment in full settlement of the note. The equipment's carrying value was $80,000 and its fair value was $75,000. Kam's tax rate is 30%. What amounts should Kam report as the gain (loss) on the transfer of assets, and the gain on restructuring of debt?

	Transfer gain (loss)	Restructuring gain
a.	$(5,000)	$25,000
b.	$ 0	$30,000
c.	$ 0	$20,000
d.	$ 20,000	$0

5. Colt, Inc. is indebted to Kent under an $800,000, 10%, four-year note dated December 31, year 1. Annual interest of $80,000 was paid on December 31, year 2 and year 3. During year 4, Colt experienced financial difficulties and is likely to default unless concessions are made. On December 31, year 4, Kent agreed to restructure the debt as follows:

- Interest of $80,000 for year 4, due December 31, year 4, was made payable December 31, year 5.

- Interest for year 5 was waived.
- The principal amount was reduced to $700,000.

Assume Colt does not elect the fair value option for reporting the debt modification. How much should Colt report as a gain in its income statement for the year ended December 31, year 4?

    a. $0
    b. $100,000
    c. $ 60,000
    d. $120,000

6. Grey Company holds an overdue note receivable of $800,000 plus recorded accrued interest of $64,000. The effective interest rate is 8%. As the result of a court-imposed settlement on December 31, year 3, Grey agreed to the following restructuring arrangement:

- Reduced the principal obligation to $600,000.
- Forgave the $64,000 accrued interest.
- Extended the maturity date to December 31, year 5.
- Annual interest of $40,000 is to be paid to Grey on December 31, year 4 and year 5.

The present value of the interest and principal payments to be received by Grey Company discounted for two years at 8% is $585,734. Grey does not elect the fair value option for reporting the debt modification. On December 31, year 3, Grey would recognize a valuation allowance for impaired loans of

    a. $ 14,266
    b. $184,000
    c. $278,266
    d. $0

7. On December 31, year 1, Marsh Company entered into a debt restructuring agreement with Saxe Company, which was experiencing financial difficulties. Marsh restructured a $100,000 note receivable as follows:

- Reduced the principal obligation to $70,000.
- Forgave $12,000 of accrued interest.
- Extended the maturity date from December 31, year 1 to December 31, year 3.
- Reduced the interest rate from 12% to 8%. Interest is payable annually on December 31, year 2 and year 3.

Present value factors:

Single sum, two years @ 8%	.85734
Single sum, two years @ 12%	.79719
Ordinary annuity, two years @ 8%	1.78326
Ordinary annuity, two years @ 12%	1.69006

In accordance with the agreement, Saxe made payments to Marsh on December 31, year 2 and year 3. Marsh does not elect the fair value option for reporting the modification of debt. How much interest income should Marsh report for the year ended December 31, year 3?

    a. $0
    b. $ 5,600
    c. $ 8,100
    d. $11,200

8. Casey Corp. entered into a troubled debt restructuring agreement with First State Bank. First State agreed to accept land with a carrying amount of $85,000 and a fair value of $120,000 in exchange for a note with a carrying amount of $185,000. What amount should Casey report as a gain from extinguishment of debt in its income statement?

a. $0
b. $ 35,000
c. $ 65,000
d. $100,000

Multiple-Choice Answers and Explanations

Answers

1.	a	__ __	3.	a	__ __	5.	b	__ __	7.	c	__ __
2.	d	__ __	4.	a	__ __	6.	a	__ __	8.	c	__ __

1st: __/8 = __%
2nd: __/8 = __%

Explanations

1. **(a)** In a restructuring involving only a change in terms, the total future cash payments should be compared to the carrying amount to determine if a gain should be recognized. Answers (b) and (c) are incorrect because the undiscounted future cash flows are compared to the carrying amount. Answer (d) is incorrect because the total amount of future cash flows are compared to the carrying amount.

2. **(d)** In this restructure, the debt is retired by the transfer of real estate to the creditor. A gain or loss is recognized on the transfer of real estate, and a gain or loss is recognized on the restructuring. The loss on the transfer of assets is the excess of the real estate's carrying amount over its FV ($100,000 − $90,000 = $10,000). The restructuring gain is the excess of the carrying amount of the liability over the FV of the real estate transferred. The restructuring gain is $60,000 ($150,000 − $90,000). The journal entry is

Liability	150,000	
Loss on transfer	10,000	
Real estate		100,000
Gain on restructuring		60,000

3. **(a)** In this restructure, the debt is retired by the transfer of real estate to the creditor. A gain or loss is recognized on the transfer of real estate, and a gain or loss is recognized on the restructuring. The loss on the transfer of assets is the excess of the real estate's carrying amount over its FV ($100,000 − $90,000 = $10,000). The restructuring gain is the excess of the carrying amount of the liability over the FV of the real estate transferred, net of the related tax effect. The restructuring gain is $60,000 ($150,000 − $90,000). The journal entry is

Liability	150,000	
Loss on transfer	10,000	
Real estate		100,000
Gain on restructuring		60,000

4. **(a)** In this restructure, the debt is retired by the transfer of equipment to the creditor. A gain or loss is recognized on the transfer of the equipment, and a gain or loss is recognized on the retirement of the debt. The loss on the transfer of equipment is the excess of the equipment's carrying amount over its fair value ($80,000 − $75,000 = $5,000). The gain on retirement of debt is the excess of the carrying amount of the debt over the fair value of the equipment transferred ($100,000 − $75,000 = $25,000).

5. **(b)** The requirement is to determine the amount of gain to be recognized from a troubled debt restructure. If the debt is continued with a modification of terms, a gain is recognized by the debtor if the future cash payments on the debt are less than the carrying value of the debt. For troubled debt restructures, carrying value is defined as the principal amount ($800,000) plus accrued interest ($80,000), or $880,000. The future payments total $780,000 ($700,000 reduced principal and $80,000 interest). The $100,000 dif-

ference ($880,000 − $780,000) is recognized as a restructuring gain.

6. **(a)** If the present value of future cash flows is less than the carrying amount of the loan (Principal + Accrued interest) then bad debt expense should be recorded for the total impairment, the accrued interest account should be written off, and the principal balance in the loan receivable account should be reduced to reflect any amounts forgiven. Any remaining balance should be recorded in an allowance account, as follows:

Present value of interest and principal payments to be received by Grey Company (as stated in the problem)	<u>585,734</u>
Recorded investment by Grey Company ($800,000 principal + $64,000 interest)	864,000
Less present value of future cash flows	(<u>585,734</u>)
	278,266

Bad debt expense	278,266	
Loan receivable		200,000
Accrued interest receivable		64,000
Valuation allowance for impaired loans		14,266

Thus, the valuation allowance Grey must recognize is $14,266.

7. **(c)** The requirement is to determine the amount of interest revenue to be recorded by Marsh, after a modification of terms type of troubled debt restructure on December 31, year 1.

When a modification of terms results in the present value of future cash flows being less than the carrying amount, then the interest revenue is calculated by using the effective interest method. In this problem the expected future cash flows is determined by discounting the principal and interest at the original effective rate of 12%.

70,000	×	.79719	=	55,803
5,600	×	1.69005	=	<u>9,464</u>
Present value of future cash flows				<u>65,267</u>

The interest revenue to be recognized can then be determined using the effective interest method.

PV at 12/31/Y1		$65,267
Interest income at 12/31/Y1 ($65,267 × 12%)	$7,832	
Interest receivable at 12/31/Y2 (70,000 × 8%)	<u>5,600</u>	
Increase in carrying value of loan		<u>2,232</u>
PV at 12/31/Y2		<u>67,499</u>
Interest revenue at 12/31/Y3 (67,499 × 12%)	$8,100	

8. **(c)** If a debt is settled by the exchange of assets, a restructuring gain is recognized for the difference between the carrying amount of the debt and the fair value of the consideration given to extinguish the debt. If a noncash asset is given, a separate gain or loss is recorded to revalue the nonasset to fair market value as the basis of the noncash asset given. Therefore, a gain of $35,000 ($120,000 – $85,000) will be recorded to revalue the land to fair market value, and a gain of $65,000 ($185,000 – $120,000) will be recorded for the extinguishment of the debt in Casey's income statement.

Simulations

Task-Based Simulation 1

Present Value		
	Authoritative Literature	Help

Situation

Jayson Company has an overdue note receivable from Simpson Corporation for $300,000. The note was dated January 1, year 1. It has an annual interest rate of 9%, and interest is paid December 31 of each year. Simpson paid the interest on the note on December 31, year 1, but Simpson did not pay the interest due in December of year 2. The current effective rate of interest is 6%.

On January 1, year 3, Jayson agrees to the following restructuring arrangement:

- Reduce the principal to $250,000.
- Forgive the accrued interest.
- Reduce the interest rate to 6%.
- Extend the maturity date of the note to December 31, year 5.

Assume that Jayson does not elect to use the fair value option for reporting the debt modification.

Calculate the present value of the future cash flows of the restructured note.

Calculate the net carrying amount of the prerestructured loan. (For a more realistic exam experience complete this requirement using a spreadsheet program such as Excel.)

Prepare the journal entries needed by Jayson for the restructuring of the loan and the interest payment received on December 31, year 3.

January 1, year 3

December 31, year 3

Task-Based Simulation 2

Research		
	Authoritative Literature	Help

Assume that you are assigned to the audit of Naples Corporation. Naples has just restructured a large note payable with FDE Bank that qualifies as a troubled debt restructuring. As a result of the modification of the terms, the carrying amount of the note payable on Naples' books is more than the future payments that will be made. Which section of the Professional Standards provides guidance on how Naples should account for the restructuring?

Enter your response in the answer fields below.

Simulation Solutions

Task-Based Simulation 1

Present Values		
	Authoritative Literature	Help

PVA ($15,000) at 9%, 3 periods + PV ($250,000) at 9%, 3 periods
2.53130 ($15,000) + .77218 ($250,000)
$37,969 + $193,046 = $231,015.

Prerestructured amount	$300,000
+ Accrued interest (9% × 300,000)	27,000
Prerestructured loan carrying amount	327,000
Less PV future cash flows	(231,015)
Loss on impairment (Bad debt expense)	$ 95,985

Journal entries for Jayson Company to record the loan restructure and the interest payment on 12/31/Y3

Bad debt expense	95,985	
Loan receivable		50,000
Interest receivable		27,000
Valuation allowance for loan impairment		18,985

Cash	15,000	
Valuation allowance for loan impairment (plug)	5,791	
Interest income		20,791
($250,000 – $18,985) × 9% = $20,791 interest income		

Task-Based Simulation 2

Research		
	Authoritative Literature	Help

ASC	470	60	35	6

D. Pensions

Accounting for pensions involves the use of special terminology. Mastery of this terminology is essential both to an understanding of problem requirements and to the ability to respond correctly to theory questions. In this section the key points covered are as follows:

1. The differences between a defined contribution pension plan and a defined benefit pension plan and the resulting accounting and reporting differences between these two types of plans.
2. The bookkeeping entries made to record an employer's pension expense and the funding of pension cost.
3. The benefits-years-of-service approach.
4. The calculation and reporting of the net pension asset/liability for employers who sponsor defined benefit pension plans.
5. The five elements which, if they all exist, an employer sponsoring a defined benefit pension plan must evaluate for inclusion in its pension expense each year. These factors are

   a. Service cost
   b. Interest cost
   c. Actual return on plan assets
   d. Amortization of unrecognized prior service cost
   e. Gain or loss.

6. The required disclosures in the financial statements of employers who sponsor pension plans.

1. Employer Sponsor's vs. Plan's Accounting and Reporting

a. In order to understand the accounting and reporting requirements for pension plans, you must keep in mind that there are two accounting entities involved: the employer sponsor of the plan, and the pension plan which is usually under the control of a pension trustee.

   (1) The employer sponsor reports Pension Cost (Pension Expense) in its income statement. In its balance sheet it usually reports a net Pension Asset/Liability representing the difference between the Projected Benefit Obligation and the Plan Assets; both of the latter accounts, are under the control of the pension trustee. As discussed later, another entry may be required to accumulated other comprehensive income to report the funding status of the plan.

b. A separate accounting entity, the pension plan, maintains the following accounts: Projected Benefit Obligation, Accumulated Benefit Obligation (for reporting purposes only), Vested Benefits (for reporting purposes only), and Plan Assets. The pension plan pays benefits to the retired employees.

c. The diagram below shows the relationship of the entities involved in a pension plan, the accounts usually used by each, and the flow of cash.

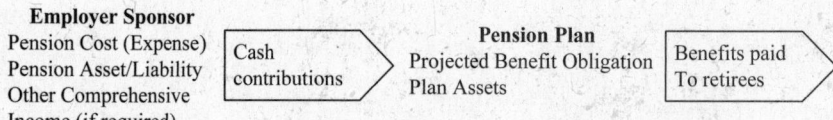

Employer Sponsor
Pension Cost (Expense)
Pension Asset/Liability
Other Comprehensive
Income (if required)

Cash contributions

Pension Plan
Projected Benefit Obligation
Plan Assets

Benefits paid
To retirees

   (1) The employer sponsor must maintain, accounts for Unrecognized Prior Service Cost and Unrecognized Gains and Losses within Other Comprehensive Income (OCI).

   > **NOTE:** The projected benefit obligations of the pension plan, the interest on these obligations, the pension plan assets available to meet these obligations, and returns (income) on these plan assets are all economic variables which impact the employer sponsor's yearly calculations of pension expense and its year-end pension asset/liability. (Key concepts are **boldfaced** to call attention to those terms and phrases that must be clearly understood.)

   (2) Plan information must be made available to the participants and beneficiaries. Furthermore, after filing under ERISA (the Employee Retirement Income Security Act of 1974), the DOL (Department of Labor) must make the annual report available to the public. Certain funding information must be filed with the PBGC (Pension Benefit Guarantee Corporation).

2. An Overview of Employer's Accounting for Pension Plans

a. Under a **defined contribution plan** the employer agrees to make a defined contribution to a pension plan as determined by the provisions of the plan. Consequently, plan participants will receive at retirement whatever benefits (i.e., payments) the contributions can provide.

(1) Accounting for a defined contribution plan is relatively straightforward. Each year the employer records an expense and a related liability for the agreed-upon contribution.

(2) Payments are charged against the liability with an offsetting reduction in cash.

(3) Additional disclosure requirements include a description of the plan including employee groups covered, the basis for determining contributions, and the nature and effects of events affecting comparability.

b. Under a **defined benefit plan** the employer agrees to provide a benefit at retirement that is defined or fixed by a formula. Because the benefits are defined, the employer accepts the risk associated with changes in the variables that determine the amounts needed to meet the obligation to plan participants. These amounts require the use of estimates that may become very complex. However, these estimates are made by actuaries hired by the management of the employer sponsor. They are not made by the sponsoring company's accountants. The remainder of our pension coverage is devoted to a discussion of the issues that arise under this type of plan.

(1) The **accrual accounting objective** for pension costs recognizes the compensation cost of an employee's pension benefits including prior service costs over that employee's service period. Under accrual accounting, pension expense should not be determined on the basis of the employer's cash payout (funding) practices.

(2) The **funding of the pension obligation** refers to the amount that the employer contributes to an independent trustee for the pension plan (plans where the fund is under the control of the employer are considered unfunded). Many factors including tax considerations, working capital management, and contractual agreements influence funding decisions.

(a) Thus, the amount selected for funding should not govern the determination of the amount to be reported as pension expense under accrual accounting; these events should be distinguished. Although both events can be recorded with one entry, we use two entries in this section to better illustrate this distinction.

Pension expense	xxxx	
Pension asset/liability		xxxx

1] This adjusting entry is to record the accrued expense. The use of the Pension asset/liability account simplifies the accounting. If the account has a net debit balance, it is an asset. If the account has a net credit balance, it is a liability.

Pension asset/liability	xxxx	
Cash		xxxx

2] This entry is to record the funding of the pension obligation at the time cash is transferred to the plan's trustee.

(b) The determination of the amounts to be used in the above entries requires the professional expertise of actuaries who assess the benefits to be provided under the pension formula and the characteristics of the employees covered under the plan (e.g., average age). With these factors as given, the actuaries must estimate the values of the variables that will influence the actual amounts to be paid at retirement by making actuarial assumptions about factors such as longevity, early retirements, turnover rate, and the rates of return to be earned on invested funds.

(3) The actuarial present value of the obligation determined under the benefits-years-of-service method is referred to as the **projected benefit obligation**. The **accumulated benefit obligation** is the amount computed using the current salary amounts instead of the estimated future salary amounts. Therefore, if the defined benefit formula is not dependent on the amount of a future salary (say a retiree receives a fixed amount for each month worked), there would be no difference between the two approaches. If the defined benefit formula is pay-related and salaries are assumed to increase over time, the projected benefit obligation will be a greater amount than the accumulated benefit obligation.

(4) The Codification requires reporting the funded status of a pension plan. Overfunded and underfunded plans must be reported on the balance sheet as either assets or liabilities.

3. **Funded Status of Pension Plan**

a. The funded status of the plan must be reported in the balance sheet. The funded status is the difference between the projected benefit obligation and the fair value of the plan assets at the measurement date.

(1) If the plan is overfunded, a noncurrent asset is recorded on the balance sheet.

(2) If the plan is underfunded, either a current liability, a noncurrent liability, or both are reported on the balance sheet.

(3) Any additional asset or liability not already recognized as pension expense is recognized in other comprehensive income (net of tax).

(4) If a plan is amended and either increases or decreases the projected benefit obligation, this amount should be recognized as either a prior service cost or credit. Prior service costs or credits should be amortized over the future periods of service of the employees expected to receive benefits.

b. For an employer with multiple plans, all overfunded plans are aggregated and disclosed as a noncurrent asset. All underfunded plans are aggregated and disclosed as a current liability, noncurrent liability, or both. **In other words, the funding status of plans may NOT be netted (overfunded plans may not be netted with underfunded plans).** The measurement date for plans is the fiscal year-end (i.e., balance sheet date) of the entity.

4. **Determination of Pension Expense**

a. The general term **Pension Cost** is preferred over pension expense because pension cost is included in overhead in the determination of product costs and therefore may be part of inventory in the balance sheet.

(1) When permissible the term "Pension Expense" is used instead because it is simpler and clearer.
(2) The disclosure of the elements included in pension expense is one of the most significant disclosures required. A comprehensive illustration is presented in Section 7 below.

(a) This illustration integrates the concepts and calculations that have been introduced in the preceding discussions.

b. Pension Expense is a net amount calculated by adding together five factors. These factors are (1) service cost, (2) interest on the projected benefit obligation, (3) return on plan assets, (4) amortization of unrecognized prior service cost or credit, and (5) the effect of gains and losses. Each of these components is discussed below.

(1) **Service cost—Increases pension expense**

(a) **Service cost** is defined as the actuarial present value of benefits attributed by the pension benefit formula to employee service during the current period.
(b) ASC Topic 715 (SFAS 87) requires that future salary levels be taken into consideration in this calculation (i.e., the benefits-years-of-service approach).

(2) **Interest on projected benefit obligation—Increases pension expense**

(a) The **interest on the projected benefit obligation** is defined as the increase in the amount of the projected benefit obligation due to the passage of time. Since the pension plan's obligation at the beginning of the year is stated in terms of present value, a provision for interest is required. By the end of the period, the plan's obligation will increase by the amount of interest that would accrue based on the discount (settlement) rate selected.

1] The discount rate selected should be determined by reference to market conditions using such rates as the return on high quality investments or the implicit rate of return in retirement annuities as a basis for comparison.
2] Also, the rate selected must be **explicit** and an unreasonable rate cannot be justified by an argument that the unreasonable rate is **implicitly** valid because of other offsetting actuarial assumptions. The selected discount rate is referred to as the **settlement rate** because it is the rate at which the plan's obligation could be settled.

EXAMPLE

Compute the "interest" component of net pension expense for year 2, if the projected benefit obligation was $4,800,000 on January 1, year 2, and the settlement rate is 9%. Answer: Net pension expense for year 2 is increased by $432,000 (9% × $4,800,000) to provide for interest on the projected benefit obligation.

---

(3) **Actual return on plan assets—Decreases or possibly increases pension expense**

(a) The **actual return on plan assets** is defined as the difference in the fair value of plan assets at the beginning and the end of the period adjusted for contributions made to the plan and benefit payments made by the plan during the period. The formula for determining the actual return is as follows:

Actual return = (End. Bal. of plan assets at fair value – Beg. bal. of plan assets at fair value) + Benefits – Contributions

(b) The **fair value or market value** of plan assets is defined as the price expected in a sales transaction between a willing buyer and seller.

1] **Plan assets** typically include marketable securities and other investments such as real estate that are held in trust for the plan participants.

2] Assets that are under the control of the employer are not considered to be plan assets.

3] In calculating the return on plan assets, considerable leeway has been allowed in measuring the fair value of plan assets.

EXAMPLE

Compute the "actual return on plan assets" component of net pension expense, if the fair value of plan assets was $3,100,000 at the beginning of the year and $3,820,000 at year-end. The employer sponsor contributed $450,000 to the plan and the plan paid benefits of $200,000 during the year. Answer: Net pension expense is decreased by $470,000 [($3,820,000 – $3,100,000) + $200,000 – $450,000] due to the actual return earned on the fair value of plan assets.

(c) Although the **actual** return on plan assets is measured and disclosed as one of the components of net pension expense, net pension expense will include only an amount equal to the **expected** return on plan assets.

1] This methodology is followed because the difference between the actual return on plan assets and the expected return on plan assets is a canceling adjustment that is included in the gain or loss calculation to be discussed below.

(4) **Prior service cost or credit—Increases or possibly decreases pension expense**

(a) **Prior service costs** are retroactive adjustments that are granted to recognize services rendered in previous periods.

1] These costs are caused by either an amendment to an existing plan or the initiation of a new plan where a **retroactive allowance** is made for past services rendered.

2] If, as a result of an amendment to an existing plan, the benefits are increased, then the amount of the plan's projected benefit obligation will increase.

a] The amount of the prior service costs is measured by the increase in the projected benefit obligation caused by the amendment or the initiation of the plan.

(b) While the prior service costs are related to the past, it is assumed that the initiation or amendment of the plan was made with the intent of benefiting the employer's future operations rather than its past operations. Because of this assumption, prior service costs should be amortized over the present and future periods affected. The unamortized portion is located in OCI. Two methods approved for use in determining the assignment of prior service costs are (1) the expected future years of service method, and (2) the straight-line basis over the average remaining service period of active employees method.

1] Under the **expected future years of service** method, the total number of employee service years is calculated by grouping employees according to the time remaining to their retirement, based on actuarial assumptions, and multiplying the number in each group by the number of periods remaining to retirement.

EXAMPLE

Eight employees expected to work ten years until retirement would contribute eighty expected future years of service to the total.

---

a] To calculate the amortization of prior service costs for a given year, the number of employee service years applicable to that period is used as the numerator of the fraction and the denominator is the total employee service years based on all the identified groups. This method produces a declining pattern similar to the amortization applicable to premiums or discounts on serial bonds and the sum-of-the-years' digits method of depreciation.

2] The **straight-line basis over the average remaining service period** of active employees is a simpler method. The projected average remaining service period for the affected participants is estimated by the use of a weighted-average method.

> **EXAMPLE**
>
> Ten employees with ten years remaining to retirement, and fifteen employees with twenty years remaining to retirement would have a weighted-average service life of sixteen years computed as follows: $(10 \times 10 + 15 \times 20)/25$. In this example, the prior service costs would be amortized and included in pension expense over sixteen years.

a] Although the costs are gradually recognized in Pension Expense over the sixteen years, the costs are fully recognized on the balance sheet in OCI immediately resulting in an adjustment to the Pension Asset/Liability account.

> **EXAMPLE**
>
> Compute the "amortization of prior service cost" component of net pension expense for the first three years after an amendment, based on the following facts. The prior service cost associated with the amendment is determined by the actuaries to be $650,000 (the difference between the projected benefit obligation before and after the amendment). The employer has 200 employees at the time of the amendment. It is expected that workers will retire or terminate at the rate of 4% per year, and the employer will use the "expected future years of service" method of amortization.
>
> **Answer:** Since the workers will leave at the rate of 8 per year (4% × 200 employees), the denominator of the amortization fraction is computed by summing $200 + 192 + 184 + ... + 8$. This series can be written as $8(25 + 24 + 23 + ... + 1)$ or $8n(n+1)/2 = 8(25)(26)/2 = 2,600$. The calculations for the first three years and the unamortized balance at year-end are presented in the table below.
>
> | Year | Amortization fraction | Annual amortization | Unamortized balances |
> |------|------------------------|----------------------|----------------------|
> | 0 | | | $650,000 |
> | 1 | 200/2,600 | $50,000 | 600,000 |
> | 2 | 192/2,600 | 48,000 | 552,000 |
> | 3 | 184/2,600 | 46,000 | 506,000 |

(5) Gain or loss—Increases or decreases pension expense

(a) Net gain or loss is defined as the change in the amount of the projected benefit obligation as well as the change in the value of plan assets (realized and unrealized), resulting from experience being different from that assumed, or from a change in an actuarial assumption. For this calculation, plan assets are valued at the market-related value, discussed under (3) above.

(b) The gain or loss component included in net pension expense consists of two items:

1] The current period difference between the actual and expected return on plan assets.

     a] (Expected rate of return on plan assets) × (Market-related value of plan assets at the beginning of the period)

2] Amortization of the unrecognized net gain or loss from **previous** periods.

     a] The current period difference is reported as a component of the current period net pension expense and the unrecognized net gain or loss is located in OCI until it is subject to amortization.

     b] In the unusual case when a gain or loss arises from an event such as the discontinuation of a business component, the gain or loss should be recognized immediately and associated with the event that was the cause (e.g., discontinued operations) rather than the pension plan.

(c) When the amortization of the cumulative unrecognized net gain or loss from previous periods is required, the procedure is comparable to the amortization of prior service cost and, in general, it requires the use of a systematic method applied on a consistent basis that is dependent on the average remaining service period for active employees.

1] Unlike past service cost, however, the amount to be amortized is not necessarily the calculated amount of the cumulative unrecognized net gain or loss.

2] Instead, the minimum amount subject to amortization is determined by the use of a method sometimes referred to as the "**corridor**" approach and is determined by computing, at the beginning of the fiscal year, the excess of the cumulative unrecognized gain or loss over 10% of the greater of the projected benefit obligation or the market-related asset value.

     a] If the cumulative unrecognized gain or loss is equal to or less than the 10% calculated value, no amount need be amortized.

EXAMPLE

Compute the "gain or loss" component of net pension expense and the other elements of pension expense based on the following facts:

At the beginning of the year the cumulative unrecognized net loss was $500,000, the fair value and market-related value of plan assets was $3,100,000, and the projected benefit obligation was $4,800,000. The expected return on assets for the year was 9% and the settlement rate was 11%. The fair value of plan assets at the end of the year was $3,400,000. There were no contributions to the plan during the year. The plan made no benefit payments during the year. Service costs for the year were $400,000. At the beginning of the year the average remaining service period of active employees was ten years. There are no other factors to be considered in computing pension expense for the year.

Answer: The elements of net pension expense are calculated as follows:

Service cost	$ 400,000	
Interest (.11 × $4,800,000)	528,000	
Actual return on plan assets	(300,000)	(1)
Amortization of unrecognized net loss	2,000	(2)
Asset gain deferred	21,000	(3)
Net pension expense	$ 651,000	

NOTE: The above components of pension expense are required to be disclosed in the employer sponsor's financial statements. This would be done in the footnotes to those statements.

(1) $3,400,000 less $3,100,000 less contributions to the plan of $0 plus benefit payments of the plan of $0.
(2) Amortization of unrecognized net loss is calculated as follows:

"Corridor" 10% × $4,800,000	$480,000
Cumulative unrecognized net loss at the beginning of the year	500,000
Excess to be amortized	$ 20,000
Amortization of unrecognized loss is: $20,000/10 years = $2,000.	

(3) The asset gain deferred of $21,000 is calculated as follows: Actual return on plan assets of $300,000 less expected return on plan assets of $279,000. The expected return on plan assets is determined by multiplying the expected return on plan assets of 9% times the market-related value of plan assets at the beginning of the year of $3,100,000. Note that in the above computation of pension expense actual return on assets of $300,000 is deducted. However, the expected return on plan assets of $279,000 ($300,000 – $21,000) is the amount that is actually included in pension expense for the year.

5. **Reconciling the Projected Benefit Obligation**

a. The projected benefit obligation (PBO) is the actuarial present value of all benefits attributed to employee service rendered prior to that date. The PBO is measured by using actuarial assumptions and estimates regarding discount rates, retirement dates, and life expectancies. Any changes in these actuarial assumptions may increase or decrease the PBO.

(1) Changes to the PBO due to changes in actuarial assumptions are referred to as actuarial gains or losses in calculating the PBO.
(2) The PBO is also affected by any changes or amendments to the plan made during the current period.
(3) The total change to the PBO caused by a plan amendment is referred to as the prior service cost or credit.

NOTE: The entire amount of the prior service cost or credit will affect the PBO in the year of the change. However, only the amortized amount of the prior service cost or credit is included in pension cost (expense) for the period.

b. The following formula is used to reconcile the projected benefit obligation:

Change in projected benefit obligation:

Beginning of year PBO
+   Service cost
+   Interest cost
±   Prior service cost or credit (from changes to plan in current year)
±   Actuarial gain or loss (from changes in actuarial or underlying assumptions)
–   Benefits paid
End of year PBO

6. **Disclosures for Pensions**

    a. The required disclosures for pensions and other postretirement benefits are as follows:

      (1) A reconciliation schedule of the benefit obligation showing the components separately

      (2) A reconciliation schedule of the fair value of plan assets with the components shown separately

      (3) The funded status of the plans, and the amounts recognized in the balance sheet showing separately the noncurrent assets, current liabilities, and noncurrent liabilities recognized

      (4) Information about plan assets including equity securities and debt securities, a narrative description of investment policies and strategies, a narrative description of the basis used to determine overall expected rate-of-return on assets, disclosure of classes of plan assets, and information about assets if information is expected to be useful

      (5) For defined benefit pension plans, the accumulated benefit obligation

      (6) The benefits expected to be paid in each of the next five fiscal years and in the aggregate for the five fiscal years thereafter

      (7) The employer's best estimate of contributions expected to be paid to the plan during the rest of the fiscal year

      (8) The net periodic benefit cost recognized with the components shown separately

      (9) The net gain or loss and net prior service cost or credit recognized in other comprehensive income (OCI) for the period, and any reclassification adjustments of OCI (amortization of items) that are recognized in pension cost

      (10) The amounts in accumulated OCI that have not yet been recognized as pension costs, showing separately the net gain or loss, the net prior service cost or credit, and net transition asset or obligation

      (11) On a weighted-average basis, the rates used for the assumed discount rate, rate of compensation increase, and expected long-term rate of return on plan assets, and the assumptions used to determine benefit obligations and net benefit cost

      (12) The assumed health care cost trend rate, a description of the pattern of change

      (13) The effect a 1-percentage-point increase or decrease would have on the aggregated service and interest cost components and the accumulated postretirement benefit obligation for health-care benefits

      (14) The amounts and types of securities of the employer and related parties included in plan assets, the approximate amount of future annual benefits of plan participants covered by insurance contracts issued by employer or related parties, and any significant transactions between the employer or related parties and the plan during the year

      (15) Any alternative method used to amortize prior service amounts or unrecognized net gains and losses

      (16) Any substantive commitments, such as past practice or history of regular benefit increases used to account for benefit obligation

      (17) The cost of providing special or contractual termination benefits recognized during the period and a description of the nature of the event

      (18) An explanation of any significant changes in the plan assets or the benefit obligation

      (19) The amounts in accumulated OCI expected to be recognized as components of pension cost over the fiscal year-end that follows the most recent balance sheet presented, showing separately net gain or loss, net prior service cost or credit, and net transition asset or obligation

      (20) The amount and timing of any plan assets expected to be returned to the employer during the next 12-month period (or operating cycle, if longer) after the most recent balance sheet

    b. The required disclosures for multiemployer plans are as follows:

      (1) The significant multiemployer plans in which an employer participates.

      (2) The level of an employer's participation (the contribution to the plan and whether that contribution represents more than 5% of the total contributions).

      (3) The financial health of the plan such as funded status, improvement plans, and surcharges.

      (4) The nature of the employer commitments to the plans such as collective bargaining agreements and minimum contribution requirements.

      (5) For plans in which users are unable to obtain additional information from outside sources:

        (a) A description of the nature of the plan benefits.

        (b) A qualitative description of the employer responsibility for plan obligations.

        (c) Other quantitative information available such as total plan assets, actuarial present value of accumulated vested benefits, and total contributions received by the plan.

7. Comprehensive Illustration

EXAMPLE

Schaefer Company has sponsored a noncontributory (i.e., employees make no contributions) defined benefit plan for its 100 employees for several years. Within this group of 100 employees, it is expected that workers will retire or terminate at the rate of 5 per year for the next twenty years starting January 1, year 5. Prior to year 5, cumulative pension expense recognized in compliance with ASC Topic 715 exceeded cumulative contributions by $150,000, resulting in a $150,000 balance sheet liability. As of January 1, year 5, the company has agreed to an amendment to its plan that includes a retroactive provision to recognize prior service. To illustrate how the provisions of ASC Topic 715 should be applied, assumptions about the facts relevant to the pension plan for year 4 and year 5 are presented in the tables that follow:

	1/1/Y4	1/1/Y5	12/31/Y5
Plan assets (at fair value = market-related value)	$ 400,000	$ 455,000	$ 760,500
Accumulated benefit obligation (ABO; 60% vested)	460,000	640,000*	710,000*
Projected benefit obligation	550,000	821,500*	1,033,650*
Unrecognized cumulative gain (loss)—due to unexpected decrease in asset value	--	(106,000)	?
Prior service cost amendment	--	105,000	?
Pension asset/(liability)	(150,000)	?	?

* Includes effects of amendment1

	12/31/Y4	12/31/Y5
Service cost	$ 117,000	$ 130,000
Employer's funding contribution	125,000	260,000
Plan assets (at fair value = market-related value)	455,000	760,500
Accumulated benefit obligation (60% vested)	620,000	710,000
Benefits paid by the plan	--	--
Unrecognized cumulative gain (loss)—due to unexpected decrease in asset value	(106,000)	(103,729)
Rate of return on assets	9%	10%
Settlement rate	9%	10%

Schedule of Changes in Plan Assets

	Year 4	Year 5
Plan assets at 12/31	$455,000	$ 760,500
Plan assets at 1/1	400,000	455,000
Increase in plan assets	55,000	305,500
Add: Benefits paid	--	--
Less: Funding contributions for the year	(125,000)	(260,000)
Actual return or (loss) on plan assets	(70,000)	45,500
Expected return on plan assets		
Year 4: 9% × $400,000	36,000	
Year 5: 10% × $455,000		45,500
Unrecognized gain (loss)	$(106,000)	$ --

Required:

A. Prepare a supporting schedule to determine the amounts to be reported as pension expense for year 4 and year 5. The company has decided to use the "expected future years of service" method to amortize the effects of the amendment made in year 5.

B. Prepare the journal entries required for year 4 and year 5 with respect to the pension plan including any entry necessary to comply with the minimum liability requirement.

C. Prepare pension worksheets for year 4 and year 5.

> **NOTE:** These worksheets summarize Schaefer's general journal entries and changes in its pension-related accounts. These worksheets also summarize the changes in the pension plan's accounts, unrecognized prior service cost, and unrecognized gain or loss. Study these worksheets as they are an excellent tool for pulling together the elements of this comprehensive illustration.

D. Indicate the pension-related amounts that should appear in the company's financial statements prepared at the end of year 4 and year 5.

E. Prepare disclosures of the funded status of the plan to the liability shown in the company's balance sheet at 1/1/Y4, 12/31/Y4, and 12/31/Y5.

EXAMPLE

Solution Part A

REQUIRED FOOTNOTE DISCLOSURE
Pension Expense

		12/31/Y4	12/31/Y5
Components of net periodic benefit cost			
1.	Service cost	$117,000	$130,000
2.	Interest cost on projected benefit obligation	49,500	82,150
3.	Actual loss or (actual return) on plan assets	70,000	(45,500)
4.	Amortization of prior service cost	--	10,000
5.	Deferral of "gain" or (loss)	(106,000)	--
6.	Loss amortization	--	2,271
7.	Recognized actuarial loss	--	--
	Net periodic benefit cost	$130,500	$178,921

Calculations

1. **Service cost** is given.
2. **Interest:** 9% × $550,000 (year 4), and 10% × $821,500 (year 5). The settlement rate times PBO.
3. **Actual return:** ($70,000) for year 4 and $45,500 (same as expected) for year 5. Note that in year 4, the $70,000 actual loss on plan assets less the $106,000 unrecognized loss equals the expected return ($36,000).
4. **Prior service cost amortization:** Compute the denominator of the fraction for amortization by calculating the sum of the estimated remaining service years by adding $100 + 95 + 90 + ... + 10 + 5$. This series can be written as $5(20 + 19 + 18 + ... + 2 + 1)$ or $5n(n+1)/2$, where $n = 100/5 = 20$, or $5(20)(21)/2 = 1,050$. For year 5 the amount is $(100/1,050) × $105,000 = $10,000$.
5. **Loss:** The $106,000 unrecognized loss that arose in year 4 is not amortized until year 5, because no unrecognized net gain or loss existed at the beginning of the year. The amortization of the unrecognized net gain or loss should be included as a component of pension expense only if the unrecognized net gain or loss existed as of the beginning of the year and the unrecognized gain or loss exceeded the corridor. At 1/1/year 5 10% of the greater of the projected benefit obligation ($821,500) or the market-related asset value ($455,000) is equal to $82,150. The minimum loss to be amortized is $106,000 − $82,150 or $23,850. The average employee service remaining as of 1/1/year 4 assuming a constant work force of 100 and an attrition rate of 5 workers per year is $(100 + 95 + 90 + ... + 10 + 5)/110$ or $1,050/110 = 10.5$ years. The amount of the loss recognized in year 5 is $23,850/11.5 = $2,271$. Since actual and expected returns are equal in year 5, no further adjustment is required.

EXAMPLE

Solution Part B

The journal entries will include three entries: (1) record pension expense for the period; (2) report the cash paid to fund the plan; and (3) report any pension asset or liability caused by overfunding or underfunding the plan. Below are the journal entries required for Schaefer for the first two entries. Below are the journal entries required for Schaefer. A compound entry is provided with the worksheet.

Journal Entries

	Year 4		Year 5	
Pension expense	130,500		178,921	
Pension asset/liability		130,500		178,921
To record pension expense				
Pension asset/liability	125,000		260,000	
Cash		125,000		260,000
To record funding				

The journal entry to record other comprehensive income for the unexpected gain/loss and prior service cost, shown net of tax, are as follows:

Assuming a 40% tax rate, the entries for year 4 and year 5 would be

Year 4 entries		
Other comprehensive income G/L	106,000	
Pension asset/liability		106,000
Deferred tax asset	42,400	
Other comprehensive income—deferred tax asset		42,400

Year 5 entries

Other comprehensive income PSC	105,000	
Other comprehensive income PSC		10,000
Other comprehensive income G/L		2,271
Pension asset/liability		92,729
Deferred tax asset	37,092	
Other comprehensive income—deferred tax asset		37,092

Therefore, in year 4, OCI would decrease by $63,600 net of tax, and in year 5, OCI would decrease $55,637 net of tax.

The total change in the pension asset/liability account resulting from the above journal entries tries to the change in the required pension asset/liability account as calculated by the change in the funded status of the plan. For example, for year 4, the entries to the pension asset/liability account include: $130,500 (CR) + 125,000 (DR) + 106,000 (CR) = $111,500. The funded status (as shown on the next page, at the beginning of the year is $150,000 (CR). The funded status at the end of the year is $261,500 (CR). The change in funded status is $261,600 – 150,000 = $111,500.

The balance sheet reflects the funded status of the plan. The status is determined by comparing the projected benefit obligation to the fair value of the plan assets. The end-of-year projected benefit obligation is calculated as shown below.

	Year 4	Year 5
Projected benefit obligation at beginning of year	$550,000	$ 821,500
Service cost	117,000	130,000
Interest cost*	49,500	82,150
Benefits paid	0	0
Projected benefit obligation at end of year	$716,500	$1,033,650

* The interest cost is determined by multiplying the Settlement rate times the beginning projected benefit obligation. ($49,500 = $550,000 × 9%) ($82,150 = $821,500 × 10%)

Then the funded status of the plan for the two years may be calculated as follows:

	12/31/Y4	12/31/Y5
Projected benefit obligation	$ 716,500	$1,033,650
Fair value of plan assets	455,000	760,500
Funded status of plan	$(261,500)	$ (273,150)

Because the plan is underfunded at the end of both years, a liability must be included on the balance sheet equal to the underfunded amount. However, the entity will often already have an accrued/prepaid pension account. To determine the liability adjustment needed, the balance in the accrued/prepaid pension cost must be considered. The balances at 12/31/Y4 and 12/31/Y5 are calculated below.

	Year 4	Year 5
Pension asset/liability at beginning of year	$(150,000)	$(155,500)
Funding contributions	125,000	260,000
Pension cost (expense)	(130,500)	(178,921)
Other comprehensive income—G/L	(106,000)	2,271
Other comprehensive income—PSC (net)		(95,000)
Pension asset/liability at end of year	$(261,500)	$(273,150)

Finally, the adjustment to establish to recognize the funding status of the plan for each year is calculated as follows:

	12/31/Y4	12/31/Y5
Liability required	$ 261,500	$ 273,150
Pension asset/liability at beginning of year	(150,000)	(261,500)
Adjustment to liability*	$ 111,500	$ (11,650)

* The adjustment must tie to the journal entries provided on previous page.

Similarly, if the pension plan were overfunded, Schaefer would record an adjusting entry to record a noncurrent asset for the amount of the plan that is overfunded.

Often, a compound journal entry will be used to reflect the changes in the pension asset/liability account. The compound journal entry can be derived from the previous information or the worksheet on the following page.

	Year 4	Year 5
Pension cost (expense)	130,500	178,921
Other comprehensive income G/L	106,000	--
Other comprehensive income PSC	--	105,000
Cash	125,000	260,000
Other comprehensive income G/L	--	2,271
Other comprehensive income PSC	--	10,000
Pension asset/liability	111,500	11,650

EXAMPLE

Solution Part C

SCHAEFER COMPANY
Pension Worksheet—Year 4

	Debit (credit)						Debit (credit)	
	General journal entries						Memo entries	
	Pension expense	**Cash**	**Accumulated OCI PSC**	**Accumulated OCI G/L**	**Deferred tax asset (liab)**	**Pension asset (liab)**	**Projected benefit obligation**	**Plan assets**
Bal. 1/1/Y4						(150,000)	(550,000)	400,000
Service cost	117,000						(117,000)	
Interest cost	49,500						(49,500)	
Actual loss	70,000							(70,000)
Deferred gain (loss)	(106,000)			106,000				
Contribution		(125,000)						125,000
Journal entry for year 4	130,500	(125,000)		106,000		(111,500)		
Def. tax adjustment				42,400	42,400			
Bal. 12/31/Y5				(63,600)	42,400	(261,500)	(716,500)*	455,000

* Before plan amendment on 1/1/11

SCHAEFER COMPANY
Pension Worksheet—Year 5

	Debit (credit)						Debit (credit)	
	General journal entries						Memo entries	
	Pension expense	**Cash**	**Accumulated OCI PSC**	**Accumulated OCI G/L**	**Deferred tax asset (liab)**	**Pension asset (liab)**	**Projected benefit obligation**	**Plan assets**
Bal. 1/1/Y5						(261,500)	(716,500)	455,000
Prior service cost amendment			105,000				(105,000)	
Service cost	130,000						(130,000)	
Interest cost	82,150						(82,150)	
Actual return	(45,500)							45,500
Prior service cost amortization	10,000		(10,000)					
Loss amortization	2,271			(2,271)				
Contribution		(260,000)						260,000
Journal entry for year 5	178,921	(260,000)	95,000	(2,271)		(11,650)		
OCI 12/31/Y4 Bal				63,600	42,400			
Def. tax adjustment			(38,000)	908	37,092			
Bal. 12/31/Y5			57,000	62,237	79,492	(273,492)	(1,033,650)	760,500

EXAMPLE

Solutions Part D and E

Required Footnote Disclosure
(Pension expense disclosure shown in Part A)

	12/31/Y4	12/31/Y5
Change in projected benefit obligation		
Benefit obligation at beginning of year*	$ 550,000	$ 716,500*
Service cost	117,000	130,000
Interest cost	49,500	82,150
Amendment (prior service cost)	--	105,000
Actuarial loss (gain)	--	--
Benefits paid	--	--
Benefit obligation at end of year	$ 716,500	$1,033,650

* Before effect of plan amendment

	12/31/Y4	12/31/Y5
Change in plan assets		
Fair value of plan assets at beginning of year	$ 400,000	$ 455,000
Actual return (loss) on plan assets	(70,000)	45,500
Employer contribution	125,000	260,000
Benefits paid	--	--
Fair value of plan assets at end of year	$ 455,000	$ 760,500
Funded status	$(261,500)	$ (273,150)
Other changes recognized in other comprehensive income		
Net actuarial loss	$(150,000)	$ --
Amortization of net loss		2,271
Plan amendment for PSC		(105,000)
Amortization of PSC		10,000
Deferred tax	42,400	37,092
Total recognized change in other comprehensive income	$ (63,600)	$ (55,637)
Amounts recognized in the statement of financial position (balance sheet) consists of		
Pension asset/liability	$(261,500)	$ (273,150)
Deferred tax asset	42,400	79,492
Other comprehensive income G/L	(63,600)	(62,237)
Other comprehensive income PSC	--	(57,000)

NOW REVIEW MULTIPLE-CHOICE QUESTIONS 1 THROUGH 35

---

8. **Postretirement Benefits other than Pensions (OPEB)**

   a. ASC Subtopic 715-60 (refer to outline) establishes the standard for employers' accounting for other (than pension) postretirement benefits (OPEB). This standard requires a single method for measuring and recognizing an employer's accumulated postretirement benefit obligation (APBO). It applies to all forms of postretirement benefits, although the most material benefit is usually postretirement health care. To the extent that the promised benefits are similar, the accounting provisions are similar. Only when there is a compelling reason is the accounting different. Companies must disclose the status of overfunded and underfunded postretirement plans on their balance sheets.

   b. There are, however, some fundamental differences between defined benefit pension plans and postretirement benefits other than pensions. The following list presents these differences.

Differences between Pensions and Postretirement Health Care Benefits*

Item	Pensions	Health care benefits
Funding	Generally funded.	Generally *NOT* funded.
Benefit	Well-defined and level dollar amount.	Generally uncapped and great variability.
Beneficiary	Retiree (maybe some benefit to surviving spouse).	Retiree, spouse, and other dependents.
Benefit payable	Monthly.	As needed and used.
Predictability	Variables are reasonably predictable.	Utilization difficult to predict. Level of cost varies geographically and fluctuates over time.

* D. Gerald Searfoss and Naomi Erickson, "The Big Unfunded Liability: Postretirement Health Care Benefits," **Journal of Accountancy**, November 1988, pp. 28-39.

c. OPEB requires accrual accounting and adopts the three primary characteristics of pension accounting: (1) delayed recognition (changes are not recognized immediately, but are subsequently recognized in a gradual and systematic way), (2) reporting net cost (aggregates of various items are reported as one net amount), and (3) offsetting assets and liabilities (assets and liabilities are sometimes shown net).

d. The Codification distinguishes between the **substantive** plan and **written** plan. Although generally the same, the substantive plan (the one understood as evidenced by past practice or by communication of intended changes) is the basis for the accounting if it differs from the written plan.

e. OPEBs are considered to be deferred compensation earned in an exchange transaction during the time periods that the employee provides services. The expected cost generally should be attributed in equal amounts (unless the plan attributes a disproportionate share of benefits to early years) over the periods from the employee's hiring date (unless credit for the service is only granted from a later date) to the date that the employee attains full eligibility for all benefits expected to be received. This accrual should be followed even if the employee provides service beyond the date of full eligibility.

(1) The transition obligation is the unrecognized and unfunded APBO (accumulated postretirement benefit obligation) for all of the participants in the plan. This obligation can either (1) be recognized immediately as the effect of an accounting change, subject to certain limitations, or (2) be recognized on a delayed basis over future service periods with disclosure of the unrecognized amount. The delayed recognition has to result in, at least, as rapid a recognition as would have been recognized on a pay-as-you-go basis.

EXAMPLE

A sample illustration of the basic accounting for OPEB follows: Firstime Accrual Co. plans to adopt accrual accounting for OPEB as of January 1, year 31. All employees were hired at age 30 and are fully eligible for benefits at age 60. There are no plan assets. This first calculation determines the unrecognized transition obligation (UTO).

Firstime Accrual Co.
December 31, Year 30

Employee	Age	Years of service	Total years when fully eligible	Expected retirement age	Remaining service to retirement	EPBO	APBO
A	35	5	30	60	25	$ 14,000	$ 2,333
B	40	10	30	60	20	22,000	7,333
C	45	15	30	60	15	30,000	15,000
D	50	20	30	60	10	38,000	25,333
E	55	25	30	65	10	46,000	38,333
F	60	30	30	65	5	54,000	54,000
G	65	RET	--		--	46,000	46,000
H	70	RET	--		--	38,000	38,000
					85	$288,000	$226,332

Calculations

1. EPBO (expected postretirement benefit obligation) is usually determined by an actuary, although it can be calculated if complete data is available.

2. APBO is calculated using the EPBO. Specifically, it is EPBO × (Years of service/total years when fully eligible)

3. The unrecognized transition obligation (UTO) is the APBO at 12/31/Y30 since there are no plan assets to be deducted. The $226,332 can be amortized over the average remaining service to retirement of 14.17 (85/6) years or an optional period of twenty years, if longer. Firstime Accrual selected the twenty-year period of amortization.

4. Note that Employee F has attained full eligibility for benefits and yet plans to continue working.

5. Note that the above year 30 table is used in the calculation of the year 31 components of OPEB cost that follows.

After the establishment of UTO, the next step is to determine the benefit cost for the year ended December 31, year 31. The discount rate is assumed to be 10%.

Firstime Accrual Co.
OPEB COST
December 31, Year 31

1.	Service Cost	$ 5,000
2.	Interest Cost	22,633
3.	Actual Return on Plan Assets	--
4.	Gain or Loss	--
5.	Amortization of Unrecognized Prior Service Cost	--
6.	Amortization of UTO	11,317
	Total OPEB Cost	$38,950

Calculations

1. Service cost calculation uses only employees not yet fully eligible for benefits.

Employee	1/1/Y31 EPBO	Total years when fully eligible	Service cost
A	$14,000	30	$ 467
B	22,000	30	733
C	30,000	30	1,000
D	38,000	30	1,267
E	46,000	30	1,533
Total service cost			$5,000

2. Interest cost is the 1/1/Y31 APBO of $226,332 × 10% = $22,633.
3. There are no plan assets so there is no return.
4. There is no gain (loss) since there are no changes yet.
5. There is no unrecognized prior service cost initially.
6. Amortization of UTO is the 1/1/Y31 UTO of $226,332/20 year optional election = $11,317.

Assume that Firstime Accrual makes a year-end cash benefit payment of $20,000. Firstime Accrual's year-end entry to record other postretirement benefit cost for year 31 would be as follows:

Postretirement benefit cost	38,950	
Cash		20,000
Accrued postretirement benefit cost		18,950

f. Required disclosures for a postretirement benefit plan are stated in ASC Subtopic 715-60. The requirements are the same as the requirements for pensions, which have already been covered in this module.

9. **Nonretirement Postemployment Benefits**

a. Benefits made available to former/inactive employees after employment but before retirement. Examples include continuation of health care and life insurance coverage, severance pay, and disability-related benefits. Criteria for accrual of these benefits are the same as for compensated absences.

   (1) Obligation relates to **services already provided** by the employee,
   (2) Rights to compensation **vest or accumulate,**
   (3) Payment of obligation is **probable,** and
   (4) Amount to be paid is **reasonably estimable**.

NOTE: The last two are the general criteria for recognizing a loss contingency per ASC Topic 450. If is not possible to reliably estimate benefits, disclosure of that fact is required in the footnotes to the financial statements.

10. **Deferred Compensation**

   Deferred compensation is the payment at a future date for work done in an earlier period(s). Account for these contracts individually on an accrual basis that reflects the terms of the agreement. Accrue amounts to be paid in future over the employment period from date agreement is signed to full eligibility date. The rationale for this treatment is matching.

NOW REVIEW MULTIPLE-CHOICE QUESTIONS 36 THROUGH 41

11. **Research Component—Accounting Standards Codification**

In the Codification, the accounting rules for pensions are found in Expenses under Compensation, which is labeled 71X. Topic 71X includes Topics 710, 712, 715, and 718. Topic 710 is Compensation—General. Topic 712 is Compensation—Nonretirement Postemployment Benefits. Topic 715 is Compensation—Retirement Benefits. Topic 715 is organized by subtopics as shown in the following table:

Subtopic	Title
715-10	Overall
715-20	Defined Benefit Plans—General
715-30	Defined Benefit Plans—Pensions
715-60	Defined Benefit Plans—Other Postretirement Plans
715-70	Defined Contribution Plans
715-80	Multiemployer Plans

12. **International Financial Reporting Standards (IFRS)**

The area of employee benefits, and more specifically pensions, is where there are many similarities between US GAAP and IFRS.

a. In a defined contribution pension plan, the accounting is similar to US GAAP. The employer recognizes an expense for the period equal to the required contribution. If payment is made to the plan, then cash is credited. If the contribution is not made by the end of the accounting period, then the entity would recognize a liability for the accrued contributions.

b. With respect to defined benefit plans, some vocabulary is different.

(1) In US GAAP, the benefits-years-of-service method is used to calculate the projected benefit obligation (PBO). Under IFRS, the Projected Unit Credit Method is used to calculate the present value of the defined benefit obligation (PV-DBO). The concept is the same, but the terms are different.

(2) In addition, rather than the term "accumulated benefit obligation," IFRS uses the term "accrued benefit obligation."

(3) In a defined benefit pension plan, the calculation of pension cost for the period is also similar to US GAAP. Under IFRS, net periodic pension cost is comprised of six components:

(a) Current service cost,

(b) Interest cost for the current period on the accrued benefit obligation,

(c) Expected return on plan assets,

(d) Actuarial gains and losses,

(e) Past service costs, and

(f) Effects of curtailments and settlements.

(4) Under US GAAP, the discount rate used is the "settlement rate" (the rate at which the plan's obligations could be settled). With IFRS the discount rate is determined by the market yields at the end of the reporting period for high-quality corporate bonds having a similar term or maturity.

(5) Another difference in accounting for pensions is that under IFRS, for periods beginning on or after January 1, 2013, an entity must immediately recognize all actuarial gains and losses in other comprehensive income. US GAAP uses the corridor approach.

(6) Finally, IFRS has specific rules for netting the balances of pension plan assets and pension liabilities. Netting of plan assets and liability balances is only permissible when there is a legally enforceable right to use the assets of one plan to settle the obligations of another plan.

c. **Termination benefits.** When an entity provides voluntary termination benefits, a liability and expense are reported when the entity is demonstrably committed to a detailed formal plan that it cannot withdraw. The plan should include information such as location, function, number of employees, benefits provided, and when the plan will be implemented.

NOW REVIEW MULTIPLE-CHOICE QUESTIONS 42 THROUGH 43

KEY TERMS

Accumulated benefit obligation. The actuarial present value of benefits (whether vested or nonvested) attributed to employee service rendered before a specified date and based on employee service and compensation before that date.

Actual return on plan assets. The difference between the fair value of plan assets at the end of the period and the fair value at the beginning of the period, adjusted for contribution and payments of benefits during the period.

Benefit-years-of-service approach. An equal portion of the total estimated benefit is attributed to each year of service. The actuarial present value of the benefits is derived after the benefits are attributed to the periods.

Benefits. Payments to which participants may be entitled under pension plan, including pension benefits, death benefits, and benefits due on termination of employment.

Contributory plan. A pension plan under which employees contribute part of the cost.

Cost approach. Assigns net pension costs to periods as level amounts or constant percentages of compensation.

Defined benefit pension plan. A pension plan that defines an amount of pension benefit to be provided, usually as a function of one or more factors such as age, years of service, or compensation.

Defined contribution plan. A plan that provides an individual account for each participant and provides benefits that are based on amounts contributed.

Expected return on plan assets. An amount calculated as a basis for determining the extent of delayed recognition of the effects of changes in the fair value of assets. The expected return on plan assets in determined based on the expected long-term rate of return on plan assets and the market-related value of plan assets.

Gain or loss. A change in the value of either the projected benefit obligation or the plan assets resulting from experience different from that assumed or from a change in an actuarial assumption. Gains and losses that are not recognized in net periodic pension cost when they arise are recognized in other comprehensive income.

Interest cost. The amount recognized in a period determined as the increase in the projected benefit obligation due to the passage of time.

Market-related value of plan assets. A balance used to calculate the expected return on plan assets. The market-related value of plan assets is either fair value or a calculated value that recognizes changes in fair value in a systematic and rational manner over not more than five years.

Multiple-employer plan. A pension plan maintained by more than one employer but not treated as a multiemployer plan.

Net periodic pension cost. The amount recognized in an employer's financial statements as the cost of a pension plan for a period. Components of net periodic pension cost are service cost, interest cost, actual return on plan assets, gain or loss, amortization of prior service cost or credit, and amortization of the transition asset or obligation.

Pension benefits. Periodic (usually monthly) payments made pursuant to the terms of the pension plan to a person who has retired from employment or to that person's beneficiary.

Plan amendment. A change in the terms of an existing plan or the initiation of a new plan. A plan amendment may increase benefits, including those attributed to years of service already rendered.

Plan assets. Assets—usually stocks, bonds, and other investments—that have been segregated and restricted, usually in a trust, to provide for pension benefits. The amount of plan assets includes amounts contributed by the employer, and by employees for a contributory plan, and amounts earned from investing the contributions, less benefits paid.

Prior service cost. The cost of retroactive benefits granted in a plan amendment. Retroactive benefits are benefits granted in a plan amendment (or initiation) that are attributed by the pension benefit formula to employee services rendered in periods before the amendment.

Projected benefit obligation. The actuarial present value as of a date for all benefits attributed by the pension benefit formula to employee service rendered before that date.

Service cost. A component of net periodic pension cost recognized in a period determined as the actuarial present value of benefits attributed by the pension benefit formula to services rendered by employees during that period.

Single-employer plan. A pension plan that is maintained by one employer. The term also may be used to describe a plan that is maintained by related parties such as a parent and its subsidiaries.

Unfunded projected benefit obligation. The excess of the projected benefit obligation over plan assets.

Vested benefit obligation. The actuarial present value of vested benefits.

Multiple-Choice Questions (1-43)

D.1.-5. Pensions

1. The following information pertains to Lee Corp.'s defined benefit pension plan for year 2:

Service cost	$160,000
Actual and expected gain on plan assets	35,000
Unexpected loss on plan assets related to a	
year 1 disposal of a subsidiary	40,000
Amortization of unrecognized prior service cost	5,000
Annual interest on pension obligation	50,000

What amount should Lee report as pension cost in its year 2 income statement?

- a. $250,000
- b. $220,000
- c. $210,000
- d. $180,000

2. Jordon Corporation obtains the following information from its actuary. All amounts given are **as of** 1/1/Y2 (beginning of the year).

	1/1/Y2
Projected benefit obligation	$1,530,000
Market-related asset value	1,650,000
Unrecognized net loss	235,000
Average remaining service period	5.5 years

What amount of unrecognized net loss should be recognized as part of pension cost in year 2?

- a. $70,000
- b. $42,727
- c. $14,909
- d. $12,727

3. Which of the following disclosures is not required of companies with a defined benefit pension plan?

- a. A description of the plan.
- b. The amount of pension expense by component.
- c. The weighted-average discount rate.
- d. The estimates of future contributions for the next five years.

4. Bulls Corporation amends its pension plan on 1/1/Y2. The following information is available:

	1/1/Y2 amendment	1/1/Y2 after amendment
Accumulated benefit obligation	$ 950,000	$1,425,000
Projected benefit obligation	1,300,000	1,900,000

The total amount of unrecognized prior service cost to be amortized over future periods as a result of this amendment is

- a. $950,000
- b. $600,000
- c. $475,000
- d. $125,000

5. On January 2, year 2, Loch Co. established a noncontributory defined benefit plan covering all employees and contributed $1,000,000 to the plan. At December 31, year 2, Loch determined that the year 2 service and interest costs on the plan were $620,000. The expected and the actual rate of return on plan assets for year 2 was 10%. There are no other

components of Loch's pension expense. What amount should Loch report in its December 31, year 2 balance sheet as prepaid pension cost?

- a. $280,000
- b. $380,000
- c. $480,000
- d. $620,000

6. Webb Co., a publicly traded company, implemented a defined benefit pension plan for its employees on January 1, year 1. During year 1 and year 2, Webb's contributions fully funded the plan. The following data are provided for year 4 and year 3:

	Year 4 Estimated	Year 3 Actual
Projected benefit obligation, December 31	$750,000	$700,000
Accumulated benefit obligation, December 31	520,000	500,000
Plan assets at fair value, December 31	675,000	600,000
Projected benefit obligation in excess of plan assets	75,000	100,000
Pension expense	90,000	75,000
Employer's contribution	90,000	50,000

What amount should Webb report as a pension liability in its December 31, year 4 balance sheet?

- a. $ 50,000
- b. $ 60,000
- c. $ 75,000
- d. $100,000

7. Visor Co. maintains a defined benefit pension plan for its employees. The service cost component of Visor's net periodic pension cost is measured using the

- a. Unfunded accumulated benefit obligation.
- b. Unfunded vested benefit obligation.
- c. Projected benefit obligation.
- d. Expected return on plan assets.

8. Which of the following components should be included in the calculation of net pension cost recognized for a period by an employer sponsoring a defined benefit pension plan?

	Actual return on plan assets, if any	Amortization of unrecognized prior service cost, if any
a.	No	Yes
b.	No	No
c.	Yes	No
d.	Yes	Yes

9. Interest cost included in the net pension cost recognized by an employer sponsoring a defined benefit pension plan represents the

- a. Amortization of the discount on unrecognized prior service costs.
- b. Increase in the fair value of plan assets due to the passage of time.
- c. Increase in the projected benefit obligation due to the passage of time.
- d. Shortage between the expected and actual returns on plan assets.

10. On July 31, year 2, Tern Co. amended its single employee defined benefit pension plan by granting increased benefits for services provided prior to year 2. This prior service cost will be reflected in the financial statement(s) for
  a. Years before year 2 only.
  b. Year 2 only.
  c. Year 2, and years before and following year 2.
  d. Year 2, and following years only.

11. Effective January 1, year 2, Flood Co. established a defined benefit pension plan with no retroactive benefits. The first of the required equal annual contributions was paid on December 31, year 2. A 10% discount rate was used to calculate service cost and a 10% rate of return was assumed for plan assets. All information on covered employees for year 2 and year 3 is the same. How should the service cost for year 3 compare with year 2, and should the year 2 balance sheet report a pension asset or a pension liability?

	Service cost for year 3 compared to year 2	Pension cost reported on the year 2 balance sheet
a.	Equal to	Pension liability
b.	Equal to	Pension asset
c.	Greater than	Pension liability
d.	Greater than	Pension asset

12. A company that maintains a defined benefit pension plan for its employees reports an unfunded pension liability. This cost represents the amount that the
  a. Cumulative net periodic cost accrued exceeds contributions to the plan.
  b. Cumulative net periodic cost exceeds the vested benefit obligation.
  c. Vested benefit obligation exceeds plan assets.
  d. Vested benefit obligation exceeds contributions to the plan.

13. The following information pertains to Seda Co.'s pension plan:

Actuarial estimate of projected benefit obligation at 1/1/Y2	$72,000
Assumed discount rate	10%
Service costs for year 2	18,000
Pension benefits paid during year 2	15,000

If **no** change in actuarial estimates occurred during year 2, Seda's projected benefit obligation at December 31, year 2 was
  a. $64,200
  b. $75,000
  c. $79,200
  d. $82,200

14. Which of the following terms includes assumptions concerning projected changes in future compensation when the pension benefit formula is based on future compensation levels (e.g., pay-related and final pay plans)?

	Service cost component	Projected benefit obligation	Accumulated benefit obligation
a.	Yes	Yes	Yes
b.	Yes	Yes	No
c.	No	Yes	No
d.	Yes	No	Yes

15. For a defined benefit pension plan, the discount rate used to calculate the projected benefit obligation is determined by the

	Expected return on plan assets	Actual return on plan assets
a.	Yes	Yes
b.	No	No
c.	Yes	No
d.	No	Yes

16. At December 31, year 2, the following information was provided by the Kerr Corp. pension plan administrator:

Fair value of plan assets	$3,450,000
Accumulated benefit obligation	4,300,000
Projected benefit obligation	5,700,000

Assume Kerr is a publicly traded company. What is the amount of the pension liability that should be shown on Kerr's December 31, year 2 balance sheet?
  a. $5,700,000
  b. $2,250,000
  c. $1,400,000
  d. $ 850,000

17. Nome Co. sponsors a defined benefit plan covering all employees. Benefits are based on years of service and compensation levels at the time of retirement. Nome determined that, as of September 30, year 2, its accumulated benefit obligation was $380,000, and its plan assets had a $290,000 fair value. The projected benefit obligation on September 30, year 2, was $400,000. In its September 30, year 2 balance sheet, what amount should Nome report as pension liability?
  a. $110,000
  b. $ 90,000
  c. $380,000
  d. $400,000

18. Payne, Inc., a nonpublicly traded company, implemented a defined benefit pension plan for its employees on January 2, year 2. The following data are provided for year 2, as of December 31, year 2:

Projected benefit obligation	$103,000
Plan assets at fair value	78,000
Net periodic pension cost	90,000
Employer's contribution	70,000

What amount should Payne record as pension liability at December 31, year 2?
  a. $0
  b. $25,000
  c. $20,000
  d. $45,000

Items 19 and 20 are based on the following:

The following data pertains to Hall Co.'s defined-benefit pension plan at December 31, year 2:

Unfunded projected benefit obligation	$25,000
Unrecognized prior service cost	12,000
Net periodic pension cost	8,000

Hall made no contributions to the pension plan during year 2.

19. At December 31, year 2, what amount should Hall record as pension liability on the balance sheet?

    a. $ 5,000
    b. $13,000
    c. $17,000
    d. $25,000

20. In its December 31, year 2 statement of stockholders' equity, what amount should Hall report as accumulated other comprehensive income for pension liabilities before tax effects?

    a. $ 5,000
    b. $13,000
    c. $17,000
    d. $25,000

21. An employer sponsoring a defined benefit pension plan must report a liability on the balance sheet equal to

    a.   The current year pension cost that was not funded.
    b.   The difference between the fair value of plan assets less the accumulated benefit obligation.
    c.   The difference between the accumulated benefit obligation and the projected benefit obligation.
    d.   The difference between the fair value of plan assets less the projected benefit obligation.

22. Claire, a publicly traded company, has the following defined benefit pension plans with the following information as of December 31, year 2:

	Plan A	Plan B	Plan C
Projected benefit obligation	100,000	150,000	180,000
Accumulated benefit obligation	80,000	140,000	150,000
Fair value of plan assets	110,000	125,000	160,000

Assume Claire will make no payments within the next 24 months to any pension plan. How should Claire report the pension plans on the December 31, year 2 balance sheet?

    a.   A noncurrent liability of $35,000.
    b.   A noncurrent asset of $10,000 and a noncurrent liability of $45,000.
    c.   A noncurrent liability of $25,000.
    d.   A noncurrent asset of $30,000 and a noncurrent liability of $25,000.

23. Dawson Corporation, a publicly traded company, implemented a defined benefit pension plan for its employees on January 2, year 1. The following data are provided for year 3 and as of December 31, year 3:

Projected benefit obligation	$350,000
Accumulated benefit obligation	320,000
Plan assets at fair value	362,000
Pension cost for year 3	100,000
Employer's contribution for year 3	95,000

What amount should Dawson report for the pension plan on its December 31, year 3 balance sheet?

    a.   A current liability of $5,000.
    b.   No asset or liability.
    c.   A noncurrent asset of $12,000.
    d.   A noncurrent asset of $42,000.

24. Rose Corporation, a publicly traded company, implemented a defined benefit pension plan for its employees on January 2, year 1. The following data are provided for year 2 and as of December 31, year 2:

Projected benefit obligation	$400,000
Accumulated benefit obligation	360,000
Plan assets at fair value	362,000
Pension cost for year 2	150,000
Pension contribution for year 2	150,000

Assume that as of January 1, year 2, Rose's pension plan was fully funded, and there were no recorded pension assets or liabilities on the balance sheet. Ignoring tax effects, which of the following entries would be needed to properly record the funding status of Rose's pension plan at December 31, year 2?

    a.   A debit to noncurrent pension asset of $2,000.
    b.   A debit to prepaid pension for $150,000.
    c.   A credit to noncurrent pension liability for $40,000.
    d.   A debit to other comprehensive income for $38,000.

25. Tulip Corporation, a publicly traded company, implemented a defined benefit pension plan for its employees on January 2, year 1. The following data are provided for year 3 and as of December 31, year 3:

Projected benefit obligation	$700,000
Accumulated benefit obligation	550,000
Plan assets at fair value	520,000
Pension cost for year 3	180,000
Pension contribution for year 3	150,000

Assume that as of January 1, year 3, Tulip's pension plan was fully funded, and there were no recorded pension assets or liabilities on the balance sheet. Assuming a tax rate of 40%, what is the net effect of the required adjustment on accumulated other comprehensive income on December 31, year 3?

    a. $90,000 decrease.
    b. $108,000 decrease.
    c. $36,000 decrease.
    d. $0

26. On September 1, year 2, Howe Corp. offered special termination benefits to employees who had reached the early retirement age specified in the company's pension plan. The termination benefits consisted of lump-sum and periodic future payments. Additionally, the employees accepting the company offer receive the usual early retirement pension benefits. The offer expired on November 30, year 2. Actual or reasonably estimated amounts at December 31, year 2, relating to the employees accepting the offer are as follows:

- Lump-sum payments totaling $475,000 were made on January 1, year 3.
- Periodic payments of $60,000 annually for three years will begin January 1, year 4. The present value at December 31, year 2, of these payments was $155,000.
- Reduction of accrued pension costs at December 31, year 2, for the terminating employees was $45,000.

In its December 31, year 2 balance sheet, Howe should report a total liability for special termination benefits of

    a. $475,000
    b. $585,000
    c. $630,000
    d. $655,000

27. The Codification requires a reconciliation of the beginning and ending balances of the benefit obligation for both defined benefit pension plans and defined postretirement plans. Which of the following items would appear in the schedule related to defined benefit pension plans?

	Service cost	Benefits paid
a.	Yes	No
b.	Yes	Yes
c.	No	Yes
d.	No	No

28. A company with a defined benefit pension plan must disclose in the notes to its financial statements
- a. A reconciliation of the vested and nonvested benefit obligation of its pension plan with the accumulated benefit obligation.
- b. A reconciliation of the accrued or prepaid pension cost reported in its balance sheet with the pension expense reported in its income statement.
- c. A reconciliation of the accumulated benefit obligation of its pension plan with its projected benefit obligation.
- d. The funded status of its pension plan and the amounts recognized in the balance sheet showing separately the noncurrent assets, current liabilities, and noncurrent liabilities reported.

29. Which of the following items would appear in the reconciliation schedule related to defined benefit pension plans?

	Benefit payments	Actual return on plan assets
a.	No	Yes
b.	No	No
c.	Yes	No
d.	Yes	Yes

30. Which of the following defined benefit pension plan disclosures should be made in a company's financial statements?

I. The amount of net periodic pension cost for the period.
II. The fair value of plan assets.

- a. Both I and II.
- b. I only.
- c. II only.
- d. Neither I nor II.

31. Which of the following is not a required disclosure for defined benefit pension plans?
- a. An explanation of a significant change in plan assets if not apparent from other disclosures.
- b. The amount of any unamortized prior service cost or credit not recognized in the statement of financial position (balance sheet).
- c. The effect of a two-percentage-point increase in the assumed health care cost trend rate(s).
- d. Reconciliation of beginning and ending balance of the projected benefit obligation.

32. Which of the following rates must be disclosed for defined benefit pension plans?

I. Assumed discount rate.
II. Expected long-term rate of return on all of the employer's assets.

III. Rate of compensation increase.

- a. I and III.
- b. II and III.
- c. I, II, and III.
- d. III only.

33. Jan Corp. amended its defined benefit pension plan, granting a total credit of $100,000 to four employees for services rendered prior to the plan's adoption. The employees, A, B, C, and D, are expected to retire from the company as follows:

A will retire after three years.
B and C will retire after five years.
D will retire after seven years.

What is the amount of prior service cost amortization in the first year?
- a. $0
- b. $ 5,000
- c. $20,000
- d. $25,000

34. The effects of a one-percentage-point increase or decrease in the trend rates for health care costs must be disclosed for which of the following relating to defined benefit postretirement plans?

I. The aggregate of the service and interest cost components.
II. The accumulated postretirement benefit obligation.

- a. Both I and II.
- b. I only.
- c. II only.
- d. Neither I nor II.

35. A company with a defined benefit pension plan must disclose in the notes to its financial statements all of the following **except**
- a. The funded status of its pension plan with the amounts recognized in the balance sheet showing separately the noncurrent assets, current liabilities, and noncurrent liabilities recognized.
- b. Rates for assumed discount rate, rate of compensation increase, and expected long-term rate of return on plan assets.
- c. A reconciliation of the accrued or prepaid pension cost reported in its balance sheet with the pension expense reported in its income statement.
- d. The recognized amount of the net periodic benefit cost with the components shown separately.

D.8. Postretirement Benefits other than Pensions (OPEB)

36. The following information pertains to Foster Co.'s defined benefit postretirement plan for the year 2.

Service cost	$120,000
Benefit payment	55,000
Interest on the accumulated postretirement benefit obligation	20,000
Unrecognized transition obligation (to be amortized over twenty years)	200,000

Foster Co.'s year 2 net periodic postretirement benefit cost was

    a. $205,000
    b. $150,000
    c. $ 95,000
    d. $285,000

37. Kemp Company provides a defined benefit postretirement plan for its employees. Kemp adopted the plan on January 1, year 1. Data relating to the pension plan for year 2 are as follows:

Service cost for year 2	28,000
Interest on the accumulated postretirement benefit obligation	5,000
Amortization of the unrecognized transition obligation	8,000

At the end of year 2, Kemp makes a benefit payment of $10,000 to employees. In its December 31, year 2 balance sheet, Kemp should record accrued postretirement benefit cost of

    a. $35,000
    b. $31,000
    c. $51,000
    d. $15,000

38. Bounty Co. provides postretirement health care benefits to employees who have completed at least ten years service and are aged fifty-five years or older when retiring. Employees retiring from Bounty have a median age of sixty-two, and no one has worked beyond age sixty-five. Fletcher is hired at forty-eight years old. The attribution period for accruing Bounty's expected postretirement health care benefit obligation to Fletcher is during the period when Fletcher is aged

    a.   48 to 65.
    b.   48 to 58.
    c.   55 to 65.
    d.   55 to 62.

39. An employer's obligation for postretirement health benefits that are expected to be provided to or for an employee must be fully accrued by the date the

    a.   Employee is fully eligible for benefits.
    b.   Employee retires.
    c.   Benefits are utilized.
    d.   Benefits are paid.

40. Which of the following are correct regarding a transition obligation resulting from the adoption of a defined benefit postretirement plan?

  I. A transition obligation may be recognized immediately.
  II. The transition obligation represents the difference between the accumulated postretirement benefit obligation and the fair value of plan assets at the beginning of the year the plan is adopted.
  III. A transition obligation may be amortized on a straight-line basis over a maximum period of twenty years.

    a.   I and II.
    b.   II only.
    c.   I, II, and III.
    d.   II and III.

41. Which of the following information should be disclosed by a company providing health care benefits to its retirees?

  I. The assumed health care cost trend rate used to measure the expected cost of benefits covered by the plan.

  II. The accumulated postretirement benefit obligation.

    a.   Both I and II.
    b.   I only.
    c.   II only.
    d.   Neither I nor II.

D.12. International Financial Reporting Standards (IFRS)

42. Which of the following methods is used in IFRS to account for defined benefit pension plans?
    a.   Projected-unit-credit method.
    b.   Benefit-years-of-service method.
    c.   Accumulated benefits method.
    d.   Vested years of service method.

43. Utter Corporation uses IFRS for financial reporting purposes and has several pension plans covering various classes of employees. When may the company net assets and liabilities of the various plans?
    a.   Assets and liabilities may always be netted.
    b.   Assets and liabilities may be netted when there is a legally enforceable right to use the assets of one plan to settle the obligations of another plan.
    c.   When the estimated cash inflows and outflows are similar in pattern.
    d.   When the assets and liabilities are both financial.

Multiple-Choice Answers and Explanations

Answers

1. d __ __	10. d __ __	19. d __ __	28. d __ __	37. b __ __
2. d __ __	11. d __ __	20. c __ __	29. d __ __	38. b __ __
3. d __ __	12. a __ __	21. d __ __	30. a __ __	39. a __ __
4. b __ __	13. d __ __	22. b __ __	31. c __ __	40. c __ __
5. c __ __	14. b __ __	23. c __ __	32. a __ __	41. a __ __
6. c __ __	15. b __ __	24. d __ __	33. c __ __	42. a __ __
7. c __ __	16. b __ __	25. a __ __	34. a __ __	43. b __ __
8. d __ __	17. a __ __	26. c __ __	35. c __ __	1st: __/43 = __%
9. c __ __	18. b __ __	27. b __ __	36. b __ __	2nd: __/43 = __%

Explanations

1. **(d)** The six elements which an employer sponsoring a defined benefit pension plan must include in its net pension cost are service cost, interest cost, actual return on plan assets, amortization of unrecognized prior service cost, deferral of unexpected gain or loss, and amortization of the unrecognized net obligation or unrecognized net asset existing at the date of initial application. Lee Corp's pension expense is calculated as follows:

Service cost	$160,000
Gain (actual and expected) on plan assets	(35,000)
Amortization	5,000
Interest	50,000
	180,000

Gains and losses that arise from a single occurrence which is not directly related to the operation of the plan should be reported as part of that occurrence and not as part of the plan's activity. Therefore, the $40,000 unexpected loss on plan assets related to a year 2 disposal of a subsidiary should be reported as part of the "loss on disposal" and not as part of the year 2 pension cost.

2. **(d)** The requirement is to determine the amount of unrecognized net loss to be recognized as a part of pension expense in year 2. The **corridor approach** is to be used to determine gain or loss amortization. Under this approach, only the unrecognized net gain or loss in excess of 10% of the **greater** of the projected benefit obligation (PBO) or the market-related asset value (M-RAV) is amortized. In this case, the M-RAV ($1,650,000) is larger than the PBO ($1,530,000). The corridor is $165,000 (10% × $1,650,000). The unrecognized net loss ($235,000) exceeds the corridor by $70,000 ($235,000 − $165,000). This excess is amortized over the average remaining service period of active employees expected to participate in the plan ($70,000 ÷ 5.5 = $12,727).

3. **(d)** Estimates of future contributions to a defined benefit pension plan are required to be disclosed only for the next fiscal year. Answer (a) is incorrect because a description of the plan is a required disclosure. Answer (b) is incorrect because the amount of pension expense by component is a required disclosure. Answer (c) is incorrect because the weighted-average discount rate is a required disclosure.

4. **(b)** The requirement is to calculate the total amount of unrecognized prior service cost to be amortized over future periods as a result of a pension plan amendment. Prior service cost is the present value of retroactive benefits given to employees for years of service provided before the date of an amendment to the plan. The cost of these retroactive benefits is measured by the increase in the projected benefit obligation at the date of amendment ($1,900,000 − $1,300,000 = $600,000). This amount will be recognized as expense (amortized) during the service periods of those employees who are expected to receive benefits under the plan.

5. **(c)** Prepaid pension cost is the cumulative excess of the amount funded over the amount recorded as pension expense. In year 2, pension expense is $520,000.

Service cost and interest on PBO	$620,000
Actual return on plan assets ($1,000,000 × 10%)	(100,000)
Pension expense	$520,000

Since year 2 funding was $1,000,000, 12/31/Y2 prepaid pension cost is $480,000 ($1,000,000 − $520,000).

6. **(c)** As of December 31, year 3, there was a pension liability only for the current year's portion of the pension cost that was not funded. The PBO is compared with the fair value of plan assets, and a liability must be recorded in the balance sheet for the underfunded plan. Therefore, the difference between the PBO and the fair value of the plan assets as of December 31, year 4 ($750,000 minus $675,000) of $75,000 must be reported as a liability on the balance sheet.

7. **(c)** The requirement is to determine how the service cost component of the net periodic pension cost is measured in a defined benefit pension plan. The service cost component recognized shall be determined as "the actuarial present value of benefits attributed by the pension benefit formula to employee service during the period" that is known as the **projected benefit obligation**.

8. **(d)** Among the components which should be included in the net pension cost recognized for a period by an employer sponsoring a defined benefit pension plan are **both** actual return on plan assets, if any, and amortization of unrecognized prior service cost, if any.

9. **(c)** Net pension cost (expense) is comprised of six elements. One of these elements is interest on the projected benefit obligation, which is defined as the increase in the amount of the projected benefit obligation due to the passage of time. Candidates must be careful so as not to confuse "interest cost" with the "actual return" component of net pension cost which is the earnings on the plan assets. If the latter component is positive, it reduces the net pension cost for the period.

10. **(d)** Plan amendments are granted with the expectation that the employer will realize economic benefits in future periods. Therefore, the prior service cost will be reflected in the financial statements for year 2 and future years only.

11. **(d)** This question addresses the behavior of the components of pension expense over a period of time. Service cost is the actuarial present value of benefits attributed by the pension benefit formula to services rendered by employees during that period. This problem states that "all information on covered employees for year 2 and year 3 is the same," which indicates that there has been no change in Flood's work force during this two-year period. The only difference in the service cost for these two years would, therefore, be attributable to differences in the discounting of the benefits. Each year a group of employees works, the group becomes one year closer to retirement age and to collecting their retirement benefits. The present value of the benefits earned by employees each year grows as their retirement date grows nearer, because the benefits are discounted over a shorter period of time. If, for instance, the "average" retirement date for Flood's employees is January 1, year 12, the present value of the benefits for year 3's service will be greater than the present value of year 2 service, because it is discounted eleven years for year 2 versus ten years for year 3. (This is because every additional year of discounting reduces the present value of the benefits.) Therefore, the service cost for year 3 will be greater than for year 2. The problem also states that Flood intends to fund the plan in equal annual installments, and that the discount rate which was used to calculate the service cost is equal to the assumed rate of return on plan assets. Under these circumstances, to fully fund the pension obligation in equal payments, Flood will contribute an amount which exceeds the pension cost in the first years of the plan and which is less than the pension cost in later years. A pension asset is the cumulative employer contributions in excess of the pension liability cost. Since year 2's funding would exceed its pension cost, Flood would report a pension asset on its year 2 balance sheet. The journal entry to record the funding would be

Pension expense	xxx	
Pension asset/liability	xxx	
Cash		xxx

12. **(a)** The requirement is to determine what the "unfunded accrued pension cost" represents. The unfunded accrued pension cost is a liability recognized when the net periodic pension cost exceeds the amount the employer has contributed to the plan.

13. **(d)** The projected benefit obligation is the actuarial present value of the pension obligation at the end of the period. Since there were no changes in actuarial estimates during the year, the end of period projected benefit obligation is computed as follows:

Projected benefit obligation, 1/1/Y2	$72,000
Service cost	18,000
Interest on projected benefit obligation	7,200

(10% × $72,000)	
Benefit payments	(15,000)
Pension benefit obligation, 12/31/Y2	$82,200

Service cost and interest on the projected benefit obligation increase the projected benefit obligation; benefit payments decrease the projected benefit obligation.

14. **(b)** The requirement is to determine which of the listed pension terms includes assumptions concerning projected changes in future compensation levels if the pension benefit formula is based on future compensation levels. The service cost component and the projected benefit obligation reflect projected future compensation levels while the accumulated benefit obligation is measured based on employees' history of service and compensation without an estimate of projected future compensation levels.

15. **(b)** The assumed discount rate should reflect the rates at which pension benefits could be effectively settled. This rate is sometimes referred to as the "settlement rate." To determine the settlement rate, it is appropriate to look at rates implicit in current prices of annuity contracts that could be used to settle the obligation under the defined benefit plan. The expected return on plan assets is **not** used to calculate the projected benefit obligation. The actual return on plan assets is also **not** used to calculate the projected benefit obligation.

16. **(b)** The funding status of the plan is recognized as an asset or liability on the balance sheet. The difference between Kerr's fair value of plan assets and the projected benefit obligation ($3,450,000 – $5,700,000 = $2,250,000) is the amount of the plan that is underfunded and must be reported as a liability on Kerr's December 31, year 2 balance sheet.

17. **(a)** The recognition of a **pension liability** is required if the projected benefit obligation (PBO) exceeds the FV of the plan assets. In this case, the excess of the PBO over the FV of plan assets is $110,000 ($400,000 – $290,000).

18. **(b)** The reporting of a **pension liability** is required if the projected benefit obligation (PBO) exceeds the FV of the plan assets. In this case, the excess of the PBO over the FV of plan assets is $25,000 ($103,000 – $78,000).

19. **(d)** A **pension liability** must be reported for the excess of the projected benefit obligation (PBO) over the fair value of the plan assets. The unfunded projected benefit obligation is this excess. Therefore, the required liability amount is $25,000.

20. **(c)** At December 31, year 2, Hall will record a pension expense of $8,000 and a pension liability of $8,000 for the current year's pension journal entry. The overfunded or underfunded status of the plan must be recognized on the balance sheet. Therefore, the unfunded PBO of $25,000 must be recognized as a liability. An entry must be made to record the adjustment to pension liability for $17,000 (25,000 – 8,000 liability already recorded). Ignoring the tax effect, the journal entry will include a debit to OCI for $17,000 and a credit to pension liability for $17,000.

21. **(d)** An employer must recognize the overfunded or underfunded status of the pension plan. A liability is reported when the fair value of the plan assets is less than the projected benefit obligation.

22. **(b)** The funded status of the plan is recognized on the balance sheet. The fair value of plan assets is compared with the projected benefit obligation. Overfunded plans are aggregated and recognized as noncurrent assets on the balance sheet. Underfunded plans are aggregated and recognized as current, noncurrent liabilities, or both. Claire must aggregate Plans B and C, because they are both underfunded. Plan B is underfunded by $25,000 ($125,000 – $150,000), and Plan C is underfunded by $20,000 ($160,000 – $180,000). Because Claire expects to make no payments within the next 12 months, the aggregated underfunded plans are recorded as noncurrent liabilities on the balance sheet. The overfunded amount (Plan A: $110,000 – 100,000) of $10,000 is recognized as a noncurrent asset on the balance sheet. Answer (a) is incorrect because all plans cannot be aggregated. Answers (c) and (d) are incorrect because according to ASC Topic 715, the accumulated benefit obligation is no longer used to measure the funding status of the plan.

23. **(c)** The funding status of the pension plan is recorded on the balance sheet. The funding status is determined by comparing the fair value of plan assets to the projected benefit obligation. Dawson's plan assets are $12,000 higher than the projected benefit obligation ($362,000 – 350,000). Therefore, Dawson would be required to report a noncurrent asset of $12,000 on their balance sheet at December 31, year 3. Answer (a) is incorrect because the current liability of $5,000 is part of the journal entry required to record pension cost for the period, and does not reflect the overall funding status of the plan. Answer (b) is incorrect because overfunded or underfunded plans must be recognized on the balance sheet. Answer (d) is incorrect because according to ASC Topic 715, the accumulated benefit obligation is not used to measure the funding status of the plan.

24. **(d)** The funding status of the pension plan is recorded on the balance sheet. The funding status is determined by comparing the fair value of plan assets to the projected benefit obligation. Because Rose's pension plan was completely funded as of December 31, year 1, no pension assets or liabilities existed on its balance sheet. The journal entry for year 2 would include a debit to pension cost and a credit to cash for the year 2 pension contribution, which was fully funded for the current year. However, in comparing the PBO and the fair value of plan assets at the end of the year, Rose's pension plan is underfunded by $38,000 ($362,000 – 400,000). Ignoring income tax effects, the entry to record the underfunded plan is to debit other comprehensive income for $38,000 and credit pension liability for $38,000.

25. **(a)** The funded status of the plan is recognized in the balance sheet. The funding status is determined by comparing the fair value of plan assets to the projected benefit obligation. The pension plan for Rose is underfunded by a total of $180,000 ($520,000 – 700,000). As of December 31, year 3, Rose has recognized a pension liability of $30,000, which is the difference between pension cost for the period and the pension contribution for the period. This $30,000 liability has been recognized as an expense and reduces net income for the period. Because Rose must recognize a $180,000 liability in the balance sheet, an entry

must be recorded for the $150,000 needed to increase the pension liability account to the underfunded amount of $180,000. Therefore, the entry to recognize the underfunded portion of the plan would be

OCI ($150,000 × 60%)	90,000 (net of tax)	
Deferred tax asset	60,000	
Pension liability		150,000

Answer (b) is incorrect because it is necessary to adjust for any existing pension or liability that may exist at year-end. Answers (c) and (d) are incorrect because the accumulated benefit obligation is not used to determine the funded status of the plan.

26. **(c)** When special termination benefits are offered to employees, a loss and liability must be recognized when the employee accepts the offer and the amount can be reasonably estimated. The amount to be recognized shall include any lump-sum payments ($475,000) and the present value of any expected future payments ($155,000). Therefore, the total liability for special termination benefits is $630,000 ($475,000 + $155,000). Note that the reduction of accrued pension costs ($45,000) would reduce the amount of the loss, but would **not** affect the liability. Instead it would be recorded as a reduction of accrued pension costs. The journal entry would be

Loss from termination benefits	585,000	
Accrued pension costs	45,000	
Liability from termination benefits		630,000

27. **(b)** The reconciliation schedule for the benefit obligation related to defined benefit pension plans would disclose both the amounts for service cost and benefits paid. Other items that would be disclosed in this reconciliation schedule include (1) interest cost, (2) contributions by plan participants, (3) actuarial gains and losses, (4) plan amendments, (5) divestitures, curtailments, and settlements, and (6) special termination benefits.

28. **(d)** The funded status of the pension plans and the amounts are recognized in the balance sheet showing separately the assets, current liabilities, and noncurrent liabilities.

29. **(d)** The reconciliation schedule for the plan assets related to defined benefit pension plans would disclose both the benefit payments and the actual return on plan assets. Other items that would be disclosed in this reconciliation schedule include (1) contributions by the employer, (2) contributions by plan participants, and (3) settlements and divestitures.

30. **(a)** An employer sponsoring a defined benefit pension plan must disclose a great deal of information related to the plan. These disclosures include the amount of net periodic pension cost for the period and the fair value of plan assets.

31. **(c)** The effect of a one-percentage-point increase in the assumed health care cost trend rate(s) is required, not a two-percentage-point increase. An explanation of a significant change in plan assets, if not apparent from other disclosures, is required according to ASC Topic 715. The amount of any unamortized prior service cost or credit not recognized in the statement of financial position (balance sheet) is a required disclosure. Another required disclosure per ASC

Topic 715 is a reconciliation of beginning and ending balances of the projected benefit obligation.

32. (a) The assumed discount rate and the rate of compensation increase are both required disclosures. The expected long-term rate of return on all of the employer's assets is not required. The expected long-term rate of return on plan assets is required, however.

33. (c) There are two methods approved for use in determining the assignment of prior service cost: the expected years of service method, and the straight-line basis over the average remaining service period of active employees method. Under the expected future years of service method, the total number of employee service years is calculated by grouping employees according to the time remaining to their retirement and multiplying the number in each group by the number of periods remaining to retirement. [(1 person × 3) + (2 people × 5) + (1 person × 7) = 20]. To calculate the amortization of prior service costs for a given year, the number of employee service years applicable to that period is used as the numerator of the fraction, and the denominator is the total employee service years based on all the identified groups. (4/20 × $100,000 = $20,000) For the straight-line basis over the average remaining service period method, the total number of service years (calculated above) is divided by the number of employees to find the weighted-average service life of each employee. (20/4 = 5 yrs.) The $100,000 of prior service cost will be amortized over the five years, or at $20,000 ($100,000 ÷ 5 = $20,000) a year.

34. (a) A disclosure is made of the effects of a one-percentage-point increase or decrease of the trend rates for health care costs on: the aggregate of the service and interest cost components and the accumulated postretirement obligation.

35. (c) A reconciliation of the accrued or prepaid pension cost reported in its balance sheet with the pension expense reported in its income statement is not required. Answer (a) is incorrect because the funded status of the pension plan must be reported in the balance sheet as noncurrent assets, current liabilities, and noncurrent liabilities. Answer (b) is also incorrect because rates for assumed discount rate, rate of compensation increase, and expected long-term rate of return on plan assets are also required. Another required disclosure is the recognized amount of the net periodic benefit cost with the components shown separately.

36. (b) Net periodic postretirement benefit cost is a net amount calculated by adding or subtracting six components. Three components present in this problem are combined as follows:

Service cost	$120,000
Interest on the accumulated postretirement benefit obligation	20,000
Amortization of transition obligation ($200,000 ÷ 20 years)	10,000
Postretirement benefit cost	$150,000

Service cost and interest on the accumulated postretirement benefit obligation always increase postretirement benefit cost. Foster Co. has elected to amortize the unrecognized transition obligation over a twenty-year period. Amortization of the $200,000 obligation on the straight-line basis

increases postretirement benefit cost by $10,000 per year. The benefit payment represents a cash payment made for benefits by the employer; however, this is not a component of net periodic postretirement benefit cost.

37. (b) To determine the accrued postretirement benefit cost, the net periodic postretirement benefit cost must first be calculated as follows:

Service cost	$28,000
Interest on the accumulated postretirement benefit obligation	5,000
Amortization of the unrecognized transition obligation	8,000
Net periodic postretirement benefit cost	$41,000

An adjusting entry is required at year-end to record net periodic postretirement benefit cost and the cash benefit payments made to employees. An accrued postretirement benefit cost will be recorded if the net postretirement benefit cost exceeds the cash payments to employees. The journal entry would be

Postretirement benefit cost	41,000	
Cash		10,000
Accrued postretirement benefit cost		31,000

The balance in the accrued postretirement benefit cost account would be $31,000.

38. (b) The requirement is to determine the attribution period for accruing the expected postretirement health care benefit obligation. The beginning of the attribution period is generally the date of hire, and the end shall be the date of full eligibility. Fletcher's age at the date of hire is forty-eight and the period of eligibility is ten years. Thus, the attribution period is forty-eight to fifty-eight.

39. (a) An employer's obligation for postretirement benefits expected to be provided to an employee must be fully accrued by the full eligibility date of the employee, even if the employee is to render additional service beyond that date.

40. (c) A transition obligation is measured as the difference between the accumulated postretirement benefit obligation and the fair value of plan assets at the beginning of the fiscal year for which ASC Topic 715 is adopted. A transition obligation may be recognized immediately in net income of the period of the change, or recognized on a delayed basis as a component of net periodic postretirement benefit cost. If delayed recognition is elected, the transition obligation should be amortized on a straight-line basis over the average remaining service period of plan participants. If the average remaining service period is less than twenty years, the employer may elect to use a twenty-year amortization period.

41. (a) The employer must disclose the amount of the accumulated postretirement benefit obligation. The employer must also disclose the assumed health care cost trend rate used to measure the expected cost of benefits covered by the plan.

42. (a) The requirement is to identify the method that is used for defined benefit pension plans. Answer (a) is correct because IFRS requires the use of the projected-unit-credit method to calculate the present value of the defined benefit obligation (PV-DBO). Answer (b) is incorrect because the benefit-years-of-service method is used in US GAAP. Answers (c) and (d) are incorrect because these are not methods for reporting pension benefits.

43.   (b)   The requirements is to identify when pension assets and liabilities may be netted under IFRS. Answer (b) is correct because assets and liabilities may be netted only when there is a legally enforceable right to use the assets of one plan to settle the obligations of another plan.

Simulations

Task-Based Simulation 1

Concepts		
	Authoritative Literature	Help

Identify whether each of the following statements is True or False.

		True	False
1.	A defined contribution plan is a plan where an employer agrees to provide a benefit at retirement defined by a formula.	○	○
2.	The present value of the projected benefit obligation is calculated using the benefits years of service method.	○	○
3.	Pension liability is calculated by comparing the accumulated benefit obligation with the fair value of plan assets.	○	○
4.	A company is required to net overfunded pension plans with underfunded pension plans and report the net amount as either noncurrent asset or noncurrent liability on the balance sheet.	○	○
5.	Prior service costs are caused by new individuals entering the plan after the vesting date.	○	○
6.	In a defined benefit plan, interest cost represents the increase in the fair value of the plan assets due to the passage of time.	○	○
7.	Companies must disclose in the notes to the financial statements the effect that a two-percentage-point increase in interest costs would have on the aggregate service and interest costs of the accumulated postretirement benefit obligation on health-care benefits.	○	○
8.	The actual return on plan assets is defined as the difference in the fair value of plan assets at the beginning and the end of the year.	○	○

Task-Based Simulation 2

Pension Calculations		
	Authoritative Literature	Help

Situation

The following information pertains to Winger Co.'s defined benefit pension plan. The common stock of Winger is publicly traded.

Discount rate	6%

At January 1, year 2:

Projected benefit obligation	$600,000
Fair value of pension plan assets	420,000
Accumulated benefit obligation	380,000
Unrecognized prior service cost	240,000

At December 31, year 2:

Projected benefit obligation	?
Fair value of pension plan assets	470,200

Service cost for year 2 was $80,000. The actual and expected return on assets was 6%. A contribution for pension of $40,000 was made during the year, and $15,000 of benefits were paid. Winger had no pension asset/liability at December 31, year 1. Winger amortizes the unrecognized service costs at $20,000 per year. Assume no pension benefits are expected to be paid in the next 12 months.

Part I.

Calculate the following amounts for Winger's pension cost for year 2.

1. _____ Interest cost

2. _____ Actual return on plan assets

3. _____ Amortization of prior service costs or credits

4. _____ Gain or (Loss)

5. _____ Pension cost for year 2

6. _____ Projected benefit obligation at December 31, year 2

Part II.

For the following items determine whether the component Increases, Decreases, or has No effect on Winger's unfunded accrued pension liability.

	Increase	Decrease	No effect
1. Service cost	○	○	○
2. Interest cost	○	○	○
3. Actual return on plan assets	○	○	○
4. Amortization of prior service costs or credits	○	○	○
5. Gain or loss in year 2	○	○	○

Task-Based Simulation 3

Research		
	Authoritative Literature	**Help**

You have been asked to research the professional literature to determine how to account for prior service cost or credits for a single-employee defined benefit pension plan. Place the citation for the excerpt from the Professional Standards that provides this information in the answer box below.

Simulation Solutions

Task-Based Simulation 1

Concepts		
	Authoritative Literature	**Help**

		True	**False**
1.	A defined contribution plan is a plan where an employer agrees to provide a benefit at retirement defined by a formula.	○	●
2.	The present value of the projected benefit obligation is calculated using the benefits years of service method.	●	○
3.	Pension liability is calculated by comparing the accumulated benefit obligation with the fair value of plan assets.	○	●
4.	A company is required to net overfunded pension plans with underfunded pension plans and report the net amount as either noncurrent asset or noncurrent liability on the balance sheet.	○	●
5.	Prior service costs are caused by new individuals entering the plan after the vesting date.	○	●
6.	In a defined benefit plan, interest cost represents the increase in the fair value of the plan assets due to the passage of time.	○	●
7.	Companies must disclose in the notes to the financial statements the effects that a two-percentage-point increase in interest costs would have on the aggregate service and interest costs of the accumulated postretirement benefit obligation on health care benefits.	○	●
8.	The actual return on plan assets is defined as the difference in the fair value of plan assets at the beginning and the end of the year.	○	●

Explanations

1. (F) A defined contribution plan is a plan where the employer defines the contribution. No benefit is promised. The benefit is provided by a trust that is funded by the defined contribution of the employer.

2. (T) The projected benefit obligation is calculated using the benefits years of service method.

3. (F) The funded status of the pension plan is calculated by subtracting the projected benefit obligation and the fair value of plan assets at year-end.

4. (F) A company may not net the overfunded and underfunded plans. Overfunded plans must be shown as noncurrent assets on the balance sheet. Underfunded plans should be shown as current liabilities, noncurrent liabilities, or both.

5. (F) Prior service costs are caused by amendments to the plan or initiation of a new plan with a retroactive allowance.

6. (F) In a defined benefit plan, the interest cost represents the increase in the projected benefit obligation due to the passage of time.

7. (F) Companies must disclose the effect that a one percentage point increase would have on the aggregate service and interest costs of the accumulated postretirement benefit obligation on health-care benefits.

8. (F) The actual return on plan assets is defined as the difference in the fair value adjusted for contributions made to the plan and benefits paid.

Task-Based Simulation 2

Pension Calculations		
	Authoritative Literature	**Help**

Part I.

1. $ 36,000   Interest cost (PBO at BOY $600,000 × 6% = $36,000)

2. $ 25,200   Actual return on plan assets (FV of plan assets BOY $420,000 × 6% = $25,200)

3. $ 20,000   Amortization of prior service costs or credits ($240,000/12 years = $20,000 per year)

4. $ _____0   Gain or (Loss) (Actual returns = expected returns)

5. $110,800   Pension cost for year 2 ($80,000 service cost + $36,000 interest cost – $25,200 ROA + $20,000 amortization of prior service cost = $110,800)

6. $701,000   Projected benefit obligation at December 31, year 2 (PBO at BOY $600,000 + Service Costs $80,000 + Interest Cost $36,000 – Benefits Paid $15,000 = $701,000 PBO at EOY)

Part II.

		Increase	Decrease	No effect
1.	Service cost	●	○	○
2.	Interest cost	●	○	○
3.	Actual return on plan assets	○	●	○
4.	Amortization of prior service costs or credits	●	○	○
5.	Gain or loss in year 2	○	○	●

Explanations

1. **(I)** Service cost increases pension cost for the period.

2. **(I)** Interest cost increases pension cost for the period.

3. **(D)** Actual return on assets decreases pension costs for the period.

4. **(I)** Amortization of prior service cost increases pension cost for the period.

5. **(N)** Winger had no gain or loss because actual and expected return on assets were the same for year 2.

Task-Based Simulation 3

Research		
	Authoritative Literature	**Help**

ASC	715	30	35	11

E. Leases

A lease is a contract between two parties—a lessor and a lessee. A lease contract gives a lessee rights to use the lessor's property for a specified period of time in return for periodic cash payments (rent) to the lessor.

1. A major goal in accounting for leases is to recognize the economic substance of the lease agreement over its mere legal form. For example, many lease agreements are similar to the purchase of an asset financed by the issuance of debt. The economic substance of a lease agreement generally takes one of two forms:

   a. Periodic payments of rent by the lessee for the **use** of the lessor's property
   b. Periodic payments similar to an installment purchase by the lessee for the rights to **acquire** the lessor's property in the future (i.e., acquisition of property by financing)

   (1) In a., the risks and rewards of owning the asset remain with the lessor. Accordingly, the asset is **not** treated as sold by the lessor to the lessee, and remains on the lessor's books. This form of leasing arrangement is called an **operating lease**.
   (2) By contrast, in b., a lease agreement may transfer many of the risks and rewards of ownership to the lessee. This form of lease is treated as a sale by the lessor and as a purchase by the lessee. This concept is clearly stated as follows:

   > The objective of the **lease** classification criteria in the Subtopic derives from the concept that a lease that transfers **substantially all** of the benefits and risks incident to the ownership of property should be accounted for as the acquisition of an asset and the incurrence of an obligation by the lessee and as a **sale or financing** by the lessor. All other leases should be accounted for as **operating leases** (ASC 840).

   c. When the risks and rewards of ownership are deemed to have been passed from the lessor to the lessee, the lessor will account for the lease as either a **direct financing** or as a **sales-type lease,** and the lessee will account for the lease as a **capital lease**.

   (1) To determine whether the risks and rewards of ownership have been transferred to the lessee, **at least one** of the following four criteria must be met:

   (a) The lease **transfers title** to the lessee.
   (b) The lease contains a **bargain purchase** option.
   (c) The lease **term is 75% or more** of useful life and the lease is not first executed within the last 25% of the original useful life.
   (d) The **present value** of minimum lease payments **is 90% or more** of the net of the **fair value** of the asset reduced by the investment tax credit (when in effect) retained by the lessor and the lease is not executed in the last 25% of the original useful life.

   (2) These four criteria apply to both the lessor and to the lessee. The lessor, however, must meet two additional criteria:

   (a) **Collectibility** of minimum lease payments is predictable, and
   (b) There are **no important uncertainties** concerning costs yet to be incurred by the lessor under the lease.
   (c) **Both** of the above must be satisfied by the lessor in order for the lessor to treat the lease in substance as a capital lease.

   d. The classification of leases can be summarized as follows:

	Lessor	*Lessee*
Risks and rewards remain with lessor (no sale and purchase of asset)	Operating ———————————	Operating
Risks and rewards transfer to lessee (sale and purchase of asset)	Direct financing ——————— Sales-type ———	Capital

2. **Study Program for Leases**

   a. Begin by reviewing the terms peculiar to leases that appear at the beginning of the outline of ASC Topic 840 (SFAS 13) in the pronouncement outlines that begin after Module 22.
   b. Review the material in this module so that you will be familiar with the major concepts and applications in the leasing area.

c. After you have developed a solid base of understanding, you should review the outline of SFAS 13 (ASC Topic 840).

d. The discussion of accounting for leases is structured to follow the lease classification matrix listed above.

(1) Operating Lease—Lessor/Lessee

An operating lease is any lease not meeting the criteria for a direct financing or sales-type lease in the case of a lessor, or for a capital lease in the case of a lessee. Under an operating lease, leased assets continue to be carried on the lessor's balance sheet and are depreciated in the normal manner. These assets, however, are not shown on the lessee's balance sheet since the lessee cannot expect to derive any future economic benefit from the assets beyond the lease term. Several issues are frequently encountered when dealing with operating leases. These issues are discussed in the remainder of this section.

(a) Free rent/uneven payments

Some lease agreements might call for uneven payments or scheduled rent increases over the lease term. Other agreements might include, as an incentive to the lessee, several months of "free rent" during which the lessee may use the asset without owing rent to the lessor. In these cases, rental revenue (expense) is still recognized by the lessor (lessee) on a straight-line basis and is prorated over the full term of the lease during which the lessee has possession of the asset. This is due to the matching principle; if physical usage is relatively the same over the lease term, then an equal amount of benefit is being obtained by both parties to the lease.

> **NOTE:** Another method to allocate rental revenue (expense) may be used if it better represents the actual physical use of the leased asset.

1] When the pattern of actual cash received (paid) as rent is other than straight-line, it will be necessary for both parties to record accruals, or deferrals, depending upon the payment schedule.

		Accruals	**(or)**	**Deferrals**
Lessor	--	Rent receivable		Unearned rent
Lessee	--	Rent payable		Prepaid rent

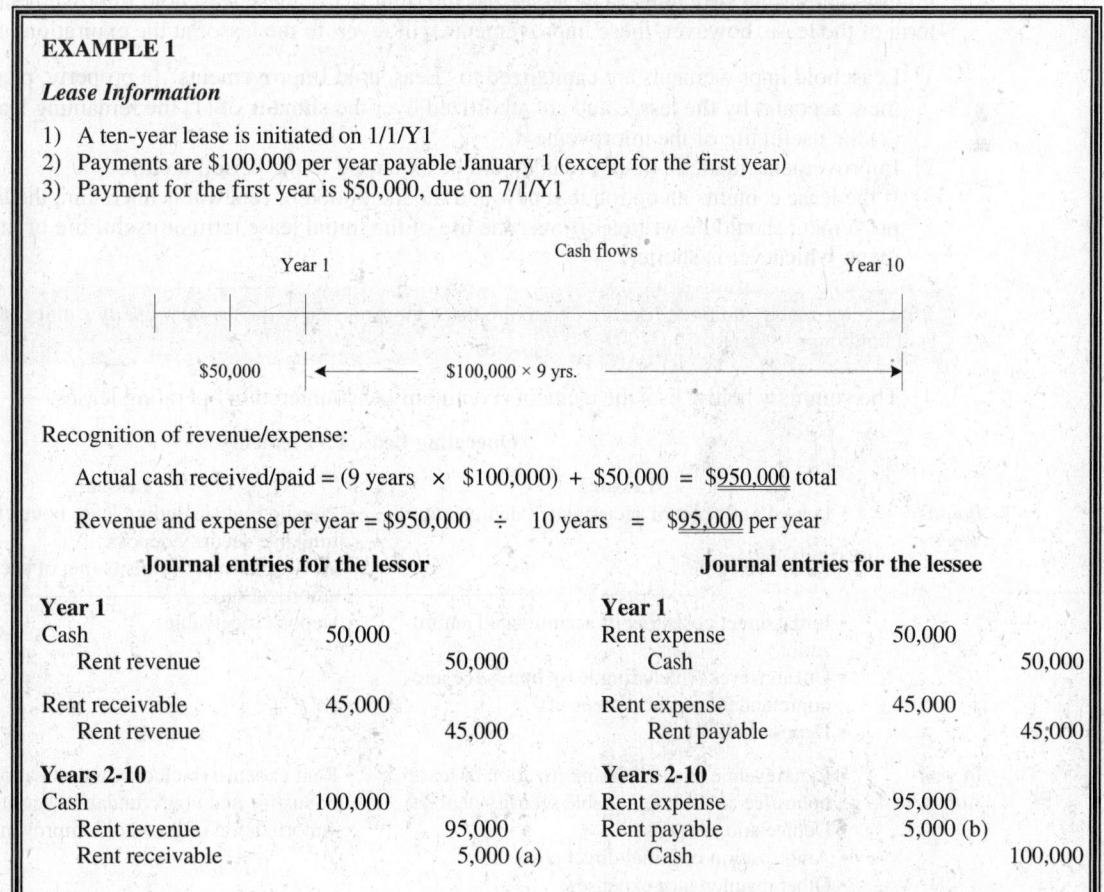

EXAMPLE 1

Lease Information

1) A ten-year lease is initiated on 1/1/Y1
2) Payments are $100,000 per year payable January 1 (except for the first year)
3) Payment for the first year is $50,000, due on 7/1/Y1

Cash flows

Year 1 ——————————————————— Year 10

$50,000 ← $100,000 × 9 yrs. →

Recognition of revenue/expense:

Actual cash received/paid = (9 years × $100,000) + $50,000 = $950,000 total

Revenue and expense per year = $950,000 ÷ 10 years = $95,000 per year

Journal entries for the lessor			Journal entries for the lessee		
Year 1			**Year 1**		
Cash	50,000		Rent expense	50,000	
Rent revenue		50,000	Cash		50,000
Rent receivable	45,000		Rent expense	45,000	
Rent revenue		45,000	Rent payable		45,000
Years 2-10			**Years 2-10**		
Cash	100,000		Rent expense	95,000	
Rent revenue		95,000	Rent payable	5,000 (b)	
Rent receivable		5,000 (a)	Cash		100,000

	Rent Receivable		(a)		(b)	Rent Payable		
yr. 1	45,000	5,000	yr. 2		yr. 2	5,000	45,000	yr. 1
		•				•		
		•				•		
		•	yr. 10		yr. 10	•		

(b) **Initial direct costs**

The lessor may incur costs in setting up the lease agreement. Such costs might include finder's fees, appraisal fees, document processing fees, negotiation fees, and any costs in closing the transaction. These costs, called initial direct costs, are carried as an asset on the lessor's balance sheet. Initial direct costs are amortized on a straight-line basis to expense over the lease term by the lessor, and are shown net of accumulated amortization on the lessor's balance sheet.

(c) **Lease bonus (fee)**

At the inception of the lease, the lessee may pay a nonrefundable lease bonus (fee) to the lessor in order to obtain more favorable leasing terms (e.g., a lease term of three years instead of five years). The lease bonus (fee) would be treated as unearned rent by the lessor and would be amortized to rental revenue on a straight-line basis over the lease term. The lessee would treat the lease bonus (fee) as pre-paid rent and would recognize it as rental expense over the lease term on a straight-line basis.

(d) **Security deposits**

Some lease agreements may require that the lessee pay the lessor a security deposit at the inception of the lease. Security deposits may be either refundable or nonrefundable. A **refundable** security deposit is treated as a liability by the lessor and as a receivable by the lessee until the deposit is returned to the lessee. A **nonrefundable** security deposit is recorded as unearned revenue by the lessor and as prepaid rent by the lessee until the deposit is considered earned by the lessor (usually at the end of the lease term).

(e) **Leasehold improvements**

Frequently, the lessee will make improvements to leased property by constructing new buildings or improving existing structures. The lessee has the right to use these leasehold improvements over the term of the lease; however, these improvements will revert to the lessor at the expiration of the lease.

1] Leasehold improvements are capitalized to "Leasehold Improvements" (a property, plant and equip-ment account) by the lessee and are amortized over the **shorter** of (1) the remaining lease term, **or** (2) the useful life of the improvement.

2] Improvements made in lieu of rent should be expensed in the period incurred.

3] If the lease contains an option to renew and the likelihood of renewal is uncertain, the leasehold im-provement should be written off over the life of the initial lease term or useful life of the improve-ment, whichever is shorter.

> **NOTE:** Moveable equipment or office furniture that is not attached to the leased property is **not** considered a leasehold improvement.

4] The summary below lists the elements commonly encountered in operating leases.

Operating Lease FS Elements

	Lessor	**Lessee**
Balance sheet:	• Leased asset (net of accumulated depreciation)	• Prepaid rent (including lease bonus/fee and nonre-fundable security deposit)
	• Rent receivable	• Leasehold improvements (net of accumulated amortization)
	• Initial direct costs (net of accumulated amorti-zation)	• Deposit receivable
	• Unearned rent (including lease bonus/fee and nonrefundable security deposit)	
	• Deposit liability	
Income statement:	• Rent revenue (including amortization of lease bonus/fee and nonrefundable security deposit)	• Rent expense (including amortization of lease bonus/fee and nonrefundable security deposit)
	• Depreciation expense	• Amortization of leasehold improvements
	• Amortization of initial direct costs	
	• Other maintenance expenses	

(f) **Modifications and terminations to capital leases**

A company may modify a capital lease in such a way that it changes the lease to an operating lease.

1] If a capital lease is modified as such, it is treated as a sales-leaseback transaction.
2] If a company terminates a capital lease, the accounting for the termination depends on whether the lease was a capital lease for real estate or for an asset other than real estate.

    a] If the capital lease was for real estate, then the criteria for recognition of gains must be met in order for the company to recognize a gain on termination of the lease. However, any loss on the transaction is recognized immediately.
    b] If the lease was for assets other than real estate, then the asset and obligation of the lease are removed from the accounts and a gain or loss is recognized for the difference.

        i] If the original lessee remains secondarily liable, the guarantee obligation is recognized.

(g) **Termination costs**

If a lessee terminates an operating lease before the end of its term, the lessee must recognize any termination costs. Termination costs may include a lump-sum payment or payments that continue during the remaining lease term. Such costs are measured and recognized at fair value on the date the agreement is terminated, the entity no longer receives rights to the assets, or the company ceases to use the assets (cease-use date).

1] If the company remains liable for payments after the cease-use date, the fair value of the termination costs is based on the remaining lease rentals reduced by the estimated sublease rentals that could be obtained for the property, even if the entity does not intend to sublease.
2] Termination costs of an operating lease are included in calculating income from continuing operations.
3] If the termination of an operating lease is associated with the exit or disposal of a discontinued operation, these costs are included in the results of discontinued operations.

NOW REVIEW MULTIPLE-CHOICE QUESTIONS 1 THROUGH 18

(2) **Direct Financing Lease—Lessor**

(a) A direct financing lease arises when a consumer needs equipment but does not want to purchase the equipment outright, and/or is unable to obtain conventional financing. In this situation, the consumer will turn to a leasing company (e.g., a bank) which will purchase the desired asset from a manufacturer (or dealer) and lease it to the consumer. Direct financing leases apply to leasing companies, as opposed to manufacturers or dealers, because leasing companies purchase the assets solely for leasing, not for resale. Leasing companies are usually involved in financing activities (e.g., banking and insurance), not in the sale of property of the type being leased. The following situation shows when a direct financing lease would arise:

EXAMPLE

ABC Company needs new equipment to expand its manufacturing operations but does not have enough capital to purchase the equipment at present. ABC Company employs Universal Leasing Company to purchase the equipment. ABC will lease the asset from Universal. Universal records a direct financing lease.

(b) The relationships in a direct financing lease arrangement are illustrated below.

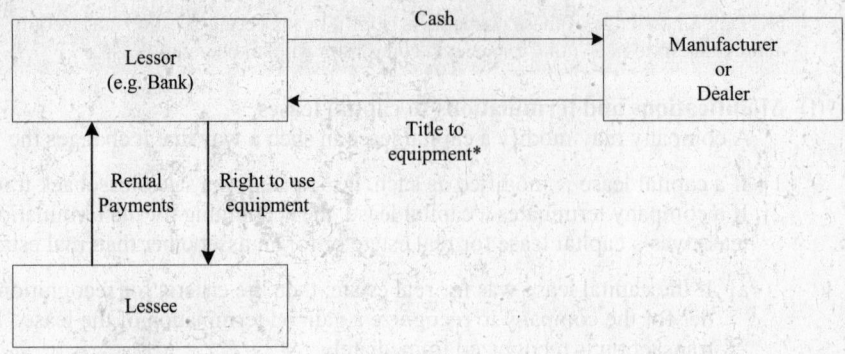

* Title would stay with the lessor unless criterion (1) or (2) previously presented is met, in which case title would pass to the lessee.

(c) As mentioned, a lease is considered to be a direct financing lease by the **lessor** if at least one of the four criteria applicable to both lessors and lessees is met, and **both** of the additional criteria applicable to lessors are met.

(d) Direct financing leases result in only interest revenue for the lessor. In essence, no product has been sold by the lessor, so no gain/loss, sales, or cost of sales is recognized from the lease transaction. Thus the FV (selling price) of the leased asset equals its cost to the lessor.

  1] The lessor's entry to record the acquisition of title to the asset to be leased is as follows:

Asset to be leased	(cost of asset = FV)	
Cash		(cash paid)

  2] At the inception of the lease, the lessor makes the following entry:

Lease receivable	xx	
Asset to be leased		xx
Unearned interest revenue		xx

  3] In effect, the asset is removed from the lessor's books; it will be transferred to the lessee's books if one of the four criteria applicable to lessees is met. It is possible that the lessee's analysis might result in an operating lease.

(e) In order to calculate the amounts in the entry above, you must first become familiar with several important terms.

  1] **Minimum lease payments (MLP)**

    MLP are the payments that the lessor/lessee is or can be required to make in connection with the leased property.

    a] Rent payments (excluding executory costs and contingent rentals)
    b] Bargain purchase option (if any)
    c] Guaranteed residual value (if any)
    d] Penalty for failure to renew (if any)
    e] Executory costs (e.g., property taxes, insurance, etc.) and contingent rentals are treated as revenues in the period earned.

  2] **Bargain purchase option (BPO)**

    This option allows the lessee to purchase leased property for an amount substantially lower than the expected FMV at the exercise date of the option.

  3] **Residual value**

    Residual value can be unguaranteed or guaranteed. Some lease contracts require lessees to guarantee residual value to lessors. The lessee can either buy the leased asset at the end of the lease term for the guaranteed residual value or allow the lessor to sell the leased asset (with the lessee paying any deficiency or receiving any excess over the guaranteed residual value).

    a] **Guaranteed residual value (GRV)** is considered part of the "minimum lease payment" and is reflected in the lessor's lease receivable account and the lessee's lease payable account. At the end of the lease term, the receivable and payable on the respective lessor's and lessee's books should be equal to the guaranteed residual value. Both lessor and lessee consider the guaranteed residual value a final lease payment. The lessee should amortize (depreciate) the asset down to the guaranteed residual value.

b] **Unguaranteed residual value** is the estimated residual value of the leased asset at the end of the lease (if a guaranteed residual value exists, the unguaranteed residual value is the excess of estimated value over the guaranteed residual value). The present value of the unguaranteed residual value should be included in the lessor's net investment in the lease unless the lease transfers title to the leased asset or there is a bargain purchase option.

i] At the end of the lease, the lessor's receivable account should be equal to the unguaranteed residual value. The lessor must review the estimated residual value annually and recognize any decreases as a loss. No upward adjustments of the residual value are permitted.

(f) Now you are ready to calculate the amounts for the lessor's entry using the following formulas:

EXAMPLE

| **Lease receivable*** (= gross investment) | = | Total MLP** | + | URV (if any) |

| **Asset to be leased** (= net investment) (= FV or cost of asset) | = | PV of gross investment |

| **Unearned interest revenue** | = | Gross investment | – | FV (or cost) of asset |

* The title **Gross investment** is used when there is an unguaranteed residual value because the lower probability of collection of the residual value makes the use of the term **Receivable** undesirable.

** Include guaranteed residual value.

Alternative methods of recording the lease transaction are shown below.

Lease receivable (gross)	xx		Lease receivable (net)	xx
Asset to be leased	xx	-or-	Asset to be leased	xx
Unearned interest revenue	xx			

NOTE: We will follow the gross method in our examples for the lessor because it is consistent with the questions on the CPA exam.

(g) Below are additional guidelines when accounting for the lessor.

1] The lease receivable should be separated into current and noncurrent components on the lessor's balance sheet.

2] Unearned interest revenue must be amortized to produce a constant periodic rate of return on the net investment using the interest method.

3] No residual value is assumed to accrue to the value of the lessor if the lease transfers ownership or contains a BPO.

4] At the termination of the lease, the balance in the receivable should equal the guaranteed or unguaranteed residual value, assuming title is not transferred and there is no bargain purchase option.

EXAMPLE 2

Lease Information

1) A three-year lease is initiated on 1/1/Y1 for equipment costing $131,858 with an expected useful life of five years. The FV of the equipment on 1/1/Y1 is $131,858.

2) Three annual payments are due to the lessor beginning 12/31/Y1. The property reverts back to the lessor upon termination of the lease.

3) The guaranteed residual value at the end of year 3 is $10,000.

4) The lessor is to receive a 10% return (implicit rate).

5) Collectivity of minimum lease payments is predictable, and there are no important uncertainties concerning costs yet to be incurred by the lessor under the lease.

6) The cost (FV) of the asset incurred by the lessor to acquire the asset for leasing is to be recovered through two components: annual rent payments and guaranteed residual value using a discount (implicit) rate of 10%.

7) The annual rent payment to the lessor is computed as follows:

   a) Find PV of guaranteed residual value

$$\underset{\text{GRV}}{\$10,000} \quad \times \quad .7513 \quad = \quad \$7,513$$

   b) Find PV of annual rent payments

$$\$131,858 \quad - \quad \$7,513 \quad = \quad \$124,345$$
$$\text{FV of asset}$$

   c) Find annual rent payment

$$\$124,345 \quad \div \quad \text{PVA}_{n=3;\, i=10\%}$$

$$\$124,345 \quad \div \quad 2.4869 \quad = \quad \$50,000$$

Lease Classification

This lease is a direct financing lease because criterion 4 (the 90% test) is satisfied.

$$\$124,345 + \$7,513 \geq (.9)(\$131,858)$$

(Since the residual value is guaranteed, the PV of the MLP is 100% of the FV.) The two additional criteria for the lessor are satisfied, and FV equals cost. If the residual value had been unguaranteed, the 90% test would still have been met because $\$124,345 \geq (.9) (\$131,858)$.

Accounting for Lease

1) The lease should be recorded at the beginning of year 1 by the lessor.
2) The lease receivable is calculated as follows:

$$\underset{\$50,000}{(\text{Annual rent payment}} \quad \times \quad \underset{\text{3 yrs.}}{\text{Lease term})} \quad + \quad \underset{\$10,000}{\text{GRV}} \quad = \$160,000$$

3) Unearned interest revenue is calculated as follows:

$$\underset{\$160,000}{\text{Lease receivable}} \quad - \quad \underset{\$131,858}{\text{FV of asset}} \quad = \$ 28,142$$

4) Unearned interest is amortized during the lease term using the following amortization schedule:

AMORTIZATION SCHEDULE

Carrying value at beg. of yr. 1 (= PV of gross investment)		$131,858
Interest revenue (10%)	$ 13,186	
Rent payment	(50,000)	(36,814)
Carrying value at beg. of yr. 2		95,044
Interest revenue	9,504	
Rent payment	(50,000)	(40,496)
Carrying value at beg. of yr. 3		54,548
Interest revenue	5,452	
Rent payment	(50,000)	(44,548)
Carrying value at end of yr. 3 (= residual value)		10,000

Lease receivable on balance sheet:

End of Year 1	–	current portion	= $40,496	principal reduction in year 2
		noncurrent portion	= $54,548	principal reductions after year 2
End of Year 2	–	current portion	= $54,548	principal reduction in the following year (includes residual value)

NOTE: As the lease expires, interest revenue decreases and the reduction of principal increases.

5) The journal entries for the lessor are shown below.

JOURNAL ENTRIES FOR THE LESSOR

Initial entries (Beg. of Yr. 1)			**End of Year 2**		
Equipment for leasing	131,858		Cash	50,000	
Cash		131,858	Lease receivable		50,000
Lease receivable	160,000		Unearned interest	9,504	
Equipment for leasing		131,858	Interest revenue		9,504
Unearned interest		28,142			

Cash	50,000		Cash	50,000	
Lease receivable		50,000	Lease receivable		50,000
Unearned interest	13,186		Unearned interest	5,452	
Interest revenue		13,186	Interest revenue		5,452

6) Assume that when the asset is returned at the end of year 3 the asset has a FV of only $4,000. The lessee will need to make a payment of $6,000 ($10,000 − $4,000) because the residual value was guaranteed. The lessor would make the following entry:

Cash	6,000	
Residual value of equipment	4,000	
Lease receivable		10,000

NOW REVIEW MULTIPLE-CHOICE QUESTIONS 19 THROUGH 20

(3) Sales-Type Lease—Lessor

A sales-type lease arises when a manufacturer or dealer leases an asset which otherwise might be sold outright for a profit. These manufacturers (dealers) use leasing as a way to market their own products (e.g., a car dealership). The leasing, or financing arrangement, is a means for the manufacturer to sell its products and realize a profit from sales. (By contrast, direct financing leases serve purely as financing arrangements.) The following situation shows when a sales-type lease would arise:

ABC Company needs equipment to expand its manufacturing operations. ABC Company enters into a lease agreement with XYZ Manufacturing, Inc. for the equipment. XYZ Manufacturing Inc. records a sales-type lease.

(a) The relationships in a sales-type lease arrangement are illustrated below.

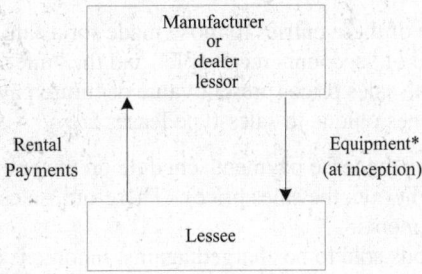

* Title stays with lessor and property will be returned to lessor at the end of the lease term unless criterion (1) or (2) previously presented is met.

(b) Sales-type leases, unlike direct financing leases, result in **both** (1) gross profit (loss) in the period of sales, **and** (2) interest revenue to be earned over the lease term using the effective interest method. The diagram below compares and contrasts direct financing leases with sales-type leases.

Direct Financing Lease (Lessor)

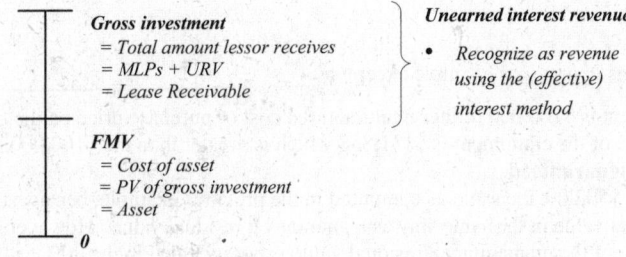

Sales-Type Lease (Lessor)

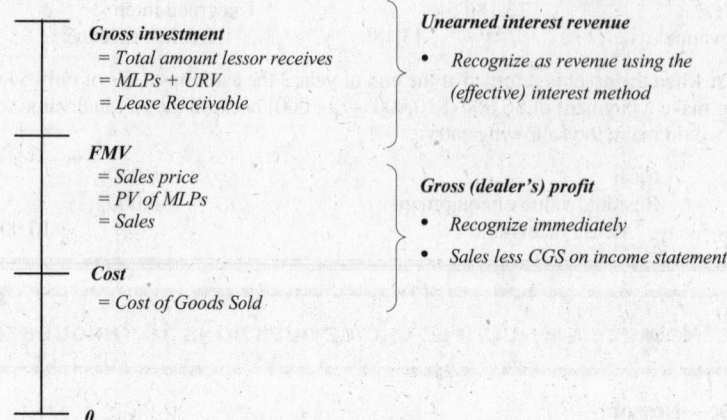

Gross investment
 = *Total amount lessor receives*
 = *MLPs + URV*
 = *Lease Receivable*

Unearned interest revenue

• *Recognize as revenue using the*
  (effective) interest method

FMV
 = *Sales price*
 = *PV of MLPs*
 = *Sales*

Gross (dealer's) profit

• *Recognize immediately*

• *Sales less CGS on income statement*

Cost
 = *Cost of Goods Sold*

0

(c) A lease is considered to be a sales-type lease from the viewpoint of the lessor if the criteria mentioned earlier for direct financing leases are satisfied. However, in the case of a sales-type lease, the FV of the asset, which is the sales price in the ordinary course of the lessor's business is **greater than** the cost or carrying value of the leased asset. Because of this difference, a sales-type lease is more complex than a direct financing lease. The journal entries to record a sales-type lease are

Lease receivable (Gross)	xx	
Sales		xx
Unearned interest		xx
CGS	xx	
Inventory		xx

Note the similarity of these entries to those made for a sale on account. The differences are "lease receivable" instead of "accounts receivable" and the "unearned interest" for the excess of the receivables over the sales price (present value of future payments).

(d) Additional guidelines unique to sales-type leases are

1] The lessor bases the lease payment schedule on the amount the lessee would have paid to purchase the asset outright (i.e., the sales price). Therefore, sales are equal to the present value of the minimum lease payments.

2] The cost of goods sold to be charged against income is equal to the historic cost or carrying value of the leased asset (most likely inventory) **less** the present value of any unguaranteed residual value.

3] The difference between the selling price and cost of goods sold is the gross profit (loss) recognized by the lessor at the inception of the lease.

4] When accounting for sales-type leases, guaranteed residual value is considered part of sales revenue because the lessor knows the entire asset has been sold. Unguaranteed residual value, however, is excluded from both sales and cost of sales at its present value because there is less certainty that unguaranteed residual value will be realized.

EXAMPLE 3

Lease Information

Assume same information as in previous example except

1) The cost of the equipment is $100,000 (either manufactured cost or purchase price paid by dealer).
2) The normal selling price of the equipment is $131,858 which is greater than the $100,000 cost.
3) The residual value is **unguaranteed**.
4) The lease payments are $50,000, the same as computed in the previous example, because the lessor treats an **un**guaranteed residual value in the same way as a guaranteed residual value. However, as mentioned below, the present value of the unguaranteed residual value is not included in the 90% test.

Lease Classification

This is a sales-type lease since the 90% test is satisfied; 90% of the $131,858 FV = $118,672, which is less than $124,345, the present value of the minimum lease payments (see Numerical Example 2); the present value of the residual value is excluded because it is unguaranteed. Additionally, the cost of the asset is less than its fair value (also the present value of the minimum lease payments plus the unguaranteed residual value). Assume the two additional criteria for the lessor have been satisfied.

Accounting for Lease

1) The gross investment is: $160,000 [3 payments of $50,000 (same as Numerical Example 2) plus a $10,000 unguaranteed residual value]

The PV of gross investment is: $131,858 [($50,000 × 2.4869) + ($10,000 × .7513)]
The unearned interest revenue is: $28,142 ($160,000 – $131,858)
Sales are: $124,345 [$131,858 – ($10,000 × .7513)*]
CGS is: $92,487 [$100,000 – ($10,000 × .7513)*]

* There is no effect on gross profit of not including the present value of the unguaranteed residual value in either sales or cost of goods sold. In both cases, the gross profit is $31,858. If the residual value were guaranteed, this adjustment would not be made.

2) The entry to record the lease is

Lease receivable**	160,000	
Cost of goods sold	92,487	
Sales		124,345
Inventory***		100,000
Unearned interest		28,142

** On the balance sheet this amount is termed gross investment since it includes an unguaranteed residual value.
*** Either acquisition cost to dealer or manufacturer's cost of production.

Interest revenue will be recognized at 10% of the outstanding net investment (lease receivable less unearned interest) each period (i.e., interest revenue in year 1 is $131,858 × 10% = $13,186).

At the end of year 1, the following entry(ies) would be made:

Cash	50,000	
Lease receivable		50,000
Unearned interest revenue	13,186	
Interest revenue		13,186

At termination, the lease receivable will have a balance of $10,000 which is the unguaranteed residual value. Note that the same amortization schedule that appears in Numerical Example 2 above is applicable to this one. The fact that the residual value is unguaranteed in this example does not affect the amortization schedule because the lessor is projecting that it will get back an asset worth $10,000. If the asset is returned to the lessor and its fair market value is only $4,000, the following entry is made on the lessor's books:

Loss	6,000	
Residual value of equipment	4,000	
Lease receivable		10,000

(e) Now that we have completed our discussion of lessor's direct financing and sales-type leases, it should be helpful to review the financial statement elements for the lessor, and to preview elements that appear on the lessee's financial statements. These elements are shown below.

Lessor

	Direct financing lease	**Sales-type lease**
Balance sheet:	Lease receivable (current and noncurrent) Initial direct costs (added to net investment causing a new implicit rate of interest)	Lease receivable (current and noncurrent)
Income statement:	Unearned interest revenue Interest revenue Amortization of initial direct costs	Unearned interest revenue Interest revenue Initial direct costs (expensed immediately) Dealer's profit

Lessee

Capital lease

Balance sheet:	Leased asset (net of accumulated depreciation) Lease obligation (current and noncurrent)
Income Statement:	Depreciation expense Interest expense Other maintenance expense

NOW REVIEW MULTIPLE-CHOICE QUESTIONS 21 THROUGH 24

(4) Capital Leases—Lessee

When a lessor records a direct financing or sales-type lease, the lessee, in turn, must record a capital lease. Capital leases reflect the transfer of risks and benefits associated with the asset to the lessee.

(a) A lease is considered to be a capital lease to the lessee if **any one** of the four criteria is satisfied.

1] Transfer of title
2] Bargain purchase
3] 75% of useful life
4] 90% of net FV

a] Lease agreements not meeting at least one of the criteria for capital leases are treated as operating leases on the lessee's books. If the lease is classified as a capital lease, the lessee must record an asset and a liability based on the present value of the minimum lease payments as follows:

Leased asset	(PV of MLP)	
Lease obligation		(PV of MLP)

b] The above entry reflects recording the transaction "net" (i.e., at present value). If the lease was recorded gross, the lease obligation would be credited for the total amount of the MLP and there would be a debit to "Discount on lease obligation."

Leased asset	(PV of MLP)	
Discount on lease obligation	(plug)	
Lease obligation		(gross MLP)

(b) The gross method is similar to the accounting for deferred payment contracts.

(c) To determine the present value of the MLP, the lessee discounts the future payments using the **lesser** of

1] The lessee's incremental borrowing rate, **or**
2] The lessor's implicit rate if known by the lessee

NOTE: Using a lower interest rate increases the present value.

(d) Leased assets, however, should **not** be recorded at an amount greater than the FV of the asset. If the FV is less than the PV of the MLP, the lease should be recorded at the FV and a new implicit interest rate calculated to reflect a constant periodic rate applied to the remaining balance of the obligation.

(e) During the term of the lease, the lessee must use the (effective) interest method to allocate cash paid between interest expense and reduction of the lease obligation. This method is the same as the one used by the lessor as previously described.

(f) Lessees must amortize leased assets recorded on the books under a capital lease. The amortization (depreciation) method used should be consistent with the lessee's normal depreciation policy. The term over which the asset is amortized may differ depending upon which criteria qualified the lease as a capital lease.

1] If the lease transfers ownership or contains a BPO (criteria 1 or 2), the asset will be amortized over its estimated useful life (since the asset actually becomes the property of the lessee at the end of the lease term and will be used for the remainder of its useful life).
2] If the 75% of useful life or the 90% test (criteria 3 or 4) is met, the leased asset is amortized over the lease term only (since the property will revert to the lessor at the end of the lease term and will be used for the remainder of its useful life).

(g) The lease term does not extend beyond the date of a bargain purchase option. Lease terms, however, may include the following:

1] Bargain renewal periods
2] Periods when the lessor has the option to renew or extend
3] Periods during which the lessee guarantees the debt of the lessor
4] Periods in which a material penalty exists for failure to renew

(h) When the lease terminates, the balance in the obligation account should equal the bargain purchase option price or the expected residual value (guaranteed residual value, or salvage value if lower).

1] Leased assets and obligations should be disclosed as such in the balance sheet. The lease obligation should be separated into both current and noncurrent components.

EXAMPLE 4

Lease Information

1) A three-year lease is initiated on 1/1/Y1 for equipment with an expected useful life of five years. The equipment reverts back to the lessor upon expiration of the lease agreement.
2) Three payments are due to the lessor in the amount of $50,000 per year **beginning 12/31/Y1**. An additional sum of $1,000 is to be paid annually by the lessee for insurance.
3) Lessee guarantees a $10,000 residual value on 12/31/Y3 to the lessor.
4) The leased asset is expected to have only a $7,000 salvage value on 12/31/Y3 despite the $10,000 residual value guarantee; therefore, the asset should be depreciated down to the $7,000 expected residual value.
5) The lessee's incremental borrowing rate is 10% (same as lessor's implicit rate).
6) The present value of the lease obligation is

PV of guaranteed residual value	=	$10,000	×	.7513	=	$ 7,513
PV of annual payments	=	$50,000	×	2.4869	=	124,345
						$131,858

Since the lessee's incremental borrowing rate is 10% and the residual value is guaranteed, the present value of $131,858 is the same amount used by the lessor in the direct financing lease example (Numerical Example 2) to determine the payments to be made by the lessee. If an incremental borrowing rate different than the lessor's is used and/or the lease contains an unguaranteed residual value, the present value computed by the lessee will differ from the lessor's present value (FV). These differences account for the fact that many leases are not capitalized by lessees because they don't meet the 90% test.

Lease Classification

The 90% test is met because the present value of the minimum lease payments ($131,858) is 100% of the FV of the leased asset.

Accounting for Lease

1) Note that executory costs (e.g., insurance, property taxes, etc.) are not included in the present value calculations
2) The entry to recognize the lease is

1/1/Y1	Leased equipment	131,858	
	Lease obligation		131,858

3) The entries to record the payments and depreciation are

	12/31/Y1	12/31/Y2	12/31/Y3	
Insurance expense	1,000	1,000	1,000	
Lease obligation*	36,814	40,496	44,548	
Interest expense*	13,186	9,504	5,452	
Cash	51,000	51,000	51,000	
Depreciation expense**	41,619	41,619	41,620	
Accumulated depreciation	41,619	41,619	41,620***	

   * Refer to the amortization table in the direct financing lease discussion (Numeric Example 2). Note that classification of the lease obligation into current and noncurrent on the lessee's books would parallel classification of the lease receivable on the lessor's books.

> **NOTE:** Classification of the lease obligation into current and noncurrent on the lessee's books would parallel classification of the lease receivable on the lessor's books.

   ** [($131,858 – 7,000) ÷ 3 years]
   *** Rounding error of $1

4) The 12/31/Y3 entry to record the guaranteed residual value payment (assuming salvage value = estimated residual value = $7,000) and to clear the lease related accounts from the lessee's books is

Lease obligation	10,000	
Accumulated depreciation	124,858	
Cash		3,000
Leased equipment		131,858

If the actual residual value were only $5,000, the credit to "cash" would be $5,000 and a $2,000 loss would be recognized by the lessee.

(i) Remember that leased assets are amortized over the lease term unless title transfers or a bargain purchase option exists—then over the useful life of the leased asset. At the end of the lease, the balance of the lease obligation should equal the guaranteed residual value or the bargain purchase option price. To illustrate, consider the following example.

EXAMPLE 5

Lease Information

1) A three-year lease is initiated on 1/1/Y1 for equipment with an expected useful life of five years.
2) Three annual $50,000 payments are due the lessor **beginning 1/1/Y1**.
3) The lessee can exercise a bargain purchase option on 12/31/Y3 for $10,000. The expected residual value at 12/31/Y5 is $1,000.
4) The lessee's incremental borrowing rate is 10% (lessor's implicit rate is unknown).

Lease Classification

Although the lease term is for only 60% of the asset's useful life, the lessee would account for this as a capital lease because it contains a bargain purchase option. Also, the PV of the minimum lease payments is greater than 90% of the FV of the leased asset.

Accounting for Lease

1) The present value of the lease obligation is

PV of bargain purchase option	=	$10,000	×	.7513	=	$ 7,513
PV of annual payments	=	$50,000	×	2.7355	=	136,775
						$144,288

2) The following amortization table summarizes the liability amortization:

AMORTIZATION TABLE

Carrying value at beg. of yr. 1		$144,288
Lease payment	$(50,000)	(50,000)
Carrying value at beg. of yr. 1 after first payment		94,288
Interest expense	9,429	
Lease payment	(50,000)	(40,571)
Carrying value at beg. of year 2 after second payment		53,717
Interest expense	5,372	
Lease payment	(50,000)	(44,628)
Carrying value at beg. of yr. 3 after third payment		9,089
Interest expense	911*	911
Bargain purchase option		10,000
Option payment	(10,000)	(10,000)
		--

* Rounding error of $2

> **NOTE:** This table reflects the fact that the lease is an annuity due with cash payments on 1/1 and interest expense accruals on 12/31; thus, the first payment does not include any interest expense.

3) The entry to record the lease is

1/1/Y1	Leased equipment	144,288	
	Lease obligation		144,288

4) The entries to record the payments, interest expense, depreciation (amortization) expense, and the exercise of the bargain purchase are

		Year 1		Year 2		Year 3	
1/1	Lease obligation	50,000		40,571		44,628	
	Accrued interest payable or						
	interest expense*			9,429		5,372	
	Cash		50,000		50,000		50,000
12/31	Interest expense	9,429		5,372		911	
	Accrued int. payable		9,429		5,372		
	Lease obligation						911
12/31	Depreciation expense**	28,658		28,658		28,658	
	Accumulated depreciation		28,658		28,658		28,658

		Year 1	Year 2	Year 3
12/31	Lease obligation			10,000
	Cash			10,000

   * If 12/31 accruals are reversed
 ** (143,288 ÷ 5 years)

3. Other Considerations

To supplement the review of lease accounting presented above, the following topics have been selected for further discussion:

  a. Initial direct costs
  b. Sale-leaseback
  c. Disclosure requirements

a. Initial direct costs

(1) Initial direct costs are the lessor's costs directly associated with negotiation and consummation of leases. These costs include commissions, legal fees, credit investigations, document preparation, etc. In operating leases, initial direct costs are capitalized and subsequently amortized to expense in proportion to the recognition of rental revenue (which is usually straight-line).

(2) Initial direct costs of direct financing and sales-type leases are accounted for differently

  (a) In sales-type leases, charge initial direct costs to operations in the year the sale is recorded;
  (b) In direct financing leases add the initial direct costs to the net investment in the lease.
  (c) Compute a new effective interest rate that equates the minimum lease payments and any unguaranteed residual value with the combined outlay for the leased asset and initial direct costs. Finally, the unearned lease (interest) revenue and the initial direct costs are to be amortized to income over the lease term so that a constant periodic rate is earned on the net investment.

b. Sale-leaseback

(1) Sale-leaseback describes a transaction where the owner of property (seller-lessee) sells the property, and then immediately leases all or part of it back from the new owner (buyer-lessor). The important consideration in this type of transaction is the recognition of two separate and distinct economic transactions. It is important, however, to note that there is not a physical transfer of property. First, there is a sale of property, and second, there is a lease agreement for the same property in which the seller is the lessee and the buyer is the lessor. This is illustrated below.

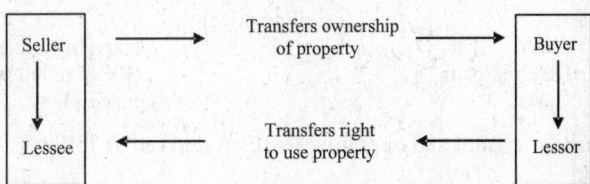

NOTE: Sale-leaseback transactions only affect accounting for the seller-lessee. Buyer-lessor accounting is unaffected.

(2) The accounting treatment from the seller-lessee's point of view will depend upon the degree of rights to use the property retained by the seller-lessee. The degree of rights may be categorized in one of three ways:

  (a) Substantially all
  (b) Minor
  (c) More than minor but less than substantially all

(3) A seller-lessee retains **substantially all** the rights to use the property if the PV of the rental payments is 90% or more of the fair value of the asset sold. This test is based on the criteria used earlier to classify leases. Since the seller-lessee retains use of the asset, this type of sale-leaseback is considered, in substance, a form of financing to the seller-lessee rather than a sale. In this case, any gain on the sale is deferred by the seller-lessee.

Cash	(selling price)	
Asset		(carrying value)
Deferred gain		(excess)

(a) The asset would be reported on the seller-lessee's balance sheet as follows:

      Leased asset   xx
      Less: Deferred gain   (xx)
                                  xx

(b) The net value of the leased asset is the same amount the asset would be if it had not been sold.

(c) If the lease is classified as a capital lease, the deferred gain is amortized over the life of the asset at the same rate as the asset is being depreciated. As deferred gain is amortized, it is charged to depreciation expense.

      Deferred gain   xx
         Depreciation expense   xx

(d) Alternatively, the gain may be recognized as income over the term of the lease.

(e) Although most leases in the "substantially all" category are capital leases, a sale-leaseback occurring in the last 25% of an asset's economic life would be classified as an operating lease.

(f) If the lease is classified as an operating lease, any deferred gain is amortized over the lease term in proportion to the related gross rental charges to expense over the lease term. Amortization in this case is charged to rent expense by the seller-lessee.

      Deferred gain   xx
         Rent expense   xx

(4) The seller-lessee retains only a **minor** portion of rights to use the property when the PV of the rental payments is 10% or less of the fair value of the asset sold. Since the seller-lessee has given up the right to use the asset, the leaseback is considered in substance a sale. Any gain on the sale is recognized in full since the earnings process is considered complete.

      Cash   (selling price)
         Asset   (carrying value)
         Gain   (excess)

(a) When only a minor portion of use is retained, the seller-lessee accounts for the lease as an operating lease.

(5) The seller-lessee retains **more than a minor portion but less than substantially all** the rights to use the property when the PV of the rental payments is more than 10% but less than 90% of the fair value of the asset sold. In this situation, gain is recognized only to the extent that it exceeds the PV of the rental payments.

      Cash   (selling price)
         Asset   (carrying value)
         Deferred gain   (PV of rental payments)
         Gain   (excess)

(6) Recognized gain for capital and operating leases is derived as follows:

(a) If the leaseback is classified as an operating lease, recognized gain is the portion of gain that exceeds the PV of the MLP over the lease term. The seller-lessee should use its incremental borrowing rate to compute the PV of the MLP. If the implicit rate of interest in the lease is known and lower, it should be used instead.

(b) If the leaseback is classified as a capital lease, recognized gain is the amount of gain that exceeds the recorded amount of the leased asset.

(7) In all cases, the seller-lessee should immediately recognize a loss when the fair value of the property at the time of the leaseback is less than its undepreciated cost (book value). In the example below, the sales price is less than the book value of the property. However, there is no economic loss because the FV which equals the PV is greater than the book value.

      Sales price   Book value   FV and PV
      $85,000 $90,000 $100,000
                         ($5,000)
                      Artificial Loss

(a) The artificial loss must be deferred and amortized as an addition to depreciation.

(8) In the following chart, when the leased asset is land only, any amortization should be on a straight-line basis over the lease term, regardless of whether the lease is classified as a capital or operating lease.

(a) The buyer-lessor should account for the transaction as a purchase and a direct financing lease if the agreement meets the criteria of **either** a direct financing lease **or** a sales-type lease. Otherwise, the agreement should be accounted for as a purchase and an operating lease.

(b) To illustrate a sale-leaseback transaction, consider the example below.

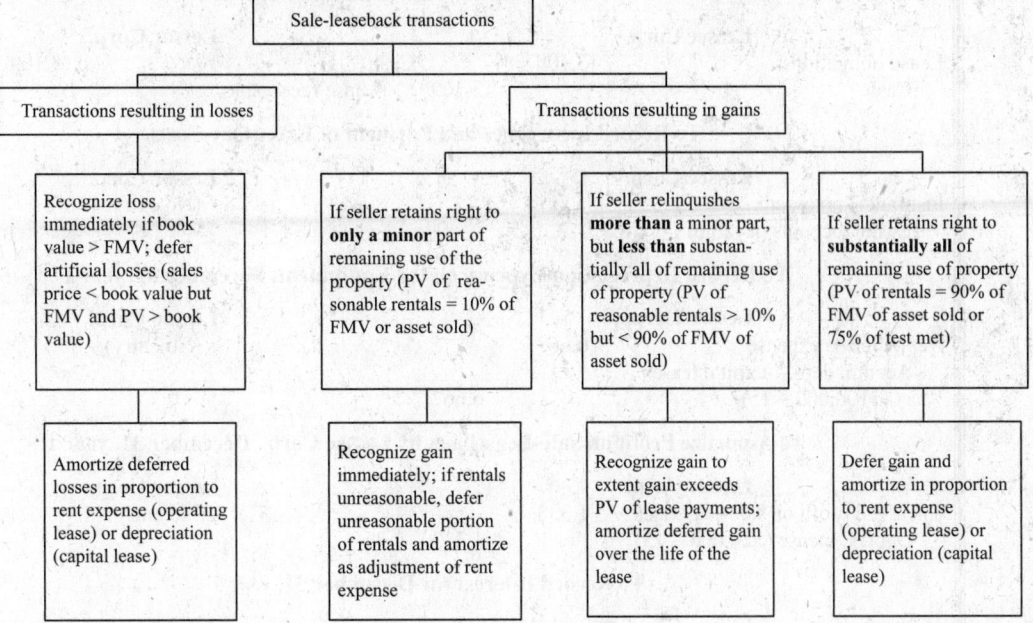

EXAMPLE 6

Lease Information

1) Lessee Corporation sells equipment that has a book value of $80,000 and a fair value of $100,000 to Lessor Corporation, and then immediately leases it back.
2) The sale date is January 1, year 1, and the equipment has a fair value of $100,000 on that date and an estimated useful life of fifteen years.
3) The lease term is fifteen years, noncancelable, and requires equal rental payments of $13,109 at the beginning of each year.
4) Lessee Corp. has the option to renew the lease annually at the same rental payments upon expiration of the original lease.
5) Lessee Corp. has the obligation to pay all executory costs.
6) The annual rental payments provide the lessor with a 12% return on investment.
7) The incremental borrowing rate of Lessee Corp. is 12%.
8) Lessee Corp. depreciates similar equipment on a straight-line basis.

Lease Classification

Lessee Corp. should classify the agreement as a capital lease since the lease term exceeds 75% of the estimated economic life of the equipment, and because the present value of the lease payments is greater than 90% of the fair value of the equipment. Assuming that collectibility of the lease payments is reasonably predictable and that no important uncertainties exist concerning the amount of unreimbursable costs yet to be incurred by the lessor, Lessor Corp. should classify the transaction as a direct financing lease because the present value of the minimum lease payments is equal to the fair market value of $100,000.

Accounting for Lease

Lessee Corp. and Lessor Corp. would normally make the following journal entries during the first year:

Upon Sale of Equipment on January 1, year 1

Lessee Corp.			Lessor Corp.		
Cash	100,000		Equipment	100,000	
Equipment		80,000	Cash		100,000
Unearned profit on sale-			Lease receivable	196,635*	
leaseback		20,000	Equipment		100,000

	Lessee Corp.			**Lessor Corp.**	
Leased equipment	100,000		Unearned interest		96,635
Lease obligations		100,000			
			* ($13,109 × 15)		

To Record First Payment on January 1, year 1

	Lessee Corp.			**Lessor Corp.**	
Lease obligations	13,109		Cash	13,109	
Cash		13,109	Lease receivable		13,109

To Record Incurrence and Payment of Executory Costs

	Lessee Corp.		**Lessor Corp.**
Insurance, taxes, etc.	xxx		(No entry)
Cash (accounts payable)		xxx	

To Record Depreciation Expense on the Equipment, December 31, year 1

	Lessee Corp.		**Lessor Corp.**
Depreciation expense	6,667		(No entry)
Accum. depr.—capital leases			
($100,000 ÷ 15)		6,667	

To Amortize Profit on Sale-Leaseback by Lessee Corp., December 31, year 1

	Lessee Corp.		**Lessor Corp.**
Unearned profit on sale-leaseback	1,333		(No entry)
Depr. Expense ($20,000 ÷ 15)		1,333	

To Record Interest for December 31, year 1

	Lessee Corp.			**Lessor Corp**	
Interest expense	10,427		Unearned interest revenue	10,427	
Accrued interest payable		10,427	Interest revenue		10,427

(Carrying value $86,891 × .12 = $10,427)

c. **Disclosure requirements**

The disclosures required of the lessor and lessee are very comprehensive and detailed. In essence, all terms of the leasing arrangement are required (i.e., contingent rentals, subleases, residual values, unearned interest revenue, etc.). There are, however, some generic disclosure requirements. First, a **general description** of the leasing arrangement is required. Second, the minimum future payments to be received (paid) by the lessor (lessee) for each of the **five succeeding fiscal years** should also be disclosed.

SUMMARY OF KEY PROBLEM SOLUTION POINTS

(1) **Lessor—direct financing and sales-type leases**

    (a) Periodic lease payments (PLP)

$$= \frac{\text{FV of leased property–PV of RV*/BPO}}{\text{PV of an annuity factor** using the lessor's implicit rate}}$$

      * Guaranteed/unguaranteed
    ** Annuity due or ordinary

    (b) Lease payments receivable/Gross investments = (Periodic lease payments × Number of rents) + Residual value/BPO

    (c) Unearned interest revenue = Gross investment – PV of PLP, PV of G/U RV, PV of BPO

    (d) Net investment = Gross investment – Unearned interest revenue

    (e) Gross profit (only for sales-type leases) = Selling price* – Cost of leased asset sold

      * (FV/PV of PLP + G/URV + BPO)

    (f) Interest revenue = Carrying value of lease receivable* × Implicit % × Time

      * (Gross investment – Unearned interest revenue)

Periodic Journal Entries

Unearned interest revenue	xxx	
Interest revenue		xxx
Cash	xxx	
Lease payments receivable		xxx

(2) Lessee—capital lease

   (a) Determine capital   =   (Periodic lease payment [PLP] × Present value factor *) +
        lease liability   (G/URV or BPO × PV of 1.00 factor)

       * Annuity due or ordinary annuity

- Use lessee's incremental borrowing %, unless lessor's implicit % is lower and lessee knows it
- PLP is exclusive of executory costs

   (b) Leased asset   =   Capital lease liability at inception of lease as computed above—PV × MLP [Exception: where FV of leased asset < PV of MLP (PLP + GRV or BPO), then leased asset and capital lease liability are recorded at the FV of leased asset.]

   (c) Depreciation (amortization) of leased asset

- Over useful life, regardless of lease term, if either criterion (1) or (2) is met: title transfer or bargain purchase option.
- Over lease term if criterion (3) or (4) is met: $\geq 75\%$ test or $\geq 90\%$ test

   (d) Lease liability   =

(1) Carrying value at inception of lease	$xxx
(2) Less first payment (usually the first payment is all principal because the lease liability is the PV of an annuity due)	(xx)
(3) Carrying value (CV)	$xxx
(4) Less principal part of second payment [PLP – (CV × interest %)]	(xxx)
(5) Carrying value	$xxx
	etc.

   (e) CV × % = Interest expense

NOW REVIEW MULTIPLE-CHOICE QUESTIONS 25 THROUGH 56

---

4. Research Component—Accounting Standards Codification

a. The accounting rules for leases are found in the area of the Codification labeled "Broad Transactions" under Topic 840 Broad Transactions—Leases is divided into the following subtopics:

Broad Transactions

840-10	Overall
840-20	Operating Leases
840-30	Capital Leases
840-40	Sales-Leaseback Transactions

b. Care should be taken when researching this area of the standards, as the rules for lessee and lessor are intertwined throughout each section of the Codification. Candidates should take special care to read the titles of each subtopic and section to ensure the question is answered appropriately for either the lessee or lessor. Typical research questions may include determining whether a lease is an operating lease or a capital lease or determining which items to include in calculating the minimum lease payments.

c. Keywords are shown below.

Bargain purchase option	Lease modification	Sales-type lease
Capital lease	Leasehold improvement	Substantial rights
Costs to terminate	Minimum lease payments	Termination costs
Direct financing lease	Modified lease	Termination of agreement
Guaranteed residual	New agreement operating lease	Transfer title
Initial direct costs	Operating lease	Unguaranteed residual
Lease bonus	Sale-leaseback	

5. International Financial Reporting Standards (IFRS)

a. Leasing is a topic where the IASB rules focus on substance over form. Unlike US GAAP, which uses certain thresholds to determine whether a lease should be classified as a capital lease, IAS 17 classifies leases based on whether substantially all the risks or benefits of ownership have been transferred. Leasing is also a topic where subtle terminology differences exist, for example, capital lease (US GAAP) versus finance lease (IFRS).

b. **Criteria for treatment of leases.** Under US GAAP, a lessee classifies a lease as either an operating lease or a capital lease. For the lessor, the lease is classified as an operating lease, a direct-financing lease, or a sales-type lease. However, under IAS 17 the lease is classified as either an operating lease or a finance lease for the lessee and the lessor. Of course, with a finance lease, the lessor is usually financing the item, or, if the lessor is a manufacturer or dealer, the lessor is selling the item through the leasing process.

c. Lease payments under an operating lease are recognized as expense on a straight-line basis over the lease term. The lessee must disclose in the footnotes the total future minimum payments for the next 12 months, payments due in Years 2-5, and payments due after five years, as well as a general description of the lease terms and restrictions imposed by the lease.

d. IFRS provides that a lease is a finance lease if substantially all of the risks or benefits of ownership have been transferred to the lessee. If any one of the four criteria is met, the lease is considered a finance lease.

   (1) The lease transfers ownership to the lessee by the end of the lease term or the lease contains a bargain purchase option, and it is reasonably certain that the option will be exercised.

   (2) The lease term is for the major part of the economic life of the asset (title may or may not pass to the lessee).

   (3) The present value of the minimum lease payments at the inception of the lease is at least equal to substantially all of the fair value of the leased asset.

   (4) The leased assets are of a specialized nature such that only the lessee can use them without modifications.

      (a) Although these four criteria are similar to the rules under US GAAP, notice that these rules do not carry specific thresholds such as 75% of the economic life or 90% of the fair value of the leased asset. Therefore, the proper classification is determined based on judgments about the substance of the transaction.

      (b) In addition, the following three other circumstances may indicate that the lease should be treated as a finance lease:

         1] If the lessee can cancel the lease, and the lessor's losses are borne by the lessee.
         2] Gains or losses resulting from the fluctuations in fair value will accrue to the lessee.
         3] The lessee has the ability to continue the lease for a supplemental term at a rent substantially lower than market value.

e. Under IFRS, a lease is classified as either an operating or a finance lease at the inception of the lease. The inception of the lease is the earlier of the date of the lease agreement or the date of commitment to the lease agreement. The commencement date of the lease term is the date on which the lessee is entitled to use the leased asset. Although the lease must be classified as either an operating or a finance lease on the date of inception, the lease is not recognized in the financial statements until the commencement date when the lessee is entitled to use the asset.

f. Another significant difference in classifying leases arises when land and buildings are leased together. Because land has an indefinite life, if title does not pass by the end of the lease term, the substantial risks and rewards of ownership do not transfer. Thus, in such cases the land lease cannot be classified as a finance lease. Under IFRS, the land and building would be treated as separate components; the land lease would be classified as an operating lease, and the building lease would be classified as a finance lease (assuming substantially all risks and rewards of ownership transferred). The minimum lease payments would be allocated between the land and the buildings elements in proportion to the relative fair values of the leasehold interests of each element. If both elements of the lease are expected to pass to the lessee at the end of the lease term, then the entire lease is classified as a finance lease.

   (1) **Accounting by lessees.** Under IFRS, the finance lease is recorded as an asset and as a liability by the lessee at the fair value of the leased property at the inception of the lease or the present value of the minimum lease payments. For the lessee, the minimum lease payments include the payments over the lease term that are required to be made, the bargain purchase option, and amounts guaranteed by the lessee. For the lessor, the minimum lease payments also include any residual value guaranteed by a third party not related to the lessor.

      (a) The interest rate used to calculate the present value of the minimum lease payments is the implicit rate. However, if the implicit rate cannot be determined, then the lessee's incremental borrowing rate is used. Any indirect costs incurred by the lessee in connection with negotiating and arranging the lease are added to the cost of the asset.

      (b) Each period the minimum lease payments are apportioned between the finance charge and the reduction of the principal outstanding. Any contingent rents are charged to expense as they are incurred. In addition, depreciation expense should be recognized for the leased asset. If ownership transfers at the end of the lease term, then the asset is depreciated over its useful life. If ownership does not transfer, then the finance lease is depreciated over the shorter of the lease term or the asset's useful life.

(c) Disclosures required for leases include the net carrying amount at the end of the reporting period, the future minimum lease payments at the end of the reporting period, and the present value of the lease payments due within one year, due after one year and less than five years, and after five years. Disclosures should also indicate the contingent rents recognized as expense during the period, a description of the lease, and its terms and restrictions.

(2) **Accounting by lessors.** In a finance lease, the asset is removed from the lessor's balance sheet, and the net investment in the lease is recorded as an asset. The net investment in the lease is calculated as gross lease receivables less the unearned finance income (interest income).

(a) Similar to US GAAP, a manufacturer or dealer will recognize the sale, cost of goods sold, lease receivable, and unearned finance income.

(b) **Sales and leaseback.** A sale and leaseback transaction may be classified as either an operating lease or a finance lease. The same criteria (risk and benefits of ownership, substance over form) determine whether the sale and leaseback is an operating or a finance lease. If it is classified as a finance lease, the gain is deferred and amortized over the lease term. If it is classified as an operating lease, the profit or loss is recognized immediately. If it is an operating lease and the fair value at the time of the sale and leaseback transaction is less than the carrying amount of the asset, then a loss is recognized immediately.

NOW REVIEW MULTIPLE-CHOICE QUESTIONS 57 THROUGH 60

KEY TERMS

Bargain purchase option (BPO). Allows the lessee to purchase leased property for an amount substantially lower than the expected FMV at the exercise date of the option.

Capital lease. A lease that transfers substantially all of the benefits and risks incident to the ownership of property.

Guaranteed residual value (GRV). A guaranteed residual value of the leased asset at the end of the lease.

Initial direct costs. Costs in setting up the lease agreement.

Lease. A contract between two parties—a lessor and a lessee that gives a lessee rights to use the lessor's property for a specified period of time in return for periodic cash payments (rent) to the lessor.

Minimum lease payments (MLP). The payments that the lessor/lessee is or can be required to make in connection with the leased property.

Operating lease. The risks and rewards of owning the asset remain with the lessor.

Unguaranteed residual value. The estimated residual value of the leased asset at the end of the lease.

E.2.d.(1) Operating Lease: Lessor/Lessee

1. Rapp Co. leased a new machine to Lake Co. on January 1, year 1. The lease is an operating lease and expires on January 1, year 6. The annual rental is $90,000. Additionally, on January 1, year 1, Lake paid $50,000 to Rapp as a lease bonus and $25,000 as a security deposit to be refunded upon expiration of the lease. In Rapp's year 1 income statement, the amount of rental revenue should be

   a. $140,000
   b. $125,000
   c. $100,000
   d. $ 90,000

2. Wall Co. leased office premises to Fox, Inc. for a five-year term beginning January 2, year 1. Under the terms of the operating lease, rent for the first year is $8,000 and rent for years two through five is $12,500 per annum. However, as an inducement to enter the lease, Wall granted Fox the first six months of the lease rent-free. In its December 31, year 1 income statement, what amount should Wall report as rental income?

   a. $12,000
   b. $11,600
   c. $10,800
   d. $ 8,000

3. On January 1, year 1, Wren Co. leased a building to Brill under an operating lease for ten years at $50,000 per year, payable the first day of each lease year. Wren paid $15,000 to a real estate broker as a finder's fee. The building is depreciated $12,000 per year. For year 1, Wren incurred insurance and property tax expense totaling $9,000. Wren's net rental income for year 1 should be

   a. $27,500
   b. $29,000
   c. $35,000
   d. $36,500

4. On July 1, year 1, Gee, Inc. leased a delivery truck from Marr Corp. under a three-year operating lease. Total rent for the term of the lease will be $36,000, payable as follows:

12 months at $ 500 = $ 6,000
12 months at $ 750 = 9,000
12 months at $1,750 = 21,000

All payments were made when due. In Marr's June 30, year 3 balance sheet, the accrued rent receivable should be reported as

   a. $0
   b. $ 9,000
   c. $12,000
   d. $21,000

5. On January 1, year 1, Glen Co. leased a building to Dix Corp. under an operating lease for a ten-year term at an annual rental of $50,000. At inception of the lease, Glen received $200,000 covering the first two years' rent of $100,000 and a security deposit of $100,000. This deposit will not be returned to Dix upon expiration of the lease but will be applied to payment of rent for the last two years of the lease. What portion of the $200,000 should be shown as

a current and long-term liability, respectively, in Glen's December 31, year 1 balance sheet?

	Current liability	Long-term liability
a.	$0	$200,000
b.	$ 50,000	$100,000
c.	$100,000	$100,000
d.	$100,000	$ 50,000

6. As an inducement to enter a lease, Graf Co., a lessor, granted Zep, Inc., a lessee, twelve months of free rent under a five-year operating lease. The lease was effective on January 1, year 1, and provides for monthly rental payments to begin January 1, year 2. Zep made the first rental payment on December 30, year 1. In its year 1 income statement, Graf should report rental revenue in an amount equal to

   a. Zero.
   b. Cash received during year 1.
   c. One-fourth of the total cash to be received over the life of the lease.
   d. One-fifth of the total cash to be received over the life of the lease.

7. Quo Co. rented a building to Hava Fast Food. Each month Quo receives a fixed rental amount plus a variable rental amount based on Hava's sales for that month. As sales increase so does the variable rental amount, but at a reduced rate. Which of the following curves reflects the monthly rentals under the agreement?

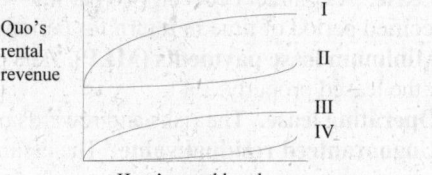

   a. I
   b. II
   c. III
   d. IV

8. As an inducement to enter a lease, Arts, Inc., a lessor, grants Hompson Corp., a lessee, nine months of free rent under a five-year operating lease. The lease is effective on July 1, year 1 and provides for monthly rental of $1,000 to begin April 1, year 2. In Hompson's income statement for the year ended June 30, year 2, rent expense should be reported as

   a. $10,200
   b. $ 9,000
   c. $ 3,000
   d. $ 2,550

9. On January 1, year 1, Park Co. signed a ten-year operating lease for office space at $96,000 per year. The lease included a provision for additional rent of 5% of annual company sales in excess of $500,000. Park's sales for the year ended December 31, year 1, were $600,000. Upon execution of the lease, Park paid $24,000 as a bonus for the lease. Park's rent expense for the year ended December 31, year 1, is

   a. $ 98,400
   b. $101,000

c. $103,400

d. $125,000

10. On July 1, year 1, South Co. entered into a ten-year operating lease for a warehouse facility. The annual minimum lease payments are $100,000. In addition to the base rent, South pays a monthly allocation of the building's operating expenses, which amounted to $20,000 for the year ended June 30, year 2. In the notes to South's June 30, year 2 financial statements, what amounts of subsequent years' lease payments should be disclosed?

a. $100,000 per annum for each of the next five years and $500,000 in the aggregate.

b. $120,000 per annum for each of the next five years and $600,000 in the aggregate.

c. $100,000 per annum for each of the next five years and $900,000 in the aggregate.

d. $120,000 per annum for each of the next five years and $1,080,000 in the aggregate.

11. On January 1, year 1, Mollat Co. signed a seven-year lease for equipment having a ten-year economic life. The present value of the monthly lease payments equaled 80% of the equipment's fair value. The lease agreement provides for neither a transfer of title to Mollat nor a bargain purchase option. In its year 1 income statement Mollat should report

a. Rent expense equal to the year 1 lease payments.

b. Rent expense equal to the year 1 lease payments less interest expense.

c. Lease amortization equal to one-tenth of the equipment's fair value.

d. Lease amortization equal to one-seventh of 80% of the equipment's fair value.

12. A twenty-year property lease, classified as an operating lease, provides for a 10% increase in annual payments every five years. In the sixth year compared to the fifth year, the lease will cause the following expenses to increase

	Rent	Interest
a.	No	Yes
b.	Yes	No
c.	Yes	Yes
d.	No	No

E.2.d.(1)(e) Leasehold Improvements

13. On December 1, year 1, Clark Co. leased office space for five years at a monthly rental of $60,000. On the same date, Clark paid the lessor the following amounts:

First month's rent	$ 60,000
Last month's rent	60,000
Security deposit (refundable at lease expiration)	80,000
Installation of new walls and offices	360,000

What should be Clark's year 1 expense relating to utilization of the office space?

a. $ 60,000

b. $ 66,000

c. $120,000

d. $140,000

14. Star Co. leases a building for its product showroom. The ten-year nonrenewable lease will expire on December 31, year 11. In January year 6, Star redecorated its showroom and made leasehold improvements of $48,000. The estimated useful life of the improvements is eight years. Star uses the straight-line method of amortization. What

amount of leasehold improvements, net of amortization, should Star report in its June 30, year 6 balance sheet?

a. $45,600

b. $45,000

c. $44,000

d. $43,200

15. On January 2, year 1, Ral Co. leased land and building from an unrelated lessor for a ten-year term. The lease has a renewal option for an additional ten years, but Ral has not reached a decision with regard to the renewal option. In early January of year 1, Ral completed the following improvements to the property:

Description	Estimated life	Cost
Sales office	10 years	$47,000
Warehouse	25 years	75,000
Parking lot	15 years	18,000

Amortization of leasehold improvements for year 1 should be

a. $ 7,000

b. $ 8,900

c. $12,200

d. $14,000

16. On January 1, year 1, Nobb Corp. signed a twelve-year lease for warehouse space. Nobb has an option to renew the lease for an additional eight-year period on or before January 1, year 5. During January year 3, Nobb made substantial improvements to the warehouse. The cost of these improvements was $540,000, with an estimated useful life of fifteen years. At December 31, year 3, Nobb intended to exercise the renewal option. Nobb has taken a full year's amortization on this leasehold. In Nobb's December 31, year 3 balance sheet, the carrying amount of this leasehold improvement should be

a. $486,000

b. $504,000

c. $510,000

d. $513,000

17. During January year 1, Vail Co. made long-term improvements to a recently leased building. The lease agreement provides for neither a transfer of title to Vail nor a bargain purchase option. The present value of the minimum lease payments equals 85% of the building's market value, and the lease term equals 70% of the building's economic life. Should assets be recognized for the building and the leasehold improvements?

	Building	Leasehold improvements
a.	Yes	Yes
b.	No	Yes
c.	Yes	No
d.	No	No

18. A lessee incurred costs to construct office space in a leased warehouse. The estimated useful life of the office is ten years. The remaining term of the nonrenewable lease is fifteen years. The costs should be

a. Capitalized as leasehold improvements and depreciated over fifteen years.

b. Capitalized as leasehold improvements and depreciated over ten years.

c. Capitalized as leasehold improvements and expensed in the year in which the lease expires.

d. Expensed as incurred.

E.2.d.(2) Direct Financing Lease: Lessor

19. Glade Co. leases computer equipment to customers under direct-financing leases. The equipment has no residual value at the end of the lease and the leases do not contain bargain purchase options. Glade wishes to earn 8% interest on a five-year lease of equipment with a fair value of $323,400. The present value of an annuity due of $1 at 8% for five years is 4.312. What is the total amount of interest revenue that Glade will earn over the life of the lease?

a. $ 51,600
b. $ 75,000
c. $129,360
d. $139,450

20. On January 1, year 1, JCK Co. signed a contract for an eight-year lease of its equipment with a ten-year life. The present value of the sixteen equal semiannual payments in advance equaled 85% of the equipment's fair value. The contract had no provision for JCK, the lessor, to give up legal ownership of the equipment. Should JCK recognize rent or interest revenue in year 2, and should the revenue recognized in year 2 be the same or smaller than the revenue recognized in year 1?

	Year 2 revenues recognized	Year 2 amount recognized compared to year 1
a.	Rent	The same
b.	Rent	Smaller
c.	Interest	The same
d.	Interest	Smaller

E.1.d.(3) Sales-Type Leases: Lessor

21. Peg Co. leased equipment from Howe Corp. on July 1, year 1 for an eight-year period expiring June 30, year 9. Equal payments under the lease are $600,000 and are due on July 1 of each year. The first payment was made on July 1, year 1. The rate of interest contemplated by Peg and Howe is 10%. The cash selling price of the equipment is $3,520,000, and the cost of the equipment on Howe's accounting records is $2,800,000. The lease is appropriately recorded as a sales-type lease. What is the amount of profit on the sale and interest revenue that Howe should record for the year ended December 31, year 1?

	Profit on sale	Interest revenue
a.	$720,000	$176,000
b.	$720,000	$146,000
c.	$ 45,000	$176,000
d.	$ 45,000	$146,000

22. Howe Co. leased equipment to Kew Corp. on January 2, year 1, for an eight-year period expiring December 31, year 8. Equal payments under the lease are $600,000 and are due on January 2 of each year. The first payment was made on January 2, year 1. The list selling price of the equipment is $3,520,000 and its carrying cost on Howe's books is $2,800,000. The lease is appropriately accounted for as a sales-type lease. The present value of the lease payments is $3,300,000. What amount of profit on the sale should Howe report for the year ended December 31, year 1?

a. $720,000
b. $500,000
c. $ 90,000
d. $0

23. The excess of the fair value of leased property at the inception of the lease over its cost or carrying amount should be classified by the lessor as

a. Unearned income from a sales-type lease.
b. Unearned income from a direct-financing lease.
c. Manufacturer's or dealer's profit from a sales-type lease.
d. Manufacturer's or dealer's profit from a direct-financing lease.

24. In a lease that is recorded as a sales-type lease by the lessor, interest revenue

a. Should be recognized in full as revenue at the lease's inception.
b. Should be recognized over the period of the lease using the straight-line method.
c. Should be recognized over the period of the lease using the interest method.
d. Does **not** arise.

E.2.d.(4) Capital Leases: Lessee

25. Lease M does not contain a bargain purchase option, but the lease term is equal to 90% of the estimated economic life of the leased property. Lease P does not transfer ownership of the property to the lessee at the end of the lease term, but the lease term is equal to 75% of the estimated economic life of the leased property. How should the lessee classify these leases?

	Lease M	Lease P
a.	Capital lease	Operating lease
b.	Capital lease	Capital lease
c.	Operating lease	Capital lease
d.	Operating lease	Operating lease

26. On December 31, year 1, Day Co. leased a new machine from Parr with the following pertinent information:

Lease term	6 years
Annual rental payable at beginning of each year	$50,000
Useful life of machine	8 years
Day's incremental borrowing rate	15%
Implicit interest rate in lease (known by Day)	12%
Present value of annuity of 1 in advance for 6 periods at	
12%	4.61
15%	4.35

The lease is not renewable, and the machine reverts to Parr at the termination of the lease. The cost of the machine on Parr's accounting records is $375,500. At the beginning of the lease term, Day should record a lease liability of

a. $375,500
b. $230,500
c. $217,500
d. $0

27. On January 1, year 1, Day Corp. entered into a ten-year lease agreement with Ward, Inc. for industrial equipment. Annual lease payments of $10,000 are payable at the end of each year. Day knows that the lessor expects a 10% return on the lease. Day has a 12% incremental borrowing rate. The equipment is expected to have an estimated useful life of ten years. In addition, a third party has guaranteed to pay Ward a residual value of $5,000 at the end of the lease.

The present value of an ordinary annuity of $1 at

12% for ten years is 5.6502
10% for ten years is 6.1446

The present value of $1 at

12% for ten years is .3220
10% for ten years is .3855

In Day's October 31, year 1 balance sheet, the principal amount of the lease obligation was

a. $63,374
b. $61,446
c. $58,112
d. $56,502

28. Robbins, Inc. leased a machine from Ready Leasing Co. The lease qualifies as a capital lease and requires ten annual payments of $10,000 beginning immediately. The lease specifies an interest rate of 12% and a purchase option of $10,000 at the end of the tenth year, even though the machine's estimated value on that date is $20,000. Robbins' incremental borrowing rate is 14%.

The present value of an annuity due of one at

12% for ten years is 6.328
14% for ten years is 5.946

The present value of one at

12% for ten years is .322
14% for ten years is .270

What amount should Robbins record as lease liability at the beginning of the lease term?

a. $62,160
b. $64,860
c. $66,500
d. $69,720

29. Neal Corp. entered into a nine-year capital lease on a warehouse on December 31, year 1. Lease payments of $52,000, which includes real estate taxes of $2,000, are due annually, beginning on December 31, year 2, and every December 31 thereafter. Neal does not know the interest rate implicit in the lease; Neal's incremental borrowing rate is 9%. The rounded present value of an ordinary annuity for nine years at 9% is 5.6. What amount should Neal report as capitalized lease liability at December 31, year 1?

a. $280,000
b. $291,200
c. $450,000
d. $468,000

30. East Company leased a new machine from North Company on May 1, year 1, under a lease with the following information:

Lease term	10 years
Annual rental payable at beginning of each lease year	$40,000
Useful life of machine	12 years
Implicit interest rate	14%
Present value of an annuity of one in advance for ten periods at 14%	5.95
Present value of one for ten periods at 14%	0.27

East has the option to purchase the machine on May 1, year 11 by paying $50,000, which approximates the expected fair value of the machine on the option exercise date. On May 1, year 1, East should record a capitalized lease asset of

a. $251,500
b. $238,000

c. $224,500
d. $198,000

31. On January 1, year 1, Babson, Inc. leased two automobiles for executive use. The lease requires Babson to make five annual payments of $13,000 beginning January 1, year 1. At the end of the lease term, December 31, year 5, Babson guarantees the residual value of the automobiles will total $10,000. The lease qualifies as a capital lease. The interest rate implicit in the lease is 9%. Present value factors for the 9% rate implicit in the lease are as follows:

For an annuity due with five payments	4.240
For an ordinary annuity with five payments	3.890
Present value of $1 for five periods	0.650

Babson's recorded capital lease liability immediately after the first required payment should be

a. $48,620
b. $44,070
c. $35,620
d. $31,070

32. On December 30, year 1, Rafferty Corp. leased equipment under a capital lease. Annual lease payments of $20,000 are due December 31 for ten years. The equipment's useful life is ten years, and the interest rate implicit in the lease is 10%. The capital lease obligation was recorded on December 30, year 1, at $135,000, and the first lease payment was made on that date. What amount should Rafferty include in current liabilities for this capital lease in its December 31, year 1 balance sheet?

a. $ 6,500
b. $ 8,500
c. $11,500
d. $20,000

33. Oak Co. leased equipment for its entire nine-year useful life, agreeing to pay $50,000 at the start of the lease term on December 31, year 1, and $50,000 annually on each December 31 for the next eight years. The present value on December 31, year 1, of the nine lease payments over the lease term, using the rate implicit in the lease which Oak knows to be 10%, was $316,500. The December 31, year 1 present value of the lease payments using Oak's incremental borrowing rate of 12% was $298,500. Oak made a timely second lease payment. What amount should Oak report as capital lease liability in its December 31, year 2 balance sheet?

a. $350,000
b. $243,150
c. $228,320
d. $0

34. On December 31, year 1, Roe Co. leased a machine from Colt for a five-year period. Equal annual payments under the lease are $105,000 (including $5,000 annual executory costs) and are due on December 31 of each year. The first payment was made on December 31, year 1, and the second payment was made on December 31, year 2. The five lease payments are discounted at 10% over the lease term. The present value of minimum lease payments at the inception of the lease and before the first annual payment was $417,000. The lease is appropriately accounted for as a capital lease by Roe. In its December 31, year 2 balance sheet, Roe should report a lease liability of

    a. $317,000
    b. $315,000
    c. $285,300
    d. $248,700

35. In the long-term liabilities section of its balance sheet at December 31, year 1, Mene Co. reported a capital lease obligation of $75,000, net of current portion of $1,364. Payments of $9,000 were made on both January 2, year 2, and January 2, year 3. Mene's incremental borrowing rate on the date of the lease was 11% and the lessor's implicit rate, which was known to Mene, was 10%. In its December 31, year 2 balance sheet, what amount should Mene report as capital lease obligation, net of current portion?

    a. $66,000
    b. $73,500
    c. $73,636
    d. $74,250

36. For a capital lease, the amount recorded initially by the lessee as a liability should normally
    a.   Exceed the total of the minimum lease payments.
    b.   Exceed the present value of the minimum lease payments at the beginning of the lease.
    c.   Equal the total of the minimum lease payments.
    d.   Equal the present value of the minimum lease payments at the beginning of the lease.

37. At the inception of a capital lease, the guaranteed residual value should be
    a.   Included as part of minimum lease payments at present value.
    b.   Included as part of minimum lease payments at future value.
    c.   Included as part of minimum lease payments only to the extent that guaranteed residual value is expected to exceed estimated residual value.
    d.   Excluded from minimum lease payments.

38. A six-year capital lease entered into on December 31, year 1, specified equal minimum annual lease payments due on December 31 of each year. The first minimum annual lease payment, paid on December 31, year 1, consists of which of the following?

	Interest expense	Lease liability
a.	Yes	Yes
b.	Yes	No
c.	No	Yes
d.	No	No

39. A six-year capital lease expiring on December 31 specifies equal minimum annual lease payments. Part of this payment represents interest and part represents a reduction in the net lease liability. The portion of the minimum lease payment in the fifth year applicable to the reduction of the net lease liability should be
    a.   Less than in the fourth year.
    b.   More than in the fourth year.
    c.   The same as in the sixth year.
    d.   More than in the sixth year.

40. A lessee had a ten-year capital lease requiring equal annual payments. The reduction of the lease liability in year two should equal

    a.   The current liability shown for the lease at the end of year one.
    b.   The current liability shown for the lease at the end of year two.
    c.   The reduction of the lease obligation in year one.
    d.   One-tenth of the original lease liability.

41. On January 2, year 1, Cole Co. signed an eight-year noncancelable lease for a new machine, requiring $15,000 annual payments at the beginning of each year. The machine has a useful life of twelve years, with no salvage value. Title passes to Cole at the lease expiration date. Cole uses straight-line depreciation for all of its plant assets. Aggregate lease payments have a present value on January 2, year 1, of $108,000 based on an appropriate rate of interest. For year 1, Cole should record depreciation (amortization) expense for the leased machine at
    a. $0
    b. $ 9,000
    c. $13,500
    d. $15,000

42. On January 2, year 1, Nori Mining Co. (lessee) entered into a five-year lease for drilling equipment. Nori accounted for the acquisition as a capital lease for $240,000, which includes a $10,000 bargain purchase option. At the end of the lease, Nori expects to exercise the bargain purchase option. Nori estimates that the equipment's fair value will be $20,000 at the end of its eight-year life. Nori regularly uses straight-line depreciation on similar equipment. For the year ended December 31, year 1, what amount should Nori recognize as depreciation expense on the leased asset?
    a. $48,000
    b. $46,000
    c. $30,000
    d. $27,500

43. The lessee should amortize the capitalizable cost of the leased asset in a manner consistent with the lessee's normal depreciation policy for owned assets for leases that

	Contain a bargain purchase option	Transfer ownership of the property to the lessee by the end of the lease term
a.	No	No
b.	No	Yes
c.	Yes	Yes
d.	Yes	No

44. On January 1, year 1, Harrow Co. as lessee signed a five-year noncancelable equipment lease with annual payments of $100,000 beginning December 31, year 1. Harrow treated this transaction as a capital lease. The five lease payments have a present value of $379,000 at January 1, year 1, based on interest of 10%. What amount should Harrow report as interest expense for the year ended December 31, year 1?
    a. $37,900
    b. $27,900
    c. $24,200
    d. $0

45. On January 1, year 1, West Co. entered into a ten-year lease for a manufacturing plant. The annual minimum lease payments are $100,000. In the notes to the December 31, year 2 financial statements, what amounts of subsequent years' lease payments should be disclosed?

	Amount for appropriate required period	Aggregate amount for the lease term
a.	$100,000	$0
b.	$300,000	$500,000
c.	$500,000	$800,000
d.	$500,000	$0

46. Cott, Inc. prepared an interest amortization table for a five-year lease payable with a bargain purchase option of $2,000, exercisable at the end of the lease. At the end of the five years, the balance in the leases payable column of the spreadsheet was zero. Cott has asked Grant, CPA, to review the spreadsheet to determine the error. Only one error was made on the spreadsheet. Which of the following statements represents the best explanation for this error?

  a. The beginning present value of the lease did **not** include the present value of the bargain purchase option.

  b. Cott subtracted the annual interest amount from the lease payable balance instead of adding it.

  c. The present value of the bargain purchase option was subtracted from the present value of the annual payments.

  d. Cott discounted the annual payments as an ordinary annuity, when the payments actually occurred at the beginning of each period.

E.3.b. Sale-Leaseback

47. On December 31, year 1, Lane, Inc. sold equipment to Noll, and simultaneously leased it back for twelve years. Pertinent information at this date is as follows:

Sales price	$480,000
Carrying amount	360,000
Estimated remaining economic life	15 years

At December 31, year 1, how much should Lane report as deferred gain from the sale of the equipment?

  a. $0
  b. $110,000
  c. $112,000
  d. $120,000

48. The following information pertains to a sale and lease-back of equipment by Mega Co. on December 31, year 1:

Sales price	$400,000
Carrying amount	$300,000
Monthly lease payment	$ 3,250
Present value of lease payments	$ 36,900
Estimated remaining life	25 years
Lease term	1 year
Implicit rate	12%

What amount of deferred gain on the sale should Mega report at December 31, year 1?

  a. $0
  b. $ 36,900
  c. $ 63,100
  d. $100,000

49. On December 31, year 1, Parke Corp. sold Edlow Corp. an airplane with an estimated remaining useful life of ten years. At the same time, Parke leased back the airplane for three years. Additional information is as follows:

Sales price	$600,000
Carrying amount of airplane at date of sale	$100,000
Monthly rental under lease	$ 6,330
Interest rate implicit in the lease as computed by Edlow and known by Parke (this rate is lower than the lessee's incremental borrowing rate)	12%
Present value of operating lease rentals ($6,330 for 36 months @ 12%)	$190,581

The leaseback is considered an operating lease. In Parke's December 31, year 1 balance sheet, what amount should be included as deferred revenue on this transaction?

  a. $0
  b. $190,581
  c. $309,419
  d. $500,000

50. On June 30, year 1, Lang Co. sold equipment with an estimated useful life of eleven years and immediately leased it back for ten years. The equipment's carrying amount was $450,000; the sale price was $430,000; and the present value of the lease payments, which is equal to the fair value of the equipment, was $465,000. In its June 30, year 1 balance sheet, what amount should Lang report as deferred loss?

  a. $35,000
  b. $20,000
  c. $15,000
  d. $0

51. On January 1, year 1, Hooks Oil Co. sold equipment with a carrying amount of $100,000, and a remaining useful life of ten years, to Maco Drilling for $150,000. Hooks immediately leased the equipment back under a ten-year capital lease with a present value of $150,000 and will depreciate the equipment using the straight-line method. Hooks made the first annual lease payment of $24,412 in December year 1. In Hooks' December 31, year 1 balance sheet, the unearned gain on equipment sale should be

  a. $50,000
  b. $45,000
  c. $25,588
  d. $0

52. In a sale-leaseback transaction, the seller-lessee has retained the property. The gain on the sale should be recognized at the time of the sale-leaseback when the lease is classified as a(n)

	Capital lease	Operating lease
a.	Yes	Yes
b.	No	No
c.	No	Yes
d.	Yes	No

53. Able sold its headquarters building at a gain, and simultaneously leased back the building. The lease was reported as a capital lease. At the time of sale, the gain should be reported as

  a. Operating income.
  b. An extraordinary item, net of income tax.
  c. A separate component of stockholders' equity.
  d. An asset valuation allowance.

54. On January 1, year 1, Goliath entered into a five-year operating lease for equipment. In January year 3, Goliath decided that it no longer needs the equipment and terminates the contract by paying a penalty of $3,000. How should Goliath account for the lease termination costs?

    a.   Recognize $3,000 termination cost in year 3 as a loss from continuing operations.

    b.   Recognize $1,000 termination cost each year for the remaining three years of the lease term.

    c.   Recognize the $3,000 termination cost as an extraordinary item in year 3.

    d.   Recognize the $3,000 termination cost as a discontinued operation in year 3.

55. In January year 1, Hopper Corp. signed a capital lease for equipment with a term of twenty years. In year 3, Hopper negotiated a modification to a capital lease that resulted in the lease being reclassified as an operating lease. Hopper calculated the company had a gain of $8,000 on the lease modification. Hopper retains all rights to use the property during the remainder of the lease term. How should Hopper account for the lease modification?

    a.   Recognize an $8,000 gain from lease modification during year 3.

    b.   Defer the gain and recognize it over the life of the operating lease.

    c.   Recognize the $8,000 gain as an extraordinary item in year 3.

    d.   Recognize the $8,000 gain as a discontinued operation in year 3.

56. On January 1, year 1, Belkor entered into a 10-year capital lease for equipment. On December 1, year 4, Belkor terminates the capital lease and incurs a $20,000 loss. How should Belkor recognize the lease termination on their financial statements?

    a.   Recognize a $20,000 loss in year 4 as a discontinued operation.

    b.   Recognize a $20,000 loss in year 4 as an extraordinary item.

    c.   Recognize a $20,000 loss from continuing operations in year 4.

    d.   Defer recognition of the loss and recognize pro rata over the life of the lease term.

E.4. International Financial Reporting Standards (IFRS)

57. Morgan Corp. signs a lease to rent equipment for ten years. The lease payments of $10,000 per year are due on January 2 each year. At the end of the lease term, Morgan may purchase the equipment for $50. The equipment is estimated to have a useful life of 12 years. Morgan prepares its financial statements in accordance with IFRS. Morgan should classify this lease as a(n)

    a.   Operating lease.

    b.   Capital lease.

    c.   Finance lease.

    d.   Sales-type lease.

58. Santiago Corp. signs an agreement to lease land and a building for 20 years. At the end of the lease, the property will not transfer to Santiago. The life of the building is estimated to be 20 years. Santiago prepares its financial statements in accordance with IFRS. How should Santiago account for the lease?

    a.   The lease is recorded as a finance lease.

    b.   The lease is recorded as an operating lease.

    c.   The land is recorded as an operating lease, and the building is recorded as a finance lease.

    d.   The land is recorded as a finance lease, and the building is recorded as an operating lease.

59. Which of the following is not true regarding lease accounting under IFRS?

    a.   Lease payments under operating leases are recognized on a straight-line basis over the life of the lease.

    b.   Leases are classified as either operating or finance leases by both the lessee and the lessor.

    c.   For a finance lease, the asset is removed from the lessor's balance sheet.

    d.   IFRS uses the same thresholds as US GAAP to determine if a lease is an operating lease or a finance lease.

60. Under IFRS what is the interest rate used by lessees to capitalize a finance lease when the implicit rate cannot be determined?

    a.   The prime rate.

    b.   The lessor's published rate.

    c.   The lessee's average borrowing rate.

    d.   The lessee's incremental borrowing rate.

Answers

1.	c	__ __	14.	c	__ __	27.	b	__ __	40.	a	__ __	53.	d	__ __
2.	c	__ __	15.	d	__ __	28.	c	__ __	41.	b	__ __	54.	a	__ __
3.	a	__ __	16.	b	__ __	29.	a	__ __	42.	d	__ __	55.	b	__ __
4.	b	__ _·	17.	b	__ __	30.	b	__ __	43.	c	__ __	56.	c	__ __
5.	b	__ __	18.	b	__ __	31.	a	__ __	44.	a	__ __	57.	c	__ __
6.	d	__ __	19.	a	__ __	32.	b	__ __	45.	c	__ __	58.	c	__ __
7.	a	__ _·	20.	d	__ __	33.	b	__ __	46.	a	__ __	59.	d	__ __
8.	a	__ _·	21.	b	__ __	34.	d	__ __	47.	b	__ __	60.	d	__ __
9.	c	__ __	22.	b	__ __	35.	b	__ __	48.	a	__ __			
10.	c	__ __	23.	c	__ __	36.	d	__ __	49.	b	__ __			
11.	a	__ __	24.	c	__ __	37.	a	__ __	50.	b	__ __			
12.	d	__ __	25.	b	__ __	38.	c	__ __	51.	b	__ __	1st: __/60 = __%
13.	b	__ __	26.	b	__ __	39.	b	__ __	52.	b	__ __	2nd: __/60 = __%

Explanations

1. (c) In an operating lease, the lessor should recognize rental revenue on a straight-line basis. This means that the lease bonus ($50,000) should be recorded as unearned revenue on 1/1/Y1, and recognized as rental revenue over the five-year lease term. Therefore, year 1 rental revenue should be $100,000 [$90,000 + ($50,000 ÷ 5)]. The security deposit ($25,000) does not affect rental revenue. Since it is to be refunded to the lessee upon expiration of the lease, it is recorded as a deposit, a long-term liability when received.

2. (c) Rental revenue on operating leases should be recognized on a straight-line basis unless another method more reasonably reflects the pattern of use given by the lessor. When the pattern of cash flows under the lease agreement is other than straight-line, this will result in the recording of rent receivable or unearned rent. Wall's total rent revenue [(1/2 × $8,000) + (4 × $12,500) = $54,000] should be recognized on a straight-line basis over the five-year lease term ($54,000 × 1/5 = $10,800). Since cash collected in year 1 is only $4,000 (one-half of $8,000, since the first six months are rent-free), Wall would accrue rent receivable and rental revenue of $6,800 ($10,800 – $4,000) at year-end to bring the rental revenue up to $10,800.

3. (a) Net rental income on an operating lease is equal to rental revenue less related expenses, as computed below.

Rental revenue	$50,000
Depreciation expense	(12,000)
Executory costs	(9,000)
Finder's fee ($15,000 ÷ 10)	(1,500)
Net rental income	$27,500

The finder's fee ($15,000) is capitalized as a deferred charge at the inception of the lease and amortized over ten years to match the expense to the revenues it enabled the lessor to earn.

4. (b) For an operating lease, rental revenue should be recognized on a straight-line basis unless another method more reasonably reflects the pattern of use given by the lessor. When the pattern of cash flows under the lease agreement is other than straight-line, this will result in the recording of rent receivable or unearned rent. Gee's total rent revenue ($36,000) should be recognized on a straight-line basis over the thirty-six-month lease, resulting in monthly

entries debiting **rent receivable** and crediting **rent revenue** for $1,000. Cash collections will result in entries debiting **cash** and crediting **rent receivable** for $500 per month for the first twelve months and $750 per month for the second twelve months. Therefore, rent receivable at 6/30/Y3 is $9,000, as indicated by the T-account below.

Rent Receivable		
Accruals (24 × $1,000) 24,000	6,000	Collections (12 × $500)
	9,000	Collections (12 × $750)
6/30/Y3 Balance 9,000		

An alternative way to analyze this problem if Gee records the entry as the customer pays at the beginning of the month. During year 1, the entry each month will be

Cash	500	
Rent receivable	500	
Rent revenue		1,000

During year 2, the entry each month will be

Cash	750	
Rent receivable	250	
Rent revenue		1,000

The Rent receivable account will accrue as follows:

Rent Receivable		
Accruals year 1	6,000	(500 × 12 mo.)
Accruals year 2	3,000	(250 × 12 mo.)
6/30/Y3 balance	9,000	

5. (b) At 1/1/Y1, Glen would record as a current liability unearned rent of $50,000, and as a long-term liability unearned rent of $150,000. During year 1, the current portion of unearned rent was earned and would be recognized as revenue. At 12/31/Y1, the portion of the long-term liability representing the second year's rent ($50,000) would be reclassified as current, leaving as a long-term liability the $100,000 representing the last two years' rent.

6. (d) Rental revenue on operating leases should be recognized on a straight-line basis unless another method more reasonably reflects the pattern of use given by the lessor. When the pattern of cash flows under the lease agreement is other than straight-line, this will result in the recording of rent receivable or unearned rent. Therefore, even though Graf received only one monthly payment in year 1

(1/48 of the total rent to received over the life of the lease), they would accrue as rent receivable and rent revenue an amount sufficient to increase the rent revenue account to a balance equal to one-fifth of the total cash to be received over the five-year life of the lease.

7.   (a)   The graph presented in the problem can be interpreted as follows:

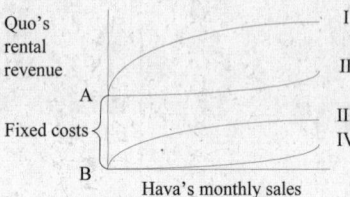

Line AB is considered to be fixed rental costs per month. Therefore, answers (c) and (d) are incorrect because lines III and IV do not include the fixed portion of the rental payment, in its graphical representation. The problem states that as the variable rental amount increases, it does so at a decreasing rate. Answer (b) is incorrect because line II is increasing, but at an increasing rate, not a decreasing rate, as line I represents. Therefore, answer (a) is the correct answer because line I is increasing, at a decreasing rate.

8.   (a)   Rent on operating leases should be expensed on a straight-line basis unless another method is better suited to the particular benefits and costs associated with the lease. In this lease, the lessee must pay rent of $1,000 monthly for five years excluding the first nine months, or fifty-one months (60 – 9). Therefore, total rent expense for the five years is $51,000 (51 × $1,000). Recognizing rent expense on a straight-line basis, rent expense for the first year is $10,200 ($51,000 ÷ 5 years).

9.   (c)   In an operating lease, the lessee should recognize rent expense on a straight-line basis unless another method is better suited to the particular lease. Therefore, the lease bonus should be recognized as rent expense on a straight-line basis over the ten-year lease term ($24,000 ÷ 10 = $2,400). However, the contingent rentals, which are based on company sales, shall be expensed in the period to which they relate. Therefore, in year 1, contingent rentals of $5,000 [5% × ($600,000 – $500,000)] should be included in rent expense. Total rent expense is $103,400, as computed below.

Base rental	$ 96,000
Lease bonus ($24,000 ÷ 10)	2,400
Cont. rental [5% × ($600,000 – $500,000)]	5,000
	$103,400

10.   (c)   For operating leases having noncancelable remaining lease terms of more than one year, the lessee must disclose future minimum lease payments in the aggregate and for each of the five succeeding fiscal years. Since the annual **minimum** lease payments are $100,000, South must disclose subsequent years' lease payments of $100,000 per annum for each of the next five years and $900,000 (nine remaining payments × $100,000) in the aggregate.

11.   (a)   To qualify for treatment as a capital lease, a lease must meet one or more of the following criteria:

1. Transfers ownership to lessee.
2. Contains bargain purchase option.

3. Lease term is ≥ 75% of the economic life of the leased asset.
4. Present value of minimum lease payments is ≥ 90% of the FV of the leased asset.

Since the lease signed by Mollat Company does not meet any of these criteria, it must be classified as an operating lease. For operating leases, the lessee's lease payments are recorded as debits to rent expense. Mollat would report rent expense equal to the year 1 lease payments in its year 1 income statement.

12.   (d)   When a leasing agreement is accounted for as an operating lease, the lessor and the lessee recognize rental revenue and rental expense respectively on a straight-line basis unless another systematic and rational basis more clearly reflects the time pattern in which use benefit is given (received) by the respective parties. The straight-lining of uneven lease payments includes scheduled rent increases. Even though the amount of the annual lease payment increases in year six, rental expense would not change. Interest is not an element of revenue (expense) in operating leases.

13.   (b)   The first month's rent ($60,000) should be expensed in year 1. The prepayment of the last month's rent (also $60,000) should be deferred and recognized as an expense in November year 6. The security deposit ($80,000) should be recorded as a long-term receivable, since Clark can expect to receive the deposit back at lease end. The installation of new walls and offices ($360,000) is recorded as a leasehold improvement at 12/1/Y1. At 12/31/Y1, amortization must be recorded for one month ($360,000 × 1/60 = $6,000). Therefore, year 1 expense is $66,000 ($60,000 + $6,000). The journal entries are

Rent expense	60,000	
Prepaid rent	60,000	
Sec. deposit receivable	80,000	
Leasehold improvements	360,000	
Cash		560,000
Amortization expense	6,000	
Leasehold improvements		6,000

14.   (c)   Leasehold improvements are capitalized and amortized over the shorter of the remaining life of the lease (six years from 1/1/Y6 to 12/31/Y11) or the useful life of the improvements (eight years). Therefore, the $48,000 cost is amortized over six years, resulting in annual amortization of $8,000 ($48,000 ÷ 6). For the period 1/1/Y6 to 6/30/Y6, amortization is $4,000 ($8,000 × 6/12), so the 6/30/Y6 net amount for leasehold improvements is $44,000 ($48,000 – $4,000).

15.   (d)   Leasehold improvements are properly capitalized and amortized over the shorter of the remaining life of the lease or the useful life of the improvement. If the lease contains an option to renew and the likelihood of renewal is uncertain (as it is in this case), then the remaining life of the lease is based on the initial lease term. In this case, the remaining life of the lease is therefore ten years. Since the estimated lives of all improvements in this case are greater than or equal to ten years, the appropriate amortization period is ten years. The year 1 amortization is thus computed as the total cost of $140,000 ($47,000 + $75,000 + $18,000 = $140,000), divided by ten years, or $14,000. There is no salvage value for leasehold improvements, because the assets revert to the lessor at the end of the lease term. Note that if the renewal of the lease for an additional ten years were considered a certainty, the amortization periods would be as follows: ten years for the sales office (estimated life); twenty years for the warehouse (lease term); and fifteen years for the parking lot (estimated life).

16. (b) The cost of the leasehold improvements ($540,000) should be amortized over the remaining life of the lease, or over the useful life of the improvements, whichever is **shorter**. The remaining life of the lease should include periods covered by a renewal option **if** it is probable that the option will be exercised. In this case, the remaining life of the lease is eighteen years (12 years of original lease + 8 years in option period – 2 years gone by), and the useful life of the improvements is fifteen years. Therefore, amortization is based on a fifteen-year life ($540,000 ÷ 15 = $36,000). The 12/31/Y1 carrying amount is $504,000 ($540,000 – $36,000).

17. (b) A lease should be classified as a capital lease by the lessee if the lease terms meet any one of the following four criteria: (1) the lease transfers ownership of the property to the lessee by the end of the lease term, (2) the lease contains a bargain purchase option, (3) the lease term is greater than or equal to 75% of the economic life of the leased property, or (4) the present value of the minimum lease payments is greater than or equal to 90% of the fair market value of the leased property. In this question, the terms of Vail's lease do not meet any of the four criteria for treatment as a capital lease, so the lease should be accounted for as an operating lease. Vail should therefore **not** recognize the building as an asset. In an operating lease, the lessee should capitalize the cost of the leasehold improvements, recognizing them as assets, and amortize their cost over the shorter of their useful lives or the term of the lease.

18. (b) Leasehold improvements are properly capitalized and amortized over the remaining life of the lease, or the useful life of the improvements, whichever is shorter. Since the useful life of the office is only ten years and the remaining term of the lease is fifteen years, the cost should be depreciated over the ten-year period.

19. (a) The annual lease payment is $75,000 ($323,400 ÷ 4.312). After five years, total lease payments will be $375,000 (5 × $75,000). The total interest revenue over the life of the lease is the excess of total lease payments over the fair value of the leased asset ($375,000 – $323,400 = $51,600).

20. (d) This lease qualifies as a direct financing lease; therefore interest revenue will be recognized rather than rent revenue. Had the lease qualified as an operating lease, rent revenue would have been recognized. The lessor's criteria for direct financing classification is as follows:

1. The lease transfers ownership to the lessee, at the end of the lease
2. The lease contains a bargain purchase option
3. The lease term is ≥ 75% of an asset's economic life
4. The present value of the minimum lease payments is ≥ 90% of the fair market value of the leased asset.

Note that the question is silent concerning the two additional criteria that apply to lessors: (1) collectibility of minimum lease payments is predictable, and (2) no important uncer-

tainties exist concerning costs yet to be incurred by the lessee. Recall that if one of the four criteria are met, the lease is treated as a capital lease. In this case, since the lease term is for 80% of the asset's economic life, test (3) is met, and the lease is properly treated as a capital lease. In addition, the amount of interest revenue will be smaller in year 2 than the revenue in year 1. This result occurs because the present value of the minimum lease payments or carrying value of the obligation decreases each year as lease payments are received. As this occurs, the amount of interest revenue on the outstanding amount of the investment will decrease as well. Over the course of time, the investment reduction portion of each level payment increases and the amount of interest declines.

21. (b) This is a sales-type lease, so at the inception of the lease, the lessor would recognize sales of $3,520,000 and cost of goods sold of $2,800,000, resulting in a **profit on sale of $720,000**. In addition, interest revenue is recognized for the period July 1, year 1, to December 31, year 1. The initial net lease payments receivable on 7/1/Y1 is $3,520,000. The first rental payment received on 7/1/Y1 consists entirely of principal, reducing the net receivable to $2,920,000 ($3,520,000 – $600,000). Therefore, year 1 **interest revenue for the six months from 7/1/Y1 to 12/31/Y1 is $146,000** ($2,920,000 × 10% × 6/12).

22. (b) This is a sales-type lease, so at the inception of the lease, the lessor would recognize sales of $3,300,000 (the PV of the lease payments), and cost of goods sold of $2,800,000, resulting in profit on the sale of $500,000 ($3,300,000 – $2,800,000). Note that the list selling price of an asset ($3,520,000 in this case) is not always representative of its FV. An asset can often be purchased for less than its list price.

23. (c) The excess of the fair value of leased property at the inception of the lease over the lessor's cost is defined as the manufacturer's or dealer's profit. Answer (a) is incorrect because the unearned income from a sales-type lease is defined as the difference between the gross investment in the lease and the sum of the present values of the components of the gross investment. Answer (b) is incorrect because the unearned income from a direct-financing lease is defined as the excess of the gross investment over the cost (also the PV of lease payments) of the leased property. Answer (d) is incorrect because a sales-type lease involves a manufacturer's or dealer's profit while a direct financing lease does not.

24. (c) Revenue is to be recognized for a sales-type lease over the lease term so as to produce a **constant rate** of return on the net investment in the lease. This requires the use of the **interest method**. Interest revenue **does** arise in a sales-type lease. Answer (a) is incorrect because the interest is to be earned over the life of the lease, not in full at the lease's inception.

25. (b) If **any** of the criteria for classification as a capital lease are met, the lease is classified as such. One of the capital lease criterion is that the lease term is equal to 75% or more of the estimated economic life of the leased property. Thus, both leases M and P should be classified as capital leases.

26. (b) This is a capital lease for the lessee because the lease term is 75% of the useful life of the machine [6 years = (75% × 8 years)]. For a capital lease, the lessee records as a **leased asset** and a **lease obligation** the lower of the PV of the minimum lease payments or the FV of the leased asset (not given in this problem). The PV of the minimum lease payments is computed using the lower of the lessee's incremental borrowing rate (15%) or the implicit rate used by the lessor if known by the lessee (12%). Since the implicit rate is lower, and known by the lessee, it is used to compute the PV ($50,000 × 4.61 = $230,500). The cost of the asset on the lessor's books ($375,500) is irrelevant.

27. (b) This is a capital lease since the lease term (ten years) is the same as the useful life of the leased asset. In a capital lease, the lessee records an asset and a liability based on the PV of the minimum lease payments. The minimum lease payments includes rentals and a guaranteed residual value, **if guaranteed by the lessee**. In this case the minimum lease payments include only the rentals, since the residual value is guaranteed by a third party. The minimum lease payments are discounted using the **lower** of the lessee's incremental borrowing rate or the implicit rate used by the lessor, if known. In this case, the lessee knows the implicit rate is 10%, which is lower than the incremental borrowing rate of 12%. Thus, the present value or principal amount of the lease obligation is $61,446 ($10,000 × 6.1446) through the first year. Although accrued interest would be recognized at 10/31/Y1, the principal amount does not change until 1/1/Y2.

28. (c) The lessee records a capital lease at the present value of the minimum lease payments. The minimum lease payments includes rental payments and bargain purchase options (among other items). The $10,000 purchase option is a **bargain** purchase option because it allows the lessor to purchase the leased asset at an amount **less** than its expected fair value. The lessee computes the present value using its incremental borrowing rate (14%), unless the lessor's implicit rate (12%) is lower and is known by the lessee. This question indicates that the implicit rate is stated in the lease; therefore it would be known to the lessee. At the beginning of the lease term, Robbins should record a leased asset and lease liability at $66,500.

PV of rentals	($10,000 × 6.328)	=	$63,280
PV of BPO	($10,000 × .322)	=	3,220
PV at 12%			$66,500

29. (a) The annual executory costs (real estate taxes of $2,000) are **not** an expense or liability until incurred; therefore they are excluded from the minimum lease payments and are **not** reflected in the initial lease liability. The 12/31/Y1 capital lease liability is recorded at the PV of the minimum lease payments [5.6 × ($52,000 – $2,000) = $280,000].

30. (b) The requirement is to determine the amount to be recorded as a capitalized leased asset. This is a capital lease for the lessee because the lease term exceeds 75% of the economic life of the leased asset (10/12 > 75%). In a capital lease, the lessee records as an asset and liability the present value (PV) of the minimum lease payments (unless the PV exceeds the asset's FV, in which case the FV is recorded). The minimum lease payments include rentals, and a lessee-guaranteed residual value or a bargain purchase

option. Only rentals apply in this case. Note that the $50,000 purchase option is not a **bargain** purchase option that the lessee would be compelled to exercise. A bargain purchase option is an option to purchase the leased asset at an amount **less** than its expected fair value. Therefore, the present value of the minimum lease payments is $238,000 ($40,000 × 5.95).

31. (a) The initial lease liability at 1/1/Y1, before the 1/1/Y1 payment, is the present value of the five rental payments (an **annuity due** since the first payment is made on 1/1/Y1) plus the present value of the guaranteed residual value. The computation is below.

PV of rentals ($13,000 × 4.240)	$55,120
PV of residual ($10,000 × 0.650)	6,500
Initial liability	$61,620

The 1/1/Y1 payment consists entirely of principal, bringing the 1/1/Y1 liability down to $48,620 ($61,620 – $13,000).

32. (b) The initial lease obligation at 12/30/Y1 was $135,000. The first lease payment was made the same day, and therefore consisted entirely of principal reduction. After the payment, the lease obligation was $115,000 ($135,000 – $20,000). This balance will be reported as current (for the portion to be paid in year 2) and long-term (for the portion to be paid beyond year 2). The next lease payment of $20,000 will be paid 12/31/Y2, and will consist of both interest ($115,000 × 10% = $11,500) and principal reduction ($20,000 – $11,500 = $8,500). Thus, the portion of the $115,000 lease obligation to be paid in the next year (and therefore reported as a current liability) is $8,500. Note that the interest to be paid next year ($11,500) is not a liability at 12/31/Y1 because it has not yet been incurred.

33. (b) This is a capital lease for the lessee because the lease term (nine years) exceeds 75% of the useful life of the machine (also nine years). For a capital lease, the lessee records as a **leased asset** and a **lease obligation** at the lower of the PV of the minimum lease payments or the FV of the leased asset (not given in this problem). The PV of the minimum lease payments is computed using the lower of the lessee's incremental borrowing rate (12%) or the implicit rate used by the lessor if known by the lessee (10%). Since the implicit rate is lower, and known by the lessee, it is used to compute the PV ($316,500). The initial lease payment ($50,000) is entirely principal because it was made at the inception of the lease. Therefore, after the 12/31/Y1 payment, the lease liability is $266,500 ($316,500 – $50,000). The 12/31/Y2 payment consists of interest incurred during year 2 ($266,500 × 10% = $26,650) and principal reduction ($50,000 – $26,650 = $23,350). Therefore, the 12/31/Y2 capital lease liability is $243,150 ($266,500 – $23,350).

34. (d) The initial lease liability at 12/31/Y1 is $417,000 (the PV of the minimum lease payments). The annual executory costs ($5,000) are **not** an expense or liability until incurred; therefore, they are excluded from the minimum lease payments and are **not** reflected in the initial lease liability. The 12/31/Y1 payment of $105,000 includes $5,000 of executory costs; the remainder ($100,000) is entirely principal since the payment was made at the inception of the lease. Therefore, after the 12/31/Y1 payment, the lease liability is $317,000 ($417,000 – $100,000). The 12/31/Y2 payment consists of executory costs ($5,000), interest incurred during year 2 ($317,000 × 10% = $31,700), and reduction of principal ($105,000 – $5,000 – $31,700 = $68,300). Therefore, the 12/31/Y2 balance sheet should include a lease liability of $248,700 ($317,000 – $68,300).

35. **(b)** On 1/2/Y2, Mene made a lease payment of $9,000, which included payment of the current portion of the lease obligation ($1,364) and interest ($9,000 – $1,364 = $7,636). After this payment, the total lease obligation was $75,000. The 1/2/Y3 payment would include interest of $7,500 ($75,000 × 10%), and principal of $1,500 ($9,000 – $7,500). This $1,500 amount would represent the current portion of the lease obligation at 12/31/Y2, so the long-term lease obligation net of the current portion at 12/31/Y2 is $73,500 ($75,000 – $1,500).

36. **(d)** If a lease is classified as a capital lease, the lessee must record an asset and a liability, each for an amount equal to the present value of the minimum lease payments at the beginning of the lease.

37. **(a)** At the inception of a capital lease, the lessee must record an asset and a liability based on the PV of the minimum lease payments. The minimum lease payments are the payments that lessee is required to make in connection with the leased property, including rent payments, bargain purchase option, and guaranteed residual value. Minimum lease payments (MLP) are recorded at present value. The whole guaranteed residual value is included in MLP.

38. **(c)** In a capital lease where the first annual lease payment is made immediately upon signing the lease (annuity due), the first payment consists solely of lease liability reduction, since no time has transpired during which interest expense could be incurred. Subsequent payments include both interest expense and reduction of the liability.

39. **(b)** Each minimum lease payment shall be allocated between a reduction of the obligation and interest expense so as to produce a constant periodic rate of interest on the remaining balance of the obligation. Since the interest will be computed based upon a **declining** obligation balance, the interest component of each payment will also be declining. The result will be a relatively larger portion of the minimum lease payment allocated to the reduction of the lease obligation in the latter portion of the lease term.

40. **(a)** When a leasing agreement is accounted for as capital lease, the lessee recognizes a liability on its books equal to the present value of the minimum lease payments. The liability should be divided between current and noncurrent based upon when each lease payment is due. At the end of year one, the current lease liability should equal the principal portion of the lease payment due in year two. Therefore, when the lease payment is made in year two, the reduction of the lease liability will equal the current liability shown at the end of year one.

41. **(b)** This is a capital lease since title passes to Cole, the lessee, at the end of the lease. At the inception of the lease on 1/2/Y1, the lessee records the PV of the lease payments ($108,000) as an asset and a liability. The asset is depreciated on a straight-line basis over its useful life of twelve years, resulting in a yearly depreciation charge of $9,000 ($108,000 ÷ 12). The asset is depreciated over its useful life rather than over the lease term (eight years) because title transfers to the lessee, allowing the lessee to use the asset for twelve years.

42. **(d)** A leased asset acquired in a capital lease should be depreciated over the period of time the lessee expects to use the asset (either the lease term or the useful life, depending on the situation). In this case, Nori expects to use the leased asset for its entire eight-year useful life, due to the expected exercise of the bargain purchase option at the end of the five-year lease term. Therefore, Nori's year 1 depreciation expense is $27,500

$$\frac{(\$240,000 \text{ cost}) - (\$20,000 \text{ salvage})}{8 \text{ years}} = \$27,500$$

43. **(c)** The requirement is to determine whether a lessee should amortize the capitalizable cost of a leased asset in a manner consistent with the lessee's normal depreciation policy for owned assets for leases that contained a bargain purchase option and/or transferred ownership at the end of the lease term. Transfer of ownership of the property to the lessee by the end of the lease term and a lease that contains a bargain purchase option are properly classified as capital leases. If the lease meets either of the above criteria, the asset shall be amortized in a manner consistent with the lessee's normal depreciation policy for owned assets.

44. **(a)** At the inception of the lease on 1/1/Y1, the capitalized liability is $379,000 (the present value of the lease payments). Since the first payment is not due until the **end** of the first year, year 1 interest expense is based on the full initial liability ($379,000 × 10% = $37,900).

45. **(c)** The future minimum lease payments (MLP) for each of the next five years and the aggregate amount of MLP for the lease term must be disclosed. At 12/31/Y2, eight annual payments of $100,000 each have not yet been paid. Therefore, future MLP are $800,000 (8 × $100,000). The amount for the appropriate required period (five years) is $500,000 ($100,000 per year for 5 years).

46. **(a)** At the end of the lease, the balance in the lease payable column should equal the bargain purchase option price. Failure to include the present value of the bargain purchase option price in the beginning present value of the lease would result in an ending balance in the lease payable column of zero. Both answers (b) and (c) would have resulted in an ending balance of less than zero, while answer (d) would have resulted in an ending balance greater than zero.

47. **(d)** Sale-leaseback arrangements are treated as though two transactions were a single financing transaction, if the lease qualifies as a capital lease. Any gain or loss on the sale is deferred and amortized over the lease term (if possession reverts to the lessor) or the economic life (if ownership transfers to the lessee). In this case, the lease qualifies as a capital lease because the lease term (twelve years) is 80% of the remaining economic life of the leased property (fifteen years). Therefore, at 12/31/Y1, all of gain ($480,000 – $360,000 = $120,000) would be deferred and amortized over twelve years. Since the sale took place on 12/31/Y1, there is no amortization for year 1.

48. **(a)** A sale-leaseback is generally treated as a single financing transaction in which any profit on the sale is deferred and amortized by the seller. However, there is an exception to this general rule when either **only a minor part** of the remaining use of the leased asset is retained (case one) or when **more than a minor part but less than substan-**

tially all of the remaining use of the leased asset is retained (case two). Case one occurs when the PV of the lease payments is 10% or less of the FV of the sale-leaseback property. Case two occurs when the leaseback is more than minor but does **not** meet the criteria of a capital lease. This problem is an example of case one, because the PV of the lease payments ($36,900) is less than 10% of the FV of the asset (10% × $400,000 = $40,000). Under these circumstances, the full gain ($400,000 − $300,000 = $100,000) is recognized, and **none is deferred**.

49.   (b) A sale-leaseback is generally treated as a single financing transaction in which any profit on the sale is deferred and amortized by the seller. However, there is an exception to this general rule when either **only a minor part** of the remaining use of the leased asset is retained (case one) or when **more than a minor part but less than substantially all** of the remaining use of the leased asset is retained (case two). Case one occurs when the PV of the lease payments is 10% or less of the FV of the sale-leaseback property. Case two occurs when the leaseback is more than minor but does **not** meet the criteria of a capital lease. This is an example of case two because while the PV of the lease payments ($190,581) is more than 10% of the FV of the asset ($600,000), the lease falls into the operating lease category. Under these circumstances, the gain on sale ($600,000 − $100,000 = $500,000) is recognized to the extent that it exceeds the PV of the lease payments ($190,581). The gain reported would be $309,419 ($500,000 − $190,581). The portion of the gain represented by the $190,581 PV of the lease payments is deferred and amortized on a straight-line basis over the life of the lease.

50.   (b) On a sale-leaseback, generally **losses** are recognized immediately. However, there can be two types of losses in sale-leasebacks. The type that is **recognized immediately** is a **real economic loss,** where the carrying amount of the asset is higher than its FV. The type that is **deferred** is an **artificial loss** where the sale price ($430,000) is below the carrying amount ($450,000), but the FV ($465,000) is above the carrying amount ($450,000). The loss in this problem ($450,000 − $430,000 = $20,000) is an artificial loss that must be deferred.

51.   (b) Sale-leaseback transactions are treated as though two transactions were a single financing transaction, if the lease qualifies as a capital lease. Any gain on the sale is deferred and amortized over the lease term (if possession reverts to the lessor) or the economic life (if ownership transfers to the lessee); both are ten years in this case. Since this is a capital lease, the entire gain ($150,000 − $100,000 = $50,000) is deferred at 1/1/Y1. At 12/31/Y1, an adjusting entry must be prepared to amortize 1/10 of the unearned gain (1/10 × $50,000 = $5,000), because the lease covers ten years. Therefore, the unearned gain at 12/31/Y1 is $45,000 ($50,000 − $5,000).

52.   (b) Any profit related to a sale-leaseback transaction in which the seller-lessee retains the property leased (i.e., the seller-lessee retains substantially all of the benefits and risks of the ownership of the property sold), shall be deferred and amortized in proportion to the amortization of the leased asset, if a capital lease. If it is an operating lease, the profit will be deferred in proportion to the related gross rental charged to expense over the lease term. It is important to note that **losses,** however, are recognized immediately for

either a capital or operating lease. Since the gain on the sale should be deferred in either case, no gain is recognized at the time of the sale.

> **NOTE:** An example of an operating lease in which substantially all of the remaining use of the leased asset is retained by the lessee occurs when the lease term begins within the last 25% of the asset's original useful life.

53.   (d) In a sale-leaseback transaction, if the leaseback is recorded as a capital lease and the lessee has retained **substantially all** of the rights to use the property, then any gain on the sale must be deferred and amortized over the life of the property in proportion to the amortization of the leased asset. This deferred gain acts as an asset valuation allowance resulting in the net amount shown for the leased asset being equal to the same carrying value as if the sale and leaseback transaction had not occurred.

54.   (a) A termination of an operating lease requires that the fair value of the termination costs be recognized as an expense or loss in calculating income from continuing operations in the year the lease was terminated.

55.   (b) A modification to a capital lease that changes the classification of the lease to an operating lease requires the transaction be accounted for as a sales-leaseback transaction. Since Hopper retains substantially all rights to use the property (and the property is not within the last 25% of its useful life), the gain will be deferred and recognized over the remaining lease term.

56.   (c) A loss on a capital lease termination is recognized immediately as a loss from continuing operations.

57.   (c) The requirement is to identify how the lease should be classified. Answer (c) is correct because IFRS requires a lease to be classified as a finance lease if substantially all the risks or benefits of ownership have been transferred to the lessee. Because the lease contains a bargain purchase option, it meets the criteria for a finance lease. Answer (a) is incorrect because the lease does not qualify as an operating lease since the risks and benefits of ownership have been transferred. Answer (b) is incorrect because US GAAP uses the term "capital lease," whereas IFRS uses the term "finance lease." Answer (d) is incorrect because IFRS does not use the term "sales-type lease."

58.   (c) The requirement is to identify how Santiago should account for the lease. Answer (c) is correct because IFRS provides that because land has an indefinite life, if title is not expected to pass by the end of the lease term, then the substantial risks and rewards of ownership do not transfer. Thus, the lease should be separated into two components. The land should be recorded as an operating lease and the building should be recorded as a finance lease.

59.   (d) The requirement is to identify the incorrect statement regarding lease accounting under IFRS. Answer (d) is correct because IFRS does not use the same thresholds as US GAAP. IFRS standards require more judgment.

60.   (d) The requirement is to identify the rate used to capitalize a finance lease when the implicit rate cannot be determined. Answer (d) is correct because the lessee's incremental borrowing rate is used.

Simulations

Task-Based Simulation 1

Journal Entries		
	Authoritative Literature	Help

Situation

On January 2, year 1, Nesbitt Co. leased equipment from Grant, Inc. Lease payments are $100,000, payable annually every December 31 for twenty years. Title to the equipment passes to Nesbitt at the end of the lease term. The lease is noncancelable.

- The equipment has a $750,000 carrying amount on Grant's books. Its estimated economic life was twenty-five years on January 2, year 1.
- The rate implicit in the lease, which is known to Nesbitt, is 10%. Nesbitt's incremental borrowing rate is 12%.
- Nesbitt uses the straight-line method of depreciation.

The rounded present value factors of an ordinary annuity for twenty years are as follows:

12%	7.5
10%	8.5

Prepare the necessary journal entries, without explanations, to be recorded by Nesbitt for

1. Entering into the lease on January 2, year 1.
2. Making the lease payment on December 31, year 1.
3. Expenses related to the lease for the year ended December 31, year 1.

Task-Based Simulation 2

Concepts		
	Authoritative Literature	Help

The terms listed below refer to lessee and lessor accounting for operating, capital, direct financing, and sales-type leases.

For each term, select the **best** phrase or description from the answers listed A–Q below. An answer may be used once, more than once, or not at all.

Answer list

A. The substance of this transaction is that it consists of two separate and distinct transactions.
B. Rental payments are recognized on a straight-line basis, even though the lease calls for payments that increase over the term of the lease.
C. Depreciation expense related to the leased asset is reported on the lessee's income statement over the lease term.
D. Sales revenue (the present value of the minimum lease payments) less the carrying amount of the leased asset is reported on the lessor's income statement at the inception of the lease.
E. The rate used by the lessee to determine the present value of the minimum lease payments if the lessee's incremental borrowing rate is less than the lessor's implicit rate.
F. Initial direct costs should be treated as an asset and amortized over the life of the lease on a straight-line basis.
G. The difference between the fair value of the asset leased and the total payments to be received over the lease term.
H. Included in the lessor's gross investment, whether guaranteed or unguaranteed.
I. Interest revenue is the only item reported on the income statement over the lease term.
J. The excess of the sales price over the carrying amount of the leased equipment is considered profit and is included in income over the duration of the lease term.
K. Should be recorded as both an asset and a liability by the lessee when the lease contains a bargain purchase option.
L. Produces a constant periodic rate of return on the net investment.
M. The principal portion of the lease liability which must be paid within the next operating cycle.
N. Produces a desired rate of return which causes the aggregate present value of the minimum lease payments to be equal to the fair value of the leased property.
O. Lessee's right to purchase leased property for an amount substantially lower than the expected FV at exercise date.
P. Costs, such as appraisal fees, incurred by the lessor in setting up the lease agreement.
Q. A lease agreement which requires the annual payments to be made at the beginning of each period.

	(A)	(B)	(C)	(D)	(E)	(F)	(G)	(H)	(I)	(J)	(K)	(L)	(M)	(N)	(O)	(P)	(Q)
1. Sales-type lease	O	O	O	O	O	O	O	O	O	O	O	O	O	O	O	O	O
2. Direct financing lease	O	O	O	O	O	O	O	O	O	O	O	O	O	O	O	O	O
3. Operating lease—lessee	O	O	O	O	O	O	O	O	O	O	O	O	O	O	O	O	O
4. Operating lease—lessor	O	O	O	O	O	O	O	O	O	O	O	O	O	O	O	O	O
5. Unearned interest revenue	O	O	O	O	O	O	O	O	O	O	O	O	O	O	O	O	O
6. Residual value	O	O	O	O	O	O	O	O	O	O	O	O	O	O	O	O	O
7. Capital lease	O	O	O	O	O	O	O	O	O	O	O	O	O	O	O	O	O
8. Implicit rate	O	O	O	O	O	O	O	O	O	O	O	O	O	O	O	O	O
9. Interest method	O	O	O	O	O	O	O	O	O	O	O	O	O	O	O	O	O
10. Present value of the minimum lease payments	O	O	O	O	O	O	O	O	O	O	O	O	O	O	O	O	O
11. Bargain purchase option	O	O	O	O	O	O	O	O	O	O	O	O	O	O	O	O	O
12. Sale-leaseback	O	O	O	O	O	O	O	O	O	O	O	O	O	O	O	O	O
13. Annuity due	O	O	O	O	O	O	O	O	O	O	O	O	O	O	O	O	O
14. Initial direct costs	O	O	O	O	O	O	O	O	O	O	O	O	O	O	O	O	O
15. Current lease obligation	O	O	O	O	O	O	O	O	O	O	O	O	O	O	O	O	O

Task-Based Simulation 3

Classification		
	Authoritative Literature	Help

Ward Co. has the following rental agreements. You have been asked to advise the accounting treatment for each of these items.

In the space provided, indicate whether each of these agreements is an operating lease or a capital lease.

		Operating lease	Capital lease
1.	Ward rents equipment for three years for $20,000 per year. The equipment is valued at $200,000. At the end of the rental term the equipment must be returned to the dealer.	O	O
2.	Ward rents equipment for five years for $80,000 per year. At the end of the rental term Ward can purchase the equipment for $500. At the date the contract was signed the equipment had a value of $300,000. At the end of five years, it is expected the equipment will have a value of $42,000.	O	O
3.	Ward received six months of free rent on an office building it was leasing for two years. Rent is normally $1,500 per month.	O	O
4.	Ward rents equipment for eight years. The present value of the lease payments are $80,000. The market value of the equipment is $90,000 and the useful life of the equipment is ten years.	O	O
5.	Ward rents equipment for ten years. At the end of the lease Ward receives title to the equipment.	O	O
6.	Ward rents equipment for seven years. The life of the equipment is ten years. The fair value of the equipment is $100,000. The present value of the minimum lease payments is $85,000.	O	O

Task-Based Simulation 4

Research		
	Authoritative Literature	Help

Assume that you are assigned to the audit of Carter Corporation. Carter leases a building from Urton, Inc., and management of Carter has decided to cancel the lease. Which section of the Professional Standards addresses the issue of valuing the liability for the termination costs related to canceling the lease?

Enter your response in the answer fields below.

Task-Based Simulation 5

Amortization Schedule		
	Authoritative Literature	Help

Situation

On December 30, year 1, Kelty Corporation signed an agreement to lease equipment for ten years. The lease payments of $70,000 are due each year on December 30. Kelty paid its first lease payment immediately after the lease was signed. The interest rate was 6%. The fair market value of the leased equipment on December 30, year 1, was $600,000. At the end of the lease term, Kelty may exercise a bargain purchase option to purchase the equipment for $10,000. The asset has a useful life of twelve years. Kelty uses the net method for recording lease obligations. The present value of the minimum lease payments is $551,702.

Prepare an amortization table for the lease through December 30, year 4.

Year ending	Interest expense	Lease payment	Amounts applied to carrying value	Carrying value of lease
At signing of note	Not applicable	Not applicable	Not applicable	
December 30, year 1				
December 30, year 2				
December 30, year 3				
December 30, year 4				

Task-Based Simulation 6

Financial Statement Disclosures		
	Authoritative Literature	Help

Situation

On December 30, year 1, Kelty Corporation signed an agreement to lease equipment for ten years. The lease payments of $70,000 are due each year on December 30. Kelty paid its first lease payment immediately after the lease was signed. The interest rate was 6%. The fair market value of the leased equipment on December 30, year 1, was $600,000. At the end of the lease term, Kelty may exercise a bargain purchase option to purchase the equipment for $10,000. The asset has a useful life of twelve years. Kelty uses the net method for recording lease obligations. The present value of the minimum lease payments is $551,702.

Determine the following amounts to be recognized in the financial statements.

Interest expense for year 2	
Interest expense for year 3	
Carrying value of lease on 12/31/Y3	
Depreciation expense for year 2	

Task-Based Simulation 7

Research		
	Authoritative Literature	Help

Assume that you are assigned to the audit of Toole Corporation. Toole leases a building from Mason, Inc. that qualifies as a capital lease. Which section of the Professional Standards addresses the issue of determining the amount of the lease liability to be recorded by Toole at the inception of the lease?

Enter your response in the answer fields below.

Task-Based Simulation 8

Leasing Concepts		
	Authoritative Literature	Help

Identify whether each statement is True or False.

		True	False
1.	Free or uneven lease payments should be recognized by the lessor when the lease payment is received.	○	○
2.	Initial direct costs are expensed by the lessor when the lease is signed.	○	○
3.	A refundable security deposit is treated as an asset by the lessor.	○	○
4.	Leasehold improvements should be amortized over the longer of the remaining lease term or the useful life of the asset.	○	○
5.	The minimum lease payment includes any penalty for failure to renew.	○	○
6.	The unguaranteed residual value is considered part of the minimum lease payment for the lessee's liability.	○	○
7.	If a seller-lessee retains substantially all rights to use the property in a sales-leaseback transaction, the gain on sale is deferred by the seller-lessee.	○	○
8.	If a capital lease is modified in such a way that it qualifies as an operating lease, it should be treated as a sales-leaseback transaction.	○	○

Task-Based Simulation 9

Research		
	Authoritative Literature	Help

Assume that you are assigned to the audit of White Corporation. White has just entered into the lease of a major piece of equipment. Which section of the Professional Standards addresses the criteria for determining whether the lease is an operating or a capital lease?

Enter your response in the answer fields below.

Simulation Solutions

Task-Based Simulation 1

Journal Entries		
	Authoritative Literature	**Help**

		Debits	**Credits**
1.	January 2, year 1—to record lease:		
	Equipment	850,000	
	Capital lease liability		850,000
2.	December 31, year 1—to record payment:		
	Capital lease liability	100,000	
	Cash		100,000
3.	December 31, year 1—to record depreciation:		
	Depreciation expense	34,000	
	Accumulated depreciation		34,000
	Interest expense	85,000	
	Capital lease liability		85,000

Explanations

1. This problem requires preparation of the lessee's journal entries for the first year of a lease. The lease is a capital lease because title passes to the lessee at the end of the lease and the lease term (twenty years) is greater than 75% of the useful life (twenty-five years).

2. In a capital lease, the lessee records a **leased asset** and a **lease obligation** at the present value of the minimum lease payments. The lessee's incremental borrowing rate (12%) should be used to determine the present value unless the lessor's implicit rate is lower and is known by the lessee. The lessor's 10% rate is lower and is known by the lessee, so it is used to compute the PV of $850,000 ($100,000 × 8.5).

3. The first lease payment on 12/31/Y1 consists of interest expense incurred during year 1 ($850,000 × 10% = $85,000) and reduction of lease obligation ($100,000 payment – $85,000 interest = $15,000). The $100,000 credit to cash is offset by debits to interest expense ($85,000) and lease obligation ($15,000).

    The only other expense related to this lease is depreciation of the leased asset. Leased assets are depreciated over the lease term (twenty years) unless the lease transfers ownership (as this one does) or contains a bargain purchase option. If either of these is present, then the asset is depreciated over the estimated useful life of the asset (twenty-five years). Depreciation expense is cost ($850,000) divided by useful life ($850,000 ÷ 25 years = $34,000). If a salvage value had been given, it would be subtracted from cost before dividing by useful life.

Task-Based Simulation 2

Concepts		
	Authoritative Literature	**Help**

		(A)	(B)	(C)	(D)	(E)	(F)	(G)	(H)	(I)	(J)	(K)	(L)	(M)	(N)	(O)	(P)	(Q)
1.	Sales-type lease	○	○	○	●	○	○	○	○	○	○	○	○	○	○	○	○	○
2.	Direct financing lease	○	○	○	○	○	○	○	○	●	○	○	○	○	○	○	○	○
3.	Operating lease—lessee	○	●	○	○	○	○	○	○	○	○	○	○	○	○	○	○	○
4.	Operating lease—lessor	○	○	○	○	○	●	○	○	○	○	○	○	○	○	○	○	○
5.	Unearned interest revenue	○	○	○	○	○	○	●	○	○	○	○	○	○	○	○	○	○
6.	Residual value	○	○	○	○	○	○	○	●	○	○	○	○	○	○	○	○	○
7.	Capital lease	○	○	●	○	○	○	○	○	○	○	○	○	○	○	○	○	○

		(A)	(B)	(C)	(D)	(E)	(F)	(G)	(H)	(I)	(J)	(K)	(L)	(M)	(N)	(O)	(P)	(Q)
8.	Implicit rate	○	○	○	○	○	○	○	○	○	○	○	○	○	●	○	○	○
9.	Interest method	○	○	○	○	○	○	○	○	○	○	○	●	○	○	○	○	○
10.	Present value of the minimum lease payments	○	○	○	○	○	○	○	○	○	○	●	○	○	○	○	○	○
11.	Bargain purchase option	○	○	○	○	○	○	○	○	○	○	○	○	○	○	●	○	○
12.	Sale-leaseback	●	○	○	○	○	○	○	○	○	○	○	○	○	○	○	○	○
13.	Annuity due	○	○	○	○	○	○	○	○	○	○	○	○	○	○	○	○	●
14.	Initial direct costs	○	○	○	○	○	○	○	○	○	○	○	○	○	○	○	●	○
15.	Current lease obligation	○	○	○	○	○	○	○	○	○	○	○	●	○	○	○	○	○

Task-Based Simulation 3

Classification		
	Authoritative Literature	**Help**

1. Ward rents equipment for three years for $20,000 per year. The equipment is valued at $200,000. At the end of the rental term the equipment must be returned to the dealer.

   Operating lease. Does not meet any of the four criteria.

2. Ward rents equipment for five years for $80,000 per year. At the end of the rental term Ward can purchase the equipment for $500. At the date the contract was signed the equipment had a value of $300,000. At the end of five years, it is expected the equipment will have a value of $42,000.

   Capital lease. The lease has a bargain purchase option.

3. Ward received six months of free rent on an office building it was leasing for two years. Rent is normally $1,500 per month.

   Operating lease. The building is only leased for two years, and it is doubtful that it is greater than 75% of the building's economic life.

4. Ward rents equipment for eight years. The present value of the lease payments are $80,000. The market value of the equipment is $90,000 and the useful life of the equipment is ten years.

   Capital lease. The present value of the lease payments is not greater than 90% of the fair market value of the leased asset; however, the rental term is 80%, which is greater than 75% of the economic life of the asset.

5. Ward rents equipment for ten years. At the end of the lease Ward receives title to the equipment.

   Capital lease. Transfer of title.

6. Ward rents equipment for seven years. The life of the equipment is ten years. The fair value of the equipment is $100,000. The present value of the minimum lease payments is $85,000.

   Operating lease. The lease is not greater than 75% of the economic life of the asset, and the present value of the minimum lease payments is not greater than 90% of the fair market value of the asset.

Task-Based Simulation 4

Research		
	Authoritative Literature	**Help**

ASC	420	10	30	7-8

Task-Based Simulation 5

Amortization Schedule		
	Authoritative Literature	**Help**

Prepare an amortization table for the lease through December 30, year 4.

Year ending	Interest expense	Lease payment	Amounts applied to carrying value	Carrying value of lease
At signing of note	Not applicable	Not applicable	Not applicable	$551,702
December 30, year 1	$0	$70,000	$70,000	481,702
December 30, year 2	28,902	70,000	41,098	440,604
December 30, year 3	26,436	70,000	43,564	397,040
December 30, year 4	23,822	70,000	46,178	350,863

Task-Based Simulation 6

Financial Statement Disclosures | **Authoritative Literature** | **Help**

Interest expense for year 2	28,902
Interest expense for year 3	26,436
Carrying value of lease on 12/31/Y3	397,040
Depreciation expense for year 2	45,975

Explanations

Interest expense recognized in year 2

$28,902 (6% × $481,702)

Interest expense recognized in year 3

$26,436 (6% × $440,604)

Carrying value of the lease on December 31, year 3

$397,040 (See table in solution to Simulation 5)

Depreciation expense for year 2

$551,702 / 12 years = $45,975
The leased asset is depreciated over the asset's life because there is a bargain purchase option.

Task-Based Simulation 7

Research | **Authoritative Literature** | **Help**

ASC	840	30	30	1

Task-Based Simulation 8

Leasing Concepts | **Authoritative Literature** | **Help**

		True	False
1.	Free or uneven lease payments should be recognized by the lessor when the lease payment is received.	○	●
2.	Initial direct costs are expensed by the lessor when the lease is signed.	○	●
3.	A refundable security deposit is treated as an asset by the lessor.	○	●
4.	Leasehold improvements should be amortized over the longer of the remaining lease term or the useful life of the asset.	○	●
5.	The minimum lease payment includes any penalty for failure to renew.	●	○
6.	The unguaranteed residual value is considered part of the minimum lease payment for the lessee's liability.	○	●

	True	False
7. If a seller-lessee retains substantially all rights to use the property in a sales-leaseback transaction, the gain on sale is deferred by the seller-lessee.	●	○
8. If a capital lease is modified in such a way that it qualifies as an operating lease, it should be treated as a sales-leaseback transaction.	●	○

Explanations

1. **(F)** Free or uneven lease payments received by the lessor should be recognized as revenue on a straight-line basis and prorated over the life of the lease.

2. **(F)** Initial direct costs should be capitalized and amortized straight-line over the life of the lease.

3. **(F)** A refundable security deposit is a liability to the lessor and a receivable to the lessee.

4. **(F)** Leasehold improvements should be amortized over the shorter of the remaining lease term or the useful life of the asset.

5. **(T)** The minimum lease payment includes any penalty.

6. **(F)** The unguaranteed residual is considered part of the lessor's net investment in lease unless there is a transfer of title or a bargain purchase option. The unguaranteed residual is not part of the minimum lease payment for the lessee; it is ignored.

7. **(T)** Gain is deferred in these situations.

8. **(T)** Sales-leaseback treatment is appropriate.

Task-Based Simulation 9

Research		
	Authoritative Literature	Help

ASC	840	.10	25	1

Module 14: Deferred Taxes

Overview

Income for financial reporting purposes (book income) and income for tax purposes (taxable income) usually differ. Differences are due to the fact that for financial reporting, firms are required to follow GAAP. However, for tax purposes, firms must follow the Internal Revenue Code. The differences can either (1) permanently differ, in which case there is no deferral, or (2) reverse over time (e.g., straight line depreciation is used for book purposes and MACRS is used for tax purposes) which leads to a temporary difference or deferred tax.

ASC Topic 740, *Income Taxes* (SFAS 109), requires an asset and liability (balance sheet) approach to recognizing and measuring deferred taxes. This means that Income Tax Expense reporting in a firm's GAAP financial statements is a function of the current taxes owed to the Internal Revenue Service (Income Tax Payable) and the deferred taxes. To understand the basic concepts of deferred taxes, study this module and the outlines of SFAS 109 and APB 23 (ASC Topic 740).

A. Overview of Deferred Tax Theory

1. There are numerous differences between the recognition and measurement of pretax financial (book) income and asset/liability valuation under GAAP and the recognition and measurement of taxable income and asset/liability valuation under the Internal Revenue Code. Because of these differences between the two bodies of promulgated rules, pretax financial (book) income usually differs from taxable income. The amount of Income Tax Expense and the amount of Income Taxes Payable are, therefore, often different amounts.

2. Financial income tax expense (the **current and deferred** tax consequences of **all** events that have been recognized in the financial statements) is charged to Income Tax Expense.

   a. Income Tax Expense equals the taxes actually owed (a current tax liability) for the current period plus or minus the change during the current period in amounts payable in the future and in future tax benefits.

      (1) By using this procedure, any possible income statement or balance sheet distortion that may result from differences in the timing of revenue recognition or expense deductibility and asset or liability valuation between GAAP and the Internal Revenue Code is avoided.

      (2) The Income Tax Expense reported in the entity's income statement reflects the amount of taxes related to transactions recognized in the financial statements prepared under GAAP for the specific period.

      (3) The deferred tax asset or liability (the difference between Income Tax Expense and Income Tax Payable) reported in the entity's balance sheet clearly reflects the amount of taxes that the entity has prepaid (an asset) or will have to pay in the future (a liability) because of temporary differences that result from differences in timing of revenue recognition or expense deductibility between GAAP and the Internal Revenue Code.

B. Permanent and Temporary Differences Defined

Differences between pretax financial (book) income and taxable income can be divided into two types: temporary differences or permanent differences. The Codification does **not** use the term permanent differences. However, to ease our explanation and your comprehension, the term "permanent difference" will be used in this module, as it is in several intermediate accounting textbooks.

1. **Temporary Differences**

   A temporary difference is "a difference between the tax basis of an asset or liability and its reported amount in the financial statements that will result in taxable or deductible amounts in future years when the reported amount of the asset or liability is recovered or settled, respectively."

   a. This definition of a temporary difference is based on the assumption that assets and liabilities reported on an entity's balance sheet will eventually be recovered or settled at their net reported (book) value.

      (1) This recovery or settling process will create income statement items (revenues/gains or expenses/losses) as the life of the asset or liability progresses.

      (2) If the reported financial (book) value of the balance sheet item differs from its tax basis, the correct period for recognition of the related income statement item will differ between the entity's financial statements and the entity's tax return. Thus, from an income statement perspective, a temporary difference occurs when a revenue or expense item: (1) is included in both financial accounting income and taxable income, **and,** (2) is recognized in one period for financial accounting purposes and in another period for income tax purposes because of differences between the promulgated rules of GAAP and the Internal Revenue Code.

         (a) If such a temporary difference exists, an amount will be recorded and reported as either a deferred tax liability or a deferred tax asset depending upon the relationship between the reported net financial (book) value and the tax basis of the related asset or liability.

         (b) When the temporary difference reverses, the recorded deferred tax amount is removed from the balance sheet; the amount removed results in an increase or decrease in income tax expense. Some examples of temporary differences are presented below.

            1] **Estimated warranty liability:** Expense recognized in the financial statements when the liability is incurred. Deduction recognized for tax purposes when the work is actually performed.

            2] **Unearned rent (royalty) revenue:** Recognized in the financial statements as a liability when the rent (royalty) is received and as revenue when earned. Recognized as revenue for tax purposes when the cash is received. (Note that the Internal Revenue Code refers to revenue received in advance as "prepaid income," not "unearned revenue.")

            3] **Plant assets and accumulated depreciation:** Changes in these assets and the related contra asset are recognized in the financial statements according to depreciation methods acceptable to GAAP. Changes in these assets and the related contra asset are usually recognized for tax purposes according to accelerated methods acceptable to the IRS such as ACRS and MACRS. Note that recovery of these assets occurs as the asset is used in the entity's operations to generate revenue. In essence, a portion of the investment in the asset is being recovered as the product or service is sold.

            4] **Donated asset:** According to GAAP, initial valuation in the financial statements of a donated asset is based upon fair market value, and revenue is recognized for the same amount. Depreciation on the asset is computed according to the entity's normal policies. Upon sale of the asset, a gain is recognized for the difference between cash received and net book value. According to the Internal Revenue Code, a donated asset has the same basis for the donee as it did in the donor's hands. Thus, no tax deductions for depreciation are allowed for the asset if the tax basis is zero. When the asset is sold, the entire amount received is a taxable gain.

            5] **Involuntary conversion of assets:** According to GAAP, a gain (loss) must be recognized when a nonmonetary asset is involuntarily converted into a monetary asset, even though the entity reinvests the monetary assets in replacement nonmonetary assets. The replacement asset is valued at its cost or fair value on date of acquisition. According to the Internal Revenue Code, no gain is recognized on an involuntary conversion if the amount reinvested in replacement property equals or exceeds the amount realized from the converted property. The tax basis of the replacement asset is valued at its cost less the deferred gain.

            6] **Goodwill:** Under GAAP, goodwill is not amortized. The Internal Revenue Code however, mandates an amortization period of fifteen years.

2. **Permanent Differences**

   A permanent difference occurs when a revenue or expense item is only included in pretax financial (book) income or in taxable income but will never be included in both. For example, interest income on municipal bonds is included in pretax financial (book) income but is never included in taxable income because it is tax exempt by law.

   a. No deferred taxes need to be recognized because no future tax consequences are created.

   b. The tax exempt income (or deduction not allowed for taxes) is simply subtracted from (or added to) book income in the book to tax reconciliation. Thus, a permanent difference affects only the current reconciliation of book income to taxable income, and has no effect on the computation of deferred taxes. Some common permanent differences are

(1) **State and municipal bond interest income:** included in book income but not included in taxable income.
(2) **Life insurance premium expense when the corporation is the beneficiary:** deducted for book income but not for taxable income; proceeds received on such policies result in a book gain but are not taxable.
(3) **Federal income tax expense:** deducted for book income but not for taxable income.
(4) **Payment of penalty or fine:** deducted for book income but not for taxable income.
(5) **Dividend received deduction (DRD):** deducted for taxable income but not for book income.

c. The example below shows how permanent and temporary differences are used in calculating taxable income, given a corporation's pretax financial (book) income.

EXAMPLE 1

A corporation has pretax financial accounting (book) income of $146,000 in year 3. Additional information is as follows:

1. Municipal bond interest income is $35,000.
2. Life insurance premium expense, where the corporation is the beneficiary, per books is $4,000.
3. Accelerated depreciation is used for tax purposes, while straight-line is used for books. Tax depreciation is $10,000; book depreciation is $5,000.
4. Estimated warranty expense of $500 is accrued for book purposes.

Taxable income can be determined as follows:

Financial (book) income before income taxes	$146,000
Permanent differences	
Life insurance premium	4,000
Municipal bond interest	(35,000)
Temporary differences	
Amount added to tax accum. depr. and deducted on the tax return >	
Amount added to book accum. deprec. and deprec. exp.	(5,000)
Amount recognized for book estimated warranty	
liability and warranty exp. not recognized on the tax return	500
Taxable income	$110,500

The above schedule is known as the reconciliation of book income to taxable income. It is similar to the Schedule M-1 of the US Corporate Income Tax Return (Form 1120) except it starts with pretax financial accounting income instead of net income as Schedule M-1 does.

NOTE: The permanent differences only impact the current year (year 3 in this case) whereas the temporary differences will have future tax consequences.

NOW REVIEW MULTIPLE-CHOICE QUESTIONS 1 THROUGH 5

C. Deferred Tax Assets and Liabilities

A **deferred tax asset** is the deferred tax consequences attributable to deductible temporary differences and carryforwards. The deferred tax asset must be reduced by a valuation account if a portion or all of the deferred tax asset will not be realized in the future. A **deferred tax liability** is defined as an amount that is recognized for the deferred tax consequence of temporary differences that will result in taxable amounts in future years. Discounting of these deferred tax assets and liabilities is not permitted.

1. Identification and Measurement of Deferred Tax Items

NOTE: The candidate's ability to work an income tax accounting problem depends upon his/her ability to correctly identify permanent and temporary differences. In order to recognize the tax consequences of a temporary difference, it must be the result of event(s) that have already been recognized in the entity's financial statements for the current or previous years. With regard to a fixed asset, this means that the fixed asset has been acquired before the end of the year for which income taxes are being determined. Thus, planned asset acquisitions for future years cannot result in temporary differences and thereby affect the determination of deferred income taxes.

a. A **temporary difference** between pretax financial (book) income and taxable income occurs when the tax basis of an asset (or liability) differs from its reported financial statement amount. As shown in Example 1, a temporary difference resulting from timing of GAAP recognition vs. timing of recognition for tax purposes can create the need for additions to or subtractions from book income in order to arrive at taxable income.

(1) These **additions (taxable amounts) or subtractions (deductible amounts)** can occur in the year an event takes place and a deferred asset or liability is incurred as well to account for future years when the asset is recovered or the liability is settled.

(2) The table below presents the various possible relationships between financial statement (book) and tax recognition of revenue and expense and assets and liabilities as well as the nature of the resulting future tax consequences.

Acctg. Income > or < taxable income*	B/S relationships	Temp. differ.** Cur.	Fut.	Type of BS tax deferral	Current deferred tax expense effect	Future deferred tax expense effect
	Assets					
>	(1) on books > tax return	D	T	Liability	(+)	(−)
<	(2) on books < tax return	T	D	Asset	(−)	(+)
	Liabilities					
<	(3) on books > tax return	T	D	Asset	(−)	(+)
	(4) on books < tax return	D	T	Liability	(+)	(−)

  * Relationship in the year the temporary difference originates.
 ** Deductible (D) /Taxable (T).

(a) For example, a type 1 temporary difference (such as the difference between the financial statement amount and the **zero** tax basis of an asset obtained by a donation) creates a deferred tax liability.

1] If the donated asset is sold for more than its tax basis, recognition of the difference between the asset's financial statement amount and its tax return basis results in a gain for taxable income and either a smaller gain or a loss for book income depending on the amount of book depreciation taken on the asset since it was received by the enterprise. The amount of cash that will be needed to pay the taxes due will be increased because the entire amount of cash received for the donated asset will be reported as gain (taxable amount) on the tax return.

2] A liability is defined in SFAC 6 as "probable future sacrifices of economic benefits arising from present obligations of a particular entity to transfer assets...as a result of past transactions or events." The increase in cash paid out for taxes (a sacrifice of economic benefits) will result when the donated asset (from a past transaction or event) is disposed of; therefore, the future tax impact of the current period difference between financial statement value and tax basis represents a deferred liability. When the liability is recognized, deferred income tax expense is also recognized.

(b) In contrast, a contingent liability recognized in the current period financial statements represents a type 3 temporary difference because a contingent liability has a zero basis for tax accounting. The amount of expense stemming from this contingent liability must be added back to financial (book) income to arrive at taxable income. Therefore, a deferred tax asset is created.

1] When the probable and measurable future event does actually occur, the contingent liability will then represent a loss (deductible amount) on the tax return. Because the tax loss recognized will reduce taxable income and income taxes payable, the amount of cash that will be needed to pay the taxes due will be decreased.

2] Remember, an asset is defined in SFAC 6 as a "probable future economic benefit obtained or controlled by a particular entity as a result of past transactions or events." The reduction of current tax expense and the resulting future decrease in cash paid out for taxes (an economic benefit) will result from the contingent liability (a past transaction or event). Therefore, the future tax impact of the current period difference between the financial statement value and tax basis represents a deferred tax asset in the year the contingency is recognized.

NOTE: The deferred tax expense recorded in this situation is a credit because it represents a current period benefit.

2. Scheduling and Recording Deferred Tax Amounts

a. An entity's total income statement provision for income taxes is the sum of that entity's current and deferred tax amounts.

(1) The **current tax expense or benefit** is defined by ASC Topic 740 (SFAS 109) as "the amount of income taxes paid or payable (or refundable) for a year as determined by applying the provisions of the tax law to the taxable income or excess of deductions over revenues for that year."

(2) The **deferred tax expense or benefit** is defined as "the change during the year in an enterprise's deferred tax liabilities or assets."

(3) Current and deferred tax amounts are computed independently.

b. The deferred tax amount (the future tax consequences of temporary differences) should be recorded in the current financial statements at the amounts that will be paid or recovered based upon tax laws and rates that are already in place and due to be in effect at the date of payment or recovery.

   (1) These are known as **enacted** tax laws and **enacted** tax rates. An entity must, therefore, determine when the identified and measured temporary differences will become taxable or deductible.
   (2) Future **taxable amounts** cause taxable income to be greater than financial (book) income in future periods. They are a result of existing temporary differences and are reported as deferred tax liabilities in the current year.
   (3) Future **deductible amounts** cause taxable income to be less than financial (book) income in future periods. They are a result of existing temporary differences and are reported as a deferred tax asset in the current year.
   (4) For illustrative purposes, the following examples show the scheduling of future temporary differences.

   > **NOTE:** In practice and on the CPA exam, extensive scheduling is generally not necessary unless (1) there is a change in future enacted tax rates or (2) the problem requires the use of a valuation allowance account.

c. Deferred tax liabilities and assets are determined separately for each tax-paying component (an individual entity or group of entities that is consolidated for tax purposes) in each tax jurisdiction. That determination includes the following procedures:

   (1) Identify the types and amounts of existing temporary differences.
   (2) Identify the nature and amount of each type of operating loss and tax credit carryforward and the remaining length of the carryforward period.
   (3) Measure the total deferred tax liability for taxable temporary differences using the applicable tax rate.
   (4) Measure the total deferred tax asset for deductible temporary differences and operating loss carryforwards using the applicable tax rate.
   (5) Measure deferred tax assets for each type of tax credit carryforward.
   (6) Reduce deferred tax assets by a valuation allowance if, based on the weight of available evidence, it is *more likely than not* (a likelihood of more than 50%) that some portion or all of the deferred tax assets will not be realized. The valuation allowance should be sufficient to reduce the deferred tax asset to the amount that is more likely than not to be realized.
   (7) Deferred tax assets and liabilities are **not** discounted to reflect their present value.

EXAMPLE 2

This example shows the **deferred tax accounting in year 3, year 4, and year 5** for the temporary differences included in Example 1 earlier in this module. Additional details are

   a. On 1/1/Y1 the enterprise acquired a depreciable asset for $30,000 that had an estimated life of six years and is depreciated on a straight-line basis for book purposes. For tax purposes, the asset is depreciated using the straight-line election under MACRS and qualifies as a three-year asset.
   b. The enterprise deducted warranty expense of $500 for book purposes in year 3 that is expected to be deductible for tax purposes in year 4.
   c. Taxable income was $110,500 in year 3, $112,000 in year 4, and $113,500 in year 5.
   d. The applicable tax rate is 40% for all years affected.

The deferred component of income tax expense for year 3 is computed as follows. First, a schedule of **the temporary depreciation differences** for all affected years is prepared:

	Year 1	Year 2	Year 3	Year 4	Year 5	Year 6
Book depreciation	$ 5,000	$ 5,000	$ 5,000	$5,000	$5,000	$5,000
Tax depreciation	5,000*	10,000	10,000	5,000*	--	--
Temporary difference:						
No difference	$ 0			$ 0		
Book deprec. < Tax deprec.		$(5,000)	$(5,000)			
Book deprec. > Tax deprec.					$5,000	$5,000

  *   Due to MACRS half-year convention

Then, a schedule of **future taxable (deductible) amounts** is prepared.

	Year 4 Taxable (deductible)	Year 5 Taxable (deductible)	Year 6 Taxable (deductible)	Tax rate	Deferred tax liability (asset)
Scheduled taxable (deductible) amounts:					
Depreciation differences:					
taxable amounts		$5,000	$5000	40%	$4,000 Noncurrent
Warranty differences:					
deductible amounts	$(500)			40%	$(200) Current

The above schedule shows that the future tax benefit (deductible amount) in year 4 of the $500 temporary difference resulting from the Warranty Expense Liability must be recognized automatically as a deferred tax asset in year 3. The deferred tax asset of $200 ($500 × 40%) should be reported as a current asset at 12/31/Y3 because the classification of the temporary difference is based on the related asset or liability, in this case a warranty liability that is expected to be satisfied in the next year. The amount of future taxes payable (deferred tax liability) associated with the total temporary difference of $10,000 resulting from excess depreciation [$5,000 (year 3) + $5,000 (year 4)] is $4,000 [($5,000 + 5,000) × 40%]. The $4,000 amount is reported as a noncurrent deferred tax liability at 12/31/Y3, because classification as current or noncurrent is based on the classification of the related asset or liability, in this case a depreciable asset that is noncurrent.

Once the deferred tax asset and deferred tax liability have been measured at year-end, a journal entry is necessary to adjust the deferred tax account balances to the current year-end amount. As stated earlier, income tax expense for the year will consist of the taxes currently payable (based on taxable income) plus or minus any change in the deferred tax accounts.

EQUATION FOR DETERMINING INCOME TAX EXPENSE

$$\begin{array}{ccccc} \text{Income tax} & & \text{Income tax} & & \text{Change in} \\ \text{expense for} & = & \text{payable from} & \pm & \text{deferred} \\ \text{financial reporting} & & \text{the tax return} & & \text{taxes (net)*} \end{array}$$

* Ending balance of deferred tax liability/asset (net) less beginning balance of deferred tax liability/asset (net)

Notes:
1. Income Tax Expense is the sum of the two numbers on the right side of the equation. Each of these two numbers is determined directly using independent calculations. It is not possible to derive Income Tax Expense from pretax financial accounting income adjusted for permanent differences, unless the tax rate is constant for all years affected.
2. The ± refers to whether the change is a credit or additional liability (+) or a debit or additional asset (–).
3. Income Tax Payable is the amount of taxes calculated on the corporate tax return. It is the amount legally owed the government (after credits).
4. One deferred tax (net) balance sheet account may be used in practice. If separate asset and liability accounts are used, the changes in each account would all be netted to determine the deferred tax component of income tax expense.

EXAMPLE

To illustrate, we will use the deferred tax liability computed in Example 2 above and the taxable income derived in Example 1. Note that at the end of year 3, but prior to adjustment, the deferred tax asset account had a zero balance and the deferred tax liability account had a balance of $2,000 ($5,000 × 40%) that was recognized as a result of the accumulated depreciation temporary difference that originated in year 1. (Refer to the schedule following the additional information given in Example 2 showing depreciation and the pattern of temporary differences and to the T-account under (c) below.) To focus on the two components of income tax expense, two entries rather than the typical combined entry will be used.

Income tax expense—current	44,200	
Income tax payable (a)		44,200

(a) $110,500 taxable income (from Example 1) × 40% = $44,200

Income tax expense—deferred (d)	1,800	
Deferred tax asset—current (b)	200	
Deferred tax liability—noncurrent (c)		2,000

(b) $500 × 40% = $200 needed Ending balance; $200 Ending balance – $0 Beginning balance = $200 increase needed in the account

```
                              Deferred Tax Asset
           Beg. bal.                    0
           Increase (b)               200
           End. bal.                  200
```

(c) $10,000 × 40% = $4,000 needed Ending balance; $4,000 Ending balance – $2,000 Beginning balance = $2,000 increase needed in the account

```
                              Deferred Tax Liability
                                   2,000      Beg. bal.
                                   2,000      Increase (c)
                                   4,000      End. bal.
```

(d) $2,000 increase in noncurrent deferred tax liability account – $200 increase in current deferred tax asset account = $1,800

The bottom of the income statement for year 3 would appear as follows:

Income before income tax		$146,000
Income tax expense		
Current	$44,200	
Deferred	1,800	46,000
Net income		$100,000

To determine the deferred component of income tax expense for **year 3,** a schedule of future taxable (deductible) amounts is prepared.

	Year 4 Taxable (deductible)	Year 5 Taxable (deductible)	Year 6 Taxable (deductible)	Tax rate	Deferred tax liability (asset)
Scheduled taxable (deductible) amounts:					
Depreciation differences:					
taxable amounts	-0-	$5,000	$5,000	40%	$4,000 Noncurrent

The temporary depreciation difference of $10,000 results in future taxes payable (a deferred tax liability) of $4,000 [($5,000 + 5,000) × 40%]. Note that the amount of the deferred tax liability in this example does not change from year 3 to year 4. The $4,000 amount would be reported as a noncurrent deferred tax liability at 12/31/11, based upon the noncurrent classification of the related depreciable asset. The $500 warranty expense deducted in year 3 for book purposes is deducted in year 4 for tax purposes. Therefore, the deferred tax asset related to warranty expense is realized in year 4 and the temporary difference related to warranty expense no longer exists.

Once the deferred tax amounts have been measured at year-end, a journal entry is required to adjust the deferred tax account balances to the current year-end amount. Income tax expense for the year consists of the taxes currently payable plus or minus any change in the deferred tax accounts. The following journal entries are needed to record income tax expense for year 4:

```
           Income tax expense—current              44,800
               Income tax payable (a)                        44,800
```

(a) $112,000 taxable income x 40% = $44,800

```
           Income tax expense deferred (c)            200
               Deferred tax asset current (b)                  200
```

(b) The credit to the deferred tax asset is the adjustment necessary to reduce the existing balance to the desired ending balance.

```
                              Deferred Tax Asset
           Beg. bal.          200
                                            200    Decrease (b)
           End. bal.            0
```

(c) Income tax expense—deferred results from the decrease in the deferred tax asset. There is no adjustment to the deferred tax liability account.

```
                              Deferred Tax Liability
                                   4,000      Beg. bal.
                                       0
                                   4,000      End. bal.
```

To determine the deferred component of income tax expense for **year 5** the following journal entries are required:

```
           Income tax expense—current              45,400
               Income tax payable (a)                        45,400
```

(a) $113,500 taxable income × 40% = $45,400

Deferred tax liability—noncurrent (b)	2,000	
Income tax expense—deferred (c)		2,000

(b)   The debit to the deferred tax liability is the adjustment necessary to reduce the existing balance to the desired ending balance.

Deferred Tax Liability

	4,000	Beg. bal.
2,000		Decrease (b)
	2,000	End. bal.

(c)   Income tax expense—deferred results from the decrease in the deferred tax liability. The deferred tax asset account was closed in year 4 because all temporary differences have reversed.

The income tax liability per the tax return in year 5 is higher than total tax expense reported on the income statement since depreciation is not deducted for tax purposes anymore. In effect, the income tax liability in year 5 includes a portion of the tax deferred from year 3- year 5 that was recorded as a liability; therefore, the deferred tax liability is reduced in year 5. There is a corresponding decrease in income tax expense—deferred that will reconcile the income tax liability per the tax return to income tax expense on the books.

Income tax expense—current	45,400
Income tax expense—deferred	(2,000)
Income tax expense per income statement	43,400

d.   **Changing tax rates.** The previous examples assumed a constant enacted tax rate of 40%.

(1) Under the **liability method**, future taxable or deductible amounts (deferred tax assets or liabilities) must be measured using enacted tax rates expected to be in effect in the periods such amounts will impact taxable income.
(2) However, when tax rates change, adjustments to reflect such changes are automatically included in the journal entry amount to increase or decrease the deferred tax accounts to the balances needed to properly reflect balance sheet amounts and to recognize the deferred component of income tax expense.

(a) The rate change effect would be included because the amount of the journal entry is determined by comparing the needed balance in deferred taxes at the end of the period which would be based on the newly enacted rates with the balance at the beginning of the period and taking the difference.

EXAMPLE 3

Assume that in June year 5 a new income tax law is passed which lowers the corporate tax rate to 35% effective January 1, year 6. The entry debiting income tax expense—current and crediting income tax payable for year 5 is identical to that above.

However, the debit to the deferred tax liability account is the adjustment necessary to reduce the existing balance to the desired ending **balance under the new tax rate**.

Deferred tax liability—noncurrent	2,250	
Income tax expense—deferred		2,250

Deferred Tax Liability

	4,000	Beg. bal.
2,250		Decrease
	1,750	End. bal.

The $1,750 is the necessary balance for the year 6 reversal of the remaining $5,000 at 35%.

EXAMPLE 4

Dart Corporation has the following temporary differences from its first year of operations:

		Treatment in the book to tax reconciliation
1. **Long-term contracts:**		
Year 1 (Current year):	Book contract income > tax contract in-	$300 subtraction
Year 2:	come	$300 addition
	Book contract income < tax contract income	
2. **Accumulated depreciation:**		
Year 1 (Current year):	Book deprec. < tax deprec.	$1,000 subtraction
Year 2:	Book deprec. < tax deprec.	$500 subtraction
Year 3:	Book deprec. > tax deprec.	$600 addition
Year 4:	Book deprec. > tax deprec.	$400 addition
Year 7:		$500 addition
3. **Estimated expense liability:**	Book est. exp./loss > tax deduction	$200 addition
Year 1 (Current year):	Book exp./loss < tax deduction	$200 subtraction
Year 7:		
4. **Rent revenue:**		
Year 1 (Current year):	Book rev. < tax rev.	$500 addition
Year 4:	Book rev. > tax rev.	$200 subtraction
Year 7:	Book rev. > tax rev.	$300 subtraction
5. **Tax rates:**	Current year: 40%	
	Years 2-4: 35%	
	Years 5-7: 30%	

The schedule below combines (1) the pretax accounting income to taxable income reconciliation and (2) the future taxable (deductible) amounts schedule. Remember that **taxable amounts** are added to financial (book) income in the book to tax reconciliation schedule in the future years in which they increase taxable income. **Deductible amounts** are subtracted from financial (book) income in the book to tax reconciliation schedule in the future years in which they decrease taxable income. Taxable income and deferred tax liability (asset) balances for year 1 (the current year) would be determined as follows:

	Current year		**Future years**			
		Year 2 taxable (deductible)	**Year 3 taxable (deductible)**	**Year 4 taxable (deductible)**	**Year 7 taxable (deductible)**	**Deferred tax liability (asset)**
	Year 1					
Tax rate	40%	35%	35%	35%	30%	
Pretax accounting income	$ 1,600					
Temporary differences:						
LT contracts	(300)	300				$ 105 Current
Accumulated deprec.	(1,000)	(500)*	600	400	500	$ 325 Noncurrent
Estimated expense liability	200			(200)		$ (60) Noncurrent
Rent revenue	500			(200)	(300)	$(160) Noncurrent
Taxable income	$ 1,000					
Income tax payable ($1,000 × 40%)	$ 400					

* Note that in year 2 there is excess tax depreciation as there was in year 1.

Income tax expense would be computed as follows:

$$\text{Income tax expense } = \text{ Income taxes } \pm \text{ Change in deferred taxes (net)}$$

Under ASC Topic 740, deferred tax assets and liabilities are classified as current or long-term based on the related asset or liability, rather than on the expected timing of the future deductible or taxable amounts. However, if a deferred tax asset or liability is not related to an asset or liability for financial reporting purposes, it is classified based upon its expected reversal date. Presented below is a solution for Example 4.

Temporary difference	**Deferred tax asset or liability**	**Related account**	**Classification***
LT contracts	$300 × 35% = $105 liability	Const-in-Progress	Current
Depreciation	[(500) + 600 + 400] × 35% + $500 × 30% = $325 liability	Accumulated depr.	Noncurrent
Est. expense	$200 × 30% = $60 asset	Estimated liability	Noncurrent
Rent revenue	$200 × 35% + $300 x 30% = $160 asset	Unearned rent	Noncurrent

* Balance sheet disclosure is explained for this example in Section F.3.

The journal entries required are as follows:

Income tax expense current	400	
Income tax payable		400 (a)

(a) $1,000 taxable income × 40% = $400

Income tax expense deferred (e)	210	
Deferred tax asset noncurrent (b)	220	
Deferred tax liability current (c)		105
Deferred tax liability noncurrent (d)		325

(b) $200 × 30% + $200 × 35% + $300 × 30%= $220 needed Ending balance; $220 Ending balance – $0 Beginning balance = $220 increase needed in the account.

Deferred Tax Asset—Noncurrent

	-0-	Beg. bal.
	220	Increase (b)
	220	End. bal.

(c) $300 × 35% = $105 Ending balance; $105 Ending balance – $0 Beginning balance = $105 increase needed in the account

Deferred Tax Liability—Current

Beg. bal.	-0-	
Increase (c)	105	
End. bal.	105	

(d) $1,000 × 35% + ($500) × 35% + $500 × 30% = $325 Ending balance; $325 Ending balance –$0 Beginning balance = $325 increase needed in the account.

Deferred Tax Liability—Noncurrent

Beg. bal.	-0-	
Increase (c)	325	
End. bal.	325	

(e) $105 increase in current deferred tax liability amount + $325 increase in noncurrent deferred tax liability account – $220 increase in noncurrent deferred tax asset account = $210.

> **NOTE:** Since this is the firm's first year of operations, there are no beginning balances in the deferred tax accounts. If there were any permanent differences, such differences would affect only the current year as they did in Example 1. In addition, the need for a valuation allowance to reduce the deferred tax asset to its net realizable value would need to be considered.

e. **Deferred tax asset valuation allowance.** A deferred tax asset is reduced by a valuation allowance if, based on the weight of available evidence, it is more likely than not (a likelihood of more than 50%) that some portion or all of the deferred tax asset will not be realized.

(1) All available evidence, both positive and negative, should be considered to determine whether a valuation allowance is needed. The need for a valuation allowance ultimately depends on the existence of sufficient taxable income (necessary to receive the benefit of a future deductible amount) within the carryback/ carryforward period, as described in Section E of this module. If any one of the following sources is sufficient to support a conclusion that a valuation allowance is not necessary, other sources need not be considered.

(2) Possible sources of taxable income

  (a) Future reversals of existing taxable temporary differences

  (b) Future taxable income exclusive of reversing temporary differences and carryforwards

  (c) Taxable income in prior carryback year(s) if carryback is permitted under the tax law

  (d) **Tax-planning strategies** that would, if necessary, be implemented to

    1] Accelerate taxable amounts to utilize expiring carryforwards

    2] Change the character of taxable or deductible amounts from ordinary income or loss to capital gain or loss

    3] Switch from tax-exempt to taxable investments.

(3) Examples of evidence to be considered when evaluating the need for a valuation allowance are summarized as follows:

(a) Negative evidence—Indicates need for a valuation allowance

    1] Cumulative losses in recent years

    2] A history of operating loss or tax credit carryforwards expiring unused

    3] Losses expected in early future years (by a presently profitable entity)

    4] Unsettled circumstances that, if unfavorably resolved, would adversely affect future operations and profit levels on a continuing basis in future years

    5] A carryback/carryforward period that is so brief that it would limit realization of tax benefits if (1) a significant deductible temporary difference is expected to reverse in a single year or (2) the enterprise operates in a traditionally cyclical business.

(b) Positive evidence—Can offset the impact of negative evidence

    1] Existing contracts or firm sales backlog that will produce more than enough taxable income to realize the deferred tax asset based on existing sales prices and cost structures

    2] An excess of appreciated asset value over the tax basis of the entity's net assets in an amount sufficient to realize the deferred tax asset

    3] A strong earnings history exclusive of the loss that created the future deductible amount (tax loss carryforward or deductible temporary difference) coupled with evidence indicating that the loss (for example, an unusual, infrequent, or extraordinary item) is an aberration rather than a continuing condition.

EXAMPLE

Valuation allowance

Assume Jeremiah Corporation has determined it has a noncurrent deferred tax asset of $800,000. Note that in the current and prior periods when this asset was recognized, income tax expense was reduced. Based on the weight of available evidence, Jeremiah feels it is more likely than not that $300,000 of this deferred tax asset will not be realized. Jeremiah would prepare the following journal entry:

Income tax expense	300,000	
Allowance to reduce deferred tax asset to expected		
realizable value		300,000

The balance sheet presentation is

Other Assets (Noncurrent)		
Deferred tax asset		$ 800,000
Less Allowance to reduce deferred tax asset		
to expected realizable value		(300,000)
		$ 500,000

At each year-end, the balance on the allowance account is adjusted upward or downward based on the evidence available at that time, resulting in an increase or decrease of income tax expense. For example, if $600,000 was deemed to be the net realizable value at the end of the next year, the following entry would be made:

Allowance to reduce deferred tax asset to expected		
realizable value	100,000	
Deferred income tax expense		100,000

D. Deferred Tax Related to Business Investments

One additional issue concerns temporary differences from income on long-term investments that are accounted for using the equity method. For these investments a corporation may assume that the temporary difference (the undistributed income since date of acquisition) will ultimately become taxable in the form of a dividend or in the form of a capital gain. Obviously, the tax expense and deferred tax liability recorded when the difference originates will be a function of whichever of these assumptions is made.

EXAMPLE

Assume Parent Company owns 70% of the outstanding common stock of Subsidiary Company and 30% of the outstanding common stock of Investee Company. Additional data for Subsidiary and Investee Companies for the year year 1 are as follows:

	Investee Co	Subsidiary Co
Net income	$50,000	$100,000
Dividends paid	20,000	60,000

Income Tax Effects from Investee Co.

The pretax accounting income of Parent Company will include equity in Investee income equal to $15,000 ($50,000 × 30%). Parent's taxable income, however, will include dividend income of $6,000 ($20,000 × 30%), and a dividends received deduction of 80% of the $6,000, or $4,800, will also be allowed for the dividends received. This 80% dividends received deduction is a permanent difference between pretax accounting and taxable income and is allowed for dividends received from domestic corporations in which the ownership percentage is less than 80% and equal to or greater than 20%. The originating temporary difference results from Parent's equity ($9,000 = $30,000 × 30%) in Investee's undistributed income of $30,000 ($50,000 – $20,000). The amount by which the deferred tax liability account would increase in year 1 depends upon the expectations of Parent Co. as to the manner in which the $9,000 of undistributed income will be received. If the expectation of receipt is via dividends, then the temporary difference is 20% of $9,000 because 80% of the expected dividend will be excluded from taxable income when received. This temporary difference in year 1 of $1,800, multiplied by the tax rate, will give the amount of the increase in the deferred tax liability. If the expectation of receipt, however, is through future sale of the investment, then the temporary difference is $9,000, and the change in the deferred tax liability is the capital gains rate (currently the same as ordinary rate) times the $9,000.

The entries below illustrate these alternatives. A tax rate of 34% is used for both ordinary income and capital gains. Note that the amounts in the entries below relate only to Investee Company's incremental impact upon Parent Company's tax accounts.

	Expectations for undistributed income	
	Dividends	**Capital gains**
Income tax expense	1,020	3,468
Deferred taxes (net)	612[b]	3,060[c]
Income taxes payable	408[a]	408[a]

[a]*Computation of income taxes payable*

Dividend income—30% ($20,000)	*$ 6,000*
Less: 80% dividends received deduction	*(4,800)*
Amount included in Parent's taxable income	*$ 1,200*
Tax liability—34% ($1,200)	*$ 408*

[b]*Computation of deferred tax liability (dividend assumption)*

Temporary difference—Parent's share of undistributed income—	
30% ($30,000)	*$ 9,000*
Less: 80% dividends received deduction	*$(7,200)*
Originating temporary difference	*$ 1,800*
Deferred tax liability—34% ($1,800)	*$ 612*

[c]*Computation of deferred tax liability (capital gain assumption)*

Temporary difference—Parent's share of undistributed income—	
30% ($30,000)	*$9,000*
Deferred tax liability—34% ($9,000)	*$3,060*

Income Tax Effects from Subsidiary Co.

The pretax accounting income of Parent will also include equity in Subsidiary income of $70,000 (70% of $100,000). Note also that this $70,000 will be included in pretax consolidated income if Parent and Subsidiary consolidate. For tax purposes, Parent and Subsidiary cannot file a consolidated tax return because the minimum level of control (80%) is not present. Consequently, the taxable income of Parent will include dividend income of $42,000 (70% of $60,000) and there will be an 80% dividends received deduction of $33,600. The temporary difference results from Parent's equity ($28,000 = $40,000 × 70%) in Subsidiary's undistributed earnings of $40,000 ($100,000 – $60,000). Remember that the undistributed income of Subsidiary has been recognized for book purposes, but only distributed income (dividends) has been included in taxable income. The amount of the deferred tax liability in year 1 depends upon the expectations of Parent Company as to the manner in which this $28,000 of undistributed income will be received in the future. The same expectations can exist as previously discussed for Parent's equity in Investee's undistributed earnings (i.e., through future dividend distributions or capital gains). Determination of the amounts and the accounts affected for these two assumptions would be similar. The following diagram illustrates the accounting and income tax treatment of the undistributed investee/subsidiary earnings by corporate investors under different levels of ownership.

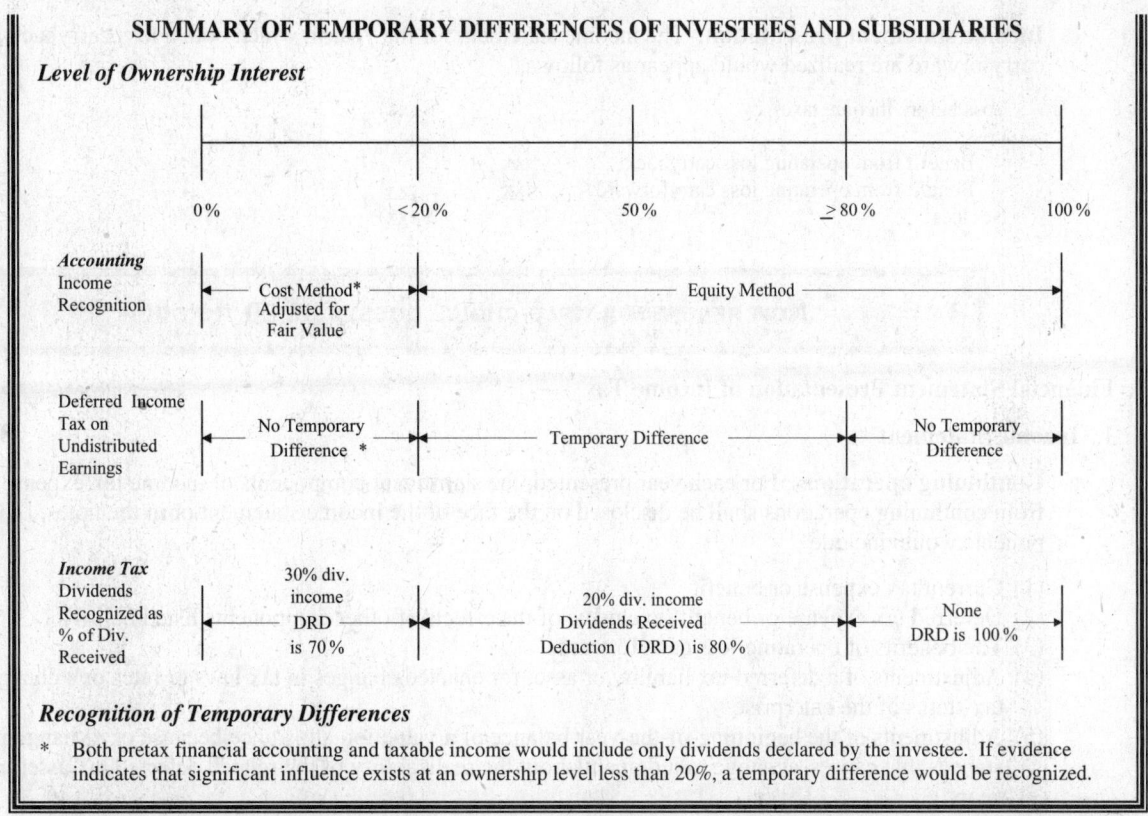

SUMMARY OF TEMPORARY DIFFERENCES OF INVESTEES AND SUBSIDIARIES

Level of Ownership Interest

Recognition of Temporary Differences

* Both pretax financial accounting and taxable income would include only dividends declared by the investee. If evidence indicates that significant influence exists at an ownership level less than 20%, a temporary difference would be recognized.

> **NOW REVIEW MULTIPLE-CHOICE QUESTIONS 6 THROUGH 29**

E. Loss Carryforwards and Carrybacks

1. Operating losses of a particular period can be carried back to the two immediate past periods' income resulting in a refund. Losses still remaining after carrybacks may also be carried forward for twenty years to offset income if income arises in any of those twenty years. Companies may at the time of the loss elect to use only the carryforward provision.

   a. **Loss carrybacks** occur when losses in the current period are carried back to periods in which there was income. Loss carrybacks result in tax refunds in the loss period and thus should be recognized in the year of the loss. The entry to record the benefit is

Tax refund receivable	(based on tax credit due to loss)
Tax loss benefit (income tax expense)	(same)

   (1) The tax loss benefit account would be closed to revenue and expense summary in the year of the loss.

   b. **Tax loss carryforwards** are recognized in the year the loss occurs. Under ASC Topic 740 (SFAS 109), the benefit of a loss carryforward is **always** recognized as a deferred tax asset which may be reduced by a valuation allowance if necessary.

EXAMPLE

Assume Caleb Corporation has a loss carryforward of $300,000 which could result in future tax savings of $120,000 (40% × $300,000). Caleb feels that based on the weight of available evidence it is more likely than not that $50,000 of these savings will not be realized. Caleb's entries to record the benefit and the valuation allowance are

Deferred tax asset	120,000	
Tax loss benefit (income tax expense)		120,000
Tax loss benefit (income tax expense)	50,000	
Allowance to reduce deferred tax asset to expected realizable value		50,000

---

c. **Income statement presentation.** The income statement for the year in which both a loss carryback and carryforward are realized would appear as follows:

Loss before income taxes		$ (xx)
Less:		
Benefit from operating loss carryback	xx	
Benefit from operating loss carryforward	xx	xx
Net loss		$ (xx)

> **NOW REVIEW MULTIPLE-CHOICE QUESTIONS 30 THROUGH 33**

F. Financial Statement Presentation of Income Tax

1. Income Statement

a. **Continuing operations.** For each year presented, the significant components of income tax expense arising from continuing operations shall be disclosed on the face of the income statement or in the notes. These components would include

(1) Current tax expense or benefit
(2) Deferred tax expense or benefit (exclusive of the effects of other components listed below).
(3) The benefits of operating loss carryforwards
(4) Adjustments of a deferred tax liability or asset for enacted changes in tax laws or rates or a change in the tax status of the enterprise
(5) Adjustments of the beginning-of-the-year balance of a valuation allowance because of a change in circumstances that causes a change in judgment about the realizability of the related deferred tax asset in future years.

b. **Other components of net income.** Income tax expense must be allocated within an accounting period between continuing operations and other components of net income (i.e., discontinued operations, extraordinary items, etc.).

(1) The amount of income tax expense allocated to continuing operations is equal to the tax on pretax income or loss from continuing operations.

(a) However, if net income includes "special items" such as discontinued operations, extraordinary items, and accounting changes, the amount of income tax expense allocated to continuing operations must consider these items.

(2) The amount allocated to an item other than continuing operations (e.g., discontinued operations, extraordinary items, and accounting changes) is equal to the incremental effect on income taxes resulting from that item.

EXAMPLE

Benjamin Corporation's ordinary loss from continuing operations is $1,000. Benjamin also has an extraordinary gain of $1,800 that is a capital gain for tax purposes. The tax rate is 40% on ordinary income and 30% on capital gains. Income taxes currently payable are $240 [($1,800 – $1,000) × 30%]. Since the effect of the $1,000 loss was to offset a capital gain, the benefit allocated to continuing operations is $300 (30% × $1,000) rather than $400 (40% × $1,000). The incremental tax expense allocated to the extraordinary gain is $540 (difference between the $300 tax benefit and the $240 total tax expense).

EXAMPLE

Alco Co. has income from continuing operations of $2,000,000, an extraordinary gain of $450,000, and no permanent or temporary differences. The current tax rate is 34%. Total income tax expense is $833,000 ($2,450,000 × 34%). This amount will first be allocated to income from continuing operations, and the remainder (incremental tax consequences attributable to the remaining components of net income) will be allocated to the extraordinary gain.

Total income tax expense	$ 833,000
Tax consequences associated with income from continuing operations ($2,000,000 × 34%)	680,000
Remainder to extraordinary gain	$ 153,000

The bottom of the income statement would appear as follows:

Income from continuing operations	$2,000,000
Income tax expense	680,000
Income before extraordinary item	$1,320,000
Extraordinary gain (net of $153,000 tax)	297,000
Net income	$1,617,000

c. **Other comprehensive income.** Components of other comprehensive income may be displayed net of related deferred tax effects or before related deferred tax effects with one amount shown for the aggregate income tax effect (with detail shown in notes). Refer to Module 9D for more information regarding comprehensive income.

2. **Retained Earnings**

Any income tax effects associated with adjustments of the opening balance of retained earnings for a **special type** change in accounting principle or correction of an error are to be charged or credited directly to retained earnings. The income tax effects of other stockholders' equity items (e.g., cumulative translation adjustment) are charged or credited to stockholders' equity.

3. **Balance Sheet**

a. The classification of deferred tax liabilities and assets is a two-stage process.

   (1) First, all deferred tax liabilities and assets are classified as current or noncurrent.

      (a) Deferred tax liabilities and assets are classified as current or long-term based on the related asset or liability.

         1] A deferred tax liability or asset is related to an asset or liability if reduction of the asset or liability will cause the temporary difference to reverse.

      (b) If the deferred tax liability or asset is **not** related to any asset or liability for financial reporting purposes (such as a deferred tax asset caused by a loss carryforward), it is classified based on the timing of its expected reversal or utilization date.

   (2) Once classification has been determined, all current amounts are netted to get a net current asset or liability and the noncurrent amounts are likewise netted to obtain a net noncurrent amount.

   (3) This process is illustrated in Example 4 that appeared earlier in this module. In Example 4, the only current deferred tax asset/liability is the $105 current liability. Thus the net current amount is a $105 liability. The other amounts are netted to find the net noncurrent amount. In this case the net noncurrent amount is a $105 liability ($325 – $220).

b. If an allowance account has been recognized for a deferred tax asset, it would be deducted from the related deferred tax asset before the netting process described above is done. If the allowance account balance relates to a deferred tax asset that is classified partially as current and partially as noncurrent, the allowance balance should be allocated between them in the ratio of each asset balance to the total asset balance.

> **NOTE:** If a tax refund receivable results from a loss carryback in the current period, this element would not be included in the netting process; only deferred tax assets and liabilities are netted.

> **NOW REVIEW MULTIPLE-CHOICE QUESTIONS 34 THROUGH 41**

G. Treatment of Selected Temporary Differences

The table on the next page summarizes the treatment of selected temporary differences from the period of origination to the period of reversal.

TREATMENT OF SELECTED TEMPORARY DIFFERENCES

	Book value		Tax basis		Previous and current reconciliations of book income to tax income	Future years(s) reconciliation of book income to tax income	Deferred consequence
a. Estimated liability under warranties	56,000	Less	--	=	56,000 addition(s)	56,000 subtraction(s)	Asset
b. Unearned rent (royalty) revenue received (liability)	40,000	Less	--	=	40,000 addition(s)	40,000 subtraction(s)	Asset
c. Long-term contracts:							
Construction in process (asset)	1,125,000	Less	1,000,000	=	125,000 subtraction	125,000 addition	Liability
d. Plant assets and accumulated depreciation:							
Equipment (asset)	50,000		50,000				
Accumulated depreciation (contra asset)	10,000	Less	18,500	Less			
End of period basis	40,000		31,500	=	8,500 subtraction(s)	8,500 addition(s)	Liability
e. Donated assets:							
Year of acquisition:							
Machinery (asset)	90,000	Less	--	=	Not included because donat. recorded in S/E	See deprec. below	Liability
Depreciation:							
Machinery (asset)	90,000		--				
Accumulated depreciation (contra asset)	18,000	Less	--	Less			
End of period basis	72,000		--	=	18,000 addition(s)	18,000 addition(s)	Reduction of liability
Sale of asset:							
Cash received	80,000		80,000				
Basis of asset	72,000	Less	80,000	Less			
Gain (revenue)	8,000		80,000	=	72,000 addition	72,000 addition	Reduction of liability
f. Replacement asset for involuntarily converted asset:							
Year of acquisition:							
Building (asset)	280,000		280,000				
Deferred gain from involuntary conversion	280,000		(110,000)	Less			
Initial basis of asset	280,000	Less	170,000	=	110,000 subtraction		Liability
Depreciation:							
Building (asset)	280,000		170,000				
Accumulated depreciation (contra asset)	(14,000)	Less	(28,900)	Less			
End of period basis	266,000		141,100	=	14,900 subtraction		Liability
Sale of replacement asset:							
Cash received	270,000		270,000				
Basis of asset	(266,000)	Less	(141,100)	Less			
Gain (revenue)	4,000		128,900	=		124,900 addition	Reduction of liability

* The $110,000 gain was recognized in the financial statements in the period the involuntary conversion occurred.

H. Research Component—Accounting Standards Codification

ASC Topic 740 addresses most research questions on deferred taxes. An important concept is that SFAS 109 uses the asset/liability method in recognizing deferred taxes. The most likely research questions are defining temporary differences, identifying the tax rates used to calculate deferred taxes, classifying items as current or noncurrent, and the use of valuation accounts. ASC Topic 740 defines temporary differences and lists examples. An important point is that the statement does not define the term "permanent differences," nor does it use this term in the standard.

Keywords for researching the most important issues in deferred taxes are shown below.

Carrybacks	Deferred tax consequences	Income taxes currently payable
Carryforwards	Deferred tax expense	Negative evidence
Change tax rates	Deferred tax liability	Positive evidence
Current tax expense	Enacted tax rates	Taxable income
Deductible temporary differences	Future deductible amount(s)	Taxable temporary differences
Deferred tax asset	Future taxable amount(s)	Valuation allowance tax
Deferred tax benefit	Income tax expense	

I. International Financial Reporting Standards (IFRS)

1. IFRS requires the use of the "liability method" to account for income taxes. Similar to US GAAP, its primary purpose is to focus on the statement of financial position and report deferred tax assets and deferred tax liabilities.

    a. IAS 12 prohibits deferred tax assets or deferred tax liabilities from being classified as current. Therefore, deferred taxes are classified as noncurrent items in the statement of financial position.

2. Current tax is the amount of income taxes payable or recoverable on the taxable profit or loss for the period.
3. Deferred tax assets and liabilities arise due to temporary differences.

    a. Temporary differences are either taxable temporary differences or deductible temporary differences.

      (1) A taxable temporary difference will result in an increase in taxable amounts in a future period.
      (2) A deductible temporary difference will result in amounts that can be deducted in future periods.

    b. A deferred tax asset arises when there is a deductible temporary difference. A deferred tax asset also arises when an entity has unused tax losses that can be deducted in the future or tax credits which can be used in the future.
    c. An entity can recognize a deferred tax asset if it is probable (more likely than not) that the tax benefit can be used.

4. Deferred tax assets and liabilities are measured using the enacted rate or substantially enacted rate (unlike US GAAP which requires the use of the enacted tax rate).
5. The liability method requires an entity to identify all temporary differences. The differences are then classified as those giving rise to deferred tax liabilities, and those giving rise to deferred tax assets.

    a. This distinction is important because all deferred tax liabilities are reported, whereas deferred tax assets can only be recognized if it is probable (more likely than not) that the asset will be realized.
    b. Similar to US GAAP, tax expense is the sum of current tax expense and the deferred tax expense.

6. One of the significant differences in accounting for income taxes between US GAAP and IFRS is the classification of deferred taxes on the balance sheet.

    a. Recall that for US GAAP, the netting procedures involve netting current deferred tax assets (DTA) with current deferred tax liabilities (DTL) to present one amount, and netting noncurrent DTA with noncurrent DTL to present another amount.
    b. Under IFRS, deferred tax assets and liabilities may not be classified as current.
    c. The netting rules are also different.

      (1) Netting of the components of deferred taxes is only permissible in certain situations.

        (a) The rules for presentation and disclosure require that a current tax payable and a current tax recoverable (receivable) can be offset only if it relates to the same taxing authority.
        (b) Likewise, the netting of deferred tax assets and deferred tax liabilities must relate to the same taxing authority. Therefore, in order to net these amounts, the entity must have a legal right to offset the amounts, and the amounts must relate to the same taxing authority.

NOW REVIEW MULTIPLE-CHOICE QUESTIONS 42 THROUGH 44

KEY TERMS

Asset. A "probable future economic benefit obtained or controlled by a particular entity as a result of past transactions or events: (SFAC 6).

Current tax expense or benefit. "The amount of income taxes paid or payable (or refundable) for a year as determined by applying the provisions of the tax law to the taxable income or excess of deductions over revenues for that year" (ASC Topic 740).

Deferred tax asset. The deferred tax consequences attributable to deductible temporary differences and carryforwards.

Deferred tax expense or benefit. "The change during the year in an enterprise's deferred tax liabilities or assets" (ASC Topic 740).

Deferred tax liability. An amount that is recognized for the deferred tax consequence of temporary differences that will result in taxable amounts in future years.

Liability. A "probable futures sacrifices of economic benefits arising from present obligations" (SFAC 6).

Loss carrybacks. Occur when losses in the current period are carried back to periods in which there was income.

Tax loss carryforwards. Occurs when losses in the current period are carried forward to future years.

Temporary difference. "A difference between the tax basis of an asset or liability and its reported amount in the financial statements that will result in taxable or deductible amounts in future years when the reported amount of the asset or liability is recovered or settled, respectively."

Multiple-Choice Questions (1-44)

A. Overview of Deferred Tax Theory

1. Justification for the method of determining periodic deferred tax expense is based on the concept of
   a. Matching of periodic expense to periodic revenue.
   b. Objectivity in the calculation of periodic expense.
   c. Recognition of assets and liabilities.
   d. Consistency of tax expense measurements with actual tax planning strategies.

B. Permanent and Temporary Differences Defined

2. Among the items reported on Cord, Inc.'s income statement for the year ended December 31, year 1, were the following:

Payment of penalty	$ 5,000
Insurance premium on life of an officer with Cord as owner and beneficiary	10,000

Temporary differences amount to
   a. $0
   b. $ 5,000
   c. $10,000
   d. $15,000

3. Caleb Corporation has three financial statement elements for which the December 31, year 1 book value is different than the December 31, year 1 tax basis.

	Book value	Tax basis	Difference
Equipment	$200,000	$120,000	$80,000
Prepaid officers insurance policy	75,000	0	75,000
Warranty liability	50,000	0	50,000

As a result of these differences, future taxable amounts are
   a. $ 50,000
   b. $ 80,000
   c. $155,000
   d. $205,000

4. Temporary differences arise when revenues are taxable

	After they are recognized in financial income	Before they are recognized in financial income
a.	Yes	Yes
b.	Yes	No
c.	No	No
d.	No	Yes

5. Which of the following differences would result in future taxable amounts?
   a. Expenses or losses that are deductible after they are recognized in financial income.
   b. Revenues or gains that are taxable before they are recognized in financial income.
   c. Expenses or losses that are deductible before they are recognized in financial income.
   d. Revenues or gains that are recognized in financial income but are never included in taxable income.

C. Deferred Tax Assets and Liabilities

6. Dunn Co.'s year 1 income statement reported $90,000 income before provision for income taxes. To compute the provision for federal income taxes, the following year 1 data are provided:

Rent received in advance	$16,000
Income from exempt municipal bonds	20,000
Depreciation deducted for income tax purposes in excess of depreciation reported for financial statements purposes	10,000
Enacted corporate income tax rate	30%

If the alternative minimum tax provisions are ignored, what amount of current federal income tax liability should be reported in Dunn's December 31, year 1 balance sheet?
   a. $18,000
   b. $22,800
   c. $25,800
   d. $28,800

7. Pine Corp.'s books showed pretax income of $800,000 for the year ended December 31, year 1. In the computation of federal income taxes, the following data were considered:

Gain on an involuntary conversion (Pine has elected to replace the property within the statutory period using total proceeds.)	$350,000
Depreciation deducted for the tax purposes in excess of depreciation deducted for book purposes	50,000
Federal estimated tax payments, year 1	70,000
Enacted federal tax rates, year 1	30%

What amount should Pine report as its current federal income tax liability on its December 31, year 1 balance sheet?
   a. $ 50,000
   b. $ 65,000
   c. $120,000
   d. $135,000

8. For the year ended December 31, year 1, Tyre Co. reported pretax financial statement income of $750,000. Its taxable income was $650,000. The difference is due to accelerated depreciation for income tax purposes. Tyre's effective income tax rate is 30%, and Tyre made estimated tax payments during year 1 of $90,000. What amount should Tyre report as current income tax expense for year 1?
   a. $105,000
   b. $135,000
   c. $195,000
   d. $225,000

9. Tower Corp. began operations on January 1, year 1. For financial reporting, Tower recognizes revenues from all sales under the accrual method. However, in its income tax returns, Tower reports qualifying sales under the installment method. Tower's gross profit on these installment sales under each method was as follows:

Year	Accrual method	Installment method
Year 1	$1,600,000	$ 600,000
Year 2	2,600,000	1,400,000

The income tax rate is 30% for year 1 and future years. There are no other temporary or permanent differences. In its December 31, year 2 balance sheet, what amount should Tower report as a liability for deferred income taxes?

a. $840,000
b. $660,000
c. $600,000
d. $360,000

10. On June 30, year 1, Ank Corp. prepaid a $19,000 premium on an annual insurance policy. The premium payment was a tax deductible expense in Ank's year 1 cash basis tax return. The accrual basis income statement will report a $9,500 insurance expense in year 1 and year 2.

Ank's income tax rate is 30% in year 1 and 25% thereafter. In Ank's December 31, year 1 balance sheet, what amount related to the insurance should be reported as a deferred income tax liability?
  a. $5,700
  b. $4,750
  c. $2,850
  d. $2,375

11. Mill, which began operations on January 1, year 1, recognizes income from long-term construction contracts under the percentage-of-completion method in its financial statements and under the completed-contract method for income tax reporting. Income under each method follows:

Year	Completed-contract	Percentage-of-completion
Year 1	$ --	$300,000
Year 2	400,000	600,000
Year 3	700,000	850,000

The income tax rate was 30% for year 1 through year 3. For years after year 3, the enacted tax rate is 25%. There are no other temporary differences. Mill should report in its December 31, year 3 balance sheet a deferred income tax liability of
  a. $ 87,500
  b. $105,000
  c. $162,500
  d. $195,000

Items 12 and 13 are based on the following:

Zeff Co. prepared the following reconciliation of its pretax financial statement income to taxable income for the year ended December 31, year 1, its first year of operations:

Pretax financial income	$160,000
Nontaxable interest received on municipal securities	(5,000)
Long-term loss accrual in excess of deductible amount	10,000
Depreciation in excess of financial statement amount	(25,000)
Taxable income	$140,000

Zeff's tax rate for year 1 is 40%.

12. In its year 1 income statement, what amount should Zeff report as income tax expense—current portion?
  a. $52,000
  b. $56,000
  c. $62,000
  d. $64,000

13. In its December 31, year 1 balance sheet, what should Zeff report as deferred income tax liability?
  a. $2,000
  b. $4,000

c. $6,000
d. $8,000

14. West Corp. leased a building and received the $36,000 annual rental payment on June 15, year 1. The beginning of the lease was July 1, year 1. Rental income is taxable when received. West's tax rates are 30% for year 1 and 40% thereafter. West had no other permanent or temporary differences. West determined that no valuation allowance was needed. What amount of deferred tax asset should West report in its December 31, year 1 balance sheet?
  a. $ 5,400
  b. $ 7,200
  c. $10,800
  d. $14,400

15. Black Co., organized on January 2, year 1, had pretax accounting income of $500,000 and taxable income of $800,000 for the year ended December 31, year 1. The only temporary difference is accrued product warranty costs that are expected to be paid as follows:

Year 2	$100,000
Year 3	50,000
Year 4	50,000
Year 5	100,000

Black has never had any net operating losses (book or tax) and does not expect any in the future. There were no temporary differences in prior years. The enacted income tax rates are 35% for year 1, 30% for year 2 through year 4, and 25% for year 5. In Black's December 31, year 1 balance sheet, the deferred income tax asset should be
  a. $ 60,000
  b. $ 70,000
  c. $ 85,000
  d. $105,000

16. A temporary difference that would result in a deferred tax liability is
  a. Interest revenue on municipal bonds.
  b. Accrual of warranty expense.
  c. Excess of tax depreciation over financial accounting depreciation.
  d. Subscriptions received in advance.

17. Orleans Co., a cash-basis taxpayer, prepares accrual basis financial statements. In its year 2 balance sheet, Orleans' deferred income tax liabilities increased compared to year 1. Which of the following changes would cause this increase in deferred income tax liabilities?

I. An increase in prepaid insurance.
II. An increase in rent receivable.
III. An increase in warranty obligations.

  a. I only.
  b. I and II.
  c. II and III.
  d. III only.

18. At the end of year one, Cody Co. reported a profit on a partially completed construction contract by applying the percentage-of-completion method. By the end of year two, the total estimated profit on the contract at completion in year three had been drastically reduced from the amount estimated at the end of year one. Consequently, in year two, a loss equal to one-half of the year one profit was recognized. Cody used the completed-contract method for income tax purposes and had no other contracts. The year two balance sheet should include a deferred tax

	Asset	Liability
a.	Yes	Yes
b.	No	Yes
c.	Yes	No
d.	No	No

19. A deferred tax liability is computed using
a. The current tax laws, regardless of expected or enacted future tax laws.
b. Expected future tax laws, regardless of whether those expected laws have been enacted.
c. Current tax laws, unless enacted future tax laws are different.
d. Either current or expected future tax laws, regardless of whether those expected laws have been enacted.

20. For the year ended December 31, year 1, Grim Co.'s pretax financial statement income was $200,000 and its taxable income was $150,000. The difference is due to the following:

Interest on municipal bonds	$70,000
Premium expense on keyman life insurance	(20,000)
Total	$50,000

Grim's enacted income tax rate is 30%. In its year 1 income statement, what amount should Grim report as current provision for income tax expense?
a. $45,000
b. $51,000
c. $60,000
d. $66,000

Items 21 and 22 are based on the following:

Venus Corp.'s worksheet for calculating current and deferred income taxes for year 1 follows:

	Year 1	Year 2	Year 3
Pretax income	$1,400		
Temporary differences:			
Depreciation	(800)	$(1,200)	$2,000
Warranty costs	400	(100)	(300)
Taxable income	$1,000		
Enacted rate	30%	30%	25%
Deferred tax accounts			

	Asset	Liability
Current	$ (30)[a]	
Noncurrent (before netting)	$ (75)[b]	$ 140[c]

[a] [($100) × 30%]
[b] [($300) × 25%]
[c] [($1,200) × 30%] + [$2,000 × 25%]

Venus had no prior deferred tax balances. In its year 1 income statement, what amount should Venus report as

21. Current income tax expense?
a. $420
b. $350
c. $300
d. $0

22. Deferred income tax expense?
a. $350
b. $300
c. $120
d. $ 35

23. Shear, Inc. began operations in year 1. Included in Shear's year 1 financial statements were bad debt expenses of $1,400 and profit from an installment sale of $2,600. For tax purposes, the bad debts will be deducted and the profit from the installment sale will be recognized in year 2. The enacted tax rates are 30% in year 1 and 25% in year 2. In its year 1 income statement, what amount should Shear report as deferred income tax expense?
a. $300
b. $360
c. $650
d. $780

24. Quinn Co. reported a net deferred tax asset of $9,000 in its December 31, year 1 balance sheet. For year 2, Quinn reported pretax financial statement income of $300,000. Temporary differences of $100,000 resulted in taxable income of $200,000 for year 2. At December 31, year 2, Quinn had cumulative taxable differences of $70,000. Quinn's effective income tax rate is 30%. In its December 31, year 2, income statement, what should Quinn report as deferred income tax expense?
a. $12,000
b. $21,000
c. $30,000
d. $60,000

25. Rein Inc. reported deferred tax assets and deferred tax liabilities at the end of year 1 and at the end of year 2. For the year ended 12/31/Y2, Rein should report deferred income tax expense or benefit equal to the
a. Decrease in the deferred tax assets.
b. Increase in the deferred tax liabilities.
c. Amount of the current tax liability plus the sum of the net changes in deferred tax assets and deferred tax liabilities.
d. Sum of the net changes in deferred tax assets and deferred tax liabilities.

26. On its December 31, year 2 balance sheet, Shin Co. had income taxes payable of $13,000 and a current deferred tax asset of $20,000 before determining the need for a valuation account. Shin had reported a current deferred tax asset of $15,000 at December 31, year 1. No estimated tax payments were made during year 2. At December 31, year 2, Shin determined that it was more likely than not that 10% of the deferred tax asset would not be realized. In its year 2 income statement, what amount should Shin report as total income tax expense?
a. $ 8,000
b. $ 8,500
c. $10,000
d. $13,000

27. Under current generally accepted accounting principles, which approach is used to determine income tax expense?
a. Asset and liability approach.
b. A "with and without" approach.
c. Net of tax approach.
d. Periodic expense approach.

D.   Deferred Tax Related to Business Investments

28. Bart, Inc., a newly organized corporation, uses the equity method of accounting for its 30% investment in Rex Co.'s common stock. During year 1, Rex paid dividends of $300,000 and reported earnings of $900,000. In addition

- The dividends received from Rex are eligible for the 80% dividends received deductions.
- All the undistributed earnings of Rex will be distributed in future years.
- There are no other temporary differences.
- Bart's year 1 income tax rate is 30%.
- The enacted income tax rate after year 1 is 25%.

In Bart's December 31, year 1 balance sheet, the deferred income tax liability should be

a. $10,800
b. $ 9,000
c. $ 5,400
d. $ 4,500

29. Leer Corp.'s pretax income in year 1 was $100,000. The temporary differences between amounts reported in the financial statements and the tax return are as follows:

- Depreciation in the financial statements was $8,000 more than tax depreciation.
- The equity method of accounting resulted in financial statement income of $35,000. A $25,000 dividend was received during the year, which is eligible for the 80% dividends received deduction.

Leer's effective income tax rate was 30% in year 1. In its year 1 income statement, Leer should report a current provision for income taxes of

a. $26,400
b. $23,400
c. $21,900
d. $18,600

E.   Loss Carryforwards and Carrybacks

30. Dix, Inc., a calendar-year corporation, reported the following operating income (loss) before income tax for its first three years of operations:

Year 1	$100,000
Year 2	(200,000)
Year 3	400,000

There are no permanent or temporary differences between operating income (loss) for financial and income tax reporting purposes. When filing its year 2 tax return, Dix did not elect to forego the carryback of its loss for year 2. Assume a 40% tax rate for all years. What amount should Dix report as its income tax liability at December 31, year 3?

a. $160,000
b. $120,000
c. $ 80,000
d. $ 60,000

31. Town, a calendar-year corporation incorporated in January year 1, experienced a $600,000 net operating loss (NOL) in year 3 due to a prolonged strike. Town never had a strike in the past that significantly affected its income and does not expect such a strike in the future. Additionally, there is no other negative evidence concerning future operating income. For years 1–2, Town reported a taxable

income in each year, and a total of $450,000 for the two years. Assume that: (1) there is no difference between pretax accounting income and taxable income for all years, (2) the income tax rate is 40% for all years, (3) the NOL will be carried back to the profit years 1–2 to the extent of $450,000, and $150,000 will be carried forward to future periods. In its year 3 income statement, what amount should Town report as the reduction of loss due to NOL carryback and carryforward?

a. $240,000
b. $180,000
c. $270,000
d. $360,000

32. Bishop Corporation began operations in year 1 and had operating losses of $200,000 in year 1 and $150,000 in year 2. For the year ended December 31, year 3, Bishop had pretax book income of $300,000. For the three-year period year 1 to year 3, assume an income tax rate of 40% and no permanent or temporary differences between book and taxable income. Because Bishop began operations in year 1, the entire amount of deferred tax assets recognized in year 1 and year 2 were offset with amounts added to the allowance account. In Bishop's year 3 income statement, how much should be reported as current income tax expense?

a. $0
b. $ 40,000
c. $ 60,000
d. $120,000

33. Mobe Co. reported the following operating income (loss) for its first three years of operations:

Year 1	$ 300,000
Year 2	(700,000)
Year 3	1,200,000

For each year, there were no deferred income taxes, and Mobe's effective income tax rate was 30%. In its year 2 income tax return, Mobe elected to carry back the maximum amount of loss possible. Additionally, there was more negative evidence than positive evidence concerning profitability for Mobe in year 3. In its year 3 income statement, what amount should Mobe report as total income tax expense?

a. $120,000
b. $150,000
c. $240,000
d. $360,000

F.   Financial Statement Presentation of Income Tax

34. In year 1, Rand, Inc. reported for financial statement purposes the following items, which were not included in taxable income:

Installment gain to be collected equally in year 2 through year 4	$1,500,000
Estimated future warranty costs to be paid equally in year 2 through year 4	2,100,000

There were no temporary differences in prior years. Rand's enacted tax rates are 30% for year 1 and 25% for year 2 through year 4.

In Rand's December 31, year 1 balance sheet, what amounts of the deferred tax asset should be classified as current and noncurrent?

	Current	Noncurrent
a.	$60,000	$100,000
b.	$60,000	$120,000
c.	$50,000	$100,000
d.	$50,000	$120,000

35. Thorn Co. applies ASC Topic 740, *Income Taxes*. At the end of year 1, the tax effects of temporary differences were as follows:

	Deferred tax assets (liabilities)	Related asset classification
Accelerated tax depreciation	$(75,000)	Noncurrent asset
Additional costs in inventory for tax purposes	25,000	Current asset
	$(50,000)	

A valuation allowance was not considered necessary. Thorn anticipates that $10,000 of the deferred tax liability will reverse in year 2. In Thorn's December 31, year 1 balance sheet, what amount should Thorn report as noncurrent deferred tax liability?

a. $40,000
b. $50,000
c. $65,000
d. $75,000

36. Because Jab Co. uses different methods to depreciate equipment for financial statement and income tax purposes, Jab has temporary differences that will reverse during the next year and add to taxable income. Deferred income taxes that are based on these temporary differences should be classified in Jab's balance sheet as a

a. Contra account to current assets.
b. Contra account to noncurrent assets.
c. Current liability.
d. Noncurrent liability.

37. At the most recent year-end, a company had a deferred income tax liability arising from accelerated depreciation that exceeded a deferred income tax asset relating to rent received in advance which is expected to reverse in the next year. Which of the following should be reported in the company's most recent year-end balance sheet?

a. The excess of the deferred income tax liability over the deferred income tax asset as a noncurrent liability.
b. The excess of the deferred income tax liability over the deferred income tax asset as a current liability.
c. The deferred income tax liability as a noncurrent liability.
d. The deferred income tax liability as a current liability.

38. On December 31, year 5, Oak Co. recognized a receivable for taxes paid in prior years and refundable through the carryback of all of its year 5 operating loss. Also, Oak had a year 5 deferred tax liability derived from the temporary difference between tax and financial statement depreciation, which reverses over the period year 6–year 10. The amount of this tax liability is less than the amount of the tax asset. Which of the following year 5 balance sheet sections should report tax-related items?

I. Current assets.
II. Current liabilities.
III. Noncurrent liabilities.

a. I only.
b. I and III.
c. I, II, and III.
d. II and III.

39. The amount of income tax applicable to transactions that are not reported in the continuing operations section of the income statement is computed

a. By multiplying the item by the effective income tax rate.
b. As the difference between the tax computed based on taxable income without including the item and the tax computed based on taxable income including the item.
c. As the difference between the tax computed on the item based on the amount used for financial reporting and the amount used in computing taxable income.
d. By multiplying the item by the difference between the effective income tax rate and the statutory income tax rate.

40. No net deferred tax asset (i.e., deferred tax asset net of related valuation allowance) was recognized in the year 1 financial statements by the Chaise Company when a loss from discontinued operations was carried forward for tax purposes because it was more likely than not that none of this deferred tax asset would be realized. Chaise had no temporary differences. The tax benefit of the loss carried forward reduced current taxes payable on year 2 continuing operations. The year 2 income statement would include the tax benefit from the loss brought forward in

a. Income from continuing operations.
b. Gain or loss from discontinued operations.
c. Extraordinary gains.
d. Cumulative effect of accounting changes.

41. Which of the following statements is correct regarding the provision for income taxes in the financial statements of a sole proprietorship?

a. The provision for income taxes should be based on business income using individual tax rates.
b. The provision for income taxes should be based on business income using corporate tax rates.
c. The provision for income taxes should be based on the proprietor's total taxable income, allocated to the proprietorship at the percentage that business income bears to the proprietor's total income.
d. No provision for income taxes is required.

I. International Financial Reporting Standards (IFRS)

42. Klaus corporation prepares its financial statements in accordance with IFRS. Klaus locates its business in two jurisdictions, France and Germany. Assume that in each country Klaus has the legal right to offset the taxes receivable and payable. Klaus prepares its taxes based on taxing authority and has the following information related to its deferred tax assets and liabilities.

Classification	Amount	Taxing jurisdiction
Deferred tax asset	$4,000	France
Deferred tax liability	$2,500	Germany
Deferred tax liability	$3,000	France

How should Klaus present its deferred taxes on its December 31, year 1 statement of financial position?

	Deferred tax asset	Deferred tax liability
a.	$4,000	$5,500
b.	$1,000	$2,500
c.	$0	$1,500
d.	$1,500	$3,000

43. Which of the following is true regarding reporting deferred taxes in financial statements prepared in accordance with IFRS?

   a.   Deferred tax assets and liabilities are classified as current and noncurrent based on their expiration dates.

   b.   Deferred tax assets and liabilities may only be classified as noncurrent.

   c.   Deferred tax assets are always netted with deferred tax liabilities to arrive at one amount presented on the balance sheet.

   d.   Deferred taxes of one jurisdiction are offset against another jurisdiction in the netting process.

44. Toller Corp. reports in accordance with IFRS. The controller of the company is attempting to prepare the presentation of deferred taxes on Toller's financial statements. Which of the following is correct about the presentation of deferred tax assets and liabilities under IFRS?

   a.   Current deferred tax assets are netted against current deferred tax liabilities.

   b.   All noncurrent deferred tax assets are netted against noncurrent deferred tax liabilities.

   c.   Deferred tax assets are never netted against deferred tax liabilities.

   d.   Deferred tax assets are netted against deferred tax liabilities if they relate to the same taxing authority.

Multiple-Choice Answers and Explanations

Answers

1. c __ __	11. c __ __	21. c __ __	31. a __ __	41. d __ __	
2. a __ __	12. b __ __	22. d __ __	32. a __ __	42. b __ __	
3. b __ __	13. c __ __	23. a __ __	33. c __ __	43. b __ __	
4. a __ __	14. b __ __	24. c __ __	34. c __ __	44. d __ __	
5. c __ __	15. c __ __	25. d __ __	35. d __ __		
6. b __ __	16. c __ __	26. c __ __	36. d __ __		
7. a __ __	17. b __ __	27. a __ __	37. c __ __		
8. c __ __	18. b __ __	28. b __ __	38. b __ __		
9. b __ __	19. c __ __	29. b __ __	39. b __ __	1st: __/44 = __%	
10. d __ __	20. a __ __	30. b __ __	40. a __ __	2nd: __/44 = __%	

Explanations

1. (c) The objective of accounting for income taxes is to recognize the amount of current and deferred taxes payable or refundable at the date of the financial statements. The standard further states that this objective is implemented through recognition of deferred tax liabilities or assets. Deferred tax expense results from changes in deferred tax assets and liabilities.

2. (a) **Temporary** differences are differences between taxable income and accounting income which originate in one period and reverse in one or more subsequent periods. The payment of a penalty ($5,000) and insurance premiums where the corporation is the beneficiary ($10,000) are **not** temporary differences because they never reverse. These are examples of **permanent** differences, which are items that either enter into accounting income but never into taxable income (such as these two items), or enter into taxable income but never into accounting income.

3. (b) The officer insurance policy difference ($75,000) is a permanent difference which does not result in future taxable or deductible amounts. The warranty difference ($50,000) is a temporary difference, but it results in future **deductible** amounts in future years when tax warranty expense exceeds book warranty expense. However, the equipment difference ($80,000) is a temporary difference that results in future taxable amounts in future years when tax depreciation is less than book depreciation.

4. (a) Examples of temporary differences are revenues which are taxable both before and after they are recognized in financial income. Note that emphasis is placed on the difference between book and tax, not the chronological order of the reporting.

5. (c) Expenses or losses that are deductible before they are recognized in financial income would result in future taxable amounts. For example, the cost of an asset may have been deducted for tax purposes faster than it was depreciated for financial reporting. In future years, tax depreciation will be less than financial accounting depreciation, meaning future taxable income will exceed future financial accounting income. Answers (a) and (b) are temporary differences that would result in future deductible amounts. Answer (d) is a permanent difference that does not result in either future taxable or future deductible amounts.

6. (b) To determine the current federal tax liability, **book** income ($90,000) must be adjusted for any temporary or permanent differences to determine **taxable** income.

Book income	$ 90,000
Rent received in advance	16,000
Municipal interest	(20,000)
Excess tax depreciation	(10,000)
Taxable income	$ 76,000

Rent received in advance (temporary difference) is added to book income because rent is taxable when received, but is not recognized as book revenue until earned. Municipal interest (permanent difference) is subtracted from book income because it is excluded from taxable income. The excess tax depreciation (temporary difference) is subtracted because this excess amount is an additional tax deduction beyond accounting depreciation. The current tax liability is computed by multiplying taxable income by the tax rate ($76,000 × 30% = $22,800).

7. (a) The **current** federal income tax liability is based on **taxable** income, which is computed in the "book to tax reconciliation" below.

Accounting income	$ 800,000
Nontaxable gain	(350,000)
Excess tax depreciation	(50,000)
Taxable income	$ 400,000

The gain on involuntary conversion was included in accounting income but is deferred for tax purposes. Depreciation deducted for tax purposes in excess of book depreciation also causes taxable income to be less than accounting income. Taxes payable before considering estimated tax payments is $120,000 ($400,000 × 30%). Since tax payments of $70,000 have already been made, the 12/31/Y1 current federal income tax liability is $50,000 ($120,000 – $70,000).

8. (c) Income tax expense must be reported in two components: the amount currently payable (current portion) and the tax effects of temporary differences (deferred portion). The current portion is computed by multiplying taxable income by the current enacted tax rate ($650,000 × 30% = $195,000). The deferred portion is $30,000 ($100,000 temporary difference × 30%). The estimated tax payments ($90,000) do not affect the amount of tax expense, although the payments would decrease taxes payable.

9. (b)   Over the two years, accounting income on the accrual basis is $4,200,000 ($1,600,000 + $2,600,000) and taxable income using the installment method is $2,000,000 ($600,000 + $1,400,000). This results in future taxable amounts at 12/31/Y2 of $2,200,000 ($4,200,000 – $2,000,000). Therefore, at 12/31/Y2, Tower should report a deferred tax liability of $660,000 ($2,200,000 × 30%).

10. (d)   For accounting purposes, prepaid insurance is $9,500 at 12/31/Y1. For tax purposes, there was no prepaid insurance at 12/31/Y1, since the entire amount was deducted on the year 1 tax return. Therefore, the temporary difference is $9,500. This temporary difference will result in a future taxable amount in year 2, when the tax rate is 25%. Therefore, at 12/31/Y1, a deferred tax liability of $2,375 (25% × $9,500) must be reported.

11. (c)   Mill's total accounting income using percentage-of-completion ($300,000 + $600,000 + $850,000 = $1,750,000) will eventually be subject to federal income taxes. However, by 12/31/Y3, only $1,100,000 of income ($400,000 + $700,000) has been reported as taxable income using the completed-contract method. The amount of accounting income which has not yet been taxed ($1,750,000 – $1,100,000 = $650,000 temporary difference) will be taxed eventually when the related contracts are completed. The resulting future taxable amounts will all be taxed after year 3 when the enacted tax rate is 25%. Therefore, the 12/31/Y3 deferred tax liability is $162,500 ($650,000 × 25%). To record the liability, the following entries would be made each year:

Year 1		
Income tax expense—deferred	90,000	
Deferred tax liability		90,000
Year 2		
Income tax expense—deferred	60,000	
Deferred tax liability		60,000
Year 3		
Income tax expense—deferred	12,500	
Deferred tax liability		12,500

The total in the deferred tax liability account on 12/31/Y3 should be $162,500. Therefore, the entry in year 3 is the amount needed to correctly state the deferred tax liability account. Since $150,000 was already accrued in the deferred tax liability account in year 1 and year 2, the entry for year 3 is $162,500 – $150,000, or $12,500.

12. (b)   Income tax expense must be reported in two components: the amount currently payable (current portion) and the tax effects of temporary differences (deferred portion). The amount currently payable, or current income tax expense, is computed by multiplying taxable income by the current enacted tax rate ($140,000 × 40% = $56,000).

13. (c)   The deferred tax liability reported at 12/31/Y1 results from future taxable (and possibly deductible) amounts which exist as a result of past transactions, multiplied by the appropriate tax rate. The nontaxable interest received on municipal securities ($5,000) is a **permanent** difference that does **not** result in future taxable or deductible amounts. The Codification requires the netting of current deferred tax assets and liabilities, and noncurrent deferred tax assets and liabilities. The future deductible amount ($10,000) resulting from a loss accrual results in a **long-term** deferred tax asset of $4,000 ($10,000 × 40%) because

it is related to a **long-term** loss accrual. The future taxable amount ($25,000) caused by depreciation results in a **long-term** deferred tax liability of $10,000 ($25,000 × 40%) because it is related to a **long-term** asset (property, plant, and equipment). Since these are both long-term, they are netted and a long-term deferred tax liability of $6,000 is reported in the balance sheet ($10,000 liability less $4,000 asset).

14. (b)   At 12/31/Y1, unearned rent for financial accounting purposes is $18,000 ($36,000 × 6/12). The amount of rent revenue recognized on the income statement is six of twelve months (36,000 × 6/12) = 18,000. Rental income on the tax return is $36,000 because rental income is taxed when received. Therefore, the timing difference is $18,000 ($36,000 – $18,000 = $18,000) giving rise to a deferred tax asset on the balance sheet of $18,000 × 40% = $7,200. The deferred tax asset to be recorded is measured using the future enacted tax rate of 40%.

15. (c)   A deferred tax asset is recognized for all deductible temporary differences. The computation of the deferred tax asset for Black Co. arising from the accrued product warranty costs of $300,000 is shown below.

	Year 2	Year 3	Year 4	Year 5	Total
Future deductible amounts	$100,000	$50,000	$50,000	$100,000	$300,000
Tax rate	30%	30%	30%	25%	
Deferred tax asset	$ 30,000	$15,000	$15,000	$ 25,000	$ 85,000

Thus, the total deferred tax asset at the end of year 1 is $85,000.

16. (c)   An excess of tax depreciation over financial accounting depreciation results in future taxable amounts and, therefore, a deferred tax liability. Answer (a) is an example of a permanent difference that does not result in future taxable or deductible amounts. Answers (b) and (d) are examples of temporary differences that result in future deductible amounts and a possible deferred tax asset.

17. (b)   The increase in prepaid insurance in year 2 creates a deductible amount for income tax reporting purposes for the insurance paid; however, for financial reporting purposes the expense is not recognized until years subsequent to year 2. As a result, net taxable income for future years is increased, thus, the deferred income tax liability increases. The increase in rent receivable in year 2 also increases the deferred tax liability. For income tax purposes, rents are not included in income until received (i.e., years subsequent to year 2). However, the amount of the receivable is earned and recognized in the income statement in year 2. The increase in warranty obligations results in warranty expense for year 2 and will provide future deductible amounts, because under the IRC, a deduction for warranty cost is not permitted until such cost is incurred. Future deductible amounts lead to deferred tax assets.

18. (b)   A deferred tax liability is recognized for temporary differences that will result in **net** taxable amounts (taxable income exceeds book income) in future years. Although Cody Co. has recognized a loss (per books) in year two of the construction contract, the contract is still profitable over the three years. Therefore, in year three when the contract is completed, Cody will recognize the total profit on its tax return, and only a portion of the profit will be recorded in its income statement. Thus, the contract will result in a taxable amount in year three and a deferred tax liability exists. Note that this liability was recorded at the end of year 1 and reduced by one-half at the end of year two due to the change in estimated profit. Answers (a) and (c) are incorrect because no deferred tax asset is created. Answer (d) is incorrect because Cody will include a deferred tax liability on its balance sheet.

19. **(c)** A deferred tax liability is recognized for the amount of taxes payable in **future** years as a result of the deferred tax consequences (as measured by the provisions of **enacted** tax laws) of events recognized in the financial statements in the current or preceding years.

20. **(a)** Income tax provision (expense) must be reported in two components: the amount currently payable (current portion) and the tax effects of temporary differences (deferred portion). The current portion is computed by multiplying taxable income by the current enacted tax rate ($150,000 × 30% = $45,000). Note that in this case, the deferred portion is $0, because both differences are permanent differences, which do not result in a deferred tax liability. Therefore, the current provision for income taxes should be reported at $45,000. It is important to note that if temporary differences did exist the tax effects would have been included in the tax expense for the current period.

21. **(c)** Income tax expense must be reported in two components: the amount currently payable (current portion) and the tax effects of temporary differences (deferred portion). The amount currently payable, or current income tax expense, is computed by multiplying taxable income by the current enacted tax rate ($1,000 × 30% = $300).

22. **(d)** Income tax expense must be reported on the IS in two components: the amount currently payable (current portion) and the tax effects of temporary differences (deferred portion). Note that scheduling is required in this question because the tax rates are not the same in all future years. The worksheet indicates two temporary differences: depreciation and warranty costs. The scheduling contained in the worksheet shows that these two temporary differences will result in a deferred tax asset of $105 ($30 + $75) and deferred tax liability of $140. The liability has the effect of increasing year 1 tax expense while the asset has the effect of decreasing year 1 tax expense. The net effect is deferred income tax expense of $35 for year 1 [$140 – ($30 + $75)].

Not required:

The balance sheet presentation would show a current deferred tax asset of $30 and a noncurrent deferred tax liability of $65 ($140 – $75).

23. **(a)** The deferred portion of income tax expense can be computed by determining the tax effect of the two temporary differences. The installment sale profit results in a future taxable amount in year 2 of $2,600, and the bad debt expense results in a future deductible amount of $1,400. The deferred tax consequences of these temporary differences will be measured by Shear in year 1 using the enacted tax rate expected to apply to taxable income in the year the deferred amounts are expected to be settled. The following journal entry is necessary to record the deferred tax liability related to the installment sale:

Deferred tax expense	650	
Deferred tax liability		650
[$2,600 × .25]		

To record the deferred tax asset related to the bad debt expense, the following journal entry is required:

Deferred tax asset	350	
Deferred tax expense		350
[$1,400 × .25]		

The amount of deferred tax expense to be reported by Shear in its year 1 income statement is $300 ($650 – $350). Note that one journal entry could have been used. Using two entries more clearly shows the opposite effect of an asset versus a liability on deferred tax expense.

24. **(c)** Income tax expense must be reported in two components: the amount currently payable (current portion) and the tax effects of temporary differences (deferred portion). The current portion is computed by multiplying taxable income by the current enacted tax rate ($200,000 × 30% = $60,000). The deferred portion is $30,000 ($100,000 temporary difference × 30%). An alternative computation for the deferred portion is shown below.

DT asset at 12/31/Y2	$ 0	
DT asset at 12/31/Y1	9,000	
Decrease in DT asset		$ 9,000
DT liability at 12/31/Y2		
($70,000 × 30%)	$21,000	
DT liability at 12/31/Y1	0	
Increase in DT liability		21,000
Deferred portion of tax expense		$30,000

25. **(d)** The deferred income tax expense or benefit is the net change during the year in an enterprise's deferred tax liabilities or assets. The deferred income tax expense or benefit must consider the net effect of changes (both increases and decreases) in both deferred tax assets and deferred tax liabilities. The decrease in deferred tax assets alone or the increase in deferred tax liabilities alone will not be equal to the deferred income tax expense. The amount of income tax liability (current portion which comes off the tax return) plus the sum of the net changes in deferred tax assets and deferred tax liabilities is the total amount of income tax expense or benefit for the year. The question asks only for the deferred portion.

26. **(c)** From 12/31/Y1 to 12/31/Y2, the deferred tax asset increased by $5,000 (from $15,000 to $20,000). Income taxes payable at 12/31/Y2 are $13,000. Based on this information, the following journal entries can be recreated.

Income tax expense—current	13,000	
Income tax payable		13,000
Deferred tax asset	5,000	
Income tax expense— deferred		5,000

An additional entry would be prepared by Shin to record an allowance to reduce the deferred tax asset to its realizable value (10% × $20,000 = $2,000).

| Income tax expense—deferred | 2,000 | |
| Allowance to reduce deferred tax asset to realizable value | | 2,000 |

Based on these three entries, total year 2 income tax expense is $10,000 ($13,000 – $5,000 + $2,000).

27. (a) Income tax expense is the sum of income taxes currently payable or refundable and the deferred tax expense or benefit which is the change during the year in an enterprise's deferred tax liabilities and assets. This method is more commonly called the asset and liability approach.

28. (b) The deferred income tax liability is the result of the undistributed earnings of an equity investee, which are expected to be distributed as dividends in future periods. For accounting purposes, investment revenue is $270,000 ($900,000 × 30%). For tax purposes, dividend revenue is $90,000 ($300,000 × 30%), which will be partially offset by the 80% dividends received deduction. Because of this 80% deduction, the difference ($270,000 – $90,000 = $180,000) is partially a permanent difference (80% × $180,000 = $144,000 which will never be subject to taxes) and partially a temporary difference (20% × $180,000 = $36,000 which will be taxable in future years). This future taxable amount of $36,000 will become taxable after 2010, when the expected tax rate is 25%. Therefore, the deferred tax liability is $9,000 (25% × $36,000). The entry to record the liability is as follows:

Income tax expense—deferred	9,000	
Deferred tax liability		9,000

29. (b) The **current** provision for income taxes is computed by multiplying taxable income on the Form 1120 by the current tax rate. Since taxable income is not given, pretax book income must be adjusted to compute taxable income.

Pretax book income	$100,000
Excess book depreciation	8,000
Excess book investment revenue	
[$35,000 – (20% × $25,000)]	(30,000)
Taxable income	$ 78,000

Excess book depreciation is added because it causes book income to be lower than taxable income. For book purposes, investment revenue of $35,000 was recognized using the equity method; for tax purposes, net dividend revenue of $5,000 was recognized [$25,000 – (80% × $25,000)]. The excess book revenue ($35,000 – $5,000 = $30,000) is deducted to compute taxable income. Therefore, the **current** provision for income taxes is $23,400 ($78,000 × 30%).

30. (b) Dix did **not** elect to forego the loss carryback, so $100,000 of the $200,000 loss will be carried back to offset year 1 income, resulting in a tax refund of $40,000 (40% × $100,000). The remaining $100,000 of the year 2 loss will be carried forward to offset part of year 3 income. Thus, the income tax **liability** at 12/31/Y3 will be $120,000 [40% × ($400,000 – $100,000)].

31. (a) The requirement is to determine the amount to be reported in year 3 as the reduction of loss due to NOL carryback and carryforward (i.e., benefit [negative tax expense] on the face of the IS). A deferred tax liability or asset is recognized for all temporary differences, operating losses, and tax credit carryforwards.

Income Tax Return Analysis

	Year 1-Year 2	Year 3
Inc (loss)	450,000	$(600,000)
Carryback	(450,000)	450,000
Unused NOL		$ 150,000

Town can thus recognize tax benefits from both the NOL carryback and carryforward. Town may carryback $450,000 of the NOL which will provide a tax benefit of $180,000 ($450,000 × .40). The journal entry to recognize the loss carryback would be as follows:

Tax refund receivable	180,000	
Benefit due to loss		
carryback		180,000

The additional $150,000 NOL can be carried forward to future periods to provide a benefit of $60,000 ($150,000 × .40). The following journal entry reflects the loss carryforward:

Deferred tax asset	60,000	
Benefit due to loss		
carryforward		60,000

Therefore, the reduction of the loss due to NOL carryback and carryforward is $240,000. Note that an allowance for nonrealization of the deferred tax asset is not necessary because the information given about the strike indicates that it is not more likely than not that part of the deferred tax asset may not be recognized.

The carryback and carryforward would be shown in the income statement as follows:

Loss before income taxes		$(600,000)
Less:		
Benefit from operating		
loss carryback	$180,000	
Benefit from operating		
loss carryforward	60,000	240,000
Net loss		$(360,000)

32. (a) The requirement is to determine the amount of year 3 current income tax expense (or income taxes payable from tax return) to be reported in the income statement. For tax purposes, loss carryforwards should not be recognized until they are actually realized.

Income Tax Return Analysis

	Year 1	Year 2	Year 3
Income or loss	$(200,000)	$(150,000)	$300,000
Carryforward	200,000	100,000	(300,000)
Unused Carry-			
forward	0	$ 50,000	0

Bishop would recognize, in the income statement, income tax expense of $0 as the loss carryforward fully offsets the year 1 income.

Not required:

The deferred tax component for year 3 would be as follows:

Balance in the deferred tax asset and allowance accounts at 1/1/Y3

	Deferred Tax Asset		Allow for Reduction, etc.	
12/31/Y1	80,000		80,000	12/31/Y1
12/31/Y2	60,000		60,000	12/31/Y2
12/31/Y2				12/31/Y2
balance	140,000		140,000	balance

The deferred tax entry for year 3 would be

Allow for reduction, etc.	140,000	
Deferred tax asset		120,000
Income tax expense—deferred		20,000

The bottom of the income statement would be

Income before taxes	$300,000	
Income tax expense or benefit		
Current		0
Deferred **benefit**		20,000
Net income	$320,000	

33. (c) A deferred tax liability or asset is recognized for all temporary differences and operating loss carryforwards. In year 2, Mobe would prepare the following entries:

Tax refund receivable ($300,000 × 30%)	90,000	
Deferred tax asset ($400,000 × 30%)	120,000	
Tax loss benefit (income tax expense)		210,000
Tax loss benefit (income tax expense)	120,000	
Allowance to reduce deferred tax asset to realizable value		120,000

The tax refund receivable results from carrying $300,000 of the year 2 loss **back** to offset year 1 taxable income. The deferred tax asset results from the potential **carryforward** of the remaining $400,000 loss ($700,000 – $300,000). However, the inconsistent performance of the company (profitable operations in the first year, loss in the second year) coupled with the lack of positive evidence concerning future operations indicate that at the end of year 2 it is more likely than not that none of the deferred tax asset will be realized. Therefore, Mobe must establish a valuation allowance to reduce this asset to its expected realizable value. In year 3, the entries are

Income tax expense ($1,200,000 × 30%)	360,000	
Deferred tax asset		120,000
Income taxes payable [($1,200,000 – $400,000) × 30%]		240,000
Allowance to reduce deferred tax asset to realizable value	120,000	
Benefit due to loss carryforward (income tax expense)		120,000

Income taxes payable is year 3 income of $1,200,000 less the $400,000 loss carryforward, times 30%. Total income tax expense for year 3 is $240,000 ($360,000 – $120,000). Note that if the facts had indicated positive evidence following year 2 for year 3 operations, the allowance account would not have been recognized and year 3 expense would have been $360,000.

34. (c) The warranty temporary difference results in future deductible amounts of $700,000 per year in year 2 through year 4 ($2,100,000 ÷ 3). The installment temporary difference results in future taxable amounts of $500,000 per year in year 2 through year 4 ($1,500,000 ÷ 3). The portions of the resulting deferred tax asset and deferred tax liability that will be netted to find the amount of the current asset/current liability to be presented on the BS are shown below.

Deferred tax asset:		
$(700,000) × 25% =		$(175,000)
Deferred tax liability:		
$500,000 × 25% =		125,000
Current deferred tax asset (CDTA) shown on BS		$ (50,000)

The noncurrent deferred tax asset is $100,000 [25% × ($2,100,000 – $1,500,000)] – $50,000 CDTA.

35. (d) Deferred tax liabilities and assets are classified as current or noncurrent based on the classification of the related asset or liability for financial reporting. The deferred tax liability resulting from accelerated tax depreciation should be considered noncurrent because the related asset is classified as noncurrent. The deferred tax asset resulting from additional costs in inventory for tax purposes is classified as current because the related asset is classified as current. Therefore, Thorn would report a **noncurrent deferred tax liability** of **$75,000**.

36. (d) Deferred tax liabilities and assets are classified as current or noncurrent based on the related asset or liability. A deferred tax liability or asset is considered to be related to an asset or liability if reduction of the asset or liability will cause the temporary difference to reverse. If the deferred tax liability or asset is **not** related to any asset or liability, then it is classified based on the timing of its expected reversal or utilization date. This deferred tax liability is related to equipment, which is noncurrent, so the deferred tax liability should also be classified as a noncurrent liability. Deferred taxes are always classified as assets or liabilities, rather than as contra accounts.

37. (c) Deferred tax assets and liabilities are classified as current or noncurrent based on the classification of the related asset or liability for financial reporting. Therefore, a deferred tax liability relating to depreciation of a fixed asset would be noncurrent in nature. The deferred tax asset relating to rent received in advance that is expected to reverse in the following year would be classified as current. No netting of net current amounts and net noncurrent amounts can occur.

38. (b) A **deferred** tax liability or asset should be classified in two categories (the current amount and the noncurrent amount) on the balance sheet based on the classification of the related asset or liability for financial reporting. The receivable for taxes paid in prior years and refundable through the carryback of the year 5 operating loss is **not** considered a **deferred** tax asset. A current asset should be reported on the balance sheet for the amount of the refund due to Oak Co. Note that if there was a current deferred tax liability it would not be netted with the refund receivable. However, a current deferred tax asset would be so netted. A noncurrent deferred tax liability should be reported on the balance sheet for temporary differences related to depreciation of fixed assets.

39. (b) Income tax expense must be associated with (i.e., allocated among) income from continuing operations, discontinued operations, extraordinary items, cumulative effect of an accounting change, and prior period adjustments. The tax effect to be associated with any of the special items (other than income from continuing operations) is computed by determining the income tax on overall taxable income and comparing it with the income tax on continuing operations. If more than one special item exists, the difference between tax on ordinary operations and tax on overall taxable income must be allocated proportionately among the special items.

40. **(a)** The tax benefit of an operating loss carryforward or carryback shall be reported in the same manner as the **source of income (loss) in the current year**. Thus, in year 1, the tax benefit shall be reported under income from continuing operations.

41. **(d)** Sole proprietorships do not pay any income taxes as the tax items related to a sole proprietorship flow through to the owner's tax return. Because the sole proprietorship is not a taxable entity, no provision for income taxes would be included in the financial statements of the sole proprietorship. Although answer (a) illustrates the correct formula for calculating the taxes payable related to a sole proprietorship's operations, it is an incorrect response because the tax provision would not be shown on the sole proprietorship's financial statements since it flows through to the owner and is a liability of the owner. The income tax expense would be calculated using the owner's tax rates, as it is the owner's personal liability, not the entity's. The proprietorship would have **no** provision for income taxes on its books. The entire income tax liability is the personal responsibility of the owner.

42. **(b)** The requirement is to determine how deferred taxes should be presented. Answer (b) is correct because IFRS provides that the netting of deferred tax assets and liabilities may only occur if the accounts relate to the same taxing authority and the entity has a legal right to offset the taxes. Therefore, the deferred tax asset of $4,000 and the deferred tax liability of $3,000 related to France may be offset, which results in a $1,000 deferred tax asset. The deferred tax liability of $2,500 related to Germany may not be netted and is shown as a deferred tax liability of $2,500 on the balance sheet.

43. **(b)** The requirement is to identify the true statement about accounting for deferred taxes. Answer (b) is correct because IFRS does not permit deferred tax assets or liabilities to be classified as current. Therefore, deferred tax assets and liabilities are reported in the noncurrent section of the statement of financial position. Answer (a) is incorrect because deferred taxes may not be classified as current. Answers (c) and (d) are incorrect because deferred tax assets and liabilities may only be netted if there is a legal right to offset the amounts and they relate to the same taxing authority.

44. **(d)** The requirement is to identify the correct statement about the presentation of deferred tax assets and liabilities under IFRS. Answer (d) is correct because deferred tax assets are netted against deferred tax liabilities if they relate to the same taxing authority.

Simulations

Task-Based Simulation 1

Tax Calculations		
	Authoritative Literature	
		Help

The following partially completed worksheet contain Lane Co.'s reconciliation between financial statement income and taxable income for the three years ended April 30, year 3, and additional information.

Lane Co.
INCOME TAX WORKSHEET
For the Three Years Ended April 30, Year 3

	April 30, Year 1	April 30, Year 2	April 30, Year 3
Pretax financial income	$900,000	$1,000,000	$1,200,000
Permanent differences	100,000	100,000	100,000
Temporary differences	200,000	100,000	150,000
Taxable income	$600,000	$ 800,000	$ 950,000
Cumulative temporary differences (future taxable amounts)	$200,000	$(2)	$ 450,000
Tax rate	20%	25%	30%
Deferred tax liability	$ 40,000	$ 75,000	$ (4)
Deferred tax expense	--	$ (3)	--
Current tax expense	$ (1)	--	--

The tax rate changes were enacted at the beginning of each tax year and were not known to Lane at the end of the prior year.

Items 1 through 4 represent amounts omitted from the worksheet. For each item, determine the amount omitted from the worksheet. Select the amount from the following list. An answer may be used once, more than once, or not at all.

Amount

A.	$ 25,000	H.	$135,000
B.	$ 35,000	I.	$140,000
C.	$ 45,000	J.	$160,000
D.	$ 75,000	K.	$180,000
E.	$100,000	L.	$200,000
F.	$112,500	M.	$300,000
G.	$120,000	N.	$400,000

Specific audit objective	(A) (B) (C) (D) (E) (F) (G) (H) (I) (J) (K) (L) (M) (N)
1. Current tax expense for the year ended April 30, year 1.	O O O O O O O O O O O O O O
2. Cumulative temporary differences at April 30, year 2.	O O O O O O O O O O O O O O
3. Deferred tax expense for the year ended April 30, year 2.	O O O O O O O O O O O O O O
4. Deferred tax liability at April 30, year 3.	O O O O O O O O O O O O O O

Task-Based Simulation 2

Tax Differences		
	Authoritative Literature	
		Help

Items 1 through 7 describe circumstances resulting in differences between financial statement income and taxable income. For each numbered item, determine whether the difference is

List
A. A temporary difference resulting in a deferred tax asset.
B. A temporary difference resulting in a deferred tax liability.
C. A permanent difference.

Indicate the classification of each item. An answer may be selected once, more than once, or not at all.

	A Temporary difference DTA	B Temporary difference DTL	C Permanent difference
1. For plant assets, the depreciation expense deducted for tax purposes is in excess of the depreciation expense used for financial reporting purposes.	O	O	O
2. A landlord collects some rents in advance. Rents received are taxable in the period in which they are received.	O	O	O
3. Interest is received on an investment in tax-exempt municipal obligations.	O	O	O
4. Costs of guarantees and warranties are estimated and accrued for financial reporting purposes.	O	O	O
5. Life insurance proceeds are collected on the death of a key officer.	O	O	O
6. Bad debts are estimated and expensed on the income statement. No bad debts were charged to the allowance account and written off during the year.	O	O	O
7. Goodwill is deducted on the tax return.	O	O	O

Task-Based Simulation 3

Deferred Tax Classification		
	Authoritative Literature	Help

Identify whether each item would create a deferred tax asset or a deferred tax liability, and whether each item would be classified as current or noncurrent.

	Deferred tax asset	Deferred tax liability	Current	Noncurrent
1. Tax depreciation in excess of book depreciation	O	O	O	O
2. Bad debts expense in excess of actual write-offs	O	O	O	O
3. Rent collected in advance for next 12 months	O	O	O	O

Task-Based Simulation 4

Research		
	Authoritative Literature	Help

Assume that you are assigned to the audit of Yee Corporation. The CFO has asked you to explain what is meant by a temporary difference with respect to deferred taxes. Which section of the Professional Standards provides the definition of a temporary difference? Enter your response in the answer fields below.

Task-Based Simulation 5

Temporary and Permanent Differences		
	Authoritative Literature	Help

Lindy is a corporation with a calendar year-end for tax purposes. Identify for Lindy which of the following items create temporary differences and which create permanent differences.

	Temporary	Permanent
Premiums on life insurance of key officer	O	O
Depreciation	O	O
Interest on municipal bonds	O	O
Warranties	O	O
Bad debts	O	O
Rent received in advance from clients	O	O

Task-Based Simulation 6

Deferred Tax Schedule		
	Authoritative Literature	Help

Jasco Corporation is in its first year of operations. The company has pretax income of $400,000. The company has the following items recorded in its records. No estimated tax payments were made during year 1.

Premiums on life insurance of key officer	$10,000
Depreciation on tax return in excess of book depreciation	12,000
Interest on municipal bonds	5,300
Warranty expense	4,000
Actual warranty repairs	3,250
Bad debt expense	1,400
Beginning balance in allowance for uncollectible accounts	0
End balance for allowance for uncollectible accounts	800
Rent received in advance from clients that will be recognized evenly over the next three years	24,000
Tax rate for year 1 and future years	40%

Prepare the following schedule for the deferred tax amounts for the year. Choose items from the following list:

Items

Premium on life insurance	Warranties
Depreciation	Bad debts
Interest on municipal bonds	Rent received

Item	Difference between taxable amount and income statement amount	Classification: Deferred tax asset Deferred tax liability	Current or noncurrent	Deferred tax amount

Complete the following table to calculate taxable income. If no adjustment is needed for a particular item enter 0 as your calculation.

Pretax financial income	
Premiums on life insurance of key officer	
Interest on municipal bonds	
Depreciation for tax in excess of book depreciation	
Adjustment for warranties	
Adjustment for bad debts	
Adjustment for rent received in advance	
Taxable income	

Task-Based Simulation 7

Research		
	Authoritative Literature	Help

    Assume that you are assigned to the audit of Carson Corporation. The CFO of Carson is unsure of the tax rate that should be used to calculate deferred taxes. Which section of the Professional Standards provides guidance on the tax rate that should be used to calculate deferred taxes? Enter your response in the answer fields below.

Task-Based Simulation 8

Research		
	Authoritative Literature	Help

    Using the authoritative literature from the accounting standards, identify the appropriate paragraph that provides the definition for deferred tax expense. Enter the exact section number and paragraphs and subparagraphs in the following fields.

FAS ACS

Simulation Solutions

Task-Based Simulation 1

Tax Calculations		
	Authoritative Literature	
		Help

	Specific audit objective	(A) (B) (C) (D) (E) (F) (G) (H) (I) (J) (K) (L) (M) (N)
1.	Current tax expense for the year ended April 30, year 1.	○ ○ ○ ○ ○ ○ ● ○ ○ ○ ○ ○ ○ ○
2.	Cumulative temporary differences at April 30, year 2.	○ ○ ○ ○ ○ ○ ○ ○ ○ ○ ○ ○ ● ○
3.	Deferred tax expense for the year ended April 30, year 2.	○ ● ○ ○ ○ ○ ○ ○ ○ ○ ○ ○ ○ ○
4.	Deferred tax liability at April 30, year 3.	○ ○ ○ ○ ○ ○ ○ ● ○ ○ ○ ○ ○ ○

Explanations

1. **(G)** Current tax expense for FY 1 is equal to taxable income (Form 1120) of $600,000 times 20% or $120,000.

2. **(M)** The $100,000 temporary difference for FY 2 is deducted from pretax financial income to arrive at taxable income. Therefore, cumulative temporary differences or future taxable amounts are increased. Thus, $300,000 ($200,000 + $100,000) will be added to pretax financial income in future reversal years.

3. **(B)** Deferred tax expense is equal to the increased rate on future taxable amounts outstanding at the beginning of FY 2 plus the amount related to the $100,000 of temporary differences that originated in FY 2. Thus, deferred tax expense is equal to $35,000 [$200,000 × (.25 − .20) + $100,000 × .25]. The entry is

Deferred tax expense   35,000
    Deferred tax liability   35,000

4. **(H)** In FY 3 cumulative temporary differences (future taxable amounts) increased by $150,000. The deferred tax liability account for three years is shown below.

Deferred Tax Liability	
	Year 1
40,000	(200,000 × .20)
	Year 2
10,000	[200,000 × (.25 − .20)]
25,000	(100,000 × .25)
	Year 3
15,000	[300,000 × (.30 − .25)]
45,000	(150,000 × .30)
	Bal. 135,000

The $135,000 is equal to the cumulative temporary differences of $450,000 ×.30.

Task-Based Simulation 2

Tax Differences		
	Authoritative Literature	
		Help

		A Temporary difference DTA	B Temporary difference DTL	C Permanent difference
1.	For plant assets, the depreciation expense deducted for tax purposes is in excess of the depreciation expense used for financial reporting purposes.	○	●	○
2.	A landlord collects some rents in advance. Rents received are taxable in the period in which they are received.	●	○	○

		A Temporary difference DTA	B Temporary difference DTL	C Permanent difference
3.	Interest is received on an investment in tax-exempt municipal obligations.	○	○	●
4.	Costs of guarantees and warranties are estimated and accrued for financial reporting purposes.	●	○	○
5.	Life insurance proceeds are collected on the death of a key officer.	○	○	●
6.	Bad debts are estimated and expensed on the income statement. No bad debts were charged to the allowance account and written off during the year.	●	○	○
7.	Goodwill is deducted on the tax return.	○	●	○

Explanations

1. (B) In cases in which tax depreciation is greater than accounting (book) depreciation, taxable income will be less than accounting income and a deferred tax liability results. The reason is that in future years tax depreciation will be less than book depreciation and taxable income will be greater than book income. This will result in future cash flows for the income tax liability shown on the Form 1120 exceeding those that would occur based on pretax accounting income. Thus a deferred tax liability will result. The entry is

        Deferred income tax expense   xx
            Deferred tax liability   xx

In the reversal year, the entry would be

        Deferred tax liability   xx
            Deferred tax expense   xx

2. (A) Taxable income will exceed pretax accounting (book) income in the year in which the rents are received. In effect, income taxes on the portion of the rent that is unearned for financial reporting under GAAP must be prepaid under the Internal Revenue Code. Thus, a deferred tax asset would result because in future years when the rent received in advance is earned, no taxes will be payable on the amount earned, because the taxes were paid in the year rent was received. The entry is

        Deferred tax asset   xx
            Deferred tax expense   xx

3. (C) Interest earned on a tax-exempt municipal obligation is a permanent difference. The interest is deducted in the year received from pretax accounting income to arrive at taxable income. However, it will never be reported as income on the firm's Form 1120. Therefore, such a difference does not result in deferred income taxes.

4. (A) Costs of guarantees and warranties are not deductible under the Internal Revenue Code until incurred. Under ASC Topic 450, however they are estimated and recorded as an expense (loss) and a liability in the period of sale. In effect, income taxes are prepaid because in later years a benefit is received when these costs are incurred and deducted on the tax return. The entry in the origination year is

        Deferred tax asset   xx
            Deferred tax expense   xx

The entry when the warranty costs are deducted is

        Deferred tax expense   xx
            Deferred tax asset   xx

5. (C) life insurance proceeds are not taxable under the Internal Revenue Code. This gives rise to a permanent difference.

6. (A) The Internal Revenue Code requires the direct write-off method for bad debts. Therefore, bad debts cannot be deducted until the debt becomes uncollectible and is written off. Since no deduction is allowed in the current year, this leads to a future deductible amount and is a deferred tax asset.

7. (B) Goodwill is amortized for tax purposes and tested for impairment for GAAP purposes. Therefore, it results in a temporary difference.

Task-Based Simulation 3

Deferred Tax Classification		
	Authoritative Literature	Help

	Deferred tax asset	Deferred tax liability	Current	Noncurrent
1. Tax depreciation in excess of book depreciation	○	●	○	●
2. Bad debts expense in excess of actual write-offs	●	○	●	○
3. Rent collected in advance for next 12 months	●	○	●	○

Task-Based Simulation 4

Research		
	Authoritative Literature	Help

ASC	740	10	05	7

Task-Based Simulation 5

Temporary and Permanent Differences		
	Authoritative Literature	Help

	Temporary	Permanent
Premiums on life insurance of key officer	○	●
Depreciation	●	○
Interest on municipal bonds	○	●
Warranties	●	○
Bad debts	●	○
Rent received in advance from clients	●	○

Task-Based Simulation 6

Deferred Tax Schedule		
	Authoritative Literature	Help

Item	Difference between taxable amount and income statement amount	Classification: Deferred tax asset Deferred tax liability	Current or noncurrent	Deferred tax amount
Depreciation	12,000	Deferred tax liability	Noncurrent	4,800
Warranties	750	Deferred tax asset	Current	300
Bad debts	800	Deferred tax asset	Current	320
Rent received	8,000	Deferred tax asset	Current	3,200
Rent received	16,000	Deferred tax asset	Noncurrent	6,400

Explanations

The adjustment to warranties is the difference between warranty expense deducted on the income statement and the actual warranty work performed during the period ($4,000 – $3,250 = $750). The adjustment to bad debt is the difference between bad debt expense subtracted on the balance sheet, and the actual bad debts written off during the period ($1,400 – $600 = $800). Note that rent received is taxable in the period received, and for deferred tax purposes, it must be fragmented into two components, current and noncurrent.

Pretax financial income	$400,000
Premiums on life insurance of key officer	10,000
Interest on municipal bonds	(5,300)
Depreciation for tax in excess of book depreciation	(12,000)
Adjustment for warranties	750
Adjustment for bad debts	800
Adjustment for rent received in advance	24,000
Taxable income	$418,250

Task-Based Simulation 7

Research			
	Authoritative Literature	Help	

ASC	740	10	30	8

Task-Based Simulation 8

Research			
	Authoritative Literature	Help	

FAS ACS	740	10	30	4

Module 15: Stockholders' Equity

Overview

Stockholders' equity is the residual of assets minus liabilities (i.e., net assets). Due to the number of fraudulent manipulations involving stocks, many states have legislated accounting for stockholders' equity transactions, and they are controlled to some degree (e.g., conditions under which dividends may be paid).

This module covers accounts located within stockholders' equity (e.g., common stock) and events affecting stockholders' equity (e.g., bankruptcy).

Common stockholders' equity consists of two major categories: contributed capital and retained earnings. Retained earnings are either appropriated or unappropriated. Paid-in capital consists of paid-in excess and legal capital. Legal capital is the par or stated value of stock.

When significant changes occur in stockholders' equity accounts, enterprises are required to disclose them. Most companies satisfy this requirement by issuing a statement of changes in stockholders' equity (illustrated below). These statements show changes in the number of shares (not included due to space limits) as well as dollars between balance sheet dates. The statement of changes in stockholders' equity may also be used to report comprehensive income.

Northern Corporation
STATEMENT OF CHANGES IN STOCKHOLDERS' EQUITY
For the Year Ended December 31, Year 2

	Common stock	Comprehensive income	Retained earnings	Accumulated other comprehensive income	Total
Balances, January 1, year 2	$1,500,000		$213,675	$ (3,450)	$1,710,225
Comprehensive income					
Net income		$63,250	63,250		
Other comprehensive income:					
Foreign currency translation adjustments, net of tax		8,000			
Unrealized gains on securities:					
Unrealized holding gains arising during period, net of tax		13,000			
Less: reclassification adjustment, net of tax, for gain included in net income		(4,000)			

	Common stock	Comprehensive income	Retained earnings	Accumulated other comprehensive income	Total
Other comprehensive income		17,000		17,000	
Comprehensive income		80,250			80,250
Proceeds from issuance of shares	200,000				200,000
Dividends paid	--		(24,825)		(24,825)
Balances, December 31, year 2	$1,700,000		$252,100	$13,550	$1,965,650

A. Common Stock

1. The entry to record the issuance of common stock is

Cash	(amount received)
Common stock	(par or stated value)
Paid-in capital in excess of par	(forced)

a. If stock is sold for less than par, a discount account is debited.

b. Very little stock is issued at a discount because of the resulting potential liability to the original purchaser for the difference between the issue price (when less than par) and par which in many states is legal capital. This liability has been avoided by the use of stated value and no par stock, but is mainly avoided by establishing par values below market.

2. Control accounts are occasionally used to control unissued stock.

a. At authorization

Unissued common stock	(total par or stated value)
Common stock authorized	(same)

b. At issuance

Cash	(cash received)
Unissued common stock	(par or stated value)
Paid-in capital in excess of par	(forced)

(1) The credit balance in the authorized account is the total available for issuance. The debit balance in the unissued account is the amount not issued. Thus, authorized (cr) – unissued (dr) = issued (cr). The unissued account is an offset account to the authorized account.

3. No-par stock is occasionally issued (i.e., no par or stated value exists). All of the proceeds from issuance of no-par stock are credited to "common stock."

4. Costs of registering and issuing common stock are generally netted against the proceeds (i.e., reduce "paid-in capital in excess of par"). An alternative method is to consider stock issue costs an organizational cost.

Legal expenses	(FMV)
Assets	(FMV)
Common stock	(par)
Paid-in capital in excess of par	(forced)

B. Preferred Stock

As implied, preferred stock has preferential rights: most commonly the right to receive dividends prior to common stockholders. Generally the dividend payout is specified (e.g., 7% of par). Additional possible features are

1. **Participating**—share with common stockholders in dividend distributions after both preferred and common stockholders receive a specified level of dividend payment

a. Participation with common stockholders in dividends is usually specified in terms of a percentage of legal capital. For example, 7% preferred receive 7% of their par value in dividends before common stockholders receive dividends. Fully participating preferred would receive the same percentage dividend as common stockholders if the common stockholders received over a 7% (of par value) dividend.

2. **Cumulative**—dividends not paid in any year (dividends in arrears) must be made up before distributions can be made to common stockholders

a. However, dividends in arrears are not a liability until declared. They should be disclosed parenthetically or in the footnotes.

3. **Convertible**—preferred stockholders have an option of exchanging their stock for common stock at a specified ratio

   a. Conversion is usually accounted for at book value

Preferred stock	(par converted)
Preferred paid-in accounts	(related balances)
Common stock	(par)
Paid-in capital in excess of par	(forced)

   b. If market value is used, common stock and paid-in excess are credited for the market value, usually resulting in a large debit to retained earnings. (Plug figure in the journal entry.)

4. **Callable**—the corporation has the option to repurchase the preferred stock at a specified price

   a. If called, no gain or loss is recognized on the income statement. Gains are taken to a paid-in capital account; losses are charged to retained earnings.

Preferred stock	(par)
Preferred paid-in accounts	(related balances)
Retained earnings	(if dr. needed)
Cash	(amount paid)
Paid-in capital from preferred retirement	(if cr. needed)

5. Any of the above features present in a preferred stock issuance should be disclosed parenthetically in the balance sheet next to the account title.

6. Any financial instrument that imposes an obligation on the issuer to transfer assets or issue equity shares is classified as a liability.

   a. Therefore, mandatorily **redeemable preferred stock** must be classified as liabilities on the balance sheet.

   b. The SEC requires that preferred securities redeemable for cash or other assets should be classified outside of permanent equity (as temporary equity) if the preferred stock is redeemable at a fixed or determinable price on a fixed or determinable date; at the option of the holder, or upon the occurrence of an event not within the control of the issuer.

C. Stock Subscriptions

   Stock (common/preferred) can be subscribed by investors. A receivable is established and "stock subscribed" credited. When the total subscription price is received, the stock (common/preferred) is issued.

1. At subscription

Cash	(any cash received)
Subscription receivable	(balance)
Common stock subscribed	(par)
Paid-in capital in excess of par	(subscription price > par)

2. Cash receipt and issuance

Cash	(balance)
Subscriptions receivable	(balance)
Common stock subscribed	(par)
Common stock*	(par)

   * Unissued common stock, if unissued and authorized accounts are being used.

3. Upon default of subscription agreements, depending on the agreement, the amount paid to date may be

   a. Returned to subscriber

   b. Kept by company

   c. Held to cover any losses on resale and balance returned

4. If returned

Common stock subscribed	(par)
Paid-in capital in excess of par	(subscription price > par)
Cash	(any cash received)
Subscriptions receivable	(balance)

   a. If kept by the company, no cash would be paid and "paid-in from subscription default" credited instead of cash.

   b. If held to cover any losses on resale, a "refundable subscription deposit" liability would be credited instead of cash. If the stock were resold at less than the original subscription price, the difference would be debited to "refundable subscription deposit."

Cash	(payment)	
Refundable subscription deposit	(forced)	
Stock		(par)
Paid-in capital in excess of par		(amount from original sale)

(1) The balance in the refundable subscription account would be paid (possibly in an equivalent number of shares) to the original subscriber.

> **NOW REVIEW MULTIPLE-CHOICE QUESTIONS 1 THROUGH 11**

D. Treasury Stock Transactions

A firm's own stock repurchased on the open market is known as treasury stock. Treasury stock is **not** an asset, as a firm may not own shares of itself. Instead it is treated as a reduction of stockholders' equity. Furthermore, a firm may only recognize a gain or loss on assets, not on transactions with its own stockholders. Therefore the terms "above cost" and "below cost" will be used instead of gain or loss. There are two methods of accounting for treasury stock: cost and par value.

1. **Cost Method**

   a. Under the **cost method,** treasury stock is debited for the cost of treasury stock.
   b. Any difference between the cost of the treasury stock and the resale price is recognized at the point of resale. However, such amounts are not included in the determination of periodic income.

   (1) Resale amounts **above cost** are credited to "paid-in capital from treasury stock transactions."
   (2) Resale amounts **below cost** should be charged first to "paid-in capital from treasury stock (TS) transactions" or "paid-in capital from stock retirement" to the extent that either of these exists for that class of stock. The remainder of any amount from sales below cost is to be charged to retained earnings.
   (3) In essence a one-transaction viewpoint is used, as the firm is treated as a middle "person" for the transfer of stock between two shareholders.

2. **Par Value Method**

   Under the **par value** method, all capital balances associated with the treasury shares are removed upon acquisition.

   a. Any excess of treasury stock cost over par value is accounted for by charging "paid-in capital from common stock" for the amount in excess of par received when the shares were originally issued.
   b. Any excess of the cost of acquiring the treasury stock over the original issue cost is charged to retained earnings.
   c. If treasury stock is acquired at a cost equal to or less than the original issue cost, "paid-in capital from common stock" is charged (debited) for the original amount in excess of par and "paid-in capital from treasury stock" is credited for the difference between the original issue price and the cost to acquire the treasury stock.
   d. When the treasury stock is resold, it is treated as a typical issuance, with the excess of selling price over par credited to "paid-in capital from common stock."

> **NOTE:** The par value method takes on a two-transaction viewpoint. The purchase is treated as a "retirement" of the shares, while the subsequent sale of the shares is treated as a "new" issue.

EXAMPLE

100 shares ($50 par) are originally sold at $60, reacquired at $70, and subsequently resold at $75.

Cost method			Par value method		
Treasury stock	7,000		Treasury stock	5,000	
Cash		7,000	Paid-in capital—common		
			stock	1,000	
			Retained earnings	1,000	
			Cash		7,000
Cash	7,500		Cash	7,500	
Treasury stock		7,000	Treasury stock		5,000
Paid-in capital—			Paid-in capital—		
treasury stock		500	common stock		2,500

If the shares had been resold at $65:

Cost method			Par value method		
Cash	6,500		Cash	6,500	
Retained earnings*	500		Treasury stock		5,000
Treasury stock		7,000	Paid-in capital—		
			common stock		1,500

* "Paid-in capital—treasury stock" or "paid-in capital—retired stock" of that issue would be debited first to the extent it exists.

NOTE: Total stockholders' equity is not affected by the method selected; only the allocation among the equity accounts is different.

E. Retirement of Stock

Formal retirement or constructive retirement (purchase with no intent of reissue) of stock is handled very similarly to treasury stock.

1. When formally retired

Common stock	xx	
Paid-in capital in excess of par*	xx	
Retained earnings*	xx	
Treasury stock*		xx

* Assuming a loss on the retirement of treasury stock

a. "Paid-in capital from treasury stock transactions" may be debited to the extent it exists
b. A pro rata portion of all paid-in capital existing for that issue (e.g., if 2% of an issue is retired, up to 2% of all existing paid-in capital for that issue may be debited)

(1) Alternatively, the entire or any portion of the loss may be debited to retained earnings. Any gains are credited to a "paid-in capital from retirement" account.

NOW REVIEW MULTIPLE-CHOICE QUESTIONS 12 THROUGH 22

F. Dividends

1. At the date of declaration, an entry is made to record the dividend liability.

Retained earnings (dividends)	xx	
Dividends payable		xx

2. No entry is made at the date of record. Those owning stock at the date of record will be paid the previously declared dividends.

a. The stockholder records consist of

(1) General ledger account
(2) Subsidiary ledger

(a) Contains names and addresses of stockholders

(3) Stock certificate book

b. Outside services: (usually banks)

(1) Transfer agent issues new certificates, canceling old, and maintains stockholder ledger
(2) Registrar validates new certificates and controls against overissuance
(3) Functions are now becoming combined

3. At the payment date, the liability is paid.

Dividends payable	xx	
Cash		xx

4. **Property dividends** are dividends payable in an asset other than cash, but the entries are similar to those of cash dividends.

a. They are recorded at fair value (FV) of the asset transferred with a gain (loss) recognized on the difference between the asset's book value (BV) and FV at disposition.

5. **Liquidating dividends** (dividends based on other than earnings) are a return of capital to stockholders and should be so disclosed.

   a. Paid-in capital is usually debited rather than retained earnings. Common stock cannot be debited because it is the legal capital which can only be eliminated upon corporate dissolution.

6. **Scrip dividends** are issuance of promises to pay dividends in the future (and may bear interest) instead of cash.

   Retained earnings   xx
       Scrip dividends payable   xx

   Scrip dividends are a liability which is extinguished by payment.

   Scrip dividends payable   xx
   Interest expense (maybe)   xx
       Cash   xx

7. Unlike cash and property dividends, stock dividends are not a liability when declared. They can be rescinded, as nothing is actually being distributed to stockholders except more stock certificates. Current assets are not used to "pay" the dividend.

   a. After stock dividends, shareholders continue to own the same proportion of the corporation.
   b. At declaration

   Retained earnings   (FV of shares)
       Stock dividend distributable   (par)
       Paid-in capital in excess of par   (plug)

   c. At issuance

   Stock dividend distributable   xx
       Common stock   xx

   d. Charge retained earnings for FV of stock dividend if less than 20%-25% increase in stock outstanding; charge RE for **par value** of stock dividend if greater than 20-25% increase in stock outstanding.

   (1) Not required if closely held company

NOW REVIEW MULTIPLE-CHOICE QUESTIONS 23 THROUGH 35

G. Stock Splits

Stock splits change the number of shares outstanding and the par value per share.

1. Par value is reduced in proportion to the increase in the number of shares.
2. The total par value outstanding does not change and no charge is made to retained earnings.
3. If legal requirements preclude changing the par or stated value, charge retained earnings only for the par or stated value issued.

STOCK DIVIDENDS AND SPLITS: SUMMARY OF EFFECTS

	Total S.E.	Par value per share	Total par outstanding	RE	Legal capital	Additional paid-in capital	No. of shares outstanding
Stock dividend < 20-25% of shares outstanding	N/C	N/C	+	Decrease by market value of shares issued	+	+	+
Stock split effected in form of dividend > 20 – 25% of shares outstanding	N/C	N/C	+	Decrease by par value of shares issued	+	N/C	+
Stock split	N/C	Decrease proportion-ately	N/C	N/C	N/C	N/C	+

N/C = No Change
+ = Increase
Prepared by Professor John R. Simon, Northern Illinois University

H. Appropriations of Retained Earnings (Reserves)

An entry to appropriate retained earnings restricts the amount of retained earnings that is available for dividends.

RE (or Unappropriated RE)   xx
    Reserve for RE (or Appropriated RE)   xx

> **NOTE:** The restriction of retained earnings does not necessarily provide cash for any intended purpose. The purpose is to show that **assets** in the amount of the appropriation are not available for dividends. When a reserve is no longer needed it must be returned directly to unappropriated retained earnings by reversing the entry that created it.

NOW REVIEW MULTIPLE-CHOICE QUESTIONS 36 THROUGH 41

I. Share-Based Payments

Share-based payments are transactions wherein an entity acquires goods or services by issuing shares (stock), share options, or other equity instruments. It also includes transactions with an employee or supplier wherein the entity incurs a liability that is based on the price of the entity's shares or that will be settled using equity shares.

1. There are two important distinctions for applying the rules for share-based payments:

   a. Is the share-based payment to employees or nonemployees?
   b. Is the share-based payment considered equity or a liability?

2. **Share-based payments to nonemployees.** Share-based payments to nonemployees for goods and services are measured at the fair value of the equity instruments or the fair value of the goods and services, whichever is more reliable.

3. **Share-based payments to employees.** Share-based payments to employees are measured based on the fair-value-based method. The cost of the services is measured at the grant-date fair value of the equity instruments issued, or the fair value of the liability incurred. Employee service cost is based on fair value net of any amount the employee pays or is obligated to pay for the instrument.

   a. The fair value of an equity share option is measured based on the observable market price of an option with the same or similar terms and conditions, or estimated using an option-pricing model.

      (1) If it is not possible to estimate fair value at the grant date, the compensation cost is measured using the intrinsic value at the end of each reporting period, and final compensation cost is measured at the settlement date.

         (a) The intrinsic value is the difference between the market value of the stock and the price the employee must pay.

   b. Compensation cost for share-based employee compensation classified as equity is amortized on a straight-line basis over the requisite service period.

      (1) The **requisite service period** is the period in which the employee is required to provide services, which is usually the vesting period.
      (2) The **service inception date** is the beginning of the requisite service period.
      (3) Firms must estimate the number of forfeitures that will occur.

         (a) No compensation cost is recognized if an employee forfeits shares because a service or performance condition is not met.
         (b) However, if an employee renders the requisite service and the share option expires or is unexercised, previously recognized compensation cost is not reversed.

   c. Share-based payments may also be classified as liabilities.

      (1) Puttable shares are considered liabilities if the repurchase feature allows the employee to avoid bearing the risks and rewards for a reasonable period (six months or more).
      (2) The measurement date for liability instruments is the settlement date; therefore, share-based payments are remeasured at the end of each reporting period.
      (3) Compensation cost is the change in fair value of the instrument from one period to the next.

Share-Based Payments		
	Classified as Equity	**Classified as Liability**
When to measure	Grant-date fair value of equity instrument	Each reporting period Final measurement on settlement date
How to measure	Observable market price of option with same or similar terms OR Estimate using option pricing model OR Intrinsic value at end of each reporting period if no market price or estimate can be determined (net of amounts that employee must pay)	Fair value of liability incurred
How to allocate compensation expense	Straight-line over requisite service period	Straight-line over requisite service period

   d. If an option-pricing model (such as Black-Scholes model) is used, the option-pricing model should consider the following variables:

     (1) Current price of the underlying stock
     (2) Exercise price of the option
     (3) Expected life of the option
     (4) Expected volatility of the underlying stock
     (5) Expected dividends on the stock
     (6) Risk-free interest rate during the expected option term

       (a) The resulting fair value shall be applied to the number of options expected to vest (based on the grant date estimate) or the total number of options issued.

J. Accounting Entries for the Share-Based Payments to Employees

   1. **Share-based payments classified as equity**

EXAMPLE

To illustrate the recognition and measurement of stock compensation expense, suppose ABC Corporation (a public company) establishes an employee stock option plan on January 1, year 1. The plan allows its employees to acquire 10,000 shares of its $1 par value common stock at $52 per share, when the market price is also $52. The options may not be exercised until five years from the grant date. The grant-date fair value of an option with similar terms and conditions is $8.62.

Accounting for Stock-Based Compensation
Calculation of Compensation Cost

Fair Value of Option at grant-date	$ 8.62
× Number of options	10,000
Deferred comp. expense	$86,200

The journal entry to recognize the deferred compensation expense in Year 1 is shown below.

Deferred comp. expense	86,200	
Stock options outstanding		86,200

During each of the next five years which is the requisite service period, compensation expense is recognizes as follows:

Compensation expense	17,240	
Deferred comp. expense		17,240

When the option is exercised, cash is received and stock is issued as reflected in the following entry (assume exercise after the five-year period):

Cash	52,000		(option price)
Stock options outstanding	86,200		
Common stock		10,000	(par)
Additional paid-in capital		128,200	(plug)

---

    a. If modifications are made to a shared-based payment plan, the incremental compensation cost is measured by comparing the fair value of the modified plan with the fair value of the plan immediately before the modification.

    b. Deferred compensation is presented in the balance sheet by subtracting the balance in the deferred compensation expense account from stock options outstanding in the paid-in capital section of owners' equity to indicate the net contributed services on any date.

2. **Share-based payments classified as liabilities**

    a. When a share-based payment is treated as a liability, it is measured at the fair value of the liability incurred. The measurement date is the date of settlement. Therefore, the liability is remeasured at the end of each reporting period until the date of settlement.

        (1) Compensation cost for each period is based on the change in fair value of the instrument for each reporting period.

        (2) If the requisite service period has not been completed, the compensation cost recognized is equal to the percentage of the requisite service that has been rendered as of that date.

    b. An example of share-based payment classified as a liability is a stock appreciation right. **Stock appreciation rights** (SAR) allow employees to receive stock or cash equal in amount to the difference between the market value and some predetermined amount per share for a certain number of shares. SARs allow employees to receive the amount of share appreciation without having to make a cash outlay as is common in stock option plans.

    c. For financial reporting purposes, compensation expense is the excess of market value over a predetermined amount.

        (1) Compensation expense is recorded in each period prior to exercise based on the excess of market value at the end of each period over a predetermined amount.

        (2) Compensation expense is adjusted up or down as the market value of the stock changes before the measurement date (which is the exercise date). Therefore, compensation expense could be credited (reduced) if the stock's market value drops from one period to the next.

EXAMPLE

Assume a company grants 100 SAR, payable in cash, to an employee on 1/1/Y1. The predetermined amount for the SAR plan is $50 per right, and the market value of the stock is $55 on 12/31/Y1, $53 on 12/31/Y2, and $61 on 12/31/Y3. Compensation expense recorded in each year would be

Total expense – Exp. previously accrued = Current expense

Year 1	100 ($55 – $50)	=	$ 500 – $ 0	=	$ 500	
Year 2	100 ($53 – $50)	=	$ 300 – $500	=	$ (200)	
Year 3	100 ($61 – $50)	=	$1,100 – $300	=	$ 800	

The total expense recognized over the three-year period is $1,100 [100($61 – $50)]. Journal entries would be

Year 1 and Year 3		**Year 2**	
Compensation expense	$500/$800	Liability under SAR plan	$200
Liability under SAR plan	$500/$800	Compensation expense	$200

[If the SAR were to be redeemed in common stock, Stock Rights Outstanding (a paid-in capital account) would replace the liability account in the above entries.]

The above example assumes no service or vesting period, which is the period of time until the SAR become exercisable. If the above plan had a two-year service period, 50% of the total expense would be recognized at the end of the first year, and 100% at the end of the second year and thereafter until exercised. The compensation would be accrued as follows:

Year 1	$ (500) (50%)	=	$ 250 – $ 0	=	$250
Year 2	$ (300) (100%)	=	$ 300 – $250	=	$ 50
Year 3	$(1,100) (100%)	=	$1,100 – $300	=	$800

---

3. **Disclosures**

    a. Excess tax benefits are recognized as additional paid-in capital.

    b. Cash retained as a result of excess tax benefits are presented in the statement of cash flows as a cash inflow from financing activities (not as a reduction of taxes paid).

    c. Diluted earnings per share is based on the actual number of options or shares granted and not yet forfeited, unless the shares are antidilutive.

(1) If equity share options are outstanding for only a part of a period, the shares are weighted to reflect the portion of time outstanding.

d. Disclosures for share-based payments should include the following:

(1) The nature and terms of arrangements during the period and potential effects on shareholders
(2) The effect of compensation cost from share-based arrangements on the income statement
(3) The method of estimating the fair value of goods or services received, or fair value of the equity instruments granted during the period
(4) The cash flow effects from share-based payments

NOW REVIEW MULTIPLE-CHOICE QUESTIONS 42 THROUGH 54

K. Basic Earnings Per Share

NOTE: CPA candidates must be able to compute both basic and diluted earnings per share (EPS). In addition to the computations, candidates should also understand the presentation and disclosure requirements.

1. Only public entities (those who trade their stock on the major stock exchanges and over the counter) are required to present earnings per share.

a. Nonpublic companies often choose to present such information, but they are not required to do so.
b. Before continuing, it is recommended that candidates read the outline of SFAS 128, *Earnings Per Share* (ASC Topic 260), in the back of the FAR section.

2. The objective of EPS is to measure the performance of an entity over the reporting period. Required presentation calls for a **basic** EPS in all situations and a **diluted** EPS in those situations where an entity's capital structure includes potential dilutive securities. Basic and dilutive (when applicable) earnings per share amounts must be presented on the face of the income statement for two elements.

a. Income from continuing operations **and**
b. Net income

3. In those situations where an entity also reports discontinued operations, and/or extraordinary items, the entity **may report** EPS on the face of the income statement or disclose such information in the footnotes to the financial statements.

NOTE: The only required EPS presentations are for income from continuing operations and net income. All other presentations of EPS are optional.

4. Public corporations begin by computing **basic** earnings per share. In this calculation, only those shares of common stock **outstanding** are included. Any **potential** issuance of securities is **ignored**. The computational formula is as follows:

$$\text{Basic EPS} = \frac{\text{Net income available to common stockholders}}{\text{Weighted-average number of common shares \textbf{outstanding}}}$$

a. The **numerator** (net income available to common stockholders) for EPS on **net income** is computed by taking the **net income** and **subtracting**

(1) The dividends **declared** in the period on the **noncumulative preferred stock** (whether paid or not) **and**
(2) The dividends **accumulated** for the current period only on the **cumulative preferred stock** (whether or not declared).

NOTE: Dividends in arrears are excluded from this calculation.

b. The **numerator** (net income available to common stockholders) for EPS on **net income from continuing operations** is computed by taking the **net income** and subtracting any net income or adding any net loss from the following:

(1) Discontinued operations
(2) Extraordinary items
(3) The net income from continuing operations is then adjusted by subtracting the preferred stock dividends as described in points number 1. and 2. above.

c. The following example will illustrate the application of this formula:

EXAMPLE

Numerator information		**Denominator information**	
a. Net income	$100,000	a. Common shares outstanding 1/1/Y1	100,000
		b. Shares issued for cash 4/1	20,000
b. Extraordinary loss (net of tax)	30,000		
c. 6% preferred stock, $100 par, 1,000 shares issued and outstanding ($100,000 × .06)	6,000	c. Shares issued in 10% stock dividend declared in July	12,000
		d. Shares of treasury stock purchased 10/1	10,000

Earnings per common share:

$$\text{On income from continuing operations} = \frac{\$130,000 - 6,000}{\text{Common shares outstanding}}$$

$$\text{Our net income} = \frac{\$100,000 - 6,000}{\text{Common shares outstanding}}$$

---

d. When calculating the amount of the numerator, the claims of senior securities (i.e., preferred stock) should be deducted to arrive at the earnings attributable to common shareholders.

(1) In the example, the preferred stock is cumulative. Thus, regardless of whether or not the board of directors declares a preferred dividend, holders of the preferred stock have a claim of $6,000 (1,000 shares × $6 per share) against year 1 earnings. Therefore, $6,000 is deducted from the numerator to arrive at the net income attributable to common shareholders. Note that this $6,000 would have been **deducted for noncumulative preferred only if a dividend of this amount had been declared**. Cumulative preferred stock dividends for the current period are always deducted whether or not declared.

e. The numerator of the EPS calculation covers a particular time period such as a month, a quarter, or a year. It is, therefore, consistent to calculate the average number of common shares which were outstanding during this same time period. The calculation below in Table I illustrates the determination of weighted-average common shares outstanding.

> **NOTE:** For stock dividends the number of shares is adjusted retroactively for the shares which were outstanding prior to the stock dividend.

(1) Since the stock dividend was issued **after** the issuance of additional shares for cash on 4/1, the shareholders of those additional shares and the shareholders of the shares outstanding at the beginning of the year will receive the stock dividend.

(2) However, if the stock dividend had been issued **before** the issuance of additional shares of stock for cash on 4/1, only the shareholders who own the shares outstanding at the beginning of the period would have received the stock dividend.

(3) Stock splits are handled in an identical fashion.

TABLE I

Dates	Number common shares outstanding	Months outstanding	Fraction of year	Shares × Fraction of year
1/1 to 4/1	100,000 + 10% (100,000) = 110,000	3	¼	27,500
4/1 to 10/1	110,000 + 20,000 + 10% (20,000) = 132,000	6	½	66,000
10/1 to12/31	132,000 − 10,000 = 122,000	3	¼	30,500
	Weighted-average of common shares outstanding			124,000

(a) There is an exception to the general rule that stock dividends and stock splits are treated as if outstanding the entire year. If a stock dividend provides that the shareholders may receive either cash or stock, the dividend is treated as a share issuance, and weighted for the time period outstanding.

(4) In the weighted-average computation, if common shares are issued in a business combination during the year, the common shares are weighted from the date of issuance.

(5) Other complications in the weighted-average calculation are posed by actual conversions of debt and preferred stock to common during the year and by exercise of warrants and options. These situations are introduced in the example presented with diluted earnings per share in the next section.

f. To complete the basic EPS example, the weighted-average number of common shares determined in Table I is divided into the income elements previously computed to arrive at the following:

Earnings per common share

On income from continuing operations $\dfrac{\$130,000 - 6,000}{124,000 \text{ common shares}}$ = \$1,000

On net income $\dfrac{\$100,000 - 6,000}{124,000 \text{ common shares}}$ = \$ .76

(1) The above EPS numbers should be presented on the face of the income statement. Reporting a \$.24 loss per share due to the extraordinary item is optional.

NOW REVIEW MULTIPLE-CHOICE QUESTIONS 55 THROUGH 61

L. Diluted Earnings Per Share

1. **Diluted EPS** measures the performance of the entity over the reporting period (same as basic EPS) while also taking into account the effect of all dilutive potential common shares that were outstanding during the period.

    a. One difference between the computation of diluted and basic EPS is that the denominator of the diluted EPS computation is increased to include the number of additional common shares that would have been outstanding if the dilutive potential common shares had been issued.
    b. In addition, the numerator is adjusted to add back any convertible preferred dividends, the after-tax amount of interest recognized in the period associated with any convertible debt, and any other changes in income (loss) that would result from the assumed conversion of the potential common shares.
    c. Diluted EPS should be based on the security holder's most advantageous conversion rate or exercise price.
    d. Similar to basic EPS, all antidilutive securities are disregarded.

2. The following two independent examples will illustrate the procedures necessary to calculate basic and diluted EPS.

EXAMPLE 1

For both examples, assume net income is \$50,000, and the weighted-average of common shares outstanding is 10,000.

In the first example, assume the following additional information with respect to the capital structure:

1. 4% nonconvertible, cumulative preferred stock, par \$100, 1,000 shares issued and outstanding the entire year
2. Options and warrants to purchase 1,000 shares of common stock at \$8 per share. The average market price of common stock during the year was \$10 and the closing market price was \$12 per share. The options and warrants were outstanding all year.

Diluted EPS must be computed because of the presence of the options and warrants. The preferred stock is not convertible; therefore, it is not a potentially dilutive security.

The first step in the solution of this problem is the determination of the basic EPS. This calculation appears as follows:

$\dfrac{\text{Net income} - \text{Preferred dividends}}{\text{Weighted-average of common shares}} = \dfrac{\$50,000 - 4,000}{10,000 \text{ shares}}$ = \$4.60

NOTE: Preferred dividends are deducted to arrive at net income applicable to common stock. When preferred stock is cumulative, this deduction is made whether or not dividends have been declared.

The calculation of diluted EPS is based upon outstanding common stock and all dilutive common shares that were outstanding during the period. In the example, the options and warrants are the only potentially dilutive security. Options and warrants are considered to be common stock equivalents at all times. Consequently, the only question that must be resolved is whether or not the options and warrants are dilutive.

This question is resolved by comparing the average market price per common share of \$10 with the exercise price of \$8. If the average market price is > the exercise price, the effect of assuming the exercise of options and warrants is dilutive. However, if the average market price is ≤ the exercise price, the effect of assuming the exercise of options and warrants would be antidilutive (i.e., EPS would stay the same or increase). In the example, the options and warrants are dilutive (\$10 > \$8).

The method used to determine the dilutive effects of options and warrants is called the **treasury stock method**.

This method assumes:

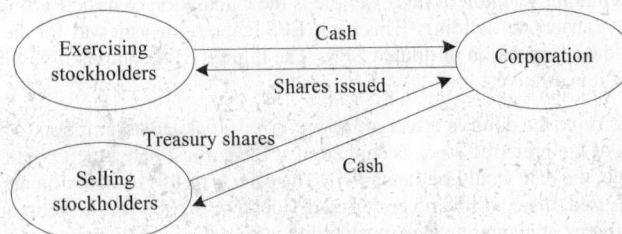

Dilutive effect = Number of shares issued to exercising stockholders − Shares acquired from selling stockholders

In the example above, all of the options and warrants are assumed to be exercised at the beginning of the year (the options and warrants were outstanding the entire year) and the cash received is used to reacquire shares (treasury stock) at the average market price. The computation below illustrates the "treasury stock" method.

Proceeds from assumed exercise of options and warrants (1,000 shares × $8)	$8,000
Number of shares issued	1,000
Number of shares reacquired ($8,000 ÷ $10)	800
Number of shares assumed issued and not reacquired	200

* An alternative approach that can be used to calculate this number for diluted EPS is demonstrated below.

$$\frac{\text{Average market price} - \text{Exercise price}}{\text{Average market price}} \times \text{Number of shares under options/warrants} = \text{Shares not reacquired}$$

$$\frac{\$10-8}{\$10} \times 1,000 \text{ shares} = 200 \text{ shares}$$

Diluted EPS can now be calculated, as follows, including the effects of applying the "treasury stock" method.

$$\frac{\text{Net income} - \text{Preferred dividends}}{\substack{\text{Weighted-average of common shares} \\ \text{outstanding} + \text{Number of shares not acquired} \\ \text{with proceeds from options and warrants}}} = \frac{\$50,000 - 4,000}{10,000 + 200 \text{ shares}} = \$4.51$$

NOTE: The incremental effects of the treasury stock method; there was no effect on the numerator of the EPS calculation while there were 200 shares added to the denominator. Note also that the options and warrants are dilutive. EPS is reduced from $4.60 to $4.51.

a. Table II summarizes the calculations made for the first example involving diluted EPS.

TABLE II

Items	Basic EPS Numerator	Denominator	Diluted EPS Numerator	Denominator
Net income	$50,000		$50,000	
Preferred div.	(4,000)		(4,000)	
Common shares out-standing		10,000 shs.		10,000 shs.
Options and warrants				200
Totals	$46,000 ÷	10,000 shs.	$46,000 ÷	10,200 shs.
EPS	$4.60		$4.51	

EXAMPLE 2

Assume net income is $50,000, and the weighted-average of common shares outstanding is 10,000.

Assume the following additional information:

1. 8% convertible debt, 200 bonds each convertible into 40 common shares. The bonds were outstanding the entire year. The average AA corporate bond yield was 10% at the date the bonds were issued. The income tax rate is 40%. The bonds were issued at par ($1,000 per bond). No bonds were converted during the year.

2. 4% convertible, cumulative preferred stock, par $100, 1,000 shares issued and outstanding. Each preferred share is convertible into 2 common shares. The preferred stock was outstanding the entire year, and the average AA corporate bond yield at the date the preferred stock was issued was 10%. The preferred stock was issued at par. No preferred stock was converted during the year.

The capital structure is **complex** in this example because of the presence of the two convertible securities. The first step in the solution of this example is the calculation of basic EPS based upon weighted-average of common shares outstanding. This basic EPS is the same as it was for the first example (i.e., $4.60). The next step is the computation of diluted EPS. The diluted EPS computation will include the convertible preferred stock if it is dilutive.

To determine the dilutive effect of the preferred stock, an assumption (called the **if-converted method**) is made that all of the preferred stock is converted at the earliest date that it could have occurred during the year. In this example, the date would be January 1. The effects of this assumption are twofold. One, if the preferred stock is converted, there will be no preferred dividend of $4,000 for the year; and, two, there will be an additional 2,000 shares of common stock outstanding during the year (the conversion rate is 2 common for 1 preferred). EPS is computed, as follows, reflecting these two assumptions.

$$\frac{\text{Net income}}{\substack{\text{Weighted-average of common shares} \\ \text{outstanding + Shares issued upon} \\ \text{conversion of preferred stock}}} = \frac{\$50,000}{10,000 + 2,000 \text{ shares}} = \$4.17$$

The convertible preferred stock is **dilutive** because it reduced EPS from $4.60 to $4.17.

In the example, the convertible bonds are assumed to have been converted at the beginning of the year. The effects of this assumption are twofold. One, if the bonds are converted, there will be no interest expense of $16,000 (8% × $200,000 face value); and, two, there will be an additional 8,000 shares (200 bonds × 40 shares) of common stock outstanding during the year. One note of caution, however, must be mentioned; namely, the effect of not having $16,000 of interest expense will increase income, but it will also increase tax expense. Consequently, the net effect of not having interest expense is $9,600 [$16,000 − (40% × $16,000)]. Diluted EPS is computed, as follows, reflecting the dilutive preferred stock and the effects noted above for the convertible bonds:

$$\frac{\text{Net income + Interest expense (net of tax)}}{\substack{\text{Weighted-average of common shares outstanding} \\ \text{+ Shares issued upon conversion of preferred and} \\ \text{conversion of bonds}}} = \frac{\$50,000 + 9,600}{10,000 + 2,000 + 8,000 \text{ shares}} = \$2.98$$

The convertible debt is **dilutive**. Both the convertible bonds and preferred stock reduced EPS from $4.60 to $2.98. Table III summarizes the computations made for the second example.

The income statement **disclosures** for EPS, as a result of the second example, would be as follows:

Earnings per common share (see Note X) $4.60
Earnings per common share assuming dilution   2.98

Note X would state the assumptions made in determining both basic and diluted EPS numbers.

b. Table III summarizes the computations made for the second example.

TABLE III

Items	Basic EPS Numerator	Basic EPS Denominator	Diluted EPS Numerator	Diluted EPS Denominator
Net income	$50,000		$50,000	
Preferred div.	(4,000)			
Common shares outstanding		10,000 shs.		10,000 shs.
Conversion of preferred				2,000
Conversion of bonds			9,600	8,000
Totals	$46,000 ÷	10,000 shs.	$59,600 ÷	20,000 shs.
EPS	$4.60		$2.98	

c. In the two examples, all of the potentially dilutive securities were outstanding the entire year and no conversions or exercises were made during the year. If a potentially dilutive security was not outstanding the entire year, then the numerator and denominator effects would have to be "time-weighted."

EXAMPLE

Suppose the convertible bonds in the second example were issued during the current year on July 1. If all other facts remain unchanged, diluted EPS would be computed as follows:

$$\frac{\text{Net income + Interest expense (net of tax)}}{\substack{\text{Weighted-average of common shares outstanding +}\\\text{Shares issued upon conversion of preferred and}\\\text{conversion of bonds}}} = \frac{\$50,000 + \frac{1}{2}(9,600)}{10,000 + 2,000 + \frac{1}{2}(8,000)} = \$3.43$$

The convertible debt is dilutive whether or not it is outstanding the entire year or for part of a year.

---

d. If actual conversions or exercises take place during a period, the common shares issued will be outstanding from their date of issuance and, therefore, will be in the weighted-average of common shares outstanding. These shares are then weighted from their respective times of issuance.

EXAMPLE

For example, assume that all the bonds in the second example are converted on July 1 into 8,000 common shares. Several important effects should be noted, as follows:

1. The weighted-average of common shares outstanding will be increased by (8,000)(.5) or 4,000. Income will increase by $4,800 net of tax because the bonds are no longer outstanding.
2. The "if converted" method is applied to the period January 1 to July 1 because it was during this period that the bonds were potentially dilutive. The interest expense, net of tax, of $4,800 is added to the income, and 4,000 shares (.5 of 8,000) are added to the denominator.
3. Interestingly, the net effect of items 1 and 2 is the same for the period whether these dilutive bonds were outstanding the entire period or converted during the period.

---

e. It should also be noted that when convertible debt is issued for a premium or discount, the interest expense net of taxes must be computed after giving effect to premium/discount amortization.
f. The benchmark used to determine if including individual securities decreases income is income from continuing operations unless an enterprise has no discontinued operations. In that case income before extraordinary items would be the benchmark number.

3. **Redemption of preferred stock.** The SEC requires that if preferred stock is redeemed, the difference between the fair value of the consideration transferred and the carrying amount of the preferred stock should be treated the same as a divided to preferred shareholders in calculating earnings per share.

   a. If the consideration transferred is greater than the carrying amount of the preferred stock, it should be subtracted from net income in the calculation of EPS.
   b. If the consideration transferred is less than the carrying amount, then it should be added to net income in calculating the numerator for EPS.

4. **Contingent issuances of common stock.** Also mentioned are **contingent issuances** of common stock (e.g., stock subscriptions). If shares are to be issued in the future with no restrictions on issuance other than the passage of time, they are to be considered issued and treated as outstanding in the computation of dilutive EPS. Other issuances that are dependent upon certain conditions being met are to be evaluated in a different respect.

   a. If the contingency is to merely maintain the earnings levels currently being attained, then the shares are considered outstanding for the entire period and considered in the computation of dilutive EPS if the effect is dilutive.
   b. If the requirement is to increase earnings over a period of time, the diluted EPS computation shall include those shares that would be issued based on the assumption that current amount of earnings will remain unchanged, if the effect is dilutive.

5. **EPS on comprehensive income and other comprehensive income components.** EPS numbers below net income are not required for comprehensive income components.

NOW REVIEW MULTIPLE-CHOICE QUESTIONS 62 THROUGH 70

M. Corporate Bankruptcy

1. The **going concern** assumption is one of the basic principles underlying the primary financial statements (balance sheet, income statement and statement of cash flows). However, this assumption of continued existence is threatened in corporations that are in severe financial trouble.

   a. A range of alternative actions is available to a company before it enters bankruptcy, such as seeking extensions on due dates of debt, restructuring its debt, or allowing a court-appointed trustee to manage the corporation.

      (1) These pre-bankruptcy options are presented in the following modules:

         (a) Creditor's agreements—Module 30, Bankruptcy
         (b) Troubled debt restructurings—Module 13, Present Value, Section C

2. Bankruptcy is the final legal act for a company. In bankruptcy, the accounting and financial reporting must present the information necessary for the liquidation of the business.

   a. The **Statement of Affairs** is prepared to present the current market values of the assets and the status of the various categories of the equity interests of the corporation.

      (1) The **Statement of Affairs** classifies assets in the following order of priority (highest to lowest):

         (a) Assets pledged with fully secured creditors—assets having a fair valuation equal to or greater than the debts for which they serve as collateral
         (b) Assets pledged with partially secured creditors—assets having a fair valuation less than their associated debts
         (c) Free assets—uncommitted assets available for remaining equity interests

   b. The accountant must provide a prioritization of the creditors' claims against the net assets of the corporation. The legal rights of each creditor are determined by the terms of the credit agreement it has with the company and by the National Bankruptcy Act.

      (1) The equity interests are classified in the following order (highest to lowest):

         (a) Preferred claims—these claims have priority as specified in the Bankruptcy Act
         (b) Fully secured creditors—these are claims which should be fully covered with the realizations from the assets pledged to the claims
         (c) Partially secured creditors—these are claims which may not be fully covered by the realizations of the pledged assets for these claims; the amount of the uncovered claims goes to the unsecured creditors category
         (d) Unsecured creditors—these are claims that have no priority and do not have any collateral claims to any specific assets
         (e) Stockholders' equity—this represents any residual claim

   c. The historical cost valuation principles used in a balance sheet assume a going concern assumption.

      (1) As a business enters bankruptcy, the liquidation values of the assets become the most relevant measures. In addition, anticipated costs of liquidation should be recognized.
      (2) The Statement of Affairs begins with the present book values of the company's assets in order to articulate with the balance sheet. After relating the projected proceeds from the liquidation of the assets to the various equity interests, the statement concludes with the estimated dollar amount of unsecured claims that cannot be paid (estimated deficiency).

EXAMPLE

The Vann Corporation's balance sheet for December 31, year 1, is shown below. The corporation is entering bankruptcy and expects to incur $8,000 of costs for the liquidation process. The estimated current values of the assets are determined and the various equity claims are prioritized. The Statement of Affairs for Vann Corporation is presented on the following page.

The Vann Corporation
BALANCE SHEET
December 31, Year 1

Assets	
Cash	$ 1,500
Marketable securities	10,000
Accounts receivable (net)	18,000
Merchandise inventory	41,000
Prepaid expenses	2,000

Assets	
Land	6,000
Building (net of depreciation)	65,000
Machinery (net of depreciation)	21,000
Goodwill	10,000
	$174,500
Equities	
Accounts payable	$ 30,000
Notes payable	37,000
Accrued wages	6,500
Mortgages payable	45,000
Capital stock ($10 par)	100,000
Retained earnings (deficit)	(44,000)
	$174,500

NOW REVIEW MULTIPLE-CHOICE QUESTIONS 71 THROUGH 73

N. Reorganizations

Chapter 11 of the Bankruptcy Reform Act of 1978 and The Bankruptcy Abuse and Consumer Protection Act of 2005 allow legal protection from creditors to provide time for a bankrupt corporation to return its operations to a profitable level.

1. The balance sheet, income statement, and statement of cash flows must distinguish events and transactions related with the reorganization from those related to ongoing operations.
2. Liabilities should be reported at expected amounts per the plan on the balance sheet. Liabilities should be classified as unsecured or secured liabilities before reorganization and liabilities incurred after the filing date for Chapter 11.
3. Transactions directly related to the reorganization should be reported separately on the income statement in the period incurred, and disclosure should be made of any anticipated changes in common stock or common stock equivalents.
4. Cash flows related to the reorganization should be reported separately from those related to regular operations.
5. At confirmation of the plan of reorganization, an entity may be considered a new entity for reporting purposes if the reorganization value of assets before confirmation is less than liabilities incurred after petition for Chapter 11 and voting shareholders before confirmation receive less than 50% of the voting shares of the emerging entity.
6. If the entity does not qualify as a new entity, the reorganization should be accounted for as troubled debt restructuring which is discussed in Module 13C.

O. Quasi Reorganization

The purpose of a quasi reorganization is to allow companies to avoid formal bankruptcy proceedings through an informal proceeding. The procedure is applicable for a situation where a going concern exists except for overvalued assets and a possible deficit. The overvalued assets result in high depreciation charges and losses or lower net income. The deficit precludes payment of dividends. The procedure is applicable during a period of declining price levels (normally associated with decreased economic activity), such as the 1930s.

1. The procedures involve

   a. Proper authorization including that from stockholders and creditors where required
   b. Revaluation of assets to current values
   c. Elimination of any deficit by charging paid-in capital

      (1) First, capital surplus
      (2) Second, capital stock

2. To write down assets: here the adjustments are taken directly to retained earnings. An alternative is to use an intermediary account such as "adjustment account" which would later be closed to retained earnings.

Retained earnings	(write-down)
Assets	(write-down)

3. To eliminate the deficit

Paid-in capital	(deficit)
Retained earnings	(deficit)

The Vann Corporation
STATEMENT OF AFFAIRS
December 31, Year 1

ASSETS

Book values		Estimated current values	Amount available to unsecured claims
	(1) Assets Pledged with Fully Secured Creditors:		
$ 6,000	Land	$12,000	
65,000	Building	41,000	
		$53,000	
	Less Mortgages Payable	45,000	
			$ 8,000
	(2) Assets Pledged with Partially Secured Creditors:		
10,000	Marketable Securities	$12,000	
	Notes Payable	37,000	
	(3) Free Assets		
1,500	Cash	1,500	
18,000	Accounts Receivable (net)	14,000	
41,000	Merchandise Inventory	22,500	
2,000	Prepaid Expenses	0	
21,000	Machinery	13,200	
10,000	Goodwill	0	
			51,200
	Estimated amount available		59,200
	Less: creditors with priority		(14,500)
	Net Estimated amount available to unsecured creditors		44,700
	(81 cents on the dollar)		
	Estimated deficiency to unsecured creditors		10,300
$174,500			$55,000

EQUITIES

Book values		Amount unsecured
	(1) Creditors with Priority	
$ 0	Estimated Liquidation Expenses (accounting, legal and other costs of liquidation process)	$ 8,000
6,500	Accrued Wages	6,500
		$14,500
	(2) Fully Secured Creditors	
45,000	Mortgages Payable	45,000
	(3) Partially Secured Creditors	
37,000	Notes Payable	37,000
	Less Marketable Securities	12,000
		25,000
	(4) Unsecured Creditors	
30,000	Accounts Payable	30,000
	(5) Stockholders' Equity	
100,000	Capital Stock	
(44,000)	Retained Earnings (deficit)	
$174,500		$55,000

4. In many cases, paid-in capital in excess of par value will be insufficient, and the par or stated value of the capital stock must be reduced to eliminate the deficit.

Existing paid-in capital	(amount on the books)
Capital stock	(total reduction in par)
Retained earnings	(deficit)
Paid-in capital from	
quasi reorganization	(forced figure)

    a. The paid-in capital arises from reducing the par or stated value from, for example, $100 to $50 rather than to $59.415. The $59.415 would come from dividing the shares outstanding into the retained earnings deficit.

    b. Retained earnings must be dated for ten years (less than ten years justified under exceptional circumstances) after a quasi reorganization takes place. Disclosure similar to "since quasi reorganization of June 30, 2010," would be appropriate.

> **NOW REVIEW MULTIPLE-CHOICE QUESTIONS 74 THROUGH 77**

P. Stock Rights

1. Generally, before additional stock is offered to the public, stock rights are issued to existing shareholders to prevent involuntary dilution of their voting rights (e.g., the preemptive privilege). The stock rights, evidenced by warrants, indicate the number and price at which the shares may be purchased. At issuance, the issuer makes only a memorandum entry. Upon exercise, the following entry is made:

Cash	(proceeds)
Common stock	(par)
Paid-in capital	(plug)

2. Information relating to stock rights outstanding must be disclosed. Detachable stock rights issued with preferred stock are treated like those on bonds (see Module 11, Section B.6.). Treatment of stock rights by recipients is discussed in Module 14, Section F.

Q. Employee Stock Ownership Plan (ESOP)

An employee stock ownership plan (ESOP) is a qualified stock bonus plan designed to invest primarily in qualifying employer securities, including stock and other marketable obligations.

1. In some instances, the ESOP will borrow funds from a bank or other lender in order to acquire shares of the employer's stock.

    a. If such an obligation of the ESOP is guaranteed by the employer (assumption by the employer of the ESOP's debt), it should be recorded as a liability in the employer's financial statements.

    b. The offsetting debit to the liability should be accounted for as a reduction of shareholders' equity.

        (1) Shareholders' equity will increase symmetrically with the reduction of the liability as the ESOP makes payments on the debt.

    c. Assets held by an ESOP should not be included in the employer's financial statements, because such assets are owned by the employees, not the employer.

    d. Additionally, the employer should charge to compensation expense the amount the employer contributed or committed to be contributed to an ESOP with respect to a given year. This is done regardless of whether or not the ESOP has borrowed funds.

> **NOW REVIEW MULTIPLE-CHOICE QUESTIONS 78 THROUGH 86**

R. Ratios
The following ratios use stockholders' equity components in their calculations:

1. **Dividend payout**—measures percentage of earnings distributed as dividends

$$\frac{\text{Dividends per share}}{\text{Earnings per share}}$$

2. **Book value of common stock** (at a point in time)—not a meaningful measure because assets are carried at historical costs

$$\frac{\text{Common stockholders' equity}}{\text{Common shares outstanding}}$$

3. **Rate of return on common stockholders' equity**—measures the return earned on the stockholders' investment in the firm

$$\frac{\text{Net income available to common stockholders}}{\text{Common stockholders' equity}}$$

4. **Debt to equity**—shows creditors the corporation's ability to sustain losses

$$\frac{\text{Total debt (all liabilities)}}{\text{Stockholders' equity}}$$

> **NOW REVIEW MULTIPLE-CHOICE QUESTIONS 87 THROUGH 91**

S. Research Component—Accounting Standards Codification

1. Stockholders' equity includes a variety of transactions and accounts that are addressed in several places in the Codification. The Statement of Shareholder Equity is found in ASC Topic 215. Earnings per Share rules are in ASC Topic 260. Accounting rules for specific shareholder equity transactions are found in ASC Topic 505, *Equity*. ASC Topic 505 includes accounting for stock dividends and stock splits, treasury stock, and equity-based payments to nonemployees. Although share-based payments to employees and nonemployees were previously covered by one accounting standard, SFAS 123(R), the rules for share-based payments are now located in two areas of the Codification. Share-based payments to nonemployees are located in ASC Topic 505 and are referred to as equity-based payments. Share-based payments to employees are located in ASC Topic 718, *Compensation—Stock Compensation*. Notice that Topic 718 is further divided into the following subtopics:

718-20	Awards Classified as Equity
718-30	Awards Classified as Liabilities
718-40	Employee Stock Ownership Plans
718-50	Employee Share Purchase Plans

2. A list of useful keywords for research is shown below.

   a. Basic stockholders' equity definitions and issues

Appropriation retained earnings	Earned surplus	Undistributed profits
Capital stock	Retained earnings	
Capital surplus	Retained income	

   b. Stock dividends, stock splits, property dividends, treasury stock

Gains on sales treasury stock	Sales of treasury stock	Stock retirement
Nonmonetary asset transfer	Stock dividend	Stock split-up
Nonreciprocal transfer to owners	Stock purchased	Treasury stock
Recipient stock dividend	Stock retired	

   c. Earnings per share

Antidilutive effect	Convertible securities	Numerator EPS
Basic EPS	Denominator EPS	Options EPS
Contingent issuable shares	Diluted EPS	Treasury stock method
Contingently issuable shares EPS	Dilutive potential shares	Warrants EPS
Conversion rate EPS	If-converted method	Weighted-average common shares

   d. Capital structure disclosures

Dividend liquidation preferences	Per-share amounts	Redeemable stock
Information about securities	Redeemable preferred stock	

e. Stock options, stock warrants, conversion of bonds

Black-Scholes	Grand date option	Restricted stock
Compensation cost option	Intrinsic value method	Service inception date
Compensatory plans	Measurement date option	Service period
Employee stock option	Measuring compensation	Share-based payments
Employee stock purchase plan	Noncompensatory plans	Stock-based compensation
Expected volatility	Nonvested stock options	Vested employee options
Fair value method	Option pricing model	Volatility
Fixed award	Requisite service period	

f. Comprehensive income

Classified items income	Display of income	Reclassification adjustments
Comprehensive income	Other comprehensive income	

T. International Financial Reporting Standards (IFRS)

1. Accounting for shareholders' equity may be influenced by the laws of a particular jurisdiction or country. Therefore, IFRS does not contain a comprehensive set of requirements for reporting shareholders' equity. Instead, IFRS provides some rules as to the minimum required disclosures. **Note that in this area, there may be vocabulary differences when describing certain components of shareholders' equity.**

   a. IFRS requires disclosure of the issued share capital, retained earnings, and other components of equity. The par value and the number of authorized, issued, and outstanding shares must be disclosed.

      (1) If shares were issued but not fully paid (referred to as "subscribed stock" in the US and "calls" in other countries), the amount not collected is shown as a contra account in the equity section.
      (2) A schedule must be presented that reconciles the number of shares of stock at the beginning and end of each period.

   b. Additional items that are disclosed in the shareholders' equity section are the capital contributions in excess of par (also called additional paid-in capital, or "share premium"), the revaluation reserve, reserves for other items, and retained earnings.

      (1) Mandatorily redeemable shares or puttable shares may not be treated as equity and should be classified as liabilities.
      (2) Compound financial instruments that have the features of both debt and equity must be separated into a liability component and an equity component and recognized in the appropriate section of the balance sheet.
      (3) Noncontrolling interest is included in the shareholders' equity section of the balance sheet.

2. Preferred shares that are convertible into ordinary shares are recorded in the preferred share account. Later, if the shares are converted, the book value method is used to account for the conversion of preferred stock into common stock.

3. Shares issued for services or property should be recorded at the fair value of the property or services.

   a. If the fair value of the property or services is not available, then the shares should be recorded at the fair value of the shares.
   b. However, if convertible debt is issued, the instrument is viewed as having a debt feature and an equity feature and should be allocated accordingly.

      (1) The amount allocated to liabilities is the fair value of the liability component, and the residual amount is allocated to equity.

4. Notes to the financial statements should describe the rights, preferences, and restrictions with respect to dividends for each class of stock, cumulative dividends in arrears, reacquired shares, and shares reserved for future issuances under options and sales contracts.

5. Cash dividends are recorded in the same way as US GAAP. Although IFRS does not address share (stock) dividends, guidance is based on national accounting rules.

   a. If dividends have been proposed but not declared or formally approved, such dividends must be reported in the notes to the financial statements.
   b. In addition, information regarding dividends declared after the end of the period but prior to issuance of the financial statements should be disclosed in the notes to the financial statements.

6. If ordinary and preferred shares are issued to investors as a unit (referred to as share units), the proceeds are allocated in proportion to the relative market values of the securities issued.

   a. If only one security is publicly traded, that security is valued at market value, and the residual is allocated to the other security.
   b. If the market value of neither security is known, then an appraisal value may be used.

7. For share subscriptions, the accounting relies on the laws of the particular jurisdiction. In some instances, the subscription receivable is shown as either a current or noncurrent asset based upon the payment due date. However, in other instances, the subscription receivable is a contra account and reduces shareholders' equity.

8. For US GAAP, donated assets are recognized at fair value and as revenue when the contribution is received. IFRS does not currently address donated assets.

9. Treasury shares are the entity's shares that have been reacquired. There are three methods for accounting for treasury shares: cost method, par value method, and constructive retirement method.

   a. The cost method and par method entries are the same as US GAAP.
   b. The construction retirement method is similar to the par value method except that the par value of the reacquired shares is charged to the share account instead of the treasury stock account.

      (1) The constructive retirement method is used when management does not intend to reissue the shares or the jurisdiction of incorporation requires that reacquired shares be retired.

10. Share-Based Payments. IFRS accounting for share-based payments and US GAAP are similar due to the convergence project. However, some vocabulary differences exist.

   a. IFRS has three categories for share-based payments: equity-settled, cash-settled, or a choice to settle in either cash or equity.

      (1) Equity-settled share-based payments to **nonemployees** are valued at fair value of goods or services received if it can be measured reliably. If the fair value of goods or services cannot be measured, then the fair value of the equity instrument is used.
      (2) Equity-settled payments to **employees** are valued at the fair value of the security. A debit is made to either an expense or an asset, and a credit is made to equity. For cash-settled, share-based payments, such as stock appreciation rights or options, a liability is measured at the fair value at the measurement date. The liability is then remeasured at every reporting date, and additional income or expense is recognized in profit or loss.

NOW REVIEW MULTIPLE-CHOICE QUESTIONS 92 THROUGH 94

KEY TERMS

Basic EPS. Measures the performance of the entity over the reporting period.

Book value of common stock (at a point in time). Not a meaningful measure because assets are carried at historical costs.

Callable. The corporation has the option to repurchase the preferred stock at a specified price.

Convertible. Preferred stockholders have an option of exchanging their stock for common stock at a specified ratio.

Cost method. Treasury stock is debited for the cost of treasury stock.

Cumulative. Dividends not paid in any year (dividends in arrears) must be made up before distributions can be made to common stockholders.

Debt to equity. Shows creditors the corporation's ability to sustain losses.

Diluted EPS. Measures the performance of the entity over the reporting period (same as basic EPS) while also taking into account the effect of all dilutive potential common shares that were outstanding during the period.

Dividend payout. Measures percentage of earnings distributed as dividends.

Employee Stock Ownership Plan (ESOP). A qualified stock bonus plan designed to invest primarily in qualifying employer securities, including stock and other marketable obligations.

Intrinsic value. The difference between the market value of the stock and the price the employee must pay.

Liquidating dividends (dividends based on other than earnings). A return of capital to stockholders.

Par value method. All capital balances associated with the treasury shares are removed upon acquisition.

Participating. Share with common stockholders in dividend distributions after both preferred and common stockholders receive a specified level of dividend payment.

Preferred stock. Stock with preferential rights.

Property dividends. Dividends payable in an asset other than cash; the entries are similar to those of cash dividend.

Quasi reorganization. Allows companies to avoid formal bankruptcy proceedings through an informal proceeding.

Rate of return on common stockholders' equity. Measures the return earned on the stockholders' investment in the firm.

Scrip dividends. Issuance of promises to pay dividends in the future (may bear interest) instead of cash.

Share-based payments. Transactions wherein an entity acquires goods or services by issuing shares (stock), share options, or other equity instruments.

Stock appreciation rights (SAR). Allows employees to receive stock or cash equal in amount to the difference between the market value and some predetermined amount per share for a certain number of shares.

Stock splits. Change the number of shares outstanding and the par value per share.

Treasury stock. A firm's own stock repurchased on the open market.

Multiple-Choice Questions (1-94)

A. Common Stock

1. East Co. issued 1,000 shares of its $5 par common stock to Howe as compensation for 1,000 hours of legal services performed. Howe usually bills $160 per hour for legal services. On the date of issuance, the stock was trading on a public exchange at $140 per share. By what amount should the additional paid-in capital account increase as a result of this transaction?

- a. $135,000
- b. $140,000
- c. $155,000
- d. $160,000

2. On July 1, year 1, Cove Corp., a closely held corporation, issued 6% bonds with a maturity value of $60,000, together with 1,000 shares of its $5 par value common stock, for a combined cash amount of $110,000. The market value of Cove's stock cannot be ascertained. If the bonds were issued separately, they would have sold for $40,000 on an 8% yield to maturity basis. What amount should Cove report for additional paid-in capital on the issuance of the stock?

- a. $75,000
- b. $65,000
- c. $55,000
- d. $45,000

3. Beck Corp. issued 200,000 shares of common stock when it began operations in year 1 and issued an additional 100,000 shares in year 2. Beck also issued preferred stock convertible to 100,000 shares of common stock. In year 3, Beck purchased 75,000 shares of its common stock and held it in Treasury. At December 31, year 3, how many shares of Beck's common stock were outstanding?

- a. 400,000
- b. 325,000
- c. 300,000
- d. 225,000

4. A corporation was organized in January year 1 with authorized capital of $10 par value common stock. On February 1, year 1, shares were issued at par for cash. On March 1, year 1, the corporation's attorney accepted 5,000 shares of the common stock in settlement for legal services with a fair value of $60,000. Additional paid-in capital would increase on

	February 1, year 1	March 1, year 1
a.	Yes	No
b.	Yes	Yes
c.	No	No
d.	No	Yes

B. Preferred Stock

5. On April 1, year 1, Hyde Corp., a newly formed company, had the following stock issued and outstanding:

- Common stock, no par, $1 stated value, 20,000 shares originally issued for $30 per share.
- Preferred stock, $10 par value, 6,000 shares originally issued for $50 per share.

Hyde's April 1, year 1 statement of stockholders' equity should report

	Common stock	Preferred stock	Additional paid-in capital
a.	$ 20,000	$ 60,000	$820,000
b.	$ 20,000	$300,000	$580,000
c.	$600,000	$300,000	$0
d.	$600,000	$ 60,000	$240,000

6. On March 1, year 1, Rya Corp. issued 1,000 shares of its $20 par value common stock and 2,000 shares of its $20 par value convertible preferred stock for a total of $80,000. At this date, Rya's common stock was selling for $36 per share, and the convertible preferred stock was selling for $27 per share. What amount of the proceeds should be allocated to Rya's convertible preferred stock?

- a. $60,000
- b. $54,000
- c. $48,000
- d. $44,000

7. During year 1, Brad Co. issued 5,000 shares of $100 par convertible preferred stock for $110 per share. One share of preferred stock can be converted into three shares of Brad's $25 par common stock at the option of the preferred shareholder. On December 31, year 3, when the market value of the common stock was $40 per share, all of the preferred stock was converted. What amount should Brad credit to Common Stock and to Additional Paid-in Capital— Common Stock as a result of the conversion?

	Common stock	Additional paid-in capital
a.	$375,000	$175,000
b.	$375,000	$225,000
c.	$500,000	$ 50,000
d.	$600,000	$0

8. Quoit, Inc. issued preferred stock with detachable common stock warrants. The issue price exceeded the sum of the warrants' fair value and the preferred stock's par value. The preferred stock's fair value was not determinable. What amount should be assigned to the warrants outstanding?

- a. Total proceeds.
- b. Excess of proceeds over the par value of the preferred stock.
- c. The proportion of the proceeds that the warrants' fair value bears to the preferred stock's par value.
- d. The fair value of the warrants.

9. Blue Co. issued preferred stock with detachable common stock warrants at a price that exceeded both the par value and the market value of the preferred stock. At the time the warrants are exercised, Blue's total stockholders' equity is increased by the

	Cash received upon exercise of the warrants	Carrying amount of warrants
a.	Yes	No
b.	Yes	Yes
c.	No	No
d.	No	Yes

C. Stock Subscriptions

10. When collectibility is reasonably assured, the excess of the subscription price over the stated value of the no par common stock subscribed should be recorded as

- a. No par common stock.
- b. Additional paid-in capital when the subscription is recorded.
- c. Additional paid-in capital when the subscription is collected.
- d. Additional paid-in capital when the common stock is issued.

11. On December 1, year 1, shares of authorized common stock were issued on a subscription basis at a price in excess of par value. A total of 20% of the subscription price of each share was collected as a down payment on December 1, year 1, with the remaining 80% of the subscription price of each share due in year 2. Collectibility was reasonably assured. At December 31, year 1, the stockholders' equity section of the balance sheet would report additional paid-in capital for the excess of the subscription price over the par value of the shares of common stock subscribed and

- a. Common stock issued for 20% of the par value of the shares of common stock subscribed.
- b. Common stock issued for the par value of the shares of common stock subscribed.
- c. Common stock subscribed for 80% of the par value of the shares of common stock subscribed.
- d. Common stock subscribed for the par value of the shares of common stock subscribed.

D. Treasury Stock Transactions

12. In year 1, Seda Corp. acquired 6,000 shares of its $1 par value common stock at $36 per share. During year 2, Seda issued 3,000 of these shares at $50 per share. Seda uses the cost method to account for its treasury stock transactions. What accounts and amounts should Seda credit in year 2 to record the issuance of the 3,000 shares?

	Treasury stock	Additional paid-in capital	Retained earnings	Common stock
a.		$102,000	$42,000	$6,000
b.		$144,000		$6,000
c.	$108,000	$ 42,000		
d.	$108,000		$42,000	

13. At December 31, year 1, Rama Corp. had 20,000 shares of $1 par value treasury stock that had been acquired in year 1 at $12 per share. In May year 2, Rama issued 15,000 of these treasury shares at $10 per share. The cost method is used to record treasury stock transactions. Rama is located in a state where laws relating to acquisition of treasury stock restrict the availability of retained earnings for declaration of dividends. At December 31, year 2, what amount should Rama show in notes to financial statements as a restriction of retained earnings as a result of its treasury stock transactions?

- a. $ 5,000
- b. $10,000
- c. $60,000
- d. $90,000

14. United, Inc.'s unadjusted current assets section and stockholders' equity section of its December 31, year 1 balance sheet are as follows:

Current assets	
Cash	$ 60,000
Investments in trading securities (including $300,000 of United, Inc. common stock)	400,000
Trade accounts receivable	340,000
Inventories	148,000
Total	$ 948,000

Stockholders' equity	
Common stock	$2,224,000
Retained earnings (deficit)	(224,000)
Total	$2,000,000

The investments and inventories are reported at their costs, which approximate market values. In its year 1 statement of stockholders' equity, United's total amount of equity at December 31, year 1, is

- a. $2,224,000
- b. $2,000,000
- c. $1,924,000
- d. $1,700,000

15. Cyan Corp. issued 20,000 shares of $5 par common stock at $10 per share. On December 31, year 1, Cyan's retained earnings were $300,000. In March year 2, Cyan reacquired 5,000 shares of its common stock at $20 per share. In June year 2, Cyan sold 1,000 of these shares to its corporate officers for $25 per share. Cyan uses the cost method to record treasury stock. Net income for the year ended December 31, year 2, was $60,000. At December 31, year 2, what amount should Cyan report as retained earnings?

- a. $360,000
- b. $365,000
- c. $375,000
- d. $380,000

16. Victor Corporation was organized on January 2, year 1, with 100,000 authorized shares of $10 par value common stock. During year 1 Victor had the following capital transactions:

January 5—issued 75,000 shares at $14 per share.
December 27—purchased 5,000 shares at $11 per share.

Victor used the par value method to record the purchase of the treasury shares. What would be the balance in the paid-in capital from treasury stock account at December 31, year 1?

- a. $0
- b. $ 5,000
- c. $15,000
- d. $20,000

17. On incorporation, Dee Inc. issued common stock at a price in excess of its par value. No other stock transactions occurred except treasury stock was acquired for an amount exceeding this issue price. If Dee uses the par value method of accounting for treasury stock appropriate for retired stock, what is the effect of the acquisition on the following?

	Net common stock	Additional paid-in capital	Retained earnings
a.	No effect	Decrease	No effect
b.	Decrease	Decrease	Decrease
c.	Decrease	No effect	Decrease
d.	No effect	Decrease	Decrease

18. Posy Corp. acquired treasury shares at an amount greater than their par value, but less than their original issue price. Compared to the cost method of accounting for treasury stock, does the par value method report a greater amount for additional paid-in capital and a greater amount for retained earnings?

	Additional paid-in capital	Retained earnings
a.	Yes	Yes
b.	Yes	No
c.	No	No
d.	No	Yes

E. Retirement of Stock

19. In year 1, Rona Corp. issued 5,000 shares of $10 par value common stock for $100 per share. In year 3, Rona reacquired 2,000 of its shares at $150 per share from the estate of one of its deceased officers and immediately canceled these 2,000 shares. Rona uses the cost method in accounting for its treasury stock transactions. In connection with the retirement of these 2,000 shares, Rona should debit

	Additional paid-in capital	Retained earnings
a.	$ 20,000	$280,000
b.	$100,000	$180,000
c.	$180,000	$100,000
d.	$280,000	$0

20. The following accounts were among those reported on Luna Corp.'s balance sheet at December 31, year 1:

Available-for-sale securities (market value $140,000)	$ 80,000
Preferred stock, $20 par value, 20,000 shares issued and outstanding	400,000
Additional paid-in capital on preferred stock	30,000
Retained earnings	900,000

On January 20, year 2, Luna exchanged all of the available-for-sale securities for 5,000 shares of Luna's preferred stock. Market values at the date of the exchange were $150,000 for the available-for-sale securities and $30 per share for the preferred stock. The 5,000 shares of preferred stock were retired immediately after the exchange. Which of the following journal entries should Luna record in connection with this transaction?

	Debit	Credit
a. Preferred stock	100,000	
Additional paid-in capital on preferred stock	7,500	
Retained earnings	42,500	
Available-for-sale securities		80,000
Gain on exchange of securities		70,000
b. Preferred stock	100,000	
Additional paid-in capital on preferred stock	30,000	
Available-for-sale securities		80,000
Additional paid-in capital from retirement of preferred stock		50,000

c. Preferred stock		150,000	
Available-for-sale securities			80,000
Additional paid-in capital on preferred stock			70,000
d. Preferred stock		150,000	
Available-for-sale securities			80,000
Gain on exchange of securities			70,000

21. On December 31, year 1, Pack Corp.'s board of directors canceled 50,000 shares of $2.50 par value common stock held in treasury at an average cost of $13 per share. Before recording the cancellation of the treasury stock, Pack had the following balances in its stockholders' equity accounts:

Common stock	$540,000
Additional paid-in capital	750,000
Retained earnings	900,000
Treasury stock, at cost	650,000

In its balance sheet at December 31, year 1, Pack should report a common stock balance of

a. $0
b. $250,000
c. $415,000
d. $540,000

22. In year 1, Fogg, Inc. issued $10 par value common stock for $25 per share. No other common stock transactions occurred until March 31, year 3, when Fogg acquired some of the issued shares for $20 per share and retired them. Which of the following statements correctly states an effect of this acquisition and retirement?

a. Year 3 net income is decreased.
b. Year 3 net income is increased.
c. Additional paid-in capital is decreased.
d. Retained earnings is increased.

F. Dividends

23. Plack Co. purchased 10,000 shares (2% ownership) of Ty Corp. on February 14, year 1. Plack received a stock dividend of 2,000 shares on April 30, year 1, when the market value per share was $35. Ty paid a cash dividend of $2 per share on December 15, year 1. In its year 1 income statement, what amount should Plack report as dividend income?

a. $20,000
b. $24,000
c. $90,000
d. $94,000

24. Arp Corp.'s outstanding capital stock at December 15, year 1, consisted of the following:

- 30,000 shares of 5% cumulative preferred stock, par value $10 per share, fully participating as to dividends. No dividends were in arrears.

- 200,000 shares of common stock, par value $1 per share.

On December 15, year 1, Arp declared dividends of $100,000. What was the amount of dividends payable to Arp's common stockholders?

a. $10,000
b. $34,000
c. $40,000
d. $47,500

25. At December 31, year 2 and year 3, Apex Co. had 3,000 shares of $100 par, 5% cumulative preferred stock outstanding. No dividends were in arrears as of December 31, year 1. Apex did not declare a dividend during year 2. During year 3, Apex paid a cash dividend of $10,000 on its preferred stock. Apex should report dividends in arrears in its year 3 financial statements as a(n)

    a. Accrued liability of $15,000.
    b. Disclosure of $15,000.
    c. Accrued liability of $20,000.
    d. Disclosure of $20,000.

26. East Corp., a calendar-year company, had sufficient retained earnings in year 1 as a basis for dividends, but was temporarily short of cash. East declared a dividend of $100,000 on April 1, year 1, and issued promissory notes to its stockholders in lieu of cash. The notes, which were dated April 1, year 1, had a maturity date of March 31, year 2, and a 10% interest rate. How should East account for the scrip dividend and related interest?

    a. Debit retained earnings for $110,000 on April 1, year 1.
    b. Debit retained earnings for $110,000 on March 31, year 2.
    c. Debit retained earnings for $100,000 on April 1, year 1, and debit interest expense for $10,000 on March 31, year 2.
    d. Debit retained earnings for $100,000 on April 1, year 1, and debit interest expense for $7,500 on December 31, year 1.

27. On January 2, year 2, Lake Mining Co.'s board of directors declared a cash dividend of $400,000 to stockholders of record on January 18, year 2, payable on February 10, year 2. The dividend is permissible under law in Lake's state of incorporation. Selected data from Lake's December 31, year 1 balance sheet are as follows:

Accumulated depletion	$100,000
Capital stock	500,000
Additional paid-in capital	150,000
Retained earnings	300,000

The $400,000 dividend includes a liquidating dividend of

    a. $0
    b. $100,000
    c. $150,000
    d. $300,000

28. On June 27, year 1, Brite Co. distributed to its common stockholders 100,000 outstanding common shares of its investment in Quik, Inc., an unrelated party. The carrying amount on Brite's books of Quik's $1 par common stock was $2 per share. Immediately after the distribution, the market price of Quik's stock was $2.50 per share. In its income statement for the year ended June 30, year 1, what amount should Brite report as gain before income taxes on disposal of the stock?

    a. $250,000
    b. $200,000
    c. $ 50,000
    d. $0

29. On December 1, year 1, Nilo Corp. declared a property dividend of marketable securities to be distributed on December 31, year 1, to stockholders of record on December 15, year 1. On December 1, year 1, the trading securities had a carrying amount of $60,000 and a fair value of $78,000. What is the effect of this property dividend on Nilo's year 1 retained earnings, after all nominal accounts are closed?

    a. $0.
    b. $18,000 increase.
    c. $60,000 decrease.
    d. $78,000 decrease.

30. Long Co. had 100,000 shares of common stock issued and outstanding at January 1, year 1. During year 1, Long took the following actions:

March 15	—	Declared a 2-for-1 stock split, when the fair value of the stock was $80 per share.
December 15	—	Declared a $.50 per share cash dividend.

In Long's statement of stockholders' equity for year 1, what amount should Long report as dividends?

    a. $ 50,000
    b. $100,000
    c. $850,000
    d. $950,000

31. A company declared a cash dividend on its common stock on December 15, year 1, payable on January 12, year 2. How would this dividend affect stockholders' equity on the following dates?

	December 15, Year 1	December 31, Year 1	January 12, Year 2
a.	Decrease	No effect	Decrease
b.	Decrease	No effect	No effect
c.	No effect	Decrease	No effect
d.	No effect	No effect	Decrease

32. Ole Corp. declared and paid a liquidating dividend of $100,000. This distribution resulted in a decrease in Ole's

	Paid-in capital	Retained earnings
a.	No	No
b.	Yes	Yes
c.	No	Yes
d.	Yes	No

33. Instead of the usual cash dividend, Evie Corp. declared and distributed a property dividend from its overstocked merchandise. The excess of the merchandise's carrying amount over its market value should be

    a. Ignored.
    b. Reported as a separately disclosed reduction of retained earnings.
    c. Reported as an extraordinary loss, net of income taxes.
    d. Reported as a reduction in income before extraordinary items.

34. The following stock dividends were declared and distributed by Sol Corp.:

Percentage of common share outstanding at declaration date	Fair value	Par value
10	$15,000	$10,000
28	40,000	30,800

What aggregate amount should be debited to retained earnings for these stock dividends?

a. $40,800
b. $45,800
c. $50,000
d. $55,000

35. Ray Corp. declared a 5% stock dividend on its 10,000 issued and outstanding shares of $2 par value common stock, which had a fair value of $5 per share before the stock dividend was declared. This stock dividend was distributed sixty days after the declaration date. By what amount did Ray's current liabilities increase as a result of the stock dividend declaration?

a. $0
b. $ 500
c. $1,000
d. $2,500

G. Stock Splits

36. How would total stockholders' equity be affected by the declaration of each of the following?

	Stock dividend	Stock split
a.	No effect	Increase
b.	Decrease	Decrease
c.	Decrease	No effect
d.	No effect	No effect

37. On July 1, year 1, Bart Corporation has 200,000 shares of $10 par common stock outstanding and the market price of the stock is $12 per share. On the same date, Bart declared a 1-for-2 reverse stock split. The par of the stock was increased from $10 to $20 and one new $20 par share was issued for each two $10 par shares outstanding. Immediately before the 1-for-2 reverse stock split, Bart's additional paid-in capital was $450,000. What should be the balance in Bart's additional paid-in capital account immediately after the reverse stock split is effected?

a. $0
b. $450,000
c. $650,000
d. $850,000

38. How would a stock split in which the par value per share decreases in proportion to the number of additional shares issued affect each of the following?

	Additional paid-in capital	Retained earnings
a.	Increase	No effect
b.	No effect	No effect
c.	No effect	Decrease
d.	Increase	Decrease

H. Appropriations of Retained Earnings (Reserves)

39. At December 31, year 1, Eagle Corp. reported $1,750,000 of appropriated retained earnings for the construction of a new office building, which was completed in year 2 at a total cost of $1,500,000. In year 2, Eagle appropriated $1,200,000 of retained earnings for the construction of a new plant. Also, $2,000,000 of cash was restricted for the retirement of bonds due in year 3. In its year 2 balance sheet, Eagle should report what amount of appropriated retained earnings?

a. $1,200,000
b. $1,450,000
c. $2,950,000
d. $3,200,000

40. The following information pertains to Meg Corp.:

- Dividends on its 1,000 shares of 6%, $10 par value cumulative preferred stock have not been declared or paid for three years.
- Treasury stock that cost $15,000 was reissued for $8,000.

What amount of retained earnings should be appropriated as a result of these items?

a. $0
b. $1,800
c. $7,000
d. $8,800

41. A retained earnings appropriation can be used to

a. Absorb a fire loss when a company is self-insured.
b. Provide for a contingent loss that is probable and reasonably estimable.
c. Smooth periodic income.
d. Restrict earnings available for dividends.

I.   Share-Based Payments

42. On January 1, year 1, Doro Corp. granted an employee an option to purchase 3,000 shares of Doro's $5 par value common stock at $20 per share. The option became exercisable on December 31, year 2, after the employee completed two years of service. The option was exercised on January 10, year 3. The market prices of Doro's stock and stock options were as follows:

Date	Market price of stock	Market price of similar stock option
January 1, year 1	$30	$8
December 31, year 2	50	9
January 10, year 3	45	11

For year 1, Doro should recognize compensation expense of

a. $45,000
b. $30,000
c. $15,000
d. $12,000

43. In connection with a stock option plan for the benefit of key employees, Ward Corp. intends to distribute treasury shares when the options are exercised. These shares were bought in year 1 at $42 per share. On January 1, year 2, Ward granted stock options for 10,000 shares at $38 per share as additional compensation for services to be rendered over the next three years. The options are exercisable during a four-year period beginning January 1, year 5, by grantees still employed by Ward. Market price of Ward's stock was $47 per share at the grant date. The fair value of a similar stock option with the same terms was $12 at the grant date. No stock options were terminated during year 2. In Ward's December 31, year 2 income statement, what amount should be reported as compensation expense pertaining to the options?

a. $90,000
b. $40,000
c. $30,000
d. $0

Items 44 and 45 are based on the following:

On January 2, year 1, Kine Co. granted Morgan, its president, compensatory stock options to buy 1,000 shares of Kine's $10 par common stock. The options call for a price of $20 per share and are exercisable for three years following the grant date. Morgan exercised the options on December 31, year 1. The market price of the stock was $50 on January 2, year 1, and $70 on December 31, year 1. The fair value of a similar stock option with the same terms was $28 on the grant date.

44. What is compensation expense for year 1 for the share-based payments?

a. $ 9,333
b. $10,000
c. $20,000
d. $28,000

45. By what net amount should stockholders' equity increase as a result of the grant and exercise of the options?

a. $20,000
b. $30,000
c. $50,000
d. $70,000

46. On January 2, year 1, Morey Corp. granted Dean, its president, 20,000 stock appreciation rights for past services. Those rights are exercisable immediately and expire on January 1, year 4. On exercise, Dean is entitled to receive cash for the excess of the stock's market price on the exercise date over the market price on the grant date. Dean did not exercise any of the rights during year 1. The market price of Morey's stock was $30 on January 2, year 1, and $45 on December 31, year 1. As a result of the stock appreciation rights, Morey should recognize compensation expense for year 1 of

a. $0
b. $100,000
c. $300,000
d. $600,000

47. Wall Corp.'s employee stock purchase plan specifies the following:

- For every $1 withheld from employees' wages for the purchase of Wall's common stock, Wall contributes $2.
- The stock is purchased from Wall's treasury stock at market price on the date of purchase.

The following information pertains to the plan's year 1 transactions:

Employee withholdings for the year	$ 350,000
Market value of 150,000 shares issued	1,050,000
Carrying amount of treasury stock issued (cost)	900,000

Before payroll taxes, what amount should Wall recognize as expense in year 1 for the stock purchase plan?

a. $1,050,000
b. $ 900,000
c. $ 700,000
d. $ 550,000

48. In accounting for stock-based compensation, what interest rate is used to discount both the exercise price of the option and the future dividend stream?

a. The firm's known incremental borrowing rate.
b. The current market rate that firms in that particular industry use to discount cash flows.
c. The risk-free interest rate.
d. Any rate that firms can justify as being reasonable.

49. In what circumstances is compensation expense immediately recognized?

a. In all circumstances.
b. In circumstances when the options are exercisable within two years for services rendered over the next two years.
c. In circumstances when options are granted for prior service, and the options are immediately exercisable.
d. In no circumstances is compensation expense immediately recognized.

50. Compensation cost for a share-based payment to employees that is classified as a liability is measured as

a. The change in fair value of the instrument for each reporting period.
b. The total fair value at grant date.
c. The present value of cash payments due over the life of the grant.
d. The actual cash outlay for the period.

51. What is the measurement date for a share-based payment to employees that is classified as a liability?

a. The service inception date.
b. The grant date.
c. The settlement date.
d. The end of the reporting period.

52. Shafer Corporation (a nonpublic company) established an employee stock option plan on January 1, year 1. The plan allows its employees to acquire 20,000 shares of its $5 par value common stock at $70 per share, when the market price is $75. The options may not be exercised until five years from the grant date. The risk-free interest rate is 6%, and the stock is expected to pay dividends of $3 annually. The fair value of a similar option at the grant date is $6.40. What is the amount of deferred compensation expense that should be recorded in year one?

a. $ 20,000
b. $ 25,000
c. $100,000
d. $128,000

53. Galaxy has a tax benefit and cash retained of $20,000 as a result of share-based payments to employees. How is this tax benefit disclosed in the financial statements?

a. As a component of other comprehensive income.
b. As a prior period adjustment.
c. As a current liability on the balance sheet.
d. As a cash inflow from financing activities on the statement of cash flows.

54. On July 1, year 1, Jordan Corp. granted employees share-based payments in the form of compensatory stock options. How should Jordan account for the outstanding options in calculating earnings per share for year 1 if the options are not antidilutive?

a. Include the options in the denominator of basic and diluted earnings per share for the entire year.
b. Include the options in the denominator of diluted earnings per share for the entire year.
c. Include the options in the denominator of diluted earnings per share weighted by number of months outstanding.
d. Ignore the options in the calculation of diluted earnings per share.

K. Basic Earnings Per Share

55. At December 31, year 2 and year 1, Gow Corp. had 100,000 shares of common stock and 10,000 shares of 5%, $100 par value cumulative preferred stock outstanding. No dividends were declared on either the preferred or common stock in year 2 or year 1. Net income for year 2 was $1,000,000. For year 2, basic earnings per share amounted to

    a. $10.00
    b. $ 9.50
    c. $ 9.00
    d. $ 5.00 .

56. Ute Co. had the following capital structure during year 1 and year 2:

Preferred stock, $10 par, 4% cumulative, 25,000 shares issued and outstanding	$ 250,000
Common stock, $5 par, 200,000 shares issued and outstanding	1,000,000

Ute reported net income of $500,000 for the year ended December 31, year 2. Ute paid no preferred dividends during year 1 and paid $16,000 in preferred dividends during year 2. In its December 31, year 2 income statement, what amount should Ute report as basic earnings per share?

    a. $2.42
    b. $2.45
    c. $2.48
    d. $2.50

57. The following information pertains to Jet Corp.'s outstanding stock for year 1:

Common stock, $5 par value

Shares outstanding, 1/1/Y1	20,000
2-for-1 stock split, 4/1/Y1	20,000
Shares issued, 7/1/Y1	10,000

Preferred stock, $10 par value, 5% cumulative

Shares outstanding, 1/1/Y1	4,000

What are the number of shares Jet should use to calculate year 1 basic earnings per share?

    a. 40,000
    b. 45,000
    c. 50,000
    d. 54,000

58. Timp, Inc. had the following common stock balances and transactions during year 1

1/1/Y1	Common stock outstanding	30,000
2/1/Y1	Issued a 10% common stock dividend	3,000
7/1/Y1	Issued common stock for cash	8,000
12/31/Y1	Common stock outstanding	41,000

What were Timp's year 1 weighted-average shares outstanding?

    a. 30,000
    b. 34,000
    c. 36,750
    d. 37,000

59. Strauch Co. has one class of common stock outstanding and no other securities that are potentially convertible into common stock. During year 1, 100,000 shares of common stock were outstanding. In year 2, two distributions of additional common shares occurred: On April 1, 20,000 shares

of treasury stock were sold, and on July 1, a 2-for-1 stock split was issued. Net income was $410,000 in year 2 and $350,000 in year 1. What amounts should Strauch report as basic earnings per share in its year 2 and year 1 comparative income statements?

	Year 2	Year 1
a.	$1.78	$3.50
b.	$1.78	$1.75
c.	$2.34	$1.75
d.	$2.34	$3.50

60. Earnings per share data must be reported on the income statement for

	Cumulative effect of a change in accounting principle	Extraordinary items
a.	Yes	No
b.	No	No
c.	No	Yes
d.	Yes ·	Yes

61. On January 31, year 2, Pack, Inc. split its common stock 2 for 1, and Young, Inc. issued a 5% stock dividend. Both companies issued their December 31, year 1 financial statements on March 1, year 2. Should Pack's year 1, basic earnings per share (BEPS) take into consideration the stock split, and should Young's year 1 BEPS take into consideration the stock dividend?

	Pack's year 1 BEPS	Young's year 1 BEPS
a.	Yes	No
b.	No	No
c.	Yes	Yes
d.	No	Yes

L. Diluted Earnings Per Share

62. Mann, Inc. had 300,000 shares of common stock issued and outstanding at December 31, year 1. On July 1, year 2, an additional 50,000 shares of common stock were issued for cash. Mann also had unexercised stock options to purchase 40,000 shares of common stock at $15 per share outstanding at the beginning and end of year 2. The average market price of Mann's common stock was $20 during year 2. What is the number of shares that should be used in computing diluted earnings per share for the year ended December 31, year 2?

    a. 325,000
    b. 335,000
    c. 360,000
    d. 365,000

63. Peters Corp.'s capital structure was as follows:

	December 31	
	Year 1	Year 2
Outstanding shares of stock:		
Common	110,000	110,000
Convertible preferred	10,000	10,000

During year 2, Peters paid dividends of $3.00 per share on its preferred stock. The preferred shares are convertible into 20,000 shares of common stock and are considered common stock equivalents. Net income for year 2 was $850,000. Assume that the income tax rate is 30%. The diluted earnings per share for year 2 is

    a. $6.31
    b. $6.54

c. $7.08
d. $7.45

64. Cox Corporation had 1,200,000 shares of common stock outstanding on January 1 and December 31, year 2. In connection with the acquisition of a subsidiary company in June year 1, Cox is required to issue 50,000 additional shares of its common stock on July 1, year 3, to the former owners of the subsidiary. Cox paid $200,000 in preferred stock dividends in year 2, and reported net income of $3,400,000 for the year. Cox's diluted earnings per share for year 2 should be

a. $2.83
b. $2.72
c. $2.67
d. $2.56

65. On June 30, year 1, Lomond, Inc. issued twenty $10,000, 7% bonds at par. Each bond was convertible into 200 shares of common stock. On January 1, year 2, 10,000 shares of common stock were outstanding. The bondholders converted all the bonds on July 1, year 2. The following amounts were reported in Lomond's income statement for the year ended December 31, year 2:

Revenues	$977,000
Operating expenses	920,000
Interest on bonds	7,000
Income before income tax	50,000
Income tax at 30%	15,000
Net income	$ 35,000

What is Lomond's year 2 diluted earnings per share?

a. $2.50
b. $2.85
c. $2.92
d. $3.50

66. West Co. had earnings per share of $15.00 for year 1 before considering the effects of any convertible securities. No conversion or exercise of convertible securities occurred during year 1. However, possible conversion of convertible bonds, not considered common stock equivalents, would have reduced earnings per share by $0.75. The effect of possible exercise of common stock options would have increased earnings per share by $0.10. What amount should West report as diluted earnings per share for year 1?

a. $14.25
b. $14.35
c. $15.00
d. $15.10

67. In determining diluted earnings per share, dividends on nonconvertible cumulative preferred stock should be

a. Disregarded.
b. Added back to net income whether declared or not.
c. Deducted from net income only if declared.
d. Deducted from net income whether declared or not.

68. The if-converted method of computing earnings per share data assumes conversion of convertible securities as of the

a. Beginning of the earliest period reported (or at time of issuance, if later).
b. Beginning of the earliest period reported (regardless of time of issuance).

c. Middle of the earliest period reported (regardless of time of issuance).
d. Ending of the earliest period reported (regardless of time of issuance).

69. In determining earnings per share, interest expense, net of applicable income taxes, on convertible debt that is dilutive should be

a. Added back to weighted-average common shares outstanding for diluted earnings per share.
b. Added back to net income for diluted earnings per share.
c. Deducted from net income for diluted earnings per share.
d. Deducted from weighted-average common shares outstanding for diluted earnings per share.

70. For contingent issue agreements requiring passage of time or earnings threshold that is met, before issuing stock, these should be

	Included in basic earnings per share	Included in computing diluted earnings per share
a.	No	No
b.	No	Yes
c.	Yes	No
d.	Yes	Yes

M. Corporate Bankruptcy

71. Kent Co. filed a voluntary bankruptcy petition on August 15, year 1, and the statement of affairs reflects the following amounts:

	Book value	Estimated current value
Assets		
Assets pledged with fully secured creditors	$ 300,000	$370,000
Assets pledged with partially secured creditors	180,000	120,000
Free assets	420,000	320,000
	$ 900,000	$810,000
Liabilities		
Liabilities with priority	$ 70,000	
Fully secured creditors	260,000	
Partially secured creditors	200,000	
Unsecured creditors	540,000	
	$1,070,000	

Assume that the assets are converted to cash at the estimated current values and the business is liquidated. What amount of cash will be available to pay unsecured nonpriority claims?

a. $240,000
b. $280,000
c. $320,000
d. $360,000

72. Seco Corp. was forced into bankruptcy and is in the process of liquidating assets and paying claims. Unsecured claims will be paid at the rate of 40 cents on the dollar. Hale holds a $30,000 noninterest-bearing note receivable from Seco collateralized by an asset with a book value of $35,000 and a liquidation value of $5,000. The amount to be realized by Hale on this note is

a. $ 5,000
b. $12,000
c. $15,000
d. $17,000

73. Kamy Corp. is in liquidation under of the Federal Bankruptcy Code. The bankruptcy trustee has established a new set of books for the bankruptcy estate. After assuming custody of the estate, the trustee discovered an unrecorded invoice of $1,000 for machinery repairs performed before the bankruptcy filing. In addition, a truck with a carrying amount of $20,000 was sold for $12,000 cash. This truck was bought and paid for in the year before the bankruptcy. What amount should be debited to estate equity as a result of these transactions?

a. $0
b. $1,000
c. $8,000
d. $9,000

N. Reorganizations

74. On December 30, year 1, Hale Corp. paid $400,000 cash and issued 80,000 shares of its $1 par value common stock to its unsecured creditors on a pro rata basis pursuant to a reorganization plan under Chapter 11 of the bankruptcy statutes. Hale owed these unsecured creditors a total of $1,200,000. Hale's common stock was trading at $1.25 per share on December 30, year 1. As a result of this transaction, Hale's total stockholders' equity had a net increase of

a. $1,200,000
b. $ 800,000
c. $ 100,000
d. $ 80,000

O. Quasi Reorganization

75. The primary purpose of a quasi reorganization is to give a corporation the opportunity to
a. Obtain relief from its creditors.
b. Revalue understated assets to their fair values.
c. Eliminate a deficit in retained earnings.
d. Distribute the stock of a newly created subsidiary to its stockholders in exchange for part of their stock in the corporation.

76. When a company goes through a quasi reorganization, its balance sheet carrying amounts are stated at
a. Original cost.
b. Original book value.
c. Replacement value.
d. Fair value.

77. The stockholders' equity section of Brown Co.'s December 31, year 1 balance sheet consisted of the following:

Common stock, $30 par, 10,000 shares
  authorized and outstanding $300,000
Additional paid-in capital   150,000
Retained earnings (deficit)   (210,000)

On January 2, year 2, Brown put into effect a stockholder-approved quasi reorganization by reducing the par value of the stock to $5 and eliminating the deficit against additional paid-in capital. Immediately after the quasi reorganization, what amount should Brown report as additional paid-in capital?

a. $ (60,000)
b. $150,000
c. $190,000
d. $400,000

P. Stock Rights

78. On July 1, year 1, Vail Corp. issued rights to stockholders to subscribe to additional shares of its common stock. One right was issued for each share owned. A stockholder could purchase one additional share for 10 rights plus $15 cash. The rights expired on September 30, year 1. On July 1, year 1, the market price of a share with the right attached was $40, while the market price of one right alone was $2. Vail's stockholders' equity on June 30, year 1, comprised the following:

Common stock, $25 par value, 4,000 shares
  issued and outstanding $100,000
Additional paid-in capital   60,000
Retained earnings   80,000

By what amount should Vail's retained earnings decrease as a result of issuance of the stock rights on July 1, year 1?
a. $0
b. $ 5,000
c. $ 8,000
d. $10,000

79. In September year 1, West Corp. made a dividend distribution of one right for each of its 120,000 shares of outstanding common stock. Each right was exercisable for the purchase of 1/100 of a share of West's $50 variable rate preferred stock at an exercise price of $80 per share. On March 20, year 3, none of the rights had been exercised, and West redeemed them by paying each stockholder $0.10 per right. As a result of this redemption, West's stockholders' equity was reduced by
a. $ 120
b. $ 2,400
c. $12,000
d. $36,000

80. On November 2, year 1, Finsbury, Inc. issued warrants to its stockholders giving them the right to purchase additional $20 par value common shares at a price of $30. The stockholders exercised all warrants on March 1, year 2. The shares had market prices of $33, $35, and $40 on November 2, year 1; December 31, year 1; and March 1, year 2, respectively. What were the effects of the warrants on Finsbury's additional paid-in capital and net income?

	Additional paid-in capital	Net income
a.	Increased in year 2	No effect
b.	Increased in year 1	No effect
c.	Increased in year 2	Decreased in year 1 and year 2
d.	Increased in year 1	Decreased in year 1 and year 2

81. A company issued rights to its existing shareholders to purchase, for $30 per share, unissued shares of $15 par value common stock. Additional paid-in capital will be credited when the

	Rights are issued	Rights lapse
a.	Yes	No
b.	No	No
c.	No	Yes
d.	Yes	Yes

Q.   Employee Stock Ownership Plan (ESOP)

Items 82 and 83 are based on the following:

On January 1, year 1, Fay Corporation established an employee stock ownership plan (ESOP). Selected transactions relating to the ESOP during year 1 were as follows:

- On April 1, year 1, Fay contributed $30,000 cash and 3,000 shares of its $10 par common stock to the ESOP. On this date the market price of the stock was $18 a share.
- On October 1, year 1, the ESOP borrowed $100,000 from Union National Bank and acquired 5,000 shares of Fay's common stock in the open market at $17 a share. The note is for one year, bears interest at 10%, and is guaranteed by Fay.
- On December 15, year 1, the ESOP distributed 6,000 shares of Fay common stock to employees of Fay in accordance with the plan formula.

82. In its year 1 income statement, how much should Fay report as compensation expense relating to the ESOP?
- a. $184,000
- b. $120,000
- c. $ 84,000
- d. $ 60,000

83. In Fay's December 31, year 1 balance sheet, how much should be reported as a reduction of shareholders' equity and as an endorsed note payable in respect of the ESOP?

	Reduction of shareholders' equity	Endorsed note payable
a.	$0	$0
b.	$0	$100,000
c.	$100,000	$0
d.	$100,000	$100,000

Stockholders' Equity: Comprehensive

84. Zinc Co.'s adjusted trial balance at December 31, year 1, includes the following account balances:

Common stock, $3 par	$600,000
Additional paid-in capital	800,000
Treasury stock, at cost	50,000
Net unrealized loss on available-for-sale securities	20,000
Retained earnings: appropriated for uninsured earthquake losses	150,000
Retained earnings: unappropriated	200,000

What amount should Zinc report as total stockholders' equity in its December 31, year 1 balance sheet?
- a. $1,680,000
- b. $1,720,000
- c. $1,780,000
- d. $1,820,000

85. Rudd Corp. had 700,000 shares of common stock authorized and 300,000 shares outstanding at December 31, year 1. The following events occurred during year 2:

January 31	Declared 10% stock dividend
June 30	Purchased 100,000 shares
August 1	Reissued 50,000 shares
November 30	Declared 2-for-1 stock split

At December 31, year 2, how many shares of common stock did Rudd have outstanding?

- a. 560,000
- b. 600,000
- c. 630,000
- d. 660,000

86. Nest Co. issued 100,000 shares of common stock. Of these, 5,000 were held as treasury stock at December 31, year 1. During year 2, transactions involving Nest's common stock were as follows:

May 3	1,000 shares of treasury stock were sold.
August 6	10,000 shares of previously unissued stock were sold.
November 18	A 2-for-1 stock split took effect.

Laws in Nest's state of incorporation protect treasury stock from dilution. At December 31, year 2, how many shares of Nest's common stock were issued and outstanding?

	Shares	
	Issued	Outstanding
a.	220,000	212,000
b.	220,000	216,000
c.	222,000	214,000
d.	222,000	218,000

R.   Ratios

87. The following information pertains to Ali Corp. as of and for the year ended December 31, year 1:

Liabilities	$ 60,000
Stockholders' equity	$500,000
Shares of common stock issued and outstanding	10,000
Net income	$ 30,000

During year 1, Ali's officers exercised stock options for 1,000 shares of stock at an option price of $8 per share. This transaction is reflected in the above balances. What was the effect of exercising the stock options?
- a. Debt to equity ratio decreased to 12%.
- b. Earnings per share increased by $0.33.
- c. Asset turnover increased to 5.4%.
- d. No ratios were affected.

88. Selected information for Irvington Company is as follows:

	December 31	
	Year 1	Year 2
Preferred stock, 8%, par $100, nonconvertible, noncumulative	$125,000	$125,000
Common stock	300,000	400,000
Retained earnings	75,000	185,000
Dividends paid on preferred stock for year ended	10,000	10,000
Net income for year ended	60,000	120,000

Irvington's return on common stockholders' equity, rounded to the nearest percentage point, for year 2 is
- a. 17%
- b. 19%
- c. 23%
- d. 25%

89. Hoyt Corp.'s current balance sheet reports the following stockholders' equity:

5% cumulative preferred stock, par value $100 per share; 2,500 shares issued and outstanding	$250,000
Common stock, par value $3.50 per share; 100,000 shares issued and outstanding	350,000
Additional paid-in capital in excess of par value of common stock	125,000
Retained earnings	300,000

Dividends in arrears on the preferred stock amount to $25,000. If Hoyt were to be liquidated, the preferred stockholders would receive par value plus a premium of $50,000. The book value per share of common stock is

   a. $7.75
   b. $7.50
   c. $7.25
   d. $7.00

90. Grid Corp. acquired some of its own common shares at a price greater than both their par value and original issue price but less than their book value. Grid uses the cost method of accounting for treasury stock. What is the impact of this acquisition on total stockholders' equity and the book value per common share?

	Total stockholders' equity	Book value per share
a.	Increase	Increase
b.	Increase	Decrease
c.	Decrease	Increase
d.	Decrease	Decrease

91. How are dividends per share for common stock used in the calculation of the following?

	Dividend per share payout ratio	Earnings per share
a.	Numerator	Numerator
b.	Numerator	Not used
c.	Denominator	Not used
d.	Denominator	Denominator

T.   International Financial Reporting Standards (IFRS)

92. Logan Corporation issues convertible bonds for $500,000. At the date of issuance, it is determined that the fair value of the bonds is $480,000. Logan prepares its financial statements in accordance with IFRS. How should the issuance of the bonds be recognized?

   a.   As a bond liability for $500,000.
   b.   As a bond liability for $480,000 and other comprehensive income of $20,000.
   c.   As a bond liability for $480,000 and an equity component of $20,000.
   d.   As a bond liability for $500,000 and a contra liability of $20,000.

93. Vestre Corporation prepares its financial statements under IFRS. Recently the company issued convertible debt. How should the company record this debt?

   a.   The instrument should be presented solely as debt.
   b.   The instrument should be presented between debt and equity.
   c.   The instrument should be presented solely as equity.
   d.   The instrument should be presented as part debt and part equity.

94. Under IFRS, which of the following is not a method that may be used to account for treasury stock?

   a.   Cost method.
   b.   Par value method.
   c.   Retained earnings method.
   d.   Constructive retirement method.

Multiple-Choice Answers and Explanations

Answers

1. a __ __	21. c __ __	41. d __ __	61. c __ __	81. b __ __
2. b __ __	22. c __ __	42. d __ __	62. b __ __	82. c __ __
3. d __ __	23. b __ __	43. b __ __	63. b __ __	83. d __ __
4. d __ __	24. c __ __	44. d __ __	64. d __ __	84. a __ __
5. a __ __	25. d __ __	45. a __ __	65. b __ __	85. a __ __
6. c __ __	26. d __ __	46. c __ __	66. a __ __	86. a __ __
7. a __ __	27. b __ __	47. c __ __	67. d __ __	87. a __ __
8. d __ __	28. c __ __	48. c __ __	68. a __ __	88. c __ __
9. a __ __	29. c __ __	49. c __ __	69. b __ __	89. d __ __
10. b __ __	30. b __ __	50. a __ __	70. b __ __	90. c __ __
11. d __ __	31. b __ __	51. c __ __	71. d __ __	91. b __ __
12. c __ __	32. d __ __	52. d __ __	72. c __ __	92. c __ __
13. c __ __	33. d __ __	53. d __ __	73. d __ __	93. d __ __
14. d __ __	34. b __ __	54. c __ __	74. b __ __	94. c __ __
15. a __ __	35. a __ __	55. b __ __	75. c __ __	
16. c __ __	36. d __ __	56. b __ __	76. d __ __	
17. b __ __	37. b __ __	57. b __ __	77. c __ __	
18. c __ __	38. b __ __	58. d __ __	78. a __ __	
19. c __ __	39. a __ __	59. b __ __	79. c __ __	1st: __/94 = __%
20. a __ __	40. a __ __	60. b __ __	80. a __ __	2nd: __/94 = __%

Explanations

1. (a) When stock is issued for services, the transaction should be recorded at either the FV of the stock issued or the FV of the services received, whichever is more clearly determinable. The FV of stock traded on a public exchange is a more objective, reliable measure than a normal billing rate for legal services, which is likely to be negotiable. If the transaction is valued at $140 per share, legal expense would be debited for $140,000 (1,000 × $140), common stock would be credited for the par value of $5,000 (1,000 × $5), and additional paid-in capital would be credited for the difference ($140,000 − $5,000 = $135,000).

2. (b) When stock is issued in combination with other securities (lump sum sales), the proceeds can be allocated by the **proportional method** or by the **incremental method**. If the FV of each class of securities is determinable, the proceeds should be allocated to each class of securities based on their relative FV. In the instances where the FV of all classes of securities is not determinable, the incremental method should be used. The market value of the securities is used as a basis for those classes that are known, and the remainder of the lump sum is allocated to the class for which the market value is not known. In this problem, the FV of the stock is unknown. As such, the incremental method must be used as follows:

Lump sum receipt	$110,000
FV of bonds	40,000
Balance allocated to common stock	$ 70,000

As the par value of the common stock is $5,000 (1,000 shares × $5), $65,000 ($70,000 − $5,000) should be reported as additional paid-in capital on the issuance of the stock.

3. (d) The number of common shares outstanding is equal to the issued shares less treasury shares. Beck Corp. had 300,000 shares outstanding at 1/1/Y1. The purchase of treasury shares in year 3 reduced the number of shares out-

standing to 225,000 (300,000 − 75,000). The preferred stock convertible into 100,000 shares of common stock is recorded as preferred stock until it is **converted** by the stockholder.

4. (d) On February 1, year 1, when shares were issued at par for cash, the following journal entry would have been made:

Cash	(cash received)	
Common stock		(par)

On March 1, year 1, however, the issuance of 5,000 shares in settlement for legal services rendered would have been recorded as follows:

Legal fees	60,000	
Common stock ($10 × 5,000		
shares)		50,000
Addl. paid-in capital		10,000

Stock issued for services (i.e., in a nonmonetary transaction) should be recorded at the fair market value of those services (in this case $60,000).

5. (a) When the common stock was issued, it was recorded at stated value with the excess recorded as additional paid-in capital.

Cash	600,000	
Common stock		20,000
Addl. paid-in capital		580,000

The preferred stock was recorded at par value with the excess credited to additional paid-in capital.

Cash	300,000	
Preferred stock		60,000
Addl. paid-in capital		240,000

Therefore, at 4/1/Y1, the balances are common stock ($20,000), preferred stock ($60,000), and additional paid-in capital ($580,000 + $240,000 = $820,000).

6. (c) In a lump-sum issuance of common and preferred stock, the proceeds ($80,000) are generally allocated based on the relative fair market values of the securities issued. The FV of the convertible preferred stock is $54,000 ($27 × 2,000) and the FV of the common stock is $36,000 ($36 × 1,000). The proceeds are allocated as follows:

$$\text{Convertible preferred} \quad \frac{\$54,000}{\$90,000} \times \$80,000 = \underline{\$48,000}$$

$$\text{Common} \quad \frac{\$36,000}{\$90,000} \times \$80,000 = \underline{\$32,000}$$

7. (a) All 5,000 shares of convertible preferred stock were converted to common stock at a rate of 3 shares of common for every share of preferred. Therefore, 15,000 shares of common stock were issued (5,000 × 3). The common stock account is credited for the par value of these shares (15,000 × $25 = $375,000). APIC – CS ($550,000 – $375,000 = $175,000) is credited for the difference between the carrying amount of the preferred stock (5,000 × $110 = $550,000) and the par value of the common stock. The journal entry is

Preferred stock	500,000	
APIC-PS	50,000	
Common stock		375,000
APIC-CS		175,000

Note that the $40 market value of the common stock is ignored. The book value method must be used for conversion of preferred stock, so no gains or losses can be recognized.

8. (d) When an issuance of debt, or in this case preferred stock, contains detachable common stock warrants the total proceeds from the sale should be allocated to both the preferred stock and the detachable stock warrants. This treatment arises due to the separability of the stock and the detachable warrants. The allocation of the proceeds is based on the relative fair values of both the stock and the warrants at the time of the issuance. However, in instances where only one of the fair values is known, the known fair value will be used to allocate proceeds to the security in which the fair value is determinable. The remainder is then allocated to the security for which the fair value is unknown. Therefore, because only the fair value of the warrants is known, answer (d) is correct. Answers (a) and (b) are incorrect because fair market value is used to allocate proceeds to the warrants, not the total proceeds or excess proceeds over par value. Answer (c) is incorrect because proceeds are allocated in proportion to both fair values, if determinable, not the fair market value and par value.

9. (a) When the preferred stock and detachable warrants are issued, the following journal entry is made:

Cash	(cash received)
Preferred stock	(par value)
APIC—preferred stock	(FV of preferred stock – par value)
APIC—stock warrants	(plug)

When the stock warrants are exercised, the following journal entry is made:

Cash	(cash received)
APIC—stock warrants	(original amount credited)
Common stock	(par value)
APIC—common stock	(plug)

Therefore, stockholders' equity is increased by the cash received upon the exercise of the common stock warrants. The carrying amount of the warrants increased total stockholders' equity when the preferred stock was issued, not when the warrants were issued.

10. (b) When no par common stock is sold on a subscription basis at a price above the stock's stated value, the stock is not issued until the full subscription price is received. The journal entry on the subscription contract date would be

Cash	(amount received—if any)
Subscription receivable	(balance due)
Common stock subscribed	(stated value)
Additional paid-in capital	(plug)

The journal entry on the date the balance of the subscription is collected and the common stock issued would be

Cash	(balance due)
Common stock subscribed	(stated value)
Common stock	(stated value)
Subscription receivable	(balance due)

Additional paid-in capital increases on the date that the stock is subscribed, not paid for or issued.

11. (d) When stock is sold on a subscription basis, the full price of the stock is not received initially, and the stock is not issued until the full subscription price is received. On the subscription contract date of December 1, year 2, the journal entry would be

Cash	(amount received)
Subscriptions receivable	(balance due)
Common stock subscribed	(par)
Additional paid-in capital	(plug)

12. (c) Under the cost method, the treasury stock account is debited for the cost of the shares acquired. If the treasury shares are reissued at a price in excess of the acquisition cost, the excess is credited to an account titled Paid-in Capital from Treasury Stock. This question refers to it as Additional Paid-in Capital because typically companies do not segregate the two accounts on the balance sheet for reporting purposes. If the treasury shares are reissued at less than the acquisition cost, the deficiency is treated first as a reduction to any paid-in capital related to previous reissuances or retirements of treasury stock of the same class. If the balance in Paid-in Capital from Treasury Stock is not sufficient to absorb the deficiency, the remainder is recorded as a reduction of retained earnings. As the shares in this question were reissued at a price in excess of the acquisition price, the following journal entry would be made at the time of reissue:

Cash (3,000 × $50)	150,000	
Treasury stock (3,000 × $36)		108,000
Additional paid-in capital ($150,000 – $108,000)		42,000

13. (c) The entry that Rama made on acquisition of treasury stock was as follows using the **cost method:**

Treasury stock		
(20,000 × $12)	240,000	
Cash		240,000

When some of the shares are later reissued, the entry is

Cash (15,000 × $10)	150,000	
Retained earnings	30,000	
Treasury stock		
(15,000 × $12)		180,000

It is assumed there was no balance in APIC—Treasury stock prior to this entry. If the problem had stated there was a credit balance, APIC—Treasury stock would be debited before retained earnings to the extent a credit balance existed in APIC—Treasury stock. When retained earnings are legally restricted the restriction must be disclosed. In this case, the net treasury stock account balance is $60,000 ($240,000 – $180,000), and this is the amount of retained earnings that must be disclosed as legally restricted.

14. (**d**) The unadjusted stockholders' equity section shows a total of $2,000,000. However, analysis of the current asset section reveals that United has incorrectly classified $300,000 of treasury stock as a current asset. Although this account has a debit balance, it is **not an asset**. Treasury stock should be reported as a reduction of stockholders' equity. Therefore, total equity at 12/31/Y1 should be $1,700,000 ($2,000,000 – $300,000).

15. (**a**) Under the cost method, when treasury stock is acquired, **treasury stock** is debited and **cash** is credited for the cost.

Treasury stock	100,000	
Cash		100,000

When the treasury stock is resold at an amount above cost, **cash** is debited for the proceeds, **treasury stock** is credited at cost, and the difference is credited to **additional paid-in capital—treasury stock**.

Cash	25,000	
Treasury stock		20,000
APIC—TS		5,000

Neither of these two transactions affect **retained earnings**. Therefore, 12/31/Y2 retained earnings consists of the 12/31/Y1 balance ($300,000) plus year 2 net income ($60,000), or $360,000.

16. (**c**) The requirement is to determine the balance in the paid-in capital from treasury stock account at 12/31/Y1. Using the par value method, treasury stock is debited for par value (5,000 × $10, or $50,000) when purchased. Any excess over par from the original issuance (5,000 × $4, or $20,000) is removed from the appropriate paid-in capital account. In effect, the total original issuance price (5,000 × $14, or $70,000) is charged to the two accounts. Any difference between the original issue price ($70,000) and the cost of the treasury stock (5,000 × $11, or $55,000) is credited to paid-in capital from treasury stock, as illustrated below.

Treasury stock	50,000		(5,000 × $10)
APIC	20,000		(5,000 × $ 4)
Cash		55,000	(5,000 × $11)
PIC—Treasury stock		15,000	($70,000 – $55,000)

17. (**b**) When Dee Inc. issued common stock at a price in excess of its par value, the following journal entry was made:

Cash	(Cash received)
Common stock	(Par)
Additional paid-in	(Excess of cash
capital	capital
	received over
	par)

When Dee Inc. acquires treasury stock using the par method for an amount exceeding the issue price the following journal entry is made:

Treasury stock	(Par)
Additional paid-in	(Excess of original issue price
capital	over par)
Retained earnings	(Excess of acquisition price over
	issue price)
Cash	(Cash paid)

Net common stock decreases by the par value of treasury stock acquired. Additional paid-in capital decreases by the excess of the original issue price over the par value. Retained earnings decreases by the excess of the acquisition price over the original issue price.

18. (**c**) In this case, the par value method does not report a greater amount for additional paid-in capital or retained earnings than the cost method. The entries for an acquisition of treasury shares at greater than par but less than the original issue price are as follows:

Cost method		Par value method	
Treasury stock xxx		Treasury stock xxx	
Cash	xxx	PIC in excess of par xxx	
		Cash	xxx
		PIC from trea-	
		sury stock	xxx

Since under the par value method the original paid-in capital in excess of par must be removed from the accounts upon reacquisition, the par value method actually reports a decrease in additional paid-in capital. On the other hand, under the cost method no change in additional paid-in capital is recorded. There is no change in retained earnings under either method.

19. (**c**) When accounting for the retirement of stock, common stock and additional paid-in capital are removed from the books based on the original issuance of the stock. Cash is credited for the cost of the shares. Any difference is debited to **retained earnings** or credited to **paid-in capital from retirement**. The entry in this case is

Common stock	20,000 (2,000 × $10)	
APIC	180,000 (2,000 × $90)	
Retained earnings	100,000 (2,000 × $50)	
Cash		300,000

Therefore, APIC should be debited for $180,000 and retained earnings should be debited for $100,000.

20. (**a**) In this problem, Luna Corp. is exchanging its available-for-sale securities (AFS) for its preferred stock (i.e., they are retiring some of their preferred stock by exchanging AFS). Upon disposition of the AFS, a gain of $70,000, which is the difference between the carrying amount ($80,000) and the FV ($150,000), must be recognized. Upon retirement of the stock, the preferred stock is debited for the $100,000 par amount (5,000 shares × $20 par). The additional paid-in capital (APIC) is debited for $7,500, which is 1/4 of the original APIC (i.e., 5,000 of the 20,000 shares were retired). The remainder of the FV of the preferred stock ($42,500 = $150,000 – $100,000 – $7,500) is debited to retained earnings.

21. (c) When accounting for the retirement of treasury stock that was initially recorded using the cost method, common stock and additional paid-in capital are removed from the books based on the original issuance of the stock. Treasury stock is credited for the cost of the shares acquired. Any difference is debited to retained earnings or credited to paid-in capital from retirement. In this problem, common stock should be debited for $125,000 (50,000 shares × $2.50), and the common stock balance at December 31, year 1, is $415,000 ($540,000 – $125,000).

22. (c) The requirement is to determine which of the statements correctly identifies an effect of the acquisition and retirement of common stock. The entry to record the retirement of common stock appears as follows:

Common stock (par)	xxx	
Additional paid-in capital	xxx	
Retained earnings	xxx	
Cash		xxx

Additional paid-in capital is debited to the extent it exists. In this case, based on the original issuance, the additional paid-in capital (APIC) balance was $15 per share on the shares retired. When stock is repurchased, if the APIC balance is depleted to zero, retained earnings must also be debited. In this case, retained earnings would not be needed, however. Common stock would be debited for $10 per share and additional paid-in capital would be debited for $10 a share. Excess APIC remains, so retained earnings are not needed to retire the stock. When common stock is repurchased and retired, additional paid-in capital decreases. When common stock is retired, net income is never affected; only stockholders' equity balances are affected. If retained earnings are needed to retire stock, the account decreases, not increases.

23. (b) Since this is an investment accounted for on the cost basis, the dividend income should be the amount of cash dividends received. Since Plack Co. had 12,000 shares at the time the cash dividend was paid, the total amount of cash dividends received is $24,000 (12,000 × $2.00).

24. (c) When preferred stock is participating, there may be different agreements as to how the participation feature is to be executed. However, in the absence of any specific agreement, the following procedure should be used:

After the preferred stock is allocated its current year dividend, the common stock will receive a "like" percentage of par value outstanding. If there are remaining declared dividends, this amount should be shared by both the preferred and common stock in proportion to the par value dollars outstanding of each stock as follows:

Current year's dividend:

Preferred, 5% of $300,000		
(30,000 shares × $10 Par)	$15,000	
Common, 5% of $200,000		
(200,000 shares × $1 Par)	10,000	$ 25,000

Amount available for participation		
($100,000 – $25,000)		$ 75,000
Par value of stock that is to participate		
($300,000 + $200,000)		$500,000

Proportional share of participating dividend:

Preferred	$\dfrac{\$300,000}{\$500,000}$	×	75,000	=	$ 45,000
Common	$\dfrac{\$200,000}{\$500,000}$	×	75,000	=	$ 30,000

Thus, the dividends payable to common shareholders is $40,000 ($10,000 + $30,000).

25. (d) For **cumulative** preferred stock, dividends not paid in **any** year will accumulate and must be paid in a later year before any dividends can be paid to common stockholders. The unpaid prior year dividends are called "dividends in arrears." The balance of dividends in arrears should be disclosed in the financial statements rather than accrued, as they are not considered a liability until they are declared. Dividends in arrears at 12/31/Y3 total $20,000, as computed below.

Year 2 $300,000 × 5%	=	$15,000
Year 3 $300,000 × 5%	=	15,000
Total cumulative preferred dividends		$30,000
Less year 3 dividend payment		(10,000)
Balance of dividends in arrears		$20,000

Answer (c) is incorrect because dividends in arrears are not considered to be a liability until they are declared. They should be disclosed parenthetically or in the notes to the financial statements. Answer (b) is incorrect because the total dividends amount needs to reflect both the year 2 and year 3 unpaid dividends since it is cumulative preferred stock. Answer (a) is incorrect because the dividends in arrears would not be considered a liability until they are declared and the $15,000 amount is the incorrect balance as discussed above.

26. (d) The interest is not an expense or liability until incurred, thus, none of it is recorded on April 1. The April 1 entry would be

Retained earnings	100,000	
Scrip dividends payable		100,000

By December 31 (the year-end for this calendar-year company), nine months' interest had been incurred, which would not be paid until the maturity date of 3/31/Y2. The $7,500 of interest expense ($100,000 × 10% × 9/12) must be accrued at 12/31/Y1 with the following entry:

Interest expense	7,500	
Interest payable		7,500

27. (b) Dividends that are based on funds other than retained earnings are considered to be liquidating dividends. The cash dividend declared of $400,000 is first assumed to be a return **on** capital for the distribution of the retained earnings balance of $300,000. The excess $400,000 dividend – $300,000 RE = $100,000 is considered to be a return **of** capital or a liquidating dividend rather than a return **on** capital. Note that the amount of liquidating dividend also equals the balance in accumulated depletion. Companies in the extractive industries may pay dividends equal to the accumulated income **and** depletion.

28. (c)   A transfer of a nonmonetary asset to a stock-holder or to another entity in a nonreciprocal transfer should be recorded at the fair value of the asset transferred, and a gain or loss should be recognized on the disposition of the asset. The fair value of the nonmonetary asset distributed is measured by the amount that would be realized in an out-right sale at or near the time of distribution. In this case, a gain should be recognized for the difference between the fair value of $2.50 per share and the carrying amount of $2 per share, or a total gain of $50,000 [100,000 × ($2.50 – $2.00)].

29. (c)   A transfer of a nonmonetary asset to a stock-holder or to another entity in a nonreciprocal transfer should be recorded at the fair market value of the asset transferred, and a gain or loss should be recognized on the disposition of the asset. At the date of declaration, Nilo records

Trading securities	18,000	
Gain on disposition of securities		18,000
Retained earnings (dividends)	78,000	
Property dividends payable		78,000

At the date of distribution, Nilo records

Property dividends payable	78,000	
Trading securities		78,000

After all nominal accounts are closed, the effect on retained earnings from the above entries would be $60,000 ($78,000 debit to retained earnings less $18,000 credit to retained earnings when the "gain on disposition" account is closed out).

30. (b)   A stock split is **not** a dividend. Stock splits change the number of shares outstanding and the par value per share. Par value per share is reduced in proportion to the increase in the number of shares. Therefore, the total par value outstanding does not change, and no journal entry is required. The only dividend to be reported in Long's year 1 statement of stockholders' equity is the 12/15 cash dividend. The stock split increased the number of shares outstanding to 200,000 (100,000 × 2), so the amount of the cash divi-dend is $100,000 (200,000 × $.50).

31. (b)   The requirement is to determine the effect of a cash dividend on stockholders' equity at the three dates listed. On the date of declaration, December 15, year 1, the following entry should be made:

Retained earnings	xxx	
Dividends payable		xxx

Thus, at December 15, year 1, stockholders' equity is reduced due to the debit to retained earnings. On December 31, year 1, there is no effect on stockholders' equity because an entry would not be recorded. On January 12, year 2, the following entry would be made:

Dividends payable	xxx	
Cash		xxx

The net effect of this entry is to decrease assets and liabili-ties by an equal amount. Thus, stockholders' equity (or net assets) would be unaffected.

32. (d)   Any dividend not based on earnings must be a reduction of corporate paid-in capital and, to that extent, it is a liquidating dividend. The following journal entries would be made for this situation:

At date of declaration:

Additional paid-in capital	100,000	
Dividends payable		100,000

At date of payment:

Dividends payable	100,000	
Cash		100,000

Thus, a liquidating dividend would decrease Ole's paid-in capital, not its retained earnings.

33. (d)   A property dividend is a nonreciprocal transfer of nonmonetary assets between an enterprise and its owners. A nonreciprocal transfer of nonmonetary assets to a stock-holder or another entity shall be recorded at the fair value of the asset transferred. Additionally, a gain or loss shall be recognized on the disposition of the asset. Accordingly, Evie Corp. should record the following journal entries to reflect the property dividend:

At the date of declaration:

Loss on decline in inventory value		
(Carrying amount – Market value)	xxx	
Merchandise inventory		xxx
Retained earnings (market value)	xxx	
Property dividends payable		xxx

At the date of distribution:

Property dividends payable	xxx	
Merchandise inventory		xxx

The loss recorded in the above journal entry does not qualify as unusual and infrequent, thus it is not an extraordinary item. The loss should be reported as a reduction in income before discontinued operations and extraordinary items.

34. (b)   The requirement is to determine the amount to be debited to retained earnings for these stock dividends. The issuance of a stock dividend less than **20-25%** (a "small" stock dividend) requires that the **market value** of the stock be transferred from retained earnings, and a divi-dend greater than **20-25%** (a "large" stock dividend) re-quires the **par value** of the stock to be transferred from re-tained earnings. Thus, a 10% stock dividend is considered to be "small" and should be transferred from retained earn-ings at the FV of $15,000. A 28% stock dividend is consid-ered to be "large" and should be transferred at the par value of $30,800. The aggregate amount to be transferred from retained earnings is $45,800.

35. (a)   When the stock dividend is less than 20-25% of the common shares outstanding at the time of the declara-tion, generally accepted accounting principles require that the FV of the stock issued be transferred from retained earnings. At the date of declaration, the following entry would be made:

Retained earnings (Stock dividends		
declared) (.05 × 10,000 shares × $5)	2,500	
Common stock dividend distribut-		
able (.05 × 10,000 × $2)		1,000
Additional paid-in capital (plug)		1,500

Note from the entry above that no asset or liability has been affected. The entry merely reflects a reclassification within the equity accounts. When a balance sheet is prepared be-tween the dates of declaration and distribution, the common stock dividend distributable should be shown in the stockholders' equity section as an addition to capital stock.

36. (d)   A stock dividend is an issuance by a corporation of its own common shares to its common shareholders without consideration to give the recipient shareholders evidence of a part of their respective interests in accumulated corporate earnings without distribution of cash or other property. A stock split is defined as an issuance by a corporation of common shares to its common shareholders without consideration...prompted mainly by a desire to increase the number of outstanding shares for the purpose of effecting a reduction in their unit market price and, thereby, of obtaining wider distribution and improved marketability of the shares. Thus, neither of these transactions results in a transfer of assets among the shareholders and the corporation. While the allocation of stockholders' equity among the various accounts (retained earnings, common stock, and additional paid-in capital) will change, the **total** stockholders' equity is **not** affected.

37. (b)   The requirement is to determine the balance of additional paid-in capital immediately after a reverse stock split. Stock splits change the number of shares outstanding and the par value per share, but the total par value outstanding does not change. Stock splits do not affect any account balances, including additional paid-in capital. Therefore, the balance of additional paid-in capital remains at $450,000.

38. (b)   A stock split does not affect either the balance of the additional paid-in capital or the retained earnings accounts. The number of shares outstanding and the par value per share merely change in proportion to each other. When this occurs, only a memorandum entry is made.

39. (a)   The requirement is to determine the amount of appropriated retained earnings Eagle should report in its year 2 balance sheet. The entry to record the appropriation of retained earnings in year 2 for the construction of a new plant is as follows:

RE (or Unappropriated RE) $1,200,000	
RE Appropriated for plant expansion	$1,200,000

The cash restricted for the retirement of bonds due in year 2 should **not** be reported as an appropriation of retained earnings because the facts in the question do not indicate that appropriation was made by management. When an appropriation is no longer needed, it must be returned directly to unappropriated retained earnings by reversing the entry that created it. Therefore, when the office building was completed in year 2, the following entry was made:

RE Appropriated for plant expansion $1,750,000	
RE (or Unappropriated RE)	$1,750,000

The total cost to complete the building has no effect on appropriated retained earnings.

40. (a)   Retained earnings are typically appropriated due to legal requirements, contractual requirements, or through the discretion of the board of directors. Dividends in arrears are not considered a liability to the company, and retained earnings would not be appropriated for this amount. In many cases, retained earnings must be appropriated for an amount equal to the cost of treasury stock acquired. However, this appropriation would be removed upon reissuance of the treasury stock.

41. (d)   Appropriations of retained earnings are not prohibited provided that the appropriation is clearly identified as such in the stockholders' equity section of the balance sheet. Costs or losses cannot be charged to an appropriation of retained earnings. A contingent loss that is probable and reasonably estimable should be accrued as a loss and liability.

42. (d)   Employee compensation expense as the result of a stock option plan is calculated as the fair value of the equity instrument **at the date of grant** times the number of option shares.

3,000 shares × $8 fair value of option = $24,000

The total compensation expense must be recognized over the requisite service period for which the option plan represents compensation. If not otherwise specified, the required service period (two years) is assumed to be the period benefited. Therefore, year 1 compensation expense is $12,000 ($24,000 ÷ 2). Note that compensation expense is not affected by changes in the market value of the stock after the measurement date.

43. (b)   Total compensation expense as a result of a stock option plan is calculated as the fair value of the equity instruments at the date of grant times the number of options.

10,000 options × $12 fair value of option = $120,000

The total compensation expense must be recognized over the requisite service period for which the option plan represents compensation. Therefore, year 2 compensation expense is $40,000 ($120,000 ÷ 3 years). Note that the cost of treasury stock distributed in an option plan does not determine compensation expense.

44. (d)   The fair value of the stock option at date of grant was $28 ($28 × 1,000 shares = $28,000). The entire amount is recognized because the options are exercisable immediately for three years after the grant date.

45. (a)   The net increase in stockholders' equity (SE) as a result of the grant and exercise of the options is equal to the increase in cash (1,000 shares × $20 option price = $20,000). The journal entry to record the options has no effect on SE because a SE account will be credited while a contra SE account will be debited as follows:

Deferred compensation	28,000	
Paid-in capital stock options		28,000
(1,000 shares × $28 per option)		

The entry to recognize compensation expense has no effect on SE because the debit decreases SE while the credit increases SE by reducing the contra account as follows:

Compensation expense	28,000	
Deferred compensation		28,000

The only entry which does affect SE is the entry for the exercise of the options, which decreases SE by $28,000 while increasing it by $48,000 (a net increase of $20,000).

Cash (1,000 × $20)	20,000	
Paid-in capital stock options (1,000 × $28)	28,000	
Common stock (1,000 × $10)		10,000
Paid-in capital in × of PV (plug)		38,000

Thus, the net increase in stockholders' equity is $20,000.

46. (c) The 20,000 stock appreciation rights (SAR) each entitle the holder to receive cash equal to the excess of the market price of the stock on the exercise date over the market price of the stock on the grant date ($30). Since these SAR are payment for past services and are exercisable immediately, there is no required service period. Therefore, the expense computed at 12/31/Y1 does **not** have to be allocated to more than one period. At 12/31/Y1, compensation expense is measured based on the excess of the 12/31/Y1 market price ($45) over the predetermined price ($30), resulting in compensation expense of $300,000 [20,000 ($45 − $30)]. Note that **if** Dean were **required** to work three years **before** the SAR could be exercised, the expense would be allocated over the three years of required service ($300,000 × 1/3 = $100,000).

47. (c) When accounting for stock compensation plans, total compensation expense is computed as the excess of the fair value of the equity instrument over the amount contributed by employees. In this case, the fair value of the 150,000 shares issued in year 1 is $1,050,000, and the employees' contributions for these shares is $350,000. Therefore, Wall should recognize $700,000 ($1,050,000 − $350,000) as expense in year 1 for the stock compensation plan.

48. (c) The rate of interest used to discount both the exercise price and dividends is the risk-free interest rate.

49. (c) If the stock options are for past services, as indicated when the options are immediately exercisable by the holders, compensation cost must be fully expensed at the grant date. Answer (a) is incorrect because usually deferred compensation expense is recognized. Answer (b) is incorrect because deferred compensation expense is recognized when service has not yet been provided. Answer (d) is incorrect because when options are provided for prior service compensation expense must immediately be recognized.

50. (a) Compensation cost for a share-based payment to employees that is classified as a liability is measured by the change in fair value of the instrument for each reporting period.

51. (c) The final measurement date is the settlement date for share-based payments to employees classified as liabilities.

52. (d) Accounting for stock-based compensation using the fair value method is as follows:

Fair value of option at grant date	6.40
Times # of options	× 20,000
Deferred compensation expense	$128,000

53. (d) Cash retained as a result of excess tax benefits in connection with share-based payments to employees should be recognized as a cash inflow from financing activities in the statement of cash flows.

54. (c) The options should be included in the denominator of diluted earnings per share unless the shares are antidilutive. If the equity share options are outstanding for only a part of a period, the shares are weighted to reflect the period of time outstanding.

55. (b) The formula for basic earnings per share (BEPS) is

$$\frac{\$1,000,000 \text{ net income} - \$50,000 \text{ preferred dividends}}{100,000 \text{ common shares outstanding}} = \$9.50$$

In calculating the numerator, the claims of preferred shareholders against year 2 earnings should be deducted to arrive at the year 2 earnings attributable to common shareholders. This amount is 50,000 (5% × $100 × 10,000 shares). The $50,000 preferred dividends in arrears is not deducted to compute the numerator in determining year 2 BEPS. This is because the $50,000 dividends in arrears is a claim of preferred shareholders against year 1 earnings and would reduce year 1 BEPS.

56. (b) The formula for basic earnings per share (BEPS) is

$$\frac{\$500,000 \text{ net income} - 10,000 \text{ preferred dividends}}{200,000 \text{ common shares outstanding}} = \$2.45$$

In calculating the numerator, the claims of preferred shareholders against year 2 earnings should be deducted to arrive at the year 2 earnings attributable to common shareholders. This amount is $10,000 ($250,000 × 4%). During year 1, the BEPS numerator would have been reduced by $10,000 even though no preferred dividends were declared, because the cumulative feature means that $10,000 of year 1 earnings are reserved for, and will ultimately be paid to, preferred stockholders. In year 2, the year 1 dividends in arrears are paid, as well as $6,000 of the $10,000 year 2 preferred dividend. Even though only $6,000 is paid, the entire $10,000 is subtracted for reasons explained above.

57. (b) For EPS purposes, shares of stock issued as a result of stock dividends or splits should be considered outstanding for the entire period in which they were issued. Therefore, both the original 20,000 shares and the additional 20,000 issued in the 4/1 stock split are treated as outstanding for the entire year (20,000 × 2 = 40,000). The 7/1 issuance of 10,000 shares results in a weighted-average of 5,000 shares (10,000 × 6/12) because the shares were outstanding for only six months during the year. Therefore, Jet should use 45,000 shares (40,000 + 5,000) to calculate EPS.

58. (d) The computation of weighted-average shares outstanding is

Date	# of shares		Fraction		WA
1/1	30,000	×	12/12	=	30,000
2/1	3,000	×	12/12	=	3,000
7/1	8,000	×	6/12	=	4,000
					37,000

The 3,000 shares issued as a result of a stock dividend are weighted at 12/12 instead of 11/12 because for EPS purposes stock dividends are treated as if they occurred at the beginning of the year.

59. (b) The formula for computing BEPS for a simple capital structure is

$$\frac{\text{Net income} - \text{Applicable pref. stock dividends}}{\text{Weighted-average \# of common shares outstanding}}$$

Net income is $410,000 and $350,000 in year 2 and year 1, respectively, and there are no preferred dividends. The weighted-average number of common shares outstanding must be computed for year 2. Stock dividends and stock splits are handled retroactively for comparability. The year 2 computation is

Dates	Number of Shares	Fraction	WA
1/1 to 3/31	100,000 × 2 = 200,000	3/12	50,000
4/1 to 6/30	(100,000 + 20,000) × 2 = 240,000	3/12	60,000
7/1 to 12/31	120,000 × 2 = 240,000	6/12	120,000
			230,000

The year 1 weighted-average of 100,000 is retroactively restated to 200,000 for comparability. Therefore, the BEPS amounts are

Year 2 $\dfrac{\$410,000}{230,000} = \$1.78$ **Year 1** $\dfrac{\$350,000}{200,000} = \$1.75$

60. **(b)** Earnings per share must be shown on the face of the income statement for income from continuing operations and net income. EPS for discontinued operations and extraordinary items may be shown on the income statement or in the notes.

61. **(c)** If the number of common shares outstanding increases as a result of a stock dividend or stock split or decreases as a result of a reverse split, the computations of EPS should give retroactive recognition for all periods presented. If these events take place after the close of the period but before completion of the financial report, the per share computations should be based on the new number of shares. Note that when per share computations reflect such changes in the number of shares after the close of the period, this fact should be disclosed.

62. **(b)** The requirement is to determine the number of shares that should be used in computing year 2 diluted earnings per share. The first step is to compute the weighted-average number of common shares outstanding. 300,000 shares were outstanding the entire year, and 50,000 more shares were outstanding for six months, resulting in a weighted-average of 325,000 [300,000 + (50,000 × 6/12)]. Second, the stock options increase the number of shares used in the computation **only** if they are dilutive. The stock options are dilutive because the exercise price is less than the market value. Thus, the denominator effect of the options must be computed. This is done using the **treasury stock method,** as illustrated below.

Assumed proceeds (40,000 × $15)	$600,000
Shares issued	40,000
Shares reacquired ($600,000 ÷ $20)	(30,000)
Shares issued, not reacquired	10,000

Therefore, the number of shares used for computing diluted earnings per share is 335,000 (325,000 + 10,000).

63. **(b)** Diluted earnings per share is based on common stock and all dilutive potential common shares. To determine if a security is dilutive, EPS, including the effect of the dilutive security, must be compared to the basic EPS. In this case, basic EPS is $7.45.

$$\frac{850,000\ (NI) - 30,000\ (pref.\ div.)}{110,000\ shares} = \$7.45$$

The effect of the convertible preferred stock is to increase the numerator by $30,000 ($3.00 dividend per share × 10,000 shares) for the amount of the preferred dividends that would not be paid (assuming conversion) and increase the

denominator by 20,000 shares. This security is dilutive because it decreases the EPS from $7.45 to $6.54.

$$\frac{850,000 - 30,000 + 30,000}{110,000 + 20,000} = \$6.54$$

If the EPS increases due to the inclusion of a security, that security is antidilutive and should not be included.

64. **(d)** The requirement is to compute the diluted earnings per share for year 2. Therefore, **all** potential common shares that **reduce** current EPS must be included in the computation. The formula for diluted EPS is

$$\frac{Net\ income\ available\ to\ common\ shareholders}{Weighted\text{-}average\ common\ shares\ outstanding}$$

The net income available to common shareholders is $3,200,000. This is the net income of $3,400,000 less the preferred stock dividend of $200,000. The weighted-average common shares outstanding is 1,250,000. This is computed as the actual common shares outstanding for the full year of 1,200,000 plus the contingent common shares of 50,000 that were outstanding for the full year because the contingency was incurred in year 1. Thus,

$$Diluted\ EPS = \frac{\$3,200,000}{1,250,000} = \$2.56$$

65. **(b)** The effect of convertible bonds is included in diluted EPS under the if converted method, if they are dilutive. The bonds are dilutive as shown below.

$$Basic\ EPS = \frac{\$35,000}{(1/2)\ 10,000 + (1/2)\ 14,000} = \$2.92$$

Incremental per share effect $= \dfrac{(7\% \times \$10,000) - 30\% (7\% \times \$10,000)}{200\ shares\ per\ bond} = \dfrac{\$490}{200} = \$2.45$

Since $2.45 < $2.92, the bonds are dilutive. Under the if converted method, the assumption is made that the bonds were converted at the beginning of the current year (1/1) or later in the current year if the bonds were issued during the current year. In this case, conversion is assumed for the first six months of year 2 only because the bonds were actually converted on July 1. Under their assumed conversion, the numerator would increase because bond interest expense would not have been incurred for the first six months of the year [1/2 ($14,000 – 30% × $14,000) = $4,900]. The denominator would increase because the 4,000 shares (20 × 200) would have been outstanding for the first six months of the year (4,000 × 6/12 = 2,000). Therefore, diluted EPS is $2.85.

$$\frac{\$35,000 + \$4,900}{12,000 + 2,000} = \frac{\$39,900}{14,000} = \$2.85$$

66. **(a)** Diluted EPS takes into account the effect of all dilutive potential common shares that were outstanding during the period. Thus, the possible conversion of convertible bonds would be included because they are dilutive (i.e., EPS would be reduced), but the possible exercise of common stock options would not be included because they are antidilutive (i.e., EPS would be increased). Diluted EPS = $15.00 – $.75 = $14.25.

67. **(d)** The requirement is to determine the treatment of nonconvertible cumulative preferred dividends in determining diluted EPS. Dividends on nonconvertible cumulative preferred shares should be deducted from net income whether an actual liability exists or not. This is because cumulative preferred stock owners must receive any dividends in arrears before future dividend distributions can be made to common stockholders.

68. (a) The if-converted method of computing earnings per share assumes that convertible securities are converted at the beginning of the earliest period reported or, if later, at the time of issuance.

69. (b) If convertible securities are deemed to be dilutive, then interest expense should be added back to net income when computing diluted earnings per share.

70. (b) The effect of contingent issue agreements are not included in basic earnings per share. They are included in diluted earnings per share if the contingency is met.

71. (d) The total cash available to pay **all** unsecured claims, including priority claims, is the cash obtained from free assets ($320,000) and any excess cash available from assets pledged with fully secured creditors after they are used to satisfy those claims ($370,000 – $260,000 = $110,000). Therefore, total cash available is $430,000 ($320,000 + $110,000). After paying priority claims, $360,000 will remain to pay all unsecured nonpriority claims ($430,000 – $70,000).

72. (c) Bankruptcy law requires that the claims of secured creditors be satisfied before any unsecured claims are paid. Hale is a secured creditor in the amount of $5,000 (the liquidation value of the collateral). The remainder of Hale's claim ($30,000 – $5,000 = $25,000) is an unsecured claim, because it is not secured by any collateral. Therefore, Hale will receive a total of $15,000 on this note: $5,000 received in full as a secured creditor, and $10,000 received as an unsecured creditor ($25,000 × $.40).

73. (d) A bankruptcy trustee may establish a new set of accounting records to maintain accountability for the bankruptcy estate. Once the trustee assumes custody of the estate, the trustee will enter any unrecorded assets or liabilities in the estate equity account. Any gains or losses and liquidation expenses incurred will also be recorded. In the Kamy Corp. bankruptcy, both the $8,000 loss on sale of the truck ($20,000 carrying value – $12,000 cash selling price) and the $1,000 unrecorded liability would be debited to the estate equity account as follows:

Estate equity	1,000	
Accounts payable		1,000

Cash	12,000	
Estate equity	8,000	
Truck		20,000

74. (b) The requirement is to determine the net increase in total stockholders' equity as a result of the payments to unsecured creditors pursuant to a reorganization plan under Chapter 11. The net increase in stockholders' equity can be determined as follows:

Fair value of liabilities owed to unsecured creditors	$1,200,000
Cash paid	(400,000)
Common stock issued (80,000 × $1.25)	(100,000)
Gain on settlement of debt	$ 700,000

The gain on the settlement of debt would be included in the income statement and closed to retained earnings. The net increase in stockholders' equity would equal $800,000 ($700,000 gain + $100,000 FV of stock issued).

75. (c) Although assets are often revalued to fair value during a quasi reorganization, the **primary** purpose of a quasi reorganization is to eliminate a deficit in retained earnings so that dividends may be paid without waiting years to eliminate the deficit through future earnings. A quasi reorganization does not directly allow a corporation to obtain relief from creditors or result in a distribution of stock.

76. (d) In certain instances an entity may elect to restate its assets, capital stock, and surplus through a readjustment (or "quasi reorganization") and thus avail itself of permission to relieve its future income account or earned surplus account of charges which would otherwise be made there against. In such instances, the entity should present a **fair (value)** balance sheet as of the date of the reorganization.

77. (c) A quasi reorganization generally involves (1) revaluing assets, (2) reducing par, and (3) writing the deficit off against additional paid-in capital. In this case, no mention is made of the first step, revaluing assets. The second step, reducing par, results in a decrease to **common stock** and an increase to **additional paid-in capital** of $250,000 [10,000 × ($30 – $5)]. The third step, writing off the deficit, increases **retained earnings** by $210,000 (creating a $0 balance) and decrease **additional paid-in capital** by the same amount. Immediately after the quasi reorganization, Brown should report additional paid-in capital of $190,000 ($150,000 + $250,000 – $210,000).

78. (a) When a corporation issues rights to its stockholders, it only makes a memorandum entry. If rights are later exercised, the corporation would make the following entry:

Cash	xxx	
Common stock		xxx
Additional paid-in capital		xxx

79. (c) The only time a journal entry is recorded for the issuance and exercise of stock rights is on the date of exercise. At the date of issuance, only a memorandum entry is recorded. The redemption of the rights issued to the shareholders should be treated like a dividend. Accordingly, retained earnings will be decreased by the amount paid to the shareholders (120,000 × $0.10 = $12,000).

80. (a) The requirement is to determine the effects of the stock warrants on the additional paid-in capital account and on net income. When a corporation issues stock warrants to its stockholders it only makes a memorandum entry. Then, when the warrants are exercised, the following entry is made:

Cash	xxx	
Common stock		xxx
Additional paid-in capital		xxx

Net income is not affected by the exercise of stock warrants because the transaction represents a process of raising capital and is not related to the earnings process. Additional paid-in capital is not affected until the exercise date in year 2.

81. (b) Note that the only time an entry related to the issuance and exercise of stock rights, which affects the equity accounts of a corporation, is recorded is on the date of exercise. At the date of issuance, only a memorandum entry is recorded, and on the date of the rights lapsing, no entry is recorded which would affect the company's equity accounts. Thus, the correct answer is (b): the additional paid-in capital account would not be credited at the time the rights are issued or at the date on which the rights lapse.

82. (c) The amount contributed or committed to be contributed to an employee stock ownership plan (ESOP) in a given year should be the measure of the amount to be charged to expense by the employer. Therefore, Fay should record year 1 compensation expense of $84,000 [contribution of $30,000 cash and common stock with a FV of $54,000 (3,000 × $18)].

83. (d) An obligation of an Employee Stock Ownership Plan (ESOP) should be recorded as a liability in the financial statements of the employer when the obligation is covered by either a guarantee of the employer or a commitment by the employer to make future contributions to the ESOP sufficient to meet the debt service requirements. Therefore, the note payable of $100,000 (which is guaranteed by Fay) should be reported in Fay's 12/31/Y1 balance sheet. The offsetting debit to the employer's liability should be reported as a reduction of stockholders' equity. Therefore, Fay should also report $100,000 as a reduction of stockholders' equity.

84. (a) All of the accounts given are stockholders' equity accounts. Total stockholders' equity is computed below.

Paid-in capital		
Common stock		$ 600,000
Addl. paid-in capital		800,000
		1,400,000
Retained earinings		
Appropriated	$150,000	
Unappropriated	200,000	350,000
		1,750,000
Accumulated other comprehensive income		
Unrealized loss on available-for-sale securities		(20,000)
Less: Treasury stock		(50,000)
		$1,680,000

Both **treasury stock** and **net unrealized loss on available-for-sale securities** are contra stockholders' equity accounts.

85. (a) The number of shares outstanding is equal to the issued shares less treasury shares (TS). The table below shows the effects of each of the stock transactions on the common shares outstanding.

	Outstanding shares
1/1/Y2	300,000
1/31/Y2 declaration of 10% stock dividend	30,000
6/30/Y2 purchase of TS	(100,000)
8/1/Y2 sale of TS	50,000
Subtotal	280,000
11/30/Y2 stock split	× 2
12/31/Y2	560,000

86. (a) Shares issued and outstanding are computed below.

	Issued	Outstanding
12/31/Y1	100,000	95,000
5/3/Y2		1,000
8/6/Y2	10,000	10,000
Subtotal	110,000	106,000
11/18/Y2	110,000	106,000
12/31/Y2	220,000	212,000

At 12/31/Y1, shares issued were 100,000 and outstanding 95,000 (100,000 issued less 5,000 treasury). The reissuance of treasury stock does not increase shares issued, but does increase shares outstanding by 1,000 to 96,000 (100,000 issued less 4,000 treasury). The issuance of previously unissued stock on 8/6/Y2 increases both issued and outstanding shares by 10,000, bringing the totals to 110,000 issued and 106,000 outstanding prior to the stock split. Since treasury stock is protected from dilution, shares issued, treasury shares, and outstanding shares are all doubled by the stock split.

87. (a) The requirement is to determine the effect on Ali Corp. of exercising the stock options. First, the debt to equity ratio is calculated as follows:

$$\text{Debt to equity} = \frac{\text{Total liabilities}}{\text{Common stockholders' equity}}$$

The figures given in the problem reflect the account balances **after** the exercise of the stock options. Thus, Ali's debt to equity ratio after the exercise is

$$\frac{\$60,000}{\$500,000} = 12\%$$

When the options were exercised, total stockholders' equity would have increased by the amount of the option price as follows:

Common stock	↑	by par value × 1,000 shares
Paid-in capital	↑	by (option price-par) × 1,000 shares

Note that the information given is incomplete as to whether compensation was recorded under the stock option plan. However, even if compensation was recorded, the entries are made only to accounts that impact stockholders' equity, and the net effect is no change. Thus, the only change is an increase resulting from the exercise of the options. Since common stockholders' equity increased, the denominator of the debt to equity ratio also increased. As the denominator becomes larger and the numerator remains constant, the quotient becomes smaller. Therefore, the debt to equity ratio must have **decreased** to its current level of 12%. Answer (b) is incorrect because earnings per share decreased by $0.33. Answer (c) is incorrect because not enough information is given to calculate the asset turnover. Answer (d) is incorrect because the debt to equity ratio, rate of return on common stock, earnings per share, price earnings ratio, and book value per share were all affected by exercising the stock options.

88. (c) The requirement is to determine Irvington's return on common stockholders' equity for year 2, which is computed by dividing net income available to common stockholders (net income less preferred dividends) by average common stockholders' equity.

$$\frac{\$120,000 - \$10,000}{(\$375,000 + \$585,000) / 2} = 23\%$$

89. **(d)** The requirement is to determine the book value per common share. The book value per common share is the amount each share would receive if the company were liquidated. The book value per common share is calculated as follows:

	Preferred	Common
Preferred stock, 5%	$250,000	
Common stock		$350,000
APIC in excess of par value of common stock		125,000
Retained earnings:		
Dividends in arrears	25,000	
Liquidation premium	50,000	
Remainder to common (Plug)		225,000
Totals	$325,000	$700,000
Shares outstanding		100,000
Book value per share		$ 7.00

Note that when calculating the remainder to common, total stockholders' equity before the liquidation must be equal to the amount after the assumed liquidation.

90. **(c)** Under the cost method, treasury stock is debited for the cost of the treasury stock, thus decreasing total stockholders' equity. However, the book value per share will increase due to the acquisition of the treasury stock. Book value per share is calculated by dividing common stockholders' equity by the shares outstanding. An example will help illustrate.

Stockholders' equity	
Common stock (30,000 shares)	
$5 par	$150,000
Additional paid-in capital	550,000
Retained earnings	250,000
	$950,000

$$\text{Book value per share} = \frac{\$950,000}{30,000} = \$31.67$$

Per the facts in the question, treasury stock was acquired at more than par and original issue price, but less than book value per share. Therefore, the acquisition price must be greater than $23.33 per share (700,000 ÷ 30,000) and less than $31.67 per share.

Let's say 1,000 shares of treasury stock were acquired at $27.00 per share.

$$\text{Book value per share} = \frac{\$950,000 - (1,000 \times \$27)}{30,000 - 1,000}$$

$$= \frac{\$923,000}{29,000}$$

$$= \$31.83$$

The book value per share increased after the acquisition of the treasury stock.

91. **(b)** Dividends per share is used in the numerator of the dividend payout ratio as shown below.

$$\frac{\text{Dividend}}{\text{payout ratio}} = \frac{\text{Dividends per share}}{\text{Earnings per share}}$$

However, dividends per share are not used in the calculation of earnings per share.

$$\frac{\text{Earnings}}{\text{per share}} = \frac{\text{Net income} - \text{Preferred dividends}}{\text{Weighted-average number of shares outstanding}}$$

92. **(c)** The requirement is to identify how Logan should recognize the issuance of the bonds. Answer (c) is correct because IFRS provides that financial instruments with characteristics of both debt and equity are compound instruments and must be separated into its respective components. The liability is valued at the fair value at the date of issuance and the residual value is assigned to the equity component. Therefore, the bond should be recorded at its fair value of $480,000 and an equity component should be recorded for 20,000. Answers (a), (b), and (d) are incorrect.

93. **(d)** The requirement is to identify the correct statement about recording convertible debt under IFRS. Answer (d) is correct because IFRS requires the proceeds to be allocated between debt and equity.

94. **(c)** The requirement is to identify the item that does not describe a method that may be used to account for treasury stock under IFRS. Answer (c) is correct because the retained earnings method is not a method that is used to account for treasury stock. The cost method, par value method, and constructive retirement method are all methods that may be used to account for treasury stock under IFRS.

Simulations

Task-Based Simulation 1

Concepts		
	Authoritative Literature	Help

Items 1 through 10 require you to select the best response from the responses to be selected.

Responses to be selected
A. Contains no potentially dilutive securities
B. A form of compensation which allows employees to receive stock or cash for the difference between the stated value and the market value
C. Legal or contractual restrictions on the number of shares an employee may own
D. Issuance of additional shares in order to reduce the market value
E. Purchase by the corporation of its own stock
F. The value of treasury shares are recorded at cost of acquisition
G. A dividend paid which is considered a return of the shareholders' investment
H. Actions by the board of directors to disclose amounts not available for dividends
I. The balance of the treasury stock account reflects the par value
J. A form of compensation which allows employees to purchase shares at a specified price
K. A dividend issued in the form of a note payable
L. A stock transaction resulting in a reduced number of shares outstanding and a higher market value
M. Assumes convertible securities were converted at the beginning of the period

	(A)	(B)	(C)	(D)	(E)	(F)	(G)	(H)	(I)	(J)	(K)	(L)	(M)
1. Par value method	O	O	O	O	O	O	O	O	O	O	O	O	O
2. Appropriations of retained earnings	O	O	O	O	O	O	O	O	O	O	O	O	O
3. Stock split	O	O	O	O	O	O	O	O	O	O	O	O	O
4. Simple capital structure	O	O	O	O	O	O	O	O	O	O	O	O	O
5. If-converted method	O	O	O	O	O	O	O	O	O	O	O	O	O
6. Scrip dividend	O	O	O	O	O	O	O	O	O	O	O	O	O
7. Stock appreciation rights	O	O	O	O	O	O	O	O	O	O	O	O	O
8. Stock option	O	O	O	O	O	O	O	O	O	O	O	O	O
9. Liquidating dividend	O	O	O	O	O	O	O	O	O	O	O	O	O
10. Treasury stock	O	O	O	O	O	O	O	O	O	O	O	O	O

Task-Based Simulation 2

Statement of Retained Earnings		
	Authoritative Literature	Help

Min Co. is a publicly held company whose shares are traded in the over-the-counter market. The stockholders' equity accounts at December 31, year 1, had the following balances:

Preferred stock, $100 par value, 6% cumulative; 5,000 shares authorized; 2,000 issued and outstanding	$ 200,000
Common stock, $1 par value, 150,000 shares authorized; 100,000 issued and outstanding	100,000
Additional paid-in capital	800,000
Retained earnings	1,586,000
Total stockholders' equity	$2,686,000

Transactions during year 2 and other information relating to the stockholders' equity accounts were as follows:

- February 1, year 2—Issued 13,000 shares of common stock to Ram Co. in exchange for land. On the date issued, the stock had a market price of $11 per share. The land had a carrying value on Ram's books of $135,000, and an assessed value for property taxes of $90,000.

- March 1, year 2—Purchased 5,000 shares of its own common stock to be held as treasury stock for $14 per share. Min uses the cost method to account for treasury stock. Transactions in treasury stock are legal in Min's state of incorporation.
- May 10, year 2—Declared a property dividend of marketable securities held by Min to common shareholders. The securities had a carrying value of $600,000; fair value on relevant dates were

Date of declaration (May 10, year 2)	$720,000
Date of record (May 25, year 2)	758,000
Date of distribution (June 1, year 2)	736,000

- October 1, year 2—Reissued 2,000 shares of treasury stock for $16 per share.
- November 4, year 2—Declared a cash dividend of $1.50 per share to all common shareholders of record November 15, year 2. The dividend was paid on November 25, year 2.
- December 20, year 2—Declared the required annual cash dividend on preferred stock for year 2. The dividend was paid on January 5, year 3.
- January 16, year 3—Before closing the accounting records for year 2, Min became aware that no amortization had been recorded for year 1 for a patent purchased on July 1, year 1. Amortization expense was properly recorded in year 2. The patent was properly capitalized at $320,000 and had an estimated useful life of eight years when purchased. Min's income tax rate is 30%. The appropriate correcting entry was recorded on the same day.
- Adjusted net income for year 2 was $838,000.

Calculate the following amounts to be reported on Min's financial statements at December 31, year 2.

		Amount
1.	Prior period adjustment, year 2	____
2.	Preferred dividends, year 2	____
3.	Common dividends—cash, year 2	____
4.	Common dividends—property, year 2	____
5.	Number of common shares issued at December 31, year 2	____
6.	Amount of common stock issued	____
7.	Additional paid-in capital, including treasury stock transactions	____
8.	Treasury stock	____

Items 9 and 10 represent other financial information for year 1 and year 2.

		Amount
9.	Book value per share at December 31, year 1, before prior period adjustment	____
10.	Numerator used in calculation of year 2 earnings per share for the year	____

Task-Based Simulation 3

Research		
	Authoritative Literature	Help

Kerry Company issued a property dividend. You have been asked to research the professional literature to determine at what amount the property dividend should be valued. Place the citation for the excerpt from professional standards that provides this information in the answer box below.

Task-Based Simulation 4

Analysis of Transactions		
	Authoritative Literature	Help

Situation

M Corporation was incorporated in year 1. During year 1, the company issued 100,000 shares of $1 par value common stock for $27 per share. During year 2, the company had the following transactions.

1/2/Y2	Issued 10,000 shares of $100 par value cumulative preferred stock at par. The preferred stock was convertible into five shares of common stock and had a dividend rate of 6%.
3/1/Y2	Issued 3,000 shares of common stock for legal service performed. The value of the legal services was $100,000. The stock was actively traded on a stock exchange and valued on 3/1/Y2 at $32 per share.
7/1/Y2	Issued 40,000 shares of common stock for $42 per share.
10/1/Y2	Repurchased 16,000 shares of treasury stock for $34 per share. M Corp. uses the cost method to account for treasury shares.
12/1/Y2	Sold 3,000 shares of treasury stock for $29 per share.
12/30/Y2	Declared and paid a dividend of $0.20 per share on common stock and a 6% dividend on the preferred stock.

During year 1, M Corporation had net income of $250,000 and paid dividends of $28,000. During year 2, M Corporation had net income of $380,000.

Indicate the impact that the transactions for M Company have on its owner equity accounts. Place the appropriate amounts in the table below. If an amount is negative, show the amount in parentheses.

Date	Transaction	Preferred stock	APIC— Preferred stock	Common stock	APIC— Common stock	Retained earnings	Treasury stock	APIC— Treasury stock
1/01	Beginning balance							
1/2/Y2	Issue preferred stock at par							
3/1/Y2	Issue common stock for services							
7/1/Y2	Issue common stock for cash							
10/1/Y2	Repurchase treasury stock							
12/1/Y2	Sell treasury stock							
12/30/Y2	Declare and pay dividends							
12/31/Y2	Net income							
12/31/Y2	Ending Balance							

Task-Based Simulation 5

Calculation EPS		
	Authoritative Literature	Help

M Corporation was incorporated in year 1. During year 1, the company issued 100,000 shares of $1 par value common stock for $27 per share. During year 2, the company had the following transactions.

1/2/Y2	Issued 10,000 shares of $100 par value cumulative preferred stock at par. The preferred stock was convertible into five shares of common stock and had a dividend rate of 6%.
3/1/Y2	Issued 3,000 shares of common stock for legal service performed. The value of the legal services was $100,000. The stock was actively traded on a stock exchange and valued on 3/1/Y2 at $32 per share.
7/1/Y2	Issued 40,000 shares of common stock for $42 per share.
10/1/Y2	Repurchased 16,000 shares of treasury stock for $34 per share. M Corp. uses the cost method to account for treasury shares.
12/1/Y2	Sold 3,000 shares of treasury stock for $29 per share.
12/30/Y2	Declared and paid a dividend of $0.20 per share on common stock and a 6% dividend on the preferred stock.

During year 1, M Corporation had net income of $250,000 and paid dividends of $28,000. During year 2, M Corporation had net income of $380,000.

Calculate basic earnings per share. Show the components of your solution in the following table:

Numerator	
Denominator	
Basic earnings per share	

Calculate diluted earnings per share. Show the components of your solution in the following table:

Numerator	
Denominator	
Diluted earnings per share	

Task-Based Simulation 6

Research		
	Authoritative Literature	**Help**

Robar Corporation sold treasury shares at a price in excess of the shares' cost. You have been asked to research the professional literature to determine how this transaction is recorded. Place the citation for the excerpt from professional standards that provides this information in the answer box below.

Task-Based Simulation 7

Concepts		
	Authoritative Literature	**Help**

Identify whether each of the following statements is True or False.

		True	**False**
1.	Mandatorily redeemable preferred stock is classified as owners' equity and is disclosed after common stock.	○	○
2.	Property dividends are valued at the book value of the property.	○	○
3.	When a company makes a liquidating dividend, it debits the common stock account.	○	○
4.	Scrip dividends are a liability on the date of declaration.	○	○
5.	Stock dividends of 40% of the outstanding shares of stock are valued at fair market value on the date of declaration.	○	○
6.	If a company has cumulative preferred stock, all dividends in arrears must be subtracted from net income in the numerator of basic earnings per share.	○	○
7.	Cash dividends become a liability to the corporation when declared.	○	○
8.	Stock issued for services should be recorded at the fair market value of the services rendered if that value is greater than the fair market value of the stock traded on the exchange.	○	○

Task-Based Simulation 8

Journal Entries		
	Authoritative Literature	**Help**

Field Co.'s stockholders' equity account balances at December 31, year 5, were as follows:

Common stock	$ 800,000
Additional paid-in capital	1,600,000
Retained earnings	1,845,000

The following year 6 transactions and other information relate to the stockholders' equity accounts:

- Field had 400,000 authorized shares of $5 par common stock, of which 160,000 shares were issued and outstanding.
- On March 5, year 6, Field acquired 5,000 shares of its common stock for $10 per share to hold as treasury stock. The shares were originally issued at $15 per share. Field uses the cost method to account for treasury stock. Treasury stock is permitted in Field's state of incorporation.
- On July 15, year 6, Field declared and distributed a property dividend of inventory. The inventory had a $75,000 carrying value and a $60,000 fair market value.
- On January 2, year 1, Field granted stock options to employees to purchase 20,000 shares of Field's common stock at $18 per share, which was the market price on that date. The options may be exercised within a three-year period beginning January 2, year 6. The measurement date is the same as the grant date. On October 1, year 6, employees exercised all 20,000 options when the market value of the stock was $25 per share. Field issued new shares to settle the transaction. The stock options were accounted for in accordance with the intrinsic value method, which was in effect at the time.
- Field's net income for year 6 was $240,000.

Prepare journal entries for the following transactions in year 6.

1.   Treasury stock purchased on March 5, year 6

2.   Declaration and distribution of a property dividend on July 15, year 6

3.   Issue of common stock on October 1, year 6

Task-Based Simulation 9

Retained Earnings		
	Authoritative Literature	**Help**

Field Co.'s stockholders' equity account balances at December 31, year 5, were as follows:

Common stock	$ 800,000
Additional paid-in capital	1,600,000
Retained earnings	1,845,000

The following year 6 transactions and other information relate to the stockholders' equity accounts:

- Field had 400,000 authorized shares of $5 par common stock, of which 160,000 shares were issued and outstanding.
- On March 5, year 6, Field acquired 5,000 shares of its common stock for $10 per share to hold as treasury stock. The shares were originally issued at $15 per share. Field uses the cost method to account for treasury stock. Treasury stock is permitted in Field's state of incorporation.
- On July 15, year 6, Field declared and distributed a property dividend of inventory. The inventory had a $75,000 carrying value and a $60,000 fair market value.
- On January 2, year 1, Field granted stock options to employees to purchase 20,000 shares of Field's common stock at $18 per share, which was the market price on that date. The options may be exercised within a three-year period beginning January 2, year 6. The measurement date is the same as the grant date. On October 1, year 6, employees exercised all 20,000 options when the market value of the stock was $25 per share. Field issued new shares to settle the transaction. The stock options were accounted for in accordance with the intrinsic value method, which was in effect at the time.
- Field's net income for year 6 was $240,000.

Complete the following schedules for retained earnings and for the stockholders' equity section of the balance sheet for Field Company.

Field Company
STATEMENT OF RETAINED EARNINGS
For the Year Ending December 31, Year 6

Beginning retained earnings, 1/1/Y6	
Net income	
Dividends	
End retained earnings, 12/31/Y6	

Field Company
STOCKHOLDERS' EQUITY SECTION OF BALANCE SHEET
December 31, Year 6

Common stock	
Additional paid-in capital	
Retained earnings	
Treasury stock	
Accumulated other comprehensive income	
Total stockholders' equity	

Task-Based Simulation 10

Research		
	Authoritative Literature	**Help**

You have been asked to research the professional literature to determine how to calculate diluted earnings per share. Place the citation for the excerpt from professional standards that provides this information in the answer box below.

Simulation Solutions

Task-Based Simulation 1

Concepts		
	Authoritative Literature	Help

		(A)	(B)	(C)	(D)	(E)	(F)	(G)	(H)	(I)	(J)	(K)	(L)	(M)
1.	Par value method	○	○	○	○	○	○	○	○	●	○	○	○	○
2.	Appropriations of retained earnings	○	○	○	○	○	○	○	●	○	○	○	○	○
3.	Stock split	○	○	○	●	○	○	○	○	○	○	○	○	○
4.	Simple capital structure	●	○	○	○	○	○	○	○	○	○	○	○	○
5.	If-converted method	○	○	○	○	○	○	○	○	○	○	○	○	●
6.	Scrip dividend	○	○	○	○	○	○	○	○	○	○	●	○	○
7.	Stock appreciation rights	○	●	○	○	○	○	○	○	○	○	○	○	○
8.	Stock option	○	○	○	○	○	○	○	○	○	●	○	○	○
9.	Liquidating dividend	○	○	○	○	○	○	●	○	○	○	○	○	○
10.	Treasury stock	○	○	○	○	●	○	○	○	○	○	○	○	○

Explanations

1. (I) In accordance with the par value method, treasury shares are recorded at par value by debiting treasury stock when acquired. Any additional paid-in capital from the original issue of the acquired shares is also debited, cash is credited, and either additional paid-in capital—treasury stock is credited or retained earnings are debited for the difference between cash and the other two debits previously mentioned.

2. (H) Appropriations of retained earnings are actions by the board of directors to disclose amounts not available for dividends.

3. (D) A stock split changes the number of shares outstanding and the par value per share. The purpose of a stock split is to reduce the market price per share.

4. (A) A simple capital structure for a corporation exists if there are no potentially dilutive securities.

5. (M) The if-converted method for convertible securities assumes that the securities were converted at the later of the beginning of the period or the date of issue. The method thus increases the weighted-average number of shares in the denominator of the EPS equation. Since the method assumes conversion at the beginning of the period, no preferred dividends or interest would be considered to have been paid.

6. (K) A scrip dividend is a dividend issued by the corporation in the form of a note payable.

7. (B) A stock appreciation right allows an employee to receive the excess of the market value of the stock over a preestablished value in the form of cash, shares of stock, or both on the exercise date.

8. (J) A stock option is a form of compensation given to employees which allows them to purchase shares of stock at a specified price.

9. (G) A dividend paid to shareholders in excess of the retained earnings balance which is considered to be a return of capital and a liquidating dividend.

10. (E) When a corporation purchases its own stock in the market, the stock is termed treasury stock. Treasury stock is not an asset as a corporation cannot invest in itself. Treasury stock is recorded in a contra equity account.

Task-Based Simulation 2

Statement of Retained Earnings		
	Authoritative Literature	Help

This problem is a collection of miscellaneous stockholders' equity problems. The candidate should start the problem by scanning the required information to determine the amounts to be calculated. While scanning, the candidate should recognize that some of the required items are related, such as number 2 (preferred dividends) in the Statement of Retained Earnings, and numbers 1,2,4 and 6 in the Financial Statement Disclosures. These relationships require that the candidate label each answer, so that it will be possible to quickly find that answer when it is used in a subsequent problem.

Unlike many previous exam problems, the order of the information concerning the transactions does not coincide with the order of the required answers. This arrangement makes it necessary to read the required amount and then hunt for the transaction information needed to calculate that required amount.

1. **($14,000)** Prior period adjustment is the term generally applied to corrections of errors of prior periods. In this problem no amortization had been recorded in a prior year—an error. Since this is not a self-correcting error, it still existed in year 2. The calculation is cost ($320,000) ÷ useful life (eight years) for 1/2 year (purchased July 1). Prior period adjustments are disclosed net of tax (30%). $320,000/8 × 1/2 × (1 − .3) = $14,000.

2. **($12,000)** Preferred dividends are 6% and cumulative. They were declared during year 2 and paid in year 3. The declaration is sufficient to record and recognize the dividends legally; they do not have to be paid in the current year to be recognized during that time period. These dividends will be used in the numerator in question 20 when calculating the year 2 EPS. Since these dividends are cumulative, they would be used in the calculation of EPS even if they had not been declared. The amount of preferred dividends is derived by multiplying the par value of the stock by its rate. 6% × $200,000 par = $12,000 dividends.

3. **($165,000)** Common dividends—cash is calculated by the formula: Common shares outstanding × Dividend per share. In this problem the number of shares outstanding is affected by the beginning shares (100,000), shares issued (13,000), and treasury shares purchased and sold (5,000 purchased, 2,000 sold) prior to the dividend date of November 4. 100,000 + 13,000 − 5,000 + 2,000 = 110,000 shares outstanding × dividend rate $1.50 = $165,000.

4. **($720,000)** Common dividends—property differs from cash dividends because the property may be carried in the accounts at an amount which does not equal its fair value (cash is always at its fair value). Management intends to distribute the property at its fair value, therefore it is necessary to bring the property to fair value on the date management is legally forced to distribute it (the declaration date). Value fluctuations beyond that date are irrelevant.

5. **(113,000)** The number of shares issued differs from the number of shares outstanding which was used in question 3 under Calculations. Shares issued include those outstanding as well as those held in the treasury. Shares outstanding from question 3 above, 110,000 plus 3,000 treasury shares = 113,000 shares.

6. **($113,000)** Amount of common stock issued—This question takes the answer from question 1 above (113,000 shares) and multiplies that figure by the par value of each share, $1.

7. **($934,000)** The additional paid-in capital, including treasury stock transactions, is derived by adding the beginning balance ($800,000) to the excess ($10) of issue price ($11) over par value ($1) for the shares issued (13,000) to acquire land on February 1, year 2. In addition, the sale of the treasury stock (2,000 shares) at an amount ($16) greater than cost ($14) gives rise to a nonoperating gain that cannot be included in net income since it was both not related to operations and is a transaction in the company's own stock. $800,000 + (13,000 × $10) + [2,000 × ($16 − $14)] = $934,000.

8. **($42,000)** Treasury stock—Since Min Co. follows the cost method of accounting for treasury stock, this answer is derived by multiplying the shares of treasury stock (3,000) by their cost ($14). 3,000 × $14 = $42,000.

9. **($24.86)** Book value per share is a concept that relates common stockholders' equity to shares of common stock. The "per share" referred to is always the **common** shares unless the problem states some other type of shares. In this case it is to be calculated before the prior period adjustment. It is necessary to subtract preferred stock's total liquidating value ($100 × 2,000 sh = $200,000) from total stockholders' equity ($2,686,000) to obtain common stockholders' equity. In this problem no liquidating value is given, so par value is used. The resulting amount ($2,686,000 − $200,000 = $2,486,000) is divided by the common shares outstanding (100,000) to obtain book value per share ($24.86). ($2,686,000 − $200,000) ÷ 100,000 = $24.86.

10. **($826,000)** The formula for calculating earnings per share is (NI − Preferred dividends) ÷ Wtd.-avg. shares outstanding. The numerator is income available to common stockholders. The problem states that adjusted net income for year 2 was $838,000. The word "adjusted" tells the candidate that net income includes all information concerning transactions in the problem and need not be changed in any way. Preferred dividends ($12,000) were calculated in question 2. above. $838,000 − $12,000 = $826,000.

Task-Based Simulation 3

Research		
	Authoritative Literature	**Help**

ASC	845	10	30	1

Task-Based Simulation 4

Analysis of Transactions								
	Authoritative Literature	Help						

Date	Transaction	Preferred stock	APIC—Preferred stock	Common stock	APIC—common stock	Retained earnings	Treasury stock	APIC—treasury stock
1/01/Y2	Beginning balance			1,000,000	2,600,000	222,000		
1/2/Y2	Issue preferred stock at par	1,000,000						
3/1/Y2	Issue common stock for services			3,000	93,000			
7/1/Y2	Issue common stock for cash			40,000	1,640,000			
10/1/Y2	Repurchase treasury stock						(544,000)	
12/1/Y2	Sell treasury stock					(15,000)	102,000	
12/30/Y2	Declare and pay dividends					(86,000)		
12/31/Y2	Net income					380,000		
12/31/Y2	Ending balance	1,000,000	0	143,000	4,333,000	501,000	(442,000)	0

Explanations

- Preferred stock 10,000 × $100 = $1,000,000
- Value of services = Fair value of stock which is more reliable since stock is traded on the open market. 3,000 shares × $32 per share = $96,000
- Common stock: 40,000 shares of common stock × $1 par = $40,000 to common stock account; $40,000 × 41 = $1,640,000 to APIC
- Treasury stock is recorded at cost. 16,000 shares × $34 per share = $544,000
- Treasury stock is reduced by the cost paid 3,000 × $34 per share = $102,000. There is a $5 per share loss on the treasury shares which is debited to retained earnings 3,000 shares × $5 = $15,000
- Dividends to preferred shareholders = 10,000 × $100 par = $1,000,000 × 6% = $60,000 preferred dividends
- Dividends to common shareholders. Number of common shares outstanding equals 100,000 shares + 3,000 shares issued + 40,000 shares issued – 16,000 treasury shares purchased + 3,000 treasury shares reissued = 130,000 outstanding shares × $0.20 = $26,000. Therefore, total dividend is $86,000

Ending Balances

- Preferred stock: Issued at par. 10,000 shares × $100 = $1,000,000
- Common stock: $100,000 + $3,000 + $40,000 = $143,000
- Additional paid-in capital—Common stock: $2,600,000 + $93,000 + $1,640,000 = $4,333,000
- Retained earnings: $250,000 – $28,000 = $222,000 at end of year 1
- Retained earnings for year 2: $222,000 – $15,000 – $86,000 + $380,000 = $501,000
- Treasury stock: $544,000 – $102,000 = $442,000

Task-Based Simulation 5

Calculation EPS		
	Authoritative Literature	Help

Numerator	320,000
Denominator	118,750
Basic earnings per share	2.6947

Explanations

Numerator: $380,000 net income – $60,000 in preferred dividends = $320,000. Denominator – Weighted-average common shares.

Date	# shares	Time outstanding	WACS
1/1	100,000	12/12	100,000
3/1	3,000	10/12	2,500
7/1	40,000	6/12	20,000

Date	# shares	Time outstanding	WACS
10/1	(16,000) treasury shares	3/12	(4,000)
12/1	3,000 treasury shares sold	1/12	250
	Total WACS outstanding		118,750

Numerator	380,000
Denominator	168,750
Diluted earnings per share	2.2519

WACS outstanding: Basic EPS 118,750 + Convertible preferred (10,000 shares preferred × 5 shares common) 50,000 = 168,750.

Task-Based Simulation 6

Research

	Authoritative Literature	Help

ASC	505	30	30	10

Task-Based Simulation 7

Concepts

	Authoritative Literature	Help

		True	False
1.	Mandatorily redeemable preferred stock is classified as owners' equity and is disclosed after common stock.	○	●
2.	Property dividends are valued at the book value of the property.	○	●
3.	When a company makes a liquidating dividend, it debits the common stock account.	○	●
4.	Scrip dividends are a liability on the date of declaration.	●	○
5.	Stock dividends of 40% of the outstanding shares of stock are valued at fair market value on the date of declaration.	○	●
6.	If a company has cumulative preferred stock, all dividends in arrears must be subtracted from net income in the numerator of basic earnings per share.	○	●
7.	Cash dividends become a liability to the corporation when declared.	●	○
8.	Stock issued for services should be recorded at the fair market value of the services rendered if that value is greater than the fair market value of the stock traded on the exchange.	○	●

Explanations

1. **(F)** Mandatorily redeemable preferred is classified as a liability on the balance sheet.

2. **(F)** Property dividends are valued at fair market value of the property at the date of declaration.

3. **(F)** When a company makes a liquidating dividend, a company usually debits additional paid-in capital rather than retained earnings. Common stock cannot be debited because it is considered legal capital which is only eliminated upon the dissolution of the corporation.

4. **(T)** All dividends are liabilities on the dates declared.

5. **(F)** Large stock dividends are recorded at par. A stock dividend of 40% of the shares outstanding is considered a large stock dividend.

6. **(F)** If a company has cumulative preferred stock, only the current year dividends in arrears are subtracted from net income in the numerator of basic earnings per share.

7. **(T)** All dividends are liabilities on the dates declared.

8. **(F)** The more objective measurement of the value of the goods or services exchanged for stock is the fair market value of the stock if the stock is traded on a stock exchange.

Task-Based Simulation 8

Journal Entries		
	Authoritative Literature	Help

1. Treasury stock purchased on March 5, year 6

Treasury stock	50,000	
Cash		50,000

    (5,000 shares at $10 per share)

2. Declaration and distribution of a property dividend on July 15, year 2

Loss on inventory	15,000	
Inventory		15,000
Retained earnings	60,000	
Inventory		60,000

3. Issue of common stock on October 1, year 6

Cash	360,000	
Common stock (20,000 × $5)		100,000 (par)
Additional paid-in capital		260,000 (plug)

    (20,000 shares × $18 exercise price)

Task-Based Simulation 9

Retained Earnings		
	Authoritative Literature	Help

Field Company
STATEMENT OF RETAINED EARNINGS
For the Year Ending December 31, Year 6

Beginning retained earnings, 1-1-Y6	1,845,000
Net income	240,000
Dividends	(60,000)
End retained earnings, 12-31-Y6	2,025,000

Field Company
STOCKHOLDERS' EQUITY SECTION OF BALANCE SHEET
December 31, Year 6

Common Stock [1]	900,000
Additional paid-in capital [2]	1,860,000
Retained earnings	2,025,000
Treasury stock	(50,000)
Accumulated other comprehensive income	0
Total stockholders' equity	4,735,000

[1] Shares issued: 160,000 + 20,000 = 180,000 × $5 = $900,000
[2] Additional paid-in capital $1,600,000 + [20,000 × ($18 – $5)] = $1,860,000 ($1,600,000 + $260,000)

Explanations

To prepare the stockholders' equity section of Field's December 31, year 6 balance sheet, certain computations need to be made first.

1. The common stock authorized does not change throughout the problem; it is 400,000 shares. The number of shares outstanding increases by the 20,000 shares issued when the stock options were exercised. The balance in the common stock account is the number of shares issued times the par value of the common stock (180,000 × $5 = $900,000).

2. The treasury stock is accounted for by the cost method, which means the treasury stock is recorded at cost (5,000 shares × $10 = $50,000). The journal entry for the treasury stock is

    Treasury stock   50,000
         Cash   50,000

3. The information given indicates that the intrinsic value method is used. Because the intrinsic value method is used, compensation cost is zero and no entry is made until the options are recognized. Additional paid-in capital is the amount of money received for stock above the par value. The exercise or option price of the stock options exercised was $18 per share. The $13 per share paid above the par value of the stock needs to be added to the additional paid-in capital account, so $260,000 ($13 × 20,000 shares) should be added to the beginning balance of $1,600,000 for a total of $1,860,000 in the additional paid-in capital account.

4. The formula for retained earnings is

> Beginning balance
> Add: Net income
> <u>Less: Dividends</u>
> Ending balance

The amount of the dividends is the fair market value of the property distributed, which is $60,000 in this case. A $15,000 loss is recognized from the property dividend for the difference between the $75,000 carrying value and market value of the inventory. However, this loss would already be included in year 2 net income. Retained earnings is calculated as follows:

Beginning balance	$1,845,000
Add: Net income	240,000
Less: Dividend	(60,000)
Ending balance	$2,025,000

Task-Based Simulation 10

Research

	Authoritative Literature		Help	

ASC	260	10	45	16

Module 16: Investments

Overview

Investments in debt and equity securities are accounted for using ASC Topics 320, 323, 325, and 825 (SFAS 115, APB 18, or SFAS 159). The accounting treatment for investments is different depending upon the percentage of ownership, the classification of the security, and the election of the fair value option for reporting financial assets. This module will begin by covering the rules for trading, available-for-sale, and held-to-maturity securities. The coverage includes discussions on the initial recording of the securities, subsequent accounting, transfers between categories, and financial statement presentation.

This module also covers the equity method of accounting for investments where significant influence exists. After you understand the reporting rules for investments the fair value option will be discussed.

A. Concepts of Accounting and Investment Percentage

1. **Debt securities** are "any security representing a creditor relationship with an entity."

   a. This includes corporate debt, convertible bonds, US Treasury and municipal securities, redeemable preferred stock, commercial paper, and other secured debt instruments.
   b. Excluded are unsecured trade receivables and consumer loans and notes receivable because they are not normally traded on organized exchanges and because of cost/benefit considerations.
   c. Investments in debt securities are classified into three categories: trading securities, available-for-sale securities, and held-to-maturity securities.

   (1) Debt securities are discussed in Section B of this module and also in Module 13, Section B.

2. **Equity securities** include ownership interests (common, preferred, and other capital stock), rights to acquire ownership interests (rights, warrants, call options), and rights to dispose of ownership interests (put options).

   a. The accounting rules for investments in the common stock of another corporation are generally based on the percentage of the voting stock obtained.

   (1) *Investments of less than 20% of the outstanding stock*
       In most cases, "small" investments in marketable equity securities are classified into two categories: trading securities and available-for-sale securities. Discussion of these smaller investments is presented in Section B of this module.
   (2) *Investments between 20% and 50% of the outstanding stock*
       At 20% or more ownership, the investor is presumed to be able to significantly influence the operating or financial decisions of the investee. Most investments in this range will result in significant influence; however, the 20% level is just a guide.

       (a) An example in which an investor owning between 20% and 50% may not be able to exercise influence over the investee is when the majority ownership is concentrated among a small group of investors who ignore the views of the minority investor.
       (b) The equity method of accounting is used for investments resulting in significant influence.
       (c) Investments where significant influence does exist are discussed in Section C of this module.

(3) *Investments of more than 50% of the outstanding stock*

At more than 50% ownership, the investor has control because of its majority ownership of the voting stock.

    (a) Most of these investments will require the preparation of consolidated financial statements. Consolidations are discussed in Module 18.

3. Securities are originally recorded at cost, including any broker's fees, taxes, etc.; this amount is the best estimate of fair value at acquisition.

    a. Cost equals the cash paid or, in noncash transactions, the fair value of either the securities received or the resources sacrificed, whichever is more clearly determinable.

        (1) The fair value of debt securities equals the present value of their future cash inflows.

            (a) The present value is calculated using the current market rate of interest for similar instruments with similar risk.
            (b) Any accrued interest is accounted for separately.

        (2) The fair value of equity securities must be readily determinable from quotes obtainable from a securities exchange registered with the SEC or from the over-the-counter market.

            (a) Investments which are considered to be nontradeable or investments which do not have determinable fair values should be carried at cost and adjusted only for permanent declines in value.

    b. The exhibit that follows illustrates the major concepts of accounting for investments in equity securities.

PERCENTAGE OF OUTSTANDING VOTING STOCK ACQUIRED

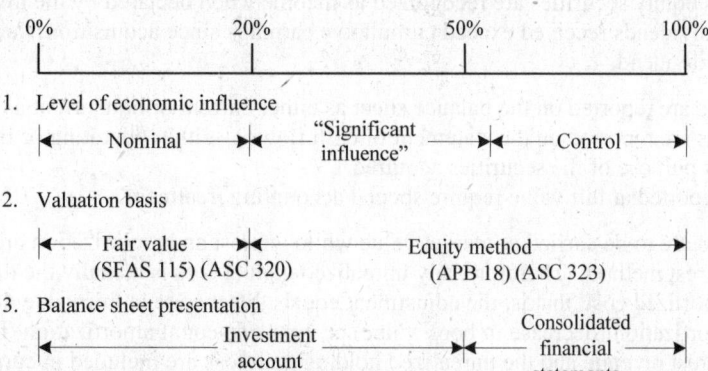

        (1) Several exceptions to these general concepts exist. These exceptions are noted in the following discussions.

B. Investments in Which Significant Influence Does *Not* Exist

Investments which do not confer significant influence over the operating or financial decisions of the investee consist of all debt securities and generally all small (less than 20%) investments in equity securities. Such investments should be segregated into held-to-maturity securities (debt securities only), trading securities, and available-for-sale securities; the appropriateness of the classification should be reviewed at each reporting date.

1. Held-to-Maturity Securities (amortized cost)

    a. This category includes only debt securities and requires the positive intent and ability to hold the securities to maturity (not simply an absence of intent to sell).
    b. Held-to-maturity securities are carried at amortized cost (acquisition cost adjusted for amortization of premium or discount) using effective interest method; thus, unrealized holding gains and losses are not reported.

        (1) However, realized gains and losses are included in earnings, as are interest income and premium and discount amortization.

    c. These securities are classified on the balance sheet as current or noncurrent on an individual basis, and on the statement of cash flows as investing activities.
    d. In rare instances, the investor company's intent to hold a security to maturity may change without casting doubt on its intent to hold other debt securities to maturity.

        (1) The circumstances must be nonrecurring and unforeseeable, such as the continuing deterioration of the issuer's credit.

(2) Premature sale of held-to-maturity securities may be considered as maturities if either of the following conditions are met:

(a) The sale occurs so close to the maturity date that interest rate risk is virtually eliminated, or
(b) The sale occurs after at least 85% of the principal has been collected.

e. Investments in held-to-maturity securities are accounted for under the cost method (unless the fair value option is elected), which requires that they be carried at amortized cost (acquisition cost adjusted for amortization of premium or discount). Coverage of accounting for these appears under bond investments in Module 13B.

2. **Trading Securities (subsequently measured at fair value)**

a. Debt and equity securities purchased and held principally for the purpose of generating gains on current resale are classified as trading securities.
b. Trading securities are accounted for according to the cost adjusted for fair value method, under which the carrying amount is adjusted at financial statement dates for subsequent changes in fair value (i.e., they are carried at fair value). (See Module 9D for a discussion of ASC Topic 820 [SFAS 157] and fair value measurements.)
c. Trading securities are generally held by brokers, bankers, and other financial institutions which engage in active buying and selling activities.
d. Both unrealized and realized gains and losses are included in income.

(1) However, to the extent that realized gains/losses have been previously reported as unrealized, only changes in the current period shall be reported as realized in the period of sale.

e. Other components of earnings include dividend and interest revenue.

(1) Dividends on equity securities are recognized as income when declared by the investee.
(2) However, if dividends received exceed cumulative earnings since acquisition, the excess is accounted for as a liquidating dividend.

f. Trading securities are reported on the balance sheet as either current or noncurrent as appropriate.
g. Trading securities are reported on the statement of cash flows as either operating or investing activities based on the nature and purpose of the securities acquired.
h. Debt securities reported at fair value require special accounting treatment.

(1) The securities are to be carried at market value while interest and amortization are to be calculated using the effective interest method. Therefore, any unrealized gain or loss is actually the difference between fair value and amortized cost, that is, the adjustment equals the change in fair value during the period, plus premium amortization (decrease in book value) or minus discount amortization (increase in book value).
(2) Both the interest revenue and the unrealized holding gain/loss are included in current earnings.
(3) An example of accounting for trading debt securities is presented in the comprehensive example at the end of Section B.

3. **Available-for-Sale Securities (subsequently measured at fair value)**

a. Available-for-sale securities include debt and equity securities not categorized as either held-to-maturity securities or trading securities. For example, a company such as a manufacturing firm may purchase securities to make use of idle cash. These securities are not actively traded, nor will they necessarily be held to maturity.
b. Included in earnings are realized gains and losses (which include previously unrealized holding gains and losses) and dividend and interest income.
c. Available-for-sale securities are accounted for according to the cost adjusted for fair value method, under which the carrying amount is adjusted at financial statement dates for subsequent changes in fair value (i.e., they are carried at fair value).
d. Unrealized gains and losses on available-for-sale debt and equity securities are calculated in the same manner as those on trading securities.

(1) These gains and losses, however, are not recognized in income of the period. Instead, the changes in fair value during a period (unrealized gains/losses) are reported as other comprehensive income (see Module 9D), and the accumulated unrealized gain/loss on marketable securities account is presented as accumulated other comprehensive income in stockholders' equity.

e. The following chart summarizes the three categories of marketable securities and the accounting treatment of each.

ACCOUNTING AND REPORTING OF MARKETABLE DEBT AND EQUITY SECURITIES

Category	Definition	How the security is reported on the balance sheet	How unrealized holding gains and losses are reported on the income statement*	How realized gains and losses are reported on the income statement
Trading (trading securities)	**Debt and equity** securities bought and held principally for the purpose of selling them in the near term	Reported at fair value and grouped with current assets on the balance sheet	Unrealized gains and losses are included in earnings in the period they occur	Realized gains and losses not already recognized as unrealized components are recognized
Available-for-sale	**Debt and equity** securities not classified as trading or held-to-maturity	Reported at fair value and may be classified as current or noncurrent	Unrealized gains and losses for a period are excluded from earnings and reported as other comprehensive income (If decline is "other than temporary" then recognized in earnings)	Realized gains and losses are recognized (which include unrealized holding gains and losses recognized previously as unrealized)
Held-to-maturity	**Debt** securities that the organization has the positive intent and ability to hold to the maturity date	Reported at amortized cost and may be classified as current or noncurrent	Unrealized gains and losses are excluded from earnings (unless decline is "other than temporary")	Realized gains and losses are recognized in accordance with amortized cost method

* Or on the statement where items of other comprehensive income are reported.

f. The fair value of a debt security minus its amortized cost represents the correct unrealized gain or loss for this security in the accumulated other comprehensive income account at year-end.

(1) The adjusting entry for this account at the end of the period will equal the difference between the account's balance before adjustment and the cumulative unrealized gain or loss on the debt and equity securities at the end of the period.

g. Available-for-sale securities are classified on the balance sheet as current or noncurrent on an individual basis based on management's intent concerning the holding period and appear on the statement of cash flows as investing activities.

EXAMPLE

On 1/01/Y1, when interest rates were 12%, STC Corp. purchased the following securities:

Security description	Acquisition cost
• Shaner Enterprise ten-year, 10%, $1,000 face value bonds (STC Corp. intends to hold the bond until it matures)	$ 887
• Harmony Corporation five-year, 14%, $5,000 face value bond (STC Corp. expects that interest rates will fall and the bond will be sold at a profit)	$5,360
• 100 shares Keswick Corporation common stock (STC anticipates that the price of the stock will rise 10%, at which time the stock will be sold)	$2,200
• 150 shares Rusell Inc. common stock (STC has no immediate plans to sell this stock)	$5,600

The Shaner bond must be classified as held-to-maturity and carried at amortized cost since management has the ability and intent to hold the investment to the maturity date. The Harmony and Keswick securities are classified as trading securities because STC intends to hold these investments for only a short period of time expressly to realize a quick profit. The Rusell Inc. stock is classified as available-for-sale because STC has not expressed an intent to hold the stock for current resale. The Harmony, Keswick, and Rusell investments are all carried at fair value.

At the end of year 1, the fair values of the Keswick and Rusell stock are $2,700 and $5,190, respectively. Interest rates have fallen to 10%, boosting the value of the Harmony bond to $5,634. Interest income, premium amortization, and unrealized gain on this bond are calculated as

Date	14% Cash interest	12% Effective interest	Premium amortization	Carrying value	Fair value	Unrealized gain (loss)
1/01/Y1				$5,360	$5,360	
12/31/Y1	$700	$643	$57	5,303	5,634	$331

NOTE: The unrealized gain ($331) equals the increase in fair value ($274) plus the premium amortization ($57).

Interest income and discount/premium amortization must be recorded for the bonds in any of the three portfolios. Both the Harmony and Shaner bonds were purchased to yield 12%. The adjusting journal entries required at 12/31/Y1 are

Interest receivable	100	
Investment in Shaner bond—held-to-maturity	6	
Interest income ($887 × 12%)		106
Interest receivable	700	
Investment in Harmony securities—trading		57
Interest income		643

On 12/31/Y1 after the two adjusting entries above are posted, the carrying values and fair values are

	12/31/Y1 Carrying amount	12/31/Y1 Fair value
Held-to-maturity:		
Shaner bond	$ 893	NA
Trading:		
Harmony bond	5,303	$5,634
Keswick stock	2,200	2,700
Available-for-sale:		
Rusell stock	5,600	5,190

At this time, the adjusting journal valuation entries are made for the trading and the available-for-sale portfolios of securities, as follows:

Investment in Harmony securities—trading	331	
Unrealized gain on holding debt securities (income statement)		331
($5,634 FV – $5,303 CV)		
Investment in Keswick securities—trading	500	
Unrealized gain on holding equity securities (income statement)		
($2,700 FV – $2,200 CV)		500
Unrealized loss on Rusell securities—available-for-sale (other comprehensive income account)	410	
Investment in Rusell securities—available-for-sale		
($5,600 CV – $5,190 FV)		410

The unrealized holding gain on trading securities is a nominal account which is closed to income at 12/31/Y1. The unrealized loss on available-for-sale securities is closed out to the "accumulated other comprehensive income" account at year-end, which is presented in the stockholders' equity section of the 12/31/Y1 balance sheet. It is important to note that the increases and decreases in fair value recorded above may alternatively be recorded in a separate fair value adjustment account (contra asset account). If a fair value adjustment account is used to carry the holding gains and losses, then the fair value adjustment account and the investment account would be netted for presentation purposes. The carrying amount of the Shaner bond at 12/31/Y1 is $893 ($887 + $6).

Now assume that in July year 2, 75 of the 150 shares of Rusell stock were sold for $30 per share. The entry to record the sale is

Cash ($30 × 75)	2,250	
Loss on sale of securities	550	
Investment in Rusell securities—available-for-sale*		2,595
Reclassification adjustment of unrealized loss on Rusell securities—available-for-sale		205

* Carrying value = $5,190 ($5,600 – 410) fair value on books ÷ 150 shares = $34.60/share. $2,595 = $34.60 × 75 shares

The loss on sale of securities equals the initial acquisition cost of the securities less the sales price. Because the Rusell securities are classified as available-for-sale, the proportionate amount of unrealized holding gains or losses ($205 = ½ × $410) which had accumulated in the stockholders' equity account would be reclassified and becomes part of the realized loss for inclusion in earnings of the period of the sale.

> **NOTE:** The accumulated other comprehensive income account in stockholders' equity is a "holding account" for the difference between the initial acquisition cost of the available-for-sale security and its current fair value at the balance sheet date.

No other holding gains or losses beyond the $410 holding loss recognized on December 31, year 1, had accumulated since December 31, year 1. When the available-for-sale security is sold, the amount of the previously recognized unrealized holding gain or loss is reclassified and becomes part of the realized gain or loss on the sale of available-for-sale securities. The realized gain or loss on the sale is then the difference between the selling price and the initial acquisition cost ($550 = $2,250 – $2,800 acquisition cost of 75 shares).

In September year 2, Keswick Corp. declared a 10% stock dividend. Stock dividends should not be reflected in income. The stock's current carrying value of $2,700 should be allocated to the additional shares received from the dividend. Since STC holds 100 shares, the dividend will be 10 shares, resulting in a total of 110 shares. After the dividend, the 110 shares will each have a carrying value of $24.55 ($2,700 ÷ 110) which will be adjusted to fair value at the end of the reporting period.

STC Corp. periodically reviews its intent to hold or actively trade its securities. At 12/31/Y2, when interest rates are 8%, STC decides that it will hold the Harmony bond indefinitely. Because this bond was originally classified as trading, it must be transferred to available-for-sale. Fair value on this date is $5,773. The entries to record interest income and to transfer the bond are

Interest receivable	700	
Investment in Harmony securities—trading		64
Interest income		636
Investment in Harmony securities—trading	204	
Unrealized gain on holding debt securities		204
Investment in Harmony securities—available-for-sale	5,773	
Investment in Harmony securities—trading		5,773

The holding gain of $204 ($5,773 FV 12/Y2 – $5,634 FV 12/Y1 plus premium amortization of $64) is recognized in current earnings, and the value recorded in the available-for-sale portfolio reflects the fair value of $5,773 at the transfer date. Note that from this point forward any holding gains or losses should be recognized as other comprehensive income and included in accumulated other comprehensive income in stockholders' equity in accordance with the available-for-sale classification.

Also on 12/31/Y2, STC sold its held-for-trading Keswick stock for $32 per share. This transaction was recorded as follows:

Cash ($32 × 110 shares)	3,520	
Investment in Keswick securities—trading		2,700
Gain on sale of securities		820

On 12/31/Y2, STC also recorded the appropriate entries for amortization of the Shaner bond ($7 discount amortization and $107 interest income) and to adjust the Rusell stock to its current fair value of $29 per share.

Finally, on 12/31/Y2 STC discovered that Shaner Enterprise is experiencing financial difficulty due to mismanagement, and the full amount of the bond will not be collected. This impairment would be considered other than temporary, so the investment in Shaner Enterprise bonds must be reduced to its current fair value of $500. The realized loss of $400 ($900 12/31/Y2 current carrying value – $500 FV) is reported in earnings, and no write-up will be allowed if a recovery is made at a later date.

To summarize STC Corp.'s marketable securities transactions for year 1 and year 2, T-accounts for each security are shown below, followed by earnings information relating to the investments.

Harmony Bond—Trading					Harmony Bond—Available-for-Sale		
1/01/Y1 Acquisition	5,360	57	12/31/Y1 Amort.		12/31/Y2 Transfer	5,773	
12/31/Y1 Adj. to FV	331	64	12/31/Y2 Amort.				
12/31/Y2 Adj. to FV	204	5,773	12/31/Y2 Transfer				
Bal. 12/31/Y2	0				Bal. 12/31/Y2	5,773	

Shaner Bond—Held-to-Maturity					Keswick Stock—Trading		
1/01/Y1 Acquisition	887				1/01/Y1 Acquisition		
12/31/Y1 Amort.	6				(100 shares)	2,200	
12/31/Y2 Amort.	7	400	12/31/Y2 Write-down		12/31/Y1 Adj. to FV	500	
Bal. 12/31/Y2	500				(9/Y1 Stock div.—10 shares)		2,700 12/31/Y2 Sale
					Bal. 12/31/Y2	0	

Rusell Stock—Available-for-Sale				
1/01/Y1 Acquisition				
(150 shares)	5,600	410	12/31/Y1 Adj. to FV	
		2,595	7/Y2 Sale (75 shares)	
		420	12/31/Y2 Adj. to FV	
Bal. 12/31/Y2	2,175			

Year	Transaction	Income/Gain	Loss	Net earnings	Other comprehensive income
Year 1	Harmony adj. to FV				$ 331
	Keswick adj. to FV				500
	Interest on Shaner bond	106			
	Interest on Harmony bond	643			

	Rusell adj. to FV				$(410)
	Year 1 total	$1,580		$1,580	(410)
Year 2	Write-down of Shaner bond		$(400)		
	Sale of one-half of Rusell securities		(550)		$ 205
	Gain on Keswick securities	$ 820			
	Harmony adj. to FV	203			
	Interest on Shaner bond	107			
	Interest on Harmony bond	636			
	Rusell adj. to FV				(420)
	Year 2 total	$1,766	$(950)	$ 816	$(215)

4. **Transfers between Categories**

   a. The classification of securities should be reviewed at each balance sheet date. Although a reclassification should be rare, a company may deem it necessary to transfer a security from one category to another.

   (1) Such transfers are accounted for at fair value, taking into consideration any unrealized holding gains or losses.

   (a) For example, when a security is transferred **from** trading securities, any recognized unrealized gain or loss as of the date of transfer should not be reversed.
   (b) On the other hand, in a transfer **to** trading securities, unrealized holding gains and losses are recognized immediately.
   (c) Held-to-maturity securities reclassified **to** available-for-sale securities must be restated to fair value; any unrealized holding gain or loss that results is reported as accumulated other comprehensive income in stockholders' equity.
   (d) However, transfers **from** held-to-maturity should be rare.
   (e) Unrealized holding gain or loss on securities transferred **to** held-to-maturity from available-for-sale is also reported as accumulated other comprehensive income in stockholders' equity, but this gain or loss is then amortized over the remaining life of the security as an adjustment to yield.

   (2) The treatment of securities transfers is summarized in the chart that follows.

Securities transferred to:

		Held-to-maturity	**Available-for-sale**	**Trading**
Securities transferred from:	Held-to-maturity		Report unrealized G/L as accumulated other comprehensive income in SE	Recognize unrealized G/L immediately
	Available-for-sale	Report unrealized G/L as accumulated other comprehensive income in SE & amortize the gain or loss over remaining life of security		Recognize unrealized G/L immediately
	Trading	Do not reverse unrealized G/L previously recognized in income	Do not reverse unrealized G/L previously recognized in income	

5. **Income Statement Presentation**

   a. Since held-to-maturity and available-for-sale securities are held for some length of time, these securities may become impaired at some point.

   (1) If the decline in value is other than temporary, then the impaired security must be written down to fair value and the realized loss included in earnings.
   (2) Any subsequent recovery would not be recognized in earnings unless realized through sale of the security.
   (3) An other than temporary impairment cannot occur in the context of trading securities because holding gains and losses are recognized in current earnings without limitation.

   b. Cash dividends or interest income should be included in the current period's income.
   c. Stock dividends should not be reflected in income.

   (1) Additional shares received from a stock dividend should be added to the original shares and the per share value should be calculated upon the original shares' carrying value.
   (2) At the end of the period the carrying value of the stock is adjusted to the fair value, and any unrealized holding gain or loss is recorded.

d. Realized and **unrealized** gains and losses on trading securities are included in the current period's earnings.

(1) Only realized gains and losses on sales of available-for-sale and held-to-maturity securities should be included in earnings.

(2) Unrealized gains (losses) on available-for-sale securities are reported as other comprehensive income in one of three ways (see Module 9D).

(3) Amortization of any unrealized holding gain or loss on securities transferred to held-to-maturity from available-for-sale is included in income.

> **NOW REVIEW MULTIPLE-CHOICE QUESTIONS 1 THROUGH 31**

C. Investments Where Significant Influence *Does* Exist

Use of the **equity method** is required for investments which give the investor the ability to exercise significant influence over the operating and financial policies of the investee.

1. Ownership of 20% or more of the outstanding stock will result in that ability.

a. Exceptions to the use of the equity method (i.e., the cost adjusted for fair value method) are related to an assessment of the investor's level of influence over the investee.

(1) The cost adjusted for fair value method should be used if an investment of more than 20% is judged to be temporary, if the investment is in a company operating in a foreign country which has severe restrictions on the operations of companies and on the transfer of monies outside the country, and for other investments of more than 20% that do not result in significant influence.

b. There may be unusual circumstances in which a less than 20% investor may have significant influence over the investee, in which case the equity method must be used to account for the investment.

2. **Cost adjusted for fair value method**—The cost adjusted for fair value and the equity methods differ in the treatment of the investment account and in the recognition of earnings from the investment.

a. The cost adjusted for fair value method first records the cost of the investment in the investment account.

b. Income is recognized for dividends distributed from income of the investee earned since the date the investor acquired the stock.

(1) Any dividends distributed by the investee which exceed earnings since the acquisition date are classified as return of capital and recorded as a reduction of the investment account.

c. Under the cost adjusted for fair value method, equity securities must be adjusted for subsequent changes in fair value, and the unrealized holding gain or loss on equity securities for the period equals the current fair value minus the previous period's fair value on the books.

3. **Equity method**—The equity method also begins with recording the cost of the investment in the investment account but the two methods differ from this point on.

a. A basic concept of the equity method is the reciprocal relationship formed between the investment account on the investor's books and the book values of the net assets on the investee's books.

b. As changes in the investee's net assets occur (e.g., earnings, dividends, etc.), the investor will recognize in the investment account the percentage of ownership share of those changes.

c. Another aspect of the equity method is the computation and accounting for the difference between the cost of the investment and the book value of the acquired asset share at the investment date.

(1) The abundance of advanced accounting texts currently in print use an assortment of terms to describe the characteristics of this concept. For purposes of uniformity, the following boldfaced terms shall be used throughout this module.

Differential: The difference between the cost of the investment and the underlying book value of the net assets of the investee. This difference can be either positive or negative, as follows:

Excess of Cost over Book Value, which is generally attributable to

- **Excess of fair value over book value,** when the fair values of the investee's assets are greater than their book values, and
- **Goodwill,** when the investee has high earnings potential for which the investor has paid more than the fair values of the other net assets

Excess of Book Value over Cost, which is generally attributable to

- **Excess of book value over fair value,** when the book values of the net assets of the investee are greater than their fair values, and
- **Excess of fair value over cost,** when the cost of the investment is less than even the fair values of the investee's net assets. Some authors term this "negative goodwill."

If the differential is related to assets with finite useful lives, it will be amortized to the investment account. Goodwill will not be amortized; it will be written down if the investment is determined to be impaired.

EXAMPLE

A Company purchased 20 shares of B Company's 100 shares of common stock outstanding for $25,000. The book value of B's total net worth (i.e., stockholders' equity) at the date of the investment was $120,000. Any excess of cost over book value is due to equipment that has a ten-year remaining useful life.

Investment cost		$ 25,000
Book value of B Company	$120,000	
Percentage owned	20%	
Investor's share		24,000
Excess of cost over book value (due to equipment)		$ 1,000

Amortization over forty years
$1,000 ÷ 10 years = $100

---

d. Under the equity method, the Income from Investment account is a parallel income statement account to the Investment in Stock balance sheet account. These two accounts should include all the income recognition and amortization resulting from the investment.

> **NOTE:** Under the equity method, dividends received from the investee are a reduction in the Investment balance sheet account and are **not** part of the Income from Investment account.

e. Alternative levels of recording the results of intercompany transactions and amortization in both the investment and investment income accounts are used in accounting practice. The alternatives are presented below.

(1) **Cost adjusted for fair value method**—No intercompany transactions or amortization are recognized in either the investment account or investment income account under this method.

(2) **"Partial" equity**—Includes recognition of percentage share of income or loss, dividends, and any changes in the investment percentage. This method is often used for investments that will be consolidated. Thus, amortization and other adjustments are made on the worksheets, not in the investment account.

(3) **"Full" equity**—In addition to the factors above, this level includes any necessary amortization or write-off of the differential between the investment cost and book value of the investment. This level also recognizes the effects of any intercompany transactions (e.g., inventory, fixed assets, and bonds) between the investor and investee corporations. All unconsolidated investments are reported in the financial statements using the "full" equity method.

EXAMPLE

Assume the same facts for A Company and B Company as stated above. In addition, B Company earned $10,000 income for the year and paid $6,000 in dividends. There were no intercompany transactions. If A Company does not have significant influence over B Company, the investment would be accounted for by the cost adjusted for fair value method. If A Company can significantly influence B Company, the equity method is used to account for and report the investment. The appropriate entries are

Cost adjusted for fair value method			Equity method		
1. To record purchase of 20% interest					
Investment in stock of B	25,000		Investment in stock of B	25,000	
Cash		25,000	Cash		25,000
2. To record percentage of share of investee's reported income					
No entry			Investment in stock of B	2,000	
			Income from investment		2,000
			(20% × $10,000)		

3. To record percentage share of dividend received as distribution of income

Cash	1,200		Cash	1,200	
Dividend income from investment (20% × $6,000)		1,200	Investment in stock of B		1,200

4. To record amortization of equipment in accordance with ASC Topic 323

No entry (no differential amortization under this method)	Income from investment	100	
	Investment in stock of B		100

The differences in the account balances under the equity method vs. the cost adjusted for fair value method reflect the different income recognition processes and underlying asset valuation concepts of the two methods. The investment account balance under the cost adjusted for fair value method remains at the investment cost of $25,000 (although subsequent changes in fair value would require that the investment account be adjusted to fair value), while under the equity method, the investment balance increases to $25,700. The $700 difference is the investor's share of the increase in the investee's undistributed earnings less the investor's amortization of the differential (excess of cost over the book value of the investment).

The amount of the investment income to be recognized by the investor also depends upon the length of time during the year the investment is owned.

For example, assume that A Company acquired the 20% interest on July 1, year 2, and B Company earned $10,000 of income ratably over the period from January 1 to December 31, year 2. The entry to record A Company's percentage share of B Company's income for the period of July 1 to December 31, year 2, would be

Cost adjusted for fair value method		**Equity method**	
No entry		Investment in stock of B	1,000
		Income from investment (20% × $10,000 × 6/12)	1,000

The receipt of the $1,200 dividends after the acquisition date would require additional analysis since the $1,200 dividend received is greater than the investor's share of the investee's income ($1,000) since acquisition. The difference of $200 ($1,200 – $1,000) is a return of capital under the cost adjusted for fair value method, and is recorded as follows:

Cost adjusted for fair value method		**Equity method**	
Cash	1,200	Cash	1,200
Dividend income from investment	1,000	Investment in stock of B	1,200
Investment in stock of B	200		

The amortization of equipment will also be prorated to the time period the investment was held.

4. **Changes to or from the equity method**—when an investor changes from the cost adjusted for fair value to the equity method, the investment account must be adjusted retroactively and prior years' income and retained earnings must be retroactively restated.

a. A change to the equity method would be made if an investor made additional purchases of stock and, for the first time, is able to exercise significant influence over the operating and financial decisions of the investee.

(1) Remember that ASC Topic 323 (APB 18) states that investments of 20% or more of the investee's outstanding stock carry the "presumption" that the investor has the ability to exercise significant influence. Therefore, in most cases, when an investment of less than 20% increases to more than 20%, the investor will retroactively change from the cost adjusted for fair value method to the equity method.

(a) The retroactive change to the equity method requires a prior period adjustment for the difference in the investment account and retained earnings account between the amounts that were recognized in prior periods under the cost adjusted for fair value method and the amounts that would have been recognized if the equity method had been used.

1] In the full-year investment example on the previous page where A Company had a $25,000 balance in its Investment in B account under the cost adjusted for fair value method and $25,700 under the equity method, if A changed from the cost to the equity method because of its increased influence over B, the change entry would be

Investment in B Company	700	
Retained earnings		700
($700 = $2,000 – $1,200 – $100)		

(b) In addition, any balance in the Unrealized holding gain or loss account must be reversed.

1] Assume that the fair value of the B Company stock had increased from $25,000 to $27,000 as of the end of the year of acquisition. The investment account would have been debited for $2,000 and the

Unrealized gain on MES account credited for $2,000 to bring the carrying value of the stock up to its fair value. Upon retroactive change to the equity method, the following reversing entry would be made:

Unrealized gain on MES	2,000	
Investment in stock of B		2,000

(2) If the change is made at any time point other than the beginning of the fiscal period, the change entry would also include an adjustment to the period's Income from investment account to record the difference between the cost adjusted for fair value and equity methods handling of the investor's share of the investee's income for the current period.

b. When an investor discontinues using the equity method because of an inability to influence the investee's financial and operating policies, no retroactive restatement is allowed.

(1) An example of this would be a disposal of stock resulting in a decrease in the percentage of stock owned from more than 20% to less than 20%.

(2) The earnings or losses that relate to the shares retained by the investor that were previously recognized by the investor should remain as a part of the carrying amount.

(a) However, if dividends received by the investor in subsequent periods exceed the investor's share of the investee's earnings for such periods, the excess should be accounted for as a return of capital and recorded as a reduction in the investment carrying amount.

c. A T-account is used to exhibit the major changes in the Investment in stock account under the equity method.

Investment in Stock

Original cost of investment	Percentage share of investee's losses since acquisition
Percentage share of investee's income since acquisition	Percentage share of dividends received
Amortization of excess of book value over cost	Amortization of excess of cost over book value
Increase above "significant influence" ownership—retroactive adjustment for change to equity	Disposal or sales of investment in stock

d. In addition to the above, several adjustments may be added if the "full equity" method is used. This method eliminates the effects of intercompany profits from transactions such as sales of inventory between the investor and investee corporations. This method is rarely required on the exam but candidates should briefly review these additions in association with the discussion of the elimination entries required for consolidated working papers presented later in Module 18.

Investment in Stock (continued)

Realized portion of intercompany profit from last period confirmed this period	Elimination of unrealized portion of intercompany profit transactions from current period

---

NOW REVIEW MULTIPLE-CHOICE QUESTIONS 32 THROUGH 48

D. Equity Method and Deferred Income Taxes

1. Recognition of deferred taxes may be required when the equity method is used.

a. The difference between the income recognized using the equity method and the dividends received from the investee represents a temporary difference for which interperiod allocation is necessary.

> **NOTE:** Companies are allowed to exclude 80% of the dividend income from domestic investees. If an investor owns 80% or more of the investee's stock, the dividend exclusion is increased to 100% (i.e., no taxes are due on investee dividend distributions). The dividend exclusion (dividends received deduction) is a permanent difference.

2. A discussion of deferred income taxes arising from equity method investments and several examples are provided in Module 14, Deferred Taxes.

E. The Fair Value Option

1. An entity may elect to value its securities at fair value.

a. A firm can elect the fair value option on an instrument-by-instrument basis.

b. If the firm elects the fair value option for reporting available-for-sale or held-to-maturity securities, the security is revalued to fair value and any gain or loss is recorded in earnings for the period.

c. Likewise, if the fair value option is elected for instruments that would otherwise be reported using the equity method, the securities are revalued to fair value. Any gain or loss is recorded in earnings for the period.

d. If the fair value option is elected for instruments that would normally use the equity method, it must be applied to all interests in that entity (i.e., both debt and equity instruments would be valued at fair value).

2. The fair value option can be elected on the date an investment is first recognized, or when the investment no longer qualifies for fair value treatment.

a. For example, if Company A has a trading security in Company B stock and acquires more than 20% of Company B, the rules of the equity method of reporting would normally be applied. However, if the fair value option is elected, Company A is no longer required to use the equity method, but instead values the security at year-end at fair value. Any unrealized gain or loss is recognized in earnings for the period.

3. The rules for the statement of cash flows continue to apply for determining the classification of a purchase or sale of security on the statement of cash flows. Additional disclosures in the notes to the financial statements are required if the fair value option is elected. Refer to the outline of SFAS 159 (ASC Topic 825) for these disclosures.

F. Stock Dividends and Splits

Stock dividends and stock splits are not recorded as income. The recipient continues to own the same proportion of the investee as before the stock split or stock dividend. The investor should make a memo entry to record the receipt of the additional shares and recompute the per share cost of the stock.

G. Stock Rights

1. Investors in common stock occasionally receive stock rights to purchase additional common stock below the existing market price. The investee company has probably issued the stock rights to satisfy the investor's preemptive right to maintain an existing level of ownership of the investee. It is possible to waive these preemptive rights in some jurisdictions.

2. Rights are issued below the existing market price to encourage the exercise of the rights (i.e., the investor's use thereof resulting in acquisitions of additional shares of stock).

a. The rights are separable, having their own markets, and should be accounted for separately from the investment in common stock.

b. The rights represent a possible dilution of investor ownership and should be recorded by allocating the cost of the stock between the market value of the rights and the market value of the stock.

(1) This is accomplished by multiplying the following ratio by the cost basis of the stock:

$$\frac{\text{Market value of right}}{\text{Market value of right} + \text{Market value of stock}}$$

3. The following entry is made to record the receipt of the rights:

Investment in stock rights	xx	
Investment in common stock		xx

4. The rights can be sold or exercised. The entry for exercise is

Investment in common stock	xx	
Investment in stock rights		xx
Cash		xx

5. If the stock rights lapse

Loss on expiration of stock rights	xx	
Investment in stock rights		xx

EXAMPLE

A Company acquired 1,000 shares of common stock in B Company for $12,000. A Company subsequently received two stock rights for every share owned in B Company. Four rights and $12 are required to purchase one new share of common stock. At the date of issuance the market value of the stock rights and the common stock is $5 and $20, respectively. The entry to record the receipt of the rights is as follows:

Investment in stock rights	4,000	
Investment in common stock		4,000

The $4,000 above was computed as follows:

Total market value of rights	2,000 rights × $ 5 =	$10,000
Total market value of shares	1,000 shares × $20 =	$20,000
Combined market value		$30,000

$$\text{Cost allocated to stock rights} \quad \frac{\$10,000}{\$30,000} \times \$12,000 = \$4,000$$

$$\text{Cost allocated to common stock} \quad \frac{\$20,000}{\$30,000} \times \$12,000 = \$8,000$$

NOTE: $2 ($4,000 ÷ 2,000 rights) of cost is assigned to each stock right and $8 ($8,000 ÷ 1,000 shares) of cost to each share of stock.

If A uses 800 rights to purchase 200 additional shares of stock, the following entry would be made to record the transaction.

Investment in common stock	4,000	
Investment in stock rights		1,600*
Cash		2,400**

* (800 rights × $2/right)
** (200 shares × $12/share)

If 1,000 stock rights are sold outright for $5 per right, the following entry would be made to record the transaction.

Cash	5,000*	
Investment in stock rights		2,000**
Gain on sale of rights		3,000

* (1,000 rights × $5/right)
** (1,000 rights × $2/right)

If the 200 remaining stock rights are permitted to expire, the following entry would be made:

Loss on expiration of stock rights	400*	
Investment in stock rights		400*

* (200 rights × $2/right)

The journal entries above can be summarized as follows:

	Investment in common stock				Investment in stock rights		
Purchase, 1,000 shares @ $12	12,000	4,000	← Cost allocated to stock rights →	4,000	1,600	Exercise of 800 rights
Purchase, 200 shares by exercise of rights	4,000				2,000	Sale of 1,000 rights
					400	Expiration of 200 rights
	12,000				--	

NOW REVIEW MULTIPLE-CHOICE QUESTIONS 49 THROUGH 52

H. Cash Surrender Value of Life Insurance

1. The cash surrender value of life insurance policies represents a noncurrent investment when the company is the beneficiary (rather than insured employees). The entry to record insurance premiums that increase cash surrender value is

Insurance expense	(plug)
Cash surrender value	(increase in CSV)
Cash	(total premium)

a. Cash surrender value remains a noncurrent asset unless the company plans to cash in the policy within the next period.

2. During the first few years of a policy, no cash surrender value may attach to the policy. During this period, the entire insurance premium would be expense. In addition, any dividends received from the life insurance policy are not recorded as revenue, but instead are offset against insurance expense.

I. Research Component—Accounting Standards Codification

1. Research for investments is found in three topics in the Codification: ASC Topics 320, 323, and 825. ASC Topic 320, *Investments—Debt and Equity Securities*, outlines the rules for trading securities, available-for-sale securities, and held-to-maturity securities. ASC Topic 323, *Investments—Equity Method and Joint Ventures*, covers the accounting rules for securities where significant influence exists and the equity method of accounting is required. ASC Topic 825, *Financial Instruments*, outlines the rules for electing the fair value option for reporting investments in debt and equity.

2. Keywords for research are listed below.

Asset-liability management	Fair value investment	Other comprehensive income loss
Available-for-sale	Fair value option	Readily determinable fair value
Carrying amount investment	Fair value security	Security maturity date
Cash flows securities	50% or less	Shares of investee
Classified securities	Held-to-maturity	Significant influence
Change intent	Increase in ownership investee	Trading
Debt equity securities	Intent indefinite period	Transfer between categories
Decline in fair value	Intercompany profits	Unrealized holding gains
Disclosure securities	Interest income	Unrealized holding losses
Dividend income	Investments equity securities	Voting privileges
Enterprise disclose	Loss temporary decline	
Equity method investment	Other comprehensive income gain	

> **NOW REVIEW MULTIPLE-CHOICE QUESTIONS 53 THROUGH 59**

J. International Financial Reporting Standards (IFRS)

1. As discussed earlier in fixed assets, the term investment is used in the area of investment property as well as investments in financial instruments of other entities. The accounting rules for investment property were covered under the section on fixed assets.

2. The term "investments" refers to investments that are held for trading (HFT), available for sale (AFS), and held to maturity (HTM), as well as investments accounted for using the equity method, and investments that require consolidated financial statements. The accounting for investments is covered by various IASs, depending upon the type of investment.

3. A financial instrument should be classified as either fair value through profit or loss (FVTPL), held to maturity (HTM), available for sale (AFS), or loans and receivables.

   a. The FVTPL category includes financial assets in the held for trading (HFT) category.
   b. HTM instruments have fixed and determinable payments and fixed maturity dates.
   c. Held for trading (HFT) securities are securities that the entity has the intent to sell in the near term.
   d. Available for sale financial assets are those that are not classified as FVTPL, HTM, or loans and receivables.

4. If an asset is classified as fair value through profit or loss (FVTPL), it is remeasured to fair value at the end of each accounting period, and any profit or loss is recorded in that period.

   a. An election can be made to use the FVTPL method for accounting purposes for an asset normally classified as available for sale (AFS) or held to maturity (HTM).

      (1) However, if an equity security has no active market in which to determine fair value, then the equity security may not be classified as FVTPL.

   b. Once the item is classified as FVTPL, it may not be subsequently reclassified.
   c. Any equity instrument that does not have a quoted market price or a determinable fair value should be accounted for using the cost method.

5. If FVTPL is not elected, different rules apply.

    a. If the investment is classified as held to maturity (HTM), the investment is recorded at cost, and is subsequently measured at amortized cost using the effective interest method.

    b. Similarly, if a financial asset is classified as loans or receivables, it is accounted for by using amortized cost and the effective interest method.

    c. If the investment is classified as available-for-sale (AFS), the asset is measured at fair value, and any income or loss is recognized in other comprehensive income for the period.

        (1) If a debt security is classified as available-for-sale, any premium or discount must be amortized using the effective interest method on the income statement, with the increase or decrease in fair value reported in other comprehensive income.

6. Investments in associates (affiliates) are accounted for using either the equity method or the FVTPL method.

    a. To qualify for the equity method, the entity must have significant influence over the investee.

        (1) Significant influence is presumed when the investor owns between 20% and 50% of the voting power of another entity.

    b. Consistent with US GAAP, the equity method requires the investment to be recorded at cost, with the investor's share of profit or loss recognized at year-end in the investment account, and the investor's share of dividend distributions recognized as a reduction in the investment account.

        (1) If the cost of the investment is greater than the investor's share of the fair value of net assets, it is not recorded as goodwill.

            (a) However, this portion of the cost of the investment over the carrying amount is amortized as the assets are realized.

        (2) If the cost is less than the fair value of net assets (goodwill is negative), this difference is recognized as income in the year of acquisition.

        (3) An impairment of an investment is recognized if the carrying amount of the investment is greater than its recoverable amount.

> **NOW REVIEW MULTIPLE-CHOICE QUESTIONS 60 THROUGH 64**

KEY TERMS

Amortized cost. Acquisition cost adjusted for amortization of premium or discount.

Available-for-sale securities. Include debt and equity securities not categorized as either held-to-maturity securities or trading securities.

Debt securities. "Any security representing a creditor relationship with an entity."

Differential. The difference between the cost of the investment and the underlying book value of the net assets of the investee.

Equity method. Required for investments which give the investor the ability to exercise significant influence over the operating and financial policies of the investee.

Equity securities. Include ownership interests (common, preferred, and other capital stock), rights to acquire ownership interests (put options).

Fair value option. An entity may elect to value its securities at fair value.

Held-to-maturity securities (amortized cost). This category includes only debt securities and requires the positive intent and ability to hold the securities to maturity (not simply an absence of intent to sell).

Trading securities (subsequently measured at fair value). Debt and equity securities purchased and held principally for the purpose of generating gains on current resale are classified as trading securities.

Multiple-Choice Questions (1-64)

A. Concepts of Accounting and Investment Percentage

1. Puff Co. acquired 40% of Straw, Inc.'s voting common stock on January 2, year 1, for $400,000. The carrying amount of Straw's net assets at the purchase date totaled $900,000. Fair values equaled carrying amounts for all items except equipment, for which fair values exceeded carrying amounts by $100.000. The equipment has a five-year life. During year 1, Straw reported net income of $150,000. What amount of income from this investment should Puff report in its year 1 income statement if Puff uses the equity method to account for the investment?

   a. $40,000
   b. $52,000
   c. $56,000
   d. $60,000

B.1. No Significant Influence: Held-to-Maturity

2. On April 1, year 1, Saxe, Inc. purchased $200,000 face value, 9% US Treasury Notes for $198,500, including accrued interest of $4,500. The notes mature July 1, year 2, and pay interest semiannually on January 1 and July 1. Saxe uses the straight-line method of amortization and intends to hold the notes to maturity. Saxe does not elect the fair value option for recording the securities. In its October 31, year 1 balance sheet, the carrying amount of this investment should be

   a. $194,000
   b. $196,800
   c. $197,200
   d. $199,000

3. Kale Co. purchased bonds at a discount on the open market as an investment and intends to hold these bonds to maturity. Kale does not elect the fair value option for the bonds. Kale should account for these bonds at
   a. Cost.
   b. Amortized cost.
   c. Fair value.
   d. Lower of cost or market.

4. For a marketable debt securities portfolio classified as held-to-maturity, which of the following amounts should be included in the period's net income, assuming the fair value option is not elected.

  I. Unrealized temporary losses during the period.
  II. Realized gains during the period.
  III. Changes in the valuation allowance during the period.

   a. III only.
   b. II only.
   c. I and II.
   d. I, II, and III.

5. Bing Corporation purchased bonds at a discount on the open market as an investment and intends to hold these bonds to maturity. Assume that Bing elects the fair value option. Bing should account for these bonds at
   a. Cost.
   b. Amortized cost.
   c. Fair value.
   d. Lower of cost or market.

6. For a marketable debt securities portfolio classified as held-to-maturity, which of the following amounts should be included in the period's net income, assuming the company elects the fair value option of reporting all of its financial instruments in the portfolio?

  I. Unrealized temporary losses during the period.
  II. Realized gains during the period.
  III. Changes in the valuation allowance during the period.
  IV. Unrealized gains during the period.

   a. I only
   b. I and II
   c. I and III.
   d. I, II, and IV.

B.2. No Significant Influence: Trading

Items 7 and 8 are based on the following:

The following data pertains to Tyne Co.'s investments in marketable equity securities:

		Fair value	
	Cost	12/31/Y2	12/31/Y1
Trading	$150,000	$155,000	$100,000
Available-for-sale	150,000	130,000	120,000

7. What amount should Tyne report as unrealized holding gain in its year 2 income statement, assuming Tyne does not elect to use the fair value option to report its investments?
   a. $50,000
   b. $55,000
   c. $60,000
   d. $65,000

8. Assume Tyne does not elect the fair value option to report investments. What amount should Tyne report as net unrealized loss on marketable equity securities at December 31, year 2, in accumulated other comprehensive income in stockholders' equity?
   a. $0
   b. $10,000
   c. $15,000
   d. $20,000

9. Reed Insurance Co. began operations on January 1, year 1. The following information pertains to Reed's December 31, year 1 portfolio of marketable equity securities:

	Trading securities	Available-for-sale securities
Aggregate cost	$360,000	$550,000
Aggregate fair value	320,000	450,000
Aggregate lower of cost or market value applied to each security in the portfolio	304,000	420,000

Reed does not elect the fair value option. If the fair value declines are judged to be temporary, what amounts should Reed report as a loss on these securities in its December 31, year 1 income statement?

	Trading securities	Available-for-sale securities
a.	$40,000	$0
b.	$0	$100,000
c.	$40,000	$100,000
d.	$56,000	$130,000

B.3. No Significant Influence: Available-for-Sale

10. Stone does not use the fair value option to account for available-for-sale securities. Information regarding Stone Co.'s portfolio of available-for-sale securities is as follows:

Aggregate cost as of 12/31/Y2	$170,000
Unrealized gains as of 12/31/Y2	4,000
Unrealized losses as of 12/31/Y2	26,000
Net realized gains during year 2	30,000

At December 31, year 1, Stone reported an unrealized loss of $1,500 in other comprehensive income to reduce these securities to fair value. Under the accumulated other comprehensive income in stockholders' equity section of its December 31, year 2 balance sheet, what amount should Stone report?

a. $26,000
b. $22,000
c. $20,500
d. $0

11. Data regarding Ball Corp.'s available-for-sale securities follow:

	Cost	Fair value
December 31, year 1	$150,000	$130,000
December 31, year 2	150,000	160,000

Differences between cost and fair values are considered temporary. Ball does not elect the fair value option to account for available-for-sale securities. The effect on Ball's year 2 other comprehensive income would be

a. $30,000
b. $20,000
c. $10,000
d. $0

12. Alton Co. began operations on January 1, year 1. The following information pertains to Alton's December 31, year 1 portfolio of marketable equity securities:

	Trading securities	Available-for-sale securities
Aggregate cost	$360,000	$550,000
Aggregate fair value	320,000	450,000
Aggregate lower of cost or market value applied to each security in the portfolio	304,000	420,000

Alton elects the fair value option for all financial instruments. If the fair value declines are judged to be temporary, what amounts should Alton report as a loss on these securities in its December 31, year 1 income statement?

	Trading securities	Available-for-sale securities
a.	$40,000	$0
b.	$0	$100,000
c.	$40,000	$100,000
d.	$56,000	$130,000

13. Information regarding Shelton Co.'s portfolio of available-for-sale securities is as follows:

Aggregate cost as of 12/31/Y1	$150,000
Unrealized gains as of 12/31/Y1	14,000
Unrealized losses as of 12/31/Y1	26,000
Net realized gains during year 1	30,000

Shelton elects to use the fair value option for reporting all available-for-sale securities. At December 31, year 1, what total amount should Shelton report on its income statement?

a. $ 4,000 gain
b. $18,000 gain
c. $30,000 gain
d. $44,000 gain

14. Data regarding Shannon Corp.'s available-for-sale securities follow:

	Cost	Fair value
December 31, year 1	$150,000	$130,000
December 31, year 2	150,000	160,000

Differences between cost and fair values are considered temporary. Shannon elects to use the fair value option for reporting all available-for-sale securities. The effect of accounting for available-for-sale securities on other comprehensive income in year 2 would be

a. $30,000
b. $20,000
c. $10,000
d. $0

15. Antonio Corp. acquired a portfolio of marketable equity securities that it does not intend to sell in the near term. Antonio elects the fair value option for reporting its financial assets. How should Antonio classify these securities, and how should it report unrealized gains and losses?

	Classify as	Report as a
a.	Trading securities	Component of income from continuing operations
b.	Available-for-sale securities	Separate component of other comprehensive income
c.	Trading securities	Separate component of other comprehensive income
d.	Available-for-sale securities	Component of income from continuing operations

16. During year 1, Rex Company purchased marketable equity securities as a short-term investment. These securities are classified as available-for-sale. Rex does not elect the fair value option to account for available-for-sale securities. The cost and fair value at December 31, year 1, were as follows:

Security	Cost	Fair value
A—100 shares	$ 2,800	$ 3,400
B—1,000 shares	17,000	15,300
C—2,000 shares	31,500	29,500
	$51,300	$48,200

Rex sold 1,000 shares of Company B stock on January 31, year 2, for $15 per share, incurring $1,500 in brokerage commission and taxes. On the sale, Rex should report a realized loss of

a. $ 300
b. $1,800

c. $2,000
d. $3,500

17. Cap Corp. reported accrued investment interest receivable of $38,000 and $46,500 at January 1 and December 31, year 1, respectively. During year 1, cash collections from the investments included the following:

Capital gains distributions	$145,000
Interest	152,000

What amount should Cap report as interest revenue from investments for year 1?

a. $160,500
b. $153,500
c. $152,000
d. $143,500

18. Nola has a portfolio of marketable equity securities that it does not intend to sell in the near term. Assume that Nola does not elect the fair value option to report these securities. How should Nola classify these securities, and how should it report unrealized gains and losses from these securities?

	Classify as	Report as a
a.	Trading securities	Component of income from continuing operations
b.	Available-for-sale securities	Separate component of other comprehensive income
c.	Trading securities	Separate component of other comprehensive income
d.	Available-for-sale securities	Component of income from continuing operations

19. On December 29, year 2, BJ Co. sold a marketable equity security that had been purchased on January 4, year 1. BJ owned no other marketable equity security. An unrealized loss was reported in year 1 as other comprehensive income. A realized gain was reported in the year 2 income statement. Was the marketable equity security classified as available-for-sale and did its year 1 fair value decline exceed its year 2 fair value recovery?

	Available-for-sale	Year 1 fair value decline exceeded year 2 fair value recovery
a.	Yes	Yes
b.	Yes	No
c.	No	Yes
d.	No	No

20. On January 10, year 1, Box, Inc. purchased marketable equity securities of Knox, Inc. and Scot, Inc., neither of which Box could significantly influence. Box classified both securities as available-for-sale. At December 31, year 1, the cost of each investment was greater than its fair value. The loss on the Knox investment was considered other-than-temporary and that on Scot was considered temporary. How should Box report the effects of these investing activities in its year 1 income statement, assuming Box does not elect the fair value option to account for these securities?

I. Excess of cost of Knox stock over its fair value.
II. Excess of cost of Scot stock over its fair value.

a. An unrealized loss equal to I plus II.
b. An unrealized loss equal to I only.
c. A realized loss equal to I only.
d. No income statement effect.

21. On both December 31, year 1, and December 31, year 2, Kopp Co.'s only marketable equity security had the same fair value, which was below cost. Kopp considered the decline in value to be temporary in year 1 but other than temporary in year 2. At the end of both years the security was classified as a noncurrent asset. Kopp considers the investment to be available-for-sale. Assume that Kopp does not elect the fair value option to account for its available-for-sale securities. What should be the effects of the determination that the decline was other than temporary on Kopp's year 2 net noncurrent assets and net income?

a. No effect on both net noncurrent assets and net income.
b. No effect on net noncurrent assets and decrease in net income.
c. Decrease in net noncurrent assets and **no** effect on net income.
d. Decrease in both net noncurrent assets and net income.

22. For the last ten years, Woody Co. has owned cumulative preferred stock issued by Hadley, Inc. During year 2, Hadley declared and paid both the year 2 dividend and the year 1 dividend in arrears. How should Woody report the year 1 dividend in arrears that was received in year 2?

a. As a reduction in cumulative preferred dividends receivable.
b. As a retroactive change of the prior period financial statements.
c. Include, net of income taxes, after year 2 income from continuing operations.
d. Include in year 2 income from continuing operations.

Items 23 and 24 are based on the following:

Deed Co. owns 2% of Beck Cosmetic Retailers. A property dividend by Beck consisted of merchandise with a fair value lower than the listed retail price. Deed in turn gave the merchandise to its employees as a holiday bonus.

23. How should Deed report the receipt and distribution of the merchandise in its income statement?

a. At fair value for both dividend revenue and employee compensation expense.
b. At listed retail price for both dividend revenue and employee compensation expense.
c. At fair value for dividend revenue and listed retail price for employee compensation expense.
d. By disclosure only.

24. How should Deed report the receipt and distribution of the merchandise in its statement of cash flows?

a. As both an inflow and outflow for operating activities.
b. As both an inflow and outflow for investing activities.
c. As an inflow for investing activities and outflow for operating activities.
d. As a noncash activity.

25. Pal Corp.'s year 1 dividend revenue included only part of the dividends received from its Ima Corp. investment. Pal Corp. has an investment in Ima Corp. that it intends to hold indefinitely. The balance of the dividend reduced Pal's carrying amount for its Ima investment. This reflects the fact that Pal accounts for its Ima investment

a. As an available-for-sale investment, and only a portion of Ima's year 1 dividends represent earnings after Pal's acquisition.
b. As an available-for-sale investment and its carrying amount exceeded the proportionate share of Ima's fair value.
c. As an equity investment, and Ima incurred a loss in year 1.
d. As an equity investment, and its carrying amount exceeded the proportionate share of Ima's fair value.

26. In its financial statements, Pare, Inc. uses the cost method of accounting for its 15% ownership of Sabe Co. At December 31, year 1, Pare has a receivable from Sabe. How should the receivable be reported in Pare's December 31, year 1 balance sheet?

a. The total receivable should be reported separately.
b. The total receivable should be included as part of the investment in Sabe, without separate disclosure.
c. 85% of the receivable should be reported separately, with the balance offset against Sabe's payable to Pare.
d. The total receivable should be offset against Sabe's payable to Pare, without separate disclosure.

B.4. No Significant Influence: Transfers

Items 27 and 28 are based on the following:

Sun Corp. had investments in marketable debt securities costing $650,000 that were classified as available-for-sale. On June 30, year 2, Sun decided to hold the investments to maturity and accordingly reclassified them to the held-to-maturity category on that date. The investments' fair value was $575,000 at December 31, year 1, $530,000 at June 30, year 2, and $490,000 at December 31, year 2. Sun does not elect the fair value option to account for these investments.

27. What amount of loss from investments should Sun report in its year 2 income statement?

a. $ 45,000
b. $ 85,000
c. $120,000
d. $0

28. What amount should Sun report as net unrealized loss on marketable debt securities in its year 2 statement of stockholders' equity?

a. $ 40,000
b. $ 45,000
c. $160,000
d. $120,000

29. A marketable debt security is transferred from available-for-sale to held-to-maturity securities. At the transfer date, the security's carrying amount exceeds its fair value. Assume the fair value option is not elected to report this security. What amount is used at the transfer date to record the security in the held-to-maturity portfolio?

a. Fair value, regardless of whether the decline in fair value below cost is considered permanent or temporary.
b. Fair value, only if the decline in fair value below cost is considered permanent.

c. Cost, if the decline in fair value below cost is considered temporary.
d. Cost, regardless of whether the decline in fair value below cost is considered permanent or temporary.

Items 30 and 31 are based on the following:

Jill Corp. had investments in marketable debt securities purchased on January 1, year 1, for $650,000 that were classified as trading securities and accounted for using the cost adjusted to fair value method. On June 30, year 2, Jill decided to hold the investments to maturity and accordingly reclassified them to the held-to-maturity category on that date. The investments' fair value was $575,000 at December 31, year 1, $530,000 at June 30, year 2, and $490,000 at December 31, year 2. Jill elects the fair value option for reporting these held-to-maturity securities.

30. What amount of loss from investments should Jill report in its year 2 income statement?

a. $ 40,000
b. $ 85,000
c. $160,000
d. $0

31. What amount should Jill report as net unrealized loss on marketable debt securities in other comprehensive income in its year 2 statement of stockholders' equity?

a. $0
b. $ 40,000
c. $ 45,000
d. $120,000

C. Investment Where Significant Influence Does Exist

Items 32 through 34 are based on the following:

Grant, Inc. acquired 30% of South Co.'s voting stock for $200,000 on January 2, year 1. Grant's 30% interest in South gave Grant the ability to exercise significant influence over South's operating and financial policies. During year 1, South earned $80,000 and paid dividends of $50,000. South reported earnings of $100,000 for the six months ended June 30, year 2, and $200,000 for the year ended December 31, year 2. On July 1, year 2, Grant sold half of its stock in South for $150,000 cash. South paid dividends of $60,000 on October 1, year 2. Grant does not elect the fair value option to report this investment.

32. Before income taxes, what amount should Grant include in its year 1 income statement as a result of the investment?

a. $15,000
b. $24,000
c. $50,000
d. $80,000

33. In Grant's December 31, year 1 balance sheet, what should be the carrying amount of this investment?

a. $200,000
b. $209,000
c. $224,000
d. $230,000

34. In its year 2 income statement, what amount should Grant report as gain from the sale of half of its investment?

a. $24,500
b. $30,500
c. $35,000
d. $45,500

35. Moss Corp. owns 20% of Dubro Corp.'s preferred stock and 80% of its common stock. Dubro's stock outstanding at December 31, year 1, is as follows:

10% cumulative preferred stock	$100,000
Common stock	700,000

Dubro reported net income of $60,000 for the year ended December 31, year 1. Assume that Moss does not elect the fair value option to report the investment in Dubro. What amount should Moss record as equity in earnings of Dubro for the year ended December 31, year 1?
a. $42,000
b. $48,000
c. $48,400
d. $50,000

36. Sage, Inc. bought 40% of Adams Corp.'s outstanding common stock on January 2, year 1, for $400,000. The carrying amount of Adams' net assets at the purchase date totaled $900,000. Fair values and carrying amounts were the same for all items except for plant and inventory, for which fair values exceeded their carrying amounts by $90,000 and $10,000, respectively. The plant has an eighteen-year life. All inventory was sold during year 1. During year 1, Adams reported net income of $120,000 and paid a $20,000 cash dividend. Assume that Sage uses the equity method to account for this investment. What amount should Sage report in its income statement from its investment in Adams for the year ended December 31, year 1?
a. $48,000
b. $42,000
c. $36,000
d. $32,000

37. Pear Co.'s income statement for the year ended December 31, year 1, as prepared by Pear's controller, reported income before taxes of $125,000. The auditor questioned the following amounts that had been included in income before taxes:

Unrealized gain on available-for-sale investment	$40,000
Equity in earnings of Cinn Co.	20,000
Dividends received from Cinn	8,000
Adjustments to profits of prior years for arithmetical errors in depreciation	(35,000)

Pear owns 40% of Cinn's common stock. Pear accounts for its investment in Cinn in accordance with the requirements of the equity method. Pear's December 31, year 1 income statement should report income before taxes of
a. $ 85,000
b. $117,000
c. $112,000
d. $152,000

38. On January 2, year 1, Saxe Company purchased 20% of Lex Corporation's common stock for $150,000. Saxe Corporation intends to hold the stock indefinitely. This investment did not give Saxe the ability to exercise significant influence over Lex. During year 1 Lex reported net income of $175,000 and paid cash dividends of $100,000 on its

common stock. There was no change in the fair value of the common stock during the year. The balance in Saxe's investment in Lex Corporation account at December 31, year 1 should be
a. $130,000
b. $150,000
c. $165,000
d. $185,000

39. On January 2, year 1, Well Co. purchased 10% of Rea, Inc.'s outstanding common shares for $400,000. Well is the largest single shareholder in Rea, and Well's officers are a majority on Rea's board of directors. Rea reported net income of $500,000 for year 1, and paid dividends of $150,000. Well does not elect the fair value option to report its investment in Rea. In its December 31, year 1 balance sheet, what amount should Well report as investment in Rea?
a. $450,000
b. $435,000
c. $400,000
d. $385,000

40. On January 2, year 1, Kean Co. purchased a 30% interest in Pod Co. for $250,000. On this date, Pod's stockholders' equity was $500,000. The carrying amounts of Pod's identifiable net assets approximated their fair values, except for land whose fair value exceeded its carrying amount by $200,000. Pod reported net income of $100,000 for year 1, and paid no dividends. Kean accounts for this investment using the equity method. In its December 31, year 1 balance sheet, what amount should Kean report as investment in subsidiary?
a. $210,000
b. $220,000
c. $270,000
d. $280,000

41. On January 1, year 1, Mega Corp. acquired 10% of the outstanding voting stock of Penny, Inc. On January 2, year 2, Mega gained the ability to exercise significant influence over financial and operating control of Penny by acquiring an additional 20% of Penny's outstanding stock. The two purchases were made at prices proportionate to the value assigned to Penny's net assets, which equaled their carrying amounts. Mega does not elect the fair value option to report its investment in Penny. For the years ended December 31, year 1 and year 2, Penny reported the following:

	Year 1	Year 2
Dividends paid	$200,000	$300,000
Net income	600,000	650,000

In year 2, what amounts should Mega report as current year investment income and as an adjustment, before income taxes, to year 1 investment income?

	Year 2 investment income	Adjustment to year 1 investment income
a.	$195,000	$160,000
b.	$195,000	$100,000
c.	$195,000	$ 40,000
d.	$105,000	$ 40,000

42. Pare, Inc. purchased 10% of Tot Co.'s 100,000 outstanding shares of common stock on January 2, year 1, for $50,000. On December 31, year 1, Pare purchased an additional 20,000 shares of Tot for $150,000. There was no goodwill as a result of either acquisition, and Tot had not issued any additional stock during year 1. Tot reported earnings of $300,000 for year 1. Pare does not elect the fair value option to report its investment in Tot. What amount should Pare report in its December 31, year 1 balance sheet as investment in Tot?

    a. $170,000
    b. $200,000
    c. $230,000
    d. $290,000

43. When the equity method is used to account for investments in common stock, which of the following affects the investor's reported investment income?

	Equipment amortization related to purchase	Cash dividends from investee
a.	Yes	Yes
b.	No	Yes
c.	No	No
d.	Yes	No

44. Park Co. uses the equity method to account for its January 1, year 1 purchase of Tun Inc.'s common stock. On January 1, year 1, the fair values of Tun's FIFO inventory and land exceeded their carrying amounts. How do these excesses of fair values over carrying amounts affect Park's reported equity in Tun's year 1 earnings?

	Inventory excess	Land excess
a.	Decrease	Decrease
b.	Decrease	No effect
c.	Increase	Increase
d.	Increase	No effect

45. An investor in common stock received dividends in excess of the investor's share of investee's earnings subsequent to the date of the investment. How will the investor's investment account be affected by those dividends for each of the following investments?

	Available-for-sale securities	Equity method investment
a.	No effect	No effect
b.	Decrease	No effect
c.	No effect	Decrease
d.	Decrease	Decrease

46. Peel Co. received a cash dividend from a common stock investment. Should Peel report an increase in the investment account if it has classified the stock as available-for-sale or uses the equity method of accounting?

	Available-for-sale	Equity
a.	No	No
b.	Yes	Yes
c.	Yes	No
d.	No	Yes

47. On January 1, year 1, Point, Inc. purchased 10% of Iona Co.'s common stock. Point purchased additional shares bringing its ownership up to 40% of Iona's common stock outstanding on August 1, year 1. During October year 1, Iona declared and paid a cash dividend on all of its outstanding common stock. Point uses the equity method to account for its investment in Iona. How much income from

the Iona investment should Point's year 1 income statement report?

    a. 10% of Iona's income for January 1 to July 31, year 1, plus 40% of Iona's income for August 1 to December 31, year 1.
    b. 40% of Iona's income for August 1 to December 31, year 1 only.
    c. 40% of Iona's year 1 income.
    d. Amount equal to dividends received from Iona.

48. In its financial statements, Pulham Corp. uses the equity method of accounting for its 30% ownership of Angles Corp. At December 31, year 1, Pulham has a receivable from Angles. How should the receivable be reported in Pulham's year 1 financial statements?

    a. None of the receivable should be reported, but the entire receivable should be offset against Angles' payable to Pulham.
    b. 70% of the receivable should be separately reported, with the balance offset against 30% of Angles' payable to Pulham.
    c. The total receivable should be disclosed separately.
    d. The total receivable should be included as part of the investment in Angles, without separate disclosure.

F. Stock Dividends and Splits

49. Wood Co. owns 2,000 shares of Arlo, Inc.'s 20,000 shares of $100 par, 6% cumulative, nonparticipating preferred stock and 1,000 shares (2%) of Arlo's common stock. During year 2, Arlo declared and paid dividends of $240,000 on preferred stock. No dividends had been declared or paid during year 1. In addition, Wood received a 5% common stock dividend from Arlo when the quoted market price of Arlo's common stock was $10 per share. What amount should Wood report as dividend income in its year 2 income statement?

    a. $12,000
    b. $12,500
    c. $24,000
    d. $24,500

50. Stock dividends on common stock should be recorded at their fair value by the investor when the related investment is accounted for under which of the following methods?

	Cost	Equity	Fair value
a.	Yes	Yes	Yes
b.	Yes	No	No
c.	No	Yes	Yes
d.	No	No	No

G. Stock Rights

51. On March 4, year 1, Evan Co. purchased 1,000 shares of LVC common stock at $80 per share. On September 26, year 1, Evan received 1,000 stock rights to purchase an additional 1,000 shares at $90 per share. The stock rights had an expiration date of February 1, year 2. On September 30, year 1, LVC's common stock had a market value, ex-rights, of $95 per share and the stock rights had a market value of $5 each. What amount should Evan report on its September 30, year 1 balance sheet as the cost of its investment in stock rights?

a. $ 4,000
b. $ 5,000
c. $10,000
d. $15,000

52. On January 3, year 1, Falk Co. purchased 500 shares of Milo Corp. common stock for $36,000. On December 2, year 3, Falk received 500 stock rights from Milo. Each right entitles the holder to acquire one share of stock for $85. The market price of Milo's stock was $100 a share immediately before the rights were issued, and $90 a share immediately after the rights were issued. Falk sold its rights on December 3, year 3, for $10 a right. Falk's gain from the sale of the rights is

    a. $0
    b. $1,000
    c. $1,400
    d. $5,000

H. Cash Surrender Value of Life Insurance

53. In year 1, Chain, Inc. purchased a $1,000,000 life insurance policy on its president, of which Chain is the beneficiary. Information regarding the policy for the year ended December 31, year 4, follows:

Cash surrender value, 1/1/Y4	$ 87,000
Cash surrender value, 12/31/Y4	108,000
Annual advance premium paid 1/1/Y4	40,000

During year 4, dividends of $6,000 were applied to increase the cash surrender value of the policy. What amount should Chain report as life insurance expense for year 4?

    a. $40,000
    b. $25,000
    c. $19,000
    d. $13,000

54. An increase in the cash surrender value of a life insurance policy owned by a company would be recorded by

    a. Decreasing annual insurance expense.
    b. Increasing investment income.
    c. Recording a memorandum entry only.
    d. Decreasing a deferred charge.

55. Upon the death of an officer, Jung Co. received the proceeds of a life insurance policy held by Jung on the officer. The proceeds were not taxable. The policy's cash surrender value had been recorded on Jung's books at the time of payment. What amount of revenue should Jung report in its statements?

    a. Proceeds received.
    b. Proceeds received less cash surrender value.
    c. Proceeds received plus cash surrender value.
    d. None.

Miscellaneous

Items 56 through 58 are based on the following data:

Lake Corporation's accounting records showed the following investments at January 1, year 3:

Common stock:

Kar Corp. (1,000 shares)	$ 10,000
Aub Corp. (5,000 shares)	100,000
Real estate:	
Parking lot (leased to Day Co.)	300,000

Other:

Trademark (at cost, less accumulated amortization)	25,000
Total investments	$435,000

Lake owns 1% of Kar and 30% of Aub. Lake's directors constitute a majority of Aub's directors. The Day lease, which commenced on January 1, year 1, is for ten years, at an annual rental of $48,000. In addition, on January 1, year 1, Day paid a nonrefundable deposit of $50,000, as well as a security deposit of $8,000 to be refunded upon expiration of the lease. The trademark was licensed to Barr Co. for royalties of 10% of sales of the trademarked items. Royalties are payable semiannually on March 1 (for sales in July through December of the prior year), and on September 1 (for sales in January through June of the same year).

During the year ended December 31, year 3, Lake received cash dividends of $1,000 from Kar, and $15,000 from Aub, whose year 3 net incomes were $75,000 and $150,000, respectively. Lake also received $48,000 rent from Day in year 3 and the following royalties from Barr:

	March 1	September 1
Year 2	$3,000	$5,000
Year 3	4,000	7,000

Barr estimated that sales of the trademarked items would total $20,000 for the last half of year 3.

56. In Lake's year 3 income statement, how much should be reported for dividend revenue?

    a. $16,000
    b. $ 2,400
    c. $ 1,000
    d. $ 150

57. In Lake's year 3 income statement, how much should be reported for royalty revenue?

    a. $14,000
    b. $13,000
    c. $11,000
    d. $ 9,000

58. In Lake's year 3 income statement, how much should be reported for rental revenue?

    a. $43,000
    b. $48,000
    c. $53,000
    d. $53,800

59. Band Co. uses the equity method to account for its investment in Guard, Inc. common stock. How should Band record a 2% stock dividend received from Guard?

    a. As dividend revenue at Guard's carrying value of the stock.
    b. As dividend revenue at the market value of the stock.
    c. As a reduction in the total cost of Guard stock owned.
    d. As a memorandum entry reducing the unit cost of all Guard stock owned.

J. International Financial Reporting Standards (IFRS)

60. On March 1, year 1, Acadia purchased 1,000 shares of common stock of Marston Corp. for $50,000 and classified the investment as available-for-sale securities. On December 31, year 1, the Marston stock had a fair value of $53,000. Acadia Corp. prepares its financial statements in accordance with IFRS. Acadia elects to use fair value through profit or loss to record its investments in available-for-sale securities. How is the gain on the investment in Marston stock reported in Acadia's year 1 financial statements?

    a.   As a $3,000 gain in other comprehensive income.

    b.   No gain or loss is reported in year 1.

    c.   As a $3,000 prior period adjustment to retained earnings.

    d.   As a $3,000 gain in current earnings of the period.

61. Under IFRS any investment may be accounted for by fair value through profit and loss providing

    a.   It is traded in an active market.

    b.   It is an equity instrument.

    c.   It is a debt instrument.

    d.   The instrument matures within 2 years.

62. Under IFRS, investments are classified in any of the following different ways, except

    a.   Fair value through profit and loss.

    b.   Held to maturity.

    c.   Tradable.

    d.   Available for sale.

63. Under IFRS if a company uses the fair value method for accounting for an investment any changes in fair value are recognized in

    a.   Other comprehensive income.

    b.   Retained earnings.

    c.   Profit and loss.

    d.   Revaluation surplus.

64. Under IFRS an equity investment may be accounted for using the equity method if the investor has significant influence over the investee. Significant influence is indicated by ownership of

    a.   At least 10%.

    b.   From 20 to 50%.

    c.   More than 50%.

    d.   More than 70%.

Multiple-Choice Answers and Explanations

Answers

1. b __ __	15. d __ __	29. a __ __	43. d __ __	57. d __ __
2. b __ __	16. d __ __	30. b __ __	44. b __ __	58. c __ __
3. b __ __	17. a __ __	31. a __ __	45. d __ __	59. d __ __
4. b __ __	18. b __ __	32. b __ __	46. a __ __	60. d __ __
5. c __ __	19. b __ __	33. b __ __	47. a __ __	61. a __ __
6. d __ __	20. c __ __	34. b __ __	48. c __ __	62. c __ __
7. b __ __	21. b __ __	35. a __ __	49. c __ __	63. c __ __
8. d __ __	22. d __ __	36. b __ __	50. d __ __	64. b __ __
9. a __ __	23. a __ __	37. c __ __	51. a __ __	
10. b __ __	24. d __ __	38. b __ __	52. c __ __	
11. a __ __	25. a __ __	39. b __ __	53. c __ __	
12. c __ __	26. a __ __	40. d __ __	54. a __ __	
13. b __ __	27. d __ __	41. c __ __	55. b __ __	1st: __/64= __%
14. d __ __	28. d __ __	42. c __ __	56. c __ __	2nd: __/64= __%

Explanations

1. **(b)** The investment should be accounted for on the equity basis and the calculation of Puff's income from the investment is shown below.

Straw's net income		$150,000
	×	40%
Puff's share of Straw's net income		$ 60,000
Less: Puff's depreciation of excess		
value of equipment		
Excess cost	$100,000	
	×	40%
Puff's share	$ 40,000	
Remaining useful life	÷	5
Puff's share of excess		
depreciation for year 1		(8,000)
Income from investment on the equity		
basis		$ 52,000

2. **(b)** Held-to-maturity securities are to be carried at amortized cost. Therefore, the investment is recorded on 4/1/Y1 at its cost of $194,000 ($198,500 less accrued interest of $4,500). The carrying amount is calculated as cost plus amortized discount, which at 10/31/Y1 is $196,800 [$194,000 + ($6,000 × 7/15)].

3. **(b)** **Held-to-maturity** securities, which include only debt securities, are reported on the balance sheet at **amortized cost** without adjustment to fair value. If the investment in bonds had been classified as trading or available-for-sale, answer (c) would be correct. **Trading** securities are reported at **fair value** with holding gains or losses flowing through the income statements. **Available-for-sale** securities are reported at **fair value** with holding gains or losses reported as a component of other comprehensive income. Cost and lower of cost or market are not used as reporting bases for bond investments.

4. **(b)** Held-to-maturity securities are carried at cost, so unrealized holding gains and losses are not reported. However, realized gains and losses on held-to-maturity securities should always be included in the income statement of the appropriate period. No valuation allowance exists for any marketable debt or equity securities. Realized gains for the period are the only item listed that is included in that period's net income.

5. **(c)** A company may elect to value held-to-maturity securities at fair value. Any increase or decrease in value is reported as a gain or loss and included in earnings for the period. Answer (a) is incorrect because bonds are recorded at cost, but reported at amortized cost at year-end. Answer (b) is incorrect because Bing elected the fair value option. Answer (d) is incorrect because investments are not recorded at lower of cost or market.

6. **(d)** A company may elect to value held-to-maturity securities at fair value. Any increase or decrease in value, whether realized or unrealized, is reported in earnings for the period. Therefore, I, II, and IV should be reported in earnings if the fair value option of reporting is elected. Changes in the valuation allowance are not relevant because when an election is made to use the fair value option, any related allowance accounts are removed from the balance sheet.

7. **(b)** Debt and equity securities that are classified as **trading securities** are reported at fair value with unrealized gains and losses included in earnings. During year 2, Tyne had an unrealized holding gain of $55,000 ($155,000 − $100,000) on its trading securities. The unrealized holding gain on **available-for-sale** securities ($130,000 − $120,000 = $10,000) is excluded from earnings and reported as other comprehensive income.

8. **(d)** The requirement is to determine the accumulated other comprehensive income to be reported in the December 31, year 2 statement of stockholders' equity. Unrealized gains and losses on **trading securities** are included in earnings. Unrealized gains and losses on **available-for-sale** securities are excluded from earnings and reported as accumulated other comprehensive income in a separate component of shareholders' equity. This amount is the net unrealized loss on available-for-sale securities at 12/31/Y2 which is $20,000 ($150,000 − $130,000).

9. **(a)** Unrealized holding gains and losses for trading securities are to be reported in earnings. On the other hand, this statement also states that unrealized gains or losses on available-for-sale securities should be excluded from earnings and reported as other comprehensive income. There-fore, only the $40,000 ($360,000 – $320,000) unrealized loss on trading securities is included in income.

10. (b) Available-for-sale securities are reported at fair value on the balance sheet. At 12/31/Y2, Stone has incurred gross unrealized gains of $4,000 and gross unrealized losses of $26,000 on its available-for-sale securities. Therefore, at 12/31/Y2, the net unrealized loss is $22,000 ($26,000 – $4,000). Stone would have to increase the balance in ac-cumulated other comprehensive income from $1,500 to $22,000 at 12/31/Y2.

11. (a) Unrealized holding gains and losses on available-for-sale securities should be reported as other comprehensive income. At 12/31/Y1, available-for-sale securities would have been reported in the balance sheet at their fair value of $130,000, with a corresponding unrealized loss of $20,000. At 12/31/Y2, the fair value of these securi-ties is $160,000. Therefore, an unrealized gain of $30,000 ($160,000 – $130,000) would result in other comprehensive income of $30,000 as **accumulated** other comprehensive income.

12. (c) A $40,000 loss is recorded on the income state-ment for the loss on trading securities. An election can be made to value available-for-sale securities at fair value. Therefore, the available-for-sale securities are valued at fair value, and the loss of $100,000 is reported on the income statement.

13. (b) A company may elect the fair value option for reporting available-for-sale securities. If the fair value op-tion is elected, realized and unrealized gains and losses from available-for-sale securities are included in earnings of the period. Therefore, the net gain of $18,000 ($14,000 unre-alized gains + $30,000 realized gains – $26,000 unrealized losses) is reported on the income statement for the period.

14. (d) If Shannon elects the fair value option for report-ing available-for-sale securities, any unrealized gains or losses are recorded in earnings for the period. In year 1, Shannon would report a loss on the income statement of $20,000, and the available-for-sale securities would be car-ried on the balance sheet at the fair value of $130,000. On December 31, year 2, the securities would be valued at $160,000 and an unrealized gain of $30,000 ($160,000 – $130,000) would be recognized on the year 2 income state-ment. Therefore, under the provisions of ASC Topic 825 (SFAS 159), there would be no entry to other comprehensive income for available-for-sale securities.

15. (d) Marketable equity securities that are not in-tended to be sold in the near future are classified as available-for-sale securities. A company may elect to record an available-for-sale security at its fair value, and any unre-alized gains or losses may be recognized as a component of income from continuing operations on the income statement. Answer (a) is incorrect because Antonio does not intend to sell the asset in the near future; therefore, it cannot be classi-fied as a trading security. Answer (b) is incorrect because when the fair value option is elected, the unrealized gain or loss is reported in earnings, not in other comprehensive in-come. Answer (c) is incorrect because the securities are not classified as trading and the gain is not recognized in OCI.

16. (d) The securities purchased by Rex are classified as available-for-sale securities and accounted for at fair value. At 12/31/Y1, the fair value of security B was $15,300; an unrealized loss of $1,700 resulted in other comprehensive income in that amount. At 1/31/Y2, the stock was sold when its fair value was $15,000 and the following entry would have been made:

Cash (net)	13,500	
Loss on sale of stock	3,500	
Investment in		
Security B		15,300
Unrealized loss on		
Sec. B.		1,700

The unrealized loss of $1,700 on Security B is a credit. It would be netted with unrealized gains and/or losses recog-nized in year 2. The effect is to offset the $1,700 loss recog-nized in year 1 that was closed to other comprehensive in-come, net retained earnings, thus avoiding double counting.

17. (a) The capital gains distribution ($145,000) would not be reported as interest revenue. The solutions approach is to set up a T-account for interest receivable.

Interest Receivable			
Beg. bal.	38,000		
Int. rev.	?	152,000	Int. collected
End. bal.	46,500		

Beginning and ending balances are given in the question. Interest receivable would be credited for cash collections to reduce the receivable.

Cash	152,000	
Interest receivable		152,000

Interest receivable would be debited for interest revenue.

Interest receivable	xxx	
Interest revenue		xxx

Solve for interest revenue ($46,500 + $152,000 – $38,000 = $160,500).

18. (b) Marketable equity securities (MES) are classi-fied as either trading (held for current resale) or available-for-sale (if not categorized as trading). Since Nola does not intend to sell these securities in the near term, they should be classified as available-for-sale. MES are carried at fair value. The unrealized gains or losses of available-for-sale MES are reported as a separate component of other compre-hensive income. It is important to note that unrealized gains or losses on **trading** securities would be reported as a com-ponent of income from continuing operations on the income statement. Thus, answer (b) is correct because the securities would be classified as available-for-sale and unrealized gains and losses from these securities would be reported as other comprehensive income.

19. (b) Unrealized losses on available-for-sale securities are reported as a separate component of other comprehen-sive income, while unrealized gains and losses on trading securities are recognized in income and unrealized gains and losses on held-to-maturity securities are ignored. Thus, this security is classified as available-for-sale. A realized gain will be reported only if the security was sold for a price in excess of its cost. Therefore, the year 1 price decline was **less than** the year 2 price recovery. For example, assume that the investment was purchased for $1,000 on 1/07/Y1.

At 12/31/Y1, its fair value was $800, and on 12/29/Y2 its fair value was $1,200. The following entries would have been made:

1/07/Y1	Investment	1,000	
	Cash		1,000
12/31/Y1	Unrealized loss	200	
	Investment		200
12/29/Y2	Cash	1,200	
	Investment		800
	Unrealized loss		200
	Gain on sale of securities		**200**

20. (c) The requirement is to determine how the losses on the securities classified as available-for-sale should be reported. A decline in fair value of a security which is considered to be **other-than-temporary** should be reported on the income statement in the current period. A decline in fair value which is considered to be **temporary** would be recorded as an unrealized loss, and recognized as other comprehensive income. Therefore, answer (c) is correct as the loss on the Knox stock is considered to be other-than-temporary and it would be reported on the income statement. Answer (a) is incorrect because the unrealized loss on the Scot stock would be reported as other comprehensive income. Answer (b) is incorrect because the loss on the Knox stock is considered to be a realized loss as it is other-than-temporary. Answer (d) is incorrect because the other-than-temporary decline in Knox stock results in a realized loss that is reported on the income statement.

21. (b) The carrying amount of a marketable equity security classified as available-for-sale shall be the fair value and the unrealized holding gain or loss should be reported as other comprehensive income. In year 1 when the value declined, the portfolio was reported at fair value with an unrealized holding loss recorded as other comprehensive income. In year 2, the decline is considered to be other than temporary. Thus, the security must be written down to fair value and a realized loss recognized. However, since there is no actual change in value, in year 2 the security will be reported at the same amount (Cost – Write-down of asset) as in year 1. Therefore, there is no effect on **net** noncurrent assets in year 2. However, net income will be affected because a realized loss is recorded on the income statement. Note that the unrealized loss account charged to other comprehensive income in year 1 would be credited and the realized loss account would be debited for the same amount. The allowance accounts will be closed against each other because the new basis after the write-down will equal the lower FV amount. Answer (a) is incorrect because net income is affected. Note that if the decline was merely temporary, there would be no net income effect because temporary declines in value of noncurrent portfolios are reported as other comprehensive income, rather than net income. Answer (c) is incorrect because there is no net decrease in noncurrent assets, but there is a net income effect. Answer (d) is incorrect because only net income decreases.

22. (d) Dividends in arrears are not a receivable to the cumulative preferred stockholder until the issuing corporation's board of directors formally declares the dividend. In this case, Hadley, Inc. did not declare the year 1 dividends in arrears until year 2. At the year 2 dividend declaration date, Woody Co. records dividends receivable and dividend income. Dividend income is included in income from continuing operations.

23. (a) A nonmonetary asset (the merchandise in this case) received in a nonreciprocal transfer should be recorded at the fair value of the asset received. Additionally, the transfer of a nonmonetary asset to a stockholder or other entity (Deed's employees in this case) should be recorded at the fair value of the asset received.

24. (d) Noncash transactions should be excluded from the statement of cash flows to better achieve the statement's objectives. However, information about noncash investing and financing transactions be must reported in related disclosures.

25. (a) An investor carries an investment in the stock of an investee at fair value, and recognizes as income dividends received that are distributed from the net accumulated earnings of the investee **since the date of acquisition** by the investor. Dividends received in excess of earnings subsequent to the date of investment are considered to be return of investment or a liquidating dividend and are recorded as reductions of the cost of the investment. Therefore, Pal Corp.'s accounting treatment of the dividend it received from Ima Corp. indicates that Pal is accounting for the securities as an available-for-sale investment in Ima. Answer (b) is incorrect because Ima's fair value does not impact Pal's treatment of dividends received. Answers (c) and (d) are incorrect because all dividends received are treated as reductions in an investee's carrying value under the equity method.

26. (a) Intercompany receivables and payables are not eliminated unless consolidated financial statements are prepared. Since Pare only has a 15% interest in Sabe, consolidated financial statements would not be prepared. Thus, on the 12/31/Y1 balance sheet, Pare should separately report the total amount of the receivable.

27. (d) The requirement is to determine the amount of loss on investments to be reported in Sun's year 2 income statement. This transfer is accounted for at fair value and any holding gains or losses on securities that are transferred to held-to-maturity from available-for-sale be reported as accumulated other comprehensive income. This amount is then amortized over the remaining life of the security as an adjustment to yield. Since cost is greater than fair value by $75,000 at 12/31/Y1 ($650,000 cost – $575,000 fair value), the following entry would be recorded:

Unrealized loss	75,000	
Marketable debt securities		75,000

Then on June 30, year 2, when Sun decides to hold the investments to maturity, an additional $45,000 will be recorded in the valuation account ($575,000 value on books – $530,000 FV) to reflect the change in FV. The following entry would be recorded:

Unrealized loss	45,000	
Marketable debt securities		45,000

Each year the unrealized loss would be reported as other comprehensive income that would be closed to "accumulated other comprehensive income."

28. (d) When a security is transferred to held-to-maturity from available-for-sale the unrealized holding gain or loss continues to be reported as a separate component of stockholders' equity. Held-to-maturity securities are carried at amortized cost, and any unrealized holding gains or losses are not reported. Thus, the balance in the "accumulated other comprehensive income" in stockholders' equity on the year 2 statement of stockholders' equity would be $120,000 ($75,000 amount reported at 12/31/Y1 plus the $45,000 amount reported at June 30, year 2). The $120,000 will be amortized over the remaining life of the security as an adjustment to yield. The additional decline in value from 6/30/Y2 to 12/31/Y2 would not be reported, as held-to-maturity securities do not report unrealized losses.

29. (a) The transfer of a security between categories of investments shall be accounted for at fair value." If fair value is less than the security's carrying amount at the date of transfer, it is irrelevant whether the decline is temporary or permanent.

30. (b) An election can be made to use the fair value option when financial assets cease to qualify for fair value treatment due to specialized accounting rules. On June 30, year 2, the trading securities were reclassified to the held-to-maturity category, and an election was made to report them at fair value. On June 30, year 2, the held-to-maturity securities were valued at $530,000, and Jill would recognize a loss of $45,000 ($575,000 – $530,000). At December 31, year 2, the securities declined in value an additional $40,000. Therefore, the total loss recognized in year 2 was $85,000 ($45,000 + $40,000). Answer (a) is incorrect because the entire amount of loss in fair value should be recognized in year 2. Answer (c) is incorrect because the loss from January 1, year 1 to December 31, year 1, would have been recognized in year 1 because it was classified as a trading security. Answer (d) is incorrect because if the fair value option is elected, unrealized gains and losses are recognized in the current year's earnings.

31. (a) Jill would recognize the unrealized loss on trading securities in the income statement. On June 30, year 2, when the securities were classified as held-to-maturity, Jill elected the fair value option for reporting the investment. Therefore, any unrealized gain or loss on the held-to-maturity securities would be reported in earnings for the period. An unrealized gain or a temporary loss on available-for-sale securities would be reported in other comprehensive income only if the fair value option were not elected. Held-to-maturity securities would be valued at amortized cost if the fair value option of reporting were not elected. Therefore, answers (b), (c), and (d) are incorrect because Jill elects the fair value option on the held-to-maturity securities.

32. (b) This investment should be accounted for using the equity method since Grant owns a 30% interest and can exercise significant influence over South. Grant's share of South's year 1 earnings (30% × $80,000 = $24,000) would be recognized as investment revenue under the equity method. If there was any excess of cost over book value of assets with finite useful lives, resulting from the purchase of the investment, it would be amortized, reducing investment revenue. However, not enough information was given to determine if there was an excess. The dividends received by Grant (30% × $50,000 = $15,000) do not affect investment revenue using the equity method; they are recorded as a reduction of the investment account.

33. (b) The equity method is used because Grant owns a 30% interest and can exercise significant influence. Under this method, the investment account is increased by Grant's equity in South's earnings (30% × $80,000 = $24,000) and is decreased by Grant's dividends received from South (30% × $50,000 = $15,000). This results in a 12/31/Y1 carrying amount for the investment of $209,000, as indicated in the following T-account.

	Investment in South		
1/2/Y1	200,000		
Equity in earnings	24,000	15,000	Dividends
12/31/Y1	209,000		

34. (b) The equity method is used because Grant owns a 30% interest and can exercise significant influence. Under this method, the investment account is increased by Grant's equity in South's earnings (30% × $80,000 = $24,000 in year 1; 30% × $100,000 = $30,000 for first six months of year 2) and is decreased by Grant's dividends received from South (30% × $50,000 = $15,000 in year 2; none in first six months of year 1). This results in a 7/1/Y2 carrying amount of $239,000, as indicated in the T-account below.

	Investment in South		
1/2/Y1	200,000		
Equity in earnings	24,000	15,000	Dividends
Equity in earnings	30,000		
7/1/Y2	239,000		

The gain on sale is the excess of the proceeds ($150,000) over the carrying amount of the shares sold (1/2 × $239,000 = $119,500), or $30,500 ($150,000 – $119,500).

35. (a) An investor's share of the income of a company in which it holds a 20% or greater investment is referred to as the investor's equity in earnings of the investee. The investor's share of the investee's earnings should be computed after deducting the investee's cumulative preferred dividends (whether declared or not). In this case, the income available to common stockholders is $50,000 [$60,000 income – (10% × $100,000 total pref. div.)], so Moss Corp.'s equity in earnings is $40,000 (80% ownership × $50,000). Since $40,000 is not one of the answer choices, apparently the candidate is expected to include the preferred dividend revenue of $2,000 [20% ownership × ($100,000 × 10% total pref. div.)] on the income statement in the equity in earnings line item. Although preferred dividends are usually classified separately, answer (a) is the best answer given. The answer, therefore, is $42,000.

Equity in earnings	$40,000
Dividend revenue	2,000
	$42,000

36. (b) Sage paid $400,000 for its 40% investment in Adams when Adams' net assets had a carrying amount of $900,000. Therefore, the book value Sage purchased is $360,000 (40% × $900,000), resulting in an excess of cost over book value of $40,000 ($400,000 – $360,000). This excess must be attributed to specific assets of Adams; any amount not attributed to specific assets is attributed to goodwill. In this case, the excess is attributed to plant assets (40% × $90,000 = $36,000) and inventory (40% × $10,000 = $4,000). The portion attributed to plant assets is amortized over eighteen years, while the portion attributed to inventory is expensed immediately (since all inventory was sold during year 1). Therefore, Sage's investment income is $42,000, as computed below.

Share of income (40% × $120,000)	$48,000
Excess amortization [($36,000/18) + $4,000]	(6,000)
	$42,000

37. (c) The unrealized gain on the available-for-sale securities is improperly included in Pear's $125,000 income before taxes. Unrealized holding gains and losses on available-for-sale securities are reported as a separate component of stockholders' equity. The equity in Cinn's earnings is properly included in Pear Co.'s pretax income. However, the dividends from Cinn are also improperly included in income because under the equity method, dividends received are a reduction of the investment account rather than dividend revenue. The adjustments to profits of prior years for arithmetic errors in depreciation ($35,000) should be recorded as a retroactive adjustment to beginning retained earnings and should **not** have been deducted when computing year 1 income before taxes. Therefore, year 1 income before taxes should be $112,000 as computed below.

Tentative income	$125,000
Unrealized holding gain	(40,000)
Dividends received	(8,000)
Prior period adjustment	35,000
Correct income	$112,000

38. (b) The equity method is to be used when the investor owns 20% or more of the investee's voting stock, unless there is evidence that the investor does **not** have the ability to exercise significant influence over the investee. Since this is the case, Saxe must carry the stock at fair value in the available-for-sale category. Under this method, dividends received are to be recognized as income to the investor, and the investment account is unaffected. Also, under this method, the investor's share of the investee's net income is not recognized. Any changes in the fair value of the stock would be reflected in the book value of the stock with a corresponding amount in a separate account in stockholders' equity. As there has been no change in the fair value, the investment account would still have a balance of $150,000 at 12/31/Y1. Note that the dividends received by Saxe were distributed from Lex's net accumulated earnings since the date of acquisition by Saxe. However, if dividends received had been in excess of earnings subsequent to the investment date, they are considered a return of capital and would be recorded as a reduction in the investment account.

39. (b) Ownership of less than 20% leads to the presumption of **no substantial influence** unless evidence to the contrary exists. Well's position as Rea's largest single shareholder and the presence of Well's officers as a **majority** of Rea's board of directors constitute evidence that Well **does have significant influence** despite less than 20% ownership. Therefore, the equity method is used. The investment account had a beginning balance of $400,000 (purchase price). This amount is increased by Well's equity in Rea's earnings (10% ownership × $500,000 income = $50,000) and decreased by Well's dividends received from Rea (10% share × $150,000 total div. = $15,000), resulting in a balance of $435,000 (see T-account below).

Investment in Rea			
1/2/Y1	400,000		
Equity in earnings	50,000	15,000	Dividends
12/31/Y1	435,000		

40. (d) The investment should have been originally recorded at the $250,000 purchase price. This amount would be increased by Kean's share of Pod's earnings (30% × $100,000 = $30,000), decreased by the amortization of excess of cost over book value, and decreased by dividends received by Kean (none in this case). The book value Kean purchased is $150,000 (30% × $500,000), resulting in an excess of cost over book value of $100,000 ($250,000 – $150,000). This excess must be attributed to the specific assets of Pod that have a fair value greater than their book value; any amount not attributed to specific assets is attributed to goodwill. In this case, the excess would be attributed first to land (30% × $200,000 = $60,000) and the remainder to goodwill ($100,000 – $60,000 = $40,000). The portion attributed to land and goodwill should not be amortized. Therefore, Kean's 12/31/Y1 balance of the investment in subsidiary is $280,000 as computed below.

Original cost	$250,000
Share of income (30% × $100,000)	30,000
	$280,000

41. (c) When an investment that has been accounted for using another method qualifies for the use of the equity method due to a change in ownership level (such as from 10% to 30%), the change to the equity method should be reported **retroactively**. At the date of the change (1/2/Y2), the **investment** account and **retained earnings** are adjusted as if the equity method had been used all along, and the results of operations in prior years are restated to reflect the equity method. In year 2, use of the equity method results in recognition of investment income of $195,000 (30% × $650,000 investee income). Year 1 investment income must be restated from the previously reported dividend income (10% × $200,000 = $20,000) to equity method income (10% × $600,000 = $60,000), an adjustment of $40,000 ($60,000 – $20,000 = $40,000).

42. (c) The requirement is to determine the balance in the December 31, year 1 investment account. When an investment that has been accounted for using another method qualifies for the use of the equity method due to a change in ownership level (in this case, from 10% to 30%), the change to the equity method should be applied retroactively. At the date of the change (12/31/Y1), the accounts are adjusted as if the equity method had been used all along. If the equity method had been used beginning at 1/2/Y1, Pare would have recorded its share of Tot's earnings (10% × $300,000 = $30,000) as investment revenue and as an increase in the investment account. Therefore, at 12/31/Y1, Pare's investment in Tot would be reported at $230,000.

Investment in Tot		
1/2/Y1 purchase	50,000	
12/31/Y1 purchase	150,000	
Equity in earnings	30,000	
	230,000	

43. (d) Under the equity method, a reciprocal relationship is formed between the investment account on the investor's books and the book values of the net assets on the investee's books. As changes in the investee's net assets occur (earnings, dividends, etc.), the investor will recognize the percentage of ownership share of that change in the investment account. Therefore, cash dividends from the investee will be recorded in the investment account, not the investment income account. The entry includes a debit to cash and a credit to the investment account. Another aspect of the equity method is the amortization of the equipment related to the purchase. The investment income account and the investment in stock account should include all the income recognitions and amortizations resulting from the investment. The entry to record the equipment amortization is a debit to Investment income and a credit to Investment in stock.

44. (b) When the equity method is used, the investor should amortize any portion of the excess of fair values over carrying amounts (differential) that relates to depreciable or amortizable assets held by the investee. Amortization of the differential results in a reduction of the investment account and a reduction in the equity of the investee's earnings. For inventory, an excess of FV over cost, FIFO cost in this case, has the same effect on the investment account and equity in investee earnings in the period in which the goods are sold. Therefore, the portion of the differential that relates to inventory would decrease Park's reported equity in Tun's earnings, and answers (c) and (d) are incorrect. Land is not a depreciable asset, so there would be no amortization of the differential related to land, and answer (a) is incorrect.

45. (d) Dividends received in excess of earnings subsequent to the date of investment are considered a return of investment and are recorded as reductions of cost of the investment. Additionally, under the equity method, "dividends received from an investee reduce the carrying amount of the investment."

46. (a) The requirement is to determine the effects of a cash dividend on an investors investment account, accounted for both as an available-for-sale security, and under the equity method. Dividends received on available-for-sale securities are to be recognized as income to the investor and the investment account is unaffected. If the dividends received are in excess of earnings to date, then they would be considered a return of the investment and would result in a reduction of the investment account. Under the equity method, the receipt of cash dividends reduces the carrying value of the investment. Therefore, answer (a) is correct as the receipt of a cash dividend would not result in an increase in the investment account under either method.

47. (a) The requirement is to determine the amount of investment income to be reported in the year 1 income statement. When an investment which has been accounted for using a different method qualifies for the use of the equity method, due to a change in ownership level (such as 10% to 40%), then the change to the equity method should be reported **retroactively**. At the date of the change, the investment account and the retained earnings account are adjusted as if the equity method had been used all along. Therefore answer (a) is correct as Point owned 10% of Iona's stock from January 1 to July 31, year 1, and 40% of Iona's stock from August 1 to December 31, year 1. Answers (b) and (c) are incorrect because income should be recognized under the equity method according to the percentage of ownership existing during each of the periods. Answer (d) is incorrect because when Iona reports its earnings to Point, Point will

record its share of the revenue. When Point receives the dividends, (which may be in a different period than Point recognized its share of Iona's income), the carrying amount of the investment will be reduced by the amount received. Therefore, the income recognized does not usually equal the dividends received.

48. (c) The equity method is used when accounting for investments in which the investor has the ability to exercise significant influence over the operating and financial policies of the investee. Ownership of 20% or more of the outstanding common stock demonstrates this ability. In this case, Pulham Corp. owns 30% of Angles and properly uses the equity method. Under the equity method intercompany profits and losses are eliminated. However, receivables and payables are not eliminated as they are in the case of consolidated financial statements. On the December 31, year 1 balance sheet, Pulham should separately disclose the total amount of the receivable. Additionally, this receivable should be shown separately from other receivables.

49. (c) Arlo's annual preferred stock dividend is $120,000 ($2,000,000 × 6%). The $240,000 dividend paid includes $120,000 dividends in arrears from year 1 and $120,000 for year 2. Therefore, Wood would receive **$24,000 of cash dividends** ($200,000 × 6% × 2) which would be reported as **dividend income** in year 2 (preferred dividends in arrears are not recognized as income until declared). No dividend income is recognized when an investor receives a proportional **stock** dividend, because the investor continues to own the same proportion of the investee as before the stock dividend, and the investee has not distributed any assets to the investor.

50. (d) Regardless of the accounting method used, no dividend revenue is recognized when an investor receives a proportional **stock** dividend, because the investor continues to own the same proportion of the investee as before the stock dividend. In addition, the investee has not distributed any assets to the investor. Therefore, **no entry** is prepared to record the receipt of a stock dividend. The investor simply makes a memo entry to record the additional number of shares owned, while leaving the balance in the investment account unchanged. The balance is then spread over the total number of shares (Previous holdings + Stock dividend) to determine the new per share cost of the stock.

51. (a) When stock rights are received, the cost of the investment (1,000 × $80 = $80,000) is allocated between the stock and the rights based on the relative fair market value of each, as calculated below.

FMV of stock	1,000 × $95	=	$ 95,000
FMV of rights	1,000 × $ 5	=	5,000
Total FMV			$100,000

The cost allocated to the stock is $76,000 ($80,000 × 95/100) and the cost allocated to the rights is $4,000 ($80,000 × 5/100).

52. (c) When the rights are received, the cost of the investment ($36,000) is allocated between the stock and the rights based on their relative fair market values, calculated below.

FMV of stock	500 × $90	=	$45,000
FMV of rights	500 × $10	=	5,000
Total FMV			$50,000

The cost allocated to the stock is $32,400 ($45,000/ $50,000, or 90%, of $36,000) and to the rights is $3,600 ($5,000/ $50,000, or 10%, of $36,000). The net proceeds from the sale of the rights is $5,000 (500 × $10), so the gain on the sale of the rights is $1,400 ($5,000 – $3,600).

53. (c) The cash surrender value (CSV) of the life insurance policy increased by $21,000 during year 4 ($108,000 – $87,000). Therefore, part of the premium paid is not expense but a payment to increase the CSV. The formula to compute insurance expense is

Cash paid – (Ending CSV – Beginning CSV) – Cash divs. received
$40,000 –   ($108,000 – $87,000)   – $0 = $19,000

The dividends in this problem are **not** cash dividends received. They are dividends that the insurance company applied to increase the CSV. They are not separately considered in the formula above because the effect of the dividends is reflected in the increase in CSV, which **is** included in the formula. Year 4 journal entries are presented below.

Cash surr. value	$15,000	($21,000 – $6,000)
Ins. expense	25,000	
Cash		$40,000
Cash surr. value	$ 6,000	
Ins. expense		$ 6,000

54. (a) When a company insures the lives of employees and names itself the beneficiary, the cash surrender value of the policies is considered an asset. During the first few years of a policy, no cash surrender value may accrue. If no increase in cash surrender value (CSV) occurs, the journal entry to record a premium paid would be

Insurance expense	xxx	
Cash		xxx

However, if cash surrender value increases, part of the cash paid is recorded as an increase in the CSV. The entry is

Insurance expense	xx	
Cash surrender value	xx	
Cash		xxx

Therefore, the increase in CSV decreases insurance expense because the same amount of cash paid must be allocated between the two accounts. The increase in CSV does **not** affect investment income or deferred charges.

55. (b) When a company insures the lives of employees and names itself as the beneficiary, the cash surrender value (CSV) of the policy is considered an asset. Premiums paid are debited to CSV for the increase in CSV that year and to insurance expense for the excess of cash paid over increase in CSV. Upon the death of the insured employee, the company recognizes a gain for the excess of proceeds received over CSV.

56. (c) In determining the amount which should be reported in Lake's year 3 income statement as dividend revenue, the first step is to determine what method should be used in accounting for Lake's investments. The equity method of accounting for an investment in common stock should be followed by an investor whose investment in common stock gives it the ability to exercise significant influence over the operating and financial policies of an investee even though the investor may hold 50% or less of the voting stock. Ability to exercise that influence may be indicated in several ways, such as representation on the board of directors. Another important consideration is the extent of ownership by an investor. The Board concluded that an investment of 20% or more of the voting stock of an investee should lead to a presumption, in the absence of evidence to the contrary, that an investor has the ability to exercise significant influence over an investee. Conversely, an investment of less than 20% of the voting stock of an investee should lead to a presumption that an investor does **not** have the ability to exercise significant influence unless such ability can be demonstrated. Lake's 30% ownership of Aub and its representation on Aub's board of directors clearly indicate that the investment in Aub should be accounted for using the equity method. Lake's 1% ownership in Kar and lack of evidence in this problem that Lake has "significant influence" over Kar indicate that this investment should be accounted for using the cost adjusted for fair value method. When the **equity** method is used, dividends received from an investee reduce the carrying amount of the investment (i.e., are **not** reported as dividend revenue). However, the investor recognizes dividends received from investees as **income** under the **cost adjusted for fair value** method. Therefore, the $1,000 of cash dividends from Kar would be reported as dividend revenue by Lake, while the $15,000 of cash dividends from Aub would reduce the carrying amount of Lake's investment in Aub.

57. (d) Lake's royalty revenue results from the licensing of their trademark to Barr Co. Lake receives royalties of 10% of Barr's sales of trademarked items. To determine royalty revenue for year 3, it must first be realized that the royalty payment on September 1, year 3, is for sales in January through June of year 3. This royalty payment of $7,000 is the first portion of royalty revenue for year 3. The second portion of royalty revenue is for Barr's sales of trademarked items for July through December of year 3. This second portion consists of 10% of Barr's estimated sales of trademarked items for the last half of year 3. Royalty revenue for the second half of year 3 is then $2,000 (10% × $20,000). Therefore, answer (d) is correct because royalty revenue would be $9,000 for year 3 and is comprised of the $7,000 royalty payment received on September 1, year 3, plus 10% of estimated sales for months July through December.

58. (c) Lake receives rental revenue from leasing a parking lot to Day Co. The annual rental payment made by Day Co. to Lake is $48,000. However, Day Co. also paid a nonrefundable deposit of $50,000 on January 1, year 1. This $50,000 deposit, since it is nonrefundable, is considered unearned revenue that must be recognized over the life of the lease on a straight-line basis. Therefore, in addition to the $48,000 annual rental payment, $5,000 ($50,000 ÷ 10 years) of the nonrefundable deposit will be recognized as rental revenue in year 3. Thus, answer (c) is correct because $53,000 will be recognized as rental revenue in year 3. Note that the $8,000 security deposit will not be revenue because it is to be refunded at the end of the lease period. It is deferred in its entirety and recorded as a long-term liability. Only a nonrefundable deposit would be recognized as rental revenue over the life of the lease.

59. (d) Stock dividends are not income to the recipient, but rather, are an adjustment of the per share basis of the investment. Answer (c) is incorrect because no change in the total investment cost is made when an investor receives stock dividends. Answer (d) is correct because some companies make a memorandum journal entry to note the receipt of the stock dividend and the adjustment of the per share basis of the investment.

60. (d) The requirement is to identify how the gain is reported. Answer (d) is correct because IFRS requires that if an asset is classified as fair value through profit or loss, it is remeasured to fair value and any profit or loss is recorded in the period. Therefore, Acadia should recognize a $3,000 gain in current earnings of the period. Answers (a), (b), and (c) are incorrect.

61. (a) The requirement is to identify for an investment to be accounted for using fair value through profit and loss. Answer (a) is correct because the investment must be traded in an active market to be accounted for using fair value through profit and loss.

62. (c) The requirement is to identify the item that does not represent a category of investments under IFRS. Answer (c) is correct because IFRS includes the classifications of fair value through profit and loss, held to maturity, and available for sale. It does not include tradable.

63. (c) The requirement is to identify how changes in fair value are recognized for an investment accounted for under IFRS. Answer (c) is correct because gains or losses are recognized in profit and loss of the period.

64. (b) The requirement is to identify the percentage of ownership that indicates significant influence under IFRS. Answer (b) is correct because like US GAAP the percentage is from 20 to 50%.

Simulations

Task-Based Simulation 1

Concepts		
	Authoritative Literature	Help

The following questions relate to investments in debt securities and in equity securities that do not involve significant influence. For each item, match the accounting treatment with the appropriate concept. Concepts may be used once, more than once, or not at all. Assume the fair value option is not elected.

Concept

A. Available-for-sale securities
B. Valuation allowance
C. Transfer from trading to available-for-sale
D. Held-to-maturity securities
E. Permanent impairment

F. Other-than-temporary securities
G. Amortization of differential
H. Trading securities
I. Transfer from available-for-sale to held-to-maturity

Accounting treatment

	(A)	(B)	(C)	(D)	(E)	(F)	(G)	(H)	(I)
1. Cash flows from purchases and sales of these securities are reported as an operating activity on the statement of cash flows.	O	O	O	O	O	O	O	O	O
2. Include unrealized holding gains/losses in earnings of current period.	O	O	O	O	O	O	O	O	O
3. Amortize unrealized holding gain/loss over life of security.	O	O	O	O	O	O	O	O	O
4. Report at amortized cost.	O	O	O	O	O	O	O	O	O
5. Report unrealized holding gains/losses as other comprehensive income and close to accumulated other comprehensive income, a separate component of stockholders' equity.	O	O	O	O	O	O	O	O	O
6. Classify as a current asset.	O	O	O	O	O	O	O	O	O
7. Subsequent recovery not recognized unless realized.	O	O	O	O	O	O	O	O	O

Task-Based Simulation 2

Accounting Treatment		
	Authoritative Literature	Help

Determine whether each statement is True or False.

	True	False
1. Held-to-maturity securities are classified as current or noncurrent on an individual basis.	O	O
2. For trading securities, some realized gains/losses are excluded from earnings.	O	O
3. A premature sale of held-to-maturity securities may be considered maturity if at least 80% of the principal has already been collected.	O	O
4. Dividends received on available-for-sale securities decrease the investment account.	O	O
5. A company that owns more than 50% of the outstanding shares of stock of another company must use the fair value method.	O	O

Task-Based Simulation 3

Financial Statement Disclosures		
	Authoritative Literature	Help

The following information pertains to Dayle, Inc.'s portfolio of marketable investments for the year ended December 31, year 2:

	Cost	Fair value 12/31/Y1	Year 2 activity Purchases	Year 2 activity Sales	Fair value 12/31/Y2
Held-to-maturity securities					
Security ABC			$100,000		$95,000
Trading securities					
Security DEF	$150,000	$160,000			155,000
Available-for-sale securities					
Security GHI	190,000	165,000			
Security JKL	170,000	175,000		$175,000	160,000

Security ABC was purchased at par. All declines in fair value are considered to be temporary. Dayle does not elect the fair value option for any of its financial assets.

For the following questions, choose from the answer list below.

Answer List

A. $0   D. $ 15,000   G. $100,000   J. $160,000
B. $ 5,000   E. $ 25,000   H. $150,000   K. $170,000
C. $ 10,000   F. $ 95,000   I. $155,000

Items 1 through 6 describe amounts to be reported in Dayle's year 2 financial statements. For each item, select from the following list the correct numerical response. An amount may be selected once, more than once, or not at all. Ignore income tax considerations.

Amount
(A) (B) (C) (D) (E) (F) (G) (H) (I) (J) (K)

1. Carrying amount of security ABC at December 31, year 2.   O O O O O O O O O O O

2. Carrying amount of security DEF at December 31, year 2.   O O O O O O O O O O O

3. Carrying amount of security JKL at December 31, year 2.   O O O O O O O O O O O

Items 4 through 6 require a second response. For each item, indicate whether a gain or a loss is to be reported.

Amount   Gain   Loss
(A) (B) (C) (D) (E) (F) (G) (H) (I) (J) (K)

4. Recognized gain or loss on sale of security GHI.   O O O O O O O O O O O   O   O

5. Unrealized gain or loss to be reported in year 2 net income.   O O O O O O O O O O O   O   O

6. Unrealized gain or loss to be reported at December 31, year 2, as a separate component of stockholders' equity entitled "accumulated other comprehensive income."   O O O O O O O O O O O   O   O

Task-Based Simulation 4

Research		
	Authoritative Literature	Help

Assume that you are assigned to the audit of Millet Corporation. The CFO of Millet is trying to determine how to account for a transfer of investment securities between the trading portfolio and the available-for-sale portfolio. Which section of the Professional Standards addresses the issue of how to account for the transfer?

Enter your response in the answer fields below.

Task-Based Simulation 5

Classification of Securities		
	Authoritative Literature	Help

Items 1 through 4 are based on the following:

Cane Co. purchased various securities during year 1 to be classified as held-to-maturity securities, trading securities, or available-for-sale securities.

Items 1 through 4 describe various securities purchased by Cane. For each item, select from the following list the appropriate category for each security. A category may be used once, more than once, or not at all.

Categories

H. Held-to-maturity
T. Trading
A. Available-for-sale

	Category (H) (T) (A)
1. Debt securities bought and held for the purpose of selling in the near term.	○ ○ ○
2. US Treasury bonds that Cane has both the positive intent and the ability to hold to maturity.	○ ○ ○
3. $3 million debt security bought and held for the purpose of selling in three years to finance payment of Cane's $2 million long-term note payable when it matures.	○ ○ ○
4. Convertible preferred stock that Cane does not intend to sell in the near term.	○ ○ ○

Task-Based Simulation 6

Journal Entries		
	Authoritative Literature	Help

Situation

Harold Johnson, an investor in Acme Co., asked you for advice on the propriety of Acme's financial reporting for two of its investments. Assume that Acme does not elect the fair value option for reporting its financial assets and liabilities. You obtained the following information related to the investments from Acme's December 31, year 1 financial statements:

- 20% ownership interest in Kern Co., represented by 200,000 shares of outstanding common stock purchased on January 2, year 1, for $600,000.
- 20% ownership interest in Wand Co., represented by 20,000 shares of outstanding common stock purchased on January 2, year 1, for $300,000.
- On January 2, year 1, the carrying values of the acquired shares of both investments equaled their purchase price.
- Kern reported earnings of $400,000 for the year ended December 31, year 1, and declared and paid dividends of $100,000 during year 1.
- Wand reported earnings of $350,000 for the year ended December 31, year 1, and declared and paid dividends of $60,000 during year 1.
- On December 31, year 1, Kern's and Wand's common stock were trading over-the-counter at $18 and $20 per share, respectively.
- The investment in Kern is accounted for using the equity method.
- The investment in Wand is accounted for as available-for-sale securities.

You recalculated the amounts reported in Acme's December 31, year 1 financial statements, and determined that they were correct. Stressing that the information available in the financial statements was limited, you advised Johnson that, assuming Acme properly applied generally accepted accounting principles, Acme may have appropriately used two different methods to account for its investments in Kern and Wand, even though the investments represent equal ownership interests.

1. Prepare the journal entry for Acme's investment in Kern Co. on January 2, year 1.

2. Prepare the journal entry for the dividends received from Kern in year 1.

3. Prepare the journal entry required for Kern's reported income for the year ending on December 31, year 1.

Task-Based Simulation 7

Financial Statement Disclosures		
	Authoritative Literature	Help

Situation

Harold Johnson, an investor in Acme Co., asked you for advice on the propriety of Acme's financial reporting for two of its investments. Assume that Acme does not elect the fair value option for reporting its financial assets and liabilities. You obtained the following information related to the investments from Acme's December 31, year 1 financial statements:

- 20% ownership interest in Kern Co., represented by 200,000 shares of outstanding common stock purchased on January 2, year 1, for $600,000.
- 20% ownership interest in Wand Co., represented by 20,000 shares of outstanding common stock purchased on January 2, year 1, for $300,000.
- On January 2, year 1, the carrying values of the acquired shares of both investments equaled their purchase price.
- Kern reported earnings of $400,000 for the year ended December 31, year 1, and declared and paid dividends of $100,000 during year 1.
- Wand reported earnings of $350,000 for the year ended December 31, year 1, and declared and paid dividends of $60,000 during year 1.
- On December 31, year 1, Kern's and Wand's common stock were trading over-the-counter at $18 and $20 per share, respectively.
- The investment in Kern is accounted for using the equity method.
- The investment in Wand is accounted for as available-for-sale securities.

You recalculated the amounts reported in Acme's December 31, year 1 financial statements, and determined that they were correct. Stressing that the information available in the financial statements was limited, you advised Johnson that, assuming Acme properly applied generally accepted accounting principles, Acme may have appropriately used two different methods to account for its investments in Kern and Wand, even though the investments represent equal ownership interests.

Identify the following amounts on Acme's financial statements.

Carrying value of Kern investment	
Carrying value of Wand investment	
Income on Income Statement	
Kern investment	
Wand investment	
Other comprehensive income	
Kern investment	
Wand investment	

Task-Based Simulation 8

Research		
	Authoritative Literature	Help

Assume that you are assigned to the audit of Health Corporation. The Controller of Health has asked you in which section of the statement of cash flows should the proceeds from the sale of available-for-sale securities be presented. Which section of the Professional Standards addresses this issue?

Enter your response in the answer fields below.

Task-Based Simulation 9

Concepts		
	Authoritative Literature	Help

Identify whether each of the following statements is True or False. Assume the fair value option is not elected.

	True	False
1. Unrealized gains from trading securities are reported in other comprehensive income.	O	O
2. Investments in stocks and bonds may be classified as trading securities, available-for-sale securities, and held-to-maturity securities.	O	O
3. X Company has significant influence over Y Company and owns 35% of the voting stock of Y Company. X Company must use the equity method of accounting for the investment in Y Company.	O	O
4. Unrealized gains and losses from available-for-sale securities that result from the change in fair value during the period should be reported as other comprehensive income.	O	O
5. The temporary unrealized gain or loss from held-to-maturity securities must be reported in income for the current period.	O	O
6. If a security is transferred from available-for-sale to trading securities classification, unrealized holding gains and losses are recognized immediately in the income statement.	O	O
7. The equity method of accounting requires a company to include the percent of income of the investee in the investor company's net income for the period.	O	O
8. The equity method of accounting requires that a company adjust the cost of the investee to fair value at the end of each period.	O	O
9. A company that receives stock dividends records income equal to the fair value of the stock on the date the dividend is declared.	O	O
10. Held-to-maturity securities are carried at amortized cost using the effective interest method.	O	O

Task-Based Simulation 10

Available-for-Sale Securities		
	Authoritative Literature	Help

At December 31, year 1, Poe Corp. properly reported as available-for-sale securities the following marketable equity securities:

	Cost	Fair value
Axe Corp., 1,000 shares, $2.40 convertible preferred stock	$ 40,000	$ 42,000
Purl, Inc., 6,000 shares of common stock	60,000	66,000
Day Co., 2,000 shares of common stock	55,000	40,000
Total available-for-sale securities	$155,000	$148,000

On January 2, year 2, Poe purchased 100,000 shares of Scott Corp. common stock for $1,700,000, representing 30% of Scott's outstanding common stock and an underlying equity of $1,400,000 in Scott's net assets on January 2. Poe had no other financial transactions with Scott during year 2. As a result of Poe's 30% ownership of Scott, Poe has the ability to exercise significant influence over Scott's financial and operating policies.

During year 2, Poe disposed of the following securities:

- January 18—sold 2,500 shares of Purl for $13 per share.
- June 1—sold 500 shares of Day, after a 10% stock dividend was received, for $21 per share.
- October 1—converted 500 shares of Axe's preferred stock into 1,500 shares of Axe's common stock, when the market price was $60 per share for the preferred stock and $21 per share for the common stock.

The following year 2 dividend information pertains to stock owned by Poe:

- February 14—Day issued a 10% stock dividend, when the market price of Day's common stock was $22 per share.
- April 5 and October 5—Axe paid dividends of $1.20 per share on its $2.40 preferred stock, to stockholders of record on March 9 and September 9, respectively. Axe did not pay dividends on its common stock during year 2.
- June 30—Purl paid a $1.00 per share dividend on its common stock.
- March 1, June 1, September 1, and December 1 —Scott paid quarterly dividends of $0.50 per share on each of these dates. Scott's net income for the year ended December 31, year 2, was $1,200,000.

At December 31, year 2, Poe's management intended to hold Scott's stock on a long-term basis. The remaining investments were considered temporary. Market prices per share of the marketable equity securities were as follows:

	At December 31	
	Year 1	Year 1
Axe Corp.—preferred	$56	$42
Axe Corp.—common	20	18
Purl, Inc.—common	11	11
Day Co.—common	22	20
Scott Corp.—common	16	18

All of the foregoing stocks are listed on major stock exchanges. Declines in fair value from cost would not be considered permanent. Poe does not elect the fair value option for reporting its financial assets and liabilities.

 Complete the following schedule for the available-for-sale securities of Poe Corp. as of December 31, year 2.

Poe Corp.
**SCHEDULE OF AVAILABLE-FOR-SALE
SECURITIES**
December 31, Year 2

	Number of shares	Cost	Beginning carrying amount at fair value	Ending market price per share	Fair value	Cumulative gain or (loss)	Unrealized gain or (loss) in year 2
Axe— preferred							
Axe— common							
Purl— common							
Day— common							

Task-Based Simulation 11

Research		
	Authoritative Literature	**Help**

 Assume that you are assigned to the audit of Swartz Corporation. The Controller of Swartz has asked you to describe the guidance in the professional standards that indicate when the equity method of accounting for an investment is generally required. Which section of the Professional Standards provides guidance on percentage of ownership that generally results in the use of the equity method for the investment?

 Enter your response in the answer fields below.

Simulation Solutions

Task-Based Simulation 1

Concepts		
	Authoritative Literature	Help

Accounting treatment

	(A)	(B)	(C)	(D)	(E)	(F)	(G)	(H)	(I)
1. Cash flows from purchases and sales of these securities are reported as an operating activity on the statement of cash flows.	○	○	○	○	○	○	○	●	○
2. Include unrealized holding gains/losses in earnings of current period.	○	○	○	○	○	○	○	●	○
3. Amortize unrealized holding gain/loss over life of security.	○	○	○	○	○	○	○	○	●
4. Report at amortized cost.	○	○	○	●	○	○	○	○	○
5. Report unrealized holding gains/losses as other comprehensive income and close to accumulated other comprehensive income, a separate component of stockholders' equity.	●	○	○	○	○	○	○	○	○
6. Classify as a current asset.	○	○	○	○	○	○	○	●	○
7. Subsequent recovery not recognized unless realized.	○	○	○	○	●	○	○	○	○

Explanations

1. **(H)** Purchases and sales of trading portfolio securities be classified as operating activities on the statement of cash flows due to the short-term, profit-seeking nature of the investment. In contrast, available-for-sale and held-to-maturity securities are classified as investing activities.

2. **(H)** Unrealized holding gains and losses on trading securities are included in income of the period.

3. **(I)** Unrealized holding gains and losses on securities transferred to held-to-maturity from available-for-sale are reported as a separate component of stockholders' equity (accumulated other comprehensive income) and amortized over the remaining life of the security.

4. **(D)** Held-to-maturity securities are carried at amortized cost.

5. **(A)** Unrealized holding gains and losses on available-for-sale securities are reported as other comprehensive income, whereas those on trading securities are included in income and those on held-to-maturity securities are not reported.

6. **(H)** Trading securities appear on the balance sheet as current assets.

7. **(E)** When a decline in value of a security is deemed to be other than temporary, the impaired security is written down to fair value. Any subsequent recovery may not be recognized in earnings unless realized through sale of the security.

Task-Based Simulation 2

Accounting Treatment		
	Authoritative Literature	Help

	True	False
1 Held-to-maturity securities are classified as current or noncurrent on an individual basis.	●	○
2. For trading securities, some realized gains/losses are excluded from earnings.	●	○
3. A premature sale of held-to-maturity securities may be considered maturity if at least 80% of the principal has already been collected.	○	●
4. Dividends received on available-for-sale securities decrease the investment account.	○	●
5. A company that owns more than 50% of the outstanding shares of stock of another company must use the fair value method.	○	●

Explanations

1.   **(T)** Held-to-maturity securities are classified as current or noncurrent according to how soon they will mature, (i.e., a security maturing within one year is classified as current, while one with a more distant maturity date is considered noncurrent).

2.   **(T)** Some unrealized holding gains and losses on trading securities could have already been included in income as unrealized components. Thus, to recognize them again upon realization would result in an erroneous doubling of the actual gain/loss.

3.   **(F)** Premature sale of held-to-maturity securities are considered at maturity if either (1) the sale occurs so close to maturity that interest rate risk is virtually eliminated, or (2) the sale occurs after at least 85% of the principal has been collected.

4.   **(F)** Dividends received on available-for-sale securities are treated as dividend income on the income statement.

5.   **(F)** A company that owns more than 50% of the outstanding shares of stock should use the equity method and prepare consolidated financial statements (assuming the company exercises control).

Task-Based Simulation 3

Financial Statement Disclosures		
	Authoritative Literature	Help

	Amount										
	(A)	**(B)**	**(C)**	**(D)**	**(E)**	**(F)**	**(G)**	**(H)**	**(I)**	**(J)**	**(K)**
1. Carrying amount of security ABC at December 31, year 2.	O	O	O	O	O	O	●	O	O	O	O
2. Carrying amount of security DEF at December 31, year 2.	O	O	O	O	O	O	O	O	●	O	O
3. Carrying amount of security JKL at December 31, year 2.	O	O	O	O	O	O	O	O	O	●	O

	Amount											**Gain**	**Loss**
	(A)	**(B)**	**(C)**	**(D)**	**(E)**	**(F)**	**(G)**	**(H)**	**(I)**	**(J)**	**(K)**		
4. Recognized gain or loss on sale of security GHI.	O	O	O	●	O	O	O	O	O	O	O	O	●
5. Unrealized gain or loss to be reported in year 2 net income.	O	●	O	O	O	O	O	O	O	O	O	O	●
6. Unrealized gain or loss to be reported at December 31, year 2, as a separate component of stockholders' equity entitled "accumulated other comprehensive income."	O	O	●	O	O	O	O	O	O	O	O	O	●

Explanations

1.   **(G; $100,000)** Held-to-maturity securities shall be measured at amortized cost. Since this debt security was purchased at par, there is neither a discount nor a premium to amortize, therefore amortized cost equals par or $100,000. Ignore fair value.

2.   **(I; $155,000)** Investments in securities that are not classified as held-to-maturity and that have readily determinable fair values shall be measured at fair value. $155,000 is fair value.

3.   **(J; $160,000)** Same explanation as question 2. Since security JKL is not a debt security classified as held-to-maturity and since it has a readily determinable fair value it shall be . . .measured at fair value.

4.   **(D, L)** Recognized gains and losses on the sale of available-for-sale securities are measured as the difference between original cost ($190,000) and the selling price of the securities ($175,000). The unrealized loss that existed in accumulated other comprehensive income in the equity section prior to the sale ($25,000) will be reversed as a credit to unrealized loss and that reversal will be reported as other comprehensive income and closed to accumulated other comprehensive income that is reported in the equity section of the balance sheet (see question 10 below). The journal entry to record the sale would be

Cash	175,000	
Realized loss on sale of A-F-S securities	15,000	
A-F-S securities		165,000
Unrealized loss on A-F-S securities		25,000

5.   **(B, L)** The only unrealized gains or losses on securities reported in the net income relate to value changes in trading securities. In this case the value of the JKL securities has decreased from $160,000 to $155,000.

6. **(C, L)** The 1/1/Y2 balance of the unrealized gain or loss on A-F-S securities reported in the equity section was $20,000, the difference between the 1/1/Y2 $25,000 unrealized loss of GHI ($190,000 – $165,000) and the 1/1/Y2 $5,000 unrealized gain of JKL ($175,000 – $170,000). The changes during the year were (1) the $25,000 reversal (credit) of the unrealized loss of GHI when it was sold and (2) the $15,000 loss ($175,000 – $160,000) in value during the year of JKL. The Other Comprehensive Income account would appear as follows:

Other Comprehensive Income			
Beg. bal.	--		
12/31/Y2 JKL	15,000	12/31/Y2 Reverse GHI	25,000
Close to Accumulated Other			
Comprehensive Income	10,000		

The Accumulated Other Comprehensive Income account would appear as follows:

Accumulated Other Comprehensive Income			
1/1/Y2		20,000	
		10,000	12/31/Y2 Close from Other Comprehensive Income
12/31/Y2 Balance		10,000	

Task-Based Simulation 4

Research		
	Authoritative Literature	Help

ASC	320	10	35	10

Task-Based Simulation 5

Classification of Securities		
	Authoritative Literature	Help

	Category		
	(H)	**(T)**	**(A)**
1. Debt securities bought and held for the purpose of selling in the near term.	○	●	○
2. US Treasury bonds that Cane has both the positive intent and the ability to hold to maturity.	●	○	○
3. $3 million debt security bought and held for the purpose of selling in three years to finance payment of Cane's $2 million long-term note payable when it matures.	○	○	●
4. Convertible preferred stock that Cane does not intend to sell in the near term.	○	○	●

Explanations

1. **(T)** Trading. Securities that are bought and held principally for the purpose of selling them in the near term (thus held for only a short period of time) shall be classified as **trading securities**.

2. **(H)** Held-to-maturity. Investments in debt securities shall be classified as **held-to-maturity** and measured at amortized cost only if the reporting enterprise has the positive intent and ability to hold those securities to maturity. Both conditions are met in this case.

3. **(A)** Available-for-sale. The company does not have the positive intent to hold this debt security to maturity, therefore the security cannot be classified as held-to-maturity. Also, since it will be sold beyond the "near term," it cannot be classified as "trading." Investments not classified as trading (nor as held-to-maturity securities) shall be classified as **available-for-sale securities**.

4. **(A)** Available-for-sale. Since this security is neither a debt security nor a security that will be sold in the near term, it is classified as available-for-sale.

Task-Based Simulation 6

Journal Entries		
	Authoritative Literature	**Help**

1. Prepare the journal entry for the investment in Kern Co. on January 2, year 1.

Investment in Kern	600,000	
Cash		600,000

2. Prepare the journal entry for the dividends received from Kern in year 1.

Cash	20,000	
Investment in Kern		20,000
[100,000 × 20% = 20,000]		

3. Prepare the journal entry required for Kern's reported income for the year ending December 31, year 1.

Investment in Kern	80,000	
Income from Kern		80,000
[400,000 × 20% = 80,000]		

Task-Based Simulation 7

Financial Statement Disclosures		
	Authoritative Literature	**Help**

Identify the following amounts on Acme's financial statements.

Carrying value of Kern investment	$660,000
Carrying value of Wand investment	$400,000
Income on Income Statement	
Kern investment	$ 80,000
Wand investment	$ 12,000
Other comprehensive income	
Kern investment	$ --
Wand investment	$100,000

Explanations

Carrying value of Kern.

Kern

Balance sheet–Acme reported its investment in Kern at a carrying amount of $660,000

> *Calculations:*
>
> Equity in earnings = $80,000 ($400,000 × 20%)
>
> Dividend rec'd = $20,000 ($100,000 × 20%)
>
> Carrying amount = $600,000 + $80,000 – $20,000 = $660,000

Carrying value of Wand.

Wand

Balance sheet–Acme reported its investment in Wand at a fair value of $400,000

> *Calculation:*
>
> 20,000 shares × $20 per share = $400,000

Income Statement Amounts

Income from Kern	$400,000 × 20% = $80,000
Income from Wand	$12,000 dividend income
	Dividend income $12,000

Calculation:

$$\$60,000 \times 20\% = \$12,000$$

Other Comprehensive Income

Kern Investment	$0	
Wand investment	Unrealized gain	$100,000

Calculation:

$$\$400,000 - \$300,000 = \$100,000$$

Task-Based Simulation 8

Research		
	Authoritative Literature	**Help**

ASC	320	10	45	11

Task-Based Simulation 9

Concepts		
	Authoritative Literature	**Help**

Identify whether each of the following statements is True or False.

		True	False
1.	Unrealized gains from trading securities are reported in other comprehensive income.	○	●
2.	Investments in stocks and bonds may be classified as trading securities, available-for-sale securities, and held-to-maturity securities.	○	●
3.	X Company has significant influence over Y Company and owns 35% of the voting stock of Y Company. X Company must use the equity method of accounting for the investment in Y Company.	●	○
4.	Unrealized gains and losses from available-for-sale securities that result from the change in fair value during the period should be reported as other comprehensive income.	●	○
5.	The temporary unrealized gain or loss from held-to-maturity securities must be reported in income for the current period.	○	●
6.	If a security is transferred from available-for-sale to trading securities classification, unrealized holding gains and losses are recognized immediately in the income statement.	●	○
7.	The equity method of accounting requires a company to include the percent of income of the investee in the investor company's net income for the period.	●	○
8.	The equity method of accounting requires that a company adjust the cost of the investee to fair value at the end of each period.	○	●
9.	A company that receives stock dividends records income equal to the fair value of the stock on the date the dividend is declared.	○	●
10.	Held-to-maturity securities are carried at amortized cost using the effective interest method.	●	○

Explanations

1. **(F)** Unrealized gains from trading securities are reported in income for the period.

2. **(F)** Stocks cannot be classified as held-to-maturity because they have no maturity date.

3. **(T)** The equity method is required when an investor exercises significant influence over the investee.

4. **(T)** Unrealized gains and losses are reported as other comprehensive income.

5. **(F)** The temporary unrealized gain from held-to-maturity securities is excluded from earnings; instead, the held-to-maturities are reported at amortized cost.

6.   (T) Unrealized gains or losses are recognized when transferred.

7.   (T) The investor recognizes its share of income as earned.

8.   (F) In the equity method, the investor does not revalue the stock to fair value. The equity method requires that the investor record the percentage share of net income and percentage share of dividends of the investee.

9.   (F) Stock dividends require a memo entry to show receipt of additional shares of stock. The company then recomputes the cost per share based upon the new number of shares.

10. (T) Held-to-maturity securities are carried at amortized cost.

Task-Based Simulation 10

Available-for-Sale Securities		
	Authoritative Literature	Help

Complete the following schedule for the available-for-sale securities of Poe Corp. as of December 31, year 2.

Poe Corp.
SCHEDULE OF AVAILABLE-FOR-SALE SECURITIES
December 31, Year 2

	Number of shares	Cost	Beginning carrying amount at fair value	Ending market price per share	Fair value	Cumulative gain or (loss)	Unrealized gain or (loss) in year 2
Axe—preferred	500	$ 20,000	$ 21,000	$56	$ 28,000	$ 8,000	$ 7,000
Axe—common	1,500	20,000	21,000	20	30,000	10,000	9,000
Purl—common	3,500	35,000	38,500	11	38,500	3,500	--
Day—common	1,700	42,500	30,900	22	37,400	(5,100)	6,500
		$117,500	$111,400		$133,900	$16,400	$22,500

Task-Based Simulation 11

Research		
	Authoritative Literature	Help

ASC	323	10	15	8

Overview

The primary purposes of the statement of **cash flows** are to provide information about an entity's cash receipts and cash payments and to disclose information about the financing and investing activities of an entity. As such, the statement divides cash receipts and cash payments into three sections: operating, investing, and financing.

1. **Operating activities** include delivering or producing goods for sale and providing services. Generally, operating activities are related to net income and the current asset and current liability sections of the balance sheet.
2. **Investing activities** include the acquisition or disposition of long-term productive assets or securities. Investing activities are generally related to the noncurrent section of the balance sheet.
3. **Financing activities** include obtaining resources from creditors and repaying amounts borrowed. Generally, financing activities are related to the noncurrent liability and equity sections of the balance sheet.

This module also covers the two methods of presenting cash flows from operating activities: direct or indirect. The FASB prefers the direct method. Cash flow presentations for investing and financing activities do not differ between the two methods.

A. Objectives of the Statement of Cash Flows (See outline of SFAS 95, [ASC Topic 230])

1. The primary purposes of this statement are to provide information about an entity's cash receipts and cash payments and to disclose information about the financing and investing activities of an entity. This statement should help the users of the statement assess:

   a. An entity's ability to generate positive future cash flows;
   b. An entity's ability to meet its obligations and pay dividends;
   c. The reasons for differences between income and associated cash receipts and payments; and
   d. The cash and noncash aspects of an entity's investing and financing transactions.

2. In order to facilitate the users in making those assessments, a statement of cash flows shall report cash receipts and cash payments of an entity's operations, its investing transactions, and its financing transactions. A separate schedule accompanying the statement should also report the effects of investing and financing transactions that **do not affect cash**.

3. The statement of cash flows is required to be prepared based on changes during the period in cash and cash equivalents. Cash equivalents include short-term, highly liquid investments that (1) are readily convertible to known amounts of cash and (2) are so near their maturity (original maturity of three months or less from **date of purchase** by the enterprise) that they present negligible risk of changes in value because of changes in interest rates. Treasury bills, commercial paper, and money market funds are all examples of cash equivalents.

B. Statement of Cash Flows Classification

1. Cash receipts and cash payments are to be classified into operating, financing, and investing activities.

   a. Operating activities include delivering or producing goods for sale and providing services.

      (1) Operating activities include all transactions that are **not** investing and financing activities.

(2) More specifically, cash flows from operations should not include cash flows from transactions whose effects are included in income but are investing and financing activities.

    (a) For example, a gain (loss) on extinguishment of debt should properly be classified as a financing activity, and a gain (loss) from disposal of property should be classified as an investing activity.

  b. Investing activities include the acquisition and disposition of long-term productive assets or securities that are not considered cash equivalents.

    (1) Investing activities also include the lending of money and collection on loans.

  c. Financing activities include obtaining resources from owners and returning the investment.

    (1) Also included is obtaining resources from creditors and repaying the amount borrowed.

2. The FASB has listed the following as examples of classifications of transactions.

ACTIVITIES REPORTED ON THE STATEMENT OF CASH FLOWS

Description of the activity	Positive cash flow	Negative cash flow
Operating activities (direct method):		
• Cash received from customers	xx	
• Cash received from interest	xx	
• Cash received from dividends	xx	
• Cash received from sales of securities classified as trading	xx	
• Cash paid to suppliers		xx
• Cash paid for operating expenses		xx
• Cash paid for interest		xx
• Cash paid for income taxes		xx
• Cash paid for securities classified as trading (based on nature and purpose acquired)		xx
Investing activities		
• Proceeds from sales of property, plant, and equipment	xx	
• Proceeds from sales of investments in stocks (available for sale) and bonds (available for sale)	xx	
• Cash paid for securities classified as trading (based on nature and purpose acquired)		xx
• Proceeds from the sale or redemption of investments in bonds classified as held to maturity	xx	
• Proceeds from collection of loans (principal only)	xx	
• Proceeds from selling components of the company	xx	
• Acquisition of property, plant, and equipment (capital expenditures)		xx
• Acquisition of investments in stocks and bonds (available for sale or held to maturity)		xx
• Making loans to other entities		xx
• Acquiring other businesses		xx
Financing activities:		
• Proceeds from issuing common and preferred stock	xx	
• Proceeds from reissuing treasury stock	xx	
• Proceeds from issuing short-term debt	xx	
• Proceeds from issuing long-term debt	xx	
• Paying cash dividends		xx
• Repurchasing common stock (treasury stock)		xx
• Repaying short-term loans (principal only)		xx
• Repaying long-term loans, including capital lease obligations (principal only)		xx

Noncash investing and financing activities (reported in a separate schedule)
- Acquiring an asset through a capital lease
- Conversion of debt to equity
- Exchange of noncash assets or liabilities for other noncash assets or liabilities
- Issuance of stock to acquire assets

  a. Cash flows from trading securities are classified as operating or investing activities based on the nature and purpose for which the securities were acquired.

> **NOTE:** Noncash investing and financing activities should be excluded from the statement itself. These transactions involve no cash inflows and outflows, but they have a significant effect on the prospective cash flows of a company. Therefore, they must be distinguished from activities that involved cash receipts and payments and must be reported in a separate schedule or in the footnotes to the financial statements.

b. In the statement, the inflows and outflows for each category (operating, investing, and financing) should be shown separately, and the **net** cash flows (the difference between the inflows and outflows) should be reported.

> **NOW REVIEW MULTIPLE-CHOICE QUESTIONS 1 THROUGH 15**

C. Direct or Indirect Presentation in Reporting Operating Activities

1. The FASB decided that the preferable method of presenting net cash flows from operating activities is by **directly** showing major classes of operating cash receipts and payments.

   a. However, the **indirect (reconciliation) method** is also permitted.
   b. When the direct method is used, it is also necessary to present a separate accompanying schedule showing the indirect method.
   c. The **direct method** is discussed first, followed by a discussion of the **indirect method**.

2. Under the direct approach, cash flow elements of operating activities are derived from the accrual basis components of net income.

   a. In converting to the cash basis, accounts that should be analyzed under operating activities are those which are debited or credited when recording transactions that affect the income statement.

      (1) These transactions include transactions with outsiders and adjusting entries.
      (2) For example, these accounts include sales, cost of sales, operating expenses, and tax expense, as well as assets and liabilities which are related to them, such as accounts receivable, inventory, accounts payable, accrued expenses, and prepaid expenses.

      > **NOTE:** Interest expense and interest revenue are included within operating activities.

      (3) Formulas for conversion of various income statement amounts from the accrual basis to the cash basis are summarized in the following table:

Accrual basis		Additions		Deductions		Cash basis
Net sales	+	Beginning AR	–	Ending AR AR written off	=	Cash received from customers
Cost of goods sold	+	Ending inventory Beginning AP	–	Depreciation and amortization* Beginning inventory Ending AP	=	Cash paid to suppliers
Operating expenses	+	Ending prepaid expenses Beginning accrued expenses payable	–	Depreciation and amortization Beginning prepaid expenses Ending accrued expenses payable	=	Cash paid for operating expenses

* Applies to a manufacturing entity

   b. A T-account analysis method may be used instead of the above formulas to determine cash received and cash paid. T-account analysis provides a quick, systematic way to accumulate the information needed to prepare the statement.
   c. The direct approach would be presented in the statement of cash flows as follows:

> *Cash flows from operating activities*
> | | | |
> |---|---|---|
> | Cash received from dividends | $ 500 | |
> | Cash received from interest | 1,000 | |
> | Cash received from sale of goods | 9,000 | |
> | Cash provided by operating activities | | $10,500 |
> | Cash paid to suppliers | 5,000 | |
> | Cash paid for operating expenses | 500 | |
> | Cash paid for interest | 500 | |
> | Cash paid for taxes | 500 | |
> | Cash disbursed from operating activities | | 6,500 |
> | Net cash flows from operating activities | | $ 4,000 |

3. The other way of reporting net cash flows from operations is known as the **indirect method**.

   a. This is done by starting with income from continuing operations and adjusting for changes in operating related accounts (e.g., inventory and accounts payable) and noncash expenses, revenues, losses, and gains.

(1) Noncash items that were subtracted in determining income must be added back in determining net cash flows from operations. Each of these noncash items is a charge against income but does not decrease cash.

(2) Items to be added back include depreciation, amortization of intangibles, amortization of discount on bonds payable, bad debt expense, and any increase in the deferred tax liability. Note each of these items is charged against income but does not decrease cash.

(3) Noncash items that were added in determining income must be subtracted from net income in determining net cash flows from operations. Each of these noncash items is an increase to income but does not increase cash.

(4) Items to be deducted from income include decreases in the deferred tax liability and amortization of the premium on bonds payable.

(5) Finally, gains (losses) on fixed assets require adjustment, since the cash received is not measured by the gain (loss), that is, a fixed asset with a book value of $10, sold for $15 in cash, provides $15 in cash but is reported as only a $5 gain on the income statement. The $15 is shown as a separate item on the cash flow statement under investing activities and the $5 gain is subtracted from income. Losses on asset disposals are added back to income.

b. When preparing the cash flows from operating activities section of a Statement of Cash Flows under the indirect method, reconstructing journal entries may help in determining if an item should be added or subtracted to net income.

EXAMPLE

If accounts receivable increased by $20,000 over the year, the journal entry that would result in an increase to accounts receivable would be

| Accounts receivable | xx | |
| Sales | | xx |

This entry results in an increase to net income (through sales), but cash is not affected. Therefore, the amount of the increase is deducted from net income in determining cash flows from operating activities.

If accounts payable decreased by $35,000, the entry for a decrease in accounts payable would be

| Accounts payable | xx | |
| Cash | | xx |

Since the corresponding credit results in a decrease to cash, the amount of this decrease should be deducted from net income in determining cash flows from operating activities.

---

c. When the **indirect** method is used, separate disclosure of cash flows related to extraordinary items and discontinued operations is permitted, but is not required.

(1) If an entity chooses to disclose this information, disclosure must be consistent for all periods affected.

(2) Extraordinary items, if disclosed, should be added to (or subtracted from) operating activities (adjustment to net income) at the gross amount, not the net-of-tax amount.

(a) Under either method, the extraordinary item should be included in financing or investing activities, whichever is appropriate.

ADJUSTMENTS TO NET INCOME FOR INDIRECT METHOD

Add to net income	**Deduct from net income**
Decreases in:	**Increases in:**
Accounts receivable (net)	Accounts receivable (net)
Inventories	Inventories
Prepaid expenses	Prepaid expenses
Deferred tax asset	Deferred tax asset
Increases in:	**Decreases in:**
Accounts payable	Accounts payable
Income taxes payable	Income taxes payable
Deferred tax liability	Deferred tax liability
Interest payable	Interest payable
Other accrued payables	Other accrued payables
Unearned revenue	Unearned revenue

Other items:
- Losses from disposals of property, plant, and equipment and available-for-sale investments
- Depreciation expense
- Amortization expense related to intangible assets and bond discounts
- Bad debts expense (if adjustment for accounts receivable is based upon the gross, not the net, change in accounts receivable)
- Losses from early extinguishments of debt

Other items:
- Gains from disposals of property, plant and equipment and available-for-sale investments
- Undistributed income from equity method investments (equity income less the cash dividends received during the period)
- Amortization of a bond premium
- Gains from early extinguishments of debt

5. The direct and indirect approaches will both be illustrated throughout the remainder of this module.

> **NOW REVIEW MULTIPLE-CHOICE QUESTIONS 16 THROUGH 29**

D. Example of Statement of Cash Flows

The following information pertains to the Haner Company at December 31, year 1. Comparative balance sheets for year 1 and year 2 are as follows:

EXAMPLE

	Year 2	Year 1	Net change
Cash	$ 9,000	$ 8,000	$ 1,000
Treasury bills	4,000	3,000	1,000
Accounts receivable	4,000	5,000	(1,000)
Inventory	1,000	2,000	(1,000)
Prepaid insurance	2,000	3,000	(1,000)
Investment in Simba Co. (held-for-trading)	15,000	15,000	--
Market increase adjustment (trading)	3,000	--	3,000
Investment in ABC Co. (available-for-sale)	15,400	22,000	(6,600)
Market decrease adjustment (available-for-sale)	(3,500)	--	(3,500)
Fixed assets	22,000	17,000	5,000
Deferred tax asset	1,400	--	1,400
	$68,300	$71,000	$(2,700)
Accounts payable	$ 4,000	$ 7,000	$(3,000)
Income tax payable	3,000	1,000	2,000
Deferred tax liability	6,360	3,000	3,360
Bonds payable	5,000	10,000	(5,000)
Common stock	20,000	20,000	--
Accumulated other comprehensive income Unrealized loss on available-for-sale securities (net of tax)	(2,100)	--	(2,100)
Retained earnings	32,040	30,000	2,040
	$68,300	$71,000	$(2,700)

Income Statement for year 2 is as follows:

Net sales	$50,000
Cost of goods sold	(20,000)
Gross profit	30,000
Operating expenses	(17,000)
Income from operations	13,000
Other revenue and gains	$5,000
Other expenses and losses	(2,560) 2,440
Income before extraordinary item and income taxes	15,440
Income tax expense:	
Current portion	5,000
Deferred portion	3,360 8,360
Net income	$ 7,080

Statement of Comprehensive Income for year 2 is as follows:

Net income		$7,080
Other comprehensive income		
Unrealized loss on available-for-sale securities, (net of tax of $2,000)	$(3,000)	
Less:		
Reclassification on sale of available-for-sale securities, (net of tax of $600)	(900)	(2,100)
Comprehensive income		$4,980

Additional information includes

- Treasury bills have a maturity of less than three months from date of purchase
- Fixed assets costing $5,000 with a book value of $2,000 were sold for $4,000
- Three-year insurance policy was purchased in year 1
- At 12/31/Y2, available-for-sale investments with a book value of $6,600 at 12/31/Y1 and $5,100 at 12/31/Y2 sold for $5,100.
- Additional bonds were issued on 12/31/Y2 for $4,000. There was no premium or discount.
- Bonds with a book value of $9,000 were retired on 12/31/Y2.
- Other revenue and gains include a $3,000 unrealized gain recognized for trading securities
- Other expenses and losses consist of $1,060 interest paid and $1,500 realized loss on available-for-sale securities
- Changes in investments:

  - No changes in fair value of the investments occurred prior to year 2
  - There were no sales or purchases of trading securities during year 2
  - The tax rate is 40%

1. **Procedural Steps**

   a. The first step is to calculate the change in cash and cash equivalents.

	Year 2	**Year 1**	**Change**
Cash	$9,000	$8,000	+$1,000
Treasury bills	4,000	3,000	+ 1,000
Net change in cash and cash equivalents			+$2,000

   b. Calculate net cash flows from operating activities

      (1) Indirect approach

Net income	$ 7,080	
Decrease in accounts receivable	1,000	(a)
Decrease in inventory	1,000	(b)
Decrease in prepaid insurance	1,000	(c)
Decrease in accounts payable	(3,000)	(d)
Increase in income tax payable	2,000	(e)
Increase in deferred tax liability	3,360	(f)
Unrealized gain on trading securities	(3,000)	(g)
Realized loss on available-for-sale securities	1,500	(h)
Gain on sale of fixed assets	(2,000)	(i)
Depreciation expense	4,000	(j)
Net cash flows from operating activities	$12,940	

      Reconstructing journal entries may serve to explain the effect on net income of an increase or decrease of a particular account.

      (a) **Accounts receivable.** For accounts receivable to decrease, the journal entry must have been

Cash	xx	
Accounts receivable		xx

      Cash increased as a result of the collection of accounts receivable. The $1,000 decrease in accounts receivable should be added to net income.

      (b) **Inventory.** For inventory to decrease, the entry must have been

Cost of goods sold	xx	
Inventory		xx

      Expenses (CGS) increased without an additional cash outlay for inventory, so the $1,000 decrease is added back to net income.

      (c) **Prepaid insurance.** For prepaid insurance to decrease, the entry must have been

Insurance expense	xx	
Prepaid insurance		xx

      Because expenses increased without a corresponding cash outlay, the $1,000 decrease in prepaid insurance should be added to net income.

      (d) **Accounts payable.** For accounts payable to decrease, the entry must have been

Accounts payable	xx	
Cash		xx

      The entry involves a cash outlay, so the $3,000 decrease in accounts payable is deducted from net income.

(e) **Income tax payable.** For income tax payable to increase, the entry must have been

Income tax expense	xx	
Income tax payable		xx

Expenses increased without an actual cash outlay; therefore the $2,000 increase in the liability is added back to net income.

(f) **Deferred tax liability.** For deferred tax liability to increase, the entry must have been

Income tax expense	xx	
Deferred tax liability		xx

Expenses increased without an actual cash outlay; therefore the $3,360 increase in the liability, which is a noncash expense, is added back to net income.

(g) **Unrealized gain on trading securities.** The entry to record the unrealized gain on trading securities would have been

Investment in Simba Co.—held-for-trading	3,000	
Unrealized holding gain		3,000

Since unrealized gains on trading securities are recognized as income but do not involve a cash inflow, such gains must be subtracted from net income.

(h) **Realized loss on available-for-sale securities.** When $5,100 stock in ABC Co. was sold, the previously unrealized loss of $1,500 ($5,100 FV at 12/31/Y2 – $6,600 FV at 12/31/Y1) which arose in year 2 became realized. The entry to record the sale would have been

Cash	5,100	
Realized loss	1,500	
Available for sale		6,600

Because the realized loss does not involve any cash outflow, it must be added back to net income. Note that a $1,500 unrealized loss would have been recognized in financial statements prepared during year 2. The entry to remove this amount from the other comprehensive income account entitled "Unrealized loss on available-for-sale securities account" and the tax effect is

Adjustment to market (available-for-sale securities)	1,500	
Deferred tax benefit—unrealized loss	600	
Unrealized loss on available-for-sale securities		1,500
Deferred tax asset		600

Since an unrealized loss on AFS securities of $3,500 was recognized during year 2 (from year 1 to year 2), a $5,000 decline in FV must have occurred in year 2, as shown below. The deferred tax asset of $1,400 came from recognizing the future benefit of the unrealized loss of $3,500. The entry was

Deferred tax asset	1,400	
Deferred tax expense (benefit)		1,400

Market Adjustment (Available-for-Sale Securities)				Available-for-Sale Securities		
		--	Year 1 Bal.	Year 1 Bal.	22,000	
Sale	1,500	5,000	Year 2 Unreal. loss			6,600 Sale
		3,500	Year 2 Bal.	Year 2 Bal.	15,400	

Accumulated Other Comprehensive Income				Unrealized Loss on AFS Securities		
		--		Year 1 Bal.	--	1,500 Realized upon sale
		1,400	Closing entry	Unreal. Loss recog. During year	5,000	
Closing entry	3,500					3,500 Closing entry
Year 2 Bal.	2,100			Year 2 Bal.	--	

Deferred Tax Benefit— Unrealized Loss				Deferred Tax Asset		
Sale	600	--		Year 1 Bal.	--	600 Sale
Closing entry	1,400	2,000	Year 2 adj.	Year 2 Adj.	2,000	
Year 2 Bal.	--			Year 2 Bal.	1,400	

Because unrealized gains/losses on available-for-sale securities do not affect cash flows, no adjustment for this change is necessary on the statement of cash flows.

(i) **Gain on sale of fixed assets.** The entry to record the sale would have been

Cash	4,000	
Accumulated depreciation	3,000	
Gain on sale		2,000
Asset		5,000

The total amount of cash received in payment for the asset, not just the amount of the gain, represents the cash inflow. Since cash inflow from the sale (including the amount of the gain) appears in the investing section, the gain should be subtracted from net income.

(j) **Depreciation expense.** The entry to record depreciation is

Depreciation expense	4,000	
Accumulated depreciation		4,000

Because expenses increased without a corresponding cash outlay, the amount recorded for depreciation expense should be added to net income. In this case, the increase in accumulated depreciation must take into consideration the accumulated depreciation removed with the sale of the asset.

```
                          AD
AD of sold asset   3,000*  |  4,000    Beg. bal.
                           | [4,000]   Depreciation (plug)
                           |  5,000    End. bal.
```

* $5,000 Cost – $2,000 book value

(2) **Direct approach**

Cash received from customers		$51,000 (a)
Cash provided by operating activities		
Cash paid to suppliers	22,000 (b)	
Cash paid for operating expenses	12,000 (c)	
Cash paid for interest	1,060 (d)	
Cash paid for income taxes	3,000 (e)	
Cash disbursed for operating activities		38,060
Net cash flows from operating activities		$12,940

(a) **Cash received from customers.** Net sales + Beginning AR – Ending AR = Cash received from customers ($50,000 + $5,000 – $4,000 = $51,000). Cash received from customers also may be calculated by analyzing T-accounts.

```
                    Accounts Receivable
Beg. bal.    5,000  |
Sales       50,000  | [51,000]   Cash collected
End. bal.    4,000  |
```

(b) **Cash paid to suppliers.** Cost of goods sold + Beginning AP – Ending AP + Ending inventory – Beginning inventory = Cash paid to suppliers ($20,000 + $7,000 – $4,000 + $1,000 – $2,000 = $22,000). This is a two-account analysis. The amount for cash paid to suppliers equals the debit to accounts payable, but to solve for that amount, you must first determine purchases. To calculate purchases you must analyze the inventory account.

Step 1. Calculate purchases

```
                        Inventory
Beg. bal.      2,000   |  20,000   CGS
Purchases   [19,000]   |
End. bal.      1,000   |
```

Step 2. Calculate cash payments to suppliers

```
                     Accounts Payable
                            |   7,000    Beg. bal.
Cash paid to suppliers [22,000] | 19,000    Purchases
                            |   4,000    End. bal.
```

Note that the $2,000 difference between the $20,000 CGS (accrual-basis amount) and the $22,000 cash payments made to suppliers (cash-basis amount) equals the difference between the $1,000 decrease in inventory and the $3,000 decrease in accounts payable when the indirect method is used. However, under the indirect method the difference is deducted from net income. This is because when the direct method is used, expenses such as CGS are examined as **outflows** of cash, whereas when the indirect method is used, net income (revenue-expenses, including CGS) is treated as a net cash **inflow**.

(c) **Cash paid for operating expenses.** Operating expenses + Ending prepaid expenses – Beginning prepaid expenses – Depreciation expense (and other noncash operating expenses) = Cash paid for operating expenses ($17,000 + $2,000 – $3,000 – $4,000 = $12,000). The two accounts in this problem that relate to operating expenses are accumulated depreciation and prepaid insurance.

	Prepaid Insurance						Accumulated Depreciation	
Beg. bal.	3,000						4,000	Beg. bal.
		Error!	Insurance expense	AD of sold asset	3,000		4,000	Depreciation expense
End. bal.	2,000						5,000	End. bal.

Since neither the expiration of prepaid insurance nor depreciation expense required a cash outlay, cash basis operating expenses are accrual expenses of $17,000 less depreciation ($4,000) and insurance expense ($1,000), or $12,000.

(d) **Cash paid for interest.** No analysis needed; amount was given in problem
(e) **Cash paid for income taxes.** Current portion of income tax expense + Beginning income tax payable – Ending income tax payable = Cash paid for income taxes ($5,000 + $1,000 – $3,000 = $3,000). The journal entry for income tax expense is

Income tax expense—current	5,000	
Income tax expense—deferred	1,360	
Income tax payable (current portion)		5,000
Deferred tax liability		1,360

Therefore, taxes paid are $3,000, as shown in the T-account below.

	Income Tax Payable		
		1,000	Beg. bal.
Income taxes paid	3,000	5,000	Current portion
		3,000	End. bal.

c. Analyze other accounts and determine whether the change is a cash inflow or outflow and whether it is a financing, an investing, or a noncash investing and financing activity.

(1) Investments in ABC Co. decreased by $5,100 when this portion was sold (cash inflow, investing activity). The entry to record the sale was

Cash	5,100	
Investment in ABC Co.— available-for-sale		5,100

(2) Fixed assets increased by $5,000 after $5,000 of assets were sold for $4,000 (cash inflow, investing activity). Thus, $10,000 of fixed assets were purchased (cash outflow, investing activity).

	Fixed Assets		
Beg. bal.	$17,000		
Purchase of new assets	10,000	5,000	Sold asset
End. bal.	22,000		

(3) Bonds payable increased by $4,000 when additional bonds were issued (cash inflow, financing activity).
(4) Bonds payable decreased by $9,000 when they were retired (cash outflow, financing activity). The entry to record the retirement of debt was

Bonds payable	9,000	
Cash		9,000

(5) Common stock had no change.
(6) Retained earnings increased $2,040 after net income of $7,080, indicating a dividend of $5,040 (cash outflow, financing activity).

Retained Earnings		
	30,000	Beg. bal.
Cash dividend 5,040	7,080	Net income
	32,040	End. bal.

d. Prepare formal statement

Haner Company
STATEMENT OF CASH FLOWS
For the Year Ended December 31, Year 2

Cash flows from operating activities:		
Cash received from customers	$51,000	
Cash provided by operating activities		$ 51,000
Cash paid to suppliers	22,000	
Cash paid for operating expenses	12,000	
Cash paid for income taxes	3,000	
Cash paid for interest expense	1,060	
Cash disbursed for operating activities		38,060
Net cash flows from operating activities		$ 12,940
Cash flows from investing activities:		
Proceeds from sale of investments	$ 5,100	
Proceeds from sale of fixed assets	4,000	
Acquisition of fixed assets	(10,000)	
Net cash used by investing activities		(900)
Cash flows from financing activities:		
Proceeds from sale of bonds	$ 4,000	
Repayment of long-term debt	(9,000)	
Dividends paid	(5,040)	
Net cash used by financing activities		(10,040)
Net increase in cash and cash equivalents		$ 2,000
Cash and cash equivalents at beginning of year		11,000
Cash and cash equivalents at end of year		$ 13,000

Reconciliation of net income to cash provided by operating activities:
[This schedule would include the amounts from D.1.b.(1) (near the beginning of this example) starting with "net income" and ending with Net cash flows from operating activities of $13,040.]

Disclosure of accounting policy:
For purposes of the statement of cash flows, the Company considers all highly liquid debt instruments purchased with a maturity of three months or less to be cash equivalents.

NOTE: If the reconciliation approach for operating activities had been shown in the body of the statement instead of the direct approach, an additional schedule showing interest paid and income taxes paid would be necessary.

NOW REVIEW MULTIPLE-CHOICE QUESTIONS 30 THROUGH 37

E. Capital Leases

In the period an entity enters into a capital lease, a noncash financing and investing activity in the amount of the present value of the minimum lease payments is reported following the cash flow statement. As payments are made by the lessee, the principal reduction component is reported as a cash outflow under financing activities. The interest component is reported in the operating activities section under the direct method. Under the indirect method, interest paid must be disclosed as supplementary information.

F. Research Component—Accounting Standards Codification

1. ASC Topic 230 outlines the accounting rules for the statement of cash flows. Typical research issues may involve determining the cash equivalents of the enterprise; classifying items as either operating, investing, or financing activities; and identifying significant noncash transactions. Note that ASC Topic 230 specifically prohibits reporting cash flow per share information on the statement of cash flows.

2. Below are keywords for researching issues on the statement of cash flows. Note that in some paragraphs in FARS, the word "transaction" or "transactions" (rather than "activity") is used to discuss whether an item is included in the operating, investing, or financing section of the statement of cash flows.

Cash equivalents	Noncash activities
Financing activities	Noncash transactions
Financing transactions	Operating activities
Investing activities	Operating transactions
Investing transactions	Reconciliation of net income

G. International Financial Reporting Standards (IFRS)

1. **Statement of cash flows.** The accounting rules for the statement of cash flows are similar to US GAAP.

   a. For IFRS, cash flows include the inflows and outflows of both cash and cash equivalents.

   (1) Cash equivalents include cash on hand, bank balances for immediate use, other demand deposits, and short-term investments with maturities of three months or less.

   b. Both the direct method and indirect method are acceptable methods for preparing the statement of cash flows.

   (1) However, for the indirect method, operating activities may be presented using a modified approach.
   (2) This modified indirect method shows revenues and expenses in operating activities, and then reports the changes in working capital accounts.

2. As in US GAAP, the statement of cash flows is divided into three parts: operating, investing, and financing activities. At the bottom of the statement of cash flows, a reconciliation must be made with the amounts in the statement of cash flows and the cash and cash equivalents reported in the statement of financial position.

3. The most significant difference between IFRS and US GAAP is where certain items are presented on the statement of cash flows.

   a. For example, interest and dividends received may be reported on the statement of cash flows as operating or investing activities.
   b. Interest and dividends paid may be reported either in the operating activities or the financing activities sections.

   (1) Although the entity has discretion on where interest and dividends are reported, it must be reported on a consistent basis.

   c. Cash from the purchase and sale of trading securities are classified as operating activities.
   d. Cash advances and loans (bank overdrafts) are also usually classified as operating activities.
   e. Taxes paid on income must be disclosed separately in operating activities.

   (1) However, cash flows from certain taxes may be classified elsewhere if they are related to investing or financing activities.

   f. In addition, the effects of noncash transactions are not reported on the statement of cash flows. Instead, significant noncash activities must be disclosed in the notes to the financial statements.

> **NOW REVIEW MULTIPLE-CHOICE QUESTIONS 38 THROUGH 39**

KEY TERMS

Cash equivalents. Short-term, highly liquid investments that (1) are readily convertible to known amounts of cash and (2) are so near their maturity (original of three months or less from **date of purchase** by the enterprise) that they present negligible risk of changes in value because of changes in interest rates.

Direct approach. Cash flow elements of operating activities are derived from the accrual basis components of net income.

Indirect method. Starts with income from continuing operations and adjusts for changes in operating related accounts (e.g., inventory and accounts payable) and noncash expenses, revenues, losses, and gains.

Statement of Cash Flow. Provides information about an entity's cash receipts and cash payments and discloses information about the financing and investing activities of an entity.

Multiple-Choice Questions (1-39)

A.   *Objectives of the Statement of Cash Flows*

1.   At December 31, year 1, Kale Co. had the following balances in the accounts it maintains at First State Bank:

Checking account #101	$175,000
Checking account #201	(10,000)
Money market account	25,000
90-day certificate of deposit, due 2/28/Y2	50,000
180-day certificate of deposit, due 3/15/Y2	80,000

Kale classifies investments with original maturities of three months or less as cash equivalents. In its December 31, year 1 balance sheet, what amount should Kale report as cash and cash equivalents?

   a. $190,000
   b. $200,000
   c. $240,000
   d. $320,000

2.   The primary purpose of a statement of cash flows is to provide relevant information about

   a.   Differences between net income and associated cash receipts and disbursements.
   b.   An enterprise's ability to generate future positive net cash flows.
   c.   The cash receipts and cash disbursements of an enterprise during a period.
   d.   An enterprise's ability to meet cash operating needs.

3.   Mend Co. purchased a three-month US Treasury bill. Mend's policy is to treat as cash equivalents all highly liquid investments with an original maturity of three months or less when purchased. How should this purchase be reported in Mend's statement of cash flows?

   a.   As an outflow from operating activities.
   b.   As an outflow from investing activities.
   c.   As an outflow from financing activities.
   d.   Not reported.

B.   *Statement of Cash Flows Classification*

4.   Alp, Inc. had the following activities during year 1:

- Acquired 2,000 shares of stock in Maybel, Inc. for $26,000. Alp intends to hold the stock as a long-term investment.
- Sold an investment in Rate Motors for $35,000 when the carrying value was $33,000.
- Acquired a $50,000, four-year certificate of deposit from a bank. (During the year, interest of $3,750 was paid to Alp.)
- Collected dividends of $1,200 on stock investments.

In Alp's year 1 statement of cash flows, net cash used in investing activities should be

   a. $37,250
   b. $38,050
   c. $39,800
   d. $41,000

5.   In year 1, a tornado completely destroyed a building belonging to Holland Corp. The building cost $100,000 and had accumulated depreciation of $48,000 at the time of the loss. Holland received a cash settlement from the insurance company and reported an extraordinary loss of $21,000. In Holland's year 1 cash flow statement, the net change reported in the cash flows from investing activities section should be a

   a. $10,000 increase.
   b. $21,000 decrease.
   c. $31,000 increase.
   d. $52,000 decrease.

6.   In a statement of cash flows, if used equipment is sold at a gain, the amount shown as a cash inflow from investing activities equals the carrying amount of the equipment

   a.   Plus the gain.
   b.   Plus the gain and less the amount of tax attributable to the gain.
   c.   Plus both the gain and the amount of tax attributable to the gain.
   d.   With **no** addition or subtraction.

7.   On September 1, year 1, Canary Co. sold used equipment for a cash amount equaling its carrying amount for both book and tax purposes. On September 15, year 1, Canary replaced the equipment by paying cash and signing a note payable for new equipment. The cash paid for the new equipment exceeded the cash received for the old equipment. How should these equipment transactions be reported in Canary's year 1 statement of cash flows?

   a.   Cash outflow equal to the cash paid less the cash received.
   b.   Cash outflow equal to the cash paid and note payable less the cash received.
   c.   Cash inflow equal to the cash received and a cash outflow equal to the cash paid and note payable.
   d.   Cash inflow equal to the cash received and a cash outflow equal to the cash paid.

Items 8 and 9 are based on the following:

A company acquired a building, paying a portion of the purchase price in cash and issuing a mortgage note payable to the seller for the balance.

8.   In a statement of cash flows, what amount is included in investing activities for the above transaction?

   a.   Cash payment.
   b.   Acquisition price.
   c.   Zero.
   d.   Mortgage amount.

9.   In a statement of cash flows, what amount is included in financing activities for the above transaction?

   a.   Cash payment.
   b.   Acquisition price.
   c.   Zero.
   d.   Mortgage amount.

10.   Fara Co. reported bonds payable of $47,000 at December 31, year 1, and $50,000 at December 31, year 2. During year 2, Fara issued $20,000 of bonds payable in exchange for equipment. There was no amortization of bond premium or discount during the year. What amount should Fara report in its year 2 statement of cash flows for redemption of bonds payable?

a. $ 3,000
b. $17,000
c. $20,000
d. $23,000

Items 11 and 12 are based on the following:

In preparing its cash flow statement for the year ended December 31, year 1, Reve Co. collected the following data:

Gain on sale of equipment	$ (6,000)
Proceeds from sale of equipment	10,000
Purchase of A.S., Inc. bonds (par value $200,000)	(180,000)
Amortization of bond discount	2,000
Dividends declared	(45,000)
Dividends paid	(38,000)
Proceeds from sale of treasury stock (carrying amount $65,000)	75,000

In its December 31, year 1 statement of cash flows,

11. What amount should Reve report as net cash used in investing activities?
a. $170,000
b. $176,000
c. $188,000
d. $194,000

12. What amount should Reve report as net cash provided by financing activities?
a. $20,000
b. $27,000
c. $30,000
d. $37,000

13. On July 1, year 1, Dewey Co. signed a twenty-year building lease that it reported as a capital lease. Dewey paid the monthly lease payments when due. How should Dewey report the effect of the lease payments in the financing activities section of its year 1 statement of cash flows?
a. An inflow equal to the present value of future lease payments at July 1, year 1, less year 1 principal and interest payments.
b. An outflow equal to the year 1 principal and interest payments on the lease.
c. An outflow equal to the year 1 principal payments only.
d. The lease payments should **not** be reported in the financing activities section.

14. Which of the following should be reported when preparing a statement of cash flows?

	Conversion of long-term debt to common stock	Conversion of preferred stock
a.	No	No
b.	No	Yes
c.	Yes	Yes
d.	Yes	No

15. Which of the following information should be disclosed as supplemental information in the statement of cash flows?

	Cash flow per share	Conversion of debt to equity
a.	Yes	Yes
b.	Yes	No

c.	No	Yes
d.	No	No

C. Direct or Indirect Presentation in Reporting Operating Activities

16. Which of the following is **not** disclosed on the statement of cash flows when prepared under the direct method, either on the face of the statement or in a separate schedule?
a. The major classes of gross cash receipts and gross cash payments.
b. The amount of income taxes paid.
c. A reconciliation of net income to net cash flow from operations.
d. A reconciliation of ending retained earnings to net cash flow from operations.

Items 17 through 21 are based on the following:

Flax Corp. uses the direct method to prepare its statement of cash flows. Flax's trial balances at December 31, year 2 and year 1 are as follows:

	December 31	
	Year 2	**Year 1**
Debits		
Cash	$ 35,000	$ 32,000
Accounts receivable	33,000	30,000
Inventory	31,000	47,000
Property, plant, & equipment	100,000	95,000
Unamortized bond discount	4,500	5,000
Cost of goods sold	250,000	380,000
Selling expenses	141,500	172,000
General and administrative expenses	137,000	151,300
Interest expense	4,300	2,600
Income tax expense	20,400	61,200
	$756,700	$976,100
Credits		
Allowance for uncollectible accounts	$ 1,300	$ 1,100
Accumulated depreciation	16,500	15,000
Trade accounts payable	25,000	17,500
Income taxes payable	21,000	27,100
Deferred income taxes	5,300	4,600
8% callable bonds payable	45,000	20,000
Common stock	50,000	40,000
Additional paid-in capital	9,100	7,500
Retained earnings	44,700	64,600
Sales	538,800	778,700
	$756,700	$976,100

- Flax purchased $5,000 in equipment during year 2.
- Flax allocated one third of its depreciation expense to selling expenses and the remainder to general and administrative expenses. There were no write-offs of accounts receivable during year 2.

What amounts should Flax report in its statement of cash flows for the year ended December 31, year 2, for the following:

17. Cash collected from customers?
a. $541,800
b. $541,600
c. $536,000
d. $535,800

18. Cash paid for goods to be sold?
    a. $258,500
    b. $257,500
    c. $242,500
    d. $226,500

19. Cash paid for interest?
    a. $4,800
    b. $4,300
    c. $3,800
    d. $1,700

20. Cash paid for income taxes?
    a. $25,800
    b. $20,400
    c. $19,700
    d. $15,000

21. Cash paid for selling expenses?
    a. $142,000
    b. $141,500
    c. $141,000
    d. $140,000

22. In a statement of cash flows, which of the following would increase reported cash flows from operating activities using the direct method? (Ignore income tax considerations.)
    a. Dividends received from investments.
    b. Gain on sale of equipment.
    c. Gain on early retirement of bonds.
    d. Change from straight-line to accelerated depreciation.

23. A company's wages payable increased from the beginning to the end of the year. In the company's statement of cash flows in which the operating activities section is prepared under the direct method, the cash paid for wages would be
    a. Salary expense plus wages payable at the beginning of the year.
    b. Salary expense plus the increase in wages payable from the beginning to the end of the year.
    c. Salary expense less the increase in wages payable from the beginning to the end of the year.
    d. The same as salary expense.

24. Metro, Inc. reported net income of $150,000 for year 1. Changes occurred in several balance sheet accounts during year 1 as follows:

Investment in Videogold, Inc. stock, carried on the equity basis	$5,500 increase
Accumulated depreciation, caused by major repair to projection equipment	2,100 decrease
Premium on bonds payable	1,400 decrease
Deferred income tax liability (long-term)	1,800 increase

In Metro's year 1 cash flow statement, the reported net cash provided by operating activities should be
    a. $150,400
    b. $148,300
    c. $144,900
    d. $142,800

25. Lino Co.'s worksheet for the preparation of its year 1 statement of cash flows included the following:

	December 31	January 1
Accounts receivable	$29,000	$23,000
Allowance for uncollectible accounts	1,000	800
Prepaid rent expense	8,200	12,400
Accounts payable	22,400	19,400

Lino's year 1 net income is $150,000. What amount should Lino include as net cash provided by operating activities in the statement of cash flows?
    a. $151,400
    b. $151,000
    c. $148,600
    d. $145,400

26. In a statement of cash flows (using indirect approach for operating activities) an increase in inventories should be presented as a(n)
    a. Outflow of cash.
    b. Inflow and outflow of cash.
    c. Addition to net income.
    d. Deduction from net income.

27. How should a gain from the sale of used equipment for cash be reported in a statement of cash flows using the indirect method?
    a. In investment activities as a reduction of the cash inflow from the sale.
    b. In investment activities as a cash outflow.
    c. In operating activities as a deduction from income.
    d. In operating activities as an addition to income.

28. Would the following be added back to net income when reporting operating activities' cash flows by the indirect method?

	Excess of treasury stock acquisition cost over sales proceeds (cost method)	Bond discount amortization
a.	Yes	Yes
b.	No	No
c.	No	Yes
d.	Yes	No

29. Which of the following should **not** be disclosed in an enterprise's statement of cash flows prepared using the indirect method?
    a. Interest paid, net of amounts capitalized.
    b. Income taxes paid.
    c. Cash flow per share.
    d. Dividends paid on preferred stock.

D.   Example of Statement of Cash Flows

Items 30 through 32 are based on the following:

The differences in Beal Inc.'s balance sheet accounts at December 31, year 2 and year 1, are presented below.

	Increase (Decrease)
Assets	
Cash and cash equivalents	$ 120,000
Available-for-sale securities	300,000
Accounts receivable, net	--
Inventory	80,000
Long-term investments	(100,000)
Plant assets	700,000
Accumulated depreciation	--
	$1,100,000

Liabilities and Stockholders' Equity

Accounts payable and accrued liabilities	$ (5,000)
Dividends payable	160,000
Short-term bank debt	325,000
Long-term debt	110,000
Common stock, $10 par	100,000
Additional paid-in capital	120,000
Retained earnings	290,000
	$1,100,000

The following additional information relates to year 2:

- Net income was $790,000.
- Cash dividends of $500,000 were declared.
- Building costing $600,000 and having a carrying amount of $350,000 was sold for $350,000.
- Equipment costing $110,000 was acquired through issuance of long-term debt.
- A long-term investment was sold for $135,000. There were no other transactions affecting long-term investments.
- 10,000 shares of common stock were issued for $22 a share.

In Beal's year 2 statement of cash flows,

30. Net cash provided by operating activities was
   a. $1,160,000
   b. $1,040,000
   c. $ 920,000
   d. $ 705,000

31. Net cash used in investing activities was
   a. $1,005,000
   b. $1,190,000
   c. $1,275,000
   d. $1,600,000

32. Net cash provided by financing activities was
   a. $ 20,000
   b. $ 45,000
   c. $150,000
   d. $205,000

Items 33 through 36 relate to data to be reported in the statement of cash flows of Debbie Dress Shops, Inc. based on the following information:

Debbie Dress Shops, Inc.
BALANCE SHEETS

	December 31	
	Year 2	Year 1
Assets		
Current assets:		
Cash	$ 300,000	$ 200,000
Accounts receivable—net	840,000	580,000
Merchandise inventory	660,000	420,000
Prepaid expenses	100,000	50,000
Total current assets	1,900,000	1,250,000
Long-term investments	80,000	--
Land, buildings, and fixtures	1,130,000	600,000
Less accumulated depreciation	110,000	50,000
	1,020,000	550,000
Total assets	$3,000,000	$1,800,000
Equities		
Current liabilities:		
Accounts payable	$ 530,000	$ 440,000
Accrued expenses	140,000	130,000
Dividends payable	70,000	--
Total current liabilities	740,000	570,000

Note payable—due year 4	500,000	--
Stockholders' equity:		
Common stock	1,200,000	900,000
Retained earnings	560,000	330,000
	1,760,000	1,230,000
Total liabilities and stock-holders' equity	$3,000,000	$1,800,000

Debbie Dress Shops, Inc.
INCOME STATEMENTS

	Year ended December 31	
	Year 2	Year 1
Net credit sales	$6,400,000	$4,000,000
Cost of goods sold	5,000,000	3,200,000
Gross profit	1,400,000	800,000
Expenses (including income taxes)	1,000,000	520,000
Net income	$ 400,000	$ 280,000

Additional information available included the following:

- All accounts receivable and accounts payable are related to trade merchandise. Accounts payable are recorded net and always are paid to take all of the discount allowed. The allowance for doubtful accounts at the end of year 2 was the same as at the end of year 1; no receivables were charged against the allowance during year 2.
- The proceeds from the note payable were used to finance a new store building. Capital stock was sold to provide additional working capital.

33. Cash collected during year 2 from accounts receivable amounted to
   a. $5,560,000
   b. $5,840,000
   c. $6,140,000
   d. $6,400,000

34. Cash payments during year 2 on accounts payable to suppliers amounted to
   a. $4,670,000
   b. $4,910,000
   c. $5,000,000
   d. $5,150,000

35. Net cash provided by financing activities for year 2 totaled
   a. $140,000
   b. $300,000
   c. $500,000
   d. $700,000

36. Net cash used in investing activities during year 2 was
   a. $ 80,000
   b. $530,000
   c. $610,000
   d. $660,000

37. Bee Co. uses the direct write-off method to account for uncollectible accounts receivable. During an accounting period, Bee's cash collections from customers equal sales adjusted for the addition or deduction of the following amounts:

	Accounts written off	Increase in accounts receivable balance
a.	Deduction	Deduction
b.	Addition	Deduction
c.	Deduction	Addition
d.	Addition	Addition

G. *International Financial Reporting Standards (IFRS)*

38. Rice Corporation prepares its financial statements in accordance with IFRS. Rice must report amounts paid for interest on a note payable on the statement of cash flows

- a. In operating activities.
- b. In financing activities.
- c. Either in operating activities or financing activities.
- d. Either in investing activities or financing activities.

39. Filigree Corporation prepares its financial statements in accordance with IFRS. Filigree acquired equipment by issuing 5,000 shares of its common stock. How should this transaction be reported on the statement of cash flows?

- a. As an outflow of cash from investing activities and an inflow of cash from financing activities.
- b. As an inflow of cash from financing activities and an outflow of cash from operating activities.
- c. At the bottom of the statement of cash flows as a significant noncash transaction.
- d. In the notes to the financial statements as a significant noncash transaction.

Multiple-Choice Answers and Explanations

Answers

1. c	__ __	10. b	__ __	19. c	__ __	28. c	__ __	37. a	__ __
2. c	__ __	11. a	__ __	20. a	__ __	29. c	__ __	38. c	__ __
3. d	__ __	12. d	__ __	21. c	__ __	30. c	__ __	39. d	__ __
4. d	__ __	13. c	__ __	22. a	__ __	31. a	__ __		
5. c	__ __	14. c	__ __	23. c	__ __	32. d	__ __		
6. a	__ __	15. c	__ __	24. c	__ __	33. c	__ __		
7. d	__ __	16. d	__ __	25. a	__ __	34. d	__ __		
8. a	__ __	17. d	__ __	26. d	__ __	35. d	__ __	1st: __/39 = __%
9. c	__ __	18. d	__ __	27. c	__ __	36. c	__ __	2nd: __/39 = __%

Explanations

1.   (c)   The 12/31/Y1 cash and cash equivalents balance is $240,000, as computed below.

Checking account #101	$175,000
Checking account #201	(10,000)
Money market account	25,000
90-day CD	50,000
Total cash and cash equivalents	$240,000

Bank overdrafts (like account #201) are normally reported as a current liability. However, when available cash is present in another account **in the same bank,** as in this case, offsetting is required. The money market account of $25,000 and the 90-day CD of $50,000 are considered cash equivalents because they had original maturities of three months or less. The 180-day CD of $80,000 is excluded because its original maturity was more than three months.

2.   (c)   The **primary** purpose of a statement of cash flows is to provide relevant information about the enterprise's cash receipts and cash payments during a period. Answers (a), (b), and (d) are incorrect because, although they represent uses of the statement of cash flows, they are not the primary use.

3.   (d)   The statement of cash flows is required to be prepared based on inflows and outflows of cash and cash equivalents during the period. The purchase of a cash equivalent using cash is **not** an outflow of cash and cash equivalents; it is merely a change in the composition of cash and cash equivalents. Cash has decreased and cash equivalents have increased, but total cash and cash equivalents is unchanged. Therefore this purchase is **not** reported in the statement of cash flows.

4.   (d)   Investing activities include all cash flows involving **assets,** other than operating items. The investing activities are

Purchase of inv. in stock	$(26,000)
Sale of inv. in stock	35,000
Acquisition of CD	(50,000)
Net cash used	(41,000)

The gain on sale of investment in Rate Motors ($35,000 – $33,000 = $2,000), the interest earned ($3,750), and dividends earned ($1,200) are all operating items. Note that the sale of investment is reported in the investing section at the cash inflow amount ($35,000), not at the carrying value of the investment ($33,000). If the CD had been for three months instead of four years, it would be part of "Cash and

Cash equivalents" and would not be shown under investing activities.

5.   (c)   The building which was destroyed had a book value of $52,000 ($100,000 – $48,000). The cash settlement from the insurance company resulted in a loss of $21,000. Therefore, the cash inflow from this investing activity must be $31,000 as shown below.

Proceeds	–	Book value	=	Loss
?	–	$52,000	=	($21,000)
$31,000	–	$52,000	=	($21,000)

Note that the $21,000 extraordinary loss must be before any income tax effect because ASC Topic 230 requires that any tax effect be left in operating activities.

6.   (a)   The cash inflow from the sale of equipment is the carrying amount plus the gain. Answers (b) and (c) are incorrect because the tax attributable to the gain is a cash outflow in the operating activities section of the statement of cash flows. Note that when using the indirect method, the gain is deducted from operating activities, as to not double count the gain.

7.   (d)   The requirement is to determine how the equipment transactions should be reported in the statement of cash flows. Companies are required to report the gross amounts of cash receipts and cash payments, rather than net amounts. Therefore, the gross cash inflow from the sale of equipment and the gross outflow for the payment of new equipment should be reported. Answer (a) is incorrect because both gross inflow and outflow should be reported, rather than reporting the net cash flow from the transaction. Answer (b) is incorrect because gross cash flows, not net, are reported and because a note payable is not reported since the transaction results in no actual inflow or outflow in the period in which the payable occurs. This noncash activity would be reported in a separate schedule or in the footnotes. Noncash transactions commonly recognized in a separate schedule in the financial statements include: conversion of debt to equity and acquisition of assets by assuming liabilities, including lease obligations. Answer (c) is incorrect because the note payable is not reported on the statement of cash flows; rather it is shown in a separate schedule.

8.   (a)   Payments at the time of purchase or soon before or after purchase to acquire property, plant, and equipment and other productive assets are categorized as cash outflows for investing activities. Generally, these payments only include advance payments, down payments, or payments made at the time of purchase or soon before or after purchase. Therefore, only the cash payment is considered a cash outflow for investing activities.

9. (c) Noncash investing and financing activities include acquiring assets by assuming directly related liabilities, such as purchasing a building by incurring a mortgage to the seller. This type of transaction does not involve the flow of cash. Therefore, cash flows for financing activities related to this transaction would be zero. Note that the cash down payment would be reported as a cash outflow for **investing** activities. The amount of the mortgage payment would be included in the noncash activities at the bottom of the statement of cash flows.

10. (b) To determine the cash paid for redemption of bonds payable, the solutions approach is to set up a T-account for bonds payable.

Bonds Payable		
	47,000	12/31/Y1
Bonds redeemed ?	20,000	Bonds issued
	50,000	12/31/Y2

The amount of bonds redeemed can be computed as $17,000. ($47,000 + $20,000 − $50,000 = $17,000)

11. (a) Investing activities include all cash flows involving **assets** other than operating items. The investing activities are

Proceeds from sale of equipment	$ 10,000
Purchase of A.S., Inc. bonds	(180,000)
Net cash used in investing activities	$(170,000)

The gain on sale of equipment ($6,000) and amortization of bond discount ($2,000) are net income adjustments in the operating section, while dividends paid ($38,000) and proceeds from sale of treasury stock ($75,000) are financing items. The excess of dividends declared over dividends paid is a noncash financing activity.

12. (d) Financing activities include all cash flows involving **liabilities and owners' equity** other than operating items. The financing activities are

Dividends paid	$(38,000)
Proceeds from sale of treasury stock	75,000
Net cash provided by financing activities	$ 37,000

The excess of dividends declared over dividends paid is a **noncash** financing activity. The gain on sale of equipment ($6,000) and amortization of bond discount ($2,000) are net income adjustments in the operating section, while the proceeds from sale of equipment ($10,000) and purchase of A.S., Inc. bonds ($180,000) are investing items.

13. (c) Financing activities include the repayment of debt principal or, as in this case, the payment of the capital lease obligation. Thus, the cash outflow is equal to the year 1 principal payments only. The interest on the capital lease is classified as an operating cash outflow.

14. (c) Information about all investing and financing activities of an enterprise during a period that affect recognized assets and liabilities but that do not affect cash receipts or cash payments in the period should be reported in a supplemental schedule to the financial statements. This schedule includes all noncash investing and financing

activities for the period. The conversion of long-term debt into common stock does not have any effect on cash flow, and it also results in a reduction of liabilities and an increase in stockholders' equity. Therefore, the conversion of long-term debt into common stock should be reported as a noncash financing activity in the supplemental schedule. Mandatorily redeemable preferred stock should be classified as a liability. On the date the preferred stock is redeemable, it is considered liability. Therefore, when the preferred stock is converted into common stock, the conversion should be reported as a noncash financing activity in the supplemental schedule.

15. (c) Noncash investing and financing activities are reported as supplemental information to the statement of cash flows because while they do not affect cash in the current year, they may have a significant effect on the prospective cash flows of the company. Therefore, conversion of debt to equity is disclosed as supplemental information to the statement of cash flows. However, cash flow per share should **not** be reported on the statement of cash flows because it may be misleading and may be incorrectly used as a measure of profitability.

16. (d) Under either the direct method or indirect method, the major classes of gross cash receipts and gross cash payments must be reported in the statement of cash flows. Under the direct method, the amount of income taxes paid is one of the components of net cash flows from operating activities; under the indirect method, it is a required supplemental disclosure. A reconciliation of net income to net cash flow from operations is a required supplemental disclosure under the direct method, and is included in the body of the statement under the indirect method. Only a reconciliation of ending retained earnings to net cash flow from operations is **not** required under either method.

17. (d) Cash collected from customers can be computed using either a formula or a T-account. The formula is

Sales −	[End AR −	(Beg AR −	Write-offs)] =	Collections
$538,800 −	[$33,000 −	($30,000 −	$0)] =	$535,800

In the formula above, sales is adjusted for the **change in AR, exclusive of write-offs,** because write-offs represent sales (and AR) which will never be collected in cash. In this problem, there were no write-offs, so it must be assumed that the change in the allowance account results solely from bad debt expense (no write-offs). Since there are no write-offs, the increase in AR ($33,000 − $30,000 = $3,000) is subtracted from sales because those sales increased AR instead of cash. The T-account solution is below.

	Accounts Receivable		
12/31/Y1	30,000		
Sales	538,800	0	Write-offs
		?	Collections = 535,800
12/31/Y2	33,000		

18. (d) Cash paid for goods to be sold can be computed using either a formula or T-accounts. The formula is

CGS	+ (End. inv. − Beg. inv.) −	(End. AP − Beg. AP) =	Cash paid
$250,000	+ ($31,000 − $47,000) −	($25,000 − $17,500) =	Cash paid
$250,000	− $16,000	− $7,500 =	$226,500

The decrease in inventory ($16,000) is subtracted from CGS because that portion of CGS resulted from a use of inventory purchased in prior years, rather than from a cash payment. The increase in AP is subtracted because that portion of

CGS was not paid this year. Using T-accounts, first purchases are computed using the inventory account, then payments are computed using the accounts payable account.

Inventory			
12/31/Y1	47,000		
Purchases	?	250,000	CGS
12/31/Y2	31,000		

1. Purchases = $234,000

Accounts Payable			
		17,500	12/31/Y1
Payments	?	234,000	Purchases
		25,000	12/31/Y2

2. Payments = $226,500

19. (c) The trial balance does **not** include prepaid interest or interest payable, both of which would affect the computation of cash paid for interest. In the absence of those accounts, cash paid for interest is equal to interest expense plus (minus) bond premium (discount) amortization.

Interest expense	–	Discount amortization	=	Cash paid
$4,300	–	($5,000 – $4,500)	=	$3,800

Flax's year 2 entry to record interest expense was

Interest expense	4,300	
Cash		3,800
Discount on bonds payable		500

20. (a) Cash paid for income taxes can be computed using the following formula:

Inc. tax expense	–	(End. inc. tax payable – Beg. inc. tax payable)	–	(End. def. tax liability – Beg. def. tax liability)	=	Cash paid for inc. tax
$20,400	–	($21,000 – $27,000)	–	($5,300 – $4,600)	=	Cash paid
$20,400	+	$6,100	–	$700	=	$25,800

The decrease in income taxes payable is added to income tax expense because cash was used to decrease the liability as well as to pay tax expense. The increase in the deferred tax liability is deducted from income tax expense because that portion of tax expense was deferred (not paid in cash). Flax's summary journal entry to record income taxes for year 2 is

Inc. tax expense	20,400	
Inc. tax payable	6,100	
Cash		25,800
Deferred taxes		700

21. (c) In general, cash paid for selling expenses is affected by prepaid selling expenses, accrued selling expenses, depreciation and/or amortization expense, and possibly bad debts expense. In this case, there are no prepaid or accrued selling expenses in the trial balances, and bad debts expense is apparently included in general and administrative expenses (see discussion below). Therefore, cash paid for selling expenses is $141,000 ($141,500 selling expenses less $500 depreciation expense). Total depreciation expense can be determined from the change in the accumulated depreciation account ($16,500 – $15,000 = $1,500), and 1/3 of that amount is selling expense (1/3 × $1,500 = $500). Note that bad debt expense ($1,300 – $1,100 = $200) must be included in general and administrative expenses, because the answer obtained by assuming it is part of selling expenses

($141,000 – $200 = $140,800) is not given as one of the four choices.

22. (a) Businesses are encouraged to use the direct method of reporting operating activities under which major classes of cash receipts and cash payments are shown. The minimum cash flows to be disclosed under this method are cash collected from customers, interest and dividends received, cash paid to employees and suppliers, income taxes paid, and interest paid.

23. (c) In a statement of cash flows in which the operating activities section is prepared using the direct method, the cash paid for wages would be equal to the accrual-basis salary expense, plus/minus any decrease/increase in the wages payable account. (The logic is essentially the same as an accrual-basis to cash-basis adjustment.)

24. (c) Net income was $150,000. Three of the four items given are net income adjustments (the major repair to projection equipment [$2,100] is a cash outflow under investing activities), resulting in net cash provided by operating activities of $144,900.

Net income	$150,000
Equity method income	(5,500)
Premium amortization	(1,400)
Increase in def. tax liability	1,800
Cash provided by operating activities	$144,900

When equity method income is recorded, the offsetting debit is to the investment account, not cash; when premium on bonds payable is amortized, the credit to interest expense is offset by a debit to the premium account, not cash. Therefore, both of these items **increase** income without increasing cash, and must be **deducted** as a net income adjustment. For the deferred tax items, when income tax expense is debited, the offsetting credit is to deferred tax liability, not cash. Therefore, this item **decreases** net income without decreasing cash, and it must be **added back** as a net income adjustment. Note that there should normally be depreciation expense as a net income adjustment, but it is not given.

25. (a) Based only on the items given, net cash provided by operating activities is $151,400, as computed below.

Net income	$150,000
Increase in net AR	
[($29,000 – 1,000) – ($23,000 – $800)]	(5,800)
Decrease in prepaid rent ($12,400 – $8,200)	4,200
Increase in AP ($22,400 – $19,400)	3,000
Cash provided by ops.	$151,400

The increase in net AR is deducted from net income because it indicates that cash collected is less than sales revenue. The decrease in prepaid rent is added because it reflects rent expense that was **not** a cash payment, but an allocation of previously recorded prepaid rent. Finally, the increase in AP is added because it also represents an expense (cost of goods sold) that was not yet paid.

26. (d) The objective of a statement of cash flows is to explain what caused the change in the cash balance. The first step in this process is to determine cash provided by operations. When presenting cash from operating activities under the indirect approach, net income must be adjusted for changes in current assets other than cash and in current liabilities. These adjustments are required because items that resulted from noncash events must be removed from accrual-based income. For example, when inventory increases during the period, inventory sold is less than inventory purchased. Considering only the increase in the inventory account, cost of goods sold on an accrual basis is less than it would have been if cash basis were being used. In converting to the cash basis, the increase in inventory must be subtracted from net income to arrive at cash from operations. Answer (a) is incorrect because even though an increase in inventories requires an outflow of cash, inventories are shown as adjustments to net income under the indirect method. Answer (b) is incorrect because changes in inventories are shown as adjustments to net income under the indirect method. Answer (c) is incorrect because an increase in an inventory would be a deduction from net income, not an addition.

27. (c) When using the indirect method for reporting net cash flows from operations, you start with net income from continuing operations and adjust for changes in operating related accounts (i.e., inventory, accounts payable) and noncash expenses, revenues, gains and losses. The proceeds from the sale of equipment is reported as an inflow in the investing section of the statement of cash flows, at its gross amount. This gross amount includes the gain. Therefore, to avoid double counting and to properly classify cash inflows, the gain is subtracted from net income to show the proper cash balance from operating activities.

28. (c) Under the indirect method of reporting cash flows from operations, income from continuing operations is adjusted for changes in operating related accounts and noncash expenses, revenues, losses, and gains. Noncash items that were subtracted in determining income must be added back in. This would include amortization of bond discount, as it is a charge against income but does not decrease cash. The excess of treasury stock acquisition cost over sales proceeds would not be added back to net income. Under the cost method, this loss would not be included in net income but would be charged back to a paid-in capital account or retained earnings. The acquisition and sale of treasury stock, furthermore, would be financing activities.

29. (c) Cash flow per share should **not** be reported on the statement of cash flows because it may be misleading and may be incorrectly used as a measure of profitability. Answers (a) and (b) are incorrect because, when the indirect method is used, separate disclosure is required for **interest paid** (net of amounts capitalized) and **income taxes paid**. Answer (d) is incorrect because, regardless of the method used, **dividends paid** on preferred stock are reported as a **financing activity**.

30. (c) Net cash provided by operating activities can be computed by using either the **direct** or **indirect** approach. In this case, there is not enough information to use the direct approach. In the indirect approach, net income is adjusted for noncash items, as shown below.

Net income	$790,000
Gain on sale of LT investment	(35,000)
Increase in inventory	(80,000)
Depreciation expense	250,000
Decrease in AP and accrued liabs.	(5,000)
	$920,000

The additional information indicates that a LT investment was sold for $135,000. The listing of accounts shows a de-

crease in LT investments of $100,000. The gain on sale ($135,000 – $100,000 = $35,000) is deducted because the total cash effect of this transaction ($135,000) will be reported as an investing activity. Two of the working capital accounts that changed are related to net income. The increase in inventory ($80,000) is deducted because cash was used to increase inventory. The decrease in accounts payable and accrued liabilities is deducted because cash was used to pay these liabilities. The increase of $300,000 for Available-for-Sale Securities is an investing activity. The only other information or account given which affects net income is accumulated depreciation. Although this account did not show any net decrease or increase during year 2, we know it was decreased by $250,000 when the building was sold ($600,000 cost less $350,000 carrying amount equals $250,000 accumulated depreciation). Therefore, depreciation expense of $250,000 must have increased the accumulated depreciation account to result in a net effect for the year of $0. Depreciation expense is added because it is a noncash expense.

An alternative method of computing net cash provided by operating activities is to back into the answer after determining cash used in investing activities and cash provided by financing activities.

Cash provided by Operating Activities	$?
Cash used in Investing Activities	(1,005,000)
Cash provided by Financing Activities	205,000
Net increase in Cash	$ 120,000

The problem tells us that cash and cash equivalents increased by $120,000. Therefore, cash provided by operating activities is $920,000 ($920,000 – $1,005,000 + $205,000 = $120,000).

31. (a) **Investing** activities include all cash flows involving **assets,** other than operating items. **Financing** activities include all cash flows involving **liabilities and equity,** other than operating items. The common stock issued is a financing activity. In this case, the changes in the inventory and accumulated depreciation accounts are operating items. The cash flows involving the other assets, listed below, are investing activities

Purchase of AFS securities	$ (300,000)
Sale of LT investments	135,000
Sale of plant assets	350,000
Purchase of plant assets	(1,190,000)
	$(1,005,000)

The amounts above were given, except for the purchase of plant assets, the amount of which can be determined from the following T-account:

Plant Assets			
Cost of equip. acquired	110,000	600,000	Cost of
Cost of plant assets purchased	?		bldg. sold
Net increase	700,000		

The equipment acquired through issuance of LT debt is a **noncash** investing and financing activity so it does not affect net **cash** used in investing activities.

32. (d) **Financing** activities include all cash flows involving **liabilities and equity,** other than operating items. **Investing** activities include all cash flows involving **assets,** other than operating items. In this case, the change in the **accounts payable and accrued liabilities** account is an operating item. The part of the change in **retained earnings** caused by net income ($790,000) is also an operating item. The cash flows involving the other liability and equity accounts, listed below, are financing activities.

Payment of dividends ($500,000 – $160,000)	$(340,000)
Issuance of ST debt	325,000
Issuance of common stock (10,000 × $22)	220,000
	$ 205,000

The problem states that $500,000 of dividends were **declared**, and this is confirmed by the change in the retained earnings account ($790,000 net income – $500,000 dividends declared = $290,000 net increase). However, since dividends payable increased by $160,000, only $340,000 of dividends were paid ($500,000 – $160,000). The issuance of common stock (10,000 shares × $22 per share = $220,000) is confirmed by the increases in the common stock and additional paid-in capital accounts ($100,000 + $120,000 = $220,000). The issuance of LT debt for equipment ($110,000) is a noncash financing and investing activity, so it does not affect net cash provided by financing activities. Note that the answers to the three related questions can be verified by comparing them to the increase in cash and cash equivalents ($120,000) given in the problem.

Cash provided by oper. acts.	$ 920,000
Cash used in inv. acts.	(1,005,000)
Cash provided by fin. acts.	205,000
Increase in cash and cash equivalents	$ 120,000

33. **(c)** The requirement is to calculate the amount of cash collected during year 2 from accounts receivable. The solutions approach is to prepare a T-account for accounts receivable. The allowance account has no effect on this analysis, because the problem states that the balance in this account has not changed and no accounts receivable were written off. Net credit sales are the only debit to accounts receivable because all accounts receivable relate to trade merchandise. In the T-account below, you must solve for the missing credit to determine that $6,140,000 was collected on account during year 2.

AR—Net

12/31/Y1 balance	580,000	?	Year 2 Collections
Year 2 net credit sales	6,400,000		
12/31/Y2 balance	840,000		

> **NOTE:** Based on the information given in this problem, no bad debt expense was recorded during year 2. However unrealistic this assumption might be, it is important to simply work with the information as given.

34. **(d)** The requirement is to calculate the amount of cash payments during year 2 on accounts payable. The solutions approach is to visualize the accounts payable T-account.

Accounts Payable

		440,000	12/31/Y1
Payments	?	?	Purchases
		530,000	12/31/Y2

It is apparent that to determine payments to suppliers, purchases of trade merchandise must first be computed. The cost of goods sold statement can be used to compute purchases.

Beginning inventory	$	420,000
+ Purchases	+	?
– Ending inventory	–	660,000
Cost of goods sold		$5,000,000

Purchases = $5,000,000 – ($420,000 – $660,000)
        = $5,240,000

Finally, the purchases are entered into the accounts payable T-account, and payments to suppliers of $5,150,000 can be plugged in.

Accounts Payable

		440,000	12/31/Y1
Payments	5,150,000	5,240,000	Purchases
		530,000	12/31/Y2

35. **(d)** The requirement is to determine net cash flows provided by financing activities in year 2. The solutions approach is to work through the comparative balance sheets noting increases and decreases in liability accounts other than those related to operations and increases or decreases in stockholders' equity accounts. The additional information given must be considered in connection with these changes. Notice the note payable was issued for cash and the proceeds were used to purchase a building. Cash inflows from financing activities include proceeds from long-term borrowing, and issuance of capital stock.

Proceeds from long-term note	$500,000
Proceeds from issuance of common stock	300,000
	$800,000

To determine the amount of dividends paid, it is necessary to analyze both the retained earnings and the dividends payable accounts.

Dividends Payable					Retained Earnings			
			--	12/31/Y1			330,000	12/31/Y1
Dividends paid	?		?	Dividends declared		?	400,000	Net income
			70,000	12/31/Y2			560,000	12/31/Y2

Dividends declared = $330,000 + 400,000 – 560,000 = $170,000
Dividends paid   = $0 + 170,000 – 70,000 = $100,000

Net cash flows provided by financing activities is $700,000 ($800,000 – $100,000).

36. **(c)** The requirement is to compute the cash used in investing activities during year 2. The two assets other than those related to operations shown on the balance sheet (long-term investments and land, building, and fixtures) have increased from 12/31/Y1 to 12/31/Y2, indicating cash purchases since the additional information does not suggest any other means of acquisition. Therefore, cash outflows from investing activities include $80,000 for long-term investments and $530,000 ($1,130,000 – $600,000) for land, building, and fixtures. Notice that the building was purchased for $500,000, so fixtures or land must have been acquired for $30,000.

37. **(a)** The solutions approach is to set up T-accounts for the related accounts.

Sales			AR		
	Sales		Beg. Bal.	Collections	
			Sales	Write-offs	
			End. Bal.		

Sales are debited to AR and credited to sales; collections are debited to cash and credited to AR. Under the direct write-off method, write-offs of customer accounts are debited to bad debts expense, and credited to AR. To adjust sales to cash collections from customers, Bee must subtract the increase in accounts receivable (because Bee has not yet received cash for the sales remaining in AR). Bee must also subtract the accounts written off, because these sales have not resulted in cash receipts (and probably never will).

38. (c) The requirement is to identify where finance costs are presented in the statement of cash flows. Answer (c) is correct because under IFRS finance costs (interest expense) may be reported in either the operating or financing section of the statement of cash flows. However, once it is disclosed in a particular section, it must be reported on a consistent basis. Therefore, answers (a), (b) and (d) are incorrect.

39. (d) The requirement is to identify how the transaction should be reported on the statement of cash flows. Answer (d) is correct because this transaction did not involve an exchange of cash; therefore, it is not included on the statement of cash flows. IFRS requires that significant noncash transactions be reported in the notes to the financial statements. (Note that for US GAAP, if there are only a few significant noncash transactions, they may be reported at the bottom of the statement of cash flows, or they may be reported in a separate schedule in the notes to the financial statements.)

Simulations

Task-Based Simulation 1

Statement of Cash Flows—Indirect Method		
	Authoritative Literature	Help

Situation

The following is a condensed trial balance of Probe Co., a publicly held company, after adjustments for income tax expense.

Probe Co.
CONDENSED TRIAL BALANCE

	12/31/Y10 Balances Dr. (Cr.)	12/31/Y9 Balances Dr. (Cr.)	Net change Dr. (Cr.)
Cash	$ 484,000	$ 817,000	$(333,000)
Accounts receivable, net	670,000	610,000	60,000
Property, plant, and equipment	1,070,000	995,000	75,000
Accumulated depreciation	(345,000)	(280,000)	(65,000)
Dividends payable	(25,000)	(10,000)	(15,000)
Income taxes payable	(60,000)	(150,000)	90,000
Deferred income tax liability	(63,000)	(42,000)	(21,000)
Bonds payable	(500,000)	(1,000,000)	500,000
Unamortized premium on bonds	(71,000)	(150,000)	79,000
Common stock	(350,000)	(150,000)	(200,000)
Additional paid-in capital	(430,000)	(375,000)	(55,000)
Retained earnings	(185,000)	(265,000)	80,000
Sales	(2,420,000)		
Cost of sales	1,863,000		
Selling and administrative expenses	220,000		
Interest income	(14,000)		
Interest expense	46,000		
Depreciation	88,000		
Loss on sale of equipment	7,000		
Gain on extinguishment of bonds	(90,000)		
Income tax expense	105,000		
	$ 0	$ 0	$ 300,000

Additional information

- During year 10 equipment with an original cost of $50,000 was sold for cash, and equipment costing $125,000 was purchased.
- On January 1, year 10, bonds with a par value of $500,000 and related premium of $75,000 were redeemed. The $1,000 face value, 10% par bonds had been issued on January 1, year 1, to yield 8%. Interest is payable annually every December 31 through year 20.
- Probe's tax payments during year 10 were debited to Income Taxes Payable. Probe recorded a deferred income tax liability of $42,000 based on temporary differences of $120,000 and an enacted tax rate of 35% at December 31, year 9; prior to year 9 there were no temporary differences. Probe's year 10 financial statement income before income taxes was greater than its year 10 taxable income, due entirely to temporary differences, by $60,000. Probe's cumulative net taxable temporary differences at December 31, year 10, were $180,000. Probe's enacted tax rate for the current and future years is 35%.
- 60,000 shares of common stock, $2.50 par, were outstanding on December 31, year 9. Probe issued an additional 80,000 shares on April 1, year 10.
- There were no changes to retained earnings other than dividends declared.

Prepare a statement of cash flows using the **indirect method**. Select the titles and the numbers from the lists provided. You may use a number more than once, if necessary. You should also enter the following amounts:

- Subtotals for each class of activity.
- Net change in cash for the year.
- Reconciliation to cash amounts.

Complete the following statement of cash flows using the **indirect method**. (Select from titles and amounts from the tables that follow.)

Probe Co. STATEMENT OF CASH FLOWS For the Year Ending 12/31/Y10	
	Cash Source (Use)
From Operating Activities	
From Investing Activities	
From Financing Activities	

Titles

Increase in accounts receivable	Decrease in bonds payable	Net income
Decrease in accounts receivable	Issue bonds	Net loss
Increase in property, plant, equipment	Redeem bonds	Taxes paid
Decrease in property, plant, equipment	Amortization of premium on bonds	Interest paid
Purchase of equipment	Gain on extinguishment of bonds	Depreciation expense
Sale of equipment	Payment of dividends	Cash collections from customers
Loss on sale of equipment	Increase in common stock	Cash paid for expenses
Increase in accumulated depreciation	Decrease in common stock	Net cash flows from operating activities
Decrease in accumulated depreciation	Issue common stock	Net cash flows from investing activities
Increase in income taxes payable	Repurchase common stock	Net cash flows from financing activities
Decrease in income taxes payable	Increase in additional paid-in capital	Other significant noncash transactions
Increase in deferred income tax liability	Decrease in additional paid-in capital	Net increase in cash
Decrease in deferred income tax liability	Increase in retained earnings	Net decrease in cash
Increase in bonds payable	Decrease in retained earnings	Cash at beginning of year
		Cash at end of year

Amounts

4,000	46,000	88,000	255,000	610,000
7,000	50,000	90,000	300,000	670,000
10,000	55,000	95,000	333,000	780,000
13,000	60,000	120,000	350,000	817,000
14,000	63,000	125,000	410,000	1,000,000
15,000	65,000	150,000	484,000	2,360,000
20,000	74,000	174,000	485,000	2,420,000
21,000	75,000	185,000	500,000	2,480,000
23,000	79,000	195,000	515,000	3,030,000
25,000	80,000	200,000	575,000	
42,000	85,000	240,000	590,000	

Task-Based Simulation 2

Concepts— Direct Method		
	Authoritative **Literature**	**Help**

Below is a list of accounts and transactions. Prepare the outline of a statement of cash flows using the **direct method** by placing the appropriate items in the correct location on the statement of cash flows. Indicate whether each item selected for use in the statement of cash flows would be a cash inflow or a cash outflow.

Amortization of patents	Dividends received on trading securities	Issue of common stock
Borrow on long-term note payable	Gain on sale of land	Loss on sale of equipment
Cash collected on account	Increase in accounts receivable	Net income
Cash paid for inventory	Increase in dividends payable	Payment of dividend
Cash paid for supplies	Increase in inventories	Purchase of held-to-maturity securities
Cash sales	Increase in taxes payable	Purchase of treasury stock
Decrease in accounts payable	Interest accrued at December 31	Redemption of bonds
Decrease in prepaid expenses	Interest expense	Sale of land
Depreciation expense	Interest paid on note	Taxes paid

Probe Co. STATEMENT OF CASH FLOWS *For the Year Ending 12/31/Y2*	
	Cash Inflow or Cash Outflow
From Operating Activities	
From Investing Activities	
From Financing Activities	

Task-Based Simulation 3

Research		
	Authoritative Literature	Help

Easton Company purchased 4,000 shares of its own stock for $20 per share and immediately retired the shares. You have been asked to research the professional literature to determine how the item is presented in Easton's statement of cash flows, using the indirect method. Place the citation for the excerpt from Professional Standards that provides this information in the answer box below.

Task-Based Simulation 4

Concepts		
	Authoritative Literature	Help

Indicate whether each of the following should be classified as an operating, investing, or financing activity on the statement of cash flows.

		Operating	Investing	Financing
1.	Payment for inventory	○	○	○
2.	Payment of dividend	○	○	○
3.	Cash received from sale of equipment	○	○	○
4.	Cash sales	○	○	○
5.	Issuance of stock to investors	○	○	○
6.	Payment of utility bill	○	○	○
7.	Payment of interest on long-term note payable	○	○	○
8.	Purchase of treasury stock	○	○	○

Task-Based Simulation 5

Calculations		
	Authoritative Literature	Help

Situation

The following is a condensed trial balance of Clark Co., a publicly held company, after adjustments for income tax expense.

Clark Co.
CONDENSED TRIAL BALANCE

	12/31/Y10 Balances Dr. (Cr.)	12/31/Y9 Balances Dr. (Cr.)	Net change Dr. (Cr.)
Cash	$ 484,000	$ 817,000	$(333,000)
Accounts receivable, net	670,000	610,000	60,000
Property, plant, and equipment	1,070,000	995,000	75,000
Accumulated depreciation	(345,000)	(280,000)	(65,000)
Dividends payable	(25,000)	(10,000)	(15,000)
Income taxes payable	(60,000)	(150,000)	90,000
Deferred income tax liability	(63,000)	(42,000)	(21,000)
Bonds payable	(500,000)	(1,000,000)	500,000
Unamortized premium on bonds	(71,000)	(150,000)	79,000
Common stock	(350,000)	(150,000)	(200,000)
Additional paid-in capital	(430,000)	(375,000)	(55,000)
Retained earnings	(185,000)	(265,000)	80,000
Sales	(2,420,000)		
Cost of sales	1,863,000		

	12/31/Y10 Balances Dr. (Cr.)	12/31/Y9 Balances Dr. (Cr.)	Net change Dr. (Cr.)
Selling and administrative expenses	220,000		
Interest income	(14,000)		
Interest expense	46,000		
Depreciation	88,000		
Loss on sale of equipment	7,000		
Gain on extinguishment of bonds	(90,000)		
Income tax expense	105,000		
	$ 0	$ 0	$ 300,000

Additional information

- During year 10 equipment with an original cost of $50,000 was sold for cash, and equipment costing $125,000 was purchased.
- On January 1, year 10, bonds with a par value of $500,000 and related premium of $75,000 were redeemed. The $1,000 face value, 10% par bonds had been issued on January 1, year 1, to yield 8%. Interest is payable annually every December 31 through year 19.
- Clark's tax payments during year 10 were debited to Income Taxes Payable. Clark recorded a deferred income tax liability of $42,000 based on temporary differences of $120,000 and an enacted tax rate of 35% at December 31, year 9; prior to year 9 there were no temporary differences. Clark's year 10 financial statement income before income taxes was greater than its year 10 taxable income, due entirely to temporary differences, by $60,000. Clark's cumulative net taxable temporary differences at December 31, year 10, were $180,000. The enacted tax rate for the current and future years is 35%.
- 60,000 shares of common stock, $2.50 par, were outstanding on December 31, year 9. Clark issued an additional 80,000 shares on April 1, year 10.
- There were no changes to retained earnings other than dividends declared.

For each transaction in **items 1 through 7**

- Determine the amount to be reported in Clark's year 10 statement of cash flows prepared using the **direct method**.
- Select from the list the appropriate classification of the item on the statement of cash flows.
- Indicate whether the item is a cash inflow or cash outflow.

Calculate the amount, and select the classification and direction from the items shown below.

Classification of Activity	**Direction of Cash Flow**
Operating	Inflow
Investing	Outflow
Financing	
Supplementary information	
Not reported on Clark's statement of cash flows	

	Amount	Classification of Activity	Direction of Cash Flow
1. Cash paid for income taxes			
2. Cash paid for interest			
3. Redemption of bonds payable			
4. Issuance of common stock			
5. Cash dividends paid			
6. Proceeds from sale of equipment			
7. Cash collections from customers			

Task-Based Simulation 6

Research		
	Authoritative Literature	Help

The holders of Dexter Company's convertible bonds converted the bonds to common stock. You have been asked to research the professional literature to determine how the item is presented in Dexter's statement of cash flows, using the indirect method. Place the citation for the excerpt from Professional Standards that provides this information in the answer box below.

Simulation Solutions

Task-Based Simulation 1

Statement of Cash Flows—Indirect Method	Authoritative Literature	Help

Probe Co. STATEMENT OF CASH FLOWS For the Year Ending 12/31/Y10	
	Cash Source (Use)
From Operating Activities	
Net income	195,000
Loss on sale of equipment	7,000
Gain on extinguishments of bonds	(90,000)
Depreciation Expense	88,000
Increase in Account Receivable	(60,000)
Decrease in Income Taxes Payable	(90,000)
Increase in Deferred Taxes Payable	21,000
Amortization of Premium on Bonds	(4,000)
Net cash flows from operating activities	67,000
From Investing Activities	
Sale of equipment	20,000
Purchase of equipment	(125,000)
Net cash flow from investing activities	(105,000)
From Financing Activities	
Redeem bonds	(485,000)
Issue common stock	255,000
Payment of dividends	(65,000)
Net cash flows from financing activities	(295,000)
Net decrease in cash	(333,000)
Cash at beginning of year	817,000
Cash at end of year	484,000

Task-Based Simulation 2

Concepts— Direct Method	Authoritative Literature	Help

Probe Co. STATEMENT OF CASH FLOWS For the Year Ending 12/31/Y2	
	Cash Inflow or Cash Outflow
From Operating Activities	
Cash paid for inventory	Outflow
Cash paid for supplies	Outflow
Cash collected on account	Inflow
Cash sales	Inflow
Dividends received on trading securities	Inflow
Interest paid on note	Outflow
Taxes paid	Outflow
From Investing Activities	
Purchase of held-to-maturity securities	Outflow
Sale of land	Inflow

From Financing Activities	
Borrow on long-term note payable	Inflow
Issue of common stock	Inflow
Payment of dividend	Outflow
Purchase of treasury stock	Outflow
Redemption of bonds	Outflow

Task-Based Simulation 3

Research			
	Authoritative Literature	Help	

ASC	230	10	45	15

Task-Based Simulation 4

Concepts		
	Authoritative Literature	Help

Indicate whether each of the following should be classified as an operating, investing, or financing activity on the statement of cash flows.

		Operating	Investing	Financing
1.	Payment for inventory	●	○	○
2.	Payment of dividend	○	○	●
3.	Cash received from sale of equipment	○	●	○
4.	Cash sales	●	○	
5.	Issuance of stock to investors	○	○	●
6.	Payment of utility bill	●	○	○
7.	Payment of interest on long-term note payable	●	○	○
8.	Purchase of treasury stock	○	○	●

Task-Based Simulation 5

Calculations		
	Authoritative Literature	Help

	Item	Amount	Classification on Statement of Cash Flows	Cash Inflow/Cash Outflow
1.	Cash paid for income taxes	174,000	Operating Activity	Outflow
2.	Cash paid for interest	50,000	Operating Activity	Outflow
3.	Redemption of bonds payable	485,000	Financing Activity	Outflow
4.	Issuance of common stock	255,000	Financing Activity	Inflow
5.	Cash dividends paid	65,000	Financing Activity	Outflow
6.	Proceeds from sale of equipment	20,000	Investing	Inflow
7.	Cash collections from customers	2,360,000	Operating Activity	Inflow

Explanations

1. **($174,000, O)** The payments for income taxes during the year were debited to the income taxes payable account. To arrive at the amount of payments, a T-account can be used as follows:

Income Taxes Payable

		150,000	12/31/Y9
Payments	174,000	84,000	Income Tax Accrual
		60,000	12/31/Y10

Note that the deferred tax liability account increased by $21,000 ($120,000 × 35%). Therefore, the entry for tax expense for year 10 would have been

Tax Expense	105,000	
Deferred Tax Liability		21,000
Taxes Payable		84,000

Using the direct method, the payment of taxes would appear in the operating section of the cash flow statement.

2. **($50,000, O)** Interest paid on the bonds in year 10 would be $50,000 ($500,000 × 10%). Alternatively, the $46,000 plus the $4,000 premium amortization (see explanation for the next item below) also results in $50,000 as the amount paid for interest. The amount paid for interest would be included in the operating activities section of the cash flow statements if the direct method is used. (Note: The amount of cash paid for interest would be reported separately as supplementary information for a statement of cash flows using the indirect method.)

3. **($485,000, F)** Through the following T-account analyses, a journal entry for the redemption of the bonds payable can be determined:

Bonds Payable

		1,000,000	12/31/Y9
Redemption	500,000		
		500,000	12/31/Y10

Unamortized Premium on Bonds

Amortization	4,000	150,000	12/31/Y9
Redemption	75,000		
		71,000	12/31/Y10

Gain on Extinguishment of Bonds

	90,000	12/31/Y10

Cash

	?

Journal entry for redemption

Bonds payable	500,000	
Unamortized premium on bonds	75,000	
Gain on extinguishment of bonds		90,000
Cash		485,000

This amount paid for the redemption of the bonds would be separately reported in the financing section on the statement of cash flows prepared using the indirect method. Financing activities include obtaining resources from owners and returning the investment, as well as obtaining resources from creditors and **repaying the amounts borrowed**.

4. **($255,000, F)** An additional 80,000 shares of $2.50 par value common stock were issued during year 10. The following T-accounts depict the changes in the common stock and additional paid-in capital accounts:

Common Stock

		150,000	12/31Y9
		200,000	Issuance (80,000 × $2.50)
		350,000	12/31Y10

Additional Paid-in Capital

		375,000	12/31/Y9
		55,000	Issuance
		430,000	12/31/Y10

The journal entry for the issuance of the stock would have been

Cash	255,000	
Common stock		200,000
Additional paid-in capital		55,000

This amount received for the issuance of the common stock would be reported separately in the financing section of the statement of cash flows prepared using the indirect method. Financing activities include **obtaining resources from owners** and returning the investment, as well as obtaining resources from creditors and repaying the amounts borrowed.

5. **($65,000, F)** The problem states that there were no changes to retained earnings during the year other than dividends declared. Therefore, the following T-account analyses depict the dividend activity during the year:

Retained Earnings

		265,000	12/31/Y9
Dividends declared	80,000		
		185,000	12/31/Y10

Dividends Payable					Cash	
		10,000	12/31/Y9		?	
Dividends paid	?	80,000	Accrual during year 10			
		25,000	12/31/Y10			

The following journal entry would have been made:

Retained earnings	80,000	
Dividends payable		80,000
Dividends payable	65,000	
Cash		65,000

This amount paid for the dividends would be reported separately in the financing section of the statement of cash flows prepared using the indirect method. Financing activities include obtaining resources from owners and **returning the investment,** as well as obtaining resources from creditors and repaying the amounts borrowed.

6. **($20,000, I)** The following T-account analyses depict the sale of the equipment during year 10:

Property, Plant and Equipment

12/31/Y9	995,000		
		50,000	Sale
Purchase	125,000		
12/31/Y10	1,070,000		

Accumulated Depreciation

		280,000	12/31/Y9
Depreciation on sold asset	23,000	88,000	Depreciation expense
		345,000	12/31/Y10

Loss on Sale of Equipment			Cash	
12/31/Y10	7,000		?	

The following journal entry would have been made for the sale of the equipment:

Cash	20,000	
Accumulated depreciation	23,000	
Loss on sale of equipment	7,000	
Property, plant and equipment		50,000

The proceeds from the sale of equipment would be reported separately in the investing section of the statement of cash flows. Included in the investing section are the acquisition and disposition of long-term productive assets or securities (not considered cash equivalents), as well as the lending of money and collection of loans.

7. **($2,360,000, O)** The following T-account analysis depicts the cash received from customers. Assume all sales are made on account.

Accounts Receivable

12/31/Y10	610,000		
Sale on Account	2,420,000		
		2,360,000	Collections on account
12/31/Y2	670,000		

Therefore, the cash collections on account were 610,000 + 2,420,000 – 670,000 = 2,360,000.

Task-Based Simulation 6

Research		
	Authoritative Literature	Help

ASC	230	10	50	3

Module 18: Business Combinations and Consolidations

Overview

This module covers business combinations and consolidations. To qualify for treatment as a business combination, the entity must meet the definition of a business. If an entity is not considered a business, the transaction is accounted for as an asset acquisition and goodwill is not recognized.

Acquisition accounting is the method to account for a business combination and it consists of four steps: (1) identifying the acquirer; (2) determining the acquisition date; (3) recognizing and measuring assets acquired, liabilities assumed, and noncontrolling interest in the acquirer; and (4) recognizing goodwill. Each of these steps is discussed in detail. Numerous examples relating to variations in acquisition accounting are presented along with the calculation of goodwill and intercompany eliminating entries.

This module also discusses required disclosures, combined financial statements, and push-down accounting. Push-down accounting is required by the SEC. It requires the subsidiary to revalue its assets and liabilities to fair value.

A. Scope—Acquisition Method

1. ASC Topic 805 (SFAS 141[Revised]) applies to business acquisitions.

   a. It does not apply to the formation of joint ventures, the acquisition of assets or groups of assets that do not constitute a business, or the combination of entities under common control.

2. **Asset acquisition** scope exception

   a. If the assets and liabilities acquired do not constitute a business, then the transaction is accounted for as an asset acquisition.

   b. In an asset acquisition, the assets are recorded at the amount of cash paid, or the cost of the assets.

      (1) If the assets are not acquired with cash, then the assets are recorded at either fair value of the assets given up (transferred) by the acquiring entity, or the fair value of the assets acquired, whichever is more reliable.

   c. If assets are acquired in a group, the cost of each asset is determined by allocating the total cost to the individual assets based on their relative fair values.

   d. **No goodwill is recorded in an asset acquisition.**

3. Common control scope exception

    a. ASC Topic 805 (SFAS 141[R]) also does not apply to entities under common control.

       (1) For example, an entity may create a new corporation and transfer some or all of its assets to the new corporation, or a parent may transfer the net assets of a wholly owned subsidiary into the parent and then liquidate the subsidiary.

    b. These types of changes are considered a change in legal organization, not a change in the reporting entity.

       (1) In situations where entities are under common control, the assets and liabilities transferred are recorded at their carrying amounts at the date of the transfer.

4. Definition of a business

    a. To qualify for treatment as a business combination, the entity must meet the definition of a business.

       (1) A **business** is defined as "an integrated set of activities and assets that is capable of being conducted and managed for the purpose of providing a return in the form of dividends, lower costs, or other economic benefits directly to investors or other owners, members or participants."

       (2) A business normally consists of inputs, processes, and outputs. However, outputs are NOT required for the entity to qualify as a business.

5. Common terminology

    a. The **acquiree** is the business that is being acquired.
    b. The **acquirer** is the entity that obtains control of the acquiree.
    c. The **acquisition date** is the date on which the acquirer obtains control of the acquiree.
    d. A **business combination** is a transaction or event in which the acquirer obtains control of one or more businesses.
    e. **Control** is defined as a controlling financial interest by ownership of a majority of the voting shares of stock. The general rule is that ownership either directly or indirectly by one company of more than 50% of the outstanding voting shares of another company constitutes control.

B. The Acquisition Method for Business Combinations

1. If an acquisition qualifies as a business combination, then the acquisition method is used. The four steps in applying the acquisition method are as follows:

    a. Identify the acquirer.
    b. Determine the acquisition date.
    c. Recognize and measure identifiable assets acquired, liabilities assumed, and noncontrolling (minority) interest in the acquiree.
    d. Recognize and measure goodwill, or recognize a gain from a bargain purchase.

2. Acquirer identification.

    a. Acquirer identification is the first step in a business combination.
    b. Distinguishing between the acquirer and the acquiree is important because only the acquiree's assets are revalued to fair value at the acquisition date.
    c. Normally the acquirer is the entity that obtains control of the acquiree.

       (1) The acquirer is usually the entity that transfers cash or incurs the liabilities in order to acquire the other firm.
       (2) However, if it is unclear which entity is the acquirer, one of the combining entities must be identified as the acquirer by examining the facts and circumstances.

          (a) The entity that retains the largest portion of voting rights is usually the acquirer.
          (b) The acquirer may also be determined by identifying the company that retains more individuals on its governing body or in its senior management.
          (c) If the business was acquired by exchanging equity interests, the acquirer is usually the entity that pays a premium over the fair value of the equity interests of the other firm.
          (d) The acquirer may also be determined by identifying the entity that is significantly larger in size, measured by its assets, revenues, or earnings.

3. Acquisition date identification.

    a. Acquisition date identification is the second step in a business combination.
    b. The acquisition date is important for two reasons:

    (1) The acquisition date is the date when the identifiable assets and the liabilities of the acquiree are measured at fair values, and

    (2) The acquirer recognizes net income of the acquiree only after the date of acquisition.

  c. Acquisition date determination:

    (1) The date on which the acquirer obtains control over the acquiree. Usually, the date on which the acquirer transfers the consideration, acquires the assets, and assumes the liabilities of the acquiree.

      (a) However, it is possible that the acquirer could obtain control either before or after the closing date when the consideration is transferred. In that case, the facts and circumstances should be examined to determine the date at which control was acquired.

4. Recognition and Measurement.

  a. Recognition and measurement of identifiable assets, liabilities and noncontrolling interest is the third step in a business combination.

  b. On the acquisition date, the identifiable assets acquired, the liabilities assumed, and any noncontrolling interest (previously referred to as minority interest) are measured at fair value. The acquirer also recognizes assets that were not previously recognized on the acquiree's books if the assets are identifiable.

    (1) An asset is an **identifiable asset** if it arises from a contractual or legal right, or if it is separable.

    (2) An asset is separable if it can be separated or divided from the entity and sold, transferred, licensed, rented, or exchanged.

  c. At the acquisition date, the acquirer must classify the assets acquired and liabilities assumed so that GAAP can be applied.

    (1) Examples of items that must be classified include trading, available-for-sale, and held-to-maturity securities, derivatives, and embedded derivative instruments.

    (2) Leases, however, are classified as either an operating or a capital lease based upon their contractual terms at the inception of the contracts.

      (a) Therefore, if the lease was a capital lease for the acquiree, then it is classified as a capital lease on the books of the acquirer.

      (b) Similarly, if the lease was an operating lease on the books of the acquiree, then the lease continues to be an operating lease on the books of the acquirer.

      (c) An exception to this rule occurs when a lease contract is modified. If a lease contract is modified at the date of acquisition, the new terms of the modified contract are used to classify the lease.

  d. On the date of acquisition, the acquirer should recognize any newly identified intangible assets of the acquiree that meet the contractual-legal or separability criteria. Examples of items that meet the contractual-legal or separability criteria include the following items:

    (1) Marketing-related intangibles, such as trademarks, trade names, service marks, certification marks, newspaper mastheads, internet domain names, and noncompetition agreements.

    (2) Customer-related intangibles, such as customer lists, order or production backlog, customer contracts, and noncontractual customer relationships.

    (3) Artistic-related intangible assets, such as plays, operas, ballets, books, magazines, newspapers, literary works, musical works, pictures, photographs, videos, motion pictures, films, music videos, and television programs.

    (4) Contract-based intangibles, such as licensing, royalty, advertising, construction, management, lease, or franchise agreements. Other examples include construction permits, operating and broadcast rights, supply or service contracts, employment contracts, and drilling, water, air, and timber cutting rights.

    (5) Technology-based intangibles, such as patented technology, computer software and mask works, unpatented technology, and databases. Another example is trade secrets, such as secret formulas, processes, and recipes.

    (6) Items that do not meet the contractual-legal or separability criteria may not be recognized as assets.

      (a) Nonqualifying assets include the value of an assembled workforce, intellectual capital, and potential contracts.

5. Recognize goodwill

  a. Goodwill recognition is the fourth step in a business combination.

  b. At the date of acquisition, the assets and liabilities of the acquiree are measured at fair value.

(1) If the acquirer has previously held equity interests in the acquiree, these shares are revalued to fair value at acquisition date.

(2) Any noncontrolling interest is also valued at fair value at acquisition date.

(3) After the assets, liabilities, previously held interests, and noncontrolling interest are valued at fair value, the goodwill or gain from a bargain purchase is calculated, as illustrated below.

> Fair value of consideration transferred (cost to the acquirer)
> Plus: Fair value of previously held equity interests in acquiree
> Plus: Fair value of noncontrolling interest
> Less: Fair value of net identifiable assets
> Goodwill or gain from bargain purchase

(4) If the fair value of net identifiable assets is less than the aggregate of the consideration transferred, plus the acquisition date fair value of previously held interests, plus the fair value of noncontrolling interest, goodwill is recognized.

    (a) **Goodwill** is defined as "an asset representing the future economic benefits that arises from other assets acquired in a business combination that are not individually identified and separately recognized."

    (b) Although an intangible asset is defined as an asset that lacks physical substance for purposes of business combinations, goodwill is not considered an intangible asset. Instead, goodwill is classified separately, and the accounting rules for goodwill apply.

(5) If the fair value of net identifiable assets exceeds the aggregate of the consideration transferred, plus the acquisition date fair value of previously held interests, plus the fair value of the noncontrolling interest, then a bargain purchase occurs. A gain is recognized by the acquirer in the current period for the bargain purchase.

  c. The consideration transferred is measured at fair value at the acquisition date.

    (1) Consideration may include assets transferred, liabilities incurred, and equity interests issued by the acquirer.

    (2) If the fair values of the acquirer's assets or liabilities transferred are different from their carrying values, the acquirer should recognize a gain or loss on the assets transferred in earnings of the current period.

    (3) However, if the acquirer retains control of the transferred assets or liabilities, then the assets and liabilities are measured at their carrying amounts immediately before the acquisition date.

    (4) If the acquirer transfers contingent consideration, then the fair value of the contingent consideration is included as part of the consideration paid for the acquiree. Measurement of contingent consideration is discussed later in this module.

6. Step acquisition.

  a. Sometimes the acquirer obtains control through a step acquisition, wherein the acquirer invests in less than 50% of the voting shares of the acquiree, and at a later date, acquires enough shares to obtain voting control.

  b. Depending upon the percentage of ownership previously acquired, the acquirer may have accounted for shares of stock using the cost adjusted for fair value method, the equity method, or the fair value option.

  c. In a step acquisition, the acquisition date fair value of the previously held shares is also included in the acquisition cost. If the fair values of the previously held shares at the acquisition date are not equal to their carrying values, a gain or loss is recognized in the current period.

  d. If the acquirer had previously recognized any changes in fair value of the securities in other comprehensive income, then the amounts recognized in other comprehensive income should be reclassified and included as a gain or loss on the income statement in the current period.

7. Noncontrolling interest.

  a. Noncontrolling interest is measured by using the active market prices on the acquisition date for the equity shares not held by the acquirer.

> **NOTE:** The fair values of the acquirer's investment and the noncontrolling interest may not be the same on a per-share basis.

    (1) This difference can be attributed to the acquirer paying a premium to obtain control of the acquiree, or to a noncontrolling interest discount due to lack of control.

    (2) This difference should be ignored, and the noncontrolling interest should be valued by multiplying the active market price on the acquisition date times the number of shares held by the noncontrolling parties.

  b. Noncontrolling interest should be classified as equity in the statement of financial position of the consolidated financial statements. On the statement of earnings, consolidated net income is adjusted to disclose the net income or loss attributed to the noncontrolling interest. Comprehensive income is also adjusted to include the comprehensive income attributed to the noncontrolling interest.

8. Acquisition-related costs

 a. Acquisition-related costs for a business acquisition are normally treated as an expense in the period in which the costs are incurred or the services are received.
 b. Acquisition-related costs may include finder's, advisory, legal, accounting, valuation, consulting and other professional fees. They also include general administrative costs.
 c. Although the costs of registering and issuing debt and equity securities are considered part of acquisition costs, these costs are not expensed in the period of the acquisition, but are recognized in accordance with other GAAP.

 (1) Costs of registering and issuing common stock are normally netted against the proceeds of the stock and reduce the paid-in capital in excess of par account.
 (2) Bond issue costs are treated as a deferred charge and amortized on a straight-line basis over the life of the bond.

C. Consolidated Financial Statements

1. An acquisition of more than 50% of the outstanding voting stock will normally result in control and require the preparation of consolidated financial statements.

 a. The complete consolidation process is presented in the next section of this module.
 b. The investment account will be eliminated in the consolidation working papers and will be replaced with the specific assets and liabilities of the investee corporation.
 c. Consolidation is generally required for investments of more than 50% of the outstanding voting stock except when the control is not held by the majority owner, Examples of noncontrol include

 (1) The investee is in legal reorganization or bankruptcy.
 (2) The investee operates in a foreign country, which has severe restrictions on the financial transactions of its business firms or is subject to material political or economic uncertainty that casts significant doubt on the parent's ability to control the subsidiary.

 (a) In these limited cases, the investment will be reported as a long-term investment in an unconsolidated subsidiary on the investor's balance sheet.
 (b) The cost method is used unless the acquirer qualifies to use the equity method or elects to use the fair value option for reporting financial assets. As you recall from Module 16 on investments, the equity method is used in cases where the investor has significant influence over the investee.

2. Variable interest entities

 a. In certain instances, control over an entity may be achieved through arrangements that do not involve ownership or voting interests.
 b. Special rules apply to **variable interest entities** (VIEs, also referred to as special-purpose entities) in which control is achieved based on contractual, ownership, or other pecuniary interests that change with changes in the entity's net asset value.
 c. The initial determination of whether a legal entity is a VIE is made on the date the reporting entity becomes involved with the legal entity.

 (1) The status of a VIE is reconsidered if certain events occur such as a change in the legal entity's contractual arrangements or characteristics, a change in the equity investment by investors, or changes in facts and circumstances that change the power from voting rights or similar rights to direct the activities of the VIE.

 d. If an entity has a controlling financial interest in the VIE, the entity is considered **the primary beneficiary** of the VIE. A primary beneficiary is required to consolidate the VIE in its financial statements.

 (1) An entity has a controlling financial interest in a VIE if both of the following conditions exist:

 (a) The entity has the power to direct the activities of a VIE that most significantly impact the VIE's economic performance.
 (b) The entity has the obligation to absorb losses of the VIE that could potentially be significant to the VIE, or has the right to receive benefits from the VIE that could potentially be significant to the VIE.

 (2) A qualitative approach is used to determine if the entity has the power to control the VIE.

 (a) If power is shared among unrelated parties and consent of the other parties is required to direct the activities of the VIE, then no one party has the power to direct the activities of the VIE. In such cases where power is shared, none of the parties is required to consolidate the VIE.

1] If power is shared by unrelated parties and the nature of the activities directed by each party is not the same, then the entities must identify which party has the power to direct the activities that most significantly affect the VIE's economic performance.

2] If the party that has the power to direct the economic performance is also obligated to absorb the losses or receive the benefits, that entity is the primary beneficiary and must consolidate the VIE.

(b) An entity should determine whether it is the primary beneficiary on the date it becomes involved with a VIE. The reporting entity must also reassess whether it is the primary beneficiary throughout its involvement with the VIE.

(c) Kick-out rights are the ability to remove the reporting entity who has the power to direct the activities that most significantly impact the VIE's economic performance.

(d) Participating rights are the ability to block the actions of a reporting entity with power to direct the activities of the VIE.

(e) Kick-out and participating rights will not affect an entity from being considered the primary beneficiary unless those rights are held by a single equity holder who has the ability to exercise those rights.

e. Additional disclosures are required for entities that have interests in VIEs.

(1) The primary beneficiary that is required to consolidate the VIE must present separately on the face of the statement of financial position the assets of the VIE that can be used only to settle obligations of the consolidated VIE and the liabilities of the VIE for which creditors do not have recourse to the general credit of the primary beneficiary. Disclosures in the notes to financial statements by the primary beneficiary that consolidates the VIE are

(a) The carrying amounts and classification of the VIE's assets and liabilities that are consolidated, as well as qualitative information about the assets and restrictions on the assets.

(b) Lack of recourse if creditors have no recourse to the general credit of the primary beneficiary.

(c) Terms of arrangements.

(2) A reporting entity that is not the primary beneficiary is not required to consolidate the VIE, but must disclose the following:

(a) The carrying amounts and classification of the assets and liabilities that relate to the reporting entity's variable interest in the VIE.

(b) The maximum exposure to loss from involvement with the VIE.

(c) A comparison of the carrying amounts of assets and liabilities and the maximum exposure to loss, together with supporting information explaining the differences in amounts.

(d) Information about any liquidity arrangements, guarantees, or other commitments by third parties that may affect the fair value or risk of the interest in the VIE.

(e) If applicable, significant factors considered and judgments in determining that the power to direct the activities of the VIE is shared.

(3) All entities with interests in VIEs (both primary beneficiaries and other holders of variable interests in VIEs that are not required to consolidate) must disclose the following:

(a) The methodology for determining whether the reporting entity is the primary beneficiary of a VIE.

(b) If facts and circumstances regarding consolidation of VIE have changed.

(c) Whether the reporting entity has provided financial or other support to the VIE that was not contractually required during the periods presented.

(d) Qualitative and quantitative information about the reporting entity's involvement with the VIE, including nature, purpose, size, and activities of the VIE, and how the VIE is financed.

3. The concept of consolidated statements is that the resources of two or more companies are under the control of the parent company.

a. Consolidated statements are prepared as if the group of legal entities were one economic entity group.

b. Consolidated statements are presumed to be more meaningful for management, owners, and creditors of the acquirer company and they are required for fair presentation of the financially-related companies.

c. Individual company statements should continue to be prepared for noncontrolling ownership and creditors of the acquiree companies.

4. The accounting principles used to record and report events for a single legal entity are also applicable to a consolidated economic entity of two or more companies.

a. The concept of the reporting entity is expanded to include more than one company, but all other accounting principles are applied in the same way as for an individual company.

    b. The consolidation process eliminates reciprocal items that are shown on both the acquirer's and acquiree's books. These eliminations are necessary to avoid double counting the same items, which would misstate the financials of the combined economic entity.

5. Consolidated financial statements are prepared from worksheets, which begin with the trial balances of the acquirer and acquiree companies.

    a. Eliminating worksheet entries are made to reflect the two separate companies' results of operations and financial position as one combined economic entity.

    b. The entire consolidation process takes place **only on a worksheet;** no consolidation elimination entries are ever recorded on either the parent's or subsidiary's books.

6. Consolidated balance sheets are typically prepared at the date of combination to determine the initial financial position of the economic entity.

    a. Any intercompany accounts between the acquirer and acquiree must be eliminated against each other.

    b. The "Investment in acquiree's stock" account from the acquirer's books will be eliminated against the reciprocal accounts of the acquiree's stockholders' equity.

    c. The remaining accounts are then combined to prepare the consolidated balance sheet.

7. The preparation of consolidated statements after the date of combination becomes a little more complex because the acquirer and acquiree income statements may include reciprocal intercompany accounts, which must be eliminated.

8. The next section of the module will present an example of the preparation of a consolidated balance sheet at the date of combination for the acquisition method. You should carefully review the date of combination consolidation process before proceeding to the preparation of consolidation statements subsequent to combination.

> **NOW REVIEW MULTIPLE-CHOICE QUESTIONS 1 THROUGH 15**

D. Pelican Corp. and Swan Corp.—Acquisition of Swan, 100% Acquisition

    A presentation of the date of combination entries for the acquisition method will be made first for a 100% acquisition. This problem will be expanded to present the method for preparing the income statement, statement of retained earnings, and balance sheet at year-end for a 100% acquisition. The example will then be modified to apply the accounting for less than a 100% acquisition with noncontrolling interest.

EXAMPLE

On January 1, year 2, Pelican Corporation acquired Swan Corporation by acquiring all of Swan's outstanding stock by issuing 16,000 shares of Pelican $1 par value common stock, with a fair value of $10 per share. The balance sheets for Pelican and Swan immediately before the acquisition are shown below.

Pelican Company and Swan Company
BALANCE SHEETS 1/1/Y2
(Immediately before combination)

Assets	Pelican Corp.	Swan Corp.
Cash	$ 30,000	$ 24,000
Accounts receivable	35,000	9,000
Inventories	23,000	16,000
Equipment	240,000	60,000
Accumulated depreciation	(40,000)	(10,000)
Patents	--	12,000
Total assets	$288,000	$111,000

Liabilities and Equity		
Accounts payable	$ 6,000	$ 7,000
Bonds payable	80,000	--
Capital stock ($10 par)	120,000	60,000
Additional paid-in capital	20,000	10,000
Retained earnings	62,000	34,000
Total liabilities and equity	$288,000	$111,000

Additional Information:

1. At the time of the acquisition, it was determined that Swan had a client list with a fair value of $5,000, and a trademark with a fair value of $14,000. The client list has a remaining life of five years, and the trademark has a remaining life of ten years.

2. The fair values of Swan's assets and liabilities on the date of the acquisition are shown below.
3. The existing equipment of Swan will be depreciated over its remaining useful life of four years.
4. The patent on Swan's books will be depreciated over a remaining life of six years.

Swan Corporation
BALANCE SHEETS 1/1/Y2
(Immediately before combination)

Assets	Book value	Fair value	Difference between BV and FV
Cash	$ 24,000	24,000	$ --
Accounts receivable	9,000	9,000	--
Inventories	16,000	17,000	1,000
Equipment	60,000	72,000	12,000
Less: Accumulated depreciation	(10,000)	(12,000)*	(2,000)
Patents	12,000	15,000	3,000
Client list	--	5,000	5,000
Trademark	--	14,000	14,000
Total assets	$111,000	$144,000	

Liabilities and Equity			
Accounts payable	$ 7,000	$ 7,000	--
Bonds payable	--	--	
Capital stock ($10 par)	60,000		
Additional paid-in capital	10,000		
Retained earnings	34,000		
Total liabilities and equity	$111,000		

* When the asset is revalued and increased by 20% ($60,000 × 20% = $12,000), there is also a corresponding increase in the accumulated depreciation account ($10,000 × 20% =$2,000).

> **NOTE:** Although there are no previously held interests or noncontrolling interest in this example, these items are shown in the following formulas for completeness.

The entry to record the investment in Swan is

Investment in Swan	160,000	
Common stock (Pelican)		16,000
Additional paid-in capital		144,000

To record the issuance of 16,000 shares of Pelican's $1 par value stock with a fair value of $10 per share to acquire Swan Corp.

Goodwill should be calculated using a three-step process.

Step 1: Compute the difference between (1) the aggregate of acquisition cost, the fair value of previously held shares, and the fair value of noncontrolling interest and (2) the book value of Swan's net assets:

Acquisition cost	$160,000
Plus: Fair value of previously held shares	--
Plus: Fair value of noncontrolling interest	--
Less: Book value of Swan ($111,000 assets – $7,000 liabilities)	104,000
Differential	$ 56,000

This differential can be attributed to assets written up to fair value, newly identified intangible assets, and goodwill.

Step 2: Compute the fair value of net identifiable assets.

Book value ($111,000 assets – $7,000 liability)	$104,000
Plus: Asset write-ups ($1,000 + $12,000 – $2,000 + $3,000)	14,000
Plus: Newly identified Intangibles ($5,000 + $14,000)	19,000
Fair value of net identifiable assets	$137,000

Step 3: Compute goodwill.

Acquisition cost	$160,000
Plus: Fair value of previously held shares	--
Plus: Fair value of noncontrolling interest	--
Less: Fair value of net identifiable assets	(137,000)
Goodwill	$ 23,000

If the cost of acquisition is greater than the fair value of the net identifiable assets acquired, then goodwill is recorded as a noncurrent asset on the balance sheet. In this situation, Pelican would report goodwill of $23,000 on the date of acquisition. After the date of acquisition, goodwill is tested for impairment each year.

Assuming Pelican paid $120,000 for Swan

Acquisition cost	$120,000
Plus: Fair value of previously held shares	--
Plus: Fair value of noncontrolling interest	--
Less: Fair value, net identifiable assets	(137,000)
Bargain Purchase	$ (17,000)

The $17,000 bargain purchase would be recorded as a gain in the current period on Pelican's income statement.

E. Pelican Corp. and Swan Corp.—Date of Combination Consolidated Balance Sheet—Acquisition Method (100% Acquisition)

At the date of acquisition, a consolidated balance sheet is prepared. This section continues our example of Pelican's 100% acquisition of Swan. The entry below is the entry recorded on Pelican's books at the date of acquisition.

EXAMPLE

1. Investment Entry on Pelican Company's Books

The entry to record the 100% acquisition on Pelican Company's books was

Investment in stock of Swan Corp.	160,000	
Common stock		16,000
Additional paid-in capital		144,000

To record the issuance of 16,000 shares of Pelican's $1 par value stock with a fair value of $10 per share to acquire 100% of Swan Corp.

Although common stock is used for the consideration in our example, Pelican could have used debentures, cash, or any other form of consideration acceptable to Swan's stockholders to make the business acquisition.

The following is the worksheet to prepare the consolidated balance sheet immediately after Pelican's acquisition of Swan. Notice that the balance sheet of Pelican has changed from the balance sheet issued prior to the acquisition of Swan. The investment account increased Pelican's assets by $160,000, the acquisition cost of the investment. Also the capital stock and additional paid-in capital account of Pelican (the acquirer) have increased for the 16,000 shares of $1 par value Pelican stock issued. Common stock increased $16,000 ($1 par × 16,000 shares), and additional paid-in capital increased by $144,000 ($9 × 16,000 shares).

PELICAN CORP. AND SWAN CORP.—CONSOLIDATED WORKING PAPERS
For Date of Acquisition—1/1/Y2
Acquisition Method—100% Acquisition

	Pelican	Swan	Adjustments and eliminations Debit		Adjustments and eliminations Credit		Consolidated balances
Balance sheet 1/1/Y2							
Cash	30,000	24,000					54,000
Accounts receivable	35,000	9,000					44,000
Inventories	23,000	16,000	(b)	1,000			40,000
Equipment	240,000	60,000	(b)	12,000			312,000
Accumulated depreciation	(40,000)	(10,000)			(b)	2,000	(52,000)
Investment in stock of Swan	160,000				(a)	160,000	--
Difference between cost and book value			(a)	56,000	(b)	56,000	--
Goodwill	--		(b)	23,000			23,000
Patents	--	12,000	(b)	3,000			15,000
Client list	--		(b)	5,000			5,000
Trademark	--		(b)	14,000			14,000
Total assets	448,000	111,000					455,000
Accounts payable	6,000	7,000					13,000
Bonds payable	80,000	--					80,000
Capital stock	136,000	60,000	(a)	60,000			136,000
Additional paid-in capital	164,000	10,000	(a)	10,000			164,000
Retained earnings	62,000	34,000	(a)	34,000			62,000
Total liabilities and equity	448,000	111,000		218,000		218,000	455,000

2. **Difference between Acquisition Cost and Book Value of Acquiree**
   To prepare the consolidated balance sheet, calculate the difference between (1) the aggregate of the acquisition cost, plus the fair value of previously held shares, plus the fair value of noncontrolling interest, and (2) the acquirer's interest in the net book value of the assets of the acquiree. This difference can be attributed to undervalued assets, newly identified intangible assets, and goodwill as shown below:

Swan Corp.

Undervalued assets	
Inventory	1,000
Equipment	12,000
Accumulated depreciation	(2,000)
Patents	3,000
New identifiable intangible assets	
Client list	5,000
Trademark	14,000
Goodwill	<u>23,000</u>
Total undervalued assets, new intangible assets, and goodwill	<u>56,000</u>

The difference of $56,000 will be accounted for by preparing consolidated working paper entries to eliminate the acquiree's equity accounts, revalue the acquiree's existing assets to fair values, record any newly identified intangible assets, and record goodwill. Note that the book value of the acquiree can also be calculated by adding the equity accounts of the acquiree at date of acquisition. A reconciliation of the cost to acquire Swan and the book value of Swan can also be calculated by using the equity accounts of Swan as shown below.

Acquisition cost		$ 160,000
Plus: Fair value of previously held shares		
Plus: Fair value of noncontrolling interest		
Less: Book value at date of acquisition		
Swan Corp.'s:		
Capital stock	(60,000)	
Additional paid-in capital	(10,000)	
Retained earnings	(34,000)	
Total		(104,000)
Differential		$ 56,000

Again, this difference is due to undervalued assets, newly identified intangible assets, and unrecorded goodwill.

3. **Completing the Consolidated Trial Balance Worksheet**

The worksheet on the date of acquisition is completed in two steps.

Step 1: Eliminate the acquiree's equity accounts, the acquirer's investment account, and establish the differential (the difference between acquisition cost and the book value of the acquiree's net assets).

Step 2: Eliminate the differential account and record asset write-ups to fair value, new identifiable intangible assets, and goodwill.

The elimination entries are then posted to the worksheet, and the consolidated worksheet is totaled.

The Step 1 entry is to eliminate the acquiree's equity account, eliminate the investment account on the acquirer's books, and record the differential as shown below.

(a)	Capital stock—B Co.	60,000	
	Additional paid-in capital—Swan Corp.	10,000	
	Retained earnings—Swan Corp.	34,000	
	Differential	56,000	
	Investment in stock of Swan Corp.		160,000

> **NOTE:** Swan's stockholders' equity accounts are eliminated. Also an account called "Differential" is debited in the workpaper entry. The differential account is a temporary account to record the difference between the cost of the investment in Swan on the Pelican's books and the book value of Pelican's 100% interest in Swan.

The next step is to allocate the differential to the specific accounts by making the following workpaper entry:

(b)	Inventories	1,000	
	Equipment	12,000	
	Patents	3,000	
	Goodwill	23,000	
	Client list	5,000	
	Trademark	14,000	
	Accumulated depreciation		2,000
	Differential		56,000

This entry reflects the allocations prepared in Step 2 and recognizes the Pelican's revaluation of assets to fair value, the newly identified intangible assets, and goodwill.

Our example does not include any other intercompany accounts as of the date of combination. If any existed, they would be eliminated to fairly present the consolidated entity. Examples of other reciprocal accounts will be shown later in this module.

When the consolidated worksheet is finished, check the worksheet for possible errors. First, you should reduce the investment in Swan's account to zero. If the entries for write-up of existing assets to fair value, recording newly identified intangible assets, and recording goodwill are done accurately, the differential account will also be zero. The common stock account and additional paid-in capital account in the consolidated worksheet should reflect only the balances of the acquirer's accounts. At date of acquisition, the retained earnings account will only reflect the balance of the acquirer's account. Finally, check to see that the acquiree's equity accounts are eliminated.

NOW REVIEW MULTIPLE-CHOICE QUESTION 16 THROUGH 25

F. Consolidated Financial Statements Subsequent to Acquisition

1. The concepts used to prepare subsequent consolidated statements are essentially the same as those used to prepare the consolidated balance sheet at the acquisition date.

   a. The income statement and statement of retained earnings are added to reflect the results of operations since the acquisition date.
   b. Furthermore, some additional reciprocal accounts may have to be eliminated because of intercompany transactions between the acquirer and the acquiree.
   c. Please note that the financial statements of a consolidated entity are prepared using the same accounting principles that would be employed by a single, unconsolidated enterprise. The only difference is that some reciprocal accounts appearing on both companies' books must be eliminated against each other before the two corporations may be presented as one consolidated economic entity.
   d. Your review should concentrate on the accounts and amounts appearing on the consolidated statements (amounts in the last column of the worksheet). This "end-result" focus will help provide the understanding of why certain elimination entries are necessary.

2. An expanded version of the consolidated worksheet is necessary if the income statement and retained earnings statement must also be prepared.

   a. A comprehensive format often called "the three statement layout" is an integrated vertical array of the income statement, the retained earnings statement, and the balance sheet.
   b. The net income of the period is carried to the retained earnings statement and the ending retained earnings are carried down to the balance sheet.
   c. If you are required to prepare just the consolidated balance sheet, then eliminating entries involving nominal accounts (income statement accounts and the "Dividends declared" account) would be made directly against the ending balance of retained earnings presented on the balance sheet.

3. The following discussion assumes the acquirer is using the partial equity method to account for the majority investment.

   a. Some firms may use the cost method during the period to account for investment income because it requires fewer book adjustments to the investment account.

      (1) In cases where the cost method is used during the period, one approach is to adjust the investment and investment income accounts to the equity method through an entry on the workpaper and the consolidation process may then be continued.
      (2) Assuming that an income statement and retained earnings statement are being prepared in addition to the balance sheet, the general form of this restatement from cost to equity entry is made on the workpapers.

Dividend income (for income recognized using cost method)	xx	
Investment in acquiree (% of undistributed income of sub)	xx	
Equity in subsidiary's income (for income recognized using equity method)		xx

      (3) Additional workpaper restatement entries would be required to recognize the equity income in prior periods if the investment were owned for more than one period and to recognize the amortizations of any differential for all periods the investment was held. After these entries are made, the investment and equity in the acquiree's income accounts would be stated on the equity basis and the consolidation process may be continued.

   > **NOTE:** The formal consolidated statements will be the same regardless of the method used by the acquirer to account for the investment on its books.

   b. The concept of measurement used in the preparation of the consolidated statements is equivalent to the full equity method and the elimination process will result in statements presented under that concept. Regardless of which method was used to initially record the investment, when the consolidated worksheet is finished, the investment in acquiree must be zero.

NOW REVIEW MULTIPLE-CHOICE QUESTIONS 26 THROUGH 41

G. Intercompany Transactions and Profit Confirmations

1. Three general types of intercompany transactions may occur between the acquirer and acquiree companies:

    a. Intercompany sales of merchandise,
    b. Transactions in fixed assets, and
    c. Intercompany debt/equity transactions.

      (1) Intercompany transactions require special handling because the profit or loss from these events must be properly presented on the consolidated financial statements.
      (2) These events may generate "unrealized profit" (also referred to as unconfirmed profit) which is a profit or gain shown in the trial balance from one of the company's books that should not be shown in the consolidated financial statements.
      (3) Intercompany bond transactions may require recognition of a gain or loss on the consolidated financials, which is not in the trial balances of either the acquirer or acquiree companies.

2. **Intercompany Inventory Transactions**

    a. Unrealized profit in ending inventory arises through intercompany sales above cost that are not resold to third parties prior to year-end.

      (1) The profit on the selling corporation's books is overstated, because an arm's-length transaction has not yet taken place.
      (2) The inventory is overstated on the purchaser's books for the amount of the unrealized intercompany profit.
      (3) An exhibit of the relationships is shown below.

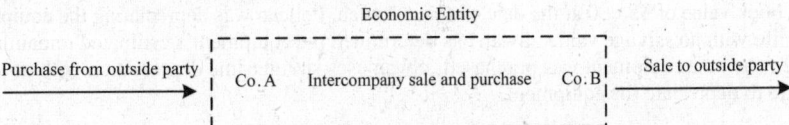

      (a) Companies A and B are two separate legal entities and will each record the sale or purchase of goods. From a consolidated or economic entity viewpoint, however, the intercompany transaction is a transfer of assets which cannot result in revenue recognition until these goods are sold to a third party.
      (b) Assuming a sale from Company A to Company B (a "downstream" intercompany sale), the sale income of Company A cannot be recognized until the goods are sold to third parties by Company B.
      (c) In addition, the ending inventory of Company B is overstated by the amount of profit in the inventory acquired from Company A.
      (d) Once intercompany sales have been sold to third parties, the earning process has been verified by an arm's-length transaction with third parties. Thus, recognition of previously unrecognized profit may occur at that time.

3. **Intercompany Fixed Asset Transactions**

    a. Unrealized profits on fixed assets arise through intercompany sales of fixed assets above undepreciated cost. From a consolidated viewpoint, the transaction represents the internal transfer of assets and no gain (loss) should be recognized. Any gain (loss) must be eliminated and the carrying value of the transferred asset must be returned to its initial book value basis.

      (1) In subsequent periods, in the case of an intercompany gain, depreciation expense is overstated, because an overvalued asset is being depreciated on the books of the company showing the asset. This overstatement of depreciation must also be eliminated in the consolidation process. In essence, the company that acquired the intercompany asset is including the intercompany gain (loss) in its depreciation expense.

4. **Intercompany Bond Transactions**

    a. When one consolidated company buys bonds of another consolidated company, there are several reciprocal items to eliminate: investment in bonds and bonds payable, interest income and interest expense, and interest payable and interest receivable. Intercompany gains and losses **cannot** arise from direct intercompany bond purchases. The book value would be the same on both books and the interest accounts would be reciprocal.

The effective interest method for debt transactions between acquirer and acquiree companies is not required. Straight-line amortizations of premiums or discounts are sometimes used in these instances.

b. Gains and losses on intercompany bond holdings occur when

   (1) Already outstanding bonds of the acquirer (acquiree) are purchased by an acquiree (acquirer),
   (2) From a third party, and
   (3) For an amount different from the carrying value of the issuer.

c. From a consolidated viewpoint, these bonds are viewed as retired. However, the bonds are still recorded as liabilities on the issuer's separate books and as investment in bonds on the purchasing corporation's books.

   (1) The eliminating entry is to recognize the imputed gain (loss) on the consolidated "retirement of debt" in the year of intercompany bond purchase. Gains on early extinguishment of debt are no longer routinely considered extraordinary.

H. Pelican Corp. and Swan Corp. — Subsequent Consolidated Financial Statements

The following information extends the basic example of Pelican and Swan begun earlier in this module. The example illustrates the major consolidation concepts and procedures most likely to appear on the CPA exam. The following intercompany transactions occurred during year 2.

EXAMPLE

During year 2, Pelican sold merchandise to Swan for $30,000. The merchandise originally cost Pelican $24,000. During year 2, Swan sold 40% of the merchandise purchased from Pelican to third parties for $15,000. On December 31, year 2, Swan's inventory included 60% of the merchandise purchased from Pelican.

During year 2, Swan sold merchandise to Pelican for $16,000. The cost of goods sold to Swan was $11,000. During year 2, Pelican subsequently sold all of these goods to an unrelated third party for $23,000.

Swan reduced its intercompany account payable to Pelican to a balance of $3,000 as of December 31, year 2, by making a payment of $1,000 on December 30. This $1,000 payment was still in transit on December 31, year 2.

On January 2, year 2, Swan acquired equipment from Pelican for $8,000. The equipment was originally purchased by Pelican for $12,000 and had a book value of $5,000 at the date of sale to Swan. Pelican was depreciating the equipment over an estimated ten-year useful life with no salvage value. Swan has determined the equipment's estimated remaining life is four years as of January 2, year 2, when the equipment was purchased. Swan uses straight-line depreciation with no salvage value and a four-year remaining life to depreciate the equipment.

On December 31, year 2, Swan purchased for $39,000, 50% of the $80,000 of outstanding bonds issued by Pelican to third parties. The bonds mature on December 31, year 7, and were originally issued at par. The bonds pay interest annually on December 31 of each year and the interest was paid to the prior investor immediately before Swan's purchase of the bonds.

The consolidated worksheet for the preparation of consolidated financial statements as of December 31, year 2, is presented on the next page.

To begin the problem, the investment account balance at the statement date should be reconciled to ensure the acquirer made the proper entries under the method of accounting used to account for the investment.

NOTE: Pelican is using the partial equity method, without amortizations. The amortizations of the excess of cost over book value will be recognized only on the worksheets. This method is the one typically followed on the CPA exam; however, be sure you determine the method used in the exam problem—do not assume!

The "proof" of the investment account of Pelican is

	Investment in Stock of Swan Corp.		
Original cost	160,000		
100% of Swan Corp.'s Income	38,000	15,000	100% of Swan Corp.'s dividends declared
Bal. 12/31/Y2	183,000		

Any errors will require correcting entries before the consolidation process is continued. Correcting entries will be posted to the books of the appropriate company; eliminating entries are **not** posted to either company's books. Eliminating entries are only recorded on the worksheet in order to prepare consolidated financial statements.

The difference between the investment cost and the book value of the net assets acquired was determined and allocated in the preparation of the date of acquisition consolidated statements presented earlier in this section. For purposes of brevity, that process will not be duplicated here since the same computations are used in preparing financial statements for as long as the investment is owned.

PELICAN CORP. AND SWAN CORP. CONSOLIDATED WORKING PAPERS
Year Ended December 31, Year 2

Acquisition Method—100% Acquisition
Subsequent, partial equity

	Pelican	Swan	Adjustments and eliminations Debit				Credit		Consolidated balances
Income statement for year ended 12/31/Y2									
Sales	800,000	400,000	(c)	30,000					1,154,000
			(d)	16,000					
Cost of sales	580,000	250,000				26,400	(c)		787,600
						16,000	(d)		
Gross margin	220,000	150,000							366,400
Depreciation and amort. expense	28,000	14,000	(k)	5,400		800	(f)		46,600
Other operating expenses	115,000	98,000							213,000
Net income from operations	77,000	38,000							106,800
Gain on sale of equipment	3,000		(e)	3,000					--
Gain on bonds						1,000	(g)		1,000
Income from acquiree	38,000		(h)	38,000					--
Net income	118,000	38,000		92,400		44,200			107,800
Statement of retained earnings for year ended 12/31/Y2									
1/1/Y2 Retained earnings									
Pelican Corp.	62,000								62,000
Swan Corp.		34,000	(i)	34,000					--
Add net income (from above)	118,000	38,000		92,400		44,200			107,800
Total	180,000	72,000							169,800
Deduct dividends	(26,000)	(15,000)				15,000	(h)		(26,000)
Balance December 31, year 2	154,000	57,000		126,400		59,200			143,800
Balance sheet 12/31/Y2									
Cash	50,000	21,000	(a)	1,000					72,000
Accounts receivable (net)	42,000	8,000				1,000	(a)		46,000
						3,000	(b)		
Inventories	34,000	14,000	(j)	1,000		3,600	(c)		45,400
Equipment	290,000	68,000	(e)	4,000					374,000
			(j)	12,000					
Accumulated depreciation	(50,000)	(17,000)	(f)	800		7,000	(e)		(77,700)
						2,000	(k)		
						2,500	(j)		
Investment in stock of Swan Corp.	183,000					23,000	(i)		--
						160,000	(h)		
Differential			(i)	56,000		56,000	(j)		--
Goodwill			(j)	23,000					23,000
Investment in bonds of Pelican Corp.		39,000				39,000	(g)		--
Patents	--	12,000	(j)	3,000		500	(k)		14,500
Client list			(j)	5,000		1,000	(k)		4,000
Trademarks			(j)	14,000		1,400	(k)		12,600
Total assets	549,000	145,000							513,800
Accounts payable	15,000	18,000	(b)	3,000					30,000
Bonds payable	80,000	--	(g)	40,000					40,000
Capital stock	136,000	60,000	(i)	60,000					136,000
Additional paid-in capital	164,000	10,000	(i)	10,000					164,000
Retained earnings (from above)	154,000	57,000		126,400		59,200			143,800
Total liabilities and equity	549,000	145,000		359,200		359,200			513,800

The following adjusting and eliminating entries will be required to prepare consolidated financials as of December 31, year 2.

NOTE: A consolidated income statement is required and, therefore, the nominal accounts are still "open." The number or letter in parentheses to the left of the entry corresponds to the key used on the worksheet.

Step 1. Complete the transaction for any intercompany items in transit at the end of the year.

| (a) Cash | 1,000 | |
| Accounts receivable | | 1,000 |

This entry eliminates the cash in transit at year-end.

Step 2. Prepare the eliminating entries.

(b) Accounts payable   3,000
   Accounts receivable   3,000

This eliminates the remaining intercompany receivable/payable owed by Swan to Pelican. This eliminating entry is necessary to avoid overstating the consolidated entity's balance sheet. The receivable/payable is not extinguished and Swan must still transfer $3,000 to Pelican in the future.

(c) Sales   30,000
   Cost of goods sold   26,400
   Inventory   3,600

This eliminates the effects of the intercompany sale of merchandise by Pelican to Swan. When Swan purchased the inventory, Swan recorded the items in its inventory account at a cost of $30,000. Swan sold 40% of the goods to third parties for $15,000. Therefore, the revenue recognized for the period should be $15,000. Swan's cost of goods sold related to the sale to third parties was $12,000 (40% × $30,000). The remaining inventory, which is 60% of the amount purchased, is $18,000 (60% × $30,000). Although Swan has $18,000 of goods remaining in its ending inventory, the value of the inventory is overstated. A reconstruction of the entries for the sales, cost of goods sold, and inventory related to the intercompany sale is shown below.

	Pelican Corp.	Swan Corp.
Sales	$30,000	$15,000
Cost of goods sold	(24,000)	(12,000)
Gross profit	6,000	3,000
Inventory purchased	24,000	$30,000
Inventory sold	(24,000)	12,000
Ending inventory	--	18,000

Since 60% of the inventory remains, the original cost to Pelican for the remaining inventory is $14,400 (60% × $24,000). If 40% of the inventory has been sold, then the actual cost of the inventory sold should be $9,600 (40% × $24,000 [Pelican's cost]). Therefore, an adjusting entry must be made to eliminate the overstatement of sales, cost of goods sold, and inventory. Analyzing the calculations above, the sale made to third parties was $15,000. This is the only sale amount that should be reflected in the consolidated financial statements. Therefore, the $30,000 sale recorded by Pelican must be eliminated. The total cost of goods sold without eliminations is $36,000, but this amount must be reduced by $26,400 to $9,600 (40% × $24,000), which is the cost to Pelican. Inventory is currently stated at $18,000, but the actual cost (Pelican's cost) of the remaining inventory is $14,400 (60% × 24,000). Therefore, inventory must be reduced by the difference $3,600 ($18,000 – $14,400).

(d) Sales   16,000
   Cost of goods sold   16,000

This entry eliminates the effects of the sale of merchandise by Swan to Pelican. Since all of the goods were sold to third parties, there is no effect on ending inventory. The effects of the sale are illustrated below.

	Swan Corp.	Pelican Corp.
Sales	$16,000	$23,000
Cost of goods sold	(11,000)	(16,000)

An elimination entry must be made to prevent double counting sales and cost of goods sold by Swan to Pelican. The sale by Pelican to third parties for $23,000 must remain on the books. The cost of goods sold of $11,000, the original cost of purchasing the inventory, is the correct cost of goods sold. Therefore, the sale of $16,000 and the cost of goods sold of $16,000 must be eliminated.

(e) Equipment   4,000
  Gain on sale of equipment   3,000
   Accumulated depreciation   7,000

This entry eliminates the gain on the intercompany sale of the equipment, eliminates the overstatement of equipment, and restores accumulated depreciation to its balance as of the date of acquisition. To understand this entry, reconstruct the accounts for both Pelican and Swan.

Pelican's books		**Swan's books**
Historical cost	$12,000	Historical cost $8,000
Less: Accum. depr.	(7,000)	
Book value	$ 5,000	
Fair value received	$ 8,000	
Less: Book value	(5,000)	
Gain on sale of asset	$ 3,000	

If the intercompany sale had not occurred, Pelican would not have recorded a gain of $3,000. The asset would continue to be valued at historical cost of $12,000 (instead of $8,000) with accumulated depreciation of $7,000. Because Swan recorded the asset at $8,000 in its records, the equipment account is not recorded at cost. The entry adjusts the accounts to eliminate the effects of the intercompany transaction.

| (f) Accumulated depreciation | 800 | |
| Depreciation expense | | 800 |

This entry eliminates the excess depreciation taken on the equipment by Swan. The depreciation recorded when Pelican owned the equipment was $12,000 cost divided by ten years, or $1,200 per year. Swan acquired the asset at a cost of $8,000 and depreciates the asset over a four-year useful life. The depreciation recorded by Swan for the asset was $8,000 divided by 4 years, or $2,000 depreciation expense per year. The excess depreciation of $800 ($2,000 – $1,200) must be eliminated.

(g) Bonds payable	40,000	
Investment in bonds of Pelican Corp.		39,000
Gain on extinguishment of debt		1,000

This entry eliminates the book value of Pelican's debt against the bond investment account of Swan. To the consolidated entity, this transaction must be shown as a retirement of debt even though Pelican still has the outstanding intercompany debt to Swan. In future periods, Swan will amortize the discount, thereby bringing the investment account up to par value and a retained earnings account will be used in the eliminating entry instead of the gain account.

(h) Income from Swan	38,000	
Dividends declared—Swan Corp.		15,000
Investment in stock of Swan Corp.		23,000

This elimination entry adjusts the investment account back to its balance at the beginning of the period and also eliminates the income from subsidiary account and the dividends from subsidiary account.

(i) Capital stock—Swan Corp.	60,000	
Additional paid-in capital—Swan Corp.	10,000	
Retained earnings—Swan Corp.	34,000	
Differential	56,000	
Investment in stock of Swan Corp.		160,000

This entry eliminates Swan's stockholders' equity at the beginning of the year, 1/1/Y2.

NOTE: The changes **during** the year were eliminated in entry (f) above. The differential account reflects the excess of investment cost greater than the book value of the assets acquired on the date of acquisition. Notice that in a three-part worksheet with an income statement, statement of retained earnings, and balance sheet, the eliminating entry for beginning retained earnings is posted to the retained earnings section of the worksheet.

(j) Inventories	1,000	
Equipment	12,000	
Patents	3,000	
Goodwill	23,000	
Client List	5,000	
Trademark	14,000	
Accumulated depreciation		2,000
Differential		56,000

This entry allocates the differential (excess of investment cost over the book values of the assets acquired). Note that this entry is the same as the allocation entry made to prepare consolidated financial statements for January 1, year 2, the date of acquisition.

(k) Depreciation and amortization expense	5,400	
Accumulated depreciation		2,500
Patents		500
Client list		1,000
Trademarks		1,400

This records depreciation on the net write-up on the equipment to fair value of $10,000 (equipment less accumulated depreciation). The entry also amortizes the write-up on the patent to fair value, and amortizes the newly acquired identifiable intangible assets.

As indicated earlier in the problem, the existing equipment has a remaining useful life of four years, and the patent has a remaining useful life of six years. The depreciation and amortization expense entry of $5,400 is calculated by totaling the following amounts:

Depreciation expense on equipment write-up ($10,000/4 years)	$2,500
Patent amortization ($3,000/ 6 years)	500
Client list amortization ($5,000/ 5 years)	1,000
Trademark amortization ($14,000/11 years)	1,400
Total depreciation and amortization	$5,400

After all adjusting and eliminating entries are made and posted to the worksheet, the worksheet is totaled. Notice that the total adjustments to the income statement (debit of $92,400 and credit of $42,200) are posted as adjustments to net income in the retained earnings section of the worksheet. Notice that the total adjustments to retained earnings (debit of $126,400 and credit of $59,200) are carried down and posted as adjustments to retained earnings on the balance sheet. The consolidated balances are then totaled. In the consolidated balance column, notice that net income flows into the retained earnings part of the worksheet, and the ending balance in retained earnings flows to the balance sheet.

NOW REVIEW MULTIPLE-CHOICE QUESTIONS 42 THROUGH 54

I. Noncontrolling Interest

1. The acquirer often acquires less than 100% (but more than 50%) of the acquiree's outstanding stock. Under the acquisition method, the consolidated financial statements will include all of the assets, liabilities, revenues, and expenses of these less than wholly owned businesses.
2. The percentage of the stock not owned by the acquirer represents the noncontrolling interest's share of the fair values of the acquiree.
3. Noncontrolling interest is disclosed as a separate line item on the balance sheet in owner's equity. In addition, the portion of net income and comprehensive income attributed to the noncontrolling interest must be disclosed on the acquirer's income statement.
4. The following procedures apply to cases of less than 100% business acquisition.

   a. The equity accounts of the acquiree are eliminated in consolidation, and a noncontrolling interest is established for the fair value of the shares of stock held by the noncontrolling interest at the date of acquisition.
   b. The effects of intercompany transactions are eliminated.
   c. A portion of net income and dividends of the acquiree are allocated to the noncontrolling interest.

5. The financial statements are consolidated and combined with the parent including 100% of the acquiree's revenues and expenses after the date of acquisition. The noncontrolling interest's share of the acquiree's income is shown as a deduction on the consolidated income statement.
6. The following problem illustrates the worksheets for a company that acquires less than 100% of the acquiree.

EXAMPLE

On January 1, year 2, Pearl purchases 90% of Sapphire by issuing 15,000 shares of Pearl's $1 par value common stock with a fair value of $10 per share on the date of acquisition. At the date of acquisition Sapphire had 6,000 shares of stock outstanding with a value of $17.50 per share. Assume the book values of Sapphire's assets are equal to their fair values on the acquisition date. The financial statements at the date of acquisition for Pearl and Sapphire were as follows:

Pearl Corp. and Sapphire Corp.
BALANCE SHEETS 1/1/Y2
(Immediately before combination)

Assets	Pearl Corp.	Sapphire Corp.
Cash	$ 30,000	$ 24,000
Accounts receivable	35,000	9,000
Inventories	23,000	16,000
Equipment	240,000	60,000
Accumulated depreciation	(40,000)	(10,000)
Patents	--	12,000
Total assets	$288,000	$111,000
Liabilities and Equity		
Accounts payable	$ 6,000	$ 6,000
Bonds payable	80,000	--
Capital stock ($10 par)	120,000	60,000
Additional paid-in capital	20,000	10,000
Retained earnings	62,000	35,000
Total liabilities and equity	$288,000	$111,000

The entry to record the investment in Sapphire is

Investment in Sapphire	150,000	
Common stock (Pearl)		15,000
Additional paid-in capital		135,000

To calculate goodwill, we use the three-step process.

Step 1:   Compute the difference between (1) the acquisition cost, plus the fair value of previously acquired shares, plus the fair value of the noncontrolling interest, and (2) the book value of Sapphire's net assets. This is referred to as the differential or difference between fair value and book value.

Acquisition cost	$150,000	
Plus: Fair value of previously acquired shares*	--	
Plus: Fair value of noncontrolling interest	10,500	(600 shares × $17.50 fair value)
Less: Book value of Sapphire	105,000	($111,000 total assets – $6,000 liability)
Differential	$ 55,500	

* In this example, no shares of stock were previously acquired.

Step 2:   Compute the fair value of net identifiable assets.

Book value of Sapphire	$105,000
Plus: Asset write-ups*	--
Plus: Newly identified intangibles*	--
Fair value of net identifiable assets	$105,000

* In this case, the fair value of net identifiable asset is equal to the book value because there are no asset write-ups or newly identified intangibles.

Step 3:   Compute goodwill.

Acquisition cost	$150,000	
+ Fair value of previously acquired shares	--	
Plus: FV of noncontrolling interest	10,500	(600 shares × $17.50 per share)
Less: Fair value, net identifiable assets	(105,000)	
Goodwill	$ 55,500	

Goodwill is then allocated between the controlling interest and noncontrolling interest, as shown below.

	Pearl (90%)	Sapphire (10%)
FV of consideration given and noncontrolling interest shares	$150,000	$ 10,500
Less: FV of net identifiable assets ($105,000)	(94,500)	(10,500)
Goodwill allocation	$ 55,500	$ 0

Goodwill is allocated to the controlling interest and noncontrolling interest, so that it may be tested for impairment at the end of each reporting period. In this case, no goodwill is allocated to the noncontrolling interest because the fair value of the noncontrolling interest is equal to the noncontrolling interest's share of the fair value of net identifiable assets. If the noncontrolling interest's share of net identifiable assets were less than the fair value of the noncontrolling interest's shares, then a portion of the goodwill would be allocated to the noncontrolling interest. If the consideration paid by the acquirer plus the fair value of noncontrolling interest is less than the fair value of the net identifiable assets, then a **bargain purchase** occurs. The entire gain on the bargain purchase is recognized by the acquirer. No gain on the bargain purchase is recognized by the noncontrolling interest.

a. On the date of acquisition, the working paper eliminations for a less-than-100% acquisition are similar to a 100% acquisition. However, entries must be made for the noncontrolling interest. When there is a noncontrolling interest, the entries required at date of acquisition are modified slightly.

(1) Step 1:   Eliminate the acquiree's equity accounts and the acquirer's investment account, establish the differential (the difference between acquisition cost and the book value of the acquiree's net assets), and record the fair value of the noncontrolling interest.

(2) Step 2:   Eliminate the differential account, and record the asset write-ups to fair value, the new identifiable intangible assets, and goodwill.

EXAMPLE

Using the information from the prior example, the Step 1 entry is illustrated below.

(a) Capital stock—Sapphire Corp.	60,000		
Additional paid-in capital—Sapphire Corp.	10,000		
Retained earnings—Sapphire Corp.	35,000		
Differential	55,500		
Investment in stock of Sapphire Corp.		150,000	
Noncontrolling interest in Sapphire		10,500	

NOTE: 100% of Sapphire's stockholders' equity accounts are eliminated. Also, an account called "Differential" is debited in the workpaper entry.

Step 2 allocates the differential to the specific accounts. In this case, all of the differential is attributed to goodwill. The following entry is made to record goodwill:

(b)	Goodwill	55,500	
	Differential		55,500

These entries are then posted to the worksheet in order to prepare consolidated financial statements.

PEARL CORP. AND SAPPHIRE CORP.—CONSOLIDATED WORKING PAPERS
For Date of Acquisition—1/1/Y2

Acquisition Method—90% Acquisition

	Pearl	Sapphire	Adjustments and eliminations Debit		Adjustments and eliminations Credit		Noncontrolling interest	Consolidated balances
Balance sheet 1/1/Y2								
Cash	30,000	24,000						54,000
Accounts receivable	35,000	9,000						44,000
Inventories	23,000	16,000						39,000
Equipment	240,000	60,000						300,000
Accumulated depreciation	(40,000)	(10,000)						(50,000)
Investment in stock of Sapphire Corp.	150,000				(a)	150,000		--
Difference between cost and book value			(a)	55,500	(b)	55,500		--
Goodwill	--		(b)	55,500				55,500
Patents	--	12,000						12,000
Total assets	438,000	111,000						454,500
Accounts payable	6,000	6,000						12,000
Bonds payable	80,000	--						80,000
Capital stock	135,000	60,000	(a)	60,000				135,000
Additional paid-in capital	155,000	10,000	(a)	10,000				155,000
Noncontrolling interest in Sapphire						10,500	10,500	10,500
Retained earnings	62,000	35,000	(a)	35,000				62,000
Total liabilities and equity	438,000	111,000		216,000		216,000		454,500

When consolidated financial statements are prepared in subsequent years, the working paper eliminations are similar to the 100% acquisition method with a few exceptions. The next worksheet is a continuation of our 90% acquisition of Sapphire for the end of the year subsequent to acquisition. Assume the following additional facts for Pearl and Sapphire:

1. During year 2, Sapphire has $38,000 of net income and pays a dividend of $15,000.
2. Pearl sold $30,000 of goods to Sapphire. Pearl's cost of goods sold was $18,000. All of the goods remain in Sapphire's inventory.
3. At December 31, year 2, Sapphire owes Pearl $5,000 for a portion of the inventory purchased in 2.

Step 1. Eliminate the acquiree's equity accounts, write-up assets to fair value, recognize newly acquired intangibles, and record noncontrolling interests.

(a)	Capital stock—Sapphire Corp.	60,000	
	Additional paid-in capital—Sapphire Corp.	10,000	
	Retained earnings—Sapphire Corp.	35,000	
	Differential	55,500	
	Investment in stock of Sapphire Corp.		150,000
	Noncontrolling interest in Sapphire		10,500
(b)	Goodwill	55,500	
	Differential		55,500

Note that in this problem, the book value of assets equals the fair value, so no asset write-ups and no newly acquired intangible assets are recorded.

Step 2. Prepare the eliminating entries for intercompany transactions.

(c)	Accounts payable	5,000	
	Accounts receivable		5,000

This entry eliminates the remaining intercompany receivable/payable owed by Sapphire to Pearl.

(d)	Sales	30,000	
	Cost of goods sold		18,000
	Inventory		12,000

This entry eliminates the intercompany sale of merchandise by Pearl to Sapphire for $30,000, eliminates the cost of goods sold, and restores the inventory to its original historical cost. Also, note that this is a "downstream" sale from the parent to the subsidiary; therefore, the entire transaction must be eliminated.

After the intercompany transactions are eliminated, the income and dividend accounts of the subsidiary must be eliminated.

(e) Income from Sapphire	34,200	
Dividend from Sapphire		13,500
Investment in Sapphire		20,700

This entry eliminates the income from Sapphire recorded on Pearl's books under the equity method, and eliminates the dividends from Sapphire. Note that since only 90% of Sapphire's income was recorded by Pearl, only $34,200 (90% × $38,000) is included in the elimination entry. Also, note that since only 90% of Sapphire's $15,000 dividends declared were paid to Pearl, only $13,500 (90% × $15,000) in dividends are eliminated. The portion that is not eliminated will be included in the balance of the noncontrolling interest in acquiree. Notice that in a three-part worksheet with an income statement, statement of retained earnings, and balance sheet, the debit to income from Sapphire is posted in the income statement portion of the worksheet. The credit to dividends from Sapphire is posted in the retained earnings section of the balance sheet.

There are several differences in the worksheet for a less-than-100% acquisition. Notice that in our example for the 90% acquisition, the initial noncontrolling interest is established by crediting noncontrolling interest for the fair value of the shares of the Sapphire stock at date of acquisition. Also, notice in the income statement portion of the worksheet, that the net income attributable to the noncontrolling interest is subtracted to determine the amount of net income attributable to the acquirer. In the retained earnings section, the net income attributable to the noncontrolling interest less the dividends paid to the noncontrolling interest will be the change in the noncontrolling interest account. The change in noncontrolling interest is added to the beginning balance in noncontrolling interest to arrive at end-of-year controlling interest.

To check for accuracy, it is important to reconcile the noncontrolling interest account. In our example, the noncontrolling interest deduction on the income statement is computed as follows:

Sapphire Corp.'s reported income	$ 38,000
Noncontrolling interest share (10%)	(3,800)
Acquirer's interest in acquiree's income	$34,200

The noncontrolling interest's share of the fair value of net identifiable assets at date of acquisition is shown on the consolidated balance sheet in the owners' equity section. The computation for the noncontrolling interest shown in the balance sheet for our example is

Fair value of noncontrolling interest at date of acquisition	$10,500
Plus: % of noncontrolling interest's share of net income	3,800
Less: % of noncontrolling interest's share of dividends	(1,500)
End of year balance, noncontrolling interest	$12,800

PEARL CORP. AND SAPPHIRE CORP. CONSOLIDATED WORKING PAPERS
Year Ended December 31, Year 2

Acquisition Method—90% Acquisition
Subsequent, partial equity

			Adjustments and eliminations			
	Pearl	**Sapphire**	**Debit**	**Credit**	**Noncontrolling interest**	**Consolidated balances**
Income statement for year ended 12/31/Y2						
Sales	800,000	400,000	(d) 30,000			1,170,000
Cost of sales	580,000	250,000		18,000 (d)		(812,000)
Gross margin	220,000	150,000				358,000
Depreciation and amort. expense	25,000	14,000				39,000
Other operating expenses	115,000	98,000				213,000
Income from operations	80,000	38,000	30,000	18,000		106,000
Income from Sapphire	34,200		(e) 34,200			--
Net income	114,200	38,000	64,200	18,000		106,000
Net income attributable to noncontrolling interest in acquiree					3,800	(3,800)
Net income attributable to acquirer						102,200
Statement of retained earnings for year ended 12/31/Y2						
1/1/Y1 Retained earnings						
Pearl Corp.	62,000					62,000
Sapphire Corp.		35,000	(a) 35,000			--
Add net income (from above)	114,200	38,000	64,200	18,000	3,800	102,200
Total	176,200	73,000	99,200	18,000	3,800	164,200
Deduct dividends	(26,000)	(15,000)		13,500 (e)	(1,500)	(26,000)
Balance December 31, year 2	150,200	58,000	99,200	31,500	2,300	138,200
Balance sheet 12/31/Y2						
Cash	48,500	21,000				69,500
Accounts receivable (net)	42,000	8,000		5,000 (c)		45,000

	Pearl	Sapphire		Debit		Credit	Noncontrolling interest	Consolidated balances
Inventories	34,000	14,000			12,000 (d)			36,000
Equipment	290,000	107,000						397,000
Accumulated depreciation	(50,000)	(17,000)						(67,000)
Investment in stock of Sapphire Corp.	170,700				20,700 (e) 150,000 (a)			--
Differential			(a)	55,500	55,500 (b)			--
Goodwill	--	--	(b)	55,500				55,500
Patents	--	12,000						12,000
Total assets	535,200	145,000						548,000
Accounts payable	15,000	17,000	(b)	5,000				27,000
Bonds payable	80,000	--						80,000
Capital stock	135,000	60,000	(a)	60,000				135,000
Additional paid-in capital	155,000	10,000	(a)	10,000				155,000
Retained earnings (from above)	150,200	58,000		99,200	31,500	(2,300)		138,200
Noncontrolling interest in Sapphire					10,500 (a)	2,300		12,800
Total liabilities and equity	535,200	145,000		285,200	285,200	2,300		548,000

7. The remainder of the consolidation process is just worksheet techniques, as described below.

   a. Take all income items across horizontally and foot the adjustments, noncontrolling interest, and consolidated columns down to the net income line.

   b. Take the amounts on the net income line (on income statement) in the adjustments, noncontrolling interest, and consolidated balances columns **down to** retained earnings items across the consolidated balances column. Foot and crossfoot the retained earnings statement.

   c. Take the amounts of ending retained earnings in each of the four columns down to the ending retained earnings line in the balance sheet. Foot the noncontrolling interest column and place its total in the consolidated balances column. Take all the balance sheet items across to consolidated balances column.

8. Take a few minutes to study this worksheet so that you understand how to subtotal and total the three areas of the worksheet.

   NOTE: The totals flow from the income statement section to the retained earnings section of the worksheet. Notice how the adjustments to retained earnings flow to the balance sheet.

9. Business consolidation problems may require only the completion of a balance sheet. If you encounter only a balance sheet in a simulation exercise, remember that the entries posted to net income and retained earnings can be posted directly to the appropriate accounts in the stockholders' equity and noncontrolling interest accounts on the balance sheet. Intercompany transactions that involve nominal accounts on the income statement, as well as dividends declared, would be posted to the retained earnings account.

10. More complex business combination problems with noncontrolling interests involve the write-up of assets to fair value, the subsequent depreciation of the increase in fair value on depreciable assets, intercompany sales of inventory by the subsidiary to the parent (upstream sales), and gains and losses from the intercompany sale of fixed assets. ASC Topic 805 states the following:

    The amount of intra-entity income or loss to be eliminated in accordance with paragraph 810-10-45-1 is not affected by the existence of a noncontrolling interest. The complete elimination of the intercompany income or loss is consistent with the underlying assumption that consolidated financial statements represent the financial position and operating results of a single economic entity. The elimination of the intercompany income or loss may be allocated between the parent and noncontrolling interests.

11. Currently, alternative methods for eliminating intercompany transactions may be used when a noncontrolling interest exists.

    a. The entire intercompany transaction may be eliminated (similar to the 100% acquisition problem earlier in this module for Pelican and Swan).

    b. Another alternative for an acquisition of less than 100% is to allocate the income or loss on intercompany transactions between the parent and the noncontrolling interest. This would apply to situations in which the subsidiary sold inventory or fixed assets to the parent (upstream sales).

    c. Another issue that was not addressed by the FASB is whether the depreciation on asset write-ups should be allocated to the acquirer and the noncontrolling interest. Current practice and accounting texts discuss the logic of allocating the additional depreciation between the acquirer and the noncontrolling interest.

    d. Inasmuch as there are alternative approaches for these transactions, either answer would be acceptable.

NOW REVIEW MULTIPLE-CHOICE QUESTIONS 55 THROUGH 67

J. Additional Issues Regarding Business Combinations

1. **Incomplete Information**—At the date of acquisition, the accounting for a business combination may be incomplete. For example, the acquirer may not have complete information on valuing certain assets or liabilities.

    a. If the information is not yet complete by the end of the reporting period, then provisional amounts are recorded for those items.

        (1) These provisional amounts may be retrospectively adjusted during the **measurement period**.
        (2) The measurement period ends when the acquirer receives information or learns the information is not obtainable.
        (3) The measurement period may not exceed one year from date of acquisition.

    b. Any changes in the provisional amounts are recognized by retrospectively adjusted the provisional amounts recognized at acquisition date and making a corresponding adjustment to goodwill.

    c. Once the measurement period has ended, the acquirer accounts for changes as a correction of an error by making a prior period adjustment and restating the financial statements.

2. **Transfer of assets**—As discussed earlier, consideration transferred may include cash, assets, liabilities incurred by the acquirer, equity interests of the acquirer, and contingent consideration.

    a. Any assets transferred by the acquirer as part of the consideration in a business acquisition should be remeasured to fair value. Any gain or loss on the remeasurement should be included in earnings for the period.

    b. If the assets remain within the combined entity after the business combination or the acquirer retains control of those assets, then the assets are measured at their carrying values.

3. **Contingent Consideration**—Contingent consideration may be transferred in a business acquisition by promising to pay additional cash or to issue additional shares of the equity of the acquirer. The contingent consideration is measured at fair value at acquisition date.

    a. After the date of acquisition, additional information may indicate the initial value has changed.

        (1) If the changes in value occur during the measurement period, then it is treated as a change in a provisional amount and accounted for by an adjustment to goodwill.
        (2) After the measurement date, a change in the fair value of contingent consideration classified as an asset or liability is reported in earnings of the period.

    b. Any contingent consideration classified as equity is not remeasured.

    c. Any settlement of contingent consideration classified as equity is accounted for within owner's equity.

4. **Recognition and Measurement Issues**—Normally, assets and liabilities are measured at fair values and classified at date of acquisition so that the appropriate GAAP rules are applied. Other accounting exceptions exist for recognition and measurement of certain items. Below is a discussion of each of these items.

    a. **Lease classification.** As we discussed earlier, an exception exists for leases. A lease should be recorded on the acquirer's book based on its classification at the inception of the lease. However, if the lease terms are modified or changed at date of acquisition, then the lease is classified as required by the modified terms.

    b. **Operating lease.** If the acquiree is a lessee in operating leases, the acquirer determines whether the lease terms are favorable or unfavorable compared to market terms at the acquisition date. If the terms are favorable, an intangible asset can be recognized apart from goodwill. If the terms are unfavorable, then a liability should be recognized.

        (1) If the acquiree is the lessor in an operating lease, the underlying asset is measured at fair value. The acquirer may also recognize a separate asset or liability if the lease terms are favorable or unfavorable with regard to market terms.

    c. **Contingencies.** Contingencies of the acquiree are considered as contractual contingencies or noncontractual contingencies.

        (1) The acquirer should recognize any contractual contingencies at fair value at the acquisition date.
        (2) For noncontractual contingencies, the acquirer must assess whether it is "more likely than not" that the contingency gives rise to either an asset or a liability as defined in SFAC 6.

            (a) If the noncontractual contingency is more likely than not to meet the definition of an asset, then it is measured at fair value at date of acquisition.

      (b) If the noncontractual contingency is not likely to give rise to either an asset or a liability, the rules for contingencies are applied.

   (3) Recall, that the rules for contingencies use the distinction of probable, reasonably possible, or remote to determine the appropriate accounting.

      (a) Subsequent to acquisition date, if new information is obtained about the possible outcome of the contingency, the acquirer would measure the asset at the lower of its acquisition-date fair value, or the best estimate of its future settlement amount.

      (b) A liability is subsequently measured at the higher of its acquisition-date fair value or the amount recognized by applying the rules for accounting for contingencies.

   (4) The acquirer may only derecognize an asset or liability arising from a contingency when the contingency is resolved.

  d. **Income taxes.** Income taxes of the acquiree are measured at the acquisition date.

  e. **Employee benefits.** Employee benefits of the acquiree are recognized at date of acquisition. This includes compensated absences, pensions, other postemployment benefits, and deferred compensation agreements.

  f. **Indemnification contracts.** Occasionally, the seller of a business may contractually indemnify (guarantee against loss) the acquirer for some uncertainty of contingency. If the seller indemnifies the acquirer, then the acquirer has an indemnification asset, which is measured at fair value at acquisition date.

  g. **Reacquired rights**—Occasionally, the seller of the business may reacquire a right that has been transferred previous to the business acquisition. Examples of reacquired right include rights to use a trade name under a franchise agreement or rights to use technology.

   (1) For example, assume that Company A licenses a trade name to Company B. Company A may or may not have recognized this right as an asset on its books. Later, Company A reacquires the right to the license when it acquires Company B in a business acquisition. At the date of acquisition, Company A, the acquirer, would measure the fair value of this reacquired right and recognize it as an intangible asset on the balance sheet. The reacquired right would be amortized over the remaining contract period.

  h. **Valuation allowances.** At the date of acquisition, the assets of the acquiree are measured at fair value. Uncertainties about cash flows should be considered in the fair value measurements. Therefore, the acquirer would not recognize a separate valuation allowance for cash flows that are considered uncollectible or uncertain at the acquisition date.

  i. **Share-based payment awards.** If the acquirer is required to replace the acquiree's share-based payment awards with new share-based payment awards of the acquirer, then the fair value of the replacement awards are included in the consideration transferred in the business acquisition. If the acquirer is not required to replace the awards, but voluntarily chooses to do so, then the fair value of the replacement awards is recognized as compensation cost in the postcombination financial statements.

  j. **Assets held for sale.** If the acquiree has assets held for sale at the acquisition date, the acquirer measures the assets held for sale at fair value less cost to sell.

K. Additional Disclosures

1. The following items should be disclosed in the notes to the financial statements for business combinations that occur during the reporting period.

  a. Name and description of the acquiree.
  b. Acquisition date.
  c. Percentage of voting equity shares acquired.
  d. Primary reasons for the business combination and how acquirer obtained control of acquiree.
  e. Qualitative description of the factors that make up the goodwill recognized.
  f. Acquisition-date fair value of total consideration transferred and the fair value of each major class of consideration including cash, other assets, liabilities assumed, contingent consideration, and equity instruments (including the number of instruments issued and method of determining fair value).
  g. For contingent consideration and indemnification assets, the amount recognized, a description of arrangement, basis for determining amount of payment, and an estimate of the range of outcomes.
  h. The amounts recognized at the acquisition date for each major class of assets acquired and liabilities assumed.
  i. For assets and liabilities arising from contingencies, the amounts recognized and the nature of recognized and unrecognized contingencies, together with a range of outcomes for the contingencies.
  j. The total amount of goodwill expected to be deducted for tax purposes.
  k. If segment information is reported, the amount of goodwill by reportable segment.
  l. For transactions recognized separately from the business combination, description, accounting, amounts and line items where it is recognized.

m. Amounts of acquisition-related costs recognized as expense and where those expenses are recognized in the income statement. Amounts of acquisition-related costs not recognized in the income statement.

n. The gain recognized from bargain purchase and the reason for the gain.

o. The fair value of any noncontrolling interest in the acquiree at acquisition date, and the valuation techniques used to measure fair value of the noncontrolling interest.

p. If the business was acquired in stages, the acquisition-date fair value of the equity interest in the acquiree held immediately before the acquisition date, as well as the amount of gain or loss recognized as a result of remeasuring those securities to fair value, valuation techniques, and information on valuation inputs.

q. If the acquirer is a public company, the amount of revenue and earnings of the acquiree since acquisition date that is included in the consolidated income statement. Also, supplemental pro forma information for revenue and earnings as if the combination had occurred at the beginning of the period, and pro forma comparative statements for the prior reporting period as if the combination had occurred in the beginning of the prior period.

r. If the acquisition occurs after the reporting date but before the financial statements are issued, the acquirer should make the disclosures of the business combination information listed above.

s. Any information that enables users of financial statements to evaluate the financial effects of adjustments recognized in the current reporting period related to business combinations that occurred in the current or previous period.

t. If accounting for a business combination is incomplete, the reason why it is incomplete, and the assets, liabilities, equity interests or items that are incomplete, and the nature and amount of any measurement period adjustments recognized during the period.

u. Any changes in a contingent consideration asset or liability, differences arising from settlement, and changes in the range of outcomes and reasons for changes.

v. A reconciliation of the carrying amount of goodwill at the beginning and end of the period.

L. Combined Financial Statements

1. **Combined financial statements** is the term used to describe financial statements prepared for companies that are owned by the same parent company or individual. These statements are often prepared when several subsidiaries of a common parent are not consolidated. Combined financial statements are prepared by combining all of the separate companies' financial statement classifications. Intercompany transactions, balances, and profit (loss) should be eliminated in the same way as in consolidated statements.

> **NOW REVIEW MULTIPLE-CHOICE QUESTIONS 68 THROUGH 77**

M. Push-Down Accounting

1. "Push-down accounting" describes the method used to prepare the separate financial statements for significant, very large subsidiaries that are either wholly owned or substantially owned (≥ 90%). For publicly traded companies, the SEC requires a onetime adjustment under the acquisition method to revalue the subsidiary's assets and liabilities to fair value, and this entry is made directly on the books of the subsidiary.

2. Push-down accounting requires the subsidiary to record an entry revaluing all assets and liabilities with a balancing entry to a revaluation capital account. The revaluation capital account will be eliminated in consolidation against the investment in subsidiary account.

3. Push-down accounting will have no effect on the presentation of the consolidated financial statements or the separate financial statements of the parent company. However, the subsidiary's financial statements would be reported at fair value rather than historical cost.

4. Advocates of push-down accounting believe that a change of ownership through an acquisition-combination justifies the use of a new basis for the acquired entity. Thus, the new basis should be pushed down or directly recorded on the acquired entity's books.

N. Research Component—Accounting Standards Codification

ASC Topic 805 applies to business combinations. ASC topic 810 provides the rules for consolidation. Below is a list of keywords for searching business combination issues.

Acquired research and development	Contingent consideration	Intercompany balances
Acquirer	Contractual rights	Intercompany profit or loss
Acquiree	Contractual-legal criterion	Legal rights
Allocate cost assets	Controlling interest	Noncontrolling interest
Allocating cost asset	Costs registering securities	Obtains control
Asset apart from goodwill	Date of acquisition	Parent-company
Assigning amounts to assets	Derecognized	Purchase method

Bargain purchase	Disclosure financial statement	Reportable segment
Business combinations	Fair value exchanged	Reporting unit
Combined entity notes to financial statements	Financial assets	Rights transferable or separable
	Goodwill	Separability criterion
Combined financial statements	Initial measurement	Stock dividends subsidiary
Commonly controlled companies	Initial recognition	Subsequent accounting acquisition
Consolidated financial statements	Intangible asset class	
Consolidation purposes	Intangible assets acquired	
Contingency	Intangible assets subject to amortization	

O. International Financial Reporting Standards (IFRS)

1. IFRS requires business combinations to be accounted for using the acquisition method. Although the accounting for business combinations is similar for US GAAP and IFRS, it is different in several respects.
2. Under US GAAP noncontrolling interest is recorded at its fair value. IFRS, on the other hand, allows noncontrolling interest to be valued at either fair value or the proportionate share of the value of the identifiable net assets of the acquiree.

   a. If the noncontrolling interest is valued at fair value, the noncontrolling interest is calculated by determining the market price for equity shares not held by the acquirer. If the market value is not available, other valuation techniques may be used to measure the fair value.
   b. The second method for valuing noncontrolling interest is to calculate the fair value of net assets acquired and multiply that amount times the percentage of shares owned by the noncontrolling interest. Note that these two methods may result in different amounts of goodwill being recognized by the acquirer.
   The calculation of goodwill is

   Consideration transferred
   + Noncontrolling interest in acquiree (valued at % of FV or % share of net assets)
   + Fair value of previously held interests in acquiree
   – <u>Fair value of net assets acquired</u>
   Goodwill

   c. If goodwill is negative, a gain from bargain purchase should be recognized in the current period on the income statement.

3. Consolidated financial statements are required for all parent and subsidiaries wherein the parent has control. Similar to US GAAP, control is presumed if the entity has more than 50% of the voting shares of another entity. However, under IFRS, a parent may exclude a subsidiary only if three conditions are met: (1) is it wholly or partially owned and its other owners do not object to nonconsolidation; (2) it does not have any debt or equity instruments publicly traded; and (3) its parent prepares consolidated financial statements that comply with IFRS.
4. The SEC requires the use of "push-down" accounting as described in M. above whereas IFRS disallows its use.

> **NOW REVIEW MULTIPLE-CHOICE QUESTIONS 78 THROUGH 79**

KEY TERMS

Business. "An integrated set of activities and assets that is capable of being conducted and managed for the purpose of providing a return in the form of dividends, lower costs, or other economic benefits directly to.

Acquiree. The business that is being acquired.

Acquirer. The entity that obtains control of the acquire.

Acquisition date. The date on which the acquirer obtains control of the acquiree.

Business combination. A transaction or event in which the acquirer obtains control of one or more businesses.

Control. A controlling financial interest by ownership of a majority of the voting shares of stock. The general rule is that ownership either directly or indirectly by one company or more than 50% of the outstanding voting shares of another company constitutes control.

Identifiable asset. Arise from a contractual or legal right, or if it is separable.

Separable. It can be separated or divided from the entity and sold, transferred, licensed, rented, or exchanged.

Goodwill. "An asset representing the future economic benefits that arises from other assets acquired in a business combination that are not individually identified and separately recognized"

Variable interest entities (VIE). Control is achieved based on contractual, ownership, or other pecuniary interest that change with changes in the entity's net asset value.

Primary beneficiary. An entity that has a controlling financial interest in a VIE.

Combined financial statements. The term used to describe financial statements prepared for companies that are owned by the same parent company or individual.

Contingent consideration. A promise to pay additional cash or to issue additional shares of the equity of the acquirer.

Bargain purchase. If the consideration paid by the acquirer plus the fair value of noncontrolling interest is less than the fair value of the net identifiable assets.

Multiple-Choice Questions (1-79)

A-C. Accounting for the Combination

1. On April 1, year 1, Dart Co. paid $620,000 for all the issued and outstanding common stock of Wall Corp. The recorded assets and liabilities of Wall Corp. on April 1, year 1, follow:

Cash	$ 60,000
Inventory	180,000
Property and equipment (net of accumulated depreciation of $220,000)	320,000
Goodwill	100,000
Liabilities	(120,000)
Net assets	$ 540,000

On April 1, year 1, Wall's inventory had a fair value of $150,000, and the property and equipment (net) had a fair value of $380,000. What is the amount of goodwill resulting from the business combination?

- a. $150,000
- b. $120,000
- c. $ 50,000
- d. $ 20,000

2. Which of the following expenses related to the business acquisition should be included, in total, in the determination of net income of the combined corporation for the period in which the expenses are incurred?

	Fees of finders and consultants	Registration fees for equity securities issued
a.	Yes	Yes
b.	Yes	No
c.	No	Yes
d.	No	No

3. On August 31, year 1, Wood Corp. issued 100,000 shares of its $20 par value common stock for the net assets of Pine, Inc., in a business combination accounted for by the acquisition method. The market value of Wood's common stock on August 31 was $36 per share. Wood paid a fee of $160,000 to the consultant who arranged this acquisition. Costs of registering and issuing the equity securities amounted to $80,000. No goodwill was involved in the acquisition. What amount should Wood capitalize as the cost of acquiring Pine's net assets?

- a. $3,600,000
- b. $3,680,000
- c. $3,760,000
- d. $3,840,000

Items 4 and 5 are based on the following:

On December 31, year 1, Saxe Corporation was acquired by Poe Corporation. In the business combination, Poe issued 200,000 shares of its $10 par common stock, with a market price of $18 a share, for all of Saxe's common stock. The stockholders' equity section of each company's balance sheet immediately before the combination was

	Poe	Saxe
Common stock	$3,000,000	$1,500,000
Additional paid-in capital	1,300,000	150,000
Retained earnings	2,500,000	850,000
	$6,800,000	$2,500,000

4. In the December 31, year 1 consolidated balance sheet, additional paid-in capital should be reported at

- a. $ 950,000
- b. $1,300,000
- c. $1,450,000
- d. $2,900,000

5. In the December 31, year 1 consolidated balance sheet, common stock should be reported at

- a. $3,000,000
- b. $3,500,000
- c. $4,000,000
- d. $5,000,000

6. On December 31, year 1, Neal Co. issued 100,000 shares of its $10 par value common stock in exchange for all of Frey Inc.'s outstanding stock. The fair value of Neal's common stock on December 31, year 1, was $19 per share. The carrying amounts and fair values of Frey's assets and liabilities on December 31, year 1, were as follows:

	Carrying amount	Fair value
Cash	$ 240,000	$ 240,000
Receivables	270,000	270,000
Inventory	435,000	405,000
Property, plant, and equipment	1,305,000	1,440,000
Liabilities	(525,000)	(525,000)
Net assets	$1,725,000	$1,830,000

What is the amount of goodwill resulting from the business combination?

- a. $175,000
- b. $105,000
- c. $ 70,000
- d. $0

7. Consolidated financial statements are typically prepared when one company has a controlling financial interest in another **unless**

- a. The subsidiary is a finance company.
- b. The fiscal year-ends of the two companies are more than three months apart.
- c. The investee is in bankruptcy.
- d. The two companies are in unrelated industries, such as manufacturing and real estate.

8. On January 1, year 1, Lake Corporation acquired 100% of the outstanding common stock of Shore Corporation for $800,000. On the date of acquisition, the fair value of Shore's net identifiable assets is $820,000. The book value of Shore Corporation's net assets is $760,000. In Lake's year 1 financial statements, Lake should recognize

- a. Goodwill on the balance sheet.
- b. A gain from bargain purchase.
- c. A reduction in certain noncurrent assets on the balance sheet.
- d. An extraordinary gain.

9. A business combination is accounted for appropriately as an acquisition. Which of the following should be deducted in determining the combined corporation's net income for the current period?

	Direct costs of acquisition	General expenses related to acquisition
a.	Yes	No
b.	Yes	Yes
c.	No	Yes
d.	No	No

10. Which of the following situations would require the use of the acquisition method in a business combination?
   a. The acquisition of a group of assets.
   b. The formation of a joint venture.
   c. The purchase of more than 50% of a business.
   d. All of the above would require the use of the acquisition method.

11. ASC Topic 805 (SFAS 141[R]) sets forth certain steps in accounting for an acquisition. Which of the following is not one of those steps?
   a. Prepare pro forma financial statements prior to acquisition.
   b. Determine the acquisition date.
   c. Identify the acquirer.
   d. Expense the costs and general expenses of the acquisition in the period of acquisition.

12. Kennedy Company is acquiring Ross Company in an acquisition. What date should be used as the acquisition date for the transaction?
   a. The date Kennedy signs the contract to purchase the business.
   b. The date Kennedy obtains control of Ross.
   c. The date that all contingencies related to the transaction are resolved.
   d. The date Kennedy purchased more than 20% of the stock of Ross.

13. Lebow Corp. acquired control of Wilson Corp. by purchasing stock in steps. Which of the following regarding this type of acquisition is true?
   a. The cost of acquisition equals the amount paid for the previously held shares plus the fair value of shares issued at the date of acquisition.
   b. The previously held shares should be remeasured at fair value on the acquisition date, and any gain on previously held shares should be included in other comprehensive income for the period.
   c. The previously held shares should be remeasured at fair value on the acquisition date and the gain recognized in earnings of the period.
   d. The acquisition cost includes only the newly issued shares measured at fair value on the date of acquisition.

14. In accounting for a business combination, which of the following intangibles should not be recognized as an asset apart from goodwill?
   a. Trademarks.
   b. Lease agreements.
   c. Employee quality.
   d. Patents.

15. With respect to the allocation of the cost of a business acquisition, ASC Topic 805 (SFAS 141[R]) requires
   a. Cost to be allocated to the assets based on their carrying values.
   b. Cost to be allocated based on relative fair values.

   c. Cost to be allocated based on original costs.
   d. None of the above.

D. and E. Date of Combination Consolidated Balance Sheet—Acquisition Accounting

Items 16 through 20 are based on the following:

On January 1, year 1, Polk Corp. and Strass Corp. had condensed balance sheets as follows:

	Polk	Strass
Current assets	$ 70,000	$20,000
Noncurrent assets	90,000	40,000
Total assets	$160,000	$60,000
Current liabilities	$ 30,000	$10,000
Long-term debt	50,000	--
Stockholders' equity	80,000	50,000
Total liabilities and stockholders' equity	$160,000	$60,000

On January 2, year 1, Polk borrowed $60,000 and used the proceeds to purchase 90% of the outstanding common shares of Strass. This debt is payable in ten equal annual principal payments, plus interest, beginning December 30, year 1. The excess cost of the investment over Strass' book value of acquired net assets should be allocated 60% to inventory and 40% to goodwill. On January 1, year 1, the fair value of Polk shares held by noncontrolling parties was $10,000.

On Polk's January 2, year 1 consolidated balance sheet,

16. Current assets should be
   a. $ 90,000
   b. $ 99,000
   c. $100,000
   d. $102,000

17. Noncurrent assets should be
   a. $130,000
   b. $136,000
   c. $138,000
   d. $140,000

18. Current liabilities should be
   a. $50,000
   b. $46,000
   c. $40,000
   d. $30,000

19. Noncurrent liabilities should be
   a. $115,000
   b. $109,000
   c. $104,000
   d. $ 55,000

20. Stockholders' equity including noncontrolling interests should be
   a. $ 80,000
   b. $ 85,000
   c. $ 90,000
   d. $130,000

21. On November 30, year 1, Parlor, Inc. purchased for cash at $15 per share all 250,000 shares of the outstanding common stock of Shaw Co. At November 30, year 1, Shaw's balance sheet showed a carrying amount of net assets of $3,000,000. At that date, the fair value of Shaw's property, plant and equipment exceeded its carrying amount by $400,000. In its November 30, year 1 consolidated balance sheet, what amount should Parlor report as goodwill?

- a. $750,000
- b. $400,000
- c. $350,000
- d. $0

22. On April 1, year 1, Parson Corp. purchased 80% of the outstanding stock of Sloan Corp. for $700,000 cash. Parson determined that the fair value of the net identifiable assets was $800,000 on the date of acquisition. The fair value of Sloan's stock at date of acquisition was $18 per share. Sloan had a total of 50,000 shares of stock issued and outstanding prior to the acquisition. What is the amount of goodwill that should be recorded by Parson at date of acquisition?

- a. $0
- b. $ 60,000
- c. $ 80,000
- d. $120,000

23. A subsidiary, acquired for cash in a business combination, owned inventories with a market value greater than the book value as of the date of combination. A consolidated balance sheet prepared immediately after the acquisition would include this difference as part of

- a. Deferred credits.
- b. Goodwill.
- c. Inventories.
- d. Retained earnings.

24. Company J acquired all of the outstanding common stock of Company K in exchange for cash. The acquisition price exceeds the fair value of net assets acquired. How should Company J determine the amounts to be reported for the plant and equipment and long-term debt acquired from Company K?

	Plant and equipment	Long-term debt
a.	K's carrying amount	K's carrying amount
b.	K's carrying amount	Fair value
c.	Fair value	K's carrying amount
d.	Fair value	Fair value

25. In a business combination accounted for as an acquisition the appraised values of the identifiable assets acquired exceeded the acquisition price. How should the excess appraised value be reported?

- a. As negative goodwill.
- b. As additional paid-in capital.
- c. As a reduction of the values assigned to certain assets and an extraordinary gain for any unallocated portion.
- d. As a gain in net income for the period.

F. Consolidated Financial Statements Subsequent to Acquisition

26. Wright Corp. has several subsidiaries that are included in its consolidated financial statements. In its December 31, year 1 trial balance, Wright had the following intercompany balances before eliminations:

	Debit	Credit
Current receivable due from Main Co.	$ 32,000	
Noncurrent receivable from Main Co.	114,000	
Cash advance to Corn Corp.	6,000	
Cash advance from King Co.		$ 15,000
Intercompany payable to King Co.		101,000

In its December 31, year 1 consolidated balance sheet, what amount should Wright report as intercompany receivables?

- a. $152,000
- b. $146,000
- c. $ 36,000
- d. $0

27. Shep Co. has a receivable from its parent, Pep Co. Should this receivable be separately reported in Shep's balance sheet and in Pep's consolidated balance sheet?

	Shep's balance sheet	Pep's consolidated balance sheet
a.	Yes	No
b.	Yes	Yes
c.	No	No
d.	No	Yes

Items 28 through 30 are based on the following:

Selected information from the separate and consolidated balance sheets and income statements of Pard, Inc. and its subsidiary, Spin Co., as of December 31, year 1, and for the year then ended is as follows:

	Pard	Spin	Consolidated
Balance sheet accounts			
Accounts receivable	$ 26,000	$ 19,000	$ 39,000
Inventory	30,000	25,000	52,000
Investment in Spin	67,000	--	--
Goodwill	--	--	30,000
Noncontrolling interest	--	--	10,000
Stockholders' equity	154,000	50,000	154,000
Income statement accounts			
Revenues	$200,000	$140,000	$308,000
Cost of goods sold	150,000	110,000	231,000
Gross profit	50,000	30,000	77,000
Equity in earnings of Spin	20,000	--	--
Net income	36,000	20,000	40,000

Additional information

- During year 1, Pard sold goods to Spin at the same markup on cost that Pard uses for all sales. At December 31, year 1, Spin had not paid for all of these goods and still held 37.5% of them in inventory.
- Pard acquired its interest in Spin on January 2, year 1.

28. What was the amount of intercompany sales from Pard to Spin during year 1?

- a. $ 3,000
- b. $ 6,000
- c. $29,000
- d. $32,000

29. At December 31, year 1, what was the amount of Spin's payable to Pard for intercompany sales?

- a. $ 3,000
- b. $ 6,000
- c. $29,000
- d. $32,000

30. In Pard's consolidated balance sheet, what was the carrying amount of the inventory that Spin purchased from Pard?

a. $ 3,000
b. $ 6,000
c. $ 9,000
d. $12,000

31. On January 1, year 1, Palm, Inc. purchased 80% of the stock of Stone Corp. for $4,000,000 cash. Prior to the acquisition, Stone had 100,000 shares of stock outstanding. On the date of acquisition, Stone's stock had a fair value of $52 per share. During the year Stone reported $280,000 in net income and paid dividends of $50,000. What is the balance in the noncontrolling interest account on Palm's balance sheet on December 31, year 1?

a. $1,000,000
b. $1,040,000
c. $1,086,000
d. $1,096,000

32. On January 1, year 1, Owen Corp. purchased all of Sharp Corp.'s common stock for $1,200,000. On that date, the fair values of Sharp's assets and liabilities equaled their carrying amounts of $1,320,000 and $320,000, respectively. During year 1, Sharp paid cash dividends of $20,000.

Selected information from the separate balance sheets and income statements of Owen and Sharp as of December 31, year 1, and for the year then ended follows:

	Owen	Sharp
Balance sheet accounts		
Investment in subsidiary	$1,320,000	--
Retained earnings	1,240,000	560,000
Total stockholders' equity	2,620,000	1,120,000
Income statement accounts		
Operating income	420,000	200,000
Equity in earnings of Sharp	140,000	--
Net income	400,000	140,000

In Owen's December 31, year 1 consolidated balance sheet, what amount should be reported as total retained earnings?

a. $1,240,000
b. $1,360,000
c. $1,380,000
d. $1,800,000

33. When a parent-subsidiary relationship exists, consolidated financial statements are prepared in recognition of the accounting concept of

a. Reliability.
b. Materiality.
c. Legal entity.
d. Economic entity.

34. A subsidiary was acquired for cash in a business combination on January 1, year 1. The consideration given exceeded the fair value of identifiable net assets. The acquired company owned equipment with a market value in excess of the carrying amount as of the date of combination. A consolidated balance sheet prepared on December 31, year 1, would

a. Report the unamortized portion of the excess of the market value over the carrying amount of the equipment as part of goodwill.
b. Report the unamortized portion of the excess of the market value over the carrying amount of the equipment as part of plant and equipment.

c. Report the excess of the market value over the carrying amount of the equipment as part of plant and equipment.
d. Not report the excess of the market value over the carrying amount of the equipment because it would be expensed in the year of the acquisition.

35. Pride, Inc. owns 80% of Simba, Inc.'s outstanding common stock. Simba, in turn, owns 10% of Pride's outstanding common stock. What percentage of the common stock cash dividends declared by the individual companies should be reported as dividends declared in the consolidated financial statements?

	Dividends declared by Pride	Dividends declared by Simba
a.	90%	0%
b.	90%	20%
c.	100%	0%
d.	100%	20%

36. It is generally presumed that an entity is a variable interest entity subject to consolidation if its equity is

a. Less than 50% of total assets.
b. Less than 25% of total assets.
c. Less than 10% of total assets.
d. Less than 10% of total liabilities.

37. Morton Inc., Gilman Co., and Willis Corporation established a special-purpose entity (SPE) (variable interest entity) to perform leasing activities for the three corporations. If at the time of formation the SPE is determined to be a variable interest entity subject to consolidation, which of the corporations should consolidate the SPE?

a. The corporation with the largest interest in the entity.
b. The corporation that is the primary beneficiary.
c. The corporation that has the most voting equity interest.
d. Each corporation should consolidate one-third of the SPE.

38. The determination of whether an interest holder must consolidate a variable interest entity is made

a. By reassessing on an ongoing basis.
b. When the interest holder initially gets involved with the variable interest entity.
c. Every time the cash flows of the variable interest entity change.
d. Interests in variable interest entities are never consolidated.

39. Matt Co. included a foreign subsidiary in its year 5 consolidated financial statements. The subsidiary was acquired in year 1 and was excluded from previous consolidations. The change was caused by the elimination of foreign exchange controls. Including the subsidiary in the year 5 consolidated financial statements results in an accounting change that should be reported

a. By footnote disclosure only.
b. Currently and prospectively.
c. Currently with footnote disclosure of pro forma effects of retroactive application.
d. By restating the financial statements of all prior periods presented.

40. On June 30, year 1, Purl Corp. issued 150,000 shares of its $20 par common stock for which it received all of Scott Corp.'s common stock. The fair value of the common stock issued is equal to the book value of Scott Corp.'s net assets. Both corporations continued to operate as separate businesses, maintaining accounting records with years ending December 31. Net income from separate company operations and dividends paid were

	Purl	Scott
Net income		
Six months ended 6/30/Y1	$750,000	$225,000
Six months ended 12/31/Y1	825,000	375,000
Dividends paid		
March 25, year 1	950,000	--
November 15, year 1	--	300,000

On December 31, year 1, Scott held in its inventory merchandise acquired from Purl on December 1, year 1, for $150,000, which included a $45,000 markup. In the year 1 consolidated income statement, net income should be reported at

    a. $1,650,000
    b. $1,905,000
    c. $1,950,000
    d. $2,130,000

41. On January 1, year 2, Pane Corp. exchanged 150,000 shares of its $20 par value common stock for all of Sky Corp.'s common stock. At that date, the fair value of Pane's common stock issued was equal to the book value of Sky's net assets. Both corporations continued to operate as separate businesses, maintaining accounting records with years ending December 31. Pane uses the equity method to account for its investment in Sky. Information from separate company operations follows:

	Pane	Sky
Retained earnings— 12/31/Y1	$3,200,000	$925,000
Net income—six months ended 6/30/Y2	800,000	275,000
Dividends paid—3/25/Y2	750,000	--

What amount of retained earnings would Pane report in its June 30, year 2 consolidated balance sheet?

    a. $5,200,000
    b. $4,450,000
    c. $3,525,000
    d. $3,250,000

G. and H. Intercompany Transactions and Profit Confirmation and Subsequent Consolidated Financial Statements

Items 42 and 43 are based on the following:

Scroll, Inc., a wholly owned subsidiary of Pirn, Inc., began operations on January 1, year 1. The following information is from the condensed year 1 income statements of Pirn and Scroll:

	Pirn	Scroll
Sales to Scroll	$100,000	$ --
Sales to others	400,000	300,000
	500,000	300,000
Cost of goods sold:		
Acquired from Pirn	--	80,000
Acquired from others	350,000	190,000
Gross profit	150,000	30,000
Depreciation	40,000	10,000
Other expenses	60,000	15,000
Income from operations	50,000	5,000
Gain on sale of equipment to Scroll	12,000	--
Income before income taxes	$ 62,000	$ 5,000

Additional information

- Sales by Pirn to Scroll are made on the same terms as those made to third parties.
- Equipment purchased by Scroll from Pirn for $36,000 on January 1, year 1, is depreciated using the straight-line method over four years.

42. In Pirn's December 31, year 1, consolidating worksheet, how much intercompany profit should be eliminated from Scroll's inventory?

    a. $30,000
    b. $20,000
    c. $10,000
    d. $ 6,000

43. What amount should be reported as depreciation expense in Pirn's year 1 consolidated income statement?

    a. $50,000
    b. $47,000
    c. $44,000
    d. $41,000

44. Clark Co. had the following transactions with affiliated parties during year 1:

- Sales of $60,000 to Dean, Inc., with $20,000 gross profit. Dean had $15,000 of this inventory on hand at year-end. Clark owns a 15% interest in Dean and does not exert significant influence.
- Purchases of raw materials totaling $240,000 from Kent Corp., a wholly owned subsidiary. Kent's gross profit on the sale was $48,000. Clark had $60,000 of this inventory remaining on December 31, year 1.

Before eliminating entries, Clark had consolidated current assets of $320,000. What amount should Clark report in its December 31, year 1 consolidated balance sheet for current assets?

    a. $320,000
    b. $317,000
    c. $308,000
    d. $303,000

45. Parker Corp. owns 80% of Smith Inc.'s common stock. During year 1, Parker sold Smith $250,000 of inventory on the same terms as sales made to third parties. Smith sold all of the inventory purchased from Parker in year 1. The following information pertains to Smith and Parker's sales for year 1:

	Parker	Smith
Sales	$1,000,000	$700,000
Cost of sales	400,000	350,000
	$ 600,000	$350,000

What amount should Parker report as cost of sales in its year 1 consolidated income statement?

a. $750,000
b. $680,000
c. $500,000
d. $430,000

46. Selected information from the separate and consolidated balance sheets and income statements of Pare, Inc. and its subsidiary, Shel Co., as of December 31, year 1, and for the year then ended is as follows:

	Pare	Shel	Consolidated
Balance sheet accounts			
Accounts receivable	$ 52,000	$ 38,000	$ 78,000
Inventory	60,000	50,000	104,000
Income statement accounts			
Revenues	$400,000	$280,000	$616,000
Cost of goods sold	300,000	220,000	462,000
Gross profit	$100,000	$ 60,000	$154,000

Additional information:

During year 1, Pare sold goods to Shel at the same markup on cost that Pare uses for all sales.

In Pare's consolidating worksheet, what amount of unrealized intercompany profit was eliminated?

a. $ 6,000
b. $12,000
c. $58,000
d. $64,000

47. During year 1, Pard Corp. sold goods to its 80%-owned subsidiary, Seed Corp. At December 31, year 1, one-half of these goods were included in Seed's ending inventory. Reported year 1 selling expenses were $1,100,000 and $400,000 for Pard and Seed, respectively. Pard's selling expenses included $50,000 in freight-out costs for goods sold to Seed. What amount of selling expenses should be reported in Pard's year 1 consolidated income statement?

a. $1,500,000
b. $1,480,000
c. $1,475,000
d. $1,450,000

48. On January 1, year 1, Poe Corp. sold a machine for $900,000 to Saxe Corp., its wholly owned subsidiary. Poe paid $1,100,000 for this machine, which had accumulated depreciation of $250,000. Poe estimated a $100,000 salvage value and depreciated the machine on the straight-line method over twenty years, a policy which Saxe continued. In Poe's December 31, year 1 consolidated balance sheet, this machine should be included in cost and accumulated depreciation as

	Cost	Accumulated depreciation
a.	$1,100,000	$300,000
b.	$1,100,000	$290,000
c.	$ 900,000	$ 40,000
d.	$ 850,000	$ 42,500

49. Wagner, a holder of a $1,000,000 Palmer, Inc. bonds, collected the interest due on March 31, year 1, and then sold the bonds to Seal, Inc. for $975,000. On that date, Palmer, a

75% owner of Seal, had a $1,075,000 carrying amount for the bonds. What was the effect of Seal's purchase of Palmer's bond on the retained earnings and noncontrolling interest amounts reported in Palmer's March 31, year 1 consolidated balance sheet?

	Retained earnings	Noncontrolling interest
a.	$100,000 increase	$0
b.	$ 75,000 increase	$ 25,000 increase
c.	$0	$ 25,000 increase
d.	$0	$100,000 increase

50. Sun, Inc. is a wholly owned subsidiary of Patton, Inc. On June 1, year 1, Patton declared and paid a $1 per share cash dividend to stockholders of record on May 15, year 1. On May 1, year 1, Sun bought 10,000 shares of Patton's common stock for $700,000 on the open market, when the book value per share was $30. What amount of gain should Patton report from this transaction in its consolidated income statement for the year ended December 31, year 1?

a. $0
b. $390,000
c. $400,000
d. $410,000

51. Perez, Inc. owns 80% of Senior, Inc. During year 1, Perez sold goods with a 40% gross profit to Senior. Senior sold all of these goods in year 1. For year 1 consolidated financial statements, how should the summation of Perez and Senior income statement items be adjusted?

a. Sales and cost of goods sold should be reduced by the intercompany sales.
b. Sales and cost of goods sold should be reduced by 80% of the intercompany sales.
c. Net income should be reduced by 80% of the gross profit on intercompany sales.
d. No adjustment is necessary.

52. Winston Co. owns 80% of the outstanding common stock of Foster Co. On December 31, year 2, Winston sold equipment to Foster at a price in excess of Winston's carrying amount, but less than its original cost. On a consolidated balance sheet at December 31, year 2, the carrying amount of the equipment should be reported at

a. Foster's original cost.
b. Winston's original cost.
c. Foster's original cost less Winston's recorded gain.
d. Foster's original cost less 80% of Winston's recorded gain.

53. Port, Inc. owns 100% of Salem, Inc. On January 1, year 6, Port sold Salem delivery equipment at a gain. Port had owned the equipment for two years and used a five-year straight-line depreciation rate with no residual value. Salem is using a three-year straight-line depreciation rate with no residual value for the equipment. In the consolidated income statement, Salem's recorded depreciation expense on the equipment for year 6 will be decreased by

a. 20% of the gain on sale.
b. 33 1/3% of the gain on sale.
c. 50% of the gain on sale.
d. 100% of the gain on sale.

54. P Co. purchased term bonds at a premium on the open market. These bonds represented 20% of the outstanding class of bonds issued at a discount by S Co., P's wholly owned subsidiary. P intends to hold the bonds until matu-

rity. In a consolidated balance sheet, the difference between the bond carrying amounts in the two companies would
- a. Decrease retained earnings.
- b. Increase retained earnings.
- c. Be reported as a deferred debit to be amortized over the remaining life of the bonds.
- d. Be reported as a deferred credit to be amortized over the remaining life of the bonds.

I. Noncontrolling Interest

55. Planet Company acquired a 70% interest in the Star Company in year 1. For the year ended December 31, year 2, Star reported net income of $80,000. During year 2, Planet sold merchandise to Star for $10,000 at a profit of $2,000. The merchandise remained in Star's inventory at the end of year 2. For consolidation purposes what is the noncontrolling interest's share of Star's net income for year 2?
- a. $23,400
- b. $24,000
- c. $24,600
- d. $26,000

Items 56 and 57 are based on the following:

On January 1, year 1, Ritt Corp. purchased 80% of Shaw Corp.'s $10 par common stock for $975,000. On this date, the carrying amount of Shaw's net assets was $1,000,000. The fair values of Shaw's identifiable assets and liabilities were the same as their carrying amounts except for plant assets (net) with fair values of $100,000 in excess of their carrying amount. The fair value of the non-controlling interest in Shaw on January 1, year 1, was $250,000. For the year ended December 31, year 1, Shaw had net income of $190,000 and paid cash dividends totaling $125,000.

56. In the January 1, year 1 consolidated balance sheet, goodwill should be reported at
- a. $0
- b. $ 75,000
- c. $ 95,000
- d. $125,000

57. In the December 31, year 1 consolidated balance sheet, noncontrolling interest should be reported at
- a. $200,000
- b. $213,000
- c. $233,000
- d. $263,000

Items 58 through 60 are based on the following:

On January 2, year 1, Pare Co. purchased 75% of Kidd Co.'s outstanding common stock. On that date, the fair value of the 25% noncontrolling interest was $35,000. During year 1, Kidd had net income of $20,000. Selected balance sheet data at December 31, year 1, is as follows:

	Pare	Kidd
Total assets	$420,000	$180,000
Liabilities	$120,000	$ 60,000
Common stock	100,000	50,000
Retained earnings	200,000	70,000
	$420,000	$180,000

During year 1 Pare and Kidd paid cash dividends of $25,000 and $5,000, respectively, to their shareholders. There were no other intercompany transactions.

58. In its December 31, year 1 consolidated statement of retained earnings, what amount should Pare report as dividends paid?
- a. $ 5,000
- b. $25,000
- c. $26,250
- d. $30,000

59. In Pare's December 31, year 1 consolidated balance sheet, what amount should be reported as noncontrolling interest in net assets?
- a. $30,000
- b. $35,000
- c. $38,750
- d. $40,000

60. In its December 31, year 1 consolidated balance sheet, what amount should Pare report as common stock?
- a. $ 50,000
- b. $100,000
- c. $137,500
- d. $150,000

61. In a business acquisition, consideration transferred includes which of the following?

- I. The fair value of assets transferred by the acquirer.
- II. The fair value of the liabilities incurred by the acquirer.
- III. The fair value of contingent consideration transferred by the acquirer.
- IV. The fair value of the equity interests issued by the acquirer as a part of the acquisition.
- V. The fair value of share-based payments voluntarily exchanged for outstanding share-based payment awards of the acquiree.

- a. I and II.
- b. I, II, and IV.
- c. I, II, IV, and V.
- d. I, II, III, and IV.

62. On June 30, year 1, Wyler Corporation acquires Boston Corporation in a transaction properly accounted for as a business acquisition. At the time of the acquisition, some of the information for valuing assets was incomplete. How should Corporation Wyler, account for the incomplete information in preparing its financial statements immediately after the acquisition?
- a. Do not record the uncertain items until complete information is available.
- b. Record a contra account to the investment account for the amounts involved.
- c. Record the uncertain items at the book value of the acquiree.
- d. Record the uncertain items at a provisional amount measured at the date of acquisition.

63. When does the measurement period end for a business combination in which there was incomplete accounting information on the date of acquisition?
- a. When the acquirer receives the information or one year from the acquisition date, whichever occurs earlier.

b. On the final date when all contingencies are re-solved.

c. Thirty days from the date of acquisition.

d. At the end of the reporting period in the year of acquisition.

64. Ross Corporation recorded a provisional amount for an identifiable asset at the date of its acquisition of Layton Inc. because the asset's fair value was uncertain. Before the measurement period ends, Ross obtains new information that indicates that the asset was overvalued by $20,000. How should Ross report the effects of this new information?

a. As an expense in the current period income statement.

b. As an extraordinary loss on the current period income statement.

c. As a reduction in recorded goodwill.

d. As a gain from bargain purchase.

65. Able Corp. acquires Bailey Company in a transaction that is properly accounted for as a business acquisition. The acquisition contract and Bailey's share-based compensation agreement require Able stock to be exchanged for Bailey common stock issued to Bailey's employees as share-based payments. No further service is required by the employees of Bailey to qualify for the replacement awards. How should Able account for the shares of stock issued as replacement awards to employees of Bailey?

a. As a cost of acquisition.

b. As an expense in the current period.

c. As a loss in the current period.

d. As an extraordinary loss in the period.

66. On January 1, year 1, Post Inc. acquires Sam Company in a transaction properly accounted for as a business combination. Sam's employees have share-based payments that will expire as a consequence of the business combination. In order to maintain employee morale, Post voluntarily replaces the awards to employees 30 days after the date of acquisition. How should Post account for the replacement awards given to Sam's employees?

a. Post should include the fair value of the awards as consideration paid in the cost of acquisition.

b. Post should recognize compensation expense for the value of the awards in the postcombination financial statements.

c. Post should recognize an extraordinary loss for the fair value of the replacement awards in its financial statements.

d. Post should capitalize the cost of the awards and amortize the cost over the remaining service years of the employees.

67. When should an acquirer derecognize a contingent liability recognized as the result of an acquisition?

a. When it becomes more likely than not that the firm will not be liable.

b. When the contingency is resolved.

c. At the end of the year of acquisition.

d. When it is reasonably possible that the liability will not require payment.

J. Additional Issues Regarding Business Combinations

68. On September 1, year 1, Phillips, Inc. issued common stock in exchange for 20% of Sago, Inc.'s outstanding common stock. On July 1, year 2, Phillips issued common stock

for an additional 75% of Sago's outstanding common stock. Sago continues in existence as Phillips' subsidiary. How much of Sago's year 2 net income should be reported as attributable to Phillips?

a. 20% of Sago's net income to June 30 and all of Sago's net income from July 1 to December 31.

b. 20% of Sago's net income to June 30 and 95% of Sago's net income from July 1 to December 31.

c. 95% of Sago's net income.

d. All of Sago's net income.

L. Combined Financial Statements

69. Mr. & Mrs. Dart own a majority of the outstanding capital stock of Wall Corp., Black Co., and West, Inc. During year 1, Wall advanced cash to Black and West in the amount of $50,000 and $80,000, respectively. West advanced $70,000 in cash to Black. At December 31, year 1, none of the advances was repaid. In the combined December 31, year 1 balance sheet of these companies, what amount would be reported as receivables from affiliates?

a. $200,000

b. $130,000

c. $ 60,000

d. $0

70. Selected data for two subsidiaries of Dunn Corp. taken from December 31, year 1 preclosing trial balances are as follows:

	Banks Co. debit	Lamm Co. credit
Shipments to Banks	$ --	$150,000
Shipments from Lamm	200,000	--
Intercompany inventory profit on total shipments	--	50,000

Additional data relating to the December 31, year 1 inventory are as follows:

Inventory acquired from outside parties	$175,000	$250,000
Inventory acquired from Lamm	60,000	--

At December 31, year 1, the inventory reported on the combined balance sheet of the two subsidiaries should be

a. $425,000

b. $435,000

c. $470,000

d. $485,000

71. Ahm Corp. owns 90% of Bee Corp.'s common stock and 80% of Cee Corp.'s common stock. The remaining common shares of Bee and Cee are owned by their respective employees. Bee sells exclusively to Cee, Cee buys exclusively from Bee, and Cee sells exclusively to unrelated companies. Selected year 1 information for Bee and Cee follows:

	Bee Corp.	Cee Corp.
Sales	$130,000	$91,000
Cost of sales	100,000	65,000
Beginning inventory	None	None
Ending inventory	None	65,000

What amount should be reported as gross profit in Bee and Cee's combined income statement for the year ended December 31, year 1?

    a. $26,000
    b. $41,000
    c. $47,800
    d. $56,000

72. The following information pertains to shipments of merchandise from Home Office to Branch during year 1:

Home Office's cost of merchandise	$160,000
Intracompany billing	200,000
Sales by Branch	250,000
Unsold merchandise at Branch on	
December 31, year 1	20,000

In the combined income statement of Home Office and Branch for the year ended December 31, year 1, what amount of the above transactions should be included in sales?

    a. $250,000
    b. $230,000
    c. $200,000
    d. $180,000

73. Mr. and Mrs. Gasson own 100% of the common stock of Able Corp. and 90% of the common stock of Baker Corp. Able previously paid $4,000 for the remaining 10% interest in Baker. The condensed December 31, year 1 balance sheets of Able and Baker are as follows:

	Able	Baker
Assets	$600,000	$60,000
Liabilities	$200,000	$30,000
Common stock	100,000	20,000
Retained earnings	300,000	10,000
	$600,000	$60,000

In a combined balance sheet of the two corporations at December 31, year 1, what amount should be reported as total stockholders' equity?

    a. $430,000
    b. $426,000
    c. $403,000
    d. $400,000

74. Mr. Cord owns four corporations. Combined financial statements are being prepared for these corporations, which have intercompany loans of $200,000 and intercompany profits of $500,000. What amount of these intercompany loans and profits should be included in the combined financial statements?

	Intercompany	
	Loans	**Profits**
a.	$200,000	$0
b.	$200,000	$500,000
c.	$0	$0
d.	$0	$500,000

75. Combined statements may be used to present the results of operations of

	Companies under common management	**Commonly controlled companies**
a.	No	Yes
b.	Yes	No
c.	No	No
d.	Yes	Yes

76. Which of the following items should be treated in the same manner in both combined financial statements and consolidated statements?

	Income taxes	**Noncontrolling interest**
a.	No	No
b.	No	Yes
c.	Yes	Yes
d.	Yes	No

77. Which of the following items should be treated in the same manner in both combined financial statements and consolidated statements?

	Different fiscal periods	**Foreign operations**
a.	No	No
b.	No	Yes
c.	Yes	Yes
d.	Yes	No

O. International Financial Reporting Standards (IFRS)

78. Under IFRS the asset goodwill may be recognized
    a.   When it is acquired by purchase.
    b.   When it is internally generated or acquired by purchase.
    c.   When it is clear that it exists and has value.
    d.   When it has future economic benefits.

79. Under IFRS a parent may exclude a subsidiary from consolidation only if all of the following conditions exist, except
    a.   It is wholly or partially owned and its owners do not object to nonconsolidation.
    b.   It does not have any debt or equity instruments publicly traded.
    c.   It has one class of stock.
    d.   Its parent prepares consolidated financial statements that comply with IFRS.

Multiple-Choice Answers and Explanations

Answers

1. a __ __	18. b __ __	35. a __ __	52. c __ __	69. d __ __
2. b __ __	19. c __ __	36. c __ __	53. b __ __	70. c __ __
3. a __ __	20. c __ __	37. b __ __	54. a __ __	71. b __ __
4. d __ __	21. c __ __	38. a __ __	55. b __ __	72. a __ __
5. d __ __	22. c __ __	39. d __ __	56. d __ __	73. b __ __
6. c __ __	23. c __ __	40. b __ __	57. d __ __	74. c __ __
7. c __ __	24. d __ __	41. d __ __	58. b __ __	75. d __ __
8. b __ __	25. d __ __	42. d __ __	59. c __ __	76. c __ __
9. b __ __	26. d __ __	43. b __ __	60. b __ __	77. c __ __
10. c __ __	27. a __ __	44. c __ __	61. d __ __	78. a __ __
11. a __ __	28. d __ __	45. c __ __	62. d __ __	79. c __ __
12. b __ __	29. b __ __	46. a __ __	63. a __ __	
13. c __ __	30. c __ __	47. d __ __	64. c __ __	
14. c __ __	31. c __ __	48. a __ __	65. a __ __	
15. b __ __	32. a __ __	49. a __ __	66. b __ __	
16. d __ __	33. d __ __	50. a __ __	67. b __ __	1st: __/79 = __%
17. c __ __	34. b __ __	51. a __ __	68. b __ __	2nd: __/79 = __%

Explanations

1. **(a)** In an acquisition, the net assets of the acquired firm are recorded at their FV. The excess of the cost of the investment over the FV of the net assets acquired is allocated to goodwill. The cost of the investment is $620,000, and the FV of the net assets acquired, **excluding goodwill,** is $470,000, as computed below.

	FMV
Cash	$ 60,000
Inventory (BV = $180,000)	150,000
Prop. and equip.	
(BV = $320,000)	380,000
Liabilities	(120,000)
Total FV	$ 470,000

Therefore, the amount allocated to goodwill is $150,000 ($620,000 – $470,000).

2. **(b)** Acquisition costs such as finder's fees are expensed in the period incurred. Registration fees for equity securities are a reduction in the issue price of the securities. Therefore, answer (b) is correct.

3. **(a)** In a business combination accounted for as an acquisition, the fair market value of the net assets is used as the valuation basis for the combination. In this case, the net assets of the subsidiary have an implied fair market value of $3,600,000 which is the value of the common stock issued to Pine's shareholders (100,000 shares × $36). The direct cost of acquisition should not be included as part of the cost of a company acquired, and the cost of registering equity securities should be a reduction of the issue price of the securities (i.e., additional paid-in capital). Thus, the $160,000 paid for a consultant who arranged the acquisition should be expensed, and the $80,000 cost for registering and issuing the equity securities should be treated as a reduction of additional paid-in capital. Answer (a) is correct because the total amount to be capitalized is $3,600,000.

4. **(d)** In a business combination accounted for as an acquisition, the fair market value of the net assets is used as the valuation basis for the combination. In this case, the net assets of the subsidiary have an implied fair market value of $3,600,000 which is the value of the common stock issued to Saxe's shareholders (200,000 × $18). Since $3,600,000 is the basis for recording this purchase, the common stock issued is recorded at $2,000,000 (200,000 shares × $10 par value per share) and additional paid-in capital is recorded at $1,600,000 ($3,600,000 – $2,000,000). Therefore, answer (d) is correct because additional paid-in capital should be reported at $2,900,000 ($1,300,000 + $1,600,000).

5. **(d)** In a business combination, the common stock account of the combined entity is the number of shares outstanding multiplied by the par value of the stock. The total common stock account of the combined entity is equal to $5,000,000, the $3,000,000 originally outstanding plus the total par value of the stock issued in the acquisition, $2,000,000 (200,000 × $10).

6. **(c)** In a business combination accounted for as an acquisition, the fair market value of the net assets is used as the valuation basis for the combination. In this case, Frey's assets have an implied fair market value of $1,900,000 which is the market value of the common stock issue (100,000 shares × $19). The value assigned to goodwill is $70,000, which is the value of the stock minus the fair value of Frey's identifiable assets ($1,900,000 – $1,830,000).

7. **(c)** A subsidiary should not be consolidated when it is in bankruptcy. Consolidation of all majority-owned subsidiaries is required regardless of the industry or business of the subsidiary. A difference in fiscal periods of a parent and a subsidiary does not of itself justify the exclusion of the subsidiary from consolidation.

8. **(b)** The consideration paid plus the fair value of the noncontrolling interest plus the fair value of any previous purchases of common stock is less than the fair value of the net identifiable assets acquired, the acquirer should recognize a gain from bargain purchase on the income statement.

The gain would be equal to $20,000 ($820,000 – 800,000). Answer (a) is incorrect because goodwill is only recognized when the purchase price is greater than the fair value of the recorded assets. Answer (c) is incorrect because it describes an inappropriate method. Answer (d) is incorrect because the gain is not treated as extraordinary.

9. (b) The direct costs of acquisition should be an expense of the period in a business combination accounted for by the acquisition method. General expenses related to the acquisition are also deducted as incurred in determining the combined corporation's net income for the current period.

10. (c) Answer (c) is correct because the acquisition method applies only to acquisitions of a business. Answers (a), (b), and (d) are incorrect because none of these situations would constitute an acquisition,

11. (a) Preparing pro forma financial statements prior to acquisition is not required in the application of the acquisition method. Answers (b) and (c) are incorrect because identifying the acquirer and determining the acquisition date are both steps in applying the acquisition method. Answer (d) is incorrect because direct costs of acquisitions and general expenses related to an acquisition should be expensed in the period of acquisition.

12. (b) The acquisition date is the date the acquirer obtains control of the acquiree. Answer (a) is incorrect because the date a contract is signed usually does not correspond with the date control is acquired. Answer (c) is incorrect because the acquisition may occur before all contingencies are resolved. Answer (d) is incorrect because control constitutes owning more than 50% of the shares of stock outstanding.

13. (c) Any previously held shares should be remeasured at fair value as of the date control is acquired, and the gain is recognized in earnings of the period. If an unrealized gain was previously recognized in other comprehensive income, the amount recognized in other comprehensive income should also be recognized as a gain in the current period. Answer (a) is incorrect because previously held shares are remeasured to fair value on the acquisition date. Answer (b) is incorrect because any gain is recognized in earnings of the period. Answer (d) is incorrect because the previously issued shares must be revalued at the acquisition date and included as part of the cost of the acquisition.

14. (c) Intangibles are recognized as assets apart from goodwill if they arise from contractual or legal rights, regardless of whether those rights are transferable or separable from the acquired entity or from other rights and obligations. If an intangible asset does not arise from contractual or other legal rights, it is recognized as an asset apart from goodwill only if it is separable (i.e., capable of being sold, transferred, or licensed). Trademarks, lease agreements, and patents all arise from contractual or legal rights. Employee quality does not and is not separable.

15. (b) The acquisition method is required for all business combinations. In applying the acquisition method, the acquisition cost is allocated to acquired assets and liabilities based on their relative fair values. Any excess of cost over the fair value of net identifiable assets is allocated to goodwill.

16. (d) The cost of the investment is $60,000. The fair value of the noncontrolling interest, $10,000, is added to the cost of the investment of $60,000, to get the fair value of the net assets of the business, $70,000. Next, the book value ($50,000) is subtracted from the fair value to arrive at the differential of $20,000 ($70,000 – $50,000), which represents the amount used to write up undervalued assets and recognize goodwill. Inventory is increased by 60% of the $20,000, or $12,000. Therefore, current assets should be reported at $102,000, as calculated below.

Current assets—Polk	$ 70,000
Current assets—Strass	20,000
Excess allocated to inventory	12,000
Total current assets	$102,000

17. (c) The acquisition method requires the assets of the acquired firm to be recorded at their fair values. The fair value of the net assets of the acquiree is determined by adding the acquirer's cost to the fair value of noncontrolling interest. In this case the fair value would be equal to $70,000 ($60,000 + $10,000). The excess of the fair value over book value is allocated 60% to inventory and 40% to goodwill. Goodwill would be recorded at $8,000 ($20,000 × 40%). Therefore, noncurrent assets should be reported at $138,000 as calculated below.

Noncurrent assets—Polk	$ 90,000
Noncurrent assets—Strass	40,000
Excess allocated to goodwill	8,000
Total noncurrent assets	$138,000

18. (b) In the consolidated balance sheet, the parent company's "investment in subsidiary" account should be eliminated and replaced by the assets and liabilities of the subsidiary. Therefore, the consolidated balance sheet should include the current liabilities of both companies, plus the current portion of the debt incurred on 1/2/Y1 ($60,000 ÷ 10 = $6,000). Thus, current liabilities should be reported at $46,000 as computed below.

Current liabilities—Polk	$30,000
Current liabilities—Strass	10,000
Current portion of new debt	6,000
Total	$46,000

19. (c) In the consolidated balance sheet, the parent company's "investment in subsidiary" account should be eliminated and replaced by the assets and liabilities of the subsidiary. Therefore, the consolidated balance sheet should include the noncurrent liabilities of both companies, plus the noncurrent portion of the debt incurred on 1/2/Y1 ($60,000 – $6,000 = $54,000).

Noncurrent liabilities—Polk	$ 50,000
Noncurrent liabilities—Strass	0
Noncurrent portion of new debt	54,000
Total	$104,000

20. (c) In the consolidated balance sheet, neither the parent company's investment account nor the subsidiary's stockholders' equity is reported. These amounts are eliminated in the same journal entry that records the excess of cost over book value. The portion of the subsidiary's stockholders' equity that is **not** eliminated is reported as noncontrolling interest in the equity section of the consolidated balance sheet. Therefore, the parent's stockholders' equity ($90,000) equals the consolidated stockholders' equity plus the minority interest. Note that once the candidate has completed items 16 through 20, the answers can be checked using the balance sheet equation.

Current assets		Non-current assets		Current liabilities		Non-current liabilities		Stock-holders' equity
	+		=		+		+	
$102,000	+	$138,000	=	$46,000	+	$104,000	+	$90,000

21. (c) In an acquisition, the net assets of the acquired firm are recorded at their FV. The excess of the cost of the investment over the FV of the net assets acquired is allocated to goodwill. The cost of this investment is $3,750,000 (250,000 shares × $15), and the FV of the net assets acquired, **excluding goodwill** is $3,400,000 ($3,000,000 + $400,000). Therefore, the amount allocated to goodwill is $350,000 ($3,750,000 – $3,400,000).

22. (c) The correct answer is calculated as illustrated below.

Assets transferred	$ 700,000
Plus: Noncontrolling interest in Sloan 10,000 shares × $18	180,000
Less: Fair value of net identifiable assets of Sloan	(800,000)
Goodwill recognized	$ 80,000

23. (c) The assets acquired would be revalued to their fair market value. Answer (c) is correct because the inventory account would then include the difference between the market value and book value. Answer (a) is incorrect because a deferred credit is never recorded. Answer (b) is incorrect because goodwill represents the excess of cost plus the fair value of previously held interests plus the fair value of noncontrolling interest less the fair value of net identifiable assets. Answer (d) is incorrect because the retained earnings account is not affected by this transaction when acquisition accounting is used.

24. (d) Answer (d) is correct because all assets and liabilities (including plant and equipment and long-term debt) should be reported at fair value.

25. (d) When the fair value of identifiable assets acquired in a business acquisition exceeds the sum of the consideration given and the fair value of previously held interest plus the fair value of noncontrolling interests, the difference is recorded as a bargain purchase. Answer (d) is correct because a gain is recognized on the income statement in the current period. Answer (a) is incorrect because negative goodwill is not recorded. Answer (b) is incorrect because the difference is not treated as a part of additional paid-in capital. Answer (c) is incorrect because it describes the accounting treatment no longer allowed.

26. (d) Consolidated statements are prepared as if the parent and subsidiaries were one economic entity. From the point of view of the consolidated entity, any intercompany receivables or payables from parent to subsidiary or vice versa are **not** payable to or receivable from any **outside** company. In other words, the consolidated entity does not have a receivable or payable. Therefore, all of Wright's intercompany receivables, payables and advances are eliminated. None are reported as intercompany receivables.

27. (a) When a subsidiary prepares separate financial statements, intercompany receivables (and payables) should be reported in the balance sheet as a separate line item.

When consolidated financial statements are prepared by the parent company, all intercompany receivables (and payables) should be eliminated to avoid overstating assets and liabilities.

28. (d) Pard's separate revenues are $200,000, and Spin's separate revenues are $140,000, resulting in a total of $340,000 ($200,000 + $140,000). Since the consolidated income statement shows sales of only $308,000, intercompany sales of $32,000 ($340,000 – $308,000) from Pard to Spin must have been eliminated during consolidation.

29. (b) Pard's separate accounts receivable is $26,000, and Spin's separate accounts receivable is $19,000, resulting in a total of $45,000 ($26,000 + $19,000). Since the consolidated balance sheet shows accounts receivable of only $39,000, intercompany receivables of $6,000 ($45,000 – $39,000) must have been eliminated during consolidation. Since Pard sold goods to Spin that Spin had not fully paid for by 12/31/Y1, the eliminated receivable must be Pard's receivable from Spin. Therefore, Spin's 12/31/Y1 payable to Pard is also $6,000.

30. (c) Pard's intercompany sales to Spin totaled $32,000 during year 1. Therefore, Spin recorded a purchase of inventory of $32,000. At 12/31/Y1, Spin still held 37.5% of these goods in inventory; in Spin's books, this inventory was carried at $12,000 (37.5% × $32,000). In the consolidated balance sheet, the intercompany profit would be eliminated, and this inventory would be carried at Pard's original cost. Pard's sales to Spin were at the same markup on cost that Pard uses for all sales. In Pard's income statement, cost of sales is 75% of sales ($150,000 ÷ $200,000). Therefore, Pard's original cost for the $12,000 of goods in Spin's inventory is $9,000 (75% × $12,000).

31. (c) The fair value of the 20,000 (100,000 × 20%) shares of noncontrolling interest in Stone on the date of acquisition is $1,040,000 (20,000 shares × $52 per share). This amount is adjusted for the noncontrolling interest's share of net income and dividends received as calculated below.

Fair value of noncontrolling interest, acquisition date	$1,040,000
Plus: Share of net income (20% × $280,000)	56,000
Less: Share of dividends (20% × 50,000)	(10,000)
Noncontrolling interest 12/31/Y1	$1,086,000

32. (a) When the equity method of accounting is used the parent company's retained earnings will be equal to the consolidated retained earnings balance. It can be determined that the equity method is being followed because the account "Equity in earnings of Sharp" appears in the parent's income statement. In addition it is important to note that the balance sheet accounts presented are dated as of the end of the year; therefore, the parent company's retained earnings of $1,240,000, should already include **all** income statement balance account adjustments. Thus, no additional income amounts will need to be added to the $1,240,000 retained earnings balance, in order to determine the total retained earnings balance.

33. (d) The requirement is to determine which accounting concept relates to the preparation of consolidated financial statements. Answer (d) is correct because when a parent-subsidiary relationship exists, the financial statements of each separate entity are brought together, or consolidated. When financial statements represent a consolidated entity, the concept of economic entity applies. Answer (a) is incorrect because reliability is a concept that applies to all financial statements, not just consolidated financial statements. Reliability is a primary quality that makes accounting information useful for decision making. This quality should be found in all statements. Answer (b) is incorrect because the concept of materiality applies to all financial statements, not just consolidated financial statements. The concept of materiality, as applied to financial statements, deals with the impact an item in the financial statements will have on a user's decision-making process. Answer (c) is incorrect because the concept of legal entity refers to the form or type of combination that takes place between entities (i.e., mergers, consolidations or acquisitions), not the basis on which financial statements are prepared.

34. (b) In general, all assets and liabilities (including equipment) should be reported at market value. The excess of the equipment's market value over its carrying amount is allocated to the equipment and amortized over the equipment's useful life. The unamortized portion of the excess of the market value over the carrying amount of the equipment is then reported as part of plant and equipment. Only the excess of the acquisition cost over the market value of the net identifiable assets acquired is reported as goodwill. The excess of the market value over the carrying amount of the equipment is capitalized and subsequently amortized over the equipment's useful life, **not** expensed on the date of the acquisition.

35. (a) When two companies own stock in each other, a reciprocal ownership relationship exists. In this case, Pride (the parent) owns 80% of Simba (the sub), and Simba owns 10% of Pride. When Pride declares a cash dividend, 90% of it is distributed to outside parties and 10% goes to Simba. Because Simba is part of the consolidated entity, its 10% share of Pride's dividend is eliminated when determining consolidated dividends declared. Thus, only 90% of dividends declared by Pride will be reported in the consolidated financial statements. When Simba declares a dividend, 80% of the dividend is distributed to Pride (the parent), and 20% is distributed to outside parties (the noncontrolling interest of Simba stock). The 80% share to Pride is eliminated when determining consolidated dividends declared because it represents an intercompany transaction. The remaining 20% to the noncontrolling interest is likewise not included in consolidated dividends declared because, from the parent company's point of view, subsidiary dividends do not represent dividends of the consolidated entity and must be eliminated.

36. (c) It is presumed that an entity with equity of less than 10% of total assets does not have sufficient funding to finance its activities unless there is definitive evidence to the contrary (e.g., a source of outside financing).

37. (b) A variable interest entity should be consolidated by the primary beneficiary. A primary beneficiary has the power to direct the activities of the VIE that most significantly impact the VIE's economic performance, and has the obligation to absorb the majority of the entity's expected losses if they occur, or receive the majority of the residual returns if they occur, or both.

38. (a) The determination of whether an entity is a variable interest entity and which enterprise should consolidate that entity is made at the time the enterprise initially gets involved with the variable interest entity and is reassessed on an ongoing basis.

39. (d) Accounting changes that result in financial statements that are, in effect, financial statements of a different reporting entity (such as presenting consolidated statements in place of statements of individual companies) should be reported by restating the financial statements of all prior periods presented so that the resulting restated prior periods' statements on a consolidated basis are the same as if the subsidiary had been consolidated since it was acquired.

40. (b) In an acquisition, the consolidated financial statements reflect the combined operations of the parent and subsidiary **from the date of combination**. Earnings of the subsidiary prior to the combination are **not** included with the parent's income. The parent's year 1 income is $1,575,000 ($750,000 + $825,000), while the subsidiary's income after the combination is $375,000 for a total of $1,950,000 ($1,575,000 + $375,000). The unrealized inventory profit of $45,000 must be eliminated, because from a consolidated viewpoint, revenue cannot be recognized until these goods are sold to a third party (i.e., a sale has not yet occurred). Therefore, year 1 consolidated net income is $1,905,000 ($1,950,000 – $45,000). Note that the net income amounts given are from **separate company operations,** so no elimination of equity earnings or dividend income is necessary.

41. (d) In combined financial statements, the statements include only the adjusted retained earnings of the parent. The subsidiary's retained earnings are **not** included. Since Pane uses the equity method to account for its investment in Sky, Pane's net income will include its share of the net earnings of Sky. Therefore, 6/30/Y2 consolidated retained earnings is equal to $3,250,000 ($3,200,000 + $800,000 – $750,000).

42. (d) Unrealized profit in ending inventory arises when intercompany sales are made at prices above cost and the merchandise is not resold to third parties prior to year-end. The profit is unrealized because the inventory has not yet been sold outside of the consolidated entity. In this case, Pirn sold goods to Scroll for $100,000, which would become Scroll's cost. However, Scroll's cost of goods sold includes only $80,000 of goods acquired from Pirn. Therefore, $20,000 of original $100,000 remains in Scroll's ending inventory. Since Pirn's gross profit rate is 30% ($150,000 ÷ $500,000), the gross profit Pirn recognized on the original $20,000 amount in Scroll's inventory was $6,000 (30% × $20,000). This intercompany profit must be eliminated on the consolidating worksheet.

43. (b) When computing consolidated income, the objective is to restate the accounts as if the intercompany transactions had not occurred. When Scroll recorded depreciation, it included depreciation on the asset purchased from Pirn for $36,000. Since Pirn recorded a $12,000 gain when it sold the asset to Scroll, Pirn's book value at the time of sale must have been $24,000. Therefore, consolidated depreciation expense should be based on $24,000 rather than on $36,000. Depreciation expense for year 1 must be decreased by $3,000 ($12,000 excess ÷ 4 years). Depreciation expense in Pirn's year 1 consolidated income statement should therefore be $47,000, as computed below.

Pirn's recorded depr.	$40,000
Scroll's recorded depr.	10,000
Less adjustment ($12,000 ÷ 4)	(3,000)
	$47,000

44. (c) Unrealized profit in ending inventory arises when intercompany sales are made at prices above cost and the merchandise is not resold to third parties prior to year-end. The profit is unrealized because the inventory has not yet been sold outside of the consolidated entity. In this case, there is no unrealized profit on the sales to Dean because the consolidated statements would not include Dean, and the equity method is not applicable. (Clark owns only 15% of Dean). However, there is unrealized profit on the materials sold by Kent, a wholly owned subsidiary, to Clark. Sixty thousand dollars of the $240,000 of materials sold by Kent to Clark remains in ending inventory. The gross profit Kent recognized on this $60,000 of materials at the time of sale was $12,000 ($48,000 ÷ $240,000 = 20% gross profit rate; 20% × $60,000 = $12,000). For the consolidated entity, this $12,000 gross profit has not been earned and must be eliminated. Therefore, consolidated current assets should be $308,000 ($320,000 – $12,000).

45. (c) When preparing the consolidated income statement, the objective is to restate the accounts as if the intercompany transactions had not occurred. As a result of the intercompany sale, Parker has recorded $250,000 of sales and Smith has recorded $250,000 cost of sales which should be eliminated (note that Parker's **cost of sales** on the original sale is the amount left in consolidated cost of sales, and Smith's **sales** when the goods were sold to outside parties is the amount left in consolidated sales). Therefore, Parker should report $500,000 as cost of sales in the year 1 consolidated income statement ($400,000 + $350,000 – $250,000).

46. (a) Pare's separate gross profit is $100,000, and Shel's separate gross profit is $60,000, resulting in a total of $160,000. Since the consolidated income statement shows gross profit of only $154,000, unrealized intercompany profit of $6,000 ($160,000 – $154,000) must have been eliminated.

47. (d) The requirement is to determine the amount of **selling** expenses to be reported in Pard's year 1 consolidated income statement. Pard's selling expenses for year 1 include $50,000 in freight-out costs for goods sold to Seed, its subsidiary. This $50,000 becomes part of Seed's inventory because it is a cost directly associated with bringing the goods to a salable condition. None of the $50,000 represents a selling expense for the consolidated entity, and $1,450,000 ($1,100,000 + $400,000 – $50,000) should be reported as selling expenses in the consolidated income statement.

48. (a) When preparing consolidated financial statements, the objective is to restate the accounts as if the intercompany transactions had not occurred. Therefore, the year 1 gain on sale of machine of $50,000 [$900,000 – ($1,100,000 – $250,000)] must be eliminated, since the consolidated entity has not realized a gain. In effect, the machine must be reflected on the consolidated balance sheet at 1/1/Y1 at Poe's cost of $1,100,000, and accumulated depreciation of $250,000, instead of at a new "cost" of $900,000. For consolidated statement purposes, year 1 depreciation is

based on the original amounts [($1,100,000 – $100,000) × 1/20 = $50,000]. Therefore, in the 12/31/Y1 **consolidated** balance sheet, the machine is shown at a cost of $1,100,000 less accumulated depreciation of $300,000 ($250,000 + $50,000).

49. (a) When Seal purchased the bonds from Wagner, the bonds were viewed as retired from a consolidated viewpoint since there is no longer any obligation to an outside party. Therefore, the consolidated entity would recognize a $100,000 gain ($1,075,000 carrying amount – $975,000 cash paid), which would increase consolidated retained earnings. This transaction has no effect on noncontrolling interest, since the subsidiary (Seal) has merely exchanged one asset for another (cash for investment in bonds).

50. (a) The requirement is to determine the amount of gain to be reported on the consolidated income statement when a wholly owned subsidiary purchases parent company stock. A parent company reports no gain or loss when a wholly owned subsidiary purchases its common stock. In effect, the consolidated entity is purchasing treasury stock when the purchase is made, and gains are not recognized on treasury stock transactions. The dividends paid by the parent to the subsidiary also do not affect income because such intercompany transactions are eliminated when consolidated financial statements are prepared. Therefore, $0 gain should be reported by the consolidated entity.

51. (a) When computing consolidated income, the objective is to restate the accounts as if the intercompany transactions had not occurred. As a result of the intercompany sales, sales and cost of goods sold are overstated and an eliminating entry is needed to reduce these accounts by the entire amount of the intercompany sales. Therefore, answer (a) is correct. Answer (b) is incorrect because sales and cost of goods sold need to be reduced by the entire amount of the intercompany sales in order to arrive at their proper consolidated amounts. Answer (c) is incorrect because net income is not affected by the intercompany sale. Sales and cost of goods sold are overstated by the same amount; thus, net income is correct for consolidated purposes. Answer (d) is incorrect because an adjustment is necessary.

52. (c) The key to this problem is that the equipment must be revalued at Winston's carrying amount (Winston's original cost less accumulated depreciation) in the consolidation process. Assume the following potential scenario:

Winston buys a piece of equipment on 1/1/Y2 for $1,000. At 12/31/Y2, the equipment was depreciated $200, and Winston's carrying value is $800 ($1,000 – $200). On 12/31/Y2, Winston sells the equipment to Foster for $900. Foster's original cost is therefore $900, and Winston will record a $100 gain that must be eliminated. After consolidation, the equipment is reported at $800, Winston's carrying value. Winston's carrying value is also equal to Foster's original cost ($900) less Winston's recorded gain ($100). Answer (a) is incorrect because Foster's original cost includes an unrealized gain that must be eliminated. Answer (b) is incorrect because revaluing the equipment at Winston's original cost would not take into consideration the depreciation already recorded by Winston. Answer (d) is incorrect because the entire gain, not 80% of the gain, must be eliminated because this is a downstream sale from the parent to the subsidiary.

53. (b)   The requirement is to determine by how much depreciation will be reduced. Use the solutions approach and set up a simple numerical example.

> Port's original cost = $1,000
> Depreciation per yr = $200
> Selling price = $810

If Port sells equipment for $810, it recognizes a $210 gain on the sale (selling price of $810 – carrying value of the equipment $600). Salem, Inc. will now depreciate the equipment on their books at $810, the price that they paid. Because the gain was not realized with an entity outside of the consolidated entity, it must be eliminated. In the consolidated financial statements, equipment will be reported at its original carrying value, the gain on the sale will be removed and depreciation expense must be recorded at Port, Inc. original amount ($200), not the amount of depreciation that Salem, Inc. records. Salem would record depreciation of $270 ($810/3). Therefore, depreciation must be reduced by $70 on the consolidated financial statements to reflect the original depreciation recorded by Port. Depreciation is reduced by $70, which as shown by the example, is 33 1/3% of the gain ($70/$210).

54. (a)   This question is silent as to which year consolidated financial statements are being prepared. However, answer (a) is correct for either the year of acquisition or a subsequent year. If financial statements were being prepared for the current year the loss would be reported as an ordinary loss on the income statement. P Co. acquired the 20% interest in S Company bonds and incurred a loss on them. This loss would be carried through to the consolidated balance sheet as a decrease in retained earnings. In subsequent years, the unamortized portion of the loss would also decrease retained earnings.

55. (b)   Because Planet owns 70% interest in Star, the noncontrolling interest in star is 30%. Therefore, the noncontrolling interest's share in Star's net income of $80,000 is 30% × $80,000 = $24,000. Planet's sale of merchandise to Star for $10,000 will be eliminated on the consolidated worksheet, and Planet's income will be reduced by the intercompany profit of $2,000. This will not affect the noncontrolling interest's share of income because it was a downstream sale from the parent to the subsidiary and is eliminated by the parent.

56. (d)   The cost of acquisition is $975,000. The fair value of Shaw's assets is equal to their book values plus the amount of the write-up, or $1,100,000 ($1,000,000 + 100,000). Goodwill is calculated as follows:

Consideration transferred	$ 975,000
Plus: Fair value of noncontrolling	
interest	250,000
Less: Fair value of net identifiable assets	$(1,100,000)
Amount of goodwill	$ 125,000

57. (d)   The percentage of the subsidiary's stockholders' equity not owned by the parent represents the noncontrolling interest's share of the fair value of net assets of the subsidiary. The fair value of the noncontrolling interest is measured at the acquisition date, and adjusted in future periods for the portion of the acquiree's income and dividends attributable to the noncontrolling interest. Therefore, the noncontrolling interest at 12/31/Y1 is calculated as follows:

Fair value of noncontrolling interests	$250,000
Plus: Share of net income ($190,000 × 20%)	38,000
Less: Share of dividends ($125,000 × 20%)	(25,000)
Noncontrolling interest 12/31/Y1	$263,000

58. (b)   Pare paid cash dividends of $25,000 and Kidd, the 75%-owned subsidiary, paid cash dividends of $5,000. The dividends paid by Pare are all payments to owners of the consolidated company and are reported as dividends paid in the consolidated statement of retained earnings. The $5,000 dividend paid by Kidd is paid 75% to Pare, and 25% to outside parties (the noncontrolling interest in Kidd's stock). The 75% share to Pare is eliminated when determining consolidated dividends declared because it is an intracompany transaction. The remaining 25% to the noncontrolling interest is likewise not included in consolidated dividends declared because, from the parent company's point of view, subsidiary dividends do not represent dividends of the consolidated entity.

59. (c)   The percentage of the subsidiary's stockholders' equity not owned by the parent represents the noncontrolling interest's share of the fair value of net assets of the subsidiary. The fair value of the noncontrolling interest is measured at the acquisition date, and adjusted in future periods for the portion of the acquiree's income and dividends attributable to the noncontrolling interest. Therefore, the noncontrolling interest at 12/31/Y1 is calculated as follows:

Fair value of noncontrolling interest	$35,000
Plus: Share of net income (25% × 20,000)	5,000
Less: Share of dividends (25% × $5,000)	(1,250)
Noncontrolling interest 12/31/Y1	$38,750

60. (b)   In the consolidated balance sheet, neither the parent company's investment account nor the subsidiary's stockholders' equity is reported. These amounts are eliminated in the same journal entry that records the excess of cost over book value. The portion of the subsidiary's stockholders' equity that is **not** eliminated is reported as noncontrolling interest. Therefore, the amount reported as common stock in the 12/31/Y1 consolidated balance sheet consists solely of Pare's common stock ($100,000). Kidd's common stock ($50,000) is eliminated along with the rest of its stockholders' equity.

61. (d)   Consideration includes the fair value of the assets transferred, the fair value of the liabilities incurred by the acquirer, the fair value of any contingent consideration, and any equity interest issued by the acquirer. Consideration does not include share-based payments exchanged voluntarily by the acquirer.

62. (d)   If information is incomplete at the acquisition date, the items should be recorded at a provisional amount measured at the date of acquisition. Answers (a), (b), and (c) are incorrect because they do not describe appropriate ways to account for situations in which there is incomplete information.

63. (a)   If the acquirer has incomplete accounting information on the date of acquisition, the measurement period ends when the acquirer receives the information or one year from the date of acquisition, whichever occurs first. Answer (b) is incorrect because contingent consideration is recorded at a provisional amount during the measurement period, and is remeasured each reporting period until the contingency is resolved. Remeasuring the contingency does not affect the measurement period. Answers (c) and (d) are incorrect because they do not describe the end of the measurement period.

64. (c) If it is determined during the measurement period that a provisional amount is not accurate, the change is recognized by retrospectively adjusting the provisional amount and making a corresponding adjustment to goodwill. Answers (a), (b), and (d) are incorrect because they describe inappropriate ways of handling the new information.

65. (a) If the acquirer is required to replace share-based payments, and no further service is required of the employees, the share-based payments are treated as part of the consideration transferred in the acquisition. The amount should be capitalized as a cost of acquisition of the acquiree. Answers (b), (c), and (d) are incorrect because the amount should not affect the income statement.

66. (b) If no further service is required to be provided and Post voluntarily replaces the awards, compensation expense is recognized in the postcombination financial statements when the awards are made. Answers (a), (c), and (d) are incorrect because they describe inappropriate ways to account for the awards.

67. (b) A liability for a contingency should be derecognized only after the contingency has been resolved. Answers (a), (c), and (d) are incorrect because they represent inappropriate points in time to derecognize a contingent liability.

68. (b) The requirement is to determine how much of Sago's year 2 net income should be reported as accruing to Phillips. In an acquisition, consolidated net income reflects the parent's net income to the date of combination and both entities' income after the combination. Phillips, Inc. can only recognize the net income of Sago, based on their 20% interest, up to the date of combination. However, after the date of combination they will recognize 95% of Sago's net income, their new ownership interest.

69. (d) **Combined financial statements** are financial statements prepared for companies that are owned by the same parent company or individual. Combined financial statements are prepared by combining all the companies' financial statement classifications. Intercompany transactions and profits should be eliminated in the same way as for consolidated statements. Therefore, **none** of the intercompany receivables should be included in the combined financial statements.

70. (c) The inventory reported on the 12/31/Y1 combined balance sheet should reflect the **original cost** to the companies of any inventory on hand. The inventory on hand that was acquired from outside parties should be reported at its cost ($175,000 + $250,000 = $425,000). The Banks inventory on hand that was acquired from Lamm must be restated back to the cost Lamm originally paid when it was purchased from outside parties. This must be done to eliminate intercompany profits. During year 1, Lamm shipped inventory that originally cost $150,000 to Banks at a billing price of $200,000. Therefore, the original cost is 75% of Banks' carrying amount. Therefore, the correct inventory amount is $470,000 [$175,000 + $250,000 + ($60,000 × 75%)].

71. (b) Combined financial statements are prepared for companies that are owned by the same parent company or individual but are not consolidated. These statements are prepared by combining the separate companies' financial statement classifications. Intercompany transactions, balances, and profit (loss) should be eliminated. Therefore, to determine the gross profit in Bee and Cee's combined income statement, the intercompany profit resulting from Bee's sales to Cee should be eliminated. Cee sold to outsiders 50% ($65,000/$130,000) of the inventory purchased from Bee. The cost of sales to the combined entity is thus 50% of the $100,000 cost of sales reported by Bee. Gross profit of the combined entity amounts to $41,000, which is $91,000 of sales to unrelated companies less $50,000 cost of sales.

72. (a) When computing sales to be reported in the combined income statement, the objective is to restate the accounts as if the intercompany transaction had not occurred. Assuming that there were no sales between Home Office and Branch, the correct amount of sales to be included in the combined income statement is the $250,000 sold by Branch to unrelated customers.

73. (b) Combined financial statements is the term used to describe financial statements prepared for companies that are owned by the same parent company or individual. Combined financial statements are prepared by combining all of the subsidiaries' financial statement classifications. Intercompany transactions should be eliminated in the same way as for consolidated statements. Combining the stockholders' equity accounts of Able and Baker results in a total of $430,000 ($100,000 + $20,000 + $300,000 + $10,000). The intercompany balances (Investment in Baker, $4,000; and Common Stock, $4,000) must be eliminated, which reduces combined stockholders' equity to $426,000 ($430,000 – $4,000).

74. (c) **Combined financial statements** are financial statements prepared for companies that are owned by the same parent company or individual. Combined financial statements are prepared by combining all the companies' financial statement classifications. Intercompany transactions and profits should be eliminated in the same way as for consolidated statements. Therefore, **none** of the intercompany loans or profits should be included in the combined financial statements.

75. (d) Combined statements may be used to present the financial position and results of operations of commonly controlled companies, companies under common management, and of a group of unconsolidated subsidiaries.

76. (c) Where combined statements are prepared for a group of related companies, intercompany transactions and profit and losses should be eliminated. Matters such as noncontrolling interests, income taxes, foreign operations, or different fiscal periods should be treated in the same manner for both combined financial statements and consolidated statements.

77. (c) When combined statements are prepared for a group of related companies, and there are issues in connection with such matters as noncontrolling interests, foreign operations, different fiscal periods, or income taxes, they should be treated in the same manner as in consolidated statements.

78. **(a)** The requirement is to identify the statement that correctly describes how goodwill may be recognized under IFRS. Answer (a) is correct because goodwill can only be recognized if it is acquired by purchase.

79. **(c)** The requirement is to identify the item that is not a condition to exclude a subsidiary from consolidation under IFRS. Answer (c) is correct because it is not required that the subsidiary have only one class of stock.

Simulations

Task-Based Simulation 1

Concepts		
	Authoritative Literature	Help

On January 1, year 1 Rain acquires 90% of the stock in Snow in a transaction properly accounted for as a business combination. **Items 1 through 6** below refer to accounts that may or may not be included in Rain and Snow's consolidated financial statements. The list below refers to the various possibilities of those amounts to be reported in Rain's consolidated financial statements for the year ended December 31, year 2. Both Rain and Snow paid dividends to investors. Ignore income tax considerations.

Responses to be selected
A. Sum of amounts on Rain and Snow's separate unconsolidated financial statements
B. Less than the sum of amounts on Rain and Snow's separate unconsolidated financial statements but not the same as the amount on either
C. Same as amount for Rain only
D. Same as amount for Snow only
E. Eliminated entirely in consolidation
F. Shown in consolidated financial statements but not in separate unconsolidated financial statements
G. Neither in consolidated nor in separate unconsolidated financial statements

	(A)	(B)	(C)	(D)	(E)	(F)	(G)
1. Cash	O	O	O	O	O	O	O
2. Investment in subsidiary	O	O	O	O	O	O	O
3. Noncontrolling interest	O	O	O	O	O	O	O
4. Common stock	O	O	O	O	O	O	O
5. Beginning retained earnings	O	O	O	O	O	O	O
6. Dividends paid	O	O	O	O	O	O	O

Task-Based Simulation 2

Journal Entries		
	Authoritative Literature	Help

On January 1, year 2, Near purchases 100% of the stock of Far in a transaction that was properly accounted for as a business combination. **Items 1 through 3** below represent transactions between Near and Far during year 2. Prepare the eliminating entries in general journal format for each of these transactions.

1. On January 3, year 2, Near sold equipment with an original cost of $30,000 and a carrying value of $15,000 to Far for $36,000. The equipment had a remaining life of three years and was depreciated using the straight-line method by both companies.

2. During year 2, Near sold merchandise to Far for $60,000, which included a profit of $20,000. At December 31, year 2, half of this merchandise remained in Far's inventory.

3. On December 31, year 2, Near paid $91,000 to purchase $100,000 of the outstanding bonds issued by Far. The bonds mature on December 31, year 6, and were originally issued at par ($100,000). The bonds pay interest annually on December 31 of each year, and the interest was paid to the prior investor immediately before Near's purchase of the bonds.

Task-Based Simulation 3

Financial Statement Amounts		
	Authoritative Literature	Help

Presented below are selected amounts from the separate unconsolidated financial statements of Poe Corp. and its 90%-owned subsidiary, Shaw Co., at December 31, year 2. Additional information follows:

	Poe	Shaw
Selected income statement amounts		
Sales	$ 710,000	$ 530,000
Cost of goods sold	490,000	370,000
Gain on sale of equipment	--	21,000
Earnings from investment in subsidiary	63,000	--
Interest expense	--	16,000
Depreciation	25,000	20,000
Selected balance sheet amounts		
Cash	$ 50,000	$ 15,000
Inventories	229,000	150,000
Equipment	440,000	360,000
Accumulated depreciation	(200,000)	(120,000)
Investment in Shaw	191,000	--
Investment in Shaw bonds	100,000	--
Discount on bonds	(9,000)	--
Bonds payable	--	(200,000)
Common stock	(100,000)	(10,000)
Additional paid-in capital	(250,000)	(40,000)
Retained earnings	(404,000)	(140,000)
Selected statement of retained earnings amounts		
Beginning balance, December 31, year 1	$ 272,000	$ 100,000
Net income	212,000	70,000
Dividends paid	80,000	30,000

Additional information

- On January 2, year 2, Poe, Inc. purchased 90% of Shaw Co.'s 100,000 outstanding common stock for cash of $155,000. On that date the fair value of the noncontrolling interest was $1.70 per share. On that date, Shaw's stockholders' equity equaled $150,000 and the fair values of Shaw's identifiable assets and liabilities equaled their carrying amounts. Poe has accounted for the purchase as an acquisition.
- On January 3, year 2, Poe sold equipment with an original cost of $30,000 and a carrying value of $15,000 to Shaw for $36,000. The equipment had a remaining life of three years and was depreciated using the straight-line method by both companies.
- During year 2, Poe sold merchandise to Shaw for $60,000, which included a profit of $20,000. At December 31, year 2, half of this merchandise remained in Shaw's inventory.
- On December 31, year 2, Poe paid $91,000 to purchase 50% of the outstanding bonds issued by Shaw. The bonds mature on December 31, 2015, and were originally issued at par. The bonds pay interest annually on December 31 of each year, and the interest was paid to the prior investor immediately before Poe's purchase of the bonds.
- On September 4, year 2, Shaw paid cash dividends of $30,000.
- On December 31, year 2, Poe recorded its equity in Shaw's earnings.

Calculate the amounts that will appear on Poe's consolidated financial statement on December 31, year 2.

1. Cash

2. Goodwill

3. Equipment

4. Common stock

5. Investment in Shaw

6. Dividends

7. Bonds payable

8. Noncontrolling interest

Task-Based Simulation 4

Research		
	Authoritative Literature	Help

Webster Corporation is acquiring Urton Company. You have been asked to research the professional literature to determine at what amounts the assets and liabilities of Urton should be recorded on the books of Webster Corporation. Place the citation for the excerpt from Professional Standards that provides this information in the answer box below.

Task-Based Simulation 5

Concepts		
	Authoritative Literature	Help

Answer True or False to each of the following questions by checking the correct box.

		True	False
1.	A company can use either the purchase or the pooling method for business combinations.	O	O
2.	Total revenues for a consolidated entity are calculated by adding the total revenue of the parent for the year and the total revenue of the subsidiary from the date of acquisition.	O	O
3.	Goodwill is amortized over a period of forty years.	O	O
4.	Goodwill is classified and included with other intangible assets for purposes of measuring impairment.	O	O
5.	Intangible assets with indefinite lives are not amortized.	O	O
6.	The stockholder equity accounts in the consolidated balance sheet are those of the parent company.	O	O
7.	The effect of unrealized profits and sales between the acquirer and acquiree is classified as an intercompany transaction and must be eliminated.	O	O
8.	A newly identified intangible asset must meet the contractual legal or the separability criterion to be recognized as an intangible asset at the time of consolidation.	O	O

Task-Based Simulation 6

Consolidation at Date of Acquisition		
	Authoritative Literature	Help

On January 1, year 2, Arcelia Corporation acquired Gavino corporation by purchasing 100% of the stock of Gavino in exchange for 20,000 shares of Arcelia stock. On the date of acquisition Arcelia stock traded for $18 per share on the stock exchange. The fair market value of Gavino's inventory is $10,000 higher than the book value.

The book values of each company on January 1, year 2, are shown below.

	Arcelia Corp.	Gavino Corp.
Current assets	$320,000	$ 70,000
Noncurrent assets	640,000	380,000
Current liabilities	210,000	50,000
Noncurrent liabilities	150,000	90,000
Owners' equity	600,000	310,000

Calculate each of the following balance sheet amounts for Arcelia Corporation immediately following the acquisition of Gavino.

Total current assets	
Total noncurrent assets	
Total current liabilities	
Total noncurrent liabilities	
Total owners' equity	

Task-Based Simulation 7

Intercompany Transactions & Eliminations		
	Authoritative Literature	**Help**

On January 1, year 4, Arcelia Corporation acquired Gavino corporation by purchasing 100% of the stock of Gavino in exchange for 20,000 shares of Arcelia stock. On the date of acquisition Arcelia stock traded for $18 per share on the stock exchange. The fair market value of Gavino's inventory is $10,000 higher than the book value.

The book values of each company on January 1, year 4, are shown below.

	Arcelia Corp.	Gavino Corp.
Current assets	$320,000	$ 70,000
Noncurrent assets	640,000	380,000
Current liabilities	210,000	50,000
Noncurrent liabilities	150,000	90,000
Owners' equity	600,000	310,000

Additional information

- During year 4, the following transactions occurred:

  1. Arcelia sold inventory to Gavino for $50,000 on account. The normal profit on sales for Arcelia is 40%. At December 31, year 4, Gavino had 20% of the goods remaining in ending inventory. At December 31, year 4, Gavino had not paid Arcelia for $8,000 of the inventory.
  2. On October 1, year 4, Gavino Corp. sold equipment to Arcelia for $24,000. The equipment was purchased by Gavino on 1/1/Y1 for $60,000 and was depreciated straight-line over five years with no salvage value. Arcelia depreciated the new equipment over three years with no salvage value.

- During year 4, Arcelia did not make entries to record the income of Gavino.
- At December 31, year 4, totals from the preclosing trial balances of both firms are as follows:

Arcelia Corporation & Subsidiaries
UNADJUSTED TRIAL BALANCE
December 31, Year 4

	Arcelia Corp.	Gavino Corp.
Revenues	1,000,000	400,000
Expenses	780,000	335,000
Current assets	400,000	110,000
Noncurrent assets	1,260,000	420,000
Current liabilities	300,000	70,000
Noncurrent liabilities	180,000	85,000
Owners' equity	960,000	310,000

Below is a consolidation worksheet dated December 31, year 4 (before closing the books of Arcelia and Gavino). Prepare the following worksheet with working paper eliminations and entries.

Arcelia Corporation
CONSOLIDATION WORKSHEET
December 31, Year 4

| | Arcelia Corp. | Gavino Corp. | Elimination entries | | End balance |
			Debit	Credit	
Revenues and gains	1,000,000	400,000			
Expenses	780,000	335,000			
Current assets	400,000	110,000			
Noncurrent assets	1,260,000	420,000			
Current liabilities	300,000	70,000			
Differential					
Noncurrent liabilities	180,000	85,000			
Owners' equity	960,000	310,000			

Task-Based Simulation 8

Research		
	Authoritative Literature	Help

Wilson Corporation has several consolidated subsidiaries. You have been asked to research the professional literature to determine how intercompany transactions are treated for financial reporting purposes. Place the citation for the excerpt from Professional Standards that provides this information in the answer box below.

Simulation Solutions

Task-Based Simulation 1

Concepts		
	Authoritative Literature	**Help**

	(A)	(B)	(C)	(D)	(E)	(F)	(G)
1. Cash	●	○	○	○	○	○	○
2. Investment in subsidiary	○	○	○	○	●	○	○
3. Noncontrolling interest	○	○	○	○	○	●	○
4. Common stock	○	○	●	○	○	○	○
5. Beginning retained earnings	○	○	●	○	○	○	○
6. Dividends paid	○	○	●	○	○	○	○

Explanations

1. **(A)** Consolidated statements are prepared as if the parent and subsidiaries are one economic entity. Therefore, cash is included in the consolidated balance sheet at their full amounts regardless of the percentage ownership held by the parent.

2. **(E)** In the consolidated balance sheet, the parent company's "Investment in subsidiary" should be eliminated completely and replaced by the net assets of the subsidiary.

3. **(F)** The percentage of the subsidiary's stockholders' equity not owned by the parent company represents the noncontrolling interest's share of the net assets of the subsidiary. This amount is only reported in the consolidated balance sheet in the equity section.

4. **(C)** In the consolidated balance sheet the subsidiary's common stock is not reported. Therefore, the parent's common stock equals the consolidated common stock.

5. **(C)** In the consolidated balance sheet, the subsidiary's beginning retained earnings is not reported. Therefore, the parent's beginning retained earnings equals the consolidated beginning retained earnings.

6. **(C)** The dividends paid by the subsidiary are eliminated in the consolidated financial statements. Ninety percent of the dividends paid are eliminated along with the "Investment in subsidiary" elimination. The remaining 10% is reflected in "Noncontrolling Interest." Therefore, only the parent's dividends paid are included on the consolidated financial statements.

Task-Based Simulation 2

Journal Entries		
	Authoritative Literature	**Help**

1.

Gain on equipment	21,000	
Accumulated depreciation		15,000
Equipment		6,000
Accumulated depreciation	7,000	
Depreciation expense		7,000

2.

Sales	60,000	
Cost of goods sold		50,000
Ending inventory		10,000

3.

Bonds payable	100,000	
Discount on bonds	9,000	
Gain on retirement of bonds		9,000
Investment in bonds		100,000

Explanations

1. **($14,000)** When preparing consolidated financial statements, the objective is to restate the accounts as if the intercompany transactions had not occurred. Therefore, the year 2 gain on sale of equipment of $21,000 ($36,000 – $15,000) must be eliminated, since the consolidated entity has not realized any gain. In addition, for consolidated statement purposes, year 2 depreciation is based on the original cost of the equipment to Near. This elimination entry can be made in two separate entries. The first entry eliminated the gain, and restores the accumulated depreciation and equipment accounts as if the intercompany sale were never made. The second entry adjusts the current year depreciation expense to the amount that would have been recorded if the sale were never made. New depreciation is $36,000 ÷ 3 years = $12,000 for Far. Near's depreciation was book value $15,000 ÷ 3 years = $5,000 per year. Therefore, depreciation expense must be adjusted by $12,000 – $5,000 = $7,000.

2. **($10,000)** Unrealized profit in ending inventory arises when intercompany sales are made at prices above cost and the merchandise is not resold to third parties prior to year-end. The profit is unrealized because the inventory has not yet been sold outside the consolidated entity. In this case, one half of the merchandise was left in Far's inventory at year-end. For the consolidated entity, one half of the $20,000 profit has not been earned and must be eliminated.

3. **($9,000)** When Near purchased the bonds from an investor outside the consolidated entity, the bonds are viewed as retired from a consolidated viewpoint since there is no longer any obligation to an outside party. Therefore, the consolidated entity would recognize an ordinary gain of $9,000 ($100,000 carrying value of the bonds – $91,000 purchase price) on the retirement of the debt.

Task-Based Simulation 3

Financial Statement Amounts		
	Authoritative Literature	Help

Calculate the amounts that will appear on Poe's consolidated financial statement in December 31, year 2.

1.	Cash	$ 65,000
2.	Goodwill	$ 22,000
3.	Equipment	$794,000
4.	Common stock	$100,000
5.	Investment in Shaw	$0
6.	Dividends	$ 80,000
7.	Bonds payable	$100,000
8.	Noncontrolling interest	$ 21,000

Explanations

1. $50,000 + $15,000 = $65,000

2. The goodwill from Poe's 90% purchase of Shaw can be determined as follows:

Acquisition cost	$ 155,000
+ Fair value of noncontrolling interest (10,000 shares × $1.70)	17,000
Fair value of interests	172,000
– Fair value of net identifiable assets	(150,000)
Goodwill	$ 22,000

3. $440,000 + $360,000 – $6,000 = $794,000

4. $100,000, common stock of parent

5. The investment in Shaw account is eliminated.

6. Dividends paid of the subsidiary are eliminated.

7. $100,000. $200,000 bonds payable – $100,000 bonds payable eliminated

8. Noncontrolling interest

Fair value at acquisition date	$17,000
+ 10% net income	7,000
– 10% dividend	(3,000)
End of year noncontrolling interest	$21,000

Task-Based Simulation 4

Research				
	Authoritative Literature	Help		

ASC	805	20	30	1

Task-Based Simulation 5

Concepts		
	Authoritative Literature	Help

		True	False
1.	A company can use either the acquisition method or the pooling method for business combinations.	○	●
2.	Total revenues for a consolidated entity are calculated by adding the total revenue of the parent for the year and the total revenue of the subsidiary from the date of acquisition.	●	○
3.	Goodwill is amortized over a period of forty years.	○	●
4.	Goodwill is classified and included with other intangible assets for purposes of measuring impairment.	○	●
5.	Intangible assets with indefinite lives are not amortized.	●	○
6.	The stockholder equity accounts in the consolidated balance sheet are those of the parent company.	●	○
7.	The effect of unrealized profits and sales between the acquirer and the acquiree is classified as an intercompany transaction and must be eliminated.	●	○
8.	A newly identified intangible asset must meet the contractual legal or the separability criterion to be recognized as an intangible asset at the time of consolidation.	●	○

Task-Based Simulation 6

Consolidation at Date of Acquisition		
	Authoritative Literature	Help

Total current assets	$400,000
Total noncurrent assets	1,060,000
Total current liabilities	260,000
Total noncurrent liabilities	240,000
Total owners' equity	960,000

Explanations

Current assets: $320,000 parent + $70,000 book value subsidiary + $10,000 inventory write-up = $400,000

Noncurrent assets: $640,000 parent + $380,000 book value subsidiary + $40,000 goodwill = $1,060,000

Total current liabilities: $210,000 parent + $50,000 subsidiary = $260,000

Noncurrent liabilities: $150,000 parent + $90,000 subsidiary = $240,000

Total owners' equity: $600,000 parent + $360,000 new stock of parent issued in acquisition = $960,000

Task-Based Simulation 7

Intercompany Transactions & Eliminations		
	Authoritative Literature	Help

Arcelia Corporation
CONSOLIDATION WORKSHEET
December 31, Year 4

	Arcelia Corp.	Gavino Corp.		Debt	Credit		End balance
				Elimination entries			
Revenues & gains	1,000,000	400,000	(c)	50,000			1,341,000
			(e)	9,000			
Expenses	780,000	335,000	(f)	1,000	46,000	(c)	1,070,000
Current assets	400,000	110,000	(b)	10,000	4,000	(c)	508,000
					8,000	(d)	
Noncurrent assets	1,260,000	420,000	(b)	40,000	360,000	(a)	1,350,000
			(e)	36,000	45,000	(e)	
					1,000	(f)	
Differential			(a)	50,000	50,000	(b)	
Current liabilities	300,000	70,000	(d)	8,000			362,000
Noncurrent liabilities	180,000	85,000					265,000
Owners' equity	960,000	310,000	(a)	310,000			960,000

Elimination entries in journal entry form

a. Eliminate subsidiary equity accounts

Common stock & APIC	310,000	
Differential	50,000	
Investment in Gavino		360,000

b. To record asset write-up and goodwill. Goodwill = Acquisition cost $360,000 – FMV of net identifiable assets $320,000 ($460,000 – $140,000) = $40,000 goodwill.

Inventory	10,000	
Goodwill	40,000	
Differential		50,000

c. Eliminate the excess sales and costs of sales and profits in inventory not sold. The intercompany sales of $50,000 must be eliminated, along with the $50,000 in cost of sales reduced by the amount by which ending inventory is overstated. Ending inventory is carried on Gavino's books at $10,000. Ending inventory should be 20% × $30,000 cost to manufacture = $6,000. Therefore, inventory is overstated by $4,000 and cost of sales is overstated by $46,000 ($50,000 – $4,000).

Sales	50,000	
Cost of goods sold		46,000
Ending inventory		4,000

d. Eliminate intercompany receivable and payable

Accounts payable	8,000	
Accounts receivable		8,000

e. Eliminate sale of equipment

Gain on sale of equipment	9,000	
Equipment	36,000	
Accumulated depreciation		45,000

f. Restore depreciation expense as if equipment had not been sold. Normally Gavino depreciates equipment $60,000/5 years = $12,000 per year. Equipment sold on 10/1/Y4; therefore, Gavino recorded depreciation of 3/4 × $12,000 = $9,000. Arcelia's cost is $24,000 and depreciation is recorded straight-line over 3 years = $8,000 per year. However, Arcelia depreciated equipment 3/12 months = $2,000 per year. Total depreciation by both firms = $11,000. Total depreciation if the asset was not sold = $12,000. Therefore, an additional $1,000 depreciation must be recorded.

Depreciation expense	1,000	
Accumulated depreciation		1,000

Task-Based Simulation 8

Research			
	Authoritative Literature	**Help**	

ASC	810	10	45	1

Module 19: Derivative Instruments and Hedging Activities

Overview

This module covers foreign currency **transactions** (foreign currency **translations** are discussed in Module 20), derivative instruments, and hedging activities. A **foreign currency transaction** is a transaction denominated in a currency other than the entity's functional currency. Foreign currency transactions are discussed in this module because exchange rate risk can be hedged.

A **derivative instrument** derives its value as a financial instrument from something else and must meet three specific criteria to qualify as such. These criteria are discussed in this module. The most relevant measure for reporting derivatives is fair value. Some instruments, hybrid instruments, must be bifurcated (separated) between the derivative and the basic contract.

Hedging instruments are derivative instruments that meet two primary criteria: (1) sufficient documentation relating to the objective of the hedge, identification of the hedge, and the assessment of the hedge must be provided and (2) the hedge must be highly effective. Hedges are classified as fair value hedges, cash flow hedges, or foreign currency hedges.

Derivative accounting and reporting can be very complex. It requires the adherence to many specific criteria to distinguish how to account for certain derivatives. The candidate is urged to spend considerable time reading through and understanding the definitions in the key terms before studying this module.

A. Foreign Currency Transactions

1. A foreign currency transaction, according to ASC Topic 830, is a transaction denominated in a currency other than the entity's functional currency. **Denominated** means that the balance is fixed in terms of the number of units of a foreign currency regardless of changes in the exchange rate. When a US company purchases or sells goods or services (or borrows or lends money) to a foreign entity, and the transaction is denominated in foreign currency units, the US company has a foreign currency transaction in which the US dollar is the functional currency.

   a. In these situations, the US company has "crossed currencies" and directly assumes the risk of fluctuating foreign exchange rates of the foreign currency units.
   b. This exposed foreign currency risk may lead to recognition of foreign exchange transaction gains or losses in the income statement of the US company.
   c. If the US company pays or receives US dollars in import and export transactions, the risk resulting from fluctuating foreign exchange rates is borne by the foreign supplier or customer, and there is no need to apply the procedures outlined in ASC Topic 830 to the transaction reported in US dollars on the US company's books.
   d. The following example illustrates the terminology and procedures applicable to the translation of foreign currency transactions.

EXAMPLE

Assume that US Company, an exporter, sells merchandise to a customer in Germany on December 1, year 1, for 10,000 euros (€). Receipt of €10,000 is due on January 31, year 2, and US Company prepares financial statements on December 31, year 1. At the transaction date (December 1, year 1), the spot rate for immediate exchange of foreign currencies indicates that €1 is equivalent to $.90. This quotation is referred to as a direct quotation since the exchange rate is stated in terms of a direct translation of the currency in which the debt is measured. To find the US dollar equivalent of this transaction, simply multiply the foreign currency amount, €10,000, by $.90 to get $9,000. Occasionally, spot rates are quoted indirectly (e.g., $1 is equivalent to €1.1111). In the example used, since $1 is equivalent to €1.1111, the foreign currency amount would be divided by €1.1111 to get the US dollar amount of $9,000 (assuming the calculation is performed using four decimal places and rounded to the nearest dollar).

At December 1, year 1, the foreign currency transaction should be recorded by US Company in the following manner:

Accounts receivable (€)	9,000	
Sales		9,000

The accounts receivable and sales are measured in US dollars at the transaction date using the spot rate at the time of the transaction. While the accounts receivable is measured and reported in US dollars, the receivable is also denominated or fixed in euros. This characteristic can result in foreign exchange transaction gains or losses if the spot rate for euros changes between the transaction date and the date the transaction is settled.

2. If financial statements are prepared between the transaction date and the settlement date, the FASB requires that receivables and liabilities denominated in a currency other than the functional currency be restated to reflect the spot rates in existence at the balance sheet date.

EXAMPLE

Assume the same facts as the previous example and that, on December 31, year 1, the spot rate for euros is €1 = $.93. This means that €10,000 are worth $9,300, and that the accounts receivable denominated in euros are increased by $300. The following journal entry should be recorded as of December 31, year 1:

Accounts receivable (€)	300	
Foreign currency transaction gain		300

NOTE: The sales account, which was credited on the transaction date for $9,000, is not affected by changes in the spot rate.

---

a. This treatment exemplifies the "two-transaction" viewpoint adopted by the FASB. In other words, making the sale is the result of an operating decision, while bearing the risk of fluctuating spot rates is the result of an investment decision. Therefore, the amount determined as sales revenue at the transaction date should not be altered because of an investment decision to wait until January 31, year 2, for payment of the account.

   (1) The risk of a foreign exchange transaction loss can be avoided either by demanding immediate payment on December 1 or by entering into a forward exchange contract to hedge the exposed asset (accounts receivable).

   (2) The fact that US Company in the example did not act in either of these two ways is reflected by the required recognition of foreign currency transaction gains or losses on this type of transaction. These gains or losses are reported on US Company's income statement as financial (nonoperating) items in the period during which the exchange rates changed.

   NOTE: Reporting transaction gains or losses before the transaction is settled results in reporting unrealized gains or losses. This represents an exception to the conventional realization principle which normally applies. This practice also results in a temporary difference between pretax accounting income and taxable income because foreign exchange transaction gains and losses do not enter into the determination of taxable income until the year they are realized. Thus, the recognition of foreign currency transaction gains and losses on unsettled foreign currency transactions results in deferred tax assets/liabilities (depending on whether the temporary differences result in future taxable or future deductible amounts).

EXAMPLE

To complete the previous illustration, assume that on January 31, year 2, the foreign currency transaction is settled when the spot rate is €1 = $.91. Note that the account receivable is still valued at $9,300 at this point. The receipt of euros and their conversion into dollars should be journalized as follows:

Foreign currency (€)	9,100	
Foreign currency transaction loss	200	
Accounts receivable (€)		9,300
Cash	9,100	
Foreign currency (€)		9,100

The net effect of this foreign currency transaction was the receipt of $9,100 from a sale which was measured originally at $9,000. This realized net foreign currency transaction gain of $100 is reported on the income statements of more than one period—a $300 gain in year 1 and a $200 loss in year 2.

---

3. The financial statement disclosures required by ASC Topic 830 include the following:

   a. Aggregate transaction gain (loss) that is included in the entity's net income
   b. Significant rate changes subsequent to the date of the financial statements including effects on unsettled foreign currency transactions

---

> **NOW REVIEW MULTIPLE-CHOICE QUESTIONS 1 THROUGH 9**

B. Derivative Instruments and Hedging Activities

1. Financial instruments include cash, accounts/notes receivable, accounts/notes payable, bonds, common stock, preferred stock, stock options, foreign currency forward contracts, futures contracts, various financial swaps, etc. Other contracts which are also considered financial instruments meet the following two criteria:

   a. The contract imposes a contractual obligation on one party (to the contract) to deliver cash or another financial instrument to the second party, or to exchange financial instruments on potentially unfavorable terms with the second party;
   b. The contract conveys a contractual right to the second party to receive cash or another financial instrument from the first party, or to exchange financial instruments on favorable terms with the first party.

   A glossary of derivative-related terms is presented at the end of this section.

   c. It is from the above universe of financial instruments and other contracts that a subset is identified that qualifies as derivative instruments. **Derivative instruments** are so called because they derive their value as a financial instrument from something outside the instrument itself.

      (1) For example, a call option to purchase an exchange-traded stock would qualify as a derivative instrument. The value of the call option can only be determined by the market price of the related stock.

      > **EXAMPLE**
      >
      > A call option allows the holder to purchase 1,000 shares of stock at $50 per share, but no determination can be made as to the value of the call option until the stock price is determined. If the market value of the stock is $58 per share, the value of the call option is easily determined to be $8,000 [1,000 shares × ($58 – $50)].

      (a) The stock price is called the **"underlying,"** the rate or price that exists outside the derivative instrument that is used to determine the value of the derivative instrument.
      (b) The 1,000 shares of stock is known as the **"notional amount,"** that is the number of units related to the derivative instrument.
      (c) Both of these terms are important for two reasons:

         1] Their existence is a necessary condition for determining whether or not a financial instrument or other contract is a derivative instrument;
         2] They are determining factors in calculating the "settlement amount" of a derivative instrument.

      (d) All of these terms are discussed in more detail later in this section, but this basic understanding of derivative instruments may be helpful in working through the remaining definitions, explanations, and examples.

2. **Foundation Principles for Accounting for Derivatives and Hedging**—The basic principles driving the structure of accounting for derivatives and hedging are

   a. **Fair value measurement.** Derivative instruments meet the definition of assets and liabilities (probable future economic benefits or sacrifices of future economic benefits resulting from past transactions or events). As such they should be reported on an entity's financial statements. The most relevant measure for reporting financial instruments is "fair value."

      (1) ASC Topic 820 defines **fair value** as "the price that would be received to sell an asset or paid to transfer a liability in an orderly transaction between market participants at the measurement date."
      (2) As a corollary to this principle, gains and losses that result from the change in the fair value of derivative instruments are **not** assets and liabilities. Therefore, gains and losses should not be reported on the balance sheet but rather should either appear in comprehensive income or be reported in current earnings.
      (3) The details for reporting gains and losses appear in a subsequent section.

b. **Hedging.** Certain derivative instruments will qualify under the definition of hedging instruments. Those that qualify will be accounted for using hedge accounting, which generally provides for matching the recognition of gains and losses of the hedging instrument and the hedged asset or liability. (More details about hedge accounting are provided in a later section.) Three kinds of hedges have been defined in the standard.

(1) **Fair value hedge**—A hedge of the exposure to changes in the fair value of (a) a recognized asset or liability, or (b) an unrecognized firm commitment.

(2) **Cash flow hedge**—A hedge of the exposure to variability in the cash flows of (a) a recognized asset or liability, or (b) a forecasted transaction.

(3) **Foreign currency hedge**—A hedge of the foreign currency exposure of (a) an unrecognized firm commitment, (b) an available-for-sale security, (c) a forecasted transaction, or (d) a net investment in a foreign operation.

If a derivative instrument does not qualify as a hedging instrument under one of the three categories shown above, then its gains or losses must be reported and recognized in current earnings.

3. **Definition of a Derivative Instrument**—Three distinguishing characteristics of a derivative instrument, must be present for a financial instrument or other contract to be considered a derivative instrument. All three characteristics must be present.

a. The financial instrument or other contract must contain (a) one or more **underlyings,** and (b) one or more **notional amounts** (or payment provisions or both).

(1) An **underlying** is any financial or physical variable that has either observable changes or objectively verifiable changes. Therefore, underlyings would include traditional financial measures such as commodity prices, interest rates, exchange rates, or indexes related to any of these items. More broadly, measures such as an entity's credit rating, rainfall, or temperature changes would also meet the definition of an underlying.

(2) **Notional** amounts are the "number of currency or other units" specified in the financial instrument or other contract. In the case of options, this could include bushels of wheat, shares of stock, etc.

(3) The **settlement amount** of a financial instrument or other contract is calculated using the underlying(s) and notional amount(s) in some combination.

(a) Computation of the settlement amount may be as simple as multiplying the fair value of a stock times a specified number of shares.

(b) On the other hand, calculation of the settlement amount may require a very complex calculation, involving ratios, stepwise variables, and other leveraging techniques.

> **NOTE:** The term "notional amount" is sometimes used interchangeably with "settlement amount." Watch to determine if the context in which the term is used is calling for a number of units (notional amount), or a dollar value (settlement amount).

b. The financial instrument or other contract requires no initial net investment or an initial net investment that is smaller than would be required for other types of contracts that would be expected to have a similar response to changes in market factors.

(1) Many derivative instruments require no net investment or simply a premium as compensation for the time value of money.

(a) Futures contracts may require the establishment of a margin account with a balance equal to a small percentage (2 – 3%) of the value of the contract.

(b) A call option on a foreign currency contract would again only cost a small fraction of the value of the contract.

(c) These are typical contracts that would meet this definition and would be included in the definition of derivative instruments.

c. The terms of the financial instrument or other contract do one of the following with regard to settlement:

(1) Require or permit net settlement, either within the contract or by a means outside the contract.

(a) Net settlement means that a contract can be settled through the payment of cash rather than the exchange of the specific assets referenced in the contract.

(b) This type of settlement typically occurs with a currency swap or an interest rate swap.

(c) This definition may have some unanticipated consequences. For example, a contract with a liquidating damages clause for nonperformance, the amount of which is determined by an underlying, would meet this criterion.

(2) Provide for the delivery of an asset that puts the recipient in a position not substantially different from net settlement.

    (a) This might include a futures contract where one party to the contract delivers an asset, but a "market mechanism" exists (such as an exchange) so that the asset can be readily converted to cash.

        1] Convertibility to cash requires an active market and is a determining factor in whether or not a financial instrument or other contract will be treated as a derivative instrument.

> **NOW REVIEW MULTIPLE-CHOICE QUESTIONS 10 THROUGH 18**

4. **Inclusions in and Exclusions from Derivative Instruments**

    The following table provides a list of those financial instruments and other contracts that meet the definition of derivative instruments and those that do not meet the definition of derivative instruments or because they are specifically excluded from treatment.

Included	Excluded
• Options to purchase (call) or sell (put) exchange-traded securities • Futures contracts • Interest rate swaps • Currency swaps • Swaptions (an option on a swap) • Credit indexed contracts • Interest rate caps/floors/collars	• Normal purchases and sales (does not exclude "take or pay" contracts with little or no initial net investment and products that are readily convertible to cash) • Equity securities • Debt securities • Regular-way (three-day settlement) security trades (this exclusion applies to "to be announced" and "when issued" trades) • Leases • Mortgage-backed securities • Employee stock options • Royalty agreements and other contracts tied to sales volumes • Variable annuity contracts • Adjustable rate loans • Guaranteed investment contracts • Nonexchanged traded contracts tied to physical variables • Derivatives that serve as impediments to sales accounting (e.g., guaranteed residual value in a leasing arrangement)

    a. **Interest rate swaps** are one of the most commonly used derivative instruments in business. The following discussion first describes an interest rate swap and then shows how it meets the definition of a derivative instrument.

    (1) In a common example, two parties may agree to swap interest payments on debt. Usually this occurs when one party (Company F) has issued fixed-rate debt and believes that interest rates are going to drop, while a second party (Company V) has issued variable-rate debt and believes that interest rates are going to rise. In this case, both companies would be interested in exchanging interest payments since both believe that their interest expense would decrease as a result of the swap. Variable-rate interest may be determined by any number of indices (e.g., London Interbank Offered Rate [LIBOR], S&P 500 index, some fixed relationship to T-bill rates, AAA corporate bonds, etc.).

        (a) In this example, the **notional amount** is defined as the principal portion of the debt, which would be the same for both the fixed and variable rate debt. The **underlying** is the index that determines the variable interest rate, for example, six-month LIBOR. There is no initial **net investment** required for this contract since the first payment will not occur until the first interest date arrives, and net settlement can be achieved through the payment of interest and principal at the maturity date. Therefore, all three of the criteria for a derivative instrument are present, and it is accounted for as an interest rate swap. Similar examples could be developed for the other financial instruments listed in the "included" column below.

5. **Embedded Derivative Instruments and Bifurcation**

    Financial instruments and other contracts may contain features which, if they stood alone, would meet the definition of a derivative instrument. These financial instruments and other contracts are known as **"hybrid instru-**

ments." This means that there is a basic contract, known as the **"host contract,"** that has an embedded derivative instrument. In these circumstances, the embedded derivative instrument may have to be separated from the host contract, a process known as **bifurcation,** and treated as if it were a stand-alone instrument. In this case, the host contract (excluding the embedded derivative) would be accounted for in the normal manner (as if it had never contained the embedded derivative), and the now stand-alone derivative instrument would be accounted for using the rules for derivatives.

a. Three criteria are used to determine if **bifurcation** must occur. **All** criteria must be met.

   (1) The embedded derivative meets the definition of a derivative.
   (2) The hybrid instrument is **not** regularly recorded at fair value, with changes reported in current earnings as they occur under other GAAP. If the hybrid instrument is regularly recorded at fair value, then there is no need to bifurcate the embedded derivative since the same end result is being accomplished already.
   (3) The economic characteristics and risks of the embedded derivative instrument are **not** "clearly and closely related" to the economic characteristics and risks of the host contract.

b. Below are listed a number of hybrid instruments that would normally require bifurcation:

   (1) A bond payable with an interest rate based on the S&P 500 index.
   (2) An equity instrument (stock) with a call option, allowing the issuing company to buy back the stock.
   (3) An equity instrument with a put option, requiring the issuing company to buy back the stock at the request of the holder.
   (4) A loan agreement that permits the debtor to pay off the loan prior to its maturity with the loan payoff penalty based on the short-term T-bill rates.
   (5) Loans with term-extending options whose values are based on the prime rate at the time of the extension.
   (6) Convertible debt (from the investor's viewpoint)

c. The holder of a hybrid instrument normally requiring bifurcation can make an election **not** to bifurcate the instrument. Instead, the entire instrument is valued at fair value.

   (1) This election is irrevocable and is made on an instrument-by-instrument basis.
   (2) Changes in fair value of the hybrid instruments are recognized each year in earnings.
   (3) If a company elects to use fair value measurement on selected hybrid instruments, the balance sheet disclosure may be presented in one of two ways:

      (a) As separate line items for the fair value and non–fair value instruments on the balance sheet,
      (b) As an aggregate amount of all hybrid instruments with the amount of the hybrid instruments at fair value shown in parentheses.

d. The fair value option may be applied to host financial instruments resulting from separation of an embedded nonfinancial derivative instrument from a nonfinancial hybrid instrument. If the fair value option is elected, the disclosure rules for fair value apply.

NOW REVIEW MULTIPLE-CHOICE QUESTIONS 19 THROUGH 27

6. **Hedging Instruments—General Criteria**
   Two primary criteria must be met in order for a derivative instrument to qualify as a hedging instrument.

a. Sufficient documentation must be provided at the beginning of the process to identify at a minimum (1) the objective and strategy of the hedge, (2) the hedging instrument and the hedged item, and (3) how the effectiveness (see below) of the hedge will be assessed on an ongoing basis.

b. The hedge must be **"highly effective"** throughout its life.

   (1) Effectiveness is measured by analyzing the hedging instrument's (the derivative instrument) ability to generate changes in fair value that offset the changes in value of the hedged item.
   (2) At a minimum, its effectiveness will be measured every three months and whenever earnings or financial statements are reported.
   (3) A "highly effective" hedge has been interpreted to mean that "the cumulative change in the value of the hedging instrument should be between 80 and 125% of the inverse cumulative changes in the fair value or cash flows of the hedged item."
   (4) The method used to assess effectiveness must be used throughout the hedge period and must be consistent with the approach used for managing risk.
   (5) Similar hedges should usually be assessed for effectiveness in a similar manner unless a different method can be justified. (Even though a hedging instrument may meet the criterion for being highly effective, it

may not eliminate variations in reported earnings, because to the extent that a hedging instrument is not 100% effective, the difference in net loss or gain in each period must be reported in current earnings.)

7. **Fair Value Hedges**

A fair value hedge is the use of a derivative instrument to hedge the exposure to changes in the fair value of an asset or a liability.

a. **Specific criteria.** The hedged asset/liability must meet certain criteria in order to qualify as a fair value hedge. The hedged item must be either **all** or a **specific portion** (e.g., a percentage, a contractual cash flow) of a recognized asset/liability or an unrecognized firm commitment.

(1) Both of these situations arise frequently in foreign currency transactions.

> **EXAMPLE**
>
> A company may enter into a firm commitment with a foreign supplier to purchase a piece of equipment, the price of which is denominated in a foreign currency and both the delivery date and the payment date are in the future. The company may decide to hedge the commitment to pay for the equipment in a foreign currency in order to protect itself from currency fluctuations between the firm commitment date and the payment date. For the period between the firm commitment date and the delivery date, the company will be hedging against an unrecognized firm commitment. For the period between the delivery date and the payment date, the company is hedging against a recognized liability. (See Section 9 of this module for the accounting associated with this example.)

(2) For an unrecognized firm commitment to qualify it must be (1) binding on both parties, (2) specific with respect to all significant terms, and (3) contain a nonperformance clause that makes performance probable.

b. **Accounting for a fair value hedge.** Gains and losses on the hedged asset/liability and the hedging instrument will be recognized in current earnings.

> **EXAMPLE**
>
> On 10/1/Y1, Dover Corp. purchases 20 shares of Porter, Inc. stock at $40. The securities are classified as available-for-sale. The market price moves to $45 by the end of the year. Assume Dover does not elect the fair value option to report its shares of Porter stock. In order to protect itself from a possible decline in the stock value of its available-for-sale security, Dover purchases an at-the-money put option for $300 on 12/31/Y1. The put option gives Dover the right, but not the obligation, to sell 200 shares of Porter stock at $45 per share, and the option expires on 12/31/Y3. Dover designates the hedge as a fair value hedge because it is hedging changes in the security's fair value. The fair value of an option is made up of two components, the time value and the intrinsic value. At the time of purchase, the time value is the purchase price of the options and the intrinsic value is $0 (because the option was purchased at-the-money).
>
> Over the life of the option, the time value will drop to $0. This is due to the fact that time value relates to the ability to exercise the option over a specified period of time. As the option moves toward the expiration date, the perceived value of the time value portion of the option will decrease as a function of the time value of money (TVM) issues and other market forces. The time value will generally decrease over the life of the option, but not necessarily in a linear fashion. The intrinsic value will vary based on the difference between the current stock price vs. the stock price on the date the option was purchased. As shown in the table below, the intrinsic value of the option increases from $0 to $200 between 12/31/Y1 and 12/31/Y2 because the stock price has dropped by $1 (× 200 shares), and the hedge has been effective for that same amount. As can be seen by analyzing the two components of the put option, the market is the primary driver of the value that should be assigned to the option. As is often the case, the intrinsic value of the option is considered to be a "highly effective" hedge against changes in the stock price, while the time value is ineffective and is reflected in current earnings. Additional information is provided below.
>
> | Item | 1/1/Y1 | 12/31/Y1 | 12/31/Y2 | 12/31/Y3 |
> |---|---|---|---|---|
> | Porter stock price | $40 | $ 45 | $ 44 | $ 42 |
> | Put option | | | | |
> | Time value | | $300 | $160 | $ 0 |
> | Intrinsic value | | $ 0 | $200 | $600 |
> | | | | (200 × $1) | (200 × $3) |
>
> **1/1/Y1**
>
> 1. Available-for-sale securities ... 8,000
>   Cash ... 8,000
> *Record the purchase of Porter stock (200 × $40).*

12/31/Y1

2. Available-for-sale securities   1,000
       Other comprehensive income   1,000
   Record the unrealized gain on Porter stock (accounting prior to the hedge in accordance with ASC Topic 320. (200 ×
   $5 valuation increase from holding gain to market value)

3. Put option   300
       Cash   300
   Record the purchase of at-the-money put option.

12/31/Y2

4. Put option   200
       Gain on hedge activity   200
   Record the increase in the intrinsic value (fair value) of the option.

5. Loss on hedge activity   200
       Available-for-sale securities   200
   Record the decrease in the fair value of the securities (accounting after the hedge is established) $200 = 200 shares ×
   $1 holding loss.

NOTE: The $200 gain on hedge activity from the put option is balanced effectively against the $200 loss on hedge activity from the hedged available-for-sale security. The portion of the unrealized holding gain or loss on an available-for-sale security that is designated as a hedged item in a fair value hedge is recognized in earnings during the period of the hedge. This is why the $200 holding loss on the available-for-sale securities is recognized in the period's earnings.

6. Loss on hedge activity   140
       Put option   140
   Record the loss related to the time value of the option. $140 = $300 – $160

12/31/Y3

7. Put option   400
       Gain on hedge activity   400
   Record the increase in the intrinsic value of the put option.

8. Loss on hedge activity   400
       Available-for-sale securities   400
   To record the decrease in the fair value of the securities (accounting after the hedge is established); $400 = 200 shares
   × $2 holding loss on available-for-sale securities.

9. Loss on hedge activity   160
       Put option   160
   Record the loss related to the time value of the option. $140 = $300 – $160

10. Cash   9,000
        Put option   600
        Available-for-sale securities   8,400
    Record the exercise of the put option (sell the 200 shares of stock @ $45) and close out the put option investment.

11. Other comprehensive income   1,000
        Gain on Porter stock   1,000
    To reclassify the unrealized holding gain recognized in entry 2., from other comprehensive income to earnings,
    because the securities were sold.

8. **Cash Flow Hedges**

   Cash flow hedges use derivative instruments to hedge the exposure to variability in expected future cash flows.

   a. **Specific criteria.** Additional criteria must be met in order to qualify as a **cash flow hedge**.

      (1) The primary criterion is that the hedged asset/liability and the hedging instrument must be **"linked."**

          (a) **Linking** is established if the basis (the specified rate or index) for the change in cash flows is the same for the hedged asset/liability and the hedging instrument.

      (2) Cash flows do not have to be identical, but they must meet the **highly effective** threshold discussed above.

      (3) In addition, if the hedged asset/liability is a **forecasted transaction,** it must be considered **probable,** based on appropriate facts and circumstances (i.e., past history).

      (4) Also, if the forecasted hedged asset/liability is a series of transactions, they must "share the same risk exposure."

          (a) Purchases of a particular product from the same supplier over a period of time would meet this requirement.

b. **Accounting for a cash flow hedge.** For the hedging instrument:

(1) The effective portion is reported in other comprehensive income, and
(2) The ineffective portion and/or excluded components are reported on a cumulative basis to reflect the lesser of

  (a) The cumulative gain/loss on the derivative since the creation of the hedge, or
  (b) The cumulative gain/loss from the change in expected cash flows from the hedged instrument since the creation of the hedge.

    1] The above amounts need to be adjusted to reflect any reclassification of other comprehensive income to current earnings. This will occur when the hedged asset/liability affects earnings (e.g., when hedged inventory is sold and the cost of inventory passes through to cost of goods sold).

EXAMPLE

A commercial bakery believes that wheat prices may increase over the next few months. To protect itself against this risk, the bakery purchases call options on wheat futures to hedge the price risk of their forecasted inventory purchases. If wheat prices increase, the profit on the purchased call options will offset the higher price the bakery must pay for the wheat. If wheat prices decline, the bakery will lose the premium it paid for the call options, but can then buy the wheat at the lower price. On June 1, year 1, the bakery pays a premium of $350 to purchase a September 30, year 1 call for 1,000 bushels of wheat at the futures price of $16.60 per bushel. The call option is considered a cash flow hedge because the designated risk that is being hedged is the risk of changes in the cash flows relating to changes in the purchase price of the wheat. On September 30, the bakery settles its call options and purchases wheat on the open market. Pertinent wheat prices are shown below.

Spot price (June 1)	$16.50
Futures price (as of June 1 for September 30)	$16.60
Spot price (September 30)	$17.30

June 1
1. Call option   350
       Cash   350
   Record the purchase of the call option.

September 30
2. Loss on hedge activity   350
       Call option   350
   Record the expiration (change in time value) of the call option.

3. Call option   700
       Other comprehensive income   700
   Record the increase in intrinsic value of the call option. $700 = {1,000 bushels × [$17.30 (the spot price per bushel on September 30) – $16.60 (the futures price as of June 1 for September 30)]}

4. Cash   700
       Call option   700
   Record the cash settlement of the call option.

5. Inventory   17,300
       Cash   17,300
   Record the purchase of the wheat at the spot price. $17,300 = 1,000 bushels × $17.30

---

9. **Foreign Currency Hedges**

Foreign currency denominated assets/liabilities that arise in the course of normal business are often hedged with offsetting forward exchange contracts. This process, in effect, creates a natural hedge. Normal accounting rules apply, and the FASB did not change this accounting treatment in the implementation of hedge accounting. Hedge accounting is required in four areas related to foreign currency hedges. The four foreign currency hedges are discussed below.

a. **Unrecognized firm commitment.** Either a derivative instrument or a nonderivative financial instrument (such as a receivable in a foreign currency) can be designated as a hedge of an unrecognized firm commitment attributable to changes in foreign currency exchange rates. If the requirements for a fair value hedge are met, then this hedging arrangement can be accounted for as a **fair value hedge,** discussed above.

b. **Available-for-sale securities.** Hedge accounting is not used for trading and held-to-maturity securities. The use of hedge accounting for transactions for securities designated as available-for-sale may be allowed in some instances. Derivative instruments can be used to hedge debt or equity available-for-sale securities. However, equity securities must meet two additional criteria.

(1) They cannot be traded on an exchange denominated in the investor's functional currency.
(2) Dividends must be denominated in the same foreign currency as is expected to be received on the sale of the security.

If the above criteria are met, hedging instruments related to available-for-sale securities can be accounted for as **fair value hedges,** discussed above.

c. **Foreign currency denominated forecasted transactions.** Only derivative instruments can be designated as hedges of foreign currency denominated forecasted transactions. A forecasted export sale with the price denominated in a foreign currency might qualify for this type of hedge treatment.

(1) Forecasted transactions are distinguished from firm commitments (discussed in a. above) because the timing of the cash flows remains uncertain.

   (a) This additional complexity results in hedging instruments related to foreign currency denominated forecasted transactions being accounted for as cash flow hedges, discussed above.
   (b) Hedge accounting is permissible for transactions between unrelated parties, and under special circumstances (not discussed here) for intercompany transactions.

d. **Net investments in foreign operations.** The accounting for net investments in foreign operations has not changed from the ASC Topic 830 rules, except that the hedging instrument has to meet the new "effective" criterion. The change in the fair value of the hedging derivative is recorded in a manner consistent with a translation adjustment in other comprehensive income which is then closed to the accumulated other comprehensive income account in the equity section of the balance sheet.

Hedge Accounting ASC Topic 815 (SFAS 133)

		Type of Hedge	
Attribute	**Fair Value**	**Cash Flow**	**Foreign Currency (FC)**
Types of hedging instruments permitted	Derivatives	Derivatives	Derivatives or nonderivatives depending on the type of hedge
Balance sheet valuation of hedging instrument	Fair value	Fair value	Fair value
Recognition of gain or loss on changes in value of hedging instrument	Currently in earnings	Effective portion currently as a component of other comprehensive income (OCI) and reclassified to earnings in future period(s) that forecasted transaction affects earnings	**FC denominated firm commitment** Currently in earnings **Available-for-sale security (AFS)** Currently in earnings
		Ineffective portion currently in earnings	**Forecasted FC transaction** Same as cash flow hedge **Net investment in a foreign operation** OCI as part of the cumulative translation adjustment to the extent it is effective as a hedge
Recognition of gain or loss on changes in the fair value of the hedged item	Currently in earnings	Not applicable; these hedges are not associated with recognized assets or liabilities	**FC denominated firm commitment** Currently in earnings **Available-for-sale security (AFS)** Currently in earnings **Forecasted FC transaction** Not applicable; same as cash flow hedge

> **NOW REVIEW MULTIPLE-CHOICE QUESTIONS 28 THROUGH 37**

10. **Forward Exchange Contracts**

   It was stated previously that foreign currency transaction gains and losses on assets and liabilities which are denominated in a currency other than the functional currency can be hedged if a US company enters into a forward exchange contract.

   a. The following example shows how a forward exchange contract can be used as a hedge, first against a firm commitment and then, following delivery date, as a hedge against a recognized liability.
   b. The general rule for estimating the fair value of forward exchange contracts is to use the forward exchange rate for the remaining term of the contract.

EXAMPLE

Baker Simon, Inc. enters into a firm commitment with Dempsey Ing., Inc. of Germany, on October 1, year 1, to purchase a computerized robotic system for €6,000,000. The system will be delivered on March 1, year 2, with payment due sixty days after delivery (April 30, year 2). Baker Simon, Inc. decides to hedge this foreign currency firm commitment and enters into a forward exchange contract on the firm commitment date to receive €6,000,000 on the payment date. The applicable exchange rates are shown in the table below.

Date	Spot rates	Forward rates for April 30, year 1
October 1, year 1	€1 = $.90	€1 = $ .91
December 31, year 1	€1 = $.92	€1 = $ .94
March 1, year 2	€1 = $.92	€1 = $.935
April 30, year 2	€1 = $.96	

---

c. The following example separately presents both the forward contract receivable and the dollars payable liability in order to show all aspects of the forward contract.

(1) For financial reporting purposes, most companies present just the net fair value of the forward contract, which would be the difference between the current value of the forward contract receivable and the dollars payable accounts.

(2) The transactions which reflect the forward exchange contract, the firm commitment and the acquisition of the asset and retirement of the related liability appear as follows:

Forward contract entries   **Hedge against firm commitment entries**

(1) 10/1/Y1 (forward rate for 4/30/Y2
       €1 = $.91)

Forward contract receivable (€)	5,460,000	
Dollars payable		5,460,000

This entry recognizes the existence of the forward exchange contract using the gross method. Under the net method, this entry would not appear at all, since the fair value of the forward contract is zero when the contract is initiated. The amount is calculated using the 10/1/Y1 forward rate for 4/30/Y2 (€6,000,000 × $.91 = $5,460,000). Note that the **net** fair value of the forward exchange contact on 10/1/Y1 is zero because there is an exact amount offset of the forward contract receivable with the dollars payable liability.

(2) 12/31/Y1 (forward rate for 4/30/Y1   (3) 12/31/Y1
       €1 = $.94)

Forward contract receivable (€)	180,000	
Gain on hedge activity		180,000

Loss on hedge activity	180,000	
Firm commitment		180,000

€6,000,000 × ($ .94 – $ .91) = $180,000. The dollar values for this entry reflect, among other things, the change in the forward rate from 10/1/Y1 to 12/31/Y2. However, the actual amount recorded as gain or loss (gain in this case) will be determined by all market factors.

The dollar values for this entry are identical to entry (2), reflecting the fact that the hedge is highly effective (100%) and also the fact that the market recognizes the same factors in this transaction as for entry (2). This entry reflects the first use of the firm commitment account, a temporary liability account pending the receipt of the asset against which the firm commitment has been hedged.

(4) 3/1/Y2 (forward rate for 4/30/Y2 €1   (5) 3/1/Y2
       = $.935)

Loss on hedge activity	30,000	
Forward contract receivable (€)		30,000

Firm commitment	30,000	
Gain on hedge activity		30,000

€6,000,000 × ($ .935 – $ .94) = $30,000. These entries again will be driven by market factors, and they are calculated the same way as entries (2) and (3) above. Notice that the decline in the forward rate from 12/31/Y1 to 3/1/Y2 resulted in a loss against the forward contract receivable and a gain against the firm commitment.

(6) 3/1/Y2 (spot rate €1 = $.92)

Equipment	5,370,000	
Firm commitment	150,000	
Accounts payable (€)		5,520,000

This entry records the receipt of the equipment (recorded at fair value determined on a discounted net present value basis), the elimination of the temporary liability account (firm commitment), and the recognition of the payable, calculated using the spot rate on the date of receipt (€6,000,000 × $.92 = $5,520,000).

(7) 4/30/Y2 (spot rate €1 = $.96)

Forward contract receivable (€)	150,000	
Gain on forward contract		150,000

The gain or loss (gain in this case) on the forward contract is calculated using the change in the forward to the spot rate from 3/1/Y2 to 4/30/Y2 [€6,000,000 × ($..96 – $.935) = $150,000]

(9) 4/30/Y2

Dollars payable	5,460,000	
Cash		5,460,000
Foreign currency units (€)	5,760,000	
Forward contract receivable (€)		5,760,000

This entry reflects the settlement of the forward contract at the 10/1/Y1 contracted forward rate (€6,000,000 × $.91 = $5,460,000) and the receipt of foreign currency units valued at the spot rate (€6,000,000 × $.96 = $5,760,000).

(8) 4/30/Y2

Transaction loss	240,000	
Accounts payable (€)		240,000

The transaction loss related to the accounts payable reflects only the change in the spot rates and ignores the accrual of interest. [€6,000,000 × ($.96 – $.92) = $180,000]

(10) Accounts payable (€) 5,760,000
      Foreign currency units 5,760,000

This entry reflects the use of the foreign currency units to settle the account payable.

d. In the case of using a forward exchange contract to speculate in a specific foreign currency, the general rule to estimate the fair value of the forward contract is to use the forward exchange rate for the remainder of the term of the forward contract.

11. **Disclosures**

Disclosures related to financial instruments, both derivative and nonderivative, that are used as hedging instruments must include the following information:

a. Objectives and the strategies for achieving them,
b. Context to understand the instrument,
c. Risk management policies, and
d. A list of hedged instruments.

   (1) These disclosures have to be separated by type of hedge and reported every time a complete set of financial statements is issued.
   (2) In addition, disclosure requirements exist for derivative instruments that are not designated as hedging instruments.

> **NOW REVIEW MULTIPLE-CHOICE QUESTIONS 38 THROUGH 41**

12. **Fair Value and Concentration of Credit Risk Disclosures of Financial Instruments other than Derivatives**

Disclosure of fair values of financial instruments is required if it is practicable to estimate fair value. This requirement pertains to both asset and liability financial instruments, whether recognized in the balance sheet or not. Disclosure of concentrations of credit risk is required.

a. Credit risk is the risk that a loss will occur because parties to the instrument do not perform as expected.

   (1) Such concentrations exist when a number of an entity's financial instruments are associated with similar activities and economic characteristics that could be affected by changes in similar conditions (e.g., an entity whose principal activity is to supply parts to one type of industry).

Lenaburg, Inc.
Notes to Financial Statements
FAIR VALUE OF FINANCIAL INSTRUMENTS HELD OR ISSUED FOR PURPOSES OTHER THAN TRADING (*in thousands*)

	December 31, year 2	
	Carrying amount	Fair value
Assets		
Cash and cash equivalents	32,656	32,656
Long-term investments	12,719	14,682
Liabilities		
Short-term debt	3,223	3,223
Long-term debt	150,000	182,500

FAIR VALUE OF FINANCIAL INSTRUMENTS HELD FOR TRADING PURPOSES (in thousands)

	December 31, year 2	
	Carrying amount	**Fair value**
Assets		
Short-term investments	4,074	4,074

Cash and cash equivalents—The carrying amount of cash and cash equivalents approximates fair value due to their short-term maturities.

Long-term investments—The fair value is estimated based on quoted market prices for these or similar investments.

Short-term investments—The Company holds US Treasury notes and highly liquid investments for trading purposes. The carrying value of these instruments approximates fair value.

Short- and long-term debt—The fair value of short- and long-term debt is estimated using quoted market prices for the same or similar instruments or on the current rates offered to the Company for debt of equivalent remaining maturities.

Summary of Disclosure Standards for Financial Instruments other than Derivatives

ASC	Pertains to	Required disclosures
825-10-50	Financial Instruments (Assets and Liabilities), Whether on Balance Sheet or Not	• Fair value, when practicable to estimate • Information pertinent to estimating fair value (carrying value, effective interest rate, maturity) if not practicable to estimate, and reasons for impracticability of estimation • Distinguish between instruments held or issued for trading purposes and instruments held or issued for purposes other than trading • Do not net or aggregate fair values of derivative financial instruments with fair values of nonderivative financial instruments or with fair values of other derivative financial instruments
	Financial Instruments with Concentrations of Credit Risk	• Information about similar activity, region, or economic characteristics • Maximum potential accounting loss • Information about collateral or security requirements

> **NOW REVIEW MULTIPLE-CHOICE QUESTIONS 42 THROUGH 50**

C. Research Component—Accounting Standards Codification

ASC Topic 815, *Derivatives and Hedging*, contains the accounting and disclosure rules for derivatives and hedging. ASC Topic 830, *Foreign Currency Matters*, contains the rules for foreign currency transactions and foreign currency translations. ASC Topic 825, *Financial Instruments*, covers the accounting rules for reporting financial instruments.

A list of research terms is listed below.

At the money	Financial instrument	Insurance contracts
Bifurcation	Firm commitment hedge	Intrinsic value
Call option	Forecasted transaction hedge	LIBOR
Cash flow hedge	Foreign currency derivative	Net settlement
Changes in fair value	Foreign currency hedge	Notional amounts
Derivative instrument	Forward contract	Out of the money
Designation as hedged item	Forward exchange contract	Payment provision hedge
Discount forward contract	Futures contract	Premium forward contract
Embedded derivative	Hedged item	Put option
Embedded derivative instruments	Hybrid instrument	Regular way securities trades
Fair value financial instruments	Impediments to sales accounting	Swaption
Fair value hedge	In the money	Transaction gain or loss
Financial guarantee contracts	Initial net investment	Underlyings

D. International Financial Reporting Standards (IFRS)

1. A derivative is a financial instrument that (1) requires little or no initial investment, (2) changes in value in response to a change in the value of another instrument or index (called an underlying), and (3) is settled in the future.

    a. Examples of derivatives include options, futures, forward contracts, and swaps. Derivatives are recognized in the financial statements using the fair value through profit and loss method (FVTPL).

    b. Derivatives are remeasured at fair value, with gains and losses recorded in profit or loss for the period.

2. A hedging instrument is a type of derivative that is classified as a fair value hedge, a cash flow hedge, or a hedge of a net investment in operations.

    a. Hedge accounting allows the optional treatment to offset profits and losses on hedged items.

    b. If a company elects to use hedge accounting, the accounting treatment differs depending on the type of hedge.

        (1) A fair value hedge is accounted for by recognizing the gains and losses in profit and loss of the period.

        (2) A cash flow hedge and a hedge of a net investment are accounted for by reporting gains and losses in other comprehensive income for the period.

NOW REVIEW MULTIPLE-CHOICE QUESTION 51

KEY TERMS

At the money. An at-the-money option is one in which the price of the underlying is equal to the strike or exercise price.

Bifurcation. The process of separating an embedded derivative from its host contract. This process is necessary so that hybrid instruments (a financial instrument or other contract that contains an embedded derivative) can be separated into their component parts, each being accounted for using the appropriate valuation techniques.

Call option. An American call option provides the holder the right to acquire an underlying at an exercise or strike price, anytime during the option term. A premium is paid by the holder for the right to benefit from the appreciation in the underlying.

Derivative instruments. Derivative instruments are defined by their three distinguishing characteristics. Specifically, derivative instruments are financial instruments or other contracts that have

1. One or more underlyings and one or more notional amounts (or payment provisions or both);
2. No initial net investment or a smaller net investment than required for contracts expected to have a similar response to market changes; and
3. Terms that require or permit

    a. Net settlement

    b. Net settlement by means outside the contract

    c. Delivery of an asset that results in a position substantially the same as net settlement

Discount or premium on a forward contract. The foreign currency amount of the contact multiplied by the difference between the contracted forward rate and the spot rate at the date of inception of the contract.

Embedded derivative. A feature on a financial instrument or other contract, which if the feature stood alone, would meet the definition of a derivative.

Fair value. Defined as the amount at which the asset or liability could be bought or settled in an arm's-length transaction; measured by reference to market prices or estimated by net present value of future cash flows, options pricing models, or by other techniques.

Financial instrument. Financial instruments include cash, accounts/notes receivable, accounts/notes payable, bonds, common stock, preferred stock, stock options, foreign currency forward contracts, futures contracts, various financial swaps, etc. Other contracts which are also considered financial instruments meet the following two criteria: (1) the contract imposes a contractual obligation on one party (to the contract) to deliver cash or another financial instrument to the second party or to exchange potentially unfavorable terms with the second party; (2) the contract conveys a contractual right to the second party to receive cash or another financial instrument from the first party or to exchange financial instruments on favorable terms with the first party.

Firm commitment. An agreement with an unrelated party, binding on both, usually legally enforceable, specifying all significant terms and including a disincentive for nonperformance sufficient to make performance likely.

Forecasted transaction. A transaction expected to occur for which there is no firm commitment, and thus, which gives the entity no present rights or obligations. Forecasted transactions can be hedged and special hedge accounting can be applied.

Foreign currency transactions. Transactions whose terms are denominated in a currency other than the entity's functional currency. Foreign currency transactions arise when an enterprise (1) buys or sells on credit goods or services whose prices are denominated in foreign currency, (2) borrows or lends funds and the amounts payable or receivable are denominated in foreign currency, (3) is a party to an unperformed forward exchange contract, or (4) for other reasons, acquires or disposes of assets, or incurs or settles liabilities denominated in foreign currency.

Forward contract. A forward contract is an agreement between two parties to buy and sell a specific quantity of a commodity, foreign currency, or financial instrument at an agreed-upon price, with delivery and/or settlement at a designated future date. Because a forward contract is not formally regulated by an organized exchange, each party to the contract is subject to the default of the other party.

Forward exchange contract. An agreement to exchange at a specified future date currencies of different countries at a specified rate (forward rate).

Futures contract. A futures contract is a forward-based contract to make or take delivery of a designated financial instrument, foreign currency, or commodity during a designated period, at a specified price or yield. The contract frequently has provisions for cash settlement. A futures contract is traded on a regulated exchange and, therefore, involves less credit risk than a forward contract.

In the money. A call option is in the money if the price of the underlying is greater than the strike or exercise price of the underlying.

Initial net investment. A derivative instrument is one where the initial net investment is zero or is less than the notional amount (possibly plus a premium or minus a discount). This characteristic refers to the relative amount of investment. Derivative instruments allow the opportunity to take part in the rate or price change without owning the asset or owing the liability. If an amount approximating the notional amount must be invested or received, it is not a derivative instrument. The two basic forms of derivative instruments are futures contracts and options. The futures contract involves little or no initial net investment. Settlement is usually near the delivery date. Call options, when purchased, require a premium payment that is less than the cost of purchasing the equivalent number of shares. Even though this distinguishing characteristic is the result of only one of the parties, it determines the application for both.

Intrinsic value. With regard to call (put) options, it is the larger of zero or the spread between the stock (exercise) price and the exercise (stock) price.

LIBOR. London Interbank Offer Rate. A widely used measure of average interest rates at a point in time.

Net settlements. To qualify as derivative instruments, one of the following settlement criteria must be met:

1. No delivery of an asset equal to the notional amount is required. For example, an interest rate swap does not involve delivery of the instrument in which the notional amount is expressed.
2. Delivery of an asset equal to the notional amount is required of one of the parties, but an exchange (or other market mechanism, institutional arrangement or side agreement) facilitates net settlement. For example, a call option has this attribute.
3. Delivery by one of the parties of an asset equal to the notional amount is required but the asset is either readily convertible to cash (as with a contract for the delivery of a marketable equity security), or is required but that asset is itself a derivative instrument (as is the case for a swaption [an option on a swap]).

This characteristic means that the derivative instrument can be settled by a net delivery of assets (the medium of exchange does not have to be cash). Contract terms based on changes in the price or rate of the notional amount that implicitly or explicitly require or permit net settlement qualify. Situations where one of the parties can liquidate their net investment or be relieved of the contract rights or obligations without significant transaction costs because of a market arrangement (broadly interpreted) or where the delivered asset can be readily converted to cash also meet the requirements for net settlement. It is assumed that an exchange traded security is readily converted to cash. Thus, commodity-based contracts for gold, oil, wheat, etc. are now included under this standard. The convertible to cash condition requires an active market and consideration of interchangeability and transaction volume. Determining if delivery of a financial asset or liability equal to the notional amount is a derivative instrument may depend upon whether it is readily convertible into cash. Different accounting will result if the notional amount is not readily converted to cash. Using the notional amount as collateral does not necessarily mean it is readily convertible to cash.

Notional amount. The notional amount (or payment provision) is the referenced associated asset or liability. A notional amount is commonly a number of units such as shares of stock, principal amount, face value, stated value, basis points, barrels of oil, etc. It may be that amount plus a premium or minus a discount. The interaction of the price or rate (underlying) with the referenced associated asset or liability (notional amount) determines whether settlement is required and, if so, the amount.

Out of the money. A call option is out of the money if the strike or exercise price is greater than the price of the underlying. A put option is out of the money if the price of the underlying is greater than the strike or exercise price.

Put option. An American put option provides the holder the right to sell the underlying at an exercise or strike price, anytime during the option term. A gain accrues to the holder as the market price of the underlying falls below the strike price.

Swap. A swap is a forward-based contract or agreement generally between two counterparties to exchange streams of cash flows over a specified period in the future.

Swaption. A swaption is an option on a swap that provides the holder with the right to enter into a swap at a specified future date at specified terms (freestanding option on a swap) or to extend or terminate the life of an existing swap (embedded option on a swap). These derivatives have characteristics of an option and an interest rate swap.

Time value. The difference between an option's price and its intrinsic value.

Transaction gain or loss. Transaction gains or losses result from a change in exchange rates between the functional currency and the currency in which a foreign currency transaction is denominated. They represent an increase or decrease in (1) the actual functional currency cash flows realized upon settlement of foreign currency transactions, and (2) the expected functional currency cash flows on unsettled foreign currency transactions.

Underlyings. An underlying is commonly a specified price or rate such as a stock price, interest rate, currency rate, commodity price, or a related index. However, any variable (financial or physical) with (1) observable changes or (2) objectively verifiable changes such as a credit rating, insurance index, climatic or geological condition (temperature, rainfall) qualifies. Unless it is specifically excluded, a contract based on any qualifying variable is accounted for under ASC Topic 815 (SFAS 133) if it has the distinguishing characteristics stated above.

Multiple-Choice Questions (1-51)

A. Foreign Currency Transactions

1. On September 1, year 1, Bain Corp. received an order for equipment from a foreign customer for 300,000 local currency units (LCU) when the US dollar equivalent was $96,000. Bain shipped the equipment on October 15, year 1, and billed the customer for 300,000 LCU when the US dollar equivalent was $100,000. Bain received the customer's remittance in full on November 16, year 1, and sold the 300,000 LCU for $105,000. In its income statement for the year ended December 31, year 1, Bain should report as part of net income a foreign exchange transaction gain of

  a. $0
  b. $4,000
  c. $5,000
  d. $9,000

2. On September 1, year 1, Cano & Co., a US corporation, sold merchandise to a foreign firm for 250,000 Botswana pula. Terms of the sale require payment in pula on February 1, year 2. On September 1, year 1, the spot exchange rate was $.20 per pula. At December 31, year 1, Cano's year-end, the spot rate was $.19, but the rate increased to $.22 by February 1, year 2, when payment was received. How much should Cano report as foreign exchange transaction gain or loss as part of year 2 income?

  a. $0.
  b. $2,500 loss.
  c. $5,000 gain.
  d. $7,500 gain.

3. Lindy, a US corporation, bought inventory items from a supplier in Argentina on November 5, year 1, for 100,000 Argentine pesos, when the spot rate was $.4295. At Lindy's December 31, year 1 year-end, the spot rate was $.4245. On January 15, year 2, Lindy bought 100,000 pesos at the spot rate of $.4345 and paid the invoice. How much should Lindy report as part of net income for year 1 and year 2 as foreign exchange transaction gain or loss?

	Year 1	Year 2
a.	$ 500	$(1,000)
b.	$0	$ (500)
c.	$ (500)	$0
d.	$(1,000)	$ 500

4. Hunt Co. purchased merchandise for £300,000 from a vendor in London on November 30, year 1. Payment in British pounds was due on January 30, year 2. The exchange rates to purchase one pound were as follows:

	November 30, Year 1	December 31, Year 2
Spot-rate	$1.65	$1.62
30-day rate	1.64	1.59
60-day rate	1.63	1.56

In its December 31, year 1, income statement, what amount should Hunt report as foreign exchange transaction gain as part of net income?

  a. $12,000
  b. $ 9,000
  c. $ 6,000
  d. $0

5. Ball Corp. had the following foreign currency transactions during year 1:

- Merchandise was purchased from a foreign supplier on January 20, year 1, for the US dollar equivalent of $90,000. The invoice was paid on March 20, year 1, at the US dollar equivalent of $96,000.
- On July 1, year 1, Ball borrowed the US dollar equivalent of $500,000 evidenced by a note that was payable in the lender's local currency on July 1, year 3. On December 31, year 1, the US dollar equivalents of the principal amount and accrued interest were $520,000 and $26,000, respectively. Interest on the note is 10% per annum.

In Ball's year 1 income statement, what amount should be included as foreign exchange transaction loss as part of net income?

  a. $0
  b. $ 6,000
  c. $21,000
  d. $27,000

6. On November 30, year 1, Tyrola Publishing Company, located in Colorado, executed a contract with Ernest Blyton, an author from Canada, providing for payment of 10% royalties on Canadian sales of Blyton's book. Payment is to be made in Canadian dollars each January 10 for the previous year's sales. Canadian sales of the book for the year ended December 31, year 2, totaled $50,000 Canadian. Tyrola paid Blyton his year 2 royalties on January 10, year 3. Tyrola's year 2 financial statements were issued on February 1, year 3. Spot rates for Canadian dollars were as follows:

November 30, year 1	$.87
January 1, year 2	$.88
December 31, year 2	$.89
January 10, year 3	$.90

How much should Tyrola accrue for royalties payable at December 31, year 2?

  a. $4,350
  b. $4,425
  c. $4,450
  d. $4,500

7. Shore Co. records its transactions in US dollars. A sale of goods resulted in a receivable denominated in Japanese yen, and a purchase of goods resulted in a payable denominated in euros. Shore recorded a foreign exchange transaction gain on collection of the receivable and an exchange transaction loss on settlement of the payable. The exchange rates are expressed as so many units of foreign currency to one dollar. Did the number of foreign currency units exchangeable for a dollar increase or decrease between the contract and settlement dates?

	Yen exchangeable for $1	Euros exchangeable for $1
a.	Increase	Increase
b.	Decrease	Decrease
c.	Decrease	Increase
d.	Increase	Decrease

8. On October 1, year 1, Mild Co., a US company, purchased machinery from Grund, a German company, with payment due on April 1, year 2. If Mild's year 1 operating income included no foreign exchange transaction gain or loss, then the transaction could have

 a. Resulted in an extraordinary gain.
 b. Been denominated in US dollars.
 c. Caused a foreign currency gain to be reported as a contra account against machinery.
 d. Caused a foreign currency translation gain to be reported as other comprehensive income.

9. On October 1, year 1, Velec Co., a US company, contracted to purchase foreign goods requiring payment in Qatari riyals, one month after their receipt at Velec's factory. Title to the goods passed on December 15, year 1. The goods were still in transit on December 31, year 1. Exchange rates were one dollar to twenty-two riyals, twenty riyals, and twenty-one riyals on October 1, December 15, and December 31, year 1, respectively. Velec should account for the exchange rate fluctuation in year 1 as

 a. A loss included in net income before extraordinary items.
 b. A gain included in net income before extraordinary items.
 c. An extraordinary gain.
 d. An extraordinary loss.

B.2.-3. Derivative Instruments and Hedging Activities

10. Derivatives are financial instruments that derive their value from changes in a benchmark based on any of the following except

 a. Stock prices.
 b. Mortgage and currency rates.
 c. Commodity prices.
 d. Discounts on accounts receivable.

11. Derivative instruments are financial instruments or other contracts that must contain

 a. One or more underlyings, **or** one or more notional amounts.
 b. No initial net investment or smaller net investment than required for similar response contacts.
 c. Terms that do not require or permit net settlement or delivery of an asset.
 d. All of the above.

12. The basic purpose of derivative financial instruments is to manage some kind of risk such as all of the following except

 a. Stock price movements.
 b. Interest rate variations.
 c. Currency fluctuations.
 d. Uncollectibility of accounts receivables.

13. Which of the following statements is(are) true regarding derivative financial instruments?

 I. Derivative financial instruments should be measured at fair value and reported in the balance sheet as assets or liabilities.
 II. Gains and losses on derivative instruments not designated as hedging activities should be reported and recognized in earnings in the period of the change in fair value.

 a. I only.
 b. II only.
 c. Both I and II.
 d. Neither I nor II.

14. Which of the following is an underlying, according to ASC Topic 815?

 a. A credit rating.
 b. A security price.
 c. An average daily temperature.
 d. All of the above could be underlyings.

15. If the price of the underlying is greater than the strike or exercise price of the underlying, the call option is

 a. At the money.
 b. In the money.
 c. On the money.
 d. Out of the money.

16. Which of the following is **not** a distinguishing characteristic of a derivative instrument?

 a. Terms that require or permit net settlement.
 b. Must be "highly effective" throughout its life.
 c. No initial net investment.
 d. One or more underlyings and notional amounts.

17. An example of a notional amount is

 a. Number of barrels of oil.
 b. Interest rates.
 c. Currency swaps.
 d. Stock prices.

18. Disclosures related to financial instruments, both derivative and nonderivative, used as hedging instruments must include

 a. A list of hedged instruments.
 b. Maximum potential accounting loss.
 c. Objectives and strategies for achieving them.
 d. Only a. and c.

B.4. Inclusions in and Exclusions from Derivative Instruments

19. Which of the following financial instruments or other contracts is not specifically excluded from the definition of derivative instruments in ASC Topic 815?

 a. Leases.
 b. Call (put) option.
 c. Adjustable rate loans.
 d. Equity securities.

20. Which of the following is **not** a derivative instrument?

 a. Futures contracts.
 b. Credit indexed contracts.
 c. Interest rate swaps.
 d. Variable annuity contracts.

B.5.   Embedded Derivative Instruments and Bifurcation

21. Which of the following criteria must be met for bifurcation to occur?
  a. The embedded derivative meets the definition of a derivative instrument.
  b. The hybrid instrument is regularly recorded at fair value.
  c. Economic characteristics and risks of the embedded instrument are "clearly and closely" related to those of the host contract.
  d. All of the above.

22. Financial instruments sometimes contain features that separately meet the definition of a derivative instrument. These features are classified as
  a. Swaptions.
  b. Notional amounts.
  c. Embedded derivative instruments.
  d. Underlyings.

23. The process of bifurcation
  a. Protects an entity from loss by entering into a transaction.
  b. Includes entering into agreements between two counterparties to exchange cash flows over specified period of time in the future.
  c. Is the interaction of the price or rate with an associated asset or liability.
  d. Separates an embedded derivative from its host contract.

24. Alvarez Corporation has two hybrid financial instruments. According to ASC Topic 815, how can Alvarez account for these instruments?
  a. Alvarez must bifurcate all hybrid financial instruments and record the components separately.
  b. Alvarez can elect to not disclose the financial instruments on the balance sheet.
  c. Alvarez can elect not to bifurcate the hybrid instruments on an instrument by instrument basis.
  d. Alvarez can make an election that requires all hybrid financial instruments not to be bifurcated.

25. According to ASC Topic 815, when a company elects not to bifurcate a hybrid financial instrument, the entire hybrid instrument should be valued at
  a. Fair value.
  b. Net present value.
  c. Net realizable value.
  d. Book value.

26. When an election is made not to bifurcate a hybrid financial instrument, how should this be disclosed on the financial statements?

  I. As separate line items for the fair value and non–fair value instruments on the balance sheet.
  II. As an aggregate amount of all hybrid instruments with the amount of the hybrid instruments at fair value shown in parentheses.
  III. As a footnote disclosure.

  a. I only.
  b. II and III only.
  c. III only.
  d. I and II only.

27. If a company elects not to bifurcate a hybrid financial instrument and records the entire instrument at fair value, which of the following is true?
  a. No changes in value are recorded until the hybrid instrument is sold.
  b. Changes in fair value of the hybrid instrument are recognized each year in other comprehensive income.
  c. Changes in fair value of the hybrid instrument are recognized each year in earnings.
  d. Changes in fair value of the hybrid instrument are recognized each year by recognizing a cumulative effect adjustment to the beginning balance of retained earnings for the period.

B.6.-9   Hedging Instruments

28. Hedge accounting is permitted for all of the following types of hedges except
  a. Trading securities.
  b. Unrecognized firm commitments.
  c. Available-for-sale securities.
  d. Net investments in foreign operations.

29. Which of the following is a general criterion for a hedging instrument?
  a. Sufficient documentation must be provided at the beginning of the process.
  b. Must be "highly effective" only in the first year of the hedge's life.
  c. Must contain a nonperformance clause that makes performance probable.
  d. Must contain one or more underlyings.

30. For an unrecognized firm commitment to qualify as a hedged item it must
  a. Be binding on both parties.
  b. Be specific with respect to all significant terms.
  c. Contain a nonperformance clause that makes performance probable.
  d. All of the above.

31. A hedge of the exposure to changes in the fair value of a recognized asset or liability, or an unrecognized firm commitment, is classified as a
  a. Fair value hedge.
  b. Cash flow hedge.
  c. Foreign currency hedge.
  d. Underlying.

32. Gains and losses on the hedged asset/liability and the hedged instrument for a fair value hedge will be recognized
  a. In current earnings.
  b. In other comprehensive income.
  c. On a cumulative basis from the change in expected cash flows from the hedged instrument.
  d. On the balance sheet either as an asset or a liability.

33. Gains and losses of the effective portion of a hedging instrument will be recognized in current earnings in each reporting period for which of the following?

	Fair value hedge	Cash flow hedge
a.	Yes	No
b.	Yes	Yes

c.   No   No
d.   No   Yes

34. Which of the following risks are inherent in an interest rate swap agreement?

I. The risk of exchanging a lower interest rate for a higher interest rate.
II. The risk of nonperformance by the counterparty to the agreement.

    a.   I only.
    b.   II only.
    c.   Both I and II.
    d.   Neither I nor II.

35. Which of the following meet the definition of assets and/or liabilities?

	Derivative instruments	G/L on the fair value of derivatives
a.	Yes	No
b.	No	Yes
c.	Yes	Yes
d.	No	No

36. Which of the following is **not** a type of foreign currency hedge?
    a.   A forecasted transaction.
    b.   An available-for-sale security.
    c.   A recognized asset or liability.
    d.   An unrecognized firm commitment.

37. Which of the following foreign currency transactions is not accounted for using hedge accounting?
    a.   Available-for-sale securities.
    b.   Unrecognized firm commitments.
    c.   Net investments in foreign operations.
    d.   Foreign currency denominated forecasted transactions.

B.10. Forward Exchange Contracts

Items 38 through 41 are based on the following:

On December 12, year 1, Imp Co. entered into three forward exchange contracts, each to purchase 100,000 euros in ninety days. The relevant exchange rates are as follows:

	Spot rate	Forward rate (for March 12, year 2)
November 30, year 1	$.87	$.89
December 12, year 1	.88	.90
December 31, year 1	.92	.93

38. Imp entered into the first forward contract to hedge a purchase of inventory in November year 1, payable in March year 2. At December 31, year 1, what amount of foreign currency transaction gain from this forward contract should Imp include in net income?
    a. $0
    b. $ 3,000
    c. $ 5,000
    d. $10,000

39. At December 31, year 1, what amount of foreign currency transaction loss should Imp include in income from the revaluation of the Accounts Payable of 100,000 euros incurred as a result of the purchase of inventory at November 30, year 1, payable in March year 2?

    a. $0
    b. $3,000
    c. $4,000
    d. $5,000

40. Imp entered into the second forward contract to hedge a commitment to purchase equipment being manufactured to Imp's specifications. The expected delivery date is March year 2 at which time settlement is due to the manufacturer. The hedge qualifies as a fair value hedge. At December 31, year 1, what amount of foreign currency transaction gain from this forward contract should Imp include in net income?
    a. $0
    b. $ 3,000
    c. $ 5,000
    d. $10,000

41. Imp entered into the third forward contract for speculation. At December 31, year 1, what amount of foreign currency transaction gain from this forward contract should Imp include in net income?
    a. $0
    b. $ 3,000
    c. $ 5,000
    d. $10,000

B.12. Fair Value and Credit Risk Disclosures

42. The risk of an accounting loss from a financial instrument due to possible failure of another party to perform according to terms of the contract is known as
    a.   Off-balance-sheet risk.
    b.   Market risk.
    c.   Credit risk.
    d.   Investment risk.

43. Examples of financial instruments with off-balance-sheet risk include all of the following except
    a.   Outstanding loan commitments written.
    b.   Recourse obligations on receivables.
    c.   Warranty obligations
    d.   Futures contracts.

44. Off-balance-sheet risk of accounting loss does not result from
    a.   Financial instruments recognized as assets entailing conditional rights that result in a loss greater than the amount recognized in the balance sheet.
    b.   Financial instruments not recognized as either assets or liabilities yet still expose the entity to risk of accounting loss.
    c.   Financial instruments recognized as assets or liabilities where the amount recognized reflects the risk of accounting loss to the entity.
    d.   Financial instruments recognized as liabilities that result in an ultimate obligation that is greater than the amount recognized in the balance sheet.

45. If it is not practicable for an entity to estimate the fair value of a financial instrument, which of the following should be disclosed?

I. Information pertinent to estimating the fair value of the financial instrument.
II. The reasons it is not practicable to estimate fair value.

a. I only.
b. II only.
c. Both I and II.
d. Neither I nor II.

46. Disclosure requirements for financial instruments include

a. Method(s) and significant assumptions used in estimating fair value.
b. Distinction between financial instruments held or issued for trading purposes and purposes other than trading.
c. A note containing a summary table cross-referencing the location of other financial instruments disclosed in another area of the financial statements.
d. All of the above should be disclosed.

47. Disclosure of credit risk of financial instruments with off-balance-sheet risk does **not** have to include

a. The amount of accounting loss the entity would incur should any party to the financial instrument fail to perform.
b. The entity's policy of requiring collateral or security.
c. The class of financial instruments held.
d. The specific names of the parties associated with the financial instrument.

48. Disclosure of information about significant concentrations of credit risk is required for

a. All financial instruments.
b. Financial instruments with off-balance-sheet credit risk only.
c. Financial instruments with off-balance-sheet market risk only.
d. Financial instruments with off-balance-sheet risk of accounting loss only.

49. Kline Bank has large amounts of notes receivable from companies with high debt-to-equity ratios as a result of buyout transactions. Kline is contemplating the following disclosures for the notes receivable in its year-end financial statements:

I. Information about shared activity, region, or economic characteristic.
II. A brief description of collateral supporting these financial instruments.

Which of the above disclosures are required under GAAP?

a. I only.
b. II only.
c. Neither I nor II.
d. Both I and II.

50. Whether recognized or unrecognized in an entity's financial statements, disclosure of the fair values of the entity's financial instruments is required when

a. It is practicable to estimate those values.
b. The entity maintains accurate cost records.
c. Aggregated fair values are material to the entity.
d. Individual fair values are material to the entity.

D. *International Financial Reporting Standards (IFRS)*

51. Under IFRS, a cash flow hedge and a hedge of a net investment are accounted for by

a. Not recognizing gains and losses.
b. Recognizing gains and losses in other comprehensive income.
c. Recognizing gains and losses in profit and loss.
d. Recognizing gains and losses when the hedge is closed out.

Multiple-Choice Answers and Explanations

Answers

1. c ___ ___	12. d ___ ___	23. d ___ ___	34. c ___ ___	45. c ___ ___
2. d ___ ___	13. c ___ ___	24. c ___ ___	35. a ___ ___	46. d ___ ___
3. a ___ ___	14. d ___ ___	25. a ___ ___	36. c ___ ___	47. d ___ ___
4. b ___ ___	15. b ___ ___	26. d ___ ___	37. c ___ ___	48. a ___ ___
5. d ___ ___	16. b ___ ___	27. c ___ ___	38. b ___ ___	49. d ___ ___
6. c ___ ___	17. a ___ ___	28. a ___ ___	39. d ___ ___	50. a ___ ___
7. b ___ ___	18. d ___ ___	29. a ___ ___	40. b ___ ___	51. b ___ ___
8. b ___ ___	19. b ___ ___	30. d ___ ___	41. b ___ ___	
9. b ___ ___	20. d ___ ___	31. a ___ ___	42. c ___ ___	
10. d ___ ___	21. a ___ ___	32. a ___ ___	43. c ___ ___	1st: __/51 = __%
11. b ___ ___	22. c ___ ___	33. a ___ ___	44. c ___ ___	2nd: __/51 = __%

Explanations

1. **(c)** When the **sale is made** on 10/15/Y1, Bain would record a receivable and sales at $100,000, the US dollar equivalent on that date.

Accounts receivable	100,000	
Sales		100,000

On 11/16/Y1, Bain receives foreign currency worth $105,000. Since the receivable was recorded at $100,000, a $5,000 gain must be recorded.

Foreign currency	105,000	
Accounts receivable		100,000
Foreign exchange		
transaction gain		5,000

The US dollar equivalent when the order was received on 9/1/Y1 ($96,000) is not used to compute the gain because no entry is recorded on this date. The receipt and acceptance of a purchase order from a customer is an executory commitment which is not generally recorded.

2. **(d)** On 9/1/Y1, Cano obtained a receivable which will be collected in a foreign currency. A gain (loss) will result if the exchange rate on the settlement date is different from the rate existing on the transaction date. A gain (loss) must be recognized at any intervening balance sheet dates, if necessary. Therefore, Cano would recognize a $2,500 foreign exchange transaction loss in its **year 1** income statement since a change in the exchange rate reduced the receivable (in US dollars) from $50,000 on 9/1/Y1 (250,000 × $.20) to $47,500 on 12/31/Y1 (250,000 × $.19). In year 2, a foreign exchange transaction gain of $7,500 is recognized because the receivable (in US dollars) increased from $47,500 on 12/31/Y1 to $55,000 when received (250,000 × $.22) on February 1, year 2.

3. **(a)** A transaction has occurred in which settlement will be made in Argentine pesos. Since Lindy's functional currency is the US dollar, a foreign exchange transaction gain (loss) will result if the spot rate on the settlement date is different than the rate on the transaction date. A provision must be made at any intervening year-end date if there has been a rate change. Thus, in year 1, a $500 foreign exchange transaction gain [100,000 × ($.4295 – $.4245)] would be recognized, while in year 2 a $1,000 foreign exchange transaction loss [100,000 × ($.4245 – $.4345)] would be recognized.

4. **(b)** A purchase has been made for which payment will be made in British pounds. A foreign exchange transaction gain or loss will result if the spot rate on the settlement date is different from the rate used on the transaction date. A gain or loss must also be recorded at any intervening balance sheet date if there has been a rate change. Thus, at 12/31/Y1 a foreign exchange transaction gain of $9,000 is recognized [300,000 × ($1.65 – $1.62)] as the foreign currency payable is reduced from $495,000 (300,000 × $1.65) to $486,000 (300,000 × $1.62). The thirty-day and sixty-day rates would affect Hunt only if the company had entered into forward contracts.

5. **(d)** On 1/20/Y1, Ball would record purchases and accounts payable at $90,000. When the account was paid, the equivalent of $96,000 was required to liquidate the $90,000 liability, resulting in a foreign exchange transaction loss of $6,000. Foreign exchange transaction gains (losses) are recognized at intervening balance sheet dates. The note payable originally recorded at $500,000 was equivalent to a liability of $520,000 at the balance sheet date, resulting in a year 1 loss of $20,000. The interest payable of $25,000 ($500,000 × 10% × 6/12) was equivalent to a liability of $26,000 at year-end, resulting in an additional year 1 loss of $1,000. Therefore, the total year 1 foreign exchange transaction loss is $27,000 ($6,000 + $20,000 + $1,000).

6. **(c)** The requirement is to determine the amount that Tyrola should accrue for royalties payable, 12/31/Y2. This situation is a foreign currency transaction in which settlement is denominated in other than a company's functional currency. In this case the functional currency is the US dollar because it is the currency of the primary economic environment in which the Colorado firm operates. Note that in this royalty agreement, 12/31/Y2 is the point at which the amount due to the author (50,000 Canadian dollars × 10% = 5,000 Canadian dollars) is determined. Royalty expense is measured and the related liability is denominated at 12/31/Y2. The year-end accrual would be

    .89 (10% × 50,000 Canadian dollars) = $4,450.

On January 10, year 2, Tyrola will have to purchase 5,000 Canadian dollars for payment to the Canadian author. The amount of US dollars required to accomplish this will depend on the spot rate on January 10 ($.90 in this case). The number of US dollars required to satisfy the obligation will be $50 greater [($.90 – .89) × 5,000 Canadian dollars]. This will result in a $50 foreign exchange transaction loss which would be included in year 2 net income.

7. **(b)** In the case of the receivable denominated in Japanese yen, a foreign exchange transaction gain was recorded on the collection of the receivable. This means that more yen was received than was recorded in the receivable account. For that to happen the rate of yen exchangeable for a dollar would have had to decrease, requiring more yen to be paid at the settlement date for the same amount of dollars at the contract date. On the other hand, there was a foreign exchange transaction loss on the payable denominated in euros. This means that at the settlement date Shore Co. had to pay more euros than were recorded in the payable account. For this to occur the rate of euros exchangeable for a dollar would have had to decrease, requiring more euros to be paid at the settlement date for the same amount of dollars at the contract date.

8. **(b)** A transaction that is denominated in a currency other than the entity's functional currency, which is payable at a fixed amount at a later date, may result in an increased or decreased amount payable because of a change in the exchange rate. This increase/decrease would be classified as a foreign exchange transaction gain/loss, and would be included as a component of income. The gain/loss would not be considered extraordinary.

9. **(b)** The requirement is to determine how Velec should account for the exchange rate fluctuation in year 1. A foreign currency transaction is a transaction denominated in a currency other than the entity's functional currency. Denominated means that the balance is fixed in terms of the number of units of a foreign currency, regardless of changes in the exchange rate. When a US company buys or sells to an unrelated foreign company, and the US company agrees either to pay for goods or receive payment for the goods in foreign currency units, this is a foreign currency transaction from the point of view of the US company (the functional currency is the US dollar). In these situations, the US company has "crossed currencies" and directly assumes the risk of fluctuating foreign exchange rates of the foreign currency units. As exchange rates fluctuate, a company will record an ordinary gain or loss on their income statement, **not** an extraordinary gain or loss. Velec has an accounts payable denominated in a foreign currency (Qatari riyals) as of December 15, the date the title to the goods passes to Velec. As the value of the riyal per dollar rises above twenty riyals per dollar, Velec Co. will have to come up with less dollars to pay off the payable, as of December 31, year 1, than they would have on December 15, year 1. This creates a foreign exchange transaction gain. As shown numerically, if 4000 riyals are assumed as being payable, on December 15 you would need $200 (4000/20) to pay off the payable. However, on December 31, $190 would be needed (4000/21). The difference between $200 and $190 represents the gain. A foreign exchange transaction gain should be included in net income, not a loss.

10. **(d)** Derivatives are financial instruments that derive their value from changes in a benchmark based on stock prices, interest rates, mortgage rates, currency rates, commodity prices, or some other agreed-upon base. Discounts on accounts receivable are not the basis of a benchmark for a derivative financial instrument.

11. **(b)** Derivative instruments must contain one or more underlyings **and** one or more notional amounts. Derivative instruments do contain terms that require or permit net settlement or delivery of an asset.

12. **(d)** Derivative financial instruments are contracts that are supposed to protect or hedge one or more of the parties from adverse movement in the underlying base. Answer (d) is correct because it does not fit the definition of a financial instrument. Risk of uncollectable accounts can be managed by effective credit policies.

13. **(c)** Derivative instruments meet the definition of assets and liabilities. As such they should be reported on the entity's financial statements. The most relevant measure for reporting financial instruments is fair value. Thus, statement I is true. If a derivative instrument does not qualify as a hedging instrument, then its gains or losses must be reported and recognized in current earnings. Thus, statement II is also true.

14. **(d)** All of the above meet the basic definition of an underlying, which is any financial or physical variable that has either observable changes or objectively verifiable changes.

15. **(b)** A call option is in the money if the price of the underlying is greater than the strike or exercise price of the underlying. An at-the-money option is one in which the price of the underlying is equal to the strike or exercise price. A call option is out of the money if the strike or exercise price is greater than the price of the underlying.

16. **(b)** Derivative instruments contain

1. One or more underlyings and one or more notional amounts
2. No initial net investment or smaller net investment than required for contracts with an expected similar response to market changes, and
3. Terms that require or permit net settlement, net settlement by means outside the contract, and delivery of an asset that is substantially the same as net settlement.

17. **(a)** Notional amounts are the referenced associated asset or liability that are commonly a number of units such as barrels of oil. Answers (b) and (d) are incorrect because they are examples of underlyings. Answer (c) is incorrect because it is an example of a derivative instrument.

18. **(d)** Disclosures related to financial instruments that are used as hedging instruments must include the following information:

1. Objectives and strategies for achieving them.
2. Context to understand the instrument.
3. Risk management policies.
4. A list of hedged instruments.

Disclosure of the maximum potential accounting loss is only required for financial instruments with concentrations of credit risk.

19. **(b)** Only call (put) options are included in the definition of derivative financial instruments. Leases are excluded because they require a payment equal to the value of the right to use the property. Equity securities and adjustable rate loans are excluded because they require an initial net investment equivalent to the fair value.

20. (d) Futures contracts, credit indexed contracts, and interest rate swaps are all included in derivative instruments.

21. (a) The hybrid instrument is **not** recorded at fair value. Economic characteristics and risks of the embedded instrument are **not** "clearly and closely" related to those of the host contract. The embedded derivative must meet the definition of a derivative instrument.

22. (c) An embedded derivative is a feature of a financial instrument or other contract, which if the feature stood alone, would meet the definition of a derivative.

23. (d) Bifurcation is the process of separating an embedded derivative from its host contract. This process is necessary so that hybrid instruments can be separated into their component parts, each being accounted for using the appropriate valuation techniques.

24. (c) Alvarez can elect not to bifurcate the hybrid instrument, and this election can be made on an instrument by instrument basis. Answer (a) is incorrect because an election can be made not to bifurcate an instrument. Answer (b) is incorrect because hybrid financial instruments must be disclosed. Answer (d) is incorrect because the hybrid financial instruments can be selected on an instrument by instrument basis.

25. (a) If a company elects not to bifurcate a hybrid financial instrument, the entire instrument is valued at fair value. Answers (b), (c), and (d) are incorrect because these valuation models are incorrect.

26. (d) The balance sheet disclosure may be presented in one of two ways: as a separate line item for the fair value and non–fair value instruments on the balance sheet, or as an aggregate amount of all hybrid instruments with the amount of the hybrid instruments at fair value shown in parentheses. Answers (a), (b), and (c) are incorrect because two disclosures are permissible on the balance sheet.

27. (c) If a company elects not to bifurcate a hybrid financial instrument, the entire instrument is recorded at fair value. Changes in fair value each year are recognized in earnings for the period. Answer (a) is incorrect because changes in fair value must be recognized. Answer (b) is incorrect because the changes are not recognized in other comprehensive income. Answer (d) is incorrect, because an adjustment is only made to beginning retained earnings in the year that a company initially adopts the new accounting pronouncement.

28. (a) Hedge accounting is permitted for four types of hedges.

1. Unrecognized firm commitments.
2. Available-for-sale securities.
3. Foreign currency denominated hedge forecasted transactions.
4. Net investments in foreign operations.

Trading securities is not one of the four types.

29. (a) The general criteria for a hedging instrument are that sufficient documentation must be provided at the begin-

ning of the process and the hedge must be "highly effective" throughout its life.

30. (d) For an unrecognized firm commitment to qualify as a hedged item it must

1. Be binding on both parties.
2. Be specific with respect to all significant items including quantity to be exchanged, the fixed price, and the timing of the transaction.
3. Contain a nonperformance clause that makes performance probable.

31. (a) A fair value hedge is a hedge of the exposure to changes in the fair value of a recognized asset or liability or firm commitment. Two other types of hedges are cash flow and foreign currency hedges. An underlying is commonly a specified price or rate.

32. (a) Gains and losses of a fair value hedge will be recognized in current earnings. The effective portion of a cash flow hedge is reported in other comprehensive income and the ineffective portion is reported on a cumulative basis to reflect the lesser of the cumulative gain/loss on the derivative or the cumulative gain/loss from the change in expected cash flows from the hedged instrument. Gains and losses from a change in the fair value of derivative instruments are not assets and liabilities and should not be reported on the balance sheet.

33. (a) Fair value hedges will recognize gains and losses for the effective portion of the hedging instrument in each reporting period. Cash flow hedges will recognize gains and losses for the effect portion of the hedging instrument in other comprehensive income.

34. (c) An interest rate swap agreement involves the exchange of cash flows determined by various interest rates. Fluctuations in interest rates after the agreement is entered into may result in the risk of exchanging a lower interest rate for a higher interest rate. Financial instruments, including swaps, also bear credit risk or the risk that a counterparty to the agreement will not perform as expected.

35. (a) Derivatives do meet the definition of assets/liabilities and, therefore, should be recognized and reported as such on the financial statements. In contrast, gains and losses that result from the change in the fair value of derivatives are not assets/liabilities and should either appear in other comprehensive income or be reported in current earnings.

36. (c) The four foreign currency hedges are an unrecognized firm commitment, an available-for-sale security, a foreign currency denominated forecasted transaction, and a net investment in foreign operations. A hedge of a recognized asset or liability is a fair value hedge or cash flow hedge, not a foreign currency hedge.

37. (c) The hedged net investment is viewed as a single asset. The provisions for recognizing the gain or loss on the hedged asset/liability and the hedging instrument rules do not apply to the hedges of net investments in foreign operations. Instead, hedges of net investments in foreign operations shall be reported in the same manner as a translation adjustment.

38. **(b)** Forward exchange contracts are measured at fair value. Each period this is accomplished by marking the forward exchange contract to market using the forward rate at the FS date. At 12/31/Y1 the forward rate is $.93. The difference between $.93 and $.90, the forward rate on the date the contracts were entered into, times 100,000 euros is $3,000, the forward exchange gain. The entry would be as follows:

Forward contract receivable	3,000	
Forward contract gain		3,000

The $3,000 forward exchange contract gain would be included in year 1 net income.

39. **(d)** The accounting for gains and losses from foreign currency transactions requires a revaluation of exposed net assets and liabilities denominated in foreign currency units at the current spot rate. At 12/31/Y1 there is a foreign exchange transaction loss of $5,000 [($.92 – .87) × 100,000 euros]. Note that accounts payable was created on 11/30/Y1. The entry to record the loss is as follows:

Foreign exchange loss	5,000	
Accounts payable		5,000

The loss would be reported in year 1 net income.

40. **(b)** Hedges involving firm purchase commitments are treated in the same manner as a forward exchange contract that was entered into to hedge an exposure of a liability.

Forward contract receivable	3,000	
Forward contract gain		3,000
To revalue forward contract using forward rates		
Foreign exchange loss	3,000	
Firm purchase commitment		3,000
To recognize loss on firm commitment		

Note that this hedge is 100% effective because the gain on the forward contract and the loss on the firm purchase commitment offset each other, net.

41. **(b)** Using a forward exchange contract to speculate would result in a gain or loss each period FS are prepared. The contract would be revalued each reporting period using the forward rate. The gain or loss calculated would be reported in net income. The journal entry would be as follows:

Forward contract receivable	3,000	
Forward contract gain		3,000

42. **(c)** Credit risk is the risk of accounting loss from a financial instrument due to possible failure of another party to perform according to the terms of the contract. Off-balance-sheet risk is the possible amount of loss from an instrument that is not reflected on the balance sheet. Market risk is the risk that future changes in market prices may make a financial instrument less valuable.

43. **(c)** The value of derivative financial instruments is typically derived from the value of an underlying asset or is tied to an index. As the price of the underlying asset changes, the price of the derivative changes. Outstanding loan commitments written, recourse obligations on receivables, and futures contracts are all tied to an asset account. Warranty obligations are the result of the sale of goods.

44. **(c)** Off-balance-sheet risk is the possible amount of loss from an instrument that is not reflected on the balance sheet because a loss has not yet occurred or because the item is not recognized as an asset or liability. If the amount recognized on the balance sheet reflects the accounting loss to the entity, then there is no off-balance-sheet risk to consider.

45. **(c)** If it is not practicable for an entity to estimate the fair value of a financial instrument, (1) information pertinent to estimating fair value **and** (2) the reasons why it is not practicable to estimate fair value should be disclosed.

46. **(d)** The following disclosures are required:

- Method(s) and significant assumptions used in estimating fair value.
- A distinction between financial instruments held or issued for trading purposes and purposes other than trading.
- Information pertinent to estimating the fair value of a financial instrument if it is not practicable for the entity to estimate and the reason why estimation is not practicable.
- Derivative financial instruments may not be combined, aggregated, or netted with nonderivative or other derivative financial instruments.
- If financial instruments are disclosed in more than one area in the financial statements, one note must contain a summary table cross-referencing the location of the other instruments.

47. **(d)** The following disclosures are required about credit risk for financial instruments with off-balance-sheet credit risk:

- The amount of accounting loss the entity would incur should any party to the financial instrument fail to perform according to the terms of the contract and the collateral, if any, is of no value.
- The class of financial instruments held.
- Categorization between instruments held for trading purposes and purposes other than trading.

48. **(a)** Concentrations of credit risk exist when an entity has a business activity, economic characteristic, or location that is common to most of its financial instruments. Disclosure of information about significant concentrations of credit risk for **all** financial instruments is required.

49. **(d)** Since many of Kline Bank's debtors have high debt-to-equity ratios, this group of debtors has a similar economic characteristic, and thus, would be considered a concentration of credit risk to Kline Bank. The entity must disclose the following information regarding concentrations of credit risk:

1. Information about the shared activity, region, or economic characteristic of the group.
2. Amount of accounting loss that the entity would incur as a result of the concentrated parties' failure to perform according to the terms of the contracts.
3. Information regarding entity's policy of requiring collateral.

50. **(a)** Entities must disclose the fair market value of financial instruments, both assets and liabilities whether recognized or not recognized in the statement of financial position, for which it is practicable to estimate fair value.

Pertinent descriptive information as to the fair value of the instrument is to be disclosed if an estimate of fair value cannot be made without incurring excessive costs.

51. **(b)** The requirement is to identify the appropriate accounting method for a cash flow hedge and a hedge of a net investment. Answer (b) is correct because such hedges are accounted for by recognizing gains and losses in other comprehensive income.

Simulations

Task-Based Simulation 1

Concepts		
	Authoritative Literature	**Help**

Select the **best** answer for each item from the terms listed in A–E. All terms should be used once.

Answer List

A.   Granted special hedge accounting treatment.
B.   Resulting gains or losses are taken into current earnings in the period in which they arise.
C.   Two currencies other than a functional currency expected to move relative to an entity's functional currency.
D.   A hedge against an exposed asset position created by having an account in a denomination other than the functional currency.
E.   The difference between the futures rate and the spot rate at the date of a forward contract.

		(A)	(B)	(C)	(D)	(E)
1.	Tandem currencies	O	O	O	O	O
2.	Discount or premium	O	O	O	O	O
3.	Ineffective portion of a hedge	O	O	O	O	O
4.	Effective portion of a hedge	O	O	O	O	O
5.	Forward contract	O	O	O	O	O

Task-Based Simulation 2

Applicability of SFAS 133		
	Authoritative Literature	**Help**

This question consists of 14 items that represent financial instruments and other contracts that may be included in or excluded from the requirements of ASC Topic 815 (SFAS 133), *Derivatives and Hedging*.

For the following items, determine if they are (I) included under the requirement of ASC Topic 815, or (E) excluded from ASC Topic 815 treatment.

I.   Item meets the definition of a derivative instrument and must be accounted for using ASC Topic 815.
E.   Item is not required to be accounted for under ASC Topic 815, either because it does not meet the definition of derivative instrument or because the item is specifically excluded from ASC Topic 815 treatment.

		(I)	(E)
1.	Leases	O	O
2.	Guaranteed investment contracts	O	O
3.	Futures contracts	O	O
4.	Equity securities	O	O
5.	Credit indexed contracts	O	O
6.	Mortgage-backed securities	O	O
7.	Debt securities	O	O
8.	Interest rate caps	O	O
9.	Swaptions	O	O
10.	Employee stock options	O	O
11.	Options to purchase or sell exchange-traded securities	O	O
12.	Variable annuity contracts	O	O
13.	Adjustable rate loans	O	O
14.	Interest rate swaps	O	O

Task-Based Simulation 3

Research		
	Authoritative Literature	Help

Reston Corporation has a gain on a foreign currency fair value hedge. You have been asked to research the professional literature to determine where the gain should be reported in the financial statements.

Place the citation for the excerpt from Professional Standards that provides this information in the answer box below.

Task-Based Simulation 4

Terminology		
	Authoritative Literature	Help

Select the **best** answer for each item from the terms listed in A–O. No answer should be used more than once.

Answer List

A. An agreement with an unrelated party, binding on both, usually legally enforceable, specifying all significant terms and including a disincentive for nonperformance sufficient to make performance likely.
B. A call option where the price of the underlying is greater than the strike or exercise price of the underlying.
C. A feature on a financial instrument or other contract, which if the feature stood alone, would meet the definition of a derivative.
D. A forward-based contract or agreement generally between two counterparties to exchange streams of cash flows over a specified period in the future.
E. With regard to call options, it is the larger of zero or the spread between the stock price and the exercise price.
F. Provides the holder the right to acquire an underlying at an exercise or stock price, anytime during the option term.
G. An agreement between the two parties to buy and sell a specific quantity of a commodity, foreign currency, or financial instrument at an agreed-upon price, with delivery and/or settlement at a designated future date.
H. A call option where the strike or exercise price is greater than the price of the underlying.
I. The process of separating an embedded derivative from its host contract.
J. The referenced associated asset or liability, commonly a number of units.
K. A specified price or rate such as a stock price, interest rate, or commodity price.
L. An option where the price of the underlying is equal to the strike or exercise price.
M. The difference between an option's price and its intrinsic value.
N. Provides the holder the right to sell the underlying at an exercise or strike price, anytime during the option term.
O. A forward-based contract to make or take delivery of a designated financial instrument, foreign currency, or commodity during a designated period, at a specified price or yield.

	(A)	(B)	(C)	(D)	(E)	(F)	(G)	(H)	(I)	(J)	(K)	(L)	(M)	(N)	(O)
1. At the money	O	O	O	O	O	O	O	O	O	O	O	O	O	O	O
2. Bifurcation	O	O	O	O	O	O	O	O	O	O	O	O	O	O	O
3. Call option	O	O	O	O	O	O	O	O	O	O	O	O	O	O	O
4. Embedded derivative	O	O	O	O	O	O	O	O	O	O	O	O	O	O	O
5. Forward contract	O	O	O	O	O	O	O	O	O	O	O	O	O	O	O
6. Futures contract	O	O	O	O	O	O	O	O	O	O	O	O	O	O	O
7. In the money	O	O	O	O	O	O	O	O	O	O	O	O	O	O	O
8. Notional amount	O	O	O	O	O	O	O	O	O	O	O	O	O	O	O
9. Out of the money	O	O	O	O	O	O	O	O	O	O	O	O	O	O	O
10. Put option	O	O	O	O	O	O	O	O	O	O	O	O	O	O	O
11. Swap	O	O	O	O	O	O	O	O	O	O	O	O	O	O	O
12. Underlying	O	O	O	O	O	O	O	O	O	O	O	O	O	O	O

Task-Based Simulation 5

Journal Entries		
	Authoritative Literature	Help

Situation

Logan Corporation markets their products internationally. The company buys and sells goods in Great Britain, France, and Germany. Although Logan's functional currency is the US dollar, the transactions are denominated in the currencies for each country as shown in the table below.

Country	Currency
Great Britain	£
France	€
Germany	€

The spot rates for various dates throughout the year are shown below.

Date	US $ per £1	US $ per €1
January 1, year 1	1.786	1.258
March 1, year 1	1.869	1.249
April 15, year 1	1.791	1.197
November 10, year 1	1.857	1.290
December 1, year 1	1.911	1.329
December 20, year 1	1.945	1.333
December 31, year 1	1.927	1.364
January 15, year 2	1.869	1.311
Average daily rate, year 1	1.886	1.279

The following transactions are denominated in each country's local currency.

On March 1, year 1, Logan sells goods on account to Lexington Corporation, located in London, for £370,000. The account is due in 60 days. Lexington pays the full balance due on April 15, year 1.

On November 10, year 1, Logan purchases supplies from Dietmar Corporation in Germany for €190,000. On December 1, year 1, Logan pays Dietmar for the supplies.

On December 20, year 1, Logan sells goods on account to Cordier Corporation in France for €250,000. Cordier pays for the goods on January 15, year 2.

1. Prepare the journal entry for the sale of goods to Lexington on March 1.

2. Prepare the journal entry on April 15, year 1, when Lexington pays for the goods.

3. Prepare the journal entry for the purchase of supplies from Dietmar Corporation on November 10, year 1.

4. Prepare the journal entry for the payment to Dietmar on December 1, year 1.

5. Prepare the journal entry for the sale of goods to Cordier Corporation.

6. Prepare any entries necessary on December 31, year 1, with regard to the foreign currency transactions with Lexington, Dietmar, and Cordier Corporation.

7. Prepare the journal entry for Cordier's payment of goods on January 15, year 2.

Task-Based Simulation 6

Foreign Currency Transaction Gains/Losses	Authoritative Literature	Help

Situation

Logan Corporation markets their products internationally. The company buys and sells goods in Great Britain, France, and Germany. Although Logan's functional currency is the US dollar, the transactions are denominated in the currencies for each country as shown in the table below.

Country	Currency
Great Britain	£
France	€
Germany	€

The spot rates for various dates throughout the year are shown below.

Date	US $ per £1	US $ per €1
January 1, year 1	1.786	1.258
March 1, year 1	1.869	1.249
April 15, year 1	1.791	1.197
November 10, year 1	1.857	1.290
December 1, year 1	1.911	1.329
December 20, year 1	1.945	1.333
December 31, year 1	1.927	1.364
January 15, year 2	1.869	1.311
Average daily rate, year 1	1.886	1.279

The following transactions are denominated in each country's local currency.

On March 1, year 1, Logan sells goods on account to Lexington Corporation, located in London, for £370,000. The account is due in 60 days. Lexington pays the full balance due on April 15, year 1.

On November 10, year 1, Logan purchases supplies from Dietmar Corporation in Germany €190,000. On December 1, year 1, Logan pays Dietmar for the supplies.

On December 20, year 1, Logan sells goods on account to Cordier Corporation in France for €250,000. Cordier pays for the goods on January 15, year 2.

Prepare the following schedule outlining the foreign currency transaction gains and losses for year 1 and year 2 for Logan Corporation.

Logan Corporation
SCHEDULE OF FOREIGN CURRENCY TRANSACTION GAINS/LOSSES
Year 1 and Year 2

	Year 1 gain/(loss)	Year 2 gain/(loss)
Lexington Corporation		
Dietmar Corporation		
Cordier Corporation		
Total FC gain/(loss)		

Indicate from the list below where the foreign currency transaction gain or loss in year 1 will be disclosed on the financial statements.

    A. Extraordinary gain/loss
    B. Other gain/loss
    C. Other comprehensive income
    D. Revenue
    E. Expense

                                         (A) (B) (C) (D) (E)

1. Foreign currency transaction gain/loss for year 1 will be disclosed where on the financial statement?   ○ ○ ○ ○ ○

Task-Based Simulation 7

Research			
	Authoritative Literature	Help	

    Emory Company has operations in the United States and Japan. You have been asked to research the professional literature to determine the exchange rate that should be used to translate a foreign currency transaction. Place the citation for the excerpt from professional standards that provides this information in the answer box below.

Simulation Solutions

Task-Based Simulation 1

Concepts	Authoritative Literature	Help

		(A)	(B)	(C)	(D)	(E)
1.	Tandem currencies	○	○	●	○	○
2.	Discount or premium	○	○	○	○	●
3.	Ineffective portion of a hedge	○	●	○	○	○
4.	Effective portion of a hedge	●	○	○	○	○
5.	Forward contract	○	○	○	●	○

Explanations

1. **(C)** Tandem currencies are two currencies other than a functional currency expected to move in tandem with each other relative to an entity's functional currency.

2. **(E)** A discount or premium is the difference between the futures rate and the spot rate at the date of a forward contract.

3. **(B)** The ineffective portion of a hedge has resulting gains or losses taken into income in the period in which they arise.

4. **(A)** The effective portion of a hedge is given special hedge accounting treatment. The evaluation of effectiveness is done no less than every three months. A highly effective hedge will have a value change ranging from roughly .8 to 1.2 times the variability of the cash flows being hedged.

5. **(D)** A forward contract is a hedge against an exposed asset position created by having an account in a denomination other than the functional currency.

Task-Based Simulation 2

Applicability of SFAS 133	Authoritative Literature	Help

		(I)	(E)
1.	Leases	○	●
2.	Guaranteed investment contracts	○	●
3.	Futures contracts	●	○
4.	Equity securities	○	●
5.	Credit indexed contracts	●	○
6.	Mortgage-backed securities	○	●
7.	Debt securities	○	●
8.	Interest rate caps	●	○
9.	Swaptions	●	○
10.	Employee stock options	○	●
11.	Options to purchase or sell exchange-traded securities	●	○
12.	Variable annuity contracts	○	●
13.	Adjustable rate loans	○	●
14.	Interest rate swaps	●	○

Explanations

1. **(E)** Leases are excluded from accounting for derivatives treatment.

2. **(E)** Guaranteed investment contracts are not required to be accounted for under derivative rules.

3. **(I)** Futures contracts must be accounted for using the rules for derivatives.

4. **(E)** Equity securities do not fall under the requirements of accounting for derivatives.

5. **(I)** Credit indexed contracts are required to be accounted for under the rules for derivatives.

6. **(E)** Mortgage-backed securities are excluded from derivatives treatment.

7. **(E)** Debt securities are not required to be accounted for using the rules for derivatives.

8. **(I)** Interest rate caps must be accounted for using the rules for derivatives.

9. **(I)** Swaptions meet the definition of a derivative instrument.

10. **(E)** Employee stock options are excluded from derivatives treatment.

11. **(I)** Options to purchase (call) or sell (put) exchange-traded securities are included under derivatives.

12. **(E)** Variable annuity contracts do not fall under the requirements of accounting for derivatives.

13. **(E)** Adjustable rate loans are not required to be accounted for under the rules for derivatives.

14. **(I)** Interest rate swaps must be accounted for using the rules for derivatives.

Task-Based Simulation 3

Research		
	Authoritative Literature	**Help**

ASC	815	25	35	16

Task-Based Simulation 4

Terminology		
	Authoritative Literature	**Help**

	(A)	(B)	(C)	(D)	(E)	(F)	(G)	(H)	(I)	(J)	(K)	(L)	(M)	(N)	(O)
1. At the money	○	○	○	○	○	○	○	○	○	○	○	●	○	○	○
2. Bifurcation	○	○	○	○	○	○	○	○	●	○	○	○	○	○	○
3. Call option	○	○	○	○	○	●	○	○	○	○	○	○	○	○	○
4. Embedded derivative	○	○	●	○	○	○	○	○	○	○	○	○	○	○	○
5. Forward contract	○	○	○	○	○	○	●	○	○	○	○	○	○	○	○
6. Futures contract	○	○	○	○	○	○	○	○	○	○	○	○	○	○	●
7. In the money	○	●	○	○	○	○	○	○	○	○	○	○	○	○	○
8. Notional amount	○	○	○	○	○	○	○	○	●	○	○	○	○	○	○
9. Out of the money	○	○	○	○	○	○	○	●	○	○	○	○	○	○	○
10. Put option	○	○	○	○	○	○	○	○	○	○	○	○	●	○	○
11. Swap	○	○	○	●	○	○	○	○	○	○	○	○	○	○	○
12. Underlying	○	○	○	○	○	○	○	○	○	○	○	●	○	○	○

Explanations

1. **(L)** An at-the-money option is one in which the price of the underlying is equal to the strike or exercise price.

2. **(I)** Bifurcation is the process of separating an embedded derivative from its host contract. This process is necessary so that hybrid instruments (a financial instrument or other contract that contains an embedded derivative) can be separated into their component parts, each being accounted for using the appropriate valuation techniques.

3. **(F)** An American call option provides the holder the right to acquire an underlying at an exercise or strike price anytime during the option term. A premium is paid by the holder for the right to benefit from the appreciation in the underlying.

4. **(C)** An embedded derivative is a feature on a financial instrument or other contract which, if the feature stood alone, would meet the definition of a derivative.

5. **(G)** A forward contract is an agreement between two parties to buy and sell a specific quantity of a commodity, foreign currency, or financial instrument at an agreed-upon price, with delivery and/or settlement at a designated future date. Because a forward contract is not formally regulated by an organized exchange, each party to the contract is subject to the default of the other party.

6. **(O)** A futures contract is a forward-based contract to make or take delivery of a designated financial instrument, foreign currency, or commodity during a designated period, at a specified price or yield. The contract frequently has provisions for cash settlement. A future contract is traded on a regulated exchange and, therefore, involves less credit risk than a forward contract.

7. **(B)** A call option is in the money if the price of the underlying is greater than the strike or exercise price of the underlying.

8. **(J)** The notional amount (or payment provision) is the referenced associated asset or liability. A notional amount is commonly a number of units such as shares of stock, principal amount, face value, stated value, basis points, barrels of oil, etc. It may be that amount plus a premium or minus a discount. The interaction of the price or rate (underlying) with the referenced associated asset or liability (notional amount) determines whether settlement is required and, if so, the amount.

9. **(H)** A call option is out of the money if the strike or exercise price is greater than the price of the underlying. A put option is out of the money if the price of the underlying is greater than the strike or exercise option.

10. **(N)** An American put option provides the holder the right to sell the underlying at an exercise or strike price, anytime during the option term. A gain accrues to the holder as the market price of the underlying falls below the strike price.

11. **(D)** A swap is a forward-based contract or agreement generally between two counterparties to exchange streams of cash flows over a specified period in the future.

12. **(K)** An underlying is commonly a specified price or rate such as a stock price, interest rate, currency rate, commodity price, or a related index. However, any variable (financial or physical) with (1) observable changes or (2) objectively verifiable changes such as a credit rating, insurance index, climatic or geological condition (temperature, rainfall) qualifies. Unless it is specifically excluded, a contract based on any qualifying variable is accounted for under the rules for derivatives if it has the distinguishing characteristics stated above.

Task-Based Simulation 5

Journal Entries		
	Authoritative Literature	Help

1.	Accounts receivable (£)	691,530	
	Sales		691,530

£370,000 × 1.869 = $691,530

2.	Cash	662,670	
	Loss on FC transaction	28,860	
	Accounts receivable (£)		691,530

£370,000 × 1.791 = $662,670

3.	Supplies	245,100	
	Accounts payable (€)		245,100

€190,000 × 1.290 = $245,100

4.	Accounts payable (€)	245,100	
	Loss on FC transaction	7,410	
	Cash		252,510

€190,000 × 1.329 = $252,510

5.

Accounts receivable (€)	333,250	
Sales		333,250

€250,000 × 1.333 = $333,250

6.

Accounts receivable (€)	7,750	
Gain on FC transaction		7,750

Adjust to spot rate on balance sheet date
€250,000 × (1.364 − 1.333) = $7,750 gain

7.

Cash	327,750	
Loss on FC transaction	13,250	
Accounts receivable (€)		341,000

€250,000 × 1.311 = $327,750
Original A/R of $333,250 + $7,750 gain = $341,000 balance in A/R as of 12/31/Y1
Loss is $341,000 − $327,750 = $13,250

Explanations

Foreign currency transactions are recorded at the spot rate on the date of the transaction. When the account is settled in the foreign currency, the currency is exchanged at the spot rate on the date of settlement, and any gain or loss is recognized as a transaction gain/loss.

If the account is outstanding at the balance sheet date, the account receivable or payable is adjusted to the spot rate on the balance sheet date and the gain/loss from foreign currency transaction is recognized as other income for the period.

Task-Based Simulation 6

Foreign Currency Transaction Gains/Losses		
	Authoritative Literature	Help

Prepare the following schedule outlining the foreign currency transaction gains and losses for year 1 and year 2 for Logan Corporation.

Logan Corporation
SCHEDULE OF FOREIGN CURRENCY TRANSACTION GAINS/LOSSES
Year 1 and Year 2

	Year 1 gain/(loss)	Year 2 gain/(loss)
Lexington Corporation	(28,860)	0
Dietmar Corporation	(7410)	0
Cordier Corporation	7,750	(13,250)
Total FC gain/(loss)	(28,520)	(13,250)

Indicate from the list below where the foreign currency transaction gain or loss in year 1 will be disclosed on the financial statements.

A. Extraordinary gain/loss
B. Other gain/loss
C. Other comprehensive income
D. Revenue
E. Expense

	(A) (B) (C) (D) (E)
1. Foreign currency transaction gain/loss for year 1 will be disclosed where on the financial statement?	○ ● ○ ○ ○

Task-Based Simulation 7

Research		
	Authoritative Literature	Help

ASC	830	20	30	3

Overview

This module covers personal financial statements, interim reporting, segment reporting, partnership accounting, and foreign currency translation.

The personal financial statements section covers how to report assets and liabilities and tax estimates. This topic is located in ASC Topic 274.

Interim reporting describes financial reporting for periods less than a year. This topic is located in ASC Topic 270.

Segment reporting presents disclosure standards for the components of an entity's operations, its products and services, its geographic areas, and its major customers. This topic is located in ASC Topic 280.

Partnership accounting describes and events related to formation, income allocation, dissolution, admission of a new partner, withdrawal of an existing partner, and liquidation. The ASC does not provide guidance for partnership accounting and reporting. Guidance is provided within the Uniform Partnership Acts of 1914 and 1997; and the Revised Uniform Partnership Act of 1994.

The foreign currency translation section covers translations and remeasurement. Determining if a subsidiary's transactions are denominated in a foreign currency or US Dollars establishes which method should be applied. This topic is located in ASC Topic 830.

A. Personal Financial Statements[1] (ASC Topic 274)

1. Personal financial statements may be prepared for an individual, husband and wife, or family. Personal financial statements (PFS) consist of

   a. **Statement of financial condition**—presents estimated current values of assets, estimated current amounts of liabilities, estimated income taxes, and net worth at a specified date.
   b. **Statement of changes in net worth**—presents main sources of increases (decreases) in net worth over the time period included by the statement of changes in net worth.

2. Assets and liabilities, including changes therein, should be recognized using the accrual basis of accounting. Assets and liabilities should be listed by order of liquidity and maturity, not a current/noncurrent basis.

3. In PFS, **assets** should be presented at their estimated current value. This is an amount at which the item could be exchanged assuming both parties are well informed, neither party is compelled to buy or sell, and material disposal costs are deducted to arrive at current values. **Liabilities** should be presented at the lesser of the discounted amount of cash to be paid or the current cash settlement amount. Income taxes payable should include unpaid income taxes as of the date of the statement of financial condition. Also, PFS should include the **estimated income tax** on the difference between the current value (amount) of assets (liabilities) and their respective tax

---

[1] The source of GAAP for personal financial statements is ASC Topic 274, which has been summarized in this module.

bases as if they had been realized or liquidated. The table below summarizes the methods of determining "estimated current values" for assets and "estimated current amounts" for liabilities.

4. Business interests which comprise a large portion of a person's total assets should be shown separately from other investments. An investment in a separate entity which is marketable as a going concern (e.g., closely held corporation) should be presented as one amount for its fair value. If the investment is a limited business activity, not conducted in a separate business entity, separate asset and liability amounts should be shown (e.g., investment in real estate and related mortgage). Of course, only the person's beneficial interest in the investment is included in their PFS.

Assets and liabilities	Discounted cash flow	Market price	Appraised value	Other
• Receivables	x			
• Marketable securities		x		
• Options		x		
• Investment in life insurance				Cash value less outstanding loans
• Investment in closely held business	x		x	Liquidation value, multiple of earnings, reproduction value, adjustment of book value or cost
• Real estate	x		x	Sales of similar property
• Intangible assets	x			
• Future interests (nonforfeitable rights)	x			
• Payables and other liabilities	x			Discharge amount if lower than discounted amount
• Noncancelable commitments	x			
• Income taxes payable				Unpaid income tax for completed tax years and estimated income tax for elapsed portion of current tax year to date of financial statements
• Estimated income tax on difference between current values of assets and current amounts of liabilities and their respective tax bases				Computed as if current value of assets and liabilities had been respectively realized or liquidated considering applicable tax laws and regulations, recapture provisions and carryovers

NOW REVIEW MULTIPLE-CHOICE QUESTIONS 1 THROUGH 17

Multiple-Choice Questions (1-17)

A. Personal Financial Statements

1. Green, a calendar-year taxpayer, is preparing a personal statement of financial condition as of April 30, year 2. Green's year 1 income tax liability was paid in full on April 15, year 2. Green's tax on income earned between January and April year 2 is estimated at $20,000. In addition, $40,000 is estimated for income tax on the differences between the estimated current values and current amounts of Green's assets and liabilities and their tax bases at April 30, year 2. No withholdings or payments have been made towards the year 2 income tax liability. In Green's April 30, year 2 statement of financial condition, what amount should be reported, between liabilities and net worth, as estimated income taxes?

    a. $0
    b. $20,000
    c. $40,000
    d. $60,000

2. On December 31, year 1, Shane is a fully vested participant in a company-sponsored pension plan. According to the plan's administrator, Shane has at that date the nonforfeitable right to receive a lump sum of $100,000 on December 28, year 2. The discounted amount of $100,000 is $90,000 at December 31, year 1. The right is not contingent on Shane's life expectancy and requires no future performance on Shane's part. In Shane's December 31, year 1, personal statement of financial condition, the vested interest in the pension plan should be reported at

    a. $0
    b. $ 90,000
    c. $ 95,000
    d. $100,000

3. The following information pertains to marketable equity securities owned by Kent:

Stock	Fair value at December 31, Year 3	Year 2	Cost in Year 1
City Mfg., Inc.	$95,500	$93,000	$89,900
Tri Corp.	3,400	5,600	3,600
Zee, Inc.		10,300	15,000

The Zee stock was sold in January year 3 for $10,200. In Kent's personal statement of financial condition at December 31, year 3, what amount should be reported for marketable equity securities?

    a. $93,300
    b. $93,500
    c. $94,100
    d. $98,900

4. Clint owns 50% of Vohl Corp.'s common stock. Clint paid $20,000 for this stock in year 1. At December 31, year 4, Clint's 50% stock ownership in Vohl had a fair value of $180,000. Vohl's cumulative net income and cash dividends declared for the five years ended December 31, year 4, were $300,000 and $40,000, respectively. In Clint's personal statement of financial condition at December 31, year 4, what amount should be shown as the investment in Vohl?

    a. $ 20,000
    b. $150,000

    c. $170,000
    d. $180,000

5. Jen has been employed by Komp, Inc. since February 1, year 1. Jen is covered by Komp's Section 401(k) deferred compensation plan. Jen's contributions have been 10% of salaries. Komp has made matching contributions of 5%. Jen's salaries were $21,000 in year 1, $23,000 in year 2, and $26,000 in year 3. Employer contributions vest after an employee completes three years of continuous employment. The balance in Jen's 401(k) account was $11,900 at December 31, year 3, which included earnings of $1,200 on Jen's contributions. What amount should be reported for Jen's vested interest in the 401(k) plan in Jen's December 31, year 3 personal statement of financial condition?

    a. $11,900
    b. $ 8,200
    c. $ 7,000
    d. $ 1,200

6. The following information pertains to an insurance policy that Barton owns on his life:

Face amount	$100,000
Accumulated premiums paid up to December 31, year 2	8,000
Cash value at December 31, year 2	12,000
Policy loan	3,000

In Barton's personal statement of financial condition at December 31, year 2, what amount should be reported for the investment in life insurance?

    a. $97,000
    b. $12,000
    c. $ 9,000
    d. $ 8,000

7. Ely had the following personal investments at December 31, year 1:

- Realty held as a limited business activity not conducted in a separate business entity. Mortgage payments were made with funds from sources unrelated to the realty. The cost of this realty was $500,000, and the related mortgage payable was $100,000 at December 31, year 1.
- Sole proprietorship marketable as a going concern. Its cost was $900,000, and it had related accounts payable of $80,000 at December 31, year 1.

The costs of both investments equal estimated current values. The balances of liabilities equal their estimated current amounts.

How should the foregoing information be reported in Ely's statement of financial condition at December 31, year 1?

		Assets	Liabilities
a.	Investment in real estate	$ 400,000	
	Investment in sole proprietorship	820,000	
b.	Investment in real estate	$ 500,000	
	Investment in sole proprietorship	820,000	
	Mortgage payable		$100,000

c.   Investment in real estate $ 500,000
Investment in sole
    proprietorship   900,000
    Mortgage payable $100,000
    Accounts payable   80,000
d.   Investments $1,400,000
Accounts and mortgage
    payable $180,000

8.   At December 31, year 1, Ryan had the following non-cancelable personal commitments:

Pledge to be paid to County Welfare Home
   thirty days after volunteers paint the walls
   and ceiling of the Home's recreation room $ 5,000
Pledge to be paid to City Hospital on the
   recovery of Ryan's comatose sister $25,000

What amount should be included in liabilities in Ryan's personal statement of financial condition at December 31, year 1?

   a. $0
   b. $ 5,000
   c. $25,000
   d. $30,000

9.   The estimated current values of Lane's personal assets at December 31, year 1, totaled $1,000,000, with tax bases aggregating $600,000. Included in these assets was a vested interest in a deferred profit-sharing plan with a current value of $80,000 and a tax basis of $70,000. The estimated current amounts of Lane's personal liabilities equaled their tax bases at December 31, year 1. Lane's year 1 effective income tax rate was 30%. In Lane's personal statement of financial condition at December 31, year 1, what amount should be provided for estimated income taxes relating to the excess of current values over tax bases?

   a. $120,000
   b. $117,000
   c. $ 3,000
   d. $0

10.   Shea, a calendar-year taxpayer, is preparing a personal statement of financial condition as of April 30, year 2. Shea's year 1 income tax liability was paid in full on April 15, year 2. Shea's tax on income earned from January through April year 2 is estimated at $30,000. In addition, $25,000 is estimated for income tax on the differences between the estimated current values of Shea's assets and the current amounts of liabilities and their tax bases at April 30, year 2. No withholdings or payments have been made towards the year 2 income tax liability. In Shea's statement of financial condition at April 30, year 2, what is the total of the amount or amounts that should be reported for income taxes?

   a. $0
   b. $25,000
   c. $30,000
   d. $55,000

11.   The following information pertains to Smith's personal assets and liabilities at December 31, year 1:

	Historical cost	Estimated current values	Estimated current amounts
Assets	$500,000	$900,000	
Liabilities	100,000		$80,000

Smith's year 1 income tax rate was 30%. In Smith's personal statement of financial condition at December 31, year 1, what amount should be reported as Smith's net worth?

   a. $294,000
   b. $420,000
   c. $694,000
   d. $820,000

12.   Personal financial statements usually consist of

   a.   A statement of net worth and a statement of changes in net worth.
   b.   A statement of net worth, an income statement, and a statement of changes in net worth.
   c.   A statement of financial condition and a statement of changes in net worth.
   d.   A statement of financial condition, a statement of changes in net worth, and a statement of cash flows.

13.   Personal financial statements should report assets and liabilities at

   a.   Estimated current values at the date of the financial statements and, as additional information, at historical cost.
   b.   Estimated current values at the date of the financial statements.
   c.   Historical cost and, as additional information, at estimated current values at the date of the financial statements.
   d.   Historical cost.

14.   A business interest that constitutes a large part of an individual's total assets should be presented in a personal statement of financial condition as

   a.   A separate listing of the individual assets and liabilities at cost.
   b.   Separate line items of both total assets and total liabilities at cost.
   c.   A single amount equal to the proprietorship equity.
   d.   A single amount equal to the estimated current value of the business interest.

15.   Smith owns several works of art. At what amount should these artworks be reported in Smith's personal financial statements?

   a.   Original cost.
   b.   Insured amount.
   c.   Smith's estimate.
   d.   Appraised value.

16.   For the purpose of estimating income taxes to be reported in personal financial statements, assets and liabilities measured at their tax bases should be compared to assets and liabilities measured at their

	Assets	Liabilities
a.	Estimated current value	Estimated current amount
b.	Historical cost	Historical cost
c.	Estimated current value	Historical cost
d.	Historical cost	Estimated current amount

17. In personal financial statements, how should estimated income taxes on the excess of the estimated current values of assets over their tax bases be reported in the statement of financial condition?

    a.   As liabilities.

    b.   As deductions from the related assets.

    c.   Between liabilities and net worth.

    d.   In a footnote disclosure only.

Multiple-Choice Answers and Explanations

Answers

1. c __ __	5. b __ __	9. a __ __	13. b __ __	17. c __ __	
2. b __ __	6. c __ __	10. d __ __	14. d __ __		
3. d __ __	7. b __ __	11. c __ __	15. d __ __	1st: __/17 = __%	
4. d __ __	8. a __ __	12. c __ __	16. a __ __	2nd: __/17 = __%	

Explanations

1. **(c)** Only the estimated amount of income taxes on the differences between the estimated current values and current amounts of assets and liabilities is presented between liabilities and net worth. Answer (a) is incorrect because the $40,000 estimated income taxes on the differences between the estimated current values and current amounts of assets and liabilities is presented between liabilities and net worth. Answer (b) is incorrect because the $20,000 current tax liability would be presented as a liability. Answer (d) is incorrect because the $20,000 current tax liability would be presented as a liability while the $40,000 amount would be presented between liabilities and net worth.

2. **(b)** In a personal statement of financial condition, assets are generally presented at estimated current values. Depending on the nature of the asset, current value can be estimated using fair market value, net realizable value, discounted cash flow, or appraised value. A future interest that is nonforfeitable should be valued using discounted cash flow. Therefore, the interest in the pension plan should be valued at $90,000.

3. **(d)** Assets are generally presented at their estimated current values on personal financial statements. For Kent's December 31, year 3 personal statement of financial condition, the current values of the marketable equity securities held as of that date should be used. Thus, Kent should report $98,900 ($95,500 + $3,400) for marketable equity securities.

4. **(d)** Assets are generally presented at their estimated current values. Depending on the nature of the asset, current value can be estimated using fair value (FV), net realizable value, discounted cash flow, or appraised value. In this problem, the fair value of the stock ($180,000) is known and should be shown as the investment in Vohl. Note that the net income and dividends have nothing to do with the amount shown as the investment in Vohl, and this information is irrelevant.

5. **(b)** This problem requires that we determine Jen's vested interest in the 401(k) plan to be reported in her December 31, year 3 personal statement of financial condition. The problem states that employer contributions vest after an employee completes three years of service. As Jen has not completed three years of service as of December 31, year 3, none of the employer's contributions have vested. Thus, the problem is to determine Jen's contributions and the earnings on **her** contributions as follows:

Year 1 contributions	$ 2,100
Year 2 contributions	2,300
Year 3 contributions	2,600
	$ 7,000
Earnings on above contributions	1,200
Jen's vested interest	$ 8,200

6. **(c)** Assets are generally presented at their estimated current values in personal financial statements. Specifically, investments in life insurance are to be valued at their cash surrender value less outstanding loans on the policy. Therefore, the investment should be reported at $9,000 ($12,000 cash value – $3,000 outstanding loan).

7. **(b)** When investments in a limited business activity are not conducted in a separate business entity, separate asset and liability amounts of the investment should be shown on the statement of financial condition. Thus, the realty (asset) and the mortgage (liability) should be reported separately at $500,000 and $100,000, respectively (their estimated current values). An investment in a separate entity that is marketable as a going concern (e.g., closely held corporation) should be presented as one amount. Thus, the $80,000 in accounts payable should be netted against the current value of $900,000 to report a net investment of $820,000.

8. **(a)** Noncancelable personal commitments should be reported at their discounted cash flow. A commitment must have all of the following attributes: (1) are for fixed or determinable amounts; (2) are not contingent on others' life expectancies or occurrence of a particular event (e.g., disability/death); and (3) do not require future performance of service by others. As the pledge to County Welfare Home is contingent upon the volunteers painting the walls and ceiling and the pledge to City Hospital is contingent upon the recovery of Ryan's comatose sister, both liabilities should be excluded from Ryan's personal statement of financial condition at December 31, year 1.

9. **(a)** Estimated taxes that would be paid if all the assets were converted to cash and all the liabilities were paid should be included with the liabilities. Thus, $120,000 [($1,000,000 – $600,000) × .30] should be provided for estimated income taxes relating to the excess of current values over tax bases.

10. **(d)** A personal statement of financial condition presents estimated current values of assets and liabilities, estimated income taxes, and estimated net worth at a specified date. Income taxes payable should include unpaid income taxes for completed tax years, the estimated tax for the elapsed portion of the current year, and the estimated income tax on the difference between the current value of assets and the current amounts of liabilities and their respective tax bases. Thus, the amount to be reported on Shea's statement of financial condition for income taxes is $55,000, equal to the sum of $30,000 tax on income earned from January through April and $25,000 estimated income tax on the difference between the current value and tax bases of assets and liabilities.

11. (c) Assets are generally presented at their estimated current values on personal financial statements. Therefore, the assets should be reported at their fair value of $900,000, rather than at their cost of $500,000. ASC Topic 274 also states that liabilities are presented at the lesser of the discounted amount of cash to be paid, or the current cash settlement amount. Therefore, the liabilities should be reported at $80,000. Estimated taxes that would be paid if all the assets were converted to cash and all the liabilities were paid should be included with the liabilities. Thus, 126,000 [(820,000 – 400,000) × .30] should be provided for estimated income taxes relating to the excess of current values over tax bases. Smith's net worth should be reported as $694,000 ($900,000 – $80,000 – $126,000).

12. (c) Personal financial statements consist of (1) a statement of financial condition and (2) a statement of changes in net worth.

13. (b) A personal financial statement presents the estimated current values of assets and liabilities. Additional information at historical cost is not required.

14. (d) Business interests that constitute a large part of a person's total assets should be shown separately from other investments. The estimated **current value** of an investment in a separate entity, such as a closely held corporation, a partnership, or a sole proprietorship, should be shown in **one amount** as an investment if the entity is marketable as a going concern.

15. (d) Assets are generally presented at their estimated current values in a personal statement of financial condition. Depending on the nature of the asset, current value can be estimated using fair market value, net realizable value, discounted cash flow, or appraised value. The best estimate of the fair value of art is the appraised value.

16. (a) In personal financial statements assets should be stated at their estimated current values and liabilities should be stated at the lower of the discounted value of their future cash payments or their current cash settlement amounts. These current amounts will differ from their tax bases and will give rise to **unrealized** tax gains and losses. A provision for estimated income taxes on these unrealized amounts should be incorporated into personal financial statements because when the unrealized gains and losses are realized, the related income taxes will have to be either paid or received.

17. (c) The estimated income taxes should be presented between liabilities and net worth in the statement of financial condition.

B. Interim Reporting

The term interim reporting is used to describe financial reporting for periods of less than one year, generally quarterly financial statements.

1. The primary purposes of interim reporting are to provide information which is more timely than is available in annual reports, and to highlight business turning points which could be "buried" in annual reports.
2. There are two basic conceptual approaches to interim reporting: the **discrete view** and the **integral view**.

   a. **Discrete view**—Each interim period is a separate accounting period; interim period must stand on its own; same principles and procedures as for annual reports; no special accruals or deferrals.
   b. **Integral view**—Each interim period is an integral part of an annual period; expectations for annual period must be reflected in interim reports; special accruals, deferrals, and allocations utilized.
   c. The **integral view** is used for interim reporting.

3. The table below summarizes the accounting standards.

Income statement item	General rule	Exceptions
Revenues	Same basis as annual reports	None
Cost of goods sold	Same basis as annual reports	1. Gross profit method may be used to estimate CGS and ending inventory for each interim period 2. Liquidation of LIFO base-period inventory, if expected to be replaced by year-end, is changed to CGS at its estimated replacement cost 3. Temporary declines in inventory market value need not be recognized 4. Planned manufacturing variances should be deferred if expected to be absorbed by year-end
All other costs and expenses	Same basis as annual reports	Expenditures which **clearly benefit** more than one interim period may be allocated among periods benefited (e.g., annual repairs, property taxes).
Income taxes	(Year-to-date income × Estimated annual effective tax rate) – (Expense recognized in previous quarters)	None
Discontinued operations	Recognized in interim period as incurred	None
Extraordinary items	Recognized in interim period as incurred. Materiality is evaluated based on expected annual results	None
Change in accounting principle	Retrospective application. Cumulative effect of change reflected in the carrying amounts of assets and liabilities as of the first period presented with offsetting adjustment to retained earnings for that period. Financial statements are adjusted for period-specific effects of the change.	None

   a. A key disclosure item for interim reporting is the seasonal nature of the firm's operations. This disclosure helps prevent misleading inferences and predictions about annual results.
   b. Income tax expense is estimated each period using an estimated annual effective tax rate. The example below illustrates the application of this requirement.

EXAMPLE

	(a)	(b)	(c)	(d) = (b) × (c)	(e)	(f) = (d) – (e)
	Quarterly income before income taxes	Year-to-date income before income taxes	Estimated annual effective tax rate	Year-to-date income tax expense	Previous quarter's expense	Current quarter's expense
Qtr						
1	$100,000	$100,000	30%	$ 30,000	$ 0	$ 30,000
2	150,000	250,000	32%	80,000	30,000	50,000
3	300,000	550,000	36%	198,000	80,000	118,000
4	200,000	750,000	35%	262,500	198,000	64,500

(1) In the prior chart, columns (a) and (c) are assumed to be given. Column (b) is obtained by accumulating column (a) figures. Column (e) is either the preceding quarter's entry in column (d) or the **cumulative** total of previous quarters in column (f).

4. **Research Component—Accounting Standards Codification**

   a. The research on interim reporting is found in ASC Topic 270. A general search using the term "interim" should locate the updated rules for specific areas.
   b. Keywords for research are shown below.

Costs and expenses interim	Interim reporting
Costs interim periods	Inventory interim
Costs of goods sold interim periods	Seasonal variations
Interim period	

5. **International Financial Reporting Standards (IFRS)**

   IFRS does not mandate interim reporting. However, when interim reports are required, four financial statements are required: the statement of financial position, the statement of comprehensive income, the statement of changes in equity, and the statement of cash flows. For consistency purposes, the entity must use the same accounting policies as used in year-end financial statements.

NOW REVIEW MULTIPLE-CHOICE QUESTIONS 1 THROUGH 19

KEY TERMS

Discrete view. Each interim period is a separate accounting period; interim period must stand on its own; same principles and procedures as for annual reports; no special accruals or deferrals.

Integral view. Each interim period is an integral part of an annual period; expectations for annual period must be reflected in interim reports; special accruals, deferrals, and allocations, utilized.

Interim reporting. Describe financial reporting for periods of less than one year.

Multiple-Choice Questions (1-19)

B. Interim Reporting

1. On January 1, year 1, Builder Associates entered into a $1,000,000 long-term, fixed-price contract to construct a factory building for Manufacturing Company. Builder accounts for this contract under the percentage-of-completion, and estimated costs at completion at the end of each quarter for year 1 were as follows:

Quarter	Estimated percentage-of-completion	Estimated costs at completion
1	10%	$750,000
2*	10%	$750,000
3	25%	$960,000
4*	25%	$960,000

*No work performed in the 2nd and 4th quarters.

What amounts should be reported by Builder as "Income on Construction Contract" in its quarterly income statements based on the above information?

	Gain (loss) for the three months ended			
	3/31/Y1	**6/30/Y1**	**9/30/Y1**	**12/31/Y1**
a.	$0	$0	$0	$10,000
b.	$25,000	$0	$(15,000)	$0
c.	$25,000	$0	$0	$0
d.	$25,000	$0	$ 6,000	$0

2. Kell Corp.'s $95,000 net income for the quarter ended September 30, year 1, included the following after-tax items:

- A $60,000 extraordinary gain, realized on April 30, year 1, was allocated equally to the second, third, and fourth quarters of year 1.
- A $16,000 cumulative-effect loss resulting from a change in inventory valuation method was recognized on August 2, year 1.

In addition, Kell paid $48,000 on February 1, year 1, for year 1 calendar-year property taxes. Of this amount, $12,000 was allocated to the third quarter of year 1.

For the quarter ended September 30, year 1, Kell should report net income of

- a. $ 91,000
- b. $103,000
- c. $111,000
- d. $115,000

3. Vilo Corp. has estimated that total depreciation expense for the year ending December 31, year 1, will amount to $60,000, and that year 1 year-end bonuses to employees will total $120,000. In Vilo's interim income statement for the six months ended June 30, year 1, what is the total amount of expense relating to these two items that should be reported?

- a. $0
- b. $ 30,000
- c. $ 90,000
- d. $180,000

4. On June 30, year 1, Mill Corp. incurred a $100,000 net loss from disposal of a business segment. Also, on June 30, year 1, Mill paid $40,000 for property taxes assessed for the calendar year 1. What amount of the foregoing items should be included in the determination of Mill's net income or loss for the six-month interim period ended June 30, year 1?

- a. $140,000
- b. $120,000
- c. $ 90,000
- d. $ 70,000

5. During the first quarter of year 2, Tech Co. had income before taxes of $200,000, and its effective income tax rate was 15%. Tech's year 1 effective annual income tax rate was 30%, but Tech expects its year 2 effective annual income tax rate to be 25%. In its first quarter interim income statement, what amount of income tax expense should Tech report?

- a. $0
- b. $30,000
- c. $50,000
- d. $60,000

6. Bailey Company, a calendar-year corporation, has the following income before income tax provision and estimated effective annual income tax rates for the first three quarters of year 1:

Quarter	Income before income tax provision	Estimated effective annual tax rate at end of quarter
First	$60,000	40%
Second	70,000	40%
Third	40,000	45%

Bailey's income tax provision in its interim income statement for the third quarter should be

- a. $18,000
- b. $24,500
- c. $25,500
- d. $76,500

7. Advertising costs may be accrued or deferred to provide an appropriate expense in each period for

	Interim financial reporting	Year-end financial reporting
a.	Yes	No
b.	Yes	Yes
c.	No	No
d.	No	Yes

8. A planned volume variance in the first quarter, which is expected to be absorbed by the end of the fiscal period, ordinarily should be deferred at the end of the first quarter if it is

	Favorable	Unfavorable
a.	Yes	No
b.	No	Yes
c.	No	No
d.	Yes	Yes

9. Due to a decline in market price in the second quarter, Petal Co. incurred an inventory loss. The market price is expected to return to previous levels by the end of the year. At the end of the year the decline had not reversed. When should the loss be reported in Petal's interim income statements?

a. Ratably over the second, third, and fourth quarters.
b. Ratably over the third and fourth quarters.
c. In the second quarter only.
d. In the fourth quarter only.

10. An inventory loss from a market price decline occurred in the first quarter. The loss was not expected to be restored in the fiscal year. However, in the third quarter the inventory had a market price recovery that exceeded the market decline that occurred in the first quarter. For interim financial reporting, the dollar amount of net inventory should

    a. Decrease in the first quarter by the amount of the market price decline and increase in the third quarter by the amount of the market price recovery.

    b. Decrease in the first quarter by the amount of the market price decline and increase in the third quarter by the amount of decrease in the first quarter.

    c. Not be affected in the first quarter and increase in the third quarter by the amount of the market price recovery that exceeded the amount of the market price decline.

    d. Not be affected in either the first quarter or the third quarter.

11. For external reporting purposes, it is appropriate to use estimated gross profit rates to determine the cost of goods sold for

	Interim financial reporting	Year-end financial reporting
a.	Yes	Yes
b.	Yes	No
c.	No	Yes
d.	No	No

12. For interim financial reporting, the computation of a company's second quarter provision for income taxes uses an effective tax rate expected to be applicable for the full fiscal year. The effective tax rate should reflect anticipated

	Foreign tax rates	Available tax planning alternatives
a.	No	Yes
b.	No	No
c.	Yes	No
d.	Yes	Yes

13. For interim financial reporting, a company's income tax provision for the second quarter of year 1 should be determined using the

    a. Effective tax rate expected to be applicable for the full year of year 1 as estimated at the end of the first quarter of year 1.

    b. Effective tax rate expected to be applicable for the full year of year 1 as estimated at the end of the second quarter of year 1.

    c. Effective tax rate expected to be applicable for second quarter of year 1.

    d. Statutory tax rate for year 1.

14. ASC Topic 270, *Interim Reporting*, states that interim financial reporting should be viewed primarily in which of the following ways?

    a. As useful only if activity is spread evenly throughout the year.

    b. As if the interim period were an annual accounting period.

    c. As reporting for an integral part of an annual period.

    d. As reporting under a comprehensive basis of accounting other than GAAP.

15. Conceptually, interim financial statements can be described as emphasizing

    a. Timeliness over reliability.
    b. Reliability over relevance.
    c. Relevance over comparability.
    d. Comparability over neutrality.

16. Wilson Corp. experienced a $50,000 decline in the market value of its inventory in the first quarter of its fiscal year. Wilson had expected this decline to reverse in the third quarter, and in fact, the third quarter recovery exceeded the previous decline by $10,000. Wilson's inventory did not experience any other declines in market value during the fiscal year. What amounts of loss and/or gain should Wilson report in its interim financial statements for the first and third quarters?

	First quarter	Third quarter
a.	$0	$0
b.	$0	$10,000 gain
c.	$50,000 loss	$50,000 gain
d.	$50,000 loss	$60,000 gain

17. Which of the following statements is true regarding interim reporting for companies that prepare their financial statements in accordance with IFRS?

    a. The discrete view is required for interim financial statements.

    b. Interim reports are required on a quarterly basis.

    c. Interim reports are not required for IFRS reporting.

    d. Interim reports require the preparation of only a statement of earnings and a statement of financial position.

18. Noble Corporation prepares its financial statements in accordance with IFRS. If Noble prepares interim financial statements, which statements are required?

    I. Statement of Financial Position
    II. Statement of Income
    III. Statement of Comprehensive Income
    IV. Statement of Cash Flows
    V. Statement of Changes in Equity

    a. I, II, and III.
    b. I, II, IV, and V.
    c. II, III, and IV.
    d. I, III, IV, and V.

19. Which of the following describes IFRS's requirements regarding interim financial statements?

    a. Interim financial statements are required.

    b. If interim financial statements are presented, four basic financial statements are required.

    c. If interim financial statements are presented, at least a balance sheet and profit and loss are required.

    d. Interim financial statements must be presented with the most recent annual financial statements.

Multiple-Choice Answers and Explanations

Answers

1. b	__ __	5. c	__ __	9. d	__ __	13. b	__ __	17. c	__ __
2. a	__ __	6. b	__ __	10. b	__ __	14. c	__ __	18. d	__ __
3. c	__ __	7. b	__ __	11. b	__ __	15. a	__ __	19. b	__ __
4. b	__ __	8. d	__ __	12. d	__ __	16. a	__ __	1st: __/19 = __%	
								2nd: __/19 = __%	

Explanations

1. **(b)** The requirement is to compute the income to be recognized in quarterly (interim) financial statements on a construction contract using the percentage-of-completion method. The solutions approach is to compute the income on the contract at the end of each quarter by (1) applying the estimated percentage-of-completion to the total estimated income to be recognized on the contract, and (2) subtracting the income recognized in preceding quarters to arrive at the income for the latest quarter. In the second and fourth quarters there was no work done on the contract and no change in the total estimated cost of completion. In quarter three the estimated costs of completion are revised upward. Since the cumulative income to date is less than income recognized in the first quarter, it is necessary to recognize a loss in the third quarter. The loss is handled as a change in accounting estimate rather than restating the first quarter.

> *Quarter 1:*
> 10% ($1,000,000 – $750,000) = $25,000 income recognized
>
> *Quarter 2:*
> -0-
>
> *Quarter 3:*
> 25% ($1,000,000 – $960,000) = $10,000 income earned to date
>
> $10,000 income to date – $25,000 income recognized in previous periods = $(15,000) loss for quarter
>
> *Quarter 4:*
> -0-

2. **(a)** Extraordinary items, gains or losses from disposal of a segment of a business, and unusual or infrequently occurring items should not be prorated over the balance of the fiscal year. Thus, the $20,000 ($60,000 ÷ 3) extraordinary gain that was allocated to the third quarter should be subtracted from net income as it actually occurred in the second quarter. Consistent with the view that all accounting changes should be made effective as of the beginning of the fiscal period, the cumulative effect of the accounting change on retained earnings is computed at the beginning of the fiscal year and reported in the first interim period's income statement. If a cumulative-effect type change is made during an interim period subsequent to the first one, the prior interim reports must be restated as if the changes had been effective as of the first day of the fiscal year. Thus, the $16,000 cumulative-effect loss should not be recognized in the third quarter. The prior interim reports should be restated and the $16,000 loss should be added back to income of the third quarter to correct the income to be reported for the quarter. Property taxes should be allocated among the

applicable quarters. As Kell Corp. properly allocated their property taxes, no adjustment to income is needed. Kell should report $91,000 ($95,000 – $20,000 + $16,000) as net income for the quarter ended September 30, year 1.

3. **(c)** A cost charged to expense in an annual period should be allocated among the interim periods which clearly benefit from the expense through the use of accruals and/or deferrals. Both yearly bonuses and the use of an asset (depreciation expense) benefit the entire year. The expense for the **six month** interim statement should be ($60,000 + $120,000) ÷ 2 = $90,000.

4. **(b)** Revenues and gains should be recognized in interim reports on the same basis as used in annual reports. At June 30, year 1, Mill Corp. would report the entire $100,000 loss on the disposal of its business segment since the loss was incurred during the interim period. ASC Topic 270 also states that a cost charged to an expense in an annual period should be allocated among the interim periods that clearly benefit from the expense through the use of accruals and/or deferrals. Since the $40,000 property tax payment relates to the entire year 1 calendar year, $20,000 of the payment would be reported as an expense at June 30, year 1, while the remaining $20,000 would be reported as a prepaid expense.

5. **(c)** The tax provision for an interim period is the tax for the year to date (estimated effective rate for the year times year-to-date income) less the total tax provisions reported for previous interim periods. In this case, the requirement is to calculate the tax provision for the first quarter interim income statement. The tax expense is $50,000 ($200,000 × 25%).

6. **(b)** The requirement is to calculate Bailey's income tax provision (expense) in its interim income statement for the third quarter. The tax provision for an interim period is the tax for the year-to-date (estimated effective rate for the year times year-to-date income) less the total tax provisions reported for previous interim periods.

Year-to-date tax (45%)($170,000)	$76,500
Previously reported tax (40% × $130,000)	52,000
Third quarter tax provision	$24,500

7. **(b)** Advertising costs may be deferred within a fiscal year if the benefits clearly extend beyond the interim period that the expense was paid. Also, advertising costs may be accrued and assigned to interim periods in relation to sales. Year-end accruals and deferrals of costs are also considered appropriate accounting treatment. Note, however, that deferral in year-end reporting is permitted only if the advertising has not been run in the media.

8. **(d)** A planned volume variance that is expected to be absorbed by the end of the fiscal year should be deferred at interim reporting dates.

9. **(d)** The requirement is to determine when the inventory loss should be reported. Inventory losses from market declines should not be deferred beyond the interim period in which the loss occurs. However, if the market decline is considered to be **temporary** and will be recovered by year-end, no loss needs to be recognized. A loss will be recognized in the fourth quarter only. In the second quarter the loss is considered temporary, therefore no loss is recognized. However, in the fourth quarter, when the decline does not reverse, it is deemed permanent and recognized in the fourth quarter. Losses are recognized in the period in which they occur, not ratably over several periods. Only expenses that benefit several periods (i.e., repairs and maintenance) are recognized ratably. The loss is not recorded in a period of temporary decline, only when the decline is considered to be permanent.

10. **(b)** A decline in inventory market price, expected to be other than temporary, should be recognized in the period of decline. A subsequent recovery of market value should be recognized as a cost recovery in the period of increase, but **never** above original cost. The decline should be recognized when it occurs in the first quarter. The subsequent recovery should be recognized when it occurs in the third quarter. The subsequent recovery cannot exceed the amount of decline. A nontemporary decline should be shown in the quarter of price decrease.

11. **(b)** The requirement is to determine the appropriateness of estimated gross profit rates in determining cost of goods sold for interim and year-end external financial reporting purposes. The use of estimated gross profit rates to determine the cost of goods sold for an interim period is appropriate. The method of estimation used and any significant adjustments that result from reconciliations with the annual physical inventory should be disclosed. An estimation of cost of goods sold is not allowable for year-end financial reporting. (The actual cost of the goods sold must be determined by the use of a cost flow assumption that most clearly reflects periodic income.) Thus, an estimated cost of goods sold figure may be used for interim but not year-end statements.

12. **(d)** The effective tax rate should reflect anticipated investment tax credits, foreign tax rates, percentage depletion, capital gains rates, and other available tax planning alternatives.

13. **(b)** The requirement is to determine what tax rate should be used to calculate the income tax provision for interim reporting. Each interim period is considered to be an integral part of the annual period. Therefore, expectations for the annual period must be reflected in the interim report. The income tax expense should be calculated using the estimated annual effective tax rate. The estimated tax rate should be updated as of the end of each interim period (here, as of the second quarter). The statutory tax rate is only a part of the effective tax. The effective tax rate includes the statutory tax rate and a variety of other items.

14. **(c)** The **integral view,** used for interim reporting, holds that each interim period is an integral part of an annual period, must reflect expectations for the annual period, and must utilize special accruals, deferrals, and allocations.

15. **(a)** The primary purposes of interim reporting are to provide information which is more **timely** than is available in annual reports and to highlight business turning points which could be "buried" in annual reports. This emphasis on timeliness comes at the expense of **reliability.** Accounting information pertaining to shorter periods may require more arbitrary allocations, and may not be as verifiable or representationally faithful as information contained in annual reports. Interim reports are generally more relevant and less reliable. Interim financial statements should not be any more or less comparable than annual reports.

16. **(a)** Temporary declines in inventory market values are not recognized. Only declines that are apparently permanent or other than temporary need to be recognized. In this case, Wilson expected the decline to reverse in the third quarter; therefore, the decline is temporary and no loss would be recorded in the first quarter. Because no loss was recorded for the decline, no gain will be recognized in the third quarter for the recovery of the $50,000 decline. Also, assuming that the inventory was valued at cost at the beginning of the fiscal year, no gain will be recorded for the recovery excess of $10,000 since inventory may not be valued at an amount in excess of cost.

17. **(c)** Interim reports are not required for companies who prepare statements in accordance with IFRS.

18. **(d)** IFRS does not mandate interim reporting. However, when interim reports are required by regulation, four financial statements are required: (1) the statement of financial position, (2) the statement of comprehensive income, (3) the statement of changes in equity, and (4) the statement of cash flows. For consistency purposes, the entity must use the same accounting policies as used in year-end financial statements.

19. **(b)** The requirement is to identify the statement that is correct about IFRS requirements regarding interim financial statements. Answer (b) is correct because IFRS has no requirement for the presentation of interim financial statements, but if they are presented, four basic financial statements are required.

C. Segment Reporting

1. ASC Topic 280 (SFAS 131—see outline) sets forth financial reporting standards for segment reporting, the disclosure of information about different components of an enterprise's operations as well as information related to the enterprise's products and services, its geographic areas, and its major customers.

   a. The purpose of segment disclosure is to assist investors and lenders in assessing the future potential of an enterprise. Consolidated statements give the user the overall view (results of operations, financial position, cash flows). However, trends, opportunities, risk factors, etc., can get lost when data for a diversified company are merged into consolidated statements. Additionally, most intersegment transactions that are eliminated from consolidated financial information are included in segment information.

   b. The approach used in segment reporting is a "management approach," meaning it is based on the way management organizes segments internally to make operating decisions and assess performance.

      (1) Companies can segment their financial information by products or services, by geography, by legal entity, or by type of customer.

      (2) The management approach facilitates consistent descriptions of an enterprise for both internal and external reporting and, in general, provides that external financial reporting closely conforms to internal reporting.

   c. Segment reporting does not apply to not-for-profit organizations or nonpublic enterprises.

2. **Operating Segments**

   a. An **operating segment** is defined as

      (1) A component of an enterprise engaged in business activity for which it may earn revenues and incur expenses, about which separate financial information is available that is evaluated regularly by the chief operating decision makers in deciding how to allocate resources and in assessing performance.

   b. A segment is significant (reportable) if it satisfies **at least one** of the following three 10% tests:

      (1) **Revenues**—Segment revenue (including intersegment revenue) is 10% or more of combined segment revenue (including intersegment revenue)

      (2) **Operating profit or loss**—The absolute amount of segment profit or loss is 10% or more of the **greater,** in absolute amount, of combined profit of segments reporting profit, or combined loss of segments reporting loss

      (3) **Segment assets**—Segment assets are 10% or more of total segment assets

   c. Operating profit or loss is unaffiliated revenue and intersegment revenue, less **all** operating expenses as defined by the chief operating decision maker to evaluate the performance of the segments.

      (1) Since segment revenue includes **intersegment sales, transfer pricing** becomes an issue.

         (a) FASB requires companies to use the same transfer prices for segment reporting purposes as are used internally.

         (b) Since most segments are **profit centers,** internal transfer prices generally reflect market prices.

   d. Common costs are operating expenses incurred by the enterprise for the benefit of more than one operating segment.

      (1) These costs should only be allocated to a segment for external reporting purposes if they are included in the measure of the segments profit or loss that is used internally by the chief operating decision maker.

   e. Similarly, only those assets that are included internally in the measure of the segment's assets used to make operating decisions shall be reported as assets of the segment in external financial reports.

   f. Interperiod comparability must be considered in conjunction with the results of the 10% tests. If a segment fails to meet the tests, but has satisfied the tests in the past and is expected to in the future, it should be considered reportable in the current year for the sake of comparability. Similarly, if a segment which rarely passes the tests does so in the current year as the result of an unusual event, that segment may be excluded to preserve comparability.

   g. There are some limitations to the number of segments which are to be reported.

      (1) There must be enough segments separately reported so that at least 75% of unaffiliated revenues are shown by reportable segments (75% test).

      (2) If the 75% test is not satisfied, additional segments must be designated as reportable until the test is satisfied.

      (3) Also, the number of reportable segments should not be so large (ten is a rule of thumb) as to make the information less useful.

(a) The following example illustrates the three 10% tests (revenues, operating profit or loss, and identifiable assets) and the 75% test:

EXAMPLE

Segment	Unaffiliated revenue	Intersegment revenue	Total revenue	Operating profit (loss)	Segment assets
A	$ 90	$ 90	$ 180	$ 20	$ 70
B	120		120	10	50
C	110	20	130	(40)	90
D	200		200	0	140
E	330	110	440	(100)	230
F	380		380	60	260
Total	$1,230	$220	$1,450	$ (50)	$840

Revenues test: (10%)($1,450) = $145

   Reportable segments: A, D, E, F

Operating profit or loss test: (10%)($140) = $14

   Reportable segments: A, C, E, F

> **NOTE:** Operating loss ($140) is greater than operating profit, $90

Segment assets test: (10%)($840) = $84

   Reportable segments: C, D, E, F

Reportable segments: Those segments which pass **at least one** of the 10% tests. Segments A, C, D, E, and F are reportable in this example.

75% test: (75%)($1,230) = $922.50

Segments A, C, D, E, and F have total unaffiliated revenue of $1,110, which is greater than $922.50.

The 75% test is satisfied; no additional segments need be reported.

---

(4) Certain other factors must be considered when identifying reportable segments. An enterprise may consider aggregating two or more operating segments if they have similar economic characteristics and if the segments are similar in each of the following areas:

   (a) The nature of the products and services
   (b) The nature of the production processes
   (c) The type of customer for their products and services
   (d) The methods used to distribute their products or provide their services
   (e) The nature of the regulatory environment

(5) Aggregation can occur prior to performing the 10% tests if the enterprise desires.
(6) Additionally, the enterprise may combine information on operating segments that do not meet any of the 10% tests to produce a reportable segment, but only if the segments meet a majority of the aggregation criteria presented above. It should be noted that information about operating segments that do not meet any of the 10% thresholds may still be disclosed separately, rather than as an aggregated total.

3. **Segment Disclosures**
Several disclosures are required regarding the enterprise's reportable segments. They include

a. **General information**—An explanation of how management identified the enterprise's reportable segments, including whether operating segments have been aggregated. Additionally, a description of the types of products and services from which each reportable segment derives its revenues.
b. **Certain information about reported segment profit and loss, segment assets, and the basis of measurement**—The enterprise shall disclose the following about each reportable segment if the specified amounts are reviewed by the chief operating decision maker:

   (1) Revenues from external customers
   (2) Intersegment revenues
   (3) Interest revenue and expense (reported separately unless majority of segment's revenues are from interest and management relies primarily on net interest revenue to assess performance)
   (4) Depreciation, depletion, and amortization expense

(5) Unusual items, extraordinary items
(6) Equity in the net income of investees accounted for by the equity method
(7) Income tax expense or benefit
(8) Significant noncash items

Also, the basis of measurement for these items must be disclosed, including differences in measurement practices between a segment and the complete entity and differences in measurement practices in a segment between periods.

c. **Reconciliations**—The enterprise will need to reconcile the segment amounts disclosed to the corresponding enterprise amounts.

d. **Interim period information**—Although the interim disclosures are not as extensive as in the annual financial report, certain segment disclosures are required in interim financial reports.

4. **Restatement of Previously Reported Segment Information**
Segment reporting is required on a comparative basis. Therefore, the information must be restated to preserve comparability whenever the enterprise has changed the structure of its internal organization in a manner that causes a change to its reportable segments. The enterprise must explicitly disclose that it has restated the segment information of earlier periods.

5. **Enterprise-Wide Disclosures about Products and Services, Geographic Areas, and Major Customers**
The enterprise-wide disclosures are required for all enterprises, even those that have a single reportable segment. Disclosures need to be provided only if not provided as part of the segment information. Disclosures are required regardless of whether the information is used in making operating decisions.

a. **Products and services.** Revenue from external customers for each product and service shall be reported by the enterprise, unless it is impractical to do so.

b. **Geographic areas.** An enterprise shall report revenues from external customers and long-lived assets attributable to its domestic operations and **foreign operations,** unless it is impractical to do so. If revenues or assets of an individual foreign country are material, then these amounts should be separately disclosed. In addition, the enterprise's basis for attributing revenue to individual countries shall be disclosed.

c. **Major customers.** Certain disclosures are made concerning major customers if the following 10% test is met. If 10% or more of **consolidated revenue** comes from a **single** external customer, the enterprise must disclose this fact in addition to the amount of such revenues, and the identity of the segment or segments making the sales. (A group of customers under common control, such as subsidiaries of a parent, is regarded as a single customer. Similarly, the various agencies of a government are considered to be a single customer.)

6. **Research Component—Accounting Standards Codification**
ASC Topic 280 uses a management approach to segment and enterprise reporting. A careful analysis of the vocabulary used in the standards is slightly different than most individuals would use in discussion. For example, we may use the term "total revenue" whereas the standard uses the term "combined revenue." Instead of using the word "tests," the standard refers to them as "quantitative thresholds." Although these differences seem trivial, they will affect your ability to find the material using a keyword search.

a. Below is a list of keywords that are useful in researching ASC Topic 280. If you add the word "segment" or "segments" to your search string, it may significantly reduce the number of irrelevant paragraphs.

Aggregation segments	Enterprise disclosure	Management approach
Combined assets segments	External revenue segments	Operating segment
Combined profit segments	Geographic areas	Products services segment
Combined revenue operating segments	Geographic information	Reportable segment
Enterprise disclose	Major customer	Single reportable segment

Flowchart for Identifying Reportable Operating Segments*

Identify operating segments by utilizing management approach

↓

Do some segments meet all aggregation criteria? —Yes→ Aggregate segments, if desired

↓ No

Do segments meet the 10% tests for revenue, profit, or assets? —Yes→ These are reportable segments to be separately disclosed

↓ No

Is revenue of reportable segments at least 75% of consolidated revenue (75% test)? —Yes→

↓ No

Identify additional segments until 75% test is met.

↓

Combine remaining segments/activities into "all other" category.

* Adapted from ASC Topic 280.

7. International Financial Reporting Standards (IFRS)

a. IFRS 8 on segment reporting includes guidance very similar to US GAAP. It requires a management approach to identifying operating segments. An operating segment is a reportable segment if it meets one of the following defined quantitative thresholds:

 (1) The segments revenue (including internal and external sales) is 10% or more of combined revenue of all segments,

 (2) The absolute value of the profit or loss is 10% or more than the greater (in absolute value) of the (1) combined reported profit of all segments that did not report a loss or (2) the combined reported loss of all segments that reported a loss, or

 (3) The assets are 10% or more of the combined assets of all segments.

b. In addition, the total external revenue by reportable segments must be a least 75% of the entity's revenue; otherwise additional segments must be identified and reported. Note that these thresholds are the same as for US GAAP.

NOW REVIEW MULTIPLE-CHOICE QUESTIONS 1 THROUGH 12

KEY TERMS

Management approach. Segment reporting is based on the way management organizes segments internally to make operating decisions and assess performance.

Operating segment. A component of an enterprise engaged in business activity for which it may earn revenues and incur expenses, about which separate financial information is available that is evaluated regularly by the chief operating decision makers in deciding how to allocate resources and in assessing performance.

Segment assets. Segment assets are 10% or more of total segment assets.

Segment operating profit or loss. The absolute amount of segment profit or loss is 10% or more of the greater, in absolute amount, of combined profit of segments reporting profit, or combined loss of segments reporting loss.

Segment revenues. Segment revenue (including intersegment revenue) is 10% or more of combined segment revenue (including intersegment revenue).

Multiple-Choice Questions (1-12)

C. Segment Reporting

1. Correy Corp. and its divisions (each is an operating segment) are engaged solely in manufacturing operations. The following data (consistent with prior years' data) pertain to the operations conducted for the year ended December 31, year 1:

(Industry operating segment)	Total revenue	Operating profit	Identifiable assets at 12/31/Y1
A	$10,000,000	$1,750,000	$20,000,000
B	8,000,000	1,400,000	17,500,000
C	6,000,000	1,200,000	12,500,000
D	3,000,000	550,000	7,500,000
E	4,250,000	675,000	7,000,000
F	1,500,000	225,000	3,000,000
	$32,750,000	$5,800,000	$67,500,000

In its segment information for year 1, how many reportable segments does Correy have?
- a. Three.
- b. Four.
- c. Five.
- d. Six.

2. The following information pertains to Aria Corp. and its operating segments for the year ended December 31, year 1:

Sales to unaffiliated customers	$2,000,000
Intersegment sales of products similar to those sold to unaffiliated customers	600,000
Interest earned on loans to other industry segments	40,000

Aria and all of its divisions are engaged solely in manufacturing operations and evaluates divisional performance based on controllable contribution. Aria has a reportable segment if that segment's revenue exceeds
- a. $264,000
- b. $260,000
- c. $204,000
- d. $200,000

Items 3 and 4 are based on the following:

Grum Corp., a publicly owned corporation, is subject to the requirements for segment reporting. In its income statement for the year ended December 31, year 1, Grum reported revenues of $50,000,000, operating expenses of $47,000,000, and net income of $3,000,000. Operating expenses include payroll costs of $15,000,000. Grum's combined identifiable assets of all industry segments at December 31, year 1, were $40,000,000. Reported revenues include $30,000,000 of sales to external customers.

3. In its year 1 financial statements, Grum should disclose major customer data if sales to any single customer amount to at least
- a. $ 300,000
- b. $1,500,000
- c. $4,000,000
- d. $5,000,000

4. External revenue reported by operating segments must be at least

- a. $22,500,000
- b. $15,000,000
- c. $12,500,000
- d. $37,500,000

5. Enterprise-wide disclosures include disclosures about

	Geographic areas	Allocated costs
a.	Yes	Yes
b.	Yes	No
c.	No	Yes
d.	No	No

6. Enterprise-wide disclosures are required by publicly held companies with

	Only one reportable segment	More than one reportable segment
a.	Yes	Yes
b.	Yes	No
c.	No	Yes
d.	No	No

7. An enterprise must disclose all of the following about each reportable segment if the amounts are used by the chief operating decision maker, except
- a. Depreciation expense.
- b. Allocated expenses.
- c. Interest expense.
- d. Income tax expense.

8. In financial reporting for segments of a business, an enterprise shall disclose all of the following except
- a. Types of products and services from which each reportable segment derives its revenues.
- b. The title of the chief operating decision maker of each reportable segment.
- c. Factors used to identify the enterprises reportable segments.
- d. The basis of measurement of segment profit or loss and segment assets.

9. In financial reporting for segments of a business enterprise, segment data may be aggregated
- a. Before performing the 10% tests if a majority of the aggregation criteria are met.
- b. If the segments do not meet the 10% tests but meet all of the aggregation criteria.
- c. Before performing the 10% tests if all of the aggregation criteria are met.
- d. If any one of the aggregation criteria are met.

10. The method used to determine what information to report for business segments is referred to as the
- a. Segment approach.
- b. Operating approach.
- c. Enterprise approach.
- d. Management approach.

11. Taylor Corp., a publicly owned corporation, assesses performance and makes operating decisions using the following information for its reportable segments:

Total revenues	$768,000
Total profit and loss	40,600

Included in the total profit and loss are intersegment profits of $6,100. In addition, Taylor has $500 of common costs for its reportable segments that are not allocated in reports used internally. For purposes of segment reporting, Taylor should report segment profit of

a. $35,000
b. $34,500
c. $41,100
d. $40,600

12. Rocket Corporation prepares its financial statements in accordance with IFRS. For segment reporting purposes, which tests must Rocket apply to determine if a unit or component is an operating segment?

a. Revenue test and asset test.
b. Revenue test, asset test, and profit or loss test.
c. Revenue test, asset test, and expense test.
d. Revenue test, asset test, and cash flow test.

Multiple-Choice Answers and Explanations

Answers

1. c __ __	4. a __ __	7. b __ __	10. d __ __	
2. b __ __	5. b __ __	8. b __ __	11. d __ __	1st: __/12 = __%
3. d __ __	6. a __ __	9. c __ __	12. b __ __	2nd: __/12 = __%

Explanations

1. (c) A division is a reportable segment if it is significant. A division is significant if it satisfies at least **one** of the three 10% tests:

1. **Revenue** is 10% or more of the combined segment revenue (including intersegment revenue).
2. **Operating profit** (loss) is 10% or more of the greater of the **absolute** combined segment profit or loss.
3. **Identifiable assets** are 10% or more of the combined segment identifiable assets.

Industry A, B, C, and E pass the revenue and operating profit tests, but A, B, C, D, and E all pass the identifiable assets test. Since a division only has to pass one of the three 10% tests to be considered a reportable segment, Corey Corp. has five reportable segments.

2. (b) Selected data for a segment is reported separately if one of three criteria is met. One of these criteria is met when a segment's revenue is greater than or equal to 10% of the combined revenues of all industry segments. Combined revenue includes sales to unaffiliated customers and intersegment sales or transfers. Thus, Aria has a reportable segment if that segment's revenues exceed $260,000 [($2,000,000 + $600,000) × 10%]. The $40,000 interest would not be included in combined revenue because it is not controllable at the division level.

3. (d) If 10% or more of the revenue of an enterprise is derived from sales to any single customer, that fact and the amount of revenue from each customer shall be disclosed. In this problem, Grum reported revenues of $50,000,000 and thus should disclose major customer data if sales to any single customer amount to $5,000,000 ($50,000,000 × 10%).

4. (a) There must be enough segments reported so that at least 75% of unaffiliated revenues is shown by reportable segments (75% test). Sales to external customers total $30,000,000 so external revenues reported by operating segments must be at least $22,500,000 ($30,000,000 × 75%).

5. (b) Enterprise-wide disclosures about products and services, geographic areas, and major customers are required for all enterprises.

6. (a) Enterprise-wide disclosures are to be reported by all public business enterprises, including those with a single reportable segment because the criteria for splitting the enterprise into reportable segments are not met.

7. (b) The enterprise shall disclose the following about each reportable segment if the specified amounts are reviewed by the chief operating decision maker:

a. Revenues from external customers
b. Intrasegment revenues
c. Interest revenue and expense (reported separately unless majority of segment's revenues are from interest and management relies primarily on net interest revenue to assess performance)
d. Depreciation, depletion, and amortization expense
e. Unusual items, extraordinary items
f. Equity in the net income of investees accounted for by the equity method
g. Income tax expense or benefit
h. Significant noncash items

Allocated expenses are not specifically included as a required disclosure.

8. (b) An enterprise shall disclose general information, including factors used to identify reportable segments and the types of products and services from which each reportable segment derives its revenues. An enterprise shall disclose certain information about reported segment profit and loss, assets, and basis of measurement. The accounting standards do not require disclosures about the term chief operating decision maker and specifically states that this term identifies a function, not necessarily a manager with a specific title.

9. (c) Two or more operating segments may be aggregated into a single operating segment if all of the aggregation criteria are met or if after performing the 10% test a majority of the aggregation criteria are met.

10. (d) The method chosen for determining what information to report is referred to as the management approach.

11. (d) An enterprise shall report a measure of profit and loss based on the measure reported to the chief operating decision maker for purposes of making decisions. The information used by management includes intersegment profits and should be included, but common costs are not allocated to the segments when assessing performance and should not be included.

12. (b) IFRS 8 on segment reporting includes guidance very similar to US GAAP. It requires a management approach to identifying operating segments. The three tests required include a revenue test, profit or loss test, and an asset test.

Simulations

Task-Based Simulation 1

Income, Revenue, Asset, Reportable Segment Tests		
	Authoritative Literature	Help

Caslow Co. is a new manufacturing company located in the United States, with divisions that operate in Spain, Turkey, and Thailand.

Each division has several reporting units that report its activities and financial information to the chief operating decision maker. Below is a list of the units and information for each unit of the three divisions. All amounts are in thousands.

Division	Reporting unit	Total revenue	Total income	Total assets	External revenue	Affiliated revenue
Spain	A	$100,000	$20,000	$260,000	$60,000	$40,000
	B	45,000	6,000	110,000	20,000	25,000
Turkey	C	85,000	19,000	120,000	50,000	35,000
	D	65,000	11,000	150,000	50,000	15,000
	E	25,000	5,000	60,000	25,000	0
Thailand	F	38,000	7,000	90,000	30,000	8,000
	G	120,000	39,000	290,000	50,000	70,000

Identify which reporting units meet the income threshold to be a reportable segment.

Identify which reporting units meet the revenue threshold to be a reportable segment.

Identify which reporting units meet the asset threshold to be a reportable segment.

Which segments are reportable?

	Division	Reporting unit	Income threshold	Revenue threshold	Asset threshold	Reportable segment
1.	Spain	A	O	O	O	O
2.		B	O	O	O	O
3.	Turkey	C	O	O	O	O
4.		D	O	O	O	O
5.		E	O	O	O	O
6.	Thailand	F	O	O	O	O
7.		G	O	O	O	O

Task-Based Simulation 2

Research		
	Authoritative Literature	Help

Assume that you are assigned to the audit of Whitman Corporation. The CFO of Whitman is working on developing the required information regarding business segments and has asked you to explain the tests to determine if a company must report information about a particular operating segment. Which section of the Professional Standards provides the tests that determine when a company must report information about an operating segment? Enter your response in the answer fields below.

Task-Based Simulation 3

Concepts		
	Authoritative Literature	Help

Indicate whether each of the following statements is True or False.

	Statement	True	False
1.	The method used for reporting segment information is the asset-liability approach.	O	O
2.	If management judges that an operating segment is reportable in year 1 and is of continuing significance, information about that segment should be reported in year 2 even if it does not meet the requirements for reportability in year 2.	O	O
3.	An enterprise must report separate information about an operating segment if its assets are 10% or more of the combined assets of all operating segments.	O	O
4.	An enterprise must report separately the costs and expenses incurred by each segment.	O	O
5.	One of the requirements of segment reporting is to report cash flows for each reportable segment.	O	O
6.	An enterprise must report the interest revenue for each reportable segment if this information is normally reviewed by the chief operating decision maker.	O	O

Task-Based Simulation 4

Segment Tests		
	Authoritative Literature	Help

Barnet Co. has distinct operating units in its operations. Each of these components of the business reports its activities and its financial information to the chief operating decision maker. The company has no foreign operations, sales, or major individual customers. Below is information provided by Barnet's operating units (in millions).

Reporting unit	Total revenue	External revenue	Affiliated revenue	Income	Assets
A	4,200	3,000	1,200	1,200	15,900
B	500	200	300	(300)	6,700
C	800	650	150	250	4,420
D	1,400	800	600	510	7,800
E	2,300	1,200	1,100	(900)	6,500
F	5,000	4,000	1,000	2,600	28,600

Identify which of the segments meets the quantitative threshold for revenues, profits/losses, and assets.

	Reporting unit	Revenue threshold	Profits/losses threshold	Asset threshold	Reportable segment
1.	A	O	O	O	O
2.	B	O	O	O	O
3.	C	O	O	O	O
4.	D	O	O	O	O
5.	E	O	O	O	O
6.	F	O	O	O	O

Task-Based Simulation 5

Research		
	Authoritative Literature	Help

Assume that you are assigned to the audit of Keger Corporation. The CFO of Keger has asked you to determine the information that must be disclosed about a reportable operating segment of the business. Which section of the Professional Standards provides guidance on the information that must be disclosed about a reportable segment? Enter your response in the answer fields below.

Simulation Solutions

Task-Based Simulation 1

Income, Revenue, Asset, Reportable Segment Tests		
	Authoritative Literature	**Help**

Total income = $107,000

$107,000 × 10% = $10,700

Identify which reporting units meet the income threshold to be a reportable segment.

Total revenue = $478,000

$478,000 × 10% = $47,800

Identify which reporting units meet the revenue threshold to be a reportable segment.

Total assets = $1,060,000

$1,060,000 × 10% = $106,000

Identify which reporting units meet the asset threshold to be a reportable segment.

Which segments are reportable?

	Division	Reporting unit	Income threshold	Revenue threshold	Asset threshold	Reportable segment
1.	Spain	A	●	●	●	●
2.		B	○	○	●	●
3.	Turkey	C	●	●	●	●
4.		D	●	●	●	●
5.		E	○	○	○	○
6.	Thailand	F	○	○	○	○
7.		G	●	●	●	●

Task-Based Simulation 2

Research		
	Authoritative Literature	**Help**

ASC	280	10	50	12	

Task-Based Simulation 3

Concepts		
	Authoritative Literature	**Help**

	Statement	True	False
1.	The method used for reporting segment information is the asset-liability approach.	○	●
2.	If management judges that an operating segment is reportable in year 1 and is of continuing significance, information about that segment should be reported in year 2 even if it does not meet the requirements for reportability in year 2.	●	○
3.	An enterprise must report separate information about an operating segment if its assets are 10% or more of the combined assets of all operating segments.	●	○
4.	An enterprise must report separately the costs and expenses incurred by each segment.	○	●

	Statement	True	False
5.	One of the requirements of segment reporting is to report cash flows for each reportable segment.	○	●
6.	An enterprise must report the interest revenue for each reportable segment if this information is normally reviewed by the chief operating decision maker.	●	○

Task-Based Simulation 4

Segment Tests		
	Authoritative Literature	Help

	Reporting unit	Revenue threshold	Profits/losses threshold	Asset threshold	Reportable segment
1.	A	●	●	●	●
2.	B	○	○	○	○
3.	C	○	○	○	○
4.	D	○	●	●	●
5.	E	●	●	○	●
6.	F	●	●	●	●

Explanations

Revenue threshold: Total revenues $14,200 \times 10\% = \$1,420$. Segment should be reported if it exceeds this revenue amount.

Income threshold: Total profit = $4,560. Total loss = $1,200. Segment should be reported if the profit/loss in absolute value is greater than 10% of $4,560 (the larger amount of profit or loss), $456.

Asset threshold: Total assets $69,920 \times 10\% = \$6,992$. Segment should be reported if it exceeds this asset amount.

Segment is reportable if it meets any one of the three threshold tests.

A meets all tests.

B and C do not meet any of the tests.

D meets income and asset test.

E meets revenue and income/loss test.

F meets all three tests.

Task-Based Simulation 5

Research		
	Authoritative Literature	Help

ASC	280	10	50	22

D. Partnership Accounting

There are no authoritative pronouncements concerning the accounting for partnerships; thus, all of the principles described below have evolved through accounting practice.

> **NOTE:** Partnership accounting typically is tested through a few multiple-choice questions on the Financial Accounting and Reporting Exam. Occasionally, the material is tested through a problem.

1. **Partnership Formation**

   a. The partnership is a separate **accounting entity** (not to be confused with a separate legal entity), and therefore its assets and liabilities should remain separate and distinct from the individual partner's personal assets and liabilities.

      (1) Thus, all assets contributed to the partnership are recorded by the partnership at their **fair market values**. All liabilities assumed by the partnership are recorded at their **present values**.

   b. Upon formation, the amount credited to each partner's capital account is the difference between the fair market value of the assets contributed and the present value of the liabilities assumed from that partner.

      (1) The capital accounts represent the residual equity of the partnership.
      (2) The capital account of each partner reflects all of the activity of an individual partner: contributions, withdrawals, and the distributive share of net income (loss).
      (3) In some cases, a **drawing** account is used as a clearing account for each partner's transactions with only the net effect of each period's activity shown in the capital account.

EXAMPLE

Partnership Formation

A and B form a partnership. A contributes cash of $50,000, while B contributed land with a fair market value of $50,000 and the partnership assumes a liability on the land of $25,000.

The entry to record the formation of the partnership is

Cash	50,000	
Land	50,000	
Liabilities		25,000
A Capital		50,000
B Capital		25,000

> **NOW REVIEW MULTIPLE-CHOICE QUESTIONS 1 THROUGH 4**

2. **Allocation of Partnership Income (Loss)**

   a. The partners should have a written agreement (articles of copartnership) specifying the manner in which partnership income (loss) is to be distributed.

   > **NOTE:** In the absence of a predetermined agreement, the profit and loss (P&L) is divided equally among the partners.

   b. It is important to remember that P&L should **not** be distributed using a ratio based on the partners' capital balances unless this is the ratio specified in the articles of copartnership.
   c. A number of issues arise which complicate the allocation of partnership income (loss).

      (1) Partners may receive interest on their capital balances. If so, it must be determined what will constitute the capital balance (e.g., the year-end amount or some type of weighted-average).
      (2) Some of the partners may receive a salary.
      (3) Some of the partners may receive a bonus on distributable net income. If so, you need to determine if the bonus should be computed before or after salary and interest allocations.
      (4) A formula needs to be determined for allocating the remaining income. The formula agreed upon is usually termed the **residual, remainder,** or **profit (loss) sharing ratio**.
      (5) Finally, the partners should decide upon how income is to be allocated if net income is insufficient to cover partners' salaries, bonuses, and interest allocations.

(a) These allocations are usually made even if the effect is to create a negative remainder. This remainder is usually allocated in accordance with the profit (loss) ratio.

(b) However, it is important to note that partners may choose to allocate losses (or a negative remainder) in a different manner than income.

EXAMPLE

Partnership P&L Distribution

Partners receive 5% interest on beginning capital balances
Partner B receives a $6,000 salary
Partner C receives a 10% bonus after interest and salaries
The P&L ratios are A — 50%, B — 30%, C — 20%

Assuming partnership net income of $18,250, the following distribution schedule would be prepared:

	A	B	C	Total
P&L ratio	50%	30%	20%	
Beginning capital balance	30,000	10,000	5,000	45,000
Net income				(18,250)
5% interest	1,500	500	250	2,250
Salary		6,000		6,000
Bonus			1,000*	1,000
Distribution of residual	4,500	2,700	1,800	9,000
Total	6,000	9,200	3,050	--
Ending capital balances	36,000	19,200	8,050	

* ($18,250 – $8,250) × .10 = $1,000

Note that if the interest, salary, and bonus allocation had exceeded net income, the excess would have been deducted on the distribution schedule in the P&L ratio.

NOW REVIEW MULTIPLE-CHOICE QUESTIONS 5 THROUGH 9

3. **Partnership Dissolution (Changes in Ownership)**

Partnership dissolution occurs whenever there is a change in ownership (e.g., the addition of a new partner, or the retirement or death of an existing partner). This is not to be confused with partnership liquidation, which is the winding up of partnership affairs and termination of the business. Under dissolution the partnership business continues, but under different ownership.

a. When partnership dissolution occurs a new accounting entity results.

(1) The partnership should first adjust its records so that all accounts are properly stated at the date of dissolution.

(2) After the income (loss) has been properly allocated to the existing partners' capital accounts, all assets and liabilities should be adjusted to their fair market value and their present values, respectively.

(a) The latter step is performed because the dissolution results in a new accounting entity.

(3) After all adjustments have been made, the accounting for dissolution depends on the type of transaction that caused the dissolution. These transactions can be broken down into two types:

(a) Transactions between the partnership and a partner (e.g., a new partner contributes assets, or a retiring partner withdraws assets)

(b) Transactions between partners (e.g., a new partner purchases an interest from one or more existing partners, or a retiring partner sells his/her interest to one or more existing partners).

b. **Transactions between a partner and the partnership**

(1) **Admission of a new partner**

When a new partner is admitted to the partnership essentially three cases can result. The new partner can invest assets into the partnership and receive a capital balance:

(a) Equal to his/her purchase price

1] If the new partner's capital balance is equal to the assets invested, then the entry debits the asset(s) contributed and credits the new partner's capital account for the fair value of the asset(s) contributed.

(b) Greater than his/her purchase price

(c) Less than his/her purchase price

1] If the new partner's capital balance is not equal to the assets invested [as in situation (b) and (c) above], then either the **bonus** or **goodwill** method must be used to account for the difference.

a] **Bonus method**—The old partnership capital plus the new partner's asset contribution is equal to the new partnership capital. The new partner's capital is allocated his purchase share (e.g., 40%) and the old partner's capital accounts are adjusted as if they had been paid (or as if they paid) a bonus. The adjustment to the old partners' capital accounts is made in accordance with their profit (loss) sharing ratio.

   i] The bonus method implies that the old partners either received a bonus from the new partner, or they paid a bonus to the new partner. As a result the old partners' capital accounts are either debited to reflect a bonus paid, or credited to reflect a bonus received. The new partner's capital account is **never** equal to the amount of assets contributed in a case where the bonus method is used.

b] **Goodwill method**—The old partnership capital plus the new partner's asset contribution is **not** equal to the new partnership capital. This is because goodwill is recorded on the partnership books for the difference between the total identifiable assets of the partnership (not including goodwill) and the deemed value of the partnership entity (which includes goodwill). Under the goodwill method, valuation of the new partnership is the objective.

   i] How the value of the partnership is determined depends on whether the book value acquired is greater or less than the asset(s) invested. If the book value acquired is less than the asset(s) invested, the value is determined based upon the new partner's contribution, and goodwill is allocated to the old partners' accounts. If the book value acquired is greater than the asset(s) contributed, the value is based upon the existing capital accounts, and goodwill is attributed to the new partner.

2] The decision as to whether the bonus or goodwill method should be used rests with the partners involved. In other words, the bonus and goodwill methods are alternative solutions to the same problem.

EXAMPLE

Partnership Dissolution—Bonus Method

Total old capital for ABC Partnership is $60,000.

Partner	A	B	C
Capital	$10,000	$20,000	$30,000
P&L Ratio	40%	40%	20%

Case 1

D is admitted to the partnership and is given a 20% interest in the capital in return for a cash contribution of $30,000.

Cash	30,000	
D Capital		18,000
A Capital		4,800
B Capital		4,800
C Capital		2,400

The total partnership capital to be shown on the books is $90,000 ($60,000 + $30,000) of which D is entitled to a 20% interest, or a capital balance of $18,000. The remaining $12,000 is treated as a bonus to the old partners and is allocated to their capital accounts in accordance with their P&L ratio.

Case 2

D is admitted to the partnership and is given a 20% interest in the capital in return for a cash contribution of $10,000.

Cash	10,000	
A Capital	1,600	
B Capital	1,600	
C Capital	800	
D Capital		14,000

The total partnership capital to be shown on the books is $70,000 ($60,000 + $10,000) of which D is entitled to a 20% interest, or a capital balance of $14,000. The difference of $4,000 ($10,000 – $14,000) is allocated to the old partners' accounts as if they had paid a bonus to the new partner.

EXAMPLE

Partnership Dissolution—Goodwill Method

Use the same original data as given above.

Case 1

D is admitted to the partnership and is given a 20% interest in the capital in return for a cash contribution of $20,000. The partners elect to record goodwill. The book value acquired [($60,000 + $20,000) × 20% = $16,000] is less than the asset contributed.

The value of the partnership is determined based upon the contribution of the new partner. In this case it is assumed that the partnership value is $100,000 ($20,000/20%). The resulting goodwill is $20,000 ($100,000 – $80,000). The $80,000 represents the total current capital, exclusive of goodwill, $60,000 of which is attributable to the old partners and $20,000 of which is attributable to the new partner.

Goodwill	20,000	
A Capital		8,000
B Capital		8,000
C Capital		4,000
Cash	20,000	
D Capital		20,000

Goodwill was allocated to the old partners in their P&L ratio. Also note that the capital balance of D represents 20% of the total capital of the partnership.

Case 2

D is admitted to the partnership and is given a 20% interest in the capital in return for a cash contribution of $10,000. The partners elect to record goodwill. The book value acquired [($60,000 + $10,000) × 20% = $14,000] is greater than the asset contributed.

The partnership value is based upon the capital accounts of the existing partners. Because D is entitled to a 20% interest, the $60,000 capital of the old partners must represent 80% of the capital. This means that the total value of the partnership is $75,000 ($60,000/80%). D's total contribution consists of the $10,000 in cash and $5,000 of goodwill. The goodwill is determined as the difference between the cash contribution and the 20% of the partnership capital.

Cash	10,000	
Goodwill	5,000	
D Capital		15,000

NOTE: In this last case no adjustment is made to the capital accounts of partners A, B, and C.

3] The table below summarizes the bonus and goodwill situations discussed above:

When to Apply Bonus Method	When to Apply Goodwill Method
New Old New Partner's Partnership = Partners' + Asset Capital Capital Investment	New Old New Partner's Partnership > Partners' + Asset Capital Capital Investment
Which Partner(s) Receive Bonus	**Which Partner(s) Goodwill Is Recognized**

• **New Partner**
  New Partner's New Partner's
  Capital Credit > Asset Investment
  (The difference represents the bonus.)
	• **New Partner's Goodwill**
	  New Partner's New Partner's
	  Capital Credit > Asset Investment
	  (The difference represents goodwill.)

- **Old Partners**

  New Partner's   New Partner's
  Capital Credit < Asset Investment
  (The difference represents the bonus allocated to
  old partners in their P&L Ratio.)

- **Old Partners' Goodwill**

  New Partner's   New Partner's
  Capital Credit = Asset Investment
  (Goodwill is allocated to old partners in their
  P & L Ratio.)

> **NOW REVIEW MULTIPLE-CHOICE QUESTIONS 10 THROUGH 15**

(2) Partner death or withdrawal

The death or withdrawal of a partner is treated in much the same manner as the admission of a new partner. However, there is no new capital account to be recorded; we are dealing only with the capital accounts of the original partners. Either the bonus or goodwill method may be used. The key thing to remember in regard to a partner's withdrawal from the partnership is that the withdrawing partner's capital account must be adjusted to the amount that the withdrawing partner is expected to receive.

EXAMPLE

Partner Withdrawal

Assume the same partnership data as given for the ABC partnership earlier.

Case 1

Assume that A withdraws from the partnership after reaching an agreement with partners B & C that would pay him $16,000. The remaining partners elect not to record goodwill.

B Capital	4,000	
C Capital	2,000	
A Capital		6,000
A Capital	16,000	
Cash		16,000

The $6,000 bonus is determined as the difference between the current balance of A's capital account and the amount of his buyout agreement. This "bonus" is then allocated between the remaining partners' capital accounts in proportion to their P&L ratios.

Case 2

Assume again that A withdraws from the partnership pursuant to the same agreement except that this time the partners elect to record goodwill.

The first step is to determine the amount of goodwill to be recorded. In this case we know that A's capital account must have a balance of $16,000, the agreed buyout payment he is to receive. In order to accomplish this, the total partnership assets must be increased by some amount of which $6,000 represents 40%, A's P&L ratio. Therefore, the amount of goodwill to be recorded is $15,000 ($6,000/40%).

Goodwill	15,000	
A Capital		6,000
B Capital		6,000
C Capital		3,000
A Capital	16,000	
Cash		16,000

NOTE: In this case all of the partners' capital accounts are adjusted to record the goodwill in accordance with their P&L ratios.

> **NOW REVIEW MULTIPLE-CHOICE QUESTIONS 16 THROUGH 20**

c. Transactions between partners

(1) The sale of a partnership interest is a transaction only between the partners. Thus, the treatment accorded the transaction is determined by the partners involved.

(2) There are two means of dealing with such a transaction.

(a) The first is to simply transfer a portion of the existing partners' capital to a new capital account for the buying partner.

EXAMPLE

Sale of a Partnership Interest—No Goodwill Recorded

Assume the following for the AB partnership:

Partner	A	B
Capital	$50,000	$50,000
P&L Ratio	60%	40%

Case 1

Assume that C wishes to enter the partnership by buying 50% of the partnership interest from both A and B for a total of $80,000. It is important to note that the $80,000 is being paid to the individual partners and not to the partnership. Thus, we are only concerned with the proper adjustment between the capital accounts, not the recording of the cash. This approach ignores the price that C paid for the partnership interest.

A Capital	25,000	
B Capital	25,000	
C Capital		50,000

(b) The other method available for recording a transaction between partners involves the recording of implied goodwill.

EXAMPLE

Sale of Partnership Interest—Recording Goodwill

Assume the same facts presented above for the sale of the partnership interest except that in this case the partners elect to record goodwill.

Case 1

Assuming that C paid $80,000 for a 50% interest in the partnership the implied value of the partnership assets is $160,000 ($80,000/50%). Because total capital prior to the purchase is only $100,000, the amount of goodwill that must be recorded is $60,000. The goodwill is allocated to the prior partners' accounts in proportion to their P&L ratios. Note that this entry is made before an adjustment is made to reflect C's admission to the partnership.

Goodwill	60,000	
A Capital		36,000
B Capital		24,000

Now we can record the sale of the partnership interest to C. The capital balance of A is now $86,000 ($50,000 + $36,000) while the capital balance of B is $74,000 ($50,000 + $24,000). Recall that C is to receive 50% of each balance.

A Capital	43,000	
B Capital	37,000	
C Capital		80,000

NOTE: In this situation the capital balance of C after the purchase is equal to the amount of the purchase price. Again no entry is made to record the receipt of cash because the cash goes directly to the individual partners, A and B.

---

4. **Partnership Liquidation**

a. A liquidation is the winding up of the partnership business. That is, it sells all of its noncash assets, pays its liabilities, and makes a final liquidating distribution to the remaining partners.

There are four basic steps to a partnership liquidation.

(1) Any operating income or loss up to the date of the liquidation should be computed and allocated to the partners' capital accounts on the basis of their P&L ratio.

(2) All noncash assets are sold and converted to cash. The gain (loss) realized on the sale of such assets is allocated to the partners' capital accounts on the basis of their P&L ratio.

(3) Any creditors' claims, including liquidation expenses or anticipated future claims, are satisfied through the payment or reserve of cash.

(4) The remaining unreserved cash is distributed to the remaining partners in accordance with the balance in their capital accounts. Note that this is **not** necessarily the P&L ratio.

b. Two factors that may complicate the liquidation process are the existence of loans or advances between the partnership and one or more of the partners, or the creation of a deficit in a partner's capital account because of the allocation of a loss.

(1) When loans exist between the partnership and a partner, the capital account and the loan(s) are combined to give a net amount. This is often referred to as the **right of offset**.

(2) When a deficit exists, the amount of the deficit is allocated to the remaining solvent partners' capital accounts on the basis of their relative P&L ratio.

> **NOTE:** If the partner with the capital deficit is personally solvent, he has a liability to the remaining partners for the amount of the deficit.

c. There are two topics that appear with regularity on the CPA examination in regard to the liquidation of a partnership. They are the **statement of partnership liquidation** and the determination of a **"safe payment"** in an installment liquidation.

(1) **Statement of partnership liquidation**
The statement of partnership liquidation shows in detail all of the transactions associated with the liquidation of the partnership.

(a) The liquidation of a partnership can take one of two forms: **simple** or **installment**.

1] A **simple liquidation** (illustrated below) is one in which all of the assets are sold in bulk and all of the creditors' claims are satisfied before a single liquidating distribution is made to the partners.

     a] Because the assets are sold in bulk there is a tendency to realize greater losses than if the assets were sold over a period of time. As a result, many partnerships liquidate on an installment basis.

2] In an **installment liquidation** the assets are sold over a period of time and the cash is distributed to the partners as it becomes available.

EXAMPLE

Statement of Partnership Liquidation—Simple Liquidation

Assume the following:

The capital balances are as given below.

The P&L ratio is 5:3:2 for A, B, and C, respectively.

STATEMENT OF PARTNERSHIP LIQUIDATION

	Cash	Other assets	Liabilities	Capital A (50%)	B (30%)	C (20%)
Balances	5,000	75,000	45,000	12,000	17,000	6,000
Sale of assets ($20,000 loss)	40,000	(60,000)		(10,000)	(6,000)	(4,000)
	45,000	15,000	45,000	2,000	11,000	2,000
Payment of liabilities	(45,000)		(45,000)			
	0	15,000	0	2,000	11,000	2,000
Sale of assets ($5,000 loss)	10,000	(15,000)		(2,500)	(1,500)	(1,000)
	10,000	0	0	(500)	9,500	1,000
Distribution of A's deficit				500	(300)	(200)
	10,000	0	0	0	9,200	800
Final distribution of cash	(10,000)				(9,200)	(800)

> **NOTE:** After the noncash assets have been sold and the creditors satisfied, a $500 deficit remains in A's capital account. The deficit is allocated to the remaining solvent partners on the basis of their relative P&L ratios, in this case, 3:2. A is liable to the partnership for the $500. If A is personally solvent and repays the $500, then $300 will go to B and $200 will go to C.

(b) If in the above example there had been liquidation expenses or loans between the partnership and partners, these would have to be recognized in the statement prior to any distribution to partners. A loan receivable from or payable to a partner is simply offset to (closed against) that partner's capital account.

(2) **Installment method of cash distribution**

(a) There are two keys to preparing a statement of partnership liquidation under the **installment method**:

1] The determination of the available cash balance at any given point in time and
2] The determination of which partner(s) is(are) to receive the payment of that cash.

(b) The reason that the cash is not distributed in accordance with the P&L ratio is twofold:

1] The final cash distribution is based upon the balance in each partner's capital account, **not** the P&L ratio, and
2] There will be situations, as illustrated in the previous example, where one or more partners will have deficit balances in their capital accounts. If this is the case, they should **never** receive a cash distribution, even if the deficit does not arise until late in the liquidation process.

(c) The determination of the available cash balance is generally very straightforward. The beginning cash balance (cash on hand at the start of the liquidation process) is adjusted for the cash receipts from receivables, sale of noncash assets, payment to creditors, and liquidation expenses incurred.

1] A situation may occur where a certain amount of cash is to be reserved for payment of future liabilities that may arise. If this is the case, this cash should be treated as an escrowed, or restricted, asset which makes it unavailable for current distribution to the partners.

(d) The determination of which partner(s) is(are) to receive the available cash is somewhat more difficult. There are a number of ways to make this computation, all of which are equally correct in the eyes of the examiners.

1] This determination can be made at the beginning of the liquidation process or at the time of each payment. In making this determination there are two key assumptions that must be made:

a] The individual partners are assumed to be personally insolvent, and
b] The remaining noncash assets are deemed to be worthless (thus creating a maximum possible amount of loss).

(e) One method of determining the amount of the "**safe payment**" is the use of an **Installment Cash Distribution Schedule**. This schedule is prepared by determining the amount of loss required to eliminate each partner's capital account.

1] As noted above, all of the remaining noncash assets are to be considered worthless at the time a safe payment is determined. Thus, if we determine the amount of loss required to eliminate each partner's capital balance, we can determine the order in which the partners should receive the cash payments.
2] When preparing this schedule it is important to make sure that the proper capital balance is used.

a] The capital balance used **must** be inclusive of any loans or advances between the partnership and partners. Thus, the capital balance at the beginning of the liquidation process is increased by any amount owed to the partner by the partnership, and decreased by any amount owed to the partnership by the partner.

EXAMPLE

SCHEDULE OF POSSIBLE LOSSES

	Total	A (50%)	B (30%)	C (20%)
Net capital balances	$35,000	$12,000	$17,000	$ 6,000
Loss to eliminate A	24,000	(12,000)	(7,200)	(4,800)
		0	$ 9,800	$ 1,200
Additional loss to eliminate C	3,000*		(1,800)	(1,200)
			8,000	0
Additional loss to eliminate B	8,000		(8,000)	
	$35,000		0	

* Allocated 60:40

The total capital balance of $35,000 indicates that if the noncash assets are sold for $35,000 less than their book value, then none of the partners will receive a cash distribution. The purpose of this schedule is to determine how much of a loss each partner's capital account can withstand based on that partner's P&L ratio. In this example A's capital would be eliminated if the partnership incurred a $24,000 ($12,000/50%) loss, B's would be eliminated by a $56,667 ($17,000/30%) loss, and C's by a $30,000 ($6,000/20%) loss. A is assumed to be eliminated first because it would take the smallest amount of loss to eliminate his account. Once A is eliminated as a partner, the P&L ratios change to reflect the relative P&L ratio of the remaining partners, in this case B and C. Based on the remaining capital balances and the relative P&L ratio, it would take a $16,333 ($9,800/60%) loss to eliminate B and a $3,000 ($1,200/40%) loss to eliminate C. Now that C is eliminated B will share all of the profits and losses as a sole partner (i.e., 100%). It will now take an $8,000 loss to eliminate B's capital. The resulting installment cash distribution schedule would appear as follows.

Schedule of Possible Losses and Installment Cash Distribution

Assume the same data as used for the previous example.

This schedule assumes that all creditors have already received full payment; thus, the cash amount represents available cash:

INSTALLMENT CASH DISTRIBUTION SCHEDULE

Partner		A	B	C
First	$ 8,000		100%	
Next	3,000		60%	40%
Next	24,000	50%	30%	20%
Any other		50%	30%	20%

While the example shown in section 4.a. was not an installment liquidation, the Installment Cash Distribution Schedule shown above could still be used to determine how the available cash of $10,000 is to be distributed. This is illustrated below.

Partner		A	B	C
First	$ 8,000		$8,000	
Next	2,000	——	1,200	$800
Total	$10,000	--	$9,200	$800

NOTE: It is important to note that this method is acceptable for most purposes; however, a CPA exam problem may require the "safe payment" approach where the amount of the safe payment is computed at a specific point in time.

NOW REVIEW MULTIPLE-CHOICE QUESTIONS 21 THROUGH 22

5. Incorporation of a Partnership

a. The incorporation of a partnership results in the formation of a new accounting (and legal) entity. This means that the partnership must adjust its records up to the date of incorporation.

(1) First, the partnership closes its books and recognizes any income or loss up to the date of incorporation.
(2) Second, the books of the partnership are adjusted to reflect the fair market value of the partnership assets and the present value of partnership liabilities.
(3) A corresponding adjustment is made to the capital accounts in accordance with the partners' P&L ratio. Third, common stock is distributed to the partners in accordance with the amounts in their capital accounts.

NOTE: The entries to record the receipt of stock by the corporation are different depending upon whether the corporation retains the partnership books or establishes new books.

b. Retention of the partnership books means that the issuance of common stock results in the closing of the partners' capital accounts with credits going to common stock and additional paid-in capital.
c. Establishing new books means that the assets and liabilities are closed out and the difference between their net value and the value of the corporate stock is debited to an asset "capital stock from corporation." This account is then credited and the partners' capital accounts debited to record the distribution of stock.

NOW REVIEW MULTIPLE-CHOICE QUESTION 23

6. **Research Component**

Because there are no authoritative pronouncements in the accounting standards for partnerships, research in the partnership area is limited to the concepts statements that apply for all for-profit entities. You should be prepared to answer conceptual questions on typical accounting concepts such as revenue recognition, matching, valuation, allocation, and other accrual basis accounting concepts that are applicable to all business entities.

KEY TERMS

Bonus method. The old partnership capital plus the new partner's asset contribution is equal to the new partnership capital.

Dissolution. Occurs whenever there is a change in ownership (e.g., the addition of a new partner, or the retirement or death of an existing partner).

Goodwill method. The old partnership capital plus the new partner's asset contribution is not equal to the new partnership capital.

Installment liquidation. The assets are sold over a period of time and the cash is distributed to the partners as it becomes available.

Liquidation. The winding up of partnership affairs and termination of the business.

Right of offset. When loans exist between the partnership and a partner, the capital account and the loan(s) are combined to give a net amount.

Simple liquidation. One in which all the assets are sold in bulk and all of the creditors' claims are satisfied before a single liquidating distribution is made to the partners.

Statement of partnership liquidation. Shows in detail all of the transactions associated with the liquidation of the partnership.

Multiple-Choice Questions (1-23)

D.1. Partnership Formation

1. Roberts and Smith drafted a partnership agreement that lists the following assets contributed at the partnership's formation:

	Contributed by	
	Roberts	**Smith**
Cash	$20,000	$30,000
Inventory	--	15,000
Building	--	40,000
Furniture & equipment	15,000	--

The building is subject to a mortgage of $10,000, which the partnership has assumed. The partnership agreement also specifies that profits and losses are to be distributed evenly. What amounts should be recorded as capital for Roberts and Smith at the formation of the partnership?

	Roberts	**Smith**
a.	$35,000	$85,000
b.	$35,000	$75,000
c.	$55,000	$55,000
d.	$60,000	$60,000

2. On April 30, year 1, Algee, Belger, and Ceda formed a partnership by combining their separate business proprietorships. Algee contributed cash of $50,000. Belger contributed property with a $36,000 carrying amount, a $40,000 original cost, and $80,000 fair value. The partnership accepted responsibility for the $35,000 mortgage attached to the property. Ceda contributed equipment with a $30,000 carrying amount, a $75,000 original cost, and $55,000 fair value. The partnership agreement specifies that profits and losses are to be shared equally but is silent regarding capital contributions. Which partner has the largest April 30, year 1 capital account balance?

- a. Algee.
- b. Belger.
- c. Ceda.
- d. All capital account balances are equal.

3. Abel and Carr formed a partnership and agreed to divide initial capital equally, even though Abel contributed $100,000 and Carr contributed $84,000 in identifiable assets. Under the bonus approach to adjust the capital accounts, Carr's unidentifiable asset should be debited for

- a. $46,000
- b. $16,000
- c. $ 8,000
- d. $0

4. When property other than cash is invested in a partnership, at what amount should the noncash property be credited to the contributing partner's capital account?

- a. Fair value at the date of contribution.
- b. Contributing partner's original cost.
- c. Assessed valuation for property tax purposes.
- d. Contributing partner's tax basis.

D.2. Allocation of Partnership Income (Loss)

5. Red and White formed a partnership in year 1. The partnership agreement provides for annual salary allowances of $55,000 for Red and $45,000 for White. The partners share profits equally and losses in a 60/40 ratio. The partnership had earnings of $80,000 for year 1 before any allowance to partners. What amount of these earnings should be credited to each partner's capital account?

	Red	**White**
a.	$40,000	$40,000
b.	$43,000	$37,000
c.	$44,000	$36,000
d.	$45,000	$35,000

6. Fox, Greg, and Howe are partners with average capital balances during year 1 of $120,000, $60,000, and $40,000, respectively. Partners receive 10% interest on their average capital balances. After deducting salaries of $30,000 to Fox and $20,000 to Howe, the residual profit or loss is divided equally. In year 1 the partnership sustained a $33,000 loss before interest and salaries to partners. By what amount should Fox's capital account change?

- a. $ 7,000 increase.
- b. $11,000 decrease.
- c. $35,000 decrease.
- d. $42,000 increase.

7. The partnership agreement of Axel, Berg & Cobb provides for the year-end allocation of net income in the following order:

- First, Axel is to receive 10% of net income up to $100,000 and 20% over $100,000.
- Second, Berg and Cobb each are to receive 5% of the remaining income over $150,000.
- The balance of income is to be allocated equally among the three partners.

The partnership's year 1 net income was $250,000 before any allocations to partners. What amount should be allocated to Axel?

- a. $101,000
- b. $103,000
- c. $108,000
- d. $110,000

8. The partnership agreement of Reid and Simm provides that interest at 10% per year is to be credited to each partner on the basis of weighted-average capital balances. A summary of Simm's capital account for the year ended December 31, year 1, is as follows:

Balance, January 1	$140,000
Additional investment, July 1	40,000
Withdrawal, August 1	(15,000)
Balance, December 31	165,000

What amount of interest should be credited to Simm's capital account for year 1?

- a. $15,250
- b. $15,375
- c. $16,500
- d. $17,250

9. The Flat and Iron partnership agreement provides for Flat to receive a 20% bonus on profits before the bonus. Remaining profits and losses are divided between Flat and Iron in the ratio of 2:3, respectively. Which partner has a greater advantage when the partnership has a profit or when it has a loss?

	Profit	Loss
a.	Flat	Iron
b.	Flat	Flat
c.	Iron	Flat
d.	Iron	Iron

D.3.a.(1) Admission of a New Partner

10. Blau and Rubi are partners who share profits and losses in the ratio of 6:4, respectively. On May 1, year 1, their respective capital accounts were as follows:

Blau	$60,000
Rubi	50,000

On that date, Lind was admitted as a partner with a one-third interest in capital and profits for an investment of $40,000. The new partnership began with total capital of $150,000. Immediately after Lind's admission, Blau's capital should be
- a. $50,000
- b. $54,000
- c. $56,667
- d. $60,000

11. Kern and Pate are partners with capital balances of $60,000 and $20,000, respectively. Profits and losses are divided in the ratio of 60:40. Kern and Pate decided to form a new partnership with Grant, who invested land valued at $15,000 for a 20% capital interest in the new partnership. Grant's cost of the land was $12,000. The partnership elected to use the bonus method to record the admission of Grant into the partnership. Grant's capital account should be credited for
- a. $12,000
- b. $15,000
- c. $16,000
- d. $19,000

12. Dunn and Grey are partners with capital account balances of $60,000 and $90,000, respectively. They agree to admit Zorn as a partner with a one-third interest in capital and profits, for an investment of $100,000, after revaluing the assets of Dunn and Grey. Goodwill to the original partners should be
- a. $0
- b. $33,333
- c. $50,000
- d. $66,667

Items 13 and 14 are based on the following:

The following condensed balance sheet is presented for the partnership of Alfa and Beda, who share profits and losses in the ratio of 60:40, respectively:

Cash	$ 45,000
Other assets	625,000
Beda, loan	30,000
	$700,000
Accounts payable	$120,000
Alfa, capital	348,000
Beda, capital	232,000
	$700,000

13. The assets and liabilities are fairly valued on the balance sheet. Alfa and Beda decide to admit Capp as a new

partner with 20% interest. No goodwill or bonus is to be recorded. What amount should Capp contribute in cash or other assets?
- a. $110,000
- b. $116,000
- c. $140,000
- d. $145,000

14. Instead of admitting a new partner, Alfa and Beda decide to liquidate the partnership. If the other assets are sold for $500,000, what amount of the available cash should be distributed to Alfa?
- a. $255,000
- b. $273,000
- c. $327,000
- d. $348,000

15. In the Adel-Brick partnership, Adel and Brick had a capital ratio of 3:1 and a profit and loss ratio of 2:1, respectively. The bonus method was used to record Colter's admittance as a new partner. What ratio would be used to allocate, to Adel and Brick, the excess of Colter's contribution over the amount credited to Colter's capital account?
- a. Adel and Brick's new relative capital ratio.
- b. Adel and Brick's new relative profit and loss ratio.
- c. Adel and Brick's old capital ratio.
- d. Adel and Brick's old profit and loss ratio.

D.3.a.(2) Partner Death or Withdrawal

Items 16 and 17 are based on the following:

On June 30, year 1, the condensed balance sheet for the partnership of Eddy, Fox, and Grimm, together with their respective profit and loss sharing percentages were as follows:

Assets, net of liabilities	$320,000
Eddy, capital (50%)	$160,000
Fox, capital (30%)	96,000
Grimm, capital (20%)	64,000
	$320,000

16. Eddy decided to retire from the partnership and by mutual agreement is to be paid $180,000 out of partnership funds for his interest. Total goodwill implicit in the agreement is to be recorded. After Eddy's retirement, what are the capital balances of the other partners?

	Fox	Grimm
a.	$ 84,000	$56,000
b.	$102,000	$68,000
c.	$108,000	$72,000
d.	$120,000	$80,000

17. Assume instead that Eddy remains in the partnership and that Hamm is admitted as a new partner with a 25% interest in the capital of the new partnership for a cash payment of $140,000. Total goodwill implicit in the transaction is to be recorded. Immediately after admission of Hamm, Eddy's capital account balance should be
- a. $280,000
- b. $210,000
- c. $160,000
- d. $140,000

18. On June 30, year 1, the balance sheet for the partnership of Coll, Maduro, and Prieto, together with their respective profit and loss ratios, were as follows:

Assets, at cost	$180,000
Coll, loan	$ 9,000
Coll, capital (20%)	42,000
Maduro, capital (20%)	39,000
Prieto, capital (60%)	90,000
Total	$180,000

Coll has decided to retire from the partnership. By mutual agreement, the assets are to be adjusted to their fair value of $216,000 at June 30, year 1. It was agreed that the partnership would pay Coll $61,200 cash for Coll's partnership interest, including Coll's loan which is to be repaid in full. No goodwill is to be recorded. After Coll's retirement, what is the balance of Maduro's capital account?

a. $36,450
b. $39,000
c. $45,450
d. $46,200

19. Allen retired from the partnership of Allen, Beck, and Chale. Allen's cash settlement from the partnership was based on new goodwill determined at the date of retirement plus the carrying amount of the other net assets. As a consequence of the settlement, the capital accounts of Beck and Chale were decreased. In accounting for Allen's withdrawal, the partnership could have used the

	Bonus method	Goodwill method
a.	No	Yes
b.	No	No
c.	Yes	Yes
d.	Yes	No

20. When Mill retired from the partnership of Mill, Yale, and Lear, the final settlement of Mill's interest exceeded Mill's capital balance. Under the bonus method, the excess

a. Was recorded as goodwill.
b. Was recorded as an expense.
c. Reduced the capital balances of Yale and Lear.
d. Had **no** effect on the capital balances of Yale and Lear.

D.4. Partnership Liquidation

21. The following condensed balance sheet is presented for the partnership of Smith and Jones, who share profits and losses in the ratio of 60:40, respectively:

Other assets	$450,000
Smith, loan	20,000
	$470,000
Accounts payable	$120,000
Smith, capital	195,000
Jones, capital	155,000
	$470,000

The partners have decided to liquidate the partnership. If the other assets are sold for $385,000, what amount of the available cash should be distributed to Smith?

a. $136,000
b. $156,000
c. $159,000
d. $195,000

22. On January 1, year 1, the partners of Cobb, Davis, and Eddy, who share profits and losses in the ratio of 5:3:2, respectively, decided to liquidate their partnership. On this date the partnership condensed balance sheet was as follows:

Assets	
Cash	$ 50,000
Other assets	250,000
	$300,000

Liabilities and Capital	
Liabilities	$ 60,000
Cobb, capital	80,000
Davis, capital	90,000
Eddy, capital	70,000
	$300,000

On January 15, year 1, the first cash sale of other assets with a carrying amount of $150,000 realized $120,000. Safe installment payments to the partners were made the same date. How much cash should be distributed to each partner?

	Cobb	Davis	Eddy
a.	$15,000	$51,000	$44,000
b.	$40,000	$45,000	$35,000
c.	$55,000	$33,000	$22,000
d.	$60,000	$36,000	$24,000

D.5. Incorporation of a Partnership

23. Jay & Kay partnership's balance sheet at December 31, year 1, reported the following:

Total assets	$100,000
Total liabilities	20,000
Jay, capital	40,000
Kay, capital	40,000

On January 2, year 2, Jay and Kay dissolved their partnership and transferred all assets and liabilities to a newly formed corporation. At the date of incorporation, the fair value of the net assets was $12,000 more than the carrying amount on the partnership's books, of which $7,000 was assigned to tangible assets and $5,000 was assigned to goodwill. Jay and Kay were each issued 5,000 shares of the corporation's $1 par value common stock. Immediately following incorporation, additional paid-in capital in excess of par should be credited for

a. $68,000
b. $70,000
c. $77,000
d. $82,000

Multiple-Choice Answers and Explanations

Answers

1. b __ __	6. a __ __	11. d __ __	16. c __ __	21. a __ __
2. c __ __	7. c __ __	12. c __ __	17. b __ __	22. a __ __
3. d __ __	8. b __ __	13. d __ __	18. c __ __	23. d __ __
4. a __ __	9. b __ __	14. b __ __	19. d __ __	1st: __/23 = __%
5. b __ __	10. b __ __	15. d __ __	20. c __ __	2nd: __/23 = __%

Explanations

1. **(b)** The requirement is to determine the amounts to be recorded as capital for Roberts and Smith at the formation of the partnership. Unless otherwise agreed upon by the partners, individual capital accounts should be credited for the fair market value (on the date of contribution) of the net assets contributed by that partner. It is necessary to assume that the amounts listed are fair market values. The amount of net assets that Roberts contributed is $35,000 ($20,000 + $15,000). The fair market value of the net assets Smith contributed is $75,000 ($30,000 + $15,000 + $40,000 – $10,000). The partners' profit and loss sharing ratio does not affect the initial recording of the capital accounts.

2. **(c)** The requirement is to determine which partner has the largest capital account balance. Use the solutions approach to solve the problem.

	Algee	Belger	Ceda
Partner contribution	50,000	80,000	55,000
Less: Liabilities assumed by the partnership	0	(35,000)	0
Ending capital balance	$50,000	$45,000	$55,000

Each partner values his contribution to the partnership at its fair market value. The fair market value becomes the partner's balance in his capital account and is basis to the partnership under generally accepted accounting principles. Any liabilities assumed by the partnership, reduces the partners' capital balance by the amount assumed.

3. **(d)** Under the bonus method, unidentifiable assets (i.e., goodwill) are not recognized. The total resulting capital is the FV of the tangible investments of the partners. Thus, there would be no unidentifiable assets recognized by the creation of this new partnership.

4. **(a)** Noncash assets contributed to an entity should be recorded at fair market value at the date of contribution. The creation of a new entity creates a new accountability for these assets. The partner's original cost relates to a previous accountability. The assessed valuation and the tax basis may differ from fair market value.

5. **(b)** Credits to partners' capital accounts are based upon earnings after allowance for interest, salary and bonus. The earnings before any allowance of $80,000 is reduced by the salary allowances of $100,000 and results in a loss of $20,000. The $20,000 loss is then distributed to the partners in relation to their profit and loss ratios as follows:

	Red	White	Total
Profit before allowance			$ 80,000
Salary allowances	$55,000	$45,000	(100,000)
Loss after allowances 60/40	(12,000)	(8,000)	(20,000)
Earnings credited to partners	$43,000	$37,000	$ 80,000

It is important to note that the losses are distributed 60/40 while profits are shared equally.

6. **(a)** When dividing the partnership loss of $33,000, first interest and salaries are allocated to the partners, **increasing** their capital balances. This allocation of interest and salaries will also increase the amount of loss. This increased loss amount would then be allocated to the partners, **decreasing** their capital accounts. The computations are shown below.

	Fox	Greg	Howe
Interest allowance (10% of avg. cap. balances)	$12,000	$ 6,000	$ 4,000
Salaries	30,000		20,000
Residual* ($105,000 ÷ 3)	(35,000)	(35,000)	(35,000)
Increase (decrease) in cap. account	$ 7,000	$(29,000)	$(11,000)

Thus, Fox's account increases by $7,000.

* The residual loss of $105,000 is the loss resulting after the interest and salary allowances are deducted [$33,000 loss – ($12,000 + $6,000 + $4,000) – ($30,000 + $20,000)].

7. **(c)** The distribution of the partnership net income of $250,000 occurs in three steps as follows:

Step	Axel	Berg	Cobb
1. Axel: 10% of first $100,000, 20% over $100,000	$ 10,000 30,000		
2. Berg & Cobb: 5% of remaining income over $150,000 [($250,000 – $10,000 – $30,000 – $150,000) × .05]		$ 3,000	$ 3,000

3. Remaining allocated equally:

[($250,000 – $10,000
– $30,000 – $3,000 –
$3,000) × 1/3]   68,000   68,000   68,000
     Totals $108,000 $71,000 $71,000

Thus, $108,000 would be distributed to Axel.

8. (b) We must first determine Simm's weighted-average capital balance for year 1 as follows:

Capital bal.	×	# of months/12	=	Weighted-avg.
140,000	×	6/12	=	$ 70,000
180,000	×	1/12	=	15,000
165,000	×	5/12	=	68,750
				$153,750

The problem states that interest of 10% per year is to be credited to each partner's capital account, and 10% of Simm's weighted-average capital balance of $153,750 is $15,375.

9. (b) In both the case of a profit or a loss, Flat will have a greater advantage. When there is a profit, Flat will obtain a 20% bonus on profits before the bonus, and also take 40% of the profit after the bonus. Iron on the other hand, will only receive 60% of the profit after the bonus. The following example illustrates this:

	Flat	Iron	Profit
P & L ratio	40%	60%	1,000
20% Bonus	200	0	(200)
			800
Share in profit	320	480	
Total distribution	520	480	

In the case of a loss, it can easily be seen that since Flat has a smaller percentage share in the loss that he has a greater advantage.

10. (b) The requirement is to calculate the balances in the capital accounts of a partnership after the admission of a new partner. In this case, the new partner is investing $40,000 for a 1/3 interest in the new total capital of $150,000. No goodwill is recorded because the new capital ($150,000) equals the total of the old capital ($110,000) and Carter's investment ($40,000). However, a bonus of $10,000 is being credited to the new partner's capital account because his interest (1/3 of $150,000, or $50,000) exceeds his investment ($40,000). The bonus to the new partner is charged to the old partners in their profit and loss ratios as shown below.

Blau [60,000 – 3/5 (10,000)]	$54,000
Rubi [50,000 – 2/5 (10,000)]	46,000
Lind (150,000 ÷ 3)	50,000
	$150,000

11. (d) The requirement is to determine the balance in the new partner's capital account after admission using the bonus method. In this case, Grant is investing land with a FV of $15,000 for a 1/5 interest in the new total capital of $95,000. Using the bonus method, the new capital $95,000 equals the total of the old capital plus Grant's investment ($60,000 + $20,000 + $15,000). Thus, a bonus of $4,000 is being credited to Grant's capital account because his interest (1/5 of $95,000, or $19,000) exceeds his investment ($15,000). The bonus to the new partner is charged to the old partners' capital accounts in their profit and loss ratios.

12. (c) The requirement is to determine the amount of goodwill implied by Zorn's investment. Zorn is investing $100,000 for a 1/3 interest in the partnership. Therefore, $100,000 represents 1/3 of the value of the equity of the new partnership ($100,000 ÷ 1/3 = $300,000). The tangible portion of the equity is $250,000 ($60,000 + $90,000 + $100,000). Thus, the total implied goodwill is $50,000 ($300,000 – $250,000).

13. (d) If no goodwill or bonus is to be recorded, the formula to determine the necessary contribution is

Partnership interest of new partner	×	(Capital bal. of existing partners	+	Amount to be contributed)	=	Amount to be contributed

$$20\% \times (\$580,000 + x) = x$$
$$\$116,000 + .2x = x$$
$$\$116,000 = .8x$$
$$\$145,000 = x$$

An alternative computation is to divide the old partner's capital ($580,000) by their interest after the new partner's admission. The result is the total capital after admission ($580,000 ÷ 80% = $725,000). To compute the new partner's contribution, the old partners' capital can be subtracted from total capital ($725,000 – $580,000 = $145,000), or total capital can be multiplied by 20% (20% × $725,000 = $145,000).

14. (b) To determine the amount of cash distributed during liquidation, the solutions approach is to prepare an abbreviated statement of partnership liquidation. In a partnership liquidation, cash is distributed based on the capital balances of the partners **after** adjusting them for any income (loss) to the date of liquidation and any loans or advances between the partners and the partnership. The abbreviated statement follows:

	Alfa	Beda	Total
Beg. capital balance	$348,000	$232,000	$580,000
Adj. for loans		(30,000)	(30,000)
Adj. for loss on sale of assets* (60-40)	(75,000)	(50,000)	(125,000)
Adj. capital balance	$273,000	152,000	$425,000

* ($500,000 – $625,000)

Note that the total cash available also equals $425,000.

Beginning cash	$ 45,000
Proceeds from sale	500,000
Payment of AP	(120,000)
	$425,000

Therefore, Alfa can receive $273,000 in cash in full liquidation of his capital balance.

15. (d) The bonus method implies that the old partners either received a bonus from the new partner, or they paid a bonus to the new partner. In this case, Colter, the new partner, contributed an amount in excess of the amount credited to Colter's capital account. Accordingly, the excess should be treated as a bonus to Adel and Brick. This bonus should be treated as an adjustment to the old partners' capital accounts and should be allocated by using Adel and Brick's old profit and loss ratio.

16. (c) Eddy is to be paid $180,000 for his 50% interest in the partnership. This implies that the net assets of the partnership are worth $360,000 ($180,000 ÷ 50%). Since the net assets are currently reported at $320,000, implied goodwill is $40,000 ($360,000 – $320,000). When goodwill is recorded, the goodwill account is debited and the partners' capital accounts are credited for their share of the goodwill. Therefore, the capital balances of Fox and Grimm are $108,000 and $72,000, as computed below.

	Fox	Grimm
Previous capital balance	$96,000	$64,000
Share of goodwill		
Fox (30% × $40,000)	12,000	
Grimm (20% × $40,000)	--	8,000
New capital balance	$108,000	$72,000

17. (b) Hamm will pay $140,000 for a 25% interest in the partnership. This implies that the net assets of the partnership, including the new investment, are worth $560,000 ($140,000 ÷ 25%). Net assets are currently reported at $320,000, and Hamm's cash payment of $140,000 brings that total up to $460,000. Therefore, implied goodwill is $100,000 [$560,000 – ($320,000 + $140,000)]. When goodwill is recorded, the goodwill account is debited and the partners' capital accounts are credited for their share of goodwill. Therefore, Eddy's capital balance ($160,000) is increased by his share of the goodwill (50% × $100,000 = $50,000), to result in a balance of $210,000 ($160,000 + $50,000).

18. (c) The requirement is to determine the balance in Maduro's capital account after Coll's retirement. When a partner withdraws from a partnership a determination of the fair value of the entity must be made. Since it is stated in the problem that the withdrawing partner is selling his interest to the partnership and that no goodwill is to be recorded, the bonus method must be employed after restatement of assets to FV. The capital accounts after restatement to FV would be

Coll
[$42,000 + 20%($216,000 – $180,000)] = $ 49,200

Maduro
[$39,000 + 20%($216,000 – $180,000)] = $ 46,200

Prieto
[$90,000 + 60%($216,000 – $180,000)] = $111,600

The bonus paid to Coll is the difference between the cash paid to him for his partnership interest and the balance of that interest plus his loan balance.

Bonus = [$61,200 – ($49,200 + $9,000)] = $3,000

Maduro's capital account would be reduced by his proportionate share of the bonus, based on the profit and loss ratio of the remaining partners [20%/(20% + 60%) = 25%].

Maduro's capital [$46,200 – 25% ($3,000)] = $45,450

19. (d) Under both the bonus and goodwill methods, the assets of the partnership must first be restated to their fair market value. Then, the withdrawing partner's capital account must be adjusted to the amount that the withdrawing partner is expected to receive. When the bonus method is used, no new goodwill is recorded. Instead, the existing partners' capital accounts are reduced by the amount necessary to increase the withdrawing partner's capital to the amount s/he is to be paid. When the goodwill method is used, new goodwill is recorded, and each partner's capital account is increased accordingly. Therefore, the bonus method results in a **decrease** of existing partners' capital accounts, while the goodwill method results in an **increase** of existing partners' capital accounts.

20. (c) Under the bonus method, adjustments are made only among partner's capital accounts (no goodwill is recorded on the partnership books). Since Mill's partnership interest exceeded the amount of Mill's capital balance, the excess interest would reduce the capital balances of Yale and Lear. Only under the goodwill method can the excess interest be recorded as goodwill. Under no circumstances should the excess partnership interest be recorded as an expense.

21. (a) This situation represents a simple liquidation since all assets are distributed at one point in time rather than in installments. In a simple liquidation all of the noncash assets are sold and the proceeds from their sale are compared to their book value to compute the gain or loss. The gain or loss on the assets is then distributed to the partners' accounts before any of the cash is distributed. The partner loan should not be considered a noncash asset for the purpose of determining gain or loss, thus, Smith is responsible to the partnership for the repayment of the entire amount of the loan. The repayment of the loan reduces that partner's (Smith) distribution as follows:

	Smith	Jones	Total
Partner balances before liquidation			
Loan (debit)	$ (20,000)		$ (20,000)
Capital (credit)	195,000	$155,000	350,000
Net balances	$175,000	$155,000	$330,000
Loss on sale of other assets (450 – 385)	39,000	26,000	(65,000)
Cash available for partners	$136,000	$129,000	$265,000
Cash available for credits			120,000
Total cash from sale of noncash assets			$385,000

22. (a) A schedule of safe payments must be prepared to determine the amount of cash to be distributed to each partner at January 15, year 1. The first cash sale of other assets with a total book value of $150,000 realized $120,000 in cash, resulting in a $30,000 loss. This loss is allocated among the partners based upon their profit and loss ratios. The schedule is completed based upon the assumption that the remaining other assets are totally worthless, and their book values are distributed to the partners as losses, based upon the partners' profit and loss ratios. The cash payments to each partner can be found at the bottom of the schedule.

	Cash	O/A	Liab.
Beginning	$ 50	$ 250	$ 60
Sale of assets	+ 120	– 150	--
	170	100	60
Dist. to creditors	– 60	--	– 60
	110	100	0
Disposal of other assets	--	– 100	--
Dist. to partners	–110	--	--
	0	0	0

	Capital		
	C	**D**	**E**
Beginning	$80,000	$90,000	$70,000
Sale of assets	−15,000	− 9,000	− 6,000
	65,000	81,000	64,000
Disposal of other assets	−50,000	−30,000	−20,000
	15,000	51,000	44,000
Dist. to partners	−15,000	−51,000	−44,000
	0	0	0

Thus, the cash should be distributed as follows: $15,000 to Cobb, $51,000 to Davis, and $44,000 to Eddy.

23. (d) When a partnership incorporates, assets and liabilities must be revalued to their fair market values on the date of incorporation. In this case, the net assets have a fair market value of $92,000 ($80,000 + $12,000) and the amount to be credited to Additional Paid-in Capital is $82,000 ($92,000 − $10,000 par value).

Simulations

Task-Based Simulation 1

Liquidation Schedule		
	Authoritative Literature	
		Help

Situation

On January 1, year 2, the partners of Dove, Eagle, and Falcon who share profits and losses in the ratio of 5:3:2, respectively decided to liquidate their partnership. On this date, the partnership's condensed balance sheet was as follows:

Assets	
Cash	$80,000
Note receivable—(loan to Eagle)	20,000
Plant, property, and equipment	300,000
	400,000
Liabilities and Capital	
Liabilities	120,000
Dove, capital	150,000
Eagle, capital	70,000
Falcon, capital	60,000

On January 30, year 2, the first cash sale of other assets with a carrying amount of $120,000 was sold for $150,000. On February 5, year 2, the remaining assets were sold for $100,000.

Prepare a Schedule of Partnership Liquidation for the partnership. Indicate the cash distribution to each partner. (For a more realistic exam experience, prepare the schedule using a spreadsheet program such as Excel.)

Partnership of Dove, Eagle, and Falcon
SCHEDULE OF PARTNERSHIP LIQUIDATION
February 5, Year 2

	Cash	Notes receivable	Plant, property, and equip.	Liabilities	Dove	Eagle	Falcon
Balances							
Partner loans							
Sale of assets, Jan. 30							
Sale of assets, Feb. 5							
Payment of liabilities							
Amount distributed to each partner							

Task-Based Simulation 2

Schedule of Safe Payments		
	Authoritative Literature	
		Help

Situation

On January 1, year 2, the partners of Dove, Eagle, and Falcon who share profits and losses in the ratio of 5:3:2, respectively decided to liquidate their partnership. On this date, the partnership's condensed balance sheet was as follows:

Assets	
Cash	$ 80,000
Note receivable—(loan to Eagle)	20,000
Plant, property, and equipment	300,000
	400,000
Liabilities and Capital	
Liabilities	120,000
Dove, capital	150,000
Eagle, capital	70,000
Falcon, capital	60,000

On January 30, year 2, the first cash sale of other assets with a carrying amount of $120,000 was sold for $150,000. On February 5, year 2, the remaining assets were sold for $100,000.

Suppose that on January 30, year 2, the first cash sale of other assets was sold for $180,000. The carrying value of the assets sold was $160,000.

Prepare a schedule of safe payments for the partnership after the sale on January 30, year 2.

Partnership of Dove, Eagle, and Falcon
SCHEDULE OF SAFE PAYMENTS
January 30, Year 2

	Cash	Notes receivable	Plant, property, and equip.	Liabilities	Dove	Eagle	Falcon
Balances							
Partner loans							
Sale of assets, Jan. 30							
Subtotal							
Payment of liabilities							
Subtotal							
Assume total loss on other assets							
Amount distributed to each partner							

Task-Based Simulation 3

Incorporation of Partnership		
	Authoritative Literature	Help

Situation

The partners of Ray, Shay, and Tay partnership have chosen to incorporate the partnership on January 30, year 2. After adjusting the partnership's books to fair value, the capital balances of the partners are as follows:

Ray	$175,000
Shay	$ 65,000
Tay	$ 70,000

The new company, RST Corp., is incorporated in the state of Delaware with 300,000 authorized shares of $2 par value common stock. The corporation retains the partnership's books and closes the partners' capital accounts. Ray receives 50,000 shares of stock, Shay receives 30,000 shares of stock, and Tay receives 20,000 shares of stock.

Prepare the journal entry to record the incorporation of the partnership.

Task-Based Simulation 4

Allocation of Income		
	Authoritative Literature	Help

Situation

On January 2, year 1, Alkire and Higdon drafted a partnership agreement to create a new partnership. The following items were contributed by each of the partners:

	Alkire	Higdon
Cash	$40,000	$ 60,000
Inventory		10,000
Building		180,000
Equipment	60,000	

The building is subject to a mortgage of $50,000 which the partnership has assumed. The partnership agreement specifies that each partner receives 10% interest on his beginning capital balance. Alkire receives an annual salary of $15,000; Higdon receives an annual salary of $20,000. The residual profit or loss is divided using a 2:3 ratio with 2 parts assigned to Alkire and 3 parts assigned to Higdon.

During year 1 the partnership had income of $185,000. Assume there were no drawings during year 1.

Record the journal entry for each partner's contribution to the partnership.

- Journal entry for Alkire's contribution
- Journal entry for Higdon's contribution

Complete the following schedule showing the allocation of partnership income for each partner.

	Alkire	Higdon
Beginning capital balance		
Interest on capital balance		
Annual salary		
Remainder		
Ending capital balance		

Task-Based Simulation 5

Admission of New Partner	Authoritative Literature	Help

On January 1, year 2, Kate and Lars decide to admit a new partner, Mark, for a 1/6 interest in the firm for $175,000. The bonus method is used to record the admission of the new partner. The book value of the firm before admitting Mark was $485,000, and the capital balance of Kate and Lars were $173,000 and $312,000 respectively. Kate and Lars had a 2:3 profit sharing ratio with 2 parts assigned to Kate and 3 parts assigned to Lars. After admitting the new partner, the partnership agreement is amended as follows:

> Each partner receives 10% interest on his beginning capital balance. Each partner receives an annual salary of $20,000. The residual profit or loss is divided in a ratio of 30% to Kate, 50% to Lars, and 20% to Mark.

Record the entry for admission of Mark to the partnership.

Task-Based Simulation 6

Partnership Liquidation	Authoritative Literature	Help

On 12/31/Y3, the partnership of DEF is dissolved. On that date, after closing the books, the following information is available:

Cash	$160,000
Loan to E	50,000
Other assets	700,000
Liabilities	110,000
Capital, D	200,000
Capital, E	400,000
Capital, F	200,000

Other information necessary for the liquidation is as follows:

During the month of January year 4, assets with a book value of $180,000 were sold for $210,000. The profit and loss sharing ratio is 30% to D, 50% to E, and 20% to F.

Prepare a schedule of safe payments as of January 31, year 4.

Partnership of DEF
SCHEDULE OF SAFE PAYMENTS
January 31, Year 4

	Cash	Notes receivable	Plant, property, and equip.	Liabilities	Capital—D	Capital—E	Capital—F
Balances	$160,000	$50,000	$700,000	$110,000	$200,000	$400,000	$200,000
Partner loans							
Sale of assets, Jan.							
Payment of liabilities							
Loss on other assets							
Safe payment to partners							

Simulation Solutions

Task-Based Simulation 1

Liquidation Schedule		
	Authoritative Literature	
		Help

Steps in Preparing Partnership Liquidation Schedule

1. Net out loans to partners.
2. Sale of assets on January 30: FV received minus book value given up = Gain/Loss on sale of assets $150,000 – $120,000 = $30,000 gain. Allocate gain as follows: Dove 50% × $30,000 = $15,000; Eagle $30,000 × 30% = $9,000; Falcon $30,000 × 20% = $6,000.
3. Sale of assets on February 5: $100,000 received – $180,000 carrying value = $80,000 loss. Allocate as follows: Dove $80,000 × 50% = $40,000 loss; Eagle $80,000 × 30% = $24,000 loss; Falcon $80,000 × 20% = $16,000 loss.
4. Pay liabilities $120,000.
5. Amount to distribute to partners: Dove = $125,000; Eagle = $35,000; Falcon = $50,000.

Partnership of Dove, Eagle, and Falcon
SCHEDULE OF PARTNERSHIP LIQUIDATION
February 5, Year 2

	Cash	Notes receivable	Plant, property, and equip.	Liabilities	Dove	Eagle	Falcon
Balances	$80,000	$20,000	$300,000	$120,000	$150,000	$70,000	$60,000
Partner loans		(20,000)				(20,000)	
Sale of assets, Jan. 30	150,000		(120,000)		15,000	9,000	6,000
Sale of assets, Feb. 5	100,000		(180,000)		(40,000)	(24,000)	(16,000)
Payment of liabilities	(120,000)			(120,000)			
Amount distributed to each partner	$210,000	$ --	$ --	$ --	$125,000	$35,000	$50,000

Task-Based Simulation 2

Schedule of Safe Payments		
	Authoritative Literature	
		Help

Partnership of Dove, Eagle, and Falcon
SCHEDULE OF SAFE PAYMENTS
January 30, Year 2

	Cash	Notes receivable	Plant, property, and equip.	Liabilities	Dove	Eagle	Falcon
Balances	80,000	20,000	300,000	120,000	150,000	70,000	60,000
Partner loans		(20,000)				(20,000)	
Sale of assets, Jan. 30	180,000		(160,000)		10,000	6,000	4,000
Subtotal	260,000	0	140,000	120,000	160,000	56,000	64,000
Payment of liabilities	(120,000)			(120,000)	0	0	0
Subtotal	140,000		(140,000)	0	160,000	56,000	64,000
Assume total loss on other assets			140,000		(70,000)	(42,000)	(28,000)
Amount distributed to each partner	140,000				90,000	14,000	36,000

Explanations

Steps in the schedule of safe payments

1. Net out loans to partners.
2. Sale of assets results in a $20,000 gain which is allocated on a 5:3:2 basis.

- Dove receives 50% × $20,000 = $10,000
- Eagle receives 30% × $20,000 = $6,000
- Falcon receives 20% × $20,000 = $4,000

3. Pay liabilities with cash.
4. Assume a total loss on other assets of $140,000.

- Dove receives 50% × $140,000 of loss = $70,000 loss
- Eagle receives 30% × $140,000 = $42,000 loss
- Falcon receives 20% × $140,000 = $28,000 loss

5. Safe payment is made based on balances in the capital accounts.

Task-Based Simulation 3

Incorporation of Partnership	Authoritative Literature	Help

Ray, capital	175,000	
Shay, capital	65,000	
Tay, capital	70,000	
Common stock		200,000
Additional paid-in capital		110,000

Task-Based Simulation 4

Allocation of Income	Authoritative Literature	Help

Journal entry for Alkire's contribution

Cash	40,000	
Equipment	60,000	
Capital, Alkire		100,000

Journal entry for Higdon's contribution

Cash	60,000	
Inventory	10,000	
Building	180,000	
Note payable		50,000
Capital, Higdon		200,000

	Alkire	Higdon
Beginning capital balance	$100,000	$200,000
Interest on capital balance	10,000	20,000
Annual salary	15,000	20,000
Remainder	48,000	72,000
Ending capital balance	$173,000	$312,000

Explanation

Each partner receives 10% on beginning capital balance. Each partner receives his respective income ($15,000 to Alkire and $20,000 to Higdon). The amount distributed thus far is $65,000. The remainder to be distributed is $120,000 (185,000 – 30,000 – 35,000). Two-fifths of this remainder 2/5 × 120,000 = 48,000 is allocated to Alkire; 3/5 × $120,000 = 72,000 is allocated to Higdon. The total income allocated to Alkire is $73,000; total income allocated to Higdon is $112,000.

Task-Based Simulation 5

Admission of New Partner	Authoritative Literature	Help

Entry for admission of Mark to the partnership

Cash	175,000	
Capital, Mark		110,000
Capital, Kate		26,000
Capital, Lars		39,000

Explanation

The book value of the partnership after the income distribution in year 1 was $485,000 (A = $173,000 and B = $312,000). After Mark's contribution, the value of the partnership is $485,000 + $175,000 = $660,000. A one-sixth interest in the partnership is $660,000 × 1/6 = $110,000. Using the bonus method, we calculate a bonus of $175,000 − $110,000 = $65,000. Using the 2:3 profit sharing ratio, the amount allocated to Kate is 2/5 × $65,000 = $26,000; the amount allocated to Lars is 3/5 × $65,000 = $39,000.

Task-Based Simulation 6

Partnership Liquidation		
	Authoritative Literature	Help

Partnership of DEF
SCHEDULE OF SAFE PAYMENTS
January 31, Year 4

	Cash	Notes receivable	Plant, property, and equip.	Liabilities	Capital—D	Capital—E	Capital—F
Balances	$160,000	$50,000	$700,000	$110,000	$200,000	$400,000	$200,000
Partner loans		(50,000)				(50,000)	
Sale of assets, Jan. (1)	210,000		(180,000)		9,000	15,000	(6,000)
Payment of liabilities	(110,000)			(110,000)			
Loss on other assets			(520,000)		(156,000)	(260,000)	(104,000)
Safe payment to partners	$260,000				53,000	105,000	102,000

Explanation

(1) The sale of assets produced a $30,000 dividend gain, which is distributed to the partners based on the new profit sharing ratio: 30% to D (9,000), 50% to E (15,000), and 20% to F (6,000). Liabilities are paid. A total loss is assumed on other assets and the assumed loss of $520,000 is distributed 30% to D (156,000), 50% to E (260,000), and 20% to F (104,000).

E. Foreign Currency Translation

1. **Objective of Foreign Currency Translation**

    a. The rules for the translation of foreign currency into US dollars apply to two major areas.

    (1) Foreign currency transactions which are denominated in other than a company's functional currency (e.g., exports, imports, loans), and

    (2) Foreign currency financial statements of branches, divisions, subsidiaries, and other investees which are incorporated with the financial statements of a US company by combination, consolidation, or the equity method

    b. The objectives of translation are

    (1) To provide information relative to the expected economic effects of rate changes on an enterprise's cash flows and equity, and

    (2) To provide information in consolidated statements relative to the financial results and relationships of each individual foreign consolidated entity as reflected by the functional currency of each reporting entity

    The first objective influences the rules for the translation of foreign currency transactions, while both objectives influence the rules for the translation of foreign currency financial statements. After working through this module, read through the outline of ASC Topic 830 (SFAS 52).

2. **Translation of Foreign Currency Statements**

EXAMPLE

Assume that a US company has a 100% owned subsidiary in France. The subsidiary's operations consist of leasing space in an office building. Its balance sheet at December 31, year 3, and its income statement for year 3 are presented below.

French Company
BALANCE SHEET
December 31, Year 3

Assets	Euros	Liabilities and Owners' Equity	Euros
Cash	60	Accounts payable	100
Accounts receivable (net)	100	Mortgage payable	200
Land	200	Common stock	100
Building	500	Retained earnings	360
Less accumulated depr.	(100)	Total liabilities and	
Total assets	€760	Owners' equity	€760

French Company
INCOME STATEMENT
For Year Ended December 31, Year 3

Revenues	€260
Operating Expenses (excluding depreciation expense)	140
Depreciation expense	20
Net Income	€100

In addition to the information above, the following data are also needed for the translation process:

1. Transactions involving land, building, mortgage payable, and common stock all occurred in year 1.
2. No dividends were paid during the period year 1–3.
3. Exchange rates for various dates follow.

    €1 = $.90 in year 1
    €1 = $1.05 at beginning of year 3
    €1 = $1.12 at end of year 3
    €1 = $1.10 weighted-average for year 3

---

    a. If the US company wants to present consolidated financial statements which include the results of its French subsidiary, the financial statements of the French company must be translated into US dollars. However, before this can be accomplished, the management of the US company must determine the functional currency of its French subsidiary. An entity's functional currency is the currency of the primary economic environment in which the entity operates; normally, that is the currency of the environment in which an entity primarily generates and expends cash. The decision concerning the functional currency is important because, once determined, it should be used consistently, unless it is clear that economic facts and circumstances have changed. The selection of the functional currency depends upon an evaluation of several factors. These factors include the following:

(1) Cash flows—Do the foreign entity's cash flows directly affect the parent's cash flows and are they immediately available for remittance to the parent?

(2) Sales prices—Are the foreign entity's sales prices responsive to exchange rate changes and to international competition?

(3) Sales markets—Is the foreign entity's sales market the parent's country or are sales denominated in the parent's currency?

(4) Expenses—Are the foreign entity's expenses incurred in the parent's country?

(5) Financing—Is the foreign entity's financing primarily from the parent or is it denominated in the parent's currency?

(6) Intercompany transactions—Is there a high volume of intercompany transactions between the parent and foreign entity?

b. If the answers to the questions above are predominantly yes, the functional currency would be the reporting currency of the parent (i.e., the US dollar). On the other hand, if the answers to the questions were predominantly no, the functional currency would be the foreign currency. In the example described previously, the euro would be the functional currency if the answers were no.

> **NOTE:** That the functional currency does not necessarily have to be the local currency of the foreign country when the answers to the questions are negative. In other words, it is possible for a foreign currency other than the euro to be the functional currency of our French company. For example, Swiss francs or British pounds could be the functional currency for the French company if one of these currencies is the currency of the primary economic environment in which the entity operates. However, assume these other possibilities are not alternatives in the example mentioned previously.

c. If the circumstances indicate the euro to be the functional currency, the current rate method is used for translation of the foreign currency financial statements. The rules for applying the current rate method are

(1) All assets and liabilities are translated using the current rate at the balance sheet date.

(2) All revenues and expenses are translated at the rates in effect when these items are recognized during the period. Due to practical considerations, however, weighted-average rates can be used to translate revenues and expenses which were incurred throughout the year.

(3) Owners' equity accounts are translated using historical exchange rates.

(4) Dividends are translated at the historic rate on the date of declaration.

(5) The translation adjustment for the period is reported as other comprehensive income under one of several acceptable reporting alternatives and the parent company's share of the accumulated amount is reported as accumulated other comprehensive income in the stockholders' equity section of the consolidated balance sheet.

d. This current rate method is illustrated below for the French financial statements shown previously.

EXAMPLE

Current Rate Method

French Company
BALANCE SHEET
December 31, Year 3
(Euro is Functional Currency)

	Euros	Exchange rates	US dollars
Assets			
Cash	60	1.12	67.20
Accounts receivable (net)	100	1.12	112.00
Land	200	1.12	224.00
Building (net)	400	1.12	448.00
Totals	€760		$851.20
Liabilities and Owners' Equity			
Accounts payable	100	1.12	112.00
Mortgage payable	200	1.12	224.00
Common stock	100	.90	90.00
Retained earnings, 12/31/Y3	360 see income statement		352.00
Translation adjustment (gain)	___		73.20 (plug)
Totals	€760		$851.20

French Company
COMBINED INCOME AND RETAINED EARNINGS STATEMENT
For the Year Ending December 31, Year 3

	Euros	Exchange rates	US dollars
Revenues	260	1.10	$ 286
Operating expenses (excluding €20 of depreciation expense)	(140)	1.10	(154)
Depreciation expense	(20)	1.10	(22)
Net income	100		110
Retained earnings calculation:			
Retained earnings at 1/1/Y3	260		242*
Net income	100		110
Retained earnings at 12/31/Y3	€ 360		$ 352

* The US dollar amount of retained earnings results from applying weighted-average exchange rates to translate revenues and expenses during the period year 1 through year 3. Retained earnings cannot be translated using a single exchange rate. The beginning retained earnings would be taken from the prior period's translated financial statements.

The translation adjustments result from translating all assets and liabilities at the current rate, while owners' equity is translated using historical rates. Common stock was issued in year 1 when the exchange rate was €1 = $.90. The beginning balance of retained earnings for year 3 was accumulated during the period year 1 through year 3. The new balance in ending retained earnings is placed on the balance sheet, and the translation adjustment is a plug figure to bring the balance sheet back into balance. In this situation, there is a translation gain of $73.20 that is credited to other comprehensive income.

You can use a trial balance technique as shown below. Translate all balance sheet and income statement items as indicated in the rules for the current rate method. The foreign currency translation gain/loss is the amount that will bring the trial balance back into balance.

French Company
TRIAL BALANCE
December 31, Year 3

	Euros		Exchange	US dollars	
	DR	CR	rates	DR	CR
Cash	60		1.12	67.20	
Accounts rec. (net)	100		1.12	112.00	
Land	200		1.12	224.00	
Building (net)	400		1.12	448.00	
Accounts payable		100	1.12		112.00
Mortgage payable		200	1.12		224.00
Common stock		100	.90		90.00
Retained earnings 1/1/Y3		260			242.00
Revenues		260	1.10		286.00
Expenses	140		1.10	154.00	
Depreciation exp.	20		1.10	22.00	
Totals	€920	€920		$1,027.20	$ 954.00
Translation adjustment (gain)					73.20
Totals				$1,027.20	$1,027.20

e. The previous illustration of the current rate technique assumed the euro to be the functional currency. Assume, however, that the circumstances were evaluated by the US company, and the US dollar was chosen as the functional currency. Under this alternative, the foreign currency financial statements are remeasured into US dollars.

(1) The remeasurement process is intended to produce the same result as if the entity's books of record had been maintained in the functional currency.

(2) If the US dollar is the functional currency, the remeasurement of foreign currency financial statements into US dollars results in a remeasurement gain or loss that is included in the subsidiary's income for the period.

(3) The remeasurement process begins by classifying assets and liabilities as either monetary or nonmonetary items and then applying the appropriate exchange rate depending on whether the item is monetary or nonmonetary. The following rules apply to the remeasurement process:

(a) Monetary assets and monetary liabilities are remeasured using the current rate at the balance sheet date.

(b) Nonmonetary assets and liabilities (e.g., land, building) which have historical cost balances are remeasured using historical exchange rates at the date the item entered the subsidiary.

(c) Owners' equity accounts such as common stock and additional paid in capital are translated using historic rates.

(d) Dividends is translated at the historic rate at the date of declaration

(e) Retained earnings is brought forward from the translated statement of the previous year.

(f) Revenues and most expenses that occur during a period are remeasured, for practical purposes, using the weighted-average exchange rate for the period. However, revenues and expenses that represent allocations of historical balances (e.g. depreciation) are remeasured using the same historical exchange rates as used for those items on the balance sheet.

(g) The remeasurement loss is reported on the consolidated income statement. The loss is the result of a remeasurement process which assumes that the US dollar is the functional currency.

(h) The calculation of the remeasurement loss is the result of the rules employed in the remeasurement process. In mechanical terms, the remeasurement loss is the amount needed to make the debits equal the credits in the French company's US dollar trial balance.

(4) The remeasurement process is illustrated below for the French subsidiary.

EXAMPLE

Remeasurement Method

French Company
BALANCE SHEET
December 31, Year 3
(US dollar is Functional Currency)

Assets	(Classification)	Euros	Exchange rates	US dollars
Cash	(Monetary)	60		
	(Monetary)	100	1.12	67.20
Accounts receivable (net)	(Monetary)	200	1.12	112.00
Land	(Nonmonetary)	400	.90	180.00
Building (net)	(Nonmonetary)	€760	.90	360.00
Totals				$719.20

Liabilities and Owners' Equity				
Accounts payable	(Monetary)	100	1.12	112.00
Mortgage payable	(Monetary)	200	1.12	224.00
Common stock		100	.90	90.00
Retained earnings, 12/31/Y3		360		293.20 (plug) (A)
Totals		€760		$719.20

The end retained earnings number is a plug figure to bring the balance sheet back into balance (**A**). This number is then used as end retained earnings in the statement of retained earnings to calculate net income after the remeasurement gain or loss (**B**). The remeasurement gain or loss (**C**) is the plug figure needed on the income statement to arrive at the calculated net income figure (**B**).

French Company
COMBINED INCOME AND RETAINED EARNINGS STATEMENT
For the Year Ending December 31, Year 3

	Euros	Exchange rates	US dollars	
Revenues	260	1.10	286.00	
Expenses (exclusive of depreciation)	(140)	1.10	(154.00)	
Depreciation	(20)	.90	(18.00)	
Earnings before remeasurement loss			114.00	
Remeasurement loss	--	--	(40.80)	(plug) (**C**)
Net income (loss)	100		73.20	(Taken from R/E Stmt)

Calculation of retained earnings, net Income and measurement loss:				
Retained earnings at 1/1/Y3	260		220.00*	(given in problem)
Net income			73.20	(plug) (**B**)
Retained earnings at 12/31/Y3	€360		$ 293.20	(plug from balance sheet)

* Retained earnings of $220 includes remeasured income from the period year 1 through year 2, which includes remeasurement losses applicable to those years due to the strengthening of the euro compared to the US dollar. Beginning retained earnings were taken from the prior period's financial statements.

An easier way to calculate the foreign currency translation gain or loss is to use the trial balance approach. The remeasurement gain/loss is the amount needed to bring the trial balance back into balance. The trial balance approach is shown below.

French Company
TRIAL BALANCE
December 31, Year 3

	Euro DR	Euro CR	Exchange rates	US dollars DR	US dollars CR	
Cash	60		1.12	67.20		
Accounts rec. (net)	100		1.12	112.00		
Land	200		.90	180.00		
Building (net)	400		.90	360.00		
Accounts payable		100	1.12		112.00	
Mortgage payable		200	1.12		224.00	
Common stock		100	.90		90.00	
Retained earnings 1/1/Y3		260			220.00*	(given in problem)
Revenues		260	1.10		286.00	
Expenses	140		1.10	154.00		
Depreciation exp.	20		.90	18.00		
Totals	€920	€920		$891.20	$932.00	
Remeasurement loss				40.80	--	(plug)
Totals				$932.00	$932.00	

(5) The significant points to remember about the French illustration are summarized below.

   (a) Before foreign currency financial statements can be translated into US dollars, a decision must be made regarding the functional currency.
   (b) If the functional currency is the foreign currency, the current rate method is used to translate to US dollars.

      1] All assets and liabilities are translated using the current rate at the balance sheet date.
      2] Owners' equity is translated using historical rates while revenues (and gains) and expenses (and losses) are translated at the rates in existence during the period when the transactions occurred.
      3] A weighted-average rate can be used for items occurring numerous times throughout the period.
      4] The translation adjustments (debit or credit) which result from the application of these rules are reported as a separate item in owners' equity in the consolidated balance sheet of the US parent.

   (c) If the functional currency is not the reporting currency (the US dollar), the foreign currency financial statements are **remeasured** into US dollars.

      1] All foreign currency balances are restated to US dollars using either historical or current exchange rates.
      2] Foreign currency balances which reflect prices from past transactions (e.g., inventories carried at cost, prepaid insurance, property, plant, and equipment, etc.) are remeasured using historical rates while foreign currency balances which reflect prices from current transactions (e.g., inventories and trading and available-for-sale securities carried at market, etc.) are remeasured using the current rate.
      3] Monetary assets and liabilities are remeasured using the current rate. (Deferred taxes are remeasured using the current rate.)
      4] Remeasurement gains/losses that result from the remeasurement process are reported on the consolidated income statement under "Other Income (Expense)."

(6) The above summary can be arranged in tabular form as shown below.

Functional currency	Functional currency determinants	Translation method	Reporting
Local currency of foreign company	a. Operations not integrated with parent's operations b. Buying and selling activities primarily in local currency c. Cash flows not immediately available for remittance to parent	Current Rate (All assets/ liabilities translated using current rate; revenues/expenses use weighted-average rate; equity accounts use historical rates)	Translation adjustments are reported as other comprehensive income under one of several acceptable reporting alternatives and as accumulated other comprehensive income in the equity section of consolidated balance sheet. Analysis of changes in accumulated translation adjustments disclosed via footnote
US Dollar	a. Operations integrated with parent's operations b. Buying and selling activities primarily in US and/or US dollars c. Cash flows immediately available for remittance to parent	Remeasurement (Monetary assets/ liabilities use current rate; historical cost balances use historical rates; revenues/ expenses use weighted-average rates and historical rates, the latter for allocations such as depr. exp.).	Remeasurement gain/loss is reported on the consolidated income statement.

3. A few comments concerning the translation of foreign currency financial statements in highly inflationary economies should be made. If the cumulative inflation rate is ≥ 100% over a three-year period in a foreign country, the foreign currency statements of a company located in that country are remeasured into the reporting currency (i.e., the US dollar). In other words, it is assumed the US dollar is the functional currency. The following flowchart summarizes the requirements of foreign currency financial statements.

FOREIGN CURRENCY FINANCIAL STATEMENTS

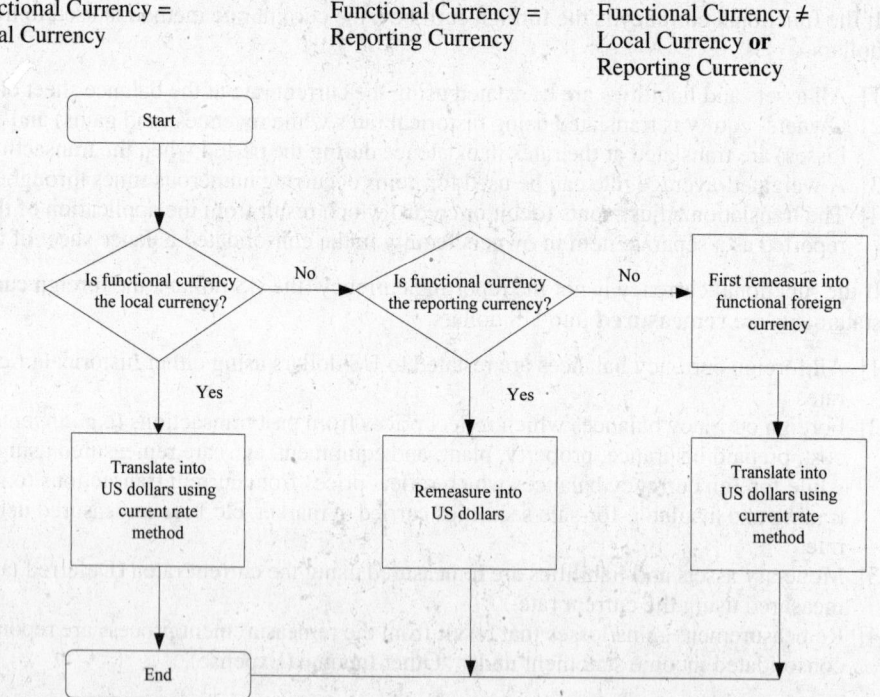

4. **Research Component—Accounting Standards Codification**

     ASC Topic 830 addresses the issues related to translation of financial statements. A list of keywords helpful in locating foreign currency translation issues is shown below.

Exchange rate	Foreign operations	Reporting currency
Foreign currency	Functional currency	Translation adjustment(s)
Foreign currency statements	Highly inflationary economy	Translation financial statement
Foreign currency translation	Primary economic environment	
Foreign entity	Remeasurement functional currency	

5. **International Financial Reporting Standards (IFRS)**

    a. Currencies are defined as either foreign, functional currency, or presentation currency. The functional currency is the currency of the primary economic environment in which the entity operates. A foreign currency is a currency other than the functional currency. The presentation currency is the currency in which financial statements are presented. Similar to US GAAP, the three-step process for translating financial statements is as follows:

        (1) Determine the functional currency.
        (2) Translate items into the functional currency.
        (3) Translate items into the presentation currency.

    b. When translating financial statement items, the items are classified into two categories: monetary and nonmonetary items.

        (1) Monetary items are translated at the year-end spot rate.
        (2) Nonmonetary items measured at historical cost are translated at the historical exchange rate.
        (3) Nonmonetary items measured at fair value are translated at the rate in effect when fair value was determined.
        (4) If the functional currency is the same as the presentation currency, any gains and losses on translation are recognized in profit or loss in the period. However, there are several exceptions to this rule.
        (5) Currency gains or losses on nonmonetary items for which gains and losses are recorded in other comprehensive income should also be reported in other comprehensive income.

    c. If the functional currency is not the same as the presentation currency, then any translation gains and losses are recorded in other comprehensive income. In this case, assets and liabilities are recorded at the closing exchange rate, and income and expenses are recorded at the rate when the transaction occurred.

KEY TERMS

    Foreign Currency Statements. Financial statements that employ as the unit of measure a functional currency that is not the reporting currency of the enterprise.

    Foreign Currency Translation. The process of expressing in the reporting currency of the enterprise those amounts that are denominated or measured in a different currency.

    Functional Currency. An entity's functional currency is the currency of the primary economic environment in which the entity operates; normally, that is the currency of the environment in which an entity primarily generates and expends cash.

    Local Currency. The currency of a particular country being referred to.

    Remeasurement. If an entity's books and records are not kept in its functional currency, remeasurement into the functional currency is required. Monetary balances are translated using the current exchange rate and nonmonetary balances are translated using historical exchange rates. If the US dollar is the functional currency, remeasurement into the reporting currency (the US dollar) makes translation unnecessary.

    Reporting Currency. The currency in which an enterprise prepares its financial statements.

    Translation Adjustments. Translation adjustments result from the process of translating financial statements from the entity's functional currency into the reporting currency.

Multiple-Choice Questions (1-13)

E.2. *Translation of Foreign Currency Statements*

1.   Certain balance sheet accounts of a foreign subsidiary of Rowan, Inc., at December 31, year 1, have been translated into US dollars as follows:

	Translated at Current rates	Historical rates
Note receivable, long-term	$240,000	$200,000
Prepaid rent	85,000	80,000
Patent	150,000	170,000
	$475,000	$450,000

The subsidiary's functional currency is the currency of the country in which it is located. What total amount should be included in Rowan's December 31, year 1 consolidated balance sheet for the above accounts?

- a. $450,000
- b. $455,000
- c. $475,000
- d. $495,000

2.   A wholly owned subsidiary of Ward, Inc. has certain expense accounts for the year ended December 31, year 3, stated in local currency units (LCU) as follows:

	LCU
Depreciation of equipment (related assets were purchased January 1, year 1)	120,000
Provision for doubtful accounts	80,000
Rent	200,000

The exchange rates at various dates are as follows:

	Dollar equivalent of 1 LCU
December 31, year 3	$.40
Average for year ended 12/31/Y3	.44
January 1, year 1	.50

Assume that the LCU is the subsidiary's functional currency and that the charges to the expense accounts occurred approximately evenly during the year. What total dollar amount should be included in Ward's year 3 consolidated income statement to reflect these expenses?

- a. $160,000
- b. $168,000
- c. $176,000
- d. $183,200

3.   Which of the following should be reported as a stockholders' equity account?

- a.   Discount on convertible bonds.
- b.   Premium on convertible bonds.
- c.   Cumulative foreign exchange translation loss.
- d.   Organization costs.

4.   A foreign subsidiary's functional currency is its local currency, which has not experienced significant inflation. The weighted-average exchange rate for the current year would be the appropriate exchange rate for translating

	Sales to customers	Wages expense
a.	No	No
b.	Yes	Yes
c.	No	Yes
d.	Yes	No

5.   The functional currency of Nash, Inc.'s subsidiary is the euro. Nash borrowed euros as a partial hedge of its investment in the subsidiary. In preparing consolidated financial statements, Nash's translation loss on its investment in the subsidiary exceeded its exchange gain on the borrowing. How should the effects of the loss and gain be reported in Nash's consolidated financial statements?

- a.   The translation loss less the exchange gain is reported as other comprehensive income.
- b.   The translation loss less the exchange gain is reported in net income.
- c.   The translation loss is reported as other comprehensive income and the exchange gain is reported in net income.
- d.   The translation loss is reported in net income and the exchange gain is reported as other comprehensive income.

6.   A balance arising from the translation or remeasurement of a subsidiary's foreign currency financial statements is reported in the consolidated income statement when the subsidiary's functional currency is the

	Foreign currency	US dollar
a.	No	No
b.	No	Yes
c.	Yes	No
d.	Yes	Yes

7.   When remeasuring foreign currency financial statements into the functional currency, which of the following items would be remeasured using historical exchange rate?

- a.   Inventories carried at cost.
- b.   Marketable equity securities reported at market values.
- c.   Bonds payable.
- d.   Accrued liabilities.

8.   Park Co.'s wholly owned subsidiary, Schnell Corp., maintains its accounting records in euros. Because all of Schnell's branch offices are in Switzerland, its functional currency is the Swiss franc. Remeasurement of Schnell's year 1 financial statements resulted in a $7,600 gain, and translation of its financial statements resulted in an $8,100 gain. What amount should Park report as a foreign exchange gain as net income in its income statement for the year ended December 31, year 1?

- a. $0
- b. $ 7,600
- c. $ 8,100
- d. $15,700

9.   In preparing consolidated financial statements of a US parent company with a foreign subsidiary, the foreign subsidiary's functional currency is the currency

- a.   In which the subsidiary maintains its accounting records.
- b.   Of the country in which the subsidiary is located.
- c.   Of the country in which the parent is located.
- d.   Of the environment in which the subsidiary primarily generates and expends cash.

E.5. International Financial Reporting Standards (IFRS)

10. For IFRS reporting purposes, currencies are defined as
    a. International and functional.
    b. Foreign, functional, and presentation.
    c. Domestic and international.
    d. Operating, international, and presentation.

11. For IFRS reporting, the functional currency is
    a. The currency in which the company reports its earnings.
    b. The currency in which the company primarily conducts banking activities.
    c. The currency in which the company primarily operates.
    d. The currency in which the company presents its financial statements.

12. For IFRS reporting, if the functional currency is the same as the presentation currency, any translation gains or losses are generally reported as
    a. A gain or loss on the statement of income.
    b. A gain or loss in other comprehensive income.
    c. A gain or loss directly in the retained earnings account.
    d. An extraordinary item on the statement of income.

13. Which of the following is not a IFRS requirement regarding foreign currency translation?
    a. Nonmonetary items measured at historical cost are translated at the historical exchange rate.
    b. Monetary items are translated at the year-end spot rate.
    c. If the functional currency is the same as the presentation currency gains or losses are reported in profit and loss for the period.
    d. If the functional currency is not the same as the presentation currency gains or losses are deferred to future periods.

Multiple-Choice Answers and Explanations

Answers

1. c __ __	4. b __ __	7. a __ __	10. b __ __	13. d __ __
2. c __ __	5. a __ __	8. b __ __	11. c __ __	1st: __/13 = __%
3. c __ __	6. b __ __	9. d __ __	12. a __ __	2nd: __/13 = __%

Explanations

1.   (c)   When the **functional currency** of a foreign subsidiary is the **foreign currency,** asset and liability accounts are **translated** using the **current** exchange rate (the rate of translation in effect at the balance sheet date). Therefore, these accounts should be included in the balance sheet at $475,000. Note that if the **functional currency** was the **US dollar,** balance sheet accounts would be **remeasured** using a combination of **historical and current rates**.

2.   (c)   The requirement is to determine the total amount of various expenses incurred by a foreign subsidiary which should be reported in the year 3 consolidated income statement. If the foreign currency is the functional currency of the subsidiary, the **current rate** method should be used to translate the financial statements. In this method, revenues and expenses are translated at the rates in effect at the time these items were recognized during the period. Because translation at the date the revenues and expenses were recognized is generally deemed impractical, An appropriate weighted-average rate may be used to translate these items. This results in a translated expense of $176,000 [($120,000 + $80,000 + $200,000) × .44].

3.   (c)   The requirement is to determine which item is reported in the stockholders' equity section. Accumulated gains and losses on certain foreign currency transactions should be reported as a component of stockholders' equity entitled other comprehensive income. Answers (a), (b), and (d) are incorrect because these items are reported on the balance sheet in the assets and liabilities sections and are amortized over their respective lives.

4.   (b)   The current rate method for the translation of foreign currency financial statements is used when a foreign subsidiary's functional currency is its local currency. Using the current rate method, revenue and expenses should be translated into US dollars at the weighted-average rate for the current year. Thus, both sales to customers and wages expense should be translated at the weighted-average rate.

5.   (a)   Translation adjustments resulting from the translation of foreign currency statements should be reported separately as components of other comprehensive income, accumulated other comprehensive income, and stockholders' equity. Additionally, gains and losses on certain foreign currency transactions should also be reported similarly. Those gains and losses which should be excluded from net income and instead reported as components of other comprehensive income and of accumulated other comprehensive income in stockholders' equity include foreign currency transactions designated as economic hedges of a net investment in a foreign entity. Thus, both the translation loss and the exchange gain are to be reported as other comprehensive income and accumulated other comprehensive income in the stockholders' equity section of the balance sheet. Because the translation loss on the investment exceeds the exchange gain on the borrowing, the translation loss less the exchange gain is the amount to be reported as separate components of other comprehensive income and accumulated other comprehensive income equity in the consolidated financial statements.

6.   (b)   **Translation** adjustments result from translating an entity's financial statements into the reporting currency. Such adjustments, which result when the entity's functional currency is the **foreign currency,** should not be included in net income. Instead, such adjustments should be reported as other comprehensive income and accumulated other comprehensive income in the stockholders' equity section of the balance sheet. If the functional currency is the **reporting currency** (US dollar), a **remeasurement** process takes place, with the resulting gain or loss included in net income.

7.   (a)   The requirement is to determine which item would be remeasured using historical exchange rates when foreign currency financial statements are being remeasured into the functional currency. When an entity's books are not maintained in the functional currency, it is necessary to use historical exchange rates in the remeasurement process of certain accounts. Among the accounts listed is inventories carried at cost. Only marketable equity securities reported at **cost** would be remeasured using historical exchange rates. Bonds payable and accrued liabilities would be remeasured at the current rate.

8.   (b)   Schnell's accounting records are kept in euros, and its functional currency is the Swiss franc. Before Schnell's financial statements can be consolidated with Park's financial statements, they must be remeasured from euros to Swiss francs, and then translated from Swiss francs to US dollars. As a result of these restatements, there is a remeasurement gain of $7,600, and a credit translation adjustment of $8,100. A remeasurement gain or loss is included in net income, but a translation adjustment is **not**. Therefore, Park would report a foreign exchange gain of $7,600 in its year 1 income statement.

9.   (d)   An entity's functional currency is the currency of the primary economic environment in which the entity operates; normally, that is the currency of the environment in which an entity primarily generates and expends cash.

10.   (b)   For IFRS reporting purposes, currencies are defined as foreign, functional, and presentation currencies.

11.   (c)   For IFRS reporting, the functional currency is the currency of the primary economic environment in which the company operates.

12.   (a)   If the functional currency is the same as the presentation currency, any translation gain or loss is reported in current earnings on the income statement. However, there are several exceptions to this rule. Currency gains or losses on nonmonetary items for which gains and losses are recorded in other comprehensive income should also be reported in other comprehensive income.

13.   (d)   The requirement is to identify the statement that is incorrect regarding foreign currency translation under IFRS. Answer (d) is correct because under IFRS, if the functional currency is not the same as the presentation currency, gains or losses are charged to other comprehensive income.

Simulations

Task-Based Simulation 1

Concepts		
	Authoritative Literature	Help

Items 1 through 9 are based on the following:

A foreign subsidiary's trial balance is translated from its functional currency to the functional currency of the parent.
For each item determine which date the exchange rate from Table A should be used for the translation. The subsidiary's functional currency is its **local** currency.

TABLE A

	Event	Date
A.	Company begins	12/31/Y1
B.	Beginning of current year	1/1/Y3
C.	1st quarter	4/1/Y3
D.	2nd quarter	7/1/Y3
E.	3rd quarter	10/1/Y3
F.	Year-end	12/31/Y3
G.	1st quarter	4/1/Y4
H.	Year average	
I.	Average since acquisition	
J.	No translation rate used	

Indicate the correct exchange rate by placing an x in the table in the appropriate box.

		A 12/31/Y1	B 1/1/Y3	C 4/1/Y3	D 7/1/Y3	E 10/1/Y3	F 12/31/Y3	G 4/1/Y4	H Year average	I Average since acquisition	J No translation rate used
1.	Cash										
2.	Inventory that had been purchased evenly throughout the year										
3.	Account payable for equipment purchased on 4/1/Y3										
4.	Cost of goods sold										
5.	Sales										
6.	Dividends declared on 10/1/Y3										
7.	Dividends declared in (6) were paid 1/2/Y4										
8.	Retained earnings										
9.	Common stock										

Task-Based Simulation 2

Translation of Financial Statements		
	Authoritative Literature	Help

Situation

Your client, Jay, Inc., prepares consolidated financial statements, which include two subsidiaries, Jay Co. of Australia (Jay A), and Jay Co. of France (Jay F). Jay A operates with US dollars, but maintains its financial statements in Australian dollars. Jay F operates primarily with euros and maintains its financial statements in euros.

Your client has asked for assistance with translating the financial statements of Jay F into US dollars. Below are the financial statements of Jay F in euros.

Jay F
INCOME STATEMENT
For the year ended December 31, Year 3

	In euros
Revenue	650,000
Cost of goods sold	(390,000)
Gross profit	260,000
Sales expense	(50,000)
General and administrative expense	(110,000)
Depreciation expense	(15,000)
Net income	85,000

Jay F
STATEMENT OF RETAINED EARNINGS
For the year ended December 31, Year 3

	In euros
Beginning retained earnings, 1/1/Y3	140,000
Add: Net income	85,000
Less: Dividends	0
End retained earnings, 12/3/Y3	225,000

Jay F
BALANCE SHEET
December 31, Year 3

	In euros
Assets:	
Cash	18,000
Accounts receivable	42,000
Inventory	137,000
Land	120,000
Building	250,000
Less: Accumulated depreciation	(30,000)
Total assets	537,000
Liabilities:	
Accounts payable	49,000
Note payable, due 12/5/Y9	100,000
Common stock	50,000
Additional paid-in capital	113,000
Retained earnings	225,000
Total liabilities and owners' equity	537,000

Additional information

Jay F began operations on January 2, year 1. All outstanding stock was issued on January 2, year 1. Jay F earned the following income since the company began operations. No dividends have been paid to date.

Year	Income
Year 1	60,000
Year 2	80,000

The exchange rates are as follows:

Date	Dollars per euro
January 2, year 1	1.10
January 1, year 3	1.24
December 31, year 3	1.36
Weighted-average rate year 1	1.15
Weighted-average rate for year 2	1.18
Weighted-average rate for year 3	1.31

Complete the following tables for the foreign currency translation into US dollars for Jay F.

Jay F
INCOME STATEMENT
For the year ended December 31, Year 3

	In euros	Exchange rate	US dollars
Revenue	650,000		
Cost of goods sold	(390,000)		
Gross profit	260,000		
Sales expense	(50,000)		
General and administrative expense	(110,000)		
Depreciation expense	(15,000)		
Net income	85,000		

Complete the following table to translate the retained earnings of Jay F into US dollars.

Jay F
STATEMENT OF RETAINED EARNINGS
For the year ended December 31, Year 3

	In euros	Exchange rate	US dollars
Beginning retained earnings, 1/1/Y3			
Year 1 net income	60,000		
Year 2 net income	80,000		
Net income for year 3	85,000		
Less: Dividends	0		
End retained earnings, 12/31/Y3	225,000		

Complete the following table to translate the balance sheet accounts of Jay F into US dollars.

Jay F
BALANCE SHEET
December 31, Year 3

	In euros	Exchange rate	Translation into US dollars
Assets:			
Cash	18,000		
Accounts receivable	42,000		
Inventory	137,000		
Land	120,000		
Building	250,000		
Less: Accumulated depreciation	(30,000)		
Total assets	537,000		
Liabilities:			
Accounts payable	49,000		
Note payable, due 12/5/Y9	100,000		
Common stock	50,000		
Additional paid in capital	113,000		
Retained earnings	225,000		
Other comprehensive income (foreign currency translation adjustment)	0		
Total liabilities and owners' equity	537,000		

Task-Based Simulation 3

Research		
	Authoritative Literature	Help

Assume that you are assigned to the audit of Daley Corporation, a multinational company. The CFO of Daley has asked you to explain the criteria to be used to identify the functional currency for consolidation purposes. Which section of the Professional Standards provides the economic indicators that are considered in determining the functional currency?

Enter your response in the answer fields below.

Simulation Solutions

Task-Based Simulation 1

Concepts		
Authoritative Literature		**Help**

		A 12/31/Y1	B 1/1/Y3	C 4/1/Y3	D 7/1/Y3	E 10/1/Y3	F 12/31/Y3	G 4/1/Y4	H Year average	I Average since acquisition	J No translation rate used
1.	Cash						x				
2.	Inventory that had been purchased evenly throughout the year						x				
3.	Account payable for equipment purchased on 4/1/Y3						x				
4.	Cost of goods sold								x		
5.	Sales								x		
6.	Dividends declared on 10/1/Y3					x					
7.	Dividends declared in (6) were paid 1/2/Y4						x				
8.	Retained earnings										x
9.	Common stock	x									

Explanations

1. (F) Assets are valued at the current rate at year-end.

2. (F) Assets are valued at the current rate at year-end.

3. (F) Liabilities are valued at the current rate at year-end.

4. (H) Expense accounts are valued at the average rate for the current year of business.

5. (H) Revenue accounts are valued at the average rate for the current year of business.

6. (E) Dividends are valued at the rate of the date of declaration.

7. (F) Liabilities (dividends payable) are valued at the current rate at year-end.

8. (J) The retained earnings are carried over from 1/1/Y3 with the translated net income added and translated dividends subtracted.

9. (A) Common stock is valued at the historical rate when it was issued.

Task-Based Simulation 2

Translation of Financial Statements		
Authoritative Literature		**Help**

Complete the following table for the foreign currency translation into US dollars for Jay F.

Jay F
INCOME STATEMENT
For the year ended December 31, Year 3

	In euros	Exchange rate	US dollars
Revenue	650,000	1.31	$ 851,500
Cost of goods sold	(390,000)	1.31	(510,000)
Gross profit	260,000	1.31	340,600
Sales expense	(50,000)	1.31	(65,500)
General and administrative expense	(110,000)	1.31	(144,100)
Depreciation expense	(15,000)	1.31	(19,650)
Net income	85,000	1.31	$ 111,350

Complete the following table to translate the retained earnings of Jay F into US dollars.

Jay F
STATEMENT OF RETAINED EARNINGS
For the year ended December 31, Year 3

	In euros	Exchange rate	US dollars
Beginning retained earnings, 1/1/Y3			
Year 1 net income	60,000	1.15	$ 69,000
Year 2 net income	80,000	1.18	94,400
Net income for year 3	85,000	1.31	111,350
Less: Dividends	0		
End retained earnings, 12/31/Y3	225,000		$274,750

Complete the following table to translate the balance sheet accounts of Jay F into US dollars.

Jay F
BALANCE SHEET
December 31, Year 3

	In euros	Exchange rate	Translation into US dollars
Assets:			
Cash	18,000	1.36	$24,480
Accounts receivable	42,000	1.36	57,120
Inventory	137,000	1.36	186,320
Land	120,000	1.36	163,200
Building	250,000	1.36	340,000
Less: Accumulated depreciation	(30,000)	1.36	(40,800)
Total assets	537,000		$730,320
Liabilities:			
Accounts payable	49,000	1.36	$66,640
Note payable, due 12/5/Y9	100,000	1.36	136,000
Common stock	50,000	1.10	55,000
Additional paid in capital	113,000	1.10	124,300
Retained earnings	225,000		274,750
Other comprehensive income (foreign currency translation adjustment)	0		73,630
Total liabilities and owners' equity	537,000		$730,320

Explanation

For Jay F, the functional currency is the foreign currency (euros).

Therefore, the current rate method is used.

The following rules apply to the current rate method:

- Assets and liabilities—use current rate at balance sheet date
- Revenues and expenses—use weighted-average rate (or rate at time of exchange if known)
- Owners' equity—use historical rates
- Dividends—use historical rates

Because Jay F's retained earnings is from three years, each year must be translated at the appropriate rate. The weighted-average rate is used for each year.

The translation gain is the plug figure to bring the balance sheet into balance, and is reported as "other comprehensive income" in the owners' equity section of the balance sheet.

Total assets = $730,320

Total liabilities + Owners' equity **before** translation adjustment = $656,690

Translation adjustment = $730,320 − 656,690 = $73,630.

Task-Based Simulation 3

Research			
	Authoritative Literature	Help	

ASC	830	10	55	5

Module 21: Governmental (State and Local) Accounting

Overview

Governmental accounting has some similarities to commercial accounting. For example, governmental accounting uses the double-entry system, journals, ledgers, trial balances, financial statements, internal control, etc. However, differences arise due to the objectives and environment of government. The major differences include

1. The absence of a profit motive, except for enterprise activities, such as utilities
2. A legal emphasis that involves restrictions both in the raising and spending of revenues
3. An inability to "match" revenues with expenditures, as revenues are often provided by persons other than those receiving the services
4. An emphasis on accountability or stewardship of resources entrusted to public officials
5. The use of fund accounting and reporting, as well as government-wide reporting
6. The recording of the budget in governmental funds which legally adopt a budget (i.e., General Fund)
7. The use of modified accrual accounting rather than full accrual accounting in some funds (governmental fund types)

Before beginning the reading you should review the key terms at the end of the module.

A. The Governmental Accounting Standards Board

The Governmental Accounting Standards Board (GASB), which has the authority to establish standards of financial reporting for all units of state and local governments, was created in 1984. It should be noted that the Financial Accounting Standards Board (FASB) has the authority to establish standards for nongovernmental not-for-profit organizations. GASB Statement No. 55 established a hierarchy of sources of generally accepted accounting principles (GAAP) for states and local governments as shown below (in descending order of authority):

1. Officially established accounting principles—GASB Statements and Interpretations.
2. GASB Technical Bulletins and AICPA Industry Audit and Accounting Guides and Statements of Position cleared by the GASB.
3. AICPA Practice Bulletins cleared by the GASB and consensus positions of groups of accountants organized by the GASB.
4. Implementation guides published by the GASB staff and practices that are widely recognized and prevalent.

In 2010, the GASB issued Statement No. 62 which incorporated into GASB's authoritative literature certain accounting and financial reporting guidance that is included in the following pronouncements issued on or before November 30, 1989:

1. FASB Statements and Interpretations
2. Accounting Principles Board Opinions
3. Accounting Research Bulletins

Major topics in GASB Statement No. 62 include

1. Capitalization of interest cost
2. Revenue recognition for exchange transactions
3. Revenue recognition when the right of return exists
4. Classification of items in the statement of net position
5. Special and extraordinary items
6. Comparative financial statements
7. Related parties
8. Prior-period adjustments
9. Accounting changes and error corrections
10. Disclosure of accounting policies
11. Contingencies
12. Long-term construction contracts
13. Extinguishment of debts
14. Troubled-debt restructuring
15. Foreign currency transactions
16. Imputation of interest costs
17. Inventory
18. Investments in common stock
19. Leases
20. Nonmonetary transactions
21. Real estate transactions
22. Research and development arrangements
23. Guidance for specialized industries, such as broadcasters and insurance entities

For these areas accounting by state and local government is similar to the accounting by business enterprises.

B. Governmental Accounting Concepts

GASB Concept Statements are much like the FASB Concepts Statements in that they set fourth fundamentals on which governmental accounting and reporting standards will be based.

1. Objectives of Financial Reporting

   a. GASB Concepts Statement No. 1 establishes the objectives of general purpose external financial reporting by state and local governmental entities and applies to both governmental-type and business-type activities.
   b. The nature of the governmental environment affects the financial reporting of governmental-type activities. The governmental environment is characterized by representative forms of government with separation of powers, a prevalence of intergovernmental revenues, and services that are provided to taxpayers. The budget is very significant in accounting for government-type activities because it expresses public policy, funding intent, and provides control over government expenditures. Control over revenues and expenditures is also provided by the use of fund accounting.
   c. Governmental business-type activities are more akin to private business activities. Generally, they involve exchanges that involve charging fees for providing particular services. However, many business-type activities receive subsidies, grants, or taxes from the general government, making them part of the government and publicly accountable.
   d. Concepts Statement No. 1 identified three primary users of the external state and local governmental financial reports:

(1) The citizenry,
(2) Legislative and oversight bodies, and
(3) Investors and creditors.

e. Government financial reports are primarily used to compare actual financial results with budgets, to assess financial condition and results of operations, to assist in determining compliance with finance-related laws and regulations, and to assist in evaluating effectiveness and efficiency.

f. State and local governmental financial reports should possess the basic characteristics of understandability, reliability, relevance, timeliness, consistency, and comparability. See Module 9A for definitions of these characteristics.

2. Service Efforts and Accomplishments Reporting (SEA Reporting)

a. GASB Concepts Statement No. 2 (as amended by Concepts Statement No. 5) describes the objective, elements and characteristics of SEA reporting. The objective of SEA Reporting is to provide more complete information about a governmental entity's performance than can be provided by traditional financial statements and schedules. Such information is necessary for assessing accountability and making informed decisions.

b. Ideally a governmental entity should (1) establish and communicate clear, relevant goals and objectives, set measureable targets for accomplishment, and develop and report indicators that measure its progress. The elements of SEA reporting include measures of service effort, measures of service accomplishments (output and outcome measures), measures that relate service efforts to service accomplishments (efficiency and cost-outcome measures) and narrative or explanatory information.

3. Communication Methods in General-Purpose External Financial Reports

a. GASB Concepts Statement No. 3 provides a conceptual basis for selecting communication methods to present items of information within general-purpose external reports that contain financial statements. The alternative methods of communication include recognition in the basic financial statements, disclosure in notes to the basic financial statements, presentation as required supplementary information, and presentation as supplementary information.

b. GASB Concepts Statement No. 4 establishes definitions for the seven elements of historically based financial statements of state and local governments. The elements of a statement of financial position are defined as

(1) Assets—resources with present service capacity that the government presently controls.
(2) Liabilities—present obligations to sacrifice resources that the government has little or no discretion to avoid.
(3) Deferred outflow of resources—a consumption of net assets by the government that is applicable to a future reporting period. This is similar to an asset (e.g., a prepaid asset).
(4) Deferred inflow of resources—an acquisition of net assets by the government that is applicable to a future reporting period. This is similar to a liability (e.g., unearned revenue).
(5) Net position—the residual of all other elements presented in a statement of financial position.

c. The elements of the resource flows statements are defined as

(1) Outflow of resources—a consumption of net assets by the government that is applicable to the reporting period.
(2) Inflow of resources—an acquisition of net assets by the government that is applicable to the reporting period.

C. The Government Reporting Model

Governmental accounting focuses on two types of accountability: operational accountability and fiscal accountability. Operational accountability is demonstrated by government-wide financial statements which illustrate how effective and efficient the organization has been at using its resources, and the resources available to meet its future obligations. Fiscal accountability is illustrated by fund financial statements which show the organization's compliance with laws and regulations affecting its spending activities. The integrated approach refers to the fact that government financial statements show operational and fiscal accountability and the relationship between the two. The integrated approach requires a reconciliation between the government-wide financial statements and the fund financial statements.

GASB Statement No. 34, as amended by GASB Statement No. 63, provides the minimum requirements for basic financial statements and required supplemental information (RSI) to be in compliance with GAAP. These requirements for **general-purpose** governmental units (i.e., states, cities, counties) are

- Management's Discussion and Analysis (MD&A) (Required Supplementary Information)
- Government-Wide Financial Statements
  Statement of Net Position
  Statement of Activities

- Fund Financial Statements
    - Governmental Funds
        - Balance Sheet
        - Statement of Revenues, Expenditures, and Changes in Fund Balances
    - Proprietary Funds
        - Statement of Net Position
        - Statement of Revenues, Expenses, and Changes in Fund Net Position
        - Statement of Cash Flows
    - Fiduciary Funds
        - Statement of Fiduciary Net Position
        - Statement of Changes in Fiduciary Net Position
- Notes to the Financial Statements
- Required Supplementary Information (RSI) other than Management's Discussion and Analysis
    - Ten-Year Schedules of Selected Information (For entities that provide pensions through pension funds that are administered through trust funds. The required information varies depending on the nature of the plan.)
    - Budgetary Comparison Schedules
    - Information about Infrastructure Assets (for Entities Reported Using the Modified Approach)
    - Claims Development Information When the Government Sponsors a Public Entity Risk Pool

In addition, general-purpose governments may choose to provide certain **other supplementary information,** including combining statements for nonmajor funds. If a government wishes to prepare a complete **Comprehensive Annual Financial Report (CAFR)**, three major sections would be included. First, an **introductory section** (unaudited) would include a letter of transmittal, organization chart, and list of principal officials. Second, a **financial section** would be prepared, including an auditor's report, the required information, and other supplementary information listed above. Finally, a **statistical section** would include a number of schedules such as net position by component, changes in net position, revenue capacity, debt capacity, and demographic and economic statistics.

Special-purpose governments include park districts, tollway authorities, school districts, and sanitation districts. GASB has categorized special-purpose governments as those that are engaged in governmental activities, business-type activities, fiduciary activities, and both governmental and business-type activities. Special-purpose governments that are engaged in governmental activities and have more than one program and special-purpose governments that are engaged in both governmental and business-type activities must prepare both the government-wide and fund financial statements. Special-purpose governments that are engaged in a single governmental activity (such as a cemetery district) may combine the government-wide and fund financial statements or use other methods allowed by GASB. Special-purpose governments that are engaged in only business-type activities or fiduciary activities are not required to prepare the government-wide statements, but only prepare the proprietary or fiduciary fund statements. All governments must include the MD&A, Notes, and RSI.

> **NOTE:** Public colleges and universities and other governmental not-for-profit organizations may choose to report as special-purpose governments engaged in only business-type activities, engaged in only governmental activities, or engaged in both governmental and business-type activities.

D. The Reporting Entity

The GASB carefully defines the **reporting entity** in an effort to ensure that all boards, commissions, agencies, etc. that are under the control of the reporting entity are included. The reporting entity consists of a primary government and appropriate component units. A **primary government** is either (1) a state government, (2) a general-purpose local government, or (3) a special-purpose local government that has a separately elected governing body, is legally separate, and is fiscally independent of other state or local governments. A **component unit** is a legally separate organization for which the elected officials of a primary government are financially accountable. As clarified by GASB Statement No. 61, financial accountability for a legally separate organization is assumed in the following circumstances:

1. The primary government appoints a voting majority of the organization's governing body and (1) it is able to impose its will on that organization, or (2) there is a potential for the organization to provide specific financial benefits to, or impose specific financial burdens on, the primary government.
2. The organization is fiscally dependent on and there is a potential for the organization to provide specific financial benefits to, or burdens on, the primary government regardless of the primary government's influence on the governing board.

A component unit is also one in which the nature and significance of their relationships with a primary government is such that omission would cause the primary government's financial statements to be misleading. Generally, the financial statements would be misleading if they excluded organizations that are closely related to, or financially integrated with, the primary unit.

Most component units are reported, in the government-wide financial statements, in a separate column or columns to the right of the information related to the primary government (**discretely presented**). However, component units should be **blended** with the primary government figures in the following circumstances:

1. The governing body of the component unit is substantially the same as that of the primary government and (1) there is a financial benefit or burden relationship between the primary government and the component unit, or (2) management of the primary government has operational responsibility for the component unit.
2. The component unit provides services entirely, or almost entirely, for the primary government or for the benefit of the primary government.
3. The component unit's total debt outstanding, including leases, is expected to be repaid entirely or almost entirely by the primary government.

GASB Statement No. 39, *Determining Whether Certain Organizations Are Component Units—An Amendment of GASB Statement No. 14*, requires that a fund-raising foundation and similar organization whose primary purpose is to raise or hold significant resources for the benefit of a specific governmental unit should be reported as a component unit of that government.

E. Management's Discussion and Analysis

The **Management's Discussion and Analysis (MD&A)** provides, in plain English terms, an overview of the government's financial activities. This section is to provide a comparison of the current year results with the results of the prior year, with emphasis on the prior year. Included will be

- A brief discussion of the financial statements
- Condensed financial information from the government-wide financial statements and individual fund statements
- An analysis of significant variations between the original budget, final budget, and actual results for the year
- A description of significant capital asset and long-term debt activity for the year
- A discussion by governments that use the modified approach to report infrastructure assets regarding the condition of these capital assets and changes from the prior year
- A description of any known facts, decisions, or conditions that would have a significant effect on the government's financial position or results of operations.

MD&A is considered to be Required Supplementary Information (RSI). The nature of RSI is described in Section G. Only items required by GASB are included.

F. Government-Wide Financial Statements

The **government-wide** statements include the Statement of Net Position and the Statement of Activities, both of which are reproduced in this module. The government-wide statements are prepared on the economic resources measurement focus and accrual basis of accounting. All activities of the primary government are included, with the exception of fiduciary activities, as well as discretely presented component units.

1. The **Statement of Net Position** is similar to a balance sheet, except that the form, "Assets + Deferred Outflows of Resources – Liabilities – Deferred Inflows of Resources = Net Position" is used. Governmental accounting standards provide that (1) deferred outflows should be reported in a separate section following assets, and (2) deferred inflows should be reported in a separate section following liabilities. The statement then arrives at net position which includes the net effects of assets, deferred outflows of resources, liabilities, and deferred inflows of resources. Remember that a deferred outflow of resources is a consumption of net assets that is applicable to a future reporting period. An example would be where a government hedges a future transaction and the fair value becomes negative. A deferred inflow of resources is an acquisition of net assets that is applicable to a future reporting period. An example would be concession arrangement that involves the sale by a government of the future income from a toll road. The payment from the toll operator represents deferred revenue that should be recognized in the applicable future periods. Therefore it is similar to a liability.

   If deferred outflows or deferred inflows are disclosed in the aggregate, the notes to the financial statements should describe the different types of deferred amounts. In addition, an explanation in the notes is required if the amount reported for a component of net position is significantly affected by the difference between deferred inflows or outflows and their related assets and liabilities.

   GASB Statement No. 65, *Items Previously Recognized as Assets and Liabilities,* clarifies which financial statement items should continue to be presented as assets and liabilities, which should be reclassified as deferred outflows and deferred inflows, and which items should be treated as current period expenditures (outflows) or current period inflows.

Examples of Deferred Outflows of Resources	**Examples of Deferred Inflows of Resources**
• Grant expenditures paid in advance of meeting timing requirements	• Grant amounts received in advance of meeting timing requirements
• Deferred amounts from refunding of debt (debits)	• Deferred amounts from refunding debt (credits)
• Cost to acquire rights to future revenues	• Proceeds from sale of future revenues

Examples of Deferred Outflows of Resources	**Examples of Deferred Inflows of Resources**

- Deferred loss from sale and leaseback
- Negative fair value of government hedge of a future transaction

- Deferred gain from a sale-leaseback transaction
- Positive fair value of government hedge of a future transaction
- Advance of revenue from imposed nonexchange transactions

Examples of Items that Continue to Be Reported as Assets	**Examples of Items that Continue to Be Reported as Liabilities**

- Prepayments
- Net pension plan position in excess of employer's total liability
- Capitalized incurred costs for regulated activities

- Advances of derived tax revenues
- Grant amounts received in advance of meeting requirements other than timing
- Receipt of prepayment
- Loan commitment fees
- Refunds imposed by a regulator

Examples of Items Reported as Current Outflows	**Examples of Items Reported as Current Inflows**

- Debt issuance costs
- Initial direct cost incurred by lessor for operating leases
- Fees related to purchased loans

- Loan origination fees related to lending activities
- Commitment fees charged to make a loan
- Loan origination fees for mortgage loans held for investment

Full accrual accounting is to be used on the statement of net position, including the recording and depreciation of fixed assets, including infrastructure. Capital assets generally are presented in the asset section of the statement of net position net of related depreciation. Note that "net position" is broken down into three categories: (1) net investment in capital assets, (2) restricted, and (3) unrestricted. The term "net investment in capital assets" is computed by taking the value of capital (fixed) assets, less accumulated depreciation, less the debt associated with the acquisition or improvement of the capital assets. Deferred outflows of resources and deferred inflows of resources that are related to the acquisition, construction, or improvement of those assets or the related debt should also be included in this component of net position. The term "restricted," as defined by GASB means "(a) externally imposed by creditors (such as through debt covenants), grantors, contributors, or laws or regulations of other governments, and (b) imposed by law through constitutional provisions or enabling legislation." Unrestricted net position is a "plug" figure, computed by taking the total net position and subtracting the net investment in capital assets and the restricted net position.

Note also that the columns are separated into (1) governmental activities, (2) business-type activities, (3) total primary government, and (4) component units. Governmental activities are those that are financed primarily through taxes and other nonexchange transactions. Business-type activities are those normally financed through user charges. The terms "primary government" and "component units" are described above. If a government has more component units than can be displayed effectively in the Statement of Net Position, then the detail of each component unit should be disclosed in the notes to the financial statements.

2. The **Statement of Activities** reports revenues and expenses on the full accrual basis. This is a consolidated statement except that interfund transactions are not eliminated, when those transactions are between governmental and business-type activities, and between the primary government and discretely presented component units. Expenses are reported by function. Revenues are also reported on the accrual basis and may be exchange revenues or nonexchange revenues. **Exchange revenues** are reported when goods or services are transferred for payment of (approximately) equal value, as is true for business enterprises. **Nonexchange transactions** are reported in accord with Section K. below.

Program revenues, those that are directly associated with the functional expense categories, are deducted to arrive at the net expense or revenue. Note that program revenues include (1) charges for services, (2) operating grants and contributions, and (3) capital grants and contributions, although program revenues are not limited to the three categories. Examples of program revenue would be the fees charged for park operations under "culture and recreation," and fines and forfeits, such as fines for traffic violations. Charges for services are deducted from the function which creates the revenues. Grants and contributions (both operating and capital) are reported in the function to which their use is restricted. The net expense or revenue is broken out between governmental activities, business-type activities, and component units, the same as in the Statement of Net Position. General revenues are deducted from the net expenses to obtain net revenues. General revenues include all taxes levied by the reporting government and other nonexchange revenues not restricted to a particular program. After that, separate additions or deductions are made for special items, extraordinary items, and transfers (between categories). If a government had contributions to term and permanent endowments and contributions to permanent fund principal, these would also be shown after general revenues. Finally, the net position at the beginning and end of the year are reconciled. (This is called an "all-inclusive activity" statement.)

Extraordinary items are those that are both unusual in nature and infrequent in occurrence (the same as for business enterprises). **Special items** are those events within the control of management that are either unusual in nature or infrequent in occurrence. An example of a special item would be the gain on sale of park land.

> Alternatively, the internal balances could be reported on separate lines as assets and liabilities. A notation would need to be added to inform the reader that the "Total" column is adjusted for those amounts.

Sample City
STATEMENT OF NET POSITION
December 31, 2013

	Governmental activities	Primary government Business-type activities	Total	Component units
Assets				
Cash and cash equivalents	$ 13,597,899	$ 10,279,143	$ 23,877,042	$ 303,935
Investments	27,365,221	--	27,365,221	7,428,952
Receivables (net)	12,833,132	3,609,615	16,442,747	4,042,290
Internal balances	175,000	(175,000)	--	--
Inventories	322,149	126,674	448,823	83,697
Capital assets, net (Note 1)	170,022,760	151,388,751	321,411,511	37,744,786
Total assets	224,316,161	165,229,183	389,545,344	49,603,660
Deferred outflow				
Payment to acquire rights to future parking revenue	--	27,520	27,520	--
Liabilities				
Accounts payable	6,783,310	751,430	7,534,740	1,803,332
Accrued and other liabilities	1,435,599	--	1,435,599	38,911
Net pension liability	4,563,789		4,563,789	
Noncurrent liabilities (Note 2):				
Due within one year	9,236,000	4,426,286	113,662,286	1,426,639
Due in more than one year	78,738,589	74,482,273	153,220,862	27,106,151
Total liabilities	100,757,287	79,659,989	180,417,276	30,375,033
Deferred inflow				
Deferred gain from sale and leaseback of building	16,300	--	16,300	--
Net position				
Net investment in capital assets	103,711,386	73,088,574	176,799,960	15,906,392
Restricted for:				
Capital projects	11,705,864	--	11,705,864	492,445
Debt service	3,020,708	1,451,996	4,472,704	--
Community development projects	4,811,043	--	4,811,043	--
Other purposes	3,214,302	--	3,214,302	--
Unrestricted (deficit)	(2,920,729)	11,056,144	8,135,415	2,829,790
Total net position	$123,542,574	$ 85,596,714	$209,139,288	$19,228,627

> *Assets restricted for capital projects* includes approximately $13 million of capital debt for which the proceeds have not yet been used to construct capital assets.

SOURCE: Revised from GASB 34, page 201.

All governments are required to report those expenses that are directly associated with each function on the appropriate line. If a government chooses to allocate some indirect expenses to functions, separate columns should show the direct, indirect, and total costs charged to each function. Direct expenses include depreciation that can be directly charged. Depreciation expense that serves all functions may be allocated as an indirect expense or charged to general government or as unallocated depreciation expense. Depreciation expense for general **infrastructure assets** (roads, bridges, storm sewers, etc.) should not be allocated but shown as an expense of that function that normally is used for capital outlay (public works, for example) or as a separate line. Interest on long-term debt would be included in direct expenses if the interest is due to a single function. Most interest, however, cannot be identified with a single function and should be shown in a separate line. Interest is capitalized for business-type activities but not for governmental activities.

A government may choose to use a **modified approach for recording eligible infrastructure assets**. Under the modified approach eligible infrastructure assets are **not required to be depreciated** as long as the following two requirements are met: (1) the government manages the eligible infrastructure assets using an asset management system and (2) the government documents that the eligible infrastructure assets are being preserved approximately at (or above) a condition level established and disclosed by the government. Under the modified approach, if a government meets the above criteria and infrastructure, assets are not depreciated and all expenditures (except for additions and improvements) made for eligible infrastructure assets should be expensed in the period incurred. Expenditures for additions and improvements of eligible infrastructure assets should be capitalized.

3. GASB No. 68, *Accounting and Financial Reporting for Pensions,* provides guidance when a state or local government has an employee pension plan administered through a trust or equivalent arrangement with the following characteristics:

- Contributions from employers or nonemployer contributing entities to the pension plan and the related earnings are irrevocable.
- Pensions plan assets are dedicated to providing pensions to plan members in accordance with the benefit terms, and
- Pension plan assets are legally protected from the creditors of employers and the pension plan administrator. If the plan is a defined benefit pension plan, plan assets also are legally protected from creditors of the plan members.

If the entity has a **single-employer defined benefit plan or an agent defined benefit plan,** the state or local government should report, in the statement of net position, a net pension liability, which is measured as the portion of the actuarial present value of projected benefit payments attributable to past periods of employee service minus the pension plan's fiduciary net position. The net pension liability should be measured as of a date (the measurement date) which should be no earlier than the end of the employer's prior fiscal year, consistently applied from year to year.

In developing the net pension liability, the entity should use the following guidance:

1. The selection of all assumptions should be in conformity with Actuarial Standards of Practice issued by the Actuarial Standards Board.
2. The projected benefits payments should include all benefits to be provided to current active and inactive employees through the pension plan in accordance with the benefit terms and any additional legal agreements to provide benefits including automatic or substantially automatic postemployement benefit changes and cost-of-living adjustments (COLAs).
3. The discount rate should be the single rate that reflects (a) the long-term expected rate of return on pension plan investments expected to be used to finance the payment of benefits to the extent that the pension plan's fiduciary net position is projected to be sufficient to make the projected benefit payments and the pension plan assets are expected to be invested to achieve that return, or (b) the yield or index rate for 20-year, tax-exempt general obligation municipal bonds with an average rating of AA/Aa or higher to the extent the conditions in (a) are not met.
4. The entry age actuarial cost method should be used to attribute the actuarial present value of projected benefit payments of each employee to periods.

GASB No. 68 requires the recording of an amount for pension expense that includes recognition of annual service cost and interest on the pension liability along with the effect on the net pension liability of changes in benefit terms. Other components of pension expense (e.g., changes in economic and demographic assumptions, and differences between assumptions and actual experience) are recognized over a closed period that is determined by the average remaining service period of the plan members. The effects on the net pension liability of differences expected and actual investment returns in recognized in pension expense over a closed period of five-years.

If the government has a **cost-sharing defined benefit plan,** it must record a liability and expense equal to its proportionate share of the collective net pension liability and expense for the plan.

If the government has a **defined contribution plan,** pension expense should be accrued equal to the amount of contributions or credits to employees' accounts that are defined by the benefit terms as attributable to current period service, net of forfeited amounts that are removed from employees' accounts. The government should record a change in pension liability equal to the difference between amounts recognized as pension expense and the amounts paid by the employer to the pension plan.

GASB 68 requires extensive note disclosure and Required Supplementary Information (RSI), including:

1. Descriptive information about the types of benefits provided.
2. A statement of how contributions to the pension plan are determined.
3. The assumptions and methods used to calculate the pension liability.

Governments with single-employer or agent defined benefit plans must disclose additional information including: (a.) the composition of the employees covered by benefits terms, and (b.) sources of changes in the components of the net pension liability for the current year. Governments with these types of plans must also provide RSI schedules covering the past 10 years regarding

1. Sources of changes in the components of the net pension liability.
2. Ratios that assist in assessing the magnitude of the net pension liability.

3. Comparisons of actual employer contributions to the pension plan with actuarially determined contribution requirements.

Governments with cost-sharing pension plans must present an RSI schedule of net pension liability, information about contractually required contributions, and related ratios.

Certain governments are legally responsible for making contributions to pension plans on behalf of another government. For example a state may be legally obligated to contribute to a pension plan that covers local school districts' teachers. In these **special funding situations,** the nonemployer contributing government must recognize in its financial statements their proportionate share of the other government's net pension liability and pension expense.

> **NOW REVIEW MULTIPLE-CHOICE QUESTIONS 1 THROUGH 25**

G. Fund Financial Statements

In addition to government-wide statements, governmental accounting standards require a number of fund financial statements. Most governments use fund accounting internally and prepare the government-wide statements with worksheet adjustments from this fund accounting base. A fund is defined by the GASB as

A fiscal and accounting entity with a self-balancing set of accounts recording cash and other financial resources, together with all related liabilities and residual equities and balances, and changes therein, which are segregated for the purpose of carrying on specific activities or attaining certain objectives in accordance with special regulations, restrictions, or limitations.

Under GASB standards there are 11 fund types, which are classified into three general categories.

Governmental funds	**Proprietary funds**	**Fiduciary funds**
(1) General	(6) Internal service	(8) Agency
(2) Special revenue	(7) Enterprise	(9) Pension and other employee benefit trust funds
(3) Debt service		(10) Investment trust funds
(4) Capital projects		(11) Private-purpose trust funds
(5) Permanent		

Fund financial statements are presented separately for the governmental, proprietary, and fiduciary fund categories. Each government has only one general fund; each other fund type may have any number of individual funds, although GASB encourages having as few funds as possible. Fixed assets and long-term debt are not reported in the fund financial statements for governmental funds. Fixed assets and long-term debt related to governmental funds only are reported in the government-wide financial statements (statement of net position).

The fund financial statements for the governmental and enterprise fund categories report **major funds,** not all funds. The general fund is always a major fund. Other funds must be considered major when both of the following conditions exist: (1) total assets, liabilities, deferred inflows and outflows, revenues, expenditures/expenses of that individual governmental or enterprise fund constitute 10% of the governmental or enterprise category **and** (2) total assets, liabilities, deferred inflows and outflows, revenues, expenditures/expenses are 5% of the total of the governmental and enterprise category combined. In addition, a government may choose to call any fund major if it feels that reporting that fund would be useful.[1] In governmental and enterprise fund statements, the nonmajor funds are aggregated and reported as a single column. Combining statements for nonmajor funds are shown as "Other supplementary information" later in the financial section of CAFR. Internal service funds are reported in a single column on the proprietary fund statements.

Fiduciary fund financial statements report a separate column for fund type (agency, pension and other employee benefit trust, investment trust, and private purpose). If separate reports are not available for each pension trust fund, then the notes must disclose this information. If separate reports are available, then the notes must disclose how readers can obtain those reports.

A reconciliation between the information presented in the governmental fund financial statements and the governmental activities column of the government-wide financial statements is required either at the bottom of the fund fi-

---

[1] The determination of whether or not a fund is major or nonmajor can be illustrated by the HUD Programs Fund, shown in the governmental funds statements as a major fund. The first step is to determine whether or not the HUD Programs Fund is 10% of the governmental funds assets ($7,504,765/51,705,690 = 14.5%), liabilities ($6,428,389/16,812,584 = 38.3%), revenues ($2,731,473/97,482,467 = 2.80%), or expenditures ($2,954,389/121,332,470 = 2.44%). The first (10%) criterion is met for assets and liabilities but not for revenues and expenditures. As a result, the 5% test will be applied for assets and liabilities only. See the statements for governmental and proprietary funds. The assets do not qualify [$7,504,765/(51,705,690 + 165,404,18) = 3.45%]. However, the liabilities do exceed 5% [$6,428,389/(16,812,584 + 79,834,989) = 6.65%]. Thus, the HUD Programs Fund must be shown as a major fund.

nancial statements or in a schedule immediately following the fund financial statements. Explanations should either accompany the reconciliation or be in the notes.

Governmental funds focus on the current financial resources raised and expended to carry out general government purposes. Governmental funds include the general, special revenue, debt service, capital projects, and permanent funds. GASB Statement No. 54 provides definitions of the governmental fund types. The **General fund** accounts for and reports all financial resources except those required to be accounted for and reported in another fund. The general fund includes expenditures for functions such as general government, public safety, culture and recreation, public works and engineering, and other activities not set aside in other funds. **Special revenue funds** are used to account for and report specific revenue sources that are restricted or committed to expenditures for specified current purposes other than debt service and capital projects. An example would include a motor fuel tax limited by law to highway and street construction and repair. **Debt service funds** are used to account for and report financial resources that are restricted, committed, or assigned to expenditures for the payment of general long-term debt principal and interest. **Capital projects funds** are used to account for and report financial resources that are restricted, committed, or assigned to expenditures for capital outlays, including the acquisition or construction of capital facilities and other capital assets. Capital projects funds exclude capital-related outflows financed by proprietary funds or for assets that will be held in trust funds. **Permanent funds** are used to account for and report resources that are restricted to the extent that only earnings, and not principal, may be used to support government programs which benefit the government or its citizens. Permanent funds exclude private purpose trust funds which benefit individuals, private organizations, or other governments.

Financial statements required for governmental fund types include (1) **Balance Sheet** and (2) **Statement of Revenues, Expenditures, and Changes in Fund Balances**. Both of these are illustrated in this module. Governmental fund financial statements are prepared on the current financial resources measurement focus and modified accrual basis of accounting (see Section H., "Measurement Focus and Basis of Accounting"). Like the government-wide statement of net position, the balance sheet of a governmental fund would include deferred outflows of resources and deferred inflow of resources. GASB Statement No. 54 established fund balance classifications that are to be used by governmental funds based on the extent to which the government is obligated to observe constraints imposed upon the use of the resources. Fund balance classifications provided by GASB Statement No. 54 are nonspendable, restricted, committed, assigned and unassigned balances. The classifications are based on the relative strength of the constraints that control how specific amounts can be spent. The **nonspendable** fund balance classification includes amounts that cannot be spent because they are either (1) not in spendable form, or (2) they are legally or contractually required to be maintained intact. "Not in spendable form" includes items that are not expected to be converted to cash, such as inventories and prepaid amounts. It also includes the long-term amount of loans and notes receivable, as well as property acquired for resale. However, if the proceeds from collection of receivables or from the sale of property is restricted, committed, or assigned, the amounts should be included in the appropriate fund balance classification, rather than in the nonspendable fund balance. **Restricted** fund balances include amounts that are restricted to specific purposes and should be reported as restricted when constraints placed upon the resources are either: (1) externally imposed by creditors, contributors, or laws or regulations of other governments or (2) imposed by law through constitutional provisions or enabling legislation. **Committed** fund balances are amounts that can only be used for specific purposes pursuant to constraints imposed by formal action of the government's highest level of decision-making authority. The **assigned** classification of fund balance includes amounts that are constrained by the government's *intent* to be used for specific purposes but are neither restricted nor committed. It also includes any remaining positive amounts that are reported in governmental funds, other than the general fund, that are not classified as nonspendable, restricted, or committed and amounts in the general fund that are intended to be used for a specific purpose. To be classified as assigned "intent" should be expressed by (1) the governing body or (2) a body (i.e., budget or finance committee) or official who has the authority to assign amounts to be used for specific purposes. Finally, the **unassigned** fund balance is the residual classification for the general fund. The unassigned classification represents the fund balance that has not been assigned to other funds and that has not been restricted, committed, or assigned to specific purposes within the general fund. GASB Statement No. 54 indicates that the general fund should be the only fund that reports a positive unassigned fund balance amount. The balance sheet or the notes to the financial statements should disclose the details of the items in each of the five fund balance classifications. GASB Statement No. 54 indicates that *encumbrances* are not a specific purpose and should not be displayed as a separate item on the balance sheet but should be included in the appropriate fund balance classification based on the definition and criteria for fund balance classifications. Significant encumbrances should be disclosed in the notes to the financial statements in conjunction with disclosures of other significant commitments.

Note in the Statement of Revenues, Expenditures, and Changes in Fund Balances that revenues are reported by source, expenditures are reported by character (current, debt service, capital outlay) and then by function (general government, public safety, etc.). The category "other financing sources and uses" includes transfers between funds and proceeds from the issuance of long-term debt and proceeds from the sale of fixed assets. Special and extraordinary items are reported in this statement in the same manner as in the government-wide Statement of Activities, and reconciliation between the beginning and ending fund balance completes the statement. Interest expenditures related to fixed assets are **not** capitalized.

Sample City
STATEMENT OF ACTIVITIES
For the Year Ended December 31, 2013

Functions/Programs	Expenses	Program revenues — Charges for services	Program revenues — Operating grants and Contributions	Program revenues — Capital grants and contributions	Net (expense) revenue and changes in net position — Primary government — Governmental activities	Net (expense) revenue and changes in net position — Primary government — Business-type activities	Net (expense) revenue and changes in net position — Total	Net (expense) revenue and changes in net position — Component units
Primary government								
Governmental activities:								
General government	$ 9,571,410	$ 3,146,915	$ 843,617	$ —	$ (5,580,878)	$ —	$ (5,580,878)	$
Public safety	34,844,749	1,198,855	1,307,693	62,300	(32,275,901)	—	(32,275,901)	
Public works	10,128,538	850,000	—	2,252,615	(7,025,923)	—	(7,025,923)	
Engineering services	1,299,645	704,793	—	—	(594,852)	—	(594,852)	
Health and sanitation	6,738,672	5,612,267	575,000	—	(551,405)	—	(551,405)	
Cemetery	735,866	212,496	—	—	(523,370)	—	(523,370)	
Culture and recreation	11,532,350	3,995,199	2,450,000	—	(5,087,151)	—	(5,087,151)	
Community development	2,994,389	—	—	2,580,000	(414,389)	—	(414,389)	
Education (payment to school district)	21,893,273	—	—	—	(21,893,273)	—	(21,893,273)	
Interest on long-term debt	6,068,121	—	—	—	(6,068,121)	—	(6,068,121)	
Total governmental activities	105,807,013	15,720,525	5,176,310	4,894,915	(80,015,263)	—	(80,015,263)	
Business-type activities:								
Water	3,595,733	4,159,350	—	1,159,909	—	1,723,526	1,723,526	
Sewer	4,912,853	7,170,533	—	486,010	—	2,743,690	2,743,690	
Parking facilities	2,796,283	1,344,087	—	—	—	(1,452,196)	(1,452,196)	
Total business-type activities	11,304,869	12,673,970	—	1,645,919	—	3,015,020	3,015,020	
Total primary government	$117,111,882	$28,394,495	$5,176,310	$6,540,834	(80,015,263)	3,015,020	(77,000,243)	
Component units								
Landfill	$ 3,382,157	$ 3,857,858	$ —	$ 11,397				487,098
Public school system	31,186,498	705,765	3,937,083	—				(26,543,650)
Total component units	$ 34,568,655	$ 4,563,623	$3,937,083	$ 11,397				$(26,056,552)
General revenues:								
Taxes:								
Property taxes, levied for general purposes					51,693,573		51,693,573	
Property taxes, levied for debt service					4,726,244		4,726,244	
Franchise taxes					4,055,505		4,055,505	
Public service taxes					8,969,887		8,969,887	
Payment from Sample City								21,893,273
Grants and contributions not restricted to specific programs					1,457,820		1,457,820	6,461,708
Investment earnings					1,958,144	601,349	2,559,493	881,763
Miscellaneous					884,907	104,925	989,832	22,464
Special item—gain on sale of park land					2,653,488		2,653,488	
Transfers					501,409	(501,409)	—	
Total general revenues, special items, and transfers					76,900,977	204,865	77,105,842	29,259,208
Change in net position					(3,114,286)	3,219,885	105,599	3,202,656
Net position—beginning					126,656,860	82,376,829	209,033,689	16,025,971
Net position—ending					$123,542,574	$85,596,714	$209,139,288	$ 19,228,627

The detail presented for government activities represents the *minimum* requirement.
Governments are encouraged to provide more details—for example, police, fire, EMS, and inspections—rather than simply "public safety."

SOURCE: Revised from GASB 34, pp. 208-9.

Proprietary funds focus on total economic resources, income determination, and cash flow presentation. Proprietary funds include internal service funds (which are reported as governmental activities in the government-wide financial statements) and enterprise funds (which are considered business-type activities in the government-wide financial statements). **Internal service funds** report any activity that provides goods or services to other funds of the primary government on a cost-reimbursement basis. Examples might include print shops, motor pools, and self-insurance activities. Internal service funds may incidentally provide services to other governments on a cost-reimbursement basis. **Enterprise funds** may be used to provide goods or services to external users for a fee. Enterprise funds must be used if (1) the activity is financed with debt that is secured solely by a pledge of the net revenues from fees and charges of that activity, (2) laws or regulations require that the activity's cost of providing services be recovered with fees and charges, rather than from taxes or similar revenues, or (3) the pricing policies of the activity establish fees and charges designed to cover its costs including capital costs (e.g., depreciation and debt service). Examples of enterprise funds would include water utilities, airports, and swimming pools.

Statements required for proprietary funds include (1) **Statement of Net Position,** (2) **Statement of Revenues, Expenses, and Changes in Fund Net Position,** and (3) **Statement of Cash Flows**. These statements are all included in this module. Note that the Statement of Net Position is prepared in the same "Assets + Deferred Outflows of Resources – Liabilities – Deferred Inflows of Resources = Net Position" format as the Statement of Net Position in the government-wide financial statements. GASB permits the more traditional balance sheet format, "Assets + Deferred Outflows of Resources = Liabilities + Deferred Inflows of Resources + Net Position" for this proprietary funds statement. The net position category has the same breakdown as the government-wide statement of net positions, "net investment in capital assets," "restricted (distinguishing between major categories of restrictions)," and "unrestricted." Note also that the internal service funds are shown separately to the right as a fund type in the proprietary fund financial statements, with all internal service funds grouped together. A classified format, with current and noncurrent assets and liabilities shown separately, is required by GASB for the proprietary fund statement of net position (or balance sheet).

The Statement of Revenues, Expenses, and Changes in Fund Net Position is an all-inclusive operating statement, with a reconciliation of the beginning and ending fund net position as the last item. Major enterprise funds are shown, along with a total of all enterprise fund activity, and the total of internal service funds is shown separately. GASB standards require an operating income figure, with operating revenues and expenses shown separately from nonoperating revenues and expenses. Capital contributions, transfers, extraordinary items, and special items are to be shown after the nonoperating revenues and expenses. GASB requires that depreciation be shown separately as an operating expense and that interest be shown as a nonoperating expense. Interest expense related to fixed assets is capitalized.

The Statement of Cash Flows is prepared in accord with the requirements of GASB Statement No. 9, as modified by GASB Statement No. 34, and contains several major differences from the familiar business cash flow statement required by FASB. First, only the direct method is acceptable, and reconciliation is required. Second, the reconciliation is from operating income to net cash flow from operating activities, not from net income as required by FASB. Third, GASB has four categories instead of the three required by FASB. The four categories of activities used are operating, noncapital financing, capital and related financing, and investing. Fourth, cash receipts from interest are classified as investing, not operating activities. Fifth, cash payments for interest are classified as financing (either noncapital or capital and related), not as operating activities. Finally, purchases of capital assets (resources provided by financing activities) are considered financing, not investing, activities.

Sample City
BALANCE SHEET
GOVERNMENTAL FUNDS
December 31, 2013

	General	HUD programs	Community redevelopment	Route 7 construction	Other governmental funds	Total governmental funds
Assets						
Cash and cash equivalents	$3,418,485	$1,236,523	$ —	$ —	$ 5,606,792	$10,261,800
Investments	—	—	13,262,695	10,467,037	3,485,252	27,214,984
Receivables, net	3,644,561	2,953,438	353,340	11,000	10,221	6,972,560
Due from other funds	1,370,757	—	—	—	—	1,370,757
Receivables from other governments	—	119,059	—	—	1,596,038	1,715,097
Liens receivable	791,926	3,195,745	—	—	—	3,987,671
Inventories	182,821	—	—	—	—	182,821
Total assets	$9,408,550	$7,504,765	$13,616,035	$10,478,037	$10,698,303	$51,705,690
Liabilities and fund balances						
Liabilities						
Accounts payable	$3,408,680	$129,975	$ 190,548	$ 1,104,632	$ 1,074,831	$ 5,908,666
Due to other funds	—	25,369	—	—	—	25,369
Payable to other governments	94,074	—	—	—	—	94,074
Total liabilities	3,502,754	155,344	190,548	1,104,632	1,074,831	6,028,109
Deferred inflows	4,266,730	6,273,045	250,000	11,000	—	10,800,775
Fund balances						
Nonspendable	958,447	—	—	—	—	958,447
Restricted	—	—	100,000	—	—	100,000
Committed	40,292	41,034	19,314	5,792,587	1,814,122	7,707,349
Assigned	—	1,035,342	13,056,173	3,569,818	7,809,350	25,470,683
Unassigned	640,327	—	—	—	—	640,327
Total fund balances	$1,639,066	$1,076,376	$13,175,487	$ 9,362,405	$ 9,623,472	$34,876,806

Amounts reported for governmental activities in the statement of net position are different because:

Capital assets used in governmental activities are not financial resources and therefore are not reported in the funds. 161,082,708

Other long-term assets are not available to pay for current-period expenditures and therefore are deferred in the funds. 9,348,876

Internal service funds are used by management to charge the costs of certain activities, such as insurance and telecommunications, to individual funds. The assets and liabilities of the internal service funds are included in governmental activities in the statement of net position. 2,994,691

Long-term liabilities, including bonds payable, are not due and payable in the current period and therefore are not reported in the funds. .... (84,760,507)

Net position of governmental activities $123,542,574

SOURCE: Revised from GASB 34, pp. 220-1.

Sample City

STATEMENT OF REVENUES, EXPENDITURES, AND CHANGES IN FUND BALANCES
GOVERNMENTAL FUNDS
For the Year Ended December 31, 2013

	General	HUD programs	Community redevelopment	Route 7 construction	Other governmental funds	Total governmental funds
Revenues						
Property taxes	$51,173,436	$ —	$ —	$ —	$ 4,680,192	$ 55,853,628
Franchise taxes	4,055,505	—	—	—	—	4,055,505
Public service taxes	8,969,887	—	—	—	—	8,969,887
Fees and fines	606,946	—	—	—	—	606,946
Licenses and permits	2,287,794	—	—	—	—	2,287,794
Intergovernmental	6,119,938	2,578,191	—	—	2,830,916	11,529,045
Charges for services	11,374,460	—	—	—	30,708	11,405,168
Investment earnings	552,325	87,106	549,489	270,161	364,330	1,823,411
Miscellaneous	881,874	66,176	—	2,939	94	951,083
Total revenues	86,022,165	2,731,473	549,489	273,100	7,906,240	97,482,467
Expenditures						
Current						
General government	8,630,835	—	417,814	16,700	121,052	9,186,401
Public safety	33,729,623	—	—	—	—	33,729,623
Public works	4,975,775	—	—	—	3,721,542	8,697,317
Engineering services	1,299,645	—	—	—	—	1,299,645
Health and sanitation	6,070,032	—	—	—	—	6,070,032
Cemetery	706,305	—	—	—	—	706,305
Culture and recreation	11,411,685	—	—	—	—	11,411,685
Community development	—	2,954,389	—	—	—	2,954,389
Education—payment to school district	21,893,273	—	—	—	—	21,893,273
Debt service						
Principal	—	—	—	—	3,450,000	3,450,000
Interest and other charges	—	—	—	—	5,215,151	5,215,151
Capital outlay	—	—	2,246,671	11,281,769	3,190,209	16,718,649
Total expenditures	88,717,173	2,954,389	2,664,485	11,298,469	15,697,954	121,332,470
Excess (deficiency) of revenues over expenditures	(2,695,008)	(222,916)	(2,114,996)	(11,025,369)	(7,791,714)	(23,850,003)
Other Financing Sources (Uses)						
Proceeds of refunding bonds	—	—	—	—	38,045,000	38,045,000
Proceeds of long-term capital-related debt	—	—	17,529,560	—	1,300,000	18,829,560
Payment to bond refunding escrow agent	—	—	—	—	(37,284,144)	(37,284,144)
Transfers in	129,323	—	—	—	5,551,187	5,680,510
Transfers out	(2,163,759)	(348,046)	(2,273,187)	—	(219,076)	(5,004,068)
Total other financing sources and uses	(2,034,436)	(348,046)	15,256,373	—	7,392,967	20,266,858
Special Item						
Proceeds from sale of park land	3,476,488	—	—	—	—	3,476,488
Net change in fund balances	(1,252,956)	(570,962)	13,141,377	(11,025,369)	(398,747)	(106,657)
Fund balances—beginning	2,908,322	1,647,338	34,110	20,387,774	10,022,219	34,999,763
Fund balances—ending	$ 1,655,366	$1,076,376	$13,175,487	$ 9,362,405	$ 9,623,472	$ 34,893,106

SOURCE: GASB 34, pp. 222-3

Sample City
STATEMENT OF NET POSITION
PROPRIETARY FUNDS
December 31, 2013

> This statement illustrates the "net position" format; the "balance sheet" format also is permitted. Classification of assets and liabilities is required in either case.

	Business-type activities—enterprise funds			Governmental activities—internal Service funds
	Water and sewer	Parking facilities	Totals	
Assets				
Current assets:				
Cash and cash equivalents	$ 8,416,653	$ 369,168	$ 8,785,821	$ 3,336,099
Investments	--	--	--	150,237
Receivables, net	3,564,586	3,535	3,568,121	157,804
Due from other governments	41,494	--	41,494	--
Inventories	126,674	--	126,674	139,328
Total current assets	12,149,407	372,703	12,522,110	3,783,468
Noncurrent assets:				
Restricted cash and cash equivalents	--	1,493,322	1,493,322	--
Capital assets:				
Land	813,513	3,021,637	3,835,150	--
Distribution and collection systems	39,504,183	--	39,504,183	--
Buildings and equipment	106,135,666	23,029,166	129,164,832	14,721,786
Less accumulated depreciation	(15,328,911)	(5,786,503)	(21,115,414)	(5,781,734)
Total noncurrent assets	131,124,451	21,757,622	152,882,073	8,940,052
Total assets	143,273,858	22,130,325	165,404,183	12,723,520
Deferred outflow				
Payment to receive rights to future parking revenue		27,520	27,520	
Liabilities				
Current liabilities:				
Accounts payable	447,427	304,003	751,430	780,570
Due to other funds	175,000	--	175,000	1,170,388
Compensated absences	112,850	8,827	121,677	237,690
Claims and judgments	--	--	--	1,687,975
Bonds, notes, and loans payable	3,944,609	360,000	4,304,609	249,306
Total current liabilities	4,679,886	672,830	5,352,716	4,125,929
Noncurrent liabilities:				
Compensated absences	451,399	35,306	486,705	--
Claims and judgments	--	--	--	5,602,900
Bonds, notes, and loans payable	54,451,549	19,544,019	73,995,568	--
Total noncurrent liabilities	54,902,948	19,579,325	74,482,273	5,602,900
Total liabilities	59,582,834	20,252,155	79,834,989	9,728,829
Net Position				
Net investment in capital assets	72,728,293	360,281	73,088,574	8,690,746
Restricted for debt service	--	1,451,996	1,451,996	--
Unrestricted	10,962,731	93,413	11,056,144	(5,696,055)
Total net position	$ 83,691,024	$ 1,905,690	$ 85,596,714	$ 2,994,691

SOURCE: Revised from GASB 34, page 227.

Fiduciary fund financial statements provide information, based on the economic resources measurement focus and accrual accounting, on resources held and used by governments for the benefit of individuals and entities other than the government. Fiduciary fund statements are the Statement of Fiduciary Net Position and the Statement of Changes in Fiduciary Net Position. Unlike the statements for the governmental and enterprise fund categories, fiduciary fund statements report totals for each of the four fund types. The fiduciary fund types are (1) pension (and other employee benefit) trust funds, (2) investment trust funds, (3) private-purpose trust funds, and (4) agency funds. However, each individual pension or employee benefit trust fund report must be reported in the notes if separate reports have not been issued. If separate reports have been issued, the notes to the financial statement must indicate how the reader might obtain such reports.

Pension (and other employee benefit) trust funds account for funds held in trust for the payment of employee retirement and other benefits. Accounting for these plans is covered by GASB Statement Nos. 25, 43, 50, and 57 (as amended by GASB 67). **Investment trust funds** are used to report the external portions of investment pools, when the reporting government is trustee. **Private-purpose trust funds** should be used to report all other trust arrangements where the principal must remain intact and the income generated is used to benefit individuals, private organizations, and other governments. An example would be a fund to report scholarship funds contributed by individuals and businesses, by a public school system. Finally, **agency funds** report resources held by the reporting government in a purely custodial capacity. Agency funds report only assets and liabilities and are not included in the Statement of Changes in Fiduciary Net Position.

Sample City
STATEMENT OF REVENUES, EXPENSES, AND CHANGES IN FUND NET POSITION
PROPRIETARY FUNDS
For the Year Ended December 31, 2013

Business-type activities—enterprise funds

	Water and sewer	Parking facilities	Totals	Governmental activities—internal service funds
Operating revenues:				
Charges for service	$11,329,883	$ 1,340,261	$12,670,144	$15,256,164
Miscellaneous	--	3,826	3,826	1,066,761
Total operating revenues	11,329,883	1,344,087	12,673,970	16,322,925
Operating expenses:				
Personal services	3,400,559	762,348	4,162,907	4,157,156
Contractual services	344,422	96,032	440,454	584,396
Utilities	754,107	100,726	854,833	214,812
Repairs and maintenance	747,315	64,617	811,932	1,960,490
Other supplies and expenses	498,213	17,119	515,332	234,445
Insurance claims and expenses	--	--	--	8,004,286
Depreciation	1,163,140	542,049	1,705,189	1,707,872
Total operating expenses	6,907,756	1,582,891	8,490,647	$16,863,457
Operating income (loss)	4,422,127	(238,804)	4,183,323	(540,532)
Nonoperating revenues (expenses):				
Interest and investment revenue	454,793	146,556	601,349	134,733
Miscellaneous revenue	--	104,925	104,925	20,855
Interest expense	(1,600,830)	(1,166,546)	(2,767,376)	(41,616)
Miscellaneous expense	--	(46,846)	(46,846)	(176,003)
Total nonoperating revenues (expenses)	(1,146,037)	(961,911)	(2,107,948)	(62,031)
Income (loss) before contributions and transfers	3,276,090	(1,200,715)	2,075,375	(602,563)
Capital contributions	1,645,919	--	1,645,919	18,788
Transfers out	(290,000)	(211,409)	(501,409)	(175,033)
Change in net position	4,632,009	(1,412,124)	3,219,885	(758,808)
Total net position—beginning	79,059,015	3,377,814	82,376,944	3,753,499
Total net position—ending	$83,691,024	$ 1,905,690	$85,596,714	$ 2,994,691

SOURCE: Revised from GASB 34, page 229.

The statements required for fiduciary funds are the **Statement of Fiduciary Net Position** and **Statement of Changes in Fiduciary Net Position**. Examples of these statements are reflected in this module. The Statement of Fiduciary Net Position is prepared in the form "Assets + Deferred Outflows of Resources – Liabilities – Deferred Inflows of Resources = Net Position." Columns are included for each fund type. The Statement of Changes in Fiduciary Net Position uses the terms "additions" and "deductions" instead of revenues and expenses, but the additions and deductions are computed on the full accrual basis. This, like all other GASB operating statements, is an "all-inclusive" statement with reconciliation of the beginning and ending net position at the bottom of the statement. Note that agency funds have only assets and liabilities (assets = liabilities) and are not reported in the Statement of Changes in Fiduciary Net Position.

H. Notes to the Financial Statements

Note disclosure requirements are found in the GASB *Codification* Section 2300 and in GASB Statement Nos. 34, 38, 40, 67, and 68. Some of the major disclosures are (1) a summary of accounting policies, (2) a description of the reporting entity, (3) disclosures on cash and investments (including securitization), (4) information relating to fixed assets, long-term debt, pensions, commitments and contingencies, (5) information on exceeding the budget at the legal level of control, (6) disclosures of individual funds with deficit fund balances, and (7) risks related to deposits and investments. Some disclosures brought about by GASB Statement No. 34 include a description of the government-wide financial statements, the policy for capitalizing fixed assets and estimating useful lives, segment information for enterprise funds, and the policy for recording infrastructure, including the use of the modified approach, if applicable.

Sample City
STATEMENT OF CASH FLOWS
PROPRIETARY FUNDS
For the Year Ended December 31, 2013

	Business-type activities—enterprise funds			Governmental activities—internal service funds
	Water and sewer	Parking facilities	Totals	
Cash flows from operating activities				
Receipts from customers	$11,400,200	$ 1,345,292	$ 12,745,492	$15,326,343
Payments to suppliers	(2,725,349)	(365,137)	(3,090,486)	(2,812,238)
Payments to employees	(3,360,055)	(750,828)	(4,110,883)	(4,209,688)
Internal activity—payments to other funds	(1,296,768)	—	(1,296,768)	—
Claims paid	—	—	—	(8,482,451)
Other receipts (payments)	(2,325,483)	—	(2,325,483)	1,061,118
Net cash provided by operating activities	1,692,545	229,327	1,921,872	883,084
Cash flows from noncapital financing activities				
Operating subsidies and transfers to other funds	(290,000)	(211,409)	(501,409)	(175,033)
Cash flows from capital and related financing activities				
Proceeds from capital debt	4,041,322	8,660,778	12,702,100	—
Capital contributions	1,645,919	—	1,645,919	—
Purchases of capital assets	(4,194,035)	(144,716)	(4,338,751)	(400,086)
Principal paid on capital debt	(2,178,491)	(8,895,000)	(11,073,491)	(954,137)
Interest paid on capital debt	(1,479,708)	(1,166,546)	(2,646,254)	41,616
Other receipts (payments)	—	19,174	19,174	131,416
Net cash (used) by capital and related financing activities	(2,164,993)	(1,526,310)	(3,691,303)	(1,264,423)
Cash flows from investing activities				
Proceeds from sales and maturities of investments	—	—	—	15,684
Interest and dividends	454,793	143,747	598,540	129,550
Net cash provided by investing activities	454,793	143,747	598,540	145,234
Net (decrease) in cash and cash equivalents	(307,655)	(1,364,645)	(1,672,300)	(411,138)
Balances—beginning of the year	8,724,308	3,227,135	11,951,443	3,747,237
Balances—end of the year	$ 8,416,653	$ 1,862,490	$ 10,279,143	$ 3,336,099
Reconciliation of operating income (loss) to net cash provided (used) by operating activities				
Operating income (loss)	$ 4,422,127	$ (238,804)	$ 4,183,323	$ (540,532)
Adjustments to reconcile operating income to net cash provided (used) by operating activities:				
Depreciation expense	1,163,140	542,049	1,705,189	1,707,872
Change in assets and liabilities:				
Receivables, net	653,264	1,205	654,469	31,941
Inventories	2,829	—	2,829	39,790
Accounts and other payables	(297,446)	(86,643)	(384,089)	475,212
Accrued expenses	(4,251,369)	(11,520)	(4,239,849)	(831,199)
Net cash provided by operating activities	$ 1,692,545	$ 229,327	$ 1,921,872	$ 883,084

SOURCE: GASB 34, pp. 230–231

I. Required Supplementary Information (RSI) other than MD&A

GASB requires four types of information that should be included immediately after the notes to the financial statements. These four items, along with MD & A (see Section C) are considered Required Supplementary Information (RSI). RSI is information presented outside the basic financial statements. While RSI is not covered in the audit opinion, omission of RSI, incomplete RSI, or misleading RSI requires a comment by the auditor. However, an auditor may not modify the report on the basic financial statements as a result of problems discovered related to RSI.

The four types of RSI other than MD&A are (1) pension schedules, (2) schedules when the government sponsors a public entity risk pool, (3) budgetary comparison schedules, and (4) certain schedules when using the modified approach for reporting infrastructure. The pension schedules vary depending on the nature of the plan as described previously.

The second type of schedule required when the government is sponsor of a public entity risk pool provides revenue and claims development information.

Sample City
STATEMENT OF FIDUCIARY NET POSITION
FIDUCIARY FUNDS
December 31, 2013

	Employee retirement plan	Private- purpose trusts	Agency funds
Assets			
Cash and cash equivalents	$ 1,973	$ 1,250	$ 44,889
Receivables:			
Interest and dividends	508,475	760	--
Other receivables	6,826	--	183,161
Total receivables	515,301	760	183,161
Investments, at fair value:			
US government obligations	13,056,037	80,000	--
Municipal bonds	6,528,019	--	--
Corporate bonds	16,320,047	--	--
Corporate stocks	26,112,075	--	--
Other investments	3,264,009	--	--
Total investments	65,280,187	80,000	--
Total assets	65,797,461	82,010	$228,050
Liabilities			
Accounts payable	--	1,234	--
Refunds payable and others	1,358	--	228,050
Total liabilities	1,358	1,234	$228,050
Net Position			
Held in trust for pension benefits and other purposes	$65,796,103	$80,776	

SOURCE: GASB 34, page 235.

Sample City
STATEMENT OF CHANGES IN FIDUCIARY NET POSITION
FIDUCIARY FUNDS
For the Year Ended December 31, 2013

	Employee retirement plan	Private-purpose trusts
Additions		
Contributions:		
Employer	$ 2,721,341	$ --
Plan members	1,421,233	--
Total contributions	4,142,574	--
Investment earnings:		
Net (decrease) in fair value of investments	(272,522)	--
Interest	2,460,871	4,560
Dividends	1,445,273	--
Total investment earnings	3,633,622	4,560
Less investment expense	216,428	--
Net investment earnings	3,417,194	4,560
Total additions	7,559,768	4,560

	Employee retirement plan	Private-purpose trusts
Deductions		
Benefits	2,453,047	3,800
Refunds of contributions	464,691	--
Administrative expenses	87,532	678
Total deductions	3,005,270	4,478
Change in net position	4,554,498	82
Net position—beginning of the year	61,241,605	80,694
Net position—end of the year	$65,796,103	$80,776

SOURCE: GASB 34, pages 235-236.

The third type of information is to provide **budgetary comparison schedules** for the general fund and all major special revenue funds for which an annual budget has been legally adopted by the governmental unit. Governments may elect to report the budgetary comparison information in a budgetary comparison statement as part of the basic financial statements, rather than as RSI. If the government has significant budgetary perspective differences that result in it not being able to present budgetary comparison information for its general fund and major special revenue funds, the government must present a budget comparison schedule based on the structure of its legally adopted budget. Budgetary comparison schedules include the original budget, the final appropriated budget, and the actual revenues and expenditures stated on the budgetary basis. A separate variance column to report the differences between the final budget and actual amounts is encouraged but not required. The format may be that of the original budget document or in the format, terminology, and classifications in the Statement of Revenues, Expenditures, and Changes in Fund Balances. Information must be provided, either in this schedule or in notes to the RSI, that reconciles budgetary information basis to GAAP information. An example of a Budget—Actual Statement is included below.

Sample City
STATEMENT OF REVENUES, EXPENDITURES, AND CHANGES IN FUND BALANCES—
BUDGET AND ACTUAL
GENERAL FUND
For the Year Ended December 31, 2013

	Budgeted amounts		Actual amounts
Revenues	Original	Final	(budgetary basis)
Property taxes	$52,017,833	$51,853,018	$51,173,436
Other taxes—franchise and public service	12,841,209	12,836,024	13,025,392
Fees and fines	718,800	718,800	606,946
Licenses and permits	2,126,600	2,126,600	2,287,794
Intergovernmental	6,905,898	6,571,360	6,119,938
Charges for services	12,392,972	11,202,150	11,374,460
Interest	1,501,945	550,000	552,325
Miscellaneous	3,024,292	1,220,991	881,874
Total revenues	91,043,549	87,078,943	86,022,165
Expenditures			
Current			
General government (including contingencies and miscellaneous)	11,837,534	9,468,155	8,621,500
Public safety	33,050,966	33,983,706	33,799,709
Public works	5,215,630	5,025,848	4,993,187
Engineering services	1,296,275	1,296,990	1,296,990
Health and sanitation	5,756,250	6,174,653	6,174,653
Cemetery	724,500	724,500	706,305
Culture and recreation	11,059,140	11,368,070	11,289,146
Education—payment to school district	22,000,000	22,000,000	21,893,273
Total expenditures	90,940,295	90,041,922	88,774,763
Excess (deficiency) of revenues over expenditures	103,254	(2,962,979)	(2,752,598)
Other Financing Sources (Uses)			
Transfers in	939,525	130,000	129,323
Transfers out	(2,970,256)	(2,163,759)	(2,163,759)
Total other financing sources and uses	(2,030,731)	(2,033,759)	(2,034,436)
Special Item			
Proceeds from sale of park land	1,355,250	3,500,000	3,476,488
Net change in fund balance	(572,227)	(1,496,738)	(1,310,546)
Fund balances—beginning	3,528,750	2,742,799	2,742,799
Fund balances—ending	$ 2,956,523	$ 1,246,061	$ 1,432,253

SOURCE: GASB 34, pages 272-273. Budget to GAAP Reconciliation Omitted.

The fourth type of information is presented only when the government is using the **modified approach for reporting infrastructure**. Governments have the option of not depreciating their infrastructure assets if they adopt the "modified" approach for recording infrastructure. Two requirements must be met to adopt this approach. First, the government must manage the eligible infrastructure assets using an asset management system that has certain characteristics. These characteristics include (1) keeping an up-to-date inventory of infrastructure assets, (2) performing condition assessments of eligible infrastructure assets, summarizing the results using a measurement scale, and (3) estimating the costs each year to preserve the infrastructure assets at the condition level established and disclosed by the government. Second, the government must document that the infrastructure assets have been preserved at the condition level prescribed by the government. Two schedules are required: (1) a schedule reflecting the condition of the government's infrastructure, and (2) a comparison of the needed and actual expenditures to maintain the government's infrastructure. Disclosures that should be included in notes to the RSI are (1) the basis of the condition measurement and the measurement scale used to assess and report the condition of the government's infrastructure assets, (2) the condition level at which the government intends to preserve its eligible infrastructure assets reported using the modified approach, and (3) factors that significantly affect trends in the information reported in the required schedules.

An example is provided to illustrate the difference between the "depreciation approach" and the "modified approach" to record infrastructure. Assume a government had $1,000,000 in ordinary maintenance expenses, $2,000,000 in expenditures to extend the life of existing infrastructure, and $3,000,000 in expenditures to add to or improve existing infrastructure. Depreciation (if recorded) amounted to $2,500,000. If the "depreciation approach" were used, $3,500,000 would be charged to expense ($1,000,000 + $2,500,000). If the modified approach were used, the amount charged to expense would be $3,000,000 ($1,000,000 + $2,000,000). In both cases, the $1,000,000 would be charged to expense, and the $3,000,000 would be capitalized. Under the "modified approach," the $2,000,000 in expenditures to extend the life of infrastructure is substituted for depreciation expense.

J. Measurement Focus and Basis of Accounting (MFBA)

GASB Standards require two types of measurement focus: *economic resources measurement focus and current financial resources measurement focus* and two types of basis of accounting: *accrual and modified accrual*. The measurement focus and basis of accounting varies depending upon the financial statement being reported. **The economic resources measurement focus and accrual basis of accounting** is a method similar to accounting for business enterprises. The objective is to measure all of the economic resources available to the governmental entity, including fixed assets and subtracting long-term debt. Full accrual accounting is used, where revenues are recognized when earned and expenses are recognized when incurred. Fixed assets are recorded and depreciated. The economic resources measurement focus and accrual basis of accounting is used for the government-wide statements, the proprietary fund statements, and the fiduciary fund statements.

The objective of the **current financial resources measurement focus and modified accrual basis of accounting** is to measure only the current financial resources available to the governmental entity. As a result governmental funds (i.e., general fund) do not account for fixed assets or long-term debt within the fund. Modified accrual accounting is used by governmental funds. Under modified accrual accounting, revenues are recognized when measurable and available to finance expenditures of the current period. Property taxes may be considered "available" when collected within sixty days of the end of the fiscal year. The recognition of expenditures (not expenses) is modified in the following way. First, expenditures may be recorded for current items (salaries, supplies), capital outlays (purchase of a police car, construction expenditures), or debt service (matured interest, matured principal). Second, payment of principal and interest on long-term indebtedness, including bonds, notes, capital leases, compensated absences, claims and judgments, pensions, special termination benefits, and landfill closure and postclosure care are recorded when due, rather than accrued. However, a government may accrue an additional amount if it has provided financial resources to a debt service fund for payment of liabilities that will mature early in the following period (not more than a month). As noted previously, the current financial resources measurement focus and modified accrual basis of accounting are used in the governmental fund financial statements and will be illustrated later.

> **NOW REVIEW MULTIPLE-CHOICE QUESTIONS 26 THROUGH 53**

K. Accounting by Governments for Certain Events and Transactions

1. **Accounting for nonexchange transactions.** The previous section indicated that, under the accrual basis of accounting, revenues are recognized when earned. Revenues and inflows of resources include **exchange transactions**, in which goods or services of equal or approximately equal values are exchanged, and **nonexchange transactions**. GASB indicates that revenues from exchange transactions are to be recognized in accordance with generally accepted accounting principles as those principles have evolved over the years and provides no special guidance. However, GASB Statement No. 33, *Accounting and Financial Reporting for Nonexchange Transactions*, defines nonexchange transactions as transactions "in which a government gives (or receives) value without directly receiving (or giving) equal value in exchange." GASB Statement No. 33 is written under the presumption that an entity is following full accrual accounting. When governmental fund financial statements are issued, modified accrual accounting "modifies" the provisions of GASB Statement No. 33 to require that resources must be measurable and available to finance the expenditures of the current period, as described in Section H. above.

GASB Statement No. 33 classifies nonexchange transactions into four categories, and revenue recognition depends upon the category. The categories are: (1) derived tax revenues, (2) imposed nonexchange revenues, (3) government-mandated nonexchange transactions, and (4) voluntary nonexchange transactions. For the government-wide financial statements, revenue from nonexchange transactions is considered to be an increase in unrestricted net position unless the revenue is restricted by the grantor, donor, or legislation. For example, a hotel-motel tax may have to be used, by legislation, for promotion of tourism. Purpose restrictions do not affect the timing of revenue recognition.

In order for a receivable and revenue to be recognized, four types of **eligibility requirements** must be met. First is the **required characteristics of the recipients**. The recipient of resources must have the characteristics required by the provider. For example, the recipient of certain state funds allocated for road repairs may have to be a county government, a municipality, or a township. Second, **time requirements** must be met, if a provider specifies that resources must be expended in a certain future period. For example, if a state indicates that funds are appropriated for water system improvements for the fiscal year ended June 30, 2012, then neither a receivable nor revenue would be recognized by the local governments receiving the funds until that fiscal year. In the absence of specified time requirements, a receivable and revenue would be recognized when a promise is unconditional. Third, certain grants from one government to another cannot be provided until the receiving government has expended the funds. This is a condition the GASB calls a **reimbursement**. Reimbursement grant revenues are recognized only when expenditures are recognized. Finally, resources pledged that have a **contingency** attached are not to be recognized until that contingency is removed.

Derived tax revenues result from taxes assessed by governments on exchange transactions. Examples include sales taxes, income taxes, and motor fuel taxes. Receivables and revenues are to be recognized when the underlying transaction (the sale, the income, etc.) takes place. For example, under accrual accounting, if a state imposed a sales tax of 6%, the state would record a revenue of $6 when a merchant recorded a sale of $100. If resources are received before the underlying transaction takes place, then the asset would be offset by revenues received in advance, a liability.

Imposed nonexchange transactions are taxes and other assessments by governments that are not derived from underlying transactions. Examples include property taxes, special assessments, and fines and forfeits. Assets from imposed nonexchange transactions should be recognized when an enforceable legal claim exists, or when the resources are received, whichever occurs first. In the case of property taxes, this would normally be specified in the enabling legislation, such as the lien or assessment date. Revenues for property taxes should be recognized, net of estimated refunds and estimated uncollectible taxes, in the period for which the taxes are levied, regardless of when the enforcement date or collection date might be. All other imposed nonexchange transactions should be recognized as revenues at the same time as the assets, or as soon as use is first permitted. On the modified accrual basis, property taxes may not be recognized unless collected within sixty days after the end of a fiscal year.

Government-mandated nonexchange transactions exist when the providing government, such as the federal government or a state government, requires the receiving government to expend funds for a specific purpose. For example, a state may require school districts to "mainstream" certain children by including them in regular classes and also to provide additional assistance in the form of extra aides. Funding for this purpose would be considered to be a government-mandated nonexchange transaction. Receiving governments should recognize assets and revenues when all eligibility requirements have been met.

Voluntary nonexchange transactions include grants and entitlements from one government to another where the providing government does not impose specific requirements upon the receiving government. For example, a state provides a grant for new technology for school districts but does not require those school districts to accept the grant or utilize that technology. Even though the use of the grant is restricted, it is a voluntary nonexchange transaction. It also includes voluntary contributions from individuals and other entities to governments. An example of this type of transaction would be the gift of funds from an individual to a school district or a college. Voluntary nonexchange transactions may or may not have purpose restrictions. The recognition of assets and revenues would be when all eligibility requirements have been met, the same as government-mandated nonexchange transactions.

If after a revenue has been recognized by a governmental entity (in a later fiscal year), and those funds must be returned to the provider, then the recipient government must record an expense and liability (or reduction of cash). If there is a difference in the provider government's and recipient government's fiscal year, then the provider's fiscal year would govern for purposes of determining eligibility requirements. If the providing government, a state, has a biennial fiscal year, then half of the grant would be recognized by the recipient government in each of the providing government's two fiscal years.

2. **Accounting for intangible assets.** GASB Statement No. 51, *Accounting and Financial Reporting for Intangible Assets,* allows only **identifiable** intangible assets to be recognized as capital assets in the statement of net position (at historical cost). Costs related to internally generated intangibles (e.g., proprietary software systems) may begin to be capitalized when

a. The government's specific **objective** for the project and the proposed **service capacity** has been determined,
b. The **feasibility** of completing the project has been demonstrated, and
c. The government's **intention** to complete or to continue the development of the asset has been demonstrated.

Intangible assets should be amortized over their useful lives. An intangible asset that has no legal, contractual, regulatory, technological, or other factors limiting its useful life should be considered to have an indefinite useful life and should not be amortized unless its useful life is later determined to be no longer indefinite.

3. **Sales and pledges of receivables and future revenues.** In some situations a state or local government may decide to sell receivables or future revenues (e.g., future tobacco settlement receipts, or delinquent tax receivables). GASB Statement No. 48, *Sales and Pledges of Receivables and Future Revenues and Intraentity Transfers of Assets and Future Revenues,* provides guidance for accounting for such transactions. Specifically, this statement provides criteria for determining when the assets have been sold and should be removed from the government's financial statements as opposed to treating the transaction as a collateralized loan.

GASB Statement No. 48 establishes that a transaction is a collateralized borrowing unless the government both transfers the receivables or future revenues and has no continued involvement with them. Circumstances that would indicate continued involvement and prevent accounting for the transaction as a sale include

- The government or the buyer can cancel the sale.
- The government can limit the buyer's ability to subsequently sell or pledge the receivables or future revenue.
- The government has access to the receivables, future revenues, or the cash collected from them.
- The government can substitute for or reacquire specific receivables without the buyer's consent.
- The government is actively involved in the future generation of sold revenues (e.g., the revenues are the product of goods or services provided by the government).

Receivables that meet the requirements for sale should be removed from the assets of the selling government's financial statements. The difference between the carrying value of the receivables and the funds received is reported as a gain or loss on accrual-basis financial statements or as revenue in modified-accrual-basis financial statements. In a sale of future revenue, the government reports the proceeds as a deferred inflow and recognizes the revenue over the life of the sales agreement.

If the transaction does not meet the requirements of a sale, it is accounted for as a collateralized loan. The proceeds represent a liability that is repaid as the receivables or revenues are collected.

4. **Accounting for derivative instruments.** GASB Statement No. 53, *Accounting and Financial Reporting for Derivative Instruments*, specifies the appropriate accounting for derivative instruments. State and local governments use derivative instruments to make investments or manage (hedge) specific risks. The rules for accounting for these instruments are similar to those for other entities under SFAS 133. Derivative instruments derive value as a financial instrument from something outside the instrument itself.

Under GASB Statement No. 53, derivative instruments are reported on the statement of net position at their fair value (except for certain Synthetic Guaranteed Investment Contracts). If the derivative is an investment or an ineffective hedge, changes in fair value should be reported as investment revenue in the flow of resources statement. Changes in the values of hedging derivatives are reported as deferred inflows or deferred outflows in the statement of net position. In proprietary or fiduciary fund-based financial statements, the fund that reports or expects to report the hedged item should report the hedging derivative instrument.

A derivative is evaluated for effectiveness as a hedge when it is acquired and reevaluated at the end of each subsequent financial reporting period. Methods used to evaluate the effectiveness include

1. Consistent critical terms method—evaluates the hedge by qualitatively evaluating the terms of the hedgeable item and the potential hedging derivative instrument. If the critical terms between the hedgeable item and the derivative instrument are the same or similar, the instrument is considered to be an effective hedge.
2. Quantitative methods

   a. Synthetic instrument method—combines the cash flow effects of the hedgeable item with the potential hedging derivative instrument to see if they offset.
   b. Dollar-offset method—compares changes in the fair value (or expected cash flows) of the hedgeable item with the potential hedging derivative.
   c. Regression analysis method—evaluates effectiveness by examining the statistical relationship between the hedgeable item and the potential hedging derivative instrument.

If in a subsequent period the derivative is determined to be no longer effective, it is terminated as a hedge and the balance in the deferral account should be reported in the flow of resources statement within the investment revenue classification. GASB No. 64 amends GASB No. 53 to clarify whether an effective hedge of a financial instrument can be maintained after the replacement of the swap counterparty or the swap counterparty's credit support provider. GASB No. 64 indicates that a hedging relationship is maintained and hedge accounting should continue if there are no changes in terms or risk of the instrument other than a replacement of the counterparty or the counterparty's credit support provider.

5. **Accounting for pollution remediation obligations.** GASB Statement No. 49, *Accounting and Financial Reporting for Pollution Remediation Obligations,* establishes rules for accounting for estimated obligations for pollution remediation. A government must estimate its expected outlays for pollution remediation if it knows a site is polluted and any of the following recognition triggers occur:

- Pollution poses an imminent danger to the public or environment and the government has little or no discretion to avoid fixing the problem.
- The government has violated a pollution prevention-related permit or license.
- A regulator (e.g., the EPA) has identified the government as responsible or potentially responsible for cleaning up pollution or paying some of the cost of the cleanup.
- The government is named in a lawsuit to compel it to address the pollution.
- The government begins or legally obligates itself to begin cleanup or post-cleanup activities.

Liabilities and expenses are estimated using an "expected cash flows" measurement technique.

6. **Service concession arrangements.** A service concession arrangement is an agreement between a government unit and an operator in which

a. The government unit conveys to the operator the right and obligation to provide public services through the operation of a facility (capital asset) in exchange for consideration;
b. The operator collects and is compensated by fees from third parties;
c. The government unit has the ability to modify or approve the services to be provided, to whom the operator is required to provide the services, and the price of the services; and
d. The government unit is entitled to significant residual interest in the facility at the end of the arrangement.

Common examples of service concession arrangements include

1. Arrangements in which an operator agrees to design and build or improve a facility and collect fees from third parties (e.g., construct a municipal complex or a tollway).
2. Arrangements in which an operator will pay the government unit for the right to operate a government facility (e.g., a parking structure) and collect fees from third party for its use.

If the facility associated with the arrangement is an existing facility, the government unit should continue to report the facility as a capital asset. If the facility is purchased, constructed or improved by the operator, the government unit should record (a) the new facility (capital asset) at its fair value when it is placed in operation, (b) any related contractual obligations as liabilities, and (c) a corresponding deferred inflow of resources equal to the difference. A contractual obligation is one that is significant and related to the facility (e.g., an obligation by the government unit to provide insurance for the facility). These obligations should be measured at their present values.

EXAMPLE

A state government through its Department of Transportation (DOT) enters into an agreement with the Local Tunnel Authority (LTA), a governmental operator, in which LTA agrees to design, build and operate a tunnel for 40 years. In exchange for building the tunnel, the LTA is entitled to collect and retain tolls generated by the tunnel for the term of the agreement. The cost of the tunnel is $1 billion. The fair value of the tunnel when it is placed in operation is $1.5 billion. When the tunnel is placed in operation, the state government would record the asset at its $1.5 billion fair value, and record $1.5 billion in deferred (revenue) inflow of resources.

In future years, the state government would apply existing capital asset guidance, including depreciation, if applicable, to the tunnel. If the state elects to use the straight-line method of amortization of revenue, it would recognize $37,500,000 ($1.5 billion ÷ 40 years) in revenue for the next 40 years and reduce the deferred inflow by the same amount.

In the Notes to the financial statements, the government should disclose

1. A general description of the arrangement, including the government's objectives for entering into the arrangement.
2. Nature of amounts of assets, liabilities, and deferred outflows and inflows of resources related to the agreement.
3. Nature and extent of rights retained by the government.
4. The details of any related guarantees and commitments.

7. **Related-party transactions.** State and local governments must disclose certain related-party transactions. In addition, if the substance of a particular transaction is significantly different from its form because of the involve-

ment of related parties, financial statements should recognize the substance of the transaction rather than merely its legal form.

8. **Subsequent events.** The requirements regarding the effect of subsequent events on financial statements are similar to those for commercial businesses under GAAP. If the event provides additional evidence about conditions that existed at the date of the statement of net position and affect the estimates in the financial statements, the effect of the event should be recognized in the financial statements. If the event provides evidence about conditions that did not exist at the date of the statement of net position but arose subsequent to that date, the event should be disclosed in the notes to the financial statements.

9. **Going concern considerations.** The guidance regarding going concern for state and local governments is similar to that for commercial business under GAAP. The financial reporting model assumes that the entity will be a going concern for a reasonable period of time (i.e., 12 months from the financial statement date). Indicators that there may be substantial doubt about the entity's ability to continue as a going concern include

    a. Negative trends (e.g., recurring losses).
    b. Other indicators of financial difficulties (e.g., defaults on loan agreements).
    c. Internal matters (e.g., work stoppages).
    d. External matters (e.g., legal proceedings).

If it is determined that there is substantial doubt about a governmental entity's ability to continue as a going concern for a reasonable period of time, the notes to the financial statements should disclose details of the sources of the concerns and the government official's plan for dealing with those concerns.

GASB Statement No. 58, *Accounting and Financial Reporting for Chapter 9 Bankruptcies,* provides accounting and financial reporting guidance when a governmental unit has been granted relief under the provisions of Chapter 9 of the US Bankruptcy Code. The standard provides that assets and liabilities should be remeasured in accordance with the court's Plan of Adjustment. In addition, the statement requires disclosure of the details of the bankruptcy and how users can obtain a copy of the Plan of Adjustment.

10. **Financial Instruments Reporting Changes.** In June 2010 the GASB issued Statement No. 59, *Financial Instruments Omnibus,* which updated and improved existing standards regarding reporting and disclosure requirements of certain financial instruments and external investment pools. The specific issues related to financial instruments addressed by GASB Statement No. 59 include

    a. Amended NCGA Statement 4 to be consistent with GASB Statement No. 53 regarding the guarantees of the indebtedness of others.
    b. Amended GASB Statements Nos. 25 and 43 to be consistent with the provisions of GASB Statement No. 31. The amendment removed the fair value exemption for unallocated insurance contracts. The effect is to report investments in unallocated insurance contracts as interest-earning investment contracts.
    c. Clarified GASB Statement No. 31 by indicating the 2a7-like investment pool is an external investment pool that operates in conformity with Security and Exchange (SEC) Rule 2a7 as promulgated under the Investment Company Act of 1940.
    d. Amended GASB Statement No. 40 to indicate that interest-rate risk information should be disclosed only for debt investment pools that do not meet the requirements to be reported as a 2a7-like pool.
    e. Amended GASB Statement No. 53 as follows:

        (1) A penalty payment for nonperformance that is dependent on the failure of the counterparty to comply with the terms of construction or purchase contract does not meet the net settlement characteristic included in the definition of a derivative instrument.
        (2) To be included with the scope of GASB Statement No. 53 a financial guarantee contract must meet the definitions of a derivative instrument and be entered into primarily for the purpose of obtaining income or profit.
        (3) The scope of GASB Statement No. 53 excludes contracts that are not exchange-traded and have reference rates based on specific volumes of sales or service revenue of one of the parties to the contract.
        (4) Provides that a hybrid instrument should be reported according to GASB Statement No. 53 if the investor's initial rate of return on the companion instrument has the potential for at least a doubled yield.

> **NOW REVIEW MULTIPLE-CHOICE QUESTIONS 54 THROUGH 68**

L. Budgetary Accounting for the General and Special Revenue Funds
The GASB, in one of its basic principles, states

1. An annual budget(s) should be adopted by every governmental unit.
2. The accounting system should provide the basis for appropriate budgetary control.
3. A common terminology and classification should be used consistently throughout the budget, the accounts, and the financial reports of each fund.

In accordance with the principle above, budgets should be prepared for each of the fund types used by governmental units. This directive, by itself, does not differentiate governmental from commercial enterprises. What is different, however, is the inclusion of budgetary accounts in the formal accounting system for the general and major special revenue funds. Inclusion of the budgetary accounts facilitates a budget-actual comparison in Required Supplementary Information (RSI) or as a basic financial statement. The budget-actual comparison is required for the general fund and all major special revenue funds that have a legally adopted annual budget. Budgetary accounts are generally used in those funds for which the budget-actual comparison is made. *As a result, CPA examination questions always assume budgetary accounts for the general fund and sometimes, but not always, assume budgetary accounts for special revenue funds.*

Budgetary accounts (Estimated Revenues, Appropriations, Estimated Other Financing Sources, Estimated Other Financing Uses, and Budgetary Fund Balance) are incorporated into governmental accounting systems to provide legislative control over revenues and other resource inflows and expenditures and other resource outflows. Recording the budget also provides an assessment of management's stewardship by facilitating a comparison of budget vs. actual. The journal entries that follow illustrate the budgetary accounts used by the general and special revenue funds.

Upon adoption of the estimated revenues and appropriations included in the legally adopted budget (at the beginning of the period), the following entry is made and posted to the general ledger:

Estimated Revenues[2] (individual items are posted to subsidiary ledger)	1,000,000	(anticipated resources/revenues)
Appropriations (individual items are posted to subsidiary ledger)	980,000	(anticipated expenditures/liabilities)
Budgetary Fund Balance	20,000	(a surplus is anticipated since estimated revenues are more the appropriations)

Estimated Revenues, Appropriations, and Budgetary Fund Balance are budgetary accounts. This budgetary entry is reversed at year-end during the closing process.

As actual resource inflows and outflows occur during the year, they are recorded in Revenues and Expenditures accounts, and the detail is posted to the revenues and expenditures subsidiary ledgers to facilitate budget vs. actual comparisons. To prevent the overspending of appropriations (which is the legal authority to spend resources) an additional budgetary account is maintained during the year. This budgetary account is called Encumbrances. When goods or services are ordered, encumbrances are recorded so that appropriations are not overspent. The following entry is used to record encumbrances:

Encumbrances (detail posted to subsidiary ledger)	5,000	(cost estimate)
Reserved for Encumbrances	5,000	(cost estimate)

The Reserved for Encumbrances is a fund equity account that is used to segregate the amount of encumbrances outstanding. When the debit in the entry is posted, the amount that can still be obligated or expended for an individual budget line item is reduced. Thereafter, when the goods or services ordered are received, the encumbrance entry is reversed and the actual resource outflow (expenditures) is recorded.

Reserved for Encumbrances	5,000	
Encumbrances (detail posted to subsidiary ledger)	5,000	
Expenditures (detail posted to subsidiary ledger)	5,200	(actual cost)
Vouchers Payable	5,200	(actual cost)

The encumbrances account does not represent an expenditure; it is a budgetary account which represents the estimated cost of goods or services which have yet to be received. In effect, the recording of encumbrances represents the recording of executory contracts, which is essential to prevent overspending of an appropriation, which is the legal authority to spend resources). As noted above, the account reserved for encumbrances is a fund equity account, not a liability account. If encumbrances are outstanding at the end of a period, the encumbrances account is closed to the fund balance, and the reserved for encumbrances account is reported in the fund balance section of the balance sheet based on GASB Statement No. 54 fund balance classifications.

At the end of the year, the following closing entries would be recorded, assuming actual revenues for the year totaled $1,005,000, actual expenditures for the year were $950,000, and encumbrances outstanding at year-end were $10,000:

1.	Budgetary Fund Balance	20,000	
	Appropriations	980,000	
	Estimated Revenues		1,000,000

---

[2] Appropriations, estimated revenues, encumbrances, revenues, expenditures, estimated other financing sources, estimated other financing uses, other financing sources, and other financing uses are **"Control"** accounts which require detail be posted to a subsidiary ledger.

2.   Revenues   1,005,000
         Expenditures   950,000
         Encumbrances   10,000
         Fund Balance—Unreserved   45,000

   If Expenditures and Encumbrances had exceeded Revenues, Fund Balance—Unreserved, an
   equity account, would have been debited in this closing entry.

   It is important to remember that Fund Balance—Unreserved and Reserved for Encumbrances are balance sheet equity accounts.

M. Expenditure Classification for Governmental Funds

Expenditure classification. The GASB *Codification* includes guidelines for the classification of governmental fund expenditure data as set forth in GASB Statement No. 1. Both internal and external management control benefit from multiple classification of expenditures. In addition, multiple classifications prove important from an accountability standpoint. This classification system provides assistance in aggregating data and performing data analysis. Internal evaluations, external reporting, and intergovernmental comparisons can be enhanced by this multiple classification system. The following chart describes each expenditure classification with examples.

Classification	Description	Examples
Function (or program)	• Provides information on the overall purposes or objectives of expenditures • Represents a major service or area of responsibility	Highways and streets Health and welfare Education General government Public safety
Organization unit (department)	• Grouped according to the government's organizational structure • The responsibility for a department is fixed	Police department Fire department Parks and recreational department Personnel department City clerk

Activity	• Specific and distinguishable line of work performed by an organizational unit as part of one of its functions or programs
	• More meaningful if the performance of each activity is fixed
		Police protection function
		Subactivities:
		   Police administration
		   Crime control and investigation
		   Traffic control
		   Police training
		   Support services

Character	• Classifies expenditures by the fiscal period benefited	Current expenditures Capital outlays Debt service
Object	• Classified according to the types of items purchased or services obtained	Personal services Supplies Rent Utilities Buildings

   The Statement of Revenues, Expenditures, and Changes in Fund Balances (earlier in this module) generally reports expenditures by function within character classifications. Budgets often report expenditures by object class at the departmental level.

N. Accounting for the General Fund

   The general fund is the most significant governmental fund. It accounts for all transactions not accounted for in any other fund. Revenues come from many sources (taxes, licenses and permits, fines and forfeits, charges for services, etc.), and the expenditures cover the major functions of government (public safety, health and welfare, highways and streets, education, etc.). The illustration below presents an overview of the general fund account structure.

GENERAL FUND ACCOUNT STRUCTURE

Real Accounts
Current Assets (DR)
Current Liabilities (CR)
Fund Balance (Fund Equity) (CR) (See note 1 below)
   Reserved (Encumbrances, Inventories, etc.)
   Unreserved

Nominal Accounts	**Budgetary Accounts**
Revenues (Control Account) (CR) (See note 2 below)	Estimated Revenues (Control Account) (DR)
Other Financing Sources (Control Account) (CR)	Estimated Other Financing
(Transfers In)	Sources (Control Account) (DR)
(Bond Issue Proceeds)	
(Sale of Capital Assets)	
Expenditures (Control Account) (DR)	Appropriations (Control Account) (CR)
	Encumbrances (Control Account) (DR)
Other Financing Uses (Control Account) (DR)	Estimated Other Financing
(Transfers Out)	Uses (Control Account) (CR)
	Budgetary Fund Balance (DR) (CR)

Note 1: For accounting purposes two fund balance classifications (reserved and unreserved) are used. However, for financial reporting under GASB Statement No. 54, five fund balance classifications (nonspendable, restricted, committed, assigned, and unassigned) are used.

Note 2: Remember that whenever a journal entry is made to a "control account" the detail needs to be posted to the subsidiary ledger.

The following represents an accounting cycle problem for the general fund. Some of these entries have been illustrated previously.

a. Adoption of a budget where estimated revenues exceed appropriations and estimated other financing uses (planned transfer out to another fund) by $10,000. (Assume it is the first year of existence for this governmental unit.)

Estimated Revenues (detail posted to subsidiary ledger)	300,000	
Appropriations (detail posted to subsidiary ledger)		240,000
Estimated Other Financing Uses		50,000
Budgetary Fund Balance		10,000

b. Transfers to a debt service fund (for general long-term debt payments) amount to $50,000.

Other Financing Uses—Transfers Out	50,000	
Due to Debt Service Fund		50,000

According to the GASB, transfers should be recognized in the accounting period in which the interfund receivable and payable arises. The account "Other Financing Uses—Transfers Out" is a temporary/nominal account that is compared with the budgetary account "Estimated Other Financing Uses." The account "Due to other funds (or Due to X fund)" is a current liability. Note that the debt service fund would record a receivable as follows:

Debt Service

Due from General Fund	50,000	
Other Financing Sources—Transfers In		50,000

The account "Due from other funds (or Due from X fund)" is a current asset account. The "Transfers" accounts are closed at the end of the year. It is important to note that the account "Transfers Out" is not an expenditure account, but is an Other Financing Use, and that the account "Transfers In" is not a revenue account, but is an Other Financing Source. (See the combined statement of revenues, expenditures, and changes in fund balance shown previously.) There is a complete discussion of interfund transactions and transfers later in this module (Section T).

c. The property tax levy is recorded as revenues, under the modified accrual basis, in the year for which the tax levy is enacted by the governmental unit, if collections will be in time to finance expenditures of the current period. The tax bills amount to $250,000, and $20,000 is estimated to be uncollectible.

Property Taxes Receivable—Current	250,000	
Allowance for Uncollectible Taxes—Current		20,000
Revenues		230,000

Under the modified accrual basis, revenues should be recorded in the period in which they are both measurable and available. The GASB requires that property taxes be recognized as a revenue if the taxes are

1. Available—collected by year-end or soon enough to pay liabilities of the current period (no more than sixty days after the end of the fiscal year)
2. To finance the budget of the current period

To the extent the modified accrual criteria for recognition are not met, the property tax levy would be recorded with a credit to Deferred Inflow of Resources Property Taxes, a liability, instead of Revenues.

If cash is needed to pay for expenditures before the property tax receivables are collected, it is not uncommon for governmental units to borrow on tax anticipation notes. The property taxes receivable serves as security for this loan and, as taxes are collected, the liability is paid (i.e., Tax Anticipation Notes Payable is debited).

The treatment of the allowance for uncollectible accounts should be noted. Expendable funds account for resource inflows (revenues) and resource outflows (expenditures). Expenses are not recorded. The Allowance for Uncollectible Accounts (contra asset account) represents an estimated reduction in a resource inflow and, accordingly, revenues are recorded net of estimated uncollectible taxes.

d. Revenues from fines, licenses, and permits amount to $40,000.

Cash	40,000	
Revenues (detail posted)		40,000

Resource inflows from fines, licenses, permits, etc. are usually not measurable until the cash is collected. Sometimes, it is possible to measure the potential resource inflow; however, because the availability is questionable, revenues are recorded when cash is collected.

e. The state owes the city $25,000 for the city's share of the state sales tax. The amount has not been received at year-end, but it is expected within the first few months of the next fiscal year (in time to pay the liabilities as of the current fiscal year).

State Sales Tax Receivable	25,000	
Revenues (detail posted)		25,000

Sales taxes, income taxes, etc. may be accrued before collection by a governmental unit, if collection is anticipated in time to pay for current year expenditures. Other firm commitments from the state or other governmental units for grants, etc. are also recorded.

f. Incurred liabilities for salaries, repairs, utilities, rent, and other regularly occurring items for $200,000.

Expenditures (detail posted)	200,000	
Vouchers Payable		200,000

Note that all resource outflows which are legally authorized appropriations are debited to Expenditures. It makes no difference whether the outflow is for a fire truck or for rent. Remember, expendable funds do not have a capital maintenance objective. Also, note that the encumbrance accounts were not used in this example. There is usually no need to encumber appropriations for items that occur regularly, and which possess a highly predictable amount (e.g., salaries, rent, etc.). It should be pointed out, however, that there is no hard and fast rule for when to use encumbrances, and encumbrance policies do vary tremendously (i.e., from every expenditure being encumbered to virtually no expenditures being encumbered).

g. Ordered one police car; estimated cost is $17,000. One month later, ordered second police car; estimated cost is $16,500.

Encumbrances	17,000	
Reserved for Encumbrances		17,000
Encumbrances	16,500	
Reserved for Encumbrances		16,500

Recording encumbrances prevents overspending line-item appropriations. In the case of the police cars, assume that appropriations were authorized in the amount of $34,000 for police vehicles. After the first police car was ordered, the unencumbered appropriation for police vehicles was reduced to $17,000. This placed a dollar limit on what could be spent on the second car.

h. Police car ordered first was received; actual cost is $16,800. Note that the encumbrance is reversed in the first journal entry in the amount of $17,000 which is the estimated cost of the police car. In the second entry the expenditures account is debited for the actual cost of the police car.

Reserved for Encumbrances	17,000	
Encumbrances		17,000
Expenditures	16,800	
Vouchers Payable		16,800

i. Property tax collections amounted to $233,000, payments to other funds amounted to $50,000 (see item b.), and payments of vouchers were $190,000.

Cash	233,000	
Property Taxes Receivable—Current		233,000
Due to Debt Service Fund	50,000	
Cash		50,000
Vouchers Payable	190,000	
Cash		190,000
Allowance for Uncollectible Taxes—Current	3,000	
Revenues		3,000

The last entry above is made because the Allowance for Uncollectible Taxes—Current was overstated. Note that the estimate was $20,000 in entry c. above. Tax revenues were estimated to be $230,000. Since property tax collections exceeded $230,000 for the current year, an increase in revenues is recorded.

j. Recorded $5,000 inventory of materials and supplies, reduced the allowance for uncollectible property taxes to $10,000, and reclassified uncollected property taxes to delinquent accounts.

Materials and Supplies Inventory[3]	5,000	
Reserved for Inventory of Materials and Supplies		5,000
Allowance for Uncollectible Taxes—Current	7,000	
Revenues		7,000
Property Taxes Receivable—Delinquent	17,000	
Allowance for Uncollectible Taxes—Current	10,000	
Allowance for Uncollectible Taxes—Delinquent		10,000
Property Taxes Receivable—Current		17,000

One of the reasons for recording the inventory of materials and supplies is to inform the preparers of the budget that items purchased during the year and charged to expenditures (item f.) are still unused. The account "Reserved for Inventory of Materials and Supplies" is a reservation of Fund Balance. In this respect, it is similar to "Reserved for Encumbrances."

The second entry adjusts the estimate of uncollectible property taxes to $10,000. This is the result of collecting more property taxes than anticipated (see entries made in c. and i. above) and of an estimate that $7,000 will now be collected.

The third entry reclassifies property taxes receivable from current to delinquent at the end of the year. Generally, interest and penalty charges accrue on the unpaid taxes from the date they become delinquent. If these items have accrued at the end of a fiscal period, they would be recorded in the following way:

Interest and Penalties Receivable on Delinquent Taxes	xx	
Allowance for Uncollectible Interest and Penalties		xx
Revenues		xx

k. Appropriate closing entries are made.

Budgetary Fund Balance	10,000	
Appropriations	240,000	
Estimated Other Financing Uses	50,000	
Estimated Revenues		300,000

The above entry reverses the entry to record the budget.

Revenues	305,000	
Expenditures		216,800
Encumbrances		16,500
Other Financing Uses—Transfers Out		50,000
Fund Balance—Unreserved		21,700

The above entry indicates that the unreserved fund balance increased by $21,700 since actual revenues exceeded expenditures, encumbrances and other financing uses.

Financial statements. Under the GASB *Codification*, individual fund statements should not be prepared that simply repeat information found in the basic or combining statements but may be prepared to present individual fund budgetary comparisons (not needed for the general or major special revenue funds), to present prior year comparative data, or to present more detailed information than is found in the basic or combining statements.

The balance sheet below would represent the general fund portion of the governmental funds balance sheet. Note the following points from the balance sheet:

1. The total fund balance (equity) is $43,200, but only $21,700 is unreserved. This $21,700 represents the appropriable component of total fund balance (i.e., the amount that can be used next period to help finance a deficit budget). The $21,700 represents unreserved net liquid resources.
2. The reason for crediting "Reserved for Inventory of Materials and Supplies" in item j. previously should now be more meaningful. The inventory of materials and supplies is not a liquid resource that can be used to finance future expenditures. Consequently, if this asset is disclosed, it must be disclosed via a fund restriction.
3. The "Reserved for Encumbrances" which is disclosed on the balance sheet relates to the second police car that was ordered but not delivered at year-end. When the car is received in the next period, the following journal entries could be made, assuming the actual cost is $16,600. It should be noted that the first journal entry reverses the encumbrances which were closed at the end of the prior year. Also note the $100 difference between the estimated cost ($16,500) and the actual cost ($16,600) of the police car is charged to current year expenditures.

---

[3] The illustration covers the "purchases method" for materials and supplies. The "consumption method" is not covered in this illustration. Consult an advanced or governmental textbook for coverage of the "consumption method."

Encumbrances—Prior Year		16,500	
Fund Balance—Unreserved			16,500
Reserved for Encumbrances		16,500	
Encumbrances—Prior Year			16,500
Expenditures—Prior Year		16,500	
Expenditure		100	
Vouchers Payable			16,600

The police car would not be recorded in the general fund as a fixed asset; rather it would be displayed as a fixed asset in the government-wide Statement of Net Position.

City of X
GENERAL FUND
BALANCE SHEET
At June 30, 2013

Assets			*Liabilities and Fund Equity*		
Cash		$33,000	*Liabilities:*		
Property Taxes Receivable—			Accounts Payable		$26,800
Delinquent	$17,000				
Less: Allowance for Uncollectible			*Fund Equity:* (See note below)		
Taxes—Delinquent	10,000	7,000	Reserved for Inventory of Materials		
State Sales Tax Receivable		25,000	and Supplies	$ 5,000	
Inventory of Materials and Supplies		5,000	Reserved for Encumbrances	16,500	
			Unreserved Fund Balance	21,700	
			Total Fund Equity		$43,200
Total Assets		$70,000	Total Liabilities and Fund Equity		$70,000

NOTE: For financial reporting purposes, GASB Statement No. 54 would require the reserve for inventory of material and supplies to be reported as nonspendable fund balance, the reserve for encumbrance would be included in the assigned fund balance classification, unless it was restricted or committed, and the unreserved fund balance would most likely be reported as unassigned fund balance.

The following would be the general fund portion of the Budgetary Comparison Schedule:

City of X
BUDGETARY COMPARISON SCHEDULE
GENERAL FUND
For the Year Ended June 30, 2013

	Budgeted amounts		Actual amounts	Variances with final budget
	Original	Final	(Budgetary basis)	positive (negative)
Budgetary Fund Balance, July 1, 2012	--	--	--	--
Resources (Inflows)	$300,000	$300,000	$305,000	$ 5,000
Amounts Available for Appropriation	300,000	300,000	305,000	5,000
Charges to Appropriations (Outflows)	240,000	240,000	233,300	6,700
Transfers to Other Funds	50,000	50,000	50,000	--
Total Charges to Appropriations	290,000	290,000	283,300	6,700
Budgetary Fund Balance, June 30, 2013	$ 10,000	$ 10,000	$ 21,700	$11,700

The Budgetary Comparison Schedule is included in Required Supplementary Information (RSI), presented after the notes to the basic statements. The format may be in accord with the budget or in accord with the Statement of Revenues, Expenditures, and Changes in Fund Balances (earlier in this module). The Budgetary Fund Balance may or may not be the same as the Unreserved Fund Balance reported in the Balance Sheet for the General Fund. (In this example, it is the same.)

One additional point needs to be covered before going to special revenue funds; that is, how to account for the inventory of materials and supplies in the second or any subsequent year. Accordingly, assume that at the end of the second year, $4,000 of materials and supplies were unused. The adjusting entry would appear as follows:

Reserved for Inventory of Materials and Supplies	1,000	
Materials and Supplies Inventory		1,000

This entry, when posted, will result in a balance of $4,000 in the inventory and reserve accounts. Note the entry at the end of the first year established a $5,000 balance in these accounts. Thereafter, the inventory and reserve accounts are adjusted upward or downward to whatever the balance is at the end of the year.[4]

---

[4] Again, this entry illustrates the "purchases method" of accounting for inventories. Consult a governmental or advanced textbook for illustration of the "consumption method."

O. Accounting for Special Revenue Funds

Special revenue funds account for and report the proceeds of specific revenue sources that are restricted or committed to expenditure for specified purposes other than debt service or capital projects. The specific revenue is then used to finance various authorized expenditures. For example, a city might place its share of the state's gasoline tax revenues into a State Gasoline Tax Fund, which could then be used to maintain streets.

> **NOTE:** A governmental unit has some discretion in terms of how many special revenue funds it creates. Sometimes separate funds are required by law or grant requirements. Many federal and state grants are reported in special revenue funds.

The accounting for special revenue funds parallels that of the general fund. One type of transaction that often takes place in a special revenue fund is a "reimbursement" grant from a federal or state government. **GASB Statement No. 33** lists reimbursement grant requirements as one of the conditions that must be satisfied before a revenue can be recognized, either for accrual or modified accrual accounting. With a reimbursement grant, the granting government will not provide resources unless the receiving government provides evidence that an appropriate expenditure has taken place; **GASB Statement No. 33** requires that the expenditure must be recognized prior to the revenue being recognized.

For example, assume a government with a calendar fiscal year receives a grant award on November 1, 2012, in the amount of $30,000. No entry would be recorded (either a receivable or revenue) until the expenditure takes place. Assume the expenditure takes place on March 1, 2013. The entries would be

Expenditures	30,000	
Cash		30,000
Grants Receivable	30,000	
Revenues—Grants		30,000

Assume cash is received on April 1, 2013; the entry would be

Cash	30,000	
Grants Receivable		30,000

The budgetary comparison schedule in RSI must include "major" special revenue funds for which annual budgets have been legally adopted.

P. Accounting for Capital Projects Funds

Capital projects funds account for and report financial resources that are restricted, committed, or assigned to expenditure for capital outlay, including the acquisition and construction of capital facilities and other capital assets. Capital projects funds exclude capital-related outflows which are financed by proprietary or fiduciary funds. Resources for construction or purchase of capital assets normally come from the issuance of general long-term debt, from government grants (federal, state, and local), and from interfund transfers.

Project budgets for estimated resources and expenditures must be approved before the project can begin. However, unlike the budgets of general and special revenue funds, an annual budget for capital projects funds may not be legally adopted and need not be recorded formally in the accounts.

The following transactions illustrate the entries encountered in a capital projects fund:

a. City Council approved the construction of a new city hall at an estimated cost of $10,000,000. General obligation long-term serial bonds were authorized for issuance in the face amount of $10,000,000. **(No formal entries are required for approval of capital projects.)**

b. $10,000,000 in 8% general obligation serial bonds were issued for $10,100,000. Assume that the premium is transferred to a debt service fund for the eventual payment of the debt. (Premiums and discounts in governmental funds are not amortized in the fund financial statements.)

Cash	10,100,000	
Other Financing Sources—Proceeds of Bonds		10,100,000
Other Financing Uses—Transfers Out	100,000	
Cash		100,000

Note the credit to Proceeds of Bonds. This is an Other Financing Source on the operating statement, whereas the Transfers Out is an Other Financing Use. Both accounts are temporary accounts that are closed to Unreserved Fund Balance at year-end.

The transfer requires an entry in the debt service fund.

Debt Service Fund

Cash	100,000	
Other Financing Sources—Transfer In		100,000

This entry will be explained in more detail later.

c. The bond issue proceeds are temporarily invested in a Certificate of Deposit (CD) and earn $50,000. The earnings are authorized to be sent to the debt service fund for the payment of bonds.

Capital Projects Fund

Investment in CD	10,000,000	
Cash		10,000,000
Cash	50,000	
Revenues—Interest		50,000

Debt Service Fund

Cash	50,000	
Other financing sources—		
Transfers in		50,000

Other financing uses—
Transfers out	50,000	
Cash		50,000

d. The lowest bid, $9,800,000, is accepted from a general contractor.

Encumbrances	9,800,000	
Reserved for Encumbrances[5]		9,800,000

e. $2,000,000 of the temporary investments are liquidated.

Cash	2,000,000	
Investment in CD		2,000,000

f. Progress billings due to the general contractor for work performed amount to $2,000,000. The contract allows 10% of the billings to be retained until final inspection and approval of the building. The contractor was paid $1,800,000.

Reserved for Encumbrances	2,000,000	
Encumbrances		2,000,000
Expenditures—Construction	2,000,000	
Contracts Payable		2,000,000
Contracts Payable	2,000,000	
Cash		1,800,000
Contracts Payable—Retained Percentage		200,000

The account "Contracts Payable—Retained Percentage" is a liability account. Note, also, that the fixed asset is not recorded in the capital projects fund because the capital projects fund is a governmental fund and governmental funds are expendable and do not have a capital maintenance objective.

g. Interest accrued on a CD at the end of the year amounted to $40,000. This was authorized to be sent to the debt service fund for the payment of debt.

Capital Projects Fund

Interest Receivable	40,000	
Revenues—Interest		40,000

Debt Service Fund

Due from Other Funds	40,000	
Other Financing Sources—		
Transfers In		40,000

Other Financing Uses—
Transfers Out	40,000	
Due to Other Funds		40,000

The interest is recognized because it is measurable and will soon be available to finance debt service fund expenditures.

h. Closing entries for the capital projects fund would appear as follows:

(1) Revenues—Interest	90,000	
Other Financing Sources—Proceeds of Bonds	10,100,000	
Fund Balance—Unreserved		10,190,000
(2) Fund Balance—Unreserved	9,800,000	
Encumbrances		7,800,000
Expenditures—Construction		2,000,000
(3) Fund Balance—Unreserved	190,000	
Other Financing Uses—Transfers Out		190,000

The GASB requires that the totals for "major" capital projects funds appear in the balance sheet and the Statement of Revenues, Expenditures, and Changes in Fund Balances, for governmental funds. Combining statements are required in the CAFR for nonmajor capital projects funds along with other nonmajor governmental funds.

A "stand-alone" Statement of Revenues, Expenditures, and Changes in Fund Balances is shown below for the capital projects fund example.

---

[5] As previously noted reserve for encumbrances is a fund equity account used to segregate the portion of fund balance related to outstanding encumbrances.

City of X
Capital Projects Fund
STATEMENT OF REVENUES, EXPENDITURES, AND CHANGES
IN FUND BALANCES
Year Ended June 30, 2013

Revenues:		
Interest on Temporary Investments		$ 90,000
Expenditures:		
Construction of City Hall		2,000,000
Excess of Expenditures over Revenues		(1,910,000)
Other Financing Sources and Uses:		
Proceeds of General Obligation Bonds	$10,100,000	
Transfer to Debt Service Fund	(190,000)	9,910,000
Excess of Revenues and Other Financing Sources over Expenditures and		
Other Financing Uses		8,000,000
Fund Balance—Beginning of Year		--
Fund Balance—End of Year		$8,000,000

At the beginning of the second year, the following entry would be made to reestablish the Encumbrances balance:

Encumbrances	7,800,000	
Fund Balance—Unreserved		7,800,000

The purpose of this entry is to permit the recording of expenditures in the normal manner (i.e., reverse the encumbrances before recording the expenditures). It should be noted that capital projects funds differ from other governmental fund types because they have a "project focus" rather than a fiscal year focus. However, closing entries are made in capital projects funds in order to facilitate the preparation of financial statements at the end of the fiscal year.

When the city hall project is finished, the capital projects fund should be closed. Assuming there are no cost overruns, the excess cash left in the fund upon project completion must be transferred to some other fund, normally a debt service fund. This entry is described along with other interfund transactions and transfers in Section S.

Impairment of capital assets. In accordance with GASB Statement No. 42, *Accounting and Financial Reporting for Impairment of Capital Assets and for Insurance Recoveries*, governments must evaluate prominent events or changes in circumstances affecting capital assets to determine whether impairment of the assets has occurred. Such events include evidence of physical damage, enactment or approval of laws or regulations, changes in environmental factors, technological changes or evidence of considered impaired if (a) the decline in service utility of the asset is large in magnitude, and (b) the event or change in circumstance is outside the normal life cycle of the capital asset (e.g., unexpected).

Impaired capital assets that are no longer used by the government should be reported at the lower of carrying value or fair value. Impairment losses on capital assets that will continue to be used by the government should be measured using the method that best reflects the asset's diminished service utility. As an example, if the asset is damaged, the loss should be measured at an estimate of the cost to restore the capital asset (the restoration approach). If the asset is affected by changes in environmental factors or obsolescence, the impairment should be measured using an approach that compares the service units provided by the asset before and after the impairment (the service units approach). If the asset is affected by a change in the manner or duration of use, the loss generally should be measured using the service units approach or the depreciated replacement cost approach which quantifies the cost of the service currently provided by the capital asset and converts that cost to historical cost.

Any insurance recovery associated with events or changes in circumstances resulting in impairment of a capital asset should be netted against the impairment loss.

Q. Debt Service Funds

Debt service funds account for and report financial resources that are restricted, committed, or assigned to expenditure for the payment of general obligation long-term debt principal and related interest. General obligation debt is secured by the full faith and taxing power of the governmental unit. Repayment of debt financed by internal service and enterprise funds (proprietary fund types) is accounted for in those individual funds. Consequently, debt service funds are normally established as the result of issuing general obligation bonds for capital projects. The bond liability to be extinguished is not recorded in the debt service fund until it matures (is legally due). Outstanding general long-term debt is reported only in the government-wide financial statements (statement of net position).

Assume the City of X authorizes a debt service fund for the general obligation serial bonds issued to finance the city hall project. The debt service fund is also authorized to pay the 8% interest on the $10,000,000 of debt on December 31 and June 30. The fiscal year-end is June 30. Note that the debt service fund has received resources from the general and capital projects funds. Transactions showing recognition and receipt of these resources were illustrated in the discussions of the general and capital projects funds. They are repeated below as follows:

(1)	Due from General Fund		50,000		(Transaction b.
	Other Financing Sources—Transfers In			50,000	in Section L.)
(2)	Cash		50,000		(Transaction i.
	Due from General Fund			50,000	in Section L.)
(3)	Cash		100,000		(Transaction b.
	Other Financing Sources—Transfers In			100,000	in Section N.)
(4)	Cash		50,000		(Transaction c.
	Other Financing Sources—Transfers In			50,000	in Section N.)
(5)	Due from Capital Projects Fund		40,000		(Transaction g.
	Other Financing Sources—Transfers In			40,000	in Section N.)

Assume the bonds were issued on July 1. In addition, assume that $250,000 of the bonds mature each six months, starting June 30.

a. The property tax levy contains $870,000 portion allocable to the debt service fund. $20,000 of this amount is estimated to be uncollectible.

Property Taxes Receivable—Current	870,000	
Allowance for Uncollectible Taxes—Current		20,000
Revenues—Property Taxes		850,000

b. $840,000 of property taxes are collected during the year. The remainder of the property taxes is reclassified as delinquent.

Cash	840,000	
Property Taxes Receivable—Current		840,000
Property Taxes Receivable—Delinquent	30,000	
Allowance for Uncollectible Taxes—Current	20,000	
Property Taxes Receivable—Current		30,000
Allowance for Uncollectible Taxes—Delinquent		20,000

c. The semiannual interest is paid on December 31 and June 30. The following entries are made on December 31:

Expenditures—Interest	400,000	
Matured Interest Payable		400,000
Matured Interest Payable	400,000	
Cash		400,000

The following entries are made on June 30:

Expenditures—Interest	400,000	
Matured Interest Payable		400,000
Matured Interest Payable	400,000	
Cash		400,000

Note that if interest were paid on dates other than December 31 and June 30, interest would not be recorded in the debt service fund until it is legally due, but would be accrued at the end of the fiscal year in the government-wide financial statements.

d. On June 30, the first $250,000 principal payment became due, and $200,000 was paid. The following entries would be made in the debt service fund:

Expenditures—Principal	250,000	
Matured Bonds Payable		250,000
Matured Bonds Payable	200,000	
Cash		200,000

If a bank were used as the fiscal agent, cash would first be transferred to a "Cash with Fiscal Agent" account, and payment would then be made from that account.

e. Appropriate closing entries are made based upon all information presented.

Revenues—Property Taxes	850,000	
Other Financing Sources—Transfers In	240,000	
Expenditures—Interest		800,000
Expenditures—Principal		250,000
Fund Balance—Reserved for Debt Service		40,000

The balance sheet for the debt service fund would appear as follows:

City of X
DEBT SERVICE FUND
BALANCE SHEET
June 30, 2013

Assets		*Liabilities and Fund Equity*	
Cash	$40,000	*Liabilities:*	
Due from Capital Projects Fund	40,000	Matured Bonds Payable	$50,000
Property taxes receivable—Delinquent (net of		*Fund Equity:* (See note below)	
$20,000 allowance for uncollectible taxes)	10,000	Fund Balance—Reserved for Debt Service	40,000
Total Assets	$90,000	Total Liabilities and Fund Equity	$90,000

> **NOTE:** For financial reporting purposes, GASB Statement No. 54 would require the fund balance—reserved for debt service to be reported as restricted, committed, or assigned.

Under modified accrual accounting, expenditures for principal and interest are generally not accrued but recorded when legally due. However, GASB Statement No. 36, *Recipient Reporting for Certain Shared Nonexchange Revenues—An Amendment of GASB Statement No. 33*, provides that if resources are available at year-end and payment is to be made within one month after year-end, an accrual may be made, if a debt service fund is used.

R. Permanent Funds

A fifth type of governmental fund, introduced by GASB Statement No. 34, is the **permanent fund** type. Permanent funds account for and report resources that are restricted to the extent that only the earnings and not the principal may be used to support government programs which benefit the government or its citizens. For illustrative purposes all revenue and expenditure transactions below are recorded in the permanent fund. An alternative approach is to record interest from investments as revenue in the permanent fund, then record the transfer of the interest as an other financing use—transfer out to the general (or a special revenue fund). The general fund (or special revenue fund) would record the transfer as an other financing source—transfer in and record the expenditures of the earnings for the specified purpose.

A common example would be a cemetery perpetual care fund. Assume a local citizen was concerned about the deplorable condition of the city cemetery and on January 2, 2012, contributed $500,000 with the stipulation that the funds be invested and held; the income is to be used for the purpose of maintaining the city cemetery. On January 2, the cash was received and invested.

Cash	500,000	
Revenues—Additions to Permanent Endowments		500,000
Investments	500,000	
Cash		500,000

During 2012, $30,000 was earned on the investment, and $25,000 was expended.

Cash (and/or interest receivable)	30,000	
Revenues—Investment Income		30,000
Expenditures	25,000	
Cash (or Vouchers Payable)		25,000

S. Accounting for Special Assessments

GASB Statement No. 52, *Land and Other Real Estate Held as Investments by Endowments,* provides that land and other real estate held by an endowment for investment purposes should be reported at fair value at each reporting date. Changes in fair value during the period should be reported as a part of investment income. GASB Statement No. 6, *Accounting and Reporting for Special Assessments,* outlines the accounting and financial reporting for special assessments. Special assessments are levied for projects to be paid primarily by the property owners who benefit from the improvement project (for example, a street lighting or sidewalk project).

Under GASB Statement No. 6, the accounting and reporting for special assessment capital projects depends on the liability of the governmental unit for the special assessment debt. If the governmental unit is not obligated in any way for the debt and merely acting in a collecting capacity, the special assessment activities will be accounted for in an agency fund. However, if the governmental unit is either **primarily** or **potentially liable** for the debt, the accounting and reporting will take place as if it were any other capital improvement and financing transaction. Construction activities will be recorded in a capital projects fund and debt principal and interest activities would be recorded in a debt service fund.

T. Accounting for Proprietary Funds

GASB standards provide two types of proprietary funds: Internal Service and Enterprise Funds. **Internal service funds** are established to account for the provision of goods and services by one department of the government to other departments within the government, generally on a cost-reimbursement basis. The extent of the use of internal service fund services are managed through the budgets of the user departments. Internal service funds are normally established for the following types of activities: central garages, motor pools, central printing and duplicating, stores departments, self-insurance, etc. **Enterprise funds,** on the other hand, account for activities for which the government provides goods and services that are (1) rendered primarily to the general public, (2) financed substantially or entirely through user charges, and (3) intended to be self-supporting. Enterprise funds are usually established for public utilities, airports, toll roads and bridges, transit systems, golf courses, solid waste landfills, etc.

Proprietary funds use the accrual basis of accounting and are nonexpendable; capital is to be maintained. Revenues and expenses are recorded generally as they would be in commercial enterprises. Fixed assets are recorded in proprietary funds, and depreciation expense is deducted from revenues. Proprietary funds also report their own long-term liabilities. The GASB has provided a special rule regarding the use of FASB pronouncements in accounting for enterprise funds of state and local governments. That rule has two parts.

1. Enterprise funds should follow FASB pronouncements issued prior to November 30, 1989, unless those FASB pronouncements conflict with GASB pronouncements.
2. Enterprise funds may or may not follow FASB pronouncements issued after November 30, 1989, which do not conflict with GASB pronouncements. The decision regarding whether or not to follow such FASB pronouncements must be applied consistently to all FASB pronouncements, and the choice must be disclosed.

When proprietary funds are initially established, a contribution or advance is usually received from the general fund. A contribution is a transfer and would be recorded by the internal service or enterprise fund as follows:

Cash	xx	
Transfer from the General Fund		xx

The transfer from the general fund would be closed to net position—unrestricted at the end of the fiscal year. The transfer would be reported in the Statement of Revenues, Expenses, and Changes in Net Position. On the other hand, an advance from the general fund is a long-term loan and would be recorded by an internal service or enterprise fund as follows:

Cash	xx	
Advance from General Fund		xx

The term "advance from" is used to indicate that the liability is long term and would be reported on the proprietary fund's balance sheet as a long-term liability. The advance would be reported as a long-term asset on the general fund's balance sheet, which requires a reservation of fund balance because it is not available for current operations.

Accounting entries for proprietary funds are similar to those for business enterprises. "Operating Revenues—Charges for Services" is a common operating revenue account for both internal service and enterprise funds. As indicated earlier, revenues and expenses are recognized on the full accrual basis and are classified as operating and nonoperating. Some features that distinguish the accounting for proprietary funds are

1. Long-term debt is recorded directly in internal service and enterprise funds. Revenue bonds are those that are backed only by the revenues of the proprietary fund activity. However, revenue bonds with general obligation backing and general obligation bonds that are to be paid with revenues of the proprietary fund activities are also recorded in the proprietary funds.
2. Interest on long-term debt is accrued as an expense, unlike interest on general long-term debt, which is generally not recorded until it is legally due (see debt service funds). Premiums and discounts on debt issuances, as well as debt issue costs, are recorded with the debt and amortized over the life of the bonds.
3. Fixed assets are capitalized and depreciated, using one of the generally accepted methods used by business enterprises. Interest incurred during construction is capitalized.
4. Revenues, expenses, capital contributions, and transfers are closed out to net position at year-end. Three categories of net position exist, as indicated earlier: (a) net investment in capital assets, (b) restricted, and (c) unrestricted. These are the same asset categories as are used in the government-wide Statement of Net Position.
5. Net position—net investment in capital assets, would be the net of fixed assets, less accumulated depreciation, less any long-term debt issued to finance capital assets. Net position—restricted would offset, for example, by any resources held for future debt service in accord with bond indenture requirements.
6. A special problem exists with self-insurance funds, which are often classified as internal service funds.[6] Governments transfer resources from other funds to self-insurance funds, from which claims are paid. To the extent that the transfers do not exceed the actuarially determined liability of the government, they are recorded as expenditures or expenses. Any transfers in addition to the actuarially determined liability are classified as transfers.

---

[6] GASB requires that, if self-insurance is to be recorded in a single fund, that fund must be an internal service or the general fund.

7. Another special problem exists with municipal waste landfills, which are often classified as enterprise funds. Many of the solid waste landfills in the US are operated by local governmental units. The problem which arises in accounting for municipal landfills is that most revenue is earned early in the useful life of the landfill, as various persons and organizations pay to dispose of waste; conversely, a significant portion of the costs, termed closure and postclosure care costs as defined by US Government regulations, occur up to twenty to thirty years later. The GASB requires that these future costs be estimated and charged against periodic revenues on a "units of production" basis according to the amount of landfill capacity consumed during each period. If a municipal waste landfill is operated as an enterprise fund, expenses and liabilities are accounted for on a full accrual basis and recorded directly in the enterprise fund. If the municipal waste landfill is operated through a governmental fund, the expenditure and fund liability would be limited to the amount that will be paid with currently available resources, and the remaining liability would be reported in the government-wide statements.

CPA exam questions sometimes portray a situation, such as a federal government grant for bus purchases, and ask candidates to provide accounting treatment for when the transaction is recorded in a governmental fund (record a revenue if expended, defer revenue if not), and for when the transaction is recorded in a proprietary fund (record as capital contributions). When uncertain, candidates should generally recall business accounting principles to record the proprietary fund transaction.

U. Accounting for Fiduciary Funds

Fiduciary funds (also referred to as "trust and agency" funds) are used to account for assets held by the governmental unit in a trustee capacity or as an agent for individuals, private organizations, and other governmental units. Fiduciary funds include private-purpose trust funds which account for resources received under a trust agreement in which the investment income of an endowment is intended to benefit an external individual, private organization, or government. (Remember that resources held and invested for the benefit of the reporting government are classified as permanent funds, a governmental fund category.) In addition to private-purpose trust funds, the fiduciary fund category includes pension (and other employee benefit) trust funds, investment trust funds, and agency funds.

Pension (and other employee benefit) trust funds are maintained when the governmental unit is trustee for the pension (or other employee benefit) plan. In addition, many state governments operate statewide Public Employee Retirement Systems (PERS) for local governments, teachers, university employees, judges, etc. These PERS are normally a part of the state government reporting entity. Full accrual accounting is used for pension trust funds, and investments are reported at fair value. Pension trust funds are required to have two financial statements. The pension trust funds are included in the (1) Statement of Fiduciary Net Position and the (2) Statement of Changes in Fiduciary Net Position. GASB No. 67 provides guidance on the presentation of financial statements of pension trust funds.

Government pension plans do not include the accrued actuarial liability in the statement of fiduciary net position. Rather, the actuarial liability is reported in the schedules and notes. Extensive note disclosures are required, both for the PERS and for the government as employer, whether or not it is trustee of the pension plan. The Notes to the financial statements should disclose:

(1) Descriptive information about the plan.
(2) Information about plan investments.
(3) Information about the terms of receivables and nature of reserves.
(4) Components of the pension liability.
(5) Significant assumptions to measure the pension liability.
(6) The measurement date.

Required Supplementary Information (RSI) includes:

(1) A ten-year schedule of changes in pension liability.
(2) A ten-year schedule of the amounts of total pension liability, fiduciary net position, net pension liability, the covered-employee payroll, and selected ratios.
(3) A ten-year schedule of the actuarial computed required contribution, the required contribution, the actual contribution to the plan, and selected ratios.
(4) A ten-year schedule of the annual money weighted return on pension plan assets.

The above requirements relate to **defined benefit** pension plans. Under **defined contribution** plans, the government is liable only for the required contributions not made, and disclosure requirements are less extensive.

Employer accounting for defined benefit plans is the same, regardless of whether or not the government is the trustee for the pension plan. Expenditures (or expenses) are charged in the appropriate funds (especially the general, special revenue, and enterprise funds) in an amount equal to the amount provided to the pension plan. The pension trust fund (or statewide PERS) would record those contributions as additions. Other additions for the pension trust fund would include employee contributions, investment income, and gains in the market value of investments. Deductions would include retirement benefit payments, disability payments, refunds to terminated (nonvested) employees, and losses in the market value of investments. However, as indicated previously, the government must include the amount of the actuarial determined net pension liability in its statement of net position.

Statewide PERS may be **agency** defined benefit, **cost-sharing** defined benefit, or defined contribution. **Agency** plans maintain separate balances for each participating government so that it is possible to determine its unfunded actuarial liability (or assets in excess of accrued actuarial benefits). **Cost-sharing** plans normally compute balances on a statewide basis only; it is not the responsibility of each participating government to fund its own liability.

A final use for pension trust funds is IRS Sec. 457 Deferred Compensation Plans (tax-deferred annuities for government employees). In many cases, these plans will not be recorded. However, when the plan meets the criteria for inclusion in a government financial statement, GASB Statement No. 34 requires that a pension trust fund be used.

The financial reporting framework for **postretirement benefits other than pensions** is covered by GASB Statement No. 45. Employers are required to measure and disclose the amount for annual other post employment benefits (OPEB) cost on the accrual basis. Annual OPEB cost is equal to the employer's annual required contribution to the plan with certain adjustments if the OPEB obligation is under- or overfunded. This is essentially the same as the accounting required by commercial enterprises under SFAS 106 (See Module 13). GASB Statement No. 45 discussed an alternative measurement method for employers with fewer than 100 total plan members. GASB Statement No. 57, *OPEB Measurements by Agent Employers and Agent Multiple-Employer Plans,* addressed issues related to the use of the alternative measurement method and the frequency and timing of measurements by employers that participate in agent multiple-employer OPEB plans. GASB Statement No. 57 amended GASB Statement No. 45 to permit an agent employer that has an individual-employer OPEB plan with fewer than 100 total plan members to use the alternative measurement method at its option regardless of the number of total plan members in the agent multiple-employer OPEB plan in which it participates. GASB Statement No. 57 also amended the GASB Statement No. 43 requirement that a defined OPEB plan obtain an actuarial valuation. GASB Statement No. 57 indicates that this requirement can be met by reporting aggregated individual-employer OPEB information determined by actuarial valuations or measurements using the alternative measurement method for individual-employer OPEB plans that are eligible. In addition, GASB Statement No. 57 indicated that actuarially determined OPEB measures should be determined at a common date and at a minimum frequency to satisfy the agent multiple-employer OPEB plan's financial reporting requirements.

A government may decide to provide **voluntary termination benefits,** such as early-retirement incentives to its employees. They may also provide **involuntary termination benefits,** such as severance pay. In governmental financial statements prepared on the accrual basis, governments should recognize a liability and expense for voluntary termination benefits when the offer has been accepted by the employees and the amount of liability can be estimated. For involuntary termination benefits, the liability should be recognized when the plan has been approved and communicated to the employees and the amount of the liability can be estimated. GASB Statement No. 47, *Accounting for Termination Benefits,* provides that the liability for termination benefits should be measured at the present value of the expected future benefit payments. In financial statements prepared on the modified accrual basis, the liability and expenditures for termination benefits should be recognized to the extent the liabilities are normally expected to be liquidated with expendable available financial resources.

Investment trust funds are required when a government sponsors an external investment pool; for example, when a county sponsors an investment pool for all cities, school districts, and other governments within its borders. The **external portion** of investment pools are to be reported (by the county) in a manner similar to pension trust funds. The Statements of Net Fiduciary Assets and of Changes in Fiduciary Net Position are required. However, Statements of Cash Flows are not required.

Private-purpose trust funds represent all other trust arrangements under which principal and income benefit external individuals, private organizations, or other governments. Private-purpose trust funds may be **nonexpendable** or **expendable**. A nonexpendable trust fund is one in which the principal cannot be expended but which provide that income may be expended for some agreed-upon purpose. Sometimes, this is called an endowment.

EXAMPLE

Assume a donor gives $500,000 to a city with instructions that the principal be invested permanently and that the income is to be used to provide scholarships for low-income children to attend a private, not-for-profit day care program. The receipt and investment of the gift would be recorded as

Cash	500,000	
Additions—Nonexpendable Donation		500,000
Investments	500,000	
Cash		500,000

Assume $30,000 is received in investment income and expended.

Cash	30,000	
Additions—Investment Income		30,000
Deductions—Awarding of Scholarships	30,000	
Cash		30,000

Expendable private-purpose trust funds are accounted for in the same manner, except that the principal as well as investment income may be expended. For example, a donor may give $10,000 to a school district with instructions that each year $2,000 plus investment income be awarded to the top student in the senior class, as a scholarship.

Another use of private-purpose trust funds, in some cases, is for **escheat property**. Escheat property is property taken over by a government, usually state government, when the property is abandoned and the legal owners cannot be found. GASB Statement No. 37 concluded that escheat property generally is recorded in the governmental or proprietary fund to which the property ultimately escheats (e.g., an educational fund). A liability is recorded for estimated amounts to potential claimants. A private-purpose trust fund is used when resources are held for individuals, private organizations, or another government.

Agency funds are used to account for activities where the government is acting as an agent for others. Agency funds have only assets and liabilities; no fund equity, revenue, or expenditure (expense) accounts are used. The GASB requires the use of agency funds for special assessments where the government is not obligated in any manner for the special assessment debt.

Another common use of agency funds is to account for property taxes. Property taxes are usually remitted to a county treasurer who places the monies in a county Tax Agency Fund. The taxes are held until such time as they are remitted to each of the other local governments located within the county. Often, a fee is charged, which decreases the amount that is distributed to the other local governments and increases the amount that is distributed to the County General Fund.

V. Reporting Interfund Activity

Under GASB Statement No. 34, interfund activity is shown between individual funds in fund financial statements and between business-type and governmental-type activities in the government-wide financial statements. GASB provides for two major types of interfund activity, each with two subtypes.

1. Reciprocal interfund activity

   a. Interfund loan and advances
   b. Interfund services provided and used

2. Nonreciprocal interfund activity

   a. Interfund transfers
   b. Interfund reimbursements

Interfund loans and advances are transactions in which one fund provides resources with a requirement for repayment. Short-term loans are recorded with "Due from" and "Due to" accounts.

EXAMPLE

Assume an enterprise fund made a short-term loan to the general fund, the entry would be

Enterprise Fund			*General Fund*		
Due from General Fund	100,000		Cash	100,000	
Cash		100,000	Due to Enterprise Fund		100,000

Long-term interfund receivables and payables use the terms "Advance to" and "Advance from." If a governmental fund makes a long-term loan to another fund, it is necessary to reserve fund balance in the amount of the advance, as the resources are not "available" for expenditure in the current period.

EXAMPLE

Assume the general fund advances $50,000 to an internal service fund. The entries would be

General Fund			*Internal Service Fund*		
Advance to Internal Service					
Fund	50,000		Cash	50,000	
Cash		50,000	Advance from General Fund		50,000
Fund Balance—Unreserved	50,000				
Fund Balance—Reserved					
for Long-Term Advances		50,000			

Loans and advances to and from component units are to be separately identified in the government-wide financial statements.

Interfund services provided and used represent transactions in which sales and purchases of goods and services between funds are made at prices approximating their external exchange price. Examples would include the sale of water from an enterprise fund to the general fund, the provision of services by an internal service fund to a governmental fund, a payment in lieu of taxes from an enterprise fund to the general fund (where payment is approximately equal to services provided), and the payment of a retirement fund contribution from the general fund to a pension trust fund. Revenues (or additions) are recognized by one fund, and an expenditure or expense is recorded by another fund. As a result, the operating statements will include these revenues and expenditures/expenses.

EXAMPLE

Assume an internal services fund charges the general fund for goods or services provided.

Internal Service Fund			*General Fund*		
Due from General Fund	30,000		Expenditures	30,000	
Operating Revenues—			Due to Internal Service		
Charges for Services		30,000	Fund		30,000

Interfund transfers are nonreciprocal transfers between funds, where payment is not expected. Examples would include an annual subsidy from an enterprise fund to the general fund or an annual transfer from the general fund to a debt service fund. To illustrate the latter in the amount of $300,000

General Fund			*Debt Service Fund*		
Other Financing Uses—Transfer					
to Debt Service Fund	300,000		Cash	300,000	
Cash		300,000	Other Financing Sources—		
			Transfer from General Fund		300,000

Transfers are reported as "Other Financing Sources (Uses)" in the governmental funds statement of revenues, expenditures, and changes in fund balance.

Interfund reimbursements are repayments from funds responsible for expenditures or expenses to those funds that initially paid for them.

EXAMPLE

Assume the general fund paid an enterprise fund for a consultant's fee that was initially paid by the enterprise fund and charged to expense.

General Fund			*Enterprise Fund*		
Expenditures	50,000		Cash	50,000	
Cash		50,000	Consultant Fee Expense		50,000

W. Accounting for Investments

GASB's rules for investment accounting are included in GASB Statement No. 31, *Accounting and Financial Reporting for Certain Investments and for External Investment Pools*. GASB Statement No. 31 provides that investments in debt securities and in equity securities with determinable fair values be reported at fair value. Changes in fair value should be reported as a part of operations, using modified accrual or accrual accounting, as appropriate. No distinction is to be made on the face of the financial statements between realized and unrealized gains and losses, although disclosure may be made of realized gains in the notes. Investment income should be reported in the fund for which investments are held, when investments are pooled.

X. Conversion from Fund Financial Statements to Government-Wide Financial Statements

Most state and local governments will keep their books on a fund basis in order to facilitate the preparation of fund financial statements and to prepare the budget-actual schedule as a part of RSI. This will mean that governments will record transactions on the modified accrual basis for governmental funds and on the accrual basis for proprietary and fiduciary funds. Many governments will make changes, on a worksheet basis, in order to prepare the government-wide financial statements (Statement of Net Position and Statement of Activities). The following are the worksheet changes that will be necessary to convert from governmental fund statements to the governmental activities portion of the government-wide statements. It should be emphasized that the journal entries illustrated below are made only for worksheet purposes and will not be posted to the funds ledger.

1. **Capitalization of Capital Outlay Expenditure**

Costs incurred for capital assets acquired or constructed by governmental funds are recorded as expenditures. Governmental funds do not record capital assets. Therefore it will be necessary to record capital outlay expenditures as capital assets in the governmental activities column of the government-wide Statement of Net Position. A worksheet adjusting entry needs to be made to reduce capital outlay expenditures to zero and capitalize the costs in appropriate capital asset accounts. These capital assets will increase the net position of the governmental activities. Assuming the amount is $10,000,000, the entry would be

Fixed Assets (Land, Buildings, Equipment, etc.)	10,000,000	
Expenditures		10,000,000

In addition, depreciation expense will be required to be recorded for the buildings and equipment.

2. **Issuance of general long-term debt**

When general long-term debt is issued, governmental funds credit Proceeds of Debt, which is an Other Financing Source. Also, premiums and discounts are not amortized but simply add to or deduct from the amount of resources available. On a worksheet it will be necessary to eliminate Other Financing Sources—Proceeds of Bonds and record the debt as a liability. Moreover, any premium or discount must be associated with the liability and amortized over the life of the bonds. The worksheet entry to convert the sale of bonds from governmental fund accounting to government-wide statements, assuming a sale of $5,000,000 bonds at par, would be

Other Financing Sources—Proceeds of Bonds	5,000,000	
Bonds Payable		5,000,000

3. **Debt service payments**

When making principal payments on long-term debt, governmental funds debit Expenditures—bond principal retirement. Those expenditures will need to be eliminated and replaced with a debit to the bond principal when preparing the government-wide statements. Bond principal retirement does not affect the government-wide Statement of Activities but reduces the bonds payable balance in the Statement of Net Position. In addition, governmental funds do not accrue interest payable but record expenditures on the maturity date. Accrual of interest payable will be required for the government-wide statements, including adjustments for amortization of premiums and discounts. Assuming that a payment of $100,000 was made for the retirement of bond principal, then the worksheet entry to convert the $100,000 principal payment from governmental fund accounting to government-wide statements would be

Bonds Payable	100,000	
Expenditures—Bond Principal Retirement		100,000

4. **Adjustment of revenue recognition**

Governmental funds recognize revenues only when measurable and available to finance expenditures of the current period. In the case of property taxes, revenues cannot be recognized if those revenues will be collected more than sixty days after the end of the fiscal year. When preparing the government-wide financial statements, some adjustments will be required to recognize all revenues, net of uncollectible receivables, in accord with revenue accounting for exchange and nonexchange transactions, as described earlier in this module. Assume a government levied $10,000,000 in property taxes for the year 2012 with 2% uncollectible. The amount to be recognized on the government-wide statements is $9,800,000. Assume that during 2012 and the first sixty days of 2013, $9,600,000 had been and was expected to be collected, limiting the amount reported as revenues in the governmental funds Statement of Revenues, Expenditures, and Changes in Fund Balances to $9,600,000. The $200,000 would have been shown as deferred inflow of resources in the Governmental Funds Balance Sheet. The worksheet entry would be

Deferred Inflow—Property Taxes	200,000	
Revenues—Taxes		200,000

5. **Accrual of expenses**

Under modified accrual accounting, expenditures are recorded for items that are current, capital outlay, and debt service. As indicated earlier, adjustments must be made to convert expenditures for capital outlay and debt service principal payments to the accrual basis. In addition, adjustments must be made to record the noncurrent portion of certain liabilities (claims and judgments, compensated absences, etc.). These worksheet entries would debit expenses and credit liabilities.

6. **Other**

Some governments use the purchases method to record governmental fund inventories, and these must be changed to the consumption method when using accrual accounting. Other governments do not record and amortize certain prepaid items, such as prepaid insurance and prepaid rent. Adjustments must also be made for these items.

7. **Reclassifications**

Fund financial statements are presented separately for governmental, proprietary, and fiduciary fund categories. Government-wide financial statements have columns for governmental activities, business-type activities, and component units. In order to make the transition from fund financial statements, the fiduciary funds will be eliminated. Internal service funds, which are proprietary funds, are to be classified as governmental activities in the government-wide statements. Discretely presented component units, which are not presented at all in the fund financial statements, will be added when preparing the government-wide financial statements.

NOW REVIEW MULTIPLE-CHOICE QUESTIONS 69 THROUGH 134

Y. Public College and University Accounting (Governmental)—GASB Statement No. 35

GASB Statement No. 35, *Basic Financial Statements—and Management's Discussion and Analysis—for Public Colleges and Universities,* established accounting and financial reporting standards for public colleges and universities within the guidelines of GASB Statement No. 34.

GASB Statement No. 35 requires that public colleges and universities follow the standards for special purpose governments outlined in GASB Statement No. 34. This means that public colleges may choose to use the guidance for special purpose governments engaged in (1) only business-type activities, (2) engaged in only governmental activities, or (3) engaged in both governmental and business-type activities.

Public colleges and universities which elect to report as special purpose governments that are engaged in only governmental activities or in governmental and business-type activities are required to follow the reporting model for state and local governments. This model requires (1) a Management's Discussion and Analysis (MD&A), (2) Government-Wide Financial Statements, (3) Fund Financial Statements, (4) Notes to the Financial Statements, and (5) Required Supplementary Information (RSI) other than MD&A.

While a number of community colleges may choose to report in the manner described in the previous paragraph, most public colleges and universities will choose to report as special entities engaged only in **business-type** activities. In this case, proprietary fund statements only are required. These institutions will report (1) an MD&A, (2) a Statement of Net Position, (3) a Statement of Revenues, Expenses, and Changes in Net Position, (4) a Statement of Cash Flows, and (5) Required Supplementary Information (RSI) other than MD&A. Public colleges and universities reporting as business-type activities present financial statements using the **economic resources measurement focus and the accrual basis of accounting**.

The **Statement of Net Position** (as illustrated) may be presented in the format: Assets + Deferred Outflows of Resources – Liabilities – Deferred Inflows of Resources = Net Position. Alternatively, a balance sheet format (Assets + Deferred Outflows of Resources = Liabilities + Deferred Inflows of Resources + Net Position) may be presented. In either case, a classified financial statement must be presented, distinguishing between current and long-term assets and between current and long-term liabilities. As is the case for state and local governments, net position must be segregated into three categories: (1) net investment in capital assets, (2) restricted, and (3) unrestricted. Restricted net position should show major categories of restrictions. It is **not** permissible to show designations of unrestricted net position.

The **Statement of Revenues, Expenses, and Changes in Net Position** is reported in an "all-inclusive" format that reconciles to the ending total net position. GASB requires that revenues be reported by major source and that a distinction be made between operating and nonoperating revenues and expenses. The general format is

	Operating Revenues
–	Operating Expenses
=	Operating Income (Loss)
±	Nonoperating Revenues and Expenses
=	Income Before Other Revenues, Expenses Gains, Losses, and Transfers
±	Capital Contributions, Additions to Permanent and Term Endowments, Special and Extraordinary Items, and Transfers
=	Increase (Decrease) in Net Position
+	Net Position, Beginning of Period
=	Net Position, End of Period

Group ASB Statement No. 35 requires that state appropriations for operating purposes be reported as nonoperating revenue. State appropriations for capital outlay are shown separately as capital appropriations. Capital grants and gifts, additions to permanent endowments, extraordinary items, and special items are also displayed separately.

The **Statement of Cash Flows** is prepared using the GASB format described earlier in this module. The direct method must be used, along with a reconciliation between net operating income (loss) and net cash provided (used) by operating activities. Four categories are used: (1) operating activities, (2) noncapital financing activities, (3) capital and related financing activities, and (4) investing activities. Note that interest paid is classified as a (capital or noncapital) financing activity and interest received is classified as cash flows from investing activities.

GASB Statement No. 35 requires that cash flows from state appropriations for operations be reported as cash flows from noncapital financing activities. It also requires that cash flows from state appropriations for construction be reported as cash flows from capital and related financing activities.

ABC University
STATEMENT OF NET POSITION
June 30, 2013

	Primary institution	Component unit hospital
Assets		
Current assets:		
Cash and cash equivalents	$ 4,571,218	$ 977,694
Short-term investments	15,278,981	2,248,884
Accounts receivable, net	6,412,520	9,529,196
Inventories	585,874	1,268,045
Deposit with bond trustee	4,254,341	--
Notes and mortgages receivable, net	359,175	--
Other assets	432,263	426,427
Total current assets	$ 31,894,372	$14,450,246
Noncurrent assets:		
Restricted cash and cash equivalents	24,200	18,500
Endowment investments	21,548,723	--
Notes and mortgages receivable, net	2,035,323	--
Other long-term investments	--	6,441,710
Investments in real estate	6,426,555	--
Capital assets, net	158,977,329	32,602,940
Total noncurrent assets	189,012,130	39,063,150
Total assets	$220,906,502	$53,513,396
Deferred outflows of assets	$1,294,500	
Liabilities		
Current liabilities:		
Accounts payable and accrued liabilities	4,897,470	2,911,419
Long-term liabilities—current portion	4,082,486	989,321
Total current liabilities	$ 8,979,956	$ 3,900,740
Noncurrent liabilities:		
Deposits	1,124,128	--
Long-term liabilities	31,611,427	2,194,236
Total noncurrent liabilities	32,735,555	2,194,236
Total liabilities	$ 41,715,511	$ 6,094,976
Deferred inflows of assets	$ 6,737,213	--
Net Position		
Net investment in capital assets	$126,861,400	$32,199,938
Restricted for:		
Nonexpendable:		
Scholarships and fellowships	10,839,473	--
Research	3,767,564	2,286,865
Expendable:		
Scholarships and fellowships	2,803,756	--
Research	5,202,732	--
Instructional department uses	938,571	--
Loans	2,417,101	--
Capital projects	4,952,101	913,758
Debt service	4,254,341	152,947
Other	403,632	--
Unrestricted	11,307,607	11,864,912
Total net position	$173,748,278	$47,418,420

SOURCE: Revised GASB 35, page 27.

ABC University
STATEMENT OF REVENUES, EXPENSES, AND CHANGES IN NET POSITION
For the Year Ended June 30, 2013

> Operating expenses may be displayed using either object or functional classification.

	Primary institution	Component unit hospital
Revenues		
Operating revenues:		
Student tuition and fees (net of scholarship allowances of $3,214,454)	$ 36,913,194	$ --
Patient services (net of charity care of $5,114,352)	--	46,296,957
Federal grants and contracts	10,614,660	--
State and local grants and contracts	3,036,953	7,475,987
Nongovernmental grants and contracts	873,740	--
Sales and services of educational departments	19,802	--
Auxiliary enterprises:		
Residential life (net of scholarship allowances of $428,641)	28,079,274	--
Bookstore (net of scholarship allowances of $166,279)	9,092,363	--
Other operating revenues	143,357	421,571
Total operating revenues	88,773,343	54,194,515
Expenses		
Operating expenses:		
Salaries:		
Faculty (physicians for the hospital)	34,829,499	16,703,805
Exempt staff	29,597,676	8,209,882
Nonexempt wages	5,913,762	2,065,267
Benefits	18,486,559	7,752,067
Scholarships and fellowships	3,809,374	--
Utilities	16,463,492	9,121,352
Supplies and other services	12,451,064	7,342,009
Depreciation	6,847,377	2,976,212
Total operating expenses	128,398,803	54,170,594
Operating income (loss)	(39,625,460)	23,921
Nonoperating Revenues (Expenses)		
State appropriations	39,760,508	--
Gifts	1,822,442	--
Investment income (net of investment expense of $87,316 for the primary institution and $19,823 for the hospital)	2,182,921	495,594
Interest on capital asset—related debt	(1,330,126)	(34,538)
Other nonoperating revenues	313,001	321,449
Net operating revenues	42,748,746	782,505
Income before other revenues, expenses, gains, or losses	3,123,286	806,426
Capital appropriations	2,075,750	--
Capital grants and gifts	690,813	711,619
Additions to permanent endowments	85,203	--
Increase in net position	5,975,052	1,518,045
Net Position		
Net position—beginning of year	167,773,226	45,900,375
Net position—end of year	$173,748,278	$47,418,420

SOURCE: GASB 35, page 28.

GASB Statement No. 39, *Determining Whether Certain Organizations Are Component Units—An Amendment of GASB Statement No. 14*, provides guidance relating to whether or not certain legally separate tax-exempt entities are to be reported in the financial statements of governments. These provisions are especially important to public colleges and universities, many of which have legally separate foundations. GASB Statement No. 39 will result in many of these foundations being reported as discretely presented component units in public college and university financial statements. All three of the following criteria must be met before these foundations are included:

1. The economic resources received or held by the separate organization are entirely or almost entirely for the benefit of the primary government, its component units, or its constituents.
2. The primary government or its component units is entitled to, or has the ability to otherwise access a majority of the economic resources received or held by the separate organization.
3. The economic resources received or held by an individual organization that the specific primary government is entitled to, or has the ability to otherwise access are significant to that primary government.

ABC University
STATEMENT OF CASH FLOWS
For the Year Ended June 30, 2013

> The direct method of reporting cash flows is required.

	Primary institution	Component unit hospital
Cash Flows from Operating Activities		
Tuition and fees	$ 33,628,945	$ --
Research grants and contracts	13,884,747	--
Payments from insurance and patients	--	18,582,530
Medicaid and Medicare	--	31,640,524
Payments to suppliers	(28,175,500)	(13,084,643)
Payments to employees	(87,233,881)	(32,988,044)
Loans issued to students and employees	(384,628)	--
Collection of loans to students and employees	291,642	--
Auxiliary enterprise charges:		
Residence halls	26,327,644	--
Bookstore	8,463,939	--
Other receipts (payments)	1,415,502	(997,502)
Net cash provided (used) by operating activities	(31,781,590)	3,152,865
Cash Flows from Noncapital Financing Activities		
State appropriations	39,388,534	--
Gifts and grants received for other than capital purposes:		
Private gifts for endowment purposes	85,203	--
Net cash flows provided by noncapital financing activities	39,473,737	--
Cash Flows from Capital and Related Financing Activities		
Proceeds from capital debt	4,125,000	--
Capital appropriations	1,918,750	--
Capital grants and gifts received	640,813	711,619
Proceeds from sale of capital assets	22,335	5,066
Purchases of capital assets	(8,420,247)	(1,950,410)
Principal paid on capital debt and lease	(3,788,102)	(134,095)
Interest paid on capital debt and lease	(1,330,126)	(34,538)
Net cash used by capital and related financing activities	(6,831,577)	(1,402,358)
Cash Flows from Investing Activities		
Proceeds from sales and maturities of investments	16,741,252	2,843,124
Interest on investments	2,111,597	70,501
Purchase of investments	(17,680,113)	(4,546,278)
Net cash provided (used) by investing activities	1,172,736	(1,632,653)
Net increase in cash	2,033,306	117,854
Cash—beginning of year	2,562,112	878,340
Cash—end of year	$ 4,595,418	$ 996,194

Reconciliation of net operating revenues (expenses) to net cash provided (used) by operating activities:

Operating income (loss)	$(39,625,460)	$ 23,921
Adjustments to reconcile net income (loss) to net cash provided (used) by operating activities:		
Depreciation expense	6,847,377	2,976,212
Change in assets and liabilities:		
Receivables, net	1,295,704	330,414
Inventories	37,284	(160,922)
Deposit with bond trustee	67,115	--
Other assets	(136,229)	75,456
Accounts payable	(323,989)	(75,973)
Deferred inflows of resources	217,630	
Deposits held for others	(299,428)	--
Compensated absences	138,406	(16,243)
Net cash provided (used) by operating activities	$(31,781,590)	$3,152,865

> **NOTE:** The required information about noncash investing, capital, and financing activities is not illustrated.

SOURCE: Revised from GASB 35, pages 29-30.

> **NOW REVIEW MULTIPLE-CHOICE QUESTIONS 135 THROUGH 138**

KEY TERMS

Agency fund. Accounts for resources held by the reporting government in a purely custodial capacity.

Agent multiple-employer defined benefit pension plan (agent pension plan). A multiple-employer defined benefit pension plan in which pension plan assets are pooled for investment purposes but separate accounts are maintained for each individual employer so that each employer's share of the pooled assets is legally available to pay the benefits of only its employees.

Capital projects fund. Accounts for financial resources that are restricted, committed, or assigned to expenditures for acquisition or construction of capital assets.

Closed period. A specific number of years that is counted from one date and declines to zero with the passage of time.

Component unit. A legally separate organization for which the elected officials of a primary government are financially accountable.

Comprehensive Annual Financial Report (CAFR). A complete annual report for a state or local government, consisting of an introductory section, a financial section, and a statistical section.

Cost-sharing multiple-employer defined benefit pension plan (cost-sharing pension plan). A multiple-employer defined benefit pension plan in which the pension obligations to the employees of more than one employer are pooled and pension plan assets can be used to pay the benefits of the employees of any employer that provides pensions through the pension plan.

Debt service fund. Accounts for resources that are restricted, committed, or assigned to expenditures for the payment of general long-term debt principal and interest.

Defined benefit pensions. Pensions for which the income or other benefits that the employee will receive at or after separation from employment are defined by the benefit terms. The pensions may be stated as a specified dollar amount or as an amount that is calculated based on one or more factors such as age, years of service, and compensation.

Enterprise fund. Accounts for activities that involve providing goods or services to external users for a fee.

Entry age actuarial cost method. A method under which the actuarial present value of the projected benefits of each individual included in an actuarial valuation is allocated on a level basis over the earnings or service of the individual between entry age and assumed exit age(s). The portion of this actuarial present value allocated to a valuation year is called the normal cost. The portion of this actuarial present value not provided for at a valuation date by the actuarial present value of future normal costs is called the actuarial accrued liability.

Exchange revenues. Transactions that involve the transfer of goods or services for payment of (approximately) equal value.

Fiduciary funds. Account for resources held and used by governments for the benefit of individuals and entities other than the government. Fiduciary funds include agency funds, pension and other employee benefit trust funds, investment trust funds, and private-purpose trust funds.

General fund. Accounts for all financial resources except those required to be accounted for in another fund.

Governmental funds. Account for the current financial resources raised and expended to carry out general government purposes. Governmental funds include the general fund, special revenue funds, debt service funds, capital projects funds, and permanent funds.

Infrastructure assets. Long-lived capital assets that normally are stationary in nature and can normally be preserved for a significant number of years, (e.g., roads, tunnels, bridges, dams, etc.).

Internal service fund. Reports activities that provide goods or services to other funds of the primary government on a cost-reimbursement basis.

Investment trust fund. Reports the external portions of investment pools, when the reporting government is the trustee.

Multiple-employer defined benefit pension plan. A defined benefit pension plan that is used to provide pensions to the employees of more than one employer.

Net pension liability. The liability of employers and nonemployer contributing entities to employees for benefits provided through a defined benefit pension plan.

Nonemployer contributing entities. Entities that make contributions to a pension plan that is used to provide pensions to the employees of other entities.

Nonexchange revenues. Transactions in which a government gives or receives value without providing equal value in return, (e.g., property taxes, income taxes, etc.).

Pension and other employee benefit trust funds. Account for funds held in trust for the payment of employee retirement and other benefits.

Permanent fund. Accounts for resources that are restricted to the extent that only earnings and not principal may be used to support specified government programs.

Primary government. A state government, a general purpose local government, or a special-purpose local government that has a separately elected governing body, is legally separate, and is fiscally independent of other state or local governments.

Private-purpose trust fund. Reports all trust arrangements where the principal must remain intact and the income generated is used to benefit individuals, private organizations, and other governments.

Proprietary funds. Account for a government's business-type activities. Proprietary funds include internal service funds and enterprise funds.

Special revenue fund. Accounts for specific revenues that are restricted or committed to expenditures for specific current purposes other than debt service or capital projects.

Multiple-Choice Questions (1-138)

A. The Government Accounting Standards Board

1. Which of the following pronouncements provides the most authoritative guidance applicable to financial reporting for state and local governments?
- a. GASB Interpretations.
- b. FASB Accounting Standards Codification.
- c. AICPA Industry Audit and Accounting Guide for state and local governments.
- d. GASB Technical Bulletins.

2. Which of the following is the least authoritative guidance based on the GAAP Hierarchy for state and local governments?
- a. AICPA Industry Audit and Accounting Guide for state and local governments.
- b. GASB Technical Bulletins.
- c. GASB Implementation Guides.
- d. AICPA Statements of Position.

B. Governmental Accounting Concepts

3. Which of the following is an accurate statement from the GASB Concepts Statements about service efforts and accomplishments reporting?
- a. Service efforts and accomplishments reporting is required for large governmental entities.
- b. Service efforts and accomplishments reporting is necessary for assessing accountability and making informed decisions.
- c. Service efforts and accomplishments reporting is not generally beneficial.
- d. Service efforts and accomplishments reporting is more appropriate for business-type activities.

4. According to GASB Concepts Statements which of the following is an essential characteristic of an asset?
- a. An asset has present service capacity.
- b. An asset is tangible.
- c. An asset is acquired through purchase.
- d. An asset provides future benefits to the citizenry.

5. According to GASB Concepts Statements, the elements of resource flows statements include
- a. Outflow of resources and inflow of resources.
- b. Outflow of resources, inflow of resources and deferred inflow of resources.
- c. Outflow of resources, inflow of resources, deferred outflow of resources.
- d. Outflow of resources, inflow of resources, deferred outflow of resources, and deferred inflow of resources.

6. Which of the following is true about service efforts and accomplishments reporting (SEA reporting) under GASB Concepts Statements?
- a. SEA reporting is required for all state and local governments with more than $100 in total assets.
- b. SEA reporting is more appropriate for governmental business-type activities than for government-type activities.
- c. The objective of SEA reporting is to provide more complete information about a governmental en-

tity's performance than can be provided in traditional financial statements and schedules.
- d. SEA reporting is particularly important to investors and creditors.

7. A deferred outflow of resources is most like which of the following financial statement elements?
- a. An asset.
- b. A liability.
- c. Equity.
- d. Revenue.

C. The Government Reporting Model

8. Which of the following statements about the statistical section of the Comprehensive Annual Financial Report (CAFR) of a governmental unit is true?
- a. Statistical tables may **not** cover more than two fiscal years.
- b. Statistical tables may **not** include nonaccounting information.
- c. The statistical section is **not** part of the basic financial statements.
- d. The statistical section is an integral part of the basic financial statements.

D. The Reporting Entity

9. What is the basic criterion used to determine the reporting entity for a governmental unit?
- a. Special financing arrangement.
- b. Geographic boundaries.
- c. Scope of public services.
- d. Financial accountability.

10. South City School District has a separately elected governing body that administers the public school system. The district's budget is subject to the approval of the city council. Major debts of the school district are expected to be paid by school taxes. The district's financial activity should be reported in the City's financial statements by
- a. Blending only.
- b. Discrete presentation.
- c. Inclusion as a footnote only.
- d. Either blending or inclusion as a footnote.

11. Marta City's school district is a legally separate entity, but two of its seven board members are also city council members and the district is financially dependent on the city. However, major debts of the school district are expected to be paid by school taxes. The school district should be reported as a
- a. Blended unit.
- b. Discrete presentation.
- c. Note disclosure.
- d. Primary government.

12. Which of the following characteristics would require a component unit to be presented on a blended rather than discretely presented basis?
- a. The primary government and the component unit are located at the same physical location.

b. Substantially all of the debt of the component unit is expected to be repaid by the primary government.

c. The chairman of the component's governing board is appointed by the governing board of the primary government.

d. The component unit provides services to the citizens of the primary government.

F. Government-Wide Financial Statements

13. Which of the following describes the required government-wide financial statements?

a. The statement of net position and the statement of activities.

b. The statement of net fund balances and statement of changes in fund balances.

c. The statement of net position, the statement of activities, and the statement of cash flows.

d. The statement of fund assets and the statement of changes in fund assets.

14. Which of the following is an example of a deferred inflow of resources?

a. Grant expenditures paid in advance of meeting timing requirements.

b. Cost to acquire rights to future revenues.

c. Proceeds from the sale of future revenues.

d. Deferred loss from sale and leaseback of assets.

15. Which of the following is an example of a deferred outflow of resources?

a. Cost to acquire rights to future revenues.

b. Grant amounts received in advance of meeting timing requirements.

c. Proceeds from the sale of future revenues.

d. Deferred gain from a sale and leaseback transaction.

16. In the government-wide financial statement, the statement of net position, deferred outflows of resources are presented

a. As a part of liabilities.

b. As a part of equity.

c. In a separate section following assets.

d. In a separate section following liabilities.

17. Hunt Community Development Agency (HCDA), a financially independent authority, provides loans to commercial businesses operating in Hunt County. This year, HCDA made loans totaling $500,000. How should HCDA classify the disbursements of loans on the cash flow statement?

a. Operating activities.

b. Noncapital financing activities.

c. Capital and related financing activities.

d. Investing activities.

18. The statement of activities of the government-wide financial statements is designed primarily to provide information to assess which of the following?

a. Operational accountability.

b. Financial accountability.

c. Fiscal accountability.

d. Functional accountability.

Items 19 and 20 are based on the following:

As of December 31, 2012, Fullerton City compiled the information below for its capital assets, exclusive of infrastructure assets.

Cost of capital assets financed with general obligation debt and tax revenues	$3,500,000
Accumulated depreciation on the capital assets	750,000
Outstanding debt related to the capital assets	1,250,000

19. On the government-wide statement of net position at December 31, 2012, under the governmental activities column, what amount should be reported for capital assets under the asset section?

a. $3,500,000

b. $1,500,000

c. $2,250,000

d. $2,750,000

20. On the government-wide statement of net position at December 31, 2012, under the governmental activities column, the information related to capital assets should be reported in the net position section at which of the following amounts?

a. $3,500,000

b. $1,500,000

c. $2,250,000

d. $2,750,000

21. Which of the following statements is correct about the accounting for infrastructure assets using the modified approach?

I. Depreciation expense on the infrastructure assets should be reported on the government-wide statement of activities, under the governmental activities column.

II. Certain information about infrastructure assets reported using the modified approach is required supplementary information in the annual report.

a. I only.

b. II only.

c. Both I and II.

d. Neither I nor II.

22. Arkansas has a single-employee defined benefit plan covered by GASB 68. What is the amount of liability that should be presented on the state government's statement of net position related to the plan?

a. The amount expected to be contributed to the plan for the next fiscal year.

b. The amount due for current pension benefits.

c. The portion of the actuarial present value of projected benefit payments attributable to past periods of employee service minus the pension plan's fiduciary net position.

d. The estimated total payments for current employees minus the pension plan's fiduciary net position.

23. In attributing the actuarial present value of projected benefit payments of each employee to periods under GASB 68, the entity should use which of the following methods?

a. The employee service method.

b. The entry age actuarial cost method.

c.   The service cost method.

d.   The projected cost method.

24. In accordance with GASB 68, the effects on the net pension liability of differences between expected and actual investment returns for a defined benefit plan is recognized in pension expense over:

a.   A closed period of five years.

b.   A closed period of ten years.

c.   A closed period equal to the average service lives of the employees.

d.   A closed period equal to the average maturity of the investments.

25. If a state government's defined benefit pension plan's net fiduciary position is not expected to be sufficient to make projected benefit payments, the government should use which of the following rates to discount projected future benefit payments?

a.   The rate for 10-year treasury notes.

b.   The rate for 20-year, tax-exempt general obligation municipal bonds with an average rating of AA/Aa or higher.

c.   The government's marginal borrowing rate.

d.   The current average prime bank rate.

G. Fund Financial Statements

26. Depreciation expense would be reported on which of the following financial statements?

I. The government-wide statement of activities.

II. The statement of revenues, expenses, and changes in fund net position prepared for proprietary funds.

a.   I only.

b.   II only.

c.   Both I and II.

d.   Neither I nor II.

27. In accordance with governmental accounting standards, governments should prepare

a.   Combined financial statements, using the modified accrual basis of accounting and the flow of economic resources.

b.   Combined financial statements, using the accrual basis of accounting and the flow of financial resources.

c.   Government-wide financial statements, using the accrual basis of accounting and the flow of financial resources.

d.   Government-wide financial statements, using the accrual basis of accounting and the flow of economic resources.

28. In accordance with governmental accounting standards, which of the following statements is true?

I. Infrastructure assets do not need to be reported on the government-wide statement of net position if the government decides to use the modified approach in its accounting for infrastructure.

II. Component units are reported on the financial statements for governmental funds.

a.   I only.

b.   II only.

c.   Both I and II.

d.   Neither I nor II.

29. Fund accounting is used by governmental units with resources that must be

a.   Composed of cash or cash equivalents.

b.   Incorporated into combined or combining financial statements.

c.   Segregated for the purpose of carrying on specific activities or attaining certain objectives.

d.   Segregated physically according to various objectives.

30. Dogwood City's water enterprise fund received interest of $10,000 on long-term investments. How should this amount be reported on the Statement of Cash Flows?

a.   Operating activities.

b.   Noncapital financing activities.

c.   Capital and related financing activities.

d.   Investing activities.

31. The primary authoritative body for determining the measurement focus and basis of accounting standards for governmental fund operating statements is the

a.   Governmental Accounting Standards Board (GASB).

b.   National Council on Governmental Accounting (NCGA).

c.   Governmental Accounting and Auditing Committee of the AICPA (GAAC).

d.   Financial Accounting Standards Board (FASB).

32. Which of the following is not one of the five fund balance classification provided by GASB Statement 54, *Fund Balance Reporting and Governmental Fund Type Definitions*?

a.   Restricted.

b.   Committed.

c.   Reserved.

d.   Assigned.

33. Which of the following is a characteristic which *differentiates* a Special Revenue Fund from a General Fund?

a.   A special revenue fund is required to be budgeted on the accrual basis.

b.   A special revenue fund is established only if a revenue source is restricted or committed to expenditure for a specified purpose.

c.   A governmental entity can only have one special revenue fund.

d.   A special revenue fund reports by using the total economic resources measurement focus.

34. For which of the following fund balance classifications is the *intent* of the governing board to use funds for a specific purpose a critical factor?

a.   Committed.

b.   Restricted.

c.   Assigned.

d.   Nonspendable.

35. Which event(s) should be included in a statement of cash flows for a governmental entity?

I. Cash inflow from issuing bonds to finance city hall construction.

II. Cash outflow from a city utility representing payments in lieu of property taxes.

a. I only.
b. II only.
c. Both I and II.
d. Neither I nor II.

36. The following transactions were among those reported by Corfe City's electric utility enterprise fund for 2012:

Capital contributed by subdividers	$ 900,000
Cash received from customer households	2,700,000
Proceeds from sale of revenue bonds	4,500,000

In the electric utility enterprise fund's statement of cash flows for the year ended December 31, 2012, what amount should be reported as cash flows from capital and related financing activities?

a. $4,500,000
b. $5,400,000
c. $7,200,000
d. $8,100,000

37. For which of the following governmental entities that use proprietary fund accounting should a statement of cash flows be presented?

	Tollway authorities	Governmental utilities
a.	No	No
b.	No	Yes
c.	Yes	Yes
d.	Yes	No

38. In accordance with governmental accounting standards, which of the following financial statements should be prepared for proprietary funds?

a. Statement of revenues, expenditures, and changes in fund balances.
b. Statement of activities.
c. Statement of changes in proprietary net position.
d. Statement of cash flows.

39. In accordance with GASB 34 (as amended), *Basic Financial Statements—and Management's Discussion and Analysis—for State and Local Governments*, which of the following statements is correct about the information reported on the balance sheet prepared for the governmental funds?

I. The focus is on reporting major funds, with all nonmajor funds aggregated and reported in a single column.
II. Fund balances are reported in two amounts—restricted and unrestricted.

a. I only.
b. II only.
c. Both I and II.
d. Neither I nor II.

40. The financial statements required for a proprietary fund include

a. The statement of fund balances, the statement of activities, and the statement of cash flows.
b. The statement of net position, the statement of revenues, expenses and changes in fund net position, and the statement of cash flows.
c. The balance sheet, the statement of income and expenses, and the statement of cash flows.
d. The statement of fund balances and the statement of changes in fund balances.

41. In accordance with governmental accounting standards, which of the following statements is correct about the information reported on the statement of net position for the proprietary funds?

I. Assets and liabilities are classified into current and non-current classifications.
II. All activities of internal service funds are aggregated and reported in a single column.

a. I only.
b. II only.
c. Both I and II.
d. Neither I nor II.

42. Which of the following financial statements is prepared using the accrual basis of accounting and the economic resources measurement focus?

I. The statement of net position for proprietary funds.
II. The statement of revenues, expenditures, and changes in fund balances for the governmental funds.

a. I only.
b. II only.
c. Both I and II.
d. Neither I nor II.

43. In accordance with governmental accounting standards, agency funds are reported on which of the following financial statements?

I. Statement of fiduciary net position.
II. Statement of changes in fiduciary net position.

a. I only.
b. II only.
c. Both I and II.
d. Neither I nor II.

44. Private-purpose trust funds are reported on which of the following financial statements?

I. Government-wide statement of net position.
II. Statement of changes in fiduciary net position.

a. I only.
b. II only.
c. Both I and II.
d. Neither I nor II.

45. In accordance with governmental accounting standards, which fund type(s) is(are) reported on the statement of cash flows?

a. Governmental and fiduciary fund types.
b. Governmental and proprietary fund types.
c. Fiduciary and proprietary fund types.
d. Proprietary fund type only.

46. In accordance with governmental accounting standards, which of the following statements is(are) true regarding the statement of cash flows?

I. The statement of cash flows is a government-wide financial statement.
II. The statement of cash flows reports cash flows from three activities—operating, investing, and financing.

a. I only.
b. II only.

c. Both I and II.
d. Neither I nor II.

47. A reconciliation must be shown of the items that cause the difference between (1) the total of the fund balances that appears on the balance sheet for the governmental funds and (2) the total net position that is disclosed for governmental activities on the government-wide statement of net position. Which of the following items would be disclosed in this reconciliation?

I. Capital assets used in governmental activities.
II. The assets and liabilities of internal service funds included in governmental activities.

    a. I only.
    b. II only.
    c. Both I and II.
    d. Neither I nor II.

48. In accordance with governmental accounting standards, a reconciliation must be shown of the items that cause the difference between (1) the net change in fund balances for the governmental funds on the statement of revenues, expenditures, and changes in fund balances, and (2) the change in net position of governmental activities on the statement of activities. Which of the following items would be disclosed in this reconciliation?

I. Revenues and expenses of internal service funds that were reported in proprietary funds.
II. The amount by which capital outlays exceeded depreciation expense for the period.

    a. I only.
    b. II only.
    c. Both I and II.
    d. Neither I nor II.

49. What measurement focus should be used for the preparation of the following financial statements?

	Statement of changes in fiduciary net position	Government-wide statement of net position
a.	Financial resources	Economic resources
b.	Economic resources	Financial resources
c.	Economic resources	Economic resources
d.	Financial resources	Financial resources

50. Which of the following statements is(are) true?

I. Pension trust funds are reported on the statement of changes in fiduciary net position.
II. Retained earnings is reported in the net position section of the statement of net position for proprietary funds.

    a. I only.
    b. II only.
    c. Both I and II.
    d. Neither I nor II.

51. In accordance with governmental accounting standards, which of the following statements is correct concerning the statement of cash flows prepared for proprietary funds?

    a. The statement format is the same as that of a business enterprise's statement of cash flows.
    b. Cash flows from capital financing activities are reported separately from cash flows from noncapital financing activities.

    c. Cash flows from operating activities may not be reported using the direct method.
    d. Cash received from interest revenue and cash paid for interest expense are both reported as operating activities.

J. Measurement Focus and Basis of Accounting

52. For governmental fund reporting, which item is considered the primary measurement focus?
    a. Income determination.
    b. Flows and balances of current financial resources.
    c. Capital maintenance.
    d. Cash flows and balances.

53. Which of the following funds of a governmental unit recognizes revenues in the accounting period in which they become available and measurable?

	General fund	Enterprise fund
a.	Yes	No
b.	No	Yes
c.	Yes	Yes
d.	No	No

K. Accounting by Governments for Certain Events and Transactions

54. Property taxes and fines represent which of the following classes of nonexchange transactions for governmental units?
    a. Derived tax revenues.
    b. Imposed nonexchange revenues.
    c. Government-mandated nonexchange transactions.
    d. Voluntary nonexchange transactions.

55. In accordance with GASB 33, *Accounting and Financial Reporting for Nonexchange Transactions*, which of the following transactions would qualify as a nonexchange transaction in the City of Geneva?
    a. The water utility (enterprise) fund billed the general fund for water usage.
    b. Property taxes were levied by the general fund.
    c. The motor pool (internal service) fund billed other departments for services rendered.
    d. The general fund sold police cars for their estimated residual value.

Items 56 and 57 are based on the following:

The general fund of Elizabeth City received a $100,000 grant from the state to be used for retraining its police force in modern crime-fighting methods. The state recently passed legislation that requires retraining for all police departments in the state. The grant was received in cash on June 15, 2012, and was used for retraining seminars during July 2012. The state mandated that the grant be spent in the fiscal year ending June 30, 2013. Elizabeth's fiscal year ends on June 30. Answer each of the questions below based upon the guidance provided by GASB 33, *Accounting and Financial Reporting for Nonexchange Transactions*.

56. What account should be credited in the general fund on the date the grant was received?
    a. Restricted revenue.
    b. Deferred inflow of resources.
    c. Revenue.
    d. Unreserved fund balance.

57. The grant from the state is an example of what type of nonexchange transaction?
    a.   Government-mandated.
    b.   Imposed.
    c.   Voluntary.
    d.   Derived.

Items 58 and 59 are based on the following:

The merchants of Eldorado City collect a sales tax of 5% on retail sales. The sales taxes are remitted by retailers to the state and distributed by the state to the various governmental units that are within the boundaries of Eldorado City. During the month of June 2012, the state received $50,000 of sales taxes from merchants in Eldorado. As of June 30, 2012, none of the sales taxes had been remitted to Eldorado or to any of the other governments that were within the boundaries of Eldorado. However, Eldorado estimated that its share of the sales taxes would be received in early July 2012, and would be used to pay for expenditures incurred during the year ended June 30, 2012. Eldorado's fiscal year ends on June 30. Answer both of the questions below using the guidance provided in GASB 33, *Accounting and Financial Reporting for Nonexchange Transactions*.

58. From the perspective of Eldorado City, the sales taxes are an example of what type of nonexchange transaction?
    a.   Imposed.
    b.   Voluntary.
    c.   Derived.
    d.   Government-mandated.

59. On the statement of revenues, expenditures, and changes in fund balance for the year ended June 30, 2012, how should the general fund of Eldorado report its share of the sales taxes that will be received in July 2012?
    a.   Deferred inflow of resources.
    b.   Restricted revenue.
    c.   Revenue.
    d.   Unreserved fund balance.

60. On July 1, 2012, the general fund of Sun City levied property taxes for the fiscal year ending June 30, 2013. According to GASB 33, *Accounting and Financial Reporting for Nonexchange Transactions*, property taxes are an example of what type of nonexchange transaction?
    a.   Voluntary.
    b.   Government-mandated.
    c.   Imposed.
    d.   Derived.

61. For the year ended December 31, 2012, the general fund of Karsten City levied property taxes of $1,000,000. The city estimated that $10,000 of the levy would not be collectible. By December 31, 2012, the city had collected $850,0000 of property taxes and expected to collect the remainder of the taxes as follows:

- $100,000 by March 1, 2013
- $40,000 during the remainder of 2013

In accordance with GASB 33, *Accounting and Reporting for Nonexchange Transactions*, how much property tax revenue should be reported by the general fund on the statement of revenues, expenditures, and changes in fund balances prepared for the year ended December 31, 2012?
    a. $ 850,000
    b. $ 950,000

    c. $ 990,000
    d. $1,000,000

62. For the year ended December 31, 2012, the general fund of Ward Village reported revenues from the following sources on the statement of revenues, expenditures, and changes in fund balances:

Sales taxes	$ 25,000
Property taxes	125,000
Income taxes	15,000
Fines	10,000

In accordance with GASB 33, *Accounting and Reporting for Nonexchange Transactions*, what is the amount of revenues that came from imposed nonexchange transactions?
    a. $175,000
    b. $150,000
    c. $140,000
    d. $135,000

63. In December 2012, the general fund of Millard City received $25,000 from the state as an advance on the city's portion of sales tax revenues, and it received $20,000 from property owners for property taxes to be levied in 2013. The advance payment of sales taxes represented the amount that the state collected in 2012 that would have been distributed to Millard in the early part of 2013. Millard used the advance to pay for expenditures incurred by the general fund in 2012. The cash received from property owners for property taxes to be levied in 2013 will be used to pay for expenditures incurred in 2013. In accordance with GASB 33, *Accounting and Reporting for Nonexchange Transactions*, what amount of revenue from these transactions should be reported by Millard's general fund on the statement of revenues, expenditures, and changes in fund balances for the year ended December 31, 2012?
    a. $25,000
    b. $20,000
    c. $0
    d. $45,000

64. In accordance with GASB 33, *Accounting and Reporting for Nonexchange Transactions*, which of the following revenues results from taxes assessed by a government on exchange transactions (a derived tax revenue)?
    a.   Property tax revenues.
    b.   Fines and forfeits.
    c.   Motor fuel taxes.
    d.   Unrestricted government grants.

65. In accordance with GASB 33, *Accounting and Reporting for Nonexchange Transactions*, which of the following revenues results from taxes and other assessments imposed by governments that are not derived from underlying transactions?
    a.   Income taxes.
    b.   Sales taxes.
    c.   Motor fuel taxes.
    d.   Fines and forfeits.

66. Devon County is developing its own software system to maintain property tax records. Which of the following is not required for Devon to begin capitalizing the software costs?
    a.   Devon has established the objective for the project and the proposed scope of the software system.
    b.   Devon has established the feasibility of creating the software system.

c.   Devon has established an accurate budget for the software system.

d.   Devon has established its intention to complete or continue developing the system.

67. The State of Texas is scheduled to receive a substantial amount of revenues as a part of a tobacco settlement. The revenues for the next five years have been sold to a commercial business for $5,000,000. Assuming that Texas has no involvement with the future revenues, how should it account for this transaction?

a.   Recognize $5,000,000 of revenue at the date of the transaction.

b.   Recognize $5,000,000 in liability to the commercial business.

c.   Recognize $5,000,000 in deferred inflow of resources and recognize the revenue over a five-year period.

d.   Recognize the difference between the cash received and the amount of future revenues sold as an expense.

68. A city government has entered into a service concession arrangement with a company that will operate the city's parking meters and retain the parking fees for a period of 30 years in exchange for a payment to the city in the amount of $3 billion. Which of the following is correct about the accounting for this arrangement?

a.   The city should write off the cost of the parking meters when the arrangement is executed.

b.   The city should recognize revenue in the amount of $3 billion at the time the agreement is executed.

c.   The city should recognize a deferred inflow of resources in the amount of $3 billion at the time the agreement is executed.

d.   The city should recognize a receivable from the operator in the amount of $3 billion at the time the agreement is executed.

L. Budgetary Accounting for the General and Special Revenue Funds

Items 69 and 70 are based on the following:

Ridge Township's governing body adopted its general fund budget for the year ended July 31, 2012, comprised of Estimated Revenues of $100,000 and Appropriations of $80,000. Ridge formally integrates its budget into the accounting records.

69. To record the appropriations of $80,000, Ridge should

a.   Credit Appropriations Control.

b.   Debit Appropriations Control.

c.   Credit Estimated Expenditures Control.

d.   Debit Estimated Expenditures Control.

70. To record the $20,000 budgeted excess of estimated revenues over appropriations, Ridge should

a.   Credit Estimated Excess Revenues Control.

b.   Debit Estimated Excess Revenues Control.

c.   Credit Budgetary Fund Balance.

d.   Debit Budgetary Fund Balance.

71. For the budgetary year ending December 31, 2012, Maple City's general fund expects the following inflows of resources:

Property Taxes, Licenses, and Fines	$9,000,000
Proceeds of Debt Issue	5,000,000
Interfund Transfers for Debt Service	1,000,000

In the budgetary entry, what amount should Maple record for estimated revenues?

a. $ 9,000,000

b. $10,000,000

c. $14,000,000

d. $15,000,000

72. In 2012, New City issued purchase orders and contracts of $850,000 that were chargeable against 2012 budgeted appropriations of $1,000,000. The journal entry to record the issuance of the purchase orders and contracts should include a

a.   Credit to Vouchers Payable of $1,000,000.

b.   Credit to Budgetary Fund Balance—Reserved for Encumbrances of $850,000.

c.   Debit to Expenditures of $1,000,000.

d.   Debit to Appropriations of $850,000.

73. During its fiscal year ended June 30, 2012, Cliff City issued purchase orders totaling $5,000,000, which were properly charged to Encumbrances at that time. Cliff received goods and related invoices at the encumbered amounts totaling $4,500,000 before year-end. The remaining goods of $500,000 were not received until after year-end. Cliff paid $4,200,000 of the invoices received during the year. What amount of Cliff's encumbrances were outstanding at June 30, 2012?

a. $0

b. $300,000

c. $500,000

d. $800,000

74. Elm City issued a purchase order for supplies with an estimated cost of $5,000. When the supplies were received, the accompanying invoice indicated an actual price of $4,950. What amount should Elm debit (credit) to Budgetary Fund Balance—Reserved for Encumbrances after the supplies and invoice were received?

a. $ (50)

b. $ 50

c. $4,950

d. $5,000

75. A budgetary fund balance reserved for encumbrances in excess of a balance of encumbrances indicates

a.   An excess of vouchers payable over encumbrances.

b.   An excess of purchase orders over invoices received.

c.   An excess of appropriations over encumbrances.

d.   A recording error.

76. Encumbrances outstanding at year-end in a state's general fund should be reported as a

a.   Liability in the general fund.

b.   Fund balance reserve in the general fund.

c.   Liability in the General Long-Term Debt Account Group.

d.   Fund balance designation in the general fund.

77. When Rolan County adopted its budget for the year ending June 30, 2012, $20,000,000 was recorded for Estimated Revenues Control. Actual revenues for the year ended June 30, 2012, amounted to $17,000,000. In closing the budgetary accounts at June 30, 2012,

    a. Revenues Control should be debited for $3,000,000.

    b. Estimated Revenues Control should be debited for $3,000,000.

    c. Revenues Control should be credited for $20,000,000.

    d. Estimated Revenues Control should be credited for $20,000,000.

78. The budget of a governmental unit, for which the appropriations exceed the estimated revenues, was adopted and recorded in the general ledger at the beginning of the year. During the year, expenditures and encumbrances were less than appropriations, whereas revenues equaled estimated revenues. The Budgetary Fund Balance account is

    a. Credited at the beginning of the year and debited at the end of the year.

    b. Credited at the beginning of the year and **not** changed at the end of the year.

    c. Debited at the beginning of the year and credited at the end of the year.

    d. Debited at the beginning of the year and **not** changed at the end of the year.

79. The following information pertains to Park Township's general fund at December 31, 2012:

Total assets, including $200,000 of cash	$1,000,000
Total liabilities	600,000
Fund balance—Reserved for encumbrances	100,000

Appropriations do not lapse at year-end. At December 31, 2012, what amount should Park report as unreserved fund balance in its general fund balance sheet?

    a. $200,000
    b. $300,000
    c. $400,000
    d. $500,000

80. The following information pertains to Pine City's general fund for 2012:

Appropriations Control	$6,500,000
Expenditures Control	5,000,000
Other Financing Sources Control	1,500,000
Other Financing Uses Control	2,000,000
Revenues Control	8,000,000

After Pine's general fund accounts were closed at the end of 2012, the fund balance increased by

    a. $3,000,000
    b. $2,500,000
    c. $1,500,000
    d. $1,000,000

81. Cedar City issues $1,000,000, 6% revenue bonds at par on April 1 to build a new water line for the water enterprise fund. Interest is payable every six months. What amount of interest expense should be reported for the year ended December 31?

    a. $0
    b. $30,000
    c. $45,000
    d. $60,000

M. Expenditure Classification for Governmental Funds

82. The expenditure element "salaries and wages" is an example of which type of classification?

    a. Object.
    b. Program.
    c. Function.
    d. Activity.

N. Accounting for the General Fund

Items 83 and 84 are based on the following information for Oak City for the calendar year 2012:

Collections during 2012	$500,000
Expected collections during the first sixty days of 2013	100,000
Expected collections during the balance of 2013	60,000
Expected collections during January 2014	30,000
Estimated to be uncollectible	10,000
Total levy	$700,000

83. What amount should Oak City report for 2012 property tax revenues in the Statement of Revenues, Expenditures, and Changes in Fund Balances prepared for governmental funds?

    a. $700,000
    b. $690,000
    c. $600,000
    d. $500,000

84. What amount should Oak City report for 2012 property tax revenues in the government-wide Statement of Activities?

    a. $700,000
    b. $690,000
    c. $600,000
    d. $500,000

85. Which of the following transactions is an expenditure of a governmental unit's general fund?

    a. Contribution of enterprise fund capital by the general fund.

    b. Transfer from the general fund to a capital projects fund.

    c. Operating subsidy transfer from the general fund to an enterprise fund.

    d. Routine employer contributions from the general fund to a pension trust fund.

86. During the year, a city's electric utility, which is operated as an enterprise fund, rendered billings for electricity supplied to the general fund. Which of the following accounts should be debited by the general fund?

    a. Appropriations.
    b. Expenditures.
    c. Due to Electric Utility Enterprise Fund.
    d. Transfers.

87. Which of the following fund types used by a government most likely would have a Fund Balance—Reserved for Inventory of Supplies?

    a. General.
    b. Internal service.
    c. Enterprise.
    d. Debt service.

88. The following revenues were among those reported by Ariba Township in 2012:

Net rental revenue (after depreciation) from a parking garage owned by Ariba	$ 40,000
Interest earned on investments held for employees' retirement benefits	100,000
Property taxes	6,000,000

What amount of the foregoing revenues should be accounted for in Ariba's governmental-type funds?

   a. $6,140,000
   b. $6,100,000
   c. $6,040,000
   d. $6,000,000

Items 89 through 91 are based on the following:

The general fund of Cliff Township acquired two police cars at the beginning of January 2012, at a total cost of $40,000. The cars are expected to last for four years and have a $10,000 residual value. Straight-line depreciation is used. Cliff adopted the provisions of governmental accounting standards, *Basic Financial Statements—and Management's Discussion and Analysis—for State and Local Governments,* for its financial statements issued for 2012.

89. On the balance sheet for the governmental funds at December 31, 2012, the police cars will be reported under assets in the general fund column at which of the following amounts?

   a. $40,000
   b. $32,500
   c. $0
   d. $22,500

90. On the government-wide statement of net position at December 31, 2012, the police cars will be reported under assets in the governmental activities column at which of the following amounts?

   a. $40,000
   b. $32,500
   c. $0
   d. $22,500

91. On the statement of revenues, expenditures, and changes in fund balances prepared for the governmental funds for the year ended December 31, 2012, the police cars will be reported as

   a. Expenditures of $40,000.
   b. Expense of $7,500.
   c. Expenditures of $7,500.
   d. Expense of $40,000.

Items 92 through 95 are based on the following:

During the year ended December 31, 2012, the general fund of the city of Vicksburg has the following selected transactions:

- Acquired police cars for $75,000 in January 2012. The cars have an estimated five-year useful life and a $15,000 salvage value. The City uses the straight-line method to depreciate all of its capital assets.
- Transferred $30,000 to the pension trust fund. The amount represented the employer's contribution.
- Levied property taxes in the amount of $800,000. Two percent of the levy was not expected to be col-

lected. At December 31, 2012, $750,000 of the property taxes were collected, but the remainder was not expected to be collected within sixty days after the end of 2012.
- Received $100,000 of sales tax revenues from the state and was owed another $25,000 by the state for sales taxes collected in 2012 that will not be remitted to Vicksburg until mid-March 2013. The sales taxes expected to be received in March will be used to pay for expenditures incurred in 2013.

92. On the statement of revenues, expenditures, and changes in fund balances prepared for the governmental funds for the year ended December 31, 2012, what amount should be reported for expenditures in Vicksburg's general fund related to the acquisition of police cars and to the pension transfer?

   a. $ 42,000
   b. $105,000
   c. $ 75,000
   d. $ 30,000

93. On the statement of revenues, expenditures, and changes in fund balances prepared for the governmental funds for the year ended December 31, 2012, what amount should be reported for revenues in Vicksburg's general fund related to property taxes and sales taxes?

   a. $884,000
   b. $909,000
   c. $850,000
   d. $875,000

94. On the government-wide statement of activities prepared for the year ended December 31, 2012, what amount should be reported for expenses for governmental activities related to the acquisition of the police cars and to the pension transfer?

   a. $ 42,000
   b. $105,000
   c. $ 75,000
   d. $ 30,000

95. On the government-wide statement of activities prepared for the year ended December 31, 2012, what amount should be reported for revenues from governmental activities related to the property taxes and the sales taxes?

   a. $884,000
   b. $909,000
   c. $850,000
   d. $875,000

O. Accounting for Special Revenue Funds

96. In November 2011, Maple Township received an unexpected state grant of $100,000 to finance the purchase of school buses, and an additional grant of $5,000 was received for bus maintenance and operations. According to the terms of the grant, the State reimbursed Maple Township for $60,000 for the purchase of school buses and an additional $5,000 for bus maintenance during the year ended June 30, 2012. The remaining $40,000 of the capital grant is expected to be spent during the next fiscal year June 30, 2013. Maple's school bus system is appropriately accounted for in a special revenue fund. In connection with the grants for the purchase of school buses and bus maintenance, what amount should be reported as grant revenues for the year ending June 30, 2012, when using modified accrual accounting?

a. $ 5,000
b. $ 60,000
c. $ 65,000
d. $100,000

97. Lake County received the following proceeds that are legally restricted to expenditure for specified purposes:

Levies on affected property owners to install sidewalks	$500,000
Gasoline taxes to finance road repairs	900,000

What amount should be accounted for in Lake's special revenue funds?

a. $1,400,000
b. $ 900,000
c. $ 500,000
d. $0

98. Should a major special revenue fund with a legally adopted budget maintain its accounts on an accrual basis and integrate budgetary accounts into its accounting system?

	Maintain on accrual basis	Integrate budgetary accounts
a.	Yes	Yes
b.	Yes	No
c.	No	Yes
d.	No	No

P. Accounting for Capital Projects Funds

99. In 2012, Menton City received $5,000,000 of bond proceeds to be used for capital projects. Of this amount, $1,000,000 was expended in 2012. Expenditures for the $4,000,000 balance were expected to be incurred in 2013. These bond proceeds should be recorded in capital projects funds for

a. $5,000,000 in 2012.
b. $5,000,000 in 2013.
c. $1,000,000 in 2012 and $4,000,000 in 2013.
d. $1,000,000 in 2012 and in the general fund for $4,000,000 in 2012.

100. Financing for the renovation of Fir City's municipal park, begun and completed during 2012, came from the following sources:

Grant from state government	$400,000
Proceeds from general obligation bond issue	500,000
Transfer from Fir's general fund	100,000

In its 2012 capital projects fund operating statement, Fir should report these amounts as

	Revenues	Other financing sources
a.	$1,000,000	$0
b.	$ 900,000	$ 100,000
c.	$ 400,000	$ 600,000
d.	$0	$1,000,000

101. An impaired capital asset that is no longer used by a government should be reported in the financial statements at

a. Historical cost.
b. Historical cost adjusted for depreciation.
c. The lower of carrying value or fair value.
d. Fair value.

102. A government should recognized the impairment of a capital asset when events or circumstances indicate that there is a significant decline in service utility and

a. The asset is not in service.
b. The event or circumstance is outside the normal life cycle of the asset.
c. The asset is not covered by insurance.
d. The asset is not fully depreciated.

Q. Debt Service Funds

103. In which of the following fund types of a city government are revenues and expenditures recognized on the same basis of accounting as the general fund?

a. Pension trust.
b. Internal service.
c. Enterprise.
d. Debt service.

104. Japes City issued $1,000,000 general obligation bonds at 101 to build a new city hall. As part of the bond issue, the city also paid a $500 underwriter fee and $2,000 in debt issue costs. What amount should Japes City report as other financing sources?

a. $1,010,000
b. $1,008,000
c. $1,007,500
d. $1,000,000

105. Dale City is accumulating financial resources that are legally restricted to payments of general long-term debt principal and interest maturing in future years. At December 31, 2012, $5,000,000 has been accumulated for principal payments and $300,000 has been accumulated for interest payments. These restricted funds should be accounted for in the

	Debt service fund	General fund
a.	$0	$5,300,000
b.	$ 300,000	$5,000,000
c.	$5,000,000	$ 300,000
d.	$5,300,000	$0

106 On April 1, 2012, Oak County incurred the following expenditures in issuing long-term bonds:

Issue costs	$400,000
Debt insurance	90,000

Oak County has established a debt service fund for the payment of interest and principal of its long-term bonds. Assuming Oak County's fiscal year ends of June 30, what amount of issue costs and debt insurance costs should be reported as an asset on the governmental funds' balance sheet at June 30, 2012?

a. $0
b. $ 90,000
c. $400,000
d. $490,000

107. Receipts from a special tax levy to retire and pay interest on general obligation bonds should be recorded in which fund?

a. General.
b. Capital projects.
c. Debt service.
d. Special revenue.

108. Wood City, which is legally obligated to maintain a debt service fund, issued the following general obligation bonds on July 1, 2012:

Term of bonds	10 years
Face amount	$1,000,000
Issue price	101
Stated interest rate	6%

Interest is payable January 1 and July 1. What amount of bond premium should be amortized in Wood's debt service fund for the year ended December 31, 2012?

a. $1,000
b. $ 500
c. $ 250
d. $0

109. The debt service fund of a governmental unit is used to account for the accumulation of resources for, and the payment of, principal and interest in connection with a

	Trust fund	Proprietary fund
a.	No	No
b.	No	Yes
c.	Yes	Yes
d.	Yes	No

110. Tott City's serial bonds are serviced through a debt service fund with cash provided by the general fund. In a debt service fund's statements, how are cash receipts and cash payments reported?

	Cash receipts	Cash payments
a.	Revenues	Expenditures
b.	Revenues	Other Financing Use
c.	Other Financing Source	Expenditures
d.	Other Financing Source	Other Financing Use

111. On March 2, 2012, Finch City issued ten-year general obligation bonds at face amount, with interest payable March 1 and September 1. The proceeds were to be used to finance the construction of a civic center over the period April 1, 2012, to March 31, 2013. During the fiscal year ended June 30, 2012, no resources had been provided to the debt service fund for the payment of principal and interest.

On June 30, 2012, Finch's debt service fund should include interest payable on the general obligation bonds for

a. 0 months.
b. Three months.
c. Four months.
d. Six months.

R. Permanent Funds

112. According to GASB 52, real estate held as an investment by a government endowment should be reported at

a. Fair value.
b. Historical cost.
c. Historical cost less accumulated depreciation.
d. A nominal value.

S. Accounting for Special Assessments

113. Fish Road property owners in Sea County are responsible for special assessment debt that arose from a storm sewer project. If the property owners default, Sea has no obligation regarding debt service, although it does bill property owners for assessments and uses the monies it collects to pay debt holders. What fund type should Sea use to account for these collection and servicing activities?

a. Agency.
b. Debt service.
c. Investment trust funds.
d. Capital projects.

T. Accounting for Proprietary Funds

114. Cy City's Municipal Solid Waste Landfill Enterprise Fund was established when a new landfill was opened January 3, 2012. The landfill is expected to reach capacity and close December 31, 2028. Cy's 2012 expenses would include a portion of which of the year 2028 expected disbursements?

I. Cost of a final cover to be applied to the landfill.
II. Cost of equipment to be installed to monitor methane gas buildup.

a. I only.
b. II only.
c. Both I and II.
d. Neither I nor II.

115. Chase City uses an internal service fund for its central motor pool. The assets and liabilities account balances for this fund that are not eliminated normally should be reported in the government-wide statement of net position as

a. Governmental activities.
b. Business-type activities.
c. Fiduciary activities.
d. Note disclosures only.

116 The billings for transportation services provided to other governmental units are recorded by an internal service fund as

a. Transportation appropriations.
b. Operating revenues.
c. Interfund exchanges.
d. Intergovernmental transfers.

117. The following information for the year ended June 30, 2012, pertains to a proprietary fund established by Burwood Village in connection with Burwood's public parking facilities:

Receipts from users of parking facilities	$400,000
Expenditures	
Parking meters	210,000
Salaries and other cash expenses	90,000
Depreciation of parking meters	70,000

For the year ended June 30, 2012, this proprietary fund should report net income of

a. $0
b. $ 30,000
c. $100,000
d. $240,000

118. A state government had the following activities:

I.	State-operated lottery	$10,000,000
II.	State-operated hospital	3,000,000

Which of the above activities should be accounted for in an enterprise fund?

a. Neither I nor II.
b. I only.
c. II only.
d. Both I and II.

119. For governmental units, depreciation expense on assets acquired with capital grants externally restricted for capital acquisitions should be reported in which type of fund?

	Governmental fund	Proprietary fund
a.	Yes	No
b.	Yes	Yes
c.	No	No
d.	No	Yes

120. An enterprise fund would be used when the governing body requires that

I. Accounting for the financing of an agency's services to other government departments be on a cost-reimbursement basis.

II. User charges cover the costs of general public services.

III. Net income information be reported for an activity.

   a. I only.
   b. I and II.
   c. I and III.
   d. II and III.

121. The following transactions were among those reported by Cliff County's water and sewer enterprise fund for 2012:

Proceeds from sale of revenue bonds	$5,000,000
Cash received from customer households	3,000,000
Capital contributed by subdividers	1,000,000

In the water and sewer enterprise fund's statement of cash flows for the year ended December 31, 2012, what amount should be reported as cash flows from capital and related financing activities?

   a. $9,000,000
   b. $8,000,000
   c. $6,000,000
   d. $5,000,000

122. The orientation of accounting and reporting for all proprietary funds of governmental units is

   a. Income determination.
   b. Project.
   c. Flow of funds.
   d. Program.

Items 123 through 124 are based on the following:

Rock County has acquired equipment through a non-cancelable lease-purchase agreement dated December 31, 2012. This agreement requires no down payment and the following minimum lease payments:

December 31	Principal	Interest	Total
2013	$50,000	$15,000	$65,000
2014	50,000	10,000	60,000
2015	50,000	5,000	55,000

123. What account should be debited for $150,000 in the general fund at inception of the lease if the equipment is a general fixed asset and Rock does **not** use a capital projects fund?

   a. Other Financing Uses Control.
   b. Equipment.
   c. Expenditures Control.
   d. Memorandum entry only.

124. If the equipment is used in enterprise fund operations and the lease payments are to be financed with enterprise

fund revenues, what account should be debited for $150,000 in the enterprise fund at the inception of the lease?

   a. Expenses Control.
   b. Expenditures Control.
   c. Other Financing Sources Control.
   d. Equipment.

125. If the equipment is used in internal service fund operations and the lease payments are financed with internal service fund revenues, what account or accounts should be debited in the internal service fund for the December 31, 2012 lease payment of $65,000?

a.	Expenditures Control	$65,000
b.	Expenses Control	$65,000
c.	Capital Lease Payable	$50,000
	Expenses Control	15,000
d.	Expenditures Control	$50,000
	Expenses Control	15,000

126. Hill City's water utility fund held the following investments in US Treasury securities at June 30, 2012:

Investment	Date purchased	Maturity date	Carrying amount
Three-month T-bill	5/31/12	7/31/12	$30,000
Three-year T-note	6/15/12	8/31/12	50,000
Five-year T-note	10/1/08	9/30/13	100,000

In the fund's balance sheet, what amount of these investments should be reported as cash and cash equivalents at June 30, 2012?

   a. $0
   b. $ 30,000
   c. $ 80,000
   d. $180,000

U. Accounting for Fiduciary Funds

127. The following fund types used by Green Township had total assets at June 30, 2012, as follows:

Agency funds	$ 300,000
Debt service funds	1,000,000

Total fiduciary fund assets amount to

   a. $0
   b. $ 300,000
   c. $1,000,000
   d. $1,300,000

128. Which of the following is not Required Supplementary Information for the financial statements of a defined-benefit pension plan under GASB 67?

   a. A ten-year schedule of changes in pension liability.
   b. A ten-year schedule of the amounts of total pension liability, fiduciary net position, net pension liability, the covered-employee payroll, and selected ratios.
   c. A ten-year schedule of the actuarial computed required contribution, the required contribution, the actual contribution to the plan, and selected ratios.
   d. A ten-year schedule of interest rates used to discount the projected future benefits for the plan.

129. Grove County collects property taxes levied within its boundaries and receives a 1% fee for administering these collections on behalf of the municipalities located in the county. In 2012, Grove collected $1,000,000 for its municipalities and remitted $990,000 to them after deducting fees of $10,000. In the initial recording of the 1% fee, Grove's agency fund should credit

    a. Net Assets—Agency Fund, $10,000.
    b. Fees Earned—Agency Fund, $10,000.
    c. Due to Grove County General Fund, $10,000.
    d. Revenues Control, $10,000.

Items 130 and 131 are based on the following:

Elm City contributes to and administers a single-employer defined benefit pension plan on behalf of its covered employees. The plan is accounted for in a pension trust fund. For the year ended December 31, 2012, employer contributions to the pension trust fund amounted to $11,000.

130. What account should be credited in the pension trust fund to record the 2012 employer contribution of $11,000?

    a. Additions.
    b. Other Financing Sources Control.
    c. Due from Special Revenue Fund.
    d. Pension Benefit Obligation.

131. To record the 2012 pension contribution of $11,000, what debit is required in the governmental-type fund used in connection with employer pension contributions?

    a. Other Financing Uses Control.
    b. Expenditures Control.
    c. Expenses Control.
    d. Due to Pension Trust Fund.

V. Reporting Interfund Activity

132. In accordance with GASB 34 (as amended), *Basic Financial Statements—and Management's Discussion and Analysis—for State and Local Governments*, what types of interfund transactions are included in the amount reported for transfers on the government-wide statement of activities?

  I. Yearly operating subsidies from the general fund to an enterprise fund.
  II. Billings from an enterprise fund to an internal service fund for services rendered.

    a. I only.
    b. II only.
    c. Both I and II.
    d. Neither I nor II.

133. During the year ended December 31, 2012, the town of Jamestown had the following selected transactions:

- The general fund made a $100,000 advance to an internal service fund. The internal service fund will repay the advance in 2013.
- The water utility enterprise fund billed the general fund $25,000 for water usage.
- The general fund transferred $30,000 to a debt service fund to pay interest on general obligation bonds.

On Jamestown's government-wide statement of activities for the year ended December 31, 2012, what amount should be reported for transfers?

    a. $125,000
    b. $ 55,000
    c. $0
    d. $130,000

134. During the year ended December 31, 2012, the town of Harrisville had the following selected transactions:

- The general fund made a permanent transfer of $100,000 to an enterprise fund. The enterprise fund used the amount transferred to acquire capital assets.
- The general fund transferred $1,000,000 to a capital projects fund for the town's portion of the cost for the renovation of the town hall.
- The general fund was reimbursed $5,000 by an enterprise fund for expenses paid by the general fund that were properly charged as operating expenses of the enterprise fund.

On Harrisville's government-wide statement of activities for the year ended December 31, 2012, what amount should be reported as transfers?

    a. $ 100,000
    b. $1,100,000
    c. $1,005,000
    d. $ 105,000

Y. Public College and University Accounting (Governmental)—GASB 35

135. In accordance with GASB 35, a public college or university that chooses to report only business-type activities should present only the financial statements required for

    a. Enterprise funds.
    b. Government funds.
    c. Internal service funds.
    d. Enterprise and internal service funds.

136. In accordance with GASB 35, a public college or university that chooses to report both governmental and business-type activities should report

	Fund financial statements	Government-wide financial statements
a.	No	Yes
b.	Yes	No
c.	Yes	Yes
d.	No	No

137. A public college had tuition and fees of $20,000,000. Scholarships, for which no services were required, amounted to $1,000,000. Employee discounts, which were provided in exchange for services, amounted to $2,000,000. The amount to be reported as net tuition and fees by the public college would be

    a. $20,000,000
    b. $19,000,000
    c. $18,000,000
    d. $17,000,000

138. Which of the following is true regarding the Statement of Revenues, Expenses, and Changes in Net Position for a public college choosing to report as a special-purpose entity engaged in business-type activities only?

    a. State appropriations should be reported as non-operating income.
    b. An operating income figure must be displayed.
    c. Both contributions for plant and for endowment purposes must be reported separately after both operating and nonoperating revenues and expenses.
    d. All of the above.

Multiple-Choice Answers and Explanations

Answers

1. a	__ __	30. d	__ __	59. c	__ __	88. d	__ __	117. d	__ __
2. c	__ __	31. a	__ __	60. c	__ __	89. c	__ __	118. d	__ __
3. b	__ __	32. c	__ __	61. b	__ __	90. b	__ __	119. d	__ __
4. a	__ __	33. b	__ __	62. d	__ __	91. a	__ __	120. d	__ __
5. a	__ __	34. c	__ __	63. a	__ __	92. b	__ __	121. c	__ __
6. c	__ __	35. b	__ __	64. c	__ __	93. c	__ __	122. a	__ __
7. a	__ __	36. b	__ __	65. d	__ __	94. a	__ __	123. c	__ __
8. c	__ __	37. c	__ __	66. c	__ __	95. b	__ __	124. d	__ __
9. d	__ __	38. d	__ __	67. c	__ __	96. c	__ __	125. c	__ __
10. b	__ __	39. a	__ __	68. c	__ __	97. b	__ __	126. c	__ __
11. b	__ __	40. b	__ __	69. a	__ __	98. c	__ __	127. b	__ __
12. b	__ __	41. c	__ __	70. c	__ __	99. a	__ __	128. d	__ __
13. a	__ __	42. a	__ __	71. a	__ __	100. c	__ __	129. c	__ __
14. c	__ __	43. a	__ __	72. b	__ __	101. c	__ __	130. a	__ __
15. a	__ __	44. b	__ __	73. c	__ __	102. b	__ __	131. b	__ __
16. c	__ __	45. d	__ __	74. d	__ __	103. d	__ __	132. a	__ __
17. a	__ __	46. d	__ __	75. d	__ __	104. a	__ __	133. c	__ __
18. a	__ __	47. c	__ __	76. b	__ __	105. d	__ __	134. a	__ __
19. d	__ __	48. c	__ __	77. d	__ __	106. a	__ __	135. a	__ __
20. b	__ __	49. c	__ __	78. c	__ __	107. c	__ __	136. c	__ __
21. b	__ __	50. a	__ __	79. b	__ __	108. d	__ __	137. b	__ __
22. c	__ __	51. b	__ __	80. b	__ __	109. a	__ __	138. d	__ __
23. b	__ __	52. b	__ __	81. c	__ __	110. c	__ __		
24. a	__ __	53. a	__ __	82. a	__ __	111. a	__ __		
25. b	__ __	54. b	__ __	83. c	__ __	112. a	__ __		
26. c	__ __	55. b	__ __	84. b	__ __	113. a	__ __		
27. d	__ __	56. b	__ __	85. d	__ __	114. c	__ __		
28. d	__ __	57. a	__ __	86. b	__ __	115. a	__ __	1st: __/138 = __%
29. c	__ __	58. c	__ __	87. a	__ __	116. b	__ __	2nd: __/138 = __%

Explanations

1. (a) GASB Statement 55 presents four categories which provide the GAAP Hierarchy for state and local governments. The pronouncements with the highest authoritative status are officially issued accounting principles—GASB Statements and Interpretations.

2. (c) According to the GAAP hierarchy provided in GASB Statement 55, the category with the least authoritative status includes implementation guides (Q & As) published by the GASB staff, as well as practices that are widely recognized and prevalent in state and local government. Answers (a), (b) and (d) are all pronouncements listed in the second highest authoritative category.

3. (b) The requirement is to identify the accurate statement about service efforts and accomplishments reporting. Answer (b) is correct because the GASB Concepts Statements indicate that service efforts and accomplishments reporting is necessary but not required.

4. (a) The requirement is to identify the statement that is true about the essential characteristics of an asset. Answer (a) is correct because according to GASB Concepts Statements, assets are resources with present service capacity that the government presently controls.

5. (a) The requirement is to identify the elements of resource flows statements. Answer (a) is correct because the elements include outflow of resources and inflow of resources. Answers (b), (c), and (d) are incorrect because deferred outflow of resources and deferred inflow of resources are elements of the statement of net position.

6. (c) The requirement is to identify the true statement about service efforts and accomplishments reporting under GASB Concepts Statements. Answer (c) is correct because GASB Concepts Statements indicate that the objective of SEA reporting is to provide more complete information about a governmental entity's performance than can be provided in traditional financial statements and schedules. Answer (a) is incorrect because SEA reporting is not required. Answer (b) is incorrect because it is not more appropriate for governmental business-type activities. Answer (d) is incorrect because the traditional financial statements are more important to investors and creditors.

7. (a) The requirement is to identify the element that is most like a deferred outflow of resources. Answer (a) is correct because a deferred outflow of resources is a consumption of net position by the government that is applicable to a future reporting period. It is similar to an asset.

8. (c) GASB 34 (as amended) indicates that the basic financial statements include only the government-wide statements, the fund statements, and the notes to the financial statements.

9. (d) The concept underlying the definition of the financial reporting entity is that elected officials are accountable to their constituents for their actions. Accordingly, the financial reporting entity consists of (1) the primary government, (2) organizations for which the primary government is **financially accountable,** and (3) other organizations for which the nature and significance of their relationship with the primary government is such that exclusion would cause the reporting entity's financial statements to be misleading or incomplete. Thus, the basic criterion used to determine the reporting entity is financial accountability.

10. (b) The requirement is to determine how the school district's financial activity should be reported. The school district is a component unit, which means it is a legally separate organization for which the elected officials of a primary government are financially accountable. Component units can be presented either discretely or blended. If the component unit is so closely tied to the primary government that the activities seem to be indistinguishable, the presentation should be blended. Specifically, the unit is blended if (1) the governing body of the component unit is substantially the same as the primary government, and (a) there is a financial benefit/burden relationship, or (b) there is common management, (2) the services provided are entirely, or almost entirely to the primary government, or (3) the component's debt will be repaid entirely or almost entirely by the primary government. None of these criteria exist in this situation and, therefore, the school district should not be presented on a blended basis. Its financial information should be presented discretely.

11. (b) The requirement is to determine how the school district should be reported. A component unit is a legally separate organization for which the elected officials of a primary government are financially accountable. The school district is a component unit, which can be presented either discretely or blended. The unit is blended if (1) the governing body of the component unit is substantially the same as the primary government, and (a) there is a financial benefit/burden relationship, or (b) there is common management, (2) the services provided are entirely, or almost entirely to the primary government, or (3) the component's debt will be repaid entirely or almost entirely by the primary government. None of these criteria exist in this situation and, therefore, the school district should not be presented on a blended basis. Its financial information should be presented discretely.

12. (b) The requirement is to identify the characteristic that would cause the component unit to be presented on a blended basis. A component unit is a legally separate organization for which the elected officials of a primary government are financially accountable. The unit is blended if (1) the governing body of the component unit is substantially the same as the primary government, and (a) there is a financial benefit/burden relationship, or (b) there is common management, (2) the services provided are entirely, or almost entirely to the primary government, or (3) the component's debt will be repaid entirely or almost entirely by the primary government. Therefore, answer (b) is correct.

13. (a) The requirement is to identify the required government-wide financial statements. Answer (a) is correct because the required financial statements are the statement of net position and the statement of activities.

14. (c) The requirement is to identify the example of a deferred inflow of resources. Answer (c) is correct because

the proceeds from the sale of future revenues is an example of a deferred inflow of resources. Answers (a), (b), and (d) are incorrect because they represent deferred outflows of resources.

15. (a) The requirement is to identify the example of a deferred outflow of resources. Answer (a) is correct because the cost to acquire rights to future revenues is an example of a deferred outflow of resources. Answers (b), (c), and (d) are incorrect because they represent deferred inflows of resources.

16. (c) The requirement is to indicate where deferred outflows of resources are presented on government-wide financial statements. Answer (c) is correct because deferred outflows of resources are presented in a separate section following assets. Answers (a), (b), and (d) are incorrect because deferred outflows of resources are presented in a separate section following assets.

17. (a) GASB 9, para 19, indicates that "cash flows from operating activities include transactions of certain loan programs." These include "program loan" programs that are undertaken to fulfill a governmental responsibility, such as the loan program mentioned in this problem.

18. (a) GASB 34 (as amended), states that "The Board concluded that a government's basic financial statements should provide operational accountability information for the government as a whole, including information about the cost of services, operating results, and financial position." Therefore, answer (a) is correct.

19. (d) In accordance with governmental accounting standards, capital assets, exclusive of infrastructure assets, are reported on the government-wide statement of net position at cost less accumulated depreciation. In the case involving Fullerton City, the amount reported under assets is $2,750,000, computed by subtracting $750,000 of accumulated depreciation from the $3,500,000 cost of the capital assets.

20. (b) In the net position section of the government-wide statement of net position, governmental accounting standards require that capital assets be reported as net investment in capital assets which is capital assets net of depreciation and related debt and any related deferred outflows of resources and deferred inflows of resources. In the case of Fullerton City, the amount reported would be $1,500,000, computed by subtracting $1,250,000 from $2,750,000.

21. (b) In accordance with governmental accounting standards, depreciation expense on infrastructure assets is not required if the government chooses the modified approach. Under the modified approach, infrastructure assets are reported on the government-wide statement of net position at their cost without reduction for accumulated depreciation. On the government-wide statement of activities, the cost to extend the life of the infrastructure assets is reported as an expense, and certain information about infrastructure assets is disclosed as required supplementary information.

22. (c) The requirement is to select the item that reflects the amount that should be presented as a liability related to the pension plan. Answer (c) is correct because GASB 68 requires recognition of the net pension liability which is equal to the portion of the actuarial present value of projected benefit payments attributable to past periods of employee service minus the pension plan's fiduciary net position.

23. **(b)** The requirement is to identify the method required by GASB 68 to attribute the actuarial present value of projected benefit payments of each employee to periods. Answer (b) is correct because GASB 68 requires use of the entry age actuarial cost method.

24. **(a)** The requirement is to identify the period over which the effects of differences in expected and actual investment returns is recognized. Answer (a) is correct because the effects are recognized over a closed period of five years.

25. **(b)** The requirement is to identify the rate that should be used to discount projected future payments if the pension plan's net fiduciary position is not expected to be sufficient to make projected benefit payments. Answer (b) is correct because GASB 68 requires the use of the rate for 20-year, tax-exempt general obligation municipal bonds with an average rating of AA/Aa or higher.

26. **(c)** According to governmental accounting standards, the government-wide statement of activities should be prepared using the accrual basis of accounting and the flow of economic resources measurement focus. As a result, capital assets are reported as assets and depreciated over their useful lives, and depreciation expense should be reported on the statement of activities. The statement of revenues, expenses, and changes in fund net position prepared for the proprietary funds is also prepared using the accrual basis of accounting and the flow of economic resources measurement focus. Therefore, capital assets are depreciated over their useful lives, and depreciation expense is reported on the statement of revenues, expenses, and changes in fund net position.

27. **(d)** According to governmental accounting standards, governments should prepare government-wide financial statements based upon the accrual basis of accounting and the economic resources measurement focus. In addition to the government-wide financial statements, governments are also required to report financial statements for governmental funds, proprietary funds, and fiduciary funds. The financial statements for governmental funds are based upon the modified accrual basis and the financial resources measurement focus, while the financial statements for proprietary and fiduciary funds are based upon the accrual basis of accounting and the flow of economic resources measurement focus.

28. **(d)** According to GASB 34 (as amended), infrastructure assets are required to be reported on the government-wide statement of net position. The use of the modified approach for infrastructure assets means that these assets are not depreciated if certain conditions are satisfied. However, infrastructure assets are reported on the statement of net position, even if they are not depreciated. According to GASB 34 (as amended), component units are reported on the entity-wide financial statements. They are not reported on the financial statements of the governmental funds.

29. **(c)** A fund is defined as a fiscal and accounting entity with a self-balancing set of accounts. These funds record cash and other financial resources, together with all related liabilities and residual equities or balances, and changes therein, **and are segregated for the purpose of carrying on specific activities or attaining certain objectives** in accordance with special regulations, restrictions, or limitations.

30. **(d)** GASB 9 indicates that cash flows from investing activities includes interest received as returns on investments. The candidate should note that this is different from SFAS 95, which classifies interest on investments as cash flows from operating activities.

31. **(a)** The Governmental Accounting Standards Board (GASB) has the authority to establish standards of financial reporting for all units of state and local government. Upon its formation in 1984, GASB adopted the past pronouncements of its predecessor organization, the National Council on Governmental Accounting (NCGA), and guidelines in the AICPA *Audits of State and Local Governmental Units*, which the GASB later modified. The FASB sets standards for profit-seeking businesses, and not governmental units.

32. **(c)** Prior to the issuance of GASB Statement 54, fund balance consisted of reserved and unreserved classifications. GASB Statement 54 establishes five fund balance classifications (nonspendable, restricted, committed, assigned and unassigned) for financial reporting purposes.

33. **(b)** GASB Statement 54 includes definitions for governmental fund types (general, special revenue, capital projects, debt service and permanent funds). Special revenue funds are used to account for the proceeds of specific revenue sources that are restricted or committed.

34. **(c)** Under GASB Statement 54, amounts that are constrained by the government's *intent* are classified in an assigned fund balance.

35. **(b)** The requirement is to determine which event(s) should be included in a statement of cash flows for a government entity. Governmental funds do not have a statement of cash flows because they are accounted for on the modified accrual basis. A statement of cash flows is included for proprietary funds because they are accounted for on the accrual basis. The cash inflow from issuing bonds to finance city hall construction is accounted for in the governmental funds. The cash outflow from a city utility representing payments in lieu of property taxes is accounted for in the proprietary funds.

36. **(b)** Cash flows from sale of revenue bonds and capital contributed by subdividers are classified as cash flows from capital and related financing activities. Both the $4,500,000 proceeds from sale of revenue bonds and $900,000 capital contributed by subdividers would be reported as cash flows from capital and related financing activities. Cash flows from customer households are operating cash flows.

37. **(c)** The statement of cash flows is applicable to proprietary funds and governmental entities that use proprietary fund accounting, including public benefit corporations and authorities, governmental utilities, and governmental hospitals. PERS (Public Employee Retirement Systems) and pension trust funds are exempt from this requirement.

38. **(d)** In accordance with governmental accounting standards, there are three financial statements that should be prepared for proprietary funds. The financial statements for proprietary funds include

1. The statement of net position
2. The statement of revenues, expenses, and changes in fund net position
3. The statement of cash flows

39. **(a)** In accordance with GASB 34 (as amended), the focus of fund financial statements is on major and nonmajor funds, not on fund types. On the balance sheet for the governmental funds, the general fund is always reported as a major fund, while other funds are evaluated as major or nonmajor based upon criteria specified in GASB 34 (as amended). A separate column is required for each major fund, while all nonmajor funds are aggregated in a single column. On the balance sheet for the governmental funds, fund balances are reported in two categories—reserved and unreserved. The terms restricted and unrestricted are not used on the balance sheet for the governmental funds.

40. **(b)** The requirement is to identify the required financial statements for a proprietary fund. Answer (b) is correct because the required financial statements are the statement of net position, the statement of revenues, expenses and changes in fund net position, and the statement of cash flows. Answer (a), (c), and (d) are incorrect because they are not correct regarding the required financial statements.

41. **(c)** In accordance with governmental accounting standards, the statement of net position for proprietary funds should (1) report assets and liabilities in current and noncurrent classifications, and (2) report all the activities of internal service funds in a single column.

42. **(a)** According to governmental accounting standards, the financial statements of proprietary funds should be based upon the accrual basis of accounting and the economic resources measurement focus. Therefore, the statement of net position for proprietary funds is prepared on the accrual basis and the economic resources measurement focus. On the other hand, the financial statements prepared for governmental funds should be based upon the modified accrual basis of accounting and the financial resources measurement focus. Therefore, the statement of revenues, expenditures, and changes in fund balances prepared for governmental funds is not prepared on the accrual basis and the economic resources measurement focus.

43. **(a)** According to governmental accounting standards, two financial statements should be prepared for fiduciary funds—the statement of fiduciary net position and the statement of changes in fiduciary net position. Fiduciary funds include pension trust, investment trust, private-purpose trust, and agency funds. Agency funds should be reported on the statement of fiduciary net position, but not on the statement of changes in fiduciary net position. Since agency funds report only assets and liabilities, they are reported on the statement of fiduciary net position, but they are not reported on the statement of changes in fiduciary net position.

44. **(b)** According to governmental accounting standards, private-purpose trust funds are fiduciary funds that should be reported on two fiduciary fund financial statements: (1) the statement of fiduciary net position and (2) the statement of changes in fiduciary net position. Therefore,

private-purpose trust funds are reported on the statement of changes in fiduciary net position. According to governmental accounting standards, the government-wide statement of net position discloses information about governmental activities, business-type activities, and component units. Fiduciary activities are not disclosed on the government-wide financial statements. This means that private-purpose trust funds would not be reported on the statement of net position for governmental and business-type activities.

45. **(d)** According to governmental accounting standards, the statement of cash flows is prepared only for the proprietary funds. The statement of cash flows is not a government-wide financial statement. Therefore, governmental and fiduciary fund types are not reported on the statement of cash flows.

46. **(d)** According to governmental accounting standards, the statement of cash flows is prepared only for the proprietary funds. The statement of cash flows is not a government-wide financial statement. The format of the statement of cash flows consists of four sections. The sections include cash flows from (1) operating activities, (2) noncapital financing activities, (3) capital and related financing activities, and (4) investing activities. This format for the statement of cash flows is different from the format used by business enterprises that discloses operating, investing, and financing activities.

47. **(c)** According to governmental accounting standards, the balance sheet prepared for the governmental funds is based on the modified accrual basis of accounting and financial resources measurement focus. However, the government-wide statement of net position is prepared based on the accrual basis of accounting and the economic resources measurement focus. The differences between these two financial statements result in a difference between the amount reported for net position for governmental activities on the statement of net position and the amount reported for fund balances on the balance sheet for the governmental funds. Governmental accounting standards require that the reasons for this difference be reported in a reconciliation schedule. One of the reasons for the difference is the acquisition of capital assets by governmental funds during the year. These capital assets do not appear under assets on the balance sheet of the governmental funds because they are recorded as expenditures using the modified accrual basis of accounting and the financial resources measurement focus. Therefore, the acquisition of capital assets has the effect of reducing the fund balances of governmental funds on the balance sheet. However, capital assets are reported as assets on the government-wide statement of net position. Capital assets acquired by governmental funds are reported on this statement as assets under governmental activities. Therefore, total assets related to governmental activities are not affected on the statement of net position when capital assets are acquired. Accordingly, capital assets used in governmental activities are items that are reported in the schedule that reconciles the net position of governmental activities with the fund balances of the governmental funds. The assets and liabilities of internal service funds are additional items that cause a difference between the fund balances of the government funds and the net position of governmental activities. The reason that the assets and liabilities of internal service funds cause a difference is that they are included with governmental activities on the statement of net position, thereby causing net position of governmental activities to increase. However, internal service fund assets and liabilities are not reported in the governmental fund financial statements; rather, they are included in the proprietary fund financial statements. Therefore, the fund balances of the governmental funds do not include these items. Accordingly, the assets and liabilities of internal service funds are reported in the schedule that reconciles the net position of governmental activities with the fund balances of the governmental funds.

48. **(c)** According to governmental accounting standards, the statement of revenues, expenditures, and changes in fund balances prepared for the governmental funds is prepared using the modified accrual basis of accounting and the financial resources measurement focus. However, the government-wide statement of activities is prepared using the accrual basis of accounting and the economic resources measurement focus. The differences between these two financial statements result in a difference between the amount reported for the change in net position for governmental activities on the statement of activities, and the amount reported for the net change in fund balances on the statement of revenues, expenditures, and changes in fund balances for the governmental funds. Governmental accounting standards require that the reasons for this difference be reported in a reconciliation schedule. One of the reasons for the difference is capital assets that were acquired by governmental funds during the year. On the statement of revenues, expenditures, and changes in fund balances, capital assets are reported as expenditures, using the modified accrual basis of accounting and the financial resources measurement focus. However, capital assets acquired by governmental funds are reported as assets and are depreciated on the government-wide statement of activities. Therefore, the difference between capital expenditures and depreciation expense is reported as a reconciling item. On the other hand, the revenues and expenses of internal service funds are additional items that cause a difference between the net change in the fund balances reported on the statement of revenues, expenditures, and changes in fund balances of the governmental funds and the change in the net position of governmental activities reported on the statement of activities. The reason that the revenues and expenses of internal service funds cause a difference is that they are included with governmental activities on the statement of activities, thereby causing the net change in fund balances of governmental activities to increase. However, internal service fund revenues and expenses are not reported in the governmental fund financial statements; rather, they are included in the proprietary fund financial statements. Therefore, the net change in fund balances of the governmental funds do not include internal service fund revenues and expenses. Accordingly, the revenues and expenses of internal service funds should be reported in the schedule that reconciles the change in net position of governmental activities with the net change in the fund balances of the governmental funds.

49. **(c)** According to governmental accounting standards, the accrual basis of accounting and the economic resources measurement focus are concepts that go together. This means that financial statements prepared using the accrual basis also are based upon the economic resources measurement focus. Both the government-wide statement of net position and the statement of changes in fiduciary net position are prepared using the accrual basis of accounting and the economic resources measurement focus. The only financial statements that use the financial resources measurement focus are those prepared for governmental funds—the balance sheet and the statement of revenues, expenditures, and changes in fund balances.

50. **(a)** According to governmental accounting standards, pension trust funds are fiduciary funds that are reported on the statement of changes in fiduciary net position. On the statement of net position for proprietary funds, net position is disclosed in three classifications: (1) net investment in capital assets, (2) restricted, and (3) unrestricted. Retained earnings is not disclosed on the statement of net position for proprietary funds; the term "net position" is used as the equity account.

51. **(b)** According to governmental accounting standards, the statement of cash flows is prepared for proprietary funds. The statement format is not the same as that for business enterprises. The format for the statement of cash flows for proprietary funds contains four sections: (1) cash flows from operating activities, (2) cash flows from noncapital financing activities, (3) cash flows from capital and related financing activities, and (4) cash flows from investing activities. The cash flows from operating activities may be presented using the direct or indirect methods. Cash paid for interest is not reported in the operating activities section. It would be disclosed either in the noncapital financing activities' section or the capital and related financing activities' section, depending upon where the debt that caused the interest payments was reported. Interest revenue received in cash is not reported in the operating activities' section. It is reported in the investing activities' section because this is where the investments were reported that resulted in the interest revenue.

52. **(b)** The governmental fund measurement focus is on determination of current financial position (sources, uses, and balances of financial resources), rather than upon income determination.

53. **(a)** Governmental fund revenues should be recognized in the accounting period in which they become available and measurable. Governmental funds include the general fund, special revenue funds, capital projects funds, debt service funds, and permanent funds. Proprietary fund revenues should be recognized in the accounting period in which they are earned and become measurable. Proprietary funds include the enterprise and internal service funds. As the question requires the funds in which revenue is recognized in the period it becomes available and measurable, this would include the general fund but not the enterprise fund.

54. **(b)** GASB 33, para 7, indicates that "imposed nonexchange revenues result from assessments by governments on nongovernmental entities, including individuals, other than assessments on nonexchange transactions. Examples include property (ad valorem) taxes; fines and penalties...."

55. **(b)** The levy of property taxes is a nonexchange transaction. GASB 33 defines nonexchange transactions as transactions "in which a government gives (or receives) value without directly receiving (or giving) equal value in exchange." Exchange transactions are transactions "in which each party receives and gives up essentially equal values." In the case of a property tax levy, the government is receiving value, the right to receive payments from property owners, without directly giving equal value in return. The government services that are financed from a property tax levy are not provided to individual taxpayers in proportion to the amount of property taxes that are paid. The other answers are incorrect because they are examples of exchange transactions.

56. (b) Deferred inflow of resources should be credited upon receipt of the grant. Cash received from government-mandated grants should be reported as a deferred inflow when cash is received prior to meeting the timing eligibility requirement. Note that, if there was no time restriction placed on the government-mandated grant by the state, Elizabeth City would have reported revenue for the year ended June 30, 2012.

57. (a) According to the guidance provided in GASB 33, the grant from the state is an example of a government-mandated type of nonexchange transaction. Government-mandated nonexchange transactions exists when the providing government, such as a state government, requires the receiving government to expend the funds for a specific purpose.

58. (c) According to the guidance provided by GASB 33, sales tax revenues are an example of a derived tax revenue. Derived tax revenues result from taxes assessed by government on exchange transactions. In the case of sales taxes, exchange transactions between merchants and consumers provide the basis for the collection of the sales tax revenues.

59. (c) The general fund of Eldorado should report the sales taxes to be received in July 2012 as revenue for the year ended June 30, 2012. Under the modified accrual measurement focus, the sales taxes should be reported as revenue for the year ended June 30, 2012, because the sales taxes are available to finance expenditures made in the year ended June 30, 2012.

60. (c) According to the guidance provided by GASB 33, property tax revenues are an example of an imposed tax revenue. Imposed revenues result from taxes and other assessments imposed by governments that are not derived from underlying transactions.

61. (b) In accordance with GASB 33, the modified accrual basis of accounting should be used for recording and reporting property tax revenues for the general fund on the statement of revenues, expenditures, and changes in fund balances. Under the modified accrual basis of accounting, revenues are recognized in the period when they are both measurable and available to pay for expenditures incurred during the current fiscal period. With respect to property tax revenues, "available" means collected during the year and within the first sixty days after the end of the year. For the general fund of Karsten City, the property taxes collected in 2012 of $850,000 as well as the $100,000 expected to be collected by March 1 of 2013 would be added to get the property tax revenues recognized in 2012. The sum of $950,000 of property tax revenues would be reported by the general fund on the statement of revenues, expenditures, and changes in fund balances for the year ended December 31,

2012. The journal entries to record the property tax levy and collections for 2012 appear below.

Property taxes receivable—Current	1,000,000	
Property tax revenues ($850,000 + 100,000)		950,000
Deferred inflow (report below liabilities on the balance sheet)		40,000
Allowance for estimated uncollectible property taxes—Current		10,000
Cash	850,000	
Property taxes receivable— Current		850,000

The deferred inflow account of $40,000 represents the property taxes expected to be collected after March 1, 2013. Because the taxes are expected to be collected after sixty days from the end of 2012, the taxes are not considered available to pay for expenditures incurred in 2012. This is the reason for crediting deferred inflow in 2012.

62. (d) In accordance with GASB 33, imposed nonexchange transactions include taxes and other assessments derived from underlying transactions. Examples include property taxes, special assessments, and fines and forfeits. For the general fund of Ward Village, imposed nonexchange transactions would include property tax revenues of $125,000 and fines of $10,000. Sales taxes and income taxes would be classified as derived tax revenues.

63. (a) In accordance with GASB 33, the modified accrual basis of accounting should be used for recording and reporting revenues reported by the general fund on the Statement of Revenues, Expenditures, and Changes in Fund Balances. The modified accrual basis of accounting for revenues results in revenues being recognized in the period in which they are both measurable and available to pay for expenditures incurred during the current fiscal period. The sales tax advance of $25,000 should be reported as revenue in 2012 because it was available to pay for expenditures incurred by the general fund in 2012. On the other hand, the cash received from property owners of $20,000 should not be reported as revenue in 2012 because the money cannot be used to pay for expenditures incurred by the general fund in 2012. The property taxes received in December 2012 should be reported as a deferred inflow of resources on the December 31, 2012 balance sheet for the general fund. Deferred inflow would appear below the liabilities classification. The entry to record both of the cash receipts in the general fund in December 2012 appears below.

Cash	45,000	
Sales tax revenues		25,000
Deferred inflow		20,000

64. (c) According to GASB 33, revenues that result from taxes assessed by government on exchange transactions are classified as derived tax revenues. Examples of derived tax revenue include sales taxes, income taxes, and motor fuel taxes. Property tax revenues and fines and forfeits are examples of revenues that come from imposed nonexchange transactions. Imposed nonexchange transactions are taxes and other assessments imposed by governments that are not derived from underlying transactions. Unrestricted government grants are an example of voluntary nonexchange transactions. This category includes grants and entitlements from one government to another where the providing government does not impose certain requirements on the receiving government.

65. **(d)** According to GASB 33, revenues that result from taxes and other assessments imposed by governments that are not derived from underlying transactions are categorized as imposed nonexchange transactions. Examples include property taxes, special assessments, and fines and forfeits. Income taxes, sales taxes, and motor fuel taxes are examples of derived tax revenues. Derived tax revenues result from taxes assessed by government on exchange transactions.

66. **(c)** The requirement is to identify the item that is not a requirement for a government to start capitalizing software costs. GASB 51 establishes three requirements to begin capitalizing the cost of an internally generated intangible asset: (1) the government must determine the objective and the service capacity of the project, (2) the government must establish the feasibility of the project, and (3) the government must establish its intention to complete or continue the project. There is no specific requirement in GASB 51 to have developed an accurate budget for the project. Therefore, answer (c) is correct.

67. **(c)** The requirement is to identify the item that correctly describes the proper accounting for the transfer of future revenue. Answer (c) is correct because a sale of future revenue should be recorded as deferred inflow of resources and recognized over the life of the agreement.

68. **(c)** The requirement is to identify the proper accounting for the arrangement. Answer (c) is correct because the city should record cash and a deferred inflow of resources in the amount of $3 billion. Answer (a) is incorrect because the city should retain the asset on its financial statements. Answer (b) is incorrect because the revenue should be recognized over the term of the agreement. Answer (d) is incorrect because the $3 billion in cash is received at the time of execution of the arrangement.

69. **(a)** To record the budget, Ridge would make the following journal entry:

Estimated Revenues Control	100,000	
Appropriations Control		80,000
Budgetary Fund Balance		20,000

Therefore, the Appropriations account is credited for the anticipated expenditures.

70. **(c)** To record the budget, Ridge would make the following journal entry:

Estimated Revenues Control	100,000	
Appropriations Control		80,000
Budgetary Fund Balance		20,000

Therefore, the Budgetary Fund Balance account is credited for the anticipated surplus of revenues over expenditures.

71. **(a)** Revenues to the general fund are defined as "increases in fund financial resources other than from interfund transfers and debt issue proceeds." Transfers to a fund and debt issue proceeds received by a fund are classified as other financing sources of the fund. Therefore, in Maple's budgetary entry, estimated revenues would be debited for the $9,000,000 expected from property taxes, licenses, and fines. The Estimated Other Financing Sources account

would be debited for the $6,000,000, consisting of the debt issue proceeds and the interfund transfers.

72. **(b)** Assuming that encumbrance accounting is utilized by the city, the journal entry to record the issuance of purchase orders and contracts is a debit to Encumbrances Control and a credit to Budgetary Fund Balance—Reserved for Encumbrances for the amount of the purchase order or estimated cost of the contracts.

73. **(c)** As Cliff approves and issues its purchase orders, the purchase order amount ($5,000,000) is recorded in the Encumbrances Control account. As the goods are received, the related purchase order amount of these goods (i.e., the amount that was originally recorded, $4,500,000) is removed from the Encumbrances Control account. Therefore, at year-end, the amount of outstanding encumbrances is $500,000. Keep in mind that the actual invoice amount is not the amount removed from the Encumbrances Control account. The invoice amount will be vouchered and charged to Expenditures Control.

74. **(d)** When Elm issued its purchase order, the following journal entry would have been made to encumber the amount:

Encumbrances Control	5,000	
Budgetary Fund Balance—Reserved for Encumbrances		5,000

When the supplies were received the following journal entries would have been made:

Budgetary Fund Balance—Reserved for Encumbrances	5,000	
Encumbrances Control		5,000
Expenditures Control	4,950	
Vouchers Payable		4,950

75. **(d)** When purchase orders for goods or services are approved and issued, the Encumbrances Control account is debited and the Budgetary Fund Balance—Reserved for Encumbrances is credited for the amount of the purchase orders. As goods are received or services are rendered the above encumbrance entry is reversed. Thus, the amount left in each would be zero. Note that the same amount is initially recorded in each of the accounts (i.e., the debit equals the credit). The same amount is also relieved from both accounts. A Budgetary Fund Balance—Reserved for Encumbrances in excess of a balance in the Encumbrances Control account indicates there has been a recording error.

76. **(b)** Encumbrances outstanding at year-end represent the estimated amount of the expenditures that could result if unperformed contracts in process at year-end are computed. Encumbrances outstanding at year-end are not expenditures or liabilities. Where appropriations do not lapse at year-end, encumbrances outstanding at year-end should be reported as reservations of fund balance for the subsequent year expenditures. Where appropriations lapse at year-end, the governmental unit may honor the contracts in progress at year-end or cancel them. If the governmental unit intends to honor them, the encumbrances outstanding at year-end should be disclosed by reservation of fund balance.

77. **(d)** When closing entries are made for a governmental unit, Estimated Revenues Control is credited for the same amount that it was debited for in the beginning of the period budget/entry. Also, Revenues Control is debited in the amount of recorded revenue for the year. In this case, Estimated Revenues Control would be credited for $20,000,000 and Revenues Control would be debited for $17,000,000 to close the books. Revenues Control and Estimated Revenues Control are not netted in the closing entry.

78. (c) The Budgetary Fund Balance account is debited upon budget adoption when the appropriations exceed the estimated revenues. The following entry is made when the budget is adopted:

Estimated Revenues Control	xx	
Budgetary Fund Balance	xx	
Appropriations Control		xx

At the end of the year, the budgetary accounts must be closed out. The budgetary closing entry is simply a reverse of the adoption entry.

Appropriations Control	xx	
Estimated Revenues Control		xx
Budgetary Fund Balance		xx

The Budgetary Fund Balance is debited at the beginning of the year when appropriations exceed the estimated revenues. An entry must be made to close the Budgetary Fund Balance account at the end of the year. Note that any differences between the budgetary revenues and appropriations and the actual revenues and expenditures and encumbrances do not affect the **Budgetary** Fund Balance account. They would, however, affect the Unreserved Fund Balance account when the operations accounts are closed out.

79. (b) The $100,000 balance in the Fund Balance—Reserved for Encumbrances account indicates that there were open purchase orders at year-end. Since the appropriations do not lapse at year-end, the Fund Balance—Reserved for Encumbrances account will not be closed but will be reported as a separate line item in the fund balance section of the balance sheet. The term "reserve" indicates that the funds are not available for expenditure. Therefore, the $100,000 cannot be included in the unreserved fund balance amount. Therefore, the amount of the Unreserved Fund Balance in the 2012 balance sheet would be $300,000 ($1,000,000 − $600,000 − $100,000).

80. (b) The closing of the general fund accounts is done by closing the budgetary accounts against each other and the actual revenue, expenditure and other accounts to the Unreserved Fund Balance. This is done most easily by reversing the beginning of the year budget entry in one entry and then using a separate entry to close the actual accounts to fund balance. The following entry would therefore be made to close the actual accounts to obtain the amount of increase in the fund balance:

General Fund

Other Financing Sources Control	1,500,000	
Revenues Control	8,000,000	
Expenditures Control		5,000,000
Other Financing Uses Control		2,000,000
Fund Balance—Unreserved		2,500,000

The Appropriations account would be closed in the reversal of the budget entry and has no effect on fund balance.

81. (c) GASB 34 (as amended), indicates that proprietary funds (including enterprise funds) are to use accrual ac-

counting. Paragraph 93 indicates that FASB pronouncements issued on or before November 30, 1989, are to be followed unless superseded by a GASB pronouncement. Accrual accounting recognizes interest expense over time; in this case, interest expense would be $1,000,000 × .06 × 9/12 = $45,000.

82. (a) Expenditure classification by object is based upon the type of items purchased or services obtained. Examples of "Current Operations" object of expenditure classifications are personal services, supplies, and other services and charges. Salaries are an example of classification by object. Function or program classifications provide information regarding the overall purpose or objectives of expenditures (i.e., police protection, sanitation, highways and streets, etc.). Activity classification provides data for calculating expenditures per unit of activity (i.e., street resurfacing).

83. (c) "When a property tax assessment is made, it is to finance the budget of a particular period, and the revenue produced from any property tax assessment should be recognized in the fiscal period for which it was levied, provided the 'available' criteria are met. 'Available' means then due, or past due and receivable within the current period, and collected within the current period or expected to be collected soon enough thereafter to pay liabilities of the current period. Such time thereafter shall not exceed sixty days." This is how property tax revenues are reported on the Statement of Revenues, Expenditures, and Changes in Fund Balances for governmental funds. Therefore, both the collections during 2012 of $500,000 and the expected collections during the first sixty days of 2013 of $100,000 would be reported as property tax revenues for 2012. Remember that the estimated uncollectible amounts are not reported on the operating statement as an offset to revenues, but rather are reported as a contra asset account. The governmental unit, in calculating the amount of the levy, factors in what has historically been uncollectible, so that the revenues in effect have already been adjusted.

84. (b) Under GASB Statement 33, imposed nonexchange revenues, including property taxes, should be recorded in the year for which budgeted. In this case, the amount would be $690,000, the total levy less the estimated uncollectible amount.

85. (d) Interfund services provided and used are transactions that would be treated as revenues or expenditures/expenses if they involved organizations external to the government (i.e., **routine employer contributions from a general fund to a pension trust fund,** internal service fund billings to departments, enterprise funds billing for services provided to the general fund). The proper accounting for interfund services provided and used is to treat them as revenues in the fund providing the goods or services and **as expenditures/ expenses in the fund receiving the goods or services,** exactly as if the transactions involved parties external to the government. Thus, answer (d) is correct because the general fund should record an expenditure for routine employer contributions to the pension trust fund. Answer (a) is incorrect because the contribution of enterprise fund capital by the general fund should be recorded in the general fund as a transfer. Answers (b) and (c) are incorrect because routine transfers between funds should also be recorded as transfers.

86. (b) Interfund services provided and used are treated as revenues or expenditures/expenses if they involved organizations external to the government (i.e., a city's electric utility providing electricity to the general fund, internal service fund billings to departments, routine employer contributions from a general fund to a pension trust fund). The proper accounting for interfund services provided and used transactions is to treat them as revenues in the fund providing the goods or services and as expenditures/expenses in the fund receiving the goods or services, exactly as if the transactions involved parties external to the government. The general fund should recognize an expenditure for the amount billed by the city's electric utility.

87. (a) The internal service fund and the enterprise fund use the accrual basis of accounting and both report net position, not fund balances. Net position is reported in the following manner: (1) net investment in capital assets, (2) restricted, and (3) unrestricted. The capital projects fund does not keep an inventory of supplies and therefore would not have a Fund Balance—Reserved for Inventory of Supplies. The general fund does maintain an inventory of supplies and would therefore have a Fund Balance—Reserved for Inventory of Supplies.

88. (d) The $6,000,000 in property taxes would be accounted for in Ariba's general fund, which is a governmental fund. The $40,000 of net rental revenue (after depreciation) from a parking garage would be accounted for in an enterprise fund, which is a proprietary fund. An enterprise fund provides products or services to the public, such as the use of the parking garage. The $100,000 interest earned on investments held for employees' retirement benefits would be included in a trust fund (more than likely a pension trust fund).

89. (c) In accordance with GASB 34 (as amended), the balance sheet prepared for the governmental funds should be based on the current financial resources measurement focus and the modified accrual basis of accounting. This means that capital assets, such as police cars, are not reported on the balance sheet for governmental funds. Instead, the police cars are reported as expenditures on the statement of revenues, expenditures, and changes in fund balances for the year ended December 31, 2012.

90. (b) In accordance with GASB 34 (as amended), the government-wide statement of net position is prepared using the economic resources measurement focus and the full accrual basis of accounting. In the column for governmental activities, the police cars would be reported at $32,500. This amount is the original cost of $40,000 less accumulated depreciation of $7,500. The use of full accrual accounting means that the police cars are depreciated. The depreciation expense is reported on the government-wide statement of activities. Depreciation expense would be $7,500, computed by taking $40,000 less the salvage value of $10,000, and dividing by the useful life of four years.

91. (a) GASB 34 (as amended) requires use of the current financial resources measurement focus and the modified accrual basis of accounting for governmental funds. On the statement of revenues, expenditures, and changes in fund balances prepared for 2012 for the governmental funds, the acquisition of the police cars is reported as expenditures of $40,000.

92. (b) According to GASB 34 (as amended), the statement of revenues, expenditures, and changes in fund balances prepared for governmental funds is based upon the modified accrual basis of accounting and the financial resources measurement focus. On the statement of revenues, expenditures, and changes in fund balances, the acquisition of police cars is reported as expenditures of $75,000. The $30,000 payment by the general fund to the pension trust fund is reported as an interfund services provided and used transaction. On the statement of revenues, expenditures, and changes in fund balances, the $30,000 should be reported as expenditures. Therefore, the acquisition of the police cars and the pension transfer result in $105,000 of expenditures being reported on the statement of revenues, expenditures, and changes in fund balances for the governmental funds.

93. (c) According to GASB 34 (as amended), the statement of revenues, expenditures, and changes in fund balances prepared for governmental funds is based upon the modified accrual basis of accounting and the financial resources measurement focus. On the statement of revenues, expenditures, and changes in fund balances, the revenue from property taxes should be reported at $750,000. The levy of $800,000 less the 2% that was not expected to be collected results in $784,000, of which $750,000 was collected in 2012. Because the remaining $34,000 was not expected to be collected within sixty days of the end of 2012, the $34,000 is not considered available in 2012, and, therefore, it is not reported as revenue in 2012. At December 31, 2012, the $34,000 should be reported as a deferred inflow on the balance sheet prepared for the governmental funds. Deferred inflows are reported below liabilities on this balance sheet. On the other hand, sales tax revenues for 2012 would be $100,000. The amount of sales taxes that are expected to be received in mid-March of 2013 is not considered available in 2012, and should not be included in revenues on the statement of revenues, expenditures, and changes in fund balances prepared for the governmental funds for the year ended December 31, 2012. Therefore, property tax revenues and sales tax revenues for 2012 would be reported at $850,000.

94. (a) According to governmental accounting standards, the government-wide statement of activities should be prepared based upon the accrual basis of accounting and the economic resources measurement focus. The statement of activities reports governmental activities, business-type activities, and component units. For the police cars that were purchased in 2012, this means that depreciation expense of $12,000 would be reported under governmental activities. The police cars would be reported as assets on the government-wide statement of net position, and the depreciation expense for 2012 would be computed by dividing five years into $75,000 less the salvage value of $15,000. The transfer to the pension trust fund would be reported under governmental activities as an expense of $30,000. The transfer is accounted for as an interfund services provided and used transaction in 2012. This means that the transfer would be reported in expenses under governmental activities for the year ended December 31, 2012. Therefore, $42,000 of expenses result from the acquisition of the police cars and the pension transfer in 2012. These expenses would be reported on the government-wide statement of activities for 2012.

95. (b) According to governmental accounting standards, the government-wide statement of activities should be prepared based upon the accrual basis of accounting and the economic resources measurement focus. The statement of activities reports governmental activities, business-type activities, and component units. For 2012, property tax revenues should be reported at the full amount of the levy of $800,000 less the 2% that was not expected to be collected. This means that $784,000 would be reported for property tax revenues in 2012. The $34,000 of property taxes that were not collected in 2012 are reported as revenues in 2012 because the statement of activities is based upon accrual accounting. For 2012, sales tax revenues should be reported at $125,000. Sales tax revenues reported for 2012 include the $100,000 collected during 2012 as well as the $25,000 that will be collected in mid-March of 2013. The $25,000 of sales taxes that will be collected in mid-March 2013 are reported as revenues in 2012 on the statement of activities because the sales taxes were collected by the state in 2012. The accrual basis of accounting mandates that the $25,000 be reported as revenue under governmental activities in 2012. Therefore, for the year ended December 31, 2012, a total of $909,000 of revenues are reported for property taxes ($784,000) and sales taxes ($125,000) on the government-wide statement of activities.

96. (c) According to GASB 33, the grant received by Maple Township is an example of a voluntary nonexchange transaction in which the providing State government imposes purpose restrictions on the grant to Maple Township. Under modified accrual accounting, grant revenue should be recognized when it is both measurable and available. Applying these criteria to the grant, revenues should be recognized in the period that Maple received reimbursement from the state for the purchase of buses ($60,000) and for bus maintenance ($5,000). It is at the point of reimbursement that the grant becomes available.

97. (b) Special revenue funds are used to account for the proceeds of specific revenue sources (other than expendable trusts or for major capital projects) that are legally restricted to expenditures for specified purposes. Thus, the gasoline taxes to finance road repairs should be accounted for in a special revenue fund. The levies to property owners to install sidewalks would be recorded either in an agency fund (if special assessment debt is not backed by the government) or by a debt service fund (if the debt is backed by the government).

98. (c) A major special revenue fund is a governmental fund and therefore uses the modified accrual basis of accounting, not the accrual basis. Budgetary accounts should be used in the general fund and special revenue fund.

99. (a) The objective of a capital projects fund is to account for the financial resources to be used for the acquisition or construction of major capital facilities. The inflow of bond proceeds should be accounted for in the year received, regardless of when the bond proceeds are expended. Therefore, the $5,000,000 of bond proceeds should be recorded in the capital projects fund in 2012, the year received. They should be treated as an "other financing source" in the operating statement of the fund. Note that the servicing of the debt will be accounted for in the debt service fund.

100. (c) Grants received by the capital projects fund from another governmental unit are considered revenues of the capital projects fund. Also, taxes or other revenues raised specifically for the capital projects fund are recorded as revenues of the fund. However, proceeds of debt issues should be recorded as proceeds of bonds/long-term debt and should be reported as another financing source in the operating statement. Similarly, resources transferred to the capital projects fund generally from the general or special revenue fund are recorded as transfers in and reported in the other financing sources section of the operating statement. Thus, Fir should report only the $400,000 from the grant as a revenue. The $600,000 consisting of the bond issue proceeds and general fund transfer should be reported as other financing sources.

101. (c) The requirement is to identify how an impaired capital asset that is no longer used by a government should be reported in the financial statements. The correct answer is (c). GASB 42 indicates that the asset should be reported at the lower of carrying value or fair value. Answers (a) and (b) are incorrect because they are often elements of the carrying value of the asset. Answer (d) is incorrect because the required valuation is the lower of carrying value or fair value.

102. (b) The requirement is to identify when impairment of a capital asset should be recognized. The correct answer is (b). GASB 42 states that impairment of a capital asset should be recognized when an event or change in circumstance causes a decline in service utility of the asset, and (1) the decline is large in magnitude and (2) the event or change in circumstance is outside the normal life cycle of the capital asset.

103. (d) Governmental fund revenues and expenditures should be recognized on the modified accrual basis. Governmental funds include the general fund, special revenue funds, capital projects funds, debt service funds, and permanent funds. Proprietary fund revenues and expenses should be recognized on the accrual basis. Proprietary funds include enterprise funds and internal service funds. Fiduciary fund additions and deductions should be recognized on the accrual basis. Pension trust funds should be accounted for on the accrual basis.

104. (a) GASB 37, para 16, indicates that proceeds of long-term issues not recorded as fund liabilities should be reported as other financing sources in governmental funds. In addition, general long-term debt issue premiums should also be reported as other financing sources. GASB 34 (as amended) indicates that debt issue costs, including underwriter fees, should be reported as expenditures.

105. (d) Debt service funds are to account for the accumulation of resources for and payment of, general long-term debt principal and interest. The general fund does not account for resources restricted for payment of general long-term debt principal and interest.

106. (a) According to governmental accounting standards, the balance sheet prepared for governmental funds is prepared using the modified accrual basis of accounting and the flow of financial resources measurement focus. Under the modified accrual basis of accounting and the financial resources measurement focus, the bond issue costs of $400,000 and the debt insurance costs of $90,000 should be charged to expenditures in the debt service fund on June 30, 2012. This means that none of the costs will be reported as an asset on the governmental funds' balance sheet prepared at June 30, 2012.

107. (c)   The requirement is to determine which fund should record receipts from a special tax levy to retire and pay interest on general obligation bonds. The correct answer is (c) because the debt service fund usually handles the repayment of general obligation long-term debt interest. A levy allocable to the debt service fund is recorded in the fund. Answer (a) is incorrect because levies for the purpose of paying interest do not get recorded in the general fund. The general fund records levies that do not have a specific purpose. Answer (b) is incorrect because capital projects funds are for construction or the purchase of fixed assets. Answer (d) is incorrect because special revenue funds are for earmarked revenue that is not to pay interest on general obligation debt.

108. (d)   The bond premium amount is usually deemed to be another financing source in a governmental fund and is recorded as such when the bonds are sold. The premium is not capitalized and amortized.

109. (a)   The GASB classifies three types of funds used in governmental accounting: governmental, proprietary, and fiduciary. Debt service funds are used to accumulate resources to pay general long-term debt of governmental funds. The debt service fund is not used in connection with either a trust fund or a proprietary fund.

110. (c)   Cash received in the debt service fund from the general fund for debt service is recorded as a transfer. Cash payments of principal and interest on the debt are then recorded as expenditures in the debt service fund. The following entries would be made in the debt service fund:

Cash	xx	
Transfers In—General Fund		xx
Expenditures—Principal	xx	
Expenditures—Interest	xx	
Cash (Payable)		xx

111. (a)   Interest on the general obligation bonds is payable on March 1 and September 1. The debt service fund accounts for the accumulation of cash to pay the interest and principal on general obligation bonds. However, interest on the bonds is not recorded until it is legally payable. On June 30, 2012, no interest is legally payable, so there would be no accrual of interest to be paid as of that date.

112. (a)   According to GASB 52, land and other real estate held by an endowment as an investment should be reported at fair value at each reporting date. Therefore, answer (a) is correct. Answers (b), (c) and (d) are incorrect because GASB 52 requires the use of fair value.

113. (a)   The debt service transactions of a special assessment issue for which the government is not obligated in any manner should be reported in an agency fund, rather than a debt service fund. The government's duties are limited to acting as an agent for the assessed property owners and the bondholders.

114. (c)   Municipal solid waste landfills that use proprietary accounting (i.e., enterprise fund) should recognize as expense (and liability) a portion of the estimated total cost of closure and post closure in each period that the landfill accepts solid waste. Estimated total costs should be assigned to periods based on use rather than on the passage of time, using a formula based on the percentage of capacity used each period. Because Cy City's landfill operates as an enterprise fund, the city's 2012 expenses should include a portion of the year 2028 expected disbursements for both the final cover (I) and cost of equipment to monitor methane gas buildup (II).

115. (a)   GASB 34 (as amended) clearly states that, in the government-wide statements, governmental activities normally include transactions that are reported in governmental and internal service funds.

116. (b)   Internal service funds account for activities that produce goods or services to be provided to other departments or governmental units on a cost reimbursement basis. Internal service funds also use the full accrual method of accounting. When the governmental units are billed, the internal service fund would record the following entry:

Billings to Departments	xx	
Operating Revenues		xx

117. (d)   A proprietary fund is created to account for goods or services the governmental unit provides to benefit the general public. It uses the accrual basis of accounting and the flow of economic resources measurement focus (i.e., capital maintenance is an objective). Fixed assets and depreciation expense on them are recorded in such funds. Therefore, the $210,000 expenditure for the parking meters would be capitalized and shown net of accumulated depreciation on Burwood's June 30, 2012 balance sheet. Burwood's net income for the year ending June 30, 2012, would be $240,000 calculated as

Receipts from users	$400,000
Expenses	
Depreciation—Parking meters	(70,000)
Salaries and other	(90,000)
Net income	$240,000

118. (d)   Enterprise funds are used to account for operations that are financed and operated in a manner similar to private business enterprises—where the intent of the government is that costs of providing goods or services to the general public on a continuing basis be financed or recovered primarily through user charges; or where the government has decided that periodic determination of net income is appropriate for accountability purposes. Accordingly, revenues from lotteries need to be matched with related expenses for prizes. Thus, lotteries should be accounted for in a fund type that uses full accrual accounting, most commonly an enterprise fund. In addition, the GASB *Codification*, Section H05, requires that hospitals be reported as a single enterprise fund when they are included as part of another government's reporting entity.

119. (d)   Depreciation of general fixed assets should **not** be recorded in the accounts of governmental funds. Depreciation of fixed assets accounted for in a proprietary fund should be recorded in the accounts of that fund. The determination of recording depreciation expense in a governmental unit's fund does not change as a result of the funding source used to acquire the asset.

120. (d) An enterprise fund is used to account for operations where the intent of the governing body is to finance the cost of the operations through user charges or where the governing body has decided revenue, expenses, and net income information is necessary. A fund that accounts for the financing of an agency's services to other government departments on a cost-reimbursement basis is an internal service fund.

121. (c) Cash flows from sale of revenue bonds and capital contributed by subdividers are classified as cash flows from capital and related financing activities. Both the $5,000,000 proceeds from sale of revenue bonds and $1,000,000 capital contributed by subdividers would be reported as cash flows from capital and related financing activities. Cash flows from customer households are operating cash flows.

122. (a) Proprietary funds are used to account for a government's ongoing organizations and activities that are similar to those often found in the private sector. The generally accepted accounting principles here are those applicable to similar businesses in the private sector; and the measurement focus is on **determination of net income,** financial position, and cash flows.

123. (c) As described in the GASB *Codification*, the aggregate lease liability is recorded as an expenditure and an "Other Financing Source" in the general fund. Therefore, Expenditures Control is debited. Answer (b) is incorrect because capital assets are not reported in the general fund. Answer (d) is incorrect because an entry needs to be recorded and posted on the books when equipment is acquired through noncancelable lease-purchase agreement. A memorandum entry is not sufficient. Answer (a) is incorrect because "Other Financing Uses" account is used for transfers out of a fund.

124. (d) The enterprise fund is a proprietary fund and all assets and liabilities of proprietary funds are accounted for and reported in their respective funds. Therefore, transactions for enterprise fund capital leases are accounted for and reported entirely within the enterprise fund. Equipment would be debited for $150,000 in the enterprise fund.

125. (c) All assets and liabilities of proprietary funds are accounted for and reported in their respective funds. The entry to establish the capital lease in the internal service fund would include a debit to Equipment for $150,000 and a credit to Capital Lease Payable for $150,000. Using general business accounting, the entry to make the December 31, 2012 payment of $65,000 would debit Capital Lease Payable for the principal of $50,000 and Expenses Control for the interest of $15,000, and credit Cash for $65,000. The internal service fund is nonexpendable and **expenses (not** expenditures) are recognized on the full accrual basis. Expenses should only be debited for the interest of $15,000, not for the principal of $50,000.

126. (c) Per the GASB *Codification*, cash includes both cash and cash equivalents. Cash equivalents are highly liquid investments readily convertible into cash, usually maturing within three months (ninety days) or less from the date the entity **purchased** the security. Maturity is not measured from the original issuance date. Therefore, in this question, the three-month treasury bill would be included in cash and cash equivalents as well as the three-year treasury

note. The three-year treasury note was purchased on 6/15/09 and matures 8/31/09. Therefore, it will be held less than ninety days. The correct answer is (c), $80,000 ($30,000 + $50,000).

127. (b) Fiduciary funds are used to account for assets held by a governmental unit in a trustee capacity or as an agent for individuals, private organizations, other governmental units, and/or other funds. They include investment trust, private-purpose trust, pension trust, and agency funds. Therefore, the total fiduciary fund assets of Green Township at June 30, 2012, is $300,000. The debt service fund is a governmental-type fund.

128. (d) The requirement is to identify the item that is not Required Supplementary Information under GASB 67. Answer (d) is correct because a ten-year schedule of interest rates used to discount the projected future benefits for the plan is not required. All of the others are Required Supplementary Information.

129. (c) Fiduciary funds (i.e., agency funds and trust funds) are used to account for assets held by a governmental unit in a trustee capacity or as an agent for individuals, private organizations, other governmental units, and/or other funds. The entry to record the 1% fee and the disbursement to the municipalities would be as follows:

Due to Various Municipalities	1,000,000	
Due to Grove County		10,000
General Fund Cash		990,000

Note that the general fund would make the following entry:

Due from Agency Fund	xxx	
Revenue from Tax Collec. Serv.		xxx

Agency funds have only assets and liabilities as accounts and do not record revenues, expenditures, or transfers. In addition, agency funds do not have net position.

130. (a) The entry to record the 2012 employer contribution in the Pension Trust Fund consists of a debit to Cash (or a "Due From" account) and a credit to Additions—Employer Contributions, both for $11,000. The GASB *Codification* classifies this contribution as an interfund services provided and used transaction that would be treated as an addition if it involved organizations external to the governmental unit. Therefore, the GASB states that it should be accounted for as an addition for the pension trust fund. Answer (b) is incorrect because Other Financing Sources include transfers to a fund which are recurring, routine transfers from one fund to another. The employer contribution is not a transfer. Answer (c) is incorrect because "Due From" is a debit account and the question asks for the credit account. Answer (d) is incorrect because Pension Benefit Obligation is the actuarial present value of credited projected benefits. It measures the present value of pension benefits adjusted for the effects of projected salary increases and any step-rate benefits estimated to be payable in the future as a result of employer service to date. The employer contribution is not included in this definition.

131. (b) The employer pension contribution is an interfund services provided and used transaction, one that would be treated as an addition, revenue, expense, or expenditure if it involved organizations external to the governmental unit. In this case, the entry for the governmental-type fund would include a debit to Expenditures Control for $11,000 and a credit to Cash (or a "Due To" account) for $11,000. Answer (a) is incorrect because Other Financing Uses include transfers out of a fund, which are routine recurring transfers of resources from one fund to another. Consequently, the employer contribution does not fall under the category of an Other Financing Use. Answer (c) is incorrect because governmental funds use modified accrual accounting and report expenditures, not expenses. Answer (d) is incorrect because Due To Pension Trust Fund could be the credit entry, and not the debit entry asked for in the question.

132. (a) On the government-wide statement of activities, transfers are reported between government activities and business-type activities. The business-type activities include the activities of enterprise funds, while the governmental activities include those of governmental funds and internal service funds. Transfers that are made to establish enterprise funds as well as yearly transfers to help subsidize enterprise funds are both reported as transfers, according to the guidance provided GASB 34 (as amended). On the other hand, billings by an enterprise fund to an internal service fund for services rendered are not reported as transfers on the statement of activities. This transition is a quasi-external transaction that should be reported on the statement of activities as an expense of governmental activities and as an operating revenue for business-type activities. The revenues and expenses of internal service funds are reported as governmental activities on the government-wide statement of activities.

133. (c) According to governmental accounting standards, the amount reported for transfers on the government-wide statement of activities represents transfers between governmental activities and business-type activities. Examples of transfers would be permanent transfers from governmental activities to business-type activities in order to establish enterprise funds and annual transfers from governmental activities to help subsidize enterprise fund activities. The activities of internal service funds are included with governmental activities, while the activities of enterprise funds are reported under business-type activities. The $100,000 advance to an internal service fund constitutes a loan, and the general fund asset and internal service fund liability that result would be eliminated in preparing the government-wide statement of net position. Therefore, the advance would not be reported in transfers on the statement of activities. The $25,000 billing by the enterprise fund to the general fund is recorded as a quasi-external transaction. Under governmental activities, $25,000 would be included in expenses, while, under business-type activities, the $25,000 would be reported as revenues. Therefore, the quasi-external transaction would not be reported in transfers. Finally, the $30,000 transferred by the general fund to a debt service fund is recorded as a transfer in by the debt service fund and as a transfer out by the general fund. However, because both of these funds are reported in governmental activities, the transfer in and transfer out are eliminated in preparing the statement of activities and are not reported in the governmental activities column on the statement of activities. Therefore, the general fund transfer to the debt service fund would not be reported as a transfer on the statement of activities.

134. (a) According to governmental accounting standards, transfers are reported on the government-wide statement of activities. For transfers to be reported, they must be between governmental activities and business-type activities. Governmental activities include the activities of internal service funds, while business-type activities include the activities of enterprise funds. Two kinds of transfers that are reported on the statement of activities include (1) permanent transfers either from governmental activities to business-type activities or from business-type activities to governmental activities and (2) recurring transfers from governmental activities to business-type activities or from business-type activities to governmental activities. Permanent transfers are typically made once, while the recurring transfers are typically made annually. The $100,000 transfer from the general fund to an enterprise fund would be reported as a transfer on the statement of activities because it is an example of a permanent transfer. The $1,000,000 transfer from the general fund to a capital project fund is a transfer made within governmental activities and, therefore, would not be disclosed as a transfer on the statement of activities. The $5,000 reimbursement from the enterprise fund to the general fund is not reported as a transfer on the statement of activities. The effect of this transaction is to increase expenses under business-type activities and to decrease expenses under governmental activities.

135. (a) According to GASB 35, public colleges and universities that choose to report only business-type activities should present only the financial statements required for enterprise funds.

136. (c) According to GASB 35, public colleges and universities that choose to report both governmental and business-type activities should report both government-wide and fund financial statements.

137. (b) Both public and private colleges report tuition and fee income net of the amount provided for scholarships, for which no services are provided. On the other hand, scholarships provided in exchange for services are reported as an expense and are not deducted from revenues. As a result, the net tuition and fees would be the $20,000,000 less the $1,000,000 scholarships provided, not in exchange for services, or $19,000,000.

138. (d) GASB Statement 35 provides that public colleges may choose to report as special-purpose entities engaged in business-type activities. GASB Statement 34 requires that special-purpose entities engaged only in business-type activities should prepare the statements required for enterprises funds, including a Statement of Revenues, Expenses, and Changes in Net Position. One requirement for that statement is that an operating income figure must be displayed (answer b). GASB Statement 34 (as amended) also indicates that contributions for plant and endowment purposes are not recorded as revenues but in separate categories; GASB Statement 35 illustrations show those items listed after revenues and expenses (answer c). GASB Statement 35 specifically requires that state appropriations must be reported as nonoperating income (answer a). Since answers (a), (b), and (c) are correct, answer (d) is the choice.

Module 22: Not-for-Profit Accounting

Overview

Nonprofit[1] organizations provide socially desirable services without the intention of realizing a profit. Nonprofit organizations are financed by user charges, contributions from donors and/or foundations, investment income, and government grants. The nature and extent of support depends upon the type of nonprofit organization.

Examples of private sector nonprofits would be private colleges (University of Chicago), private sector health care entities operated by religious or other nonprofit organizations, voluntary health and welfare organizations, and various "other" nonprofits, such as performing arts companies. Examples of government nonprofits would be public colleges (Northern Illinois University), government hospitals, and government museums. Private sector nonprofit organizations have GAAP set primarily by the FASB; governmental nonprofit organizations have GAAP set primarily by the GASB.

In June of 1993, the FASB issued SFAS 116, *Accounting for Contributions Received and Contributions Made,* and SFAS 117, *Financial Statements of Not-for-Profit Organizations.* These standards are applicable to private sector not-for-profit organizations of all types. This module presents GAAP for private sector nonprofits under SFAS 116 and 117 (FASB ASC 958). The AICPA has developed two *Audit Guides* that correspond and add to the new FASB principles: (1) Not-for-Profit Organizations, and (2) Health Care Organizations. The *Not-for-Profit Guide* applies only to private sector not-for-profits. The *Health Care Guide* applies to all health care entities, private for-profit, private not-for-profit, and governmental.

Governmental nonprofits are not permitted to follow SFAS 116 and 117 (FASB ASC 958). (The definition of a government is provided in the introductory section of Module 21.) As applied to colleges, health care entities, and other not-for-profit organizations, that guidance has been outlined through different pronouncements.

First, in November 1999, the GASB issued Statement 35, *Basic Financial Statements—and Management's Discussion and Analysis—for Public Colleges and Universities.* GASB 35 permits public colleges to report as special-purpose entities engaged in governmental or business-type activities, or both. Most four-year institutions are expected to report as special-purpose entities engaged only in business-type activities. Some community colleges may choose to report as special-purpose entities engaged in governmental activities due to the extent of state and local government tax support. The provisions of GASB 35 are outlined in Module 21.

Second, GASB 34 indicates that hospitals and other health care providers may be considered special-purpose entities that may be engaged in either governmental or business-type activities, or both. Most health care organizations will choose to report as special-purpose entities that are engaged in business-type activities. As a result, proprietary fund statements will be required for those health care entities. The AICPA Audit and Accounting Guide, *Health Care Organizations*, contains guidance for both private sector and governmental health care organizations; both are presented in this module.

Third, other governmental not-for-profit organizations (essentially governmental voluntary health and welfare and "other" not-for-profit organizations) also may be considered special-purpose entities that may be engaged in either governmental or business-type activities, or both. However, GASB 34 specifically permits these organizations that were using the "AICPA Not-for-Profit Model" upon adoption of GASB 34 to report as special-purpose entities engaged in business-type activities. These entities will present proprietary fund statements. The AICPA Audit and Accounting Guide, *Not-for-Profit Organizations*, applies only to private sector organizations and these principles are contained in this module; governmental not-for-profits are less significant and are not illustrated in this module.

The first section of this module presents the FASB and AICPA standards for all nongovernmental nonprofits, including private sector colleges, universities, and health care entities. The second section presents standards that apply primarily to private colleges and universities. The third and fourth sections present standards for health care entities; first

---

[1] The terms not-for-profit and nonprofit are used interchangeably here and in practice.

for private sector health care entities; next for governmental health care entities. Module 21 presents standards for public colleges and universities. Before beginning the reading you should review key terms at the end of the module.

A. FASB and AICPA Standards for Private Sector Nonprofits

FASB ASC 958 applies to private sector nonprofits subject to FASB guidance; they do not apply to governmental nonprofits subject to GASB guidance.

More recently, FASB issued Statement 124, *Accounting for Certain Investments Held by Not-for-Profit Organizations*. This statement requires fair value accounting for most equity and debt investments by not-for-profit organizations and requires reporting of realized and unrealized gains and losses directly in the Statement of Activities.

Most recently, FASB issued Statement 136, *Transfers of Assets to a Not-for-Profit Organization or Charitable Trust That Raises or Holds Contributions for Others*. This statement provides guidance regarding proper reporting by foundations and similar not-for-profits when funds are raised for others, as described in 1.n. and o. below.

The FASB guidance is intended to eliminate the differences in accounting and reporting standards that existed previously between four types of not-for-profit organizations. While some differences exist, for example, in functional categories reported, private sector nonprofit colleges and universities, health care entities, voluntary health and welfare organizations, and "other" organizations follow the basic guidance in the FASB standards; some differences between health care entities and other private sector not-for-profits will be illustrated later. The section lists a number of basic requirements, illustrates financial statements, and presents a few journal entries as required by SFAS 116, 117, 124, and 136 (FASB ASC 958). All illustrations are for a general nongovernmental not-for-profit organization, but remember that the principles apply to all four types (colleges and universities, health care organizations, voluntary health and welfare organizations, and "other" not-for-profit organizations).

1. **Important Features of the FASB Guidance**

   a. The standards apply to **all** nongovernmental nonprofit organizations, except those that operate for the direct economic benefit of members (such as mutual insurance companies). General FASB standards, unless specifically prohibited by those standards or do not apply because of their nature (capital stock, etc.) or unless modified by these standards, are presumed to apply.

   b. Net assets are divided into three classes: unrestricted, temporarily restricted, and permanently restricted. Fund classifications are not reported, unless the information can be shown as subdivisions of the three major classes. To be restricted, resources must be restricted by donors or grantors; internally designated resources are unrestricted. Only contributed resources may be restricted.

   c. Permanently restricted resources include (1) certain assets, such as artwork, etc. that must be maintained or used in a certain way, (2) endowments, which represent resources that must be invested permanently with income to be used for either restricted or unrestricted purposes, and (3) land, when that land must be held in perpetuity.

   d. Temporarily restricted resources include unexpended resources that are to be used for a particular purpose, at a time in the future, or are to be invested for a period of time (a term endowment). Temporarily restricted resources might also be used for the acquisition or receipt of a gift of plant and would represent the undepreciated amount. As the plant is depreciated, the amount depreciated would be reclassified from temporarily restricted net assets to unrestricted net assets and shown as a deduction from unrestricted revenues, gains, and other support on the statement of activities. Alternatively, plant may be initially recorded as unrestricted.

   e. Unrestricted resources include all other resources including unrestricted contributions, the net amount from providing services, unrestricted income from investments, etc. Resources are presumed to be unrestricted, unless evidence exists that donor-imposed restrictions exist. As mentioned above, undepreciated plant may be included as unrestricted or temporarily restricted.

   f. Statements required are (1) Statement of Financial Position, (2) Statement of Activities, and (3) Statement of Cash Flows. Certain note disclosures are also required and others recommended. In addition, voluntary health and welfare organizations are required to report a Statement of Functional Expenses that show expenses by function and by natural classifications.

   g. The Statement of Financial Position reports assets, liabilities, and net assets. Organization-wide totals must be provided for assets, liabilities and net assets, and net assets must be broken down between unrestricted, temporarily restricted, and permanently restricted.

   h. The Statement of Activities reports revenues, expenses, gains, losses, and reclassifications (between classes of net assets). Organization-wide totals must be provided. Separate revenues, expenses, gains, losses, and reclassifications for each class may or may not be reported, but the changes in net assets for each class must be reported.

   i. Revenues, expenses, gains, and losses are reported on the full accrual basis. A revenue is presumed to be unrestricted unless donor-imposed restrictions apply, either permanent or temporary. A presumption is made, in the absence of contrary information, that a given expense would use restricted resources first, rather than unrestricted resources. Revenues and expenses should be reported at gross amounts; gains and losses are often reported net. Investment gains and losses may be reported net.

j. Unconditional contributions are to be recorded as assets (contributions receivable) and as revenues (contribution revenue). However, a donor-imposed **condition** causes a not-for-profit organization to not recognize either a receivable or a revenue. A donor-imposed condition specifies a future or uncertain event whose occurrence or failure to occur gives the promisor a right of return of the assets transferred or releases the promisor from its obligation to transfer the assets promised.

> **EXAMPLE**
>
> A not-for-profit organization receives a pledge from a donor that she will transfer $1,000,000 if matching funds can be raised within a year. The $1,000,000 would not be recognized as a revenue until the possibility of raising the matching funds is reasonably certain.

k. Multiyear contributions receivable would be recorded at the present value of the future collections. Moneys to be collected in future years would be presumed to be temporarily restricted revenues (based on time restrictions) and then reclassified in the year of receipt. The difference between the previously recorded temporarily restricted revenue at present value amounts and the current value would be recorded as contribution revenue, not interest. **All** contributions are to be recorded at fair market value as of the date of the contribution.

l. Organizations making the contributions, including businesses and other nonprofits, would recognize contribution expense using the same rules as followed by the receiving organization.

m. Contributions are to be distinguished from exchange revenues. The *Not-for-Profit Guide* indicates criteria that indicate when an increase in net assets is a contribution and when it is an exchange revenue; the most important rule is that if nothing is given by the not-for-profit organization in exchange in a transaction, that transaction would be considered a contribution. Contributions are recognized as additions to any of the net asset classifications. Exchange revenues (tuition, membership dues, charges for services, etc.) are increases in unrestricted net assets and are recognized in accordance with GAAP as applied to business enterprises.

n. Accounting standards require that when a not-for-profit organization (such as a foundation) is an **intermediary** or an **agent** for the transfer of assets to another not-for-profit organization, that intermediary or agent would not recognize a contribution. Unless the intermediary or agent not-for-profit organization is granted **variance power** to redirect the resources, or unless it is financially interrelated, the receipt of resources would be offset with the recognition of a liability to the recipient organization. If variance power exists, the recipient organization would recognize contribution revenue.

o. Accounting standards also require that the recipient organization recognize a revenue when the intermediary or agent recognizes a liability. When the intermediary or agent and the beneficiary are **financially interrelated,** the intermediary or agent would recognize contribution revenue; the beneficiary would recognize its interest in the net assets of the intermediary or agent.

p. Expenses are to be reported by function either in the statements or in the notes. The FASB does not prescribe functional classifications but does describe functions as program and supporting. Major program classifications should be shown. Supporting activities include management and general, fund raising, and membership development. Other classifications may be included, such as operating income, but are not required, except for health care entities. All expenses are reported as decreases in unrestricted net assets.

q. Plant is recorded, as mentioned above, either as temporarily restricted or unrestricted, and depreciated. Depreciation is to be charged for exhaustible fixed assets.

r. An entity may or may not capitalize "collections." "Collections" are works of art, historical treasures, and similar assets if those assets meet all of the following conditions:

(1) They are held for public exhibition, education, or research in furtherance of public service rather than financial gain;

(2) They are protected, kept encumbered, cared for, and preserved;

(3) They are subject to an organizational policy that requires the proceeds from sales of collection items to be used to acquire other items for collections.

If collections are not capitalized, revenues (contributions) would not be recognized for donated collections. Extensive note disclosure regarding accessions, disposals, etc. are required.

s. Investments in all debt securities and investments in equity securities that have readily determinable fair values (except equity securities accounted for under the equity method and investments in consolidated subsidiaries) are to be reported at fair value in the Statement of Net Assets. Unlike accounting standards for business enterprises, all unrealized gains and losses are to be reflected in the Statement of Activities along with realized gains and losses, in the appropriate net asset class.

t. Contributed services, when recognized, are recognized as both revenue and expense. However, contributed services should be recognized only when the services: (1) create or enhance nonfinancial assets, or (2) require specialized skills, are provided by individuals possessing those skills, and would typically be purchased if not provided by donation.

> **EXAMPLE**
>
> Jenna Wu, an attorney, provides necessary legal services to a not-for-profit organization gratis. The value of these services may be recognized by the not-for-profit as contributed services because they require specialized skills, are provided by an individual possessing those skills, and would typically be purchased in not provided by Jenna.

u. All expenses are reported as unrestricted. Expenses using resources that are temporarily restricted, including depreciation of plant, would be matched by a reclassification of resources from temporarily restricted to unrestricted net assets.

v. The "Reclassification" category of the Statement of Activities is unique. Sometimes "Reclassifications" are called "Net Assets Released from Restrictions." Reclassifications generally include (1) satisfaction of program restrictions (a purpose restriction by a donor), (2) satisfaction of equipment acquisition restrictions (depreciation of assets classified as temporarily restricted), (3) satisfaction of time restrictions (donor actual or implied restrictions as to when funds be used), and (4) expiration of term endowment.

w. Cash Flow statements are required for nonprofit organizations. The three FASB categories (operating, investing, and financing) are to be used. As is true for business organizations, either the direct or indirect method may be used. The indirect method, or reconciliation schedule for the direct method, will reconcile the change in **total** net assets to the net cash used by operating activities. Restricted contributions for long-term purposes (endowments, plant, future program purposes, etc.) are reported as financing activities.

x. Note disclosures are required for all items required for generally accepted accounting principles that are relevant to nonprofit organizations. In addition, specific requirements of SFAS 117 (FASB ASC 958) include (1) policy disclosures related to choices related to restricted contributions received and expended in the same period, and to the recording of plant as temporarily restricted or unrestricted, and (2) more detailed information regarding the nature of temporarily and permanently restricted resources.

y. The FASB specifically encourages note disclosures on (1) detail of the reclassification, (2) detail of investments and (3) breakdown of expenses by function and natural classifications (except for Voluntary Health and Welfare Organizations, which must include this information in a Statement of Functional Expenses).

z. The *Not-for-Profit Guide* provides guidance for **split-interest agreements,** such as charitable lead trusts and charitable remainder trusts. Split-interest agreements represent arrangements whereby both a donor (or beneficiary) and a not-for-profit organization receive benefits, often at different times in a multiyear arrangement. Specific rules exist for each type of split-interest agreement. The general rule is that the not-for-profit will record revenues in an amount equal to the present value of anticipated receipts.

> **EXAMPLE**
>
> Roger Smith established a charitable lead trust for a donation to the Salvation Army. Roger put $1,000,000 in the trust to be invested for 10 years. The Salvation Army receives the trust income for the 10-year period. At the end of the 10-year period, the principal of the trust goes to Roger's children.

aa. FASB requires that fund-raising expenses be reported either on the face of the financial statements or in the notes. AICPA Statement of Position 98-2 indicates that when an activity, such as a mailing, might involve fund-raising and either program or management and general activities, it is presumed to be fund-raising unless three criteria exist. Those criteria are

   (1) **Purpose.** The activity has more than one purpose, as evidenced by whether compensation or fees for performing the activity are based strictly on the amount raised or on the performance of some program and/or management and general activity.
   (2) **Audience.** If the audience is selected on the basis of its likelihood to contribute to the not-for-profit, this criterion is not met.
   (3) **Content.** In order for this criterion to be met, the mailing or event must include a call to action other than raising money. For example, a mailing from the American Cancer Society might call for recipients to have regular check-ups, to exercise, to eat the right kinds of food, etc.

   Expenses related to soliciting funds other than contributions and membership dues (e.g., promoting sales of goods or services to customers, responding to government or foundation proposals for customer-sponsored contracts for goods and services, etc.) are not presented as fund raising. Instead they are presented as a part of management and general activities.

2. **Illustrative Financial Statements**

The FASB requires three financial statements for nongovernmental, not-for-profit organizations, including (1) Statement of Financial Position, (2) Statement of Activities, and (3) Statement of Cash Flows. Voluntary health and welfare organizations (such as the American Red Cross, a mental health association, or a Big Brothers/ Big Sisters organization) are required to prepare a fourth statement, a Statement of Functional Expenses. The first three of these statements are described and illustrated below.

a. **Statement of Financial Position.** A Balance Sheet or Statement of Financial Position must show total assets, total liabilities, and total net assets. Net assets must be broken down between those that are unrestricted, temporarily restricted, and permanently restricted. Assets and liabilities may be classified or reported in order of liquidity and payment date. Assets restricted for long-term purposes must be reported separately from those that are not. The comparative format illustrated is optional; entities may report only balances for one year. Contributions receivable are to be reported at the present value of future receipts. Investments in securities with determinable fair values are to be reported at fair value. The following reflects one of the permissible formats of FASB ASC 958:

Not-for-Profit Organization
STATEMENTS OF FINANCIAL POSITION
June 30, 20X1 and 20X0
(in thousands)

	20X1	20X0
Assets		
Cash and cash equivalents	$ 75	$ 460
Accounts and interest receivable	2,130	1,670
Inventories and prepaid expenses	610	1,000
Contributions receivable	3,025	2,700
Short-term investments	1,400	1,000
Assets restricted to investment in land, buildings, and equipment	5,210	4,560
Land, buildings, and equipment	61,700	63,590
Long-term investments	218,070	203,500
Total assets	$292,220	$278,480
Liabilities and net assets		
Accounts payable	$ 2,570	$ 1,050
Refundable advance		650
Grants payable	875	1,300
Notes payable		1,140
Annuity obligations	1,685	1,700
Long-term debt	5,500	6,500
Total liabilities	10,630	12,340
Net assets		
Unrestricted	115,228	103,670
Temporarily restricted	24,342	25,470
Permanently restricted	142,020	137,000
Total net assets	281,590	266,140
Total liabilities and net assets	$292,220	$278,480

SOURCE: SFAS 117, page 56

b. **Statement of Activities.** Note the following from the example Statement of Activities:

(1) Contributions, income on long-term investments, and net unrealized and realized gains on long-term investments may increase unrestricted, temporarily restricted, and permanently restricted net assets. All of these revenue sources increase unrestricted net assets unless restricted by donors.

(2) Fees increase unrestricted net assets. All exchange revenues increase unrestricted net assets. Exchange revenues include admissions charges, fees, and membership dues.

(3) Net unrealized gains are shown together with realized gains and investments. FASB prohibits displaying net unrealized and realized gains separately.

(4) All expenses decrease unrestricted net assets. (Losses, such as the actuarial loss, may decrease restricted net assets.)

(5) At some point net assets are released from restrictions (reclassified) from temporarily restricted to unrestricted net assets. This might be for satisfaction of program restrictions, satisfaction of equipment acquisition restrictions, expiration of time restrictions, or expiration of term endowments. Note that when net assets are released from restrictions, temporarily restricted net assets decrease and unrestricted net assets increase.

(6) Expenses are broken down between programs (A, B, C) and supporting (management and general, fundraising). While the FASB does not require these functional breakdowns, the FASB does have two requirements.

(a) Expenses must be reported by function in the notes if not in this statement, and

(b) Fund-raising expenses must be disclosed in the notes, if not in this statement.

The FASB permits other formats. For example, some entities prepare two statements.

(a) Statement of Revenues, Expenses, and Changes in Unrestricted Net Assets, and

(b) Statement of Changes in Net Assets.

Regardless of the format used, the change in net assets must be reported, by net asset class and in total.

Not-for-Profit Organization
STATEMENT OF ACTIVITIES
Year Ended June 30, 20X1
(in thousands)

	Unrestricted	Temporarily restricted	Permanently restricted	Total
Revenues, gains, and other support:				
Contributions	$ 8,640	$ 8,110	$ 280	$ 17,030
Fees	5,400			5,400
Income on long-term investments	5,600	2,580	120	8,300
Other investment income	850			850
Net unrealized and realized gains on long-term investments	8,228	2,952	4,620	15,800
Other	150			150
Net assets released from restrictions:				
Satisfaction of program restrictions	11,990	(11,990)		
Satisfaction of equipment acquisition restrictions	1,500	(1,500)		
Expiration of time restrictions	1,250	(1,250)		
Total revenues, gains, and other support	43,608	(1,098)	5,020	47,530
Expenses and losses:				
Program A	13,100			13,100
Program B	8,540			8,540
Program C	5,760			5,760
Management and general	2,420			2,420
Fund raising	2,150			2,150
Total expenses	31,970			31,970
Fire loss	80			80
Actuarial loss on annuity obligations		30		30
Total expenses and losses	32,050	30		32,080
Change in net assets	11,558	(1,128)	5,020	15,450
Net assets at beginning of year	103,670	25,470	137,000	266,140
Net assets at end of year	$115,228	$ 24,342	$142,020	$281,590

SOURCE: SFAS 117, page 59.

c. **Statement of Cash Flows.** In general, the FASB rules for cash flow statements, required for business enterprises, apply to not-for-profit organizations.

NOTE: GASB rules, illustrated in Module 21, do not apply. The only major difference is that cash receipts for contributions restricted for long-term purposes are classified as financing activities.

Not-for-Profit Organization
STATEMENT OF CASH FLOWS
Year Ended June 30, 20X1
(in thousands)

Cash flows from operating activities:	
Cash received from service recipients	$ 5,220
Cash received from contributors	8,030
Cash collected on contributions receivable	2,615
Interest and dividends received	8,570
Miscellaneous receipts	150
Interest paid	(382)
Cash paid to employees and suppliers	(23,808)
Grants paid	(425)
Net cash used by operating activities	(30)

Cash flows from investing activities:

Insurance proceeds from fire loss on building	250
Purchase of equipment	(1,500)
Proceeds from sale of investments	76,100
Purchase of investments	$(74,900)
Net cash used by investing activities	(50)

Cash flows from financing activities:

Proceeds from contributions restricted for:

Investment in endowment	200
Investment in term endowment	70
Investment in plant	1,210
Investment subject to annuity agreements	200
	1,680

Other financing activities:

Interest and dividends restricted for reinvestment	300
Payments of annuity obligations	(145)
Payments on notes payable	(1,140)
Payments on long-term debt	(1,000)
	(1,985)
Net cash used by financing activities	(305)
Net decrease in cash and cash equivalents	(385)
Cash and cash equivalents at beginning of year	460
Cash and cash equivalents at end of year	$ 75

Reconciliation of change in net assets to net cash used by operating activities:

Change in net assets	$ 15,450

Adjustments to reconcile change in net assets to net cash used by operating activities:

Depreciation	3,200
Fire loss	80
Actuarial loss on annuity obligations	30
Increase in accounts and interest receivable	(460)
Decrease in inventories and prepaid expenses	390
Increase in contributions receivable	(325)
Increase in accounts payable	1,520
Decrease in refundable advance	(650)
Decrease in grants payable	(425)
Contributions restricted for long-term investment	(2,740)
Interest and dividends restricted for long-term investment	(300)
Net unrealized and realized gains on long-term investments	(15,800)
Net cash used by operating activities	$ (30)
Supplemental data for noncash investing and financing activities:	
Gifts of equipment	$ 140
Gift of paid-up life insurance, cash surrender value	$ 80

SOURCE: SFAS 117, pages 64-65.

3. **Illustrative Transactions**

a. Unrestricted revenues and expenses.

Under FASB guidance, full accrual accounting is used. A look at the Statement of Activities indicates that revenues might include contributions, fees, investment income, and realized and unrealized gains on investments. Expenses must be reported as unrestricted and reported by function, either in the statements or in the notes.

Assume the following unrestricted revenues:

Cash	1,000,000	
Contributions Receivable	200,000	
Accounts Receivable	100,000	
Interest Receivable	50,000	
Contributions—Unrestricted		700,000
Fees—Unrestricted		300,000
Income on Long-Term Investments—Unrestricted		350,000

Income earned from investments can be unrestricted, temporarily restricted, or permanently restricted depending on the wishes of the donor. If the donor does not specify, the investment income is unrestricted, even if the investment principal itself is permanently restricted.

Assume the following expenses, reported by function:

Program A Expense	400,000	
Program B Expense	300,000	
Program C Expense	200,000	
Management and General Expense	100,000	
Fund Raising Expense	200,000	
Cash		900,000
Accounts Payable		300,000

b. Purpose restrictions—temporarily restricted resources

    Temporarily restricted resources are generally restricted by purpose, by time, and for the acquisition of plant. Assume that in 20X0 a donor gives $100,000 in cash for cancer research and that the funds are expended in 20X1. In 20X0, the following entry would be made:

Cash	100,000	
Contributions—Temporarily Restricted		100,000

At the end of 20X0 the $100,000 would be a part of the net assets of the temporarily restricted net asset class. In 20X1, the following entries would be made, assuming the funds are expended for cancer research.

Program A Expense (Research)	100,000	
Cash		100,000
Reclassifications from Temporarily Restricted Net Assets—		
Satisfaction of Program Restrictions	100,000	
Reclassifications to Unrestricted Net Assets—Satisfaction of		
Program Restrictions		100,000

> **NOTE:** The assets are released from restriction by the expense, by conducting the research. Looking at the example statement of activities, the $100,000 would be included as a part of the $11,990,000 in program reclassifications.

c. Time restrictions—temporarily restricted resources

    If a donor makes a contribution and indicates that the contribution should be used in a future period, that contribution would be recorded as a revenue in the temporarily restricted net asset class and then transferred to the unrestricted net asset class in the time period specified by the donor. In the absence of other information, if a pledge is made, the schedule of anticipated receipts would determine when the net assets are reclassified. Assume a $100,000 pledge in late 20X0, intended to be used by the nonprofit organization in 20X1; the entry in 20X0 would be

Pledges receivable	100,000	
Contributions—Temporarily Restricted		100,000

At the end of 20X0, the $100,000 would be reflected in the net assets of the temporarily restricted in class. In 20X1, the following entries would be made:

Cash	100,000	
Pledges receivable		100,000
Reclassifications from Temporarily Restricted Net Assets—		
Satisfaction of Time Restrictions	100,000	
Reclassifications to Unrestricted Net Assets—Satisfaction of		
Time Restrictions		100,000

    The $100,000 above would be a part of the $1,250,000 in reclassifications for satisfaction of time restrictions in the statement of activities. Note that time, not an expense, determines when the asset is released from restrictions. In the special case of multiyear pledges, the present value of the future payments should be recorded as a revenue in the year of the pledge. In future years, the increase in the present value, due to the passage of time, is to be recorded as contribution revenue, not interest.

    Finally, note that a time restriction might be explicit or implicit. An explicit time restriction would occur when a donor states specifically that the funds are for a certain year (this might be printed on pledge cards). An implicit time restriction reflects the provision that cash must be received from a donor during an accounting period, or the pledge will be assumed to carry a time restriction. The idea is that, if a donor wished a nonprofit to spend the money this year, the donor would have contributed the cash.

d. Plant acquisition restrictions—temporarily restricted resources

    Sometimes donors give moneys restricted for the acquisition of plant, often in connection with a fund drive. The resources, whether in the form of pledges, cash, or investments, would be held in the temporarily restricted net asset class until expended. When expended, the nonprofit organization has a choice of two options: (1) reclassify the resources to the unrestricted class and record the entire plant as unrestricted, or (2) record the plant as temporarily restricted and reclassify to unrestricted in accordance with the depreciation schedule. Under the first option, assume that a donor gives $50,000 to a nonprofit organization in 20X0 for the purchase of equipment. The equipment is purchased in 20X1. The following entry would be made in the temporarily restricted class in 20X0:

Cash	50,000	
Contributions		50,000

In 20X1, the following entries would be made:

Equipment	50,000	
Cash		50,000
Reclassifications from Temporarily Restricted Net Assets—		
Satisfaction of Equipment Acquisition Restrictions	50,000	
Reclassification to Unrestricted Net Assets—Satisfaction of		
Equipment Acquisition Restrictions		50,000

The equipment would then be depreciated as a charge to expense in the unrestricted class as would be normal in business accounting. Remember that depreciation may be allocated to functional categories. Assume a ten-year life and that the equipment was purchased at the beginning of the year and that the equipment was used solely for Program A.

Program A Expense	5,000	
Accumulated Depreciation—Equipment		5,000

The above alternative has normally been used in the CPA Examination. When this is the case, the problem often states that, "the Not-for-Profit Organization implies no restriction on the acquisition of fixed assets."

The second alternative is to record the equipment as an increase in temporarily restricted net assets and reclassify it over time. The entries are illustrated below. Assume the contribution was received but unexpended in 20X0.

Cash	50,000	
Contributions—Temporarily Restricted		50,000

Assume the equipment was acquired early in 20X1.

Equipment	50,000	
Cash		50,000

Note that the $50,000 remains in temporarily restricted net assets. At the end of 20X1, the depreciation entry is made, and $5,000 is reclassified.

Program A Expense	5,000	
Accumulated Depreciation—Equipment		5,000
Reclassification from Temporarily Restricted Net Assets—		
Satisfaction of Equipment Acquisition Restrictions	5,000	
Reclassification to Unrestricted Net Assets—Satisfaction of		
Equipment Acquisition Restrictions		5,000

Using the first alternative, at the end of 20X1, the net asset balance of $45,000 would be in the unrestricted net asset class; in the second alternative, the $45,000 net asset balance would be in the temporarily restricted net asset class.

e. Permanently restricted resources

Resources in the permanently restricted class are held permanently. An example would be an endowment, where a donor makes a contribution with the instructions that the amount be permanently invested. The income might be unrestricted or restricted for a particular activity or program. Assume that in 20X1 a donor gave $100,000 for the purpose of creating an endowment. An entry would be made in the permanently restricted class (this would be part of the $280,000 shown in the Statement of Activities).

Cash	100,000	
Contributions—Permanently Restricted		100,000

> **NOTE:** Revenues can be recorded in any of the three net asset classes but expenses are recorded only in the unrestricted class. Note also that the expiration of restrictions is recorded by reclassifications.

B. College and University Accounting—Private Sector Institutions

Private colleges and universities are subject to the same guidance as other not-for-profit organizations that are included under the *Not-for-Profit Guide*. However, a few comments that specifically impact colleges and universities are in order.

1. Student tuition and fees are reported net of those scholarships and fellowships that are provided not in return for compensation.

> **EXAMPLE**
>
> Assume a university provides a scholarship based on grades, entering ACT or SAT, etc. The scholarship would be recorded as follows:
>
> | | | |
> |---|---|---|
> | Cash | 8,000 | |
> | Revenue Deduction—Student Scholarships | 2,000 | |
> | Revenue—Student Tuition and Fees | | 10,000 |

2. Student graduate assistantships and other amounts given as tuition remissions (for example for full-time employees) that are given in return for services provided to the institution are charged as expenses, to the department and function where the services are provided.

> **EXAMPLE**
>
> Assume that an assistantship was given with services provided to the Biology Department. The assistantship would be recorded as follows:
>
> | | | |
> |---|---|---|
> | Cash | 8,000 | |
> | Expense—Instruction (Biology Department) | 2,000 | |
> | Revenue—Student Tuition and Fees | | 10,000 |

3. The AICPA *Not-for-Profit Guide* specifically states that operation and maintenance of physical plant is not to be reported as a functional expense. Those costs, including depreciation, are to be allocated to other functions.

4. The *Not-for-Profit Guide* does not include examples of financial statements for colleges and universities, or other not-for-profit organizations. The illustrative statement of activities for an educational institution is taken from the *Financial Accounting and Reporting Manual for Higher Education* published by the National Association of College and University Business Officers. Many other formats are possible, as long as the changes in net assets are shown separately for unrestricted, temporarily restricted, and permanently restricted net assets.

NOTE: All expenses are reported as decreases in unrestricted net assets; losses may be reported as decreases in any of the net asset classes.

Educational Institution
ILLUSTRATIVE STATEMENT OF ACTIVITIES
Multicolumn Format

	Unrestricted	Temporarily restricted	Permanently restricted	Total
Revenues and gains:				
Tuition and fees	$xxx	--	--	$xxx
Contributions	xxx	$xxx	$xxx	xxx
Contracts and other exchange transactions	xxx	--	--	xxx
Investment income on life income and annuity agreements	--	xxx	--	xxx
Investment income on endowment	xxx	xxx	xxx	xxx
Other investment income	xxx	xxx	xxx	xxx
Net realized gains on endowment	xxx	xxx	xxx	xxx
Net realized gains on other investments	xxx	xxx	xxx	xxx
Sales and services of auxiliary enterprises	xxx	--	--	xxx
Total revenues and gains	xxx	xxx	xxx	xxx
Net assets released from restrictions	xxx	(xxx)	--	--
Total revenues and gains and other support	xxx	xxx	xxx	xxx

	Unrestricted	Temporarily restricted	Permanently restricted	Total
Expenses and losses:				
Educational and general:				
Instruction	xxx	--	--	xxx
Research	xxx	--	--	xxx
Public service	xxx	--	--	xxx
Academic support	xxx	--	--	xxx
Student services	xxx	--	--	xxx
Institutional support	xxx	--	--	xxx
Total educational and general expenses	xxx	--	--	xxx
Auxiliary enterprises	xxx	--	--	xxx
Total expenses	xxx	--	--	xxx
Fire loss	xxx	--	--	xxx
Payments to life income beneficiaries	--	xxx	--	xxx
Actuarial loss on annuity obligations	xxx	--	--	xxx
Total expenses and losses	xxx	--	--	xxx
Increase (decrease) in net assets	xxx	xxx	xxx	xxx
Net assets at beginning of year	xxx	xxx	xxx	xxx
Net assets at end of year	$xxx	$xxx	$xxx	$xxx

SOURCE: National Association of College and University Business Officers, *Financial Accounting and Reporting Manual for Higher Education*, Chapter 500, as modified with the exclusion of Operation and Maintenance of Physical Plant and Scholarships and Fellowships as functional expenses.

NOW REVIEW MULTIPLE-CHOICE QUESTIONS 1 THROUGH 62

C. Health Care Organization Accounting—Private Sector

The AICPA has issued an AICPA Audit and Accounting Guide, *Health Care Organizations*. This *Guide* applies both to private sector and governmental health care organizations; separate illustrative statements are presented for each. This section of the module presents private sector health care principles, first by indicating the unique features (beyond part A of this module) that apply and second by presenting illustrative statements. A few of the major features are as follows:

1. Requirements of the *Guide* apply to clinics, medical group practices, individual practice associations, individual practitioners, emergency care facilities, laboratories, surgery centers, other ambulatory care organizations, continuing care retirement communities, health maintenance organizations, home health agencies, hospitals, nursing homes, and rehabilitation centers. Sometimes, a fine line is drawn between those organizations that are considered health care entities and those that are considered voluntary health and welfare organizations, which are not covered by this *Guide*. The distinction is made by the source of revenues, not by the services provided. A nonprofit organization providing health care service in return for payment (an exchange transaction) by the recipient of the service, by a third-party payor, or a government program would be considered a health care organization. A nonprofit organization providing health care service funded primarily by voluntary contributions (from persons or organizations not receiving the service) would be considered a voluntary health and welfare organization.

2. Health care organizations may be not-for-profit, investor owned, or governmental. When possible, accounting and reporting for all types should be similar.

3. Financial statements include a balance sheet, a statement of operations, a statement of changes in net assets, a cash flow statement, and notes to the financial statements.

4. The statement of operations should include a performance indicator, such as operating income, revenues over expenses, etc. The *Guide* specifically indicates that the following must be reported separately from (underneath) that performance indicator (this is a partial list):

   a. Equity transfers involving other entities that control the reporting entity, are controlled by the reporting entity, or are under the common control of the reporting entity.

   b. Receipt of restricted contributions.

   c. Contributions of (and assets released from donor restrictions related to) long-lived assets.

   d. Unrealized gains and losses on investments not restricted by donors or by law, except for those investments classified as trading securities.

   e. Investment returns restricted by donors or by law.

   f. Other items that are required by GAAP to be reported separately (such as extraordinary items, the effect of discontinued operations, accounting changes).

5. Note disclosure must indicate the policies adopted by the entity to determine what is and what is not included in the performance indicator.

6. Patient service revenue is to be reported on the accrual basis net of adjustments for contractual and other adjustments in the operating statement. Provisions recognizing contractual adjustments and other adjustments (for example, hospital employee discounts) are deducted from gross patient revenue to determine **net patient** revenue. Significant revenue under capitation agreements (revenues from third party payors based on number of employees to be covered, etc. instead of services performed) is to be reported separately. Note disclosure should indicate the methods of revenue recognition and description of the types and amounts of contractual adjustments.

7. Patient service revenue does not include charity care. Management's policy for providing charity care and the level of charity care provided should be disclosed in the notes.

8. "Other revenues, gains, and losses" (included in operative revenues) include items such as

   a. Investment income
   b. Fees from educational programs
   c. Proceeds from sale of cafeteria meals
   d. Proceeds from gift shop, parking lot revenue, etc.

9. As is true for other not-for-profit organizations, contributions restricted to long-term purposes (plant acquisition, endowment, term endowment, etc.) would not be reported in the Statement of Operations (as unrestricted revenue) but would be reported in the Statement of Changes in Net Assets as a revenue increasing temporarily restricted or permanently restricted net assets, as appropriate.

10. Expenses are decreases in unrestricted net assets. Expenses may be reported by either natural (salaries, supplies, etc.) or functional classification. Not-for-profit health care entities must disclose expenses in the notes by function if functional classification is not presented on the operating statement. Functional classifications should be based on full cost allocations. Unlike organizations subject to the *Not-for-Profit Guide,* health care organizations may report depreciation, interest, and bad debt expense along with functional categories.

11. Health care organizations, except for continuing care retirement communities, are to present a classified balance sheet, with current assets and current liabilities shown separately. Continuing care retirement communities may sequence assets in terms of nearness to cash and liabilities in accordance with the maturity date.

Two statements are presented for a private sector not-for-profit hospital, both taken from the *Guide*. The statement of operations is presented with one line shown for "excess of revenues over expenses." This is the performance indicator. Note the separation of items above and below that line. Also note the presentation separately for depreciation, interest, and provision for bad debts. In addition, note that the net assets released from restrictions includes separate amounts for those net assets released for operations and those released for other items. The statement of changes in net assets presents the other changes required by FASB ASC 958.

Sample Not-for-Profit Hospital
STATEMENTS OF OPERATIONS
Years Ended December 31, 20X7 and 20X6
(in thousands)

	20X7	20X6
Unrestricted revenues, gains and other support:		
Net patient service revenue	$85,156	$78,942
Premium revenue	11,150	10,950
Other revenue	2,601	5,212
Net assets released from restrictions used for operations	300	--
Total revenues, gains and other support	99,207	95,104
Expenses:		
Operating expenses	88,521	80,585
Depreciation and amortization	4,782	4,280
Interest	1,752	1,825
Provision for bad debts	1,000	1,300
Other	2,000	1,300
Total expenses	98,055	89,290
Operating income	1,152	5,814

	20X7	20X6
Other income:		
Investment income	3,900	3,025
Excess of revenues over expenses	5,052	8,839
Change in net unrealized gains and losses on other than trading securities	300	375
Net assets released from restrictions used for purchase of property and equipment	200	
Change in interest in net assets of Sample Hospital Foundation	283	536
Transfers to parent	(688)	(3,051)
Increase in unrestricted net assets, before extraordinary item	5,147	6,699
Extraordinary loss from extinguishment of debt	(500)	--
Increase in unrestricted net assets	$ 4,647	$ 6,699

See accompanying notes to financial statements.

SOURCE: AICPA Audit and Accounting Guide, *Health Care Organizations.*

Sample Not-for-Profit Hospital
STATEMENTS OF CHANGES IN NET ASSETS
Years Ended December 31, 20X7 and 20X6
(in thousands)

	20X7	20X6
Unrestricted net assets:		
Excess of revenues over expenses	$ 5,052	$ 8,839
Net unrealized gains on investments, other than trading securities	300	375
Change in interest in net assets of Sample Hospital Foundation	283	536
Transfers to parent	(688)	(3,051)
Net assets released from restrictions used for purchase of property and equipment	200	--
Increase in unrestricted net assets before extraordinary item	5,147	6,699
Extraordinary loss from extinguishment of debt	(500)	--
Increase in unrestricted net assets	4,647	6,699
Temporarily restricted net assets:		
Contributions for charity care	140	996
Net realized and unrealized gains on investments	5	8
Net assets released from restrictions	(500)	--
Increase (decrease) in temporarily restricted net assets	(355)	1,004
Permanently restricted net assets:		
Contributions for endowment funds	50	411
Net realized and unrealized gains on investments	5	2
Increase in permanently restricted net assets	55	413
Increase in net assets	4,347	8,116
Net assets, beginning of year	72,202	64,086
Net assets, end of year	$76,549	$72,202

See accompanying notes to financial statements.

SOURCE: AICPA Audit and Accounting Guide, *Health Care Organizations.*

D. Health Care Organization Accounting—Governmental

Governmental health care organizations, as mentioned earlier, are not allowed to use the principles established in SFAS 116 and 117 for not-for-profit organizations. The AICPA *Health Care Guide,* however, attempts to present accounting and reporting principles allowed by the GASB in as close a fashion as possible to private sector health care entities. A few major observations should be noted.

1. Governmental health care organizations are permitted by GASB 34 to report as special-purpose entities engaged in governmental or business-type activities, or both. Most will choose to report as special-purpose entities engaged in business-type activities.
2. Governmental health care organizations reporting as special-purpose entities engaged in business-type activities will prepare the statements required for proprietary funds. These are the (a) Balance Sheets, (b) Statement of Revenues, Expenses, and Changes in Net Assets, and (c) Statement of Cash Flows
3. GASB principles must be followed in the separate reports of governmental health care organizations. For example, net assets are to be categorized as (a) invested in capital assets, net of related debt; (b) restricted, and (c) unrestricted. The GASB cash flow format should be used. Refer to the proprietary fund example statements in Module 21.
4. To the extent possible, AICPA *Health Care Guide* principles should also be followed. For example, the items listed above in Section C.4. should be reported below the performance indicator, net patient revenue should be calculated in the same manner as described previously in C.6. and should not include charity care cases.

> ## NOW REVIEW MULTIPLE-CHOICE QUESTIONS 63 THROUGH 83

KEY TERMS

Contributions (of cash). A voluntary transfer of resources to a charitable organization motivated by generosity.

Contributions (of services). A voluntary providing of personal services to a charitable organization.

Permanently restricted resources. Resources such as (1) certain assets, such as artwork, etc. that must be maintained or used in a certain way, (2) endowments that represent funds that must be invested permanently, and (3) land when it must be held in perpetuity.

Split-interest agreement. An arrangement whereby both a donor (or beneficiary) and a not-for-profit organization receive benefits (e.g., charitable lead trusts and charitable remainder trusts).

Temporarily restricted resources. Resources restricted to be (1) used for a particular purpose, (2) expended at a time in the future, or (3) invested for a period of time.

Unrestricted resources. All resources that do not have restrictions by donors or grantors.

A. FASB and AICPA Standards for Private Sector Nonprofits

1. A statement of functional expenses is required for which one of the following private nonprofit organizations?
- a. Colleges.
- b. Hospitals.
- c. Voluntary health and welfare organizations.
- d. Performing arts organizations.

2. The statement of financial position (balance sheet) for Founders Library, a private nonprofit organization, should report separate dollar amounts for the library's net assets according to which of the following classifications?
- a. Unrestricted and permanently restricted.
- b. Temporarily restricted and permanently restricted.
- c. Unrestricted and temporarily restricted.
- d. Unrestricted, temporarily restricted, and permanently restricted.

3. Chicago Museum, a private nonprofit organization, has both regular and term endowments. On the museum's statement of financial position (balance sheet), how should the net assets of each type of endowment be reported?

	Term endowments	Regular endowments
a.	Temporarily restricted	Permanently restricted
b.	Permanently restricted	Permanently restricted
c.	Unrestricted	Temporarily restricted
d.	Temporarily restricted	Temporarily restricted

4. Kerry College, a private not-for-profit college, received $25,000 from Ms. Mary Smith on April 30, 2012. Ms. Smith stipulated that her contribution be used to support faculty research during the fiscal year beginning on July 1, 2012. On July 15, 2012, administrators of Kerry awarded research grants totaling $25,000 to several faculty in accordance with the wishes of Ms. Smith. For the year ended June 30, 2012, Kerry College should report the $25,000 contribution as
- a. Temporarily restricted revenues on the statement of activities.
- b. Unrestricted revenue on the statement of activities.
- c. Temporarily restricted deferred revenue on the statement of activities.
- d. An increase in fund balance on the statement of financial position.

5. Good Hope, a private not-for-profit voluntary health and welfare organization, received a cash donation of $500,000 from Mr. Charles Peobody on November 15, 2012. Mr. Peobody directed that his donation be used to acquire equipment for the organization. Good Hope used the donation to acquire equipment costing $500,000 in January of 2013. For the year ended December 31, 2012, Good Hope should report the $500,000 contribution on its
- a. Statement of activities as unrestricted revenue.
- b. Statement of financial position as temporarily restricted deferred revenue.
- c. Statement of financial position as unrestricted deferred revenue.
- d. Statement of activities as temporarily restricted revenue.

6. On the statement of activities for a private not-for-profit performing arts center, expenses should be deducted from

- I. Unrestricted revenues.
- II. Temporarily restricted revenues.
- III. Permanently restricted revenues.

- a. I, II, and III.
- b. Both I and II.
- c. I only.
- d. II only.

7. Albert University, a private not-for-profit university, had the following cash inflows during the year ended June 30, 2012:

- I. $500,000 from students for tuition.
- II. $300,000 from a donor who stipulated that the money be invested indefinitely.
- III. $100,000 from a donor who stipulated that the money be spent in accordance with the wishes of Albert's governing board.

On Albert University's statement of cash flows for the year ended June 30, 2012, what amount of these cash flows should be reported as operating activities?
- a. $900,000
- b. $400,000
- c. $800,000
- d. $600,000

8. Gamma Pi, a private nonprofit fraternal organization, should prepare a statement of financial position and which of the following financial statements?

- I. Statement of activities.
- II. Statement of changes in fund balances.
- III. Statement of cash flows.

- a. I, II, and III.
- b. III only.
- c. II and III.
- d. I and III.

9. Save the Planet, a private nonprofit research organization, received a $500,000 contribution from Ms. Susan Clark. Ms. Clark stipulated that her donation be used to purchase new computer equipment for Save the Planet's research staff. The contribution was received in August of 2012, and the computers were acquired in January of 2013. For the year ended December 31, 2012, the $500,000 contribution should be reported by Save the Planet on its
- a. Statement of activities as unrestricted revenue.
- b. Statement of activities as deferred revenue.
- c. Statement of activities as temporarily restricted revenue.
- d. Statement of financial position as deferred revenue.

10. United Ways, a private not-for-profit voluntary health and welfare organization, received a contribution of $10,000 from a donor in 2011. The donor did not specify any use restrictions on the contribution; however, the donor specified that the donation should not be used until 2012. The governing board of United Ways spent the contribution in 2012 for fund-raising expenses. For the year ended Decem-

ber 31, 2011, United Ways should report the contribution on its
  a. Statement of financial position as deferred revenue.
  b. Statement of activities as unrestricted revenue.
  c. Statement of financial position as an increase in fund balance.
  d. Statement of activities as temporarily restricted revenue.

11. The statement of cash flows for a private not-for-profit hospital should report cash flows according to which of the following classifications?

  I. Operating activities.
  II. Investing activities.
  III. Financing activities.

  a. I, II, and III.
  b. II and III.
  c. I only.
  d. I and III.

12. Pharm, a nongovernmental not-for-profit organization, is preparing its year-end financial statements. Which of the following statements is required?
  a. Statement of changes in financial position.
  b. Statement of cash flows.
  c. Statement of changes in fund balance.
  d. Statement of revenue, expenses and changes in fund balance.

13. Stanton College, a not-for-profit organization, received a building with no donor stipulations as to its use. Stanton does not have an accounting policy implying a time restriction on donated fixed assets. What type of net assets should be increased when the building is received?

  I. Unrestricted.
  II. Temporarily restricted.
  III. Permanently restricted.

  a. I only.
  b. II only.
  c. III only.
  d. II or III.

14. Sea Lion Park, a private not-for-profit zoological society, received contributions restricted for research totaling $50,000 in 2011. None of the contributions were spent on research in 2011. In 2012, $35,000 of the contributions were used to support the research activities of the society. The net effect on the statement of activities for the year ended December 31, 2012, for Sea Lion Park would be a
  a. $15,000 increase in temporarily restricted net assets.
  b. $35,000 decrease in temporarily restricted net assets.
  c. $35,000 increase in unrestricted net assets.
  d. $35,000 decrease in unrestricted net assets.

15. Clara Hospital, a private not-for-profit hospital, earned $250,000 of gift shop revenues and spent $50,000 on research during the year ended December 31, 2012. The $50,000 spent on research was part of a $75,000 contribution received during December of 2011 from a donor who stipulated that the donation be used for medical research. Assume none of the gift shop revenues were spent in 2012. For the year ended December 31, 2012, what was the in-

crease in unrestricted net assets from the events occurring during 2012?
  a. $300,000
  b. $200,000
  c. $250,000
  d. $275,000

16. Which of the following transactions of a private not-for-profit voluntary health and welfare organization would increase temporarily restricted net assets on the statement of activities for the year ended June 30, 2012?

  I. Received a contribution of $10,000 from a donor on May 15, 2012, who stipulated that the donation not be spent until August of 2012.
  II. Spent $25,000 for fund-raising on June 20, 2012. The amount expended came from a $25,000 contribution on March 12, 2012. The donor stipulated that the contribution be used for fund-raising activities.

  a. Both I and II.
  b. Neither I nor II.
  c. I only.
  d. II only.

17. Catherine College, a private not-for-profit college, received the following contributions during 2012:

  I. $5,000,000 from alumni for construction of a new wing on the science building to be constructed in 2012.
  II. $1,000,000 from a donor who stipulated that the contribution be invested indefinitely and that the earnings be used for scholarships. As of December 31, 2012, earnings from investments amounted to $50,000.

For the year ended December 31, 2012, what amount of these contributions should be reported as temporarily restricted revenues on the statement of activities?
  a. $ 50,000
  b. $5,050,000
  c. $5,000,000
  d. $6,050,000

18. On December 31, 2012, Hope Haven, a private not-for-profit voluntary health and welfare organization, received a pledge from a donor who stipulated that $1,000 would be given to the organization each year for the next five years, starting on December 31, 2013. Present value factors at 6% for five periods are presented below.

Present value of an ordinary annuity for 5 periods at 6%	4.21236
Present value of an annuity due for 5 periods at 6%	4.46511

For the year ended December 31, 2012, Hope Haven should report, on its statement of activities,
  a. Unrestricted revenues of $5,000.
  b. Temporarily restricted revenues of $4,465.
  c. Unrestricted revenues of $4,465.
  d. Temporarily restricted revenues of $4,212.

19. For Guiding Light, a nongovernmental nonprofit religious organization, net assets that can be expended in accordance with the wishes of the governing board of the organization should be reported as

I. Unrestricted.
II. Temporarily restricted.
III. Permanently restricted.

    a.   I only.
    b.   Both I and II.
    c.   I, II, and III.
    d.   Either I or II.

20. The Jackson Foundation, a private not-for-profit organization, had the following cash contributions and expenditures in 2012:

> Unrestricted cash contributions of $500,000.
> Cash contributions of $200,000 restricted by the donor to the acquisition of property.
> Cash expenditures of $200,000 to acquire property with the donation in the above item.

Jackson's statement of cash flows should include which of the following amounts?

	Operating activities	Investing activities	Financing activities
a.	$700,000	$(200,000)	$0
b.	$500,000	$0	$0
c.	$500,000	$(200,000)	$200,000
d.	$0	$500,000	$200,000

21. United Hope, a private not-for-profit voluntary health and welfare organization, received the following contributions in 2012:

I. $500 from donors who stipulated that the money not be spent until 2013.
II. $1,000 from donors who stipulated that the contributions be used for the acquisition of equipment, none of which was acquired in 2012.

Which of the above events increased temporarily restricted net assets for the year ending December 31, 2012?
    a.   I only.
    b.   Both I and II.
    c.   II only.
    d.   Neither I nor II.

22. A statement of financial position (balance sheet), which reports unrestricted, temporarily restricted, and permanently restricted net assets, is required for which one of the following organizations?

I. A public university.
II. A private, not-for-profit hospital.

    a.   Both I and II.
    b.   I only.
    c.   Neither I nor II.
    d.   II only.

23. A storm broke glass windows in the building of Lea Meditators, a not-for-profit religious organization. A member of Lea's congregation, a professional glazier, replaced the windows at no charge. In Lea's statement of activities, the breakage and replacement of the windows should
    a.   Not be reported.
    b.   Be reported by note disclosure only.
    c.   Be reported as an increase in both expenses and contributions.
    d.   Be reported as an increase in both net assets and contributions.

24. Financial statements of not-for-profit organizations focus on
    a.   Basic information for the organization as a whole.
    b.   Standardization of funds nomenclature.
    c.   Inherent differences of not-for-profit organizations that impact reporting presentations.
    d.   Distinctions between current fund and noncurrent fund presentations.

25. On December 30, 2012, Leigh Museum, a not-for-profit organization, received a $7,000,000 donation of Day Co. shares with donor-stipulated requirements as follows:

> Shares valued at $5,000,000 are to be sold, with the proceeds used to erect a public viewing building.
> Shares valued at $2,000,000 are to be retained, with the dividends used to support current operations.

As a consequence of the receipt of the Day shares, how much should Leigh report as temporarily restricted net assets on its 2012 statement of financial position (balance sheet)?
    a. $0
    b. $2,000,000
    c. $5,000,000
    d. $7,000,000

26. The Jones family lost its home in a fire. On December 25, 2012, a philanthropist sent money to the Amer Benevolent Society, a not-for-profit organization, to purchase furniture for the Jones family. During January 2013, Amer purchased this furniture for the Jones family. How should Amer report the receipt of the money in its 2012 financial statements?
    a.   As an unrestricted contribution.
    b.   As a temporarily restricted contribution.
    c.   As a permanently restricted contribution.
    d.   As a liability.

27. If the Pel Museum, a not-for-profit organization, received a contribution of historical artifacts, it need **not** recognize the contribution if the artifacts are to be sold and the proceeds used to
    a.   Support general museum activities.
    b.   Acquire other items for collections.
    c.   Repair existing collections.
    d.   Purchase buildings to house collections.

28. A large not-for-profit organization's statement of activities should report the net change for net assets that are

	Unrestricted	Permanently restricted
a.	Yes	Yes
b.	Yes	No
c.	No	No
d.	No	Yes

29. Which of the following classifications is required for reporting of expenses by all not-for-profit organizations?
    a.   Natural classification in the statement of activities or notes to the financial statements.
    b.   Functional classification in the statement of activities or notes to the financial statements.
    c.   Functional classification in the statement of activities and natural classification in a matrix format in a separate statement.
    d.   Functional classification in the statement of activities and natural classification in the notes to the financial statements.

30. Rosary Botanical Gardens, a private not-for-profit organization, established a $500,000 quasi endowment on September 1, 2012. On the garden's statement of financial position at December 31, 2012, the assets in this quasi endowment should be included in which of the following classifications?

    a. Temporarily restricted net assets.
    b. Unrestricted net assets.
    c. Permanently restricted net assets.
    d. Either temporarily or permanently restricted net assets, depending on the expected term of the quasi endowment.

31. During 2011, an alumnus of Smith College, a private not-for-profit college, transferred $100,000 to the college with the stipulation that it be spent for library acquisitions. However, the alumnus specified that none of the cash transferred could be spent until the college had matched the entire amount transferred with donations from other alumni by December 31, 2012. As of December 31, 2011, the college had received matching cash donations of only $5,000 from other alumni, and the college estimated that it was reasonably possible that it would not reach the goal of $100,000 by December 31, 2012. If the funds are not matched by December 31, 2012, the cash will be returned to the alumnus. On the college's statement of financial position at December 31, 2011, the cash transfer of $100,000 would be included in the amount reported for

    a. Liabilities.
    b. Unrestricted net assets.
    c. Temporarily restricted net assets.
    d. Permanently restricted net assets.

32. During the year ended December 31, 2012, a not-for-profit performing arts entity received the following donor-restricted contribution and investment income:

Cash contribution of $100,000 to be permanently invested.
Cash dividends and interest of $6,000 to be used for the acquisition of theater equipment.

As a result of these cash receipts, the statement of cash flows for the year ended December 31, 2012, would report an increase of

    a. $106,000 from operating activities.
    b. $106,000 from financing activities.
    c. $6,000 from operating activities and an increase of $100,000 from financing activities.
    d. $100,000 from operating activities and an increase of $6,000 from financing activities.

33. Which of the following private, nonprofit entities is required to report expenses both by function and by natural classification?

    a. Hospitals.
    b. Colleges and universities.
    c. Voluntary health and welfare organizations.
    d. Performing arts organizations.

34. On December 5, 2012, Jones Heating and Air Conditioning Service repaired the heating system in the building occupied by Good Hope, a private not-for-profit voluntary health and welfare organization. An invoice for $1,500 was received by Good Hope for the repairs on December 15, 2012. On December 30, 2012, Jones notified Good Hope that the invoice was canceled and that the repairs were being donated without charge. For the year ended December 31, 2012, how should Good Hope report these contributed services?

    a. Only in the notes to the financial statements.
    b. No disclosure is required either in the financial statements or in the notes.
    c. As an increase in unrestricted revenues and as an increase in expenses on the statements of activities.
    d. As an increase in temporarily restricted net assets on the statement of activities.

35. During the year ended December 31, 2012, the James Community Foundation, a private not-for-profit organization, received the following contributed services:

  I. Anderson & Anderson, attorneys-at-law, contributed their services which involved advice related to the foundation's regular endowments.
  II. Senior citizens participated in a telethon to raise money for a new music building.

Which of these contributed services should be included in unrestricted revenues, gains, and other support on James Community Foundation's statement of activities for the year ended December 31, 2012?

    a. Both I and II.
    b. Neither I nor II.
    c. II only.
    d. I only.

36. Child Care Centers, Inc., a not-for-profit organization, receives revenue from various sources during the year to support its day care centers. The following cash amounts were received during 2012:

$2,000 restricted by the donor to be used for meals for the children.
$1,500 received for subscriptions to a monthly child-care magazine with a fair market value to subscribers of $1,000.
$10,000 to be used only upon completion of a new playroom that was only 50% complete at December 31, 2012.

What amount should Child Care Centers record as contribution revenue in its 2012 Statement of Activities?

    a. $ 2,000
    b. $ 2,500
    c. $10,000
    d. $11,000

37. On December 20, 2012, United Appeal, a private not-for-profit voluntary health and welfare organization, received a donation of computer equipment valued at $25,000 from a local computer retailer. The equipment is expected to have a useful life of three years. The donor placed no restrictions on how long the computer equipment was to be used, and United has an accounting policy that does not imply a time restriction on gifts of long-lived assets. On United's statement of activities prepared for the year ended December 31, 2012, the donation of computer equipment should be reported

    a. As an increase in temporarily restricted net assets.
    b. Only in the notes to the financial statements.
    c. As an increase in unrestricted net assets.
    d. As either an increase in temporarily restricted net assets or as an increase in unrestricted net assets.

38. On December 30, 2012, the Board of Trustees of Henry Museum, a private not-for-profit organization, designated $4,000,000 of unrestricted net assets for the construction of an addition to its building. What effect does this designation have on the museum's unrestricted and temporarily restricted net assets which are reported on the statement of financial position (balance sheet) at December 31, 2012?

	Unrestricted net assets	Temporarily restricted net assets
a.	No effect	Increase
b.	Decrease	Increase
c.	Decrease	No effect
d.	No effect	No effect

39. Darlin Hospital, a private not-for-profit hospital, had the following cash receipts for the year ended December 31, 2012:

Patient service revenue	$300,000
Gift shop revenue	25,000
Interest revenue restricted by donor stipulation for acquisition of equipment	50,000

As a result of these cash receipts, the hospital's statement of cash flows for the year ended December 31, 2012, would report an increase in operating activities of

- a. $325,000
- b. $375,000
- c. $350,000
- d. $300,000

40. For a private, not-for-profit organization, when is a donor's conditional promise to give considered to be unconditional?

- a. When the condition is partially met.
- b. When the possibility that the condition will not be met is remote.
- c. When the conditional promise is made.
- d. When cash or other assets promised are received.

41. A not-for-profit organization receives $150 from a donor. The donor receives two tickets to a theater show and an acknowledgment in the theater program. The tickets have a fair market value of $100. What amount is recorded as contribution revenue?

- a. $0
- b. $ 50
- c. $100
- d. $150

42. On November 30, 2011, Justin Barlow, an alumnus of Murry School, a private, not-for-profit high school, contributed $15,000, with the stipulation that the donation be used for faculty travel expenses during 2012. During 2012, Murry spent all of the donation in accordance with Mr. Barlow's wishes. For the year ended December 31, 2012, what was the effect of the donation on unrestricted and temporarily restricted net assets?

	Unrestricted net assets	Temporarily restricted net assets
a.	Increase	Decrease
b.	No effect	Decrease
c.	Increase	No effect
d.	No effect	No effect

43. A private not-for-profit voluntary health and welfare organization received a cash donation in 2009 that contained a donor-imposed restriction that stipulated that the donation could not be spent until 2011. The voluntary health and welfare organization spent the donation in 2011 on fund-raising activities. On the statement of activities prepared for the year ended December 31, 2011, the expiration of the time restriction would result in reporting a(n)

- a. Increase in temporarily restricted net assets.
- b. Reclassification that decreased temporarily restricted net assets.
- c. Increase in unrestricted net assets.
- d. Expense that decreased temporarily restricted net assets.

44. In the financial statements of not-for-profit organizations, reporting reclassifications are caused by which of the following?

I. Expiration of donor-imposed conditions.
II. Expiration of donor-imposed restrictions.

- a. I only.
- b. Both I and II.
- c. II only.
- d. Neither I nor II.

45. Which of the following transactions would result in an increase in unrestricted net assets for the year ended December 31, 2012?

I. A private, not-for-profit hospital earned interest on investments that were board-designated.
II. A private, not-for-profit voluntary health and welfare organization received unconditional promises to give (pledges) which will not be received until the beginning of 2013. The donors placed no restrictions on their donations.

- a. Both I and II.
- b. I only.
- c. II only.
- d. Neither I nor II.

46. Benevolent Society, a private not-for-profit organization, should recognize contributed services on its statement of activities if which of the following conditions is(are) met?

I. The contributed services create or enhance nonfinancial assets.
II. The contributed services require specialized skills, are provided by individuals possessing those skills, and would typically need to be purchased if not provided by donation.

- a. Both I and II.
- b. Neither I nor II.
- c. I only.
- d. Either I or II.

47. During 2012, Margaret Billingsley, a prominent art collector, donated several items in her collection to the Darrwin Museum, a private, not-for-profit organization. Ms. Billingsley stipulated that her contribution be shown to the public, that it should be preserved, and not be sold. Darrwin's accounting policy is to capitalize all donations of art, historical treasures, and similar items. On the date of donation, what was the effect of Ms. Billingsley's donation on Darrwin's financial statements?

a. Temporarily restricted net assets increased.
b. Reclassifications caused a simultaneous increase in permanently restricted net assets and a decrease in temporarily restricted net assets.
c. There was no effect on any class of Darrwin's net assets.
d. Permanently restricted net assets increased.

48. Which of the following transactions or events would cause an increase in unrestricted net assets for the year ended December 31, 2012?

I. A private not-for-profit voluntary health and welfare organization spent a restricted donation that was received in 2011. In accordance with the donor's wishes, the donation was spent on public health education during 2012.
II. During 2012, a private, not-for-profit college earned dividends and interest on term endowments. Donors placed no restrictions on the earnings of term endowments. The governing board of the college intends to use this investment income to fund undergraduate scholarships for 2013.

a. II only.
b. I only.
c. Neither I nor II.
d. Both I and II.

49. Mary Egbart promised Columbus College, a private, not-for-profit college, that she would provide 80% of the funds needed to construct a new performing arts center, if the college could get the remaining 20% of the funds needed from other donors by July 1, 2012. The promise was made in 2011. At December 31, 2011, the governing board of the college had received donations from other donors for approximately 15% of the cost of the new center and believed that the probability of not getting the remaining 5% of the necessary funds was remote. For the year ended December 31, 2011, Ms. Egbart's promise would

a. Be reported as an increase in permanently restricted net assets on the statement of activities.
b. Not be reported on the statement of activities.
c. Be reported as an increase in deferred support on the statement of financial position.
d. Be reported as an increase in temporarily restricted net assets on the statement of activities.

50. How should a private not-for-profit hospital report its investments in debt securities that are classified as current assets and noncurrent assets on its statement of financial position (balance sheet)?

	Debt securities in current assets	Debt securities in noncurrent assets
a.	Fair value	Amortized cost
b.	Amortized cost	Fair value
c.	Fair value	Fair value
d.	Amortized cost	Amortized cost

51. The governing board of Crestfallen, a private not-for-profit voluntary health and welfare organization, acquired equity securities of BMZ Company at a cost of $35,000 on May 1, 2012. The governing board used unrestricted net assets to acquire this investment, and it intends to use the income from its investment in BMZ, as well as other investments, to acquire much needed computer equipment for the

organization. The investment in the equity securities of BMZ Company, which is listed on a national stock exchange, represents less than a 1% interest in the company. On November 15, 2012, Crestfallen received $1,000 of dividends from BMZ, and the fair value of the BMZ equity securities was $42,000 on December 31, 2012. As a result of Crestfallen's investment in BMZ Company, the statement of activities for the year ended December 31, 2012, would report an increase of

a. $8,000 in unrestricted net assets.
b. $8,000 in temporarily restricted net assets.
c. $1,000 in unrestricted net assets.
d. $7,000 in unrestricted net assets.

52. Jazz Planners, a private not-for-profit performing arts organization, has donor-restricted permanent endowment funds which include investments in equity securities. These equity securities all have readily determinable fair values because they are all traded on national security exchanges. Most of the equity investments represent between 1% and 3% of the common stock of the investee companies; however, a few of Jazz Planners' investments permit the organization significant influence over the operating and financing policies of the investee companies. How should the organization report these equity securities on its statement of financial position (balance sheet)?

	Equity securities: 1% to 3% ownership	Equity securities: significant influence
a.	Fair value	Fair value
b.	Fair value	Use equity method
c.	Lower of cost or market	Fair value
d.	Fair value	Lower of cost or market

53. Rose Smith made a cash donation for a specific purpose in December 2012, to United Ways, a nongovernmental, nonprofit organization that raises contributions for others. Assume United Ways was (1) not granted variance power by Rose Smith over her donation and (2) the beneficiaries of the donation are not financially related to United Ways. How should United Ways account for Rose's cash donation?

a. As an increase in contribution revenue.
b. As an increase in liabilities.
c. As either an increase in contribution revenue or liabilities.
d. As neither an increase in contribution revenue nor liabilities.

54. World-Wide Helpers Foundation, a nonprofit entity, received a cash donation in 2012 from Herold Smith. World-Wide Helpers Foundation is controlled by World-Wide Helpers, a nonprofit entity that raises resources for others. The resources of World-Wide Helpers Foundation are used for the benefit of World-Wide Helpers. How should World-Wide Helpers Foundation account for the cash donation?

a. As an increase in contribution revenues.
b. As an increase in liabilities.
c. As either an increase in contribution revenue or liabilities.
d. As neither an increase in contribution revenue or liabilities.

55. A cash donation from a resource provider should be reported as contribution revenue by a recipient organization when which of the following exists?

a. The recipient organization and beneficiary are **not** financially interrelated.

b. The resource provider does **not** allow the recipient organization to use the donation for beneficiaries other than those specified by the resource provider.

c. The resource provider does **not** grant variance power to the recipient organization to redirect the donation to other beneficiaries.

d. The resource provider grants variance power to the recipient organization to redirect the donation to other beneficiaries.

56. Peter Smith made a cash donation in January 2012, to World-Wide Helpers, a nongovernmental, nonprofit organization that raises contributions for others. Peter specified the beneficiaries for his contribution, but provided variance power to World-Wide Helpers to use the donation for beneficiaries not specified by Peter. How should World-Wide Helpers account for Peter's cash donation?

a. As an increase in contribution revenue.

b. As an increase in liabilities.

c. As either an increase in contribution revenue or liabilities.

d. As neither an increase in contribution revenue nor liabilities.

57. The Taft family lost its home in a flood in October 2012. In November of 2012, Mary Wilson donated cash to Goodbody Benevolent Society to purchase furniture for the Taft family. In December 2012, Goodbody purchased this furniture for the Taft family. How should Goodbody report the receipt of the cash donation in its 2012 financial statements?

a. As an unrestricted contribution.

b. As a temporarily restricted contribution.

c. As a liability.

d. As either a liability or as a temporarily restricted contribution.

58. An arrangement where a donor makes an initial gift to a trust or directly to the not-for-profit organization, in which the not-for-profit organization has a beneficial interest but is not the sole beneficiary is known as a

a. Donor-imposed condition.

b. Donor-imposed restriction.

c. Share-the-wealth agreement.

d. Split-interest agreement.

59. Under which of the following cases should joint costs be allocated between fund-raising and the appropriate program or management and general function?

a. An appeal for funds accompanied by a statement of the mission of the not-for-profit entity.

b. An appeal for funds accompanied by a brochure explaining why funds are needed and how they will be used.

c. An organization seeks the involvement of the public in the attainment of their missions by telling people what they should do about particular issues in addition to fund-raising appeals.

d. An appeal for funds and education materials sent to a person based on his/her presumed ability to provide financial support.

60. Which of the following are considered to be capital additions in the statement of activity of a not-for-profit organization?

I. Nonexpendable gifts, grants, and bequests restricted by donors to endowment funds.

II. Legally restricted investment income on investments held in endowment funds that must be added to the principal.

III. Donor-restricted gifts for program or supporting services.

a. I, II, and III.

b. I and III only.

c. I and II only.

d. III only.

61. Depending on the extent of discretion that the not-for-profit recipient has over the use or subsequent disposition of the assets, gifts in kind may be treated as

	Agency transactions	Contributions
a.	No	No
b.	No	Yes
c.	Yes	Yes
d.	Yes	No

62. A not-for-profit organization receives an asset for which they have little or no discretion over the use of the asset. The organization should report the asset as a(n)

a. Contribution.

b. Agency transaction.

c. Exchange.

d. Conditional transfer.

C. Health Care Organization Accounting—Private Sector

63. Elizabeth Hospital, a nonprofit hospital affiliated with a religious group, should prepare which of the following financial statements?

	Statement of changes in net assets	Statement of operations
a.	Yes	No
b.	No	Yes
c.	Yes	Yes
d.	No	No

64. Williams Hospital, a nonprofit hospital affiliated with a religious group, reported the following information for the year ended December 31, 2012:

Gross patient service revenue at the hospital's full established rates	$980,000
Bad debts expense	10,000
Contractual adjustments with third-party payors	100,000
Allowance for discounts to hospital employees	15,000

On the hospital's statement of operations for the year ended December 31, 2012, what amount should be reported as net patient service revenue?

a. $865,000

b. $880,000

c. $855,000

d. $955,000

65. For private sector health care organizations, which of the following is included in patient service revenue?

    a. Contractual adjustments.
    b. Charity care.
    c. Significant revenue under capitation agreements (premium revenue).
    d. Unrestricted contributions.

66. Which of the following is **not** covered by the AICPA Audit and Accounting Guide, *Health Care Organizations*?
    a. Nursing homes.
    b. Home health agencies.
    c. Hospitals.
    d. Voluntary health and welfare organizations.

67. Which of the following can be included in the performance indicator on the statement of operations for private sector health care organizations?
    a. Extraordinary items.
    b. Premium revenue from capitation agreements.
    c. Equity transfers.
    d. Contributions of long-lived assets.

68. If private not-for-profit health care entities do not use this expense classification on the operating statement, they must provide it in the notes.
    a. Natural.
    b. Character.
    c. Functional.
    d. Object.

69. When functional classifications are used by private sector health care organizations, they should be based on
    a. Net present value.
    b. Full cost allocations.
    c. Percentage allocations.
    d. Resale value.

70. Which of the following would be acceptable as a performance indicator on a private sector health care entity's statement of operations?
    a. Increase in unrestricted net assets.
    b. Net income.
    c. Increase in net assets.
    d. Excess of revenues over expenses.

71. How is charity care accounted for on the financial statements of a not-for-profit private sector health care organization?
    a. As patient service revenue.
    b. As bad debt expense.
    c. As a separate component of revenue.
    d. Not included on the financial statements.

72. How are nonrefundable advance fees representing payments for future services to be accounted for by nonprofit continuing care retirement communities?
    a. As revenue.
    b. As a liability.
    c. As other financing sources.
    d. In a trust fund.

73. Kash Hospital, a private sector, not-for-profit organization, has gross patient service revenues of $750,000, charity care of $75,000, amounts disallowed by third-party payors of $63,000, and donor-unrestricted contributions of $110,000. What is the amount of net patient service revenue?
    a. $687,000
    b. $722,000

    c. $785,000
    d. $797,000

74. James Hospital, a nonprofit hospital affiliated with a private university, provided $200,000 of charity care for patients during the year ended December 31, 2012. The hospital should report this charity care
    a. As net patient service revenue of $200,000 on the statement of operations.
    b. As net patient service revenue of $200,000 and as an operating expense of $200,000 on the statement of operations.
    c. As accounts receivable of $200,000 on the balance sheet at December 31, 2012.
    d. Only in the notes to the financial statements for 2012.

75. Michael Hospital, a nonprofit hospital affiliated with a private university, reported the following information for the year ended December 31, 2012:

Cash contributions received from donors for capital additions to be acquired in 2013	$150,000
Proceeds from sales at hospital gift shop and snack bar	75,000
Dividend revenue not restricted by donors or by law	25,000

Using the information provided, what amount should be reported as "other revenue and gains" on the hospital's statement of operations for the year ended December 31, 2012?
    a. $ 25,000
    b. $ 75,000
    c. $100,000
    d. $250,000

76. Swathmore Hospital, a nonprofit hospital affiliated with Swathmore University, received the following cash contributions from donors during the year ended December 31, 2011:

Contributions restricted by donors for research	$ 50,000
Contributions restricted by donors for capital acquisitions	250,000

Neither of the contributions was spent during 2011; however, during 2012, the hospital spent the entire $50,000 contribution on research and the entire $250,000 contribution on a capital asset that was placed into service during the year. The hospital has adopted an accounting policy that does not imply a time restriction on gifts of long-lived assets. On the hospital's statement of operations for the year ended December 31, 2012, what total amount should be reported for "net assets released from restrictions"?
    a. $ 50,000
    b. $300,000
    c. $250,000
    d. $0

77. The governing board of Smithson Hospital, a nonprofit hospital affiliated with a religious organization, acquired 100 BMI Company bonds for $103,000 on June 30, 2012. The bonds pay interest on June 30 and December 30. On December 31, 2012, interest of $3,000 was received from BMI, and the fair value of the BMI bonds was $105,000. The governing board acquired the BMI bonds with cash which was unrestricted, and it classified the bonds as trading securities at December 31, 2012, since it intends to sell all of the bonds in January 2013. As a result of the investment in BMI bonds, what amount should be included in revenue, gains, and other support on the statement of operations for the year ended December 31, 2012?

a. $0
b. $3,000
c. $2,000
d. $5,000

78. On the statement of operations for a nonprofit, nongovernmental hospital, which of the items below is included in the amount reported for "revenue and gains over expenses and losses" (the performance indicator)?

I. Unrealized loss on other than trading securities. The securities are included in unrestricted net assets.
II. Contribution received from a donor that cannot be used until next year.

a. I only.
b. II only.
c. Both I and II.
d. Neither I nor II.

79. Tucker Hospital, a nonprofit hospital affiliated with Tucker University, received a donation of medical supplies during the year ended December 31, 2012. The supplies cost the vendor $10,000 and had a selling price of $15,000 on the date they were donated. The vendor did not place any restrictions on how the supplies were to be used. During 2012, all of the donated medical supplies were used. On the hospital's statement of operations for the year ended December 31, 2012, how should the donation be reported?

a. The donation should be included in both revenue and operating expenses in the amount of $10,000.
b. The donation should be excluded from the statement of operations.
c. The donation should be included in both revenue and operating expenses in the amount of $15,000.
d. The donation should be included in revenue in the amount of $15,000 and in operating expenses in the amount of $10,000.

80. Wilson Hospital, a nonprofit hospital affiliated with Wilson College, had the following cash receipts for the year ended December 31, 2012:

Collections of health care receivables	$750,000
Contribution from donor to establish a term endowment	250,000
Tuition from nursing school	50,000
Dividends received from investments in permanent endowment	80,000

The dividends received are restricted by the donor for hospital building improvements. No improvements were made during 2012. On the hospital's statement of cash flows for the year ended December 31, 2012, what amount of these cash receipts would be included in the amount reported for net cash provided (used) by operating activities?

a. $ 880,000
b. $ 800,000
c. $1,050,000
d. $ 750,000

81. Which of the following financial statements of a private, nonprofit hospital reports the changes in unrestricted, temporarily restricted, and permanently restricted net assets for a time period?

	Balance sheet	Statement of operations
a.	Yes	Yes
b.	Yes	No
c.	No	Yes
d.	No	No

82. Unrealized gains on investments which are permanently restricted as to use by donors are reported by a private, nonprofit hospital on the

a. Statement of operations.
b. Statement of cash flows.
c. Statement of changes in net assets.
d. Statement of operations and statement of cash flows.

83. The statement of operations for a private, nonprofit hospital should include a performance indicator that indicates the results of operations for a period. Which of the following items would be included in a hospital's performance indicator reported on the statement of operations?

I. Proceeds from sales of cafeteria meals and guest trays to employees, medical staff, and visitors.
II. Net assets released from restrictions used for operating expenses.

a. I only.
b. Both I and II.
c. II only.
d. Neither I nor II.

Multiple-Choice Answers and Explanations

Answers

1. c __ __	19. a __ __	37. c __ __	55. d __ __	73. a __ __
2. d __ __	20. c __ __	38. d __ __	56. a __ __	74. d __ __
3. a __ __	21. b __ __	39. a __ __	57. c __ __	75. c __ __
4. a __ __	22. d __ __	40. b __ __	58. d __ __	76. b __ __
5. d __ __	23. c __ __	41. b __ __	59. c __ __	77. d __ __
6. c __ __	24. a __ __	42. b __ __	60. c __ __	78. d __ __
7. d __ __	25. c __ __	43. b __ __	61. c __ __	79. c __ __
8. d __ __	26. d __ __	44. c __ __	62. b __ __	80. b __ __
9. c __ __	27. b __ __	45. b __ __	63. c __ __	81. d __ __
10. d __ __	28. a __ __	46. d __ __	64. a __ __	82. c __ __
11. a __ __	29. b __ __	47. d __ __	65. a __ __	83. b __ __
12. b __ __	30. b __ __	48. a __ __	66. d __ __	
13. a __ __	31. a __ __	49. d __ __	67. b __ __	
14. b __ __	32. b __ __	50. c __ __	68. e __ __	
15. c __ __	33. c __ __	51. a __ __	69. b __ __	
16. c __ __	34. c __ __	52. b __ __	70. d __ __	
17. b __ __	35. d __ __	53. b __ __	71. d __ __	1st: __/83 = __%
18. d __ __	36. b __ __	54. a __ __	72. b __ __	2nd: __/83 = __%

Explanations

1. (c) According to FASB ASC 958, a statement of functional expenses is required for voluntary health and welfare organizations. Other private nonprofit organizations are encouraged to disclose this information, but they are not required to.

2. (d) According to FASB ASC 958, a statement of financial position for a nongovernmental nonprofit entity, like a library, should report net assets according to whether the net assets are unrestricted, temporarily restricted, or permanently restricted.

3. (a) According to FASB ASC 958, the net assets of term endowments should be reported as temporarily restricted, while the net assets of regular endowments should be reported as permanently restricted. The net assets of term endowments are temporarily restricted because the donor of a term endowment stipulates that the endowment last only a specific number of years. Donors of regular endowments intend that these endowments last indefinitely; hence, the net assets are permanently restricted.

4. (a) According to FASB ASC 958, contributions are reported as revenue in the year received even though there are donor-imposed use or time restrictions on the donation. Since Ms. Smith's donation was use and time restricted, the donation should be reported as a temporarily restricted revenue on the statement of activities for the year ended June 30, 2012.

5. (d) According to FASB ASC 958, contributions are reported as revenue in the year received even though there are donor-imposed use or time restrictions on the contribution. Since Mr. Peobody's contribution was use restricted, the contribution would be reported as temporarily restricted revenue on the statement of activities for the year ended December 31, 2012.

6. (c) According to FASB ASC 958, all expenses are reported as unrestricted on the statement of activities. This means that expenses are deducted only from unrestricted revenues.

7. (d) In accordance with FASB ASC 958, nongovernmental not-for-profit organizations are required to report a statement of cash flows. On this statement, cash flows are reported using the classifications of operating, investing, and financing activities. Cash flows related to revenues and expenses that are unrestricted should be reported in the operating activities section. The cash inflows from both tuition ($500,000) and the unrestricted contribution ($100,000) are both unrestricted and should be reported as operating activities. Restricted contributions for long-term purposes, like the $300,000 endowment, are reported as financing activities on the statement of cash flows.

8. (d) According to FASB ASC 958, nongovernmental, not-for-profit entities should prepare the following financial statements:

1. Statement of financial position
2. Statement of activities
3. Statement of cash flows

In addition, a voluntary health and welfare organization should also prepare a statement of functional expenses.

9. (c) Donor restricted contributions should be reported as revenue in the period received. Donor restricted contributions which are restricted according to use should be reported as either temporarily restricted revenues or as permanently restricted revenues, depending on the restriction. In the case of Save the Planet, the restriction is temporary, not permanent. Therefore, Ms. Clark's contribution should be reported as temporarily restricted revenue on the statement of activities for the year ended December 31, 2012.

10. (d) Donor restricted contributions are revenues in the year the contribution is made, not in the year the contribution is spent. Contributions that are restricted temporarily should be reported on the statement of activities as temporarily restricted revenues.

11. (a) The statement of cash flows for a nongovernmental not-for-profit entity should report its cash flows from operating, investing, and financing activities.

12. (b) FASB ASC 958 indicates that "a complete set of financial statements of not-for-profit organization shall include a statement of financial position as of the end of the reporting period, a statement of activities and a statement of cash flows for the reporting period, and accompanying notes to financial statements."

13. (a) FASB ASC 958 states

Gifts of long-lived assets received without stipulations about how long the donated asset must be used shall be reported as restricted support if it is an organization's accounting policy to imply a time restriction that expires over the useful life of the donated assets...In the absence of that policy and other donor-imposed restrictions on use of the asset, gifts of long-lived assets shall be reported as unrestricted support.

14. (b) For the year ended December 31, 2011, the contributions received for research would be reported on the statement of activities as an increase of $50,000 in temporarily restricted net assets. Contributions received from outside donors for use in research are reported as temporarily restricted net assets. For the year ended December 21, 2012, a reclassification of net assets would be reported on the statement of activities. A reclassification of $35,000 would be reported as both a decrease in temporarily restricted net assets and an increase in unrestricted net assets. In addition, research expense of $35,000 would be reported as a decrease in unrestricted net assets on the statement of activities for the year ended December 31, 2012. Therefore, as a result of the transactions in 2012, there was a decrease of $35,000 in temporarily restricted net assets and no effect on unrestricted net assets (the $35,000 reclassification to unrestricted net assets is offset by a $35,000 increase in research expense).

15. (c) Unrestricted net assets increased $250,000 for the year ended December 31, 2012. The $50,000 spent on research during 2012 would be reclassified (added) to unrestricted net assets when the money was spent for research. The $50,000 addition to unrestricted revenues, gains, and other support would be accompanied by a $50,000 reclassification (deduction) from temporarily restricted revenues. The expenses of $50,000 for research are deducted from unrestricted revenues, etc., which include the $50,000 reclassification. Therefore, the net effect on unrestricted net assets of spending $50,000 on research is zero. The $250,000 of gift shop revenue is unrestricted revenue because the governing board has control of this revenue.

16. (c) Contributions should be reported as revenue in the period of contribution, even though a donor has placed a time or use restriction on the contribution. The $10,000 and the $25,000 contributions should be reported as temporarily restricted revenues on the statement of activities for the year ended June 30, 2012. When the $25,000 is spent on fundraising, a reclassification of $25,000 should be reported as a deduction from temporarily restricted revenues. This $25,000 deduction results in a net increase in temporarily restricted net assets of $10,000 on the statement of activities for the year ended June 30, 2012. The deduction of $25,000 from temporarily restricted revenues also results in an in-

crease in unrestricted revenues, gains, and other support of $25,000. Expenses can only be deducted from unrestricted revenues on the statement of activities. Therefore, the fundraising expenses of $25,000 will be deducted from unrestricted revenues, gains, and other support that includes the $25,000 reclassification from temporarily restricted revenues. Alternatively, FASB ASC 958 also permits temporarily restricted revenues to be reported as unrestricted revenues in the year the resources are received. This alternative is allowed only for the amount of temporarily restricted revenues that are spent during the year. In the situation presented, $25,000 would be disclosed as both an unrestricted revenue and expense for 2012. There would be no need for a reclassification; however, the answer would not change because temporarily restricted net assets increase $10,000 as a result of the contribution that was not spent in 2012.

17. (b) Contributions should be reported as revenues in the period received, even though donors have placed time or use restrictions on the contributions. The $5,000,000 contribution from alumni for a new wing for the science building should be reported as a temporarily restricted revenue on the statement of activities for the year ended December 31, 2012. Also, the $50,000 of earnings related to the investments should also be reported as temporarily restricted revenues on the statement of activities for the year ended December 31, 2012. The $1,000,000 contribution from the donor, who stipulated that the contribution be invested indefinitely, should be reported as a permanently restricted revenue on the statement of activities for the year ended December 31, 2012.

18. (d) A multiyear pledge should be reported at its present value. If there is a time restriction on the pledge, the pledge should be reported as a temporarily restricted revenue in the year the pledge is given. In Hope Haven's situation, the pledge should be reported as temporarily restricted revenue in 2012. The pledge should be reported at its present value. This amount is calculated by using the present value of an ordinary annuity factor for five periods at 6% ($1,000 × 4.21236 = $4,212 rounded).

19. (a) Net assets under the control of the governing board are reported as unrestricted net assets.

20. (c) The requirement is to determine how to report three cash flows on the statement of cash flows for a nongovernmental, nonprofit entity, the Jackson Foundation. The $500,000 cash inflow from unrestricted contributions should be reported as an increase in the operating activities section. The $200,000 cash inflow restricted for the acquisition of property should be reported as an increase in the financing activities section, while the use of the $200,000 to acquire property should be shown as a decrease in the investing activities section.

21. (b) Contributions are reported as revenue in the year received, whether the donors place time or use restrictions on the resources. Net assets should be disclosed according to whether they are unrestricted, temporarily restricted, and permanently restricted. Both of the events listed would increase temporarily restricted net assets for the year ending December 31, 2012.

22. (d) FASB ASC 958 requires a statement of financial position which reports unrestricted, temporarily restricted, and permanently restricted net assets for nongovernmental, not-for-profit organizations. Therefore, the statement of financial position is required for a private, not-for-profit hospital, but not for a public university, which is supported by government.

23.   (c)   Per FASB ASC 958, contributed services which would be purchased if not donated, and which require performance by a specialist, shall be recorded as an increase in both expenses and contributions. In this case, the requirements of FASB ASC 958 are met since the window needs to be replaced and the work is performed by a professional glazier (specialist).

24.   (a)   FASB ASC 958 establishes standards for general-purpose external financial statements. This statement focuses on the basic information of the organization as a whole so as to enhance the relevance, understandability, and comparability of the financial statements by the external users. Thus, answer (a) is correct since the overall objective is the enhancement of the basic information, while answers (b), (c), and (d) address factors that are taken into consideration to achieve the objective.

25.   (c)   FASB ASC 958 requires classification of an organization's net assets and its revenues, expenses, gains, and losses based on the existence or absence of donor-imposed restrictions. It requires that the amount for **each** of three classes of net assets—permanently restricted, temporarily restricted, and unrestricted—be displayed in a statement of financial position and that the amounts of change in each of those classes of net assets be displayed in a statement of activities.

A temporary restriction is a donor-imposed restriction that permits the donee organization to use up or expend the donated assets as specified; it is satisfied either by the passage of time or by actions of the organizations involved. Accordingly, the $5,000,000 contribution of Day Co. shares represents temporarily restricted net assets until the shares are sold and the proceeds used to erect a public viewing building. The $2,000,000 contribution of Day Co. shares represents permanently restricted net assets because the shares are to be retained permanently.

26.   (d)   A liability (not revenue) is recorded when the reporting entity acts as an agent or trustee. A recipient of assets who is an agent or trustee has little or no discretion in determining how the assets transferred will be used. The receipt of cash to purchase furniture specifically for the Jones family would constitute a "transfer" of assets. Upon receipt of the asset (cash), the Amer Benevolent society must expend (i.e., purchase furniture) the contribution to comply with the restrictions of the donor. Answer (a) is incorrect because the donee restricted the use of the contribution. Answer (c) is incorrect because a permanent restriction stipulates that the resources be maintained permanently (but permits the donee organization to expend part or all of the income or other economic benefits derived from the donated assets).

27.   (b)   Per FASB ASC 958, an entity need not recognize the contributions of works of art and historical artifacts if the collection is held for public exhibition rather than financial profit, cared for and preserved, and, if sold, the proceeds are used to acquire other items for collections.

28.   (a)   A Statement of Activities reports revenues, expenses, gains, losses, and reclassifications. Resources are

divided into three classes: unrestricted, temporarily restricted, and permanently restricted. Separate revenues, expenses, gains, losses, and reclassifications for each class may or may not be reported, but the change in net assets for each class **must** be reported.

29.   (b)   The requirement is to determine what classification is required to report expenses of all not-for-profit organizations. All not-for-profit organizations must classify expenses according to their function in either the financial statement or in the notes to the financial statements.

30.   (b)   Quasi endowment funds are established by the governing board of an organization using unrestricted net assets. Therefore, the assets in the quasi endowment would be included in the unrestricted net assets category.

31.   (a)   According to FASB ASC 958, a transfer of assets with a conditional promise to contribute them shall be accounted for as a refundable advance until the conditions have been substantially met. The conditions have been substantially met when the possibility that they will not be met is remote. In this question, the chance that the condition will not be met is reasonably possible, which is a higher level of doubt than remote and thus results in reporting the cash transfer as a liability at December 31, 2011.

32.   (b)   The receipt of cash from a donor to establish a permanent endowment should be reported as a financing activity on the statement of cash flows. This same paragraph also states that receipts from investment income that by donor stipulation are restricted for the purposes of acquiring plant, equipment, and other long-lived assets should also be reported as a financing activity.

33.   (c)   Voluntary health and welfare organizations should provide a statement of functional expenses. This statement reports expenses by both function (program and supporting) and by their natural classification (salaries expense, depreciation expense, etc.).

34.   (c)   Donations of services are recognized on the statement of activities if either of the following two conditions are met: (1) the services create or enhance a nonfinancial asset, or (2) the services require specialized skills, are provided by individuals possessing those skills, and would typically need to be purchased if not provided by donation. The services provided by Jones Heating and Air Conditioning would clearly meet the second criterion. Good Hope would record the invoice in the following manner:

Supporting Expenses	1,500	
Accounts Payable		1,500

Upon notification that the invoice was canceled, Good Hope would make the following journal entry:

Accounts Payable	1,500	
Unrestricted Revenues		1,500

Therefore, the net effect of the contributed services is an increase in expenses and an increase in unrestricted revenues.

35.   (d)   Donations of services are recognized on the statement of activities if either of the following conditions are met: (1) the services create or enhance a nonfinancial asset, or (2) the services require specialized skills, are provided by individuals possessing those skills, and would typically need to be purchased if not provided by donation. The services of Anderson and Anderson, attorneys-at-law, clearly meet criterion 2 and should be reported as unrestricted revenues on James' statement of activities. However, the services provided by the senior citizens do not meet either criterion, and should not be reported on the foundation's statement of activities.

36. **(b)** The requirement is to determine what amount should be reported as contribution revenue in the 2012 statement of activities. The $2,000 restricted for meals is considered contribution revenue even though it is restricted. The amount received over the fair market value of the subscriptions is considered to be contribution revenue, which is $500 ($1,500 – $1,000). The $10,000 to be used upon completion of a new playroom is not part of 2012 revenue contribution because a condition, completion of a new playroom, has not been fulfilled. The money is only available upon completion, and the building is not complete in 2012. What is included in contribution revenue is $2,500 ($2,000 + $500).

37. **(c)** Gifts of long-lived assets should be reported as unrestricted support if the organization has an accounting policy which does not imply a time restriction on such gifts.

38. **(d)** The designation of unrestricted net assets by the board of Henry Museum for the building addition does not change the classification of the net assets which were designated. The assets designated were unrestricted before the designation, and they remain unrestricted after the designation.

39. **(a)** Cash flows from operating activities would include both the cash received from patient service revenue of $300,000 and the cash received from gift shop sales of $25,000. Cash received from investment income that is restricted by donors for the acquisition of long-lived fixed assets should be reported as financing activities.

40. **(b)** A conditional promise to give is considered unconditional if the possibility that the condition will not be met is remote.

41. **(b)** The requirement is to determine how much of the $150 from a donor in exchange for theater tickets and an acknowledgment is considered contribution revenue. Contribution revenue is the amount given above the fair market value. The amount given, $150, is $50 more than fair market value of the tickets, which is $100.

42. **(b)** The use of the cash donation for faculty travel in 2011 is reported as a reclassification on the high school's statement of activities for 2012. Reclassifications are reported on the statement of activities as "net assets released from restrictions." Net assets released from restrictions of $15,000 are reported as a negative amount for temporarily restricted net assets in 2012, while net assets released from restrictions of $15,000 are reported as a positive amount for unrestricted net assets for 2012. However, the $15,000 of travel expense is reported on the statement of activities as an expense for 2012. All expenses are reported on the statement of activities as decreases in unrestricted net assets. This means that the use of the donation for faculty travel had no effect on unrestricted net assets in 2012. Note that, when the donation was received in 2011, temporarily restricted net assets increased by $15,000 on the statement of activities prepared for 2011.

43. **(b)** Expiration of donor-imposed restrictions that simultaneously increase one class of net assets and decrease another should be reported as reclassifications on the statement of activities. Reclassifications are reported as "net assets released from restrictions." When the time restriction on the donation expired in 2011, unrestricted net assets increased while temporarily restricted net assets decreased. The spending of the donation on fund-raising should be reported as an expense, which is a deduction from unrestricted net assets. Therefore, the net effect of the reclassification and the use of the donation is zero on unrestricted net assets. However, the reclassification decreased temporarily restricted net assets for 2011.

44. **(c)** Reclassifications result from expirations of donor-imposed restrictions. The donor-imposed restrictions may be either time or purpose related. When a donor-imposed condition is satisfied, the conditional promise to give assets becomes unconditional, and there is an increase in the appropriate classification of net assets, depending on the restrictions placed upon the assets by the donors. However, this increase is reported as either revenue or support at the time the promise becomes unconditional.

45. **(b)** Interest earned on board-designated investments is reported as unrestricted revenue. When the governing board of a not-for-profit organization places limitations on assets, they are designating the use of unrestricted net assets. Therefore, income earned on board-designated investments represents an increase in unrestricted net assets. Unconditional promises to give are reported in the period the pledges are made, not in the period of cash collection. However, since the contributions will not be received until 2013, the contributions should be reported as an increase in temporarily restricted net assets on the statement of activities for 2012 because of this time restriction.

46. **(d)** Contributed services should be recognized if either of the following conditions is met: (1) the services create or enhance nonfinancial assets, or (2) the services require specialized skills, are provided by individuals possessing those skills, and would typically need to be purchased if not provided by donation.

47. **(d)** Donations of works of art for which the donor stipulated a specified purpose and which are to be preserved and not be sold, represent permanently restricted net assets. Since the museum's policy is to capitalize all donations of art, Ms. Billingsley's donation would be reported as an increase in permanently restricted net assets on the statement of activities.

48. **(a)** The restricted donation of the voluntary health and welfare organization is reported as a reclassification on the statement of activities for 2012. The net effect of the reclassification and the recognition of the expense is zero. The reclassification resulting from the expiration of the donor-imposed restriction increases unrestricted net assets; however, the expense resulting from using the funds for public health education is subtracted from this increase, causing no effect on unrestricted net assets. The interest and dividends earned on the term endowments are unrestricted, and should be reported as an increase in unrestricted revenue for 2012. Since no expenses have been incurred from the use of the investment income for 2012, the net effect is an increase in unrestricted net assets for 2012.

49.   (d)   A conditional promise to give is considered unconditional if the possibility that the condition will not be met is remote. At December 31, 2011, Ms. Egbart's promise would be considered unconditional. This means that the college should report the funds that Ms. Egbart promised as an increase in temporarily restricted net assets on its statement of activities prepared for the year ended December 31, 2011.

50.   (c)   According to FASB ASC 958, all investments in debt securities should be measured at fair value in the statement of financial position.

51.   (a)   Since Crestfallen owns less than 1% of BMZ Company, the equity method cannot be used to account for the investment.

Investments in equity securities with readily determinable market values should be reported at fair value in the statement of financial position. In order to report BMZ's equity securities at their market value of $42,000, a gain of $7,000 should be recognized on the statement of activities. This gain represents an increase in unrestricted net assets, since the gain is related to an investment made by the governing board with unrestricted net assets. In addition, the dividends of $1,000 would also be reported as an increase in unrestricted net assets, since the dividends were earned on unrestricted net assets. Therefore, the investment in BMZ would result in an $8,000 increase in unrestricted net assets on the statement of activities prepared for the year ended December 31, 2012.

52.   (b)   Jazz Planners' investments that permit it to have significant influence over the operating and financing policies of the investee companies should be reported on the statement of financial position using the equity method. On the other hand, the investments that represent 1% to 3% ownership interests should be reported on the statement of financial position at fair value.

53.   (b)   When a resource provider transfers assets to a nonprofit entity and (1) does not grant the recipient organization variance power and (2) the recipient organization and the beneficiaries are not financially interrelated, the recipient entity should record an increase in assets and liabilities as a result of the donation. In the case at hand, United Ways is the recipient entity that should record the cash donation by increasing both assets and liabilities.

54.   (a)   When the recipient organization and the beneficiary are financially interrelated organizations, and the resources held by the recipient organization must be used for the benefit of the beneficiary, the recipient entity should account for the asset transfer as an increase in assets and as an increase in contribution revenue. In the case at hand, World-Wide Helpers Foundation is the recipient entity that should record the asset transfer by increasing cash and increasing contribution revenue.

55.   (d)   A contribution from a resource provider is reported as contribution revenue if (1) the recipient organization is granted variance power by the resource provider or (2) the recipient organization and the beneficiary are financially interrelated organizations. In the case at hand, answer (d) is correct because the resource provider granted variance power to the recipient organization. Answers (b) and (c) are

incorrect because the resource provider designates the beneficiaries and does not grant the recipient organization the ability to redirect the donation to other than the specified beneficiaries. For both situations (b) and (c), the recipient organization should record the donation by increasing both assets and liabilities. Answer (a) is incorrect because contribution revenue is reported by a recipient organization if the recipient organization and the beneficiary are financially interrelated. If they are not financially interrelated, the recipient organization should report the donation as an increase in assets and an increase in liabilities.

56.   (a)   When the resource provider provides variance power over transferred assets, the recipient entity should account for the assets donated as an increase in assets and an increase in contribution revenue. Variance power means the ability of the recipient organization to redirect the resources transferred to it by a resource provider. In case at hand, World-Wide Helpers is the recipient entity that should record the cash donation by increasing both assets and contribution revenue.

57.   (c)   A recipient organization that receives a contribution from a resource provider is required to report the contribution as an asset and a liability unless one of two condition exist (1) the recipient organization is granted variance power to redirect the resources, or (2) the recipient organization and the beneficiary are financially interrelated organizations. Since Mary Wilson did not grant variance power to Goodbody to redirect her donation to other flood victims, and the Taft family and Goodbody are not financially interrelated organizations, the cash donation should be reported as a liability in Goodbody's 2012 financial statements.

58.   (d)   According to the AICPA Audit and Accounting Guide, *Not-for-Profit Organizations*,

> *Under a split-interest agreement, a donor makes an initial gift to a trust or directly to the not-for-profit organization, in which the not-for-profit organization has a beneficial interest but is not the sole beneficiary....The assets are invested and administered by the organization, a trustee, or a fiscal agent, and distributions are made to a beneficiary or beneficiaries during the term of the agreement. At the end of the agreement's term, the remaining assets covered by the agreement are distributed to or retained by either the not-for-profit organization or another beneficiary or beneficiaries.*

59.   (c)   According to the Not-for-Profit Guide, all joint costs of informational materials or activities that include a fund-raising appeal should be reported as fund-raising expense unless an appeal is designed to motivate its audience to action other than providing financial support. Answer (c) is the only alternative that requires both other action and financial support.

60.   (c)   According to the Not-for-Profit Guide, capital additions include nonexpendable gifts restricted to endowment, plant, or loan funds and the legally restricted investment income on investments in such funds. Donor-restricted gifts for programs or supporting services are not capital additions.

61.   (c)   According to the Not-for-Profit Guide, gifts in kind are noncash assets received by not-for-profit organizations from resource providers. These gifts in kind are reported as agency transactions or as contributions depending on the extent of discretion that the not-for-profit recipient has over the use or subsequent disposition of the assets.

62. (b) According to the Not-for-Profit Guide, when a not-for-profit organization has little or no discretion over the use of the asset, the transaction is an agency transaction.

63. (c) According to the AICPA Audit and Accounting Guide, *Health Care Organizations*, the basic financial statements for a hospital include a balance sheet, a statement of operations, a statement of changes in net assets, and a statement of cash flows. Accordingly, Elizabeth Hospital should prepare both a statement of changes in net assets as well as a statement of operations.

64. (a) According to the AICPA Audit and Accounting Guide, *Health Care Organizations*, the provision for contractual adjustments and discounts is recognized on the accrual basis and deducted from gross patient service revenue to determine net patient revenue. Bad debts expense is reported as an operating expense, not as a contra to gross patient service revenue. Accordingly, net patient service revenue for 2012 is $865,000. This amount is determined by subtracting the contractual adjustments of $100,000 and the discounts of $15,000 from gross patient service revenue of $980,000.

65. (a) Patient service revenue is to be reported net of adjustments for contractual and other adjustments in the operating statement. Provisions recognizing contractual adjustments and other adjustments are recorded on an accrual basis and deducted from gross service revenue to determine net service revenue.

66. (d) Voluntary health and welfare organizations are categorized as not-for-profit, nonbusiness-oriented organizations that are covered by the AICPA Audit and Accounting Guide, *Not-for-Profit Organizations*. Nursing home, home health agencies, and hospitals are all considered health care entities and are covered in the AICPA Audit and Accounting Guide, *Health Care Organizations*.

67. (b) The AICPA Audit and Accounting Guide, *Health Care Organizations*, lists the items that must be reported separately from the performance indicator. Among these are extraordinary items (and other items required by GAAP to be reported separately), equity transfers, receipt of restricted contributions, contributions of long-lived assets, restricted investment returns, and unrealized gains/losses of unrestricted investments (except trading securities). Premium revenue is included in the performance indicator.

68. (c) The AICPA Audit and Accounting Guide, *Health Care Organizations*, states that expenses may be reported on the face of the financial statements using either a natural classification or functional presentation. Not-for-profit organizations that report using a natural classification of expenses are required to disclose expenses by functional classification in the notes.

69. (b) Functional classifications should be based on full cost allocations. Health care organizations may report depreciation, interest, and bad debts along with functions.

70. (d) The performance indicator should report the results of operations. However, it should not include such items as extraordinary items, unrealized gains and losses on nontrading securities, and contributions of long-lived assets.

Increase in unrestricted net assets and increase in net assets include these items and so cannot be performance indicators. Net income is a term associated with for-profit enterprises and so is not used by health care entities.

71. (d) According to the AICPA Audit and Accounting Guide, *Health Care Organizations*,

Charity care represents health care services that are provided but are never expected to result in cash flows. As a result, charity care does not qualify for recognition as receivables or revenue in the financial statements. Distinguishing charity care from bad-debt expense requires the exercise of judgment. Charity care is provided to a patient with demonstrated inability to pay. Each organization establishes its own criteria for charity care consistent with its mission statement and financial ability. Only the portion of a patient's account that meets the organization's charity care criteria is recognized as charity. Although it is not necessary for the entity to make this determination upon admission or registration of an individual, at some point the entity must determine that the individual meets the established criteria for charity care.

Therefore, charity care is not included on the financial statements.

72. (b) According to the AICPA Audit and Accounting Guide, *Health Care Organizations*, "Under provisions of continuing-care contracts entered into by a CCRC and residents, nonrefundable advance fees represent payment for future services and should be accounted for as deferred revenue." Deferred revenue is classified as a liability.

73. (a) Patient service revenue is to be reported net of contractual adjustments. Contractual adjustments are the difference between revenue at established rates and the amounts realizable from third-party payors under contractual agreements. Charity care is not part of patient service revenue, and donor contributions are reported separately. Therefore,

	Gross patient service revenue	$750,000
−	Contractual adjustments	− 63,000
=	Net patient service revenue	$687,000

74. (d) According to the AICPA Audit and Accounting Guide, *Health Care Organizations*, charity care does not qualify for recognition as receivables or revenue in the financial statements. According to the AICPA Audit and Accounting Guide, *Health Care Organizations*, management's policy for providing charity care, as well as the level of charity care provided, should be disclosed in the financial statements. Such disclosure generally is made in the notes to the financial statement and is measured based on the providers' rates, costs, units of service, or other statistical measure.

75. (c) According to the AICPA Audit and Accounting Guide, *Health Care Organizations*, a hospital's other revenue, gains, and losses are derived from services other than providing health care services or coverage to patients. Other revenue, gains, and losses typically include interest and dividends that are unrestricted as well as proceeds from sales at gift shops and snack bars. Cash contributions from donors that are restricted to the acquisition of capital assets during 2013 are not reported on the statement of operations for 2012. The capital contribution should be reported on the statement of changes in net assets for the year ended December 31, 2012, as an increase in temporarily restricted net assets. Therefore, the amount that Michael should report as other revenue and gains on its statement of operations for 2012 is $100,000.

76. **(b)** According to the AICPA Audit and Accounting Guide, *Health Care Organizations*, expirations of donor restrictions on temporarily restricted net assets should be reported on the statement of operations as net assets released from restrictions. On Swathmore's statement of operations for 2012, the use of the $50,000 contribution for research in 2012 should be reported as "net assets released from restrictions." This amount should be included in revenues, gains, and other support on the statement of operations, and it is also included in the "performance indicator" reported on the statement of operations. The use of the $250,000 contribution to acquire a capital asset placed into service during 2012 is also reported as "net assets released from restrictions" on the 2012 statement of operations. This results because the hospital adopted an accounting policy that did not imply a time restriction on gifts of long-lived assets. However, this amount is reported after the performance indicator on the statement of operations. Accordingly, the total amount reported as net assets released from restrictions on the 2012 statement of operations is $300,000.

77. **(d)** According to the AICPA Audit and Accounting Guide, *Health Care Organizations*, unrealized gains on trading securities should be included as part of the amount reported for revenue, gains, and other support on the statement of operations. These unrealized gains are included in the performance indicator. Likewise, unrestricted revenues from interest and dividends are included as part of the amount reported for revenue, gains, and other support on the statement of operations. Therefore, Smithson Hospital should report both the $3,000 of interest revenue and the $2,000 unrealized holding gain ($105,000 less $103,000) in the amount reported for revenue, gains, and other support on its statement of operations for the year ended December 31, 2012.

78. **(d)** According to the AICPA Audit and Accounting Guide, *Health Care Organizations*, unrealized gains and losses from other than trading securities, which are not restricted by donors, are reported after the performance indicator on the statement of operations. Therefore, the unrealized loss in item I is reported on the statement of operations, but it is not included in the amount reported for revenue and gains over expenses and losses, the performance indicator. The donor contribution that cannot be used until next year is not reported on the statement of operations. The contribution represents an increase in temporarily restricted net assets and is reported on the statement of changes in net assets.

79. **(c)** According to the AICPA Audit and Accounting Guide, *Health Care Organizations*, a donation of noncash assets should be reported at fair value and reported as an increase in the appropriate net asset class. If there are no donor-imposed restrictions on the donation, the donation increases unrestricted net assets on the statement of operations. More specifically, the donation is included in the amount reported for revenue, gains, and other support if the donation is used for the operations of the hospital. The use of the donation in the operations of the hospital is reported as part of the operations expenses for the period. The donation of medical supplies to Tucker Hospital should be reported as both a revenue and as an operating expense in the

amount of $15,000 on the statement of operations for the year ended December 31, 2012.

80. **(b)** The cash flows from revenues, gains, and other support, which are reported on the hospital's statement of operations, would be included in the net cash provided (used) by operating activities on the statement of cash flows. Both net patient service revenue and tuition revenue are included in the amount reported for revenue, gains, and other support on the hospital's statement of operations. Accordingly, cash received from patient service revenue and from tuition revenue are both included in the amount reported for cash flows from operating activities. The cash received for the term endowment as well as the cash received from dividends would not be included in the amount reported for net cash provided (used) by operating activities. Both of these cash receipts would be reported as increases in cash flows provided by financing activities. According to FASB ASC 958, cash contributions that are donor-restricted for long-term purposes are reported as financing activities on the statement of cash flows. In addition, the AICPA Audit and Accounting Guide, *Health Care Organizations*, states that cash received for long-term purposes, for example, the cash received for the term endowment and the building improvements, is not reported as a current asset. So that the statement of cash flows will reconcile with the change in cash and cash equivalents reported as current assets on the balance sheet, an amount equal to the cash received for the two financing activities is included in the amount reported for cash flows from investing activities. For Wilson Hospital, this would mean that $330,000, the sum of the $250,000 for the term endowment and the $80,000 of restricted dividends, is reported as a negative amount in the investing activities' section of the statement of cash flows. Note that both of these amounts are reported as investing activities whether the cash was spent this period or in subsequent period(s).

81. **(d)** The statement of changes in net assets reports the changes in the hospital's unrestricted, temporarily restricted, and permanently restricted net assets for a time period. The statement of operations discloses only the changes in unrestricted net assets for a time period, while the balance sheet discloses the amounts of unrestricted, temporarily restricted, and permanently restricted net assets as of a specific date. Therefore, neither the balance sheet nor the statement of operations discloses the changes in unrestricted, temporarily restricted, and permanently restricted net assets for a time period.

82. **(c)** According to the AICPA Audit and Accounting Guide, *Health Care Organizations*, investment returns not restricted by donors are reported on the statement of operations. The statement of operations explains the change in the hospital's unrestricted net assets for a period. Consequently, investment returns that are permanently restricted would not be reported on the statement of operations. Investment returns that are realized in cash are reported on the statement of cash flows. However, investment returns that are not realized in cash are not reported on the statement of cash flows. Investment returns, whether realized or unrealized, that are restricted by donors are reported on the statement of changes in net assets. Unrealized gains on investments that are permanently restricted represent investment returns which would be reported as an increase in permanently restricted net assets on the statement of changes in net assets.

83. **(b)** The AICPA Audit and Accounting Guide, *Health Care Organizations,* lists proceeds from sales of cafeteria meals and guest trays to employees, medical staff, and visitors as one of the items reported as other revenue on the statement of operations. Other revenue is included in the performance indicator on the statement of operations. Net assets released from restrictions are also reported in the performance indicator if the net assets are used for operating expenses.

ARB, APB, and FASB Pronouncements

Study Program for the Accounting Pronouncements

As of July 1, 2009, the FASB Accounting Standards Codification is the only source of US GAAP, other than SEC literature. Older pronouncements, such as the Accounting Research Bulletins, Accounting Principles Board Opinions, and FASB Statements, are no longer considered authoritative. Outlines of the pronouncements that were used in the Codification are included in this edition to assist the CPA candidate in his/her transition to the Codification. The outlines of these previous sources of accounting literature are presented by Accounting Standard Codification (ASC) Topic order (e.g., ASC Topic 205, 210, 505), with cross-references to their location in the new ASC. For standards with the same ASC Topic cross-reference (e.g., both APB 6 and SFAS 129 relate to ASC Topic 505), the earlier issued standard is presented first. For standards relating to multiple ASC Topic areas (e.g., SFAS 6 is related to ASC Topic 210 and ASC Topic 470), the entire standard is presented in both locations. A cross references list by standard type precedes the outlines.

Study through the outlines as you are referred to them in the modules throughout the text. Note that on the CPA exam, it is not necessary to know the Codification Topic numbers or pronouncement numbers; however, being familiar with the numbering system will greatly aid the candidate in the research component of the FAR exam. Also, note that it is not necessary to memorize all the required disclosures. A good approach to take is to take the position of a financial analyst: What data would you want to know? Utilizing this approach will help you remember any exceptions (i.e., items you would not normally think an analyst would be interested in.)

References to FASB Materials

In studying the outlines, you might notice that parts of some pronouncements have not been outlined. The reason some sections of the pronouncements are excluded from the outlines is that they have never been tested on the exam. Also, outlines for very specialized pronouncements (e.g., SFAS 50, *Financial Reporting in the Record and Music Industry*) are not included in this manual. Several others are outlined more generally. Only those FASB Interpretations and Technical Bulletins having widespread applicability are included in this chapter. They are set apart with solid lines **only** to distinguish them from the SFAS.

ACCOUNTING RESEARCH BULLETINS

ARB 43—Chapter 1A Rules Adopted by Membership (ASC Topics 310, 505, 605, and 850)
Chapter 1B—Profits or Losses on Treasury Stock (ASC Topic 505)
Chapter 2A—Comparative Financial Statements (ASC Topic 205)
Chapter 3A—Current Assets and Current Liabilities (ASC Topics 210, 310, 340, 470)
Chapter 4—Inventory Pricing (ASC Topic 330)
Chapter 7A—Quasi Reorganization (ASC Topic 852)
Chapter 7B—Stock Dividends and Stock Splits (ASC Topic 505—Equity)
Chapter 10A—Real and Personal Property Taxes (ASC Topic 720—Other Expenses)
ARB 45—Long-Term Construction Contracts (ASC Topic 605—Revenue)
ARB 51—Consolidated Financial Statements (ASC Topic 810—Consolidation)

ACCOUNTING PRINCIPLES BOARD OPINIONS CROSS-REFERENCE

APB 6—Status of Accounting Research Bulletins (ASC Topic 505—Equity)
APB 9—Reporting the Results of Operations (ASC Topics 225, 250, 505)
APB 10—Omnibus Opinion—1966 (ASC Topics 210, 605, 740)
APB 12—Omnibus Opinion—1967 (ASC Topics 310, 360, 505, 710, 835)
APB 14—Convertible Debt and Debt Issued with Stock Warrants (ASC Topic 470—Debt)
APB 18—The Equity Method for Investments (ASC Topics 323, 325, 850)
APB 21—Interest on Receivables and Payables (ASC Topic 835—Interest)
APB 22—Disclosure of Accounting Policies (ASC Topic 235—Notes to Financial Statement)
APB 23—Accounting for Income Taxes—Special Areas (ASC Topic 740—Income Taxes) (Amended by SFAS 109)
APB 26—Early Extinguishment of Debt (ASC Topic 470—Debt) (Amended by SFAS 84 and SFAS 145)
APB 28—Interim Financial Reporting (ASC Topic 270—Interim Reporting)
APB 29—Accounting for Nonmonetary Transactions (ASC Topic 845—Nonmonetary Transactions)
APB 30—Reporting the Results of Operations (ASC Topic 225—Income Statement)

STATEMENTS OF FINANCIAL ACCOUNTING STANDARDS CROSS-REFERENCE

SFAS 2—Accounting for Research and Development Costs (R&D) (ASC Topic 730—Research & Development)

SFAS 6—Classification of Short-Term Obligations Expected to Be Refinanced (ASC Topics 210 and 470)

SFAS 7—Accounting and Reporting by Development Stage Companies (ASC Topic 915—Development Stage Entities)

SFAS 13—Accounting for Leases (ASC Topic 840—Leases)

SFAS 15—Accounting by Debtors and Creditors for Troubled Debt Restructurings (ASC Topics 310 and 470) (Superseded by SFAS 114 with regard to creditors)

SFAS 16—Prior Period Adjustments (ASC Topics 250 and 270)

SFAS 34—Capitalization of Interest Cost (ASC Topic 835—Interest)

SFAS 43—Accounting for Compensated Absences (ASC Topics 710—Compensation—General)

SFAS 45—Accounting for Franchise Fee Revenue (ASC Topic 952—Franchisors)

SFAS 47—Disclosure of Long-Term Obligations (ASC Topics 440 and 470)

SFAS 48—Revenue Recognition When Right of Return Exists (ASC Topic 605—Revenue) (Also ASC Topics 450 and 460)

SFAS 52—Foreign Currency Translation (ASC Topic 830—Foreign Currency Matters)

SFAS 57—Related-Party Disclosures (ASC Topic 850—Related-Party Disclosures)

SFAS 66—Accounting for Sales of Real Estate (ASC Topics 360, 605, and 976)

SFAS 78—Classification of Obligations That Are Callable by the Creditor (ASC Topic 470—Debt)

SFAS 86—Accounting for the Costs of Computer Software to Be Sold, Leased, or Otherwise Marketed (ASC Topic 985—Software)

SFAS 87—Employers' Accounting for Pensions (ASC Topic 715—Compensation—Retirement Benefits)

SFAS 88—Employers' Accounting for Settlements and Curtailments of Defined Benefit Pension Plans and for Termination Benefits (ASC Topic 715—Retirement Benefits)

SFAS 89—Financial Reporting and Changing Prices (ASC Topic 255—Changing Prices)

SFAS 91—Accounting for Nonrefundable Fees and Costs Associated with Originating or Acquiring Loans and Initial Direct Costs of Leases (ASC Topic 310—Receivables)

SFAS 94—Consolidation of All Majority-Owned Subsidiaries (ASC Topic 810—Consolidation)

SFAS 95—Statement of Cash Flows (ASC Topic 230—Statement of Cash Flows)

SFAS 98—Accounting for Leases (ASC Topic 840—Leases)

SFAS 106—Employers' Accounting for Postretirement Benefits other than Pensions (ASC Topic 715—Compensation—Retirement Benefits)

SFAS 107—Disclosures about Fair Value of Financial Instruments (ASC Topic 825—Financial Instruments)

SFAS 109 (I27)—Accounting for Income Taxes (ASC Topic 740—Income Taxes)

SFAS 112—Employers' Accounting for Postemployment Benefits (ASC Topic 712—Compensation—Nonretirement Postemployment Benefits)

SFAS 114—Accounting by Creditors for Impairment of a Loan (ASC Topic 310—Receivables)

SFAS 115—Accounting for Certain Investments in Debt and Equity Securities (ASC Topic 320—Investments—Debt and Equity Securities)

SFAS 116—Accounting for Contributions Received and Contributions Made (ASC Topic 958—Not-for-Profit Entities)

SFAS 117—Financial Statements of Not-for-Profit Organizations (ASC Topic 958—Not-for-Profit Entities)

SFAS 123—Revised (C36) Share-Based Payment (ASC Topic 718—Compensation—Stock Compensation and ASC Topic 505—Equity)

SFAS 124—Accounting for Certain Investments Held by Not-for-Profit Organizations (ASC Topic 958—Not-for-Profit Entities)

SFAS 128—Earnings Per Share (ASC Topic 260—Earnings per Share)

SFAS 129—Disclosure of Information about Capital Structure (ASC Topic 505—Equity)

SFAS 130—Reporting Comprehensive Income (ASC Topic 220—Comprehensive Income)

SFAS 131—Disclosures about Segments of an Enterprise and Related Information (ASC Topic 280—Segment Reporting)

SFAS 132 (Revised)—Employers' Disclosures about Pensions and Other Postretirement Benefits (ASC Topic 715—Compensation—Retirement Benefits)

SFAS 133—Accounting for Derivative Instruments and Hedging Activities (ASC Topic 815—Derivatives and Hedging)

SFAS 138—Accounting Certain Derivative Instruments and Certain Hedging Activities: (ASC Topic 815—Derivatives and Hedging)

SFAS 140—Accounting for Transfers and Servicing of Financial Assets and Extinguishment of Liabilities (ASC Topic 860—Transfers and Servicing)

SFAS 141(R)—Business Combinations (ASC Topic 805—Business Combinations)

SFAS 142—Goodwill and Other Intangible Assets (ASC Topic 350—Intangibles—Goodwill and Other)

SFAS 143—Accounting for Asset Retirement Obligations (ASC Topic 410—Asset Retirement and Environmental Obligations)

SFAS 144—Accounting for the Impairment or Disposal of Long-Lived Assets (ASC Topic 360—Property, Plant, and Equipment; ASC Topic 205—Presentation of Financial Statements; and ASC Topic 225—Income Statement)

SFAS 145—Rescission of FASB Statements No. 4, 44, and 64, Amendment of FASB Statement No. 13, and Technical Corrections (Rescinds SFAS 4, 44, and 64 and amends SFAS 13)

SFAS 146—Liabilities: Exit or Disposal Costs (ASC Topic 420—Exit or Disposal Cost Obligation)

SFAS 147—Acquisitions of Certain Financial Institutions, An Amendment of FASB Statements No. 72 and 144 and FASB Interpretation No. 9 (The authors believe that this topic is too specialized for the CPA exam)

SFAS 149—Amendment of Statement 133 on Derivative Instruments and Hedging Activities (ASC Topic 815)

SFAS 150—Accounting for Certain Financial Instruments with Characteristics of Both Liabilities and Equity (ASC Topic 480—Distinguishing Liabilities from Equity)

SFAS 151—Inventory Costs (ASC Topic 330—Inventory)

SFAS 152—Accounting for Real Estate Time Sharing Transactions—An Amendment of FASB Statements No. 66 and 67 (Amends SFAS 66 and SFAS 67)

SFAS 153—Exchanges of Nonmonetary Assets—An Amendment of APB Opinion No. 29 (ASC Topic 845—Nonmonetary Transactions)

SFAS 154—Accounting Changes and Error Corrections (ASC Topic 250—Accounting Changes and Error Corrections)

SFAS 155—Accounting for Certain Hybrid Financial Instruments (ASC Topic 815—Derivatives and Hedging)

SFAS 156—Accounting for Servicing of Financial Assets (ASC Topic 860—Transfers and Servicing)

SFAS 157—Fair Value Measurements (ASC Topic 820—Fair Value Measurement and Disclosures)

SFAS 158—Employers' Accounting for Defined Benefit Pension and Other Postretirement Plans (An Amendment of FASB Statements 87, 88, 106, and 132[R]) (ASC Topic 715—Compensation—Retirement Benefits and ASC Topic 958—Not-for-Profit Entities)

SFAS 159—The Fair Value Option for Financial Assets and Financial Liabilities—including an amendment of FASB Statement 115 (ASC Topic 825—Financial Instruments)

SFAS 160—Noncontrolling Interests in Consolidated Financial Statements—An Amendment of ARB No. 51 (ASC Topic 810—Consolidation)

SFAS 161—Disclosures about Derivative Instruments and Hedging Activities—An Amendment of FASB Statement No. 133 (ASC Topic 815—Derivatives and Hedging)

SFAS 162—The Hierarchy of Generally Accepted Accounting Principles

SFAS 163—Accounting for Financial Guarantee Insurance Contracts—An Interpretation of FASB Statement No. 60. (The authors believe that this topic is too specialized for the CPA exam.)

SFAS 164—Not-for-Profit Entities: Mergers and Acquisitions—Including an Amendment of FASB Statement No. 142 (ASC Topic 958) (The authors believe that this topic is too specialized for the CPA exam.)

SFAS 165—Subsequent Events (ASC Topic 855)

SFAS 166—Accounting for Transfers of Financial Assets—An Amendment of FASB Statement No. 140 (ASC Topic 860)

SFAS 167—Amendments to FASB Interpretation No. 46(R) (ASC Topic 810)

SFAS 168—The FASB Accounting Standards Codification and the Hierarchy of Generally Accepted Accounting Principles—A Replacement of FASB Statement No. 162 (ASC Topic 105)

GENERAL PRINCIPLES (ASC TOPIC 100)

SFAS 168—The FASB Accounting Standards Codification and the Hierarchy of Generally Accepted Accounting Principles—A Replacement of FASB Statement No. 162 (ASC Topic 105)

A. Establishes the Codification as the single source of US GAAP for nongovernmental entities, except for SEC authoritative literature which applies to SEC registrants

B. Content in SEC Sections of the Codification is provided for convenience and is not the complete SEC literature.

PRESENTATION (ASC TOPIC 200)

ARB 43—Chapter 2A Comparative Financial Statements (ASC Topics 205)

Comparative statements enhance the usefulness of financial statements and should be presented.

SFAS 144 Accounting for the Impairment or Disposal of Long-Lived Assets (ASC Topic 360—Property, Plant, and Equipment; ASC Topic 205—Presentation of Financial Statements; and ASC Topic 225—Income Statement)

A. Establishes financial and reporting requirements for the impairment or disposal of long-lived assets. In addition to property, plant, equipment, and intangible assets being amortized, SFAS 144 applies to capital leases of lessees, long-lived assets of lessors subject to operating leases, proved oil and gas properties that are being accounted for using the successful efforts method of accounting, and long-term prepaid assets.

B. If a long-lived asset (or assets) is part of a group that includes other assets and liabilities not covered by SFAS 144, the statement applies to the group.

C. Assets to be held and used

1. Reviewed for impairment when circumstances indicate that the carrying amount of a long-term asset (or group) is not recoverable and exceeds its fair value. The carrying amount of a long-lived asset (asset group) is not recoverable it if exceeds the sum of the undiscounted cash flows expected to result from its use and eventual disposal.

2. A long-lived asset (asset group) shall be tested for recoverability whenever events or changes in circumstances indicate that its carrying amount may not be recoverable. Examples of such events include

   a. Significant decrease in market value
   b. Change in way asset used or physical change in asset
   c. Legal factors or change in business climate that might affect asset's fair value or adverse action or assessment by regulator
   d. Asset costs incurred greater than planned
   e. Current-period operating or cash flow loss combined with historical or projection of such amounts demonstrates continuing losses from the asset
   f. A current expectation that, more likely than not a long-lived asset will be disposed of significantly before the end of its previously estimated useful life

3. Impaired if the expected total future cash flows are less than the carrying amount of the asset (asset group)

   a. Assets should be grouped at lowest level for which there are identifiable cash flows independent of other groupings
   b. Expected future cash flows are future cash inflows to be generated by the asset (asset group) less the future cash outflows expected to be necessary to obtain those inflows
   c. Expected future cash flows are **not** discounted and do not consider interest charges
   d. If the management has alternative courses of action to recover the carrying amount, or if a range of possible cash flows are associated with a particular course of action, a probability-weighted approach may be useful

4. Written down to fair value and loss recognized upon impairment

   a. Fair value is "the price that would be received to sell an asset or paid to transfer a liability in an orderly transaction between market participants at the measurement date." (SFAS 157)
   b. If quoted market price in active market is not available, the estimate of fair value should be based on best information available

5. An impairment loss for an asset group shall reduce only the carrying amounts of the long-lived assets. Impairment of other assets in the group should be accounted for in accordance with other applicable accounting standards

6. If an impairment loss is recognized, the adjusted carrying amount becomes its new cost basis

7. Fair value increases on assets previously written down for impairment losses may not be recognized

8. Disclosures

   a. Description of impaired asset (asset group) and circumstances which led to impairment
   b. Amount of impairment and manner in which fair value was determined
   c. Caption in income statement in which impairment loss is aggregated, if it is not presented separately thereon
   d. Business segment(s) affected (if applicable)

D. Long-lived assets to be disposed of other than by sale

1. Long-lived assets to be abandoned are disposed of when they cease to be used
2. Long-lived assets to be exchanged for similar assets or to be distributed to owners are disposed of when they are exchanged or distributed

E. Long-lived assets to be disposed of by sale

1. Long-lived assets to be sold shall be classified as "held-for-sale" in the period in which all of the following criteria are met:

   a. Management commits to a plan of disposal
   b. The assets are available for sale
   c. An active program to locate a buyer has been initiated
   d. The sale is probable
   e. The asset is being actively marketed for sale at a fair price
   f. It is unlikely that the disposal plan will significantly change

2. Reported at lesser of the carrying amount or fair value less cost to sell

    a. Cost to sell includes broker commissions, legal and title transfer fees, and closing costs prior to legal title transfer

3. In future periods, adjusted carrying amount of asset shall be revised down or up to extent of changes in estimate of fair value less cost to sell, provided that the adjusted carrying amount does not exceed the carrying amount of the asset prior to the adjustment reflecting the decision to dispose of the asset

    a. Thus, recoveries may be recognized when assets are to be **disposed of** but not on impaired assets that continue to be used

F. Reporting long-lived assets and disposal groups to be disposed of

1. Discontinued operations of a component of an entity

    a. A component of an entity comprises operations and cash flows that can be clearly distinguished, operationally and for financial reporting purposes

    b. The results of a component of an entity that either has been disposed of or is classified as held for sale shall be reported as discontinued operations if both of the following conditions are met:

        (1) The operations and cash flows of the component have been (will be) eliminated from ongoing operations

        (2) The entity will not have any significant continuing involvement in the operations of the component after disposal

    c. In reporting discontinued operations, the income statement should present the results of discontinued operations separately after income from continuing operations and before extraordinary items as shown below

Income from continuing operations before income taxes	$xxxxx
Income taxes	xxx
Income from continuing operations	$xxxx
Discontinued operations (Note X)	
Loss from operations of discontinued Component Z (including	
loss on disposal of $xxx)	xxxx
Income tax benefit	xxxx
Loss on discontinued operations	xxxx
Net income	$xxxx

2. A gain or loss recognized for long-term asset (group) classified for sale that is not a component of an entity shall be included in income from continuing operations before income taxes
3. Disclosures

    a. Description of assets to be disposed of, reasons for disposal, expected disposal date, and carrying amount of those assets

    b. Gain or loss, if any, resulting from changes in carrying amount due to further changes in market value

    c. If applicable, amounts of revenue and pretax profit or loss reported in discontinued operations

    d. If applicable, the segment of the business affected (see outline of SFAS 131)

ARB 43—Chapter 3A Current Assets and Current Liabilities (ASC Topics 210, 310, 340, 470)

Chapter 3A contains the definitions and examples of current assets and liabilities.

A. Current assets are "cash and other assets or resources commonly identified as those which are reasonably expected to be (1) realized in cash, (2) sold, or (3) consumed during the ordinary operating cycle of the business."

1. Cash available for current operations
2. Inventories
3. Trade receivables
4. Other receivables collectible in one year
5. Installment, deferred accounts, and notes receivable
6. Prepaid expenses

B. Current liabilities are "obligations whose liquidation is reasonably expected to require the use of existing resources properly classifiable as current assets or the creation of other current liabilities during the ordinary operating cycle of the business."

1. Trade payables
2. Collections received in advance of services
3. Accruals of expenses

4. Other liabilities coming due in one year
5. Note that liabilities not using current assets for liquidation are not current liabilities (e.g., bonds being repaid from a sinking fund)

C. Operating cycle is "average time intervening between the acquisition of materials or services entering this process and the final cash realization."

APB 10 Omnibus Opinion—1966 (ASC Topics 210, 605, 740)

A. ARB 43, Chapter 3B Working Capital

1. Offsetting of liabilities and assets in the balance sheet is not acceptable unless a right of offset exists.
2. Most government securities are not designed to be prepayment of taxes and thus may not be offset against tax liabilities. Only where an explicit prepayment exists may an offset be used.

FASB INTERPRETATION NO. 39 OFFSETTING OF AMOUNTS RELATED TO CERTAIN CONTRACTS

A right of setoff exists when all of the following conditions are met: (a) each of the two parties to a contract owes the other determinable amounts, (b) the reporting entity has the right to set off the amount owed with the amount owed by the other entity, (c) the reporting entity intends to set off, and (d) the right of setoff is enforceable at law.

B. Installment method of accounting

Revenues should be recognized at the point of sale unless receivables are in doubt. The installment or cost recovery method may be used.

SFAS 6 Classification of Short-Term Obligations Expected to Be Refinanced (ASC Topics 210 and 470)

A. Short-term obligations shall be classified as a current liability unless

1. Enterprise intends to refinance the obligation on a long-term basis
2. AND the intent is supported by ability to refinance

   a. Post-balance-sheet issuance of long-term debt or equity securities, or
   b. Financing agreement that clearly permits refinancing on a long-term basis

   (1) Does not expire or is not callable for one year
   (2) No violation of the agreement exists at the balance sheet date or has occurred to date

3. The amount of the short-term obligation excluded from current liability status should not exceed the

   a. Net proceeds of debt or securities issued
   b. Net amounts available under refinancing agreements

   (1) The enterprise must intend to exercise the financing agreement when the short-term obligation becomes due.

4. Refinancing of short-term obligations is a FS **classification** issue, **not** a **recognition** and **measurement** issue.

FASB INTERPRETATION NO. 8 CLASSIFICATION OF A SHORT-TERM OBLIGATION REPAID PRIOR TO BEING REPLACED BY A LONG-TERM SECURITY

Short-term obligations that are repaid after the balance sheet date but **before** funds are obtained from long-term financing are to be classified as current liabilities at the balance sheet date.

EXAMPLES

In situation 1 below, the obligation will be classified as a noncurrent liability at the balance sheet date. Why? Proceeds from refinancing were obtained prior to the due date of the obligation.

12/31 Year-end	2/1 Stock/long-term debt issued	2/15 Short-term obligation due	3/15 Financial statements issued

Situation 1: Classify obligation due 2/15 as noncurrent liability at balance sheet date.

In situation 2 below, the short-term obligation will be classified as a current liability. Why? Proceeds from the issuance of stock or long-term debt were not obtained until after the due date of the short-term obligation. Therefore, current assets must have been used to pay the short-term obligation.

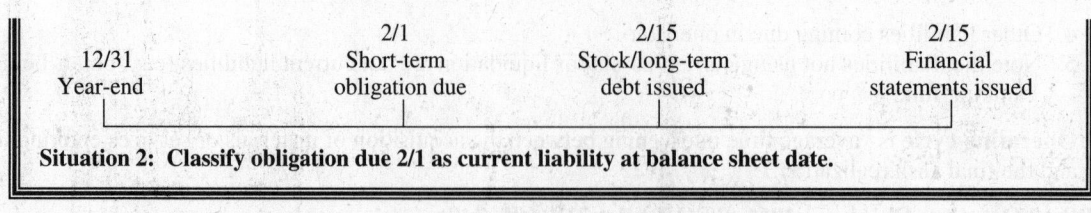

12/31	2/1	2/15	2/15
Year-end	Short-term obligation due	Stock/long-term debt issued	Financial statements issued

Situation 2: Classify obligation due 2/1 as current liability at balance sheet date.

SFAS 130 Reporting Comprehensive Income (ASC Topic 220—Comprehensive Income)

A. Establishes standards for reporting and display of comprehensive income (net income plus **other comprehensive income**) in a full set of general-purpose FS

B. Items, and changes therein, to be included as part of and separately classified in **other comprehensive income**

   1. Foreign currency items
   2. Unrealized gains (losses) on certain investments in debt and equity securities
   3. The amounts for overfunded or underfunded pension plans

C. Presentation of comprehensive income

   1. Alternative display options

     a. At the bottom of IS, continue from net income to arrive at a **comprehensive income** figure (equals net income plus other comprehensive income), or
     b. In a separate statement that starts with net income.

   2. Components of other comprehensive income may be displayed net of related tax effects or before related tax effects with one amount shown for the aggregate income tax effect (with detail shown in notes)
   3. Reclassification (recycling) adjustments

     a. Made to avoid double counting of items included in other comprehensive income in a prior year or current year that are included in net income (earnings) for the period
     b. Display separately from the balance of each item adjusted (B.1. and B.2. above) (gross display)

       (1) For reclassification adjustments related to the minimum pension liability, a single amount shall be displayed (net display)

D. Separate EPS numbers are not required for other comprehensive income or comprehensive income

APB 9 Reporting the Results of Operations (ASC Topics 225, 250, 505)

A. Designates a new format for income statement in which all normal operating items would be presented at the top of the income statement resulting in "net income before extraordinary items."

   1. "Net income before extraordinary items" is followed by extraordinary items resulting in "net income."

B. "Prior period adjustments" are excluded from the income statement and constitute adjustments of beginning retained earnings disclosed at the top of the retained earnings statement.

   1. Beginning retained earnings are adjusted by "prior period adjustments" resulting in "restated beginning retained earnings."
   2. "Restated retained earnings" is then adjusted for net income and dividends which results in ending retained earnings.

C. Prior period adjustments should be disclosed in the period of adjustment.

   1. The effect on each prior period presented should be disclosed including restated income taxes.
   2. Disclosure in subsequent periods is not normally required.
   3. Historical summary data should also be restated and disclosed in the period of adjustment.

D. The APB also reaffirmed earlier positions that the following should not affect determination of net income:

   1. Transactions in the company's own stock
   2. Transfers to or from retained earnings
   3. Quasi reorganization adjustments

APB 30 Reporting the Results of Operations (ASC Topic 225—Income Statement)

A. Extraordinary items are **both** unusual and infrequent.

1. **Unusual nature.** "The underlying event or transaction should possess a high degree of abnormality and be of a type clearly unrelated to, or only incidentally related to, the ordinary and typical activities of the entity, taking into account the environment in which the entity operates."

   a. Special characteristics of the entity

      (1) Type and scope of operations
      (2) Lines of business
      (3) Operating policies

2. **Infrequency of occurrence.** "The underlying event or transaction should be of a type that would not reasonably be expected to recur in the foreseeable future, taking into account the environment in which the entity operates."

3. Example of extraordinary presentation

Income before extraordinary items	$xxx
Extraordinary items (less applicable income taxes of $__) (Note __)	xxx
Net income	$xxx

4. Examples of gains and losses that are **not** generally extraordinary

   a. Write-downs or write-offs of receivables, inventories, R&D, etc.
   b. Translation of foreign exchange including major devaluations
   c. Disposal of a component of a business
   d. Sale of productive assets
   e. Effects of strikes
   f. Accruals on long-term contracts

5. Extraordinary items should be classified separately if material on an individual basis.

6. Gains or losses that are unusual **or** infrequent but not both should be disclosed separately (but not net of tax) in the income statement or notes.

SFAS 95 Statement of Cash Flows (ASC Topic 230—Statement of Cash Flows)

A. Statement of Cash Flows in General

1. Required for each period results of operation (income statement) are provided
2. Objectives

   a. Provide information about cash receipts and cash payments
   b. Provide information about operating, investing, and financing activities
   c. Helps users to assess

      (1) Ability to generate future net cash flows
      (2) Ability to meet obligations and pay dividends
      (3) Reasons for differences between income and associated cash receipts and payments
      (4) Both cash and noncash aspects of entity's investing and financing activities

3. Shall report

   a. Cash effects during a period from

      (1) Operating activities
      (2) Investing activities
      (3) Financing activities

   b. Noncash financing and investing activities in supplemental schedule

B. Gross and Net Cash Flows

1. Gross amount of cash receipts and payments is relevant.

   a. For example, must show issuance of bonds and retirement of bonds separately

2. Statement should explain change during the period in **cash and cash equivalents**.

   a. Cash equivalents

      (1) Short-term, highly liquid investments that are

(a) Readily convertible into known amounts of cash
(b) Near maturity (original maturity of three months or less from **date of purchase** by the enterprise) and present negligible risk of changes in value

(2) Examples

(a) Treasury bills
(b) Commercial paper
(c) Money market funds

C. Classification

1. Investing activities

a. Include

(1) Lending money and collecting on those loans
(2) Acquiring and selling, or disposing

(a) Securities that are neither cash equivalents nor held in a trading portfolio
(b) Productive assets expected to generate revenue over long periods of time

(3) Cash inflows

(a) Receipts from loans by

1] Principal repayments
2] Sale of loans made by the entity

(b) Receipts from sale of

1] Securities of other entities carried in held-to-maturity (debt only) or available-for-sale portfolios (debt or equity)
2] Property, plant, and equipment

(4) Cash outflows

(a) Loans made or purchased by the entity
(b) Payments to acquire assets

1] Securities of other entities carried in held-to-maturity (debt only) or available-for-sale portfolios (debt or equity)
2] Property, plant, and equipment

2. Financing activities

a. Include

(1) Obtaining resources from owners and providing them with a return on, and a return of, their investment
(2) Obtaining resources from creditors and repaying the amounts borrowed

b. Cash inflows

(1) Proceeds from the issuance of

(a) Equity securities
(b) Bonds
(c) Mortgages
(d) Notes
(e) Other short- or long-term borrowing

c. Cash outflows

(1) Payments of dividends
(2) Outlays to repurchase entity's shares
(3) Repayments of amounts borrowed

3. Operating activities

a. Include

(1) All transactions and other events that are not investing and financing
(2) Delivering or producing goods for sale and providing services
(3) Cash effects of transactions and other events that enter into the determination of income

b. Cash inflows

    (1) Cash receipts from sale of goods or services
    (2) Interest and dividends received
    (3) Other operating cash receipts
    (4) Sales of "trading portfolio" securities

c. Cash outflows

    (1) Payments to employees and other suppliers of goods or services
    (2) Income taxes paid
    (3) Interest paid
    (4) Other operating cash payments
    (5) Purchases of "trading portfolio" securities

D. Exchange Rate Effects

1. Report the reporting currency equivalent of foreign currency cash flows using exchange rates in effect at time of cash flows

    a. Weighted-average exchange rate may be used, if result substantially same.

E. Content and Form

1. Report net cash provided or used by operating, investing, and financing activities
2. At end of statement, reconcile beginning and ending cash and cash equivalents by showing net increase or decrease for period as addition to beginning balance to obtain ending balance
3. Cash flow from operating activities

    a. Direct presentation (encouraged by FASB)

        (1) Report major classes of operating receipts and payments (C.3.b.–c. above)
        (2) Difference between cash receipts and payments—net cash flow from operating activities
        (3) Supplemental schedule using indirect presentation must be presented when direct method used in body of statement

    b. Indirect presentation (acceptable format)

        (1) Shall separately report all major classes of reconciling items

            (a) Deferrals of past operating cash receipts and cash payments such as depreciation and changes during the period in inventory and unearned revenue
            (b) Accruals of expected future operating cash receipts and cash payments such as changes during the period in receivables and payables

        (2) Interest paid (net of amounts capitalized) and income taxes paid must appear in related disclosures

    c. Does not include cash flows from transactions or events whose effects are included in income, but which are not operating activities; for example,

        (1) Gain or loss on extinguishment of debt—financing activities
        (2) Gain or loss on sale of assets or from disposal of discontinued operations—investing activities

4. Inflows and outflows of cash from investing and financing activities

    a. Noncash aspects should be clearly identified in separate schedule; for example,

        (1) Conversion of debt to equity
        (2) Acquisition of assets by assuming liabilities

            (a) Includes capital lease obligations

        (3) Exchanges of assets or of liabilities

5. Enterprise shall disclose policy for determining items included in cash equivalent.

    a. Change in policy is change in accounting principle requiring restatement of comparative FS.

F. Cash flow per share shall not be reported.

APB 22 Disclosure of Accounting Policies (ASC Topic 235—Notes to Financial Statement)

A. Accounting policies can affect reported results significantly and the usefulness of the financial statements depends on the user's understanding of the accounting policies adopted by the reporting entity. Disclosure of accounting policies are

1. Essential to users
2. Integral part of financial statements
3. Required for one or more financial statements
4. Required for not-for-profit entities
5. Not required for unaudited interim statements

   a. If no change in accounting policy has occurred

B. Disclosure should include accounting principles and methods of applying them if material to reported amounts.

1. Generally, disclosure pertinent to principles involving recognition of revenue and expense
2. Specifically, disclosure pertinent to

   a. Selection from existing alternatives
   b. Principles peculiar to a particular industry
   c. Unusual or innovative applications

3. Examples

   a. Consolidation method
   b. Depreciation method
   c. Amortization of intangibles
   d. Inventory pricing
   e. R&D references amended by SFAS 2
   f. Translation of foreign currencies
   g. Long-term contract accounting
   h. Franchising and leasing activities

4. Accounting policy disclosure should not duplicate disclosures elsewhere in the statements.

C. Particularly useful is a separate **Summary of Significant Accounting Policies** either preceding or as the initial note.

SFAS 16 Prior Period Adjustments (ASC Topics 250 and 270)

A. All P&L items are included in the determination of net income except the correction of an error in statements of a prior period.

1. Account for and report as a prior period adjustment to beginning retained earnings

B. An exception exists for interim reporting regarding certain adjustments relating to prior interim periods of the current year.

1. These "adjustments" (affecting prior interim periods of the current fiscal year) are settlements or adjustments of

   a. Litigation or similar claims
   b. Income taxes
   c. Renegotiation proceedings
   d. Utility revenue per the rate-making process

2. These "adjustments" must also

   a. Be material to operating income, trends in income, etc.
   b. All or part of the adjustment is specifically identified with specified prior interim periods of the current fiscal year.
   c. Not subject to reasonable estimation prior to the current interim period (e.g., new retroactive tax legislation)

SFAS 154 Accounting Changes and Error Corrections (ASC Topic 250—Accounting Changes and Error Corrections)

A. Defines an accounting change as (1) change in principle; (2) change in an estimate; or (3) change in reporting entity. The correction of an error is not an accounting change.
B. Once an accounting principle is adopted, it must be used consistently for similar events and transactions. An entity may change an accounting principle only if the change is required by a new accounting pronouncement, or if the entity can justify that the alternative method is preferable.

C. Change in accounting principle

1. Is given retrospective application of the new accounting principle to all prior periods, unless it is impracticable to do so. This includes

   a. Cumulative effects of the change are presented in the carrying amounts of assets and liabilities as of the beginning of the first period presented
   b. Offsetting adjustment is made to opening balance of retained earnings for that period
   c. Financial statements of each period are adjusted to reflect period-specific effects of the new accounting principle

Only direct effects of change are recognized (i.e., changes in inventory balances, deferred taxes, impairment adjustments). Indirect effects are reported in period in which the accounting change is made.

D. If cumulative effect can be determined, but period-specific effects cannot be determined, cumulative effect is applied to the earliest period to which it can be calculated. Offsetting adjustment is made to retained earnings of that period.

E. If it is impracticable to determine the cumulative effect of the change in any prior period, treat prospectively.

F. Notes to the financial statements must include

1. The nature and reason for the change with explanation as to why the new method is preferable
2. The method of applying the change
3. A description of the prior period information retrospectively adjusted
4. Effect of change on income from continuing operations, net income, and other affected line items on financial statements, and any per share amounts for current period and all periods adjusted
5. The cumulative effect of the change on retained earnings and other components of equity or net assets as of the earliest period presented
6. If retrospective application is impracticable, the reason and a description of how the change was reported
7. A description of the indirect effects of the change and amounts recognized in the current period and related per share amounts
8. The amounts of indirect effects of the change and per share amounts

G. Disclosures for interim periods should disclose the effect of change on income from continuing operations, net income, and related per share amounts for postchange interim periods.

H. Once the change in method is disclosed, financial statements in subsequent periods do not need to repeat disclosures.

I. Change in accounting estimate

1. Treat on prospective basis in current and future periods
2. If change is effected by change in principle, treat as change in estimate
3. Change in depreciation method is treated as change in estimate
4. If change in estimate is caused by change in principle, must show footnote disclosures required by change in accounting principle

J. Change in reporting entities

1. Change is retrospectively applied to the financial statements of all periods presented
2. Previously issued interim statements presented on a retrospective basis
3. Footnote disclosures include the nature and reason for change, net income, other comprehensive income, and any related per share amounts for all periods presented

K. Correction of an error

1. Errors are errors in recognition, measurement, presentation, or disclosure (Change from non-GAAP to GAAP is a correction of error)
2. Treat as prior period adjustment by restating financial statements
3. Cumulative effect of error is reflected in carrying value of assets and liabilities at the beginning of the first period presented, with an offsetting adjustment in the opening balance in retained earnings
4. Restate financial statements to reflect period-specific effects of error
5. Footnote disclosures must disclose that previously issued statements were restated, along with description of error.
6. Effects of error and any per share amounts must also be disclosed for each period presented
7. Cumulative effect of the change on retained earnings or other components of equity should be presented for the earliest period presented.
8. Gross effects and net effects from income taxes on net income of prior period must be disclosed. Amount of income tax applicable to each prior period must be disclosed.
9. Once correction of error is disclosed, financial statements of subsequent years do not need to repeat disclosure

SFAS 89 Financial Reporting and Changing Prices (ASC Topic 255—Changing Prices)

This statement **encourages** but does not require a business enterprise that prepares its financial statements in US dollars and in accordance with US generally accepted accounting principles to disclose supplementary information on changing prices.

A. Measurement

  1. Inventory

    a. Current cost is the current cost of purchasing or manufacturing, whichever is applicable

      (1) Or recoverable amount if lower

  2. Property, plant, and equipment

    a. Current cost is current cost of acquiring same service potential (or recoverable amount if lower)

      (1) That is, the same operating costs and output
      (2) Three valuation methods

        (a) Current cost of new asset less depreciation
        (b) Cost of comparable used asset
        (c) Adjusting new asset cost for differences in

          1] Useful life
          2] Output capacity
          3] Nature of service
          4] Operating costs

  3. Recoverable amount

    a. Current worth of net amount of cash expected to be recoverable from the use or sale of an asset

  4. Increase or decrease in current cost amount of inventory and PP&E, net of inflation

    a. Differences between current cost at entry dates and exit dates

      (1) Entry dates are the later of the beginning of the year or date of acquisition
      (2) Exit dates are the earlier of date of use, sale, etc., or year-end

SFAS 128 Earnings Per Share (ASC Topic 260—Earnings per Share)

A. Presentation on Financial Statements

  1. Entities with publicly held common stock and simple capital structures (no potential common shares) need only present basic per share amounts. All other entities must present basic and diluted per share amounts with equal prominence.
  2. Must present EPS on face of income statement for

    a. Income from continuing operations
    b. Net income

  3. May present on face of income statement or in notes

    a. Discontinued operations
    b. Extraordinary items
    c. Cumulative effect of change in accounting principle

B. Basic EPS—Measures entity performance over a period of time

  1. Computed as net income minus preferred dividends divided by the weighted-average number of common shares outstanding. The claims of senior securities (nonconvertible preferred dividends) should be deducted from income prior to computing EPS to properly determine net income available to **common** shareholders. Therefore, dividends on cumulative preferred are deducted whether or not declared, while dividends on noncumulative preferred are deducted only if declared.
  2. EPS figures should be based upon consolidated income figures after consolidating adjustments and eliminations.
  3. To compute the weighted-average of common shares outstanding, treasury shares should be excluded as of date of repurchase.
  4. EPS data for all periods presented should be retroactively adjusted for all splits and dividends, even those subsequent to the period being presented.

5. For stock issued in purchase combinations, use weighted-average from date of combination. For pooling combination, shares assumed outstanding the entire period regardless of when issued.

C. For Diluted EPS, these additional procedures apply

1. The "if-converted" method is used to adjust EPS on outstanding common shares for dilutive convertible securities.

   a. The convertible securities are considered to have been converted at the beginning of the period (or at issuance if later) increasing the denominator of EPS.
   b. For convertible bonds, the interest savings net of tax is added to the numerator of EPS.
   c. For convertible preferred, the preferred dividends deducted in arriving at EPS are not deducted, thereby increasing the numerator. There is no tax effect because dividends are not an expense.

2. The "treasury stock" method is used to adjust EPS on outstanding common shares for dilutive options and warrants (i.e., those for which the exercise price is below the market price).

   a. The options and warrants are assumed to be exercised at the beginning of the period (or the date the options and warrants were issued if later). The shares assumed issued increase the denominator of EPS.
   b. The hypothetical proceeds are used to purchase treasury stock at the average price over the year.
   c. No retroactive adjustment should be made to EPS figures for options and warrants as a result of market price changes.

3. When convertible securities require payment of cash at conversion, they are considered the equivalent of warrants. The "if-converted" method is used for the conversion and the "treasury stock" method is applied to the cash proceeds.

4. Fixed awards and nonvested stock to be issued to an employee under a stock-based compensation arrangement are considered options and are considered to be outstanding as of the grant date even though their exercise may be contingent upon vesting.

5. Contingently issuable shares are shares whose issuance is contingent upon the satisfaction of certain conditions and shall be considered outstanding and included in the diluted EPS computation as follows:

   a. If all necessary conditions have been satisfied by the end of the period, the shares should be included as of the beginning of the period in which the conditions were satisfied (or as of the date of the contingent stock agreement, if later).
   b. If all necessary conditions have not been satisfied, the number of contingently issuable shares shall be based on the number of shares (if any) that would be issuable if the end of the reporting period were the end of the contingency period and if the result would be dilutive. These shares shall be included in the diluted EPS denominator as of the beginning of the period (or as of the date of the contingent stock agreement if later).

6. Antidilutive securities shall not be included in diluted EPS computations.

D. Additional Disclosure Requirements

1. A reconciliation of the numerators and denominators of the basic and diluted per share computations for income from continuing operations, including the individual income and share amount effects of all securities that affect earnings per share.

2. The effect that has been given to preferred dividends in arriving at income available to common shareholders in computing basic EPS.

3. Securities that are antidilutive for the period(s) presented but could potentially dilute basic EPS in the future.

4. A description of any transaction that occurs after the end of the most recent period but before issuance of the financial statements that would materially change the number of shares outstanding at the end of the period if the transaction had occurred before the end of the period.

APB 28 Interim Financial Reporting (ASC Topic 270—Interim Reporting)

PART I *Application of GAAP to Interim Periods*

A. APB faced basic question about interim periods

1. Are interim periods basic accounting periods?
2. Are interim periods integral parts of the annual period?

B. The APB decided interim periods are an integral part of an annual period.

1. Certain GAAP must be modified for interim reporting to better relate the interim period to the annual period.

C. Revenue should be recognized on the same basis as for the annual period.

D. Costs directly associated with revenue should be reported as in annual periods with the following exceptions:

1. Estimated gross profit rates may be used to estimate inventory. Disclose method used and significant adjustments to reconcile to later physical inventory.
2. When LIFO base period inventories are liquidated during the interim period but are expected to be replaced by the end of the annual period, cost of sales should be priced at replacement costs rather than at base period costs.
3. Declines in inventory market values, unless temporary, should be recognized. Subsequent recovery of market value should be recognized as a cost recovery in the subsequent period.
4. Unanticipated and unplanned standard cost variances should be recognized in the respective interim period.

E. The objective of reporting all other costs is to obtain fair measure of operations for the annual period. These expenses include

1. Direct expenditures—salaries
2. Accruals—vacation pay
3. Amortization of deferrals—insurance

F. These costs should be applied in interim statements as follows:

1. Charge to income as incurred, or based on time expiration, benefit received, etc. Follow procedures used in annual reports.
2. Items not identified with specific period are charged as incurred.
3. No arbitrary assignment.
4. Gains and losses of any interim period that would not be deferred at year-end cannot be deferred in the interim period.
5. Costs frequently subjected to year-end adjustments should be anticipated in the interim periods.

   a. Inventory shrinkage
   b. Allowance for uncollectibles, quantity discounts
   c. Discretionary year-end bonuses

G. Seasonal variations in above items require disclosure and one may add twelve-month reports ending at the interim date for current and preceding years.

H. The best estimate of the annual tax rate should be used to provide taxes on a year-to-date basis.

1. The best estimate should take investment credits, capital gains, etc. into account, but not extraordinary items.
2. Tax effects of losses in early portion of the year should not be recognized unless realization in subsequent interim periods is assured beyond a reasonable doubt (e.g., an established pattern of loss in early periods).

   a. When tax effects of losses in early periods are not recognized, no taxes should be accrued in later periods until loss credit has been used.

I. Extraordinary items should be disclosed separately and recognized in the interim period in which they occur.

1. The materiality of extraordinary items should be determined in relation to expected annual income.
2. Effects of disposals of a component of a business are not extraordinary items, but should be disclosed separately.
3. Extraordinary items should **not** be prorated over remainder of the year.
4. Contingencies should be disclosed in the same manner as required in annual reports.

J. Each interim report should disclose any change in accounting principle from

1. Comparable period of prior year
2. Preceding periods of current year
3. Prior annual report

K. Reporting these changes

1. SFAS 154 should be applied.
2. A change in accounting estimate (including effect on estimated tax rate) should be accounted for in period of change and disclosed in subsequent periods if material.
3. Changes in principle should be given retrospective application. Financial statements are retrospectively adjusted showing the effects of the change on the carrying amounts of assets and liabilities for the earliest period presented, with an adjustment to beginning retained earnings for that period. Period-specific effects of the change should be shown for all direct effects of the change.

PART II Required Interim Disclosures by Publicly Traded Companies

A. Minimum disclosure includes

1. Sales, provision for taxes, extraordinary items, cumulative effect of principle changes, and net income
2. BEPS and DEPS

3. Seasonal revenue, costs, and expenses
4. Significant changes in estimates of taxes
5. Disposal of a business component and extraordinary items
6. Contingent items
7. Changes in accounting principles and estimates
8. Significant changes in financial position
9. Reportable operating segments

   a. External revenues
   b. Intersegment revenues
   c. Segment profit/loss
   d. Total assets (if material change from last annual report)
   e. Description of changes from last annual report in method of determining segments or measurement of segment profit/loss
   f. Reconciliation of total of reportable segments' profit/loss to corresponding enterprise amount

B. When **summarized interim data** are reported regularly, the above should be reported for the

1. Current quarter
2. Current year-to-date or last twelve months with comparable data for the preceding year

C. If fourth quarter data are not separately reported, disclose in annual report

1. Disposal of business component
2. Extraordinary, unusual, and infrequent items
3. Aggregate year-end adjustments

D. The APB encourages interim disclosure of financial position and funds flow data.

1. If not disclosed, significant changes therein should be disclosed.

FASB INTERPRETATION NO. 18 ACCOUNTING FOR INCOME TAXES IN INTERIM PERIODS

Tax on income from continuing operations for an interim period is based on estimated annual effective rate, which reflects anticipated tax planning alternatives. Expense of interim period is (Year-to-date income) × (Estimated rate) less (Expense recognized in prior interim periods). Tax effect of special items (below continuing operations) computed as they occur.

SFAS 131 Disclosures about Segments of an Enterprise and Related Information (ASC Topic 280—Segment Reporting)

A. Requires disclosures about

1. Operating segments of an enterprise, products and services, geographic areas, major customers

   a. Disclosures are required for **public** companies in complete annual FS per GAAP and in condensed FS of interim periods including comparative presentations
   b. Purpose of disclosures is to better assist statement users in appraising past and future performance of the enterprise and assessing prospects for future net cash flows.

B. Definitions

1. **Management approach.** Method chosen by the FASB to determine what information should be reported; it is based on the way that management organizes segments internally for making operating decisions and assessing performance.
2. **Operating segment.** Component of an enterprise that may earn revenues and incur expenses, about which separate financial information is available that is evaluated regularly by the chief operating decision maker in deciding how to allocate resources and in assessing performance.
3. **Chief operating decision maker.** Person whose general function (not specific title) is to allocate resources to, and assess the performance of, the segments of an enterprise.
4. **Segment revenue.** Includes revenue from unaffiliated customers and intersegment sales (use company transfer prices to determine intersegment sales).
5. **Segment operating profit (loss).** Segment revenue less all operating expenses, including any allocated revenues or expenses.
6. **Segment assets.** Tangible and intangible assets directly associable or used by the segment, including any allocated portion of assets used jointly by more than one segment

C. To determine reportable segments

1. Identify operating segments under management approach
2. Determine if aggregation of operating segments is appropriate.
3. Perform quantitative threshold tests (10% tests).

D. Operating segments may be aggregated by management if they have similar economic characteristics and if segments are similar in each of the following areas:

1. Nature of products and services
2. Nature of production processes
3. Type of customer for their products and services
4. Methods used to distribute their products or provide their services
5. Nature of regulatory environment; for example, banking

E. Operating segments that meet any of the three quantitative thresholds (10% tests) are immediately deemed reportable segments.

1. Segment revenue is ≥ 10% of combined revenue (revenue includes intersegment revenue).
2. Segment operating profit or loss is ≥ 10% of the greater of, in absolute amount

   a. Combined operating profit of all operating segments with profit, or
   b. Combined operating loss of all operating segments with loss

3. Segment assets are ≥ 10% of combined assets of all segments.

F. Additional considerations when determining reportable segments

1. Management may combine information about operating segments that do not meet the 10% tests with information on other operating segments that do meet the 10% tests to produce reportable segment only if majority of the aggregation criteria exists.
2. Segment that was reported previously should continue to be reported if judged to be of continuing significance by management even if it does not meet the 10% tests in current period.
3. Combined sales to nonaffiliated customers of segments reporting separately must be at least 75% of total consolidated sales

   a. If not, additional segments must be identified as reportable segments

4. All other operating segments which are not reportable shall be combined with any other business activities (e.g., corporate headquarters) and disclosed in "all other" category.
5. Number of reportable segments probably should not exceed ten.

   a. Combine closely related segments if number of segments becomes impracticable

G. Information is to be presented for each reportable segment and in aggregate for remaining segments not reported separately

1. General information, including

   a. Explanation of factors used to identify the enterprise's reportable segments
   b. Types of products and services from which revenue is derived

2. An enterprise shall report a measure of profit or loss and total assets for each reportable segment. To the extent the following is included in the measure of profit or loss or assets it shall also be disclosed:

   a. Revenues from external customers
   b. Revenues from transactions with other operating segments of the same enterprise
   c. Interest revenue
   d. Interest expense
   e. Depreciation, depletion, and amortization expense
   f. Unusual items not qualifying as extraordinary items
   g. Equity in net income of investees accounted for by equity method
   h. Income tax expense or benefit
   i. Extraordinary items
   j. Significant noncash items other than depreciation, depletion, and amortization expense

3. For segment assets

    a. Total expenditures for additions to long-lived assets
    b. Amount of investment in equity method investees

4. Enterprise shall provide an explanation of the measurements of segment profit or loss and assets, including

    a. Basis of accounting
    b. Nature of any differences between measurement of profit and loss or assets for the segment and that of the consolidated enterprise
    c. Nature of any changes from prior periods
    d. Nature and effect of asymmetrical allocations (e.g., allocating depreciation, but not related assets to segment)

5. Enterprise will need to provide reconciliations for the segment amounts disclosed to the corresponding enterprise amounts.
6. Although not as extensive as in the annual report, certain disclosures are required in the interim reports.

H. Previously issued segment information must be restated (unless impractical to do so) if any enterprise changes structure of internal organization that causes composition of reportable segments to change

I. Information about products and services

1. Enterprise-wide disclosure required even if only one and segment disclosures required.
2. Revenue from external customers for each product and service shall be reported by the enterprise.

J. Information about geographic areas (individual countries)

1. Enterprise-wide disclosure required even if only one and segment disclosures required.
2. Enterprise shall report revenues from external customers and long-lived assets attributable to its domestic operations and foreign operations.
3. If enterprise functions in two or more foreign geographic areas, to the extent revenues or assets of an individual foreign geographic area are material, then these amounts should be separately disclosed.

K. Major customers

1. Enterprise-wide disclosure required even if segment disclosures are not required
2. Disclose amount of revenue to each customer accounting for $\geq$ 10% of revenue
3. Disclose similarly if $\geq$ 10% of revenue derived from sales to domestic government agencies or foreign governments
4. Identify segment making sales

ASSETS (ASC TOPIC 300)

ARB 43—Chapter 1A Rules[1] Adopted by Membership (ASC Topics 310, 505, 605, and 850)

Four rules recommended by the Committee on Cooperation with Stock Exchanges in 1934. The last rule is from another 1934 Institute committee.

1. Profit is realized at the point of sale unless collection is not reasonably assured.
2. Capital (paid-in) surplus should not be charged with losses or expenses, except in quasi reorganizations.
3. Receivables from officers, employees, and affiliates must be separately disclosed.
4. Par value of stock issued for assets cannot be used to value the assets if some of the stock is subsequently donated back to the corporation.

Chapter 3A Current Assets and Current Liabilities (ASC Topics 210, 310, 340, 470)

Chapter 3A contains the definitions and examples of current assets and liabilities.

A. Current assets are "cash and other assets or resources commonly identified as those which are reasonably expected to be (1) realized in cash, (2) sold, or (3) consumed during the ordinary operating cycle of the business."

1. Cash available for current operations
2. Inventories
3. Trade receivables
4. Other receivables collectible in one year
5. Installment, deferred accounts, and notes receivable
6. Prepaid expenses

---

[1] The references in parentheses are from the FASB Accounting Standards—Current Texts: Volumes 1 and 2, John Wiley & Sons, Inc. These are included only for facilitating the use of the Current Texts for candidates who have access to them.

B. Current liabilities are "obligations whose liquidation is reasonably expected to require the use of existing resources properly classifiable as current assets or the creation of other current liabilities during the ordinary operating cycle of the business."

1. Trade payables
2. Collections received in advance of services
3. Accruals of expenses
4. Other liabilities coming due in one year
5. Note that liabilities not using current assets for liquidation are not current liabilities (e.g., bonds being repaid from a sinking fund)

C. Operating cycle is "average time intervening between the acquisition of materials or services entering this process and the final cash realization."

APB 12 Omnibus Opinion—1967 (ASC Topics 310, 360, 505, 710, 835)

A. Allowance or contra accounts (allowance for bad debts, accumulated depreciation, etc.) should be deducted from assets or groups of assets with appropriate disclosure.

B. Disclosure of depreciable assets should include

1. Depreciation expense for the period
2. Balances of major classes of depreciable assets by nature or function
3. Accumulated depreciation either by major class or in total
4. Description of method(s) of depreciation by major classes of assets

C. Changes in the separate shareholder equity accounts in addition to retained earnings and changes in number of equity securities must be disclosed in the year of change

1. In separate statements
2. Or the financial statements
3. Or the notes

SFAS 15 Accounting by Debtors and Creditors for Troubled Debt Restructurings (ASC Topics 310 and 470)
(Superseded by SFAS 114 with regard to creditors)

A. Troubled debt restructurings occur when a creditor is compelled to grant relief to a debtor due to the debtor's inability to service the debt. This SFAS prescribes accounting for such debt restructurings if

1. By creditor-debtor agreement
2. Imposed by a court
3. Result of repossessions and foreclosures
4. But not changes in lease agreements

    a. Nor legal actions to collect receivables
    b. Nor quasi reorganizations

B. If a **debtor** transfers assets to settle fully a payable, recognize a gain on restructuring equal to the book value of the payable less FV of assets transferred.

1. Use fair value measurements as outlined by SFAS 157.
2. The difference between set FV and carrying value of the assets transferred is a gain or loss in disposition of assets per APB 30.

C. If a **debtor** issues an equity interest to settle fully a payable, account for equity issued at FV.

1. Excess of carrying value of payable over equity FV is a gain on restructuring.

D. A **debtor** having the terms of troubled debt modified should account for the restructure prospectively (i.e., no adjustment of the payable).

1. Recompute the new effective rate of interest based on the new terms

    a. Total cash payments to be paid, less carrying value of payable is the interest
    b. Amortize the payable by the interest method (APB 21) using the new interest rate

2. Exception is if restructured terms require total cash payments (including interest) which are less than the carrying value of the payable, write down the payable to the total cash to be paid

    a. Include contingent payments in calculation; this precludes recognizing a gain currently and interest expense later

   b. Recognize gain on the write-down
   c. All future cash payments reduce the payable (i.e., no interest expense is recognized)

E. If restructured by partial settlement (assets and/or equity issuance) and modified terms

   1. First account for asset and/or equity issuance per above
   2. Then account for modified terms per above

F. Related matters

   1. A repossession or foreclosure is accounted for per the above.
   2. Contingent payments on restructured debt shall be recognized per SFAS 5 (i.e., its payment is probable and subject to reasonable estimate).
   3. Legal fees on debt restructuring involving equity issuance reduce the amounts credited to the equity accounts.

      a. All other direct costs of debt restructuring reduce gain or are expenses of the period if there is no gain.

G. Disclosures by **debtors**

   1. Description of major changes in debt of each restructuring
   2. Aggregate gain on debt restructuring and related tax effect
   3. Aggregate net gain (loss) on asset transfers due to restructuring
   4. EPS amount of aggregate gain on restructuring net of tax effect

SFAS 91 Accounting for Nonrefundable Fees and Costs Associated with Originating or Acquiring Loans and Initial Direct Costs of Leases (ASC Topic 310—Receivables)

Establishes the accounting for nonrefundable fees and costs associated with lending, committing to lend, or purchasing a loan or group of loans. Applies to all types of loans.

A. Loan origination fees shall be recognized over life of related loan as adjustment of yield.
B. Certain direct loan origination costs shall be deferred over the life of the related loan as a reduction of the loan's yield.
C. All loan commitment fees shall be deferred except for certain retrospectively determined fees.

   1. Those commitment fees meeting specified criteria shall be recognized over the loan commitment period.
   2. All other commitment fees shall be recognized as an adjustment of yield over the related loan's life.
   3. If commitment expires unexercised, then recognize in income upon expiration of the commitment.

D. Loan fees, certain direct loan origination costs, and purchase premiums and discounts on loans shall be recognized as an adjustment of yield generally by the interest method based on contractual terms of the loan.

   1. Prepayments by debtors may be anticipated in certain specified circumstances.

SFAS 114 Accounting by Creditors for Impairment of a Loan (ASC Topic 310—Receivables)

A. Scope of SFAS 114

   1. Applies to all creditors and to all loans except for those specified in A.3 (a.-d.)
   2. Applies to all loans (including A.3.a.) that are restructured in a troubled debt restructuring involving a modification of terms
   3. Exceptions

      a. Large groups of smaller-balance homogeneous loans collectively evaluated for impairment
      b. Loans that are measured at fair value or at the lower of cost or fair value
      c. Leases
      d. Debt securities

   4. Does not specify how a creditor should identify loans that are to be evaluated for collectibility

B. Recognition of Impairment

   1. A loan is impaired when it is probable that a creditor will be unable to collect all amounts due according to the contractual terms.

      a. Probable—future event or events are likely to occur
      b. All amounts due according to the contractual terms include both interest and principal payments collected as scheduled in loan agreement.

   2. If a loan qualifies as exception A.3.a., the creditor may not apply the provisions of SFAS 114 until the debt is restructured.
   3. Instances when a loan is not impaired

a. Insignificant delays or shortfalls

b. A delay in which creditor expects to collect all amounts due including interest accrued for the period of delay

C. Measurement of Impairment

1. Creditor measures impairment based on present value of expected future cash flows discounted at the loan's effective interest rate

   a. Effective interest rate—rate implicit in loan at time of origination

   b. If effective interest rate varies (based on an independent index or rate)

      (1) May be calculated based on the index or rate as it changes over life of loan

      (2) Or may be fixed at rate in effect at date the loan meets impairment criterion

   c. Expected future cash flows determined as creditor's best estimate based on reasonable and supportable assumptions and projections (including estimated costs to sell)

2. Loans with common risk characteristics may be aggregated and impairment measured using historical statistics and a composite effective interest rate.

3. Alternative measures of impairment

   a. Loan's observable market price

   b. Fair value of collateral if loan is collateral dependent

      (1) Collateral dependent means repayment provided solely by the underlying collateral

      (2) This method must be used when foreclosure is probable (and loan is collateral dependent)

4. When measure of impaired loan is less than recorded investment in loan

   a. Create valuation allowance with charge to bad debt expense

   b. Or adjust existing valuation allowance with charge to bad debt expense

5. Significant changes (increases or decreases) subsequent to initial measure of impairment

   a. Recalculate impairment

   b. Adjust valuation allowance

   c. Net carrying amount of loan may never exceed recorded investment in loan

D. Income Recognition

1. The present value of an impaired loan changes over time and also changes because of revised estimates in the amount or timing of cash flows.

2. Recognition and measurement methods to reflect changes in present value are not specified in this statement as amended.

E. Disclosures

1. The recorded investment in impaired loans, total allowance for credit losses related to impaired loans, and amount for which no allowance for credit losses

2. The creditor's income recognition method, including cash receipts

3. For each period presented which relates to the impaired loans

   a. Average recorded investment

   b. Interest revenue recognized

   c. If practicable, interest revenue recognized on a cash basis

SFAS 115 Accounting for Certain Investments in Debt and Equity Securities (ASC Topic 320—Investments—Debt and Equity Securities)

A. Establishes financial accounting and reporting requirements for all investments in debt securities and for small investments in equity securities with readily determinable fair values

1. "Small" investments are those not accounted for by the equity method or involving consolidated subsidiaries

B. Segregates debt and equity securities into three categories

1. Held-to-maturity securities

   a. Applies only to debt securities

   b. Requires intent and ability to hold to maturity

    (1) Will **not** sell in response to changes in

        (a) Funding terms and sources
        (b) Interest rates and prepayment risk
        (c) Foreign currency risk
        (d) Attractiveness of alternative investments
        (e) Liquidity needs

    (2) In rare cases, intent may change due to nonrecurring and unforeseeable circumstances.

        (a) Continuing deterioration of issuer's credit
        (b) Elimination of tax-exempt status of interest
        (c) Business combination or disposition that increases interest rate risk or credit risk
        (d) Regulatory change in permissible investments
        (e) Downsizing to meet industry capital requirements
        (f) Increased risk weight of debt securities held as regulatory risk-based capital

    (3) Considered maturity if

        (a) Sale occurs so close to maturity that interest rate risk is virtually eliminated
        (b) Sale occurs after at least 85% of the principal has been collected

  c. Balance sheet

    (1) Report at amortized cost
    (2) Classify as current or noncurrent on an individual basis

  d. Income statement

    (1) Do not report unrealized holding gains and losses
    (2) Include realized G(L) in earnings
    (3) Include interest income and premium/discount amortization in earnings

  e. Statement of cash flows

    (1) Classify cash inflows from sales and outflows from purchases gross (not netted) as investing activities

2. Trading securities

  a. Applies to debt and equity securities held for current resale
  b. Balance sheet

    (1) Report at fair value (See SFAS 157 for fair value measurements)
    (2) Classify as current assets, generally

  c. Income statement

    (1) Include unrealized holding G(L) in earnings
    (2) Exclude previously recognized realized G(L) from earnings
    (3) Include dividend and interest revenue

  d. Statement of cash flows

    (1) Classify purchases and sales as operating activity

3. Available-for-sale securities

  a. Applies to debt and equity securities not categorized as held-to-maturity or trading securities
  b. Balance sheet

    (1) Report at fair value (See SFAS 157 for fair value measurements)
    (2) Classify as current or noncurrent on an individual basis
    (3) Report net unrealized holding G(L) in other comprehensive income and accumulated other comprehensive income as separate component of stockholders' equity

  c. Income statement

    (1) Include realized G(L) in earnings
    (2) Include dividend and interest revenue and premium/discount amortization in earnings

  d. Statement of cash flows

    (1) Classify sales and purchases gross (not netted) as investing activity

C. Transfers between categories are accounted for at fair value

1. From trading

   a. Do not reverse recognized unrealized holding G(L) at date of transfer

2. To trading

   a. Recognize unrealized holding G(L) immediately

3. To available-for-sale from held-to-maturity

   a. Report unrealized holding G(L) as other comprehensive income
   b. Transfers from held-to-maturity should be rare

4. To held-to-maturity from available-for-sale

   a. Report unrealized holding G(L) as other comprehensive income
   b. Amortize G(L) over remaining life of security as adjustment to yield

D. Impairment of Securities

1. Applies to held-to-maturity and available-for-sale securities
2. If permanent decline

   a. Write down to fair value
   b. Include realized loss in earnings

3. No write-up for subsequent recoveries

E. Disclosures

1. Only held-to-maturity and available-for-sale securities
2. By major security type

   a. Aggregate fair value
   b. Gross unrealized holding gains and losses
   c. Amortized cost basis

3. By maturity of debt securities

   a. All enterprises disclose contractual information.
   b. Financial institutions disclose fair value and amortized cost for four or more groups of maturities

      (1) Up to one year
      (2) Over one through five years
      (3) Over five through ten years
      (4) Over ten years

   c. Securities maturing at multiple dates

      (1) May disclose separately
      (2) May allocate over groupings

4. Available-for-sale securities

   a. Proceeds from sales
   b. Gross realized G(L)
   c. Cost basis for determining G(L)
   d. Change in net unrealized holding G(L) reported as comprehensive income in stockholders' equity

5. Trading securities

   a. Change in net unrealized holding G(L) reported in earnings

6. Transfers

   a. Gross G(L) on transfer from available-for-sale to trading
   b. Of held-to-maturity securities

      (1) Amortized cost
      (2) Realized or unrealized G(L)
      (3) Reason for sale

APB 18 The Equity Method for Investments (ASC Topics 323, 325, 850)

A. The equity method should be used for corporate joint ventures.

B. The equity method should be applied to investments where less than 50% ownership is held but the investor **can exercise significant influence over operating and financing policies of the investee.**

1. Twenty percent (20%) or more ownership should lead to presumption of substantial influence, unless there is evidence to the contrary.
2. Conversely, less than 20% ownership leads to the presumption of no substantial influence unless there is evidence to the contrary.
3. The 20% test should be based on voting stock outstanding and disregard common stock equivalents.
4. The following procedures should be used in applying the equity method:

   a. Intercompany profits should be eliminated.
   b. Difference between cost and book value of net assets acquired should be accounted for per SFAS 141 and 142.
   c. The investment account and investor's share of investee income should be presented as single amounts in investor statements with the exception of d. below.
   d. Investor's share of discontinued operations, extraordinary items, cumulative effects of accounting changes, and prior period adjustments of investee should be so presented in statements of investor.
   e. Investee capital transactions should be accounted for as are subsidiary capital transactions in consolidated statements.
   f. Gains on sale of investment are the difference between selling price and carrying value of investment.
   g. When investee and investor fiscal periods do not coincide, use most recent investee statement and have consistent time lag.
   h. Losses, not temporary in nature, of investment value should be recognized by investor.
   i. Investor's share of investee loss should not be recorded once investment account is written to zero. Subsequent income should be recognized after losses not recognized are made up.
   j. Investor's share of investee's earnings should be computed after deducting investee's cumulative preferred dividends whether declared or not.
   k. If an investor's holding falls below 20%, discontinue applying the equity method but make no retroactive adjustment.
   l. When an investor's holding increases from a level less than 20% to a level equal to or greater than 20%, the investment account and retained earnings of the investor should be adjusted retroactively to reflect balances as if the equity account had been used. This is accounted for like a prior period adjustment.

5. Statements of investors applying the equity method should disclose

   a. Investees and percentages held

      (1) Accounting policies followed
      (2) Treatment of goodwill, if any

   b. Aggregate market value of investment (not for subsidiaries)
   c. When investments are material to investor, summarized information of assets, liabilities, and results of operations of investee may be necessary
   d. Conversion of securities, exercise of warrants, or issuances of investee's common stock which significantly affects investor's share of investee's income

---

FASB INTERPRETATION NO. 35 CRITERIA FOR APPLYING THE EQUITY METHOD OF ACCOUNTING FOR INVESTMENTS IN COMMON STOCK. Interprets APB 18.

Investors owning between 20 and 50% of an investee may **not** be able to exercise significant influence over the investee's operating and financial policies. The presumption of significant influence stands until overcome by evidence to the contrary, such as (1) opposition by the investee, (2) agreements under which the investor surrenders shareholder rights, (3) majority ownership by a small group of shareholders, (4) inability to obtain desired information from the investee, (5) inability to obtain representation on investee board of directors, etc. Whether contrary evidence is sufficient to negate the presumption of significant influence is a matter of judgment requiring a careful evaluation of all pertinent facts and circumstances, in some cases over an extended period of time. Application of this interpretation resulting in changes to or from the equity method shall be treated per APB 18, paras 19l and 19m.

FASB INTERPRETATION NO. 1 ACCOUNTING CHANGES RELATED TO THE COST OF INVENTORY

Changes in the cost composition of inventory is an accounting change and must conform to APB 20, including justification for the change. Preferably should be based on financial reporting objectives rather than tax-related benefits.

Chapter 4 Inventory Pricing (ASC Topic 330)

Contains 10 statements outlining inventory valuation

1. Inventory consists of tangible personal property

   a. Held for sale in ordinary course of business
   b. In process of production for such sale
   c. To be currently consumed in the production of such goods

2. Major objective of inventory valuation is proper income determination

   a. Matching of costs and revenues

3. Primary basis is cost. Cost includes all reasonable and necessary costs of preparing inventory for sale. These costs would include expenditures to bring inventory to existing condition and location.

   a. Direct or variable costing is not acceptable (use absorption costing)

4. Cost may be determined under any flow assumption. Use method which most clearly reflects income.
5. Departure from cost to market required when utility of goods, in their disposal in the ordinary course of business, is not as great as cost.

   a. Write-down recognized as a loss of the current period
   b. Use of lower of cost or market method more fairly reflects income of the period than would the cost method
   c. Results in a more realistic estimate of future cash flows to be realized from the assets
   d. Supported by doctrine of conservatism

6. Market means current replacement cost subject to

   a. Market should not exceed net realizable value (sales price less selling and completion costs)
   b. Market should not be less than net realizable value less normal profit

7. Lower of cost or market may be applied to individual items or the inventory as a whole. Use method that most clearly reflects income.
8. Basis for stating inventories and changes therein should be consistent and disclosed.
9. Inventories may be stated above cost in exceptional cases

   a. No basis for cost allocation (e.g., meatpacking)
   b. Disposal assured and price known (e.g., precious metals)

10. Purchase commitment loss should be recognized in the same manner as inventory losses.

SFAS 151 Inventory Costs (ASC Topic 330—Inventory)

A. Requires that abnormal amounts of idle facility expense, freight, handling costs, and wasted material (spoilage) may be treated as current period charges.
B. Requires that fixed overhead allocation be based on normal capacity of production facilities.

1. Normal capacity is a range of production levels.
2. Normal capacity is production expected to be achieved over a number of periods or seasons under normal circumstances, taking into account loss of capacity due to planned maintenance.
3. Normal capacity varies on business and industry-specific factors.

C. Factors that might cause abnormally low production level include significantly reduced demand, labor and material shortages, unplanned facility or equipment downtime.
D. Actual level of production may be used if it approximates normal capacity.
E. In periods of abnormally high production, amount of fixed overhead allocated to each unit is decreased so inventories are not measured above cost.
F. Items treated as period costs include

1. Unallocated overhead costs are recognized as expense in period in which they are incurred.
2. General and administrative expenses (under most circumstances).
3. Selling expense.
4. Abnormal freight, handling costs, amount of wasted materials (spoilage).

SFAS 142 Goodwill and Other Intangible Assets (ASC Topic 350—Intangibles—Goodwill and Other)

This standard provides guidance on accounting for intangible assets including goodwill.

A. Initial Recognition and Measurement of Intangible Assets

1. Intangible assets not acquired in a business combination

    a. An intangible asset that is acquired either individually or with a group of other assets shall be initially recognized at its fair value
    b. The cost of assets acquired as a group should be allocated to the individual assets based on their relative fair values and shall not give rise to goodwill

2. Intangible assets (including goodwill) acquired in a business combination shall be recognized in accordance with SFAS 141
3. Costs of internally developing, maintaining, or restoring intangible assets that are not specifically identifiable, that have indeterminate lives, or that are inherent in a continuing business and related to an entity as a whole, shall be recognized as an expense when incurred

B. Accounting for Intangible Assets

1. The cost of an intangible asset with a finite useful life is amortized over its estimated useful life

    a. The useful life of an intangible asset should be estimated by considering factors such as

        (1) Expected use
        (2) Expected useful life of assets related to the intangible asset
        (3) Legal, regulatory, and contractual provisions that may limit or extend the useful life
        (4) The effects of obsolescence, demand, competition, and other economic factors
        (5) The level of expenditures expected to be required to maintain the asset

    b. The method of amortization shall reflect the pattern in which the economic benefits of the intangible assets are consumed; if the pattern cannot be reliable determined, a straight-line amortization method shall be used
    c. The residual value of the intangible asset will be presumed to be zero unless there is a commitment from a third party to purchase the asset at the end of its useful life, or the residual value can be determined by reference to an exchange transaction in an existing market
    d. The remaining useful life of the intangible asset should be reevaluated each reporting period—if it is no longer appropriate the carrying amount should be amortized prospectively over the revised remaining useful life
    e. Intangible assets with finite useful lives should be reviewed for impairment in accordance with SFAS 144

2. An intangible asset that is determined to have an indefinite useful life should not be amortized until its useful life is determined to be no longer indefinite

    a. An intangible asset that is not subject to amortization should be tested for impairment annually, or more frequently if events or changes in circumstances indicate that the asset might be impaired
    b. The impairment test involves comparison of the carrying amount of the asset to its fair value

3. Goodwill should not be amortized

    a. Goodwill should be examined for impairment at the level of reporting referred to as a reporting unit (an operating segment or one level below). See the outline of SFAS 131
    b. An entity has the option to first qualitatively determine if it is more likely than not (greater than 50%) that the fair value of a reporting unit is less than its carrying value, including goodwill. Circumstances to be examined include, but are not limited to, examinations of macroeconomic conditions, industry and market considerations, cost factors, overall financial performance, entity-specific events, reporting unit events, and share price decreases. If it is found that it is not more likely than not that the fair value of the reporting unit is less than its carrying value, the goodwill impairment tests are deemed unnecessary. The entity can choose to bypass the qualitative assessment and proceed directly to the first step of the goodwill impairment test. The test of impairment is a two-step process as described below.

        (1) The first step involves a comparison of the fair value of the reporting unit with its carrying amount. If the carrying amount of the unit exceeds its fair value, the second step is performed. In estimating the fair value of a reporting unit, a valuation technique based on multiples of earnings or revenue or other performance measure may be used.
        (2) The second step involves a comparison of the implied fair value of goodwill of the reporting unit with the carrying amount of that goodwill
        (3) The implied fair value of goodwill is determined in the same manner as the amount of goodwill recognized in a business combination—see outline of SFAS 141. That is, all assets in the segment are valued in accordance with SFAS 141 and the excess of the fair value of the reporting unit as a whole over the

amounts assigned to its recorded assets and liabilities is the implied goodwill. If the implied value of goodwill is less than the carrying amount, goodwill is written down to its implied value and an impairment loss is recognized.

  c. Goodwill should be tested for impairment on an annual basis and between annual dates if one or more of the following events occur:

    (1) A significant adverse change in legal factors or in the business climate
    (2) An adverse action or assessment by a regulator
    (3) Unanticipated competition
    (4) A loss of key personnel
    (5) A more-likely-than-not expectation that a reporting unit or a significant portion of a reporting unit will be sold or otherwise disposed of
    (6) The test for recoverability under SFAS 144 within a reporting unit reveals that a significant group of assets are recorded at amounts above their recoverable values
    (7) Recognition of a goodwill impairment loss in the financial statements of a subsidiary that is a component of a reporting unit

  d. A reporting unit may be tested at any time during the fiscal year as long as it is tested at the same time each year. Different reporting units may be tested at different times during the year.

  e. Initially goodwill is allocated to reporting units. Then the assets and liabilities of the reporting units are valued individually with goodwill being measured as the difference between the cost assigned to the reporting unit and the fair value of the individual assets and liabilities.

C. Disclosures

  1. In the period of acquisition

    a. For intangible assets subject to amortization

      (1) The amount assigned in total and by major intangible asset class
      (2) Significant residual value, in total and by major intangible asset class
      (3) The weighted-average amortization period, in total and by major intangible asset class

    b. For intangible assets not subject to amortization, the amount assigned in total and by major intangible asset class

    c. The amount of research and development assets acquired and written off and in which financial statement line items the amounts are included

  2. Continuing disclosures

    a. For intangible assets subject to amortization

      (1) The gross carrying amount and accumulated amortization, in total and by major intangible asset class
      (2) The aggregate amortization expense for the period
      (3) The estimated aggregate amortization expense for each of the five succeeding fiscal years

    b. For intangible assets not subject to amortization, the carrying amount in total and by each major intangible asset class

    c. The changes in the carrying amount of goodwill during the period including

      (1) The aggregate amount of goodwill acquired
      (2) The aggregate amount of impairment losses recognized
      (3) The amount of goodwill included in the gain or loss on disposal of all or a portion of a reporting unit

    d. For each other-than-goodwill impairment loss recognized (other than for goodwill)

      (1) A description of the impaired intangible asset and the facts and circumstances leading to the impairment
      (2) The amount of the impairment loss and the method of determining fair value
      (3) The caption in the income statement or the statement of activities in which the impairment loss is aggregated
      (4) If applicable, the segment in which the impaired intangible asset is reported under SFAS 131

    e. For each goodwill impairment loss recognized

      (1) A description of the facts and circumstances leading to the impairment
      (2) The amount of the impairment loss and the method of determining the fair value of the associated reporting unit

(3) If a recognized impairment loss is an estimate that has not yet been finalized, the facts and circumstances and the amount of subsequent adjustments

SFAS 66 Accounting for Sales of Real Estate (ASC Topics 360, 605, and 976)

A. Other than retail land sales

1. Use the full accrual method if the following criteria are satisfied:

   a. Sale is consummated
   b. Buyer's initial and continuing investments demonstrate a commitment to pay for the property
   c. Seller's receivable is not subject to future subordination
   d. Risks and rewards of ownership have been transferred

2. When the criteria are not met and dependent upon the particular circumstance, use one of the following methods:

   a. Installment method
   b. Cost recovery method
   c. Deposit method
   d. Reduced profit method
   e. Percentage-of-completion

B. Retail land sales (not outlined due to specialized nature)

SFAS 144 Accounting for the Impairment or Disposal of Long-Lived Assets (ASC Topic 360—Property, Plant, and Equipment; ASC Topic 205—Presentation of Financial Statements; and ASC Topic 225—Income Statement)

A. Establishes financial and reporting requirements for the impairment or disposal of long-lived assets. In addition to property, plant, equipment, and intangible assets being amortized, SFAS 144 applies to capital leases of lessees, long-lived assets of lessors subject to operating leases, proved oil and gas properties that are being accounted for using the successful efforts method of accounting, and long-term prepaid assets.

B. If a long-lived asset (or assets) is part of a group that includes other assets and liabilities not covered by SFAS 144, the statement applies to the group.

C. Assets to be held and used

1. Reviewed for impairment when circumstances indicate that the carrying amount of a long-term asset (or group) is not recoverable and exceeds its fair value. The carrying amount of a long-lived asset (asset group) is not recoverable it if exceeds the sum of the undiscounted cash flows expected to result from its use and eventual disposal.

2. A long-lived asset (asset group) shall be tested for recoverability whenever events or changes in circumstances indicate that its carrying amount may not be recoverable. Examples of such events include

   a. Significant decrease in market value
   b. Change in way asset used or physical change in asset
   c. Legal factors or change in business climate that might affect asset's fair value or adverse action or assessment by regulator
   d. Asset costs incurred greater than planned
   e. Current-period operating or cash flow loss combined with historical or projection of such amounts demonstrates continuing losses from the asset
   f. A current expectation that, more likely than not a long-lived asset will be disposed of significantly before the end of its previously estimated useful life

3. Impaired if the expected total future cash flows are less than the carrying amount of the asset (asset group)

   a. Assets should be grouped at lowest level for which there are identifiable cash flows independent of other groupings
   b. Expected future cash flows are future cash inflows to be generated by the asset (asset group) less the future cash outflows expected to be necessary to obtain those inflows
   c. Expected future cash flows are **not** discounted and do not consider interest charges
   d. If the management has alternative courses of action to recover the carrying amount, or if a range of possible cash flows are associated with a particular course of action, a probability-weighted approach may be useful

4. Written down to fair value and loss recognized upon impairment

   a. Fair value is "the price that would be received to sell an asset or paid to transfer a liability in an orderly transaction between market participants at the measurement date." (SFAS 157)
   b. If quoted market price in active market is not available, the estimate of fair value should be based on best information available

5. An impairment loss for an asset group shall reduce only the carrying amounts of the long-lived assets. Impairment of other assets in the group should be accounted for in accordance with other applicable accounting standards
6. If an impairment loss is recognized, the adjusted carrying amount becomes its new cost basis
7. Fair value increases on assets previously written down for impairment losses may not be recognized
8. Disclosures

     a. Description of impaired asset (asset group) and circumstances which led to impairment
     b. Amount of impairment and manner in which fair value was determined
     c. Caption in income statement in which impairment loss is aggregated, if it is not presented separately thereon
     d. Business segment(s) affected (if applicable)

D. Long-lived assets to be disposed of other than by sale

1. Long-lived assets to be abandoned are disposed of when they cease to be used
2. Long-lived assets to be exchanged for similar assets or to be distributed to owners are disposed of when they are exchanged or distributed

E. Long-lived assets to be disposed of by sale

1. Long-lived assets to be sold shall be classified as "held-for-sale" in the period in which all of the following criteria are met:

     a. Management commits to a plan of disposal
     b. The assets are available for sale
     c. An active program to locate a buyer has been initiated
     d. The sale is probable
     e. The asset is being actively marketed for sale at a fair price
     f. It is unlikely that the disposal plan will significantly change

2. Reported at lesser of the carrying amount or fair value less cost to sell

     a. Cost to sell includes broker commissions, legal and title transfer fees, and closing costs prior to legal title transfer

3. In future periods, adjusted carrying amount of asset shall be revised down or up to extent of changes in estimate of fair value less cost to sell, provided that the adjusted carrying amount does not exceed the carrying amount of the asset prior to the adjustment reflecting the decision to dispose of the asset

     a. Thus, recoveries may be recognized when assets are to be **disposed of** but not on impaired assets that continue to be used

F. Reporting long-lived assets and disposal groups to be disposed of

1. Discontinued operations of a component of an entity

     a. A component of an entity comprises operations and cash flows that can be clearly distinguished, operationally and for financial reporting purposes
     b. The results of a component of an entity that either has been disposed of or is classified as held for sale shall be reported as discontinued operations if both of the following conditions are met:

         (1) The operations and cash flows of the component have been (will be) eliminated from ongoing operations
         (2) The entity will not have any significant continuing involvement in the operations of the component after disposal

     c. In reporting discontinued operations, the income statement should present the results of discontinued operations separately after income from continuing operations and before extraordinary items as shown below

Income from continuing operations before income taxes	$xxxxx	
Income taxes	xxx	
Income from continuing operations		$xxxx
Discontinued operations (Note X)		
Loss from operations of discontinued Component Z (including loss on disposal of $xxx)		xxxx
Income tax benefit		xxxx
Loss on discontinued operations		xxxx
Net income		$xxxx

2. A gain or loss recognized for long-term asset (group) classified for sale that is not a component of an entity shall be included in income from continuing operations before income taxes

3. Disclosures

   a. Description of assets to be disposed of, reasons for disposal, expected disposal date, and carrying amount of those assets

   b. Gain or loss, if any, resulting from changes in carrying amount due to further changes in market value

   c. If applicable, amounts of revenue and pretax profit or loss reported in discontinued operations

   d. If applicable, the segment of the business affected (see outline of SFAS 131)

LIABILITIES (ASC TOPIC 400)

SFAS 143 Accounting for Asset Retirement Obligations (ASC Topic 410—Asset Retirement and Environmental Obligations)

This standard provides guidance on accounting for obligations associated with the retirement of tangible long-lived assets.

A. The guidance applies to legal obligations associated with the retirement of long-lived assets that result from the acquisition, construction, development and/or normal operation of a long-lived asset, except for certain obligations of lessees. Examples include

1. Costs to decommission a nuclear utility plant at the end of its useful life
2. Costs to dismantle and remove an offshore oil platform at the end of its useful life

B. Such legal obligation may arise from

1. Existing or enacted law, statute, ordinance
2. Written or oral contract
3. Legal construction of a contract under the doctrine of promissory estoppel (inferred legal obligation)

C. An asset retirement obligation is recognized at its fair value in the period in which it is incurred providing that a reasonable estimate of fair value can be made

D. Upon initial recognition of a liability, the entity shall increase the carrying amount of the related long-lived asset by the same amount as that recognized for the liability

E. The cost shall be subsequently expensed using a systematic and rational method over periods no longer than that for which the related asset is expected to provide benefits

F. Initial measurement of the liability

1. The best source of fair value of the liability would be provided by market-determined values but they will seldom be available
2. In the absence of a market, expected present value of future cash flows should be used. In determining the expected present value, the entity should

   a. Use probability-weighted present values in a range of the expected cash flows

   b. The amounts should be discounted to present value using a credit-adjusted risk-free rate

G. Subsequent to the initial measurement of the liability the obligation should be adjusted for

1. The passage of time, and
2. Revisions in estimates of timing or amounts of future cash flows

H. Adjustments to the liability for revisions in estimates of timing or amounts of cash flows should also be reflected in the carrying value of the related asset

I. Disclosures related to asset retirement obligations should include

1. Description of the obligation and related asset
2. Description of how fair value was determined
3. The funding policy, if any
4. A reconciliation of the beginning and ending aggregate carrying value

SFAS 146 Liabilities: Exit or Disposal Costs (ASC Topic 420—Exit or Disposal Cost Obligation)

A. A liability for cost associated with an exit or disposal shall be recognized and measured initially at its fair value in the period in which the liability is incurred

1. There is an exception for a liability for one-time termination benefits that involves employees providing future services
2. When fair value cannot be reasonably estimated, the liability shall be recognized initially in the period in which fair value can be reasonably estimated

B. An exit activity includes but is not limited to restructurings which are programs that are planned and controlled by management, and materially changes either

    1. The scope of a business undertaken by the company, or
    2. The manner in which that business is conducted
    3. Examples include

        a. Sale or termination of line of business
        b. Closure of business activities at a particular location
        c. Relocation of business activities from one location to another
        d. Changes in management structure
        e. Fundamental reorganization of the business

C. Exit or disposal activities covered by this statement do not include those that involve an entity acquired in a business combination, nor do they include disposals covered by SFAS 144. It also does not apply to costs associated with the retirement of a long-lived asset covered by SFAS 143. Examples of exit or disposal activities covered by this statement include

    1. Termination benefits provided to involuntarily terminated employees (other than ongoing arrangements and deferred compensation agreements)
    2. Costs to terminate a contract that is not a capital lease
    3. Costs to consolidate facilities or relocate employees

D. A liability for a cost associated with an exit or disposal activity shall be recognized and measured initially at fair value in the period in which the liability is incurred

    1. This typically is measured by determining the present value of the liability by discounting it using the entity's credit-adjusted risk-free interest rate

E. In the unusual circumstance in which fair value cannot be reasonably estimated, the liability shall be recognized initially in the period in which fair value can be reasonably estimated

F. Subsequent to initial recognition, the liability is adjusted over time by using the discount rate used to initially determine the liability

G. Measurement of onetime termination benefits

    1. A onetime termination agreement exists when the plan of termination meets the following criteria and has been communicated to the employees:

        a. Management commits to the plan
        b. The plan identifies the number of employees to be terminated, their job classifications and locations, and the expected completion date
        c. The plan establishes the terms of the benefit arrangement
        d. It is unlikely that significant changes in the plan will be made

    2. The liability is recognized and measured at the communication date if

        a. The employees are not required to perform additional services to receive termination benefits, or
        b. The employees will not be retained to render services beyond the minimum retention period (not to exceed the legal notification period)

    3. If the employees are required to render service until they are terminated in order to receive termination benefits and will render service beyond the minimum retention period

        a. The liability for termination benefits shall be initially measured at the communication date based on the fair value of the liability as of the termination date, and
        b. The liability shall be recognized ratably over the future service period

H. Measurement of contract termination costs

    1. Costs to terminate the contract before term end

        a. Recognized and measured when the contract is terminated

    2. Costs that will be incurred for the remaining term without benefit to the entity

        a. Recognized and measured when the entity ceases to use the rights conveyed by the contract (e.g., when the entity returns the leased assets)

I. Disclosure

1. A description of the exit or disposal activity
2. For each major type of cost associated with the activity

   a. The total amount expected to be incurred
   b. A reconciliation of the beginning and ending liability amounts

3. The line items in the income statements in which the costs are included
4. For each reportable segment, the total amount of costs expected to be incurred in connection with the activity
5. If a liability cannot be reasonably estimated, the reasons therefor

SFAS 47 Disclosure of Long-Term Obligations (ASC Topics 440 and 470)

A. This statement requires that firm disclose

1. Commitments under unconditional purchase obligations that are associated with suppliers (financing arrangements)
2. Future payments on long-term borrowings

B. **Unconditional purchase obligations** are obligations to transfer funds in the future for fixed or minimum amounts of goods or services at fixed or minimum prices.

C. Unconditional purchase obligations that have all the following characteristics must be disclosed; they are not recorded on the balance sheet.

1. Is noncancelable or cancelable only

   a. Upon occurrence of a remote contingency, or
   b. With permission of another party, or
   c. If a replacement agreement is signed between same parties, or
   d. Upon penalty payment such that continuation appears reasonably assured

2. Was negotiated as part of arranging financing for the facilities that will provide the contracted goods
3. Has a remaining term greater than one year

D. Disclosure of those unconditional purchase obligations not recorded on the balance sheet shall include

1. Nature and term of obligation
2. Amount of fixed and determinable portion of obligation as of most recent BS in aggregate and if determinable for each of next five years
3. Description of any variable elements of the obligation
4. Amounts purchased under the obligation(s) for each year an income statement is presented
5. Encourages disclosing imputed interest to reduce the obligation to present value using

   a. Effective interest rate, or if unknown
   b. Purchaser's incremental borrowing rate at date obligation was entered into

E. This statement **does not change** the accounting for obligations that are recorded on the balance sheet, nor does it suggest that disclosure is a substitute for accounting recognition. For recorded obligations, the following information should be disclosed for each of the next five years:

1. Aggregate amount of payments for unconditional obligations that meet criteria for balance sheet recognition
2. Combined aggregate amount of maturities and sinking fund requirements for all long-term borrowings

SFAS 5 Accounting for Contingencies (ASC Topic 450—Contingencies)

A. Contingency is "an existing condition, situation, or set of circumstances involving uncertainty as to possible gain (loss) to an enterprise that will ultimately be resolved when one or more future events occur or fail to occur."

1. Definitions

   a. Probable—future events are likely to occur
   b. Reasonably possible—chance of occurrence is more than remote, but less than likely
   c. Remote—chance of occurrence is slight

2. Loss contingency examples

   a. Receivable collection
   b. Product warranty obligations
   c. Risk of property losses by fire, explosion, etc.
   d. Asset expropriation threat

    e. Pending, threatened, etc., litigation
    f. Actual or possible claims and assessments
    g. Catastrophe losses faced by insurance companies
    h. Guarantees of indebtedness of others
    i. Banks' obligations under "standby letters of credit"
    j. Agreements to repurchase receivables, related property, etc. that have been sold
    k. Asset retirement obligations

B. Estimated loss from contingencies shall be accrued and charged to income when

    1. It is probable (at balance sheet date) that an asset has been impaired or liability incurred
    2. **And** the amount of loss can be reasonably estimated

        a. Difference between estimate recorded and actual amount determined in subsequent period is a change in accounting estimate

C. Loss contingency disclosures

    1. Nature and amount of material items
    2. Nonaccrued loss contingencies for which a reasonable possibility of loss exists

        a. Disclose nature of contingency
        b. Estimate possible range of loss

            (1) Or state estimate cannot be made

    3. If a loss contingency develops after year-end, but before statements are issued, disclosure of the nature of the contingency and amount may be necessary.

        a. If a year-end contingency results in a loss before issuance of the statements, disclosure (possibly pro forma amounts) may be necessary.

    4. Disclose nature and amount of the following loss contingencies (even if remote)

        a. Guarantees of others' debts
        b. Standby letters of credit by banks
        c. Agreements to repurchase receivables

D. General, unspecified risks are not contingencies.

E. Appropriation of RE for contingencies shown within shareholders' equity is not prohibited.

    1. Cannot be shown outside shareholders' equity
    2. Contingency costs and losses cannot be charged to appropriation.

F. Gain contingency accounting

    1. Normally not reflected in accounts until realized.
    2. Adequate disclosure should be made without misleading implications of likelihood of realization.

G. Rationale for accounting for contingencies per SFAS 5

    1. Reflects **conservatism**—recognize losses immediately (if probable and reasonably estimable), but recognize gains only when realized.
    2. Results in better matching—contingent losses are recognized in time period of origin.

FASB INTERPRETATION NO. 14 REASONABLE ESTIMATION OF THE AMOUNT OF LOSS

A range of the amount of a loss is sufficient to meet the criteria of SFAS 5 that the amount of loss be "subject to reasonable estimate." When one amount in the range is a better estimate, use it; otherwise, use the minimum of the range and disclose range.

STATEMENTS OF POSITION NO. 96-1 ENVIRONMENTAL REMEDIATION LIABILITIES

This SOP includes accounting guidance, preceded by a very detailed description of relevant laws, remediation laws, remediation provisions and other pertinent information, useful to auditors as well as clients. Auditing guidance is limited to recitation of SFAS 5 concerns about reasonable estimation of loss accruals.

Accounting guidance includes the following provisions:

A. Interprets SFAS 5 in the context of environmental obligations (e.g., threshold for accrual of liability, etc.) and sets "benchmarks" for recognition.

B. Benchmarks for accrual and evaluation of estimated liability (stages which are deemed to be important to ascertaining the existence and amount of the liability) are

1. Identification and verification of an entity as a potentially responsible party (PRP), since the proposal stipulated that accrual should be based on premise that expected costs will be borne by only the "participating potentially responsible parties" and that the "recalcitrant, unproven and unidentified" PRP will not contribute to costs of remediation
2. Receipt of unilateral administrative order
3. Participation, as a PRP, in the remedial investigation/feasibility study (RI/FS)
4. Completion of the feasibility study
5. Issuance of the Record of Decision (ROD)
6. Remedial design through operation and maintenance, including postremediation monitoring

C. The amount of liability is affected by

1. The entity's allocable share of liability for a specified site; and
2. Its share of the amounts related to the site that will not be paid by the other PRP or the government

D. Costs to be included in the accrued liability are

1. Incremental direct costs of the remediation effort itself; and

    a. Fees to outside law firms for work related to the remediation effort
    b. Costs relating to completing the RI/FS
    c. Fees to outside consulting and engineering firms for site investigations and development of remedial action plans and remedial actions
    d. Costs of contractors performing remedial actions
    e. Government oversight costs and past costs
    f. Cost of machinery and equipment dedicated to the remedial actions that do not have an alternative use
    g. Assessments by a PRP group covering costs incurred by the group in dealing with a site
    h. Costs of operation and maintenance of the remedial action, including costs of postremediation monitoring required by the remedial action plan

2. Costs of compensation and benefits for employees directly involved in the remediation effort
3. Costs are to be estimated based on existing laws and technologies, and not discounted to present value unless timing of cash payments is fixed or reliably determinable

---

ARB 43— Chapter 3A Current Assets and Current Liabilities (ASC Topics 210, 310, 340, 470)

Chapter 3A contains the definitions and examples of current assets and liabilities.

A. Current assets are "cash and other assets or resources commonly identified as those which are reasonably expected to be (1) realized in cash, (2) sold, or (3) consumed during the ordinary operating cycle of the business."

1. Cash available for current operations
2. Inventories
3. Trade receivables
4. Other receivables collectible in one year
5. Installment, deferred accounts, and notes receivable
6. Prepaid expenses

B. Current liabilities are "obligations whose liquidation is reasonably expected to require the use of existing resources properly classifiable as current assets or the creation of other current liabilities during the ordinary operating cycle of the business."

1. Trade payables
2. Collections received in advance of services
3. Accruals of expenses
4. Other liabilities coming due in one year
5. Note that liabilities not using current assets for liquidation are not current liabilities (e.g., bonds being repaid from a sinking fund)

C. Operating cycle is "average time intervening between the acquisition of materials or services entering this process and the final cash realization."

APB 14 Convertible Debt and Debt Issued with Stock Warrants (ASC Topic 470—Debt)

A. Convertible debt constitutes securities which are convertible into common stock of the user or affiliate. Terms generally include

1. Lower interest rate than on ordinary debt
2. Initial conversion price greater than the common price at time of issuance
3. A conversion price which does not decrease except to protect against dilution

B. While there are arguments to account for the debt and equity characteristics separately, the APB has concluded no proceeds of a convertible issue should be attributed to the conversion factor.

   1. Primary **reasons** are

      a. The inseparability of the debt and conversion features
      b. The practical difficulties of valuing the conversion feature

C. When debt is issued with detachable purchase warrants, the debt and warrants generally trade separately and should be treated separately.

   1. The allocation of proceeds should be based on relative market value at date of issuance.
   2. Any resulting debt discount or premium should be accounted for as such.

D. Separate valuation of debt and warrants is applicable where the debt may be used as consideration when exercising the warrants. Separate valuation is not acceptable where the debt must be tendered to exercise the warrants (i.e., the warrants are, in essence, nondetachable).

APB 26 Early Extinguishment of Debt (ASC Topic 470—Debt)
(Amended by SFAS 84 and SFAS 145)

A. Definitions

   1. **Net carrying amount.** "Amount due at maturity, adjusted for unamortized premium, discount, and cost of issuance."
   2. **Reacquisition price.** "Amount paid on extinguishment, including a call premium and miscellaneous costs of reacquisition."
   3. **Refunding.** Replacement of debt with other debt

B. Retirement is usually achieved by use of liquid assets.

   1. Currently in existence
   2. From sale of equity securities
   3. From sale of debt securities

C. **A difference** between **reacquisition price** and **net carrying amount** of the extinguished debt should be recognized in the year of extinguishment as a separate item.

   1. Gains and losses should not be amortized to future years.
   2. Gains and losses are ordinary.

SFAS 6 Classification of Short-Term Obligations Expected to Be Refinanced (ASC Topics 210 and 470)

A. Short-term obligations shall be classified as a current liability unless

   1. Enterprise intends to refinance the obligation on a long-term basis
   2. AND the intent is supported by ability to refinance

      a. Post-balance-sheet issuance of long-term debt or equity securities, or
      b. Financing agreement that clearly permits refinancing on a long-term basis

         (1) Does not expire or is not callable for one year
         (2) No violation of the agreement exists at the balance sheet date or has occurred to date

   3. The amount of the short-term obligation excluded from current liability status should not exceed the

      a. Net proceeds of debt or securities issued
      b. Net amounts available under refinancing agreements

         (1) The enterprise must intend to exercise the financing agreement when the short-term obligation becomes due.

   4. Refinancing of short-term obligations is a FS **classification** issue, **not** a **recognition** and **measurement** issue.

FASB INTERPRETATION NO. 8 CLASSIFICATION OF A SHORT-TERM OBLIGATION REPAID PRIOR TO BEING REPLACED BY A LONG-TERM SECURITY

Short-term obligations that are repaid after the balance sheet date but **before** funds are obtained from long-term financing are to be classified as current liabilities at the balance sheet date.

EXAMPLES

In situation 1 below, the obligation will be classified as a noncurrent liability at the balance sheet date. Why? Proceeds from refinancing were obtained prior to the due date of the obligation.

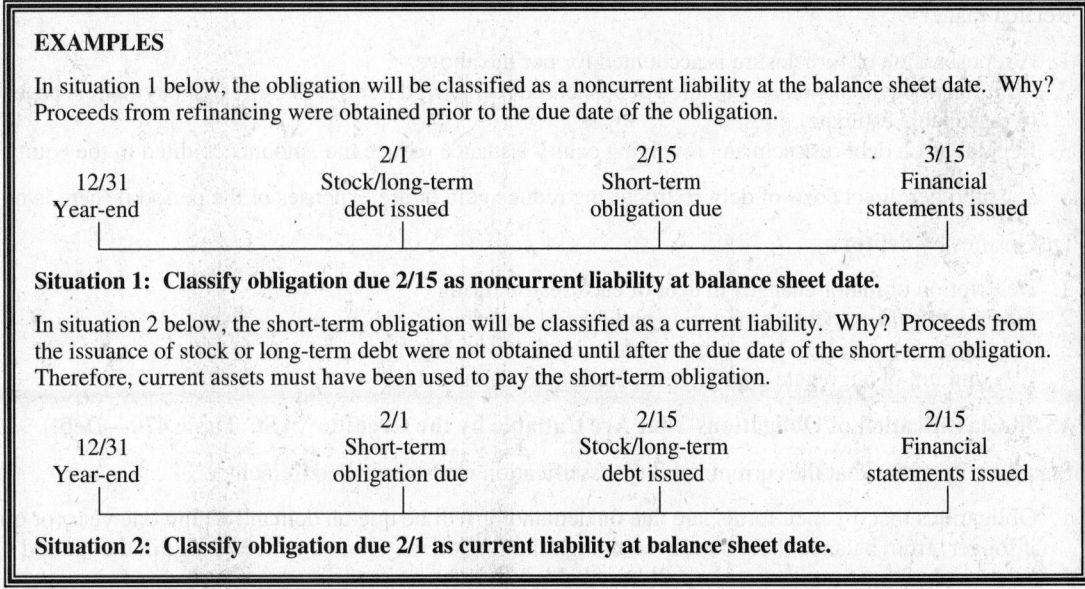

Situation 1: Classify obligation due 2/15 as noncurrent liability at balance sheet date.

In situation 2 below, the short-term obligation will be classified as a current liability. Why? Proceeds from the issuance of stock or long-term debt were not obtained until after the due date of the short-term obligation. Therefore, current assets must have been used to pay the short-term obligation.

Situation 2: Classify obligation due 2/1 as current liability at balance sheet date.

SFAS 15 Accounting by Debtors and Creditors for Troubled Debt Restructurings (ASC Topics 310 and 470)
(Superseded by SFAS 114 with regard to creditors)

A. Troubled debt restructurings occur when a creditor is compelled to grant relief to a debtor due to the debtor's inability to service the debt. This SFAS prescribes accounting for such debt restructurings if

1. By creditor-debtor agreement
2. Imposed by a court
3. Result of repossessions and foreclosures
4. But not changes in lease agreements

   a. Nor legal actions to collect receivables
   b. Nor quasi reorganizations

B. If a **debtor** transfers assets to settle fully a payable, recognize a gain on restructuring equal to the book value of the payable less FV of assets transferred.

1. Use fair value measurements as outlined by SFAS 157.
2. The difference between set FV and carrying value of the assets transferred is a gain or loss in disposition of assets per APB 30.

C. If a **debtor** issues an equity interest to settle fully a payable, account for equity issued at FV.

1. Excess of carrying value of payable over equity FV is a gain on restructuring.

D. A **debtor** having the terms of troubled debt modified should account for the restructure prospectively (i.e., no adjustment of the payable).

1. Recompute the new effective rate of interest based on the new terms

   a. Total cash payments to be paid, less carrying value of payable is the interest
   b. Amortize the payable by the interest method (APB 21) using the new interest rate

2. Exception is if restructured terms require total cash payments (including interest) which are less than the carrying value of the payable, write down the payable to the total cash to be paid

   a. Include contingent payments in calculation; this precludes recognizing a gain currently and interest expense later
   b. Recognize gain on the write-down
   c. All future cash payments reduce the payable (i.e., no interest expense is recognized)

E. If restructured by partial settlement (assets and/or equity issuance) and modified terms

1. First account for asset and/or equity issuance per above
2. Then account for modified terms per above

F. Related matters

1. A repossession or foreclosure is accounted for per the above.
2. Contingent payments on restructured debt shall be recognized per SFAS 5 (i.e., its payment is probable and subject to reasonable estimate).
3. Legal fees on debt restructuring involving equity issuance reduce the amounts credited to the equity accounts.

   a. All other direct costs of debt restructuring reduce gain or are expenses of the period if there is no gain.

G. Disclosures by **debtors**

1. Description of major changes in debt of each restructuring
2. Aggregate gain on debt restructuring and related tax effect
3. Aggregate net gain (loss) on asset transfers due to restructuring
4. EPS amount of aggregate gain on restructuring net of tax effect

SFAS 78 Classification of Obligations That Are Callable by the Creditor (ASC Topic 470—Debt)

A. Statement specifies that the current liability classification is also intended to include

1. Obligations that, by their terms, are due on demand or will be due on demand within one year (or operating cycle, if longer) from balance sheet date, even though liquidation may not be expected within that period
2. Long-term obligations that are or will be callable by creditor either because

   a. Debtor's violation of debt agreement provision at balance sheet date makes obligation callable **or**
   b. Violation, if not cured within grace period, will make obligation callable

B. Callable obligations in A.2. should be classified current unless one of the following conditions is met:

1. Creditor has waived or subsequently lost the right to demand repayment for more than one year (or operating cycle, if longer) from balance sheet date
2. For long-term obligations containing grace period within which debtor may cure violation, it is probable violation will be cured within that period

   a. If obligation meets this condition, the circumstances shall be disclosed

C. This statement does not modify SFAS 6 or 47

SFAS 84 Induced Conversions of Convertible Debt (ASC Topic 470—Debt)

A. Establishes accounting and reporting standards for conversion of convertible debt to equity securities when debtor induces conversion of the debt

1. Applies only to conversions that both

   a. Occur pursuant to changed conversion privileges exercisable only for limited period of time
   b. Include issuance of all of the equity securities issuable pursuant to the original conversion privileges for each instrument that is converted

2. Examples of changed terms to induce conversion

   a. Reduction of original conversion price
   b. Issuance of warrants or other securities not included in original conversion terms
   c. Payment of cash or other consideration to debt holders who convert during the specified time period

B. Debtor enterprise shall recognize expense equal to excess of fair value of all securities and other consideration transferred in the transaction over fair value of securities issuable pursuant to the original conversion terms.

1. Expense is not an extraordinary item.
2. Fair value of securities/other consideration measured as of inducement date

   a. Typically date converted by debt holder or binding agreement entered into

SFAS 150 Accounting for Certain Financial Instruments with Characteristics of Both Liabilities and Equity (ASC Topic 480—Distinguishing Liabilities from Equity)

A. This statement addresses how an issuer classifies and measures certain financial instruments with characteristics of both liabilities and equity. If the financial instrument embodies an obligation to the issuer, then it should be reported as a liability.

B. Terms: An obligation is a conditional or unconditional duty or responsibility to transfer assets or to issue equity shares. The duty may require a physical settlement (repurchasing its equity shares), a net cash settlement (transferring cash), or a net share settlement (issuing shares to settle).

C. This pronouncement applies to three classes of financial instruments: mandatorily redeemable preferred stock, obligations to repurchase the issuer's equity shares by transferring assets, and certain obligations to issue a variable number of shares.

1. Mandatorily redeemable preferred stock is classified as a liability unless the redemption only occurs upon liquidation or termination of the entity.
2. If a financial instrument embodies an obligation to repurchase the issuer's equity shares and requires settlement by transferring assets, then the instrument is classified as a liability.
3. If the financial instrument has an obligation that the issuer must settle by issuing a variable number of its equity shares, then it is classified as a liability if the value of the obligation is based on a fixed monetary amount or an amount tied to variations or inverse variations in something other than the issuer's securities.

D. These items are presented in the liabilities section of the statement of financial position. For EPS purposes, mandatorily redeemable preferred and forward contracts to repurchase equity shares are excluded in the calculation of earnings per share. Dividends and participation rights are deducted in computing income available to common shareholders in calculating EPS.

E. Disclosure: The following must be disclosed in the notes to financial statements:

1. The amount that would be paid or number of shares that would be issued and their fair value if settlement were to occur at reporting date
2. How changes in fair value of the shares would affect the settlement amounts
3. The maximum number of shares that could be required to be paid for a physical settlement
4. The maximum number of shares that could be required to be issued
5. That a contract does not limit the amount that the issuer could be required to pay or issue shares
6. If the forward contract or option indexed to the issuer's equity shares, the forward price or option strike price, the number of issuer's shares to which the contract is indexed and the settlement date or dates

EQUITY (ASC TOPIC 500)

ARB 43—Chapter 1A Rules[2] Adopted by Membership (ASC Topics 310, 505, 605, and 850)

Four rules recommended by the Committee on Cooperation with Stock Exchanges in 1934. The last rule is from another 1934 Institute committee.

1. Profit is realized at the point of sale unless collection is not reasonably assured.
2. Capital (paid-in) surplus should not be charged with losses or expenses, except in quasi reorganizations.
3. Receivables from officers, employees, and affiliates must be separately disclosed.
4. Par value of stock issued for assets cannot be used to value the assets if some of the stock is subsequently donated back to the corporation.

ARB 43—Chapter 1B Profits or Losses on Treasury Stock (ASC Topic 505)

Profits on treasury stock are not income and should be reflected in capital surplus.

ARB 43— Chapter 7B Stock Dividends and Stock Splits (ASC Topic 505—Equity)

A. Dividend—evidence given to shareholders of their share of accumulated earnings that are going to be retained in the business

B. Split—stock issued to increase number of outstanding shares to reduce market price and/or to obtain a wider distribution of ownership

C. To the recipient, splits and dividends are not income. Dividends and splits take nothing from the property of the corporation and add nothing to the property of the recipient.

1. Upon receipt of stock dividend or split, recipient should reallocate cost of shares previously held to all shares held.

D. Issuer of a stock dividend (issuance is small in relation to shares outstanding and consequently has no apparent effect on market price) should capitalize retained earnings equal to the fair market value of shares issued.

1. Unless retained earnings are capitalized, retained earnings thought to be distributed by the recipient will be available for subsequent distribution.

---

[2] The references in parentheses are from the FASB Accounting Standards—Current Texts: Volumes 1 and 2, John Wiley & Sons, Inc. These are included only for facilitating the use of the Current Texts for candidates who have access to them.

2. Issuances less than 20-25% of previously outstanding shares are dividends. Issuances greater than 20-25% of previously outstanding shares are splits.
3. Where stock dividend is so large it may materially affect price (a split effected in the form of a dividend), no capitalization is necessary other than that required by law.

   a. Some jurisdictions require that the par value of splits be capitalized (i.e., changes in par value are not permitted).

4. For closely held corporations, there is no need to capitalize retained earnings other than to meet legal requirements.

APB 6 Status of Accounting Research Bulletins (ASC Topic 505—Equity)

A. ARB 43, Chapter 1B Treasury Stock

1. An excess of purchase price of treasury stock, purchased for retirement or constructive retirement, over par or stated value may be allocated between paid-in capital and retained earnings.

   a. The charge to paid-in capital is limited to all paid-in capital from treasury stock transactions and retirements of the same issue and a pro rata portion of all other paid-in capital of that issue.
   b. Also, paid-in capital applicable to fully retired issues may be charged.

2. Alternatively, losses may be charged entirely to retained earnings.
3. All gains on retirement of treasury stock go to paid-in capital.
4. When the decision to retire treasury stock has not been made, the cost of such is a contra shareholders' equity item. Losses may only be charged to paid-in capital from treasury transactions and retirements of the same issue.
5. Some state laws prescribe accounting for treasury stock. The laws are to be followed where they are at variance with this APB. Disclose all statutory requirements concerning treasury stock such as dividend restrictions.

B. ARB 43, Chapter 3A Current Assets and Liabilities

Unearned interest, finance charges, etc. included in receivables should be deducted from the related receivable.

C. ARB 43, Chapter 7B Stock Dividends and Splits

States "the shareholder has no income solely as a result of the fact that the corporation has income," but does not preclude use of the equity method.

APB 9 Reporting the Results of Operations (ASC Topics 225, 250, 505)

A. Designates a new format for income statement in which all normal operating items would be presented at the top of the income statement resulting in "net income before extraordinary items."

1. "Net income before extraordinary items" is followed by extraordinary items resulting in "net income."

B. "Prior period adjustments" are excluded from the income statement and constitute adjustments of beginning retained earnings disclosed at the top of the retained earnings statement.

1. Beginning retained earnings are adjusted by "prior period adjustments" resulting in "restated beginning retained earnings."
2. "Restated retained earnings" is then adjusted for net income and dividends which results in ending retained earnings.

C. Prior period adjustments should be disclosed in the period of adjustment.

1. The effect on each prior period presented should be disclosed including restated income taxes.
2. Disclosure in subsequent periods is not normally required.
3. Historical summary data should also be restated and disclosed in the period of adjustment.

D. The APB also reaffirmed earlier positions that the following should not affect determination of net income:

1. Transactions in the company's own stock
2. Transfers to or from retained earnings
3. Quasi reorganization adjustments

APB 12 Omnibus Opinion—1967 (ASC Topics 310, 360, 505, 710, and 835)

A. Allowance or contra accounts (allowance for bad debts, accumulated depreciation, etc.) should be deducted from assets or groups of assets with appropriate disclosure.
B. Disclosure of depreciable assets should include

1. Depreciation expense for the period
2. Balances of major classes of depreciable assets by nature or function

3. Accumulated depreciation either by major class or in total
4. Description of method(s) of depreciation by major classes of assets

C. Changes in the separate shareholder equity accounts in addition to retained earnings and changes in number of equity securities must be disclosed in the year of change

1. In separate statements
2. Or the financial statements
3. Or the notes

SFAS 123 (Revised) (C36) Share-Based Payment (ASC Topic 718—Compensation—Stock Compensation and ASC Topic 505—Equity)

A. Provides a fair value based method of accounting for stock-based payment plans

1. Supersedes APB 25, amends SFAS 123
2. Applies to all transactions between an entity and its "suppliers" (whether employees or nonemployees) in which the entity acquires goods or services through issuance of equity instruments or incurrence of liabilities based on fair value of the entity's common stock or other equity instruments
3. Examples include stock purchase plans, stock options, restricted stock, and stock appreciation rights
4. Classifies share-based payment as either equity or liability

B. Transactions with Nonemployees—Accounted for based on fair value of consideration received or fair value of equity instruments given, whichever is more readily determinable.
C. Transactions with Employees—Uses fair value based method
D. Measurement Methods

1. Share-based payments recorded as equity

   a. Measured at fair value at grant date
   b. Stock options are measured at fair value which is based on the observable market price of an option with the same or similar terms and conditions, or via use of an option pricing model which considers, as of grant date, exercise price and expected life of the option, current price of underlying stock and its anticipated volatility, expected dividends on the stock, and risk-free interest rate for expected term of the option.
   c. If fair value cannot be determined as of grant date, final measure shall be based on stock price and any other pertinent factors when it becomes reasonably possible to estimate that value. Current intrinsic value shall be used as a measure until a final determination of fair value can be made.

2. Share-based payments recorded as liabilities
   Requires the recording of liability based on current stock price at end of each period. Changes in stock price during service period are recognized as compensation cost over service period. A change in stock price subsequent to service period is recognized as compensation cost of that period.

E. Recognition of Compensation Cost

1. Total compensation cost is based on the number of instruments that eventually vest

   a. Vesting is defined as moment when employee's right to receive or retain such instruments or cash is no longer contingent on performance of additional services
   b. No compensation cost shall be recognized for employees that forfeit eligibility due to failure either to achieve service requirement or performance condition
   c. Compensation cost shall not be reversed if vested employee's stock option expires unexercised
   d. Company must estimate forfeitures due to service or performance condition not being met
   e. Total compensation cost is amortized straight-line over the requisite service period

2. Acceptable accrual methods

   a. As of grant date, base accruals of compensation cost on best available estimate of the number of options or instruments expected to vest, with estimates for forfeitures
   b. As of grant date, accrue compensation cost as if all options or instruments that are subject only to a service requirement will vest

F. Tax consequences of stock-based compensation transactions shall be accounted for pursuant to SFAS 109

1. Excess tax benefits are recognized as additional paid-in capital
2. Cash retained as a result of excess tax benefits is presented on the statement of cash flows as a cash inflow from financing activities

G. Disclosures

1. The method of estimating the fair value of goods or services received or fair value of the equity instruments granted during the period
2. The cash flow effects from share-based payments
3. Vesting requirements, maximum term of options granted, and number of shares authorized for grants of options or other equity instruments
4. The number and weighted-average exercise prices of each group of options
5. The weighted-average grant-date fair value of options granted during the year, classified according to whether exercise price equals, exceeds, or is less than fair value of stock at date of grant
6. A description of methods used and assumptions made in determining fair values of the options
7. Total compensation cost recognized for the year

SFAS 129 Disclosure of Information about Capital Structure (ASC Topic 505—Equity)

A. Information to Be Disclosed about Securities within the Financial Statements

1. The rights and privileges of the various securities outstanding; for example

   a. Dividend and liquidation preferences
   b. Participation rights
   c. Call prices and dates
   d. Conversion/exercise prices/rates and dates
   e. Sinking fund requirements
   f. Unusual voting rights
   g. Significant terms of contracts to issue additional shares

2. The number of shares issued upon conversion, exercise, or satisfaction of required conditions during at least the most recent annual fiscal period and any subsequent interim period presented.

B. Disclosure of Liquidation Preference of Preferred Stock within the Financial Statements

1. Relationship between the preference in liquidation and the par/stated value of the shares when preferred stock (or other senior stock) has a preference in involuntary liquidation considerably in excess of the par/stated value of the shares. This disclosure should be made in the equity section of the balance sheet in the aggregate, either parenthetically or "in short."
2. Aggregate or per share amounts at which preferred stock may be called or is subject to redemption through sinking fund operations or otherwise.
3. Aggregate and per share amount of arrearages in cumulative preferred dividends.

C. Disclosure of Redeemable Stock within the Financial Statements

1. The amount of redemption requirements, separately by issue or combined, for all issues of capital stock that are redeemable at fixed or determinable prices on fixed or determinable dates in each of the five years following the date of the latest balance sheet presented.

REVENUE (ASC TOPIC 600)

ARB 43—Chapter 1A Rules[3] Adopted by Membership (ASC Topics 310, 505, 605, and 850)

Four rules recommended by the Committee on Cooperation with Stock Exchanges in 1934. The last rule is from another 1934 Institute committee.

1. Profit is realized at the point of sale unless collection is not reasonably assured.
2. Capital (paid-in) surplus should not be charged with losses or expenses, except in quasi reorganizations.
3. Receivables from officers, employees, and affiliates must be separately disclosed.
4. Par value of stock issued for assets cannot be used to value the assets if some of the stock is subsequently donated back to the corporation.

ARB 45 Long-Term Construction Contracts (ASC Topic 605—Revenue)

Discusses accounting for multiple-period projects

A. The percentage-of-completion method recognizes income as work progresses.

1. Recognized income based upon a percentage of estimated total income

---

[3] The references in parentheses are from the FASB Accounting Standards—Current Texts: Volumes 1 and 2, John Wiley & Sons, Inc. These are included only for facilitating the use of the Current Texts for candidates who have access to them.

    a. (Incurred costs to date)/(Total expected costs) known as cost-to-cost measure

    b. Other measure of progress based on work performed (e.g., engineering or architectural estimate)

2. Costs, for percentage-of-completion estimate, might exclude materials and subcontracts, especially in the early stages of a contract.

    a. Avoids overstating the percentage-of-completion

3. If a loss is estimated on the contract, the **entire loss** should be recognized currently.

4. Contracts should be separated into net assets and net liabilities.

    a. Current assets include costs and income (loss) in excess of billings.

    b. Current liabilities include billings in excess of costs and income (loss).

    c. Contracts should not be offset on the balance sheet.

5. Advantages of percentage-of-completion are periodic recognition of income and reflection of the status of the contract.

    a. Results in appropriate matching of costs and revenues

    b. Avoids distortions in income from year to year and thus provides more relevant information to financial statement users

6. The principal disadvantage is the reliance on estimates.

7. The percentage-of-completion method is required when total costs and percent of completion can be reasonably estimated.

B. The completed-contract method recognizes income when the contract is complete.

1. General and administrative expenses can be allocated to contracts.

    a. Not necessary if many projects are in process

    b. No excessive deferring of costs

2. Provision should be made for **entire amount of any expected loss** prior to job completion.

    a. That is, losses are recognized immediately in their entirety—conservative treatment

3. An excess of accumulated costs over related billings is a current asset. An excess of accumulated billings over related costs is a liability (current in most cases).

    a. Balance sheet accounts are determined as in A.4., except no income is included

    b. Recognized losses in B.2. reduce accumulated costs.

4. The advantage of the completed-contract method is that it is based on final results, and its primary disadvantage is that it does not reflect current performance.

    a. Overall, the completed-contract method represents a conservative approach.

APB 10 Omnibus Opinion—1966 (ASC Topics 210, 605, 740)

A. ARB 43, Chapter 3B Working Capital

1. Offsetting of liabilities and assets in the balance sheet is not acceptable unless a right of offset exists.

2. Most government securities are not designed to be prepayment of taxes and thus may not be offset against tax liabilities. Only where an explicit prepayment exists may an offset be used.

FASB INTERPRETATION NO. 39 OFFSETTING OF AMOUNTS RELATED TO CERTAIN CONTRACTS

A right of setoff exists when all of the following conditions are met: (a) each of the two parties to a contract owes the other determinable amounts, (b) the reporting entity has the right to set off the amount owed with the amount owed by the other entity, (c) the reporting entity intends to set off, and (d) the right of setoff is enforceable at law.

B. Installment method of accounting

Revenues should be recognized at the point of sale unless receivables are in doubt. The installment or cost recovery method may be used.

SFAS 48 Revenue Recognition When Right of Return Exists (ASC Topic 605—Revenue)
(Also ASC Topics 450 and 460)

A. Specifies accounting for sales in which a product may be returned for refund, credit applied to amounts owed, or in exchange for other products.

1. Right is specified by contract or is a matter of existing practice.
2. Right may be exercised by ultimate customer or party who resells product to others.
3. Not applicable to service revenue, real estate or lease transactions, or return of defective goods

B. Recognize revenue from right of return sales only if all of the following conditions are met:

1. Price is substantially fixed or determinable at date of sale.
2. Buyer has paid or is unconditionally obligated to pay.
3. Obligation is not changed by theft, destruction, or damage of product.
4. Buyer has "economic substance" apart from seller (i.e., sale is not with a party established mainly for purpose of recognizing sales revenue).
5. Seller has no significant obligation for performance to directly cause resale of product.
6. Amount of future returns can be reasonably estimated.

C. If all of the conditions in B. above are met, record sales and cost of sales **and**

1. Reduce sales revenue and cost of sales to reflect estimated returns
2. Accrue expected costs or losses in accordance with SFAS 5

D. If any condition in B. above is not met, do not recognize sales and cost of sales until either

1. All conditions are subsequently met, or
2. Return privilege has substantially expired

E. Factors which may impair ability to make a reasonable estimate of returns include

1. Susceptibility of product to significant external factors (e.g., obsolescence or changes in demand)
2. Long period of return privilege
3. Absence of experience with similar products or inability to apply such experience due to changing circumstances (e.g., marketing policies or customer relationships)
4. Absence of large volume of similar transactions

SFAS 66 Accounting for Sales of Real Estate (ASC Topics 360, 605, and 976)

A. Other than retail land sales

1. Use the full accrual method if the following criteria are satisfied:

   a. Sale is consummated
   b. Buyer's initial and continuing investments demonstrate a commitment to pay for the property
   c. Seller's receivable is not subject to future subordination
   d. Risks and rewards of ownership have been transferred

2. When the criteria are not met and dependent upon the particular circumstance, use one of the following methods:

   a. Installment method
   b. Cost recovery method
   c. Deposit method
   d. Reduced profit method
   e. Percentage-of-completion

B. Retail land sales (not outlined due to specialized nature)

EXPENSES (ASC TOPIC 700)

APB 12 Omnibus Opinion—1967 (ASC Topics 310, 360, 505, 710, 835)

A. Allowance or contra accounts (allowance for bad debts, accumulated depreciation, etc.) should be deducted from assets or groups of assets with appropriate disclosure.

B. Disclosure of depreciable assets should include

1. Depreciation expense for the period
2. Balances of major classes of depreciable assets by nature or function
3. Accumulated depreciation either by major class or in total
4. Description of method(s) of depreciation by major classes of assets

C. Changes in the separate shareholder equity accounts in addition to retained earnings and changes in number of equity securities must be disclosed in the year of change

  1. In separate statements
  2. Or the financial statements
  3. Or the notes

SFAS 43 Accounting for Compensated Absences (ASC Topics 710—Compensation—General)

A. This statement addresses the accounting for future sick pay benefits, holidays, vacation benefits, and other like compensated absences.

B. Accrual of a liability for future compensated absences is required if all of the conditions listed below exist.

  1. Obligation of employer to compensate employees arises from services already performed
  2. Obligation arises from vesting or accumulation of rights
  3. Probable payment of compensation
  4. Amount can be reasonably estimated

C. Above criteria require accrual of a liability for vacation benefits; however, other compensated absences typically may not require accrual of a liability.

  1. In spite of the above criteria, accrual of a liability is not required for accumulating nonvesting rights to receive sick pay benefits because amounts are typically not large enough to justify cost.

SFAS 112 Employers' Accounting for Postemployment Benefits (ASC Topic 712—Compensation—Nonretirement Postemployment Benefits)

A. Statement sets forth accounting standards for employers providing **postemployment** benefits to former/ inactive employees, **after employment but before retirement.**

  1. Applies to any postemployment benefits provided to former employers and their beneficiaries and dependents except

     a. Special or contractual termination benefits addressed by SFAS 88 and 106.
     b. Postemployment benefits derived from post**retirement** benefit or pension plans.
     c. Stock compensation plans covered by APB 25.
     d. Deferred compensation plans for individual employees that are covered by APB 12.

  2. Postemployment benefits may

     a. Result from death, disability, layoff, etc.
     b. Be paid in cash or in kind
     c. Be paid upon assumption of inactive status or over a period of time

B. Applicable postemployment benefits must be accounted for according to SFAS 43, which states:

  1. Liability for future compensated absences must be accrued if

     a. Obligation relates to services already provided by the employee,
     b. Rights to compensation vest or accumulate,
     c. Payment of obligation is probable, **and**
     d. Amount to be paid is reasonably estimable.

C. If conditions listed above are not met but the benefits are within scope of SFAS 43, they are accounted for according to SFAS 5, which states

  1. Estimated loss contingency accrued if

     a. It is known before FS are issued that it is probable that asset has been impaired or a liability incurred and that future events will probably confirm the loss, **and**
     b. Amount of loss is reasonably estimable.

D. Disclosure required if liability for postemployment benefits not accrued solely because amount not reasonably estimable.

SFAS 87 Employers' Accounting for Pensions (ASC Topic 715—Compensation—Retirement Benefits)

Applies to any arrangement that is similar in substance to pension plan regardless of form or means of financing. Applies to written plan and to plan whose existence may be implied from well-defined, although perhaps unwritten, practice of paying postretirement benefits. Does not apply to plan that provides only life insurance benefits or health insurance benefits, or both, to retirees. Does not apply to postemployment health care benefits.

The following terms are given specific definitions for the purposes of SFAS 87:

Accumulated benefit obligation—Actuarial present value of benefits (whether vested or nonvested) attributed by the pension benefit formula to employee service rendered before a specified date and based on employee service and compensation (if applicable) prior to that date. The accumulated benefit obligation differs from the projected benefit obligation in that it includes no assumption about future compensation levels. For plans with flat-benefit or non-pay-related pension benefit formulas, the accumulated benefit obligation and the projected benefit obligation are the same.

Actual return on plan assets component (of net periodic pension cost)—Difference between fair value of plan assets at the end of the period and the fair value at the beginning of the period, adjusted for contributions and payments of benefits during the period.

Actuarial present value—Value, as of a specified date, of an amount or series of amounts payable or receivable thereafter, with each amount adjusted to reflect (a) the time value of money (through discounts for interest) and (b) the probability of payment (by means of decrements for events such as death, disability, withdrawal, or retirement) between the specified date and the expected date of payment.

Amortization—Usually refers to the process of reducing a recognized liability systematically by recognizing revenues or reducing a recognized asset systematically by recognizing expenses or costs. In pension accounting, amortization is also used to refer to the systematic recognition in net pension cost over several periods of previously **unrecognized** amounts, including unrecognized prior service cost and unrecognized net gain or loss.

Defined contribution pension plan—Plan that provides pension benefits in return for services rendered, provides an individual account for each participant, and specifies how contributions to the individual's account are to be determined instead of specifying the amount of benefits the individual is to receive. Under a defined contribution pension plan, the benefits a participant will receive depend solely on the amount contributed to the participant's account, the returns earned on investments of those contributions, and forfeitures of other participants' benefits that may be allocated to such participant's account.

Gain or loss—Change in the value of either the projected benefit obligation or the plan assets resulting from experience different from that assumed or from a change in an actuarial assumption. See also **Unrecognized net gain or loss**.

Gain or loss component (of net periodic pension cost)—The gain or loss component is the net effect of delayed recognition of gains and losses (the net change in the unrecognized net gain or loss) except that it does not include changes in the projected benefit obligation occurring during the period and deferred for later recognition.

Interest cost component (of net periodic pension cost)—Increase in the projected benefit obligation due to passage of time.

Market-related value of plan assets—Balance used to calculate the expected return on plan assets. Market-related value can be either fair market value or a calculated value that recognizes changes in fair value in a systematic and rational manner over not more than five years. Different ways of calculating market-related value may be used for different classes of assets, but the manner of determining market-related value shall be applied consistently from year to year for each asset class.

Net periodic pension cost—Amount recognized in an employer's financial statements as the cost of a pension plan for a period. Components of net periodic pension cost are service cost, interest cost, actual return on plan assets, gain or loss, amortization of unrecognized prior service cost, and amortization of the unrecognized net obligation or asset existing at the date of initial application of SFAS 87. SFAS 87 uses the term **net periodic pension cost** instead of **net pension expense** because part of the cost recognized in a period may be capitalized along with other costs as part of an asset such as inventory.

Prior service cost or credit—Cost of retroactive benefits or credit granted in a plan amendment.

Projected benefit obligation—Actuarial present value as of a date of all benefits attributed by the pension benefit formula to employee service rendered prior to that date. The projected benefit obligation is measured using assumptions as to future compensation levels if the pension benefit formula is based on those future compensation levels (pay-related, final-pay, final-average-pay, or career-average-pay plans).

Service cost component (of net periodic pension cost)—Actuarial present value of benefits attributed by the pension benefit formula to services rendered by employees during the period. The service cost component is a portion of the projected benefit obligation and is unaffected by the funded status of the plan.

Unfunded projected benefit obligation—Excess of the projected obligation over plan assets.

Unrecognized net gain or loss—Cumulative net gain (loss) that has not been recognized as a part of net periodic pension cost. See **Gain or loss**.

Unamortized prior service cost or credit—Portion of prior service cost or credit that has not been recognized as a part of net periodic pension cost.

A. Single-Employer Defined Benefit Plans

  1. Pension benefits are part of compensation paid to employees for services

     a. Amount of benefits to be paid depends on a number of future events specified in the **plan's benefit formula**.

2. Any method of pension accounting that recognizes cost before payment of benefits to retirees must deal with two problems

   a. Assumptions must be made concerning future events that will determine amount and timing of benefits
   b. Approach to attributing cost of pension benefits to individual years of service must be selected

B. Basic Elements of Pension Accounting

1. Prior service cost

   a. Except as specified otherwise, prior service cost shall be amortized by assigning an equal amount to each future service period of each employee active at the date of a plan amendment who is expected to receive benefits under plan.
   b. If all/almost all of plan's participants are inactive, cost of retroactive plan benefits should be amortized over remaining life expectancy of those participants.
   c. Consistent use of alternative amortization approach that more rapidly reduces unrecognized cost of retroactive amendments is acceptable.

      (1) Alternative method used should be disclosed.

   d. When period during which employer expects to realize economic benefits from amendment granting retroactive benefits is shorter than entire remaining service period of active employees, amortization of prior service cost should be accelerated.
   e. Plan amendment can reduce, rather than increase, the projected benefit obligation.

      (1) Reduction should be used to reduce any existing unrecognized prior service cost.
      (2) Excess should be amortized on same basis as cost of benefit increases.

2. Gains and losses

   a. Gains (losses)

      (1) Result from changes in amount of either projected benefit obligation or plan assets due to experience different than assumed and changes in assumptions
      (2) Include both **realized** and **unrealized** amounts

   b. Asset gains (losses) include both changes reflected in the market-related value of assets and changes not yet reflected in the market-related value.

      (1) Asset gains (losses) not yet reflected in market-related value are not required to be amortized as B.2.c. below.

   c. As a minimum, amortization of unrecognized net gain (loss) should be included as a component of net pension cost for a year if, as of the beginning of the year, that unrecognized net gain (loss) $\geq$ .10 of the larger of the projected benefit obligation or the market-related value of plan assets.

      (1) Minimum amortization should be the excess divided by the average remaining service period of active employees expected to receive benefits under the plan.

         (a) Amortization must always reduce beginning-of-the-year balance.
         (b) Amortization of a net unrecognized gain (loss) results in a decrease (increase) in net periodic pension cost.

      (2) If all or almost all of plan's participants are inactive, average remaining life expectancy of inactive participants should be used instead of average remaining service.

   d. Any systematic method of amortization of unrecognized gains (losses) may be used in lieu of the minimum specified above provided that

      (1) Minimum is used in any period in which minimum amortization is greater (reduces the net balance by more)
      (2) Method is applied consistently and disclosed

3. Recognition of liabilities and assets

   a. Liability (asset) is recognized if net periodic pension cost recognized exceeds (is less than) amounts the employer has contributed to the plan and if the projected benefit obligations exceeds (is less than) plan asset.

C. Attribution

1. Pension benefits should be attributed to periods of employee service based on plan's benefit formula.
2. When employer has a present commitment to make future amendments, and substance of plan is to provide benefits attributable to prior service that are greater than benefits defined by written terms of the plan.

   a. The substantive commitment should be basis for accounting, and
   b. Existence and nature of the commitment to make future amendments should be disclosed

3. Assumptions

   a. Assumed discount rates reflect rates at which pension benefits could be effectively settled

      (1) Used in measurements of projected and accumulated benefit obligations and the service and interest cost components of net periodic pension cost

   b. Assumed compensation levels (when measuring service cost and the projected benefit obligation) should reflect an estimate of the actual future compensation levels of employees involved, including future changes attributed to general price levels, productivity, seniority, promotion, and other factors.
   c. Accumulated benefit obligation shall be measured based on employees' history of service and compensation without estimate of future compensation levels.
   d. Automatic benefit increases specified by plan that are expected to occur should be included in measurements of projected and accumulated benefit obligations and the service cost component.
   e. Retroactive plan amendments should be included in computations of projected and accumulated benefit obligations.

      (1) Once they have been contractually agreed to
      (2) Even if some provisions take effect only in future periods

D. Measurement of Plan Assets

1. For purposes of determining the funded status of the plan and required disclosures, plan investments, whether equity or debt securities, real estate, or other, should be measured at their fair value as of measurement date.
2. Market-related asset value is used for purposes of determining the expected return on plan assets and accounting for asset gains and losses.

E. Acceptable Measurement Dates

1. As of date of financial statements, or
2. If used consistently from year to year, as of a date < 3 months prior to that date
3. Measurement date is not intended to require that all procedures be performed after that date.
4. Information for items requiring estimates can be prepared as of an earlier date and projected forward to account for subsequent events (e.g., employee service).
5. The "assets and liabilities" reported in interim financial statements should be the same "assets and liabilities" recognized in previous year-end balance sheet.

   a. Adjusted for subsequent accruals and contributions unless measures of both the obligation and plan assets are available as of a current date or a significant event occurs, such as plan amendment, that would call for such measurements

6. Measurements of net periodic pension cost for both interim and annual financial statements should be based on assumptions used for previous year-end measurements.

   a. If more recent measurements are available or a significant event occurs, use these more recent measurements.

7. For fiscal years ending after December 15, 2008, the measurement date is the fiscal year-end of firm

F. Disclosures (Amended by SFAS 132[R] and SFAS 158)

SFAS 88 Employers' Accounting for Settlements and Curtailments of Defined Benefit Pension Plans and for Termination Benefits (ASC Topic 715—Retirement Benefits)

Statement applies to an employer that sponsors a defined benefit pension plan accounted for under the provisions of SFAS 87 if all or part of the plan's pension benefit obligation is settled or the plan is curtailed. It also applies to an employer that offers benefits to employees in connection with their termination of employment.

The following terms are given specific definitions for the purposes of SFAS 88:

Settlement—Transaction that (a) is an irrevocable action, (b) relieves the employer (or the plan) of primary responsibility for a pension benefit obligation, and (c) eliminates significant risks related to the obligation and the assets used to effect the settlement.

Annuity contract—Irrevocable contract in which an insurance company[4] unconditionally undertakes a legal obligation to provide specified benefits to specific individuals in return for a fixed consideration or premium. It involves the transfer of significant risk from the employer to the insurance company.

Curtailment—Event that significantly reduces the expected years of future service of present employees or eliminates for a significant number of employees the accrual of defined benefits for some or all of their future services.

A. Relationship of Settlements and Curtailments to Other Events

1. Settlement and curtailment may occur separately or together.

B. Accounting for Settlement of Pension Obligation

1. For purposes of this statement, when a pension obligation is settled, the maximum gain or loss subject to recognition is the unrecognized gain or loss defined in SFAS 87 plus any remaining unrecognized net asset existing at the date of initial application of SFAS 87.
2. If the purchase of a participating annuity contract constitutes a settlement, the maximum gain (but not the maximum loss) should be reduced by the cost of the participation right before determining the amount to be recognized in earnings.
3. If the cost of all settlements in a year is less than or equal to the sum of the service cost and interest cost components of net periodic pension cost for the plan for the year, gain or loss recognition is permitted but not required for those settlements.

C. Accounting for Plan Curtailment

1. Unrecognized prior service cost is a loss.
2. The projected benefit obligation may be decreased (a gain) or increased (a loss) by a curtailment.

D. Termination Benefits

1. Employer may provide benefits to employees in connection with their termination of employment.
2. Termination benefits may take many forms consisting of

   a. Lump-sum payments
   b. Periodic future payments

3. The cost of termination benefits recognized as a liability and a loss shall include the amount of any lump-sum payments and present value of any expected future payments.

SFAS 106 Employers' Accounting for Postretirement Benefits other than Pensions (ASC Topic 715—Compensation—Retirement Benefits)

Standard applies to all forms of postretirement benefits, particularly postretirement health care benefits. Applies to written plan and to a plan whose existence may be implied from well-defined, although perhaps unwritten, practice of paying postretirement benefits (called the substantive plan). Does not apply to pensions.

The following terms are given specific definitions for purposes of SFAS 106:

Attribution period—The period of an employee's service to which the expected postretirement benefit obligation for that employee is assigned. The beginning of the attribution period is the employee's date of hire unless the plan's benefit formula grants credit only for service from a later date, in which case the beginning of the attribution period is generally the beginning of that credited service period. The end of the attribution period is the full eligibility date.

Benefit formula—The basis for determining benefits to which participants may be entitled under a postretirement benefit plan. A plan's benefit formula specifies the years of service to be rendered, age to be attained while in service, or a combination of both that must be met for an employee to be eligible to receive benefits under the plan.

Full eligibility date—The date at which an employee has rendered all of the service necessary to have earned the right to receive all of the benefits expected to be received by that employee (including any beneficiaries and dependents expected to receive benefits).

Health care cost trend rates—An assumption about the annual rate(s) of change in the cost of health care benefits currently provided by the postretirement benefit plan, due to factors other than changes in the composition of the plan population by age and dependency status, for each year from the measurement date until the end of the period in which benefits are expected to be paid.

Incurred claims cost (by age)—The cost of providing the postretirement health care benefits covered by the plan to a plan participant, after adjusting for reimbursements from Medicare and other providers of health care benefits and for deductibles, coinsurance provisions, and other specific claims costs borne by the retiree.

---

[4] If the insurance company is controlled by the employer or there is any reasonable doubt that the insurance company will meet its obligation under the contract, the purchase of the contract does not constitute a settlement for purposes of this statement.

Net periodic postretirement benefit cost—The amount recognized in an employer's financial statements as the cost of a postretirement benefit plan for a period. Components of net periodic postretirement benefit cost include service cost, interest cost, actual return on plan assets, gain or loss, amortization of unrecognized prior service cost, and amortization of the unrecognized transition obligation or asset.

Plan amendment—A change in the existing terms of a plan. A plan amendment may increase or decrease benefits, including those attributed to years of service already rendered.

Transition asset—The unrecognized amount, as of the date this statement is initially applied, of (a) the fair value of plan assets plus any recognized accrued postretirement benefit cost or less any recognized prepaid postretirement benefit cost in excess of (b) the accumulated postretirement benefit obligation.

Transition obligation—The unrecognized amount, as of the date this statement is initially applied, of (a) the accumulated postretirement benefit obligation in excess of (b) the fair value of plan assets plus any recognized accrued postretirement benefit cost or less any recognized prepaid postretirement benefit cost.

Unrecognized transition asset—The portion of the transition asset that has not been recognized either immediately as the effect of a change in accounting or on a delayed basis as a part of net periodic postretirement benefit cost, as an offset to certain losses, or as a part of accounting for the effects of a settlement or a curtailment.

Unrecognized transition obligation—The portion of the transition obligation that has not been recognized either immediately as the effect of a change in accounting or on a delayed basis as a part of net periodic postretirement benefit cost, as an offset to certain gains, or as a part of accounting for the effects of a settlement or a curtailment.

A. Single Employer Defined Benefit Plans

1. Postretirement benefits are part of compensation paid to employees for services

   a. Amount of benefits to be paid depends on future events specified in plan's benefit formula

2. Postretirement benefits formerly were accounted for on a pay-as-you-go (cash) basis. SFAS 106 changes this practice by requiring accrual, during the years that the employee renders necessary service, of **expected** cost of providing those benefits to an employee. Any method of postretirement benefits accounting that recognizes cost before payment of benefits to retirees must deal with two problems.

   a. Assumptions must be made concerning future events that will determine amount and timing of benefits.
   b. Approach to attributing cost of postretirement benefits to individual years of service must be selected.

B. Basic Elements of Postretirement Benefits Accounting

1. Prior service cost

   a. Except as specified otherwise, prior service cost shall be amortized by assigning an equal amount to each future service period of each employee active at the date of a plan amendment who was not yet fully eligible for benefits at that date.
   b. If all or almost all of a plan's participants are fully eligible for benefits, prior service cost shall be amortized over remaining life expectancy of those participants.
   c. Consistent use of alternative amortization approach that more rapidly reduces unrecognized cost of retroactive amendments is acceptable.

      (1) Alternative method used should be disclosed.

   d. When period during which employer expects to realize economic benefits from amendment granting increased benefits is shorter than entire remaining service period of active employees, amortization of prior service cost shall be accelerated.
   e. Plan amendment can reduce, rather than increase, accumulated postretirement benefit obligation

      (1) Reduction should be used to reduce any existing unrecognized prior service cost
      (2) Then to reduce any remaining unrecognized transition obligation
      (3) Excess, if any, shall be amortized on same basis as specified for prior service cost

2. Gains and losses

   a. Gains (losses)

      (1) Result from changes in amount of either accumulated postretirement benefit obligation or plan assets due to experience different than assumed and changes in assumptions
      (2) Include both **realized** and **unrealized** amounts

   b. Asset gains (losses) include both (a) changes reflected in market-related value of assets and (b) changes not yet reflected in market-related value.

      (1) Asset gains (losses) not yet reflected in market-related value are not required to be amortized as c. below.

   c. As a minimum, amortization of unrecognized net gain (loss) should be included as a component of net postretirement benefit cost for a year if, as of the beginning of the year, that unrecognized net gain (loss) > .10 of the larger of the accumulated postretirement benefit obligation or the market-related value of plan assets.

      (1) Minimum amortization should be the excess divided by the average remaining service period of active employees expected to receive benefits under the plan

         (a) Amortization must always reduce beginning of the year balance
         (b) Amortization of a net unrecognized gain (loss) results in a decrease (increase) in net periodic pension cost

      (2) If all or almost all of plan's participants are inactive, average remaining life expectancy of inactive participants should be used instead of average remaining service.

   d. Any systematic method of amortization of unrecognized gains (losses) may be used in lieu of the minimum specified above provided that

      (1) Minimum is used in any period in which minimum amortization is greater (reduces the net balance by more)
      (2) Method is applied consistently and disclosed

3. Recognition of liabilities and assets

   a. SFAS 106 requires an employer's obligation for postretirement benefits expected to be provided to an employee be **fully** accrued by the full eligibility date of employee, even if employee is to render additional service beyond that date
   b. Transition obligations

      (1) SFAS 106 measures the transition obligation as the unfunded and unrecognized accumulated postretirement benefit obligation for all plan participants. Two options are provided for recognizing that transition obligation.

         (a) **Immediate** recognition of the transition obligation as the effect of an accounting change (i.e., include all of the obligation as part of the net periodic postretirement benefit cost)
         (b) Recognize the transition obligation in the balance sheet and income statement on a delayed basis over the plan participants' future service periods, with proper disclosure of the remaining unrecognized amount. Note that delayed recognition **cannot** result in less rapid recognition than accounting for the transition obligation on a pay-as-you-go basis.

C. Attribution

1. The expected postretirement benefit obligation shall be attributed, in equal amounts, to each year of service in the attribution period.
2. However, if a benefit plan contains a benefit formula that attributes a disproportionate share of the expected postretirement benefit obligation to employees' early years of service, the postretirement benefits should be attributed based on the plan's benefit formula.
3. Assumptions

   a. Assumed discount rates shall reflect time value of money in determining present value of future cash outflows currently expected to be required to satisfy postretirement benefit obligation

      (1) Used in measurements of expected and accumulated postretirement benefit obligations and service and interest cost components of net periodic postretirement benefit cost

   b. Assumed compensation levels (when measuring service cost and expected and accumulated postretirement benefit obligations) shall reflect estimate of actual future compensation levels of employees involved, including future changes attributed to general price levels, productivity, seniority, promotion, and other factors.
   c. Accumulated postretirement benefit obligation shall be measured based on employees' history of service and compensation without estimate of future compensation levels.
   d. Automatic benefit changes specified by plan that are expected to occur should be included in measurements of projected and accumulated benefit obligations and the service cost component.
   e. Plan amendments should be included in computations of projected and accumulated benefit obligations.

      (1) Once they have been contractually agreed to
      (2) Even if some provisions take effect only in future periods

D. Measurement of Plan Assets

1. For purposes of required disclosures, plan investments, whether equity or debt securities, real estate, or other, shall be measured at FMV as of measurement date.
2. Market-related asset value is used for purposes of determining the expected return on plan assets and accounting for asset gains and losses.

E. Acceptable Measurement Dates

1. As of date of financial statements, or
2. If used consistently from year to year, as of a date < 3 months prior to that date
3. Measurement date is not intended to require that all procedures be performed after that date
4. Information for items requiring estimates can be prepared as of an earlier date and projected forward to account for subsequent events (e.g., employee service)
5. Measurements of net periodic postretirement benefit cost for both interim and annual financial statements shall be based on assumptions used for previous year-end measurements

   a. If more recent measurements are available or a significant event occurs, use more recent measurements

F. Disclosures (amended by SFAS 132)

SFAS 132 (Revised) Employers' Disclosures about Pensions and Other Postretirement Benefits (ASC Topic 715—Compensation—Retirement Benefits)

A. Disclosures for defined benefit pensions plans and defined benefit postretirement plans

1. A reconciliation of beginning and ending balances of the benefit obligation with the effects of the following shown separately:

   a. Service cost
   b. Interest cost
   c. Contributions by plan participants
   d. Actuarial gains and losses
   e. Foreign currency exchange rate changes
   f. Benefits paid
   g. Plan amendments
   h. Business combinations
   i. Divestitures
   j. Curtailments
   k. Settlements
   l. Special termination benefits

2. A reconciliation of beginning and ending balances of the fair value of plan assets with the effects of the following shown separately:

   a. Actual return on plan assets
   b. Foreign currency exchange rate changes
   c. Contributions by the employer
   d. Contributions by plan participants
   e. Benefits paid
   f. Business combinations
   g. Divestitures
   h. Settlements

3. The funded status of the plans
4. The amounts recognized and the amounts not recognized in the statement of financial position such as

   a. Any unamortized prior service cost or credit
   b. Any unrecognized net gain or loss
   c. Any unamortized net obligation or net asset existing at the initial date of prior SFAS 87 or 106 that are still unrecognized
   d. Prepaid assets or accrued liabilities of the net pension or other postretirement benefits
   e. Any intangible asset
   f. The amount of other comprehensive income recognized

5. Information about plan assets including

    a. For each major category of plan assets, including equity securities, debt securities, real estate, and all other assets, the percentage of the fair value of total plan assets held as of the measurement date

    b. A description of investment policies and strategies, including target allocation percentages or ranges of percentages for each major category of plan assets, and other factors that are pertinent to understanding the investment policies and strategies, (i.e., investment goals, risk management practices, permitted and prohibited investments)

    c. A description of the basis used to determine the overall expected long-term rate-of-return-of-assets assumption, the general approach used, the extent to which ROA assumption was based on historical returns, adjustments made to reflect expectations of future returns, and how adjustments were determined.

    d. Disclosure of additional asset categories and additional information about specific assets is encouraged if the information is useful in understanding risks and long-term rate of return.

6. For defined benefit pension plans, the accumulated benefit obligation.

7. The benefits are expected to be paid in each of the next five fiscal years, and in the aggregate for the five fiscal years thereafter.

8. The employer's best estimate of contributions expected to be paid to the plan during the next fiscal year. The estimated contributions may be presented in the aggregate combining contributions required by funding regulations or laws, discretionary contributions, and noncash contributions.

9. The recognized amount of the net periodic benefit cost with the components shown separately

10. The amount caused from a change in the additional minimum pension liability that was included in other comprehensive income

11. On a weighted-average basis, the rates for

    a. Assumed discount rate

    b. Rate of compensation increase

    c. Expected long-term rate of return on plan assets

12. The assumptions used to determine the benefit obligation and the net benefit cost

13. Trend rates assumed for health care cost for the next year and thereafter

14. The measurement date(s) used to determine pension and other postretirement benefit measurements for plans that make up the majority of assets and benefit obligations

15. The effects of a one-percentage-point increase or decrease of the trend rates for health care costs on

    a. The aggregate of the service and interest cost components

    b. The accumulated postretirement benefit obligation

16. If applicable

    a. The amounts and types of securities of the employer or a related party in plan assets

    b. The amount of future benefits covered by insurance contracts issued by the employer or a related party

    c. Any significant transactions between the plan and the employer or a related party

    d. Any substantive commitment used as the basis for accounting for the benefit obligation

    e. The cost of special or contractual termination benefits recognized during the period with a description of the event

17. An explanation of significant changes in the benefit obligation or plan assets that is not apparent in the other disclosures required

B. Disclosures for employers with more than one plan

1. Disclosures required in this statement may be disclosed in aggregate for an employer's defined benefit pension plans and in aggregate for an employer's defined benefit postretirement plans but must still present separately prepaid benefit costs and accrued benefit liabilities recognized in the statement of financial position.

2. An employer may not combine the disclosures of plans outside the US and plans in the US if the benefit obligation of the plans outside the US represent a significant portion of the total benefit obligation and significant differences exist in the assumptions used.

C. Disclosure requirements for nonpublic entities

1. Nonpublic entities may choose to disclose the following instead of the disclosures stated in A.:

    a. Benefit obligation

    b. Fair value of plan assets

    c. Funded status of the plan

    d. Contributions by the employer and the participant

    e. Amounts recognized in the statement of financial position of

(1) Prepaid assets or accrued liabilities
(2) Any intangible asset

f. Amount of accumulated other comprehensive income recognized and the amount resulting from a change in the minimum pension liability recognized
g. Net periodic benefit cost recognized
h. Rates for

(1) Assumed discount rate
(2) Rate of compensation increase
(3) Expected long-term rate of return on plan assets

i. Trend rates assumed for health care cost for the next year and thereafter
j. If applicable

(1) Amounts and types of securities of the employer or a related party
(2) Future annual benefits covered by insurance contracts issued by the employer or a related party
(3) Any significant transactions between the plan and the employer or a related party

k. Nature and effect of significant nonroutine events

D. Disclosures for defined contribution plans

1. Amount of cost recognized for pension or postretirement benefit plans must be separate from the cost recognized for defined benefit plans
2. Nature and effect of any significant changes that affect comparability must be disclosed

E. Disclosures for multiemployer plans

1. Amount of contributions to multiemployer plans
2. Nature and effect of changes which affect comparability
3. If withdrawals made by an employer from a multiemployer plan will result in an obligation for a portion of the unfunded benefit obligation or the unfunded accumulated postretirement benefit obligation, follow the provision of SFAS 5, *Accounting for Contingencies*
4. The significant multiemployer plans in which an employer participates
5. The level of an employer's participation (the contribution to the plan and whether that contribution represents more than 5% of the total contributions).
6. The financial health of the plan, such as funded status, improvement plans, and surcharges.
7. The nature of the employer commitments to the plans, such as collective bargaining agreements and minimum contribution requirements.
8. For plans in which users are unable to obtain additional information from outside sources:

a. A description of the nature of the plan benefits
b. A qualitative description of the employer responsibility for plan obligations
c. Other quantitative information available, such as total plan assets, actuarial present value of accumulated vested benefits, and total contributions received by the plan

SFAS 158 Employers' Accounting for Defined Benefit Pension and Other Postretirement Plans (An Amendment of FASB Statements 87, 88, 106, and 132[R]) (ASC Topic 715—Compensation—Retirement Benefits and ASC Topic 958—Not-for-Profit Entities)

A. Recognize funded status of benefit plans

1. Aggregate status of all overfunded plans and show as noncurrent asset on balance sheet
2. Aggregate status of all underfunded plans, and show as current liability, noncurrent liability, or both on balance sheet.
3. Recognize as other comprehensive income the gain and loss and the prior service costs or credits that arise during the period but are not a part of pension expense.

B. Effective for fiscal years ending after December 15, 2008, the measurement date is the employer's fiscal year-end balance sheet date.
C. Disclosures

1. Funded status of the plans, and the amounts recognized in the balance sheet, showing separately the noncurrent assets, current liabilities, and noncurrent liabilities recognized.
2. Disclose the net gain or loss, net prior service cost or credit recognized in OCI for the period, and any reclassification adjustments of OCI that are recognized in pension cost.

3. The amounts in accumulated OCI that have not yet been recognized as pension costs. Show separately the following items:

    a. Net gain or loss
    b. Net prior service cost or credit
    c. Net transition asset or obligation

4. The amount and timing of any plan assets expected to be returned to the employer during the next 12-month period after the most recent balance sheet date.

SFAS 123 (Revised) (C36) Share-Based Payment (ASC Topic 718—Compensation—Stock Compensation and ASC Topic 505—Equity)

A. Provides a fair value based method of accounting for stock-based payment plans

1. Supersedes APB 25, amends SFAS 123
2. Applies to all transactions between an entity and its "suppliers" (whether employees or nonemployees) in which the entity acquires goods or services through issuance of equity instruments or incurrence of liabilities based on fair value of the entity's common stock or other equity instruments
3. Examples include stock purchase plans, stock options, restricted stock, and stock appreciation rights
4. Classifies share-based payment as either equity or liability

B. Transactions with Nonemployees—Accounted for based on fair value of consideration received or fair value of equity instruments given, whichever is more readily determinable.
C. Transactions with Employees—Uses fair value based method
D. Measurement Methods

1. Share-based payments recorded as equity

    a. Measured at fair value at grant date
    b. Stock options are measured at fair value which is based on the observable market price of an option with the same or similar terms and conditions, or via use of an option pricing model which considers, as of grant date, exercise price and expected life of the option, current price of underlying stock and its anticipated volatility, expected dividends on the stock, and risk-free interest rate for expected term of the option.
    c. If fair value cannot be determined as of grant date, final measure shall be based on stock price and any other pertinent factors when it becomes reasonably possible to estimate that value. Current intrinsic value shall be used as a measure until a final determination of fair value can be made.

2. Share-based payments recorded as liabilities
    Requires the recording of liability based on current stock price at end of each period. Changes in stock price during service period are recognized as compensation cost over service period. A change in stock price subsequent to service period is recognized as compensation cost of that period.

E. Recognition of Compensation Cost

1. Total compensation cost is based on the number of instruments that eventually vest

    a. Vesting is defined as moment when employee's right to receive or retain such instruments or cash is no longer contingent on performance of additional services
    b. No compensation cost shall be recognized for employees that forfeit eligibility due to failure either to achieve service requirement or performance condition
    c. Compensation cost shall not be reversed if vested employee's stock option expires unexercised
    d. Company must estimate forfeitures due to service or performance condition not being met
    e. Total compensation cost is amortized straight-line over the requisite service period

2. Acceptable accrual methods

    a. As of grant date, base accruals of compensation cost on best available estimate of the number of options or instruments expected to vest, with estimates for forfeitures
    b. As of grant date, accrue compensation cost as if all options or instruments that are subject only to a service requirement will vest

F. Tax consequences of stock-based compensation transactions shall be accounted for pursuant to SFAS 109

1. Excess tax benefits are recognized as additional paid-in capital
2. Cash retained as a result of excess tax benefits is presented on the statement of cash flows as a cash inflow from financing activities

G. Disclosures

1. The method of estimating the fair value of goods or services received or fair value of the equity instruments granted during the period
2. The cash flow effects from share-based payments
3. Vesting requirements, maximum term of options granted, and number of shares authorized for grants of options or other equity instruments
4. The number and weighted-average exercise prices of each group of options
5. The weighted-average grant-date fair value of options granted during the year, classified according to whether exercise price equals, exceeds, or is less than fair value of stock at date of grant
6. A description of methods used and assumptions made in determining fair values of the options
7. Total compensation cost recognized for the year

ARB 43— Chapter 10A Real and Personal Property Taxes (ASC Topic 720—Other Expenses)

Accounting for personal and real property taxes which vary in time of determination and collection from state to state

A. In practice, the dates below have been used to apportion taxes between accounting periods.

1. Assessment date
2. Beginning of fiscal period of taxing authority
3. End of fiscal period of taxing authority
4. Lien date
5. Date of tax levy
6. Date tax is payable
7. Date tax is delinquent
8. Period appearing on tax bill

B. The most acceptable basis is a monthly accrual on the taxpayer's books during the fiscal period of the taxing authority.

1. At year-end, the books will show the appropriate prepayment or accrual.
2. An accrued liability, whether known or estimated, should be shown as a current liability.
3. On income statement, property taxes may be charged to operating expense, deducted separately from income, prorated among accounts to which they apply, or combined with other taxes (but not with income taxes).

SFAS 2 Accounting for Research and Development Costs (R&D) (ASC Topic 730—Research & Development)

A. Establishes accounting standards for R&D costs with objective of reducing alternative practices. In summary, all R&D costs are expensed except intangible assets purchased from others and tangible assets that have alternative future uses (which are capitalized and depreciated or amortized as R&D expense).

1. SFAS 2 specifies

   a. R&D activities
   b. Elements of R&D costs
   c. Accounting for R&D costs
   d. Required disclosures for R&D

2. SFAS 2 does not cover

   a. R&D conducted for others under contract
   b. Activities unique to extractive industries

B. R&D activities

1. Research is "planned search or critical investigation aimed at discovery of new knowledge with the hope that such knowledge will be useful in developing a new product or service or a new process or technique in bringing about a significant improvement to an existing product or process."
2. Development is "the translation of research findings or other knowledge into a plan or design for a new product or process or for a significant improvement to an existing product or process whether intended for sale or use."
3. R&D examples

   a. Laboratory research to discover new knowledge

      (1) Seeking applications for new research findings

   b. Formulation and design of product alternatives

      (1) Testing for product alternatives
      (2) Modification of products or processes

   c. Preproduction prototypes and models

     (1) Tools, dies, etc. for new technology
     (2) Pilot plants not capable of commercial production

   d. Engineering activity until product is ready for manufacture

  4. Exclusions from R&D

    a. Engineering during an early phase of commercial production
    b. Quality control for commercial production
    c. Troubleshooting during commercial production breakdowns
    d. Routine, ongoing efforts to improve products
    e. Adaptation of existing capability for a specific customer or other requirements
    f. Seasonal design changes to products
    g. Routine design of tools, dies, etc.
    h. Design, construction, startup, etc. of equipment except that used solely for R&D
    i. Legal work for patents or litigation
    j. Items a.–h. above are normally expensed but not as R&D; i. is capitalized

C. Elements of R&D costs

  1. Materials, equipment, and facilities

    a. If acquired for a specific R&D project and have no alternative use
    b. If there are alternative uses, costs should be capitalized

     (1) Charge to R&D as these materials, etc., are used

  2. Salaries, wages, and related costs
  3. Intangibles purchased from others are treated as materials, etc. in 1. above

    a. If capitalized, amortization is covered by APB 17

  4. R&D services **performed by others**
  5. A reasonable allocation of indirect costs

    a. Exclude general and administrative costs not clearly related to R&D

D. Accounting for R&D

  1. Expense R&D as incurred

E. Disclosure required on face of IS or notes

  1. Total R&D expensed per period

APB 10 Omnibus Opinion—1966 (ASC Topics 210, 605, 740)

A. ARB 43, Chapter 3B Working Capital

  1. Offsetting of liabilities and assets in the balance sheet is not acceptable unless a right of offset exists.
  2. Most government securities are not designed to be prepayment of taxes and thus may not be offset against tax liabilities. Only where an explicit prepayment exists may an offset be used.

FASB INTERPRETATION NO. 39 OFFSETTING OF AMOUNTS RELATED TO CERTAIN CONTRACTS

  A right of setoff exists when all of the following conditions are met: (a) each of the two parties to a contract owes the other determinable amounts, (b) the reporting entity has the right to set off the amount owed with the amount owed by the other entity, (c) the reporting entity intends to set off, and (d) the right of setoff is enforceable at law.

B. Installment method of accounting

Revenues should be recognized at the point of sale unless receivables are in doubt. The installment or cost recovery method may be used.

APB 23 Accounting for Income Taxes—Special Areas (ASC Topic 740—Income Taxes)
(Amended by SFAS 109)

A. Undistributed earnings of domestic subsidiaries

1. Inclusion of undistributed earnings in pretax accounting income of parent (either through consolidation or equity method) results in temporary difference.

   a. Tax effect may be based on assumptions such as

      (1) Earnings would be distributed currently as dividends or
      (2) Earnings would be distributed in form of capital gain.

B. Foreign subsidiaries are not required to accrue deferred taxes for undistributed earnings if sufficient evidence exists that subsidiary would reinvest the undistributed earnings indefinitely or remit them tax-free.

SFAS 109 (I27) Accounting for Income Taxes (ASC Topic 740—Income Taxes)

A. Establishes financial accounting and reporting requirements for income taxes resulting from an entity's activities during the current and preceding years.

1. Continues BS-oriented asset and liability approach consistent with SFAC 6.
2. Objectives

   a. Recognize taxes payable or refundable for current year.
   b. Recognize deferred tax liabilities and assets for future tax consequences of events previously recognized in financial statements or tax returns.

B. Basic principles

1. Recognize current tax liability or asset for estimated taxes payable or refundable on tax returns for current year
2. Measure and recognize deferred tax liability or asset using enacted tax rate(s) expected to apply to taxable income in periods in which the deferred tax assets and liabilities are expected to be realized or settled
3. Adjust measurement of deferred tax assets so as to not recognize tax benefits not expected to be realized
4. Deferred tax assets and liabilities are **not** discounted to reflect their present value

C. Measurement of Deferred Taxes

1. Temporary differences

   a. Difference between tax basis of asset or liability and its reported amount for financial accounting which results in taxable or deductible amounts in future years

      (1) Includes all timing differences
      (2) Includes tax-book differences in asset's bases

   b. Future effects

      (1) **Taxable amounts** are from temporary differences that will result in lower amounts of expense or higher amounts of revenue being reported on the tax return than are reported on the books in the future period.
      (2) **Deductible amounts** are from temporary differences that will result in higher amounts of expense or lower amounts of revenue being reported on the tax return than are reported on the books in the future period.

2. Deferred tax liability or asset measured each BS date

   a. Identify types and amounts of existing temporary differences **and** nature of each type of operating loss and tax credit carryforward and the remaining length of the carryforward period
   b. Measure total deferred tax liability for taxable temporary differences using the enacted applicable tax rate
   c. Measure total deferred tax asset for deductible temporary differences and operating loss carryforwards using the enacted applicable tax rate
   d. Measure deferred tax assets for each type of tax credit carryforward
   e. Reduce deferred tax assets by a valuation allowance, **if more likely than not** (a likelihood of more than 50%) that some or all of deferred tax asset will not be realized

      (1) All available evidence (positive and negative) should be considered to determine whether valuation allowance is needed.

D. Changes in Tax Rates

 1. Change in rates

 a. Change previously recorded amounts of deferred tax liabilities or assets
 b. Net adjustments shall be reflected in tax expense on continuing operations in period that includes enactment date.

E. Business Combinations

 1. Recognize deferred tax asset or liability for differences between assigned values and tax basis of assets and liabilities recognized in a purchase combination

F. Intraperiod Tax Allocation

 1. Allocate income tax expense or benefit for the period among continuing operations, extraordinary items, other comprehensive income, and items charged or credited to stockholders' equity

 a. In cases where there is only one item after continuing operations, portion of income tax expense (benefit) remaining after allocation to continuing operations is amount allocated to that item.
 b. In cases where there are two or more items after continuing operations, portion left after allocation to continuing operations is allocated among other items in proportion to their individual effects on income tax expense (benefit).

G. Financial Statement Presentation and Disclosure

 1. Balance sheet

 a. Report deferred tax liabilities and assets as current or noncurrent based on classification of related asset or liability
 b. Classify deferred tax liabilities or assets not related to an asset or liability (i.e., one related to a carryforward) according to the expected reversal date of the temporary difference
 c. For a taxpaying component of an enterprise and within a particular tax jurisdiction

 (1) All current deferred tax liabilities and assets should be offset and reported as a single amount
 (2) All noncurrent deferred tax liabilities and assets should be offset and reported as a single amount

 2. Must disclose the following components of the net deferred tax liability or asset:

 a. The total of all deferred tax liabilities
 b. The total of all deferred tax assets
 c. The total valuation allowance for deferred tax assets

 3. Additional disclosures

 a. Disclose any net change in the total valuation allowance
 b. Disclose the types of temporary differences, carryforwards, and carrybacks

 4. Income statement

 a. Components of tax expense attributable to continuing operations shall be disclosed in financial statements or notes. For example

 (1) Current tax expense or benefit
 (2) Deferred tax expense or benefit (exclusive of other components listed below)
 (3) Investment tax credits
 (4) Government grants (to the extent recognized as a reduction of income tax expense)
 (5) Benefits of operating loss carryforwards
 (6) Tax expense resulting from allocation of certain tax benefits either directly to contributed capital or to reduce goodwill or other noncurrent intangible assets of an acquired entity
 (7) Adjustments of a deferred tax liability or asset resulting from enacted changes in tax laws, rates, or status

 b. Variances between statutory and effective tax rates must be disclosed.

 (1) Public entities should disclose reconciliation using percentages or dollar amounts.
 (2) Nonpublic entities must disclose nature of significant reconciling items.

 c. Disclose amounts and expiration dates of operating loss and tax credit carryforwards **and** any portion of the deferred tax asset valuation allowance for which subsequently recognized tax benefits will be allocated to reduce intangible assets or directly reduce accumulated other comprehensive income.

BROAD TRANSACTIONS (ASC TOPIC 800)

SFAS 141(R) Business Combinations (ASC Topic 805—Business Combinations)

A. Scope

1. Applies to transactions or events that meet the definition of a business combination.
2. Does not apply to joint venture, acquisition of group of assets that are not a business, or combination of entities or businesses under common control.
3. The acquisition method is required for all business combinations.

B. Key terms

1. Acquiree—business of which the acquirer obtains control.
2. Acquirer—entity that obtains control of acquiree.
3. Acquisition date—date which acquirer obtains control.
4. Business—integrated set of activities and assets that are capable of being conducted and managed for the purpose of providing a return in the form of dividends, lower costs, or other economic benefits directly to investors or other owners, members, or participants.
5. Business combination—transaction or other event in which acquirer obtains control of one or more businesses.
6. Contingent consideration—obligation to transfer additional assets or equity interests to the former owners as part of the exchange for control of the acquiree if certain events or conditions occur.
7. Control is ownership of more than 50% of the voting stock.
8. Equity interest is an ownership interest.
9. Fair value is the price that would be received to sell an asset or paid to transfer a liability in an orderly transaction between market participants at the measurement date.
10. Goodwill—an asset representing the future economic benefit arising from other assets acquired in a business combination that are not individually identified and separately recognized.
11. Intangible asset lacks physical substance. For purposes of SFAS 141(R), intangible assets exclude goodwill.
12. Noncontrolling interest is the equity in a subsidiary not attributable directly or indirectly to a parent.

C. Application of the acquisition method.

1. Identify the acquirer (the entity that obtains control over the acquiree). Factors to consider

   a. The relative voting rights in the combined entity after the combination.
   b. The existence of a large minority voting interest in the combined entity when no other owner or organized group of owners has a significant voting interest.
   c. The composition of the governing body of the combined entity.
   d. The composition of the senior management of the combined entity.
   e. The terms of the exchange of equity securities.
   f. Examine the facts and circumstances.

2. Determine the acquisition date.

   a. Usually the date the acquirer legally transfers consideration and acquires the assets and liabilities of the acquiree.
   b. Usually the closing date.
   c. Examine facts and circumstances if necessary.

3. Recognize and measure the identifiable assets acquired, the liabilities assumed, and any noncontrolling interest in the acquiree.

   a. Assets, liabilities, and noncontrolling interest are measured at fair value.

4. Recognize and measure goodwill or gain from a bargain purchase.

   a. Consideration transferred includes

      (1) Assets transferred.
      (2) Liabilities incurred.
      (3) Equity interests issued by acquirer.
      (4) Contingent consideration.

   b. Goodwill

      (1) Defined as an asset representing the future economic benefits that arise from other assets acquired in a business combination that are not individually identified and separately recognized.

   (2) Calculated as the aggregate of the fair value of consideration given, plus the fair value of previously held interests, plus the fair value of noncontrolling interests, less the fair value of assets acquired.
   (3) Not considered an intangible asset.
   (4) Test for impairment using rules of SFAS 142.

c. Bargain purchase

   (1) Excess of the fair value of assets acquired over the aggregate of the fair value of consideration transferred, plus the fair value of previously held interests, plus the fair value of the noncontrolling interests.
   (2) Recognized as a gain in the current period.

5. Acquisition-related costs are expensed in the period incurred (finder's fees, advisory, legal, accounting, valuation, consulting, general administrative costs, and other professional fees).
6. Cost of registering and issuing debt securities are recognized in accordance with GAAP.

   a. For equity securities, net against the proceeds of the stock and reduce additional paid-in capital.
   b. Bond issue costs are treated as deferred charge and amortized on a straight-line over life of bond.

D. Exceptions to Recognition or Measurement Principles.

1. Provisional Amounts.

   a. Record for items that have incomplete information.
   b. Adjust during the measurement period.
   c. Measurement period ends when acquirer receives information or learns information is not available.
   d. Changes in provisional amounts recognized by retrospectively adjusting provisional amounts and making an adjustment to goodwill.
   e. After measurement period ends, changes are made as error corrections in accordance with SFAS 154.

2. Transferred assets

   a. Measured at fair value.
   b. Gain or loss is reported in earnings of the period.
   c. If acquirer retains control, then measure at carrying value.

3. Contingent consideration

   a. Measure at fair value at acquisition date.
   b. Changes in value are treated as changes in provisional amounts.
   c. After measurement date, changes in value are remeasured to fair value at each reporting date until contingency is resolved, with changes reported in earnings of the period.
   d. Contingent consideration classified as equity is not remeasured.

4. Lease classification.

   a. Leases are classified based on classification at inception of lease.
   b. If lease is modified at acquisition date, classify lease by its new terms.
   c. When acquiree is lessee in an operating lease, if terms are favorable, record an intangible asset apart from goodwill. If unfavorable, record a liability.
   d. If acquiree is lessor in operating lease, measure at fair value, and recognize a separate asset or liability if lease terms are favorable or unfavorable with regard to market terms.

5. Contingencies

   a. Categorize as contractual or noncontractual.
   b. Contractual contingencies recorded at fair value at acquisition date.
   c. Noncontractual contingencies are assessed as to whether it is more likely than not that the contingency gives rise to an asset or liability. If more likely than not, record a liability.
   d. May derecognize an asset or liability from the contingency only when the contingency is resolved.

6. Income taxes measured at acquisition date in accordance with SFAS 109.
7. Employee benefits measured at acquisition date.
8. Indemnification contracts (guarantees against loss). If seller indemnifies acquirer, an indemnification asset is recorded.
9. Reacquired rights recorded as intangible asset and amortized over remaining contract period.
10. Valuation allowances of the acquiree are not recorded.
11. Share-based payments

    a. If acquirer is required to replace, then the fair value of awards are part of consideration transferred.

    b. If acquirer voluntarily replaces, then fair value of awards is recognized in compensation cost in accordance with SFAS 123(R).

12. Assets held for sale are recorded at fair value less cost to sell, as provided by SFAS 144.

E. Disclosures in Notes to Financial Statements

1. Name and description of the acquiree.
2. Acquisition date.
3. Percentage of voting equity shares acquired.
4. Primary reasons for the business combination and how acquirer obtained control of acquiree.
5. Qualitative description of the factors that make up the goodwill recognized.
6. Acquisition-date fair value of total consideration transferred and the fair value of each major class of consideration including cash, other assets, business or subsidiary of the acquirer, liabilities, contingent consideration, and equity instruments (including the number of instruments issued and method of determining fair value).
7. For contingent consideration and indemnification assets, the amount recognized, a description of arrangement, basis for determining amount of payment, and an estimate of the range of outcomes.
8. The amounts recognized at the acquisition date for each major class of assets acquired and liabilities assumed.
9. For assets and liabilities arising from contingencies, the amounts recognized and the nature of recognized and unrecognized contingencies, together with a range of outcomes for the contingencies.
10. The total amount of goodwill expected to be deducted for tax purposes.
11. If segment information is reported, the amount of goodwill by reportable segment.
12. Transaction that are recognized separately from the business combination.
13. The gain recognized from bargain purchase and a reason for the gain.
14. The fair value of any noncontrolling interest in the acquiree at acquisition date, and the valuation techniques used to measure fair value of the noncontrolling interest.
15. If the business was achieved in stages, the acquisition-date fair value of the equity interest in the acquiree held immediately before the acquisition date, as well as the amount of gain or loss recognized as a result of remeasuring those securities to fair value.
16. If the acquirer is a public company, the amount of revenue and earnings of the acquiree since acquisition date that is included in the consolidated income statement. Also, supplemental pro forma information for revenue and earnings as if the combination had occurred at the beginning of the period, and pro forma comparative statements for the prior reporting period as if the combination had occurred in the beginning of the prior period.
17. If the acquisition occurs after the reporting date but before the financial statements are issued, the acquirer should make the disclosures of the business combination information listed above.
18. Any information that enables users of financial statements to evaluate the financial effects of adjustments recognized in the current reporting period related to business combinations that occurred in the current or previous period.
19. If accounting for a business combination is incomplete, the reason why it is incomplete, and the assets, liabilities, equity interests or items that are incomplete, and the nature and amount of any measurement period adjustments recognized during the period.
20. Any changes in a contingent consideration asset or liability, differences arising from settlement, and changes in the range of outcomes and reasons for changes.
21. A reconciliation of the carrying amount of goodwill at the beginning and end of the period as required by SFAS 142.

ARB 51 Consolidated Financial Statements (ASC Topic 810—Consolidation)

A. Consolidated statements present financial statements of a parent and subsidiaries, as if the group were a single company for the benefit of the parent's stockholders and creditors.

1. Substance (effectively a single entity) takes precedence over **legal form** (legally separate entities).
2. Consolidated financial statements result in **more meaningful presentation of financial position and operating results** than if separate statements were presented for the parent and subsidiary.

B. The general condition for consolidation is over 50% ownership of subsidiaries.

1. Theoretical condition is **control** of the subsidiaries.

    a. This is generally implicit in greater than 50% ownership.

2. Subsidiaries that are a temporary investment (in reorganization, in bankruptcy, etc.) should not be consolidated.
3. Large indebtedness to bondholders should not preclude consolidation.

FASB INTERPRETATION NO. 46 CONSOLIDATION OF VARIABLE INTEREST ENTITIES

Variable interest entities are entities that must be consolidated because they do not have sufficient funding to finance their future activities without the infusion of additional subordinated investment. Entities are presumed to be variable interest entities subject to consolidation if their equity is less than ten percent of total assets. To avoid consolidation of such entities, definitive evidence must be provided that they can fund their future activities without additional subordinated investment. Entities with equity of ten percent or more of total assets may also be a variable interest entity if it appears that the entity will not be able to fund its activities without obtaining additional subordinated investment. A variable interest entity is consolidated by the primary beneficiary, which is the enterprise that is obligated to fund the majority of the variable interest entity's expected losses if they occur, or will receive the majority of the residual returns if they occur, or both.

C. A difference in fiscal periods should not preclude consolidation.

1. Differences of three months are acceptable if one discloses material intervening events.
2. Differences in excess of three months should be consolidated on the basis of interim statements of the subsidiary.

D. Consolidation policy should be disclosed by headings or footnotes.
E. Intercompany balances and transactions should be eliminated in consolidated statements.

1. Intercompany gains and losses on assets remaining in the group should be eliminated (eliminate entire gross profit or loss even on transactions with minority interest subsidiaries).

F. Retained earnings of subsidiaries at the acquisition date should not appear in the consolidated statements.
G. When a parent purchases a subsidiary in several blocks of stock, the subsidiary's retained earnings should be determined by the step method (apply equity method to subsidiary retroactively).
H. When a subsidiary is purchased in midyear, subsidiary operations may be included in the consolidated income statement for the year and then the operating results prior to acquisition would be deducted.

1. As an alternative for a subsidiary purchased in midyear, postacquisition operations can be included in the consolidated income statement.
2. For midyear disposals, omit operations from the consolidated income statement and include equity in subsidiary's operations up to disposal date as a separate item in the income statement.

> **NOTE:** F. through H. pertain only to acquisitions accounted for as purchases per APB 16.

I. Sometimes combined, as distinguished from consolidated, financial statements are appropriate for commonly owned companies and are prepared when consolidated statements are not appropriate.

SFAS 94 Consolidation of All Majority-Owned Subsidiaries (ASC Topic 810—Consolidation)

A. Precludes use of parent company FS prepared for issuance to stockholders as FS of primary reporting entity
B. Requires consolidation of all majority-owned (ownerships, directly or indirectly, of more than 50% of outstanding voting shares of another company) subsidiaries

1. Unless control

   a. Temporary
   b. Not held by majority owner (e.g., subsidiary)

      (1) Is in legal reorganization or bankruptcy
      (2) Operates under foreign exchange restrictions, controls, or other governmentally imposed uncertainties

2. Even if

   a. Subsidiary's operations nonhomogeneous
   b. Large minority interest exists
   c. Subsidiary located in foreign country

SFAS 160 Noncontrolling Interests in Consolidated Financial Statements—An Amendment of ARB No. 51 (ASC Topic 810—Consolidation)

A. Scope—Applies to all entities that prepare consolidated financial statements except for not-for-profit organizations.
B. Classification of noncontrolling interest on the balance sheet.

1. Noncontrolling interest is classified as equity.
2. Noncontrolling interest is attributed its share of income or loss.

3. The amount of net income attributable to the parent and the noncontrolling interest must be presented on the face of the consolidated income statement.
4. Noncontrolling interest is attributed losses even if it results in a deficit balance.

C. Income Statement Disclosures

1. Consolidated net income includes net income attributed to the noncontrolling interest.
2. Consolidated comprehensive income includes comprehensive income attributed to the noncontrolling interest.

D. Changes in Ownership Interests

1. Accounted for as equity transaction.
2. No gain or loss recognized in net income or comprehensive income.
3. The carrying amount of the noncontrolling interest is adjusted to reflect change in ownership in subsidiary.
4. Difference between the fair value of consideration received or paid and amount by which controlling interest is adjusted is recognized in additional paid-in capital of the parent.

E. Deconsolidation

1. The parent recognizes a gain or loss in net income when subsidiary is deconsolidated.
2. Deconsolidation occurs as of the date parent ceases to have control.
3. Gain or loss on deconsolidation of the subsidiary is measured using the fair value of the noncontrolling equity investment.
4. Gain or loss is calculated as aggregate of (1) fair value of consideration received PLUS (2) fair value of retained noncontrolling investment, PLUS (3) carrying amount of noncontrolling interest in former subsidiary LESS (4) the carrying amount of the former subsidiary's assets and liabilities.
5. If parent deconsolidates by a nonreciprocal transfer to owners (such as spin-off), then APB Opinion 29 applies for nonmonetary transactions.
6. Disclosures for deconsolidation

   a. Amount of gain or loss.
   b. Portion of gain or loss related to remeasurement of retained investment in the former subsidiary.
   c. The caption in the income statement in which gain or loss is recognized.

F. Disclosures in Consolidated Financial Statements
   A parent with a less than wholly owned subsidiary shall disclose the following:

1. On the face of the financial statements, the amounts of consolidated net income and consolidated comprehensive income attributed to the parent and the noncontrolling interests.
2. In the notes or on the face of the income statement, amounts attributable to the parent for the following:

   a. Income from continuing operations.
   b. Discontinued operations.
   c. Extraordinary items.

3. In either the consolidated statement of changes in equity or the notes to the financial statements, a reconciliation at the beginning and end of the period carrying amount of total equity, equity attributable to the parent, and equity attributable to the noncontrolling interest. The reconciliation must disclose separately

   a. Net income.
   b. Transactions with owners, contributions from and distributions to owners.
   c. Each component of other comprehensive income.
   d. In the notes to financial statements, a schedule showing effects of changes in parent's ownership interest in subsidiary.

SFAS 167—Amendments to FASB Interpretation No. 46(R) (ASC Topic 810)

A. Eliminates the quantitative-based risks and rewards calculation for determining if an enterprise has a controlling financial interest in a variable interest entity
B. Approach focuses on identifying which entity has the power to direct the activities of a variable interest entity that can significantly impact the entity's performance and

1. The obligation to absorb the losses of the entity, or
2. The rights to receive benefits from the entity

C. Amends FASB Interpretation 46(R) to require additional disclosures about an enterprise's involvement in variable interest entities

SFAS 133 Accounting for Derivative Instruments and Hedging Activities (ASC Topic 815—Derivatives and Hedging)

A. Foundation principles for SFAS 133

1. Financial instruments should be measured at fair value (See SFAS 157 for fair value measurements)
2. Changes in fair value, or gains and losses, should be reported in comprehensive income or in current earnings
3. Hedging instrument criteria

    a. Fair value hedge

        (1) Recognized asset or liability
        (2) Unrecognized firm commitment

    b. Cash flow hedge

        (1) Recognized asset or liability
        (2) Forecasted transaction

    c. Foreign currency hedge

        (1) Unrecognized firm commitment
        (2) Available-for-sale security
        (3) Forecasted transaction
        (4) Net investment in foreign operations

B. Definition of derivative instrument

1. Contract must contain one or more underlyings and one or more notional amounts
2. Contract requires no initial net investment, or a smaller initial net investment than required for contracts with an expected similar response to market changes
3. Terms that require or permit net settlement, net settlement by means outside the contract, or delivery of an asset that results in a position no substantially different from net settlement

C. Embedded derivative instruments

1. Financial instruments which contain features which separately meet the definition of a derivative instrument
2. Three criteria used to determine whether the instrument should be separated from the host contract

    a. The embedded derivative instrument meets the definition of a derivative instrument (e.g., strips)
    b. The hybrid instrument is not regularly recorded at fair value
    c. The economic characteristics and risks of the embedded instrument are not clearly and closely related to the economic characteristics of the host contract

3. An election can be made not to bifurcate the instrument. See outline of SFAS 155.

D. Hedging instruments criteria

1. Sufficient documentation must be provided at the beginning of the process

    a. Identify the objective and strategy of the hedge
    b. Identify the hedging instrument and the hedged item
    c. Identify how the effectiveness of the hedge will be assessed on an ongoing basis

2. The hedge must be highly effective throughout its life

    a. Measured every three months and whenever earnings or financial statements are reported

E. Fair value hedges

1. Specific criteria

    a. Hedged item must be a specific portion of a recognized asset/liability or an unrecognized firm commitment
    b. An unrecognized firm commitment must be binding on both parties, specific with respect to all significant terms, and contain a nonperformance clause that makes performance probable.

2. Gains and losses will be recognized in current earnings

F. Cash flow hedges

  1. Specific hedges

    a. The change in cash flows must be the same, or linked, for the hedge's asset/liability and the hedging instrument
    b. A forecasted transaction's cash flows must be considered probable
    c. A forecasted series of transactions must share the same risk exposure

  2. Accounting for

    a. Effective portion reported in other comprehensive income
    b. Ineffective portion reported in earnings

G. Foreign currency hedge

  1. Unrecognized firm commitment

    a. Accounted for as fair value hedge if requirements met

  2. Available-for-sale securities

    a. Accounted for as fair value hedge if requirements met and

      (1) Cannot be traded on exchange denominated in investor's functional currency
      (2) Dividends must be denominated in same foreign currency as expected sale proceeds

  3. Foreign currency denominated forecasted transactions

    a. Accounted for as cash flow hedges

  4. Net investments in foreign operations

    a. Must meet hedge effectiveness criterion
    b. Change in fair value recorded in other comprehensive income

H. Forward exchange contracts

  1. Mark to market using the forward exchange rate at each reporting date
  2. Recognize changes in fair value in current earnings

I. Disclosures

  1. Objectives and strategies for achieving financial instruments
  2. Context to understand the instrument
  3. Risk management policies
  4. A list of hedged instruments
  5. Disclosure of fair value of financial instruments required when practicable to estimate fair value

SFAS 138 Accounting Certain Derivative Instruments and Certain Hedging Activities: (ASC Topic 815— Derivatives and Hedging)

A. Amended four specific items in SFAS 133

  1. Normal purchases and sales exception extended

    a. Applies to contracts that require delivery of nonfinancial assets to be used in the normal operations of an entity
    b. These contracts need not be accounted for as derivative instruments unless the contracts require net settlements of gains or losses

  2. Redefined the interest rate risk

    a. Permits a benchmark interest rate to be designated as the hedged risk in a hedge of interest rate risk
    b. This benchmark presents the risk-free rate and is the interest rate on direct Treasury obligations of the US government, or the London Interbank Offered Rate (LIBOR)
    c. A company's actual interest rate above the benchmark interest rate reflects that company's credit risk which is separate from the risk-free rate of interest

  3. Hedging recognized foreign currency denominated assets or liabilities

    a. Permits a recognized foreign currency denominated asset or liability, for which a foreign currency transaction gain or loss is recognized in earnings under the provisions of SFAS 52, to be the hedged item in a fair value or cash flow hedge.

    b. The foreign currency denominated asset or liability continues to be remeasured using the spot exchange rates to compute the transaction gain or loss for the period.

    c. In the case of cash flow hedges, the transaction gain or loss would be offset by an equal amount of reclassified from other comprehensive income. In the case of fair market value hedges, the hedging instrument would be a hedge of both interest rate risk and foreign exchange rate risk. The foreign currency denominated asset or liability would be adjusted for changes in fair value attributable to changes in foreign interest rates before remeasurement at the spot exchange rate. This eliminates the differences on earnings related to the use of different measurement criteria for the hedged item and the hedging instrument

4. Hedging with intercompany derivatives

    a. Permits derivative instruments entered into with another member of the consolidated group to qualify as hedging instruments in the consolidated financial statements if those internal derivatives are offset by unrelated third-party contracts on a net basis

    b. Previously, the internal derivative had to be offset on an individual derivative contract basis with a third party

SFAS 149 Amendment of Statement 133 on Derivative Instruments and Hedging Activities (ASC Topic 815)

A. This statement clarifies under what circumstances a contract with an initial net investment meets the characteristics of a derivatives. It also clarifies when a derivative contains a financing component, and amends the definition of an underlying to conform to language used in FASB Interpretation 45, and amends other existing pronouncements.

B. This statement amended existing pronouncements to clarify that the use of the term "expected cash flows" does not have the same meaning as the term is defined and used in SFAC 7, *Using Cash Flow Information and Present Value in Accounting Measurements*.

SFAS 155 Accounting for Certain Hybrid Financial Instruments (ASC Topic 815—Derivatives and Hedging)

SFAS 155, issued in February 2006, amends SFAS 133. SFAS 155 changes the accounting for hybrid financial instruments that would normally be required to be bifurcated.

A. An election can be made **not** to bifurcate the instrument

B. The election is irrevocable and is made on an instrument-by-instrument basis

C. Changes in fair value of the hybrid instruments are recognized in earnings each year

D. Balance sheet disclosure may be presented in one of two ways

1. As a separate line item for the fair value and non–fair value instruments, **or**
2. As an aggregate amount of all hybrid instruments with the amount of the hybrid instruments at fair value shown in parentheses

E. Initial adoption of SFAS 155 requires the difference between the total carrying amount of the components of the bifurcated hybrid instruments and the fair value of the hybrid instruments to be recognized as a cumulative effect adjustment to the beginning balance of retained earnings

F. Notes to financial statements should indicate the gross gains and losses of the cumulative effect adjustments. Prior periods are not restated

G. SFAS 155 does not apply to hedging instruments

SFAS 161 Disclosures about Derivative Instruments and Hedging Activities—An Amendment of FASB Statement No. 133 (ASC Topic 815—Derivatives and Hedging)

A. Additional disclosures required for derivative instruments

1. How and why an entity uses derivatives
2. How derivatives and hedges are accounted for
3. How derivatives and hedges affect the financial position, financial performance, and cash flows

B. Type of information disclosed

1. Risk exposure such as interest rate, credit, foreign exchange rate, and price risk
2. Purpose of instrument, (i.e., risk management or other)
3. Location and fair value amounts of derivative instruments reported in balance sheet
4. Location and amounts recognized on the income statement

SFAS 157 Fair Value Measurements (ASC Topic 820—Fair Value Measurement and Disclosures)

A. Fair value is the price that would be received to sell an asset or paid to transfer a liability in an orderly transaction between market participants at the measurement date (an exit price).

B. Applying the fair value measurement approach involves

1. Identify the asset or liability to be measured
2. Determine the principal or most advantageous market *(highest and best use)*
3. Determine the valuation premise *(in-use or in-exchange)*
4. Determine the appropriate valuation technique *(market, income, or cost approach)*
5. Obtain inputs for valuation *(Level 1, Level 2, or Level 3)*
6. Calculate the fair value of the asset

C. Assumes the asset or liability is sold or transferred in either the principal market or most advantageous market

1. Principal market has greatest volume and level of activity
2. Most advantageous market minimizes price received for the asset or minimizes amount paid to transfer liability
3. Market participants have the following characteristics:

    a. Be independent of the reporting entity (not related parties)
    b. Knowledgeable
    c. Able to transact
    d. Willing to transact (motivated, but not compelled to transact)

4. Do not adjust prices for costs to sell
5. If location is attribute of asset or liability, price is adjusted for costs necessary to transport asset or liability to market

D. Assumes the highest and best use of the asset

1. Highest and best use maximizes the value of asset or group of assets
2. Highest and best use must be

    a. Physically possible
    b. Legally permissible
    c. Financially feasible at measurement date

3. Highest and best use determines the valuation premise used

E. Valuation Premise

1. In use:

    a. Asset provides maximum value by using it with other assets as a group
    b. Valuation based on price to sell asset assuming it is used with other assets

2. In-exchange:

    a. Asset provides maximum value on stand-alone basis
    b. Valuation based on price to sell the asset stand-alone

F. Valuation Techniques

1. Market approach

    a. Uses prices and relevant information from market transaction for identical or comparable assets or liabilities

2. Income approach

    a. Uses present value techniques to discount cash flows or earnings to present value amounts

3. Cost approach

    a. Relies on current replacement cost to replace the asset with a comparable asset, adjusted for obsolescence.

G. Levels of Input for Valuation

1. Use fair value hierarchy to prioritize inputs to valuation techniques
2. Fair value hierarchy is Level 1, Level 2, and Level 3
3. Inputs should be based on lowest level of input (i.e., highest priority is lowest level)
4. Level 1 inputs—lowest level, highest priority

    a. Uses quoted prices (unadjusted prices) from active markets
    b. Examples are quotes from NYSE, quotations from dealer markets

5. Level 2 inputs

   a. Inputs that are directly or indirectly observable other than quoted prices of Level 1.
   b. Examples are quoted prices for similar assets or liabilities, observable inputs such as yield curves, bank prime rates, interest rates, volatilities, loss severities, credit risks, and default rates.

6. Level 3 inputs

   a. Unobservable inputs
   b. May only be used if observable inputs are not available
   c. May reflect reporting entity's own assumptions about market
   d. Based on best information available

H. Change in Valuation Premise or Technique

1. Treat as change in estimate on a prospective basis
2. Requirements of SFAS 154 do not apply

I. Disclosures

1. For assets measured at fair value on recurring basis

   a. Valuation techniques used
   b. Identify level of hierarchy or measurements used
   c. The amount of significant transfers between Level 1 and Level 2 and reason for the transfer along with the entity's transfer policy.
   d. If Level 2 or Level 3 using significant other observable inputs and unobservable inputs respectively, the valuation techniques and the inputs used.
   e. If Level 3 used, the effect of measurements on earnings for the period, purchases, sales, issuances, and settlements, and any transfers in or out of Level 3 are disclosed

2. For assets and liabilities measured at fair values on a nonrecurring basis (i.e., impaired assets), identify the following:

   a. The fair value measurements used
   b. The reasons for the measurements
   c. The level within the hierarchy
   d. For Level 2 or Level 3, the inputs and valuation techniques used to measure fair value.
   e. A description of nonfinancial assets with a current use differing from the highest and best use.

SFAS 107 Disclosures about Fair Value of Financial Instruments (ASC Topic 825—Financial Instruments)

A. Statement requires entities to disclose the fair value of financial instruments, both assets and liabilities whether recognized or not recognized in the statement of financial position, for which it is practicable to estimate fair value.

1. Applies to all entities
2. Does not change any recognition, measurement, or classification requirements for financial instruments in financial statements
3. Fair value disclosures of financial instruments previously prescribed by GAAP meet the requirements of this statement.

B. Financial instruments include

1. Cash
2. Evidence of ownership interest in an entity, or
3. A contract that both

   a. Imposes contractual obligation on one entity to deliver cash or another financial instrument to second entity or to exchange financial instruments on potentially unfavorable terms with second entity, and
   b. Conveys contractual right to second entity to receive cash or another financial instrument from first entity or to exchange financial instruments on potentially favorable terms with first entity

C. Fair value of a financial instrument is defined by SFAS 157 as "the price that would be received to sell an asset or paid to transfer a liability in an orderly transaction between market participants at the measurement date."

D. Standard lists a number of areas for which the disclosure requirements are not applicable, including pensions and other deferred compensation arrangements and leases.

E. Disclosure Requirements

1. When practicable (i.e., without incurring excessive costs), an entity must disclose the fair value of financial instruments in either the body of the financial statements or in the accompanying notes.

   a. Disclosure must include the method(s) and significant assumptions used in estimating fair value

      (1) Quoted market price is generally the best estimate of fair value.
      (2) If quoted market price is not available, management must estimate fair value based upon similar financial instruments or valuation techniques.
      (3) No disclosure is required for trade receivables and payables when carrying amount approximates fair value.

   b. Disclosure must distinguish between financial instruments held or issued for

      (1) Trading purposes
      (2) Purposes other than trading

2. If estimation of the fair value of financial instruments is not practicable, entity must disclose

   a. Information pertinent to estimating the fair value (i.e., the carrying amount, effective interest rate, and maturity), and
   b. The reason why estimation of fair value is not practicable.

3. Derivative financial instruments may not be combined, aggregated or netted with nonderivative or other derivative financial instruments.
4. If financial instruments disclosed in more than one area in FS, one note must contain a summary table cross-referencing the location of the other instruments.
5. Disclosure of concentrations of credit risk of all financial instruments

   a. Disclose all significant concentrations of credit risk from **all** financial instruments, whether from an individual counterparty or groups of counterparties.
   b. Group concentrations exist if a number of counterparties are engaged in similar activities and have similar economic characteristics such that they would be similarly affected by changes in conditions.
   c. Disclose for each significant concentration

      (1) Information about the (shared) activity, region, or economic characteristics
      (2) The amount of accounting loss the entity would incur should any party to the financial instrument fail to perform according to the terms of the contract and the collateral or security, if any, is of no value.
      (3) The entity's policy of requiring collateral or security, the entity's access to that collateral or security, and the nature and brief description of the collateral or security.

SFAS 159 The Fair Value Option for Financial Assets and Financial Liabilities—including an amendment of FASB Statement 115 (ASC Topic 825—Financial Instruments)

A. Scope

1. Applies to

   a. Financial assets and financial liabilities (includes available-for-sale, held-to-maturity, and equity method investments, and liabilities)
   b. Firm commitments that involve financial instruments
   c. Written loan commitments
   d. Nonfinancial insurance contracts that can be settled by paying third party
   e. Warranties that can be settled by paying third party
   f. Host financial instruments resulting from separation of embedded nonfinancial derivative instrument from a nonfinancial hybrid instrument

2. Does **not** apply to consolidations, pensions, share-based payments, stock options, OPEB, exit or disposal activities, leases, and financial instruments that are component of equity

B. Definitions

1. **Fair value**—The price that would be received to sell an asset or paid to transfer a liability in an orderly transaction between market participants at the measurement date
2. **Financial asset**—Cash, evidence of an ownership interest in an entity or a contract that conveys a right to receive cash or another financial instrument or to exchange other financial instruments on potentially favorable items
3. **Financial liability**—A contract that imposes an obligation to deliver cash or another financial instrument to exchange other financial instruments on potentially favorable terms

4. **Firm commitment**—An agreement, usually legally enforceable, that specifies all significant terms, including quantity, fixed price, and timing of transaction. The agreement includes a disincentive for nonperformance that makes performance probable

C. Fair Value Option (FVO)

1. Can elect to measure financial asset or financial liability at fair value
2. Must elect to use fair value method on specific items

   a. Can be elected on instrument-by-instrument basis

      (1) If multiple advances to one borrower for single contract, fair value options is applied to larger balance and not each individual advance
      (2) If fair value applied to investment that can use equity method, it must be applied to all interests in same entity (i.e., debt and equity)
      (3) If applied to insurance contracts, must be applied to all claims and obligations for that contract

   b. Is irrevocable
   c. Must apply to entire instrument, not a portion of instrument

3. Report unrealized gains and losses in earnings
4. Classification on statement of cash flows—rules of FAS 95 apply

D. Election Dates

1. The date an eligible item is first recognized
2. The date the entity enters into a firm commitment
3. When financial assets cease to qualify for fair value treatment due to specialized accounting rules, can elect to use fair value (i.e. equity method for investments)
4. Percentage of ownership change and can no longer consolidate
5. Modifications of debt

E. Financial Statement Disclosure Requirements—two methods permissible

1. Present aggregate fair value and non–fair value amounts in same line, with amounts measured at fair value parenthetically disclosed
2. Present two separate line items for fair value and non–fair value carrying amounts

F. Disclosures to Notes to Financial Statements—Balance Sheet

1. Management's reasons for electing fair value option for each item or group of items
2. If fair value option is elected for some but not all items

   a. Description of similar items and reason for partial election
   b. Information to understand how group of similar items relates to individual line items on balance sheet

3. Information to understand how line items relate to major categories of assets and liabilities presented in SFAS 157 fair value disclosure requirements
4. Aggregate carrying amount of items included in each line item in balance sheet that are not eligible for fair value option
5. Difference between aggregate fair value and aggregate unpaid principal balance of

   a. Loans and long-term receivables using FVO
   b. Long-term debt instruments using FVO
   c. Aggregate fair value of loans that are 90 days or more past due
   d. Aggregate fair value of loans in nonaccrual status if interest is recognized separately from changes in fair value
   e. Difference between aggregate fair value and aggregate unpaid principal balance for loans 90 days or more past due

6. For investments that would have used equity method, the information required by APB 18 for equity method

G. Required Disclosures for Income Statement Items

1. Amounts of gains/losses included in earnings for each line item in balance sheet
2. Description of how interest and dividends are measured and reported on the income statement
3. For loans and receivables held as assets

   a. Estimated amount of gains/losses in earnings that is attributed to changes in credit risk
   b. How the gains/losses were determined

4. For liabilities affected by credit risk

     a. Amount of gains/losses attributable to changes in credit risk
     b. Qualitative information about reasons for changes
     c. How gains/losses were determined

5. Methods and significant assumptions to estimate fair value

H. Transition Requirements

1. Report as cumulative effect adjustment to opening balance of retained earnings
2. Remove balance sheet effects such as

     a. Amortized deferred costs, fees, premiums, discounts
     b. Valuation allowances (such as allowance for loan losses)
     c. Accrued interest

SFAS 52 Foreign Currency Translation (ASC Topic 830—Foreign Currency Matters)

A. Primary objectives of foreign currency translation

1. Should provide information disclosing effects of rate changes on enterprise cash flows and equity
2. Should also provide information in consolidated statements as to financial results and relationships of individual consolidated entities measured in their respective functional currencies in accordance with US GAAP

B. Functional currency is the currency of the primary economic environment in which a foreign entity operates (i.e., the environment in which the entity generates and spends cash).

1. A foreign entity's assets, liabilities, revenues, expenses, gains, and losses shall be measured in that entity's functional currency.
2. The functional currency could be the currency of the country in which the entity operates if the entity is a self-contained unit operating in a foreign country.

> **EXAMPLE**
>
> An entity (1) whose operations are not integrated with those of the parent, (2) whose buying and selling activities are primarily local, and (3) whose cash flows are primarily in the foreign currency.

3. There may be several functional currencies if there are many self-contained entities operating in different countries.
4. The functional currency might be the US dollar if the foreign entity's operations are considered to be a direct and integral part of the US parent's operations.

> **EXAMPLE**
>
> An entity (1) whose operations are integrated with those of the parent, (2) whose buying and selling activities are primarily in the parent's country and/or the parent's currency, and (3) whose cash flows are available for remittance to the parent.

5. Functional currency for a foreign entity, once determined, shall be used consistently unless it is clear that economic facts and circumstances have changed.

     a. If a change is made, do not restate previously issued financial statements

6. If a foreign entity's bookkeeping is not done in the functional currency, the process of converting from the currency used for the books and records to the functional currency is called remeasurement.

     a. Remeasurement is intended to produce the same result (e.g., balances for assets, expenses, liabilities, etc.) as if the functional currency had been used for bookkeeping purposes.
     b. In highly inflationary economies (cumulative inflation over a 3-year period is > 100%), the remeasurement of a foreign entity's financial statements shall be done as if the functional currency were the reporting currency (i.e., the US dollar).

7. The functional currency (if not the US dollar) is translated to the reporting currency (assumed to be the US dollar) by using appropriate exchange rates (see item C. below).

     a. If the functional currency is the US dollar, there is no need to translate (if the books and records are maintained in US dollars).

C. The translation of foreign currency FS (those incorporated in the FS of a reporting enterprise by consolidation, combination, or the equity method of accounting) should use a current exchange rate if the foreign currency is the functional currency.

1. Assets and liabilities—exchange rate at the balance sheet date is used to translate the functional currency to the reporting currency
2. Revenues (expenses) and gains (losses)—exchange rates when the transactions were recorded shall be used to translate from the functional currency to the reporting currency

   a. Weighted-averages for exchange rates may be used for items occurring numerous times during the period.

3. Translation adjustments will result from the translation process if the functional currency is a foreign currency.

   a. Translation adjustments are not an element of net income of the reporting entity.
   b. Effects of current translation adjustments are reported in other comprehensive income for the period with the accumulated amount reported as part of the reporting entity's owners' equity and labeled accumulated other comprehensive income.
   c. Accumulated translation adjustments remain part of the owners' equity until the reporting entity disposes of the foreign entity.

      (1) In period of disposal, these adjustments are reported as part of the gain (loss) on sale or liquidation.

D. **Foreign currency transactions** are those which are denominated (fixed) in other than the entity's functional currency.

1. Receivables and/or payables which are fixed in a currency other than the functional currency may result in transaction gains (losses) due to changes in exchange rates after the transaction date.
2. Transaction gains or losses generally are reported on the income statement in the period during which the exchange rates change.
3. Deferred taxes may have to be provided for transaction gains or losses that are realized for income tax purposes in a time period different than that for financial reporting.

E. **A forward exchange contract** represents an agreement to exchange different currencies at a specified future rate and at a specified future date. (Accounting and reporting now specified by SFAS 133)

F. FS disclosures required

1. Aggregate transaction gain (loss) that is included in the entity's net income
2. Analysis of changes in accumulated translation adjustments which are reported as part of other comprehensive income
3. Significant rate changes subsequent to the date of the financial statements including effects on unsettled foreign currency transactions

---

FASB INTERPRETATION NO. 37 ACCOUNTING FOR TRANSLATION ADJUSTMENTS UPON SALE OF PART OF AN INVESTMENT IN A FOREIGN ENTITY

If an enterprise sells part of its ownership interest in a foreign entity, a pro rata portion of the accumulated translation adjustment component of equity attributable to that investment shall be recognized in measuring the gain (loss) on the sale.

SFAS 34 Capitalization of Interest Cost (ASC Topic 835—Interest)

A. Interest costs, when material, incurred in acquiring the following types of assets, shall be capitalized:

1. Assets constructed or produced for a firm's own use

   a. Including construction by others requiring progress payments

2. Assets intended for lease or sale that are produced as discrete projects

   a. For example, ships and real estate developments

3. But not on

   a. Routinely produced inventories
   b. Assets ready for their intended use
   c. Assets not being used nor being readied for use
   d. Land, unless it is being developed (e.g., as a plant site, real estate development, etc.)

   4. The objective of interest capitalization is to

     a. Reflect the acquisition cost of assets
     b. Match costs to revenues in the period benefited

   5. Capitalized interest shall be treated as any other asset cost for depreciation and other purposes.
   6. Required interest cost disclosures

     a. Total interest cost incurred
     b. Interest capitalized, if any

B. Amount of interest to be capitalized

   1. Conceptually, the interest that would have been avoided if the expenditures had not been made
   2. Based on the average accumulated expenditures on the asset for the period

     a. Includes payment of cash, transfer of other assets, and incurring interest-bearing liabilities
     b. Reasonable approximations are permitted

   3. Use the interest rates incurred during period

     a. First, the rates on specific new borrowings for the asset
     b. Second, a weighted-average of other borrowings

       (1) Use judgment to identify borrowings

   4. Interest cost capitalized in any period cannot exceed interest cost incurred in that period.

     a. On a consolidated basis for consolidated statements
     b. On an individual company basis for individual company statements

   5. Capitalized interest should be compounded.

C. Interest capitalization period

   1. Begins when all the following three conditions are present:

     a. Asset expenditures have been made
     b. Activities to ready asset for intended use are in progress

       (1) Includes planning stages

     c. Interest cost is being incurred

   2. If activities to ready asset for intended use cease, interest capitalization ceases

     a. Not for brief interruptions that are externally imposed

   3. Capitalization period ends when asset is substantially complete

     a. For assets completed in parts, interest capitalization on a part of the asset ends when that part is complete
     b. Capitalize all interest on assets required to be completed in entirety until entire project is finished

   4. Interest capitalization continues if capitalized interest raises cost above market values

     a. Apply impairment accounting per SFAS 144

APB 12 Omnibus Opinion—1967 (ASC Topics 310, 360, 505, 710, 835)

A. Allowance or contra accounts (allowance for bad debts, accumulated depreciation, etc.) should be deducted from assets or groups of assets with appropriate disclosure.

B. Disclosure of depreciable assets should include

   1. Depreciation expense for the period
   2. Balances of major classes of depreciable assets by nature or function
   3. Accumulated depreciation either by major class or in total
   4. Description of method(s) of depreciation by major classes of assets

C. Changes in the separate shareholder equity accounts in addition to retained earnings and changes in number of equity securities must be disclosed in the year of change

   1. In separate statements
   2. Or the financial statements
   3. Or the notes

APB 21 Interest on Receivables and Payables (ASC Topic 835—Interest)

Accounting for receivables and payables whose face value does not approximate their present value

A. Applies to receivables and payables except

1. Normal course of business receivables and payables maturing in less than one year
2. Amounts not requiring repayment in the future (will be applied to future purchases or sales)
3. Security deposits and retainages
4. Customary transactions of those whose primary business is lending money
5. Transactions where interest rates are tax affected or legally prescribed (e.g., municipal bonds and tax settlements)
6. Parent-subsidiary transactions
7. Estimates of contractual obligations such as warranties

B. Notes exchanged for cash are recorded at their present value. Present value equals the cash paid/received. If face value of note ≠ cash paid/received, difference is a discount/premium.

1. If unstated **rights or privileges** are exchanged in issuance of note for cash, adjust cash payment to obtain present value of the note and unstated rights.

C. Notes exchanged for goods or services in arm's-length transaction are recorded at face amount (presumption that face amount = present value).

1. Presumption not valid if note is

   a. Noninterest-bearing
   b. Stated interest rate is unreasonable
   c. Face amount of the note differs materially from sales price of goods or services

2. When presumption not valid, record note at fair value of goods or services

   a. Compute **implicit** rate (rate that discounts the future value [face of note plus cash interest, if any] to fair value of goods and services) for interest expense/revenue recognition

3. When no established market price for goods and services exists, record note at its fair market value.

   a. Compute **implicit** rate (rate that discounts the future value [face of note plus cash interest, if any] to fair [present] value of note) for interest expense/revenue recognition

4. When no fair market value exists for either the goods and services or the note, record note at approximation of market value.

   a. Use **imputed** rate to compute present value of (and discount on) note.
   b. Imputed rate should approximate the rate an independent borrower and lender would negotiate in a similar transaction. Consider

      (1) Credit standing of issuer
      (2) Restrictive covenants
      (3) Collateral
      (4) Payment and other terms
      (5) Tax consequences to buyer and seller
      (6) Market rate for sale or assignment
      (7) Prime rate
      (8) Published rates of similar bonds
      (9) Current rates charged for mortgages on similar property

D. Discount or premium should be amortized by the interest method (constant rate of interest on the amount outstanding).

1. Other methods (e.g., straight-line) may be used if the results are not materially different from those of the interest method.

E. Discount or premium should be netted with the related asset or liability and **not** shown as separate asset or liability.

1. Issue costs should be reported as deferred charges.

SFAS 13 Accounting for Leases (ASC Topic 840—Leases)

Applies to agreements for use of property, plant, and equipment, but not natural resources and not for licensing agreements such as patents and copyrights.

The major issue in accounting for leases is whether the benefits and risks incident to ownership have been transferred from lessor to lessee. If so, the lessor treats the lease as a sale or financing transaction and the lessee treats it as a purchase. Otherwise, the lease is accounted for as a rental agreement. These different treatments recognize the **substance** of a transaction rather than its **form;** that is, what is legally a lease may be effectively the same as or similar to an installment purchase by the lessee and a sale or financing transaction by the lessor.

The following terms are given specific definitions for the purpose of SFAS 13:

Bargain purchase option—A provision allowing the lessee the option of purchasing the leased property for an amount that is sufficiently lower than the expected fair value of the property at the date the option becomes exercisable. Exercise of the option must appear reasonably assured at the inception of the lease.

Contingent rentals—Rentals that represent the increases or decreases in lease payments which result from changes in the factors on which the lease payments are based occurring subsequent to the inception of the lease.

Estimated economic life of lease property—The estimated remaining time which the property is expected to be economically usable by one or more users, with normal maintenance and repairs, for its intended purpose at the inception of the lease. This estimated time period should not be limited by the lease term.

Estimated residual value of leased property—The estimated fair value of the leased property at the end of the lease term.

Executory costs—Those costs such as insurance, maintenance, and taxes incurred for leased property, whether paid by the lessor or lessee. Amounts paid by a lessee in consideration for a guarantee from an unrelated third party of the residual value are also executory costs. If executory costs are paid by the lessor, any lessor's profit on those costs is considered the same as executory costs.

Fair value of leased property—The price that would be received to sell the property in an orderly transaction between market participants at the measurement date.

When the lessor is a manufacturer or dealer, the fair value of the property at the inception of the lease will ordinarily be its normal selling price net of volume or trade discounts.

When the lessor is not a **manufacturer or dealer,** the fair value of the property at the inception of the lease will ordinarily be its costs net of volume or trade discounts.

Implicit interest rate—The discount rate that, when applied to the minimum lease payments, excluding that portion of the payments representing executory costs to be paid by the lessor, together with any profit thereon, and the unguaranteed residual value accruing to the benefit of the lessor, causes the aggregate present value at the beginning of the lease term to be equal to the fair value of the leased property to the lessor at the inception of the lease.

Inception of the lease—The date of the written lease agreement or commitment (if earlier) wherein all principal provisions are fixed and no principal provisions remain to be negotiated.

Incremental borrowing rate—The rate that, at the inception of the lease, the lessee would have incurred to borrow over a similar term (i.e., a loan term equal to the lease term) the funds necessary to purchase the leased asset.

Initial direct costs—(See outline of SFAS 91)

Lease term—The fixed, noncancelable term of the lease plus all renewal terms when renewal is reasonably assured.

> **NOTE:** The lease term should not extend beyond the date of a bargain purchase option.

Minimum lease payments—For the **lessee:** The payments that the lessee is or can be required to make in connection with the leased property. Contingent rental guarantees by the lessee of the lessor's debt, and the lessee's obligation to pay executory costs are excluded from minimum lease payments. If the lease contains a bargain purchase option, only the minimum rental payments over the lease term and the payment called for in the bargain purchase option are included in minimum lease payments. Otherwise, minimum lease payments include the following:

1. The minimum rental payments called for by the lease over the lease term
2. Any guarantee of residual value at the expiration of the lease term made by the lessee (or any party related to the lessee), whether or not the guarantee payment constitutes a purchase of the leased property. When the lessor has the right to require the lessee to purchase the property at termination of the lease for a certain or determinable amount, that amount shall be considered a lessee guarantee. When the lessee agrees to make up any deficiency below a stated amount in the lessor's realization of the residual value, the guarantee to be included in the MLP is the stated amount rather than an estimate of the deficiency to be made up.
3. Any payment that the lessee must or can be required to make upon **failure to renew or extend** the lease at the expiration of the lease term, whether or not the payment would constitute a purchase of the leased property

For the **lessor:** The payments described above plus any guarantee of the residual value or of the rental payments beyond the lease term by a third party unrelated to either the lessee or lessor (provided the third party is financially capable of discharging the guaranteed obligation).

Unguaranteed residual value—the estimated residual value of the leased property exclusive of any portion guaranteed by the lessee, by any party related to the lessee, or any party unrelated to the lessee. If the guarantor is related to the lessor, the residual value shall be considered as unguaranteed.

A. Classification of leases by lessees. Leases that meet one or more of the following criteria are accounted for as capital leases; all other leases are accounted for as operating leases:

1. Lease transfers ownership (title) to lessee during lease term.
2. Lease contains a bargain purchase option.
3. Lease term is 75% or more of economic useful life of property.
4. Present value of minimum lease payments equals 90% or more of FV of the leased property.

    a. Present value is computed with lessee's incremental borrowing rate, unless lessor's implicit rate is known and is less than lessee's incremental rate (then use lessor's implicit rate).

    b. FMV is cash selling price for sales-type lease; lessor's cost for direct financing of lease. (If not recently purchased, estimate FV)

> **NOTE:** 3. and 4. do not apply if lease begins in last 25% of asset's life.

B. Classification of leases by lessors

1. Sales-type leases provide for a manufacturer or dealer profit (i.e., FV of leased property is greater than lessor cost or carrying value).

    a. Sales-type leases must meet one of the four criteria for lessee capital leases (A.1. to A.4. above) and **both** of the following two criteria:

        (1) Collectibility is reasonably predictable, and

        (2) No important uncertainties regarding costs to be incurred by lessor exist, such as unusual guarantees of performance. Note estimation of executory expense such as insurance, maintenance, etc., is not considered.

2. Direct financing leases must meet same criteria as sales-type leases (just above) but do not include a manufacturer's or dealer's profit.
3. Operating leases are all other leases that have not been classified as sales-type, direct financing, or leveraged.

C. Lease classification is determined at the inception of the lease.

1. If changes in the lease are subsequently made which change the classification, the lease generally should be considered a new agreement and reclassified and accounted for as a new lease. Exercise of renewal options, etc., are not changes in the lease. However, if the terms of a capital lease are modified such that it should be reclassified as an operating lease, the lessee should account for it under the sale-leaseback provisions of SFAS 98
2. Changes in estimates (e.g., economic life or residual value) or other circumstances (e.g., default) do not result in a new agreement but accounts should be adjusted and gains or losses recognized.
3. An important goal of SFAS 13 was to achieve **symmetry** in lease accounting (i.e., an operating lease for the lessee will be an operating lease for the lessor) and likewise for capital leases.

D. Accounting and reporting by lessees

1. Record capital leases as an asset and liability

    a. Leased asset shall not be recorded in excess of FV. If the present value of the lease payments is greater than the FV, the leased asset and related liability are recorded at FV and the effective interest rate is thereby increased.

    b. Recognize interest expense using the effective interest method.

    c. If there is a transfer of ownership or a bargain purchase option, the asset's depreciation/amortization period is its economic life. Otherwise, depreciate/amortize assets to the expected residual value at the end of the lease term.

2. Rent on operating leases should be expensed on a straight-line basis unless another method is better suited to the particular benefits and costs associated with the lease.
3. Contingent rentals are reported as rent expense in the period incurred.
4. Disclosures by lessees include

    a. General description of leasing arrangement including

        (1) Basis of computing contingent payments

        (2) Existence and terms of renewal or purchase options and escalation clauses

        (3) Restrictions imposed by the lease agreement such as limitations on dividends and further leasing arrangements

    b. Capital lease requirements

        (1) Usual current/noncurrent classifications

        (2) Depreciation/amortization should be separately disclosed

(3) Future minimum lease payments in the aggregate and for each of the five succeeding fiscal years with separate deductions being made to show the amounts representing executory cost and interest
(4) Total minimum sublease rentals to be received in the future under noncancelable subleases
(5) Total contingent rental actually incurred for each period for which an income statement is presented

c. Operating leases which have initial or remaining noncancelable term > 1 year

(1) Future minimum lease payments in the aggregate and for each of the five succeeding fiscal years
(2) Total minimum sublease rentals to be received in the future under noncancelable subleases
(3) All operating leases—rent expense of each IS period

    (a) Present separate amounts for minimum rentals, contingent rentals, and sublease rentals
    (b) Rental payments for leases with a term of a month or less may be excluded

E. Accounting and reporting by lessors

1. Sales-type leases

a. Lease receivable is charged for the gross investment in the lease (the total net minimum lease payments plus the unguaranteed residual value). Sales is credited for the present value of the minimum lease payments.
b. Cost of sales is the carrying value of the leased asset plus any initial direct costs less the present value of the unguaranteed residual value. Note that in a sales-type lease, initial direct costs are deducted in full in the period when the sale is recorded. Unearned interest income is credited for the difference between the gross investment and the sales price.
c. Recognize interest revenue using the effective interest method
d. At the end of the lease term, the balance in the receivable account should equal the amount of residual value guaranteed, if any.
e. Contingent rental payments are reported as income in the period earned.

2. Direct financing leases

a. Accounting is similar to sales-type lease except that no manufacturer's or dealer's profit is recognized.
b. Lease receivable is charged for the gross investment in the lease, the asset account is credited for the net investment in the lease (cost to be acquired for purpose of leasing) and the difference is recorded as unearned income.
c. Initial direct costs are recorded in a separate account. A new effective interest rate is computed that equates the minimum lease payments and any unguaranteed residual value with the combined outlay for the leased asset and initial direct costs. The initial direct costs and unearned lease revenue are both amortized so as to produce a constant rate of return over the life of the lease.
d. The remaining requirements are the same as those for the sales-type lease.

3. Operating leases

a. Leased property is to be included with or near PP&E on the BS, and lessor's normal depreciation policies should be applied.
b. Rental revenue should be recognized on a straight-line basis unless another method is better suited to the particular benefits and costs associated with the lease.
c. Initial direct costs should be deferred and allocated over the lease term in proportion to the recognition of rental revenue.

F. Related-party leases shall be accounted for as unrelated-party leases except when terms have been significantly affected by relationship.
G. Sale-leasebacks

1. Legally two separate transactions
2. Lessee (seller) accounts for the gain (loss) as follows:

a. Loss (when FV < Book value) on the sale should be recognized immediately.
b. Gain treatment

(1) Seller relinquishes the right to substantially all of the remaining use of the property sold (PV of reasonable rentals < 10% of fair value of asset sold)—then separate transactions, and entire gain is recognized.
(2) Seller retains more than a minor part, but less than substantially all of the remaining use (PV of reasonable rentals are > 10% but < 90% of fair value of asset sold)—then gain on sale is recognized to the extent of the excess of gain over the present value of minimum lease payments (operating) or the recorded amount of the leased asset (capital).
(3) Seller retains right to substantially all of the remaining use—then entire gain on sale is deferred.

    c. If the gain is deferred and lease is accounted for as

       (1) Capital lease—defer and amortize gain over lease term using same method and life used for depreciating/amortizing cost of leased asset

         (a) Deferral and amortization of the gain are required because the sale and leaseback are components of a single transaction and are interdependent.

       (2) Operating lease—recognize gain on straight-line basis

         (a) Treat as a reduction of rent expense.

3. Lessor records as a purchase of asset to be leased and as a direct financing or operating lease

---

FASB TECHNICAL BULLETIN 85-3 ACCOUNTING FOR OPERATING LEASES WITH SCHEDULED RENT INCREASES

    SFAS 13 requires lessees or lessors to recognize rent expense or rental income for an operating lease on a straight-line basis. Certain operating lease agreements specify scheduled rent increases over the lease term. The effects of these scheduled rent increases, which are included in minimum lease payments under SFAS 13, should also be recognized by lessors and lessees on a straight-line basis over the lease term.

SFAS 98 Accounting for Leases (ASC Topic 840—Leases)

> **NOTE:** The outline below includes those changes that relate to all leases. The remainder of SFAS 98 deals with real estate leases that are not outlined since they are not expected to be tested on the exam.

A. Lease term, as redefined, includes

1. All periods covered by bargain renewal options
2. All periods for which failure to renew the lease imposes a penalty
3. All periods during which a loan, directly or indirectly related to the leased property, is outstanding
4. All periods covered by ordinary renewal options preceding the exercisable date of a bargain purchase option
5. All periods representing renewals or extensions of the lease at the lessor's option

APB 29 Accounting for Nonmonetary Transactions (ASC Topic 845—Nonmonetary Transactions)

A. Definitions

1. **Monetary assets and liabilities.** "Assets and liabilities whose amounts are fixed in terms of units of currency by contract or otherwise. Examples are cash, short- or long-term accounts and notes receivable in cash, and short- or long-term accounts and notes payable in cash."
2. **Nonmonetary assets and liabilities.** "Assets and liabilities other than monetary ones. Examples are inventories; investments in common stocks; property, plant, and equipment; and liabilities for rent collected in advance."
3. **Exchange.** "A reciprocal transfer between an enterprise and another entity that results in the enterprise's acquiring assets or services or satisfying liabilities by surrendering other assets or services or incurring other obligations. A reciprocal transfer of a nonmonetary asset shall be deemed an exchange only if the transferor has no substantial continuing involvement in the transferred asset such that the usual risks and rewards of ownership of the asset are transferred."
4. **Nonreciprocal transfer.** "Transfer of assets or services in one direction, either from an enterprise to its owners (whether or not in exchange for their ownership interests) or another entity or from owners or another entity to enterprise. An entity's reacquisition of its outstanding stock is an example of a nonreciprocal transfer."
5. **Productive assets.** "Assets held for or used in the production of goods or services by the enterprise. Productive assets include an investment in another entity if the investment is accounted for by the equity method but exclude an investment not accounted for by that method."

B. APB 29 does **not** apply to

1. Business combinations
2. Transfer of nonmonetary assets between companies under common control
3. Acquisition of nonmonetary assets with capital stock of an enterprise
4. Stock dividends and splits, issued or received
5. A transfer of assets for an equity interest
6. A transfer of a financial asset under SFAS 140

C. APB 29 does apply to

   1. Nonreciprocal transfers with owners. Examples are distributions to stockholders

     a. Dividends
     b. To redeem capital stock
     c. In liquidation
     d. To settle rescission of a business combination

   2. Nonreciprocal transfer with other than owners. Examples are

     a. Contribution to charitable institutions
     b. Contribution of land by governmental unit to a business

   3. Nonmonetary exchange

D. Nonmonetary transactions should generally be accounted for as are monetary transactions.

   1. Cost of a nonmonetary asset is the fair value of the asset surrendered to obtain it.

     a. The difference between fair value and book value is a gain or loss.
     b. Fair value of asset received, if clearer than that of asset given, should value transaction.

   2. Recorded (book) value shall be used for exchanges in which

     a. Fair value is not determinable
     b. Exchange transaction is to facilitate sales to customers
     c. Exchange transaction lacks commercial substance

   3. A nonmonetary transaction has commercial substance if the entity's future cash flows are expected to significantly change as a result of the exchange. Tax cash flows that arise solely because the tax business purpose is based on achieving a specified financial reporting result are not considered in cash flows.

E. If a nonmonetary exchange, which is recorded at book value, contains boot received, the portion of the gain recognized should be limited to the ratio [Boot ÷ (Boot received + FMV of asset received)] times the gain.

   1. Firm paying boot should not recognize gain.

F. Liquidation distributions to owners should not be accounted for at fair value if a gain results (loss may be recognized).

   1. Use historical cost
   2. Other nonreciprocal distributions to owners should be accounted for at fair value if fair value

     a. Is objectively measurable
     b. Would be clearly realizable if sold

G. Fair value should be determined in accordance with SFAS 157, *Fair Value Measurements*

   1. If one party could elect to receive cash instead of monetary asset, the amount of cash is evidence of fair value

H. Nonmonetary transaction disclosures should include

   1. Nature of the transactions
   2. Basis of accounting
   3. Gains and losses recognized

FASB INTERPRETATION NO. 30 ACCOUNTING FOR INVOLUNTARY CONVERSIONS OF NONMONETARY ASSETS TO MONETARY ASSETS

When involuntary conversions of nonmonetary assets (e.g., fixed assets) to monetary assets (e.g., insurance proceeds) occur, the difference between the assets' cost and the monetary assets received should be reported as a gain or loss. If an unknown amount of monetary assets are to be received in a later period, gain (loss) is estimated per SFAS 5. Could be extraordinary per APB 30.

SFAS 153 Exchanges of Nonmonetary Assets—An Amendment of APB Opinion No. 29 (ASC Topic 845— Nonmonetary Transactions)

A. Requires that nonmonetary exchanges should be measured based on fair values unless certain conditions are met. It removes the distinction of "similar" and "dissimilar" assets found in APB 29 and outlines exceptions to fair value treatment. The statement also clarifies when APB 29 does not apply. The provisions of the statement are to be applied prospectively.

B. A nonmonetary exchange is a reciprocal transfer only if the transferor has no substantial continuing involvement in the asset, and the risks and rewards of ownership are transferred.

C. APB 29, *Accounting for Nonmonetary Exchanges,* does not apply to

1. Business combination accounted for under SFAS 141
2. Transfer of nonmonetary assets between companies under common control
3. Acquisition of nonmonetary assets or services on the issuance of capital stock
4. Stock issued or received in stock dividends and stock splits
5. A transfer of assets in exchange for an equity interest in entity
6. A pooling of assets in a joint undertaking to find, develop, or produce gas or oil
7. Exchange of a part of an operating interest owned for a part of another operating interest owned by another party
8. Transfers of financial assets within the scope of SFAS 140

D. Measure exchange based on fair value unless

1. Fair value is not determinable
2. It is an exchange transaction to facilitate sales to customers
3. The transaction lacks commercial substance

E. Commercial Substance

1. A nonmonetary change has commercial substance if the entity's future cash flows are expected to be significantly changed as a result of the exchange of assets.

   a. Configuration (risk, timing, and amount) of future cash flows differs significantly from that of the asset transferred.
   b. Entity-specific value of the asset differs from the entity-specific value of asset transferred, and that difference is significant in relation to fair values exchanged. Entity specific value can be computed per SFAC 7 by using expectations about use

2. If transaction has commercial substance, the exchange is measured at fair value.
3. If transaction lacks commercial substance, measure based on recorded amount of nonmonetary asset relinquished.
4. Cash flows from tax effect are not considered in determining if the transaction has commercial substance.

ARB 43—Chapter 1A Rules[5] Adopted by Membership (ASC Topics 310, 505, 605, and 850)

Four rules recommended by the Committee on Cooperation with Stock Exchanges in 1934. The last rule is from another 1934 Institute committee.

1. Profit is realized at the point of sale unless collection is not reasonably assured.
2. Capital (paid-in) surplus should not be charged with losses or expenses, except in quasi reorganizations.
3. Receivables from officers, employees, and affiliates must be separately disclosed.
4. Par value of stock issued for assets cannot be used to value the assets if some of the stock is subsequently donated back to the corporation.

APB 18 The Equity Method for Investments (ASC Topics 323, 325, 850)

A. The equity method should be used for corporate joint ventures.
B. The equity method should be applied to investments where less than 50% ownership is held but the investor **can exercise significant influence over operating and financing policies of the investee.**

1. Twenty percent (20%) or more ownership should lead to presumption of substantial influence, unless there is evidence to the contrary.
2. Conversely, less than 20% ownership leads to the presumption of no substantial influence unless there is evidence to the contrary.
3. The 20% test should be based on voting stock outstanding and disregard common stock equivalents.
4. The following procedures should be used in applying the equity method:

   a. Intercompany profits should be eliminated.
   b. Difference between cost and book value of net assets acquired should be accounted for per SFAS 141 and 142.
   c. The investment account and investor's share of investee income should be presented as single amounts in investor statements with the exception of d. below.
   d. Investor's share of discontinued operations, extraordinary items, cumulative effects of accounting changes, and prior period adjustments of investee should be so presented in statements of investor.

   e. Investee capital transactions should be accounted for as are subsidiary capital transactions in consolidated statements.

   f. Gains on sale of investment are the difference between selling price and carrying value of investment.

   g. When investee and investor fiscal periods do not coincide, use most recent investee statement and have consistent time lag.

   h. Losses, not temporary in nature, of investment value should be recognized by investor.

   i. Investor's share of investee loss should not be recorded once investment account is written to zero. Subsequent income should be recognized after losses not recognized are made up.

   j. Investor's share of investee's earnings should be computed after deducting investee's cumulative preferred dividends whether declared or not.

   k. If an investor's holding falls below 20%, discontinue applying the equity method but make no retroactive adjustment.

   l. When an investor's holding increases from a level less than 20% to a level equal to or greater than 20%, the investment account and retained earnings of the investor should be adjusted retroactively to reflect balances as if the equity account had been used. This is accounted for like a prior period adjustment.

5. Statements of investors applying the equity method should disclose

   a. Investees and percentages held

      (1) Accounting policies followed
      (2) Treatment of goodwill, if any

   b. Aggregate market value of investment (not for subsidiaries)

   c. When investments are material to investor, summarized information of assets, liabilities, and results of operations of investee may be necessary

   d. Conversion of securities, exercise of warrants, or issuances of investee's common stock which significantly affects investor's share of investee's income

---

FASB INTERPRETATION NO. 35 CRITERIA FOR APPLYING THE EQUITY METHOD OF ACCOUNTING FOR INVESTMENTS IN COMMON STOCK. Interprets APB 18.

Investors owning between 20 and 50% of an investee may **not** be able to exercise significant influence over the investee's operating and financial policies. The presumption of significant influence stands until overcome by evidence to the contrary, such as: (1) opposition by the investee, (2) agreements under which the investor surrenders shareholder rights, (3) majority ownership by a small group of shareholders, (4) inability to obtain desired information from the investee, (5) inability to obtain representation on investee board of directors, etc. Whether contrary evidence is sufficient to negate the presumption of significant influence is a matter of judgment requiring a careful evaluation of all pertinent facts and circumstances, in some cases over an extended period of time. Application of this interpretation resulting in changes to or from the equity method shall be treated per APB 18, paras 19l and 19m.

FASB INTERPRETATION NO. 1 ACCOUNTING CHANGES RELATED TO THE COST OF INVENTORY

Changes in the cost composition of inventory is an accounting change and must conform to APB 20, including justification for the change. Preferably should be based on financial reporting objectives rather than tax-related benefits.

SFAS 57 Related-Party Disclosures (ASC Topic 850—Related-Party Disclosures)

A. Definitions

1. **Affiliate**—Party is controlled by another enterprise that controls, or is under common control with another enterprise, directly or indirectly

2. **Control**—Power to direct or cause direction of management through ownerships contract, or other means

3. **Immediate family**—Family members whom principal owners or management might control/influence or be controlled/influenced by

4. **Management**—Persons responsible for enterprise objectives who have policy-making and decision-making authority

   a. For example, board of directors, chief executive and operating officers, and vice-presidents
   b. Includes persons without formal titles

5. **Principal owners**—Owners of more than 10% of a firm's voting interests

   a. Includes known beneficial owners

6. **Related parties**—Affiliates, equity method investees, employee benefit trusts, principal owners, management or any party that can significantly influence a transaction

B. FS shall include disclosures of material transactions between related parties except

1. Compensation agreements, expense allowances, and other similar items in the ordinary course of business
2. Transactions which are eliminated in the preparation of consolidated/combined FS

C. Disclosures of material transactions shall include

1. Nature of relationship(s)
2. Description of transaction(s), including those assigned zero or nominal amounts
3. Dollar amounts of transactions for each income statement period and effect of any change in method of establishing terms
4. Amounts due to/from related parties, including terms and manner of settlement

D. Representations concerning related-party transactions shall not imply that terms were equivalent to those resulting in arm's-length bargaining unless such statement can be substantiated.
E. When a **control** relationship exists, disclose such relationship even though no transactions have occurred.

ARB 43— Chapter 7A Quasi Reorganization (ASC Topic 852)

Describes what is permitted before and after quasi reorganization.

A. Procedure in readjustment

1. A clear report should be made to shareholders to obtain consent for the proposed restatements of assets and shareholders' equity.
2. Write-down of assets should not go below fair value.
3. If potential losses exist, provide for maximum probable loss.
4. When determined, amounts should be written off first to retained earnings and then to capital surplus.

B. Procedure after readjustment

1. After readjustment, accounting should be similar to that appropriate for a new company
2. A new, dated retained earnings account should be created

   a. Dated for ten years to indicate when the reorganization occurred.

SFAS 165—Subsequent Events (ASC Topic 855)

A. Scope—applies to accounting and disclosure for subsequent events not addressed in other GAAP
B. Defines subsequent events as transactions that occur after the balance sheet date but before financial statements are issued or available to be issued

1. Two types of subsequent events

   a. Recognized subsequent events are conditions that existed as of the balance sheet date
   b. Unrecognized subsequent events are conditions that did not exist as of the balance sheet date

C. Effects of recognized subsequent events should be recognized at the balance sheet date (warranty estimates, litigation settlement, and bankruptcy of client with receivables)
D. Effects of nonrecognized subsequent events should be disclosed in a footnote if the financial statements would be misleading if not disclosed
E. Entity must disclose the date through which the subsequent events have been evaluated and the date the financial statements were issued or available to be issued

SFAS 166—Accounting for Transfers of Financial Assets—An Amendment of FASB Statement No. 140 (ASC Topic 860)

A. Modifies SFAS 140 and eliminates the concept of a qualifying special-purpose entity
B. Limits the portions of financial assets that are eligible for derecognition

SFAS 140 Accounting for Transfers and Servicing of Financial Assets and Extinguishment of Liabilities (ASC Topic 860—Transfers and Servicing)

A. Provides accounting and reporting standards for transfers and servicing of financial assets and extinguishment of liabilities

B. Transfer of Assets

1. Necessary conditions to qualify as a sale

   a. Transferred assets have been isolated from the transferor or its creditors,
   b. Transferee has the unconstrained right to pledge or exchange the transferred assets, and
   c. Transferor does not maintain effective control over the transferred assets through

      (1) An agreement that obligates the transferor to repurchase or redeem them before their maturity, or
      (2) The ability to unilaterally cause the holder to return specific assets
      (3) An agreement that requires the transferor to repurchase the assets at a favorable price

2. Upon any transfer of assets, the transferor shall

   a. Initially recognize and measure at fair value the servicing assets and servicing liabilities that require recognition
   b. Allocate the previous carrying amount between the assets sold and the interests that continue to be held by the transferor based on relative fair values at the date of transfer
   c. Continue to carry in its balance sheet any interest it continues to hold in the transferred assets

3. Upon any completion of a transfer of assets which satisfies the conditions of a sale, the transferor shall

   a. Derecognize all assets sold
   b. Recognize all assets obtained and liabilities incurred in consideration as sale proceeds
   c. Initially measure at fair value assets obtained and liabilities incurred in a sale
   d. Recognize in earnings any gain (loss) on sale

4. Upon any completion of a transfer of assets which satisfies the conditions of a sale, the transferee shall

   a. Recognize all assets obtained and liabilities incurred at fair value

5. If transfer of assets does not meet the criteria for a sale, the transfer shall be accounted for as a secured borrowing with pledge of collateral

C. Servicing Assets and Liabilities

1. Recognize and initially measure at fair value a servicing asset or servicing liability if enter into a servicing contract in any of the following situations:

   a. Transfer of the servicer's financial assets that meets the requirements for sale accounting
   b. Transfer of the servicer's financial assets to a qualifying SPE in a guaranteed mortgage securitization in which transferor retains the securities and classifies them as available-for-sale or trading securities
   c. An acquisition or assumption of an obligation that does not relate to the financial assets of the servicer or its consolidated affiliates

2. If entity transfers financial assets to a qualified SPE in a guaranteed mortgage securitization and transferor retains all securities and classifies them as held-to-maturity securities, may either recognizing the servicing assets or servicing liabilities separately or report them with the asset being serviced

3. Measure servicing assets and servicing liabilities with one of two methods

   a. Amortization method

      (1) Initially record at fair value
      (2) Amortize in proportion to and over the period of estimated net servicing income or net servicing loss
      (3) Assess for impairment or increased obligation based on fair value.

   b. Fair value method

      (1) Initially record at fair value
      (2) Measure at fair value at each reporting date
      (3) Report changes in fair value in earnings in the period in which the change occurs

4. Election must be made for each class of servicing assets and servicing liabilities
5. Once an election is made to use the fair value method, election cannot be reversed
6. Report servicing assets and servicing liabilities measured at fair value separately on the balance sheet from amortized assets in one of two ways

   a. Display separate line items for amounts valued at fair value and amounts measured by amortization method, **or**
   b. Present aggregate amounts for all servicing assets and liabilities, and disclose parenthetically the amount that is measured in fair value that is included in the aggregate amount

D. Financial Assets Subject to Prepayment

1. Shall be measured like investments in debt securities classified as available-for-sale or trading

E. Secured Borrowing and Collateral

1. Pledge

   a. Debtor grants a security interest in certain assets
   b. Collateral is transferred to the secured party

2. Accounting for noncash collateral

   a. Debtor to separate asset on balance sheet into an encumbered asset section if secured party has right to sell or repledge collateral
   b. Secured party recognizes the proceeds from sale and obligation to return collateral if it sells collateral pledged to it
   c. Debtor defaults under terms of agreement and is no longer entitled to redeem the pledged asset

      (1) Derecognize the pledged asset
      (2) Secured party recognizes collateral as an asset at fair value
      (3) If collateral already sold, secured party derecognizes its obligation to return collateral.

F. Extinguishment of Liabilities

1. Debtor shall derecognize a liability when it has been extinguished

   a. Debtor pays the creditor and is relieved of its obligation for the liability
   b. Debtor is legally released from being obligor under the liability, either judicially or by the creditor.

G. Required Disclosures

1. Collateral

   a. Policy for requiring collateral or other security due to repurchase agreements or securities lending transactions
   b. Carrying amount and classification of pledged assets as collateral that are not reclassified and separately reported in the balance sheet
   c. The fair value of collateral that can be sold or repledged and information about the sources and uses of that collateral

2. Extinguished debt

   a. General description of transaction
   b. Amount of debt that was considered extinguished at end of period

3. Description of assets set aside for satisfying scheduled payments of a specific obligation
4. Nonestimable fair value of assets

   a. Description of the assets or liabilities
   b. The reasons why it is not practicable to estimate the assets or liabilities

5. For all servicing assets and servicing liabilities

   a. Management's basis for determining its classes
   b. Description of risks, the instruments used to mitigate income statement effect of changes in fair value (Quantitative information, including fair value at beginning and end of period is encouraged but not required)
   c. Amount of contractually specified servicing fees, late fees, and ancillary fees for each period on income statement, with description of where each amount is reported in income statement

6. For servicing assets and servicing liabilities measured at fair value

   a. For each class, the activity including

      (1) Beginning and ending balances
      (2) Additions
      (3) Disposals
      (4) Changes in fair value from changes in valuation inputs or assumptions used, other changes in fair value
      (5) Other changes that affect balance and description of changes

   b. Description of the valuation techniques used to estimate fair value, with qualitative and quantitative information about assumptions used in the model

7. For servicing assets and servicing liabilities amortized

   a. For each class, the activity including

      (1) Beginning and ending balances
      (2) Additions
      (3) Disposals
      (4) Amortization
      (5) Application of valuation allowance to adjust carrying value
      (6) Other than temporary impairments
      (7) Other changes that affect balance and description of changes

   b. For each class, the fair value at the beginning and end of period if practicable to estimate the value
   c. Description of the valuation techniques used to estimate fair value, with qualitative and quantitative information about assumptions used in the model
   d. The risk characteristics of the underlying financial assets used to stratify servicing assets for measuring impairment
   e. The activity by class in any valuation allowance for impairment of servicing assets, including beginning and ending balances, additions charged, recoveries made, and write-downs charged against the allowance for each period

8. Transfer of securitized financial assets accounted for as a sale

   a. Accounting policies for measuring the retained interest
   b. Characteristics of securitizations and the gain (loss) from sale
   c. Key assumptions used in measuring the fair value of retained interests at time of securitization
   d. Cash flows between the securitization SPE and the transferor

9. Retained interests in secured financial assets

   a. Accounting policies for subsequently measuring retained interests
   b. Key assumptions used in subsequently measuring fair value of retained interests
   c. Sensitivity analysis or stress test showing hypothetical effect of unfavorable variations on the retained interest's fair value, including limitations of analysis
   d. Securitized assets

      (1) Total principal outstanding, portion derecognized, and portion that continues to be recognized
      (2) Delinquencies at end of period
      (3) Credit losses, net of recoveries

SFAS 156 Accounting for Servicing of Financial Assets (ASC Topic 860—Transfers and Servicing)

SFAS 156, issued in March 2006, amends SFAS 140. It provides that an election may be made to use the fair value method to value servicing assets and servicing liabilities. Election must be made for each class of servicing assets and servicing liabilities. Once the election is made, it cannot be reversed. SFAS 156 allows balance sheet disclosure to be presented in one of two ways: either displayed as separate line items for amounts valued at fair value and amounts measured by the amortization method, **or** by presenting aggregate amounts for all servicing assets and liabilities with a parenthetical disclosure for the amount that is measured using fair value. Additional footnote disclosures are required for all servicing assets, with separate disclosures for servicing assets measured at fair value and servicing assets measured by the amortization method.

See the outline of SFAS 140, paragraphs B, C, and G.

INDUSTRY (ASC TOPIC 900)

SFAS 7 Accounting and Reporting by Development Stage Companies (ASC Topic 915—Development Stage Entities)

A. A company, division, component, etc., is in the development stage if

   1. Substantially all efforts are devoted toward establishing the business, or
   2. Principal operations are underway but have not produced significant revenues

B. Example activities of development stage companies

   1. Financial planning
   2. Raising capital
   3. Exploring or developing natural resources

4. R&D
5. Establishing sources of supply
6. Acquiring property, plant, equipment, etc.
7. Personnel recruitment and training
8. Developing markets
9. Production start-up

C. No special accounting standards apply to development stage companies.

1. Report revenue in the income statement as in normal operations
2. Expense costs as one would for a company in normal operations
3. Capitalize costs as one would for a company in normal operations

   a. Determine cost recoverability within entity for which statements are being prepared

D. Development stage company statements include

1. A balance sheet with cumulative net losses termed "deficit accumulated during development stage"
2. An income statement with revenues and expenses for both current period and cumulative expenses and revenues from the inception of the development stage
3. A statement of cash flows for both current period and cumulative amounts from inception
4. Statement of owner's investment including

   a. Dates of issuance and number of shares, warrants, etc.
   b. Dollar amounts must be assigned to each issuance

      (1) Dollar amounts must be assigned for noncash consideration

   c. Dollar amounts received for each issuance or basis for valuing noncash consideration

5. Identification of statements as those of a development stage company
6. During the first period of normal operations, notes to statements should disclose that company was, but is no longer, in the development stage

SFAS 45 Accounting for Franchise Fee Revenue (ASC Topic 952—Franchisors)

A. Definitions

1. **Franchisee**—Party who has been granted business rights
2. **Franchisor**—Party who grants business rights
3. **Area franchise**—Agreement transferring franchise rights within a geographical area permitting the opening of a number of franchise outlets
4. **Continuing franchise fee**—Consideration for continuing rights granted by the agreement (general or specific) during its life
5. **Franchise agreement**—Essential criteria

   a. Contractual relation between franchisee and franchisor
   b. Purpose is distribution of a product, service, or entire business concept
   c. Resources contributed by both franchisor and franchisee in establishing and maintaining the franchise
   d. Outline of specific marketing practices to be followed
   e. Creation of an establishment that will require and support the full-time business activity of the franchisee
   f. Both franchisee and franchisor have a common public identity

6. **Initial franchise fee**—Consideration for establishing the relationship and providing some initial services
7. **Initial services**—Variety of services and advice (e.g., site selection, financing and engineering services, advertising assistance, training of personnel, manuals for operations, administration and recordkeeping, bookkeeping and advisory services, quality control programs)

B. Franchise fee revenue from individual sales shall be recognized when all material services or conditions relating to the sale have been substantially performed or satisfied by the franchisor.

1. Substantial performance means

   a. Franchisor has no remaining obligation or intent to refund money or forgive unpaid debt
   b. Substantially all initial services have been performed
   c. No other material conditions or obligations exist

2. If large initial franchise fee is required and continuing franchise fees are small in relation to future services, then portion of initial franchise fee shall be deferred and amortized over life of franchise.

C. Continuing franchise fees shall be reported as revenue as fees are earned and become receivable from the franchise. Related costs shall be expensed as incurred.

D. Direct franchise costs shall be deferred until related revenue is recognized.

1. These costs should not exceed anticipated revenue less estimated additional related costs.

E. Disclosure of all significant commitments and obligations that have not yet been substantially performed are required

1. Notes to the FS should disclose whether the installment or cost recovery method is used.
2. Initial franchise fees shall be segregated from other franchise fee revenue if significant.

SFAS 116 Accounting for Contributions Received and Contributions Made (ASC Topic 958—Not-for-Profit Entities)

Establishes accounting standards for contributions received or made for all types of entities, not-for-profit, and business enterprises.

A. Contributions—defined

Contributions can be defined as an unconditional promise to give cash or other assets to an entity. A cancellation of a liability is also considered a contribution.

B. Contributions received (donee accounting)

1. Shall be capitalized by the donee at FMV of the item and recognized as revenue in period received.
2. Contributions with donor imposed restrictions shall be reported as restricted revenues or gains unless the restrictions are met in the same reporting period.
3. Receipts of unconditional promises to give the payments due in the future shall be reported as restricted support unless the donor intends the funds to be used for current operations.
4. Not-for-profit organizations shall recognize the expiration of donor-imposed restrictions as they expire.

C. Contributions made (donor accounting) shall be recognized at FMV as expense in period the item is donated

1. Donation expense should be classified under other expense on the income statement.
2. If difference exists between the FMV and book value of the item, then gain or loss on disposal will be recognized.

SFAS 117 Financial Statements of Not-for-Profit Organizations (ASC Topic 958—Not-for-Profit Entities)

Establishes the reporting standards for the general-purpose external financial statements of not-for-profit organizations.

A. A complete set of financial statement for a not-for-profit organization shall include

1. A statement of financial position
2. A statement of activities
3. A statement of cash flows
4. Accompanying notes

B. Voluntary health and welfare organizations shall also include a statement of functional expenses

C. The statement of financial position provides relevant information bout liquidity, financial flexibility, and the interrelationship of the organization's assets and liabilities

1. Assets and liabilities should be aggregated in reasonably homogenous groups
2. Cash or other assets received with a donor-imposed restriction that limits their use to long-term purposes should not be classified with cash or other assets that are available for current use
3. Information about liquidity may be provided by one or more of the following

   a. Sequencing assets according to their nearness of conversion to cash and liabilities according to maturity
   b. Classifying assets and liabilities as current and noncurrent
   c. Note disclosure about liquidity and maturity

4. A statement of position shall present

   a. Permanently restricted net assets
   b. Temporarily restricted net assets
   c. Unrestricted net assets

D. The statement of activities is designed to provide information about

1. The effects of transactions and other events that change the amount and nature of net assets
2. The relationships of those transactions and other events and circumstances to each other
3. How the organization's resources are used

E. The statement of activities should show the change in permanently restricted net assets, temporarily restricted net assets, and unrestricted net assets for the period

1. Generally, revenues and expenses shall be reported at gross amounts
2. However, gains and losses may be shown at net amounts if they result from peripheral or incidental or from events and circumstances that are beyond the control of management
3. Expenses should be presented according to their functional classification

F. The statement of cash flows is designed to provide information about cash receipts and payments of the organization during the period

SFAS 124 Accounting for Certain Investments Held by Not-for-Profit Organizations (ASC Topic 958—Not-for-Profit Entities)

A. Requires all equity investments and debt instruments to be valued at their fair values, with the exception of

1. Equity investments accounted for on the equity method.
2. Equity investments without readily determinable fair values.

B. Gains and losses on investments shall be reported in the statement of activities as increases or decreases in unrestricted net assets unless their use is temporarily or permanently restricted.

C. Dividend, interest, and other investment income shall be reported in the period earned as increases in unrestricted net assets unless the use of the assets received is limited by donor-imposed restrictions.

D. Donor-restricted investment income is reported as an increase in temporarily restricted net assets or permanently restricted net assets, depending on the type of restriction.

E. Disclosures

1. The composition of investment return
2. A reconciliation of investment return to amounts reported in the statement of activities
3. The aggregate carry amount of investments by major types
4. The basis for determining the carrying values
5. The methods and assumptions used to determine fair values
6. The aggregate amount of deficiencies for donor-restricted endowment funds
7. Significant concentrations of market risk

SFAS 158 Employers' Accounting for Defined Benefit Pension and Other Postretirement Plans (An Amendment of FASB Statements 87, 88, 106, and 132[R]) (ASC Topic 715—Compensation—Retirement Benefits and ASC Topic 958—Not-for-Profit Entities)

A. Recognize funded status of benefit plans

1. Aggregate status of all overfunded plans and show as noncurrent asset on balance sheet
2. Aggregate status of all underfunded plans, and show as current liability, noncurrent liability, or both on balance sheet.
3. Recognize as other comprehensive income the gain and loss and the prior service costs or credits that arise during the period but are not a part of pension expense.

B. Effective for fiscal years ending after December 15, 2008, the measurement date is the employer's fiscal year-end balance sheet date.

C. Disclosures

1. Funded status of the plans, and the amounts recognized in the balance sheet, showing separately the noncurrent assets, current liabilities, and noncurrent liabilities recognized.
2. Disclose the net gain or loss, net prior service cost or credit recognized in OCI for the period, and any reclassification adjustments of OCI that are recognized in pension cost.
3. The amounts in accumulated OCI that have not yet been recognized as pension costs. Show separately the following items:

   a. Net gain or loss
   b. Net prior service cost or credit
   c. Net transition asset or obligation

4. The amount and timing of any plan assets expected to be returned to the employer during the next 12-month period after the most recent balance sheet date.

SFAS 164 Not-for-Profit Entities: Mergers and Acquisitions—Including an Amendment of FASB Statement No. 142 (ASC Topic 958)

The authors believe that this topic is too specialized for the CPA exam.

SFAS 66 Accounting for Sales of Real Estate (ASC Topics 360, 605, and 976)

A. Other than retail land sales

1. Use the full accrual method if the following criteria are satisfied:

   a. Sale is consummated
   b. Buyer's initial and continuing investments demonstrate a commitment to pay for the property
   c. Seller's receivable is not subject to future subordination
   d. Risks and rewards of ownership have been transferred

2. When the criteria are not met and dependent upon the particular circumstance, use one of the following methods:

   a. Installment method
   b. Cost recovery method
   c. Deposit method
   d. Reduced profit method
   e. Percentage-of-completion

B. Retail land sales (not outlined due to specialized nature)

SFAS 86 Accounting for the Costs of Computer Software to Be Sold, Leased, or Otherwise Marketed (ASC Topic 985—Software)

A. Establishes standards of financial accounting and reporting for the costs of computer software to be sold, leased, or otherwise marketed as a separate product or as part of a product or process, whether internally developed and produced or purchased.

B. Research and development costs consist of all costs to establish technological feasibility.

1. Evidence of technological feasibility

   a. Process of creating the computer software product includes a detailed program design **or**
   b. Process of creating the computer software product includes a product design and a completed working model.

C. Capitalization costs include costs incurred subsequent to establishing technological feasibility.

1. Capitalization shall cease when product is available for general release to customers.

D. Amortization of capitalized software costs is performed on a product-by-product basis.

1. Annual amortization is the greater of

   a. The amount computed using the ratio current gross product revenues to total current and anticipated future gross product revenues **or**
   b. S-L method using the estimated economic life of the software product

2. Amortization begins when product is available for general release to customers.
3. Unamortized capitalized costs cannot exceed the net realizable value (NRV) of that software product. Any excess shall be written off at the end of the year.

E. Inventory costs include costs incurred for duplicating software materials and for physically packaging the product.

1. Costs of maintenance and customer support are charged to expense.

F. FS disclosures shall include

1. Unamortized computer software costs
2. Total amount charged to amortization expense and amounts written down to NRV

MISCELLANEOUS

SFAS 145 Rescission of FASB Statements No. 4, 44, and 64, Amendment of FASB Statement No. 13, and Technical Corrections (Rescinds SFAS 4, 44, and 64 and amends SFAS 13)

A. Rescinds SFAS 4, 44, and 64 to no longer allow treatment of extinguishment of debt as an extraordinary item in the statement of income

B. Amends SFAS 13 to require that when a modification of a capital lease terms gives rise to a new agreement classified as an operating lease, the lessee should account for the new agreement under the sale-leaseback requirements of SFAS 98 (see outline)

SFAS 147 Acquisitions of Certain Financial Institutions, An Amendment of FASB Statements No. 72 and 144 and FASB Interpretation No. 9

The authors believe that this topic is too specialized for the CPA exam.

SFAS 152 Accounting for Real Estate Time Sharing Transactions—An Amendment of FASB Statements No. 66 and 67

(Amends SFAS 66 and SFAS 67)

Requires real estate time-sharing transactions to be accounted for as nonretail land sales. AICPA SOP 04-2 provides guidance on accounting for real estate time-sharing transactions. This statement also amends SFAS 67 (*Accounting for Costs and Initial Rental Operations of Real Estate Projects*), so that SFAS 67 does not apply to real estate time-sharing transactions. Restatement of previously issued financial statements is not permitted.

SFAS 162 The Hierarchy of Generally Accepted Accounting Principles

A. Identifies the sources of accounting principles for US GAAP
B. Descending order of authority for accounting principles is as follows:

1. FASB Statements of Accounting Standards and Interpretations, FASB Staff Positions, AICPA Accounting Research Bulletins, and Accounting Principles Board Opinions not superseded by the FASB.
2. FASB Technical Bulletins, and if cleared by the FASB, the AICPA Industry Audit and Accounting Guides and Statements of Position.
3. AICPA Accounting Standards Executive Committee Practice Bulletins that have been cleared by the FASB, consensus positions of the FASB Emerging Issues Task Force (EITF), and the topics discussed in Appendix D of the EITF Abstracts.
4. Implementation guides (Q&As) published by the FASB staff; AICPA Accounting Interpretations; AICPA Industry Audit and Accounting Guides and Statements of Position not cleared by the FASB; and practices that are widely recognized and prevalent generally or in industry.

C. If accounting treatment is not specified by a pronouncement in the highest category, then use the next highest level of authority. If accounting treatment is not specified in any other category, then consider the accounting principles for similar transactions or events within the given categories, and use other accounting literature.
D. Other accounting literature includes FASB Concept Statements, AICPA Issues Papers, International Financial Reporting Standards, pronouncements of other professional associations or regulatory agencies, Technical Information Service Inquiries and Replies included in AICPA Technical Practice Aids, and accounting textbooks, handbooks, and articles.

SFAS 163 Accounting for Financial Guarantee Insurance Contracts—An Interpretation of FASB Statement No. 60

The authors believe that this topic is too specialized for the CPA exam.

STATEMENTS OF FINANCIAL ACCOUNTING CONCEPTS (SFAC)

Statements of Financial Accounting Concepts (SFAC) set forth financial accounting and reporting objectives and fundamentals that will be used by the FASB in developing standards. While practitioners may also use SFAC in areas where promulgated GAAP does not exist, it is important to note that the SFAC do not constitute authoritative GAAP. Accordingly, SFAC do not come under Ethics Rule 203.

SFAC 1 Objectives of Financial Reporting by Business Enterprises—Superseded by SFAC 8

SFAC 2 Qualitative Characteristics of Accounting Information—Superseded by SFAC 8

SFAC 3 Elements of Financial Statements—Superseded by SFAC 6

SFAC 4 Objectives of Financial Reporting of Nonbusiness Organizations

The authors believe that this concept is not on the CPA Exam.

SFAC 5 Recognition and Measurement in Financial Statements of Business Enterprises

A. Statement addresses principal items that a full set of FS should show and provides fundamental recognition criteria to use in deciding which items to include in FS.

1. Recognition criteria presented are not radical change from current practice
2. Only applies to business enterprises

B. FS

1. A principal means of communicating financial information to those outside an entity
2. Some useful information is better provided by other means of financial reporting, such as notes to the statements or supplementary information (SFAC 1).
3. Objectives of financial reporting (which encompasses FS) are detailed in SFAC 1.
4. Full set of FS should show

   a. Financial position at end of period
   b. Earnings for period
   c. Comprehensive income for period
   d. Cash flows for period
   e. Investments by and distributions to owners during period

5. Are intended as "general-purpose" statements and, therefore, do not necessarily satisfy all users equally well
6. Simplifications, condensations, and aggregations are necessary and useful, but focusing on one figure (i.e., "the bottom line") exclusively should be avoided.
7. FS interrelate and complement each other.
8. Information detailed in 4. above is provided by the following individual financial statements:

   a. **Statement of Financial Position**

      (1) Provides information about entity's assets, liabilities, and equity and their relationships to each other at a particular point in time
      (2) Does not purport to show the value of an entity

   b. **Statement of Earnings and Comprehensive Income**

      (1) Shows how the equity of an entity increased or decreased from all sources (other than from transactions with owners) during period
      (2) Item "earnings" is similar to present net income term but does not include certain accounting adjustments recognized in current period (i.e., change in accounting principle).
      (3) Earnings is a performance measure concerned primarily with cash-to-cash cycles.
      (4) Comprehensive income includes all recognized changes in equity except those from transactions with owners (SFAC 6).
      (5) The terms "gains" and "losses" are used for those items included in earnings.
      (6) The terms "cumulative accounting adjustments" and "other nonowner changes in equity" are used for those items excluded from earnings but included in comprehensive income.

   c. **Statement of Cash Flows**

      (1) Shows entity's cash flows from operating, investing, and financing activities during a period

   d. **Statement of Investments by and Distributions to Owners**

      (1) Shows capital transactions of entity which are increases and decreases in equity from transactions with owners during period

9. FS help users assess entity's liquidity, financial flexibility, profitability, and risk.
10. Full set of FS based on concept of financial capital maintenance—a return is achieved only after capital has been maintained or recovered.

C. Recognition criteria

1. Recognition is presentation of item in both words and numbers that is included in the totals of the financial statements (SFAC 6).
2. Item should meet four fundamental recognition criteria to be recognized

   a. **Definitions**—item is element of FS as defined by SFAC 6
   b. **Measurability**—item has a relevant attribute that is measurable with sufficient reliability

      (1) Five measurement attributes are used in current practice

         (a) Historical cost (historical proceeds)
         (b) Current (replacement) cost
         (c) Current market value
         (d) Net realizable (settlement) value
         (e) Present (discounted) value of future cash flows

(2) Statement suggests that use of different attributes will continue

(3) The monetary unit of measurement of nominal units of money is expected to continue to be used

   c. **Relevance**—item has capacity to make a difference in users' decisions (SFAC 2)

   d. **Reliability**—item is representationally faithful, verifiable, and neutral (SFAC 2)

      (1) Reliability may affect timing of recognition due to excessive uncertainties

      (2) A trade-off may sometimes be needed between relevance and reliability because waiting for complete reliability may make information untimely

D. Guidance in applying recognition criteria

1. Need to identify which cash-to-cash cycles are substantially complete
2. Degree of skepticism is needed (SFAC 2)
3. **Revenues** and **gains**

   a. Generally not recognized until realizable (SFAC 6)

      (1) Realizable means assets received or held are readily convertible to known amounts of cash or claims to cash

   b. Not recognized until earned (APB 4, SFAC 6)

4. **Expenses** and **losses**

   a. Generally recognized when economic benefits are consumed or assets lose future benefits

   b. Some expenses are recognized when associated revenues are recognized (e.g., cost of goods sold).

   c. Some expenses are recognized when cash is spent or liability incurred (e.g., selling and administrative salaries).

   d. Some expenses are allocated by systematic and rational procedures to periods benefited (e.g., depreciation and insurance).

E. Recognition of changes in assets and liabilities

1. Initial recognition generally based on current exchange prices at date of recognition
2. Changes can result from two types of events

   a. Inflows and outflows

   b. Changes in amounts which can be a change in utility or substance (e.g., depreciation) or changes in price

3. Current price information may only be used if it is reliable, cost justified, and more relevant than alternative information.

SFAC 6 Elements of Financial Statements
(Replaces SFAC 3)

A. Statement contains definitions of FS elements

1. Definitions provide a significant first screen in determining content of FS.

   a. Possessing characteristics of a definition of an element is necessary but not sufficient condition for including an item in FS

   b. To qualify for inclusion in FS an item must

      (1) Meet recognition criteria (e.g., revenue recognition tests)

      (2) Possess a relevant attribute which can be measured reliably (e.g., historical cost/historical proceeds)

B. Elements of FS of both business enterprises and not-for-profit organizations

1. **Assets** are probable future economic benefits controlled by a particular entity as a result of past transactions or events.

   a. Characteristics of assets

      (1) Probable future benefit by contribution to future net cash inflows

      (2) Entity can obtain and control access to benefit

      (3) Transaction or event leading to control has already occurred

   b. Asset continues as an asset until collected, transferred, used, or destroyed.

   c. Valuation accounts are part of related asset.

2. **Liabilities** are probable future sacrifices of economic benefits, arising from present obligations of a particular entity that result from past transactions or events.

a. Characteristics of liabilities

    (1) Legal, equitable, or constructive duty to transfer assets in future
    (2) Little or no discretion to avoid future sacrifice
    (3) Transaction or event obligating enterprise has already occurred

b. Liability remains a liability until settled or discharged.
c. Valuation accounts are part of related liability.

3. **Equity** (net assets) is the owner's residual interest in the assets of an entity that remains after deducting liabilities.

    a. Business enterprises

      (1) Characteristics of equity

        (a) The source of distributions by enterprise to its owners
        (b) No unconditional right to receive future transfer of assets; depends on future profitability
        (c) Inevitably affected by enterprise's operations and circumstances affecting enterprise

      (2) Transactions or events that change owners' equity include revenues and expenses; gains and losses; investments by owners; distributions to owners; and changes within owners' equity (does not change total amount)

    b. Not-for-profit organizations

      (1) Characteristics of net assets (equity)

        (a) Absence of ownership interest
        (b) Operating purposes not centered on profit
        (c) Significant receipt of contributions, many involving donor-imposed restrictions

      (2) Classes of net assets

        (a) **Permanently restricted net assets** is the part of net assets of a not-for-profit organization resulting from

          1] Contributions and other inflows of assets whose use by the organization is limited by donor-imposed stipulations that neither expire by passage of time nor can be fulfilled or otherwise removed by actions of the organization
          2] Other asset enhancements and diminishments subject to same kinds of stipulations
          3] Reclassifications from (or to) other classes of net assets as a consequence of donor-imposed stipulations

        (b) **Temporarily restricted net assets** is the part of net assets of a not-for-profit organization resulting from

          1] Contribution and other inflows of assets whose use by the organization is limited by donor-imposed stipulations that either expire by passage of time or can be fulfilled and removed by actions of the organization pursuant to those stipulations
          2] Other asset enhancements and diminishments subject to same kinds of stipulations
          3] Reclassifications to (or from) other classes of net assets as a consequence of donor-imposed stipulations, their expiration by passage of time, or their fulfillment and removal by actions of the organization pursuant to those stipulations

        (c) **Unrestricted net assets** is the part of net assets of a not-for-profit organization that is neither permanently restricted nor temporarily restricted by donor-imposed stipulations. They result from

          1] All revenues, expenses, gains, and losses that are not changes in permanently or temporarily restricted net assets and
          2] Reclassifications from (or to) other classes of net assets as a consequence of donor-imposed stipulations, their expiration by passage of time, or their fulfillment and removal by actions of the organization pursuant to those stipulations

      (3) Transactions and events that change net assets include revenues and expenses, gains and losses, and changes within net assets that do not affect assets or liabilities (including reclassifications between classes of net assets).
      (4) Changes in classes of net assets of not-for-profit organizations may be significant because donor-imposed restrictions may affect the types and levels of services that a not-for-profit organization can provide.

        (a) Characteristics of change in permanently restricted net assets

1] Most increases in permanently restricted net assets are from accepting contributions of assets that donors stipulate must be maintained in perpetuity. Only assets that are not by their nature used up in carrying out the organization's activities are capable of providing economic benefits indefinitely. Gifts of cash, securities, and nonexhaustible property are examples.

(b) Characteristics of change in temporarily restricted net assets

1] Most increases in temporarily restricted net assets are from accepting contributions of assets that donors limit to use after specified future time or for specified purpose. Temporary restrictions pertain to contributions with donor stipulations that expire or can be fulfilled and removed by using assets as specified.

(c) Characteristics of change in unrestricted net assets

1] Change in unrestricted net assets for a period indicates whether organization has maintained the part of its net assets that is fully available (free of donor-imposed restrictions) to support the organization's services to beneficiaries in the next period.

4. **Revenues** are increases in assets or decreases in liabilities during a period from delivering goods, rendering services, or other activities constituting the entity's major or central operations.

   a. Characteristics of revenues

      (1) Accomplishments of the earning process
      (2) Actual or expected cash inflows resulting from central operations
      (3) Inflows reported gross

5. **Expenses** are decreases in assets or increases in liabilities during a period from delivery of goods, rendering of services, or other activities constituting the entity's major or central operations.

   a. Characteristics of expenses

      (1) Sacrifices involved in carrying out earnings process
      (2) Actual or expected cash outflows resulting from central operations
      (3) Outflows reported gross

6. **Gains (losses)** are increases (decreases) in equity from peripheral transactions of entity excluding revenues (expenses) and investment by owners (distribution to owners).

   a. Characteristics of gains and losses

      (1) Result from peripheral transactions and circumstances that may be beyond control
      (2) May be classified according to sources or as operating and nonoperating
      (3) Change in equity reported net

7. **Accrual accounting** and **related concepts** include

   a. **Transaction**—external event involving transfer of something of value between two or more entities
   b. **Event**—a happening of consequence to an entity (internal or external)
   c. **Circumstances**—a set of conditions developed from events which may occur imperceptibly and create possibly unanticipated situations
   d. **Accrual accounting**—recording "cash consequence" transactions as they occur rather than with movement of cash; deals with process of cash movement instead of beginning or end of process (per SFAC 1)

      (1) Based on cash and credit transactions, exchanges, price changes, changes in form of assets and liabilities

   e. **Accrual**—recognizing revenues and related asset increases and expenses and related liability increases as they occur; expected future cash receipt or payment follows recognition of revenue (expense)
   f. **Deferral**—recognizing liability for cash receipt with expected future revenue or recognizing asset for cash payment with expected future expense; cash receipt (payment) precedes recognition of revenues (expenses)
   g. **Allocation**—process of assigning or distributing an amount according to a plan or formula

      (1) Includes amortization

   h. **Amortization**—process of systematically reducing an amount by periodic payments or write-downs
   i. **Realization**—process of converting noncash resources and rights into money; refers to sales of assets for cash or claims to cash

      (1) Realized—identifies revenues or gains or losses on assets sold
      (2) Unrealized—identifies revenues or gains or losses on assets unsold

    j. **Recognition**—process of formally recording an item in financial statements

       (1) Major differences between accrual and cash basis accounting is timing of recognition of income items

    k. **Matching**—simultaneous recognition of revenues with expenses which are related directly or jointly to the same transaction or events

C. Elements of FS exclusive to business enterprises

    1. **Investments by owners** are increases in net assets resulting from transfers by other entities of something of value to obtain ownership.

    2. **Distributions to owners** are decreases in net assets resulting from transferring assets, rendering services, or incurring liabilities by the enterprise to owners.

    3. **Comprehensive income** is the change in equity of an entity during a period from transactions and other events of nonowner sources (i.e., all equity amount changes except investment and distributions).

      a. Term "comprehensive" income is used instead of net earnings (net income) because the board is reserving "earnings" for a component part of comprehensive income yet to be determined.[6]

      b. Concept of capital maintenance or recovery of cost is needed in order to separate return **on** capital from return **of** capital.

      c. Financial capital maintenance concept vs. physical capital maintenance concept

        (1) Financial capital maintenance—objective is to maintain purchasing power
        (2) Physical capital maintenance—objective is to maintain operating capacity

      d. Comprehensive income is return on financial capital.

      e. Characteristics, sources, and components of comprehensive income include

        (1) Cash receipts (excluding owner investments) less cash outlays (excluding distributions to owners) over life of enterprise

          (a) Recognition criteria and choice of attributes to be measured affect timing, not amount.

        (2) Specific sources of income are

          (a) Transactions between enterprise and nonowners
          (b) Enterprise's productive efforts
          (c) Price changes, casualties, and other interactions with environment

        (3) **Earnings process** is the production and distribution of goods or services so firm can pay for goods and services it uses and provide return to owners.
        (4) Peripheral activities may also provide income.
        (5) Components of comprehensive income

          (a) Basic components—revenues, expenses, gains and losses
          (b) Intermediate components result from combining basic components

        (6) Display considerations (e.g., items included in operating income) are the subject of another SFAC.

SFAC 7 Using Cash Flow Information and Present Value in Accounting Measurements

A. Statement provides

    1. A framework for using future cash flows as the basis for accounting measurements

      a. At initial recognition
      b. In **fresh-start measurements**—measurements in period following initial recognition that establish a new carrying amount unrelated to previous amounts and accounting conventions.
      c. For the **interest method of allocation**—reporting conventions that use present value techniques in the absence of a fresh-start measurement to compute changes in the carrying amount of an asset or liability from one period to the next. Like depreciation and amortization conventions, interest methods are grounded in notion of historical cost.

    2. General principles that govern the use of present value

      a. Especially when uncertainties exist in

---

[6] Although SFAS 130 has defined comprehensive income as including net income plus other comprehensive income, it has not yet changed the components that comprise net income. Additionally, prior period adjustments are still reported in the retained earnings statement, not as comprehensive income.

(1) The amount of future cash flows
(2) The timing of future cash flows, or
(3) Both (1) and (2)

3. Common understanding of objective of present value in accounting measurements
4. **Guidance on measurement** issues **only—recognition issues are not addressed by SFAS 7.**

B. Statement does not specify when fresh-start measurements are appropriate

1. FASB expects to decide whether a particular situation requires a fresh-start measurement (or some other accounting response) on a project-by-project basis.

C. Objective of present value in an accounting measurement is to capture, to the extent possible, the economic difference between sets of estimated cash flows

1. Without present value, a $3,000 cash flow due tomorrow and a $3,000 cash flow due in fifteen years appear the same.
2. Because present value distinguishes between cash flows that might otherwise appear similar, a measurement based on the present value of estimated future cash flows provides more relevant information than a measurement based on the undiscounted sum of those cash flows.
3. A present value measurement that fully captures the economic differences between various sets of future cash flows would necessarily include the following elements:

   a. An estimate of the future cash flow (or in more complex cases, series of future cash flows at different times)
   b. Expectations about possible variations in the amount or timing of those cash flows
   c. The time value of money, represented by the risk-free rate of interest
   d. The price for bearing the uncertainty inherent in the asset or liability
   e. Other sometimes unidentifiable factors, including liquidity and market imperfections

D. To provide relevant information in financial reporting, present value must represent some observable measurement attribute of assets or liabilities.

1. In the absence of observed transaction prices, accounting measurements at initial recognition and fresh-start measurements should attempt to capture the elements that taken together would comprise a market price if one existed, that is, fair value.

   a. The **fair value** of an asset (or liability) is the amount at which that asset or liability could be bought (or incurred) or sold (or settled) in a current transaction between willing parties.

2. While the expectations of an entity's management are often useful and informative, the marketplace is the final arbiter of asset and liability values.
3. The entity must pay the market's price when it acquires an asset or settles a liability in a current transaction, regardless of its intentions or expectations.
4. For some assets and liabilities, management's estimates may be the only available information.

   a. In this case, the objective is to estimate the price likely to exist in the marketplace, if there were a marketplace.

E. The techniques used to estimate future cash flows and interest rates will vary from one situation to another depending on the circumstances surrounding the asset or liability in question. Certain general principles govern any application of present value techniques in measuring assets or liabilities.

1. To the extent possible, estimated cash flows and interest rates should reflect assumptions about the future events and uncertainties that would be considered in deciding whether to acquire an asset or group of assets in an arm's-length transaction for cash.
2. Interest rates used to discount cash flows should reflect assumptions that are consistent with those inherent in the estimated cash flows. Otherwise, the effect of some assumptions will be double-counted or ignored. For example, an interest rate of 12% might be applied to contractual cash flows of a loan. That rate reflects expectations about future defaults from loans with particular characteristics. That same 12% rate should not be used to discount expected cash flows because those cash flows already reflect assumptions about future defaults.
3. Estimated cash flows and interest rates should be free from both bias and factors unrelated to the asset, liability, or group of assets or liabilities in question. For example, deliberately understating estimated net cash flows to enhance the apparent future profitability of an asset introduces bias into the measurement.
4. Estimated cash flows or interest rates should reflect the range of possible outcomes rather than a single most-likely, minimum, or maximum possible amount.

F. An accounting measurement that uses present value should reflect the uncertainties inherent in the estimated cash flows. Otherwise items with different risks may appear similar.

G. Accounting applications of present value have typically used a single set of estimated cash flows and a single interest rate. SFAC 7 introduces the expected cash flow approach.

1. The expected cash flow approach focuses on explicit assumptions about the range of possible estimated cash flows and their respective possibilities.
2. The traditional approach treats those uncertainties implicitly in the selection of an interest rate.
3. By incorporating a range of possible outcomes, the expected cash flow approach accommodates the use of present value techniques when the timing of cash flows is uncertain.

H. The measurement of liabilities involves different problems from the measurement of assets.

1. The most relevant measurement of an entity's liabilities at initial recognition and fresh-start measurements should always reflect the credit standing of the entity.

I. Interest method of allocation

1. Present value techniques are also used in periodic reporting conventions known collectively as **interest methods of allocation**.
2. Financial statements usually attempt to represent the changes in assets and liabilities from one period to the next. By using current information and assumptions, fresh-start measurements capture all the factors that create change, including

   a. Physical consumption of assets (or reduction of liabilities)
   b. Changes in estimates, and
   c. Holding gains and losses that result from price changes

3. Accounting allocations are planned approaches designed to represent only consumption or reduction.
4. Changes in estimates may receive some recognition, but the effects of a change often have been spread over future periods.
5. Holding gains and losses are generally excluded from allocation systems.
6. In principle, the purpose of all accounting allocations is to report changes in the value, utility, or substance of assets and liabilities over time.
7. Accounting allocations attempt to relate the change in an asset or liability to some observable real-world phenomenon.

   a. An interest method of allocation relates changes in the reported amount with changes in present value of a set of future cash flows.

8. Allocation methods are only representations (not measurements) of an asset or liability.
9. While an interest method could be applied to any asset or liability, it is generally considered more relevant than other methods when applied to assets and liabilities that exhibit one or more of the following characteristics:

   a. The transaction giving rise to the asset or liability is commonly viewed as a borrowing or lending
   b. Period-to-period allocation of similar assets or liabilities employs an interest method
   c. A particular set of estimated future cash flows is closely associated with the asset or liability
   d. The measurement at initial recognition was based on present value

10. Like all allocation systems, the manner in which an interest method of allocation is applied can greatly affect the pattern of income or expense. In particular, the interest method requires a careful description of the following:

    a. The cash flows to be used (promised cash flows, expected cash flows, or some other estimate)
    b. The convention that governs the choice of an interest rate (effective rate or some other rate)
    c. How the rate is applied (constant effective rate or a series of annual rates)
    d. How changes in the amount or timing of estimated cash flows are reported

11. In most situations, the interest is based on contractual cash flows and assumes a constant effective interest rate over the life of those cash flows.

    a. That is, the method uses promised cash flows (rather than expected cash flows) and bases the interest rate on the single rate that equates the present value of the promised cash flows with the initial price of the asset or liability.

12. In reality, actual cash flows often occur sooner or later in greater or lesser amounts than expected. Changes from the original estimate of cash flows, in either timing or amount, can be accommodated in the interest amortization scheme or included in a fresh-start measurement of the asset or liability.

    a. Presently, the FASB doesn't address the conditions that might govern the choice between those two approaches.

13. If a change occurs in the amount or timing of estimated cash flows and the item is not remeasured, the interest amortization scheme must be altered to incorporate the new estimate of cash flows.

    a. The following techniques have been used to address the changes in estimated cash flows:

        (1) A prospective approach computes a new effective interest rate based on the carrying amount and remaining cash flows.

        (2) A catch-up approach adjusts the carrying amount to the present value of the revised estimated cash flows, discounted at the original effective interest rate.

        (3) A retrospective approach computes a new effective interest rate based on the original carrying amount, actual cash flows to date, and remaining estimated cash flows. The new effective interest rate is then used to adjust the carrying amount to the present value of the revised estimated cash flows, discounted at the new effective interest rate.

    b. The FASB considers the catch-up approach to be preferable to other techniques for reporting changes in estimated cash flows because

        (1) It is consistent with the present value relationships portrayed by the interest method, and

        (2) It can be implemented at a reasonable cost

    Under the catch-up approach, the recorded amount of an asset or liability (assuming estimated cash flows do not change) is the present value of the estimated future cash flows discounted at the original effective interest rate. If a change in estimate is effected through the catch-up approach, the measurement basis after the change will be the same as the measurement basis for the same asset or liability before the change in estimate (estimated cash flows discounted at the original effective rate).

    c. The prospective approach obscures the impact of changes in estimated cash flows and, as a result, produces information that is both less useful and less relevant. The interest rate that is derived under the prospective approach is unrelated to the rate at initial recognition or to current market rates for similar assets and liabilities. The amount that remains on the balance sheet can be described as "the unamortized amount," but no more.

    d. In some pronouncements, the retrospective approach has been used. Some consider it the most precise and complete of the three techniques listed above. However, the retrospective approach requires that entities retain a detailed record of all past cash flows. The costs of maintaining these detailed records usually outweigh any advantage provided by this approach.

SFAC 8 Conceptual Framework for Financial Reporting

Overview: Statements of Financial Accounting Concepts

A. Joint project between FASB and IASB

    Divided into chapters. New chapters added as project is completed
    Not part of the Accounting Standards Codification

B. Financial accounting concepts are fundamentals on which standards of financial accounting and reporting are based. Defines financial accounting concepts broader than financial statements and other data.

Chapter 1—The Objective of General-Purpose Financial Reporting

A. Objective of general-purpose financial reporting is to provide information useful to existing and potential investors, lenders, and other creditors.

    1. Primary users are investors, lenders, and other creditors.
    2. Primary users rely on financial reports.
    3. Provides information for primary users to assess prospects for future net cash flows.
    4. Managements, regulators, and other members of the public may use financial information, but are not considered primary users.

B. Information needed about

    1. Resources of the entity.
    2. Claims against the entity.
    3. Changes in economic resources and claims.
    4. How efficiently and effectively the entity's management and governing board have discharged their responsibilities to use those resources.
    5. Information is not designed to show value of an entity, but provide information for users to estimate the value of the reporting entity.

C. Financial reporting based on estimates, judgments, and models.

D. Financial reporting includes

1. Resources and claims against resources.
2. Changes in economic resources and claims.
3. Changes in resources and claims not resulting from financial performance.
4. Financial performance reflected by accrual accounting.
5. Financial performance reflected by past cash flows.

Chapter 3—Qualitative Characteristics of Useful Financial Information

A. The Hierarchy of Accounting Qualities

1. Decision usefulness.
2. Cost-benefit constraint.
3. Materiality threshold (relates to relevance).

B. Fundamental Qualitative Characteristics

1. Relevance

    a. Capable of making a difference in user's decision.
    b. Must have predictive value, confirmatory value or both.
    c. Has predictive value if it can be used as an input to predict future outcomes.
    d. Has confirmative value if it provides feedback about previous evaluations.

2. Faithful Representation

    a. Must faithfully represent phenomena that it purports to represent
    b. Must be complete, neutral, and free from error
    c. Complete all information necessary for a user to understand the phenomena depicted
    d. Neutral without bias toward a particular user
    e. Not accurate in all respects, but free from material error

C. Enhancing Qualitative Characteristics

1. Comparability enables user to identify and understand similarities and differences.
2. Verifiability occurs when different sources reach consensus or agreement on an amount of representation of an item.
3. Timeliness requires that information is available to a decision maker when it is useful to make the decision.
4. Understandability involves classifying, characterizing, and presenting information clearly and concisely.

APPENDICES

The following appendices provide you with additional practice for the exam.

Appendix A: Financial Accounting and Reporting Sample Examination

Testlet 1

Items 1 and 2 are based on the following:

The town of Silverton applies the provisions of GASB 34, *Basic Financial Statements—and Management's Discussion and Analysis—for State and Local Governments,* for its financial statements. As of December 31, 2010, Silverton compiled the information below for its capital assets, exclusive of infrastructure assets.

Cost of capital assets financed with general obli-
gation debt and tax revenues $5,000,000
Accumulated depreciation on the capital assets   1,000,000
Outstanding debt related to the capital assets   2,000,000

1. On the government-wide statement of net assets at December 31, 2010, under the governmental activities column, what amount should be reported for capital assets?
- a. $5,000,000
- b. $4,000,000
- c. $3,000,000
- d. $2,000,000

2. On the government-wide statement of net assets at December 31, 2010, under the governmental activities column, the information related to capital assets should be reported in the net assets section at which of the following amounts?
- a. $5,000,000
- b. $4,000,000
- c. $3,000,000
- d. $2,000,000

3. Tree City reported a $1,500 net increase in fund balance for governmental funds. During the year, Tree purchased general capital assets of $9,000 and recorded depreciation expense of $3,000. What amount should Tree report as the change in net assets for governmental activities?
- a. $ (4,500)
- b. $ 1,500
- c. $ 7,500
- d. $10,500

4. A not-for-profit voluntary health and welfare organization received a $500,000 permanent endowment. The donor stipulated that the income must be used for a mental health program. The endowment fund reported $60,000 net decrease in market value and $30,000 investment income. The organization spent $45,000 on the mental health program during the year. What amount of change in temporarily restricted net assets should the organization report?
- a. $75,000 decrease.
- b. $15,000 decrease.
- c. $0
- d. $425,000 increase.

5. Oz, a nongovernmental not-for-profit organization, received $50,000 from Ame Company to sponsor a play given by Oz at the local theater. Oz gave Ame 25 tickets, which generally cost $100 each. Ame received no other benefits. What amount of ticket sales revenue should Oz record?
- a. $0
- b. $2,500
- c. $47,500
- d. $50,000

6. Under Statement of Financial Accounting Concepts 8, the ability through consensus among measurers to ensure that information represents what it purports to represent is an example of the enhancing qualitative characteristic of
- a. Relevance.
- b. Verifiability.
- c. Comparability.
- d. Confirmatory value.

7. When a company changes the expected service life of an asset because additional information has been obtained, which of the following should be reported?

	Pro forma effects of retroactive application	Retrospective application
a.	Yes	Yes
b.	No	Yes
c.	Yes	No
d.	No	No

8. Gilbert Corporation issued a 40% stock split-up of its common stock that had a par value of $10 before and after the split-up. At what amount should retained earnings be capitalized for the additional shares issued?
- a. There should be no capitalization of retained earnings.
- b. Par value.
- c. Market value on the declaration date.
- d. Market value on the payment date.

9. A nonmonetary asset was received by Company Y in a nonreciprocal transfer from Company Z that has commercial substance. The asset should be recorded by Y at
- a. Z's recorded amount.
- b. Z's recorded amount or the fair value of the asset received, whichever is higher.
- c. Z's recorded amount or the fair value of the asset received, whichever is lower.
- d. The fair value of the asset received.

10. A development stage enterprise
- a. Does **not** issue an income statement.
- b. Issues an income statement that only shows cumulative amounts from the enterprise's inception.
- c. Issues an income statement that is the same as an established operating enterprise, but does **not** show cumulative amounts from the enterprise's inception as additional information.
- d. Issues an income statement that is the same as an established operating enterprise, and shows cumu-

lative amounts from the enterprise's inception as additional information.

11. During a period of inflation, an account balance remains constant. With respect to this account, a purchasing power gain will be recognized if the account is a
   a. Monetary liability.
   b. Monetary asset.
   c. Nonmonetary liability.
   d. Nonmonetary asset.

12. The summary of significant accounting policies should disclose the
   a. Pro forma effect of retroactive application of an accounting change.
   b. Basis of profit recognition on long-term construction contracts.
   c. Adequacy of pension plan assets in relation to vested benefits.
   d. Future minimum lease payments in the aggregate and for each of the five succeeding fiscal years.

13. The following items relate to the preparation of a statement of cash flows:

	2010	2009		2010
Cash	$150,000	$100,000	Net sales	$3,200,000
AR—net	420,000	290,000	CGS	(2,500,000)
Merchandise				
inventory	330,000	210,000	Expenses	(500,000)
AP	265,000	220,000	Net income $	200,000

All accounts payable relate to trade merchandise. Accounts payable are recorded net and always are paid to take all of the discount allowed. The direct approach is used for operating activities. Under operating activities, cash payments during 2010 to suppliers amounted to
   a. $2,575,000
   b. $2,500,000
   c. $2,455,000
   d. $2,335,000

14. Boa Constructors, Inc. had an operating loss carryforward of $100,000 that arose from ordinary operations in 2010. There is no evidence that indicates the need for a valuation allowance. The income tax rate is 40%. For the year ended December 31, 2010, the tax benefit should be reported in the income statement as
   a. A $40,000 reduction in income tax expense from continuing operations.
   b. An extraordinary item of $40,000.
   c. An operating gain of $40,000.
   d. An extraordinary item of $100,000.

Items 15 through 17 are based on the following information:

The December 31, 2010 balance sheet of Ratio, Inc. is presented below. These are the only accounts in Ratio's balance sheet. Amounts indicated by a question mark (?) can be calculated from the additional information given.

Assets	
Cash	$ 25,000
Accounts receivable (trade)	?
Inventory	?
Property, plant and equipment (net)	294,000
	$432,000

Liabilities and stockholders' equity	
Accounts payable (trade)	?
Income taxes payable (current)	25,000
Long-term debt	100,000
Common stock	300,000
Retained earnings	?
	?

Additional information	
Current ratio (at year-end)	1.5 to 1
Total liabilities divided by total stockholders' equity	.8
Inventory turnover based on sales and ending inventory	15 times
Inventory turnover based on cost of goods sold and ending inventory	10.5 times
Gross margin for 2010	$315,000

15. What was Ratio's December 31, 2010 balance in the inventory account?
   a. $ 21,000
   b. $ 30,000
   c. $ 70,000
   d. $135,000

16. What was Ratio's December 31, 2010 balance in trade accounts payable?
   a. $ 67,000
   b. $ 92,000
   c. $182,000
   d. $207,000

17. What was Ratio's December 31, 2010 balance in retained earnings?
   a. $ 60,000 deficit.
   b. $ 60,000
   c. $132,000 deficit.
   d. $132,000

18. Companies A and B have been operating separately for five years. Each company has a minimal amount of liabilities and a simple capital structure consisting solely of voting common stock. Company A, in exchange for 40% of its voting stock, acquires 80% of the common stock of Company B. This was a "tax free" stock for stock (type B) exchange for tax purposes. Company B identifiable assets have a total net fair market value of $800,000 and a total net book value of $580,000. The fair market value of the A stock used in the exchange was $700,000. The fair value of the shares of stock of B owned by the noncontrolling interest was $100,000 at the date of acquisition. The goodwill on this acquisition would be
   a. Zero.
   b. $ 60,000
   c. $120,000
   d. $236,000

19. Empire Corporation owns an office building and leases the offices under a variety of rental agreements involving rent paid monthly in advance and rent paid annually in advance. Not all tenants make timely payments of their rent. Empire's balance sheets contained the following information:

	2010	2009
Rentals receivable	$3,100	$2,400
Unearned rentals	6,000	8,000

During 2010, Empire received $20,000 cash from tenants. How much rental revenue should Empire record for 2010?

   a. $17,300
   b. $18,700
   c. $21,300
   d. $22,700

20. Moore Company carries product A in inventory on December 3, 2010, at its unit cost of $7.50. Because of a sharp decline in demand for the product, the selling price was reduced to $8.00 per unit. Moore's normal profit margin on product A is $1.60, disposal costs are $1.00 per unit, and the replacement cost is $5.30. Under the rule of cost or market, whichever is lower, Moore's December 31, 2010, inventory of product A should be valued at a unit cost of

   a. $5.30
   b. $5.40
   c. $7.00
   d. $7.50

21. On January 1, 2010, Richmond, Inc. signed a fixed-price contract to have Builder Associates construct a major plant facility at a cost of $4,000,000. It was estimated that it would take three years to complete the project. Also on January 1, 2010, to finance the construction cost, Richmond borrowed $4,000,000 payable in 10 annual installments of $400,000 plus interest at the rate of 11%. During 2010 Richmond made deposit and progress payments totaling $1,500,000 under the contract; the average amount of accumulated expenditures was $650,000 for the year. The excess borrowed funds were invested in short-term securities, from which Richmond realized investment income of $250,000. What amount should Richmond report as capitalized interest at December 31, 2010?

   a. $ 71,500
   b. $165,000
   c. $190,000
   d. $440,000

22. On May 1, 2010, Lane Corp. bought a parcel of land for $100,000. Seven months later, Lane sold this land to a triple-A rated company for $150,000, under the following terms: 25% at closing, and a first mortgage note (at the market rate of interest) for the balance. The first payment on the note, plus accrued interest, is due December 1, 2011. Lane reported this sale on the installment basis in its 2010 tax return. In its 2010 income statement, how much gain should Lane report from the sale of this land?

   a. $0
   b. $12,500
   c. $37,500
   d. $50,000

23. On January 1, 2010, Derby Company lent $20,000 cash to Elliott Company. The promissory note made by Elliott did not bear interest and was due on December 31, 2011. No other rights or privileges were exchanged. The prevailing interest for a loan of this type was 12%. The present value of $1 for two periods at 12% is 0.797. Derby should recognize interest income in 2010 of

   a. $0
   b. $1,913
   c. $2,030
   d. $2,400

24. Platt Co. has been forced into bankruptcy and liquidated. Unsecured claims will be paid at the rate of $.50 on the dollar. Maga Co. holds a noninterest-bearing note receivable

from Platt in the amount of $50,000, collateralized by machinery with a liquidation value of $10,000. The total amount to be realized by Maga on this note receivable is

   a. $35,000
   b. $30,000
   c. $25,000
   d. $10,000

25. Included in W. Cody's assets at December 31, 2010, are the following:

- 2,000 shares of Dart Corporation common stock purchased in 2008 for $100,000. The market value of the stock was $80 per share at December 31, 2010.
- A $500,000 whole life insurance policy having a cash value of $72,000 at December 31, 2010, subject to a $30,000 loan payable to the insurance company.

In Cody's December 31, 2010 personal statement of financial condition, the above assets should be reported at

   a. $232,000
   b. $202,000
   c. $172,000
   d. $142,000

26. Footnotes to the financial statements are beneficial in meeting the disclosure requirements of financial reporting. The footnotes should not be used to

   a.   Describe significant accounting policies.
   b.   Describe depreciation methods employed by the company.
   c.   Describe the principles and methods peculiar to the industry in which the company operates, when these principles and methods are predominantly followed in that industry.
   d.   Correct an improper presentation in the financial statements.

27. The statement of cash flows classifies cash receipts and cash payments as arising from operating, investing, and financing activities. All of the following should be classified as investing activities except

   a.   Cash outflows to purchase manufacturing equipment.
   b.   Cash inflows from the sale of bonds of other entities.
   c.   Cash outflows to lenders for interest.
   d.   Cash inflows from the sale of a manufacturing plant.

28. Initial direct costs incurred by the lessor under a sales-type lease should be

   a.   Deferred and allocated over the economic life of the leased property.
   b.   Expensed in the period incurred.
   c.   Deferred and allocated over the term of the lease in proportion to the recognition of rental income.
   d.   Added to the gross investment in the lease and amortized over the term of the lease as a yield adjustment.

29. Under IFRS which of the following is the definition of a "provision"?

   a.   A liability that is uncertain in timing or amount.
   b.   A liability that has definitely been incurred.
   c.   An asset that is uncertain as to its fair value.
   d.   An asset that is certain as to value.

30. Larson prepares its financial statements in accordance with IFRS. Larson has several cash advances and loans from bank overdrafts. How should these items be reported on the statement of cash flows?
  a.　Operating activities.
  b.　Investing activities.
  c.　Financing activities.
  d.　Other significant noncash activities.

Hints for Testlet 1

1. Capital assets are presented net of accumulated depreciation.

2. In the net assets section capital assets are presented net of related debt.

3. Net assets is increased by increase in fund balance and increase in capital assets.

4. Endowment is a permanently restricted amount.

5. Ticket revenue is at fair value.

6. Not a fundamental qualitative characteristic.

7. This is a change in an accounting estimate.

8. This constitutes a large stock dividend. It is not a stock split because par value has not changed.

9. No tricks here.

10. Must follow GAAP.

11. Monetary items are fixed in amount.

12. Entity should disclose the accounting principles followed and methods of applying those principles.

13. Cash payments to suppliers is determined by adjusting **CGS** for changes in **inventory** and **AP**.

14. The operating loss reduces income from operations.

15. Calculate inventory algebraically—Sales = (10.5)
     $$(INV) + \$315,000 = (15)(INV).$$

16. First calculate total current assets, then use current ratio.

17. Liabilities/SE = 0.8/1.0.

18. Measurement of GW.

19. Review Cash to accrual, Module 9, Section A.4.

20. Floor is NRV less normal profit.

21. Capitalized interest is avoidable interest.

22. Installment method can only be used under GAAP where collection is not reasonably assured.

23. $20,000 is both the PV and FV of this note.

24. Only $40,000 of the note is unsecured.

25. Present estimated current values of assets and current amounts of liabilities.

26. Footnotes provide additional information.

27. Investing activities relate to investments in property, plant, and equipment and securities.

28. Initial direct costs are part of cost of sales.

29. Provisions are liabilities.

30. These are not classified as financing activities.

Answers to Testlet 1

1. b	6. b	11. a	16. a	21. a	26. d
2. d	7. d	12. b	17. a	22. d	27. c
3. c	8. b	13. a	18. a	23. a	28. b
4. c	9. d	14. a	19. d	24. b	29. a
5. b	10. d	15. c	20. b	25. b	30. a

Explanations to Testlet 1

1. (b) The assets under the governmental activities column would include the capital assets of $5,000,000 less the accumulated depreciation of $1,000,000.

2. (d) The amount of net assets is equal to assets minus liabilities. Therefore, the amount would be equal to $2,000,000 ($5,000,000 total assets – $1,000,000 accumulated depreciation – $2,000,000 liabilities).

3. (c) The changes in net assets is equal to $7,500 ($9,000 expenditures for capital assets – $1,500 increase in fund balances). The depreciation expense would not be included in the funds statement.

4. (c) The endowment would be a permanently restricted asset. The income would be initially recorded as temporarily restricted funds and the expenditures would be recorded as decreases in unrestricted assets. At the end of the period, the temporarily restricted income would be reclassified as unrestricted, resulting in $0 change in temporarily restricted assets. Note that if the entity had not spent all of the endowment income in this year there would have been a change in temporarily restricted assets.

5. (b) The ticket sales revenue should be equal to the fair market value of the tickets.

6. (b) Verifiability is an enhancing qualitative characteristic.

7. (d) A change in the expected service life of an asset because of new information is reported prospectively. Prior periods are not restated.

8. (b) In a large stock dividend, retained earnings should be charged for the par value of the additional shares issued.

9. (d) If the nonmonetary exchange has commercial substance, the asset received is recorded at its fair value.

10. (d) A development stage enterprise issues an income statement that is the same as an established operating enterprise and shows cumulative amounts from the enterprise's inception as additional information.

11. (a) In a period of inflation, a gain will be recognized on a monetary liability. The liability will be paid with dollars with less purchasing power.

12. (b) The summary of significant accounting policies should disclose the basis of profit recognition on long-term construction contracts.

13. (a) The cash payments to suppliers is equal to $2,575,000 ($2,500,000 CGS + $220,000 beg. AP – $265,000 end. AP – $210,000 beg. Inv. + $330,000 end. Inv.).

14. (a) The tax benefit is $40,000 ($100,000 × 40%).

15. (c) Inventory is equal to $70,000. To calculate this amount, inventory turnover based on cost of goods sold (10.5) is deducted from inventory turnover based on sales (15), which results in 4.5. Then, divide this amount into gross margin to get $70,000 ($315,000 ÷ 4.5).

16. (a) To calculate this amount, first calculate current assets by deducting the amount of property, plant, and equipment from total assets. Current assets is equal to $138,000 ($432,000 – $294,000). If the current ratio is equal to 1.5 to 1, then current liabilities are equal to $92,000 ($138,000 ÷ 1.5). Finally, accounts payable is equal to $67,000 ($93,000 CL – $25,000 income taxes payable).

17. (a) Retained earnings is equal to $60,000 deficit ($432,000 total assets – $67,000 AP – $25,000 income taxes payable – $100,000 long-term debt – $300,000 common stock).

18. (a) Goodwill is calculated as the consideration given of $700,000 plus the fair value of the noncontrolling interest of $100,000 less the fair value of the net identifiable assets of the acquiree of $800,000, which equals zero.

19. (d) Rent earned is equal to $22,700 ($20,000 cash received – $2,400 beg. rent receivable + $3,100 end. rent receivable + $8,000 beg. unearned rent – $6,000 end. unearned rent).

20. (b) The lower of cost or market value is the floor of $5.40 ($8.00 sales price – $1.00 disposal costs – $1.60 normal profit).

21. (a) Capitalized interest is equal to $71,500 ($650,000 average amount of accumulated expenditures × 11% interest rate).

22. (d) The total gain on the sales is $50,000 ($150,000 – $100,000). Under GAAP the total gain is recognized unless there is too much uncertainty about the amount to be collected.

23. (a) Since there were no other aspects to the transaction, no interest is implicit, and none should be imputed.

24. (b) The amount realized is equal to $10,000 (collateral value) + 50% of the remaining $40,000, or $30,000.

25. (b) The assets should be reported at their fair market values of $202,000 [(2,000 × $80) + ($72,000 – $30,000)]. Note that the insurance policy value is shown net of the loan.

26. (d) Footnotes should not correct errors in the financial statements.

27. (c) Cash outflows to lenders for interest are classified as financing activities.

28. (b) Initial direct costs incurred by a lessor should be expensed as incurred.

29. (a) A "provision" is defined under IFRS as a liability that is uncertain in timing or amount.

30. (a) IFRS requires cash advances and loans from bank overdrafts to be classified as operating activities.

Testlet 2

1. For which of the following governmental entities that use proprietary fund accounting should a statement of cash flows be presented?

	Swimming pool	Government utilities
a.	No	No
b.	No	Yes
c.	Yes	Yes
d.	Yes	No

2. The Williamsburg Zoo, a private not-for-profit organization, established a $1,000,000 quasi endowment on July 1, 2010. On the zoo's financial statement of financial position at December 31, 2010, the assets in this quasi endowment should be included in which of the following classifications?
  a. Temporarily restricted net assets.
  b. Unrestricted net assets.
  c. Permanently restricted net assets.
  d. Either temporarily or permanently restricted net assets, depending on the expected term of the endowment.

3. Chase City imposes a 2% tax on hotel charges. Revenues from this tax will be used to promote tourism in the city. Chase should record this tax as what type of nonexchange transaction?
  a. Derived tax revenue.
  b. Imposed nonexchange revenue.
  c. Government-mandated transaction.
  d. Voluntary nonexchange transaction.

4. Pica, a nongovernmental not-for-profit organization, received unconditional promises of $100,000 expected to be collected within one year. Pica received $10,000, prior to year-end. Pica anticipates collecting 90% of the contributions and has a June 30 fiscal year-end. What amount should Pica record as contribution revenue as of June 30?
  a. $ 10,000
  b. $ 80,000
  c. $ 90,000
  d. $100,000

5. Why is a reclassification adjustment used when reporting other comprehensive income?
  a. Adjustment made to reclassify an item of comprehensive income as another item of comprehensive income.
  b. Adjustment made to avoid double counting of items.
  c. Adjustment made to make net income equal to comprehensive income.
  d. Adjustment made to adjust for the income tax effect of reporting comprehensive income.

6. In a statement of cash flows, interest payments to lenders and other creditors should be classified as cash outflows for
  a. Operating activities.
  b. Borrowing activities.
  c. Lending activities.
  d. Financing activities.

7. When treasury stock is purchased for cash at more than its par value, what is the effect on total stockholders' equity under each of the following methods?

	Cost method	Par value method
a.	Increase	Increase
b.	Decrease	Decrease
c.	No effect	Decrease
d.	No effect	No effect

8. When the allowance method of recognizing bad debt expense is used, the allowance for doubtful accounts would decrease when a(n)
  a. Specified account receivable is collected.
  b. Account previously written off is collected.
  c. Account previously written off becomes collectible.
  d. Specific uncollectible account is written off.

9. In computing basic earnings per share, a company would include which of the following?
  a. Dividends on nonconvertible cumulative preferred stock.
  b. Dividends on common stock.
  c. Interest on convertible bonds.
  d. Number of shares of nonconvertible cumulative preferred stock.

10. On January 2, 2008, a company established a sinking fund in connection with an issue of bonds due in 2015. At December 31, 2010, the independent trustee held cash in the sinking fund account representing the annual deposits to the fund and the interest earned on those deposits. How should the sinking fund be reported in the company's classified balance sheet at December 31, 2010?
  a. The entire balance in the sinking fund account should appear as a noncurrent asset.
  b. The entire balance in the sinking fund account should appear as a current asset.
  c. The cash in the sinking fund should appear as a current asset.
  d. The accumulated deposits only should appear as a noncurrent asset.

11. For interim financial reporting, an inventory loss from a market decline in the second quarter that is **not** expected to be restored in the fiscal year should be recognized as a loss
  a. In the fourth quarter.
  b. Proportionately in each of the second, third, and fourth quarters.
  c. Proportionately in each of the first, second, third, and fourth quarters.
  d. In the second quarter.

12. A review of the December 31, 2010 financial statements of Rhur Corporation revealed that under the caption "extraordinary losses," Rhur reported a total of $260,000. Further analysis revealed that the $260,000 in losses was comprised of the following items:

  • Rhur recorded a loss of $50,000 incurred in the abandonment of equipment formerly used in the business.
  • In an unusual and infrequent occurrence, a loss of $75,000 was sustained as a result of hurricane damage to a warehouse.
  • During 2010, several factories were shut down during a major strike by employees. Shutdown expenses totaled $120,000.

- Uncollectible accounts receivable of $15,000 were written off as uncollectible.

Ignoring income taxes, what amount of loss should Rhur report as extraordinary on its 2010 statement of income?
  a. $ 50,000
  b. $ 75,000
  c. $135,000
  d. $260,000

13. On December 30, 2009, Future, Incorporated paid $2,000,000 for land. At December 31, 2010, the current value of the land was $2,200,000. In January 2011, the land was sold for $2,250,000. Ignoring income taxes, by what amount should stockholders' equity be increased for 2010 and 2011 as a result of the above facts in current value financial statements?

	2010	2011
a.	$0	$ 50,000
b.	$0	$250,000
c.	$200,000	$0
d.	$200,000	$ 50,000

14. Kenny Company, a publicly traded company, adopted a defined benefit pension plan on January 1, 2009. The following data are available at December 31, 2010:

Pension expense 2010	$103,000
Pension funding 2010	90,000
Fair value of plan assets 12/31/10	225,000
Accumulated pension obligation 12/31/10	208,000
Projected benefit obligation 12/31/10	290,000

At December 31, 2009, Kenny reported prepaid pension cost of $11,000. Kenny's pension liability to be reported in the December 31, 2010 balance sheet is
  a. $0
  b. $ 2,000
  c. $13,000
  d. $65,000

15. On May 1, 2010, the board of directors of Edgewood, Inc. approved a plan to sell its electronic component. The plan met the criteria to classify the component as "held for sale." During 2010 the component had a loss from operations of $500,000. In addition, the carrying value of the component's assets is estimated to be $700,000 greater than their fair value less costs to sell. Edgewood's effective tax rate for 2010 is 40%. For the year ended December 31, 2010, Edgewood should report a total loss (net of taxes) from discontinued operations of
  a. $240,000
  b. $400,000
  c. $480,000
  d. $720,000

16. Tapscott, Inc., is indebted to Bush Finance Company under a $600,000, 10%, five-year note dated January 1, 2008. Interest, payable annually on December 31, was paid on the December 31, 2008 and 2009 due dates. However, during 2010 Tapscott experienced severe financial difficulties and is likely to default on the note and interest unless some concessions are made. On December 31, 2010, Tapscott and Bush signed an agreement restructuring the debt as follows:

- Interest for 2010 was reduced to $30,000 payable March 31, 2011.
- Interest payments each year were reduced to $40,000 per year for 2011 and 2012.
- The principal amount was reduced to $400,000.

What is the amount of gain that Tapscott should report on the debt restructure in its income statement for the year ended December 31, 2010?
  a. $120,000
  b. $150,000
  c. $200,000
  d. $230,000

17. Included in Kerr Corporation's liability account balances at December 31, 2010, were the following:

14% note payable issued October 1, 2010, maturing September 30, 2011	$250,000
16% note payable issued April 1, 2008, payable in 6 equal annual installments of $100,000 beginning April 1, 2009	400,000

Kerr's December 31, 2010 financial statements were issued on March 31, 2011. On January 15, 2011, the entire $400,000 balance of the 16% note was refinanced by issuance of a long-term obligation payable in a lump sum. In addition, on March 10, 2011, Kerr consummated a noncancelable agreement with the lender to refinance the 14%, $250,000 note on a long-term basis, on readily determinable terms that have not yet been implemented. Both parties are financially capable of honoring the agreement, and there have been no violations of the agreement's provisions. On the December 31, 2010 balance sheet, the amount of the notes payable that Kerr should classify as short-term obligations is
  a. $0
  b. $100,000
  c. $250,000
  d. $350,000

18. On July 1, 2010, Diamond, Inc. paid $1,000,000 for 100,000 shares (40%) of the outstanding common stock of Ashley Corporation. At that date the net assets of Ashley totaled $2,500,000 and the fair values of all of Ashley's identifiable assets and liabilities were equal to their book values. Ashley reported net income of $500,000 for the year ended December 31, 2010, of which $300,000 was for the six months ended December 31, 2010. Ashley paid cash dividends of $250,000 on September 30, 2010. Diamond does not elect the fair value option for reporting its investment in Ashley. In its income statement for the year ended December 31, 2010, what amount of income should Diamond report from its investments in Ashley?
  a. $ 80,000
  b. $100,000
  c. $120,000
  d. $200,000

19. West Company determined that it has an obligation relating to employees' rights to receive compensation for future absences attributable to employees' services already rendered. The obligation relates to rights that vest, and payment of the compensation is probable. The amounts of West's obligations as of December 31, 2010, are reasonably estimated as follows:

Vacation pay	$110,000
Sick pay	80,000

In its December 31, 2010 balance sheet, what amount should West report as its liability for compensated absences?

    a. $0
    b. $ 80,000
    c. $110,000
    d. $190,000

20. The balance in Ashwood Company's accounts payable account at December 31, 2010, was $900,000 before any necessary year-end adjustment relating to the following:

- Goods were in transit from a vendor to Ashwood on December 31, 2010. The invoice cost was $50,000, and the goods were shipped FOB shipping point on December 29, 2010. The goods were received on January 4, 2011.
- Goods shipped FOB shipping point on December 20, 2010, from a vendor to Ashwood were lost in transit. The invoice cost was $25,000. On January 5, 2011, Ashwood filed a $25,000 claim against the common carrier.
- Goods shipped FOB destination on December 21, 2010, from a vendor to Ashwood were received on January 6, 2011. The invoice cost was $15,000.

What amount should Ashwood report as accounts payable on its December 31, 2010 balance sheet?

    a. $925,000
    b. $940,000
    c. $950,000
    d. $975,000

21. At December 31, 2010, Arno Beauticians had 1,000 gift certificates outstanding that had been sold to customers during 2010 for $75 each. Arno operates on a gross margin of 60%. How much revenue pertaining to the 1,000 outstanding gift certificates should be deferred at December 31, 2010?

    a. $0
    b. $30,000
    c. $45,000
    d. $75,000

22. On January 1, 2007, Green Company purchased a machine for $800,000 and established an annual depreciation charge of $100,000 over an eight-year life. During 2010, after issuance of the 2009 financial statements, Green applied the recoverability test to the machine and concluded that: (1) the machine suffered permanent impairment of its operational value, and (2) $200,000 is a reasonable estimate of the amount expected to be recovered through use of the machine for the period January 1, 2010, to December 31, 2014. The fair value of the machine is $160,000. In Green's December 31, 2010 balance sheet, the machine should be reported at a carrying amount of

    a. $0
    b. $100,000
    c. $160,000
    d. $400,000

23. On December 1, 2010, Poplar, Inc. purchased for cash at $18 per share all 200,000 shares of the outstanding common stock of Spruce Co. At December 1, 2010, Spruce's balance sheet showed a carrying amount of net assets of $3,200,000. The carrying amounts are equal to the fair values of all the identifiable assets except property, plant, and equipment. However, the fair value of Spruce's property, plant and equipment exceeded its carrying amount by $150,000. In its

December 1, 2010 consolidated balance sheet, what amount should Poplar report as goodwill?

    a. $550,000
    b. $400,000
    c. $250,000
    d. $0

24. Cicci and Arias are partners who share profits and losses in the ratio of 7:3, respectively. On October 5, 2010, their respective capital accounts were as follows:

Cicci	$35,000
Arias	30,000
Total	$65,000

On that date they agreed to admit Soto as a partner with a one-third interest in the capital and profits and losses, upon his investment of $25,000. The new partnership will begin with a total capital of $90,000. Immediately after Soto's admission, what are the capital balances of Cicci, Arias, and Soto, respectively?

    a. $30,000; $30,000; $30,000
    b. $31,500; $28,500; $30,000
    c. $31,667; $28,333; $30,000
    d. $35,000; $30,000; $25,000

25. A not-for-profit organization receives $1,000 from a donor. The donor receives two tickets to dinner with a fair market value of $150. What amount should be recorded as contribution revenue?

    a. $0
    b. $ 150
    c. $ 850
    d. $1,000

26. The impairment rules for long-lived assets apply to all of the following **except:**

    a. Buildings currently used in the business.
    b. Financial instruments.
    c. Land.
    d. Minicomputers used to run a production process.

27. A change from the sum-of-the-years' digits depreciation method to the straight-line depreciation method is accounted for as a(n)

    a. Accounting estimate change.
    b. Accounting principle change.
    c. Error correction.
    d. Prior period adjustment.

28. On December 1, Charles Company's board of directors declared a cash dividend of $1.00 per share on the 50,000 shares of common stock outstanding. The company also has 5,000 shares of treasury stock. Shareholders of record on December 15 are eligible for the dividend, which is to be paid on January 1. On December 1, the company should

    a. Make no accounting entry.
    b. Debit retained earnings for $45,000.
    c. Debit retained earnings for $55,000.
    d. Debit retained earnings for $50,000.

29. Which of the following is not true about the presentation of financial statements under IFRS?

    a. A separate statement of comprehensive income and statement of changes in equity is required.
    b. The LIFO cost flow assumption is not allowed for inventories.
    c. Presentation of extraordinary items is required.

    d.   Impairment losses may be reversed in future periods.

30. Milan Corporation prepares its financial statements in accordance with IFRS. Milan acquires 80% of the stock of Petri Corporation in a transaction that qualifies as a business acquisition. At what amount should Milan record the noncontrolling interest in Petri in its consolidated financial statements?

   I.   The fair value of the shares of stock not held by the acquirer.
   II.   The proportionate share of the fair value of net identifiable assets of the acquiree.
 III.   The proportionate share of the book value of net identifiable assets of the acquiree
 IV.   The fair value of the shares of stock held by the noncontrolling interest plus the proportionate share of goodwill.

    a.   I or II.
    b.   I, II, or III.
    c.   I or III.
    d.   I, II, or IV.

Hints for Testlet 2

1. Required for proprietary funds and governmental entities that use proprietary fund accounting.

2. Voluntarily established endowments are still part of unrestricted net assets.

3. Taxes on exchanges are derived tax revenue.

4. Contribution revenue is reported on accrual basis.

5. Reverse amounts that have been recognized.

6. Operating activities section of SCF parallels IS.

7. Cost—subtract from stockholders' equity; par value—subtract from shares issued.

8. Allowance increases when account previously written off becomes collectible.

9. Want to find income available to common stockholders.

10. These funds have been segregated for the company's long-term needs.

11. Defer if temporary.

12. A strike is not considered extraordinary.

13. Current cost accounting discards historical cost.

14. Pension liability = FV plan assets – PBO.

15. Loss on sale is estimated.

16. Gain = Prerestructure carrying amount (including unpaid interest) – Future cash flows.

17. Account for as short-term obligations expected to be refinanced.

18. The investment was held only for the last six months of the year. Equity method was used to account for the investment.

19. Recall the four conditions for accrual.

20. Under the terms "FOB shipping point," title is transferred when goods are delivered to the common carrier.

21. Review Module 12, Section C.1.h.

22. Depreciate over remaining useful life.

23. Purchase price minus fair market value of identifiable assets. $3,600,000 – $3,350,000 = $250,000.

24. Allocate bonus according to P & L ratio.

25. Contribution is amount above fair market value.

26. ASC Topic 360 on impairment applies to fixed assets.

27. Change in method and change in estimate may be related.

28. What entry is required on the day of declaration?

29. No trick here.

30. A choice from two methods is allowed.

Answers to Testlet 2

1. c		6. a		11. d		16. b		21. d		26. b	
2. b		7. b		12. b		17. a		22. c		27. a	
3. a		8. d		13. d		18. c		23. c		28. d	
4. c		9. a		14. d		19. d		24. b		29. c	
5. b		10. a		15. d		20. d		25. c		30. a	

Explanations to Testlet 2

1. (c) A statement of cash flows is required for proprietary funds, and proprietary funds include internal service funds and enterprise funds. Examples of enterprise funds include utilities, airports, and swimming pools.

2. (b) Quasi endowments are established voluntarily by the organization and may be rescinded at any time. Therefore, they are classified as part of unrestricted net assets.

3. (a) This is an example of derived tax revenue.

4. (c) The contributions revenue is $90,000 ($100,000 × 90 %), the amount expected to be collected.

5. (b) Reclassification adjustments are necessary to keep from double counting gains and losses that have been recognized in ordinary income during the period.

6. (a) Interest payments are classified as cash flows for operating activities.

7. (b) No matter what method is used, stockholders' equity is decreased as a result of the purchase of treasury stock.

8. (d) The only item that would decrease the allowance for doubtful accounts is the write-off of an uncollectible account.

9. (a) Basic earnings per share is calculated by dividing the number of shares of common stock outstanding by net income reduced by the amount of dividends to nonconvertible cumulative preferred stock.

10. (a) The amount should be reported as a noncurrent asset because it is committed to pay a noncurrent liability.

11. (d) A loss that is not expected to be recovered should be recognized in the quarter that it is incurred.

12. (b) Extraordinary items are unusual and infrequent in occurrence.

13. (d) On current value financial statements the increase in the value of $200,000 is reported in 2010 and the $50,000 additional gain on sale is recognized in 2011.

14. (d) The required minimum liability is $65,000 ($290,000 projected benefit obligation – $225,000 fair value of plan assets).

15. (d) The amount that should be presented as the total loss from discontinued operations is $720,000 [$1,200,000 – ($1,200,000 × 40%)]. Both the operating loss and the estimated loss on sale of assets is included, net of taxes.

16. (b) The amount of the gain is $150,000. The amount owed at the date of restructuring is $660,000 ($600,000 principle + $60,000 in accrued interest). The total future payments equal $510,000 ($400,000 + $30,000 + $40,000 + $40,000). The difference is equal to $150,000 ($660,000 – $510,000).

17. (a) Since the items were refinanced prior to issuance of the financial statements, both liabilities may be classified as noncurrent.

18. (c) Diamond should report $120,000 ($300,000 × 40%) in income from the investment. This investment should be accounted for using the equity method and Diamond should recognize its share of income earned.

19. (d) West should accrue the entire amount of the compensation for future absences earned by the employees.

20. (d) The amount of accounts payable that should be presented is $975,000 ($900,000 + $50,000 + $25,000). Where title had passed prior to year-end, the liability and asset should be included on Ashwood's financial statements.

21. (d) The certificates should be reported as a liability of $75,000 (1,000 × $75), the face value of the certificates.

22. (c) The machine should be written down to $200,000 in 2009 and depreciated over a 5-year period. Therefore, the carrying value of the machine at December 31, 2010 should be $160,000 [$200,000 – ($200,000 ÷ 5)].

23. (c) Goodwill should be recorded at $250,000 [($18 × 200,000) – $3,200,000 – $150,000].

24. (b) The capital balances should be $31,500; $28,500; $30,000. Since Soto is getting a 1/3 interest in the capital of the partnership, he should have 1/3 of the capital. The total capital after Soto's investment is $90,000 ($65,000 + $25,000) and, therefore, Soto's capital becomes $30,000 which is $5,000 more than his investment. This $5,000 should be distributed to the other two partners based on their profit and loss ratio. Cicci's capital would be reduced by $3,500 ($5,000 × 7/11), and Arias' capital would be reduced by $1,500 ($5,000 × 3/11).

25. (c) The contribution is the excess of the donation over the fair market value of the goods or services received by the donor, or $850 ($1,000 – $150).

26. (b) The standard does not apply to financial instruments.

27. (a) A change in estimate effected by a change in principle is accounted for as a change in estimate.

28. **(d)**　Retained earnings is debited for the dividends on stock outstanding at the declaration date.

29. **(c)**　IFRS does not allow the presentation of extra-ordinary items.

30. **(a)**　IFRS allows noncontrolling interest to be valued either at fair value or the proportionate share of the value of the identifiable assets and liabilities of the acquiree.

Testlet 3

1. Wildlife Fund, a private not-for-profit organization, received contributions restricted for research totaling $1,000,000 in 2009. None of the contributions were spent in 2009. In 2010, $650,000 of the contributions were used to support the research activities of the organization. The net effect on the statement of activities for the year ended December 31, 2010, would be a
   a. $350,000 increase in temporarily restricted net assets.
   b. $650,000 decrease in temporarily restricted net assets.
   c. $650,000 increase in unrestricted net assets.
   d. $650,000 decrease in unrestricted net assets.

2. The statement of activities of the government-wide financial statements is designed primarily to provide information to assess which of the following?
   a. Operational accountability.
   b. Financial accountability.
   c. Fiscal accountability.
   d. Functional accountability.

3. According to GASB 34, *Basic Financial Statements— and Management's Discussion and Analysis—for State and Local Governments,* certain budgetary schedules are required supplementary information. What is the minimum budgetary information required to be reported in those schedules?
   a. A schedule of unfavorable variances at the functional level.
   b. A schedule showing the final appropriations budget and actual expenditures on a budgetary basis.
   c. A schedule showing the original budget, the final appropriations budget, and actual inflows, outflows, and balances on a budgetary basis.
   d. A schedule showing the proposed budget, the approved budget, the final amended budget, actual inflows and outflows on a budgetary basis, and variances between budget and actual.

4. Nox City reported a $25,000 net increase in the fund balances for total governmental funds. Nox also reported an increase in net assets for the following funds:

Motor pool internal service fund	$ 9,000
Water enterprise fund	12,000
Employee pension fund	7,000

The motor pool internal service fund provides service to the general fund departments. What amount should Nox report as the change in net assets for governmental activities?
   a. $25,000
   b. $34,000
   c. $41,000
   d. $46,000

5. Forkin Manor, a nongovernmental not-for-profit organization, is interested in having its financial statements reformatted using terminology that is more readily associated with for-profit entities. The director believes that the term "operating profit" and the practice of segregating recurring and nonrecurring items more accurately depict the organization's activities. Under what condition will Forkin be allowed to use "operating profit" and to segregate its recurring items from it nonrecurring items in its statement of activities?

   a. The organization reports the change in unrestricted net assets for the period.
   b. A parenthetical disclosure in the notes implies that the not-for-profit organization is seeking for-profit entity status.
   c. Forkin receives special authorization from the Internal Revenue Service that this wording is appropriate.
   d. At a minimum, the organizations reports the change in permanently restricted net assets for the period.

6. If inventory levels are stable or increasing, an argument that is not in favor of the LIFO method as compared to FIFO is
   a. Income taxes tend to be reduced in periods of rising prices.
   b. Cost of goods sold tends to be stated at approximately current cost in the income statement.
   c. Cost assignments typically parallel the physical flow of the goods.
   d. Income tends to be smoothed as prices change over time.

7. If financial assets are exchanged for cash or other consideration, but the transfer does not meet the criteria for a sale, the transferor should account for the transaction as a

	Secured borrowing	Pledge of collateral
a.	No	Yes
b.	Yes	Yes
c.	Yes	No
d.	No	No

8. In accounting for a long-term construction contract using the percentage-of-completion method, the amount of income recognized in any year would be added to
   a. Deferred revenues.
   b. Progress billings on contracts.
   c. Construction in progress.
   d. Property, plant, and equipment.

9. In calculating the carrying amount of a loan, the lender deducts from the principal

	Direct loan origination costs incurred by the lender	Loan origination fees charged to the borrower
a.	Yes	Yes
b.	Yes	No
c.	No	Yes
d.	No	No

10. How is compensation expense measured by public entities for share-based payments classified as equity-based payments?
   a. Use the normal hourly rate of the employees.
   b. Measure the intrinsic value of options difference between market price and exercise price at measurement date.
   c. Measure the fair value of options using an option-pricing model.
   d. Measure the difference between the market price and the fair value of the options.

11. A gain on the sale of a marketable equity security from the available-for-sale portfolio should be presented in a statement of cash flows in which the operating section is prepared using the direct method as a(n)
- a. Inflow of cash under investing activities only.
- b. Deduction from net income under operating activities and as an inflow of cash under investing activities.
- c. Inflow of cash under operating activities only.
- d. Deduction from net income only.

12. Lee Corporation's checkbook balance on December 31, 2010, was $4,000. In addition, Lee held the following items in its safe on December 31:

Check payable to Lee Corporation, dated January 2, 2011, not included in December 31 checkbook balance	$1,000
Check payable to Lee Corporation, deposited December 20, and included in December 31 checkbook balance, but returned by bank on December 30, stamped "NSF." The check was redeposited January 2, 2011, and cleared January 7	200
Postage stamps received from mail order customers	75
Check drawn on Lee Corporation's account, payable to a vendor, dated and recorded December 31, but not mailed until January 15, 2011	500

The proper amount to be shown as Cash on Lee's balance sheet at December 31, 2010, is
- a. $3,800
- b. $4,000
- c. $4,300
- d. $4,875

13. The books of Curtis Company for the year ended December 31, 2010, showed income of $360,000 before provision for income tax. In computing the taxable income for federal income tax purposes, the following differences were taken into account:

Depreciation deducted for tax purposes in excess of depreciation recorded on the books	$16,000
Royalty income reported for tax purposes in excess of royalty income recognized on the books	12,000

Assuming a corporate income tax rate of 40%, what should Curtis record as its current federal income tax liability at December 31, 2010?
- a. $137,600
- b. $142,400
- c. $144,000
- d. $145,600

14. Walker, Inc., a US corporation, ordered a machine from Nippon Corporation of Japan on July 15, 2010, for 1,000,000 yen when the spot rate for yen was 95 yen to the US dollar. Nippon shipped the machine on September 1, 2010, and billed Walker for 1,000,000 yen. The spot rate was 97 yen to the US dollar on this date. Walker bought 1,000,000 yen and paid the invoice on October 25, 2010, when the spot rate was 100 to the US dollar. In Walker's income statement for the year ended December 31, 2010, how much should be reported as foreign exchange gain?

- a. $0
- b. $217.04
- c. $526.32
- d. $743.36

15. On July 1, 2010, Jasmine Corporation borrowed $30,000 from the bank on a 5-year note. On July 5, Jasmine used the money as a down payment to buy equipment costing $50,000. On the statement of cash flows for the year ending December 31, 2010, how should Jasmine disclose the July transactions?
- a. Operating activities $20,000 decrease; investing activities $50,000 increase.
- b. Investing activities $50,000 decrease; financing activities $50,000 increase.
- c. Investing activities, $30,000 increase; financing activities $50,000 increase.
- d. Investing activities $50,000 decrease; financing activities $30,000 increase.

16. Howard Co. incurred research and development costs in 2010 as follows:

Materials used in research and development projects	$ 400,000
Equipment acquired that will have alternate future uses in future research and development projects	2,000,000
Depreciation for 2010 on above equipment	500,000
Personnel costs of persons involved in research and development projects	1,000,000
Consulting fees paid to outsiders for research and development projects	100,000
Indirect costs reasonably allocable to research and development projects	200,000
	$4,200,000

The amount of research and development costs charged to Howard's 2010 income statement should be
- a. $1,500,000
- b. $1,700,000
- c. $2,200,000
- d. $3,500,000

17. Kay Company, a lessor of office machines, purchased a new machine for $600,000 on January 1, 2010, which was leased the same day to Lee. The machine will be depreciated $55,000 per year. The lease is for a four-year period expiring January 1, 2014, and provides for annual rental payments of $100,000 beginning January 1, 2010. Additionally, Lee paid $64,000 to Kay as a lease bonus. In its 2010 income statement, what amount of revenue and expense should Kay report on this leased asset?

	Revenue	Expense
a.	$100,000	$0
b.	$116,000	$0
c.	$116,000	$55,000
d.	$164,000	$55,000

18. In January 2010 Bell Company exchanged an old machine, with a book value of $39,000 and a fair value of $35,000, and paid $10,000 cash for a similar used machine having a list price of $50,000. The transaction has commercial substance. At what amount should the machine acquired in the exchange be recorded on the books of Bell?
- a. $45,000
- b. $46,000

c. $49,000
d. $50,000

19. During the course of your audit of the financial statements of H Co., a new client, for the year ended December 31, 2010, you discover the following:

- Inventory at January 1, 2010, had been overstated by $3,000.
- Inventory at December 31, 2010, was understated by $5,000.
- An insurance policy covering three years had been purchased on January 2, 2009, for $1,500. The entire amount was charged as an expense in 2009.

During 2010 the company received a $1,000 cash advance from a customer for merchandise to be manufactured and shipped during 2011. The $1,000 had been credited to sales revenues. The company's gross profit on sales is 50%. Net income reported on the 2010 income statement (before reflecting any adjustments for the above items) is $20,000.

The proper net income for 2010 is
a. $26,500
b. $23,500
c. $16,500
d. $20,500

20. The following information is available for Cooke Company for 2010:

Net sales	$1,800,000
Freight-in	45,000
Purchase discounts	25,000
Ending inventory	120,000

The gross margin is 40% of net sales. What is an estimate of cost of goods available for sale?
a. $ 840,000
b. $ 960,000
c. $1,200,000
d. $1,220,000

21. Warrants exercisable at $20 each to obtain 10,000 shares of common stock were outstanding during a period when the average market price of the common stock was $25. Application of the treasury stock method for the assumed exercise of these warrants in computing diluted earnings per share will increase the weighted-average number of outstanding common stock shares by
a. 8,000
b. 8,333
c. 2,000
d. 1,667

22. Greg Corp. reported revenue of $1,250,000 in its accrual-basis income statement for the year ended June 30, 2010. Additional information was as follows:

Accounts receivable June 30, 2009	$400,000
Accounts receivable June 30, 2010	530,000
Uncollectible accounts written off during the fiscal year	15,000

Under the cash basis, Greg should report revenue of
a. $ 835,000
b. $ 850,000
c. $1,105,000
d. $1,135,000

23. On January 1, 2010, Mann Company's allowance for doubtful accounts had a credit balance of $30,000. During 2010 Mann charged $64,000 to doubtful accounts expense, wrote off $46,000 of uncollectible accounts receivable, and unexpectedly recovered $12,000 of bad debts written off in the prior year. The allowance for doubtful accounts balance at December 31, 2010, would be
a. $48,000
b. $60,000
c. $64,000
d. $94,000

24. Greene Company bought a patent from White Company on January 1, 2010, for $102,000. An independent research consultant retained by Greene estimated that the remaining useful life of the patent was four years. Its remaining legal life was six years. Its unamortized cost on White's books at January 1, 2010, was $30,000. How much should be amortized by Greene for the year ended December 31, 2010?
a. $ 5,000
b. $ 7,500
c. $17,000
d. $25,500

25. On January 1, 2010, Harry Corporation sold equipment costing $2,000,000 with accumulated depreciation of $500,000 to Anna Corporation, its wholly owned subsidiary, for $1,800,000. Harry was depreciating the equipment on the straight-line method over twenty years with no salvage value, which Anna continued. In consolidation at December 31, 2010, the cost and accumulated depreciation, respectively, should be
a. $1,500,000 and $100,000
b. $1,800,000 and $100,000
c. $2,000,000 and $100,000
d. $2,000,000 and $600,000

26. Which of the following is true about accounting for leases under IFRS?
a. All leases are treated as capital leases.
b. All leases are treated as operating leases.
c. When land and building are leased, elements of the lease are considered separately in accounting for the lease.
d. Operating leases are never recorded on the balance sheet.

27. According to ASC Topic 250, *Accounting Changes and Error Corrections*, a change in the liability for warranty costs requires
a. Presenting prior period financial statements as previously reported.
b. Presenting the effect of pro forma data on income and earnings per share for all prior periods presented.
c. Restating the financial statements of all prior periods presented.
d. Reporting current and future financial statements on the new basis.

28. Rouge Corporation prepares consolidated financial statements in accordance with International Financial Reporting Standards. Rouge has four subsidiaries, and it is considering excluding one of the subsidiaries from consolidation. Which of the following conditions are required for Rouge to exclude the subsidiary from consolidation?

I.   The other owners of the subsidiary do not object to nonconsolidation.
II. The parent makes an election to not consolidate.
III. The subsidiary does not have any publicly traded debt or equity instruments.
IV. The parent must own 100% of the subsidiary.

    a.   I and II.
    b.   I, II, and III.
    c.   I and III.
    d.   II, and IV.

Items 29 and 30 are based on the following information:

Patterson Company has the following information on one of its vehicles purchased on January 1, 2008:

Vehicle cost	$50,000
Useful life, years, estimated	5
Useful life, miles, estimated	100,000
Salvage value, estimated	$10,000
Actual miles driven, 2008	30,000
2009	20,000
2010	15,000

No estimates were changed during the life of the asset.

29. The 2010 depreciation expense for the vehicle using the sum-of-the-years' digits (SYD) method was
    a. $ 6,000
    b. $ 8,000
    c. $10,000
    d. $13,333

30. The fiscal 2009 year-end accumulated depreciation balance, using the double-declining balance method was
    a. $12,000
    b. $16,000
    c. $25,600
    d. $32,000

Hints for Testlet 3

1. Spending of funds results in decrease in restricted assets.

2. Statement of activities focuses on operations.

3. Original budget, final budget, and actual inflows, outflows, and balances.

4. Water enterprise and pension fund are excluded.

5. Unrestricted net assets must be shown.

6. Most recent purchases go to CGS first, reducing income and matching current costs to revenues.

7. What is debt?

8. Recall the account to be debited.

9. How is lender's investment affected by these?

10. Recognize compensation for stock options.

11. The direct method is **not** based on net income, which includes gains and losses.

12. Postdated check should be excluded.

13. Deduct excess tax depreciation from book income.

14. Walker was billed at $.4875, but only had to pay $.4855.

15. Borrowing from the bank increases cash from financing activities by $30,000; purchasing equipment decreases cash by the amount of the purchase $50,000.

16. Only intangibles or fixed assets purchased from others having alternative future uses may be deferred.

17. The bonus is amortized over the lease term.

18. Losses are **always** recognized when FV is determinable.

19. The portion of the cash advance representing income = **unearned** revenues.

20. Freight-in and discounts are already included in cost of sales and ending inventory.

21. Calculate number of shares that could be reacquired with proceeds.

22. The entry to write off bad debts debits the allowance account (not expense).

23. A recovery is charged back to the allowance account.

24. Review Module 11, Sec. J.

25. Intercompany transactions must be eliminated.

26. IFRS allows operating leases to be capitalized.

27. Warranty liabilities are estimated liabilities.

28. In addition to the parent preparing financial statements in accordance with IFRS, there are two other requirements.

29. Ratio is three-fifteenths.

30. DDB rate is equal to 40%.

Answers to Testlet 3

1. b	6. c	11. a	16. c	21. c	26. c
2. a	7. b	12. c	17. c	22. c	27. d
3. c	8. c	13. b	18. a	23. b	28. c
4. b	9. c	14. b	19. a	24. d	29. b
5. a	10. c	15. d	20. c	25. d	30. d

Explanations to Testlet 3

1. **(b)** The expenditure results in $650,000 being released from the temporarily restricted assets category.

2. **(a)** The statement of activities is designed to provide information to assess operational accountability.

3. **(c)** The minimum disclosure is the original budget, the final budget, and actual inflows, outflows and balances on a budgetary basis.

4. **(b)** The change in net assets for governmental activities would include the increase in the fund balances of governmental funds ($25,000) and the motor pool internal service fund. The amount for the water enterprise fund would be presented in business-type activities and the employee pension fund change would be presented in the fiduciary fund statement.

5. **(a)** This is allowed as long as the changes in net assets for each class are reported.

6. **(c)** FIFO cost assignment typically parallels the flow of goods, not LIFO.

7. **(b)** If the exchange of an asset does not meet the criteria for a sale, the transaction should be treated as a secured borrowing with pledged collateral.

8. **(c)** The amount of revenue recognized is added to construction in progress.

9. **(c)** In calculating the carrying amount of a loan, the lender deducts from the principle the loan origination fees charged to the borrower but not direct loan origination costs incurred by the lender.

10. **(c)** Compensation expense is measured at fair value, generally with the use of an option pricing model.

11. **(a)** The gain is included in the proceeds from the sale of the security in the investing activities section only. Since the operating section under the direct method does not start with net income, the gain would not be presented in the operating section.

12. **(c)** Cash is equal to $4,300 ($4,000 in the account – $200 NSF check + $500 postdated check).

13. **(b)** The current tax liability is equal to $142,400 ([$360,000 – $16,000 + $14,000] × 40%).

14. **(b)** The gain is the difference between the exchange rate when the machine title passed (shipping date) and the exchange rate when the liability is paid. Therefore the gain is equal to $309.28 [(1,000,000 yen ÷ 97 per dollar) – (1,000,000 yen ÷ 100 per dollar)].

15. **(d)** The transactions would be shown as investing activities ($50,000 decrease for the machine purchase) and financing activities ($30,000 for the loan from the bank).

16. **(c)** The total research and development costs would equal $2,200,000 ($400,000 materials + $500,000 depreciation + $1,000,000 personnel costs + $100,000 consulting fees + $200,000 indirect costs).

17. **(c)** Revenue is equal to $116,000 [$100,000 + ($64,000 ÷ 4 years)], and expense is equal to $55,000 depreciation.

18. **(a)** The machine should be recorded at the fair value of the consideration given or $45,000 ($35,000 + $10,000). The list price does not usually reflect the fair value of an item.

19. **(a)** The proper amount of income is equal to $26,500 ($20,000 + $3,000 overstatement of beginning inventory + $5,000 understatement of ending inventory – $500 insurance expense – $1,000 overstatement of revenue).

20. **(c)** Cost of goods available for sale is equal to cost of goods sold plus ending inventory. Cost of goods sold would be estimated to be $1,080,000 ($1,800,000 × 60%). Therefore, an estimate of cost of goods available for sale would be $1,2000,000 ($1,080,000 cost of goods sold + $120,000 ending inventory).

21. **(c)** The treasury stock method results in 2,000 additional shares [(10,000 × $20) ÷ $25].

22. **(c)** The cash basis revenue is equal to $1,105,000 ($1,250,000 + $400,000 – $530,000 – $15,000).

23. **(b)** The amount of the allowance for uncollectible accounts is $60,000 ($30,000 + $64,000 – $46,000 + $12,000).

24. **(d)** The amortization expense is equal to $25,500 ($102,000 ÷ 4 years).

25. **(d)** The cost and accumulated depreciation is equal to $2,000,000 and $600,000, respectively. On the consolidated financial statements the asset would have Harry's cost and accumulated depreciation.

26. **(c)** IFRS provides that when land and a building are leased, they should be considered separately in accounting for the lease.

27. **(d)** A change in warranty liability is accounted for on a prospective basis.

28. (c) IFRS states that a parent may exclude a subsidiary only if three conditions are met: (1) it is wholly or partially owned and its other owners do not object to non-consolidation; (2) it does not have any debt or equity instruments publicly traded; and (3) its parent prepares consolidated financial statements that comply with IFRS.

29. (b) The depreciation expense under the sum-of-the-years' digits method is $8,000 [($50,000 − $10,000) × 3/15].

30. (d) The accumulated depreciation balance using the double-declining balance method is equal to $32,000 [($50,000 × 40%) + ($30,000 × 40%)].

Testlet 4

Task-Based Simulation 1

Property, Plant, and Equipment		
	Authoritative Literature	Help

At December 31, 2009, Cord Company's plant asset and accumulated depreciation accounts had balances as follows:

Category	Plant assets	Accumulated depreciation
Land	$ 175,000	$ --
Building	1,500,000	328,900
Automobiles and trucks	172,000	100,325

Depreciation methods and useful lives

Buildings—150% declining balance; twenty-five years.
Automobiles and trucks—150% declining balance; five years, all acquired after 2003.
Depreciation is computed to the nearest month.
The salvage values of the depreciable assets are immaterial.

Transactions during 2010 and other information

On January 6, 2010, a plant facility consisting of land and building was acquired from King Corp. in exchange for 25,000 shares of Cord's common stock. On this date, Cord's stock has a market price of $50 a share. Current assessed values of land and building for property tax purposes are $187,500 and $562,500, respectively.

- On August 30, 2010, Cord purchased a new automobile for $12,500.
- On September 30, 2010, a truck with a cost of $24,000 and a carrying amount of $9,100 on date of sale was sold for $11,500. Depreciation for the nine months ended September 30, 2010, was $2,650.
- On November 4, 2010, Cord purchased for $350,000 a tract of land as a potential future building site.

Complete the following spreadsheet analyzing the changes in each of the plant asset accounts during 2010. Show supporting calculations in the space provided below the table.

	A	B	C	D	E	F	G
1	Cord Company						
2	ANALYSIS OF CHANGES IN PLANT ASSETS						
3	For the Year Ended December 31, 2010						
4							
5		Beginning				Ending	
6	Item	Balance	Additions		Disposals	Balance	
7							
8	Land	$ 175,000		[1]			
9	Buildings	$1,500,000		[1]			
10	Automobiles & Trucks	$172,000					
11		$1,847,000					
12							

Supporting Calculations:

Task-Based Simulation 2

Depreciation		
	Authoritative Literature	**Help**

At December 31, 2009, Cord Company's plant asset and accumulated depreciation accounts had balances as follows:

Category	Plant assets	Accumulated depreciation
Land	$ 175,000	$ --
Building	1,500,000	328,900
Automobiles and trucks	172,000	100,325

Depreciation methods and useful lives

Buildings—150% declining balance; twenty-five years.
Automobiles and trucks—150% declining balance; five years, all acquired after 2003.
Depreciation is computed to the nearest month.
The salvage values of the depreciable assets are immaterial.

Transactions during 2010 and other information

On January 6, 2010, a plant facility consisting of land and building was acquired from King Corp. in exchange for 25,000 shares of Cord's common stock. On this date, Cord's stock has a market price of $50 a share. Current assessed values of land and building for property tax purposes are $187,500 and $562,500, respectively.

- On August 30, 2010, Cord purchased a new automobile for $12,500.
- On September 30, 2010, a truck with a cost of $24,000 and a carrying amount of $9,100 on date of sale was sold for $11,500. Depreciation for the nine months ended September 30, 2010, was $2,650.
- On November 4, 2010, Cord purchased for $350,000 a tract of land as a potential future building site.

For each asset category, complete the following spreadsheet showing the amounts as indicated. **Round computations to the nearest whole dollar.** Show supporting calculations in the space provided.

	A	B	C	D	E	F	G
1	Cord Company						
2	ANALYSIS OF CHANGES IN PLANT ASSETS & DEPRECIATION						
3	For the Year Ended December 31, 2010						
4			Accumulated		Accumulated		
5			Depreciation	Current Year	Depreciation	Book	
6	Item	Cost	1/1/2010	Depreciation	12/31/2010	Value	
7							
8	Land						
9	Buildings						
10	Automobiles & Trucks						
11							
12							

Supporting Calculations:

Task-Based Simulation 3

Financial Statement Amounts		
	Authoritative Literature	Help

Moxley Co. is a publicly held company whose shares are traded in the over-the-counter market. The stockholders' equity accounts at December 31, 2009, had the following balances:

Preferred stock, $100 par value, 6% cumulative; 5,000 shares authorized; 2,000 issued and outstanding	$ 200,000
Common stock, $1 par value, 150,000 shares authorized; 100,000 issued and outstanding	100,000
Additional paid-in capital	800,000
Retained earnings	1,586,000
Total stockholders' equity	$2,686,000

Transactions during 2010 and other information relating to the stockholders' equity accounts were as follows:

- February 1, 2010—Issued 13,000 shares of common stock to Ram Co. in exchange for land. On the date issued, the stock had a market price of $11 per share. The land had a carrying value on Ram's books for $135,000, and an assessed value for property taxes of $90,000.

- March 1, 2010—Purchased 5,000 shares of its own commons stock to be held as treasury stock for $14 per share. Moxley uses the cost method to account for treasury stock. Transactions in treasury stock are legal in Moxley's state of incorporation.

- May 10, 2010—Declared a property dividend of marketable securities held by Moxley to common shareholders. The securities had a carrying value of $600,000; fair value on relevant dates were

Date of declaration (May 10, 2010)	$720,000
Date of record (May 25, 2010)	758,000
Date of distribution (June 1, 2010)	736,000

- October 1, 2010—Reissued 2,000 shares of treasury stock for $16 per share.

- November 4, 2010—Declared a cash dividend of $1.50 per share to all common shareholders of record November 15, 2010.

- December 20, 2010—Declared the required annual cash dividend on preferred stock for 2010. The dividend was paid on January 5, 2011.

- January 16, 2011—Before closing the accounting records for 2010, Moxley became aware that no amortization had been recorded for 2009 for a patent purchased on July 1, 2009. Amortization expense was properly recorded in 2010. The patent was properly capitalized at $320,000 and had an estimated useful life of eight year when purchased. Moxley's income tax rate is 30%. The appropriate correcting entry was recorded on the same day.

- Adjusted net income for 2010 was $838,000.

Items 1 through 4 represent amounts to be reported on Moxley's 2010 statement of retained earnings. Calculate the amounts requested.

1. Prior period adjustment.

2. Preferred dividends.

3. Common dividends—cash.

4. Common dividends—property.

Task-Based Simulation 4

Stockholders' Equity		
	Authoritative Literature	Help

Moxley Co. is a publicly held company whose shares are traded in the over-the-counter market. The stockholders' equity accounts at December 31, 2009, had the following balances:

Preferred stock, $100 par value, 6% cumulative; 5,000 shares authorized; 2,000 issued and outstanding	$ 200,000
Common stock, $1 par value, 150,000 shares authorized; 100,000 issued and outstanding	100,000
Additional paid-in capital	800,000
Retained earnings	1,586,000
Total stockholders' equity	$2,686,000

Transactions during 2010 and other information relating to the stockholders' equity accounts were as follows:

- February 1, 2010—Issued 13,000 shares of common stock to Ram Co. in exchange for land. On the date issued, the stock had a market price of $11 per share. The land had a carrying value on Ram's books for $135,000, and an assessed value for property taxes of $90,000.

- March 1, 2010—Purchased 5,000 shares of its own commons stock to be held as treasury stock for $14 per share. Moxley uses the cost method to account for treasury stock. Transactions in treasury stock are legal in Moxley's state of incorporation.

- May 10, 2010—Declared a property dividend of marketable securities held by Moxley to common shareholders. The securities had a carrying value of $600,000; fair value on relevant dates were

Date of declaration (May 10, 2010)	$720,000
Date of record (May 25, 2010)	758,000
Date of distribution (June 1, 2010)	736,000

- October 1, 2010—Reissued 2,000 shares of treasury stock for $16 per share.

- November 4, 2010—Declared a cash dividend of $1.50 per share to all common shareholders of record November 15, 2010.

- December 20, 2010—Declared the required annual cash dividend on preferred stock for 2010. The dividend was paid on January 5, 2011.

- January 16, 2011—Before closing the accounting records for 2010, Moxley became aware that no amortization had been recorded for 2009 for a patent purchased on July 1, 2009. Amortization expense was properly recorded in 2010. The patent was properly capitalized at $320,000 and had an estimated useful life of eight year when purchased. Moxley's income tax rate is 30%. The appropriate correcting entry was recorded on the same day.

- Adjusted net income for 2010 was $838,000.

Items 1 through 4 represent amounts to be reported on Moxley's statement of stockholders' equity at December 31, 2010. Calculate the amounts requested.

1. Number of common shares issued at December 31, 2010.

2. Amount of common stock issued.

3. Additional paid-in capital, including treasury stock transactions.

4. Treasury stock.

Items 5 and 6 represent other financial information for 2009 and 2010.

5. Book value per share at December 31, 2009, before prior period adjustment.

6. Numerator used in calculation of 2010 basic earnings per share for the year.

Task-Based Simulation 5

Riley Corp. has entered into several derivative contracts in order to manage its risk exposure. Select the **best** answer for each item from the terms listed in A-L. No term should be used more than once.

Answer List

A. A hedge of the exposure to changes in the fair value of a recognized asset or liability or an unrecognized firm commitment.

B. A hedge of the exposure to variability in the cash flows of a forecasted transaction or a recognized asset or liability.

C. A hedge of the foreign currency exposure of an unrecognized firm commitment, an available-for-sale security, a forecasted transaction, or a net investment in a foreign operation.

D. Financial instruments that contain features which, if they stood alone, would meet the definition of a derivative instrument.

E. Two or more separate derivatives traded as a set.

F. Commonly a specified price or rate such as a stock price, interest rate, currency rate, commodity price, or a related index.

G. A legally enforceable, binding agreement with an unrelated party, specifying all significant terms and including a disincentive for nonperformance sufficient to make performance likely.

H. The referenced associated asset or liability, commonly a number of units.

I. The difference between an option's price and its intrinsic value.

J. A transaction expected to occur for which there is no firm commitment, which gives the entity no present rights or obligations.

K. With regard to put options, it is the larger of zero or the spread between the exercise price and the stock price.

L. Agreement between two parties to buy and sell a specific quantity of a commodity, foreign currency, or financial instrument at an agreed-upon price, with delivery and/or settlement at a designated future date.

	(A)	(B)	(C)	(D)	(E)	(F)	(G)	(H)	(I)	(J)	(K)	(L)
1. Forward contract	O	O	O	O	O	O	O	O	O	O	O	O
2. Forecasted transaction	O	O	O	O	O	O	O	O	O	O	O	O
3. Firm commitment	O	O	O	O	O	O	O	O	O	O	O	O
4. Embedded derivative	O	O	O	O	O	O	O	O	O	O	O	O
5. Intrinsic value	O	O	O	O	O	O	O	O	O	O	O	O
6. Underlying	O	O	O	O	O	O	O	O	O	O	O	O
7. Notional amount	O	O	O	O	O	O	O	O	O	O	O	O
8. Cash flow hedge	O	O	O	O	O	O	O	O	O	O	O	O
9. Fair value hedge	O	O	O	O	O	O	O	O	O	O	O	O
10. Foreign currency hedge	O	O	O	O	O	O	O	O	O	O	O	O

Task-Based Simulation 6

Financial Statement Amounts		
	Authoritative Literature	Help

Situation

On January 2, 2011, Purl Co. purchased 90% of Strand Co.'s outstanding common stock at a purchase price that was in excess of Strand's stockholders' equity. On that date, the fair value of Strand's assets and liabilities equaled their carrying amounts. Purl has accounted for the purchase as a business acquisition. Transactions during 2011 were as follows:

- On February 15, 2011, Purl sold equipment to Strand at a price higher than the equipment's carrying amount. The equipment has a remaining life of three years and was depreciated using the straight-line method by both companies.
- During 2011, Purl sold merchandise to Strand under the same terms it offered to third parties. At December 31, 2011, one-third of this merchandise remained in Strand's inventory.
- On November 15, 2011, both Purl and Strand paid cash dividends to their respective stockholders.
- On December 31, 2011, Purl recorded its equity in Strand's earnings.

Items 1 through 10 relate to accounts that may or may not be included in Purl and Strand's consolidated financial statements. The list below refers to the possible ways those accounts may be reported in Purl's consolidates financial statements for the year ended December 31, 2011. An answer may be selected once, more than once, or not at all.

Responses to be selected

A. Sum of the amounts on Purl and Strand's separate unconsolidated financial statements

B. Less than the sum of the amounts on Purl and Stand's separate unconsolidated financial statements, but not the same as the amount on either separate unconsolidated financial statement

C. Same as the amount for Purl only

D. Same as the amount for Strand only

E. Eliminated entirely in consolidation

F. Shown in the consolidated financial statements but not in the separate unconsolidated financial statements

	(A)	(B)	(C)	(D)	(E)	(F)
1. Cash	O	O	O	O	O	O
2. Equipment	O	O	O	O	O	O
3. Investment in subsidiary	O	O	O	O	O	O
4. Noncontrolling interest	O	O	O	O	O	O
5. Common stock	O	O	O	O	O	O
6. Beginning retained earnings	O	O	O	O	O	O
7. Dividends paid	O	O	O	O	O	O
8. Cost of goods sold	O	O	O	O	O	O
9. Interest expense	O	O	O	O	O	O
10. Depreciation expense	O	O	O	O	O	O

Task-Based Simulation 7

Research		
	Authoritative Literature	Help

Worthy Corporation has self-constructed an asset for operations. Research the professional literature to determine what types of assets qualify for capitalization of interest. Place the citation for the excerpt from professional standards that provides this information in the answer box below.

Solutions to Testlet 4

Solution to Task-Based Simulation 1

Property, Plant, and Equipment	Authoritative Literature	Help

	A	B	C	D	E	F	G
1	Cord Company						
2	ANALYSIS OF CHANGES IN PLANT ASSETS						
3	For the Year Ended December 31, 2010						
4							
5		Beginning				Ending	
6	Item	Balance	Additions		Disposals	Balance	
7							
8	Land	$ 175,000	$ 312,500	[1]	$ --	$ 487,500	
9	Buildings	1,500,000	937,500	[1]	--	2,437,500	
10	Automobiles & Trucks	172,000	12,500		24,000	160,500	
11		$1,847,000	$1,262,500		$24,000	$3,085,500	
12							

Explanation of amounts

[1]   Plant facility acquired from King 1/6/10—
        allocation to Land and Building
          Fair value—25,000 shares of Cord
            common stock at $50 market price $1,250,000
          Allocation in proportion to appraised
            values at the exchange date

	Amount	% to total
Land	$187,500	25
Building	562,500	75
	$750,000	100
Land	($1,250,000 × 25%)	$ 312,500
Building	($1,250,000 × 75%)	937,500
		$1,250,000

Solution to Task-Based Simulation 2

Depreciation	Authoritative Literature	Help

Cord Company
DEPRECIATION EXPENSE
For the Year Ended December 31, 2010

Building
  Carrying amount $1,171,100
  Building acquired 1/6/10   937,500

  Total amount subject to depreciation   2,108,600
  150% declining balance rate [(100% ÷ 25) × 1.5]   ×   6%

    Depreciation on buildings for 2010 $126,516

Automobiles and trucks
  Carrying amount, 1/1/10 ($172,000 – $100,325) $ 71,675
    Deduct carrying amount, 1/1/10 on
     truck sold 9/30/10 ($9,100 + $2,650)   11,750

  Amount subject to depreciation   59,925
  150% declining balance rate [(100% ÷ 5) × 1.5]   ×   30%   17,978

Automobile purchased 8/30/10	12,500	
Depreciation for 2010 (30% × 4/12)	× 10%	1,250
Truck sold 9/30/10—depreciation		
for 2010 (1/1 to 9/30/10)		2,650
Depreciation on automobiles and trucks for 2010		$ 21,878
Total depreciation expense for 2010		$148,394

	A	B	C	D	E	F	G
1	**Cord Company**						
2	**ANALYSIS OF PLANT ASSETS & DEPRECIATION**						
3	**For the Year Ended December 31, 2010**						
4			**Accumulated**		**Accumulated**	**Book**	
5			**Depreciation**	**Current Year**	**Depreciation**	**Value**	
6	**Item**	**Cost**	**1/1/2010**	**Depreciation**	**12/31/2010**	**12/31/2010**	
7							
8	Land	$ 487,500	$0	$0	$0	$ 487,500	
9	Buildings	$2,437,500	$328,900	$126,516	$455,416	$1,982,084	
10	Automobiles & Trucks	$ 160,500	$100,325	$ 21,878	$122,203	$ 38,297	
11		$3,085,500	$429,225	$148,394	$577,619	$2,507,881	
12							

Solution to Task-Based Simulation 3

Financial Statement Amounts		
	Authoritative Literature	**Help**

1. ($14,000) Prior period adjustment is the term generally applied to corrections of errors of prior periods. In this problem no amortization had been recorded in a prior year—an error. Since this is not a self-correcting error, it still existed in 2010. The calculation is cost ($320,000) ÷ useful life (eight years) for 1/2 year (purchased July 1). Prior period adjustments are disclosed net of tax (30%). $320,000/8 × 1/2 × (1 − .3) = $14,000. An adjustment is made to the opening balance of retained earnings in 2010. In addition, the financial statements of the prior period are restated to reflect the correct amounts of assets and liabilities at the beginning of the first period presented. Financial statements for each prior period are adjusted to reflect the correction of the period-specific effects of the error.

2. ($12,000) Preferred dividends are 6% and cumulative. They were declared during 2010 and paid in 2011. The declaration is sufficient to record and recognize the dividends legally; they do not have to be paid in the current year to be recognized during that time period. These dividends will be used in the numerator in question 10 when calculating the 2010 EPS. Since these dividends are cumulative, they would be used in the calculation of EPS even if they had not been declared. The amount of preferred dividends is derived by multiplying the par value of the stock by its rate. 6% × $200,000 par = $12,000 dividends.

3. ($165,000) Common dividends—cash is calculated by the formula: Common shares outstanding × Dividend per share. In this problem the number of shares outstanding is affected by the beginning shares (100,000), shares issued (13,000), and treasury shares purchased and sold (5,000 purchased, 2,000 sold) prior to the dividend date of November 4. 100,000 + 13,000 − 5,000 + 2,000 = 110,000 shares outstanding × dividend rate $1.50 = $165,000.

4. ($720,000) Common dividends—property differ from cash dividends because the property may be carried in the accounts at an amount which does not equal its fair value (cash is always at its fair value). Management intends to distribute the property at its fair value, therefore it is necessary to bring the property to fair value on the date management is legally forced to distribute it (the declaration date). Value fluctuations beyond that date are irrelevant.

Solution to Task-Based Simulation 4

Stockholders' Equity		
	Authoritative Literature	**Help**

1. (113,000) The number of shares issued differs from the number of shares outstanding. Shares issued include those outstanding as well as those held in the treasury. Shares outstanding are equal to 110,000 plus 3,000 treasury shares = 113,000 shares.

2. ($113,000) Amount of common stock issued (113,000 shares) multiplied by the par value of each share, $1.

3. ($934,000) The additional paid-in capital, including treasury stock transactions, is derived by adding the beginning balance ($800,000) to the excess ($10) of issue price ($11) over par value ($1) for the shares issued (13,000) to acquire land on

February 1, 2010. In addition, the sale of the treasury stock (2,000 shares) at an amount ($16) greater than cost ($14) gives rise to a nonoperating gain that cannot be included in net income since it was both not related to operations and is a transaction in the company's own stock. $800,000 + (13,000 × $10) + (2,000 × $16 – $14) = $934,000.

4. **($42,000)** Treasury stock—Since the Moxley Co. follows the cost method of accounting for treasury stock, this answer is derived by multiplying the shares of treasury stock (3,000) by their cost ($14). 3,000 × $14 = $42,000.

5. **($24.86)** Book value per share is a concept that relates common stockholders' equity to shares of common stock. The "per share" referred to is always the **common** shares unless the problem states some other type of shares. In this case it is to be calculated before the prior period adjustment. It is necessary to subtract preferred stock's total liquidating value ($100 × 2,000 sh = $200,000) from total stockholders' equity ($2,686,000) to obtain common stockholders' equity. In this problem no liquidating value is given, so par value is used. The resulting amount ($2,686,000 – $200,000 = $2,486,000) is divided by the common shares outstanding (100,000) to obtain book value per share ($24.86). ($2,686,000 – $200,000) ÷ 100,000 = $24.86.

6. **($826,000)** The formula for calculating earnings per share is (NI – Preferred dividends) ÷ Wtd-avg. shares outstanding. The numerator is income available to common stockholders. The problem states that adjusted net income for 2010 was $838,000. The word "adjusted" tells the candidate that net income includes all information concerning transactions in the problem and need not be changed in any way. Preferred dividends were 12,000. $838,000 – $12,000 = $826,000.

Solution to Task-Based Simulation 5

Terminology		
	Authoritative Literature	**Help**

	(A)	(B)	(C)	(D)	(E)	(F)	(G)	(H)	(I)	(J)	(K)	(L)
1. Forward contract	○	○	○	○	○	○	○	○	○	○	○	●
2. Forecasted transaction	○	○	○	○	○	○	○	○	○	●	○	○
3. Firm commitment	○	○	○	○	○	○	●	○	○	○	○	○
4. Embedded derivative	○	○	○	●	○	○	○	○	○	○	○	○
5. Intrinsic value	○	○	○	○	○	○	○	○	○	○	●	○
6. Underlying	○	○	○	○	○	●	○	○	○	○	○	○
7. Notional amount	○	○	○	○	○	○	○	●	○	○	○	○
8. Cash flow hedge	○	●	○	○	○	○	○	○	○	○	○	○
9. Fair value hedge	●	○	○	○	○	○	○	○	○	○	○	○
10. Foreign currency hedge	○	○	●	○	○	○	○	○	○	○	○	○

Explanation of solutions

1. **(L)** Agreement for purchase and sale of a specified quantity of a commodity, foreign currency, or financial instrument at an agreed-upon price, with future delivery and/or settlement at a designated future date.

2. **(J)** A transaction expected to occur for which there is no firm commitment, which gives the entity no present rights or obligations.

3. **(G)** A legally enforceable, binding agreement with an unrelated party, specifying all significant terms and including a disincentive for nonperformance sufficient to make performance likely.

4. **(D)** Financial instruments that contain features which, if they stood alone, would meet the definition of a derivative instrument.

5. **(K)** With regard to put options, it is the larger of zero or the spread between the exercise price and the stock price.

6. **(F)** Commonly a specified price or rate such as a stock price, interest rate, currency rate, commodity price, or a related index.

7. **(H)** The referenced associated asset or liability, commonly a number of units.

8. **(B)** A hedge of the exposure to variability in the cash flows of a forecasted transaction or a recognized asset or liability.

9. **(A)** A hedge of the exposure to changes in the fair value of a recognized asset or liability or an unrecognized firm commitment.

10. **(C)** A hedge of the foreign currency exposure of an unrecognized firm commitment, an available-for-sale security, a forecasted transaction, or a net investment in a foreign operation.

Solution to Task-Based Simulation 6

Financial Statement Amounts		
	Authoritative Literature	Help

	(A)	(B)	(C)	(D)	(E)	(F)
1. Cash	●	○	○	○	○	○
2. Equipment	○	●	○	○	○	○
3. Investment in subsidiary	○	○	○	○	●	○
4. Noncontrolling interest	○	○	○	○	○	●
5. Common stock	○	○	●	○	○	○
6. Beginning retained earnings	○	○	●	○	○	○
7. Dividends paid	○	○	●	○	○	○
8. Cost of goods sold	○	●	○	○	○	○
9. Interest expense	●	○	○	○	○	○
10. Depreciation expense	○	●	○	○	○	○

Explanation of solutions

1. **(A)** The total of cash on each entity's books equals the total for the consolidated entity.

2. **(B)** The amount shown for equipment on the consolidated balance sheet is less than the sum of the amounts on Purl's and Strand's unconsolidated balance sheets because on an upstream intercompany transaction the parent's share (90%) of the gain would be eliminated. The equipment now on the parent's books would be reduced on the worksheet by subtracting 90% of the gain not realized through depreciation from equipment.

3. **(E)** The investment in subsidiary would be eliminated in the process of consolidation in the same entry in which the subsidiary's equity accounts are eliminated.

4. **(F)** Noncontrolling interest is presented only in the consolidated balance sheet.

5. **(C)** Only Purl's common stock would be included in the consolidated balance sheet. All of Strand's common stock would be eliminated. Ten percent would be included in noncontrolling interest.

6. **(C)** Beginning retained earnings would be the same as Purl's. Under the purchase method none of the acquiree's (Strand's) retained earnings is carried forward in recording the business combination.

7. **(C)** Dividends paid would include only the parent's. The dividends of the subsidiary are all eliminated in consolidation.

8. **(B)** Cost of goods would be less than the sum of that of Purl and Strand because intercompany profit would be eliminated from cost of goods sold. The amount eliminated would be 100% of the intercompany profit on two-thirds of the downstream sale from Purl to Strand.

9. **(A)** No information is given to indicate that there is any intercompany interest-bearing debt. Thus, the amount included for interest expense in the consolidated financial statements would be the sum of the two entities.

10. **(B)** Depreciation expense would be less on the consolidated financial statement than the sum of depreciation in each firm's unconsolidated financial statements because the part relating to the intercompany profit on equipment sold upstream would be eliminated in consolidation.

Solution to Task-Based Simulation 7

Research		
	Authoritative Literature	Help

ASC	835	20	15	5

1. For $50 a month, Rawl Co. visits its customers' premises and performs insect control services. If customers experience problems between regularly scheduled visits, Rawl makes service calls at no additional charge. Instead of paying monthly, customers may pay an annual fee of $540 in advance. For a customer who pays the annual fee in advance, Rawl should recognize the related revenue

   a. Evenly over the contract year as the services are performed.
   b. At the end of the contract year after all of the services have been performed.
   c. When the cash is collected.
   d. At the end of the fiscal year.

2. Simm Co. has determined its December 31 inventory on a FIFO basis to be $400,000. Information pertaining to that inventory follows:

Estimated selling price	$403,000
Estimated cost of disposal	20,000
Normal profit margin	60,000
Current replacement cost	360,000

Simm records losses that result from applying the lower of cost or market rule. At December 31, what should be the amount of Simm's inventory?

   a. $400,000
   b. $388,000
   c. $360,000
   d. $328,000

3. A bond issued on June 1, 2011, has interest payment dates of April 1 and October 1. Bond interest expense for the year ended December 31, 2011, is for a period of

   a. Three months.
   b. Four months.
   c. Six months.
   d. Seven months.

4. Governmental financial reporting should provide information to assist users in which situation(s)?

  I. Making social and political decisions.
  II. Assessing whether current-year citizens received services but shifted part of the payment burden to future-year citizens.

   a. I only.
   b. II only.
   c. Both I and II.
   d. Neither I nor II.

1. **(a)** Revenue is generally recognized when **realized or realizable** and **earned**. Revenues are considered earned when the entity has substantially accomplished what it must do to be entitled to the benefits represented by the revenues. Therefore, service revenue generally is earned as the work is performed, and it should be recognized evenly over the contract year as the monthly services are performed. Answer (c) is incorrect because accrual basis accounting is preferable; SFAC 6 explains that cash method provides little information about the results of operations. Answer (d) is incorrect because revenue should be recognized when earned. Answer (b) is incorrect because the completed-contract method should only be used when reasonable estimates of contract costs, revenues, and the extent of progress toward completion cannot be reasonably estimated.

2. **(c)** The lower of cost or market (LCM) is used for financial reporting of inventories. The market value of inventory is defined as the replacement cost (RC), as long as it is less than the ceiling (net realizable value, or NRV) and more than the floor (NRV less a normal profit, or NRV – NP). In this case, the amounts are

Ceiling: NRV = $408,000 est. sell. price –	
$20,000 dep. cost =	$388,000
Replacement cost	$360,000
Floor: NRV – NP = $388,000 – $60,000 =	$328,000

The designated market value is the replacement cost of $360,000 because it falls between the floor and the ceiling. Once market value is designated, LCM can be determined by simply picking the lower of cost ($400,000) or market ($360,000). Thus, the inventory should be reported at market.

3. **(d)** Under the accrual basis of accounting, expenses should be recognized when incurred, regardless of when cash is paid. Therefore, expense from the bond issue date (6/1/11) through year-end (12/31/11) should be recognized in 2012.

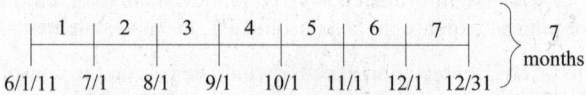

The seven months (6/1/11 - 12/31/11) of interest expense would be the net effect of entries prepared on the issuance date, the October 1 interest date, and December 31 (adjusting entry).

4. **(c)** Financial reporting by state and local governments is used in making economic, social, and political decisions and in assessing accountability. Additionally, current year citizens need information concerning when costs of current services are actually paid for. Thus, both items I and II are provided to the users of governmental reporting.

5. During the year, Jones Foundation received the following support:

- A cash contribution of $875,000 to be used at the board of directors' discretion;
- A promise to contribute $500,000 in the following year from a supporter who has made similar contributions in prior periods;
- Contributed legal services with a value of $100,000, which Jones would have otherwise purchased.

At what amounts would Jones classify and record these transactions?

	Unrestricted revenue	Temporarily restricted revenue
a.	$ 875,000	$500,000
b.	$ 975,000	$500,000
c.	$ 975,000	$0
d.	$1,375,000	$0

5. **(b)** Restricted revenues are recorded only when a restriction has been placed by the donor. One type of restricted revenue is a pledge that has not been received during the year. This is considered a time restriction; accordingly, the $500,000 would be considered a temporarily restricted revenue based on a time restriction. The $875,000 and the $100,000 would be considered unrestricted revenues. The $100,000 is considered contributed services and carries no restriction. Contributed services are recognized when the services received (1) create or enhance nonfinancial assets or (2) require specialized skills, are provided by individuals possessing those skills, and would typically need to be purchased if not provided by donation. The $100,000 contribution meets the second criterion.

NOTE: This simulation has been modified to reflect the effects of SFAS 154 and adapted to a task-based simulation format.

Task-Based Simulation 1

Treatments		
	Authoritative Literature	Help

In the table below, determine which description applies to each event by double-clicking the shaded box in the Description column and selecting the appropriate description. Then determine the appropriate accounting treatment for each event by double-clicking the shaded box in the Accounting treatment column and selecting the appropriate accounting treatment. Assume that all events are material in amount. A selected item may be used once, more than once, or not at all.

Description	Accounting treatment
Change in accounting principle	Current income
Change in accounting estimate	Cumulative effect in current income
Correction of error	Prospective treatment
Neither a change nor an error correction	Retrospective adjustment
	Restatement of previous periods
	No impact

Event	Description	Accounting treatment
Change in long-term construction contract from percentage-of-completion method to completed-contract method		
Write-off of uncollectible receivables under the direct write-off method		
Write-off of uncollectible receivables under the reserve method		
Change in salvage value of a depreciable asset		
Change in useful life of a patent		

NOTE: The solution to this testlet is based upon ASC Topic 250, *Accounting Changes and Error Corrections* (FAS 154).

Solution to Task-Based Simulation 1

Treatments		
	Authoritative Literature	Help

Event	Description	Accounting treatment
Change in long-term construction contract from percentage-of-completion method to completed-contract method	Change in accounting principle	Retrospective application
Write-off of uncollectible receivables under the direct write-off method	Change in accounting estimate	Current income
Write-off of uncollectible receivables under the reserve method	Neither a change nor an error correction	No impact
Change in salvage value of a depreciable asset	Change in accounting estimate	Current income
Change in useful life of a patent	Change in accounting estimate	Current income

Task-Based Simulation 2

Cumulative Effect		
	Authoritative Literature	
		Help

Situation

On January 1, 2008, Charleston Company purchased machinery at a cost of $150,000. The machinery was depreciated under the double-declining balance method, assuming a ten-year life and no salvage value. The company took full-year depreciation in the year of acquisition. During 2011, management decided to change depreciation methods to the straight-line method for financial reporting purposes, but it continued to use the accelerated method for tax purposes. Charleston has a 40% effective income tax rate.

Using the spreadsheet below, calculate the amount of the depreciation expense for Charleston for each year. You may record your entries as numbers or as formulas that produce the correct number. Be sure that the value of the change appears in the shaded cell at the bottom of the spreadsheet.

NOTE: To use a formula in the spreadsheet, it must be preceded by an equal sign (e.g., = B1 + B2).

A	B	C	D
		Depreciation expense	
Double-declining balance method			
	2008		
	2009		
	2010		
Straight-line method			
	2011		
Accumulated depreciation 12/31/2011			

Solution to Task-Based Simulation 2

Cumulative Effect		
	Authoritative Literature	
		Help

A	B	C	D
		Depreciation expense	
Double-declining balance method			
	2008	$30,000	
	2009	$24,000	
	2010	$19,200	
Straight-line method			
	2011	$10,971	
Accumulated depreciation 12/31/2011			$84,171

There is no cumulative effect of change in method on the income statement for a change in depreciation method. The change is treated as a change in estimate effected by a change in accounting method. A change in estimate is accounted for in the period of the change and future periods.

The machinery was depreciated using the double-declining balance method assuming a ten-year life and no salvage. Assume the machinery was acquired on January 1, 2008, and the change in depreciation method to straight-line was made in 2011. To account for the change on a prospective basis, it is necessary to calculate the book value of the machinery as of December 31, 2011, at the end of Year 3.

Double-declining balance method

Year 1 (2008)	$30,000
Year 2 (2009)	24,000
Year 3 (2010)	19,200
Total depreciation 12/31/10	$73,200

To calculate book value at 12/31/10

Historical cost	$150,000
Less: Accum. depr.	(73,200)
Book value	$ 76,800

To calculate depreciation expense for 2011, straight-line depreciation is calculated using the book value at the beginning of the year in which the change is made and the remaining useful life of the asset.

$$(\$76,800 - \$0 \text{ salvage}) \div 7 \text{ years remaining life} = \$10,971$$

Task-Based Simulation 3

Journal Entries		
	Authoritative Literature	Help

Situation

On January 1, 2008, Charleston Company purchased machinery at a cost of $150,000. The machinery was depreciated under the double-declining balance method, assuming a ten-year life and no salvage value. The company took full-year depreciation in the year of acquisition. During 2011, management decided to change depreciation methods to the straight-line method for financial reporting purposes, but it continued to use the accelerated method for tax purposes. Charleston has a 40% effective income tax rate.

Use the form below to complete the journal entries required to record Charleston's accounting change in 2011 from the double-declining balance method to the straight-line method. Enter the appropriate account title in column A by clicking the shaded box and then selecting the desired account title from the list provided. Account titles may be used once, more than once, or not at all.

Use columns B and C to record the dollar value corresponding to each journal entry. Be sure your entries appear in the appropriate shaded spaces. Some of the shaded spaces may not be used.

Column A

Accounts payable	Deferred income taxes
Accounts receivable	Depreciation expense
Accumulated depreciation	Income tax expense
Cash	Prior period adjustment
Cumulative effect of change in accounting	Retained earnings
Retained earnings	

A	B	C
	Debit	Credit

Solution to Task-Based Simulation 3

Journal Entries		
	Authoritative Literature	Help

There is no journal entry for a cumulative effect of change in accounting principle for a change in depreciation method. Since the accounting change is accounted for on a prospective basis, depreciation expense is calculated and recorded for the current year. The depreciation expense entry for Year 4 (2011) is

Depreciation expense	10,971	
Accumulated depreciation		10,971

Task-Based Simulation 4

Financial Statement		
	Authoritative Literature	Help

Situation

On January 1, 2008, Charleston Company purchased machinery at a cost of $150,000. The machinery was depreciated under the double-declining balance method, assuming a ten-year life and no salvage value. The company took full-year depreciation in the year of acquisition. During 2011, management decided to change depreciation methods to the straight-line method for financial reporting purposes, but it continued to use the accelerated method for tax purposes. Charleston has a 40% effective income tax rate. The accurate depreciation amounts for this situation are illustrated below.

A	B	C	D
		Depreciation expense	
Double-declining balance method			
	2008	$30,000	
	2009	$24,000	
	2010	$19,200	
Straight-line method			
	2011	$10,971	
Accumulated depreciation 12/31/2011			$84,171

The depreciation expense entry for Year 4 (2011) is

Depreciation expense	10,971	
Accumulated depreciation		10,971

Complete the following excerpts from Charleston's balance sheet at December 31, 2011, and income statement for the year ending December 31, 2011. Insert the appropriate values in the shaded cells in column D below. Indicate in column F whether the net cumulative effect is income or expense by clicking the shaded box in column F and then selecting either "Income" or "Expense."

NOTE: To use a formula in the spreadsheet, if must be preceded by an equal sign (e.g., = B1 + B2).

A	B	C	D	E	F	H
Charleston Company						
Balance sheet						
December 31, 2011						
	Machinery					
	Accumulated depreciation					
	Net					
Charleston Company						
Income statement						
Year ending December 31, 2011						
	Depreciation expense					

Solution to Task-Based Simulation 4

Financial Statement		
	Authoritative Literature	Help

A	B	C	D	E	F	H
Charleston Company						
Balance sheet						
December 31, 2011 (End of Year 4)						
	Machinery		$150,000			
	Accumulated depreciation		$ (84,171)			
	Net		$ 65,829			
Charleston Company						
Income statement						
Year ending December 31, 2011 (Year 4)						
	Depreciation expense		$ (10,971)			

Task-Based Simulation 5

Research		
	Authoritative Literature	Help

Use the resource materials available to you by clicking the Authoritative Literature button to find the answer to the following question in either the Current Text or Original Pronouncements. What constitutes the cumulative effect of an accounting change?

Insert the citation in the answer box below.

Solution to Task-Based Simulation 5

Research		
	Authoritative Literature	Help

ASC	250	10	05	1

1. A company has the following items on its year-end trial balance:

Net sales	$500,000
Common stock	100,000
Insurance expense	75,000
Wages	50,000
Cost of goods sold	100,000
Cash	40,000
Accounts payable	25,000
Interest payable	20,000

What is the company's gross profit?
  a. $230,000
  b. $275,000
  c. $400,000
  d. $500,000

2. Burns Corp. had the following items:

Sales revenue	$45,000
Loss on early extinguishment of bonds	36,000
Realized gain on sale of available-for-sale securities	28,000
Unrealized holding loss on available-for-sale securities	17,000
Loss on write-down of inventory	3,100

Which of the following amounts would the statement of comprehensive income report as other comprehensive income or loss?
  a. $11,000 other comprehensive income.
  b. $16,900 other comprehensive income.
  c. $17,000 other comprehensive loss.
  d. $28,100 other comprehensive loss.

3. Baler Co. prepared its statement of cash flows at year-end using the direct method. The following amounts were used in the computation of cash flows from operating activities:

Beginning inventory	$200,000
Ending inventory	150,000
Cost of goods sold	1,200,000
Beginning accounts payable	300,000
Ending accounts payable	200,000

What amount should Baler report as cash paid to suppliers for inventory purchases?
  a. $1,200,000
  b. $1,250,000
  c. $1,300,000
  d. $1,350,000

1. **(c)** The requirement is to compute the company's gross profit. Gross profit is calculated as net sales less cost of goods sold. Answer (c) is correct because $500,000–$100,000 = $400,000. Answer (a) is incorrect because it erroneously subtracts insurance expense, wages, accounts payable, and interest payable along with cost of goods sold from net sales ($500,000 – $100,000 – $75,000 – $50,000 – $25,000 – $20,000 = $230,000). Answer (b) is incorrect because it erroneously subtracts insurance expense and wages along with cost of goods sold from net sales ($500,000 – $100,000 – $75,000 – $50,000 = $275,000). Answer (d) is incorrect because it excludes subtracting cost of goods sold from net sales.

2. **(c)** The requirement is to determine which amount would appear on the statement of comprehensive income as other comprehensive income or loss. The statement of other comprehensive income requires disclosure of changes during a period of items such as unrealized gains and losses on available-for-sale securities, pension funding status adjustments, and foreign currency translation gains and losses. Answer (c) is correct because unrealized gains and losses on available-for-sale securities is the only item in the problem that would appear in a statement of other comprehensive income. Answers (a), (b) and (d) are incorrect since each includes items appearing in the income statement rather than statement of comprehensive income.

3. **(b)** The requirement is to calculate the amount to report as the cash paid to suppliers for inventory purchases. Answer (b) is correct because cash paid to suppliers is calculated as cost of goods sold less the decrease in inventory and plus the decrease in ending accounts payable, or $1,250,000 ($1,200,000 cost of goods sold – $50,000 decrease in inventory + $100,000 decrease in accounts payable). Answer (a) is incorrect because it only includes cost of goods sold in the calculation. Answer (c) is incorrect because it ignores the change in inventory for the year and only includes cost of goods sold and the decrease in accounts payable ($1,200,000 + $100,000 = $1,300,000). Answer (d) is incorrect because it incorrectly adds the decrease in inventory to cost of goods sold and the change in accounts payable ($1,200,000 + $100,000 + $50,000 = $1,350,000).

4. Which of the following transactions is included in the operating activities section of a cash flow statement prepared using the indirect method?
   a. Gain on sale of plant asset.
   b. Sale of property, plant, and equipment.
   c. Payment of cash dividend to the shareholders.
   d. Issuance of common stock to the shareholders.

4. **(a)** The requirement is to identify which transaction would be included in the operating activities section of a cash flow statement. The operating activities section of the cash flow statement includes those items related to producing goods for sale and providing services. Generally, operating activities are related to net income and the current asset and current liability sections of the balance sheet. Answer (a) is correct because a gain on the sale of plant assets would be a reconciling item from net income to operating cash flows. Answer (b) is incorrect because it would appear as an investing activity in the statement of cash flows. Answers (c) and (d) are incorrect because they would appear as financing activities in the statement of cash flows.

5. Tinsel Co.'s balances in allowance for uncollectible accounts were $70,000 at the beginning of the current year and $55,000 at year-end. During the year, receivables of $35,000 were written off as uncollectible. What amount should Tinsel report at uncollectible accounts expense at year-end?
   a. $15,000
   b. $20,000
   c. $35,000
   d. $50,000

5. **(b)** The requirement is to determine the amount to report as uncollectible accounts expense. Answer (b) is correct because uncollectible accounts expense is equal to the ending allowance balance plus accounts written off less reinstatements less the beginning allowance balance ($55,000 – $70,000 + $35,000 = $20,000). Answer (a) is incorrect because it only examines the change between the beginning and ending allowance balances ($70,000–$55,000 = $15,000) and that change is in the wrong direction. Answer (c) is incorrect because it only takes into account the accounts written off ($35,000). Answer (d) is incorrect because it incorrectly adds the beginning balance and subtracts the ending balance to accounts written off ($70,000 – $55,000 + $35,000 = $50,000).

6. Alta Co. spent $400,000 during the current year developing a new idea for a product that was patented during the year. The legal cost of applying for a patent license was $40,000. Also, $50,000 was spent to successfully defend the rights of the patent against a competitor. The patent has a life of 20 years. What amount should Alta capitalize related to the patent?
   a. $ 40,000
   b. $ 50,000
   c. $ 90,000
   d. $490,000

6. **(c)** The requirement is to determine the amount to capitalize related to the patent. Answer (c) is correct because research and development must be expensed as incurred ($400,000) but the legal costs related to applying for a patent and the legal costs related to a successful defense of a patent may be capitalized ($40,000 + $50,000 = $90,000). Answer (a) is incorrect because it only includes the legal cost of applying for the patent. Answer (b) is incorrect because it only includes the legal cost of successfully defending the patent. Answer (d) is incorrect because it incorrectly capitalizes the $400,000 spent on patent development along with the legal costs.

7. A retail store sold gift certificates that are redeemable in merchandise. The gift certificates lapse one year after they are issued. How would the deferred revenue account be affected by each of the following?

	Redemption of certificates	Lapse of certificates
a.	Decrease	Decrease
b.	Decrease	No effect
c.	No effect	Decrease
d.	No effect	No effect

7. **(a)** The requirement is to determine how the deferred revenue account would be affected by redemption of certificates and lapse of certificates. Revenue is recognized when realized or realizable and earned. A deferral results when the cash is received, but the revenue is not earned. The revenue from gift certificates is deferred until either the certificate is redeemed or the certificate expires. Answer (a) is correct because revenue is earned when the certificates are redeemed causing a reduction in the deferred revenue account, and a liability no longer exists when the certificates expire resulting in a reduction of the deferred revenue account.

8. On January 2, Vole Co. issued bonds with a face value of $480,000 at a discount to yield 10%. The bonds pay interest semiannually. On June 30, Vole paid bond interest of $14,400. After Vole recorded amortization of the bond discount of $3,600, the bonds had a carrying amount of $363,600. What amount did Vole receive upon issuing the bonds?
   a. $360,000
   b. $367,200
   c. $476,400
   d. $480,000

8. **(a)** The requirement is to calculate the amount received upon bond issuance. Answer (a) is correct because the issuance value at year 0 is equal to carrying value at the end of year 1 less the discount amortization ($363,600 – $3,600 = $360,000). Answer (b) is incorrect because it adds the discount amortization instead of subtracting the discount amortization ($363,600 + $3,600 = $367,200). Answer (c) is incorrect because it subtracts the discount from the face value of the bonds ($480,000 – $3,600 = $476,400). Answer (d) is incorrect because it provides a solution for the face value of the bonds, not the issuance value of the bonds.

9. What type of bonds mature in installments?
   a.   Debenture.
   b.   Term.
   c.   Variable rate.
   d.   Serial.

10. Balm Co. had 100,000 shares of common stock outstanding as of January 1. The following events occurred during the year:

4/1   Issued 30,000 shares of common stock.
6/1   Issued 36,000 shares of common stock.
7/1   Declared a 5% stock dividend.
9/1   Purchased as treasury stock 35,000 shares of its common stock. Balm used the cost method to account for the treasury stock.

What is Balm's weighted-average of common stock outstanding at December 31?
   a.   131,000
   b.   139,008
   c.   150,675
   d.   162,633

11. The stockholders of Meadow Corp. approved a stock-option plan that grants the company's top three executives options to purchase a maximum of 1,000 shares each of Meadow's $2 par common stock for $19 per share. The options were granted on January 1 when the fair value of the stock was $20 per share. Meadow determined that the fair value of the compensation is $300,000 and the vesting period is three years. What amount of compensation expense from the options should Meadow record in the year the options were granted?
   a. $ 20,000
   b. $ 60,000
   c. $100,000
   d. $300,000

12. At the beginning of the year, the carrying value of an asset was $1,000,000 with 20 years of remaining life. The fair value of the liability for the asset retirement obligation was $100,000. At year-end, the carrying value of the asset was $950,000. The risk-free interest rate was 5%. The credit-adjusted risk-free interest rate was 10%. What was the amount of accretion expense for the year related to the asset retirement obligation?
   a. $ 10,000
   b. $ 50,000
   c. $ 95,000
   d. $100,000

9.   (d) The requirement is to determine which type of bond matures in installments. Answer (d) is correct because serial bonds mature in installments. Answer (a) is incorrect because debenture bonds are bonds that have no collateral. Answer (b) is incorrect because term bonds have the same maturity date. Answer (c) is incorrect because variable rate bonds are bonds with a floating interest rate.

10.   (b) The requirement is to calculate the weighted-average common stock outstanding at December 31. Answer (b) is correct because weighted-average common stock outstanding is calculated as follows:

Date and Total Shares		Time		Stock Dividend		Weighted average
1/1 100,000 shares (given)	×	3/12	×	1.05	=	26,250
4/1 130,000 shares (100,000 + 30,000)	×	2/12	×	1.05	=	22,750
6/1 166,000 shares (130,000 + 36,000)	×	1/12	×	1.05	=	14,525
7/1 174,300 shares (166,000 + 8,300)	×	2/12			=	29,050
9/1 139,300 shares (174,300 – 35,000)	×	4/12			=	46,433
		12/12				139,008

Answer (a) is incorrect because it does not weight the events and does not account for the stock dividend (100,000 + 30,000 + 36,000 – 35,000 = 131,000). Answer (c) is incorrect because it omits the treasury share purchase and weights the 7/1 entry for 6 months (26,500 + 22,750 +14,525 +87,000 = 150,675). Answer (d) is incorrect because it incorrectly weights the 7/1 entry for 8 months and ignores the transactions before that entry (174,300 × 8/12 + 139,300 × 4/12 = 162,633).

11.   (c) The requirement is to determine the amount of compensation expense to record in the first year the options were granted. Answer (c) is correct because compensation expense for employee stock options allocates the fair value of the compensation (as determined by an option pricing model) over the vesting period ($300,000/3 = $100,000). Answer (a) is incorrect because it expenses the number of shares times the fair value of the stock (1000 × $20 = $20,000). Answer (b) is incorrect because it expenses three times the number of the shares times the fair number of the stock (3 × 1000 × $20 = $60,000). Answer (d) is incorrect because it expenses the entire compensation value of $300,000 rather than allocating it over the vesting period.

12.   (a) The requirement is to calculate accretion expense. Asset retirement obligations (ARO) are initially valued at fair value and an associated liability is placed on the books. The cost of the ARO is allocated over the asset's life and the interest is accrued (accreted). Answer (a) is correct because accretion expense is calculated by multiplying the adjusted interest rate by the fair value of the liability ($100,000 × 10% = $10,000). Answer (b) is incorrect because it incorrectly takes 5% of the asset value ($1,000,000 × 0.05 = $50,000). Answer (c) is incorrect because it takes 10% of the asset carrying value ($950,000 × 0.10 = $95,000). Answer (d) is incorrect because it incorrectly multiplies the 10% interest rate times the beginning of year asset carrying value ($1,000,000 × 0.10 = $100,000).

13. Blythe Corp. is a defendant in a lawsuit. Blythe's attorneys believe it is reasonably possible that the suit will require Blythe to pay a substantial amount. What is the proper financial statement treatment for this contingency?

    a.   Accrued and disclosed.

    b.   Accrued but **not** disclosed.

    c.   Disclosed but **not** accrued.

    d.   No disclosure or accrual.

14. Jones Co. had 50,000 shares of $5 par value common stock outstanding at January 1. On August 1, Jones declared a 5% stock dividend followed by a two-for-one stock split on September 1. What amount should Jones report as common shares outstanding at December 31?

    a. $105,000

    b. $100,000

    c. $ 52,500

    d. $ 50,000

15. A transaction that is unusual in nature or infrequent in occurrence should be reported as a(n)

    a.   Component of income from continuing operations, net of applicable income taxes.

    b.   Extraordinary item, net of applicable income taxes.

    c.   Component of income from continuing operations, but **not** net of applicable income taxes.

    d.   Extraordinary item, but **not** net of applicable income taxes.

16. Giaconda, Inc. acquires an asset for which it will measure the fair value by discounting future cash flows of the asset. Which of the following terms best describes this fair value measurement approach?

    a.   Market.

    b.   Income.

    c.   Cost.

    d.   Observable inputs.

17. A company owns a financial asset that is actively traded on two different exchanges (market A and market B). There is no principal market for the financial asset. The information on the two exchanges is as follows:

	Quoted price of asset	Transaction costs
Market A	$1,000	$75
Market B	1,050	150

What is the fair value of the financial asset?

    a. $ 900

    b. $ 925

    c. $1,000

    d. $1,050

13.   **(c)**   The requirement is to determine how to account for the given contingency. Answer (c) is correct because contingent liabilities that are deemed reasonably possible (estimable or not) are disclosed but not accrued. Answer (a) is incorrect because the contingent liability would have to be deemed probable and estimable in order to disclose and accrue. Answer (b) is incorrect because the contingent liability would have to be deemed probable in order to accrue it. Answer (d) is incorrect because a contingent liability would have to be deemed remote in order to take no action.

14.   **(a)**   The requirement is to calculate common shares outstanding. Answer (a) is correct because the calculation of common shares outstanding is as follows: 50,000 + (50,000 × 0.05) = 52,500 × 2 = 105,000. Answer (b) is incorrect because it ignores the stock dividend (50,000 × 2 = 100,000). Answer (c) is incorrect because it ignores the stock split (50,000 + (50,000 × 0.05) = 52,500). Answer (d) is incorrect because it ignores both the stock dividend and stock split.

15.   **(c)**   The requirement is to identify how to report an item that is unusual in nature or infrequent in occurrence, but not both. In order to be classified as extraordinary, an item must be infrequent **and** unusual in nature. If an item meets the definition of an extraordinary item, then the item is presented net of tax, below continuing operations. Answer (c) is correct because an item not meeting the extraordinary item definition would be recorded as a component of income from continuing operations. Answer (a) is incorrect because continuing operation items are not reported net of tax. Answer (b) is incorrect because the item does not meet the definition of an extraordinary item. Answer (d) is incorrect because the item fails the extraordinary item criteria.

16.   **(b)**   The requirement is to identify which fair value measurement approach is described. Three valuation techniques can be used to measure fair value: the market approach uses prices and relevant information from market transactions for identical or comparable assets or liabilities; the income approach converts future amounts to a single current (discounted) amount; and the cost approach relies on the current replacement cost to replace the asset with a comparable asset, adjusted for obsolescence. Therefore, answer (b) is correct. Answers (a) and (c) do not rely on discounting future cash flows for measurement and answer (d) is not a valuation technique.

17.   **(c)**   The requirement is to determine which value is to be used as fair value. In valuing an asset, the price in the principal or most advantageous market **shall not** be adjusted for transaction costs. However, the cost to sell is used to determine which market is the most advantageous market when a principal market does not exist. Answer (c) is correct since Market A is the most advantageous market. Market A value = $1,000 – $75 = $925. Market B value = $1,050 – $150 = $900. Since market A is the most advantageous market, its quoted price is used ($1,000). Answer (a) is incorrect because it uses the Market B quoted price less transaction costs ($1,050 – $150 = $900) as the fair value. Answer (b) is incorrect because it uses the Market A quoted price less transaction costs ($1,000 – $75 = $925) as the fair value. Answer (d) is incorrect because it ignores which market is designated to be the most advantageous market.

18. Brand Co. incurred the following research and development project costs at the beginning of the current year:

Equipment purchased for current and future projects	$100,000
Equipment purchased for current projects only	200,000
Research and development salaries for current project	400,000

Equipment has a five-year life and is depreciated using the straight-line method. What amount should Brand record as depreciation for research and development projects at December 31?

    a. $0
    b. $ 20,000
    c. $ 60,000
    d. $140,000

19. How should NSB, Inc. report significant research and development costs incurred?

    a.   Expense all costs in the year incurred.
    b.   Capitalize the costs and amortize over a five-year period.
    c.   Capitalize the costs and amortize over a 40-year period.
    d.   Expense all costs two years before and five years after the year incurred.

20. Kenn City obtained a municipal landfill and passed a local ordinance that required the city to operate the landfill so that the costs of operating the landfill, as well as the capital costs, are to be recovered with charges to customers. Which of the following funds should Kenn City use to report the activities of the landfill?

    a.   Enterprise.
    b.   Permanent.
    c.   Special revenue.
    d.   Internal service.

21. At the beginning of the current year, Paxx County's enterprise fund had a $125,000 balance for accrued compensated absences. At the end of the year, the balance was $150,000. During the year, Paxx paid $400,000 for compensated absences. What amount of compensated absences expense should Paxx County's enterprise fund report for the year?

    a. $375,000
    b. $400,000
    c. $425,000
    d. $550,000

22. Which of the following funds would be reported as a fiduciary fund in Pine City's financial statements?

    a.   Special revenue.
    b.   Permanent.
    c.   Private-purpose trust.
    d.   Internal service.

18. **(b)** The requirement is to calculate depreciation for research and development project assets. Research and development costs are expensed as incurred except for intangibles or fixed assets purchased from others having alternative future uses. Therefore, answer (b) is correct because only the equipment purchases for current and future projects may be capitalized and depreciated ($100,000/5 = $20,000). Answer (a) is incorrect because equipment purchased for current and future projects can be capitalized and depreciated. Answer (c) is incorrect because equipment purchased for current projects only must be expensed, not capitalized and depreciated ($100,000 + $200,000)/5 = $60,000. Answer (d) is incorrect because equipment purchased for current projects only and research and development salaries for the current project must be expensed as incurred ($100,000 + $200,000 + 400,000)/5.

19. **(a)** The requirement is to identify how to account for research and development costs incurred. Answer (a) is correct because research and development costs must be expensed in the period incurred.

20. **(a)** The requirement is to identify the fund that would used to account for the landfill. Answer (a) is correct because an enterprise fund is used to report activities that involve providing goods and services to individuals for a fee. Answer (b) is incorrect because a permanent fund is used to report resources that are legally restricted to the extent that the earnings, and not principal, may be used to support government programs. Answer (c) is incorrect because a special revenue fund is used to account for specific revenue sources that are legally restricted to expenditures for specified current purposes. Answer (d) is incorrect because an internal service is used to report activity that provides goods or services to other governments on a fee basis.

21. **(c)** The requirement is to calculate the amount of compensated absences expense that should be reported in an enterprise fund. Answer (c) is correct because an enterprise funds use the accrual basis of accounting. Therefore, compensated absences expense is equal to $425,000 ($400,000 paid out plus the $25,000 ($150,000 – $125,000) increase in accrued expense). Answers (a), (b), and (d) are incorrect because enterprise funds use the accrual basis of accounting,

22. **(c)** The requirement is to identify the fund that would be reported as a fiduciary fund in the financial statements. Answer (c) is correct because a private-purpose trust fund is an example of a fiduciary fund. Answer (a) is incorrect because a special revenue fund is an example of a governmental fund. Answer (b) is incorrect because a permanent fund is a governmental fund. Answer (d) is incorrect because an internal service fund is a proprietary fund.

23. Belle, a nongovernmental not-for-profit organization, received funds during its annual campaign that were specifically pledged by the donor to another nongovernmental not-for-profit health organization. How should Belle record these funds?

    a.   Increase in assets and increase in liabilities.

    b.   Increase in assets and increase in revenue.

    c.   Increase in assets and increase in deferred revenue.

    d.   Decrease in assets and decrease in fund balance.

24. Ragg Coalition, a nongovernmental not-for-profit organization, received a gift of treasury bills. The cost to the donor was $20,000, with an additional $500 for brokerage fees that were paid by the donor prior to the transfer of the treasury bills. The treasury bills had a fair value of $15,000 at the time of the transfer. At what amount should Ragg report the treasury bills in its statement of financial position?

    a. $15,000

    b. $15,500

    c. $20,000

    d. $20,500

25. In year 2, the Nord Association, a nongovernmental not-for-profit organization, received a $100,000 contribution to fund scholarships for medical students. The donor stipulated that only the interest earned on the contribution be used for the scholarships. Interest earned in year 2 of $15,000 was used to award scholarships in year 3. What amount should Nord report as temporarily restricted net assets at the end of year 2?

    a. $115,000

    b. $100,000

    c. $15,000

    d. $0

26. Which of the following characteristics of accounting information primarily allows users of financial statements to generate predictions about an organization?

    a.   Reliability.

    b.   Timeliness.

    c.   Neutrality.

    d.   Relevance.

27. Polk Co. acquires a forklift from Quest Co. for $30,000. The terms require Polk to pay $3,000 down and finance the remaining $27,000. On March 1, year 1, Polk pays the $3,000 down and accepted delivery of the forklift. Polk signed a note that requires Polk to pay principal payments of $1,000 per month for 27 months beginning July 1, year 1. What amount should Polk report as an investing activity in the statement of cash flows for the year ended December 31, year 1?

    a. $ 3,000

    b. $ 9,000

    c. $12,000

    d. $30,000

23. (a) The requirement is to identify how the organization should account for the donation. Answer (a) is correct because the donation increases assets and liabilities because it is pledged to another organization. Answer (b) is incorrect because the donation is pledged to another organization. Answer (c) is incorrect because the donation is pledged to another organization. Answer (d) is incorrect because the fund balance would not decrease.

24. (a) The requirement is to identify the amount at which the treasury bill would be reported. Answer (a) is correct because donations are reported at their fair value at the time of transfer. Answers (b), (c), and (d) are incorrect because the donation should be reported at fair value at the time of transfer.

25. (c) The requirement is to identify the amount that would be reported as temporarily restricted net assets at the end of year 2. Answer (c) is correct because the amount of temporarily restricted net assets is the amount of the earnings that cannot be spent until year 3. Answer (a) is incorrect because the principal of the gift is permanently restricted. Answer (b) is incorrect because the principal of the gift is permanently restricted and the earnings are temporarily restricted. Answer (d) is incorrect because the earnings are temporarily restricted.

26. (d) The requirement is to determine which characteristic primarily allows a user to generate predictions. Answer (d) is correct because the fundamental quality of relevance is comprised of predictive value and confirmatory value. Answer (a) is incorrect because it is not a fundamental quality. Answer (b) is incorrect because timeliness is an enhancing quality belonging to both relevance and faithful representation. It requires that information is available to a decision maker when it is useful to make a decision. Answer (c) is incorrect because it describes faithful representation. Neutrality requires the item to be depicted without bias.

27. (a) The requirement is to calculate the amount to be reported as an investing activity on the statement of cash flows. Answer (a) is correct because the investing cash outflow related to the transaction is $3,000. The financing is initially a noncash transaction and, when paid, the principal payments are considered a financing activity whereas the interest is considered an operating activity. Answer (b) is incorrect because it incorrectly classifies the 6 months of principal payments as investing and adds them to the down payment ($1,000 × 6 = $6,000 + $3,000). Answer (c) is incorrect because it incorrectly calculates 12 months of principal payments and ignores the $3,000 down payment. (12 × $1,000 = $12,000). Answer (d) is incorrect because it incorrectly classifies the total cost of the asset ($30,000) as an investing activity.

28. A company that is a large accelerated filer must file its Form 10-Q with the United States Securities and Exchange Commission within how many days after the end of the period?

   a.   30 days.
   b.   40 days.
   c.   45 days.
   d.   60 days.

29. Each of the following is a component of the changes in the net assets available for benefits of a defined benefit pension plan trust, **except**

   a.   The net change in fair value of each significant class of investments.
   b.   The net change in the actuarial present value of accumulated plan benefits.
   c.   Contributions from the employer and participants.
   d.   Benefits paid to participants.

30. During the year, Hauser Co. wrote off a customer's account receivable. Hauser used the allowance method for uncollectable accounts. What impact would the write-off have on net income and total assets?

	Net income	Total assets
a.	Decrease	Decrease
b.	Decrease	No effect
c.	No effect	Decrease
d.	No effect	No effect

31. The original cost of an inventory item is above the replacement cost. The inventory item's replacement cost is above the net realizable value. Under the lower of cost or market method, the inventory item should be valued at

   a.   Original cost.
   b.   Replacement cost.
   c.   Net realizable value.
   d.   Net realizable value **less** normal profit margin.

28. **(b)** The requirement is to state how many days a large accelerated filer has to file a Form 10-Q. There are two due dates for 10-Qs: 40 days after fiscal quarter end for large accelerated filers and accelerated filers and 45 days after fiscal quarter end for all others. Therefore, answer (b) is correct because large accelerated filers must file 10-Qs within 40 days after the end of the period.

29. **(b)** The requirement is to identify which item does not appear in the changes in net assets available for benefits in a defined benefit pension plan trust. Answer (b) is correct because the items included in the net assets available for benefits of a defined benefit pension plan trust include the net change in the fair value of each significant class of investments, contributions, and benefits paid. The net change in the actuarial present value of the accumulated plan benefits is not a component. Answers (a), (c), and (d) are components.

30. **(d)** The requirement is to identify the impact of a write-off of a customer account on net income and total assets. The journal entry for a write-off of a customer account is to debit the allowance account and credit the accounts receivable account. There is no effect on income and a net zero effect on total assets. Therefore, answer (d) is correct.

31. **(c)** The requirement is to identify which value is to be used in a lower of cost or market valuation. Designated market for comparison to cost is the middle value of the replacement cost, the ceiling/net realizable value (selling price less cost to sell and costs to complete), and the floor (ceiling less a normal profit margin). By definition, net realizable value less normal profit margin is smaller than net realizable value. Thus, market must be designated to be net realizable value because replacement cost > net realizable value > net realizable value – normal profit margin. Therefore, answer (c) is the correct answer because designated market (net realizable value) is lower than cost. Answer (a) is incorrect since original cost is higher than replacement cost and net realizable value. Answer (b) is incorrect since replacement cost is higher than net realizable value and net realizable value less normal profit margin and therefore cannot be equal to market. Answer (d) is incorrect since net realizable value less a normal profit margin, by definition, has to be less than net realizable value and net realizable value was designated as market.

32. Kauf Co. had the following amounts related to the sale of consignment inventory:

Cost of merchandise shipped to consignee	$72,000
Sales value for two-thirds of inventory sold by consignee	80,000
Freight cost for merchandise shipped	7,500
Advertising paid for by consignee, to be reimbursed	4,500
10% commission due the consignee for the sale	8,000

What amount should Kauf report as net profit (loss) from this transaction for the year?

    a. $(12,000)
    b. $ 8,000
    c. $ 14,500
    d. $ 32,000

33. A manufacturer has the following per-unit costs and values for its sole product:

Cost	$10.00
Current replacement cost	5.50
Net realizable value	6.00
Net realizable value less normal profit margin	5.20

In accordance with IFRS, what is the per-unit carrying value of inventory in the manufacturer's statement of financial position?

    a. $ 5.20
    b. $ 5.50
    c. $ 6.00
    d. $10.00

32. **(c)** The requirement is to calculate net profit (loss) from the consignment sale. Costs to include in inventory are all costs necessary to prepare the good for sale (freight in, handling costs, and normal spoilage). In this case, the items to include in inventory are the cost of inventory itself and the freight to ship the inventory. ($72,000 + $7,500 = $79,500). Period costs include advertising and commission ($4,500 + $8,000 = $12,500). Therefore, answer (c) is correct because net profit (loss) includes sales ($80,000) less cost of sales ($79,500 × 2/3 = $53,000) less period expenses ($4,500 + $8,000 = $12,500). Net profit is equal to $14,500 ($80,000 – $53,000 – $12,500). Answer (a) is incorrect because it incorrectly deducts 100% of the inventory costs and other expenses rather than two thirds of inventory costs ($80,000 – $72,000 – $7,500 – $4,500 – $8,000 = – $12,000). Answer (b) is incorrect because it incorrectly includes only the cost of the merchandise and 100% of that cost rather than two-thirds ($80,000 – $72,000 = $8,000). Answer (d) is incorrect because it incorrectly ignores all costs other than the 2/3 costs of the merchandise ($80,000 – (2/3 × $72,000) = $32,000).

33. **(c)** The requirement is to identify the inventory value under IFRS. Under IFRS, inventory is valued at lower of cost or net realizable value. Therefore, answer (c) is correct because net realizable value ($6) is less than cost ($10). Answers (a) and (b) are incorrect since replacement cost and net realizable value less normal profit margin are not part of the IFRS inventory valuation. Answer (d) is incorrect because cost ($10) is higher than net realizable value ($6).

34. At the beginning of the year, Cann Co. started construction on a new $2 million addition to its plant. Total construction expenditures made during the year were $200,000 on January 2, $600,000 on May 1, and $300,000 on December 1. On January 2, the company borrowed $500,000 for the construction at 12%. The only other outstanding debt the company had was a 10% interest rate, long-term mortgage of $800,000, which had been outstanding the entire year. What amount of interest should Cann capitalize as part of the cost of the plant addition?

 a. $140,000
 b. $132,000
 c. $ 72,500
 d. $ 60,000

35. Bondholders of Balm Co. converted their bonds into 90,000 shares of $5 par value common stock. In Balm's accounting records, the bonds had a par value of $775,000 and unamortized discount of $23,000 at the time of conversion. What amount of additional paid-in capital from the conversion should Balm record??

 a. $302,000
 b. $325,000
 c. $348,000
 d. $798,000

36. On January 1 of the current year, Barton Co. paid $900,000 to purchase two-year, 8%, $1,000,000 face value bonds that were issued by another publicly-traded corporation. Barton plans to sell the bonds in the first quarter of the following year. The fair value of the bonds at the end of the current year was $1,020,000. At what amount should Barton report the bonds in its balance sheet at the end of the current year?

 a. $ 900,000
 b. $ 950,000
 c. $1,000,000
 d. $1,020,000

34. (c) The requirement is to determine the amount of interest to capitalize. The amount of interest to capitalize is the lesser of the amount that could have been avoided if the project had not been undertaken or actual interest. Avoidable interest is equal to the average accumulated expenditures during construction times the interest rate times the construction period. The interest rate is the rate on specific borrowings for the asset or a weighted-average of other borrowings when a specific rate is not available. Answer (c) is correct because avoidable interest is less than actual interest and equals $72,250.

Date and cumulative amount		Time		Average accumulated expenditure
1/2 $200,000	×	4/12	=	$ 66,667
5/1 $800,000	×	7/12	=	$466,667
12/1 $1,100,000	×	1/12	=	$ 91,666
				$625,000

Avoidable interest:					
Specific borrowing	$500,000	×	12%	=	$60,000
Other borrowing	$125,000	×	10%	=	$12,500
					$72,250

Actual interest:					
Specific borrowing	$500,000	×	12%	=	$60,000
Other borrowing	$800,000	×	10%	=	$ 80,000
					$140,000

Answer (a) is incorrect because it erroneously uses actual interest ($140,000) which is larger than avoidable interest ($72,250). Answer (b) is incorrect because it incorrectly calculates interest as accumulated expenditure times the specific borrowing rate [($200,000 + $600,000 + $300,000) × 12% = $132,000]. Answer (d) is incorrect because it only includes the specific borrowing interest ($500,000 × 12% = $60,000).

35. (a) The requirement is to calculate the amount of additional paid-in capital from a bond conversion. Bonds are converted using the book value method. The entry to record the conversion is

Bonds	775,000	
Discount		23,000
Common stock (90,000 × $5)		450,000
Paid-in capital (plug)		302,000

Therefore, answer (a) is correct. Answer (b) is incorrect because it ignores the discount ($775,000 – $450,000 = $325,000). Answer (c) is incorrect because it incorrectly adds the value of the discount rather than subtracting it ($775,000 + $23,000 – $450,000 = $348,000). Answer (d) is incorrect because it adds the value of the discount instead of subtracting it and it ignores the value assigned to the common stock ($775,000 + $23,000 = $798,000).

36. (d) The requirement is to calculate the investment balance sheet value. Because Barton Co. plans to sell the bonds, they would be classified as trading securities. Trading securities are valued at fair value. Therefore, answer (d) is correct. Answer (a) is incorrect because the purchase price is not used to value trading securities on the balance sheet. Answer (b) is incorrect because fair value is used to value trading securities on the balance sheet. Answer (c) is incorrect because historical cost is not used to value trading securities on the balance sheet.

37. The funded status of a defined benefit pension plan for a company should be reported in
    a.   The income statement.
    b.   The statement of cash flows.
    c.   The statement of financial position.
    d.   The notes to the financial statements only.

37. (c) The requirement is to identify how to report the funded status of a defined benefit pension plan. Answer (c) is correct because the funding status of a pension plan must be reported in the balance sheet (statement of financial position). Answers (a) and (b) are incorrect because funding status is an asset or liability to be reported on the statement of financial position, not an income statement or cash flow statement item. Answer (d) is incorrect because the funding status must be reported in the statement of financial position, not only in the notes to the financial statement.

38. Martin Pharmaceutical Co. is currently involved in two lawsuits. One is a class-action suit in which consumers claim that one of Martin's best selling drugs caused severe health problems. It is reasonably possible that Martin will lose the suit and have to pay $20 million in damages. Martin is suing another company for false advertising and false claims against Martin. It is probable that Martin will win the suit and be awarded $5 million in damages. What amount should Martin report on its financial statements as a result of these two lawsuits?
    a. $0
    b. $5 million income
    c. $15 million expense.
    d. $20 million expense.

38. (a) The requirement is to determine the amount to appear in the financial statements from lawsuits. Contingent losses are accrued when probable and estimable. Contingent gains are recognized when realized. Since Martin's contingent loss is only reasonably possible, it would not be accrued. Since Martin's contingent gain is not realized, it would not be accrued. Therefore, answer (a) is correct. Answers (b), (c), and (d) are incorrect because the contingencies should not be accrued.

39. Wood Co.'s dividends on noncumulative preferred stock have been declared but not paid. Wood has not declared or paid dividends on its cumulative preferred stock in the current or the prior year and has reported a net loss in the current year. For the purpose of computing basic earnings per share, how should the income available to common stockholders be calculated?
    a.   The current-year dividends and the dividends in arrears on the cumulative preferred stock should be added to the net loss, but the dividends on the noncumulative preferred stock should **not** be included in the calculation.
    b.   The dividends on the noncumulative preferred stock should be added to the net loss, but the current-year dividends and the dividends in arrears on the cumulative preferred stock should **not** be included in the calculation.
    c.   The dividends on the noncumulative preferred stock and the current-year dividends on the cumulative preferred stock should be added to the net loss.
    d.   Neither the dividends on the noncumulative preferred stock nor the current-year dividends and the dividends in arrears on cumulative preferred stock should be included in the calculation.

39. (c) The requirement is to identify how cumulative and noncumulative preferred dividends affect income available to common stockholders. Preferred dividends on cumulative preferred stock are subtracted from net profit or added to a net loss for the current year and years in arrears if declared; if not declared, only the current year is subtracted from net profit or added to a net loss. Noncumulative dividends are only subtracted from net profit or added to a net loss if declared. In this case dividends on noncumulative stock have been declared and dividends on cumulative stock have not been declared. Additionally, Wood had a net loss. Therefore, answer (c) is correct; only the current year dividends for the cumulative and noncumulative stock would be added to the net loss. Answer (a) is incorrect because it incorrectly includes the dividends in arrears although a dividend has not been declared and it incorrectly excludes the declared dividend on the noncumulative dividend. Answer (b) is incorrect because it incorrectly excludes the current year dividend on the cumulative preferred stock. Answer (d) is incorrect because it excludes all dividends.

40. The fair value for an asset or liability is measured as
    a.   The appraised value of the asset or liability.
    b.   The price that would be paid to acquire the asset or received to assume the liability in an orderly transaction between market participants.
    c.   The price that would be received when selling an asset or paid when transferring a liability in an orderly transaction between market participants.
    d.   The cost of the asset **less** any accumulated depreciation or the carrying value of the liability on the date of the sale.

40. (c) The requirement is to identify how to measure the fair value of an asset or liability. Answer (c) is correct because the fair value for an asset or liability is the price that would be received when selling the asset or paid when transferring a liability in an orderly transaction between market participants. Answer (a) is incorrect because the appraised value is not a fair value measurement. Answer (b) is incorrect because it mismatches the term paid with acquiring an asset and received with assuming a liability. Answer (d) is incorrect because the carrying value is not a fair value measurement.

41. Hudson Corp. operates several factories that manufacture medical equipment. The factories have a historical cost of $200 million. Near the end of the company's fiscal year, a change in business climate related to a competitor's innovative products indicated to Hudson's management that the $170 million carrying amount of the assets of one of Hudson's factories may not be recoverable. Management identified cash flows from this factory and estimated that the undiscounted future cash flows over the remaining useful life of the factory would be $150 million. The fair value of the factory's assets is reliably estimated to be $135 million. The change in business climate requires investigation of possible impairment. Which of the following amounts is the impairment loss?

   a. $15 million
   b. $20 million
   c. $35 million
   d. $65 million

42. On January 1, year 1, Peabody Co. purchased an investment for $400,000 that represented 30% of Newman Corp.'s outstanding voting stock. For year 1, Newman reported net income of $60,000 and paid dividends of $20,000. At year-end, the fair value of Peabody's investment in Newman was $410,000. Peabody elected the fair value option for this investment. What amount should Peabody recognize in net income for year 1 attributable to the investment?

   a. $ 6,000
   b. $10,000
   c. $16,000
   d. $18,000

43. On June 19, Don Co., a US company, sold and delivered merchandise on a 30-day account to Cologne GmbH, a German corporation, for 200,000 euros. On July 19, Cologne paid Don in full. Relevant currency exchange rates were

	June 19	July 19
Spot rate	$.988	$.995
30-day forward rate	.990	1.000

What amount should Don record on June 19 as an account receivable for its sale to Cologne?

   a. $197,600
   b. $198,000
   c. $199,000
   d. $200,000

41. **(c)** The requirement is to calculate the amount of the impairment loss. Impairment occurs when the carrying amount of a long-lived asset or asset group exceeds its fair value. An impairment loss is recorded on that difference if the carrying value of the asset is not recoverable. The carrying value is not recoverable if its carrying value exceeds the sum of the expected value of undiscounted cash flows from use of the asset. Answer (c) is correct because it compares the carrying amount of the equipment to its fair value ($170 m – $135 m = $35 m) and the carrying value is not recoverable ($170m >$150m). Answer (a) is incorrect because it calculates the impairment loss as the difference between the estimated undiscounted cash flows and the fair value ($150 m – $135 m = $15 m). Answer (b) is incorrect because it calculates the impairment loss as the difference between carrying value and undiscounted cash flows ($170 m – $150 m = $20 m). Answer (d) is incorrect because it calculates the impairment loss as the difference between the historical cost and fair value ($200 m – $135 m = $65 m).

42. **(c)** The requirement is to calculate investment net income when the fair value option has been elected. When the fair value option is elected, changes in fair value are recorded in income. When the fair value option is elected for an investment accounted for on the equity method, dividends are recognized as income rather than the investor's share of the investee's net income. Answer (c) is correct because income is calculated as dividends plus the change in fair value (30% × $20,000 = $6,000 + $10,000 ($410,000 – $400,000) = $16,000). Answer (a) is incorrect because it only includes dividend income. Answer (b) is incorrect because it only includes the change in fair value. Answer (d) is incorrect because it uses the equity method of determining income ($60,000 × 30% = $18,000) rather than the fair value option income.

43. **(a)** The requirement is to calculate the amount to record as an account receivable for the foreign currency transaction. This qualifies as a foreign currency transaction, a transaction denominated in a currency other than the entity's functional currency. The US company directly assumes the fluctuation exchange rate risk. On the transaction date, the amount recorded in US dollars would be determined by the spot rate on that date. Therefore, answer (a) is correct (200,000 Euros × $0.988 = $197,600). Answer (b) is incorrect because it uses the 30-day forward rate instead of the spot rate on the date of the transaction. Answer (c) is incorrect because it uses the July 19th spot rate (the rate that should be used when settling the transaction). Answer (d) is incorrect because it uses the July 19th 30-day forward rate to record the transaction.

44. On June 1 of the current year, a company entered into a real estate lease agreement for a new building. The lease is an operating lease and is fully executed on that day. According to the terms of the lease, payments of $28,900 per month are scheduled to begin on October 1 of the current year and to continue each month thereafter for 56 months. The lease terms spans five years. The company has a calendar year-end. What amount is the company's lease expense for the current calendar year?

  a. $ 86,700
  b. $161,838
  c. $188,813
  d. $202,300

45. On March 21, year 2, a company with a calendar year-end issued its year 1 financial statements. On February 28, year 2, the company's only manufacturing plant was severely damaged by a storm and had to be shut down. Total property losses were $10 million and determined to be material. The amount of business disruption losses is unknown. How should the impact of the storm be reflected in the company's year 1 financial statements?

  a. Provide **no** information related to the storm losses in the financial statements until losses and expenses become fully known.
  b. Accrue and disclose the property loss with **no** accrual or disclosure of the business disruption loss.
  c. Do **not** accrue the property loss or the business disruption loss, but disclose them in the notes to the financial statements.
  d. Accrue and disclose the property loss and additional business disruption losses in the financial statements.

46. On January 1, Fonk City approved the following general fund resources for the new fiscal period:

Property taxes	$5,000,000
Licenses and permits	400,000
Intergovernmental revenues	150,000
Transfers in from other funds	350,000

What amount should Fonk record as estimated revenues for the new fiscal year?

  a. $5,400,000
  b. $5,550,000
  c. $5,750,000
  d. $5,900,000

47. Which of the following is one of the three standard sections of a governmental comprehensive annual financial report?

  a. Investment.
  b. Actuarial.
  c. Statistical.
  d. Single audit.

44. (c) The requirement is to calculate lease expense. When a lease contains future rent steps or payments are not required to start immediately, rent expense should be recognized on a straight line basis over the lease term starting when the lessee has possession of the asset. The contract was executed on June 1. Payments of $28,900 span 56 months starting on October 1. Total lease cost equals $28,900 × 56 months = $1,618,400. Converting this to a 5-year lease term results in a monthly payment of $26,973.33 ($1,618,400/60 = $26,973.33). Seven months (June 1 – Dec 31) have passed since the execution of the lease, resulting in a lease expense of $188,813 for the year ($26,973.33 × 7 months = $188,813). Therefore, answer (c) is correct. Answer (a) is incorrect because it takes the given monthly payment multiplied by the payments made during the year ($28,900 × 3 = $86,700). Answer (b) is incorrect because it incorrectly calculates the straight-line payment over six months instead of seven months ($26,973.33 × 6 = $161,838). Answer (d) is incorrect because it takes the given monthly payment and multiplies it by the months since execution ($28,900 × 7 = $202,300).

45. (c) The requirement is to identify how to record a subsequent event. Subsequent events are of two types: (1) those that relate to the current financial statements but come to light after year-end, and (2) those that come to light after year-end and relate to the next year's financial statements. The first situation may require accrual but the second situation requires disclosure only if it is material. In this case, the company's only manufacturing plant was shut down in February of year 2. Since this event occurred after year-end, no accrual is necessary. However it would qualify as a subsequent event requiring disclosure. Therefore, answer (c) is correct.

46. (b) The requirement is to calculate the amount that should be recorded as estimated revenues for the year. Answer (b) is correct because all of the items are reported as revenues except transfers in from other funds. Answer (a) is incorrect because intergovernmental revenues are part of estimated revenues. Answer (c) is incorrect because intergovernmental revenues are part of estimated revenues but transfers in from other funds are not. Answer (d) is incorrect because transfers in from other funds are not part of estimated revenues.

47. (c) The requirement is to identify the item that is one of the three standard sections of the comprehensive annual financial report. Answer (c) is correct because the three sections of the comprehensive annual financial report are introductory, financial and statistical. Answer (a), (b), and (d) are incorrect because they are not one of the three sections.

48. A government makes a contribution to its pension plan in the amount of $10,000 for year 1. The actuarially-determined annual required contribution for year 1 was $13,500. The pension plan paid benefits of $8,200 and refunded employee contributions of $800 for year 1. What is the pension expenditure for the general fund for year 1?

    a. $ 8,200
    b. $ 9,000
    c. $10,000
    d. $13,500

49. On January 1, Read, a nongovernmental not-for-profit organization, received $20,000 and an unconditional pledge of $20,000 for each of the next four calendar years to be paid on the first day of each year. The present value of an ordinary annuity for four years at a constant interest rate of 8% is 3.312. What amount of restricted net assets is reported in the year the pledge was received?

    a. $ 66,240
    b. $ 80,000
    c. $ 86,240
    d. $100,000

50. Which of the following financial categories are used in a nongovernmental not-for-profit organization's statement of financial position?

    a.   Net assets, income, and expenses.
    b.   Income, expenses, and unrestricted net assets.
    c.   Assets, liabilities, and net assets.
    d.   Changes in unrestricted, temporarily restricted, and permanently restricted net assets.

48. (c)   The requirement is to identify the pension expenditure from the general fund for the year. Answer (c) is correct because the expenditure is equal to the contribution. Answer (a) is incorrect because it is the amount of expenditure by the plan. Answer (b) is incorrect because it is the sum of the two types of expenditures by the plan. Answer (d) is incorrect because this amount represents an increase in liability for future benefits.

49. (a)   The requirement is to identify the amount that would be presented as restricted net assets. Answer (a) is correct because the restricted net assets would equal the pledged future payments reported at their net present value, or $66,240 ($20,000 x 3.312). Answer (b) is incorrect because the receivable should be presented at its present value. Answer (c) is incorrect because the $20,000 already received is not restricted. Answer (d) is incorrect because the $20,000 already received is not restricted and the future payments should be discounted to their present values.

50. (c)   The requirement is to identify the categories used in the statement of financial position. Answer (c) is correct because the statement of financial position consists of assets, liabilities, and net assets. Answer (a) is incorrect because income and expenses are presented in the statement of activities. Answer (b) is incorrect because income and expenses are presented in the statement of activities. Answer (d) is incorrect because it does not contain all of the categories in the statement of position.

Task-Based Simulation 1

Adjusted trial Balance		
	Authoritative Literature	Help

JRM Co. is in the process of closing its books for the year ended December 31, year 2.

The following business events are not properly reflected in JRM's December 31, year 2, unadjusted trial balance:

- The controller determined that half of the recorded rent expense is attributable to year 3.
- JRM depreciates its property, plant, and equipment using the straight-line method over 10 years. The property, plant, and equipment had an original cost of $20,000 and a salvage value of $5,000.
- JRM uses the percentage-of-sales method to determine the addition to bad debt expense. Uncollectible accounts receivable for year 2 was estimated to be 0.25%.
- On December 31, year 2, a customer declared bankruptcy and its account receivable of $855 is uncollectible.
- Life insurance premiums for the period ended December 31, year 2, of $650 for key members of management are included in prepaid expense.
- Interest of $300 was earned and outstanding on notes receivable during year 2. The note receivable is due at the end of year 5.
- Income taxes for year 2 are estimated to be $3,000.

Based on the business events above, calculate the adjustments necessary to JRM's unadjusted trial balance by entering the appropriate debit and credit amounts in columns D and E, respectively. Enter debit adjustments as positive values and credit adjustments as negative values.

The amounts in Column F will automatically calculate.

	A	B	C	D	E	F
1	**Account name**	**Trial balance debit**	**Trial balance (credit)**	**Adjustment debit**	**Adjustment (credit)**	**Adjusted trial balance debit/(credit) balance**
2	Cash	1,000	0			1,000
3	Interest receivable	0	0			300
4	Accounts receivable	25,000	0			24,145
5	Allowance for doubtful accounts	0	(2,500)			(2,395)
6	Prepaid expenses	1,000	0			(5,350)
7	Property, plant, and equipment	20,000	0			20,000
8	Accumulated depreciation — property, plant, and equipment	0	(10,000)			(11,500)
9	Notes receivable	20,000	0			20,000
10	Accounts payable	0	(33,000)			(33,000)
11	Taxes payable	0	(1,000)			(3,000)
12	Equity	0	(1,500)			(1,500)
13	Sales	0	(300,000)			(300,000)
14	Cost of goods sold	195,000	0			195,000
15	Salaries, officer, and general expenses	75,000	0			75,000
16	Rent expense	10,000	0			5,000
17	Tax expense	1,000	0			3,000
18	Bad debt expense	0	0			750
19	Depreciation expense	0	0			1,500
20	Insurance expense	0	0			650
21	Interest income	0	0			(300)
22		348,000	(348,000)	11,055	(11,055)	0

Solution to Task-Based Simulation 1

Adjusted Trial Balance | Authoritative Literature | Help

	A	B	C	D	E	F
1	**Account name**	**Trial balance debit**	**Trial balance (credit)**	**Adjustment debit**	**Adjustment (credit)**	**Adjusted trial balance debit/(credit) balance**
2	Cash	1,000	0			1,000
3	Interest receivable	0	0	(6) 300		300
4	Accounts receivable	25,000	0		(4) (855)	24,145
5	Allowance for doubtful accounts	0	(2,500)	(4) 855	(3) (750)	(2,395)
6	Prepaid expenses	1,000	0	(1) 5,000	(5) (650)	(5,350)
7	Property, plant, and equipment	20,000	0			20,000
8	Accumulated depreciation — property, plant, and equipment	0	(10,000)		(2) (1,500)	(11,500)
9	Notes receivable	20,000	0			20,000
10	Accounts payable	0	(33,000)			(33,000)
11	Taxes payable	0	(1,000)		(7) (2,000)	(3,000)
12	Equity	0	(1,500)			(1,500)
13	Sales	0	(300,000)			(300,000)
14	Cost of goods sold	195,000	0			195,000
15	Salaries, officer, and general expenses	75,000	0			75,000
16	Rent expense	10,000	0		(1) (5,000)	5,000
17	Tax expense	1,000	0	(7) 2,000		3,000
18	Bad debt expense	0	0	(3) 750		750
19	Depreciation expense	0	0	(2) 1,500		1,500
20	Insurance expense	0	0	(5) 650		650
21	Interest income	0	0		(6) (300)	(300)
22		348,000	(348,000)	11,055	(11,055)	0

Explanation of solutions

(1) To defer half of year 2 rent expense to year 3 ($10,000/2) = $5,000

Prepaid rent $5,000
        Rent expense $5,000

(2) To record depreciation expense for the year (cost − salvage)/n = ($20,000 − $5,000)/10 = $1,500

Depreciation expense $1,500
        Accumulated depreciation $1,500

(3) To record bad debt expense 0.25% × 300,000 (taken from trial balance) = $750

Bad debt expense $750
        Allowance for doubtful accounts $750

(4) To write off customer account due to bankruptcy

Allowance for doubtful accounts $855
        Accounts receivable $855

(5) To record life insurance expense

Insurance expense $650
        Prepaid expense $650

(6) To record accrued interest

Interest receivable $300
        Interest income $300

(7) To record income taxes ($3,000 total less $1,000 already recorded) = $2,000

Tax expense $2,000
        Taxes payable $2,000

Task-Based Simulation 2

Intangible Asset Entries	Authoritative Literature	Help

For each situation below, record the appropriate journal entry for Richter Corp.

Assume the company uses the straight-line method for amortization and depreciation and that all amortization and depreciation is recorded on December 31 of each year. Richter uses separate general ledger accounts to record accumulated amortization for each intangible asset.

To prepare each entry:

- Double-click the shaded cells in the account name column and select from the list provided the appropriate account name. If no entry is needed, select "No entry required". An account may be used once or not at all for each entry.
- Enter the corresponding debit or credit amount in the appropriate column.
- Round all amounts to the nearest dollar.
- All rows may not be required to complete each entry.

April 1, year 1:
Richter purchased a patent with a 10-year life for $50,000 from DD Co. DD incurred costs of $35,000 developing the patent. Prepare the journal entry, if any, to record the patent.

1	Account name	Debit	Credit
2			
3			
4			
5			

July 1, year 1:
Richter purchased scientific equipment used in product development studies having potential alternative uses for future products. The equipment cost $75,000 and the company paid an additional $4,000 for delivery. The equipment has an estimated useful life of 5 years. Prepare the journal entry, if any, to record the purchase of the equipment.

1	Account name	Debit	Credit
2			
3			
4			
5			

October 1, year 1:
Richter received an unfavorable judgment in defense of a trademark and paid $25,000 in fees to their law firm. Prepare the journal entry, if any, to record the legal fees.

1	Account name	Debit	Credit
2			
3			
4			
5			

December 31, year 1:
Prepare the journal entry, if any, to account for the patent purchased on April 1, year 1

1	Account name	Debit	Credit
2			
3			
4			
5			

December 31, year 1:
Prepare the journal entry, if any, to account for the scientific equipment purchased on July 1, year 1.

1	Account name	Debit	Credit
2			
3			
4			
5			

December 31, year 1:

Richter had previously recorded $300,000 of goodwill related to an acquisition.

At December 31, year 1, the carrying value of the identifiable net assets acquired exceeded their fair value by $50,000. The implied fair value of the goodwill was $310,000. Prepare the journal entry, if any, to adjust the carrying value of goodwill.

1	**Account name**	**Debit**	**Credit**
2			
3			
4			
5			

Select Item
Accumulated amortization — patent
Accumulated depreciation
Amortization expense
Cash
Depreciation expense
Equipment
Goodwill
Goodwill impairment loss
Investment
Legal expense
Patents
Prepaid patent expense
Research and development expense
Trademark
No entry required

Solution to Task-Based Simulation 2

Intangible Asset Entries		
	Authoritative Literature	Help

April 1, year 1:

Richter purchased a patent with a 10-year life for $50,000 from DD Co. DD incurred costs of $35,000 developing the patent. Prepare the journal entry, if any, to record the patent.

(1)

1	Account name	Debit	Credit
2	Patents	50,000	
3	Cash		50,000
4			
5			

July 1, year 1:

Richter purchased scientific equipment used in product development studies having potential alternative uses for future products. The equipment cost $75,000 and the company paid an additional $4,000 for delivery. The equipment has an estimated useful life of 5 years. Prepare the journal entry, if any, to record the purchase of the equipment.

(2)

1	Account name	Debit	Credit
2	Equipment	79,000	
3	Cash		79,000
4			
5			

October 1, year 1:

Richter received an unfavorable judgment in defense of a trademark and paid $25,000 in fees to their law firm. Prepare the journal entry, if any, to record the legal fees.

(3)

1	Account name	Debit	Credit
2	Legal expense	25,000	
3	Cash		25,000
4			
5			

December 31, year 1:

Prepare the journal entry, if any, to account for the patent purchased on April 1, year 1

(4)

1	Account name	Debit	Credit
2	Amortization expense	3,750	
3	Accumulated amortization — patent		3,750
4			
5			

December 31, year 1:

Prepare the journal entry, if any, to account for the scientific equipment purchased on July 1, year 1.

(5)

1	Account name	Debit	Credit
2	Research and development expense	7,900	
3	Accumulated depreciation		7,900
4			
5			

December 31, year 1:

Richter had previously recorded $300,000 of goodwill related to an acquisition.

At December 31, year 1, the carrying value of the identifiable net assets acquired exceeded their fair value by $50,000. The implied fair value of the goodwill was $310,000. Prepare the journal entry, if any, to adjust the carrying value of goodwill.

(6)

1	Account name	Debit	Credit
2	No entry required		
3			
4			
5			

Explanation of solutions

(1) Record patent — if an intangible is acquired, record at cost.

Patent	$50,000	
Cash		$50,000

(2) R&D costs are expensed as incurred except for intangibles or fixed assets purchased from others having alternative future uses. The amount to be capitalized includes all costs necessary to get the asset to the work site and to prepare it for use. $75,000 + $4,000 shipping = $79,000

Equipment	$79,000	
Cash		$79,000

(3) Legal fees to defend patents may only be capitalized in successful suits. Since this suit was uncessful, fees must be expensed.

Legal expense	$25,000	
Cash		$25,000

(4) The patent purchased on 4/1 should be amortized over its life of 10 years ($50,000/10) = $5,000 per year × 9/12 of the year = $3,750.

Amortization expense	$3,750	
Accumulated amortization – patent		$3,750

(5) The equipment purchased on 7/1 should be depreciated over its life of 5 years ($79,000/5) = $15,800 per year × 6/12 of the year = $7,900.

Research and development expense	$7,900	
Accumulated depreciation		$7,900

(6) Goodwill impairment analysis is a two-step process. First, compare the carrying amount ot its fair value and if the carrying amount exceeds the fair value, proceed to step 2. Since the carrying value exceeds fair value by $50,000, you should proceed to step 2. Compare the implied fair value of the goodwill to its carrying value and if the implied value of goodwill is less than its carrying amount, write down goodwill. In this case, the implied value ($310,000) exceeds the carrying value ($300,000). Since implied goodwill is greater than the carrying value of goodwill, no entry is required.

Task-Based Simulation 3

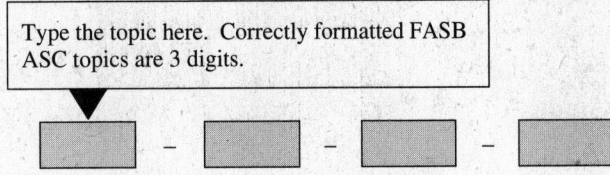

Situation 3

ABC Corp., an issuer, is planning to implement an employee share purchase plan. Substantially all employees that meet the limited employment qualifications may participate on an equitable basis. Which section of the authoritative guidance best outlines the criteria that allow a company to provide a share purchase plan that does not require compensation cost to be recognized?

Enter your response in the answer fields below. Unless specifically requested, your response should not cite implementation guidance. Guidance on correctly structuring your response appears above and below the answer fields.

Type the topic here. Correctly formatted FASB ASC topics are 3 digits.

Solution to Task-Based Simulation 3

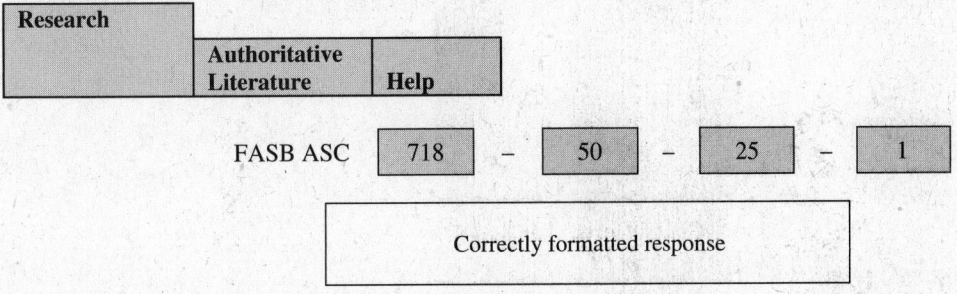

FASB ASC   718 – 50 – 25 – 1

Correctly formatted response

INDEX